lonely planet

Ireland

Tom Downs, Fionn Davenport, Des Hannigan,
Etain O'Carroll, Oda O'Carroll, Neil Wilson

Contents

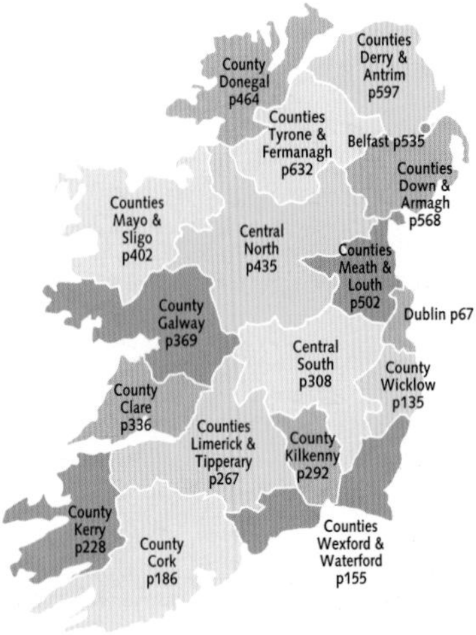

Counties Derry & Antrim p597
County Donegal p464
Counties Tyrone & Fermanagh p632
Belfast p535
Counties Down & Armagh p568
Counties Mayo & Sligo p402
Central North p435
Counties Meath & Louth p502
County Galway p369
Dublin p67
Central South p308
County Wicklow p135
County Clare p336
Counties Limerick & Tipperary p267
County Kilkenny p292
County Kerry p228
County Cork p186
Counties Wexford & Waterford p155

Destination: Ireland

Pastoral, urban, poetic, feisty, backwards, brilliant, devout and debauched: Ireland has always been more complicated than its shamrock-laden image ever let on. But the old clichés are now more inadequate than ever. The past decade has been a time of rejuvenation for the small island nation.

Ireland has finally shaken the shackles of colonisation, and in the process its cities have blossomed with commerce and culture. Dublin in particular has become one of Europe's most exciting and vibrant urban centres. Meanwhile, Galway, Belfast, Cork and Kilkenny, always fine spots for a few lazy pints, have picked up the pace, with a range of flashy clubs and international restaurants exuding a cosmopolitan *joie de vivre* never before seen this side of London. The good life is spilling out to the remotest villages, where cozy country cottages have been converted into artisans workshops and fine eateries.

Ireland's prosperity has also attracted, for the first time in its history, a wave of immigrants from Eastern Europe and Africa who have brought with them an energy and culture that add greatly to Ireland's own identity. In the North, the Troubles appear to be entering the last chapter of their turbulent history.

But Ireland has not forsaken its stunning natural beauty and proud traditions. Slate-toned lakes, green pastures, tranquil mountain retreats, magnificent cliffs overlooking the wild Atlantic coast, remote sandy beaches, ancient offshore island villages and the friendliness of the people remain untarnished. Many traces of traditional culture survive, especially in remote western areas, and there are still communities in which Irish is the first language. Ireland remains one of the most beautiful and interesting countries in Europe.

RICHARD CUMMINS

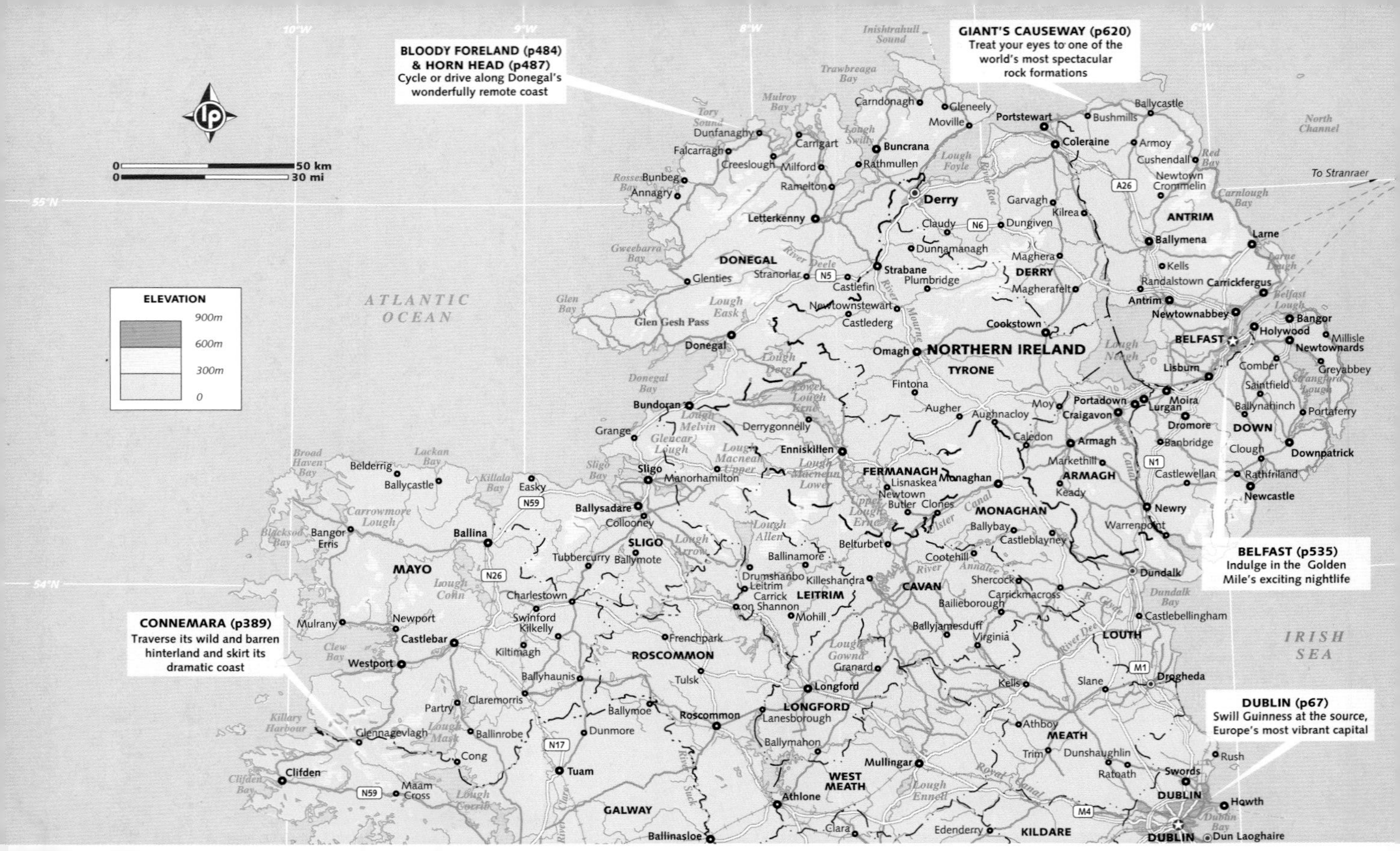

BLOODY FORELAND (p484) & HORN HEAD (p487)
Cycle or drive along Donegal's wonderfully remote coast
GIANT'S CAUSEWAY (p620)
Treat your eyes to one of the world's most spectacular rock formations
BELFAST (p535)
Indulge in the Golden Mile's exciting nightlife
DUBLIN (p67)
Swill Guinness at the source, Europe's most vibrant capital
CONNEMARA (p389)
Traverse its wild and barren hinterland and skirt its dramatic coast
ELEVATION
900m
600m
300m
0
0
50 km
0
30 mi
10°W
9°W
8°W
6°W
55°N
54°N
ATLANTIC OCEAN
IRISH SEA
North Channel
To Stranraer
NORTHERN IRELAND
DONEGAL
DERRY
ANTRIM
TYRONE
FERMANAGH
ARMAGH
DOWN
MONAGHAN
CAVAN
LOUTH
LEITRIM
SLIGO
MAYO
ROSCOMMON
LONGFORD
WEST MEATH
MEATH
GALWAY
KILDARE
DUBLIN
Derry
Belfast
Letterkenny
Buncrana
Donegal
Strabane
Omagh
Enniskillen
Sligo
Ballina
Castlebar
Westport
Clifden
Tuam
Roscommon
Longford
Athlone
Mullingar
Dundalk
Drogheda
Newry
Armagh
Coleraine
Portstewart
Ballymena
Larne
Lisburn
Bangor
Cookstown
Monaghan
Cavan
Kells
Navan
Swords
Howth
Dun Laoghaire

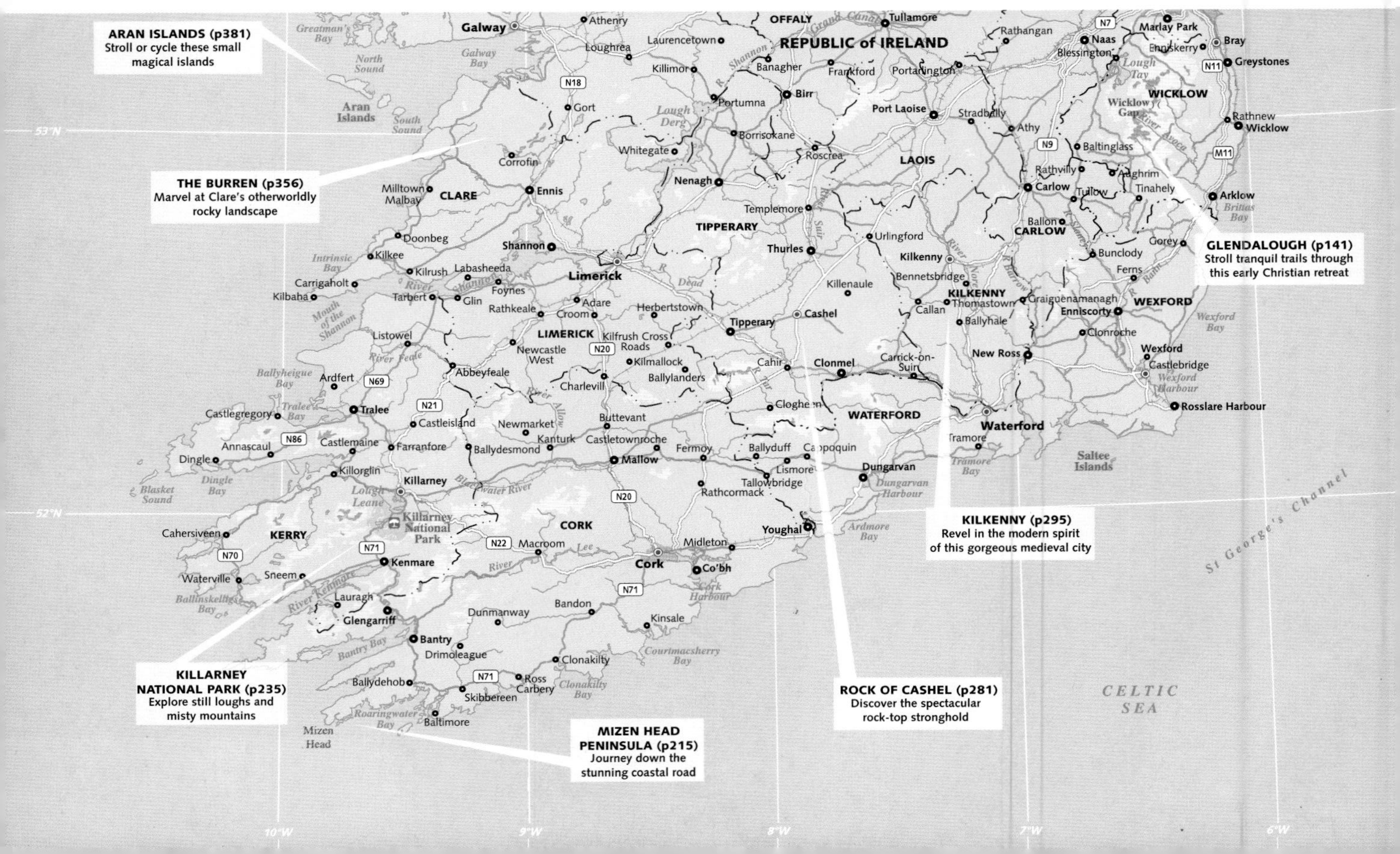
ARAN ISLANDS (p381)
Stroll or cycle these small magical islands
THE BURREN (p356)
Marvel at Clare's otherworldly rocky landscape
GLENDALOUGH (p141)
Stroll tranquil trails through this early Christian retreat
KILKENNY (p295)
Revel in the modern spirit of this gorgeous medieval city
ROCK OF CASHEL (p281)
Discover the spectacular rock-top stronghold
KILLARNEY NATIONAL PARK (p235)
Explore still loughs and misty mountains
MIZEN HEAD PENINSULA (p215)
Journey down the stunning coastal road
REPUBLIC of IRELAND
OFFALY
LAOIS
WICKLOW
CARLOW
KILKENNY
WEXFORD
TIPPERARY
CLARE
LIMERICK
WATERFORD
CORK
KERRY
CELTIC SEA
St George's Channel
Galway
Athenry
Tullamore
Loughrea
Laurencetown
Banagher
Frankford
Portarlington
Rathangan
Naas
Blessington
Marlay Park
Enniskerry
Bray
Greystones
Killimor
Birr
Portumna
Port Laoise
Stradbally
Athy
Gort
Borrisokane
Roscrea
Whitegate
Corrofin
Ennis
Nenagh
Templemore
Thurles
Urlingford
Kilkenny
Bennetsbridge
Callan
Thomastown
Ballyhale
Carlow
Tullow
Baltinglass
Rathvilly
Aughrim
Tinahely
Ballon
Bunclody
Gorey
Arklow
Ferns
Enniscorty
Graiguenamanagh
Clonroche
New Ross
Wexford
Castlebridge
Rosslare Harbour
Wicklow
Rathnew
Milltown Malbay
Doonbeg
Kilkee
Kilrush
Labasheeda
Foynes
Shannon
Limerick
Carrigaholt
Kilbaha
Tarbert
Glin
Rathkeale
Adare
Croom
Herbertstown
Killenaule
Cashel
Tipperary
Kilfrush Cross Roads
Kilmallock
Ballylanders
Newcastle West
Listowel
Abbeyfeale
Charlevill
Cahir
Clonmel
Carrick-on-Suir
Cloghe n
Waterford
Tramore
Ardfert
Tralee
Castlegregory
Castleisland
Newmarket
Buttevant
Kanturk
Castletownroche
Fermoy
Ballyduff
Cappoquin
Lismore
Tallowbridge
Dungarvan
Annascaul
Castlemaine
Farranfore
Ballydesmond
Mallow
Rathcormack
Youghal
Dingle
Killorglin
Killarney
Killarney National Park
Cahersiveen
Macroom
Midleton
Cork
Co'bh
Kenmare
Waterville
Sneem
Lauragh
Glengarriff
Bandon
Kinsale
Dunmanway
Bantry
Drimoleague
Clonakilty
Ballydehob
Ross Carbery
Skibbereen
Baltimore
Mizen Head
Saltee Islands
Aran Islands
N7
N11
M11
N9
N18
N20
N21
N22
N69
N70
N71
N86
53°N
52°N
10°W
9°W
8°W
7°W
6°W

Coasts & Islands

Ireland is blessed with more than 5000km of dramatic, ragged coastline and dozens of interesting little islands that are a short boat ride away. The stupendous variety of cliffs, rock formations and white sandy beaches leave a traveller with no dearth of options.

You can ride horseback on the white sands of **Connemara** (p389), contemplate coastal reveries and explore the lonely reaches of County Clare's **Loop Head peninsula** (p353) or follow poet WB Yeats and find your muse in County Sligo's dramatic coastal scenery, especially at **Carrowkeel Passage Tomb Cemetery** (p430), situated on a hilltop in the Bricklieve Mountains overlooking Lough Arrow. In the far north, there's seemingly no end to the sheer coastal allurement in counties **Donegal** (p464) and **Antrim** (p617), which afford superb walking, cycling and driving opportunities.

Island hoppers face some daunting decisions. How to choose between the stark beauty of **Inisheer** (p388) and **Inishmaan** (p386), both Gaeltacht islands; late night pubbing on **Inishbofin** (p394); or the colourful cultural peculiarities of **Tory Island** (p484)?

Explore the uninhabited **Blasket Islands** (p266)

GARETH MCCORMACK

Peer over the edge of the **Cliffs of Moher** (p356)

RICHARD MILLS

GARETH MCCORMACK

Enjoy the evening view across Trawbreaga Bay on **Inishowen Peninsula** (p495)

RICHARD CUMMINS

Marvel at the awesome cliffs at **Mizen Head** (p218)

Hike along the extraordinary hexagonal basalt columns of the **Giant's Causeway** (p620)

GARETH MCCORMACK

Castles, Forts & Cloisters

Ireland is littered with forts, castles and monastic sites from the Middle Ages and earlier. It's always startling to spot an ancient watch tower standing amid sheep grazing in a field. Some of these stone structures are lovingly kept up, while others are in various stages of ruination.

The medieval-mad traveller can actually spend an extravagant night in a castle such as County Kildare's **Kilkea Castle** (p317) or County Monaghan's **Castle Leslie** (p446). If that's just too decadent, the medieval banquets at **Bunratty Castle** (p345) in County Clare and **Dunguaire Castle** (p399) in Galway are good kitschy fun.

The sins of the castles are washed away by an equal abundance of monastic sites, among them the ruinous hulks of **Jerpoint Abbey** (p304) and **Kells Priory** (p304) in County Kilkenny.

Ramble around the spectacular cemetery of **Clonmacnoise** (p331)

RICHARD CUMMINS

EOIN CLARKE

Check out the ancient ring forts of **Dún Aengus** (p383)

Explore the astonishing beehive monasteries on **Skellig Michael** (p243)

RICHARD MILLS

Wander around the tranquil **Glendalough** (p141)

RICHARD CUMMINS

RICHARD CUMMINS

Stand and admire the 17th-century **Birr Castle** (p327)

Gaze at the beautifully restored **Kilkenny Castle** (p297)

RICHARD CUMMINS

There's a pub serving creamy pints on pretty much every street in the country, but even in this category some towns will always lord it over the others. **Dublin** (p117) has the world's most gorgeous old pubs alongside cutting edge nightclubs. **Galway city** (p379), too, has its dynamic collection of clubs, pubs and traditional music venues, and no visit to the North is complete without slipping into the timeworn pubs of **Belfast** (p559). For traditional music, head to **South Armagh** (p590), or **Ennis** (p342) or **Doolin** (p361) in County Clare. **Cork city** (p197) and **Kilkenny city** (p301) are also good for a night on the town. Ireland's oldest bar is **Sean's** (p462) in Athlone.

PATRICK HORTON

Soak up the history and atmosphere at Belfast's **Crown Liquor Saloon** (p559)

Wine and dine outdoors at Kinsale's **Bulman** (p207)

RICHARD CUMMINS

JULIET COOMBE

Reward yourself with a creamy pint at the end of a visit to the **Guinness Storehouse** (p94)

RICHARD CUMMINS

Stand shoulder to shoulder on a Saturday night at Ennis' **Cíaran's Bar** (p342)

Eat, drink and be merry at Dublin's **Stag's Head** (p117)

OLIVER STREWE

Drink with the masses at **Temple Bar** (p117)

DOUG MCKINLAY

The best way to soak up Ireland's greenery is to head down one of the narrow footpaths that slice through the parks, wilderness areas and countryside.

The serious walker can get away from the hustle and bustle by taking a challenging hike through County Down's **Mourne Mountains** (p584) or by exploring County Tyrone's lonely **Sperrin Mountains** (p636). The 35km walk along County Clare's **Burren Way** (p655) includes a stretch from Doolin to the Cliffs of Moher. A walk down County Cork's **Beara Peninsula** (p222) takes in ancient sights and dramatic old copper mines. Scenic riverside trails grant pleasant walking opportunities through **Graiguenamanagh** (p305) and **Inistioge** (p305) in County Kilkenny.

If you can't be bothered to leave Dublin, there are lovely urban walks to be had around the Georgian **Merrion Square** (p89) and **St Stephen's Green** (p87).

GARETH MCCORMACK

Stop the world on top of **Mt Brandon** (p261)

Walk along the Mourne Wall to the summit of **Slieve Donard** (p587)

EOIN CLA

Bushwalk through rivers, lakes and hills in **Killarney National Park** (p235)

RICHARD CUMM

Getting Started

It's fairly easy to find what you are looking for in Ireland if you know when to go and prepare adequately for your trip. Ireland is an expensive destination, so a little budgetary forethought is advisable.

WHEN TO GO

Key factors to take into account before making this important decision are the weather, crowds, events and availability of tourist amenities.

See Climate (p660) in the Directory for more information.

If you go in July or August, you can expect reasonably warm weather and longer days. Everything will be open, but this is peak season, which presents some challenges if you're wanting a bit of solitude. Many of the country's top festivals take place during summer.

Spring and autumn can also bring nice weather, and if you are so lucky the smaller crowds of tourists can make these shoulder seasons truly delightful. Spring festivities include the ever-popular St Patrick's Day.

Winter weather can be downright inhospitable, but Ireland (the west coast in particular) does look beautiful in the rain, and there's nearly always a pub nearby to duck into. However, in many Irish towns restaurants and B&Bs close down around October and don't reopen until Easter. With a few advance phone calls you can avoid getting stranded somewhere with no place to stay or eat.

HOW MUCH?

Irish Times (newspaper) €1.45

1km taxi fare €1.45

Cinema ticket €8

Admission to Gaelic football match €12-15

Aran sweater €50+

LONELY PLANET INDEX

Litre of petrol €0.90

Litre of bottled water €1.20

Pint of Guinness €4

Souvenir T-shirt €20

Street snack (pub sandwich) €3.50

COSTS

Visitors to Ireland are almost always surprised by the high cost of accommodation and dining. Per-person rates in B&Bs and hotels can favour the solo traveller (for whom €30 and up might not seem so high), but when those rates are multiplied for entire families, suddenly a budget room can be quite pricey. Hotels charging for the room, rather than per person, are often more reasonable for groups. If B&Bs are all that's available in the towns you'll be visiting, you can often negotiate a slightly reduced rate for children. Hostels in Ireland are generally very nice and typically have reasonably priced family rooms.

Very ordinary meals can cost €20 or more. Throughout this book we recommend cheaper eating options as well as those expensive places that are worth it. Sandwich shops and cafés often feature simple menus with filling dishes for less than €10, as do the majority of pubs.

Car rental is also costly in Ireland (see Hire, p678). Be sure to check your auto insurance policy back home before accepting the exorbitant insurance policies offered at car-rental agencies. If your credit card usually covers car-rental insurance, confirm that the policy applies in Ireland.

DON'T LEAVE HOME WITHOUT...

Ireland doesn't usually test a traveller's survival skills in any dramatic fashion, but there are a few essentials you'll want to bring with you to Ireland:

- Good walking shoes
- Raincoat
- UK/Ireland electrical adapter
- A finely honed sense of humour
- A hollow leg

TOP TENS

OUR FAVOURITE FESTIVALS & EVENTS

You might even plan your trip around one or more of the following events, so mark your calendars.

- Irish National Surfing Championships (County Donegal) March (p473)
- St Patrick's Day (Dublin & throughout Ireland) 17 March (p662)
- The Cat Laughs Comedy Festival (Kilkenny city) late May, early June (p299)
- Bloomsday (Dublin) 16 June (p102)
- Galway Arts Festival (Galway city) July (p377)
- Puck Fair (Killorglin, County Kerry) August (p239)
- Appalachian & Bluegrass Music Festival (Omagh, County Tyrone) September (p636)
- Ballinasloe Horse Fair (Ballinasloe, County Galway) October (p401)
- Belfast Festival at Queens (Belfast) October (p554)
- Wexford Festival Opera (Wexford) October (p159)

MUST-SEE IRISH MOVIES

Pre-departure planning is always more fun if it includes a few flicks to get you in the mood. The following films are all available on video cassette or DVD. For other information about Irish cinema and television, see p48.

- *Bloody Sunday* (2002) Director: Paul Greengrass
- *The Boxer* (1997) Director: Jim Sheridan
- *Cal* (1984) Director: Pat O'Connor
- *The Commitments* (1991) Director: Alan Parker
- *The Crying Game* (1992) Director: Neil Jordan
- *The Dead* (1987) Director: John Huston
- *The Field* (1990) Director: Jim Sheridan
- *Into the West* (1992) Director: Mike Newell
- *The Quiet Man* (1952) Director: John Ford
- *The Secret of Roan Inish* (1995) Director: John Sayles

TOP CONTEMPORARY NOVELS

Diving into a few good novels is a fantastic way to gain insight into Irish issues and culture, and it'll also provide fodder for lively discussions over pints at the pub. Here are some good reads to seek out:

- *Ulysses* (1922) James Joyce
- *Borstal Boy* (1958) Brendan Behan
- *The Third Policeman* (1967) Flann O'Brien
- *Angela's Ashes* (1996) Frank McCourt
- *Mother of Pearl* (1998) Mary Morrissy
- *The Butcher Boy* (1992) Patrick McCabe
- *Paddy Clarke Ha Ha Ha* (1993) Roddy Doyle
- *Stir Fry* (1994) Emma Donoghue
- *Ripley Bogle* (2000) Robert McLiam Wilson
- *The Untouchable* (1997) John Banville

For other information about Irish literature see p46.

TRAVEL LITERATURE

Travel in Ireland seems to inspire writers, and it is equally true that a smartly written travel journal can surely inspire one to travel well. Hence, the following suggestions.

The Crack: A Belfast Year by Sally Belfrage is a reporter's account of a series of visits to Belfast in the 1980s.

A Place Apart by Dervla Murphy tells of the author's bicycle journey through Northern Ireland in the 1970s. It's a highly readable introduction to such topics as Orangeism, Paisleyism and the problems in South Armagh.

The *Oxford Illustrated Literary Guide to Great Britain and Ireland* traces the movements of famous writers who immortalised various towns and villages in Ireland.

A Literary Guide to Dublin by Vivien Igoe delves into the Irish capital's literary haunts, with pubs and cemeteries naturally using up their share of the word count.

Joyce's Dublin: A Walking Guide to Ulysses by Jack McCarthy caters to Bloomsday junkies wanting a year-round fix. It follows the novel chapter by chapter and has clear maps.

McCarthy's Bar is a colourful account of author Pete McCarthy's attempt to rediscover Ireland by having a pint in every pub that bears his name.

'McCarthy's Bar is a colourful account of the author's attempt to rediscover Ireland by having a pint in every pub that bears his name'

INTERNET RESOURCES

The Internet has become an indispensable planning tool for travellers. Ireland is well wired, so there's a lot of useful information available online. Here are a few sites to get you started.

Blather (www.blather.net) This wry webzine dishes out healthy portions of irreverent commentary on all things Irish. It's a savvy way to get up to date on current events and attitudes.

Entertainment Ireland (www.entertainmentireland.ie) Countrywide listings for clubs, theatres, festivals, cinemas, museums and much more. It's well worth consulting this site as you plan your next move in Ireland.

Irish Tourist Board (www.ireland.travel.ie) The Republic's tourist information site has heaps of practical info. It features a huge accommodation database with photos.

Irish Times (www.ireland.com) The website of Ireland's largest daily newspaper represents a great way to get up to speed on all the latest news before you leave home.

Lonely Planet (www.lonelyplanet.com) Comprehensive travel information and advice.

Northern Ireland Tourism (www.ni-tourism.com) Northern Ireland's official tourism information site is particularly strong on activities and accommodation.

Itineraries

CLASSIC ROUTES

INTO THE WEST

1 week / Mayo to West Cork

Begin at the excavated **Céide Fields** (p418) in Mayo. Wind your way round the coast, stopping at some of Ireland's wildest beaches to the pretty village of **Pollatomish** (p418). Head to the heritage town of **Westport** (p408), with its pubs and restaurants, before heading past **Croagh Patrick** (p411) and through **Connemara National Park** (p396), then down to **Leenane** (p396), situated on Ireland's only fjord. Take the beautiful coastal route, passing **Kylemore Abbey** (p395) and **Clifden's** (p392) scenic **Sky Road** (p393) through pretty **Roundstone** (p391), or the stunning wilderness of the inland route, passing the **Twelve Bens** (p389) through Maam Cross to **Galway** (p371). Relax in Galway before moving to the fishing villages of **Kinvara** (p399) and **Ballyvaughan** (p363) in the heart of the unique **Burren** (p356) and visiting the ancient **Aillwee Caves** (p365). Enjoy a medieval banquet at **Bunratty Folk Park** (p346) before visiting **Limerick's Hunt Museum** (p270). Explore the **Dingle Peninsula** (p255) before following the **Ring of Kerry** (p239) ending with a trek in **Killarney National Park** (p235). Continue down the **Beara Peninsula** (p222) to the Italianate **Garinish Island** (p223) with its rare and exotic flowers. Follow the coast to **Cork** (p188) through Castletownsend and the fishing village of **Union Hall** (p211).

This tourist trail brings you past some of Ireland's most famous attractions and spectacular countryside. You could manage it in two days but what's the point? You won't be disappointed on this route.

GIANT LOOP

3 weeks / Starting & ending in Dublin

Start your Giant Loop of Ireland just north of Dublin at **Casino at Marino** (p98), not a place to cash your chips but a 19th-century Italianate trompe l'oeil mansion. Continue north to **Mellifont Abbey** (p527), Ireland's first Cistercian abbey, and on to the pretty village of **Carlingford** (p532) on the lough with its narrow streets and 16th-century buildings. Wind through the Mourne Mountains to the **Ards Peninsula** (p575) and **Strangford Lough** (p579). Take some time in **Belfast** (p535) to discover its culture, history and entertainment before moving northwest to the unmissable rock formation and World Heritage site, **Giant's Causeway** (p620). Continue around the stunning coastline of north Donegal, stopping at some of Ireland's finest **beaches** (p487) and passing through the beautiful **Glenveagh National Park** (p483). Stop off at Norman and Jacobean **Donegal Castle** (p468) before catching lively **Sligo** (p425) town with its Yeatsean literary connections. Climb up to the mystical Stone Age passage grave, **Carrowkeel** (p430), built on a leyline and with panoramic views of **Lough Arrow** (p430). For the west coast as far as Cork follow **Into the West** (p16). From Cork, head east to **Fota Wildlife Park** (p200) for a picnic and then on to **King John's Castle** (p271), with its unusual 12th-century shell. Drive around the picturesque **Hook Peninsula** (p166), stopping for an ice cream in the seaside town of **Dunmore East** (p179). Spot the unusual varieties of geese in the world-famous **Wexford Wildfowl Reserve** (p162) before heading up to County Wicklow with its lakes, **Wicklow Mountains National Park** (p137). Now settle into a well-deserved pint of Guinness in Dublin's **Ryan's** (p119) on Parkgate St.

This coastal loop will give you a real feel for Ireland's coastline and could take you from four days to three weeks.

HEAD TO HEEL

2 weeks / Derry to Wexford

Begin your Head to Heel trail by walking the city walls of **Derry city** (p599) and exploring its fascinating history. Walk around one of Ireland's best museums, the **Ulster American Folk Park** (p635) which reproduces a typical 19th-century Ulster village at the time of mass emigration to America. Just south of here the town of **Omagh** (p634), site of one of the worst single atrocities in the North's history (a car bomb), acts as a stark reminder of the region's tragic political history. From here, head south to **Castle Coole** (p644), a National Trust–restored 18th-century mansion, before spending an afternoon boating or fishing on **Lough Erne** (p644). For more watery pastimes you can't beat **County Cavan** (p437), which has a lake for every day of the year. Hire a boat in **Mountnugent** (p442) and fish on **Lough Sheelin** (p437 and p442) before moving on down to **Tullynally Castle's** (p460) Chinese and Tibetan garden in Westmeath. The **Seven Wonders of Fore** (p460), Westmeath's answer to the Seven Wonders of the World, while less awe-inspiring, will keep you entertained for an hour or two before a wander around the splendid **Belvedere House** (p459), overlooking Lough Ennell, with its multimedia exhibition. Place a bet at **Kilbeggan races** (p459) emboldened by a tipple of fine whiskey at **Locke's Distillery** (p460). Take a hike up the beautiful **Slieve Bloom Mountains** (p325) for the best view of the Midlands, before moving south to the delightful village of **Inistioge** (p305), in County Kilkenny, with its quaint village square and rambling estate, Woodstock Park. In County Wexford have a picnic in the **John F Kennedy Park & Arboretum** (p169) before a visit to the tranquil Cistercian **Tintern Abbey** (p166).

This north to south trail could be described as an Irish diagonal. The middle of Ulster has plenty of fine architecture and heritage. The abundance of lakes in Ireland's centre will keep fishing folk and nature lovers happy before moving on to the beautiful countryside of the southeast.

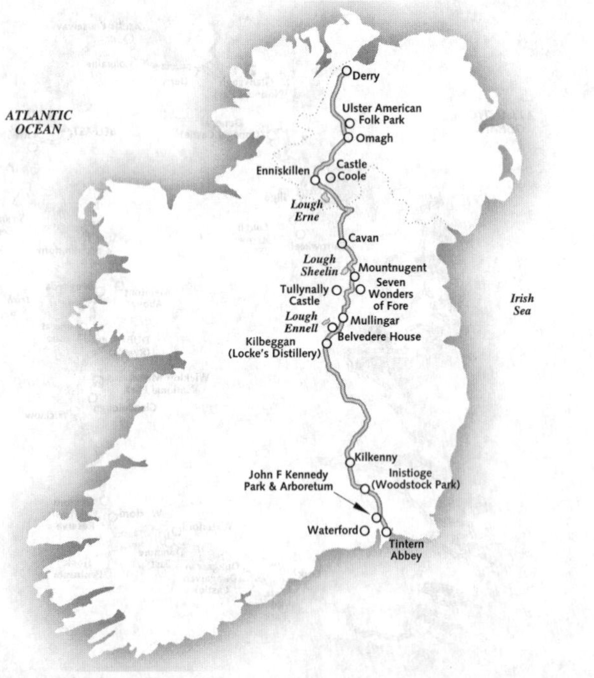

ROADS LESS TRAVELLED

IRELAND'S CENTRE

1 week / Roscommon to Offaly

To avoid the throngs in summer, consider a trail around Ireland's less populated central counties. Begin in barren north Roscommon at Arigna by taking a trip down a mining shaft at the fascinating **Arigna Mining Experience** (p451). Head south to Boyle and visit the 12th-century **Boyle Abbey** (p451) and **King House** (p451) manor and former military barracks before continuing on to the vibrant market town of **Carrick-on-Shannon** (p454) with its marina and fine architecture. Just south of Carrick at Tulsk, in the heart of Roscommon's flat land, is the **Cruachan Aí Visitor Centre** (p449), which explores the mystical Celtic site of Rathcroghan with its 60 megalithic tombs and burial sites. Learn about Ireland's terrible legacy in the **Irish Famine Museum** (p449) before crossing the Shannon to the **Corlea Trackway Visitor Centre** (p456), Europe's widest timber trackway dating from 148 BC, hidden in the tranquil Keenagh boglands. You could take a mellow trip round the Shannon on a rowing boat from beautiful **Glasson** (p463) village nearby, with its fine restaurants and pub. Heading southeast, horse-lovers, gardeners and children will all enjoy a visit to the **National Stud and Japanese Gardens** (p315) in Kildare with its equine museum, stables and sunken gardens. Looping eastward, **Birr** (p327) town with its many restaurants and the stunning 17th-century **Birr Castle** (p328), its surroundings housing a **science centre** and the **telescope** used to map the mountains of the moon, should precede a jaunt over the haunting **Slieve Bloom Mountains** (p325).

If you're after a taste of real, unpolished rural Ireland, this central tour is for you. Take your time over a week or pick 'n' mix attractions en route west from Dublin. Culture vultures and cruisers will be happy campers on this trail of the best of hidden Ireland.

BEST OF THE ISLANDS

3 weeks / Tory to West Cork

Ireland's outlying islands are many and varied and offer the visitor an insight into a traditional lifestyle rarely seen in the Western world. Start at the barren and remote **Tory** (p484), off Bloody Foreland in Donegal, a Gaeltacht (Irish-speaking) area with a school of primitive painters and a wonderful spot for bird-watching. Joined to the mainland by a bridge, **Achill** (p414) in County Mayo, with its deserted Famine village and dramatic cliffs, is Ireland's largest offshore island and is renowned for its water sports. **Inishturk** (p412), just south of Achill, with less than 100 inhabitants, gets very little tourist traffic, despite its sheltered sandy beaches. Off the coast of Galway, the three Aran Islands are probably Ireland's most visited. The largest, **Inishmór** (p383), has some fine archaeological remains, including the magical fort of Dún Aengus. The middle island **Inishmaan** (p386), favourite of the writer JM Synge, is a pleasure to walk around with its stone walls and tiny fields. The smallest and least visited **Inisheer** (p388), best accessed from Doolin in County Clare, has some wonderful wild walks. Some of the most special islands to visit are Europe's most westerly **Blasket Islands** (p266), off Kerry, uninhabited since 1953, where you can spot puffins, seals and porpoises. **Skellig Michael** (p243), off Caherciveen in Kerry, a Unesco World Heritage site and home to a 7th-century monastery, is a breathtaking, truly spiritual place and a highlight of any trip to Ireland. Ornithologists and orators alike will enjoy **Clear Island** (p214), also called Cape Clear Island, off the western coast of Cork, famous for its Manx shearwater and its lively Storytelling Festival in September.

If you're one to appreciate the cultural experience and simple pleasures of island life, you won't want to hurry this trail. Take three weeks if you can spare it and experience the unique differences of Ireland's islands properly. Otherwise try to get in at least a day trip.

TAILORED TRIPS

ADRENALINE JUNKIES

2 weeks / Kerry to Sligo

Thrill seekers should kick off their action and adventure tour of the west coast with a **quad biking** (p244) burn out through mountain passes, bog swamps and forest trails of Waterville, County Kerry. The next day, head up the coast to Ballyvaughan in County Clare for a couple of days. Start with some **sea kayaking** (p364) around Galway Bay, followed by **caving** (p359) in Poll na gColm, Ireland's longest cave, in the unique geological terrain of the Burren. Cross the wilderness of Connemara by mountain bike and head for Glassillaun Beach, County Galway to **scuba dive** (p395) in some of the country's clearest waters and see colourful marine life brought north by the Gulf Stream. Down the road in Leenane, nip by **chopper** (p396) to the summit of Connemara's highest mountain, Mweelrea, and scramble down on foot to Killary Harbour to sail its sheltered waters in a **catamaran** (p396). Then test your physical strength and endurance nearby on a cross-country **assault course** (p412) at beautiful Delphi, located next to Ireland's only fjord, before heading north to **surf** (p430) the waves on world-class near-perfect 10ft tubes at Easky, County Sligo.

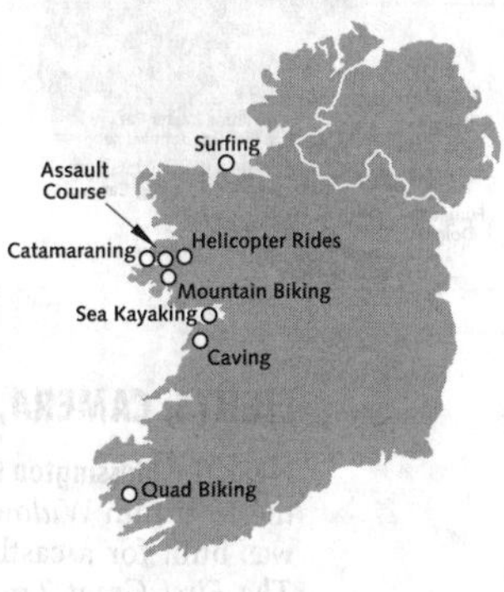

HERITAGE HIKE

1 week / Meath to Offaly

Begin your heritage hike at one of the most important sites in the country, the stunning megalithic tombs of **Newgrange** (p506) and **Knowth** (p507) in Donore, County Meath in the heart of the Boyne Valley. Not far from here, pass Navan's **Hill of Tara** (p512), the seat of the High Kings of Ireland, an important centre of religious and pre-Christian power. Veer south and visit **Castletown House** (p313) in Celbridge, County Kildare, Ireland's largest and most significant Palladian house and estate, en route to the beautiful medieval city of **Kilkenny** (p295) with its 19th-century **Castle** (p297) and parklands. After a day wandering Kilkenny you could catch the Cistercian monastery **Jerpoint Abbey** (p304) with its sculptured cloisters at the pretty village of Thomastown in County Kilkenny. From here, head west to the fine medieval **Rock of Cashel** (p281), standing out on a craggy hill in Cashel, County Tipperary. Heading north to County Galway, stop off at **Portumna Castle and gardens** (p401), a Jacobean manor on the River Shannon. and continue on to world-famous **Clonmacnoise Abbey** (p331), the 6th-century monastic site at Shannonbridge, County Offaly.

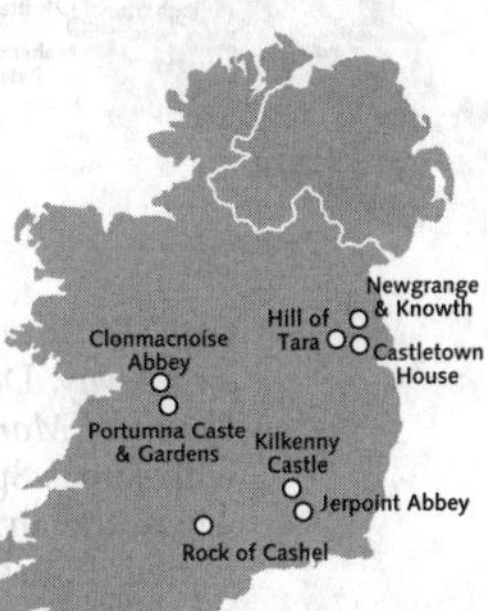

TOT'S TOUR

1 week / Kerry to East Cork

Step back in time with a multimedia tour of medieval Kerry at the **Kerry the Kingdom Museum** (p249) in Tralee. Recharge your batteries on the Tralee & Dingle light **steam train** (p250) and chug around Tralee Bay on a trip back in time. About 1km away, watch wheat being milled at Blennerville in Ireland's largest working **windmill** (p250), built in 1800. Zip on down the peninsula to Dingle to see turtles, stingrays and exotic fish up close in Dingle's **Oceanworld aquarium** (p256). For more watery adventures, catch a boat into the bay to see the friendly **Fungie the dolphin** (p256) at play. The next day make your way to Killarney and take a relaxing tour of town in a **jaunting car** (p235). From here, head east to **Fota Wildlife Park** (p200) in Carrigtwohill, East Cork where you'll see over 90 species of exotic and endangered wildlife like cheetahs, macaques and oryxes.

LIGHTS, CAMERA, ACTION

2 days / Wicklow

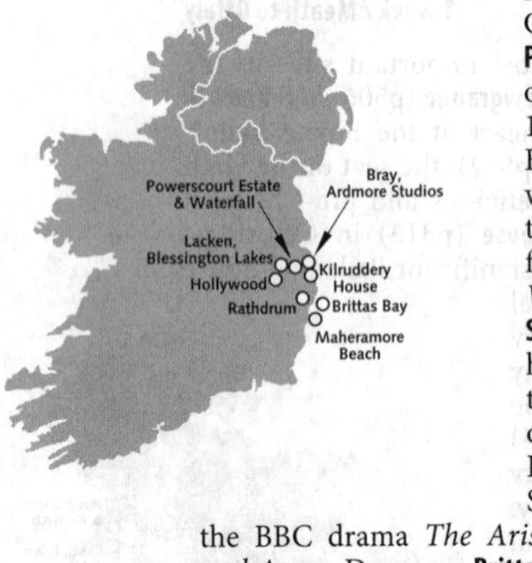

Near the **Blessington Lakes** (p146) is the location for most of the scenes for the 1992 film *Widow's Peak*, starring Mia Farrow, and where a high tower was built for a castle scene in Mel Gibson's *Braveheart*. Continuing on, *The First Great Train Robbery* (1978), starring Sean Connery, used the roof of the Glencree Peace and Reconciliation Centre for a dramatic escape scene. And nearby **Powerscourt Estate** (p138) has hosted the crews of more than 22 feature films, beginning in 1944 with Laurence Olivier's *Henry V*. John Boorman's 1981 Arthurian saga *Excalibur* was made almost exclusively here and around the nearby Powerscourt Waterfall, which also featured Mike Newell's romantic *Into the West*. The hub of indoor production is **Ardmore Studios** (p149) in Bray, host to practically every high-profile Irish film from *The Commitments* to *My Left Foot*. Taking the coastal road south of Bray you pass **Kilruddery House** (p149) and French-style garden, location for part of Stanley Kubrick's period film, *Barry Lyndon*, the BBC drama *The Aristocrats* and some opening scenes from *Far and Away*. Down on **Brittas Bay** (p148) scenes from the epic remake *The Count of Monte Cristo*, starring Guy Pearce, and the ill-fated *Driftwood*, with James Spader, took place. Further south, **Maheramore Beach** (p152) is where the airplane scene in *This is My Father* starring Aidan Quinn was filmed. Finish in **Rathdrum** (p152), where the Railway Bar can be seen in the background during Liam Neeson's impassioned speech as *Michael Collins* in Neil Jordan's historical epic.

The Authors

TOM DOWNS **Coordinating Author, Counties Kilkenny & Galway**

Tom has some Paddy blood in him and can put away Guinness until the cows come home. He likes tramping through bogs, and would live in one, inside a tent, if the situation called for it. He, his wife Fawn and their daughters Mai and Lana live in Berkeley, California.

My Favourite Day

The day before St Patrick's Day, 2003, I arrived on Inishmaan (p386) bright and early on the morning boat. I checked into Máire Mulkerrins' cosy home, filled with heartwarming breakfast scents, and set out to walk the island. Descending from Dún Chonchúir I met an old man named Dara Beag Ó Fatharta, a poet. He recited a lovely poem in Irish, and when I asked its meaning he said the poem imagined what Jaqueline Kennedy must have thought when her husband was shot in the head. That night, a bluegrass band from Dublin played in the pub, and after a couple of clean sets things started to break down. Everyone in the pub sang songs from the soundtrack to *O Brother Where Art Thou* till the wee hours. Heck of a day.

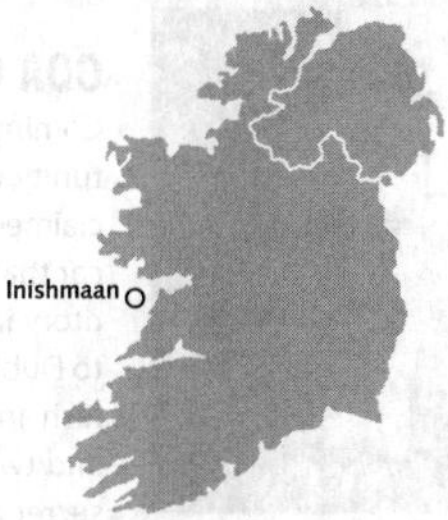

FIONN DAVENPORT **Counties Wicklow, Wexford, Waterford, Mayo, Sligo, Donegal, Meath & Louth**

In 1992 Fionn took on a job as an Irish tour guide – and he quickly discovered (to his first group's dismay) that being born in Ireland and living there most of his life did not an Irish expert make. And so he began to explore the island, beginning with the thatched-cottage pubs and the local discotheques. He realised then that Ireland outside of his hometown of Dublin was like a foreign country, but his ignorance made the process of discovery all the more exciting. Over the years he's been to every county and fallen in love with, and in, a bunch of them, especially Donegal. On a summer's day, it's the greatest place on earth.

DES HANNIGAN **Counties Cork, Kerry, Limerick & Tipperary**

Des' previous work in Ireland includes compiling a publishing database of hundreds of the country's archaeological sites, an odyssey that took him into some of the remotest parts of the west coast. He did similar work cataloguing everything from old buildings to museums, pubs and clubs in Ireland's cities and main towns and has written about Dublin, and about climbing Ireland's mountains, for other publications. In his previous incarnation as a fisherman Des even worked off Kinsale Head, usually in vicious weather, but in a fairly big boat. He lives on the Atlantic coast of Cornwall and catches Irish music on the radio when the pressure's high.

ETAIN O'CARROLL

Central South

Born and bred in the heart of the country, Etain has an insider's approach to life in the vast boggy stretches of rural Ireland. As a travel writer and photographer she has written about Ireland's landscape and culture for a wide variety of magazines and newspapers. Work on the Central South chapter combined the rally driving skills of an experienced pot holer, the elegance of some of Ireland's finest country houses and the inimitable spirit of the race track.

ODA O'CARROLL

Dublin, Central North

Coming from the lesser-known reaches of Roscommon gave Oda the opportunity to wax lyrical about her favourite hotspots of Central North, an area she claimed to know like the back of her hand...until her research. In a near-vintage car that kept breaking down, she was pleasantly surprised to discover virgin territory in her own back yard. Oda remembers the excitement of childhood trips to Dublin, trawling through the Dandelion market in search of luminous nail varnish and the thrill of eating in fast food joints! Almost two decades, one husband and two daughters later, she still loves it and was only too happy to revisit her secret haunts to give you the low-down on the best city in the world.

NEIL WILSON

Belfast, Counties Down, Armagh, Derry, Antrim, Tyrone & Fermanagh

Neil's first visit to Northern Ireland was in 1994, during the first flush of post-ceasefire optimism. His interest in the history and politics of the place intensified a few years later when he found out that most of his mum's ancestors were from Ulster. Researching the Northern Ireland chapters for this edition gave him the chance to climb Slieve Donard, hike the Causeway Coast, and track down ancestral graves in County Fermanagh, in between crawling round Belfast's bars and being impressed by the North's new wave of gourmet restaurants. Neil is a full-time travel writer based in Edinburgh, Scotland, and has written more than 35 guidebooks for half a dozen publishers.

Snapshot

Ask anyone in the world to tell you three things about Ireland and they will most likely mention Guinness, U2 (see Music, p50) and the Celtic Tiger (in Egypt, mysteriously, they're as likely to mention MP Bobby Sands – see p000). Ireland's phenomenal economic U-turn of the mid-1990s, a classic rags to riches story, has become the stuff of legend.

The nation's unprecedented growth, while now abating, meant that the Irish could enjoy a newfound level of prosperity that previous generations only ever imagined; unemployment rates hit an all-time low at the height of the boom, most young people now own a car and take a foreign holiday each year. On top of this Ireland has developed a new confidence, its society has become more secular and outward looking and the arrival of political and economic asylum seekers from around the globe has created a cosmopolitan, less homogenous society. The cease-fire and ongoing peace process in the North (see Good Friday & Beyond, p39) has led to a stability in the region and improved relations with Britain. But the most successful period in Ireland's history hasn't been without its fallout.

While no one would want to return to the brain drain of the 1980s where masses of highly educated young people were leaving for London or the USA and levels of emigration and unemployment were at their highest since the Famine (see The Great Famine, p31), the newly acquired prosperity has led to seismic changes in the Irish psyche and the country's cultural fabric. Ireland's personality has changed in the last decade: some would say for the worse. Undoubtedly it has become a more competitive, stressful and perhaps more aggressive place than before.

There's no denying that Ireland is an expensive place to live; in fact the second most expensive country in the Euro zone, just behind Finland. The introduction of the euro in 2001 led to profiteering as some unscrupulous retailers interpreted the policy of 'rounding up' a little too creatively. Another negative trend has been climbing inflation rates which are now higher than the European average. While personal taxation rates are some of the lowest in Europe, public services have paid the price with the health service in crisis and almost 30,000 people on waiting lists for treatment. The lowest interest rates in 40 years has fuelled ever-spiralling house prices and now owning your own home, especially in Dublin, is beyond most young people's reach. The greater availability of jobs and financial pressure of crippling mortgages has resulted in the return of many women to the labour force. With both parents obliged to work, in most families the availability of childcare has become a problem in both the private and public sector.

With so many people working there's been a huge increase in youth affluence and their significant disposable income has been partly to blame in creating a drink culture that far exceeds Ireland's pub-loving reputation: a nascent problem that is only now being tackled by the government. The 1990s saw a whopping 46% per capita increase in alcohol consumption. Hospital A&E departments are choked at weekends with drink-related casualties and street violence is on the increase. In an effort to control the escalating problem licensing laws have been curbed, restrictions placed on alcohol advertising and a stricter enforcement of public disorder laws effected.

The boom has literally led to overdrive with more cars on the road than the infrastructure can cope with and horrendous traffic jams a

FAST FACTS

Population: 3.9 million

Unemployment: 4.5%

Inflation: 4.3%

Territory size: 70,300 sq km

Annual earnings from tourism: €4 million

Average number of minutes Irish mobile phone users talk per month: 188 (79 minutes more than Germans and 81 minutes more than Britons)

Irish adults who live in a home with satellite TV: 25%

Irish adults who own a deep-fat fryer: 59%

Average age of maternity: 27

daily reality for commuters. Property prices have contributed to an urban sprawl around the country with commuter belts widening and people forced to spend longer amounts of time in cars. Although roads have improved dramatically over the last 10 years, with huge investment from Europe, motorways are only slowly developing and unlike other countries there isn't an efficient public transport system. Road accidents are the greatest cause of death among 15- to 24-year-old Irish men: a new penalty points system introduced by the government in 2003 – some would say belatedly – and a tighter implementation of traffic laws has had an impact in reducing these terrible statistics.

'Road accidents are the greatest cause of death among 15- to 24-year-old Irish men'

Some would say these are the growing pains of an emerging nation.

Ireland has a particularly young demographic, with almost 40% of its population under the age of 24 (see Population, p42). It doesn't take a mathematician to make the connection between this and the fact that contraception was only legalised in 1979.

By the time you read this, smoking in Irish pubs and restaurants will be a distant haze. On 1 January 2004, a nationwide ban on smoking in public places came into law; a move which was welcomed almost universally by all but – unsurprisingly – the vintners association. They cited a report in support of their resistance which alleged that exposure to smoke was not as harmful as previously thought. It later transpired that the report had been funded by the tobacco industry in the USA.

The thorny abortion issue (see Religion, p46) has been temporarily resolved in a typically Irish compromise. Abortion is still illegal but it's no longer illegal to provide information on abortion, and women who travel to Britain to terminate their pregnancies do so without fear of legal sanction.

In their defence the Irish can always point to the 'premium' of the lifestyle available. Open space, wild beaches, rolling countryside, and the fact that the horizon is always visible (the only high-rise building in Ireland – seven blocks of flats in the Dublin suburb Ballymun – began to be demolished in 2003 in a phased, five-year plan) make it an attractive place to live, as does the free, high standard of education and the generally low level of crime.

History

VERY EARLY IRISH & THE CELTS

Our turbulent tale begins about 10,000 years ago, as the last ice caps melted and the rising sea level cut Ireland off from Britain. Hunters and gatherers may first have traversed the narrowing land bridge, but many more crossed the Irish Sea in small hide-covered boats. Farming did not reach Ireland until around 4000 BC. Bronze Age goldworking was of a very high quality in Ireland and stimulated trade with the rest of Europe.

The Celtic warrior tribes who have had such an influence on Irish culture came from central Europe. They had conquered large sections of southern Europe. The Romans called them 'Galli' (Gauls) and the Greeks used the term 'Keltoi', and both societies feared the brutal Celts, who were to plunder Rome in the 4th century AD. They were an imaginative race who put great store in spirituality and the supernatural.

The Celts reached Ireland around 300 BC – they brought the Iron Age with them – and within 200 years they were well ensconced on the island. They established a sophisticated code of law, called the Brehon Law, that remained in use until the early 17th century. Their swirling, maze-like design style, evident on artefacts nearly 2000 years old, is still considered distinctively Irish today. Some excellent ancient Celtic designs survive in the Broighter Collar in the National Museum in Dublin. The Turoe Stone in County Galway is another fine representative of Celtic artwork.

Under the Celts Ireland was divided into five provinces: Leinster, Meath, Connaught, Ulster and Munster. Meath later merged with Leinster. Within the provinces there were perhaps 100 or more minor kings and chieftains controlling sections of the country but Tara in County Meath tended to be the base for Ireland's most powerful Celtic leaders.

The Celts controlled the country for 1000 years and left a legacy of language and culture that survives in Ireland, Scotland, Wales and remote parts of Europe.

Christianity, which of course would play a significant part in the island's history, reached Ireland between the 3rd and 5th centuries. Long-forgotten missionaries surely came before St Patrick, but Ireland's patron saint is traditionally credited for proselytising the native Irish. Patrick lived in the 5th century and as a teenager was kidnapped from Britain by Irish pirates. He found religion while working as a slave in Ireland and escaped back to Britain, before following powerful visions back to Ireland to introduce Christianity to the people there. His base was the town of Armagh.

While the Dark Ages engulfed much of the rest of Europe, Ireland became known as a land of saints and scholars. During the 7th and 8th centuries monks in Ireland wrought beautiful objects in semiprecious metals, and illuminated manuscripts including the famous, intricately detailed Book of Kells (held in Trinity College, Dublin). Clonmacnoise in County Offaly and Glendalough in County Wicklow are outstanding examples of such monasteries.

'While the Dark Ages engulfed much of the rest of Europe, Ireland became known as a land of saints and scholars'

TIMELINE

8,000 BC
The first humans arrive in Ireland, after the last Ice Age ends.

4,000 BC
Farming introduced to Ireland.

OF NORSE & NORMANS

At the end of the 8th century, Norse Vikings came sniffing for booty. They first landed their slim, powerful boats at Lambay Island off Dublin in AD 795. They made surprise attacks along the eastern coast and strategic advances up rivers to inland terrain, where they set up bases and began plundering the prosperous monasteries. Intertribal squabbles prevented the Irish from establishing a unified defence, and Irish weapons and soldiers proved no match for the superbly armed Norsemen.

The Oxford History of Ireland edited by RF Foster is a collection of academic essays that offer a level of insight typically lacking in more general histories.

For a recap of Ireland's history, in a mere 250 pages or less, look for *A Traveller's History of Ireland* by Peter Neville, *Ireland: A Concise History* by Máire and Conor Cruise O'Brien; both are a quick read and cover the basics.

For a concise, 10-minute read on who the Celts were see www.ibiblio.org/gaelic/celts.html

The Vikings spread throughout Ireland during the 9th and 10th centuries. They established a small Viking kingdom called Dubh Linn, which would later become the city of Dublin, and they founded the towns of Wicklow, Waterford and Wexford. In 1014 the Vikings were defeated at Clontarf by Brian Ború, king of Munster, and his forces. Viking domination was broken, but Norsemen stayed in many parts of Ireland, and would soon be joined on the island by another group of former Vikings, the Normans.

The Normans had settled large sections of what is now France and took England in 1066. Their foothold in Ireland came in a deal with Dermot MacMurrough, the king of Leinster, who had been banished by rival kings in 1166. MacMurrough fled to England, where he met Henry II and Richard Fitz-Gilbert de Clare, earl of Pembroke. De Clare, better known as Strongbow, agreed to send an army to Ireland in return for the hand of MacMurrough's daughter and succession to the kingdom of Leinster on MacMurrough's death.

In May 1169, the first Anglo-Norman forces landed in Bannow Bay, County Wexford, and with MacMurrough took Wexford town and Dublin with ease. The following year Strongbow arrived and, after a bloody battle, took Waterford as well as his new bride. Within 12 months MacMurrough had died and Strongbow claimed the final part of the bargain, his title as king of Leinster.

Henry II had taken steps to be recognised by the pope as lord of Ireland, and he watched Strongbow's activities with great interest and growing unease. Fearing Strongbow's growing power, Henry sent a huge naval force to Waterford in 1171 and assumed a semblance of control.

The Normans, like the Norsemen before them, settled and assimilated in Ireland. In 1366, the English Crown attempted to reverse this trend by enacting the Statutes of Kilkenny, which outlawed intermarriage and the Irish language and other customs, but it was too late. By this time the Anglo-Norman barons had established independent power bases. Over the following two centuries English control gradually receded to an area around Dublin known as 'the Pale'. Hence the expression 'beyond the pale' for an area beyond control.

MONARCHS TAKE CONTROL

In the 16th century Henry VIII, wary of an invasion from the French or Spanish through Ireland, moved to reinforce English authority. He set out to destroy the defiant and influential Anglo-Norman Fitzgeralds, earls of Kildare, who posed a serious threat to his supremacy.

In 1534 Silken Thomas, son of the reigning earl, stormed Dublin and its English garrisons on the false pretext that his father had been executed by Henry in England. Henry retaliated with even greater aggression. The

300 BC
Celtic people begin to settle in Ireland, beginning 1000 years of cultural and political dominance.

432 AD
St Patrick begins to convert the Irish to Christianity.

rebellion was squashed and Thomas and his followers were subsequently executed. In a pattern of retribution that was to be frequently repeated in the following centuries, the Fitzgerald estates were divided among English settlers and an English viceroy was appointed.

Henry then launched an assault on the affluent property of the Catholic Church, with whom he had fallen out over his divorce from Catherine of Aragon. Once his armies had pillaged and plundered the Irish monasteries, Henry ensured that the Irish Parliament declared him king of Ireland in 1541.

Elizabeth I further consolidated English power in Ireland, establishing jurisdiction in Connaught and Munster despite rebellions by the local ruling families. Ulster remained the last outpost of the Irish chiefs. Hugh O'Neill, earl of Tyrone, led the last serious assault on English power in Ireland for centuries. O'Neill – who supposedly ordered lead from England to reroof his castle, but instead used it for bullets – instigated open conflict with the English, and so began the Nine Years' War (1594–1603). He proved a courageous and crafty foe, and the English forces met with little success against him in the first seven years of fighting.

The Battle of Kinsale, in 1601, spelled the end for O'Neill and for Ulster. Although O'Neill survived the battle, his power was broken and he surrendered to the English Crown. In 1607, O'Neill and 90 other Ulster chiefs sailed to Europe, leaving Ireland forever. This was known as the Flight of the Earls, and it left Ulster open to English rule.

With the native chiefs gone, Elizabeth and her successor, James I, pursued a policy of colonisation known as the Plantation – an organised, ambitious confiscation of land that sowed the seeds for the division of Ulster that still exists. Huge swathes of land were taken from the Irish and given to English gentlemen 'undertakers', who carved up the land and gave it to Scottish and English settlers. Unlike previous invaders, these new Protestant landowners were not about to assimilate with the impoverished, angry population of Irish and Anglo-Norman Catholics.

THE GROWING RELIGIOUS DIVIDE

The English Civil War, which lasted for much of the 1640s, had severe repercussions for Ireland. The native Irish and Anglo-Norman Catholics, allied under the 1641 Confederation of Kilkenny, supported Charles I against the Protestant parliamentarians in the hope of restoring Catholic power in Ireland. Much blood was spilled on Irish soil during the decade-long rebellion.

After Charles' defeat and execution, the victorious Oliver Cromwell, leader of the parliamentarians, decided to 'restore order' in Ireland. He arrived in 1649 and, after a ruthless massacre in Drogheda, rampaged through the country leaving a fearsome trail of death behind him. Word of his barbaric conduct spread quickly and towns often gave up without a fight when his army approached. Many Irish were dispossessed and exiled to the harsh, infertile lands of Connaught. Two million hectares of land were confiscated – more than 25% of the country – and handed over to Cromwell's supporters.

In 1689, scarcely more than two decades after Restoration (the re-establishment of the British monarchy after the execution of Charles I),

DID YOU KNOW?

In the early 17th century Plantation, Protestants were 'planted' in Ulster; these English and Scot settlers represented a ready militia loyal to the Crown.

795

Vikings land on east coast, and later begin to settle Ireland.

1169–71

Normans, under the leadership of Strongbow, begin conquest of Ireland in 1169.

Hell or Connaught by Peter Berresford Ellis delves into the bleak years surrounding Cromwell's destructive tour of Ireland in the mid-17th century.

the openly Catholic James II was forced to flee England. He intended to raise an army in Ireland and regain his throne from the Protestant William of Orange, who had been appointed by parliament. James II arrived at Kinsale in March and headed north to Dublin, where the Irish Parliament recognised him as king and began to organise the return of expropriated land to Catholic landowners. To this end, James' forces began a siege of Derry that would cause mass starvation. The Protestant slogan 'No Surrender!', which acquired mythical status among Irish Protestants over the following centuries, dates from the siege.

The siege lasted from April to July 1690, when William's ships landed with an army of 36,000 men. The Battle of the Boyne was fought between Irish Catholics (led by James II, a Scot) and English Protestants (led by William of Orange, a Dutchman) on 12 July. William's victory was a turning point and is commemorated to this day by Northern Protestants as a pivotal victory over 'popes and popery'.

Oppressive penal laws, known collectively as the 'popery code', were enacted in 1695 to prohibit Catholics from owning land or entering any profession. Irish culture, music and education were banned in the hope that Catholicism would be eradicated. Most Catholics continued to worship at secret locations, but some prosperous Irish converted to Protestantism to preserve their careers and wealth. Land was steadily transferred to Protestant owners, and a significant majority of the Catholic population became tenants living in wretched conditions. By the late 18th century Catholics owned barely 5% of the land.

THE DAWN OF IRISH NATIONALISM

In the aftermath of the American War of Independence and the French Revolution, a Belfast organisation called the United Irishmen was formed. Its most prominent leader was a young Dublin Protestant, Theobald Wolfe Tone (1763–98). The United Irishmen started out with high ideals of bringing together men of all creeds to reform and reduce Britain's power in Ireland, but their attempts to gain power through straightforward politics proved fruitless.

For the Cause of Liberty: A Thousand Years of Ireland's Heroes by Terry Golway vividly describes the struggles of Irish Nationalism.

When war broke out between Britain and France, the United Irishmen found they were no longer tolerated by the establishment. They re-formed themselves as an underground organisation committed to bringing change by any means. Wolf Tone looked to France for help, and loyalist Protestants prepared for possible conflict by forming the Protestant Orange Society, which later became known as the Orange Order.

In 1796 a French invasion fleet, with thousands of troops and Wolfe Tone aboard, approached Bantry Bay in County Cork. On shore, the local militia were ill equipped to repel them. However, a strong offshore wind frustrated attempts to land and the ships and a disappointed Wolfe Tone were forced to return to France.

The government in Ireland began an effective nationwide campaign to hunt out United Irishmen. Floggings and indiscriminate torture sent a wave of panic through the population and sparked the 1798 Rising. Wexford, a county not noted for its rebellious tendencies, experienced the fiercest fighting, with Father John Murphy leading the resistance.

1366

Statutes of Kilkenny prohibit Anglo-Irish intermarriage, after two centuries of Norman assimilation in Ireland.

1530s

Henry VIII of England squashes Fitzgerald rebellion and distributes their vast landholdings among English settlers.

After a number of minor victories the rebels were decisively defeated at Vinegar Hill just outside Enniscorthy.

The persistent Wolfe Tone returned later in 1798 with another French fleet, but was defeated at sea. Wolfe Tone was captured and taken to Dublin where he committed suicide in his prison cell. It was the end for the United Irishmen.

The Protestant gentry, alarmed at the level of unrest, now sought the security of British authority, and in 1800 the Act of Union united Ireland politically with Britain. The Irish Parliament voted itself out of existence and around 100 of the Members of Parliament (MPs) moved to the House of Commons in London.

In the meantime, Daniel O'Connell (1775–1847), a Catholic from Kerry, had started on a course that would make him one of Ireland's most significant leaders. In 1823 O'Connell founded the Catholic Association with the aim of achieving political equality for Catholics. The association soon became a vehicle for peaceful mass protest and action. In the 1826 general election it first showed its muscle by backing Protestant candidates who were in favour of Catholic emancipation.

In 1828 O'Connell himself stood for a seat in County Clare, even though, being a Catholic, he couldn't take the seat. O'Connell won easily, putting the British Parliament in a quandary. If they didn't allow O'Connell to take his seat, there might be a popular uprising. Many in the House of Commons favoured emancipation, and the combination of circumstances led them to pass the 1829 Act of Catholic Emancipation, allowing some well-off Catholics voting rights and the right to be elected as MPs.

O'Connell then sought to secure further reforms. He turned his attentions to the repeal of the Act of Union and the re-establishment of an Irish Parliament, which this time would include Catholic MPs. In 1843 the campaign took off, with O'Connell's 'monster meetings' attracting up to half a million supporters and taking place all over Ireland. O'Connell exploited the threat that such gatherings represented to the establishment, but he balked at a genuinely radical confrontation with the British. His bluff was called when a monster meeting at Clontarf was prohibited and he called it off.

O'Connell was arrested in 1844 and served a short spell in prison. He fell out with the Young Ireland movement (which, having seen pacifism fail, favoured the use of violence) and never again posed a threat to the British. He died in 1847.

THE GREAT FAMINE

One of Ireland's worst tragedies, the Great Famine of 1845–51, during which a staggering three million people died or were forced to emigrate from Ireland is all the more inconceivable given that the scale of suffering was attributable to selfishness as much as natural causes. Potatoes were the staple food of a rapidly growing, desperately poor population and when a blight hit the crop, prices soared. The repressive penal laws ensured that farmers, already crippled with high rents, could ill afford the little subsistence potatoes provided. Inevitably, most tenants fell into arrears with little or no concession given by mostly indifferent landlords and were evicted or sent to the dire conditions of the workhouses.

The Great Hunger by Cecil Woodham-Smith is the classic study of the Great Famine of 1845–51.

The Great Shame by Thomas Keneally is a gripping tome that delves into the Great Famine and the ensuing diaspora.

1608

Bushmills, the world's oldest licensed distillery, officially opens for business.

1610

Start of Plantation, in which English colonise Ulster and assume ownership of land.

Shamefully, during this time there were abundant harvests of wheat and dairy produce – the country was producing more than enough grain to feed the entire population and it's said that more cattle were sold abroad than there were people on the island. But while millions of its citizens were starving, Ireland was forced to export its food to Britain and overseas.

DID YOU KNOW?

In 1870, after the Great Famine and ongoing emigration, more than one-third of all native-born Irish lived outside of Ireland.

The Poor Laws in place at the height of the Famine deemed landlords responsible for the maintenance of their poor and encouraged many to 'remove' tenants from their estates by paying their way to America. Many Irish were sent unwittingly to their deaths on board the notoriously scourged 'coffin ships'. British Prime Minister Sir Robert Peel made well intentioned but inadequate gestures at famine relief, and some – but far too few – landlords did their best for their tenants.

Mass emigration continued to reduce the population during the next 100 years and huge numbers of Irish emigrants who found their way abroad, particularly to the USA, carried with them a lasting bitterness.

PARNELL & THE LAND LEAGUE

In spite of the bitterness aroused by the Famine, there was little challenge to Britain's control of Ireland for quite some time. One rebellion was the abortive Fenian (Irish Republican Brotherhood) rising in March 1867.

In 1875 Charles Stewart Parnell (1846–91) was elected to Westminster. The son of a Protestant landowner from County Wicklow, he had much in common with other members of the Anglo-Irish Ascendancy (ruling classes). But Parnell's mother was American and her father had fought the British in the American War of Independence. Parnell's family supported the principle of Irish independence from Britain. He quickly became noticed in the House of Commons as a passionate, difficult member who asked awkward questions. At 31 he became leader of the new Home Rule Party, which advocated a limited form of autonomy for Ireland.

DID YOU KNOW?

The term 'boycott' comes from Charles C Boycott, a County Mayo land agent who was, yes, boycotted by Parnell's Land League in 1880.

In 1879 Ireland appeared to be facing another famine as potato crops were failing once again and evictions were becoming widespread. Cheap corn from America had pushed down grain prices and with that the earnings of the tenants who grew grain on their plots. Michael Davitt, a Fenian, began to organise the tenants and found a sympathetic ear in Parnell. Together forming the Land League, Parnell and Davitt initiated widespread agitation for reduced rents and improved working conditions. The conflict heated up and there was violence on both sides. Parnell instigated the strategy of 'boycotting' tenants, agents and landlords who didn't adhere to the Land League's aims: they were treated like lepers by the local population.

The Land War, as it became known, lasted from 1879 to 1882 and was momentous. For the first time, tenants were defying their landlords en masse. The Land Act of 1881 improved life immeasurably for tenants, creating fair rents and the possibility of tenants owning their land.

A crisis threatened in 1882 when two of the Crown's leading figures in Ireland were murdered by nationalists in Phoenix Park, Dublin, and Parnell was wrongly implicated. However, reform had been achieved, and Parnell turned his attentions to Home Rule. He had an extraordinary ally in Prime Minister William Gladstone, who was dependent on Parnell for crucial

1649

Cromwell lays waste throughout Ireland after the Irish support Charles I in English Civil War.

1690

William of Orange leads his Protestant army to victory over the Catholic forces of James II in the Battle of the Boyne.

support in Parliament. But Gladstone and Parnell had their Home Rule Bill defeated, partly as a result of defections from Gladstone's own party.

The end was drawing near for Parnell. For 10 years he had been having an affair with Kitty O'Shea, who was married to a member of his own party. When the relationship was exposed in 1890, Parnell refused to resign as party leader and the party split. Parnell married O'Shea, was deposed as leader and the Catholic Church in Ireland quickly turned against him. The 'uncrowned king of Ireland' was no longer welcome. Parnell's health deteriorated rapidly and he died less than a year later.

HOME RULE BECKONS

Gladstone was elected as prime minister for a fourth term in 1892 and this time managed to get his Home Rule for Ireland Bill through the House of Commons, only to see it thrown out by the House of Lords.

By now, eastern Ulster was quite prosperous. It had been spared the worst effects of the Famine, and heavy industrialisation meant the Protestant ruling class was doing nicely. While Gladstone had failed for the time being, the Ulster Unionists (the Unionist Party had been formed in 1885) were now acutely aware that Home Rule could resurface and were determined to fight if it became law. The unionists, led by Sir Edward Carson (1854–1935), a Dublin lawyer, formed a Protestant vigilante brigade called the Ulster Volunteer Force (UVF), which held a series of mass paramilitary rallies mustering strong opposition to Home Rule. Carson threatened an armed struggle for a separate Northern Ireland if independence was granted to Ireland. The British began to bend before this Ulster opposition and, in July 1914, Carson agreed that Home Rule could go through for Ireland, so long as Ulster was kept separate and thus Ireland's partition was established.

Ireland Since the Famine by FSL Lyons is a standard history for all students of modern Ireland.

In Britain a new Liberal government under Prime Minister Asquith had removed the House of Lords' power to veto bills and began to put another Home Rule for Ireland Bill through parliament. The bill was passed (but not enacted) in 1912 against strident unionist and Conservative British opposition.

As the UVF grew in strength, a republican group called the Irish Volunteers, led by the academic Eoin MacNeill, was set up in the south

THE GAELIC REVIVAL

While Home Rule was being debated and shunted, something of a revolution was taking place in Irish arts, literature and identity. The poet William Butler Yeats and his coterie of literary friends (including Lady Gregory, Douglas Hyde, John Millington Synge and George Russell) championed the Anglo-Irish literary revival, unearthing old Celtic tales and writing with fresh enthusiasm about a romantic Ireland of epic battles and warrior queens. For a country that had suffered centuries of invasion and deprivation, these images presented a much more attractive version of history.

Similarly, Hyde and Eoin MacNeill did much to ensure the survival of the Irish language and the more everyday Irish customs and culture, which they believed to be central to Irish identity. They formed the Gaelic League (Conradh na Gaeilge) in 1893, which, among other things, pushed for the teaching of Irish in schools. Meanwhile, the strongly politicised Gaelic Athletic Association (GAA) promoted Irish sport and culture.

1695
Penal laws prohibit Catholics from buying property; within 100 years, Catholics would own only 5% of Irish land.

1759
Guinness Brewery founded.

to defend Home Rule for the whole of Ireland. They lacked the weapons and organisation of the UVF, however, which succeeded in large-scale gunrunning, and in 1914, with widespread support from the British army, civil war loomed.

The Home Rule Act was suspended at the outbreak of WWI in August 1914 and for a time the question of Ulster was left unresolved.

THE EASTER RISING

Many Irishmen with nationalist sympathies went off to the battlefields of Europe believing their sacrifice would compel Britain to follow through on the promise of Home Rule for Ireland. However, a minority of nationalists in Ireland was not so trusting of British resolve. While many Irish Volunteers agreed with John Redmond's wait-and-see approach, a growing radical faction believed a more revolutionary course of action was necessary.

Two small groups – a section of the Irish Volunteers under Pádraig Pearse and the Irish Citizens' Army led by James Connolly – conspired in a rebellion that took the country by surprise. The insurrection was counting on a shipment of arms from Germany, but the arms were intercepted by the British navy, and Eoin MacNeill, annoyed that the rising had been planned without him, attempted to call the rebellion off. A depleted Volunteer group marched into Dublin on Easter Monday

COUNTESS MARKIEVICZ

Born Constance Georgina Gore-Booth to a wealthy family in Lissadell, County Sligo, in 1868, the Countess Markievicz (as she later became known) played a pivotal role in the 1916 Easter Rising. Having her subsequent death sentence commuted to life, she went on to become the first woman elected to British Parliament – a seat she refused to take – and later the first female government minister in any modern democracy.

As a privileged child she displayed an early solidarity with the underdog, helping the peasants on her estate with their manual chores. At 19, the strident young woman was presented at court to Queen Victoria as 'the new Irish beauty' and entered society as a member of the Anglo-Irish landed gentry. Tired of the normal social whirlwind of hunts and balls and with aspirations to be a painter, Constance left Ireland to study at the Slade School and later to Julien's in Paris where she met and married Count Casimir Markievicz, a Polish Catholic landowner. They returned to Lissadell for the birth of her daughter.

By 1908 Constance was fully immersed in the Dublin theatrical scene – a vehicle for nationalist feeling – and was propelled towards an all-consuming anti-British devotion. She joined Inghinidhe na hÉireann (Daughters of Erin) and soon established the Fianna, a nationalist boy scout movement and military training ground for later Volunteers.

As her military activities became more involved, her marriage deteriorated and, by the 1916 Rising, her husband had left a fully fledged republican activist in his wake. She was sentenced to death after the Rising but had it commuted to life imprisonment, and on her release a year later, she returned to Ireland unbroken, a Catholic and a national hero. Refusing her British Parliament seat two years later from the confines of Holloway prison, she opted instead for a seat as Minister for Labour of the newly formed Dáil Éireann under Eamon de Valera. Her continued fighting in the civil war, a spell in a workhouse and a hunger strike all contributed to her deteriorating health, and the maverick countess died in a slum hospital among Dublin's poor in 1927.

1798

Anti-English United Irishmen are hunted, leading to 1798 Rising that is squashed.

1828

Daniel O'Connell, a Catholic, wins a seat in Parliament, leading to new laws granting limited voting rights to Catholics.

1916, and took over a number of key positions in the city, claiming the General Post Office on O'Connell St as their headquarters. From its steps Pearse read out to passers-by a declaration that Ireland was now a republic and that his band was the provisional government. Less than a week of fighting ensued before the rebels surrendered to the superior British forces. The rebels weren't popular and had to be protected from angry Dubliners as they were marched to jail.

Many have speculated that Pearse, realising they didn't stand a chance, had been driven by the need for a blood sacrifice to galvanise the nation. Whether or not he actually believed this, a blood sacrifice was on the way.

'The rebels weren't popular and had to be protected from angry Dubliners as they were marched to jail'

The Easter Rising would probably have had little impact on the Irish situation had the British not unwittingly made martyrs of the leaders of the rebellion. Of the 77 given death sentences, 15 were executed. Pearse was shot three days after the surrender, and nine days later James Connolly was the last to die, shot in a chair because he couldn't stand on a gangrenous ankle. The executions provoked a sea change in public attitudes, and support for the republicans rose dramatically.

Countess Markievicz (see p34) was one of those not executed, because she was female, and Eamon de Valera's (1882–1975) death sentence was commuted to life imprisonment because of his US citizenship; he was freed after an amnesty in 1917.

In the 1918 general election, the republicans stood under the banner of Sinn Féin and won a large majority of the Irish seats. Ignoring London's Parliament, where technically they were supposed to sit, the newly elected Sinn Féin deputies – many of them veterans of the 1916 Easter Rising – declared Ireland independent and formed the first Dáil Éireann (Irish assembly or lower house), which sat in Dublin's Mansion House under the leadership of Eamon de Valera. The Irish Volunteers became the Irish Republican Army (IRA) and the Dáil authorised them to wage war on British troops in Ireland.

A lot more blood would soon seep into Irish soil.

THE ANGLO-IRISH WAR

The day the Dáil convened in Dublin in January 1919, two policemen were shot dead in County Tipperary. Thus began the bitter Anglo-Irish War, which would last 2½ years. The charismatic and ruthless Michael Collins (1890–1922) now came to the fore, masterminding the campaign of violence against the British.

The war quickly became entrenched and bloody. The IRA faced a coalition of the Royal Irish Constabulary, regular British army soldiers and two groups of quasi-military status (the Auxiliaries and the notoriously brutal Black and Tans, who were newly demobbed British soldiers), who rapidly gained a vicious reputation. The Black and Tans' use of violence and corruption compounded resentment against the British and bolstered fervent support for the nationalist cause. The hunger-strike death of Terence MacSwiney, mayor of Cork, further crystallised Irish opinion. The IRA created 'flying columns', small groups of armed volunteers to ambush British forces, and on home ground they operated successfully. A truce was eventually agreed in July 1921.

1845–51

During the Great Famine, caused by blighted potato crops, three million Irish die or are forced to emigrate.

1879–82

In the Land War, tenant farmers gain fair rents and make it possible for farmers to own their land.

To gain some insight into the mind of Michael Collins, read *In His Own Words*, a collection of Collins' writings and speeches. Neil Jordan's motion picture *Michael Collins*, starring Liam Neeson as the revolutionary, depicts the Easter Rising, the founding of the Free State and Collins' violent demise.

After months of difficult negotiations in London, the Irish delegation signed the Anglo-Irish Treaty on 6 December 1921. It gave 26 counties of Ireland independence and allowed six largely Protestant Ulster counties the choice of opting out. If they did (a foregone conclusion), a Boundary Commission would decide on the final frontiers between north and south.

The Treaty negotiations had been largely undertaken on the Irish side by Collins and Griffith. Both knew that many Dáil members wouldn't accept the loss of the North, or the fact that the British monarch would still be head of the new Irish Free State and Irish MPs would still have to swear an oath of allegiance to the Crown. Nevertheless, they signed the Treaty without checking with de Valera in Dublin.

Collins regarded the issue of the monarchy and the oath of allegiance as largely symbolic. He also hoped that the six northeastern counties wouldn't be a viable entity and would eventually become part of the Free State. During the Treaty negotiations he was convinced that the Border Commission would decrease the size of that part of Ireland remaining outside the Free State. Knowing the risks of signing the agreement he declared: 'I may have signed my death warrant tonight.'

PARTITION & CIVIL WAR

On 22 June 1921 the Northern Ireland Parliament came into being, with James Craig as the first prime minister. Catholic nationalists elected to the Parliament took up their seats with reluctance and from the start the politics of the North was divided on religious grounds.

Meanwhile, the Irish Free State, as southern Ireland was known until 1949, was established and the unpopular treaty was ratified in the Dáil in January 1922. In June the country's first general election resulted in victory for the pro-Treaty forces. Fighting broke out two weeks later. Collins failed to persuade his colleagues to accept the Treaty, and a bitter civil war broke out between comrades who, a year previously, had fought alongside each other. Collins was shot in an ambush in County Cork and Griffith died from pure exhaustion and anxiety. De Valera was briefly imprisoned by the new Free State government, under Prime Minister William Cosgrave, which went so far as to execute 77 of its former comrades. The Civil War then ground to an exhausted halt in 1923.

After boycotting the Dáil for a number of years, de Valera founded a new party, called Fianna Fáil (Warriors of Ireland), which won nearly half the seats in the 1927 election. De Valera and the other new teachta Dála (TDs; members of the Dáil) entered the Dáil without taking the oath of allegiance to the Crown.

Fianna Fáil won a majority in the 1932 election and remained in power for 16 years. De Valera introduced a new constitution in 1937, doing away with the oath and claiming sovereignty over the six counties of the North. De Valera also refused to pay land annuities, which had been agreed upon in the Anglo-Irish Treaty, to the British government. An economic war with Britain ensued, which severely crippled Irish agriculture and was resolved only shortly before the 1948 general election.

1890s

Gaelic Revival, championed by poet WB Yeats, helps intensify pride in Irish traditions and culture.

1904

June 16 is immortalised in James Joyce's *Ulysses*.

THE REPUBLIC

Fianna Fáil lost the 1948 general election to Fine Gael (the direct descendants of the first Free State government) in coalition with the new republican Clann an Poblachta. The new government declared the Free State to be a republic at last. Ireland left the British Commonwealth in 1949, and in so doing the south cut its final links to the north.

When Sean Lamass came to power in 1959, as successor to de Valera, he sought to stem the continuing emigration by improving the country's economic prospects. By the mid-1960s his policies had been successful enough to reduce emigration to less than half what it had been a decade earlier, and many who had left began to return. He also introduced free secondary education.

In 1972 the Republic (along with Northern Ireland) became a member of the European Economic Community (EEC). At first, membership brought some measure of prosperity, but by the early 1980s Ireland was once more in economic difficulties and emigration figures rose again. By the early 1990s the Irish economy had begun to recover and is now one of the strongest in Europe.

Meanwhile, the Catholic Church's grip on cultural and ethical issues began to loosen. The results of referenda in the 1980s on abortion and divorce left both illegal, but another referendum on divorce in 1995 was narrowly accepted.

'Ireland left the British Common-wealth in 1949, and in so doing the south cut its final links to the north'

Although the president's power is limited, the election of barrister Mary Robinson to the presidency in 1990 saw her modernise the institution and start to wield considerable informal influence over social policies. Her work contributed to a shift away from the traditionally conservative attitudes on issues such as divorce, abortion and gay rights.

Robinson was succeeded as president by Mary McAleese, a Belfast-born Catholic nationalist and Queen's University law lecturer. Although more conservative than Robinson, McAleese was elected on a platform of continuing Robinson's work and has shown a similarly tolerant attitude on social issues. This was illustrated in 1999 by her high-profile visit to Outhouse, a gay, lesbian and transgender community centre in southern Dublin, and the following year by controversially receiving communion at a Church of Ireland service.

In 1994 *Taoiseach* (Prime Minister) Albert Reynolds, who had helped negotiate the first IRA cease-fire with Gerry Adams, was forced to resign. His resignation mainly resulted from the appointment of a president to the High Court, Harry Whelehan, who had been criticised for not tackling sexual scandals involving the Catholic Church more vigorously. Reynolds was succeeded by Fine Gael leader John Bruton, who came to power in coalition with the Labour Party and the Democratic Left. Bruton's government was the first to take office without a general election.

When it did face one in 1997 it was ousted by Fianna Fáil under Bertie Ahern, in partnership with the Progressive Democrats and a number of independents. Mary Harney became Ireland's first female *tánaiste* (deputy prime minister).

Bertie Ahern's government has been closely involved in the peace-making process in Northern Ireland. Among other things the 1998 Good Friday Agreement made provision for a North-South Ministerial

1916

Easter Rising gains little support, but subsequent executions of Pádraig Pearse and James Connolly galvanise Irish resistance.

1919–22

Anglo-Irish War leads to partition; Northern Ireland Parliament is established in 1921 and the Irish Free State is founded in 1922.

Council, of which the Irish government would become a part, to deal with issues affecting the whole island. Another outcome of the search for a settlement in the North has been improved relations between the Republic and Britain, symbolised by the invitation from Bertie Ahern to British Prime Minister Tony Blair to address the Dáil.

THE TROUBLES

For 25 years the story of the Troubles, as the conflict between northern Catholics and Protestants became euphemistically known, was one of lost opportunities, intransigence on both sides and fleeting moments of hope.

A History of Ulster by Jonathon Bardon is a serious and far-reaching attempt to get to grips with Northern Ireland's saga.

Peter Taylor's *Provos: The IRA and Sinn Féin* examines the evolution of the IRA, with first-hand accounts from IRA members.

Many films depict events related to the Troubles, including *Bloody Sunday* (2002), *The Boxer* (1997; starring Daniel Day Lewis) and *In the Name of the Father* (1994; also starring Lewis).

By the 1960s the Northern county of Derry's population was split approximately 60% Catholic to 40% Protestant, yet through rigged electoral districts and restrictive voting rights the city's council always maintained a Protestant majority. What began as a peaceful civil rights movement quickly morphed into a violent struggle. In October 1968 a Catholic march in Derry was violently broken up by the Royal Ulster Constabulary (RUC), signalling the start of the Troubles.

In January 1969 another civil rights movement, called People's Democracy, organised a march from Belfast to Derry. As the marchers neared their destination they were attacked by a Protestant mob. The police first stood to one side and then compounded the problem with a sweep through the predominantly Catholic Bogside. Further marches, protests and violence followed, and far from keeping the two sides apart, the police were clearly part of the problem. In August British troops went to Derry and then Belfast to maintain law and order. The British army was initially welcomed in some Catholic quarters, but soon it too came to be seen as a tool of the Protestant majority. Over-reaction by the army actually fuelled recruitment into the long-dormant IRA. IRA numbers especially increased after Bloody Sunday (30 January 1972), when British troops killed 13 civilians in Derry.

Northern Ireland's Parliament was abolished in 1972, although substantial progress had been made towards civil rights. A new power-sharing arrangement, worked out in the 1973 Sunningdale Agreement, was killed stone dead by the massive and overwhelmingly Protestant Ulster Workers' Strike of 1974.

While continuing to target people in Northern Ireland, the IRA moved its campaign of bombing to mainland Britain. Its activities were increasingly condemned by citizens and parties on all sides of the political spectrum. Meanwhile, loyalist paramilitaries began a sectarian murder campaign against Catholics. Passions reached fever pitch in 1981 when republican prisoners in the North went on a hunger strike, demanding the right to be recognised as political prisoners. Ten of them fasted to death, the best known being an elected MP, Bobby Sands.

The waters were further muddied by an incredible variety of parties splintering into sub groups with different agendas. The IRA had split into 'official' and 'provisional' wings, from which sprang more extreme republican organisations such as the Irish National Liberation Army (INLA). Myriad Protestant loyalist paramilitary organisations sprang up in opposition to the IRA, and violence was typically met with violence.

1948

The Irish Free State becomes a Republic.

1969

The violent conflict between Catholics and Protestants in Northern Ireland, known as the Troubles, begins.

GOOD FRIDAY & BEYOND

In the 1990s external circumstances started to alter the picture. Membership of the EU, economic progress in Ireland and the declining importance of the Catholic Church in the South started to reduce differences between the North and South. Also American interest added an international dimension to the situation.

In December 1993 the Downing Street Declaration was signed by British Prime Minister John Major and the Irish Prime Minister Albert Reynolds. It was a crucial element in the peace process, stating that Britain had no 'selfish, strategic or economic interest in Northern Ireland' and enshrining the principle of majority consent at the heart of any talks about constitutional change.

Then, on 31 August 1994, the Sinn Féin leader, Gerry Adams, announced a 'cessation of violence' on behalf of the IRA. In October 1994 the Combined Loyalist Military Command also announced a cease-fire. Most British troops were then withdrawn to barracks, and roadblocks were removed. There followed an edgy peace while all the parties restated their agendas.

A major sticking point became the issue of decommissioning (the Unionist requirement that the IRA show good faith in a final peace settlement by surrendering its weapons before talks began). For their part Sinn Féin and the IRA argued that no arms could be given up until British troops withdrew and political prisoners were freed, and that decommissioning should be part of the final settlement. With the peace process stalled, the IRA declared the cease-fire over when it exploded bombs in Canary Wharf in London on 9 February 1996, killing two people and injuring many more.

Encouraged by the rise of Tony Blair in Britain and Bertie Ahern in the Republic of Ireland, who each stated their commitment to resolving the problems in Northern Ireland, the IRA declared another cease-fire from 20 July 1997. Six weeks later Sinn Féin joined the peace talks.

'The 94% Yes vote in the Republic accepted the end of Dublin's territorial claim to the North'

On 10 April 1998 intensive negotiations culminated in the historic Good Friday Agreement. The agreement, which states that the political future of Northern Ireland depends on the consent of the majority of the people of Northern Ireland, was overwhelmingly endorsed by simultaneous referendums held in Northern Ireland and the Republic on 22 May 1998. Just over 71% of people in Northern Ireland voted to accept devolved democracy, while the 94% Yes vote in the Republic accepted the end of Dublin's territorial claim to the North.

Under the agreement the new Northern Ireland Assembly was given full legislative and executive authority over agriculture, economic development, education, environment, finance and personnel, and health and social services. It also established the terms of reference for an independent commission on the future of policing, plans for the release of most paramilitary prisoners, the removal of security installations and a major reduction in the RUC.

Unfortunately the year of the peace agreement was also one of violence, with rioting over the Parades Commission ban on the annual Orange Order parade at Drumcree, Portadown. Escalating loyalist violence culminated in a petrol bomb attack that burned to death three young

1972

On Bloody Sunday, 30 January, 13 civilians are killed by British Troops in Derry.

1981

Republican prisoners in the North begin a hunger strike and ultimately die of starvation.

'Then on 15 August came the single worst atrocity in the entire history of the Troubles, the bombing of Omagh'

boys on 12 July. Then on 15 August came the single worst atrocity in the entire history of the Troubles, the bombing of Omagh by the Real IRA, a breakaway republican group opposed to the Good Friday Agreement. The 650kg bomb killed 29 people and injured 200. Confused telephone warnings had caused the RUC to evacuate people to the very area where the bomb exploded. Swift action by politicians, including a statement by Gerry Adams condemning the bombing, prevented a loyalist backlash.

Fruitless talks continued until 6 May 1999 when the IRA released a statement saying that it was ready to begin a process that would 'completely and verifiably' put its arms beyond use. At the end of June the arms inspectors reported that they had inspected the arms dumps and concluded that the arms couldn't be used without their detection. But in an October 2000 arms inspection the Independent International Decommissioning Commission (IIDC) declared that no progress had been made on actual disarmament.

These ongoing starts and stalls in the peace process clearly demonstrate that the main players remained hostage to the more extreme elements. Sinn Féin, although committed to the peace process, has to keep its supporters on side to prevent any growth in the dissident breakaway republican paramilitary movements. On the Unionist side, the Ulster Unionist Party faces leakage of their support to the Democratic Unionist Party (and their stated opposition to the Good Friday Agreement) unless they maintain a strong anti-IRA stance.

1990s

New tech industries set the table for the new prosperity of the 'Celtic Tiger'.

1998

Good Friday agreement is endorsed in the North and the Republic, outlining steps for peace in Northern Ireland.

The Culture

THE NATIONAL PSYCHE

The friendliness of the Irish is world renowned. Their welcoming attitude towards strangers and willingness to help or just to pass the time with conversation puts anyone who arrives in the country – whether on a business or leisure trip – at ease. The Irish are outward-looking and proud to be a significant member of the European Union.

Almost two centuries of emigration, starting with enforced emigration during the Potato Famine in the late 1840s through to the Depression of the 1930s and the recessions of the 1970s and 1980s, have given the Irish and their diaspora a sense that they are truly an international race who can influence world affairs. The influence of the Catholic Church is also deep seated and has instilled a sense of responsibility towards neighbours and the less well off. The average Irish social conscience is very strong and time and time again the Irish prove they give more to charity per capita than any other nation. Religious division, while an obvious point of difference in the North, is nonexistent in the Republic where the big divide is between those who are from Dublin and those who are not: those from the country are disparagingly referred to as 'culchies' – a byword for unsophisticated – by Dubliners. But it is a badge worn with pride by those from the country, who have an equally dismissive attitude towards Dubliners, believing that they wrongly consider themselves superior.

'Those from the country are disparagingly referred to as 'culchies' – a byword for unsophisticated – by Dubliners'

The stronghold of Catholicism is losing its grip and church attendance has fallen dramatically in the last 10 years. But the laws and the attitude of the Irish are still conservative. The repressed attitude towards sex – for Catholics, sex is only for procreation – has long gone, but sex is still not something that will be openly discussed or flaunted, especially in rural areas. In a 1995 referendum, divorce was narrowly, but finally, accepted.

The laid-back attitude towards work, however, can be infuriating: hiring equipment, getting repairs to cars, houses, or finding skilled labour quickly can be a bit of a trial with the '*mañana*' culture as strong as ever. Alcohol consumption, exacerbated by the new-found wealth of the tiger economy, is also a problem and only in 2003 did the government start to consider combating the rise in alcoholism through regulation. Drinking is the single most popular pastime, and it is no accident that the 'Irish bar' is one of the country's most successful exports. Rural Ireland has also caught up with the cities, with drugs more readily available and drinking among schoolchildren becoming an increasing concern.

LIFESTYLE

Large families of up to 13 children, not uncommon 10 years ago, have now all but disappeared. Two- and three-child families are now the norm and most parents find they both have to work to make ends meet. It is hard to imagine now, with contraceptives widely available, but in the 1980s contraception was still hard to find for unmarried couples outside of Dublin and without a doctor's prescription – a problem which led to a rash of teenage pregnancies.

The attitude towards gay people in Ireland has also changed for the better since the early 1980s, when there was only one gay nightclub in the whole country. Back then it would have been hard to imagine the current climate, with a transvestite presenting a popular primetime television programme on conservative RTE.

THE GAELTACHT

Were you to limit your travels in Ireland to what was once called the Pale (including Dublin and Counties Wexford and Waterford), or much of the east and south for that matter, you would be forgiven for thinking you were in a monolingual, English-speaking country. That's not the case in the Gaeltacht, a word used collectively to describe the pockets of the Republic where Irish (or Gaelic as it is sometimes called) remains, at least in theory, the first language of communication and commerce among the majority of the population.

Sadly, the Gaeltacht represents only a tiny area of Ireland's linguistic past. If you were to look at a map of Ireland dating from the early 19th century that had been shaded to show the areas in which Irish was spoken as a first language, and then compared it with one marking today's Gaeltacht, you would be shocked to see the extent that the language has lost ground over the past 200 years.

The older map would incorporate more than two-thirds of the island, representing some 2.4 million people. On the more recent map there would be just a dozen small smudges in seven counties, mostly along the west coast. Some 90,000 people live in the Gaeltacht today, with the majority of them – just over 70% – *Gaeilgeoirí* (Irish speakers). But according to the most recent census (2002), only 55.6% of adults there speak Irish on a daily basis.

More than 1.5 million people in the Irish Republic claim to have an ability to speak Irish, but the vast majority say so only because they were required to study it for up to 12 years at school.

The Irish are a pretty homogeneous people and while the traveller (tinker) community would have been the butt of racial intolerance in the past, that minority group has been replaced by others, particularly those with different skin colour. In Dublin especially, verbal abuse and even racially motivated attacks have unfortunately become more common. That said, most rural communities have warmly embraced the many nationalities of asylum seekers and refugees who have been dispersed around the country. The sleepy town of Ballaghadereen in County Roscommon, with a population of 1200, somewhat typically, is now home to 14 different nationalities.

DID YOU KNOW?

Females outnumber males in Dublin by 20,000.

POPULATION

The total population of Ireland is around 5.6 million. This figure is actually lower than 160 years ago. Prior to the 1845–51 Famine the population was around eight million. Death and emigration reduced the population to around five million, and emigration continued at a high level for the next 100 years. Not until the 1960s did this haemorrhaging slow down, but economic difficulties meant that even in the 1980s more than 200,000 people joined the diaspora.

The Republic's population is just more than 3.9 million. Dublin is the largest city and the capital of the Republic, with around 1.1 million people (about 40% of the population) living within commuting distance of the city centre. The Republic's next largest cities are Cork, Galway and Limerick. Ireland's population is predominantly young: 41% is aged under 25 and in fact Ireland has the highest population of 15- to 24-year-olds and second highest of under 15-year-olds in Europe.

DID YOU KNOW?

The most popular names in Ireland are Jack and Sarah.

Northern Ireland has a population of nearly 1.7 million, and Belfast, the principal settlement, around 280,000. It has the youngest population in the UK, with 25% aged under 16.

Since the early 1990s there has been less emigration than immigration, which mostly consists of returning Irish but also immigrants from Britain, other EU countries and North America. The country has also admitted a significant number of refugees from Eastern Europe and Africa.

These figures (and population counts throughout the book) are based on the last census of 2002.

SPORT

Ireland, by and large, is a nation of sports enthusiasts. Whether it's shouting the team on from the sideline or a bar stool, the Irish have always taken their sport seriously. The country played host to the Special Olympics in the summer of 2003 with 7000 athletes taking part in venues around Dublin.

Gaelic Football & Hurling

Ireland has two native games with a large, enthusiastic following – Gaelic football and hurling.

Gaelic football is a fast and exciting spectacle and is hugely popular throughout the country. In recent years, the game has been glamourised by the association of high-profile sponsors and major advertising. The ball is round like a soccer ball and the players can pass it in any direction by kicking or punching it. The goalposts are similar to rugby posts, and a goal, worth three points, is scored by putting the ball below the bar, while a single point is awarded when the ball goes over the bar.

Hurling is a ball-and-stick game something like hockey, but much faster and more physical. Visitors are often taken aback by the crash of players wielding what look like ferocious clubs, but injuries are infrequent. The goalposts and scoring method are the same as Gaelic football, but the leather ball or sliotar is the size of a baseball. A player can pick up the ball on their stick and run with it for a certain distance. Players can handle the ball briefly and pass it by palming it. The players' broad wooden sticks are called hurleys. Women's hurling is called camogie.

Hurling has an ancient history and is mentioned in many old Irish tales. The mythical Celtic hero Cúchulainn was a legendary exponent of the game. Today hurling is played on a standard field, but in the olden days the game might have been played across country between two towns or villages, the aim being to get the ball to a certain spot or goal.

Gaelic football and hurling are played nationwide by a network of town and county clubs and under the auspices of the Gaelic Athletic Association, or GAA (www.gaa.ie). The most important competitions are played at county level, and the county winners out of each of the sport's four provinces come together in the autumn for the All-Ireland Finals, the climax of Ireland's sporting year. The Gaelic football and hurling finals are both played in September at Dublin's newly revamped world-class stadium, Croke Park (see p123). In fact, a match at Croke Park (if you can get your hands on tickets), with the crowd chanting and its electric atmosphere, is a highlight of any trip to the city.

Football & Rugby

Football (soccer) and rugby enjoy considerable support all over the country, particularly around Dublin; football is very popular in Northern Ireland.

The international rugby team consists of players from the North and the Republic and has a tremendous, mostly middle-class following. The highlights of the rugby year are the international matches played against England, Scotland, Wales, France and Italy in the Six Nations championship between January and March. Home matches are played at Lansdowne Rd Stadium, Dublin. See p123 and www.irishrugby.ie for more details.

The North and the Republic field separate international football teams and the Republic's team has had a good record in competitions, making it to several World Cups, including Japan 2002. Roy Keane, the team's captain and one of Ireland's truly world-class players at the time, hit the headlines when he was sent home from the competition after a row with the team's manager, Mick McCarthy. However, the Irish team went on to qualify for the second round and are now ranked 15th in the world. International matches are played at the Lansdowne Rd Stadium, Dublin, and Windsor Park, Belfast (see p562).

Many home players from the North and the Republic play professional football in Britain and the most successful have the status of pop or movie stars. Roy Keane plays for Manchester United, Damien Duff for Blackburn, Stephen Carr and Robbie Keane for Tottenham Hotspur and Shay Given for Newcastle. English clubs Arsenal, Liverpool and Manchester United and Scottish clubs Celtic and Rangers have strong followings in Ireland.

Both the North (www.irishfa.com) and the Republic (www.fai.ie) have their own professional football league.

Golf

Golf is enormously popular in Ireland and there are many fine golf courses. The annual Irish Open takes place in June or July and the Irish Women's Open in September. For details of venues, contact the **Golfing Union of Ireland** (☎ 01-269 4111; www.gui.ie; 81 Eglinton Rd, Donnybrook, Dublin 4). Players to watch out for include Paul McGinley, Darren Clarke, Pádraig Harrington and Graeme McDowell.

'The object of road bowling is to throw a cast-iron ball along a public road (normally one with little traffic) for a designated distance'

Cycling

Cycling is a popular spectator sport and events held annually include the Des Hanlon Memorial Race at Carlow (March or April), and the gruelling Milk Rás (May), which sometimes approaches 1120km (700 miles) in length. In 1998 Ireland hosted the first section of the Tour de France. Current Irish cyclists include Ciaran Power, Aidan Duff and Tommy Evans. For information on events try www.irishcycling.com.

Road Bowling

The object of this sport is to throw a cast-iron ball along a public road (normally one with little traffic) for a designated distance, usually 1km or 2km. The person who does it in the least number of throws is the winner. The main centres are Cork and Armagh and competitions take place throughout the year, attracting considerable crowds.

Handball

Handball is another Irish sport with ancient origins and is also governed by the GAA. It is different from Olympic handball in that it is played by two individuals or two pairs who use their hands to strike a ball against a forecourt wall, rather like squash.

Athletics

Athletics is popular and the Republic has produced a few international stars, particularly in middle- and long-distance events. Cork athlete Sonia O'Sullivan consistently leads in women's long-distance track events worldwide, and Catherina McKiernan is one of the world's top marathon runners. In Ireland, the main athletic meets are held at Morton Stadium, Dublin. The Dublin Marathon is run on the last Monday in October.

Boxing

Boxing has traditionally had a strong working-class following. Irish boxers have often won Olympic medals or world championships. Barry McGuigan and Steve Collins, both now retired, were world champions in their day; Michael Carruth won the world welterweight title in 1998. Dublin's National Stadium is a popular venue.

Greyhound Racing

With fixtures year round, greyhound racing has a strong following in Ireland. There are 20 tracks across the country, administered by the **Irish Greyhound Board** (☎ 061-316 788; www.igb.ie; 104 Henry St, Limerick).

Snooker

Snooker has a cult following in Ireland. The Irish Masters takes place in Dublin in March. Top players are Fergal O'Brien and Ken Doherty, who is the only player in the sport to have ever won both the amateur and professional world championships. Ken Doherty just missed the world championship title in 2003.

Horse Racing

Horses have played a big role in Irish life over the centuries and the country has produced a large number of internationally successful race horses.

A total of 27 racecourses dot the country, including Leopardstown in County Dublin (see p123), Fairyhouse in County Meath, and Naas, Punchestown and the Curragh (p314) in County Kildare. Major annual races include the Irish Grand National (Fairyhouse, April), Irish Derby (the Curragh, June) and Irish Leger (the Curragh, September). For more information on events contact the **Irish Horseracing Authority** (☎ 01-289 2888; www.iha.ie; Leopardstown Racecourse, Foxrock, Dublin).

MEDIA

There are three national newspapers in the Republic – the *Irish Times*, the *Irish Independent* and the *Examiner* – and one national evening paper, the *Evening Herald*. In the north the three main papers are, with the highest circulation, the *Belfast Telegraph*, and the equally popular pro-Unionist *Newsletter* and pro-Nationalist *Irish News*.

Visit www.medialive.ie for everything you wanted to know about Irish media but were afraid to ask.

The *Irish Times* has long prided itself on being the paper of the liberal intelligentsia with a core readership in Dublin. But its reputation took a dent in 2002 when huge losses were incurred after unbridled expansion into the Internet and a decline in readership in the face of a fierce circulation battle with the *Independent* and London newspapers that had started creating Irish editions of their publications.

The *Irish Independent* and its sister Sunday title are owned by one of Ireland's best-known businessmen, Tony O'Reilly, the former boss of Heinz beans and owner of Waterford Glass and Wedgwood China. His papers have always had the upper hand in circulation with a large following in the countryside. And while the *Irish Press*, a paper that had Republican leanings, was around, the paper would have distinguished itself with its anti-Republican stance, a position that is patently continued through the pages of its Sunday edition. Tony O'Reilly has since got special dispensation from the Irish government to accept a knighthood from the UK government and likes to be referred to with his full title as Sir Tony O'Reilly in his own newspapers. His decision to accept the title from a foreign government brought howls of derision in some quarters who felt it was as good as saying being Irish was no longer good enough.

The real divide in the Irish newspapers, however, is between the UK and Irish newspapers. Every tabloid paper now has an Irish edition leading to accusations by media speculators that Irish culture is being coarsened. The traditions of the UK tabloids who have built circulation on the back of celebrity buy ups and salacious stories about sex and crime have inevitably been exported and are beginning to have an influence on the editorial position of the Irish titles, particularly on Sunday.

The *Daily Mail*, considered one of the most right-wing papers in the UK with its anti-immigration, anti-Europe and anti-women stance, arrived in 2002 with a Sunday newspaper, *Ireland on Sunday*, and immediately plunged itself into a bitter war with the *Sunday Independent*.

The Republic has three national television stations: the relatively conservative public broadcaster, RTE, funded by the State, advertising and the license fee; the newer purely commercial TV3; and the critically-acclaimed Irish-language station TG4, which has the most diverse and challenging output.

RELIGION

About 90% of residents in the Republic are Roman Catholic, followed by 3% Protestant, 0.1% Jewish and the rest with no religious belief. In the North the breakdown is about 60% Protestant and 40% Catholic. Most Irish Protestants are members of the Church of Ireland, an offshoot of the Church of England, and the Presbyterian and Methodist Churches.

The Catholic Church has always taken a strong conservative line on abortion, contraception, divorce and censorship, and opposed attempts to liberalise the laws on these matters. But the Church has been weakened by drastically declining attendance, the fall in the number of young men and women entering religious life and by damaging paedophile sex scandals. The Church is now treated with a curious mixture of respect and derision by various sections of the community.

Despite its declining power, the Catholic Church still wields considerable influence in the Republic. It retains control of most schools and hospitals (which are funded by the state), and in rural towns and villages large numbers attend Mass every Sunday. Oddly enough, the primates of both the Roman Catholic Church (Archbishop Sean Brady) and the Church of Ireland (Reverend Robin Eames) sit in Armagh, Northern Ireland, the traditional base of St Patrick. The country's religious history clearly overrides its current divisions.

Yeats Is Dead, edited by Joseph O'Connor and penned by 15 Irish authors from populist Marian Keyes to heavyweight Anthony Cronin and plenty in between, is a screwball comedic caper about a petty criminal who gets his hands on Joyce's last manuscript.

Patrick McCabe's *The Butcher Boy* is a brilliant, gruesome tragicomedy about an orphaned Monaghan boy's descent into madness, by one of Ireland's most imaginative authors. It has received several awards and was made into a successful film.

At Swim-Two-Birds by the late satirical columnist Flann O'Brien (also known as Myles na gCopaleen) is a funny, absurdist novel that uses inventive wordplay in telling the story within a story of a student novelist.

ARTS

Literature

The Irish have always had a distinctive way of using their adopted tongue which differs from other English speakers, and it's this great oral tradition and love of language that contributes to Ireland's legacy of world-renowned writers and storytellers. If you took all the Irish writers off the university reading lists for English literature, the degree courses could probably be shortened by a year!

The first great work of Irish literature was the Ulaid (Ulster) Cycle, written down from oral tradition between the 8th and 12th centuries. The chief story is the *Táin Bó Cúailnge*, about a battle between Queen Maeve of Connaught and Cúchulainn, the principal hero of Irish mythology. Cúchulainn appears in the work of Irish writers right up to the present day, from Samuel Beckett to Frank McCourt.

Some of the more famous names born before 1900 include *Gulliver's Travels* author Jonathan Swift (1667–1745), acclaimed dramatist Oscar Wilde (1854–1900) and, not least, James Joyce (1882–1941).

Samuel Beckett (1906–89) came from an Anglo-Irish background and studied at Trinity College before moving to Paris where he associated with Joyce. Influenced by the Italian poet Dante and French philosopher Descartes, his work centres on fundamental existential questions about the human condition and the nature of self. He is probably best known

JAMES JOYCE

James Joyce (1882–1941) is regarded as probably the most significant Irish writer of the 20th century.

In 1904 three short stories appeared in an Irish farmers' magazine, written under the pen name Stephen Dedalus; later it formed part of *Dubliners*, which was published 10 years later. The final story in this remarkable collection, *The Dead*, was turned into a memorable film by John Huston.

On leaving Ireland with Nora Barnacle in 1904, Joyce spent most of the next 10 years in self-imposed exile in Trieste, Italy. Although he despised the conservatism and repression of the Catholic Church at home, his canon of work draws directly from his experiences of everyday life and people in Ireland, particularly Dublin. It was there he dreamt up his autobiographical novel *Stephen Hero*, which evolved into *A Portrait of the Artist as a Young Man*.

In 1918 extracts of his masterpiece *Ulysses* were published in a US magazine, but notoriety was already pursuing his epic work and censors prevented further episodes from being published until 1922 when, ironically, its sensational reputation contributed to its instant success. Though considered challenging because of its experimental literary style, there is much for a reader new to Joyce to relish on its pages. A testament to its enduring relevance, *Ulysses* has inspired a whole host of Dublin guides based on the events in the novel, and to this day Joyce admirers from around the world converge annually in Dublin to celebrate the time of its setting – Bloomsday, 16 June 1904. Joyce's most daunting but enjoyable work is *Finnegan's Wake*.

Recommended for anyone who wants to know more about Joyce's life is *Nora: A Biography of Nora Joyce* by Brenda Maddox, which was made into a film in 2000. It complements Richard Ellmann's more reverential biography of James Joyce himself.

for his play *Waiting for Godot* but his unassailable reputation is based on a series of stark novels and plays. A good taster of his work might be *Krapp's Last Tape*, a monologue about an old man listening irreconcilably to a tape of himself as a young, idealistic man talking about his dreams, or the black humoured novel *Molloy*.

Playwright and novelist Brendan Behan (1923–64) led a turbulent life, which spawned powerful tragicomic writing. Grappling with alcoholism from an early age, he was expelled from school, and when caught working as a courier for the IRA was sent to reform school in Britain, from where one of his most famous works, *Borstal Boy*, originates. A further incarceration, this time in Mountjoy prison, provided the backdrop for his acclaimed *The Quare Fellow*, a vehicle for Behan's vehement objections to capital punishment. *The Hostage* is one of his most enduring works, a fantastical mixture of slapstick and human anguish. Behan died, a local legend, from alcoholism in Dublin.

CS Lewis (1898–1963), from Belfast, is best known for *The Chronicles of Narnia*, a series of allegorical children's stories. Other Northern writers have, not surprisingly, featured the Troubles in their work.

Ireland has produced its fair share of women writers and out of the Anglo-Irish Ascendancy (ruling classes), most notably, came literary team EO Somerville (1858–1949) and her cousin Violet Martin (1861–1915), who wrote under the pseudonym of Martin Ross and co-penned *The Irish RM*. Molly Keane (1904–96) wrote several books in the 1920s and 1930s under the pseudonym MJ Farrell, then had a literary second life in her 70s when *Good Behaviour* and *Time after Time* came out under her real name.

The Ireland Anthology edited by the late Seán Dunne, poet and literary editor of the *Examiner*, is a good introduction to Irish literature, though, as with any anthology, some might debate its inclusions and omissions. *The Oxford Companion to Irish Literature*, edited by Robert Welch, is a useful reference.

Reading In the Dark by Seamus Deane is thoughtful prose (the Guardian Fiction Prize winner) and recounts a young boy's struggles to unravel the truth of his own history growing up in the Troubles of Belfast.

Double Drink Story by Caitlin Thomas (nee MacNamara), who subjugated her impulse to write under the weight of husband Dylan's celebrity and her own addictions, is an eloquent, self-deprecating account of their debaucherous life, love-hate relationship and the burden of creativity, making a brilliant literary memoir.

Circle of Friends by the queen of Irish popular fiction, Maeve Binchy, ably captures the often hilarious peculiarities of the lives of two hapless country girls in the 1940s, who come to Dublin in search of romance.

Racy London-based Edna O'Brien bases her sensationalist 1997 novel *Down by the River* on the controversial true story of a 14-year-old Dublin girl who was raped and went to England for an abortion.

Ireland can boast four winners of the Nobel Prize for Literature: George Bernard Shaw in 1925, WB Yeats in 1938, Samuel Beckett in 1969 and Seamus Heaney in 1995. The prestigious annual IMPAC awards, administered by Dublin City Public Libraries, accept nominations from public libraries around the world for works of high literary merit and offer a €100,000 award to the winning novelist. Previous winners have included David Malouf (Australian) and Nicola Barker (English).

POETRY

WB Yeats (1865–1939) was both playwright and poet, but it's his poetry that has the greatest appeal. His *Love Poems*, edited by Norman Jeffares, makes a suitable introduction for anyone new to his writing.

Pádraig Pearse (1879–1916) used the Irish language as his medium and was one of the leaders of the 1916 Easter Rising. *Mise Éire* typifies his style and passion.

Patrick Kavanagh (1905–67), one of Ireland's most respected poets, was born in Inniskeen, County Monaghan. *The Great Hunger* and *Tarry Flynn* evoke the atmosphere and often grim reality of life for the poor farming community. You'll find a bronze statue of him in Dublin, sitting beside his beloved Grand Canal (see p98).

Seamus Heaney (born 1939) won the 1995 Nobel Prize for Literature. In 1997 Heaney added the Whitbread Book of the Year to his accolades for *The Spirit Level.* His translation of the 8th-century Anglo-Saxon epic *Beowulf* has been widely praised. Some of his poems reflect the hope, disappointment and disillusionment of the peace process.

Paul Durcan (born 1944) boldly tackles awkward issues such as the oppressive nature of Catholicism and Republican activity in his trademark unconventional style.

Cork-born Irish-language poet Louis de Paor has had two of his collections win Ireland's prestigious Sean O'Riordan Prize. Tom Paulin (born 1949) writes memorable poetry about the North – try *The Strange Museum* – as does Ciaran Carson (born 1948). Many of Paula Meehan's (born 1955) magical, evocative poems speak of cherished relationships.

For a taste of modern Irish poetry try *Contemporary Irish Poetry* edited by Fallon and Mahon. *A Rage for Order* edited by Frank Ormsby is a vibrant collection of the poetry of the North.

Cinema & Television

During much of the 20th century Ireland didn't have a particularly active film-making industry, partly because of the small home market, and it was often left to American or British film-makers to represent Ireland to the rest of the world.

This began to change in 1981 following the creation of the Irish Film Board and the spending of more money on a home-grown film industry, including some attractive tax-incentive packages for foreign film makers in Ireland. By the mid-1990s the Irish film industry was genuinely booming with big budget American features such as Mel Gibson's *Braveheart* and Stephen Spielberg's *Saving Private Ryan* creating ongoing industry employment and a domestic skills base. Plans are afoot to shelve the tax incentive, Section 481, at the end of 2004, which may have bleak consequences for the Irish film industry.

The adventure only begins when youngster Tony accidentally bumps off his girlfriend and tries to bury the evidence in Robert Quinn's stylish and accomplished debut thriller *Dead Bodies* (2003).

Quite a few Irish actors have achieved extraordinary international success in the last couple of decades. Young Dublin soap actor Colin Farrell shot to stardom in 2001 following his naturalistic portrayal of a pre-Vietnam GI in US boot camp *Tigerland*, followed up by *Minority Report* in 2003; Jonathan Rhys-Meyers similarly enjoyed success in glam rock drama *Velvet Goldmine* and *The Age of Innocence*, and Aiden Gillen's versatile talents can be seen in films *The Low Down*, *Mojo*, *Shanghai Knights* and Channel 4 TV drama *Queer as Folk*. Liam Neeson *(Schindler's List)* and Daniel Day-Lewis and Brenda Fricker *(My Left Foot)* have won Oscars; Belfast-born Kenneth Branagh's career has invited comparisons with Laurence Olivier's; Gabriel Byrne starred in a series of hits *(The Usual Suspects, Man in the Iron Mask)*; and Navan man Pierce Brosnan scored the coveted James Bond role. Other actors who achieved success in the same period include Aidan Quinn *(Legends of the Fall)*, Stephen Rea *(The Crying Game)* and Colm Meaney *(The Commitments)*. They have followed in the footsteps of the likes of Richard Harris *(The Guns of Navarone, The Field)*, Peter O'Toole *(Lawrence of Arabia)* and Milo O'Shea *(Barbarella)*.

To this crop of acting talent can be added the screenwriter and director Neil Jordan, whose impressive body of work includes *Mona Lisa* (1986), *The Butcher Boy* (1998) and *The Good Thief* (2003). *The Crying Game* (1992), for which Jordan won an Oscar for best screenplay, is perhaps the most intriguing commercial film to feature the IRA. Jordan's powerful *Michael Collins* (1996) stars Liam Neeson and follows the life of Collins from the Easter Rising to the Civil War and his death in 1922 at the hands of his former comrades.

Other important film-makers are producer Noel Pearson and director Jim Sheridan, who worked together on *My Left Foot* (1989) and *The Field* (1990). *My Left Foot* told the true story of Dublin writer Christy Brown, who was crippled with cerebral palsy. Jim Sheridan's *In the Name of the Father* (1993) starred Daniel Day-Lewis as Gerry Conlon and Emma Thompson as his lawyer. It tells the story of the arrest and conviction of the Guildford Four for a pub bombing in England, then of the struggle to clear their names. Jim Sheridan also wrote the screenplay for Mike Newell's *Into the West* (1993), a romantic story of two children and a mythical white horse.

Pat O'Connor's credits as film director include Bernard MacLaverty's *Cal* (1984) and Maeve Binchy's *Circle of Friends* (1994). Dubliner Damien O'Donnell's follow up to *East is East*, *Heartlands* (2003) is the empathetic story of a simple lad who breaks the mould of his northern English small town existence to win back his girlfriend.

Other young directors to watch out for are Kirsten Sheridan and Robert Quinn.

Inevitably, with the arrival of digital television, terrestrial channels have had to work much harder to maintain audiences. Not that you'd notice though, watching Irish channels. TG4 aside, Irish television is mainly derivative of British and American programming and reflects commercial rather than critical interests. The current taste for reality TV shows hasn't escaped Irish producers and programmes such as *Treasure Island, Who Wants To Be A Millionaire* and *Big Brother* have been franchised or reproduced in a thinly-veiled guise on Irish channels. The hugely successful absurd comedy drama series *Father Ted*, featuring the ridiculous exploits of two parish priests, was famously turned down by RTE before being commissioned in Britain. For a taste of Irish life, tune into the world's longest running chat show, *The Late Late Show*, now hosted by Pat Kenny and in its 42nd year. It has become more a light entertainment promotional vehicle than a serious discussion forum in recent years but still includes plenty of worthwhile material.

John Crowley's pacey, well-scripted drama *Intermission* (2003) follows a host of eccentric characters in pursuit of love, played by Colin Farrell, Colm Meaney and Ger Ryan.

Paddy Breathnach's hilarious road movie *I Went Down* (1998) follows the capers of two unlikely petty criminals sent on a mission by a low-rent loan shark.

Jim Sheridan's authentic drama *The Boxer* (1998) tells the story of a former IRA member's emergence and readjustment from a Belfast prison, to discover everyone, including his girlfriend, has moved on.

Music

The rock band U2 may be Ireland's biggest musical export but when people talk about Irish music they are generally referring to an older, more intimate style of traditional or folk music. For the visitor, the joy of Irish music lies in its sheer accessibility. The biggest names may play the same major venues as the rock stars, but almost every town and village seems to have a pub renowned for its music where you can show up and find a session in progress, or even join in if you feel so inclined.

Hot Press is a fortnightly magazine featuring local and international music interviews and listings.

Until around 1700, the harp was the most important instrument in Irish music. Traditionally, music was performed as a background to dancing, so the 17th-century penal laws did nothing to help by banning all expressions of traditional culture, including dancing. Music was forced underground, which goes some way towards explaining the homely feel of much Irish music today.

In the 1960s, Seán O'Riada (1931–71) of Cork set up Ceoltóirí Chualann, a band featuring a fiddle, flute, accordion, bodhrán and uilleann pipes, and began to perform music to listen to rather than dance to. When his band performed at the Gaiety Theatre in Dublin, it gave a whole new credibility to traditional music. Members of the band went on to form the Chieftains, who still play an important role in bringing Irish music to an international audience.

With added vocals come bands such as the Dubliners with their notorious drinking songs; the Wolfe Tones, who've been described as 'the rabble end of the rebel song tradition'; and the Fureys. Younger groups such as Clannad, Altan, Dervish and Nomos espouse a quieter, more mystical style of singing, while Kila stretch the boundaries by combining traditional music with reggae, Eastern and new-age influences.

Foggy Notions is a visually striking, subversive new magazine catering to eclectic music tastes.

Christy Moore is the most prominent of the contemporary singer-songwriters playing in a broadly traditional idiom. He has been performing since the 1960s, and although a pivotal member of the influential bands Planxty and Moving Hearts, he's probably best known for his solo albums.

The unique Van Morrison, native of Belfast, seems to have been going for ever. In the 1960s he was lead singer with Them, whose anthem *Gloria* was a Beatles-era classic. Appealing to younger audiences, Paddy Casey has been compared to David Gray for his melodic arrangements and intelligent lyrics. Songwriter Mark Geary, returned from New York, has

10 BEST IRISH ALBUMS

- *Astral Weeks* (Van Morrison) One of the seminal records of the 1960s.
- *The Big Romance* (David Kitt) Brilliant ambient-folk debut album, released in 2001.
- *All That You Can't Leave Behind* (U2) The album that sees the band back in genuine form after a few overblown albums.
- *24 Star Hotel* (Mundy) This melodic rocker checks in with some finger-clickingly catchy tunes.
- *Jailbreak* (Thin Lizzy) Famed 1976 album featuring Dublin ditty 'The Boys Are Back in Town'.
- *The Lion and the Cobra* (Sinead O'Connor) Chilling debut with poptastic single *Mandinka*.
- *The Last Man In Europe* (The Blades) The first and best album from Dublin's most underrated band.
- *Everyone Else Is Doing It So Why Can't We?* (The Cranberries) Love 'em or hate 'em, their brooding indie sound sells in its millions.
- *Undertones: Greatest Hits* (Undertones) So many short sharp classics; why not hear them all?
- *Live in Europe* (Rory Gallagher; 1972) It rocks.

been wowing audiences with his bittersweet tunes. Dublin-based soul-folk-rockers the Frames have a phenomenally loyal following and are highly rated for their live performances.

Female singer-songwriters have an equally strong following. The mystical voice of Donegal's Enya, formerly of Clannad, has huge popular appeal internationally. Among the best-known contemporary female singers to look out for are Mary Black, smoky-voiced Mary Coughlan and wild melodion-player Sharon Shannon. Gemma Hayes and Nina Hynes are two younger, more pop-driven songwriters.

No account of contemporary Irish music would be complete without reference to the popularity of country music singer and boy-next-door Daniel O'Donnell, with huge album sales under his belt. Ireland's phenomenal success rate in the Eurovision Song Contest is not to be sniffed at either. First in a long line to receive the honour was a fresh-faced, 16-year-old Dana from Derry in 1970 with 'All Kinds of Everything', followed by Johnny Logan (twice); Ireland won it for three consecutive years from 1992 to 1994, and again in 1996. It was also from that unlikely platform that *Riverdance*, a traditional Irish dance pastiche, became the outstanding success it is today.

During the 1960s when America and Britain were producing revolutionary acts like the Doors, the Beatles, Led Zeppelin and the Rolling Stones, Ireland had its own genre of popular music – the showband. Dickie Rock, Brendan Boyer and the Big Eight, and the Miami Showband gigged around the country playing covers of Top 40 hits.

It wasn't until the late 1960s and 1970s that Rory Gallagher's band Taste and Phil Lynott's Thin Lizzy put Ireland on the map.

The punk explosion of 1976 saw bands like The Boomtown Rats, fronted by an angry but eloquent Bob Geldof, emerge with hugely successful singles 'Rat Trap' and 'I Don't Like Mondays'.

In Northern Ireland, bands such as the Undertones and Stiff Little Fingers were spearheading the musical anarchy. The Undertones' radio-friendly *Teenage Kicks* stands out as an all-time classic single of that era.

In 1978 a group of friends from the Dublin suburb of Artane – Bono, The Edge, Adam Clayton and Larry Mullen Jr – formed The Hype, later known as U2. Their debut album *Boy* in 1980 was the first in a series of classic albums that decade. *War*, *The Unforgettable Fire* and *The Joshua Tree* followed as the band went from strength to strength. With Edge's idiosyncratic guitar playing, Clayton's and Mullen's driving rhythm section and Bono's fervent, emotive lyrics and vocal range, U2 were always primed to fill stadiums with their rock anthems. U2's ability to reinvent themselves from the overblown theatrics of 1993's *Zooropa* to the self-deprecating but no less indulgent *Popmart* tour of 1997 has been a factor in their enduring across-the-board popularity.

In the early 1980s, London-based Irish rabble-rousers Pogue Mahone (the name is phonetically Gaelic for 'kiss my arse') emerged. After a ban by the BBC the more tastefully rechristened Pogues, under the stewardship of singer Shane McGowan, evolved but McGowan's drunken on- and off-stage antics often overshadowded his genuine, empathetic and lucid songwriting talent.

'In the early 1980s, London-based Irish rabble-rousers Pogue Mahone (the name is phonetically Gaelic for 'kiss my arse') emerged'

The demise of guitar-based rock music in the early 1990s paved the way for the emergence of boy bands, a formula with which Ireland has had unmitigated success. First off the school bus in 1993 were Boyzone, an innocuous five-piece from Dublin, headed by Ronan Keating. The combination of good-looks and tried and tested hits to cover was a sure-fire winner. Their first 12 singles reached the Top 5 in Britain and, with a solid fanbase of adoring prepubescents, they went the way of all boy bands and split up. Boyzone's manager Louis Walsh created a second lucrative prodigy, Westlife, who have topped the Beatles' record with seven consecutive No 1 hits in the UK. Sultry half-Zambian diva Samantha Mumba is also on Walsh's books and has been more critically successful with her singles, Bowie-sampled 'Body II Body' and 'Gotta Tell You'. Easy on the eyes and ears, The Corrs, sisters and brother act from Dundalk, combine a touch of the traditional with American pop rhythms and harmonies.

The London-based baroque pop act Divine Comedy, fronted by Derry-born lyricist Neil Hannon, blend jazz, classical and pop influences with tongue-in-cheek lyrics. They've had a string of radio-friendly singles such as 'Generation Sex'.

'The Irish names for forts have ended up in the names of countless towns and villages'

The emergence of a dance scene proper in Britain came about in the late 1980s and, like the arrival of punk, signalled a dissension with the music of the day – in this case excessive stadium rock – and the need for a fresh new sound. Dance culture really only hit Ireland fully in the early 1990s, but it wasn't long before those thumping club beats were ubiquitous. Since then dance culture has evolved and fragmented into distinct identifiable subcultures.

David Holmes from Belfast is probably Ireland's most commercially successful DJ. His Sugar Sweet night (now called Shake Ya Brain) in his home town was the first serious venue for dance music in Northern Ireland. Young Dubliner Johnny Moy has been playing in clubs in Britain and Ireland and touring the major European festivals since 1990. His eclectic taste in Detroit techno, soul and funk has kept him at the fore of the notoriously fickle dance scene in Ireland.

Architecture

Ireland is packed with prehistoric graves, ruined monasteries, crumbling fortresses and many other solid reminders of its long, often dramatic, history. The principal surviving structures from Stone Age times are the graves and monuments people built for their dead, usually grouped under the heading of megalithic (great stone) tombs. Among the most easily recognisable megalithic tombs are dolmens, massive three-legged structures rather like giant stone stools, most of which are 4000 to 5000 years old. Good examples are the Poulnabrone Dolmen in the Burren (see p365) and Browne's Hill near Carlow town (see p322).

Passage graves such as Newgrange and Knowth in Meath (see p506) are huge mounds with narrow stone-walled passages leading to burial chambers. These chambers are enriched with spiral and chevron symbols and have an opening through which the rising sun penetrates on the winter or summer solstice, thus acting as a giant celestial calendar.

The Irish names for forts – *dun*, *rath*, *caiseal/cashel* and *caher* – have ended up in the names of countless towns and villages. The Irish countryside is peppered with the remains of over 30,000 of them. The earliest known examples date from the Bronze Age, most commonly the ring fort, with circular earth-and-stone banks, topped by a wooden palisade fence to keep out intruders, and surrounded on the outside by a moatlike ditch. Outside Clonakilty in County Cork, the ring fort at Lisnagun (Lios na gCon) has been reconstructed to give some idea of its original appearance (see p210).

Some forts were constructed entirely of stone; the Iron Age fort of Dún Aengus on Inishmór (the largest of the Aran Islands) is a superb example (see p383).

After Christianity arrived in Ireland in the 5th century, the first monasteries were built. The early stone churches were often very simple, some roofed with timber, such as the 6th-century Teampall Bheanáin

(Church of St Benen) on Inishmór of the Aran Islands, or built completely of stone, such as the 8th-century Gallarus Oratory on the Dingle Peninsula (see p264). Early hermitages include the small beehive huts and buildings on the summit of Skellig Michael off County Kerry (see p243).

As the monasteries grew in size and stature, so did the architecture. The 12th-century cathedral at Glendalough (p141) and the 10th- to 15th-century cathedral at Clonmacnoise (p331) are good examples, although they're tiny compared with European medieval cathedrals.

Round towers have become symbols of Ireland. These tall, stone, needle-like structures were built largely as lookout posts and refuges in the event of Viking attacks in the late 9th or early 10th centuries.

With the Normans in 1169 came the Gothic style of architecture, characterised by tall vaulted windows and soaring V-shaped arches. Fine examples of this can be seen in the 1172 Christ Church Cathedral in Dublin (see p83), and the 13th-century St Canice's Cathedral in Kilkenny (see p297).

Authentic traditional thatched Irish cottages were built of limestone or clay to suit the elements, but weren't durable and have become rare, the tradition dying out around the middle of the 20th century.

In Georgian times, Dublin became one of the architectural glories of Europe, with simple, beautifully built Georgian terraces of red brick, with delicate glass fanlights over large, elegant, curved doorways. From the 1960s Dublin's Georgian heritage suffered badly but you can see fine examples around Merrion Square (p89).

The Anglo-Irish Ascendancy built country houses such as the 1722 Castletown House near Celbridge (see p313), and the 1741 Russborough House near Blessington (see p147), which are both excellent examples of the Palladian style, with their regularity and classical correctness. Prolific German architect Richard Cassels (also known as Richard Castle) came to Ireland in 1728 and designed many landmark buildings including Powerscourt House in County Wicklow (see p138) and Leinster House (home to Dáil Éireann, the Irish government) in Dublin (see p86).

Ireland has little modern architecture of note. For much of the 20th century the pace of change was slow, and it wasn't until the construction of Dublin's Busáras Station in the 1950s that modernity began to really express itself. It was designed by Michael Scott, who was to have an influence on architects in Ireland for the next two decades. The poorly regulated building boom of the 1960s and 1970s, however, paid little attention to the country's architectural heritage and destroyed more than it created. From that period Paul Koralek's 1967 brutalist-style Berkeley Library in Trinity College, Dublin, has been hailed as Ireland's best example of modern architecture.

'Berkeley Library in Trinity College, Dublin, has been hailed as Ireland's best example of modern architecture'

Since the 1980s more care has been given to architectural heritage and context, the best example of which has been the redevelopment of Dublin's previously near-derelict Temple Bar area (p80). Ireland's recent boom at the turn of the last century spawned a huge growth of building work around Dublin of inevitably mixed quality. Some good examples in the Docklands area include the imposing Financial Services Centre and Custom House Square. The Millenium Wing of the National Gallery (p85) opened the same year and is another terrific example of modern civic architecture with its sculpted Portland stone façade and tall, light-filled atrium. Celebrated Spanish architect Santiago Calatrava was commissioned to build a new bridge over Dublin's Liffey due to be completed by mid-2004. Probably the most controversial piece of modern architecture to be unveiled in recent years has been the Monument of

Light (rechristened simply The Spire) on Dublin's O'Connell St (see p90). At seven times the height of the GPO (120m in total) the brushed steel hollow cone was always going to face opposition but since its unveiling in spring 2003, its awe-inspiring structure and beautifully reflective surface have won over all but a few hardened cynics.

Visual Arts

Ireland's painting doesn't receive the kind of recognition that its literature and music do. Nevertheless, painting in Ireland has a long tradition dating back to the illuminated manuscripts of the early Christian period, most notably the Book of Kells.

The National Gallery (p85) has an extensive Irish School collection, much of it chronicling the people and pursuits of the Anglo-Irish aristocracy.

'Ireland has a theatrical history almost as long as its literary one'

Like other European artists of the 18th century, Roderic O'Conor featured portraits and landscapes in his work. His postimpressionist style stood out for its vivid use of colour and sturdy brush strokes. James Malton captured 18th-century Dublin in a series of line drawings and paintings.

In the 19th century there was still no hint of Ireland's political and social problems in the work of its major artists. The most prominent landscape painter was James Arthur O'Connor.

Just as WB Yeats played a seminal role in the Celtic literary revival, his younger brother, Jack Butler Yeats (1871–1957), inspired an artistic surge of creativity in the early 20th century, taking Celtic mythology and Irish life as his subjects. (Their father, John Butler Yeats, had also been a noted portrait painter.) William John Leech (1881–1961) was fascinated by changing light, an affection reflected in his expressionistic landscapes and flower paintings. Born to English parents in Dublin, Francis Bacon (1909–92) emerged as one of the most powerful figurative artists of the 20th century with his violent depictions of distorted human bodies.

The pioneering work of Irish cubist painter Mainie Jellett (1897–1944) and her friend, modernist stained-glass artist Evie Hone (1894–1955), had an influence on later modernists Barrie Cooke (born 1931) and Camille Souter (born 1929). Together with Louis Le Brocquy (born 1916), Jellett and Hone set up the Irish Exhibition of Living Art in 1943 to foster the work of nonacademic artists. Estella Solomons (1882–1968) trained under William Orpen and Walter Osborne in Dublin and was a noted portrait and landscape painter. The rural idyll of the west of Ireland was also a theme of Paul Henry's (1876–1958) landscapes. In the 1950s and 1960s, a school of naive artists including James Dixon appeared on Tory Island, off Donegal.

Contemporary artists to watch out for include Nick Miller, New York-based Sean Scully and Fionnuala Ní Chíosain.

Experimental photographer Clare Langan's work has gained international recognition with her trademark ethereal images of elemental landscapes.

Murals have been an important way of documenting Ireland's more recent political history. Wall murals can be seen in Belfast (p550) and Derry (p606).

Theatre & Dance

Dublin and Belfast are the main centres, but most sizable towns, such as Cork, Derry, Donegal, Limerick and Galway, have their own theatres. Ireland has a theatrical history almost as long as its literary one. Dublin's first theatre was founded in Werburgh St in 1637, although it was closed only four years later by the Puritans. Another theatre, named the Smock Alley Playhouse or Theatre Royal, opened in 1661 and continued to stage plays for more than a century. The literary revival of the late 19th century resulted in the establishment of Dublin's Abbey Theatre, now Ireland's national theatre (see p91). Its role is to present works by former greats such as WB Yeats, George Bernard Shaw (1856–1950), JM Synge (1871–1909) and Sean O'Casey (1880–1964), as well as to promote modern Irish dramatists. Also in Dublin, the Gate Theatre (p92) produces classics and comedies, while the Gaiety and Olympia Theatres (p123) present a range of productions, as does the Grand Opera House in Belfast (see p543). Dublin's Project Arts Centre (p124) offers a more experimental programme.

One of the most outstanding playwrights of the last two decades is Frank McGuinness (born 1956), who has had a prolific output since the 1970s. His plays, such as *The Carthaginians*, explore the consequences of 1972's Bloody Sunday on the people of Derry. London-Irish young playwright Martin McDonagh (born 1971) uses the darker side of a romantic rural Irish idyll as his inspiration. Among his work, *The Leenane Trilogy* has been performed by Britain's National Theatre and on Broadway, where he has won a number of Tony Awards. *Dancing at Lughnasa* by Brian Friel (born 1929) was a great success on Broadway and in London and has been made into a film.

Other talented young playwrights to watch out for include Dubliner Conor McPherson (whose acclaimed play *The Weir* was commissioned by the Royal Court), who also scripted three Irish films, Donal O'Kelly *(Catalpa)* and Enda Walsh *(Disco Pigs)*.

The work of playwright and poet Damian Gorman (born 1962) has received considerable praise. *Broken Nails*, his first play, received four Ulster Theatre awards. Mark O'Rowe (who also wrote the film script *Intermission*) received commendable reviews for his graphically violent third and most controversial play *Crestfall* in 2003 at the Gate.

'Riverdance has popularised the real art and given a new lease of life to dancing schools around the country'

The most important form of dance in Ireland is traditional Irish dancing, performed communally at ceilidh (*kay*-lees), often in an impromptu format and always accompanied by a traditional Irish band. Dances include the hornpipe, jig and reel. Irish dancing has received international attention and success through shows such as *Riverdance* and its offshoots, and while this glamorised style of dance is only loosely based on traditional dancing, it has popularised the real art and given a new lease of life to the moribund Irish dancing schools around the country.

Ireland doesn't have a national dance school, but there are a number of schools and companies around the country teaching and performing ballet and modern dance. The Dance Theatre of Ireland and the Irish Modern Dance Theatre are based in Dublin, while the Firkin Crane Centre in Cork is Ireland's only venue devoted solely to dance.

Environment

THE LAND

Ireland is an island lying off the northwestern edge of the Eurasian landmass, separated from the island of Britain by the Irish Sea and the St George's and North channels. The island's area is 84,421 sq km (14,139 sq km in the North and 70,282 sq km in the Republic). It stretches 486km north to south and 275km east to west.

Ireland is divided into 32 counties. The Republic of Ireland consists of 26 counties, and Northern Ireland of six. The northernmost point in the Republic (Malin Head in Donegal) is actually further north than anywhere in Northern Ireland. The island has traditionally been divided into four provinces: Leinster, Ulster, Connaught and Munster.

Most of the island's higher ground is close to the coast, while the central regions are mostly flat. Almost the entire western seaboard from

DID YOU KNOW?

Of the nine counties that originally comprised the province of Ulster, six are now part of Northern Ireland while three are part of the Republic.

Look for *Reading the Irish Landscape* by Frank Mitchell and Michael Ryan to catch up on Ireland's geology, archaeology, urban growth, agriculture and afforestation.

THE BOGS

Bogs, or peatlands, are believed to once have covered nearly 20% of Ireland, and although today the bogs have been significantly reduced (to about 2000 sq km), Ireland's bogs still occupy a greater area than in any other European nation.

Peat is soil formed from partly decomposed plants, mainly sphagnum moss, heathers, grasses and sedges, which have piled up in waterlogged places over thousands of years. The micro-organisms that cause decay are starved of oxygen, and decomposition is never complete. Ample rain and poor drainage help create conditions for peat formation. Peat stores energy, and the Irish have long used it as a fuel. (Walking in a small town on a chilly afternoon, you might recognise the smell of a turf fire coming from someone's chimney.) The bogs of the midlands have been harvested by the Bord na Móna (Irish Turf Board) to create electricity, fireplace briquettes and, to a lesser extent, garden compost since 1932.

Bogs come in three varieties. Raised bogs form in low-lying, waterlogged areas. The centres of these bogs are higher than the edges, hence the name. The most famous example in Ireland is the Bog of Allen, which once covered as much as 1000 sq km. The bogs found covering hills and valleys are known as blanket bogs. These develop on acidic soil in a very wet climate. There are good examples of still-surviving blanket bogs in Wicklow, Sligo, Antrim and the Slieve Bloom Mountains. Fens are flat bogs found at the edges of lakes and in waterlogged areas supplied by mineral-rich waters. When that water supply is cut off, raised bogs develop over the top of fens.

The preservation properties of bogs also make them a vital historical resource. Due to the acidity and lack of oxygen in the peat, fragile organic artefacts and pollen that would otherwise have disintegrated long ago are occasionally preserved. The countless relics recovered, some of them 5000 years old, include Iron Age wooden highways, preserved bodies, wooden wheels, buckets and a tub of 300-year-old butter.

Now that so many of these bogs have been almost obliterated, there is a conservation movement to protect some of what's left. Many of Ireland's bogs are now secured in National Nature Reserves, mostly managed by National Parks and Wildlife. Some people argue that all bogs should be conserved, especially since they are home to their own unique family of plants and insects and provide an important habitat for birdlife.

Cork to Donegal is a continuous bulwark of cliffs, hills and mountains, with few safe anchorages. The highest mountains are in the southwest; the tallest mountain in Ireland is Carrantuohil (1041m) in Kerry's MacGillycuddy's Reeks.

The Shannon is the longest river in Ireland. It runs for 370km from its source in Cavan's Cuilcagh Mountains down through the midlands before emptying into the wide Shannon Estuary west of Limerick town. Lough Neagh in Northern Ireland is the island's largest lake, covering 396 sq km.

The midlands of Ireland lie above Carboniferous limestone deposited between 300 and 400 million years ago. On the surface, the flat landscape is mostly rich farmland and raised bogs.

As you travel west from the midlands, the soil becomes poorer, the fields smaller and stone walls more numerous. The Cromwellian cry 'To hell or to Connaught' wasn't without foundation, as the land west of the Shannon can't compare with fertile counties such as Meath and Tipperary.

DID YOU KNOW?

In 1821 the body of an Iron Age man was found in a bog in Galway, his cape, shoes and beard still intact.

WILDLIFE

Animals

MAMMALS

The most common native land mammals of any size are the fox and badger, but although there are plenty about you're unlikely to see any on a casual visit. Smaller mammals include rabbit, hare, hedgehog and shrew. Of the seven species of bat present, two common varieties – the lesser horseshoe bat and Leisler's bat – are considered rare in other parts of Europe. Red deer roam the hillsides in many of the wilder parts of the country, particularly the Wicklow Mountains (p137), and in Killarney National Park (p235), which holds the country's largest herd of native red deer. Other deer have been introduced from abroad, including the Japanese sika deer.

An illustrated pocket guide called *The Animals of Ireland* by Gordon D'Arcy is a handy, inexpensive introduction.

Less common in Ireland are the elusive otter, stoat and pine marten, which are usually found in remote areas such as the Burren in County Clare (see p358) or Connemara in County Galway.

Sea mammals include the grey and common seal, which are often easily spotted around the coast. There are some substantial colonies of grey seals living on the uninhabited islands off County Mayo and around the shores of Strangford Lough in Northern Ireland (see p579). Dolphins often swim close to land, particularly in the bays and inlets off the western coast.

BIRDS

Ireland possesses fewer breeding species than mainland Europe because of its relative isolation, but its westerly location on the fringe of Europe makes it an ideal stopover point for birds migrating from North America and the Arctic. In autumn the southern counties become temporary home to the American waders (mainly sandpipers and plovers) and warblers. Migrants from Africa, such as shearwaters, petrels and auks, begin to arrive in spring in the southwestern counties.

The reasonably rare corncrake, which migrates from Africa, can be found in the western counties, in Donegal (p498) and around the Shannon Callows, and on islands such as Inishbofin in Galway. In late spring and early summer, the rugged coastlines, particularly cliff areas and islands, become a haven for breeding seabirds, mainly puffin, gannet, kittiwake, Manx shearwater, fulmar, cormorant and heron. Sightings of rarer species such as cory and skua have also been recorded.

Irish Birds by David Cabot is a pocket guide that describes birds and their habitats and outlines the best places for serious bird-watching.

The lakes and low-lying wetlands attract large numbers of Arctic and northern European waterfowl and waders such as whooper swans, lapwing, barnacle, white-fronted geese and golden plover. The important Wexford Wildfowl Reserve (p162) holds half the world's population of Greenland white-fronted geese, and little tern breed on the beach there, protected by the dunes. Also found during the winter are teal, redshank and curlew. The main migration periods are April to May and September to October.

Birds of prey include hen harrier, sparrowhawk, falcon (peregrine, merlin and kestrel) and the odd buzzard. The magnificent peregrine falcon has been making something of a recovery and can be found nesting on cliffs in Wicklow and elsewhere. In 2001, a number of golden eagle chicks from Scotland were released into Glenveagh National Park in Donegal (see p483) in an effort to reintroduce the species.

Puffins, resembling penguins with their tuxedo colour scheme, nest in large colonies on coastal cliffs.

ENDANGERED SPECIES

The chough, an unusual crow with bright-red feet and beak, is still seen in the west along coastlines with extensive sand dunes and on Clare Island in Mayo (see p412). Other endangered birds are the barn owl, Canadian brent goose, roseate tern, little tern and red-throated diver.

In the Ring of Kerry, the Kerry Bog pony is officially designated a rare breed. Other endangered mammals are the whiskered bat, hedgehog, Irish hare, badger and otter. A rare ancient Irish fish and glacial relic, the pollan, found in Lough Derg among other places, is in danger of becoming extinct partly because the invasive zebra mussel, which was introduced to Irish waters attached to foreign boats, has colonised the pollan's spawning ground.

Plants

After the end of the last Ice Age about 10,000 years ago, a shrubby flora similar to that found in modern Arctic tundra took hold. This was eventually replaced by sessile (without a leafstalk) oak forest, which established itself on most of the island. In the upland regions and on more exposed hillsides, the oak was mixed with or replaced by birch and pine. In the lower regions where the soil was richer there were also elm, alder, hawthorn and ash. Underneath the oak trees were smaller plants such as holly, hazel, ferns, mosses and brambles, which provided a rich habitat for animals. Many species of European flora failed to reach Ireland before it became an island.

Today, however, the predominant flora is mostly that which has been introduced by humans. Only 1% of genuine native oak forest survives, making Ireland the least wooded country in Europe. There are remnants in Killarney National Park (p235) and in southern Wicklow near Shillelagh. Regimental columns of pine plantations are now a major feature of the Irish countryside and add little in the way of beauty.

In the 17th century hedges were introduced to the landscape to act as land boundaries. Native plants survive in the hedgerows and in the wilder parts of the country. Because intensive agriculture arrived only comparatively recently, the range of surviving plant species is larger than in many other European countries.

The Burren limestone region in County Clare was covered in light woodland before the early settlers arrived. Now the area is almost all bare rock, but many of the original plants live on, a remarkable mixture of Mediterranean, alpine and arctic species (see p358).

The bogs of Ireland are home to a unique flora adapted to wet, acidic, nutrient-poor conditions and whose survival is threatened by the depletion of bogs for energy use. Sphagnum moss is the key bog plant and is joined by plants such as bog rosemary, bog cotton, black-beaked sedge (whose spindly stem grows up to 30cm high) and various types of heather and lichen. Carnivorous plants also thrive, such as the sundew, whose sticky tentacles trap insects, and bladderwort whose tiny explosive bladders trap aquatic animals in bog pools.

NATIONAL PARKS

Ireland has five national parks: The Burren (Clare, see p356, and Galway), Connemara (Galway, see p396), Glenveagh (Donegal, see p483), Killarney (Kerry, see p235) and Wicklow Mountains (Wicklow, see p137). These have been developed to protect, preserve and make accessible areas of significant natural heritage. The parks open year round and each has its own information office.

For information on parks, gardens, monuments and inland waterways see www.heritageireland.ie

Forests & Forest Parks

Coillte Teoranta (Irish Forestry Board) administers about 4000 sq km of forested land, which includes designated picnic areas and 12 forest parks. These parks open year round and have a range of wildlife and habitats. Some also have chalets and/or caravan parks, shops, cafés and play areas for children. For further information contact **Coillte Teoranta** (☎ 01-661 5666; pr@coillte.ie; Leeson Lane, Dublin).

National Nature Reserves

There are 66 state-owned and 10 privately owned National Nature Reserves (NNRs) in the Republic, represented by Dúchas (government department in charge of parks, monuments and gardens in the Republic). In Northern Ireland there are more than 40 NNRs, which are leased or owned by the Department of the Environment. These reserves are defined as areas of importance for their special flora, fauna or geology and include the Giant's Causeway (p620) and Glenariff Glen (p627) in Antrim, Marble Arch in County Fermanagh (see p649) and North Strangford Lough in County Down (see p579). More information is available from the **Environment & Heritage Service** (☎ 028-9054 6533; Commonwealth House, 35 Castle St, Belfast).

For more information see www.nics.gov.uk/ehs

ENVIRONMENTAL ISSUES

Forests

At one time Ireland was largely covered by forests. Then, about 6000 years ago, the first farmers cleared small areas for their crops, the beginning of a long process of deforestation. Substantial tracts of natural oak wood survived until the mid-16th century, but the following 200 years resulted in the country being stripped of its oak for ship timbers, charcoal, tanning and barrels, and by the mid-18th century almost all the country's timber was being imported.

In the 20th century, pine plantations were born out of the need for local timber and the desire to do something with what many people considered to be wasteland. There are now state subsidies for plantations, although the most widely used species – sitka spruce and lodgepole pine – are so fast growing and soft as to be unsuitable for high-quality wood products.

To get information from the Irish Wildlife Trust see www.iwt.ie

Today forests cover about 5.5% of the country and the percentage is slowly increasing, although much of the wood grown is for commercial purposes. Recognition of the need for native forest is found in places such as Glencree in County Wicklow (see p140), where there's a project to reforest part of the area with oak trees.

Agriculture

In the past, Ireland experienced limited industrialisation compared to other developed countries, leaving the beautiful Irish countryside mostly untouched. However, in the 1970s, the EU encouraged intensive, specialised farming and the use of pesticides and chemical fertilisers. These caused serious pollution and land degradation in areas such as the Burren in County Clare. More recently, the EU and the Irish government have promoted environmental protection, less-intensive farming methods and the adoption of alternative practices or crops. The result has been a reduction in pollution, though it continues to occur in rivers and lakes.

In the same period the trend towards larger farms led to the destruction of many ring forts and stone walls.

Beaches

Unfortunately a number of Irish beaches suffer from pollution and despite EU directives on waste management, plastic containers and other landfill debris have found their way onto beaches. As part of a scheme to improve the situation, clean beaches are awarded the EU Blue Flag and encouragingly in 2001, more than 70 beaches, including seven in Northern Ireland, were awarded a Blue Flag. An Taisce (National Trust for Ireland) keeps a list of these, or you can check them on www.blueflag.org.

Food & Drink

Irish food is great until it's cooked, laughed generations of travellers who for aeons visited these shores *in spite* of the grub. The cuisine was thrown together by an indifferent, almost penitent race and so it came to be known for charred chops and mushy vegetables.

Ironically, Ireland has always been blessed with a wealth of staples and specialities – with meat, seafood and dairy produce the envy of the world – but it was what to do with these riches that baffled Irish mothers for so long. Then, in the twilight of the 20th century, a remarkable renaissance took place at the Irish table and a new wave of cooks began producing a New Irish Cuisine. In truth, there was very little new about this cuisine at all; it was more a confident return to tradition which combined the simple cooking techniques with the finest local ingredients.

Nevertheless, it aroused the nation's taste buds. Irish diners became more discerning; they banged on their tables, refused the old crap and suddenly food became something to savour (rather than soak up the drink). Pretty soon, cooks had to look outside Ireland for new influences to satisfy their adventurous appetites and, in the space of a decade, Ireland's gastronomy was transformed. Of course, you can still find leathery meat, shrivelled fish and vegetables so overcooked that they can barely cling to the fork but – by following our recommendations – you're as likely to experience hearty fare that will make your head spin and your palate sing.

The Potato Year by Lucy Madden and Peter Bland. An intriguing cookbook (if you like spuds) with 365 traditional and novel ways to cook the potato; it has titbits of folklore and local history.

STAPLES & SPECIALITIES

Potatoes

It's a wonder the Irish retain their good humour amid the perpetual potato-baiting they endure. But, despite the stereotyping, and however much we'd like to disprove it, potatoes are still paramount here and you will see lots of them on your travels. The mashed potato dishes colcannon and champ (with cabbage and spring onion respectively) are two of the tastiest potato recipes in the country.

Meat & Seafood

Irish meals are usually meat based, with beef, lamb and pork common options. Seafood, long neglected, is finding a place on the table in Irish homes. It's widely available in restaurants and is often excellent, especially in the west. Oysters, trout and salmon are delicious, particularly if they're direct from the sea or river rather than a fish farm. The famous Dublin Bay Prawn isn't actually a prawn, but a lobster, sometimes called langoustine. At its best, the Dublin Bay Prawn is superlative, but it is priced accordingly. If you're going to splurge, do so here but make sure you choose live Dublin Bay Prawns because once these fellas die, they quickly lose their flavour.

DID YOU KNOW?

More than 100,000 oysters are consumed each year at the Galway Oyster Festival (p377).

Cheese

One of the most exciting culinary developments here in recent decades has been the emergence of local cheese making, and Ireland's farmhouse cheeses have won many awards and plaudits around the world and feature on platters in some of Europe's top restaurants. Specialist producers abound, particularly in Munster (the southern counties), and you should check out notables like Ardrahan, Durrus and Gubbeen from Cork and Tipperary's Cashel Blue.

Bread

The most famous Irish bread, and unquestionably one of the tastes of Ireland, is soda bread. Because Irish flour is so soft it doesn't take well to yeast as a raising agent. In the 19th century, bread soda (bicarbonate of soda) was introduced for leavening bread, and combined with buttermilk it makes a superbly light-textured and tasty bread.

The Cork Cook Book edited by Nuala Fenton, Angie Shanahan and Damhnait Sweeney. An excellent selection of favourites from the many decent restaurants in the culinary capital and from gastrophile West Cork; all proceeds go to the Cork Simon Community, a local charity for the homeless.

The Fry

Perhaps the most feared Irish speciality is the traditional fry – the heart attack on a plate that is the second part of every B&B deal in the country. In spite of the hysterical health fears, the fry is still one of the most common traditional meals in the country. Who can say no to a plate of fried bacon, sausages, black pudding, white pudding, eggs and tomatoes? For the famous Ulster fry, common throughout the North, simply add fadge (potato bread).

DRINKS

Nonalcoholic Drinks

TEA

The Irish drink more tea, per capita, than any other nation in the world and you'll be offered a cup of it as soon as you cross the threshold of any Irish home. It's a leveller and an icebreaker, and an appreciation for 'at least a cup in your hand' is your passport to conviviality here. Preferred blends are very strong, and nothing like the namby-pamby versions that pass for Irish breakfast tea elsewhere.

RED LEMONADE

This product, basically white lemonade with colouring, has been produced in Ireland since the end of the 19th century and is still made to virtually the same recipe today. Always more popular in the Republic than the North, it is still a favourite for adults and children alike. It is commonly used as a mixer with brandy and rye whiskeys such as Canadian Club and Southern Comfort.

Alcoholic Drinks

Drinking in Ireland is more important than a mere social activity: it's the foundation on which Irish culture is built. Along with its wonderful drinks, this helps to explain why through centuries of poverty and oppression the Irish retained their reputation for unrivalled hospitality and good humour.

DID YOU KNOW?

Stout originated in London in the 18th century and only became associated with Ireland during WWI, when rationing laws in Britain meant that brewers there were unable to produce 'the black stuff'.

STOUT

Of all of Ireland's drinks, the 'black stuff' is the most celebrated. It is simply a way of life in Ireland, as much a part of the culture as the weather, though more fondly regarded. As Irish pubs are the focus of the country's social existence, stout (or 'plain') is the fuel that drives it. Unlike whiskey, stout has always been a sociable drink, to be enjoyed with company in a pub and very rarely drunk at home.

While Guinness has become synonymous with stout the world over, few outside Ireland realise that there are two other major stout producers competing for the favour of the Irish drinker: Murphy's and Beamish & Crawford, both based in Cork city in the south of Ireland.

THE PERFECT PINT OF GUINNESS?

What makes a perfect pint of Guinness? This much-debated question has no complete, definitive answer, but we can offer a few indications.

Everyone agrees that proximity to Dublin's St James's Gate Guinness Brewery (p94) is one requirement, for although a pint in Kuala Lumpur can still be a fine thing, Guinness at its best can be found only in Ireland.

The proper pour is also essential. First, you need a good, experienced bartender who has ensured that the pipes are clean and free-flowing (there's nothing worse than dirty pipes). Once everything is in place, the pour can begin. The glass is tilted to about 45 degrees, then the tap is pulled forwards so that the liquid is poured against the back of the glass. When it is about three-quarters full, the glass is left to 'settle', which means that the heavier black liquid settles underneath the lighter, creamy head. After a few minutes, the pint is topped up by pushing the tap backwards, allowing only the black beer into the glass. When the pint is full, it is left to settle a second time, and then it's ready to drink. It takes time but, as Guinness is fond of telling us, good things come to those who wait.

Now's the time to test the quality of the pint. When you're about halfway through, look at the sides of the glass: if there are rings of white foam round the inside (the thicker the better), you can be sure that the pint is a good one. In which case, best order another...

OTHER IRISH BEERS

Beamish Red Ale

This traditional-style red ale is sweet and palatable, brewed in Cork city by Beamish & Crawford (p193).

Caffrey's Irish Ale

One of the most exciting additions to Ireland's beer map, this creamy ale has only been around since 1994. It's a robust cross between a stout and an ale. Brewed in County Antrim.

The Book of Guinness Advertising by Jim Davies. My Goodness! A collection of Guinness' finest posters from the 1920s to the end of the 20th century.

Smithwicks

Smithwicks is a lovely, refreshing full 'scoop' with a charming history. It is brewed in Kilkenny (see p298), on the site of the 14th-century St Francis Abbey in what is Ireland's oldest working brewery. John Smithwick set up his brewery in 1710, and the monks brewed ale there since the 14th century. A stronger, drier version is exported worldwide as Kilkenny Irish Beer.

Harp Lager

This golden lager is neither here nor there.

McCardles Traditional Ale

This wholesome, dark, nutty ale is hard to come by, but worthy of an exploration.

Kaliber

This nonalcoholic lager was made popular by famous Irish athlete Eamon O'Coughlan. Even in the name of research we couldn't be bothered trying it but it seems to have some credibility among Ireland's hard drinkers.

WHISKEY

While whiskey shares only equal billing with stout as the national drink of Ireland, in the home it is paramount. At last call, there were almost 100 different brands of Irish whiskey, with most of them available in the Irish market. Jameson and Bushmills are two great ambassadors but not necessarily Irish whiskey's showcase. A visit to the country reveals a depth of excellence which will make the connoisseur's palate spin, while winning over many new friends to what the Irish call *uisce beatha*, the 'water of life'.

The Irish were pioneers in the development of distilling whiskey (distilled three times and spelled with an 'e' as opposed to twice-distilled Scotch whisky). Established in 1608, Bushmills in County Antrim is the world's oldest legal distillery (see p619).

The Whiskeys of Ireland by Peter Mulryan. Informative tippler's companion, with a comprehensive history of distillation and production and tasting notes to 55 Irish brands.

IRISH COFFEE

Stories of Irish coffee's origination abound but the most common one credits Joe Sheridan, a barman at Shannon airport, with the creation in the 1940s. All travellers arriving in Ireland from the USA would stop over in Shannon for an hour or two before heading onto their final destination. Landing in the bracing cold, shivering passengers used to approach Sheridan looking for an alcoholic drink and something that might heat them up. He hit upon the winning blend of Irish whiskey and piping hot coffee, topped with rich cream. It was just the trick then, and still is today.

POITÍN

The making of *poitín* (potch-een), illicit whiskey, has a folkloric respect in Ireland. Those responsible came to be regarded as heroes of the people rather than outlaws of the land as the authorities tried to tar them. In tourist and duty-free shops you'll see a commercial brand of *poitín* which is strictly a gimmick for tourists. Don't bother; it is just an inferior spirit with little to its credit. There are still *poitín* makers plying their trade in the quieter corners of Ireland. It is not uncommon in Donegal, the *poitín* capital, for deals to be sealed or favours repaid with a drop of the 'cratur'. In the quiet, desolate, peaty bogs of Connemara a plume of smoke rising into the sky may not just be a warming fire. Or in West Cork, one of the most fiercely patriotic and traditional pockets of Ireland, a friend of a friend may know something about it.

Jameson Guide: The Best Places to Eat, Drink & Stay by Georgina Campbell. Annual guides with over 900 recommendations for munching, supping and snoozing on the Emerald Isle.

WHERE TO EAT & DRINK

It's easy to eat well in the cities and you'll find whatever cuisine your taste buds desire, from Irish seafood to foreign fusion. Along the west coast, you'll be spoilt for choice when it comes to seafood restaurants.

If you ask a local for 'somewhere to eat', you'll probably be directed to his or her favourite pub because, outside the cities, the best place for a feed, particularly lunch, *is* often the pub. Virtually every drinking house will offer the simple fare of soup, potatoes, vegetables, steaks and chicken. Some extend themselves and have separate dining rooms where you can get fresh soda breads, and hearty meals like shepherd's pie, stews and casseroles, and seafood dishes. Normally only pubs with separate dining rooms serve food at night.

The Bridgestone Guides by John and Sally McKenna. A well-respected series of Irish food guides written by a husband-and-wife team; books include the *Vegetarian Guide to Ireland; Food Lover's Guide to Northern Ireland; Traveller's Guide; Shopper's Guide* and the annual *100 Best Restaurants*.

VEGETARIANS & VEGANS

Oh boy, you're a long way from home now. Ireland provides so few vegetarian options that your convictions might be tested. In the cities and bigger towns there will be enough dedicated eateries to keep your spirits up, but once you head out into rural Ireland you enter the vegetarian's wilderness.

We trust vegans have brought packed lunches; Ireland really won't be your cup of black tea. Save yourself time and heartache and buy the most up-to-date restaurant guide as soon as your plane touches down. And get used to the incredulous question, 'What, you don't eat any dairy produce!?!'

FOOD FOR THE FAMILY

You can bring *na páiste* (the children) to just about any Irish eatery, including the pub. However, after 7pm, the kids are banished from most boozers and the smarter restaurants. You will sometimes see children's menus but normally small portions of the adult fare will do. For more information on travelling with children, see p659.

HABITS & CUSTOMS

How the Irish Eat

The Irish have hefty appetites and eat almost 150% of the recommended daily calorie intake according to the EU. This probably has as much to do with their penchant for snacks as the size of their meals (which *are* big).

When Ireland was predominantly agricultural, breakfast was a leisurely and communal meal shared with family and workers around midmorning, a few hours after rising. As with most of the developed world, it's now a fairly rushed and bleary-eyed affair usually involving toast and cereals. The traditional fry is a weekend indulgence while the contracted version of bacon and eggs is still popular whenever time allows. The day's first cup of tea comes after breakfast and most people will admit to not being themselves until they've had their first cuppa.

Café Paradiso Cookbook is a creative and modern vegetarian cookbook with ne'er a brown lentil stew in sight; from the eponymous Cork restaurant (p196).

Elevenses is the next culinary pit stop and involves tea and snacks to tide appetites over until the next main meal. Afternoon tea takes the same form and serves the same function, breaking up the afternoon.

Lunch was traditionally the biggest meal of the day, which was probably a throwback to farming Ireland, when the workers would return home around 1pm, ravenous after a day's work. The timing of the main meal today is one of the most visible rural/urban divides. Outside the cities, lunch is still usually the most substantial meal every day of the week while the workers in urban areas have succumbed to the nine-to-five drudgery and usually eat lunch on the run. However, on weekends, everybody has dinner mid-afternoon, usually around 4pm on Saturday and before 2pm Sunday. They might call it 'lunch' but don't be deceived, it's the most substantial meal of the week.

Avoca Café Cookbook by Hugo Smith Ireland. Hearty, wholesome recipes from the family-run Avoca Handweaver restaurants originally based in Wicklow (see p150) and now with five establishments across the Republic.

'Supper' is increasingly becoming the main meal for urbanites, and it takes place as soon as the last working parent gets home, usually after 6pm. Whatever time it takes place, main meals are still held as precious occasions for catching up on the news and sharing ideas and plans with family, friends and loved ones.

Etiquette

Conviviality is the most important condiment at the Irish table. Meal times are about taking the load off your feet, relaxing and enjoying the company of your fellow diners. There is very little prescribed or restrictive etiquette. In fact, the only behaviour likely to cause offence could be your own haughtiness. The Irish will happily dismiss any faux pas but if they think you have ideas above your station, they'll gleefully bring you back down to earth.

EAT YOUR WORDS

Bacon and Cabbage Slices of boiled bacon or gammon with boiled cabbage on the side served with boiled potatoes.

Barm Brack A spicy, cake-like bread, traditionally served at Halloween with a ring hidden inside (careful!).

Blaa Soft and floury bread roll.

Visit www.foodisland.com, a site run by Bord Bia, the state food board, for recipes, a short culinary history of Ireland and links to producers of Irish food, from whom you can purchase that prized truckle of farmhouse cheese or whiskey flavoured fruit cake.

Black and White Pudding Black pudding is traditionally made from pig's blood, pork skin and seasonings, shaped like a big sausage and cut into discs and fried. There are many gourmet versions available, the best of which is from Clonakilty in Cork (see Edward Twomey, p210). White pudding is the same without the blood.
Boxty A potato pancake, becoming rarer on menus.
Carrigeen A seaweed dish.
Champ A Northern Irish dish of potatoes mashed with spring onions (scallions).
Coddle A Dublin dish of semithick stew made with sausages, bacon, onions and potatoes.
Colcannon Mashed potato, cabbage and onion fried in butter and milk.
Crubeens A Cork dish of pigs' trotters.
Dulse A dried seaweed that's sold salted and ready to eat, mainly in Ballycastle, County Antrim.
Fadge Northern Irish potato bread.
Farl General name for triangular-shaped baking.
Guinness Cake A popular fruitcake flavoured with Guinness.
Irish Stew This quintessential Irish dish is a stew of mutton (preferably lamb), potatoes and onions, flavoured with parsley and thyme and simmered slowly.
Potato Bread Thin bread made out of spuds.
Soda Bread This wonderful bread, white or brown, sweet or savoury, is made from very soft Irish flour and buttermilk and found throughout the country.
Yellowman A hard, chewy toffee made in County Antrim.

Dublin

CONTENTS

Dublin is one of Europe's most compelling capitals. In fact, against stiff competition, it was recently voted fourth as Europe's most popular city destination after London, Paris and Rome. If you've never been, now is the time; if you've already experienced its delights, you won't need us to tell you to return.

Visitors swarm in their droves to Dublin like moths to a lightbulb and for good reason. You can't help but enjoy the energy, humour and relaxed attitude of its people. Its many historic museums, top-class attractions and Georgian architecture aside, it's the genuine social interaction and legendary 'craic' that make the place magnetic. There's a warmth and vibrancy to the city that, in an ever fast-paced world, are worth their weight in gold. If you want to have a good time, hook up with old friends or make new ones, Dublin is the place for you.

Ireland's economic revival has now become the stuff of legend, and while the Celtic Tiger's roar may have quietened somewhat in recent years, the unparalleled optimism and positivity felt by most Dubliners is still evident all over the city. The attendant migration of people from all corners of the globe to Ireland, and particularly to Dublin, has added a cosmopolitan and culturally diverse element to the city's personality. New hotels, restaurants, bars and cafés continue to crop up almost daily and, on the surface at least, there appears to be a blissful ignorance of economic down-turnings. Good times or bad, Dubliners know how to enjoy themselves – and there's no doubt they'll certainly show you how to as well.

HIGHLIGHTS

- Take a walking tour of **Trinity College** (p77), including a visit to the unmissable **Book of Kells** (p77)
- Peruse the wonderful Oriental art in the **Chester Beatty Library** (p82)
- Gaze at Georgian architecture around **Merrion Square** (p89) and **St Stephen's Green** (p87)
- Enjoy the craic on the streets during Dublin's largest four-day festival, the **St Patrick's Day Festival** (p103)
- Relax with a pint or two, or three at one of Dublin's many **pubs and clubs** (p117)

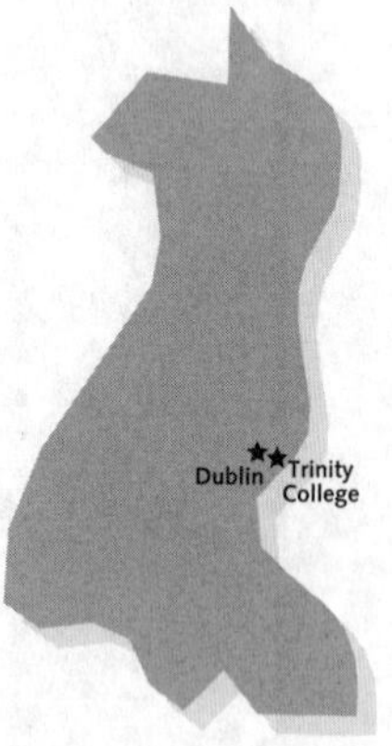

- TELEPHONE CODE: 01
- POPULATION: 1,122,821
- AREA: 921 SQ KM

HISTORY

Dublin celebrated its official millennium in 1988 but there were settlements here long before AD 988. The first early-Celtic habitation was on the banks of the River Liffey, giving rise to the city's Irish name, Baile Átha Cliath (Town of the Hurdle Ford), which comes from the ancient river crossing that can still be pinpointed today.

It wasn't until the Vikings turned up that Dublin became a permanent fixture. Its maritime situation ensured its significance as a place of trade, a likely factor in its emergence as the country's capital. By the 9th century, raids from the north had become a fact of Irish life and some of the fierce Danes chose to stay rather than simply rape, pillage and depart. They intermarried with the Irish and established a vigorous trading port at the point where the River Poddle joined the Liffey in a black pool, in Irish a 'dubh linn'. Today there's little trace of the Poddle, which has been channelled underground and flows under St Patrick's Cathedral to dribble into the Liffey by the Capel St (or Grattan) Bridge.

The boom years came with the 18th century, the period of the Protestant Ascendancy, when, for a time, London was the only larger city in the British Empire. As the city expanded, the nouveaux riches abandoned medieval Dublin and moved north across the river to a new Dublin of stately squares surrounded by fine Georgian mansions.

The city's slums soon spread north in pursuit of the rich, who returned south to new homes in Merrion Square, Fitzwilliam Square and St Stephen's Green. In 1745 when James Fitzgerald, Earl of Kildare, began building Leinster House, his magnificent mansion south of the Liffey, he was mocked for this foolish move away from the centre into the wilds. 'Where I go society will follow,' he confidently predicted, and was soon proved right. Today Leinster House is home to the Irish Parliament and is right in the centre of modern Dublin.

The Georgian boom years were followed by more trouble and unrest. The union with Britain in 1801, ending the separate Irish Parliament and returning power to London, spelled the end of Dublin's century of dramatic growth. Dublin entered the 20th century a downtrodden, dispirited place.

The 1916 Easter Rising caused considerable damage to parts of central Dublin, particularly along O'Connell St, where the General Post Office (GPO) was gutted. The continuing struggle between British forces and the IRA led to more damage, including the burning of the Custom House in 1921. A year later Ireland was independent, but then tumbled into the Civil War, which inflicted still more damage on the city, including the burning of the Four Courts in 1922 and a further bout of destruction for O'Connell St.

When peace finally came to Ireland, Dublin was exhausted – a shadow of its Georgian self. Until the 1970s it was a city in decay, but Ireland's becoming a member of what was then the European Economic Community (now the European Union) in 1972 held the prospect of better times to come. Today, Ireland's economic turnaround and cultural resurgence has transformed the city and gone a long way towards restoring its vitality.

Dublin's expansion has continued south to Dun Laoghaire and beyond, but the River Liffey remains a rough dividing line between southern 'haves' and northern 'have-nots', although that too is beginning to change as rising house prices lead to a gradual gentrification of the entire city centre.

ORIENTATION

Greater Dublin sprawls around the arc of Dublin Bay, bounded to the north by the hills at Howth and to the south by the Dalkey headland. Splitting the city in two is the unremarkable River Liffey, which traditionally also marks a psychological and social break between the poorer northside and the more affluent southside.

North of the River Liffey the important streets for visitors are O'Connell St and, just off it, Henry St, the major shopping thoroughfares. Most of the northside's B&Bs are on Gardiner St, which becomes rather rundown as it continues north. At the northern end of O'Connell St is Parnell Square. The main bus station, Busáras, and Connolly Station, one of the city's two main train stations, are near the southern end of Gardiner St.

Immediately south of the river, over O'Connell Bridge, is the Temple Bar area and the expanse of Trinity College. Nassau St, along the southern edge of the campus, and pedestrianised Grafton St are the main shopping streets. At the southern end of

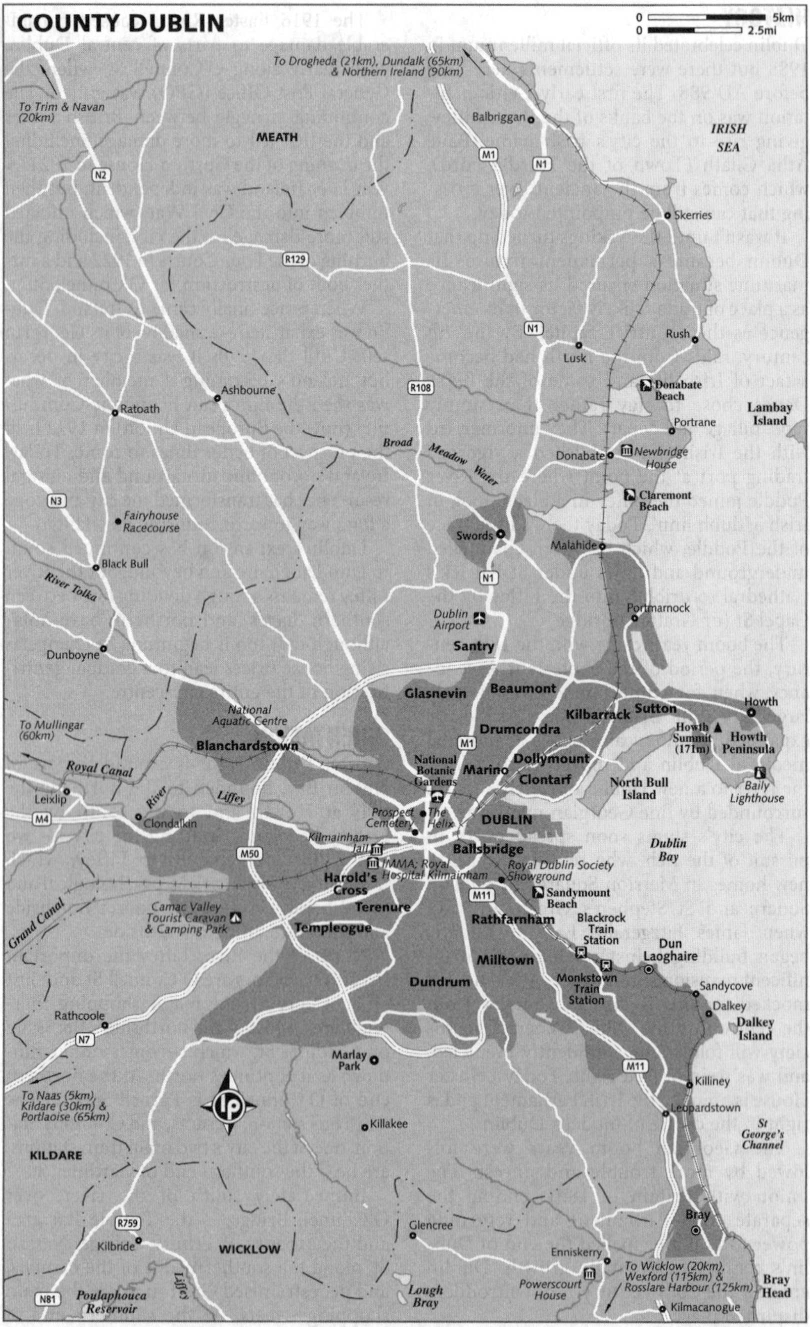
COUNTY DUBLIN
0 5km
0 2.5mi
To Drogheda (21km), Dundalk (65km) & Northern Ireland (90km)
To Trim & Navan (20km)
MEATH
Balbriggan
IRISH SEA
M1
N1
N2
Skerries
R129
N1
Rush
Lusk
Donabate Beach
Ashbourne
R108
Ratoath
Lambay Island
Portrane
Broad Meadow Water
Donabate
Newbridge House
N3
Claremont Beach
Fairyhouse Racecourse
Swords
Malahide
Black Bull
River Tolka
N1
Dublin Airport
Portmarnock
Santry
Dunboyne
Glasnevin
Beaumont
Howth
Sutton
Kilbarrack
National Aquatic Centre
Drumcondra
Howth Summit (171m)
Howth Peninsula
To Mullingar (60km)
Blanchardstown
M1
Royal Canal
National Botanic Gardens
Marino
Dollymount
Clontarf
North Bull Island
Baily Lighthouse
Leixlip
River Liffey
Prospect Cemetery
The Helix
DUBLIN
M4
Clondalkin
Kilmainham Jail
Dublin Bay
M50
Ballsbridge
IMMA; Royal Hospital Kilmainham
Royal Dublin Society Showground
Harold's Cross
M11
Sandymount Beach
Terenure
Camac Valley Tourist Caravan & Camping Park
Rathfarnham
Blackrock Train Station
Grand Canal
Templeogue
Dun Laoghaire
Milltown
Monkstown Train Station
Sandycove
Dundrum
Dalkey
Dalkey Island
Rathcoole
N7
Marlay Park
M11
Killiney
To Naas (5km), Kildare (30km) & Portlaoise (65km)
Leopardstown
Killakee
St George's Channel
KILDARE
Bray
R759
Glencree
Kilbride
WICKLOW
Enniskerry
To Wicklow (20km), Wexford (115km) & Rosslare Harbour (125km)
Powerscourt House
Bray Head
N81
Poulaphouca Reservoir
Liffey
Lough Bray
Kilmacanogue

Grafton St is St Stephen's Green. About 2km west, beside the river, is Heuston Station, the city's other main train station.

The postcodes for central Dublin are Dublin 1, immediately north of the river and Dublin 2, immediately south. The posh Ballsbridge area southeast of the centre is Dublin 4. A handy tip for postcodes is to remember that even numbers apply to the southside and odd ones to the north.

See p125 for information on transport to/from the airport and train stations.

Maps

Lonely Planet's *Dublin City Map* has a complete index of all streets and sights, a Dublin Area Rapid Transport (DART) and suburban rail plan and a unique walking tour of the city.

INFORMATION

Bookshops

Dublin Bookshop (Map p88; ☎ 677 5568; 24 Grafton St) Good Irish-interest section.
Dublin Writers' Museum (Map pp72-4; ☎ 872 2077; 18 Parnell Sq North)
Easons (Map pp72-4; ☎ 873 3811; 40 O'Connell St) One of the biggest magazine stockists in Ireland.
Forbidden Planet (Map pp80-1; ☎ 671 0688; 5-6 Crampton Quay) Science-fiction and comic-book specialist.
Fred Hanna (Map pp80-1; ☎ 677 1255; 27-29 Nassau St)
Government Publications bookshop (Map p88; ☎ 647 6879; Sun Alliance House, Molesworth St) Official publications and maps.
Hodges Figgis (Map p88; ☎ 677 4754; 56-58 Dawson St)
Hughes & Hughes (Map p88; ☎ 478 3060; St Stephen's Green Shopping Centre & Dublin airport)
Irish Museum of Modern Art (Map p70; ☎ 612 9900; IMMA; Royal Hospital, Kilmainham) Contemporary art and Irish-interest books.
Library Book Shop (Map p78; ☎ 6081171; Trinity College) Irish-interest books, including those on the *Book of Kells*.
Murder Ink (Map p88; ☎ 677 7570; 15 Dawson St) Mystery titles.
National Gallery (Map p88; ☎ 678 5450; Merrion Sq West) Traditional art and Irish interest books.
Sinn Féin Bookshop (Map pp72-4; ☎ 872 7096; 44 Parnell Sq West)
An Siopa Leabhar (Map p88; ☎ 478 3814; Harcourt St) Stocks books in Irish.
Waterstone's (Map p88; ☎ 679 1415; 7 Dawson St; ☎ 878 1311; Jervis St Centre)
Winding Stair (Map pp80-1; ☎ 873 3292; 40 Ormond Quay Lower) New and second-hand books.

> **FINDING ADDRESSES**
>
> Finding addresses in Dublin can be complicated by the tendency for street names to change every few blocks and for streets to be subdivided into upper and lower or north and south parts, which in some cases are on two different sides of the city. It doesn't seem to matter if you put the definer in front of or behind the name – thus you can have Lower Baggot St or Baggot St Lower, South Anne St or Anne St South. Street numbering often runs up one side of a street and down the other, rather than having odd numbers on one side and even on the other. Also, the use of 'south' and 'north' usually means that the two streets are on opposite sides of the river, rather than running into one another. So, while South Great George's St is to be found off Dame St on the southern side, North Great George's St is on the northern side of the river, running parallel to Upper O'Connell St.

Cultural Centres

Alliance Française (Map p88; ☎ 676 1732; 1 Kildare St)
British Council (Map p88; ☎ 676 4088; Newmount House, 22-24 Lower Mount St)
Goethe Institut (Map p88; ☎ 661 1155; 37 Merrion Sq North)
Italian Cultural Institute (Map p88; ☎ 676 6662; 11 Fitzwilliam Sq)
Spanish Cultural Institute (☎ 668 2024; 58 Northumberland Rd)

Emergency

For national emergency numbers see Emergencies inside the cover.
Confidential Line Freefone (☎ 1800 666 111) Garda confidential line to report crime.
Drugs Advisory & Treatment Centre (☎ 677 1122; Trinity Ct, 30-31 Pearse St)
Rape Crisis Centre (☎ 1800 778 888, 661 4911; 70 Lower Leeson St)
Samaritans (☎ 1850 609 090, 872 7700) For people who are depressed or suicidal.

Internet Access

Central Cyber Café (Map pp80-1; ☎ 677 8298; info@centralcafé.ie; 6 Grafton St)
Global Cyber Café (Map pp72-4; ☎ 878 0295; info@globalcafé.ie; 8 Lower O'Connell St)
Internet Exchange (Map pp80-1; ☎ 670 3000; iexch_cecilia_st@hotmail.com; 1 Cecilia St) Open 24 hours.

DUBLIN

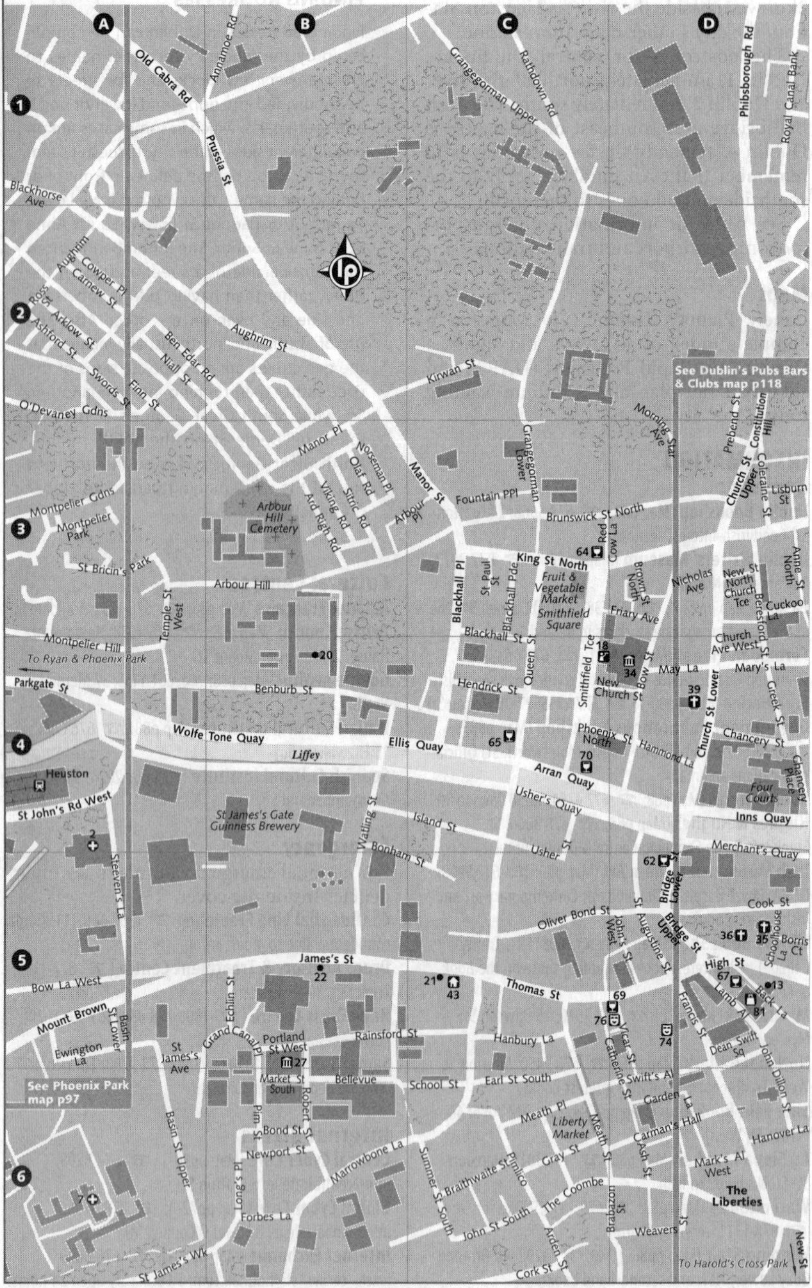

A
B
C
D
1
2
3
4
5
6
Old Cabra Rd
Annamoe Rd
Prussia St
Grangegorman Upper
Rathdown Rd
Phibsborough Rd
Royal Canal Bank
Blackhorse Ave
Aughrim St
Cowper Pl
Carnew St
Ross St
Arklow St
Ashford St
Swords St
Ben Edar Rd
Niall St
Finn St
O'Devaney Gdns
Kirwan St
See Dublin's Pubs Bars & Clubs map p118
Morning Star Ave
Prebend St
Constitution Hill
Manor Pl
Norseman Pl
Olaf Rd
Sitric Rd
Viking Rd
Ard Righ Rd
Manor St
Arbour Pl
Fountain Pl
Grangegorman Lower
Brunswick St North
Church St Upper
Coleraine St
Lisburn St
Montpelier Gdns
Montpelier Park
Arbour Hill Cemetery
King St North
Red Cow La
64
St Paul St
Blackhall Pde
Fruit & Vegetable Market
Smithfield Square
Brown St North
Nicholas Ave
New St North
Church Tce
Anne St North
Beresford St
Cuckoo La
St Bricin's Park
Arbour Hill
Blackhall Pl
Friary Ave
Temple St West
Montpelier Hill
To Ryan & Phoenix Park
20
Blackhall St
Queen St
Smithfield Tce
18
34
Bow St
May La
Church Ave West
Mary's La
Parkgate St
Benburb St
Hendrick St
New Church St
39
Church St Lower
Creek St
Wolfe Tone Quay
Ellis Quay
65
Phoenix St North
Hammond La
Chancery St
Liffey
70
Arran Quay
Heuston
St John's Rd West
St James's Gate Guinness Brewery
Usher's Quay
Four Courts
Chancery Place
Inns Quay
Watling St
Island St
2
Usher St
Bonham St
62
Merchant's Quay
Bridge St Lower
Steeven's La
Cook St
Oliver Bond St
John's St West
St Augustine St
Bridge St Upper
36
35
Schoolhouse La
Borris Ct
James's St
22
High St
21
43
67
13
Bow La West
Thomas St
69
Back La
Lamb Al
81
Mount Brown
Basin St Lower
Echlin St
Grand Canal Pl
Rainsford St
76
Vicar St
74
Francis St
Dean Swift Sq
Ewington La
St James's Ave
Portland St West
Hanbury La
27
Catherine St
Swift's Al
John Dillon St
See Phoenix Park map p97
Market St South
Robert St
Bellevue
School St
Earl St South
Garden La
Basin St Upper
Pim St
Bond St
Meath Pl
Liberty Market
Carman's Hall
Hanover La
Newport St
Marrowbone La
Summer St South
Braithwaite St
Pimlico
Gray St
Meath St
Ash St
Mark's Al West
Long's Pl
7
The Coombe
Brabazon St
The Liberties
Forbes La
John St South
Arden St
Weavers St
New St
St James's Wk
Cork St
To Harold's Cross Park

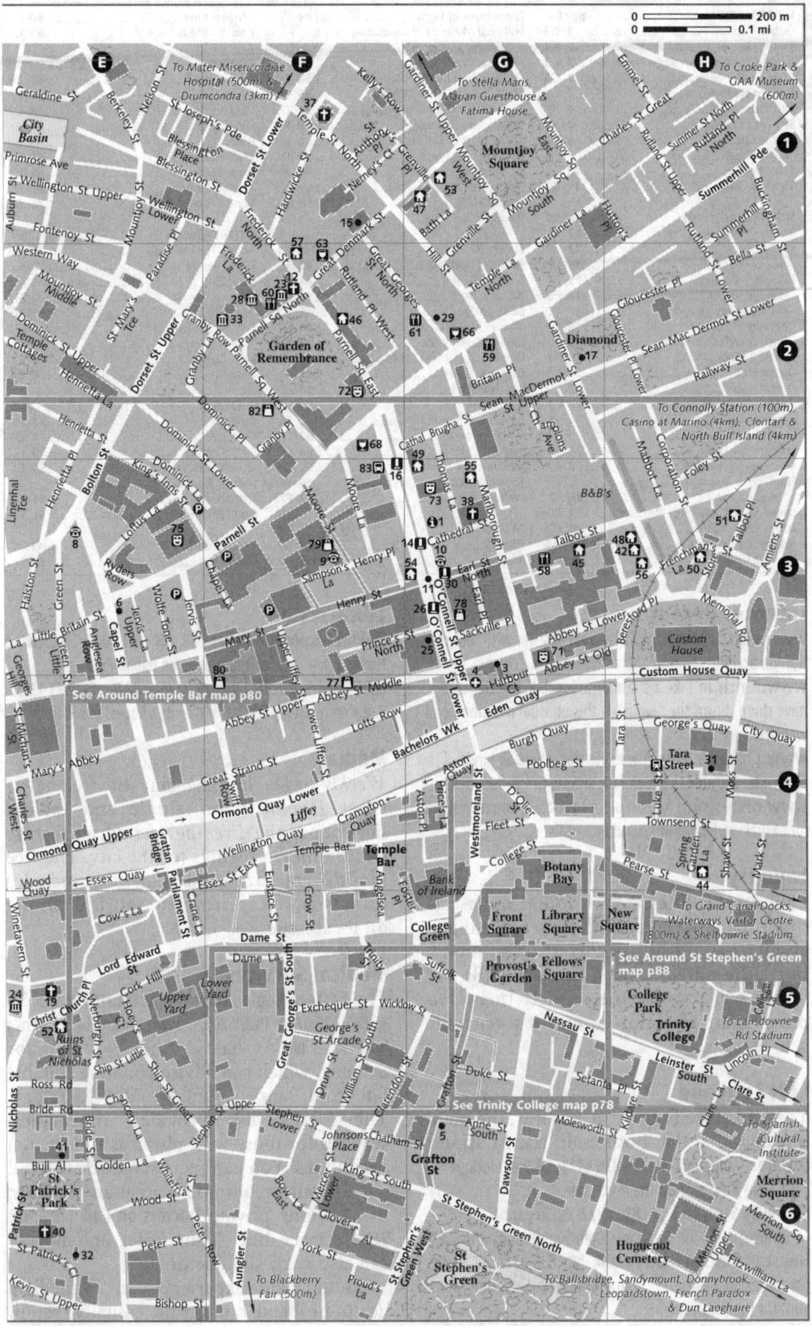
0 200 m
0 0.1 mi
E
F
G
H
1
2
3
4
5
6
To Mater Misericordiae Hospital (500m) & Drumcondra (3km)
To Stella Maris, Marian Guesthouse & Fatima House
To Croke Park & GAA Museum (600m)
To Connolly Station (100m), Casino at Marino (4km), Clontarf & North Bull Island (4km)
To Grand Canal Docks, Waterways Visitor Centre (800m) & Shelbourne Stadium
To Lansdowne Rd Stadium
To Spanish Cultural Institute
To Ballsbridge, Sandymount, Donnybrook, Leopardstown, French Paradox & Dun Laoghaire
To Blackberry Fair (500m)
See Around Temple Bar map p80
See Around St Stephen's Green map p88
See Trinity College map p78
Geraldine St
City Basin
Primrose Ave
Wellington St Upper
Auburn St
Fontenoy St
Western Way
Mountjoy Middle
Dominick St Upper
Temple Cottages
Henrietta La
Henrietta St
Henrietta Pl
Berkeley St
Nelson St
St Joseph's Pde
Blessington Place
Blessington St
Wellington Lower
Mountjoy St
Paradise Pl
St Mary's Tce
Dorset St Lower
Dorset St Upper
Granby Row
Granby La
Granby Pl
Hardwicke St
Frederick St North
Frederick La
Temple St North
Nerney's Ct
St Anthony's Pl
Grenville Pl
Kelly's Row
Great Denmark St
Rutland Pl West
Great Georges St North
Parnell Sq North
Parnell Sq West
Parnell Sq East
Garden of Remembrance
Gardiner St Upper
Mountjoy Sq West
Mountjoy Square
Mountjoy Sq East
Mountjoy Sq South
Bath La
Hill St
Grenville St
Gardiner La
Temple La North
Hutton's Pl
Emmet St
Charles St Great
Rutland St Upper
Summer St North
Rutland Pl North
Summerhill Pde
Summerhill Pl
Buckingham St
Rutland St Lower
Bella St
Gloucester Pl
Gloucester Pl Lower
Sean Mac Dermot St Lower
Diamond
Railway St
Britain Pl
Gardiner St Lower
Sean MacDermot St Upper
Champions Ave
Cathal Brugha St
Thomas La
Marlborough St
Mabbot La
Corporation St
Foley St
B&B's
Dominick Pl
Dominick St Lower
Dominick La
King's Inns St
Bolton St
Linenhall Tce
Loftus La
Parnell St
Moore St
Moore La
Cathedral St
Talbot St
Talbot Pl
Frenchman's La
Store St
Amiens St
Halston St
Green St
Ryders Row
Chapel La
Wolfe Tone St
Jervis St
Jervis La Upper
Sampson's La
Henry Pl
Henry St
Earl St North
Earl Pl
Sackville Pl
Abbey St Lower
Beresford Pl
Memorial Rd
Custom House
Little Britain St
Capel St
Anglesea Row
Little Green St
Georges Hill
Mary St
Upper Liffey St
Prince's St North
O'Connell St Upper
O'Connell St Lower
Abbey St Old
Harbour Ct
Custom House Quay
Abbey St Middle
Abbey St Upper
Lower Liffey St
Lotts Row
Eden Quay
Bachelors Wk
St Michan's St
Mary's Abbey
Great Strand St
Swift Row
Ormond Quay Lower
Ormond Quay Upper
Liffey
Grattan Bridge
Crampton Quay
Aston Quay
Aston Pl
Burgh Quay
Poolbeg St
George's Quay
City Quay
Tara St
Tara Street
Moss St
Luke St
Charles St West
Wellington Quay
Temple Bar
Price's La
Westmoreland St
D'Olier St
Fleet St
Townsend St
College St
Botany Bay
Pearse St
Spring Garden La
Shaw St
Mark St
Wood Quay
Essex Quay
Essex St East
Parliament St
Crane La
Eustace St
Crow St
Anglesea St
Foster Pl
Bank of Ireland
Front Square
Library Square
New Square
Winetavern St
Cow's La
College Green
Dame St
Dame La
Lord Edward St
Cork Hill
Upper Yard
Lower Yard
Trinity St
Suffolk St
Provost's Garden
Fellows' Square
College Park
Trinity College
College La
Christ Church Pl
Werburgh St
Hoey's Ct
Ruins of St Nicholas
Ship St Little
Ship St Great
Exchequer St
Wicklow St
George's St Arcade
Great George's St South
William St South
Drury St
Clarendon St
Grafton St
Duke St
Nassau St
Leinster St South
Lincoln Pl
Setanta Pl
Kildare St
Clare La
Clare St
Nicholas St
Ross Rd
Bride Rd
Bride St
Chancery La
Stephen St Upper
Stephen St Lower
Johnsons Place
Chatham St
Anne St South
Molesworth St
Dawson St
Bull Al
Golden La
St Patrick's Park
Whitefriar St
Wood St
Peter Row
Peter St
Mercer St Lower
King St South
Bow La East
Glover's Al
St Stephen's Green North
St Stephen's Green West
St Stephen's Green
Merrion Square
Merrion Sq South
Merrion St Upper
Huguenot Cemetery
Fitzwilliam La
Patrick St
St Patrick's Cl
Kevin St Upper
Bishop St
Aungier St
York St
Proud's La

INFORMATION	**pp71-6**	
Dublin Tourism	1	G3
Eastern Regional Health Authority	2	A4
Iarnród Éireann (Irish Railways Office)	3	G3
O'Connells Pharmacy	4	G4
O'Connells Pharmacy	5	G6
Outhouse	6	E3
St James's Hospital	7	A6
Talk Is Cheap	8	E3
Talk is Cheap	9	F3
Talk Shop	10	G3
Thomas Cook	11	G3
SIGHTS & ACTIVITIES	**pp76-100**	
Abbey Presbyterian Church	12	F2
An Taisce	13	D5
Anna Livia Statue	14	G3
Belvedere College	15	F1
Charles Parnell Statue	16	F3
Children's Playground	17	G2
Chimney	18	C4
Christ Church Cathedral	19	E5
Collins Barracks	20	B4
Digital Hub	21	C5
Digital Hub	22	B5
Dublin Writers Museum	23	F2
Dublinia	24	E5
Eason & Son	25	G3
Fr Matthew Statue	26	G3
Guinness Storehouse	27	B5
Hugh Lane Municipal Gallery of Modern Art	28	F2
James Joyce Cultural Centre	29	G2
James Joyce Statue	30	G3
Markievicz Lesiure Centre	31	H4
Marsh's Library	32	E6
Monument of Light	(see 11)	
National Museum of Decorative Arts & History	(see 20)	
National Wax Museum	33	F2
Old Jameson Distillery	34	D4
St Audoen's Catholic Church	35	D5
St Audoen's Church of Ireland	36	D5
St George's Church	37	F1
St Mary's Pro-Cathedral	38	G3
St Michan's Church	39	D4
St Patrick's Cathedral	40	E6
Synod Hall	(see 24)	
Tailor's Hall	(see 13)	
Viking Splash Tours	41	E6
SLEEPING	**pp105-11**	
Anchor Guesthouse	42	H3
Brewery Hostel	43	C5
Brown's Hotel	44	H4
Celtic Lodge	45	G3
Charles Stewart	46	F2
Clifden Guesthouse	47	G1
Globetrotters Tourist Hostel	48	H3
Gresham Hotel	49	G3
Isaac's Hostel	50	H3
Jacob's Inn	51	H3
Jurys Inn Christchurch	52	E5
Lyndon House	53	G1
Lynham's Hotel	54	G3
Marlborough Hostel	55	G3
Townhouse	56	H3
Waltons Hotel	57	F2
EATING	**pp111-17**	
101 Talbot	58	G3
Ailang	59	G2
Chapter One	60	F2
Cobalt Café & Gallery	61	G2
DRINKING	**pp117-20**	
Brazen Head	62	D5
Castle Hotel	63	F2
Cobblestone	64	C3
Dice Bar	65	C4
Forum Bar	66	G2
Mother Redcaps	67	D5
Parnell Mooney	68	F2
Thomas House	69	D5
Voodoo Lounge	70	C4
ENTERTAINMENT	**pp120-4**	
Abbey Theatre	71	G3
Gate Theatre	72	F2
Isaac Butt	(see 50)	
Peacock Theatre	(see 71)	
Savoy	73	G3
Temple Theatre	(see 37)	
Tivoli Theatre	74	D5
UGC Multiplex	75	E3
Vicar St	76	D5
SHOPPING	**pp124-5**	
Arnott's	77	F4
Clery's & Co	78	G3
ILAC Centre	79	F3
Jervis St Centre	80	F4
Mother Redcaps Market	81	D5
Sinn Féin Bookshop	82	F2
TRANSPORT	**pp125-8**	
Dublin Bus	83	F3

Internet Resources

www.visitdublin.com Fáilte Ireland's site with information on accommodation and activities in the city.

www.lunch.ie Take a stranger to lunch in the city and have them return the favour via this unusual meeting point website.

www.pigsback.com A website that offers all kinds of city-wide discounts from cinema tickets to free lunches.

www.nixers.com A good place to check if you're looking for casual work over the summer.

Laundry

Laundry facilities can be found quite easily in the city centre with prices starting at about €7.50 a load; ask at your accommodation. Alternatively, most hostels, B&Bs and hotels will provide the service. In hostels prices start at about €6 and it's generally self-service.

Left Luggage

You can store luggage at Busáras, the main bus depot, and at both main train stations.

Busáras (Map pp72-4; ☎ 836 6111; €4-9 per locker; 🕓 7am-10.45pm) On the north side.

Connolly Station (☎ 836 6222; €2.50 per bag; 🕓 7am-10pm Mon-Sat, 8am-10pm Sun) On the north side.

Heuston Station (Map pp72-4; ☎ 836 6222; €1.50-5 per locker for 24 hrs; 🕓 7am-10pm Mon-Sat, 8am-10pm Sun) On the south side.

Libraries

Dublin Corporation (Map p88; ☎ 661 9000; Cumberland House, Fenian St) For information on public libraries.

ILAC Centre Public Library (Map pp72-4; ☎ 873 4333; ILAC Centre, Henry St) One of the city's largest public libraries.

Media

Weekly In Dublin magazine, the free newssheet *Dublin Event Guide* and tabloid newspaper the *Evening Herald* all feature entertainment listings for the city. The free monthly magazine the *Slate* also includes listings as well as irreverent satirical ranting on local issues.

Medical Services

The **Eastern Regional Health Authority** (Map pp72-4; ☎ 679 0700; 1800 520520; www.erha.ie; Dr Steevens's Hospital, Dublin 8) has a Choice of Doctor Scheme, which can advise you on a suitable GP from 9am to 5pm Monday to Friday. The ERHA also provides information services for those with physical and mental disabilities. You can request a doctor to call out to your accommodation at any time on the 24-hour private **Doctors on Call** (☎ 453 9333) service line. Your hotel or embassy can also suggest a doctor.

Should you experience an immediate health problem, contact the casualty section of the nearest public hospital; in an emergency call an ambulance on ☎ 999.

Baggot St Hospital (Map p88; ☎ 668 1577; 18 Upper Baggot St) South side city centre.

Mater Misericordiae Hospital (☎ 830 1122; Eccles St off Lower Dorset St) North side city centre.

St James's Hospital (Map pp72-4; ☎ 453 7941; James St) South side.

Condoms are widely available in Dublin, in both pharmacies and in many bars and clubs. The contraceptive pill is available only on prescription. The following city centre chemists stay open till 10pm:

O'Connell's Pharmacy (Map pp72-4; ☎ 679 0467; 21 Grafton St; ☎ 873 0427; 55-56 O'Connell St)

Well Women Clinic (Map pp72-4; ☎ 661 0083; 35 Lower Liffey St; ☎ 660 9860; 67 Pembroke Rd) For female health issues. It supplies contraceptives, including the morning-after pill (€39).

Money

There are currency-exchange counters at Dublin airport in the baggage-collection area and on the arrival and departure floors, open 5.30am to 11pm.

There are numerous banks around the city centre with exchange facilities, open during regular bank hours.

First Rate (Map pp80-1; ☎ 671 3233; 1 Westmoreland St; 🕑 8am-9pm Mon-Fri, 9am-9pm Sat, 10am-9pm Sun Jun-Sep, 9am-6pm daily Oct-May)

American Express (☎ 605 7709; Dublin Tourism, Andrew's St; 🕑 9am-5pm Mon-Sat)

Thomas Cook (Map pp80-1; ☎ 677 1721, 677 1307; 118 Grafton St; 🕑 9am-5.30pm Mon- Tue & Fri-Sat, 10am-5.30pm Wed, 9am-7pm Thu)

Post

GPO (Map pp72-4; ☎ 705 7000; O'Connell St; 🕑 8am-8pm Mon-Sat) Dublin's famed general post office has a free poste restante service, a philatelic counter and a bank of telephones.

An Post (Map p88; ☎ 677 7127; Sth Anne St; 🕑 9am-6pm Mon-Fri; ☎ 705 8206; St Andrew's St; 🕑 8.30am-5pm Mon-Fri)

Telephone

Talk Shop (Map pp80-1; ☎ 672 7212; www.talkshop.ie; 20 Temple Lane; Map pp72-4; ☎ 872 0200; 5 Upper O'Connell St) For cheap international phone calls.

Talk Is Cheap (Map pp80-1; ☎ 872 2235; 87 Capel St; ☎ 874 6013; 55 Moore St)

Tourist Information

No tourist information offices in Dublin provide any information over the phone – they're exclusively walk-in services.

Dublin Tourism Centre (Map pp80-1; ☎ 605 7700; www.visitdublin.com; St Andrew's Church, 2 Suffolk St; 🕑 9am-7pm Mon-Sat, 10.30am-3pm Sun Jul & Aug, 9am-5.30pm Mon-Sat Sep-Jun) Dublin's main tourist office. There is a booking fee of €4 for serviced accommodation, €7 for self-catering and a 10% deposit is refunded through your hotel bill.

Dublin Tourism City Centre (Map pp72-4; 14 O'Connell St; 🕑 9am-5pm Mon- Sat; Map pp72-4; Wilton Tce; 🕑 9.30am-noon & 12.30-5pm Mon-Fri) Dun Laoghaire

DUBLIN IN...

Two Days

Kick-start your day with a mean brunch at **Gruel** (p112) on Dame St, a stone's throw from **Trinity College** (p77) where the walking tour includes entry to the **Book of Kells** (p77). Ramble through atmospheric **George's Street Arcade** (p125) to **Grafton St** (p87) to catch the **buskers** and splurge on Dublin's most exclusive shopping street. Round it off with a cocktail, dinner and outdoor movie on the terrace at **Eden** (p116), one of Dublin's trendiest restaurants in **Temple Bar** (p80) before falling into bed at the fashionable **Clarence Hotel** (p109). The next day marvel at the oriental art of the **Chester Beatty Library** (p82) before strolling up to the **Guinness Storehouse** (p94) for a tour that ends with a glass of 'plain' in the Gravity Bar with stunning 360 degree views of the city.

Four Days

Follow the two-day itinerary then wander around the historic **Glasnevin Cemetery** (p97) before moseying into the peaceful **Botanic Gardens** (p97). Back in town, browse the funky shops of **Cow's Lane** in Temple Bar and grab a bite in **Diep Noodle Bar** (p116) before taking the **Dublin Literary Pub Crawl** (p103). The following day take the DART along the coast to exclusive suburb **Killiney** for a stroll on the beach and stop off at the pretty village of **Dalkey** (p132) on the way home. Gather your strength with a fine meal at **Mash** (p116) before a gig at **Vicar St** (p123).

(Dun Laoghaire ferryport; 10am-6pm Mon-Sat)
Airport (Arrivals hall; 8am-10pm daily)
Fáilte Ireland head office (Map p88; ☎ 1850 230330; www.ireland.travel.com; Wilton Tce, Baggot St Bridge; 9am-5.15pm Mon-Fri)

All telephone bookings and reservations are operated by Gulliver, a computerised information and reservation service that is available at all walk-in offices or from anywhere in the world. It provides up-to-date information on events, attractions and transport, and can also book accommodation. In Ireland, call ☎ 1800 668668; from Britain call ☎ 00800 6686 6866; from the rest of the world call ☎ 00 353 669 792083.

Travel Agencies

Amex and Thomas Cook both have offices in the centre of Dublin (p75).

USIT (Map pp80-1; ☎ 602 1600; www.usit.com; 19 Aston Quay, 9.30am-6.30pm Mon-Wed & Fri, 9.30am-8pm Thu, 9.30am-6.30pm Sat) Travel agency of the Union of Students in Ireland.

DANGERS & ANNOYANCES

Despite the fact that Dublin is one of Europe's safest capitals, in recent years its good reputation has been somewhat marred by an increase in petty crime, particularly pick-pocketing, bag-snatching and car break-ins. So be sure to take the usual precautionary measures and you won't find yourself describing the contents of your bag/wallet/car to a jaded police officer. The most important of these is don't show off your valuables and don't leave anything in your car. The latter is particularly true for rental and foreign-registered vehicles, seen as an easy target by thieves. You should also bear in mind that insurance policies often don't cover losses from cars.

Certain parts of Dublin are unsafe after dark and visitors should avoid run-down, deserted-looking and poorly lit areas. Phoenix Park is not safe at night and under no circumstances should you camp there. One of the more deleterious effects of Ireland's recent economic boom has been the sharp increase in numbers of young people who drink to excess at weekends. Hospital casualty departments have had to bear the brunt of it with emergency departments clogged up with drink-related casualties. Regrettably O'Connell St has become an unpleasant place to find yourself in the small hours, when hordes of drink-fuelled revellers spill out of nightclubs in search of taxis, kebabs and sometimes trouble. Some of the hostels are also in the rougher parts of north Dublin.

As in other parts of Europe, beggars, some of them alarmingly young, are commonplace. If you don't want to give them money but would like to do something to help the homeless and long-term unemployed, you could buy a copy of the magazine the *Big Issue* (€2.50), some of the proceeds of which go to them.

Like all big cities, Dublin is choking on traffic fumes, as you'll become quickly aware if you're travelling by bike. Following New York's lead, from January 2004 a ban on smoking in bars and restaurants took effect. It was a move that, with the exception of the Vintner's Association unsurprisingly, was generally greeted with uncharacteristic acceptance.

RACISM

The influx of nonwhite immigrants and asylum seekers to Dublin has not been without its problems, especially for Africans and, to a lesser extent, Eastern Europeans. The irony is the vast majority of Dubliners deny that they have any racist feelings and that Ireland as a whole is not a racist country. That said, an overwhelming majority of blacks in Dublin have experienced some kind of racial harassment, especially taunting.

Racism does exist and is a problem. Thankfully, though, the more extreme kind of racism – punctuated by physical intimidation or violence – is infrequent and limited to a mindless minority. Still, there are enough right-minded Dubliners to ensure that in most cases sense and decency will prevail, and it is not unheard of for locals to rally to the side of the victim of racial abuse. If you do experience any problems, be sure to report them to the police.

SIGHTS

South Dublin has the fanciest shops, almost all the restaurants of note and a majority of the hotels, as well as most of the reminders of Dublin's early history and the finest

Georgian squares and houses. However, north of the Liffey, you'll still find plenty of architectural and historical significance, cheaper shops and perhaps a more authentic taste of the true character of the city.

South of the Liffey

TRINITY COLLEGE Map p78

Ireland's premier university – and one of the city's most beautiful sights – was founded by Elizabeth I in 1592 on grounds confiscated from the Augustinian priory of All Hallows, which was dissolved in 1537. By providing an alternative to education on the continent, the queen hoped the students would avoid being 'infected with popery'. Trinity is in the centre of Dublin, though at the time of foundation it was outside the city walls. Archbishop Ussher, whose scientific feats included the precise dating of the act of creation to 4004 BC, was one of the college's founders.

Officially, the university's name is the University of Dublin, but Trinity College is its sole college. Until 1793 Trinity College remained completely Protestant apart from one short break. Even when the Protestants allowed Catholics in, the Catholic Church forbade it, a restriction that wasn't completely lifted until 1970. To this day Trinity College is still something of a centre of British and Protestant influence, even though the majority of its 9500 students are Catholic. Women were first admitted in 1903, earlier than at most British universities.

A good way to see the college is on an organised **walking tour** (☎ 608 1724; admission €9; ⏰ 10.15am-3.40pm Mon-Sat, 10.15am-3pm Sun mid-May–Sep). They depart every 40 minutes from the main gate on College Green (the street in front of the college). It's good value since it includes the fee to see the *Book of Kells*.

Facing College Green, the Front Gate or Regent House **main entrance** to the college grounds was built between 1752 and 1759 and is guarded by statues of the poet Oliver Goldsmith (1730–74) and the orator Edmund Burke (1729–97).

The open area reached from Regent House is divided into Front Square, Parliament Square and Library Square. The area is dominated by the 30m-high **Campanile**, designed by Edward Lanyon and erected between 1852 and 1853 on what was believed to be the centre of the monastery that preceded the college. To the left of the Campanile is a statue of George Salmon, college provost from 1888 to 1904, who fought bitterly to keep women out of the college. He carried out his threat to permit them 'over my dead body' by promptly dropping dead when the worst came to pass.

Clockwise round Front Square from the Front Gate, the first building is the **chapel** (☎ 608 1260; Front Sq, Trinity College; admission free), built from 1798 to plans made in 1777 by the architect Sir William Chambers (1723–96) and, since 1972, open to all denominations. It's noted for its extremely fine plasterwork by Michael Stapleton, its Ionic columns and its painted, rather than

BOOK OF KELLS

For visitors, Trinity College's prime attraction is the magnificent *Book of Kells*, an illuminated manuscript dating from around AD 800, making it one of the oldest books in the world. It was probably produced by monks at St Colmcille's Monastery on the remote island of Iona, off the western coast of Scotland. Repeated looting by marauding Vikings forced the monks to flee to the temporary safety of Kells, County Meath, in Ireland in AD 806, along with their masterpiece. Around 8½ centuries later, the book was brought to the college for safekeeping and has remained there since.

The *Book of Kells* contains the four gospels of the New Testament, written in Latin, as well as prefaces, summaries and other text. If it were merely words, the *Book of Kells* would simply be a very old book – it's the extensive and amazingly complex illustrations that make it so wonderful. The superbly decorated opening initials are only part of the story, for the book has smaller illustrations between the lines.

The 680-page book was rebound in four calfskin volumes in 1953. Two volumes are usually on display, one showing an illuminated page and the other showing text. The pages are turned over regularly, but you can acquire your own reproduction copy for a mere €22,000. If that's too steep, the library bookshop has various less expensive books, including *The Book of Kells*, a paperback with some attractive colour plates costing €18 or a popular CD-ROM showing all 800 pages for €30.

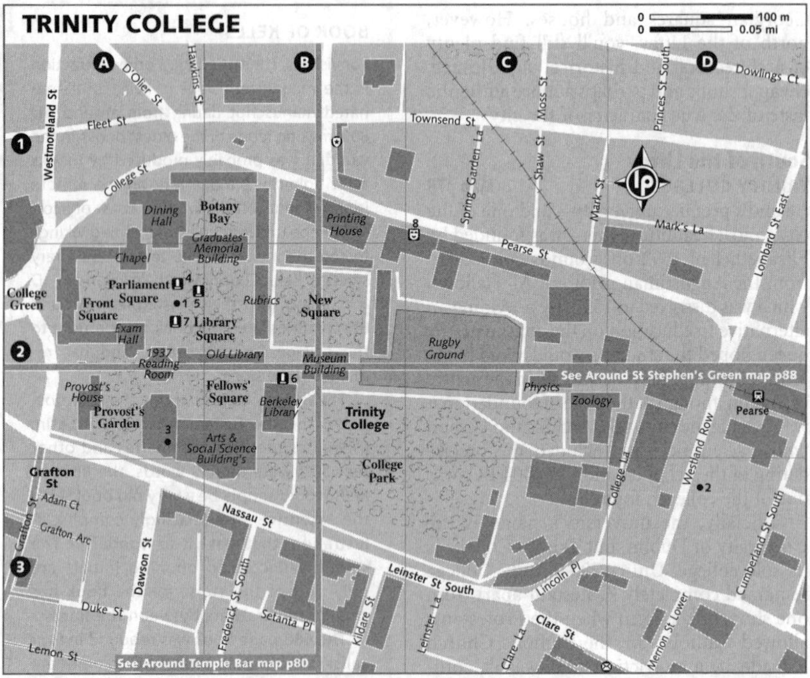

SIGHTS & ACTIVITIES pp76-100
Campanile......1 A2
Dan Dooley Car & Van Hire......2 D3
Douglas Hyde Gallery......3 A2
George Salmon Statue......4 A2
Henry Moore Statue......5 A2
Sphere within Sphere......6 B2
WEH Lecky Statue......7 A2

ENTERTAINMENT p124
Players' Theatre......8 C1

stained-glass, windows. The main one is dedicated to Archbishop Ussher.

Next to the chapel is the **dining hall** (Parliament Sq; open to students only), originally designed in 1743 by Richard Cassels (aka Castle), but dismantled 15 years later because of problems caused by inadequate foundations. The replacement was completed in 1761 and may have retained some elements of the original design. It was extensively restored after a fire in 1984.

The 1892 **Graduates' Memorial Building** (Botany Bay; closed to public) forms the northern side of Library Square. Behind it are the tennis courts in the open area known as Botany Bay. The popular legend behind this name is that the unruly students housed around the square were suitable candidates for the British penal colony at Botany Bay in Australia.

At the eastern side of Library Square, the red-brick **Rubrics Building** dates from around 1690, making it the oldest building in the college. It was extensively altered in an 1894 restoration and then underwent major structural modifications in the 1970s.

To the south of the square is the **Old Library** (☎ 608 2320; Library Sq; admission as part of Book of Kells tour), which was built in a rather severe style by Thomas Burgh between 1712 and 1732. The Old Library's 65m Long Room contains numerous unique ancient texts, and its biggest attraction **Book of Kells** (see the boxed text on p77) is displayed in the Library Colonnades. Despite Ireland's independence, the Library Act of 1801 still entitles Trinity College Library, along with four libraries in Britain, to a free copy of every book published in the UK. Housing this bounty requires nearly another 1km of shelving every year and the collection amounts to around 4½ million books. Of course these cannot all be kept at the college library, so there are now additional library storage facilities dotted around Dublin.

The **Long Room** (☎ 608 2320; East Pavilion, Library Colonnades; adult/under 12s €7.50/free; includes admission to temporary exhibitions in the East Pavilion; 9.30am-5pm Mon-Sat year round, noon-4.30pm Sun Oct-May, 9.30am-4pm Sun Jun-Sep) is mainly used for about 250,000 of the library's oldest volumes. Until 1892 the ground floor Colonnades was an open arcade, but it was enclosed at that time to increase the storage area. A previous attempt to increase the room's storage capacity had been made in 1853, when the Long Room ceiling was raised.

As well as the world-famous *Book of Kells*, on display is the so-called harp of Brian Ború, which was definitely not in use when the army of this early Irish hero defeated the Danes at the Battle of Clontarf in 1014. It does, however, date from around 1400, making it one of the oldest harps in Ireland.

Other exhibits in the Long Room include a rare copy of the Proclamation of the Irish Republic, which was read out by Pádraig Pearse at the beginning of the Easter Rising in 1916. The collection of 18th- and 19th-century marble busts around the walls features Jonathan Swift, Edmund Burke and Wolfe Tone, all former members of Trinity College.

The Long Room and *Book of Kells* exhibition is packed in high season. The Colonnades also houses a busy book and souvenir shop and a temporary exhibition hall.

Continuing clockwise around the Campanile there's the **1937 Reading Room** and the **Public Theatre** or Exam Hall, which dates from 1779 to 1791. Like the Chapel building it was the work of William Chambers and also has plasterwork by Michael Stapleton. The Exam Hall has an oak chandelier rescued from the Houses of Parliament (now the Bank of Ireland) across College Green and an organ said to have been salvaged from a Spanish ship in 1702, though evidence indicates otherwise.

Behind the Exam Hall is the 1760 **Provost's House**, a particularly fine Georgian house where the provost, or college head, still resides. The house and its adjacent garden are not open to the public.

To one side of the Old Library is Paul Koralek's 1967 **Berkeley Library** (Fellow's Sq; closed to public). This solid, square brutalist-style building has been hailed as the best example of modern architecture in Ireland, though it has to be admitted the competition isn't great. It's fronted by Arnaldo Pomodoro's 1982–83 sculpture *Sphere within Sphere*.

George Berkeley was born in Kilkenny in 1685, studied at Trinity when he was only 15 years old and went on to a distinguished career in many fields, but particularly in philosophy. His influence spread to the new English colonies in North America where, among other things, he helped to found the University of Pennsylvania. Berkeley in California, and its namesake university, are named after him.

South of the Old Library is the 1978 **Arts & Social Science Building**, which backs on to Nassau St and forms the alternative entrance to the college. Like the Berkeley Library it was designed by Paul Koralek; it also houses the **Douglas Hyde Gallery of Modern Art** (☎ 608 1116; admission free; 11am-6pm Mon-Wed & Fri, 11am-7pm Thu, 11am-4.45pm Sat).

After the *Book of Kells* the college's other big tourist attraction is the **Dublin Experience** (☎ 608 1688; Arts & Social Science Bldg; adult/student €4.20/3.50, incl Book of Kells €10.50/8.50; 10am-5pm mid-May–Sep). It's a 45-minute multimedia introduction to the city. Shows take place at the back of the Arts & Social Science Building.

Behind the Rubrics Building, at the eastern end of Library Square, is **New Square**. The highly ornate 1853–57 **Museum Building** (☎ 608 1477; New Sq; admission free; by prior arrangement only) has the skeletons of two enormous giant Irish deer just inside the entrance, and the Geological Museum upstairs.

The 1734 **Printing House**, designed by Richard Cassels to resemble a Doric temple and now used for the microelectronics and electrical engineering departments, is on the northern side of New Square.

At the eastern end of the college grounds are the rugby ground and College Park, where cricket is played. There are a number of science buildings here also. The Lincoln Place Gate at this end is usually open and makes a good entrance or exit from the college, especially if you're on a bicycle.

BANK OF IRELAND

The imposing **Bank of Ireland** (Map pp80-1; ☎ 671 1488; College Green; 10am-4pm Mon-Wed & Fri, 10am-5pm Thu), directly opposite Trinity College, was originally built in 1729 to house the Irish Parliament. When the Parliament voted itself out of existence by the Act of Union in 1801, it became a building without a role. It was sold in 1803 with instructions that the interior be altered to prevent its being used as a debating chamber in the future. Consequently, the large central House of Commons was remodelled but the smaller chamber of the House of Lords survived. After independence the Irish government chose to make Leinster House the new parliamentary building and ignored the possibility of restoring this fine building to its original use.

Inside, the banking mall occupies what was once the House of Commons, but it offers little indication of its former role. The Irish House of Lords is a much more interesting place, with its Irish-oak woodwork, late-18th-century Dublin crystal chandelier and tapestries and 10kg silver-gilt mace.

There are **tours** of the **House of Lords** (admission free), which also include an informal talk as much about Ireland, and life in general, as the building itself. Tours are on Tuesdays at 10.30am, 11.30am and 1.45am.

TEMPLE BAR

West of College Green and the Bank of Ireland, the maze of streets that make up **Temple Bar** (Map pp80–1) are sandwiched between Dame St and the river. One of the oldest areas of the city, Temple Bar's run-down buildings and cobbled streets were revitalised throughout the 1990s and it is now the most popular part of the city centre. Temple Bar has a number of interesting galleries and small museums, as well as a growing selection of trendy shops, but it is the area's pubs and restaurants that are its biggest draw, attracting tourists in their tens of thousands.

Frankly, Temple Bar has been ruined by the success it has had since it was first earmarked as the city's 'cultural quarter'. In an attempt to recreate a Left Bank atmosphere where artists' studios stood alongside cosy cafés and small boutiques selling ethnic artefacts, developers succumbed to the powerful financial draw and created an over-commercialised quarter full of overpriced

AROUND TEMPLE BAR

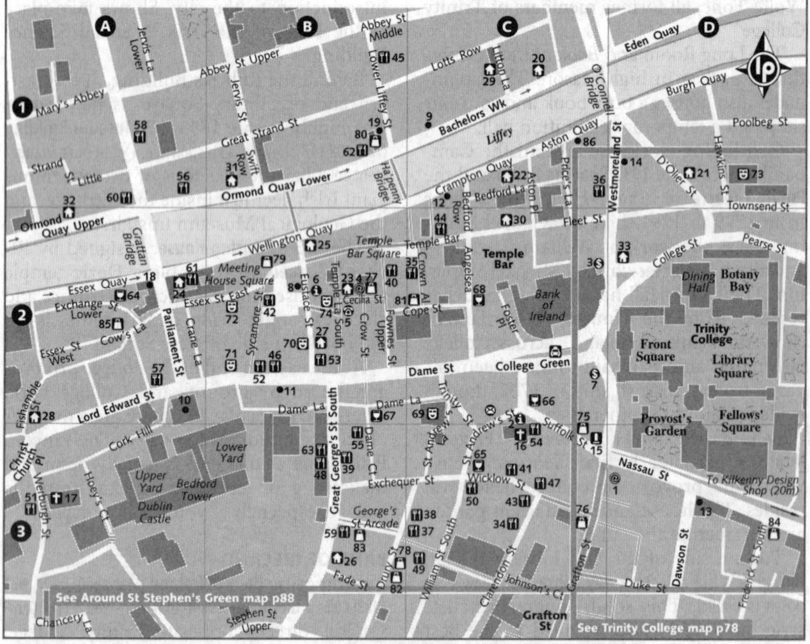

restaurants serving indifferent food aimed strictly at tourists and – with one or two exceptions – characterless bars. During the day, however, Temple Bar is pleasant enough; at night (especially at the weekend) it overflows with drunken locals and foreigners intent on renaming the area Temple Barf.

Dame St forms part of the southern boundary of Temple Bar and links new Dublin (centred around Trinity College and Grafton St) and old (stretching from Dublin Castle to encompass Christ Church and St Patrick's cathedrals). Along its route Dame St changes name to Cork Hill, Lord Edward St and Christchurch Place.

Temple Bar Properties (Map pp80-1; ☎ 677 2255; www.templebar.ie; 18 Eustace St; ⌚ 9am-5.30pm Mon-Fri) publishes the TASCQ cultural guide to Temple Bar which gives information on attractions and restaurants in the area and is available from its office or in businesses around Temple Bar. It's best to check the website for details of events and the Diversions festival, a programme of family entertainment, music and film which takes place in Meeting House Square between May and September.

The western boundary of Temple Bar is formed by **Fishamble St**, the oldest street in Dublin, dating back to Viking times – not that you'd know that to see it now. Christ Church Cathedral (see p83), beside Fishamble St, dates from 1170, but there was an earlier Viking church on this site. Brass symbols in the pavement direct you towards a mosaic laid out to show the ground plan of the sort of Viking dwelling excavated here in 1980 and 1981. Another Viking area is being excavated closer to Parliament St.

In 1742 Handel conducted the first performance of his **Messiah** in the **Dublin Music Hall**, behind Kinlay House hotel on Lord Edward St, now part of a hotel that bears the composer's name. The Music Hall, which opened in 1741, was designed by Richard Cassels; the only reminder of it today is the entrance and the original door.

On **Parliament St**, which runs south from the river to the City Hall and Dublin Castle, the Sunlight Chambers beside the river has a beautiful **frieze** around the façade. Sunlight was a brand of soap manufactured by Lever Brothers, who were responsible for the late-19th-century building. The frieze shows the Lever Brothers' view of the world and soap: men make clothes dirty, women wash them!

Eustace St is an interesting road. Buildings on the street include the 1715 Presbyterian Meeting House, now **The Ark** (☎ 670 7788; 11a Eustace St), a children's cultural centre. The

INFORMATION pp71-6
- Central Cyber Café 1 D3
- Dublin Tourism Centre 2 C2
- First Rate 3 C2
- Internet Exchange 4 B2
- Talk Shop 5 B2
- Temple Bar Properties 6 B2
- Thomas Cook 7 C2

SIGHTS & ACTIVITIES pp76-100
- Ark 8 B2
- C Harding for Bikes 9 C1
- City Hall 10 A2
- Dame St Pharmacy 11 B2
- Forbidden Planet 12 C1
- Fred Hanna 13 D3
- Harrisons 14 D1
- Molly Malone Statue 15 C3
- St Andrew's Church 16 C3
- St Werburgh's Church 17 A3
- Sunlight Chambers 18 A2
- Well Women Clinic 19 B1

SLEEPING pp105-11
- Abbey Court Hostel 20 C1
- Ashfield House 21 D1
- Aston Hotel 22 C1
- Barnacles Temple Bar House 23 B2
- Clarence 24 A2
- Eliza Lodge 25 B2
- Grafton Guesthouse 26 B3
- Irish Landmark Trust 27 B2
- Kinlay House 28 A3
- Litton Lane Hostel 29 C1
- Morgan 30 C2
- Morrison Hotel 31 B1
- Ormond Quay Hotel 32 A2
- Westin Dublin 33 D2

EATING pp111-17
- Aya 34 C3
- Bad Ass Café 35 C2
- Bewley's Oriental Café 36 C1
- Bistro 37 C3
- Blazing Salads 38 C3
- Café Bardeli 39 B3
- Café Irie 40 B2
- Cornucopia 41 C3
- Eden 42 B2
- El Bahia 43 C3
- Elephant & Castle 44 C2
- Epicurean Food Hall 45 B1
- Gruel 46 B2
- Halo (see 31)
- Imperial Chinese 47 C3
- Juice 48 B3
- La Maison des Gourmets 49 C3
- Lemon 50 C3
- Leo Burdock's 51 A3
- Mermaid Café 52 B2
- Monty's 53 B2
- Nude 54 C2
- Odessa 55 B3
- Panem 56 A1
- Queen of Tarts 57 A2
- Refectory Restaurant (see 28)
- Ristorante Romano 58 A1
- Simon's Place 59 B3
- Soup Dragon 60 A1
- Tea Rooms 61 A2
- Winding Stair Bookshop & Café 62 B1
- Yamamori 63 B3

DRINKING pp117-20
- Bar Italia 64 A2
- International 65 C3
- O'Neill's 66 C2
- Stag's Head 67 B2
- Stock Exchange 68 C2

ENTERTAINMENT pp120-4
- Andrew's Lane Theatre 69 C2
- Irish Film Centre 70 B2
- Olympia Theatre 71 B2
- Project Arts Centre 72 B2
- Screen 73 D1
- Temple Bar Music Centre 74 B2

SHOPPING pp124-5
- Avoca Handweavers 75 C3
- Brown Thomas 76 C3
- Claddagh Records 77 B2
- Costume 78 C3
- DesignYard 79 B2
- Dublin Woollen Company 80 B1
- Eager Beaver 81 C2
- George St Arcade (see 83)
- Harlequin 82 C3
- Jenny Vander 83 B3
- Knobs & Knockers 84 D3
- Smock 85 A2

OTHER
- Usit 86 C1

Dublin branch of the Society of United Irishmen, who sought parliamentary reform and equality for Catholics, was first convened in 1791 in the Eagle Tavern, now the Friends Meeting House. This should not be confused with the other Eagle Tavern, which is on Cork St.

Merchant's Arch leads to the **Ha'penny Bridge**, so called because of the ha'penny toll once demanded to cross. The Stock Exchange lives on Anglesea St, in a building dating from 1878.

DUBLIN CASTLE

The centre of British power in Ireland and originally built on the orders of King John in 1204, **Dublin Castle** (Map pp80-1; ☎ 677 7129; Cork Hill, Dame St; adult/student/senior or child €4.25/3.25/1.75; 10am-5pm Mon-Fri, 2-5pm Sat & Sun) is more palace than castle. Only the Record Tower, completed in 1258, survives from the original Norman castle. Parts of the castle's foundations remain and a visit to the excavations is the most interesting part of the castle tour. The moats, which are now completely covered by more modern developments, were once filled by the River Poddle. The castle is also home to one of Dublin's best museums, the Chester Beatty Library.

The castle, which tops Cork Hill, behind the City Hall, is still used for government business, and tours (every 20 minutes) are often tailored around meetings and conferences or sometimes cancelled altogether, so it's wise to phone beforehand.

CHESTER BEATTY LIBRARY

The world-famous **Chester Beatty Library** (Map pp80-1; ☎ 407 0750; www.cbl.ie; Dublin Castle; admission free; 10am-5pm Mon-Fri, 11am-5pm Sat, 1-5pm Sun, tours 1pm Wed, 3 & 4pm Sun) houses the collection of mining engineer Sir Alfred Chester Beatty (1875–1968) bequeathed to the Irish State on his death. The breathtaking collection includes over 20,000 manuscripts, rare books, miniature paintings, clay tablets, costumes and other objects spread across two floors. On the ground floor you'll find works of art from the Western, Islamic and East-Asian worlds, including perhaps the finest collection of Chinese jade books in the world. Also worth examining are the illuminated European texts.

The 2nd floor is devoted to the major religions of the world – Judaism, Islam, Christianity, Hinduism and Buddhism. The collection of Qur'ans dating from the 9th to the 19th centuries (the library has over 270 of them) are considered by experts to be the best example of illuminated Islamic texts in the world. And it doesn't stop there. You'll also find some marvellous examples of ancient papyri, including the renowned Egyptian love poems from the 12th century, and some of the earliest illuminated gospels in the world, dating to around AD 200. The collection is rounded off with some exquisite scrolls and artwork from China, Japan, Tibet and Southeast Asia.

There's also a full restaurant, gift shop and oriental roof garden here.

BEDFORD TOWER & GENEALOGICAL OFFICE

The **Bedford Tower & Genealogical Office** (Map pp80–1) are directly across the Upper Yard from the main entrance. In 1907 the collection known as the Irish Crown Jewels was stolen from the tower and never recovered. The Genealogical Office as an institution dates from 1552. Its present building dates from the 18th century.

The entranceway to the castle yard, beside the Bedford Tower, is topped by a statue of Justice which has always been a subject of mirth. She faces the castle and has her back to the city – seen as a sure indicator of how much justice the average Irish citizen could expect from the British. The scales of justice also had a distinct tendency to fill with rain and tilt in one direction or the other, rather than assuming the approved level position. Eventually a hole was drilled in the bottom of each pan so the rainwater could drain out.

CITY HALL & MUNICIPAL BUILDINGS

Fronting Dublin Castle on Lord Edward St, the **City Hall** (Map pp80-1; ☎ 672 2204; www.dublincity.ie/cityhall; Cork Hill; adult/student/senior or child €4/2/1.50; 10am-5.15pm Mon-Sat, 2-5pm Sun) was built by Thomas Cooley between 1769 and 1779 as the Royal Exchange and later became the offices of the Dublin Corporation. It stands on the site of the Lucas Coffee House and the Eagle Tavern, in which Dublin's infamous Hell Fire Club was established in 1735. Founded by Richard Parsons, Earl of Rosse, it was one of a number of gentlemen's clubs in Dublin where less-than-gentlemanly conduct took place. It gained a reputation for debauchery and black magic, but there's no evidence that such things took place.

A multimedia exhibition entitled 'The Story of the Capital' has opened in the basement. It traces the history of Dublin from its earliest beginnings up to 2000.

The 1781 **Municipal Buildings**, immediately west of the City Hall, were built by Thomas Ivory (1720–86), who was also responsible for the Genealogical Office in Dublin Castle.

CHRIST CHURCH CATHEDRAL

Christ Church Cathedral (Church of the Holy Trinity; Map pp72-4; ☎ 677 8099; www.cccdub.ie; Christ Church Pl; requested donation adult/student €5/2.50; ⏰ 9.45am-5pm Mon-Fri, 10am-5pm Sat, between services on Sun) is just south of the river and west of the city centre and Temple Bar. Dublin's original Viking settlement stood between the cathedral and the river. This was also the centre of medieval Dublin, with Dublin Castle, the Tholsel (Town Hall; demolished in 1809) and the original Four Courts (demolished in 1796) all close by. Nearby, on Back Lane, is the only remaining guildhall in Dublin. The 1706 Tailors Hall was due for demolition in the 1960s but survived to become the office of An Taisce (National Trust for Ireland).

Originally built in wood by the Danes in 1038, the cathedral was subsequently rebuilt in stone from 1172, by Richard de Clare, Earl of Pembroke (better known as Strongbow), the Anglo-Norman noble who invaded Ireland in 1170.

Through much of its history, Christ Church vied for supremacy with nearby St Patrick's Cathedral but, like its neighbour, it fell on hard times in the 18th and 19th centuries and was virtually derelict by the time restoration took place. Earlier, the nave had been used as a market and the crypt had housed taverns. Today both Church of Ireland cathedrals are outsiders in a Catholic nation.

From the southeastern entrance to the churchyard you walk past ruins of the chapter house, which dates from 1230. The entrance to the cathedral is at the southwestern corner and as you enter you face the northern wall. This survived the collapse of its southern counterpart but has also suffered from subsiding foundations.

The southern aisle has a monument to the legendary Strongbow. The armoured figure on the tomb is unlikely to be of Strongbow (it's more probably the earl of Drogheda) but his internal organs may have been buried here. A popular legend relates that the half-figure beside the tomb is of Strongbow's son, who was cut in two by his father when his bravery in battle was suspect.

The southern transept contains the superb baroque tomb of the 19th earl of Kildare (died 1734). His grandson, Lord Edward Fitzgerald, was a member of the United Irishmen and died in the abortive 1798 Rising.

An entrance just by the southern transept descends to the unusually large arched crypt, which dates back to the original Viking church. Curiosities in the crypt include a glass display case housing a mummified cat chasing a mummified mouse that were trapped inside an organ pipe in the 1860s! From the main entrance, a bridge, part of the 1871–78 restoration, leads to Dublinia.

DUBLINIA

Inside what was once the Synod Hall attached to Christ Church Cathedral, the Medieval Trust has created **Dublinia** (☎ 679 4611; adult/student/child €5.75/4.75/4.25; ⏰ 10am-5pm daily Apr-Sep, 11am-4pm Mon-Sat, 10am-4.30pm Sun Oct-Mar), a lively attempt to bring medieval Dublin to life. The ground floor has models of 10 episodes in Dublin's history that are explained through headsets as you walk around. On the 1st floor, finds from medieval excavations are displayed alongside a large model of the city. There are also models of the medieval quayside and of a cobbler's shop. On the top floor is the Medieval Fayre, a replica of a 12th-century fair outside the city gates. The displays include merchants' wares, a medicine stall, an armourer's pavilion, a medieval confessional booth and a bank. Finally you can climb neighbouring St Michael's Tower for views over the city to the Dublin Hills.

Your ticket gets you into Christ Church Cathedral free (via the link bridge).

ST PATRICK'S CATHEDRAL

St Patrick himself is said to have baptised converts at a well within the cathedral grounds, so the **cathedral** (Map pp72-4; ☎ 475 4817; www.stpatrickscathedral.ie; St Patrick's Close; adult/senior or student/child under 8 €4/3/free; ⏰ 9am-5pm Mon-Fri, 9am-5.30pm Sat, 9am-10.45am, 12.30-2.45pm & 4.30-5.30pm Sun Mar-Oct, 9am-4pm Sat, 9am-10.45pm & 12.30-2pm Sun Nov-Feb, closed 24-26 Dec & 1 Jan) stands on one of the earliest Christian sites in the city. Like Christ Church Cathedral it was built on unstable ground, with the subterranean River Poddle flowing under its foundations. Because of the high water table St Patrick's doesn't have a crypt.

Although a church stood on the Patrick St site from as early as the 5th century, the present building dates from 1190 or 1225 – opinions differ. Its current form dates mainly from some overenthusiastic restoration in 1864, which included the addition of the flying buttresses. St Patrick's Park, the expanse of green beside the cathedral, was a crowded slum until it was cleared and its residents evicted in the early 20th century.

Like Christ Church Cathedral, the building has suffered a rather dramatic history of storm and fire damage. Oliver Cromwell, during his 1649 visit to Ireland, converted St Patrick's to a stable for his army's horses, an indignity to which he also subjected numerous other Irish churches. Jonathan Swift was the dean of the cathedral from 1713 to 1745, but prior to its restoration it became very neglected.

Entering the cathedral from the southwestern porch you come almost immediately, on your right, to the graves of Swift and Esther Johnson, or Stella, Swift's long-term companion. On the wall nearby are Swift's own Latin epitaphs to the two of them, and a bust of him.

The huge, dusty Boyle Monument to the left was erected in 1632 by Richard Boyle, Earl of Cork, and is decorated with numerous painted figures of members of his family. The figure in the centre on the bottom level is of the earl's five-year-old son, Robert Boyle (1627–91), who became a noted scientist. His contributions to physics include Boyle's Law, which relates the pressure and volume of gases.

In 2001 a new exhibition, 'Living Stones', was inaugurated in the church. It features a comprehensive view of the church's history and symbolism, and also has sections on Jonathan Swift and the important role of music in St Patrick's. Admission to this is included in the cathedral's admission price.

The cathedral's choir school dates back to 1432 and the choir took part in the first performance of Handel's Messiah in 1742. You can hear the choir sing at 9.40am and 5.35pm Monday to Friday (no evensong on Wednesday) during the school year. A real treat are the carols performed around Christmas; call ☎ 453 9472 for details of how to obtain a hard-to-get ticket.

To get there take bus No 50, 50A or 56A from Aston Quay or No 54 or 54A from Burgh Quay.

MARSH'S LIBRARY

In St Patrick's Close, beside St Patrick's Cathedral, is **Marsh's Library** (Map pp72-4; ☎ 454 3511; www.marshlibrary.ie; St Patrick's Close; adult/student/child €2.50/2/free; 10am-1pm & 2-5pm Mon & Wed-Fri, 10.30am-1pm Sat), founded in 1701 by Archbishop Narcissus Marsh (1638–1713) and opened in 1707. It was designed by Sir William Robinson, who was also responsible for the Royal Hospital, Kilmainham. The oldest public library in the country, it contains 25,000 books dating from the 16th to early 18th centuries, as well as maps, numerous manuscripts and a collection of incunabula, the technical term for books printed before 1500. One of the oldest and finest books in the collection is a volume of Cicero's *Letters to His Friends* printed in Milan in 1472. The manuscript collection includes one in Latin dating back to 1400.

ST WERBURGH'S CHURCH

In Werburgh St, just south of Christ Church Cathedral and beside Dublin Castle, **St Werburgh's** (Map pp80-1; ☎ 478 3710; Werburgh St; admission by donation; 10am-4pm Mon-Fri) stands on ancient foundations. Its early history, however, is unknown. It was rebuilt in 1662, in 1715 and again in 1759 (with some elegance) after a fire in 1754. In 1810 the church's tall spire was ordered to be dismantled because authorities feared that rebels would use the vantage point to fire into Dublin Castle, but thankfully the order was not followed through. It is linked with the Fitzgerald family; Lord Edward Fitzgerald, a member of the United Irishmen who was a leader of the 1798 Rising, is interred in the vault. In what was an unfortunately frequent theme of Irish uprisings, compatriots betrayed him and he died from wounds received while being captured. Ironically, Major Henry Sirr, his captor, is buried in the graveyard. John Field (1782–1837), the pianist who invented the nocturne, was baptised here – he is buried in Moscow. In the porch you will notice two fire pumps which date from the time when Dublin's fire department was composed of church volunteers.

Werburgh St was also the location of Dublin's first theatre and Jonathan Swift was born just off the street at 7 Hoey's Court in 1667. Phone or see the caretaker at 8 Castle St to view inside the church.

ST AUDOEN'S CHURCHES

Lucky St Audoen has two churches to his name, both just west of Christ Church Cathedral. The smaller **Church of Ireland** (Map pp72-4; ☎ 677 0088; Cornmarket, High St; adult/student/child €2/1.25/1; 🕐 9.30am-4.45pm Jun-Sep) is the only surviving medieval parish church in the city and easily one of Dublin's most beautiful places of worship. It was built between 1181 and 1212, though recent excavations unearthing a 9th-century burial slab suggest that it was built on top of an even older church. Its tower and door date from the 12th century and the aisle from the 15th century, but the church today is mainly a 19th-century restoration.

St Anne's Chapel, the visitor centre, houses a number of tombstones of leading members of Dublin society from the 16th to the 18th centuries. At the top of the chapel is the tower, which houses the three oldest bells in Ireland, dating from 1423. Although the church's exhibits are hardly spectacular, the building itself is very beautiful and a genuine slice of medieval Dublin.

The church is entered from the north through an arch off High St. Part of the old city wall, this arch was built in 1240 and is the only surviving reminder of the city gates.

Joined onto the older Protestant St Audoen's is the newer and larger Catholic **St Audoen's** (Cornmarket, High St; admission free), a large church whose claim to local fame is Father Flash Kavanagh, who used to read Mass at high speed so that his large congregation could head off to more absorbing Sunday pursuits, such as the football.

NATIONAL MUSEUM

Designed by Sir Thomas Newenham Deane and completed in 1890, the **National Museum's** (Map p88; ☎ 677 7444; www.museum.ie; Kildare St; admission by donation; 🕐 10am-5pm Tue-Sat, 2-5pm Sun) star attraction is the Treasury, home to the finest collection of Bronze and Iron Age gold artefacts in the world and the world's most complete collection of medieval Celtic metalwork.

The centrepieces of the Treasury's unique collection are Ireland's most famous crafted artefacts, the **Ardagh Chalice** and the **Tara Brooch**. Measuring 17.8cm high and 24.2cm in diameter, the 12th-century Ardagh chalice is made of gold, silver, bronze, brass, copper and lead. Put simply, this is the finest exemplar of Celtic art ever found. The equally renowned Tara Brooch was crafted around AD 700 primarily in white bronze, but with traces of gold, silver, glass, copper, enamel and wire beading, and was used as a clasp for a cloak.

The Treasury includes many other stunning pieces, many of which are grouped together in 'hoards', after the manner in which they were found, usually uncovered by a farmer digging up a field or a bog. Be sure not to miss the Broighter and Mooghaun hoards.

Upstairs, Viking Age Dublin tells the story of Dublin's Viking era, with exhibits from the excavations at Wood Quay – the area between Christ Church Cathedral and the river, where Dublin City Council plonked its new headquarters. Other exhibits focus on the 1916 Easter Rising and the independence struggle between 1900 and 1921. Frequent short-term exhibitions are also held.

The National Museum's main annexe is at **Collins Barracks** (Map pp72-4; ☎ 677 7444; Benburb St; admission free), off Ellis Quay, on the city's north side. The unusually beautiful former army barracks, with its huge central courtyard, was completely renovated and opened in 1999 as the **National Museum of Decorative Arts & History**. Inside, you'll find artefacts ranging from silver, ceramic and glassware to weaponry, furniture and examples of folk life.

NATIONAL GALLERY

Opened in 1864, the **National Gallery** (Map p88; ☎ 661 5133; www.nationalgallery.ie; Merrion Sq West; admission free; 🕐 9.30am-5.30pm Mon-Wed & Fri-Sat, 9.30am-8.30pm Thu, noon-5.30pm Sun) looks out on Merrion Square. Its excellent collection is strong in Irish art, but there are also high-quality collections of every major school of European painting.

On the lawn in front of the gallery is a statue of the Irish railway magnate William Dargan, who organised the 1853 Dublin Industrial Exhibition at this spot; the profits from the exhibition were used to found the gallery. Nearby is a statue of George Bernard Shaw, a major benefactor of the gallery.

The gallery has four wings: the original Dargan Wing, the Milltown Rooms, the North Wing and the spectacular new Millenium Wing, opened in 2002. The Dargan Wing's ground floor has the imposing Shaw Room, lined with full-length portraits and illuminated by a series of spectacular Waterford crystal chandeliers. Upstairs, a series of rooms is dedicated to the Italian early and high Renaissance, 16th-century northern Italian art and 17th- and 18th-century Italian art. Fra Angelico, Titian and Tintoretto are among the artists represented, but the highlight is undoubtedly Caravaggio's **The Taking of Christ**, which lay undiscovered for over 60 years in a Jesuit house in Leeson St and was accidentally discovered by chief curator Sergio Benedetti.

The central Milltown Rooms were added between 1899 and 1903 to hold Russborough House's art collection, which was presented to the gallery in 1902. The ground floor displays the gallery's fine Irish collection plus a smaller British collection, with works by Reynolds, Hogarth, Gainsborough, Landseer and Turner. One highlight is the room at the back of the gallery displaying works by Jack B Yeats (1871–1957), younger brother of WB Yeats. Other rooms display specific periods and styles of Irish art, including one room of works by Irish artists painting in France.

Upstairs are works from Germany, the Netherlands and Spain. There are rooms full of works by Rembrandt and his circle and by the Spanish artists of Seville. The Spanish collection features works by El Greco, Goya and Picasso.

The North Wing was added only between 1964 and 1968 but has already undergone extensive refurbishment. It houses works by British and European artists.

The impressive new Millenium Wing with its light-filled modern design, can also be entered from Nassau St. It houses a small collection of 20th-century Irish art and high profile visiting collections (for which there is a charge to visit), an art reference library, a lecture theatre, a good bookshop and **Fitzer's Café**. There are free guided tours at 3pm Saturday and 2pm, 3pm and 4pm Sunday.

LEINSTER HOUSE

The Dáil (Lower House) and Seanad (Upper House) of the Oireachtas na Éireann (Irish Parliament) meet in **Leinster House** (Map p88; ☎ 618 3000, 618 3271 for tour information; www.irlgov.ie/oireachtas; Kildare St; admission free). The entrance to Leinster House from Kildare St is flanked by the National Library and the National Museum. Originally built as Kildare House between 1745 and 1748 for the earl of Kildare, the building had its name changed when the earl also assumed the title of duke of Leinster in 1766.

Leinster House's Kildare St frontage was designed by Richard Cassels to look like a town house, whereas the Merrion Square frontage was made to look like a country house. The obelisk in front of the building is dedicated to Arthur Griffith, Michael Collins and Kevin O'Higgins, architects of independent Ireland.

The Dublin Society, later named the Royal Dublin Society, bought the building in 1814 but moved out in stages between 1922 and 1925, when the first government of independent Ireland decided to establish Parliament there.

The Seanad meets in the north-wing saloon, while the Dáil meets in a less interesting room that was originally a lecture theatre added to the original building in 1897. When Parliament is sitting, visitors are admitted to an observation gallery. You get an entry ticket from the Kildare St entrance on production of some identification. Bags can't be taken in, or notes or photographs taken. Parliament sits for 90 days a year, usually November to May. The observation gallery is open when parliament is in session, which is usually 2.30pm to 8.30pm Tuesday, 10.30am to 8.30pm Wednesday and 10.30am to 5.30pm Thursday November to May. Prearranged guided tours are available.

GOVERNMENT BUILDINGS

On Upper Merrion St, the domed **Government Buildings** (Map p88; ☎ 662 4888; www.taoiseach.gov.ie; Upper Merrion St; free tours 10.30am-3.30pm Sat only) were opened in 1911, in a rather heavy-handed Edwardian interpretation of the Georgian style. Each 40-minute tour takes about 15 people, so you may have to wait a while for a group to assemble. Tours can't be booked in advance, but on Saturday morning you can put your name down for one later in the day. You get to see the Taoiseach's office, the cabinet room, the ceremonial staircase with a stunning stained-glass window designed by Evie Hone (1894–1955) for the 1939 New York Trade Fair, and innumerable fine examples of modern Irish arts and crafts. Tickets for the free tours are available from the National Gallery **ticket office** (☎ 661 5133).

NATIONAL LIBRARY

Flanking the Kildare St entrance to Leinster House is the **National Library** (Map p88; ☎ 603 0200; www.nli.ie; Kildare St; admission free; 🕒 10am-9pm Mon-Wed, 10am-5pm Thu-Fri, 10am-1pm Sat), which was built between 1884 and 1890, at the same time and to a similar design as the National Museum, by Sir Thomas Newenham Deane and his son Sir Thomas Manly Deane. Leinster House, the library and museum were all part of the Royal Dublin Society (formed in 1731), which aimed to improve conditions for poor people and to promote the arts and sciences. The library's extensive collection has many valuable early manuscripts, first editions, maps and other items. The library's reading room featured in James Joyce's *Ulysses*. Temporary displays are often held in the entrance area.

On the 2nd floor is the **Genealogical Office** (☎ 603 0200; National Library, Kildare St; 🕒 10am-4.30pm Mon-Fri, 10am-12.30pm Sat) where you can obtain information on how best to trace your Irish roots. A genealogist can do the trace for you (at a fee dependent on research) or simply point you in the right direction (for free).

NATURAL HISTORY MUSEUM

The **Natural History Museum** (Map p88; ☎ 677 7444; www.museum.ie; Merrion St; admission free; 🕒 10am-5pm Tue-Sat, 2-5pm Sun) has scarcely changed since 1857 when Scottish explorer Dr David Livingstone delivered the opening lecture. In the face of the city's newer high-tech museums, its Victorian charm has been beautifully preserved, making it one of Dublin's more interesting museums. Commonly referred to as the 'dead zoo', the museum's huge and well organised collection numbers about 2 million, roughly half of which are insects. That moth-eaten look often afflicting neglected stuffed-animal collections has been kept at bay and children are likely to find it fascinating.

On the ground floor, the collection of skeletons, stuffed animals and the like covers the full range of Irish fauna. It includes three skeletons of the Irish giant deer, which became extinct about 10,000 years ago. On the 1st and 2nd floors are fauna from around the world.

GRAFTON STREET & AROUND

Grafton St was the major traffic artery of south Dublin until it was turned into a pedestrian precinct in 1982. It's now Dublin's fanciest and most colourful shopping centre, with plenty of street life and the city's most entertaining buskers. The street is equally lively after dark, as some of Dublin's most interesting pubs are clustered around it.

Apart from fine shops, such as the **Brown Thomas** (Map pp80-1) department store, which opened in 1848, Grafton St also boasts **Bewley's Oriental Café** (Map p88; ☎ 677 6761; 78 Grafton St). This branch of the chain has memorabilia upstairs relating to the company's history.

Johnson's Court leads off Grafton St to the elegantly converted **Powerscourt Townhouse shopping centre** (Map p88; ☎ 679 4144; 59 South William St). Built between 1771 and 1774, this grand house has a balconied courtyard and, following its conversion in 1981, now shelters three levels of shops and restaurants. It was extensively restored between 1998 and 2000. The Powerscourt family's principal residence was **Powerscourt House** (Map p70) in County Wicklow and this city mansion was soon sold for commercial use. It survived that period in remarkably good condition and in its present incarnation forms a convenient link from Grafton St to the South City Market on South Great George St.

At the College Green end of Grafton St is the modern **statue of Molly Malone** (Map pp80–1) of song fame, rendered in such extreme *deshabille* that she's nicknamed 'the tart with the cart'.

ST STEPHEN'S GREEN & AROUND Map p88

On warm summer days the nine hectares of **St Stephen's Green** provide a popular lunchtime escape for office workers. The green was originally an expanse of open common land where public whippings, burnings and hangings took place. The green was enclosed by a fence in 1664 when the Dublin Corporation sold off the surrounding land for buildings. A stone wall replaced the fence in 1669 and trees and gravel paths soon followed within the park. By the end of that century restrictions were in force prohibiting buildings of less than two storeys or those constructed of mud and wattle around the green.

The fine Georgian buildings around the square date mainly from Dublin's mid- to late-18th-century Georgian prime. At that time the northern side was known as the

AROUND ST STEPHEN'S GREEN

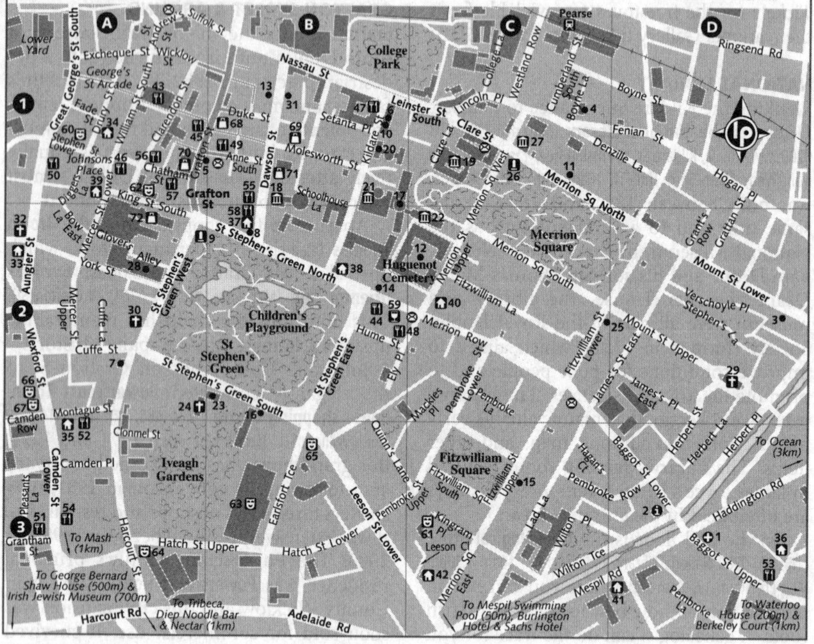

INFORMATION

- Baggot St Hospital.....1 D3
- Bord Fáilte.....2 D3
- British Council.....3 D2
- Dublin Corporation.....4 C1
- O'Connells Pharmacy.....5 A1

SIGHTS & ACTIVITIES pp76-100

- Alliance Française.....6 B1
- An Siopa Leabhar.....7 A2
- Dawson Lounge.....8 B2
- Fusiliers' Arch.....9 A2
- Genealogical Office.....10 B1
- Goethe Institute.....11 C1
- Government Buildings.....12 C2
- Hodges Figgis.....13 B1
- Huguenot Cemetery.....14 B2
- Italian Cultural Institute.....15 C3
- Iveagh House.....16 B2
- Leinster House (Irish Parliament).....17 B1
- Mansion House.....18 B1
- National Gallery.....19 C1
- National Library.....20 B1
- National Museum.....21 B1
- Natural History Museum.....22 C2
- Newman House.....23 B2
- Newman University Church.....24 A2
- No 29 Lower Fitzwilliam St.....25 C2
- Oscar Wilde Statue.....26 C1
- Oscar Wilde's House.....27 C1
- Royal College of Surgeons.....28 A2
- St Stephen's 'Peppercanister Church'.....29 D2
- Unitarian Church.....30 A2
- Waterstone's.....31 B1
- Whitefriar St Carmelite Church.....32 A2

SLEEPING pp105-11

- Avalon House.....33 A2
- Brooks Hotel.....34 A1
- Frankies Guesthouse.....35 A2
- Hibernian Hotel.....36 D3
- La Stampa.....37 B2
- Le Méridien Shelbourne.....38 B2
- Mercer Court.....39 A1
- Merrion.....40 C2
- Mespil Hotel.....41 D3
- Number 31.....42 C3

EATING pp111-17

- Ba Mizu.....43 A1
- Bang.....44 B2
- Bewley's Oriental Café.....45 A1
- Busy Feet & Coco Café.....46 A1
- Dail Bía.....47 B1
- Ely Wine Bar.....48 B2
- Gotham Café.....49 B1
- Govinda's.....50 A1
- Havana.....51 A3
- Il Primo.....52 A2
- Langkawi.....53 D3
- Listons.....54 A3
- Pizza Milano.....55 B1
- Rajdoot Tandoori.....56 A1
- Restaurant Patrick Guilbaud.....(see 40)
- Steps of Rome.....57 A1
- Tiger Becs.....58 B2

DRINKING p119

- O'Donoghue's.....59 B2

ENTERTAINMENT pp120-4

- Bodega.....60 A1
- Focus Theatre.....61 C3
- Gaiety Theatre.....62 A1
- National Concert Hall.....63 B3
- PoD.....64 A3
- Red Box.....(see 64)
- Sugar Club.....65 B3
- Village.....66 A2
- Whelan's.....67 A2

SHOPPING pp124-5

- Dublin Bookshop.....68 B1
- Government Publications bookshop.....69 B1
- HMV.....70 A1
- Murder Ink.....71 B1
- Powerscourt Townhouse Shopping Centre.....(see 43)
- St Stephen's Green Shopping Centre.....72 A2
- Tulle.....(see 43)

Beaux Walk and it's still one of Dublin society's most esteemed meeting places. Private use of the green continued until 1877 when Sir Arthur Edward Guinness, later Lord Ardilaun, pushed an act through Parliament to once again open the green to the public. He also financed the central park's gardens and ponds, which date from 1880.

The main entrance to the green is through **Fusiliers' Arch** at the northwestern corner. Modelled on the Arch of Titus in Rome, the arch commemorates the 212 soldiers of the Royal Dublin Fusiliers who died in the Boer War (1899–1902).

Across the road from the western side of the green are the 1863 **Unitarian Church** and the **Royal College of Surgeons** with its fine façade. In the 1916 Easter Rising, the building was occupied by the colourful Countess Markievicz (1868–1927), an Irish nationalist married to a Polish count (see p34). The columns still bear bullet marks.

Other notable buildings around the green include the imposing 1867 **Le Méridien Shelbourne** on the northern side and, just beyond, a small **Huguenot cemetery** dating from 1693, when many French Huguenots fled here from persecution under Louis XIV.

On the southern side is **Newman House** (☎ 716 7422; 85-86 St Stephen's Green; adult/child €4/3; ⌚ Jun-Aug as part of 40-min tour: on the hour noon, 2-4pm Tue-Fri, 2-5pm Sat), now part of University College, Dublin. These buildings have some of the finest plasterwork in the city. The Catholic University of Ireland, predecessor of University College, Dublin, acquired No 85 in 1865, and then passed it to the Jesuits. Some of the plasterwork was a little too detailed for Jesuit tastes, however, so cover-ups were prescribed. On the ceiling of the upstairs saloon, previously naked female figures were clothed in what can best be described as furry swimsuits. One survived the restoration process.

Next to Newman University Church is the **Catholic University Church**, or Newman Chapel, built between 1854 and 1856 with a colourful neo-Byzantine interior that attracted a great deal of criticism at the time. Today it's one of the most fashionable churches in Dublin for weddings.

One of Dublin's most beautiful parks is the landscaped **Iveagh Gardens** (Map p88; ⌚ dawn-dusk year round), directly behind Newman House and reached via Earlsfort Terrace or Clonmel St, just off Harcourt St. The imposing walls give the impression that they are private gardens, but they are one of the nicest places to relax on a summer's day or before a show in the National Concert Hall.

MERRION SQUARE **Map p88**

With its well-kept Archbishop Ryan Park and elegant Georgian buildings, **Merrion Square** dates back to 1762. Around this square you can find some of Dublin's best Georgian entrances, with fine doors, peacock fanlights, ornate door knockers and more than a few foot scrapers where gentlemen removed mud from their shoes before venturing indoors.

Oscar Wilde spent much of his youth at 1 North Merrion Square. WB Yeats (1865–1939) lived at 52 Merrion Square East and later, between 1922 and 1928, at 82 Merrion Square South. George (AE) Russell (1867–1935), the 'poet, mystic, painter and cooperator', worked at No 84. Daniel O'Connell (1775–1847) was a resident of No 58 in his later years. The Austrian Erwin Schrödinger (1887–1961), co-winner of the 1933 Nobel Prize for physics, lived at No 65 between 1940 and 1956. Dublin seems to attract the writers of horror stories: Joseph Sheridan Le Fanu (1814–73), who penned the vampire classic *Carmilla*, was a resident of No 70.

The UK embassy was at 39 Merrion Square East until it was burned out in 1972 in protest against Bloody Sunday in Derry, Northern Ireland. The Architectural Association is at 8 Merrion Square North, a few doors down from the Wilde residence.

The **Leinster Lawn** at the western end of the square has the 1791 Rutland Fountain and an 18m obelisk honouring the founders of independent Ireland.

Merrion Square hasn't always been merely graceful and affluent, however. During the Famine, soup kitchens were set up in the gardens, which were crowded with starving rural refugees.

Merrion Square East once continued into Lower Fitzwilliam St in the longest unbroken series of Georgian houses anywhere in Europe. In 1961 the Electricity Supply Board (ESB) knocked down 26 of the houses to build an office block.

At the southeastern corner of Merrion Square the ESB had the decency to preserve one fine old Georgian house, **29 Lower**

Fitzwilliam St (☎ 702 6165; www.esb.ie/education; 29 Lower Fitzwilliam St; adult/student/child €3.50/1.50/free; 🕑 10am-5pm Tue-Sat, 2-5pm Sun, closed 2 weeks before Christmas). It has been restored to give a good impression of genteel home life in Dublin between 1790 and 1820. A short film on its history is followed by a 30-minute guided tour in groups of nine or less.

OSCAR WILDE'S HOUSE

The very first Georgian residence that was constructed on the square, 1 North Merrion Square, was built in 1762. Today it is owned by the American College Dublin, who have converted part of the house into a **museum** (Map p88; ☎ 662 0281; www.amcd.edu/oscar/; 1 North Merrion Sq; admission €2.45) devoted to Oscar Wilde.

In 1855 the surgeon Sir William Wilde and the poet Lady 'Speranza' Wilde moved here with their one-year-old son Oscar. They occupied the house until 1876. It is likely that Oscar's literary genius was first stimulated by the creative atmosphere of the house, where Lady Wilde hosted the city's most famous (and best frequented) literary salon. Tours are available at 10.15am and 11.15am Monday, Wednesday and Thursday.

Enthusiasts should check out the **Oscar Wilde statue** at the northwestern corner of the square, as it is adorned with the witty one-liners for which Oscar Wilde became famous.

OTHER SOUTH DUBLIN MUSEUMS

Noted playwright George Bernard Shaw was born and lived until the age of 10 in Dublin in what is now home to the **George Bernard Shaw House** (Map p88; ☎ 475 0854; 33 Synge St; bus No 16, 19, 122 from Trinity College; adult/student/child €6/5/3.50; 🕑 10am-1pm & 2-5pm Mon-Sat, from 11am Sun Easter-Oct). The house re-creates a Victorian household with an audio presentation on Shaw's life. Note that it's possible to buy a combination ticket that also gives you access to the Dublin Writers' Museum and James Joyce Museum in Sandycove.

Located in an old synagogue, the **Irish-Jewish Museum** (Map p88; ☎ 453 1797; 4 Walworth Rd; bus No 16, 19 & 122 from Trinity College; admission free; 🕑 11am-3.30pm Tue, Thu & Sun May-Sep, 10.30am-2.30pm Sun only Oct-Apr) was opened in 1985 by the then Israeli president, Chaim Herzog, who was actually born in Belfast. Dublin's small, but culturally important Jewish population is remembered through photographs, paintings, certificates, books and other memorabilia.

North of the Liffey

Though south Dublin has the lion's share of the city's tourist attractions, there are still quite a few reasons to head across the Liffey.

CUSTOM HOUSE

James Gandon's first great building was the **Custom House** (Map pp72–4), constructed between 1781 and 1791 just past Eden Quay, in spite of opposition from city merchants and dock workers at the original Custom House, upriver in Temple Bar.

In 1921, during the independence struggle, the Custom House was set alight and completely gutted in a fire that burned for five days. The interior was later extensively redesigned, and a further major renovation took place between 1986 and 1988.

The glistening white building stretches for 114m along the Liffey. The best complete view is obtained from across the river, though a close-up inspection of its many fine details is also worthwhile. The building is topped by a copper dome with four clocks. Above that stands a 5m-high statue of Hope.

Beneath the dome is the **Custom House Visitor Centre** (☎ 888 2538; Custom House Quay; admission €1; 🕑 10am-12.30pm Mon-Fri, 2-5.30pm Sat & Sun mid-Mar–Oct, 10am-12.30pm Wed-Fri, 2-5pm Sun Nov–mid-Mar), which features a small museum on Gandon himself as well as the history of the building.

O'CONNELL ST — Map pp72–4

The major thoroughfare of north Dublin and probably the most important and imposing street in the city is **O'Connell St**. It started life in the early 18th century as Drogheda St, named after Viscount Henry Moore, Earl of Drogheda. There is still a Henry St, a Moore St and an Earl St nearby. The earl even managed to squeeze in an Of Lane! At that time, Capel St, further to the west, was the main traffic route, and Drogheda St, lacking a bridge to connect it with south Dublin, was of little importance.

Dublin Corporation has announced a radical overhaul of the street. Over €45 million of public money as well as several hundred million euros of private investment will result in a new plaza in front of the GPO, wider footpaths, a new street linking O'Connell St with Moore St, a major shopping centre and a thorough re-appraisal of the street's building design.

The first project was the impressive **Monument of Light** (aka the Spire), which graced the spot once occupied by Admiral Nelson. This magnificent 130m spire was originally planned to be constructed in time for New Year's Eve 1999, but it was delayed by objections and wasn't finished until January 2003.

Nearby, a **James Joyce statue** stands nonchalantly outside Café Kylemore on the corner of pedestrianised North Earl St. Northside Dubliners commonly refer to it as the 'prick with the stick'.

Further north is the **statue of Father Theobald Mathew** (1790–1856), the 'apostle of temperance' – a hopeless role in Ireland. This quixotic task, however, also resulted in a Liffey bridge bearing his name. The northern end of the street is completed by the imposing **statue of Charles Stewart Parnell** (1846–91), Home Rule advocate and victim of Irish morality. Just to the west of O'Connell St is an energetic and colourful open-air **fruit and vegetable market** (Moore St; 8am-6pm Mon-Sat).

GENERAL POST OFFICE

The **GPO building** (Map pp72-4; ☎ 705 7000; www.anpost.ie; O'Connell St; 8am-8pm Mon-Sat) is an important landmark physically and historically. The building, designed by Francis Johnston and opened in 1818, was the focus for the 1916 Easter Rising when Pádraig Pearse, James Connolly and the other leaders read their proclamation from the front steps. In the subsequent siege the building was burned out. The façade is still pockmarked from the 1916 clash and from further damage wrought at the start of the Civil War in 1922. The GPO wasn't reopened until 1929. Its central role in the history of independent Ireland has made it a prime site for everything from official parades to personal protests.

ABBEY THEATRE

Opened in 1904, **Abbey Theatre** (Map pp72-4; ☎ 878 7222; www.abbeytheatre.ie; Lower Abbey St), on the corner of Marlborough and Lower Abbey Sts, is just north of the Liffey. Here the Irish National Theatre Society soon made a name not only for playwrights such as JM Synge and Sean O'Casey but also for Irish acting ability and theatrical presentation. The 1907 premiere of JM Synge's *The Playboy of the Western World* brought a storm of protest from theatregoers, and

THE NAME'S THE GAME

It seems that Dubliners just aren't happy with the names given to the various statues, monuments and other assorted sights throughout the city, and in an effort to convey the deeper significance of what these sights represent, they are compelled to make up humorous rhyming names for them. Silly or not, they are often quite funny, perhaps a sign of how iconoclastic Dubliners really are.

Just next to the northern side of Ha'penny Bridge is a bronze sculpture of two women sitting on a bench with shopping bags at their feet – it's commonly known as 'the hags with the bags'.

At the end of Grafton St is a statue of a woman with a wheelbarrow loaded with cockles and mussels; she is Molly Malone, street vendor extraordinaire and the subject of Dublin's most famous song. But she is in such a serious state of undress that she is known as 'the tart with the cart'.

Before Dublin's newest monument was even built (a 130m-high spire to replace Nelson's Pillar, known as the Monument of Light) Dublin's wags had already taken to calling it 'the skewer by the sewer', and 'the stiletto in the ghetto'.

Just across the street from the GPO on O'Connell St is a small statue of James Joyce, his head slightly cocked, his hand leaning on a walking stick. So how do Dubliners choose to remember their greatest writer? As 'the prick with the stick'. Joyce certainly loved his rhyming word play, so we're *almost* sure he would have smiled.

The best names of all were reserved for the Anna Livia statue, which used to stand on O'Connell St. Joyce enthusiasts will know that the author gave the Liffey a woman's personality and name, Anna Livia, and the statue of a woman lying in water was swiftly rechristened 'the floozy in the Jacuzzi' and 'the hooer in the sewer' .

Sean O'Casey's *The Plough and the Stars* prompted a similar reaction in 1926. On the latter occasion WB Yeats himself came on stage after the performance to tick the audience off!

The original theatre burned down in 1951. It took 15 years to come up with a replacement and this dull building fails to live up to its famous name or the company's continuing reputation. Thankfully, plans are afoot to either completely refurbish the building or – more likely – to move it completely down to the Grand Canal Docks on the river's southern side. The smaller Peacock Theatre at the same location presents new and experimental works.

ST MARY'S PRO-CATHEDRAL

On the corner of Marlborough and Cathedral Sts, just east of O'Connell St, is Dublin's most important **Catholic church** (Map pp72-4; ☎ 874 5441; Marlborough St; admission free; 🕑 8am-6.30pm). It was built between 1816 and 1825. Unfortunately, the cramped Marlborough St location makes it difficult to stand back far enough to admire the front with its six Doric columns, modelled on the Temple of Theseus in Athens.

The 1814 competition for the church's design was won by John Sweetman, a former owner of Sweetman's Brewery. And who organised the competition? Why William Sweetman, John Sweetman's brother. And did John Sweetman design it himself? Well, possibly not. He was living in Paris at the time and may have bought the plans from a French architect who designed the remarkably similar Notre Dame de Lorette in northern France. The only clue as to the church's architect is in the ledger, which lists the builder as 'Mr P'. It's not clear what pro means, but it implies something like 'unofficial cathedral'.

You wouldn't know it now, but before Irish independence this area was once the busiest red-light district in Europe (thanks to the British garrison); it was known as Monto and featured in Joyce's *Ulysses* as Nighttown.

GATE THEATRE

In the southeastern corner of Parnell Square is the **Gate Theatre** (Map pp72-4; ☎ 874 4045; Parnell Sq East), opened in 1929 by Micheál MacLiammóir and Hilton Edwards (the actual building dates from 1784–86, when it was constructed as part of the Rotunda Hospital complex). MacLiammóir continued to act at his theatre until 1975, when he retired at the age of 76 after making his 1384th performance of the one-man show *The Importance of Being Oscar* (Oscar being Oscar Wilde, of course). The Gate Theatre was the stage for Orson Welles' first professional appearance and also featured James Mason early in his career.

Today it features a more exciting brand of theatre than its longtime rival, the Abbey, with a worthwhile mix of classic plays from Ireland and abroad, and more modern, experimental work.

MUNICIPAL GALLERY OF MODERN ART

The **Municipal Gallery of Modern Art** (Map pp72-4; ☎ 874 1903; www.hughlane.ie; 22 North Parnell Sq; admission free to permanent collection; to Francis Bacon exhibition adult/child €7/3.50, free before noon Tue; 🕑 9.30am-6pm Tue-Thu, 9.30am-5pm Fri-Sat, 11am-5pm Sun) has a fine collection of work by French Impressionists and by 20th-century Irish artists.

The gallery was founded in 1908 and moved to its present location in Charlemont House in 1933. It was established by wealthy Sir Hugh Lane, with no help from the government. He died in the 1915 sinking of the *Lusitania*, which was torpedoed off the southern coast of Ireland by a German U-boat. The lack of official funding was the subject of one of WB Yeats' most vitriolic poems *September 1913*. The Lane Bequest pictures, which formed the nucleus of the gallery, were the subject of a dispute over Lane's will between the gallery and the National Gallery in London. A settlement was finally reached in 1959, splitting the collection.

From November 1999 the gallery has displayed Manet's *Eva Gonzales*, Pissarro's *Printemps*, Berthe Morisot's *Jour d'Eté* and the most important painting of the collection, Renoir's *Les Parapluies*.

In June 2001 the gallery unveiled its most recent addition to its permanent collection, a recreation of Francis Bacon's London studio, complete with all of the painter's personal effects and several paintings.

DUBLIN WRITERS MUSEUM

This **museum** (Map pp72-4; ☎ 872 2077; 18 North Parnell Sq; adult/student/child €6/5/3.50; 🕑 10am-5pm Mon-Sat, 10am-6pm Jun-Aug, 11am-5pm Sun) celebrates the city's long and continuing history as a literary centre. The Gallery of Writers upstairs houses busts and portraits of some of Ireland's most famous writers; their letters, photographs and 1st editions are downstairs. The museum also has a bookshop and the **Chapter One** restaurant. Admission includes taped guides with readings from relevant texts in English and other languages. If you plan to visit the James Joyce Museum (see p129) and George Bernard Shaw House (see p90), bear in mind that a combined ticket is cheaper than three separate ones.

While the museum concerns itself primar ily with dead authors, next door at No 19 the Irish Writers' Centre provides a meeting and working place for their living successors.

JAMES JOYCE CULTURAL CENTRE

This **house** (Map pp72-4; ☎ 878 8547; www.jamesjoyce.ie; 35 North Great George's St; adult/student/child €4.50/3.50/free; ⏰ 9.30am-5pm Mon-Sat, 12.30-5pm Sun) was where Denis Maginni taught dance in the front room early this century. Hardly remarkable, but the fact that he and his home featured several times in Ulysses led Joycean scholar and leading gay activist Senator David Norris to take over the house in 1982. He proceeded to restore the house and convert it into a centre for the study of Joyce and his books.

Visitors see the room where Maginni taught, and a collection of pictures of the 17 different Dublin homes occupied by the nomadic Joyce family and the real individuals fictionalised in the books. Some of the fine plaster ceilings are restored originals, others careful reproductions of Michael Stapleton's designs. For information on James Joyce-related walking tours departing from the centre, see p103.

ST MICHAN'S CHURCH

Named after a Danish saint, **St Michan's Church** (Map pp72-4; ☎ 872 4154; Lower Church St; adult/student €3.50/3; ⏰ 10am-12.45pm & 2-4.45pm Mon-Fri, 10am-12.45pm Sat), near the Four Courts, was founded by the Danes in 1095, though there's little trace of the original. The battlement tower dates from the 15th century, but otherwise the church was rebuilt in the late 17th century, considerably restored in the early 19th century and again after the Civil War, during which it had been damaged.

The church contains a 1724 organ which Handel may have played for the first performance of his Messiah. The organ case is distinguished by a fine oak carving of 17 entwined musical instruments on its front. A skull on the floor on one side of the altar is said to represent Oliver Cromwell. On the opposite side, a penitent's chair was where 'open and notoriously naughty livers' did public penance. But the church's main 'attraction' lies in the subterranean crypt, where bodies have been preserved to varying degrees, not by mummification but by the constant dry atmosphere. You can visit the church any time during opening hours, but you can see the crypt only as part of a tour. Tours are organised on an ad hoc basis depending on how many people are there.

SMITHFIELD

Earmarked 10 years ago for major residential and cultural development, **Smithfield** (Map pp72–4), bordered to the east by Church St, to the west by Blackhall Place, to the north by North King St and to the south by Arran Quay, has progressed in fits and starts but never quite evolved into the cultural quarter promised. At the centre of the development is the old hay, straw, cattle and horse marketplace, Smithfield Market, which has now been replaced by a new open civic space. The flagship of the Historic Area Rejuvenation Project (HARP) whose brief is to restore the northwest inner city, it features a pedestrianised square bordered on one side by 26m-high gas lighting masts, each with a 2m-high flame. The old cobblestones were removed, cleaned up and put back along with new granite slabs that give the whole square a modern feel without sacrificing its traditional beauty.

Bordering the eastern side of the square is the Old Jameson Distillery. In keeping with its traditional past, the old **fruit and vegetable market** still plies a healthy wholesale trade on the square's western side.

THE CHIMNEY

As part of the ongoing development of the Smithfield area, an old distillery chimney, built by Jameson's in 1895, has been converted into Dublin's first and only 360-degree **observation tower** (Map pp72-4; ☎ 817 3820; Smithfield Village; adult/student €5/3.50; ⏰ 10am-5pm Mon-Sat,

11am-5.30pm Sun). A glass lift shuttles visitors to the top, where, behind the safety of glass, you can see the entire city, the sea and the mountains to the south which, on a clear day, makes for some nice photo opportunities.

OLD JAMESON DISTILLERY

Where does Irish whiskey get its particular colour and smooth bouquet from? While most people have heard the term 'single malt', how many can actually tell you what it is? These are just some of the secrets you can learn at the **Old Jameson Distillery** (Map pp72-4; ☎ 807 2355; Bow St; adult/student €7/5.75; tours every 35 min 10am-5.30pm), a museum devoted to Irish whiskey just northwest of St Michan's Church.

The compulsory guided tour is well worth it and kicks off with a short film, after which visitors are led through a re-creation of the old factory, where the guide explains the entire process of whiskey distilling from grain to bottle. Visitors are then invited into the Jameson Bar, where they are offered a complimentary glass of 'the hard stuff' (as it is referred to in Dublin vernacular). The tour finishes with a surprise competition, but you'll have to visit to find out what it is! There's also a restaurant on the premises.

FOUR COURTS

On Inns Quay beside the river the extensive **Four Courts** (Map pp72-4; ☎ 872 5555; Inn's Quay; admission free), with its 130m-long façade, was one of James Gandon's (1743–1823) masterpieces. Gandon was 18th-century Dublin's pre-eminent architect. The Custom House, King's Inns and some elements of the Parliament building (now the Bank of Ireland) are also among his masterpieces. Construction on the Four Courts began in 1786, soon engulfing the Public Offices (built a short time previously at the western end of the same site), and continued until 1802. By then it included a Corinthian-columned central block connected to flanking wings with enclosed quadrangles. The ensemble is topped by a diverse collection of statuary. The original four courts – Exchequer, Common Pleas, King's Bench and Chancery – branch off the central rotunda.

The Four Courts played a brief role in the 1916 Easter Rising, without suffering damage, but the events of 1922 were not so kind. When anti-Treaty forces seized the building and refused to leave, it was shelled from across the river. As the occupiers retreated, the building was set on fire and many irreplaceable early records were burned. This event sparked off the Civil War. The building wasn't restored until 1932.

Visitors are allowed to wander through, but not to enter courts or other restricted areas. In the lobby of the central rotunda you'll see bewigged barristers conferring and police officers handcuffed to their charges waiting to enter court.

CROKE PARK & GAA MUSEUM

About 500m northeast of Mountjoy Square is the home of the Gaelic Athletic Association (GAA; the governing body of Ireland's national sports) and the country's largest stadium, **Croke Park**, where the All-Ireland finals are played in September (see .p123). The history of Gaelic sports is the theme of a new **museum** (☎ 855 8176; www.gaa.ie; New Stand, Croke Park, Clonliffe Rd; adult/student/child €5/3.50/3; 9.30am-5pm Mon-Sat, noon-5pm Sun Apr-Oct, 10am-5pm Tue-Sat, noon-4pm Sun Nov-Mar) that is a must for sporting enthusiasts. You can also test your skills at both Gaelic football and hurling. To get there take bus Nos 3, 11, 11A, 16, 16A or 123 from O'Connell St. Tours are available twice daily.

Outside City Centre

There's still much more to see in Dublin. To the west are the Guinness Brewery in the colourful Liberties area, Kilmainham Jail and Phoenix Park. To the north and northeast are the Royal Canal, Prospect Cemetery, Botanic Gardens, the Casino at Marino and Clontarf. To the south and southeast are the Grand Canal, Ballsbridge and the Royal Dublin Society Showground.

GUINNESS BREWERY, STOREHOUSE & THE LIBERTIES

West of St Audoen's churches, Thomas St metamorphoses into James's St in the area of Dublin known as the Liberties. Along James's St stretches the historic St James's Gate Guinness Brewery, where 2.5 million pints of stout are brewed daily. From its foundation by Arthur Guinness in 1759, the operation has expanded down to the Liffey and across both sides of the street. It covers 26 hectares and for a time was the largest brewery in the world. The oldest parts of the site are south of James's St; at one time there was a gate spanning the street.

The brewery is far more than just a place where beer is manufactured. It is an intrinsic part of Dublin's history and a key element of the city's identity. Accordingly, the quasi-mythical stature of Guinness is the central theme of the brewery's new museum, the **Guinness Storehouse** (Map pp72-4; ☎ 408 4800; www.guinness-storehouse.com; St James's Gate; adult/student/child €13.50/9/3; 🕑 9.30am-5pm). It opened in December 2000 in place of the old – and much smaller – Guinness Hop Store. It is the only part of the brewery that opens to visitors. Take bus Nos 21A, 78 or 78A from Fleet St.

Undoubtedly, this is an impressive building with a beautiful central atrium. The exhibition, complete with all the latest interactive gadgets, is interesting enough, tracing the history of the brewery and giving a thumbnail sketch of how the beer is brewed. The main reason for coming here, however, is for the prize at the end of the visit: Dublin's most delicious pint of Guinness, served in the Gravity Bar at the top of the building and complete with a 360-degree panoramic view of Dublin.

Around the corner at No 1 Thomas St, a plaque marks the house where Arthur Guinness (1725–1803) lived. In a yard across the road stands St Patrick's Tower, Europe's tallest smock windmill (with a revolving top), which was built around 1757.

The Liberties is also home to the **Digital Hub** (Map pp72-4; ☎ 480 6200; www.thedigitalhub.com; 10-13 Thomas St), a government initiative to develop digital media spread over a nine-acre site next to Guinness. It hosts occasional multimedia exhibitions at its office; check the website for details.

IMMA & ROYAL HOSPITAL KILMAINHAM

The **Irish Museum of Modern Art** (IMMA; Map p70; ☎ 612 9900; Military Rd; admission free; 🕑 10am-5.30pm Tue-Sat, noon-5.30pm Sun) at the old Royal Hospital Kilmainham is close to Kilmainham Jail. The permanent collection and regular temporary exhibitions display a range of 20th-century Irish and international art. Bus Nos 24, 79 or 90 from Aston Quay will get you there.

The **Royal Hospital Kilmainham** was built between 1680 and 1687 as a home for retired soldiers and continued to fill that role until after Irish independence. At the time of its construction, it was one of the finest buildings in Ireland and there was considerable muttering that it was altogether too good a place for its residents. The building was designed by William Robinson, whose other work included Marsh's Library near St Patrick's Cathedral.

In 2001, a new **heritage itinerary** (adult/student €3.50/2; 🕑 Tue-Sun Jun-Sep) was launched to make the most of the building's treasures. Highlights include the Banqueting Hall and the stunning baroque chapel, which has papier-mâché ceilings and a set of exquisite Queen Anne gates. Also worth seeing are the fully restored formal gardens.

Free guided tours (2.30pm Wed, Fri & Sun) of the museum's exhibits include a new exhibition space in the restored Deputy Master's House at the northeastern corner of the gardens. Tours for groups are held Tuesday to Friday (10am, 11.45am, 2.30pm and 4pm) but bookings must be made two weeks in advance. There's a good café and bookshop on the grounds.

KILMAINHAM JAIL

Built between 1792 and 1795, **Kilmainham Jail** (Map p70; ☎ 453 5984; Inchicore Rd; adult/student & child €5/2; 🕑 9.30am-5pm daily Apr-Oct, 9.30am-4pm Mon-Sat, 10am-5pm Sun Oct-Mar) is a solid, grey, threatening building. During each act of Ireland's long, painful path to independence, at least one part of the performance took place at the jail.

The uprisings of 1798, 1803, 1848, 1867 and 1916 ended with the leaders' confinement here. Robert Emmet, Thomas Francis Meagher, Charles Stewart Parnell and the 1916 Easter Rising leaders were all visitors, but it was the executions in 1916 that most deeply etched the jail's name into the Irish consciousness. Of the 15 executions that took place between 3 and 12 May after the rising, 14 were conducted here. As a finale, prisoners from the Civil War struggles were held here from 1922. The jail closed in 1924.

An excellent audiovisual introduction to the building is followed by a thought-provoking tour. Incongruously sitting outside in the yard is the Asgard, the ship that successfully ran the British blockade to deliver arms to nationalist forces in 1914.

The tour finishes in the gloomy yard where the 1916 executions took place. Take bus Nos 23, 51, 51A, 78 or 79 from Aston Quay.

PHOENIX PARK

Map p97

The 700-plus hectares of **Phoenix Park** make it one of the world's largest city parks, dwarfing Central Park in New York (a mere 337 hectares) and all the London parks – Hampstead Heath is only 324 hectares. There are gardens and lakes, a host of sporting facilities, the second-oldest public zoo in Europe, a visitor centre, a castle, the Garda Síochána (police) Headquarters, various government offices, the residences of the US ambassador and the Irish president, and even a herd of deer.

Lord Ormond turned this land into a park in 1671 but it wasn't opened to the public until 1747, by Lord Chesterfield. 'Phoenix' is actually a corruption of the Irish words for 'clear water', fionn uisce. The park played a crucial role in Irish history, as Lord Cavendish, the British chief secretary for Ireland, and his assistant were murdered outside what is now the Irish president's residence in 1882 by an Irish nationalist group called the National Invincibles. Lord Cavendish's home is now called Deerfield and is used as the US ambassador's residence.

Near the Parkgate St entrance to the park is the 63m-high **Wellington Monument** obelisk. This took from 1817 to 1861 to build, mainly because the duke of Wellington fell from public favour during its construction. Nearby is the **People's Garden**, dating from 1864, and the bandstand in the Hollow. Behind the zoo, on the edge of the park, the Garda Síochána Headquarters has a small police museum.

In the centre of the park, the **Papal Cross** marks the site where Pope John Paul II preached to 1.25 million people in 1979. The **Phoenix Monument**, erected by Lord Chesterfield in 1747, looks very unphoenix-like and is often referred to as the Eagle Monument. The southern part of the park is given over to a large number of football and hurling pitches and, though they occupy about 200 acres, the area is known as Fifteen Acres. To the west, the rural-looking **Glen Pond** corner of the park is extremely attractive.

Back towards the Parkgate entrance is **Magazine Fort**, on Thomas' Hill. The fort took from 1734 to 1801 to build and never served any discernible purpose, although it was a target in the 1916 Easter Rising.

DUBLIN ZOO

Established in 1830, 12-hectare **Dublin Zoo** (Map p97; ☎ 677 1425; www.dublinzoo.ie; Phoenix Park; adult/child/family €11/7/32; 🕑 9.30am-6pm Mon-Sat, 10.30am-6pm Sun May-Sep, 9.30am-4pm Mon-Fri, 9.30am-5pm Sat, 10.30am-5pm Sun Oct-Apr) is one of the oldest in the world, but is mainly of interest to children. It used to be a run-down zoo where depressed animals used to depress visitors, but a substantial facelift, when the African Plains were added, doubled the zoo in size making it a much more pleasant place for animals to live and for you to stroll around.

Bus No 10 from O'Connell St or Nos 25 and 26 from Abbey St Middle will take you to the zoo.

ÁRAS AN UACHTARÁIN

The **residence of the Irish president** (Map p97) was built in 1751 and enlarged in 1782, then again in 1816, on the latter occasion by noted Irish architect Francis Johnston, who added the Ionic portico. From 1782 to 1922 it was the residence of the British viceroys or lord lieutenants. After independence it became the home of Ireland's governor-general until Ireland cut ties with the British Crown and created the office of president in 1937. The Phoenix Park Visitor Centre runs free one-hour tours of the house every Saturday between 10.30am and 2.30pm October to mid-March and 10.30pm to 3.30pm otherwise.

THE ROYAL CANAL

Constructed from 1790, by which time the older Grand Canal was already past its prime, the **Royal Canal** (Map p70), which encircles Dublin to the north, was a commercial failure – but its story is certainly colourful. It was founded by Long John Binns, a Grand Canal director who quit the board because of a supposed insult over his profession as a shoemaker. He established the Royal Canal principally for revenge but it never made money and actually became known as the Shoemaker's Canal. In 1840 the canal was sold to a railway company and tracks still run alongside much of the canal's route through the city.

The Royal Canal towpath makes a relaxing walk through the heart of the city. You can join it beside Newcomen Bridge at North Strand Rd, just north of Connolly Station, and follow it to the suburb of Clonsilla and beyond, more than 10km away. The walk is particularly pleasant beyond Binns Bridge in Drumcondra. At the top of Blessington St a large pond, used when the canal also supplied drinking water to the city, attracts water birds.

NATIONAL BOTANIC GARDENS

Founded in 1795, the 19.5-hectare **National Botanic Gardens** (Map p70; ☎ 837 7596, Botanic Rd, Glasnevin; admission free; 🕐 9am-6pm Mon-Sat, 11am-6pm Sun Apr-Oct, 10am-4.30pm Mon-Sat, 11am-4.30pm Sun Nov-Mar) are directly north of the centre, flanked to the north by the River Tolka.

In the gardens is a series of curvilinear glasshouses dating from 1843 to 1869. The glasshouses were created by Richard Turner, who was also responsible for the glasshouse at Belfast Botanic Gardens and the Palm House in London's Kew Gardens. Within these Victorian masterpieces you will find the latest in botanical technology, including a series of computer-controlled climates reproducing environments of different parts of the world. The gardens also have a palm house. Among the pioneering botanical work conducted here was the first attempt to raise orchids from seed, back in 1844. Pampas grass and the giant lily were first grown in Europe in these gardens.

Catch bus Nos 13, 13A or 19 from O'Connell St or take bus Nos 34 or 34A from Middle Abbey St.

PROSPECT CEMETERY

Prospect Cemetery (Glasnevin Cemetery; Map p70; ☎ 830 1133; Finglas Rd; admission free; 🕐 24 hrs, tours 2.30pm Wed & Fri), northwest of the city centre, is the largest in Ireland. It was established in 1832 as a cemetery for Roman Catholics, who faced opposition when they conducted burials in the city's Protestant cemeteries. Many monuments and memorials have staunchly patriotic overtones, with numerous high crosses, shamrocks, harps and other Irish symbols. The single most imposing memorial is the colossal monument to

PHOENIX PARK

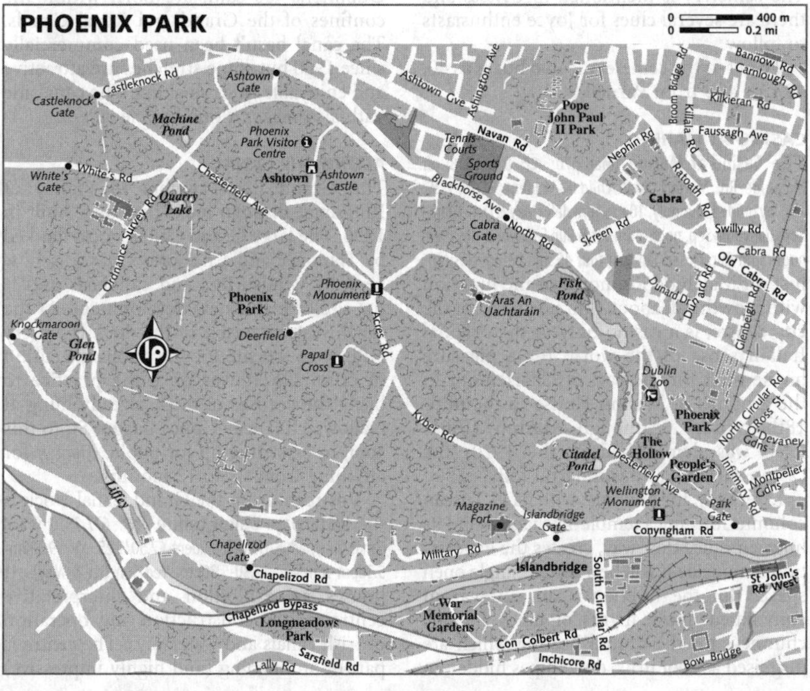

Cardinal McCabe (1837–1921), archbishop of Dublin and primate of Ireland.

A modern replica of a round tower acts as a handy landmark for locating the tomb of Daniel O'Connell, who died in 1847 and was reinterred here in 1869, when the tower was completed. Charles Stewart Parnell's tomb is topped with a huge granite rock. Other notable people buried here include Sir Roger Casement, who was executed for treason by the British in 1916 and whose remains weren't returned to Ireland until 1964; the republican leader Michael Collins, who died in the Civil War; the docker and trade unionist Jim Larkin, a prime force in the 1913 general strike; and the poet Gerard Manley Hopkins.

There's also a poignant 'class' memorial to the men who have starved themselves to death for the cause of Irish freedom over the century, including 10 men in the 1981 H Block hunger strikes.

The most interesting parts of the cemetery are at the southeastern Prospect Square end. The watch towers were once used to keep watch for body snatchers. The cemetery is mentioned in *Ulysses* and there are several clues for Joyce enthusiasts to follow.

To get to the cemetery, catch bus Nos 40, 40A or 40B from Parnell St.

CASINO AT MARINO

The **Casino at Marino** (Map p70; ☎ 833 1618; off Malahide Rd, Marino; adult/child & student €2.75/1.25; ⏰ by guided tour only, 10am-5pm daily May & Oct, 10am-6pm daily Jun-Sep, noon-4pm Sat & Sun Feb-Apr & Nov-Dec, noon-5pm Apr, closed Jan; last tour 45 min before closing), just off Malahide Rd, north of the junction with Howth Rd, about 4km northeast of the city centre, is a casino only in the original Italian sense of the word. It's a pleasure house built for the earl of Charlemont in the grounds of Marino House in the mid-18th century. Although Marino House itself was demolished in the 1920s the casino survives as a wonderful folly.

Externally, the building, with its 12 Tuscan columns forming a temple-like façade and its huge entrance doorway, creates the expectation that inside it will be a simple single open space. But the interior is an extravagant convoluted maze: flights of fancy include chimneys for the central heating which are disguised as roof urns, downpipes hidden in columns, carved draperies, ornate fireplaces, beautiful parquet floors constructed of rare woods, and a spacious wine cellar. A variety of statuary adorns the outside but it's the amusing fakes that are most enjoyable. The towering front door is a sham and a much smaller panel opens to reveal the secret interior. The windows have blacked-out panels to hide the fact that the interior is a complex of rooms, not a single chamber.

In 1870 Marino House was sold to the government. The Marino estate followed in 1881 and the casino in 1930, though it was decrepit by then. Restoration is continuing and new planting helps to hide the surrounding houses.

Bus Nos 20A, 20B, 27, 27B, 42, 42C or 123 from city centre or the DART to Clontarf Rd will get you there.

The Grand Canal Map p70

Built to connect Dublin with the River Shannon, the **Grand Canal** makes a graceful 6km loop round south Dublin. At its eastern end the canal forms a harbour connected with the Liffey at Ringsend. True Dubliners, it's said, are born within the confines of the Grand and Royal Canals. The canal hasn't been used commercially since 1960 but some stretches are attractive and enjoyable to stroll along. The canalside path also makes a fine bicycle ride.

ALONG THE CANAL

The Grand Canal enters the Liffey at Ringsend, through locks that were built in 1796. The large Grand Canal Dock, flanked by Hanover and Charlotte Quays, is now used by windsurfers and canoeists and is the site of major new development. At the northwestern corner of the dock is Misery Hill, once the site for the public execution of criminals. It was once the practice to bring the corpses of those already hung at Gallows Hill, near Upper Baggot St, to this spot, to be strung up for public display for anything from six to 12 months.

Upstream from the Grand Canal Dock is the **Waterways Visitor Centre** (☎ 677 7510; Grand Canal Quay; adult/child & student €2.50/1.25; ⏰ 9.30am-5.30pm Jun-Sep, 12.30-5.30pm Wed-Sun Oct & May). It houses an exhibition and interpretative centre on the construction and operation of Irish canals and waterways. The centre is part of an ongoing (and highly impressive) programme of urban renewal that has transformed the area. Catch the DART to Grand Canal Quay.

A **memorial to the 1916 Easter Rising** can be seen on the Mount St Bridge. A little further southwest, Baggot St crosses the canal on the 1791 Macartney Bridge.

This lovely stretch of the canal with its grassy, tree-lined banks was a favourite haunt of the poet Patrick Kavanagh. Among his compositions is the hauntingly beautiful *On Raglan Road*, which Van Morrison put to music. One Kavanagh poem requested that he be commemorated by 'a canal bank seat for passers-by' and Kavanagh's friends obliged with a seat beside the lock on the southern side of the canal. A little further along on the northern side you can sit down by Kavanagh himself, cast in bronze, comfortably lounging on a bench and watching his beloved canal.

Ballsbridge

Map p70

Southeast of central Dublin, the suburb of **Ballsbridge** was principally laid out between 1830 and 1860. Many streets have British names with a distinctly military flavour. Many embassies, including the US embassy, are in Ballsbridge. It also has some of Dublin's most luxurious B&Bs and several top-end hotels. The main attractions are the **Royal Dublin Society Showground** and the **Lansdowne Rd rugby stadium**, though **Herbert Park** is also a favourite for sport, walking or just sitting around.

ROYAL DUBLIN SOCIETY SHOWGROUND

The **Royal Dublin Society (RDS) Showground** (Map p70; ☎ 668 9878; Merrion Rd, Ballsbridge), about 15 minutes by bus from the city centre, is used for various exhibitions throughout the year. The society was founded in 1731 and had its headquarters in a number of well known Dublin buildings, including, from 1814 to 1925, Leinster House. The society was involved in the foundation of the National Museum, Library, Gallery and Botanic Gardens. The most important annual event at the showground is the August **Dublin Horse Show** (☎ 668 0866 for tickets; Ballsbridge), which includes an international showjumping contest. Ask at the tourist office or consult a listings magazine for other events. Take bus No 7 (every seven minutes) from Trinity College.

ACTIVITIES

Beaches & Swimming

Dublin is hardly the sort of place to work on your suntan and even a hot Irish summer day is unlikely to raise the water temperature much above freezing. However, there are some pleasant beaches. Many Joyce fans feel compelled to take a dip in **Forty Foot Pool** at Dun Laoghaire (see p131). Sandy beaches near the centre of Dublin include **Sutton** (11km), **Portmarnock** (11km), **Malahide** (11km), **Claremount** (14km) and **Donabate** (21km). Although the beach at Sandymount is nothing special, it is only 5km southeast of central Dublin. Take bus No 3 from Fleet St.

The fabulous new **National Aquatic Centre** (Map p70; ☎ 646 43000; www.nac.ie; Snugborough Rd, Blanchardstown, Dublin 15; adult/child/family from €9/7/25.60; 🕑 11am-10pm Mon-Fri, 9am-8pm Sat & Sun), opened in March 2003 to accommodate the Special Olympics World Summer Games, is the largest indoor water park. Besides its Olympic-size competition pool it has water roller coasters, wave and surf machines, a leisure pool and all types of flumes. It's a great day out for the family but be prepared to join the shivering line of children queuing for slides on weekends. Get bus No 38A from Hawkin St to Snugborough Rd.

There is a sad dearth of good quality pools in the city centre. Most of the pools in Dublin are small, crowded and not quite hygienic. On the plus side, they don't charge very much for a 40-minute session. The best of the lot, at least in terms of convenience to the city centre, is **Markievicz Leisure Centre** (Map pp72-4; ☎ 672 9121; cnr Tara & Townsend Sts; adult/child €4.70-5.80/2.60; 🕑 7am-9.45pm Mon-Thu, 7am-8.45pm Fri, 9am-6pm Sat, 10am-4pm Sun). For the admission price you can swim pretty much as long as you like; children are only allowed at off-peak times.

Cycling

Dublin isn't a bad place to get around by bicycle, as it is small enough and flat enough to make bike travel easy. Many visitors explore further afield by bicycle, a popular activity in Ireland despite the often less-than-encouraging weather.

Cycle lanes have thankfully proliferated around the city centre in the last five years but are often blocked by parked cars, making safe cycling a challenge. Add to that the seemingly permanent road works, buses and taxis that pull out at random and cars that chance a crossing at orange-red traffic lights and you'll get a feel for the obstacle course that awaits cyclists. Nonetheless, with your wits about you, it's the fastest way to get about the increasingly congested centre.

Many hostels offer secure bicycle parking areas, but if you're going to have a bike stolen anywhere in Ireland, Dublin is where it'll happen. Lock your bike up well. Surprisingly, considering how popular bicycles are in Dublin, there's a scarcity of suitable bike-parking facilities. Grafton St and Temple Bar are virtually devoid of places to lock a bike. Elsewhere, there are signs on many likely stretches of railing announcing that bikes must not be parked there. Nevertheless, there are some places, such as the Grafton St corner of St Stephen's Green.

Bike rental has become increasingly more difficult to find because of crippling insurance costs. Typical rental for a mountain bike is around €25 a day or €100 per week. Raleigh Rent-a-Bike agencies can be found all over Ireland, north and south of the border. Contact them at **Eurotrek** (☎ 456 8847; www.eurotrekraleighgroup.com). Raleigh agencies in Dublin include the following:

C Harding for Bikes (☎ 873 2455; 30 Bachelor's Walk)
Irish Cycling Safaris (☎ 260 0749; UCD)
Joe Daly (☎ 298 1485; Lower Main St, Dundrum)
MacDonalds Cycles (☎ 475 2586; 38 Wexford St)

Irish Cycling Safaris organises nine themed week-long tours (€565) of the countryside. Price includes hotel and B&B accommodation, bike rental and a guide.

WALKING TOUR

THE BARFLY TRAIL
Distance of Trail: 2.5km
Duration: one hour to two days!

Dubliners of old would assure their 'bitter halves' that they were 'going to see a man about a dog' before beating a hasty retreat to the nearest watering hole. Visiting barflies need make no excuse to enjoy the social and cultural education – ahem – of a tour of Dublin's finest, most charming and hardcore bars. Start in the historic **Le Méridien Shelbourne Hotel** (**1**; p109). Here you can earwig political gossip at any hour of the day among the hacks and legal eagles who prop up the **Horseshoe Bar**. Head down to Dawson St into Dublin's smallest bar, the **Dawson Lounge** (**2**), for an appropriately diminutive tipple before sinking a pint of plain in the snug at South Anne St's **Kehoes** (**3**; p117), one of the city centre's most atmospheric bars. Lament the world's woes with Dublin's frustrated poets, writers and artists in **Grogan's Castle Lounge** (**4**; p118) on Castlemarket before nipping around the corner to the new jazzy **Market Bar** (**5**; p120)

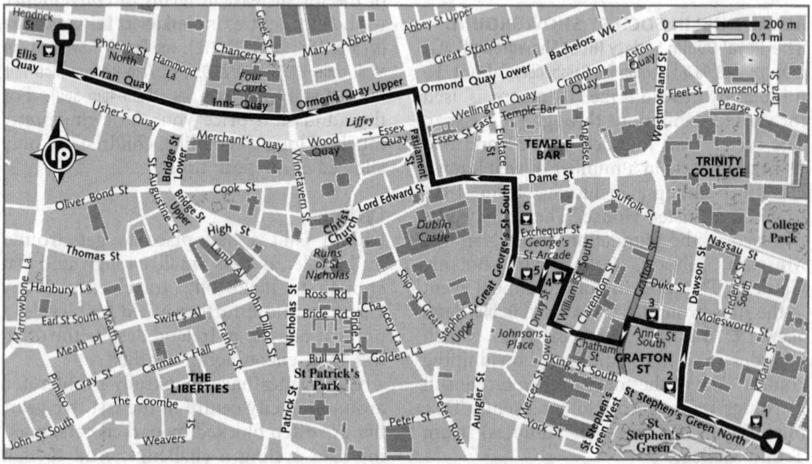

on Fade St. From here, cruise over to the **Globe** (**6**; p120) on South Great George's Street to shake your booty to funky beats with the city's young scenesters. Cross over the Liffey and (this is where the real walking bit comes in) follow the quays west to Queen St's grungy **Dice Bar** (**7**; p119), a little slice of downtown New York City, where you can regain your strength over some Long Island iced teas.

DUBLIN FOR CHILDREN

Sometimes holidaying with small children requires the organisational skills of an army boot camp, boundless energy and patience, bottomless pockets and a sense of humour, so it really helps when facilities and goodwill are there to back up your efforts.

All but a few hotels will provide cots and many have babysitting on request. While waiters may not act like your baby is the first they've ever seen, as in some southern European locations, you'll still find a warm reception for junior travellers in Dublin: at least during the day. Frustratingly many city centre restaurants are unwilling to accommodate diners under 12, especially babies, after 6pm. You'll need to check before making a booking. Most restaurants – even exclusive ones – have highchairs and will gladly heat bottles and baby food, but so-called 'kiddie menus' lack imagination and rarely stretch further than the ubiquitous chicken nuggets or sausages with chips. That said, places catering specifically for families who want to eat more nutritious food are cropping up all the time and pizza chain Milano has resourcefully added free weekend childcare facilities to its Dublin restaurants.

Nappy-changing facilities and city centre playgrounds are remarkably few and far between. Shopping centres and department stores (or a hotel if you're stuck) are good places to try. There's a reasonable sized playground on Gardiner St or in St Stephen's Green, where you can also feed the ducks, and the **Iveagh Gardens** (Map p88), while it doesn't have a playground, has a waterfall and small maze, and is a lovely quiet space to relax while your children play.

The **Ark** (Map pp80–1) is a children's cultural centre which organises plays, exhibitions and workshops for four to 14 year olds. You really need to book in advance for events.

Lambert Puppet Theatre (☎ 280 0974; www.lambertpuppettheatre.com; Clifton Lane, Monkstown) stages puppet shows for the over-threes.

The **National Museum** (p85), **Natural History Museum** (p87) and **IMMA** (p95) run fun educational programmes for children at weekends. The **National Wax Museum** (Map pp72-4; ☎ 873 6340; Granby Row, Parnell Sq; adult/child €7/4; 🕑 10am-5.30pm Mon-Sat, noon-5.30pm Sun) has slightly tired looking models but its chamber of horrors and new Star Wars exhibit should entertain. Otherwise, a swim or trip to the zoo might well keep little ones happy for at least a few hours.

A nice spot for a picnic is **Newbridge House** with its large **traditional farm** (Map p70; ☎ 843 6534; Donabate; adult/child/family €2.50/1.50/6; 🕑 10am-5pm Tue-Sat, 2-6pm Sun Apr-Sep, 2-5pm Sat & Sun Oct-Mar) northeast of swords at Donabate, 19km from the centre. It has cows, pigs and chickens, a large parkland and adventure playground. You can get there on the Suburban Rail service (€2.40, 30 minutes), which departs hourly from either Connolly or Pearse station in the city centre.

The *Irish Times* includes a column on things to do for children in its Wednesday edition.

Many hotels can provide babysitting on request (normally €7 to €10 per hour) or, though more expensive, you could try a couple of agencies that provide professional nannies. It's up to you to negotiate a fee with the nanny but €10 per hour is the average, plus taxi fare if s/he isn't driving. You'll need to sign a form beforehand that the agency will fax to your hotel.

Belgrave Agency (☎ 280 9341; 55 Mulgrave St, Dun Laoghaire; fee €13/hour plus 21% VAT)

Executive Nannies (☎ 873 1273; 43 Dominick St Lower; fee €20/hour)

QUIRKY DUBLIN

Call two fat ladies at ultra-camp bingo in the **George** (Map pp118-19; ☎ 478 2983; 89 Sth Great George's St; admission free; 🕑 8.30pm) with drag queen Shirley Temple Bar on a Sunday night. Take a thrill-seeker's safari in a speedboat around Dublin bay and its islands from Malahide to Dalkey with **Sea Safaris** (☎ 806 1626; www.seasafaris.ie; Malahide Marina; €25/hr; 🕑 daily). Join a slow food banquet for 300, or gen up on plant medicine at the annual eco-friendly **Convergence festival** (☎ 674 6415; www.sustainable.ie; 15-19 Essex St) in May. Catch some of Ireland's best known comedians doing stand-up in the intimate **International Bar** (Map pp118-19; ☎ 677 9250; 23 Wicklow St; admission €8; 🕐 8.30pm) on Wednesday nights. Root for rare original manuscripts or antique maps in cramped **Cathach Books** (☎ 671 8676; www.rarebooks.ie; 10 Duke St). Grab moving sushi from the conveyor belt counter at **Aya** (Map pp80-1; ☎ 677 1544; Clarendon St) and wash it down with a jug of sake.

TOURS

Dublin is an easy city to see on foot so a guided walking tour is an ideal way to double up on a bit of culture and exercise. For longer tours, or a cushier ride, there are numerous themed city-wide bus tours and several that do day trips further afield.

Bus Tours

DUBLIN BUS

Dublin Bus (☎ 872 0000; www.dublinbus.ie, 59 Upper O'Connell St) tours can be booked at its office or at the Bus Éireann counter at Dublin Tourism in St Andrew's Church, Suffolk St.

Dublin City hop-on hop-off City Tour (adult/child €12.50/6; every 15 min 9.30am-4.30pm; 1½ hrs) can be joined at any of the 16 designated stops covering the city centre's major attractions. Admission to the sights is not included.

Ghost Bus Tour (adult €22; 8pm Tue-Fri, 7 & 9pm Sat & Sun; 2 hrs) is a popular tour of graveyards and haunted places.

Coast & Castles Tour (adult/child €20/10; 10am daily; 3 hrs) takes in the Botanic Gardens in Glasnevin, the Casino at Marino, Malahide and Howth.

South Coast Tour (adult/child €20/10; 11am & 2pm daily; 3¾ hr) brings you along the stretch of coastline between Dun Laoghaire and Killiney.

WILD COACH TOURS

Award-winning 'wild coach' tours are run by **Aran Tours** (☎ 280 1899; www.wildcoachtours.com). Prices include admission.

Wild Powerscourt Tour (adult/child €20/16; 1.30pm daily Mar-Sep, Sat & Sun Oct-Feb; 4½ hours) departs from the Gresham Hotel and covers Sandycove, Powerscourt house and gardens.

Wild Wicklow Tour (adult/child €28/25; 9am daily; 8½ hrs) leaves from Dublin Tourism, Suffolk

BLOOMSDAY

Six days after meeting her, the writer James Joyce had his first date with Nora Barnacle, the woman he was to marry, on 16 June 1904. Later, when he came to write his masterpiece *Ulysses*, which describes a single day in the life of Dubliner Leopold Bloom, the date he chose for this latter-day odyssey was 16 June 1904. Now Dublin duly celebrates Bloomsday on 16 June each year, with a range of entertainment, some serious, some less so, at venues all around the city. Serious Bloomsdayers don Edwardian costume for the day.

In general, events are designed to follow Bloom's progress around town and in recent years festivities have expanded to continue over four days around 16 June. On Bloomsday proper you can kick things off with breakfast at the **James Joyce Cultural Centre** (Map pp72-4; ☎ 878 8547; 35 North Great George's St) where the 'inner organs of beast and fowl' come accompanied by celebratory readings.

In the morning, guided tours of Joycean sites usually leave from the GPO, on O'Connell St, and the James Joyce Cultural Centre. Lunchtime activity focuses on **Davy Byrne's** (Map pp80-1; Duke St), Joyce's 'moral pub', where Bloom paused to dine on a glass of Burgundy and a slice of Gorgonzola. Street entertainers are likely to keep you amused as you pass the afternoon, the guided walks topped up with animated readings from *Ulysses* and Joyce's other books at appropriate sites and times: **Ormond Quay Hotel** (Map pp80-1; Ormond Quay) at 4pm and **Harrisons** (Map pp80-1; Westmoreland St) later in the day.

Should you have any energy left, you can spin things out to the early hours, perhaps in **Bewley's Oriental Café** (Map p88; 78 Grafton St), where animated performances of Molly Bloom's closing (and at one time controversial) soliloquy take place.

Events also take place in the days leading up to and following Bloomsday. The best source of information about what's on in any particular year is likely to be the James Joyce Cultural Centre (www.jamesjoyce.ie) or the free Dublin Event Guide, close to the date. You don't have to know anything about Joyce or his books to enjoy the day, although it certainly helps!

St, and goes down the coast to Avoca Handweavers, Glendalough and the Sally Gap.

Walking Tours

HISTORICAL TOURS

1916 Easter Rising Walk (☎ 676 2493; www.1916rising.com; adult/child €10/free; 11.30am & 2.30pm Mon-Sat, 1pm Sun, no 2.30pm tour Mar & Oct, from International Bar; 1½ hrs) is a recommended tour run by graduates of Trinity College taking in parts of Dublin that were directly involved in the Easter Rising.

LITERARY TOURS

There are 1½-hour walking tours of north Dublin, focusing on sites associated with James Joyce, departing from the **James Joyce Cultural Centre** (Map pp72-4; ☎ 878 8547; 35 North Great George's St) at 11am and 2.30pm Monday to Saturday; phone to check departure times outside the summer months. The cost of a tour of the centre and the walk is €5.70.

Dublin Literary Pub Crawl (☎ 454 0228; www.dublinpubcrawl.com; adult/student €10/8; 7.30pm daily, noon Sun Apr-Oct; Fri-Sun Nov-Apr from the Duke pub; 2½ hrs) has an entertaining walk-and-performance led by two actors around pubs with literary connections. A drink at each stop may lead to a fuzzy memory at the end when there's a competition relating to the tour. This award-winning tour is very popular, so be sure to get to the pub by 7pm to buy tickets.

Water Tours

Viking Splash Tours (Map pp72-4; ☎ 707 6000; www.vikingsplashtours.com; adult/child from €14/8; 10 tours daily from 64-65 Patrick St; 1¼ hrs) has witty tours of Viking Dublin in reconditioned WWII amphibious boat-buses, ending in the Grand Canal Harbour.

Musical Walks

The **Dublin Musical Pub Crawl's** (☎ 478 0191; www.musicalpubcrawl.com; adult/student €10/8; 7.30pm daily May-Oct, Fri & Sat Nov & Feb-Apr; 2½ hrs) focus is on Irish traditional music: two musicians demonstrate the various styles and explain the music's history in a number of pubs in Temple Bar. The tour leaves from Oliver St John Gogarty's pub (see Map pp118–19).

Macabre Tours

In recent years there has been a growth of tours that focus on Dublin's more sinister past, both real and invented. Aside from the very popular ghost bus tour run by Dublin Bus, there are a couple of good walking tours worth checking out.

The **Walk Macabre Tour** (☎ 087 677 1512; www.ghostwalk.cjb.com; €9; 7.30pm daily; 1¼ hrs) is as much a show as a walk through the spooky corners of Georgian Dublin. Tours leave from St Stephen's Green main gate.

Carriage Tours

You can pick up a **horse and carriage** with a driver/commentator at the junction of Grafton St and St Stephen's Green. Half-hour tours cost up to €40 and the carriages can take four or five people. Tours of different lengths can be negotiated with the drivers.

FESTIVALS & EVENTS

Time was when a few trucks dressed up as floats, some tired-looking bunting and a handful of stilt walkers were all you could expect of Ireland's national festival, the St Patrick's Day parade. A cash injection and the sudden dawning that the event marked an important date in the lucrative tourist calendar has seen the parade reinvent itself into a four-day explosion of activities: street theatre, music, fireworks and family events. But that's only the half of it: Dubliners love of social interaction and rich cultural heritage is reflected in the huge number of festivals to be enjoyed the whole year round. The following list of festivals is by no means exhaustive and you should check Fáilte Ireland's website (www.boardfailte.ie) for further details. For information on Ireland's special events, see the Directory chapter. For information on Bloomsday, 16 June, see the 'Bloomsday' boxed text on p102.

St Patrick's Day Festival (☎ 676 3205; www.stpatricksday.ie) Big four-day carnival around 17 March on city streets and in venues.

Anna Livia International Opera Festival (☎ 661 7544; www.operaannalivia.com) Week-long festival in the Gaiety theatre, National Concert Hall and Bank of Ireland Arts Centre in July.

Convergence Festival (☎ 674 6415; www.sustainable.ie; 15-19 Essex St) Ten-day green festival on sustainable living with diverse programme of workshops, exhibitions, children's activities in spring in Temple Bar.

Diversions (☎ 677 2255; www.temple-bar.ie) Free outdoor music, children's and film events at weekends from May to September in Temple Bar's Meeting House Square.

GAY & LESBIAN DUBLIN

The dark days of furtively holding a same-sex partner's hand under a pub table or coyly exchanging glances across the straight nightclub floor are over. It's just over 10 years since gay sex between consenting adults over 17 was decriminalised in 1993 and Dublin's gay community could firmly slam the closet door. In the meantime a slew of gay clubs, bars and saunas have opened making Dublin – while Sydney or San Francisco it ain't – a much easier place to be gay. Most people wouldn't bat an eyelid at public displays of affection between same-sex couples, or cross dressing in the city centre, but discretion is advised in the suburbs.

Outhouse (Map pp72-4; ☎ 873 4932; www.outhouse.ie; 105 Capel St) Gay, lesbian and bisexual resource centre. Great stop-off point to see what's on, check noticeboards and meet people. It publishes the free *Ireland's Pink Pages*, a directory of gay-centric services which is also accessible on the website.

Gay Switchboard Dublin (☎ 872 1055; www.gayswitchboard.ie) A friendly and useful voluntary service that provides information from where to find accommodation to legal issues.

If you do encounter any sort of trouble or harassment on the streets don't hesitate to call the **Gay & Lesbian Garda Liaison Officer** (☎ 666 9000) or the **Sexual Assault Unit** (☎ 666 000) at the Pearse St Garda station.

Gay Community News (www.gcn.ie) is a useful nationwide news- and issues-based monthly paper, while the new glossy *Q-Life* and *Free!* are entertainment guides that can be found in Temple Bar businesses and the Irish Film Centre on Eustace St.

Although most of the city's hotels wouldn't think twice about checking in same-sex couples, the same cannot be said of many of the city's B&Bs. One central option is **Frankies Guesthouse** (Map p88; ☎ 478 3087; www.frankiesguesthouse.com; 8 Camden Pl; s €60-75, d €78-95), a comfortable B&B with pleasant rooms equipped with TV and tea and coffee facilities.

Gay & Lesbian Nightspots

Check www.gay-ireland.com for other entertainment venues.

George (Map pp118-19; ☎ 478 2983; 89 Sth Great George's St) One of the longest established and biggest gay bars/clubs in town and a good spot for cruising. Bingo on Sunday night is a mecca for divas who flock to see gorgeous drag queen Miss Shirley Temple Bar grab those rattling balls.

Out on the Liffey (Map pp118-19; ☎ 872 2480; 27 Upper Ormond Quay) A 'harder' rough and ready pub, popular with the biker or butch set of both sexes.

There are plenty of clubs that run gay and lesbian nights. The scene is constantly changing, however, and while the nights mentioned following are pretty regular and steady, we recommend that you call ahead to confirm that they're still on.

Front Lounge (Map pp118-19; ☎ 670 4112; 33 Parliament St) A lavish lounge attracting a mixed upmarket clientele. Drag queen Panti runs the cabaret and karaoke night, Casting Couch, on Tuesdays.

Gubu (Map pp118-19; ☎ 874 0483; 7-8 Capel St) One of the newer trendier gay- and lesbian-friendly bars on the north side which shows movies and hosts comedy night midweek.

PoD (Place of Dance; Map p88; ☎ 478 0166; 35 Harcourt St) Friday night's HAM, aka Homo Action Movies, is one of Dublin's most enduring gay and lesbian nights. The soundtrack is thumping house, uplifting and progressive.

Molloy's (Map pp118-19; ☎ 677 3207; 13 High St) Near Christ Church Cathedral, this bar has lesbian-only night on Saturday called Stonewallz.

Rí Rá (Map pp118-19; ☎ 677 4835; Dame Ct) Strictly Handbag is a long-running Monday night at one of Dublin's friendlier clubs. It's not exclusively gay, but it is popular with the gay community.

Spy (Map pp118-19; ☎ 677 0014; Powerscourt House, South William St) This is one the hardest places to get in to unless you're dripping with glamour, but Sunday night's Hilton Edwards club (named after the gay co-founder of the Gate Theatre) requests only that you're gay and reasonably well dressed. It's cool, chic and, at the time of writing, the hottest ticket in town.

Some annual events worth catching are the **Lesbian & Gay Film Festival** (☎ 670 6377; www.irishculture.net/filmfestival) an international film and documentary festival held in the Irish Film Centre in August and **Gay Pride** (www.gay-ireland.com) when queers, dykes, bis and fetishists take to the streets in a colourful, high energy handbag-fest.

Dublin Theatre Festival (☎ 677 8439; www.eircomtheatrefestival.com) Well-established international theatre festival over a fortnight in autumn in most Dublin venues.

Dublin Fringe Festival (☎ 872 9016; www.fringefestival.com) Comedy and alternative fringe theatre in October.

Dublin International Organ & Choral Festival (☎ 633 7392; www.dublinorganfestival.com) Ten-day international music festival in June.

Heineken Green Energy Festival (☎ 1890 925100) Four-day rock and indie music festival based outside Dublin Castle and adjacent venues.

SLEEPING

Finding a place to stay in Dublin will be one of the more important decisions you'll make while you're here, as it will play a part in dictating the kind of time you'll have. If you're only here for the weekend, you'll want to stay as close to the city centre as possible – at the heart of the action. If you're planning a longer visit, the choice becomes less important, but it'll matter nonetheless. If you're lodging in the suburbs, you'll have to plan your excursions carefully. Public transport is slow, inefficient and, more importantly, virtually nonexistent after midnight. That leaves you relying on taxis which, despite the addition of 2000 new plates in 2002, can still be a nightmare to grab.

Like every other city in the world, the closer you stay to the centre, the more you'll pay, and in Dublin, that can be a lot. The city's renaissance as a tourist magnet has radically changed the accommodation map, with new hotels of varying quality springing up almost weekly and still it can be hard to find a bed at peak times. Our advice is: book ahead or go to one of the Dublin Tourism offices and ask them to book you a room. For €4 plus a 10% deposit on the cost of the first night, they'll find you somewhere to stay. Sometimes this may require a great deal of phoning around so it can be money well spent.

It is virtually impossible to get a really cheap room in Dublin anymore, and even the city's hostels, once the backbone of dirt-cheap accommodation, have substantially raised their prices. Basically, Dublin is one of Europe's more expensive cities to sleep in.

Accommodation prices vary according to season, reaching a peak during the main holiday periods and over public holidays. Prices quoted are those for the high season. You can usually get a bed in a hostel for €15 to €28. In a typical B&B the cost per person will be around €45 to €65. More expensive B&Bs or mid-range hotels cost around €57 to €82 per person. Dublin's top hotels cost upwards of €150 per person.

North of the Liffey

BUDGET

Since there are no conveniently central camp sites in Dublin, budget travellers usually head for one of Dublin's numerous hostels. They can be heavily booked from late April to late September, but then so is everything else.

There's a large number of hostels in the north of the city.

Abbey Court Hostel (Map pp80-1; ☎ 878 0700; www.abbey-court.com; 29 Bachelor's Walk; dm/d €21/88) Spread over two buildings on the Liffey quays, this large, well-run hostel has 33 clean dorms with good storage. En suite doubles are in the newer building where a light breakfast is also provided in the adjacent café, Juice.

Globetrotters Tourist Hostel (Map pp72-4; ☎ 878 8088; gtrotter@indigo.ie; 46-48 Lower Gardiner St; dm/d €19/50) This is a really friendly, city-centre place with 94 beds in a variety of en suite dorms, all with under-bed storage. Décor is funky and there's a little patio garden to the rear for the elusive sunny day.

Isaacs Hostel (Map pp72-4; ☎ 855 6215; www.isaacs.ie; 2-5 Frenchman's Lane; dm/d from €11.50/52.50) Located just around the corner from its sister hostel, Jacob's Inn, in a 200-year-old wine vault, this busy, grungy hostel has loads of character and is probably the cheapest bed in town. Summer barbecues and live music in the foyer, provided by musicians who play the Isaac Butt venue next door, are an added feature. One of the first independent hostels in the country, facilities probably haven't changed much since it opened but, at the time of writing, a major facelift was underway with a new hangout area, Internet facilities and a disabled access room in the pipeline.

Jacob's Inn (Map pp72-4; ☎ 855 5660; www.isaacs.ie; 21-28 Talbot Pl; dm/d from €16.50/65) Just behind Busáras, this clean, modern hostel offers spacious en suite accommodation and excellent facilities, including some disabled access rooms.

Litton Lane Hostel (Map pp80-1; ☎ 872 8389; litton@irish-hostel.com; 2-4 Litton Lane; dm/d from €17/70) True to its dog-eared recording studio origins (once patronised by Van Morrison) this friendly hostel could do with a lick of paint but retains a certain grungy charm. Dorms are mixed, as are the showers down the corridor.

Marlborough Hostel (Map pp72-4; ☎ 874 7629; www.marlboroughhostel.com; 81-82 Marlborough St; dm/d from €14/52) Next to the Pro-Cathedral, this well-located hostel has 76 beds and adequate facilities. High Georgian ceilings make up for small rooms and the slightly jaded showers, in the basement, are a bit of a trek from the dorms.

MID-RANGE

If you're looking for budget accommodation, but want the kind of privacy you're unlikely to find in hostels, then a B&B is your best option. Traditionally the most popular kind of accommodation in Ireland, Dublin's B&Bs have undergone something of a renaissance in recent years, as demands for greater luxury and amenities have forced many B&B owners to renovate, upgrade and – inevitably – raise their prices. Today you'll find two kinds of B&B: the townhouse, the more traditional kind with two or three rooms in someone's home; and the guesthouse, a kind of upmarket, larger B&B which is more expensive. Though still cheap in comparison to most of the city's hotels, it's unlikely that you'll find any kind of decent room in townhouse style for less than €35 and €45 per person in a guesthouse. What you're paying for is the kind of attentive service not usually found in hotels, as well as the convivial, more homely atmosphere.

Dublin's B&B street is Gardiner St, just east of O'Connell St. Thankfully, the street's reputation for late-night danger has receded in the face of urban rejuvenation, though we still advise a modicum of caution at night, particularly on Upper Gardiner St past Mountjoy Square.

Further out, you can find a better price and quality combination north of the centre at Clontarf or in the seaside suburbs of Dun Laoghaire or Howth. The Ballsbridge area, just southeast of the centre, offers quality and convenience, but you pay more for the combination. Other suburbs to try are Sandymount (immediately east of Ballsbridge) and Drumcondra (north of the centre toward the airport).

There is a collection of places on Lower Gardiner St and Talbot St, near the bus and train stations, and another group on Upper Gardiner St, further north near Mountjoy Square. Other B&Bs are in the streets around it.

Anchor Guesthouse (Map pp72-4; ☎ 878 6913; www.anchorguesthouse.com; 49 Lower Gardiner St; s/d from €56/72) The Anchor's elegant, very comfortable en suite rooms all come with TV, and tea and coffee making facilities. This lovely Georgian guesthouse with delicious wholesome breakfasts comes highly recommended by readers.

Celtic Lodge (Map pp72-4; ☎ 677 9955; 81-82 Talbot St; s/d €65/70) This cheap and cheerful guesthouse situated above a pub has 29 simply furnished rooms. Because of the pub's live music below, you might want to ask for a room at the back if you'd rather not join in the sing-song from your bed.

Clifden Guesthouse (Map pp72-4; ☎ 874 6364; www.clifdenhouse.com; 32 Gardiner Pl; s/d from €45/80) This really is a great place to stay in the area. A very nicely refurbished Georgian house with 14 tastefully decorated rooms, all en suite, immaculately clean and extremely comfortable.

Lyndon House (Map pp72-4; ☎ 878 6950; 26 Gardiner Pl; s/d from €40/80) There are seven simple en suite rooms and two small standard rooms in this modestly furnished but very friendly Georgian house.

Old Dubliner (☎ 855 5666; 62 Amiens St; s/d from €70/100; P) This long-established guesthouse, right opposite Connolly train station, has 14 elegant and very comfortable en suite rooms. Ask for discounts midweek.

Charles Stewart (Map pp72-4; ☎ 878 0350; www.charlesstewart.ie; 5-6 Parnell Sq; s/d from €31.75/65) Just north of O'Connell St, the Charles Stewart has 76 clean, spacious and functional rooms with small bathrooms for a very good price. Rooms in the new extension to the rear are huge and very quiet.

Other modest options on Upper Gardiner St (all away from the city centre) are the friendly **Fatima House** (☎ 874 5410; 17 Upper Gardiner St; s/d from €35/70), the plain comforts of **Marian Guest House** (☎ 874 4129; 21 Upper Gardiner St; s/d from €30/54) or the pleasant **Stella Maris**

(☎ 874 0835; stellamaris@ireland.com; 13 Upper Gardiner St; s/d from €45/80).

There is a hazy line dividing B&Bs, guesthouses and the mid-range hotels. Places in this mid-range bracket usually cost from €60 to €90 per person per night. Some of the small, central hotels in this category are among the most enjoyable places to stay in Dublin.

In this range you'll find some excellent places to stay north of the river.

Browns Hotel (Map pp72-4; ☎ 855 0034; 80-90 Lower Gardiner St; s/d from €60/70) With only 22 rooms, this small, reasonable hotel books up fast. Rooms are compact and simply furnished with contemporary furnishings and en suite. Great value for such a central location.

Castle Hotel (Map pp72-4; ☎ 874 6949, fax 872 7674; Great Denmark St; s/d/t from €45/99/130) Established in 1809, the Castle Hotel claims to be Dublin's oldest and has been in the hands of only three families. Furnishings are likewise traditional and a tad antiquated throughout its 50 rooms, many of which are generous in size and still retain their lovely Georgian cornicing and proportions. There's a fabulous *palazzo*-style grand staircase, and the house, though rough around the edges, still feels like an authentic nineteenth-century home. Its owner, Fionn MacCumhaill, will happily regale you with local history from the bar.

Lynham's Hotel (Map pp72-4; ☎ 888 0886; www.lynams-hotel.com; 63-64 O'Connell St; s/d/t from €70/130/165) Bang in the middle of O'Connell St, beside the GPO, this smart little friendly hotel is a gem. All 42 rooms are nicely furnished with country pine furniture and tasteful fabrics. Room No 41 is a lovely dormer triple with an additional camp bed, handy for groups who want to share. Ask for discounts midweek.

Ormond Quay Hotel (Map pp80-1; ☎ 872 1811; www.ormondqh.com; 7-11 Upper Ormond Quay; s/d €120/200) Beside the river, this hotel has a plaque outside noting its role in the sirens episode of *Ulysses*. The 60 rooms are clean and neat, even if the décor is a little loud. This hotel is openly gay-friendly.

Townhouse (Map pp72-4; ☎ 878 8808; gtrotter@indigo.ie; 47-48 Lower Gardiner St; s/d from €60/102) The Townhouse has all the hallmarks of a great guesthouse; 80 individually designed, comfortable rooms with satellite TV, friendly and efficient staff, a city centre location and a tab that won't burn a hole in your pocket. This place comes highly recommended.

Walton's Hotel (Map pp72-4; ☎ 878 3131; waltonshotel@eircom.net; 2-5 North Frederick St; s/d from €55/109) Just north of Parnell Square, this relatively new hotel is run by the Walton family, whose legendary musical instrument shop is next door. There are 43 simply furnished rooms with TV and modern décor. Children under 12 stay for free. It's a very friendly place in the centre of town.

TOP END

Gresham Hotel (Map pp72-4; ☎ 874 6881; www.gresham-hotels.com; Upper O'Connell St; s/d from €190/255, penthouse €900) The Gresham Hotel, a landmark hotel and one of Dublin's oldest and until now, most traditional, underwent a significant facelift in 2002, shedding its cosy granny's parlour look to reveal a brighter, smarter, more modern look. The hotel's apparent clientele – well-heeled Americans and elderly groups on shopping breaks to the capital – has remained loyal. Rooms are spacious and well serviced, though the décor is a little fussy.

Morrisson Hotel (Map pp80-1; ☎ 887 2400; www.morrisonhotel.ie; Lower Ormond Quay; rooms from €270-570, penthouse €1490) Since opening its doors in 1999, the eternally-hip Morrison has been vying with The Clarence across the river in the style stakes, for Dublin's coveted title Trendiest Hotel in Town. Hong Kong–Irish fashion designer John Rocha helped create the Morrison's sophisticated-earthy look using his signature velvet throws, dark wood and contemporary white furnishings. The loosely Oriental style rooms are bright, if a little compact and feature Egyptian cotton linen, CD players, modem facilities and pieces of Rocha's own line of crystal.

South of the Liffey

BUDGET

There's plenty of hostel accommodation south of the Liffey.

Avalon House (Map p88; ☎ 475 0001; www.avalon-house.ie; 55 Aungier St; dm/d €15/64) Within spitting distance of St Stephen's Green, this 280-bed hostel has 12-bed mixed dorms nicely laid-out on two levels, offering some privacy. There's a large kitchen, several lounges with board games and a pool room.

Ashfield House (Map pp80-1; ☎ 679 7734; ashfield@indigo.ie; 19-20 D'Olier St; dm/d from €15/46)

A stone's throw from Temple Bar and O'Connell Bridge, this relatively new hostel has only one 14-bed en suite dorm, but its 25 other rooms include four-bed family rooms as well as doubles. It feels more like a small hotel, without the price tag. Maximum stay is six nights.

Barnacles Temple Bar House (Map pp80-1; ☎ 671 6277; www.barnacles.ie; 19 Temple Lane; dm/d from €17/38.50) Bright and spacious, in the heart of Temple Bar, this hostel is immaculately clean, has nicely laid-out en suite dorms and doubles with that rare beast – in-room storage. Because of its location, rooms are quieter to the back. Top facilities, comfy lounge and linen and towels provided. Probably the best hostel south of the river.

Brewery Hostel (Map pp72-4; ☎ 453 8600; breweryh@indigo.ie; 22-23 Thomas St; dm/d €15/42) A small, family-run hostel, right at the doorstep of Guinness Brewery. It has five bedrooms and seven dorms with wooden bunks, all en suite. There's a little patio to the rear with barbecue area.

Kinlay House (Map pp80-1; ☎ 679 6644; www.kinlayhouse.ie; 2-12 Lord Edward St; dm/d from €16/30) A former boarding house for boys, this busy hostel has some massive, mixed 24-bed dorms, as well as smaller rooms. Not for the faint-hearted. Its bustling location next to Christ Church Cathedral and Dublin Castle is a bonus.

From mid-June to late September only, you can stay in accommodation provided by the city's universities, so be sure to book well in advance.

Trinity College (Map p78; ☎ 608 1177; reservations@tcd.ie; Accommodations Office, Trinity College; B&B rooms €50.50-61.50) Although it's expensive, the college sometimes has wonderfully positioned accommodation on campus.

Mercer Court (Map p88; ☎ 478 2179; reservations@mercercourt.ie; Mercer St Lower; d & tw from €82-105; 5-bed self-catering apartment €820) Owned and run by the Royal College of Surgeons, this is perhaps the best student accommodation option in the city: cheaper than Trinity but just as central, close to Grafton St and St Stephen's Green. The rooms are modern and up to hotel standard.

MID-RANGE

As soon as you cross the Liffey, prices go up and what passes as a mid-range hotel here can often be considered a more expensive spot on the northside.

Aston Hotel (Map pp80-1; ☎ 677 9300; www.aston-hotel.com, 7-9 Aston Quay; s/d from €83/114) The Aston, just off O'Connell Bridge, is a small, friendly hotel with spacious, inoffensively decorated rooms all equipped with cable TV and en suite. There are two wheelchair accessible rooms available. A buffet breakfast is included.

Eliza Lodge (Map pp80-1; ☎ 671 8044; info@dublinlodge.ie; 23-24 Wellington Quay; s/d from €76/177) It's priced like a hotel, looks like a hotel, but it's still a guesthouse. Its 18 bedrooms are fabulous: comfortable, spacious and – due to its position right over the Millennium Bridge – with great views of the Liffey. It offers air-conditioning, TVs and, in the fancier rooms, Jacuzzis.

Grafton Guesthouse (Map pp80-1; ☎ 679 2041; graftonguesthouse@eircom.net; 26-27 South Great George's St; s/d from €65/120) Located in a Gothic-style building over the George's St Arcade market, just off Dame St, this friendly guesthouse has 16 bright rooms, if you don't mind the old-school chintz and brocade décor.

Jurys Inn Christchurch (Map pp72-4; ☎ 454 0000; www.bookajurysinn.com; Christchurch Pl; rooms from €96) This large limited-services hotel, opposite Christ Church Cathedral in an excellent location, offers clean but anodyne rooms that sleep up to three.

Morgan Hotel (Map pp80-1; ☎ 679 3939; www.themorgan.com, 10 Fleet St; s/d from €126/215) The relatively new Morgan is a boutique hotel on the edge of Temple Bar. Its all-cream, contemporary-designed rooms are

SOMETHING SPECIAL...

Irish Landmark Trust (Map pp80-1; ☎ 670 4733; www.irishlandmark.com; 25 Eustace St; 1/3 nights from €275/695) This fabulous heritage 18th-century house has been gloriously restored to the highest standard by the Irish Landmark Trust charity. You can have this unique house, which sleeps up to seven in its double, twin and triple bedrooms for one or any number of nights all to yourself. Furnished with tasteful antiques, authentic furniture and fittings (including a grand piano in the drawing room), this kind of period rental accommodation is rare and something really unique.

on the small side with furnishings looking a bit tired for the price, but on the plus side, come equipped with TV, video, stereo and minibar. Breakfast is extra

La Stampa Hotel (Map p88; ☎ 677 4444; www.lastampa.ie; 35 Dawson St; s/d from €100/135) La Stampa is a wonderful, atmospheric little hotel on trendy Dawson St. There are plans afoot to extend but at the moment, it has 24 lovely Asian-influenced white rooms with Oriental rattan furniture, exotic velvet throws, TV, air conditioning and minibar. One considerable drawback for those travelling with all but the kitchen sink, is that bedrooms are up two flights of very steep stairs and there's no lift. Excellent value for its location.

Waterloo House (☎ 660 1888; www.waterloohouse.ie; 8-10 Waterloo Rd; s/d €65/118) A short walk from St Stephen's Green, off Baggot St, this lovely guesthouse is spread over two ivy-clad Georgian houses. Rooms are tastefully decorated with high quality furnishings in authentic, Farrow & Ball Georgian colours and all have cable TV and kettles. Home-cooked breakfast is served in the conservatory or garden on sunny days.

Mespil Hotel (☎ 667 1222; www.leehotels.ie; Mespil Rd; rooms from €135) Nicely located on the banks of the Grand Canal, this large, rather plain hotel has bigger-than-average, comfortable rooms at a very reasonable rate. Ask for one of the bright rooms to the front and on the top floor where, because of the hotel's origin as a government office block, windows are massive and offer great views of the canal and city centre. There are plenty of disabled-access rooms. The hotel offers special discounted rates in winter and is a 10-minute walk from St Stephen's Green, along Baggot St.

TOP END

Brooks Hotel (Map p88; ☎ 670 4000; www.sinnotthotels.com; 59-62 Drury St; s/d from €190/245) Located a one-minute walk west of Grafton St, the relatively new Brooks Hotel is a small, plush place where the emphasis is on familial, friendly service. Décor is *nouveau*-classical with high-veneer panelled walls, decorative bookcases and old fashioned sofas, while bedrooms are extremely comfortable and are fitted out in subtly coloured furnishings. The clincher for us though is the king and super king size beds in all rooms, complete with a pillow menu.

> **SOMETHING SPECIAL...**
>
> **Number 31** (Map p88; ☎ 676 5011; www.number31.ie; 31 Leeson Close; s/d/t from €100/120/165) Number 31 could be a set from the zeitgeist film *The Ice Storm*. The coach house and former home of modernist architect Sam Stephenson (of Central Bank fame) still feels like a real 1960s home intact, with its sunken sitting room, leather sofas, mirrored bar, perspex lamps and ceiling to floor windows. A hidden oasis of calm, a five-minute walk from St Stephen's Green, this is one of our favourite places to stay in Dublin. Its 21 bedrooms are split between the retro coach house with its chi-chi rooms and the more gracious Georgian house, through the garden, where rooms are individually furnished with tasteful French antiques and big comfortable beds. Gourmet breakfasts with kippers, home-made breads and granola are served in the conservatory. Children under 10 are not permitted.

Clarence Hotel (Map pp80-1; ☎ 407 0800; www.theclarence.ie; 6-8 Wellington Quay; rooms from €300-320, suites from €615-2100) Its 1930s penthouse suite, with unrivalled views of the city from its rooftop hot tub, is almost continuously booked out by visiting celebs and rock star friends of hotel owners Bono and the Edge from U2. For the rest, the 50-odd lavish rooms, decorated in an ecclesiastical theme with white and cardinal colour schemes, offer the elegant comfort of Egyptian cotton linen, beautifully simple bathrooms, white American oak furniture and original artwork by band-mate, Guggi. Savour the pleasures of a Prada facial (€50) or Ayurvedic head massage (€55) in the hotel's Treatment Room before slipping down to the Octagon Bar for a bilini. A night's kip doesn't come cheap here but you'll rest well, knowing you're in one of the hottest beds in town.

Le Méridien Shelbourne (Map p88; ☎ 676 6471; www.shelbourne.ie; 27 St Stephen's Green; s/d from €305/325) Founded in 1824, the famous Shelbourne Hotel remains one of Dublin's best addresses and still retains its enduring old world grandeur. Rooms are spacious and very comfortable with every modern facility. The Irish Constitution was first drafted here in 1922 and to this day, politicians and hacks can be spotted swigging malt in its Horseshoe Bar. For the more salubrious, the leisure centre and swimming pool provide a healthy alternative. Afternoon cream teas in the drawing room, overlooking St Stephen's Green, are a Dublin institution.

Merrion (Map p88; ☎ 603 0600; www.merrionhotel.com; Upper Merrion St; s/d €300/325) This resplendent five-star hotel, in a terrace of beautifully restored Georgian townhouses, opened in 1988 but looks like it's been around a lot longer. Try to get a room in the old house, rather than the newer wing, to sample its sophisticated comforts. Its location opposite government buildings and just off Merrion Square – a predominantly business area – makes for an unusually tranquil weekend setting so close to the city centre.

Westin Dublin (Map pp80-1; ☎ 645 1000; www.westin.com; Westmoreland St; rooms from €340) The Westin began life as an Allied Irish Bank and, in keeping with its origin, uses the old bank vaults and marble counters in its basement Mint Bar. Rooms exude a classical American grandeur with an understated style that includes separate shower and bath, lap-top size safe and Westin's trademark Heavenly Bed with 10 luxurious layers to envelop you. Ask to take a look at the beautiful banqueting hall, in the former banking area, with its exquisite ceiling and gold leaf plasterwork. Breakfast will set you back €25.

Outside the City Centre

BUDGET

There's no convenient central camp site in Dublin. It is illegal (not to mention dangerous) to camp in Phoenix Park.

Camac Valley Tourist Caravan & Camping Park (Map p70; ☎ 464 0644; camacvalley@eircom.net; Naas Rd, Clondalkin; sites €6-7) Bus No 69 from city centre. Only 35 minutes by bus from the city centre, this new four-star camping ground is spread across several fields with an abundance of facilities.

MID-RANGE

About a 30-minute walk (3km, five minutes by bus) east of Upper O'Connell St (along Dorset St), on the road to the airport, is the leafy suburb of Drumcondra, a popular area for B&Bs. Most of the houses here are late-Victorian or Edwardian, and are generally extremely well kept and comfortable. As they're on the airport road, they tend to be full virtually throughout the year, so advance booking is recommended. Bus Nos 3, 11, 11A, 16 or 36A from Trinity College/O'Connell St all stop along the Drumcondra Rd.

Griffith House (☎ 837 5030; www.griffithhouse.com; 125 Griffith Ave; s/d €40/70; ⊠) This elegant house, on a beautiful, tree-lined avenue, has four double rooms, three of them en suite. Each room is tastefully appointed, with large, comfortable beds and nice furniture.

St Andrew's Guesthouse (☎ 837 4684; 1-3 Lambay Rd; s/d from €45/85) This place has 16 comfortable en suite rooms, with elegant period-style beds. It's located off the Drumcondra Rd, down Griffith Ave and the third turn to the left. Bus No 11A or 11B stops along the adjacent Home Farm Rd.

Tinode House (☎ 837 2277; www.tinodehouse.com; 170 Upper Drumcondra Rd; s/d €55/75) This comfortable Edwardian townhouse has four elegant bedrooms, all with bathrooms. A familial welcome and excellent breakfast are part of the package.

The following B&Bs are southeast of the city centre. It's only a 10-minute bus ride from the city centre; bus Nos 5, 7, 7A, 8, 18 and 45 all stop in the area.

Ariel House (☎ 668 5512; www.ariel-house.net; 52 Lansdowne Rd; s/d €105/130) With 28 rooms, all en suite, this is hardly your average B&B, but not many B&Bs are listed Victorian homes that have been given top rating by Fáilte Ireland. Recently restored to its 19th-century elegance, every room is individually decorated in period furniture, which lends the place an air of genuine luxury. This place beats almost any hotel.

Merrion Hall (☎ 668 1426; merrionhall@iol.ie; 56 Merrion Rd; s/d €99/130) Close to the Royal Dublin Showground, this award-winning Edwardian guesthouse has all the comforts of a small hotel and is popular with Americans and business people. Its 34 en suite rooms, some of which have Jacuzzis and four poster beds, are each decorated in a classical style, with excellent facilities.

TOP END

Burlington (☎ 660 5222; www.jurysdoyle.com; Upper Leeson St; s/d €223/249) With 500 rooms, The

Burlington ranks as Ireland's largest hotel, but prides itself on its familial welcome. A traditional place, it's popular with tour groups and Americans. Like its sister hotel, the Berkely Court, it's well worth checking the website for significant discounts.

Hibernian Hotel (Map p88; ☎ 668 7666; www.hibernianhotel.com; Eastmoreland Pl; rooms with breakfast €222-277.50) The Hibernian is a charming, homely but luxurious little hotel in a quiet cul-de-sac off Baggot St in Ballsbridge. Dating from 1890, the Victorian building used to be the nurse's home attached to nearby Baggot St hospital. Rooms to the back seem to be more spacious, but all are cosily furnished in a traditional way and have cable TV, dataports and lovely bathrooms.

Berkeley Court (☎ 660 1711; www.jurysdoyle.com; Lansdowne Rd; s/d from €313/333) This upmarket hotel, southeast of the city centre, in the leafy suburb of Ballsbridge, caters mainly to business travellers. Its décor is firmly traditional, while kitted out to the highest standard and rooms offer every modern amenity. Check the website for special offers, because at the time of writing, rooms were selling for less than half the quoted rate.

EATING

An increase in Dubliners' spending power in recent years which, despite warnings of economic downturn, continues unabated has spawned a proliferation of new eating possibilities around the capital. Added to this, the welcome assimilation of foreign immigrants to Ireland's previously homogenous culture has created a market for ethnically diverse eateries from specialist grocery shops to authentic and exotically-themed restaurants. Parnell St and its environs is one place where you'll find a spate of new restaurants of international origin. Many of the mid-range options for lunch and dinner are concentrated around the southside city centre, though the numbers of decent quality restaurants and cafés north of the Liffey is growing steadily.

The Temple Bar area is awash with eateries of mixed quality from the superb to the downright awful, the bulk of them catering to the constant stream of visitors to the area. Regrettably, Ireland and especially Dublin has gained a reputation for being an expensive place to eat compared to her European counterparts, but having said that, with so many places to choose from, you'll easily find a restaurant to suit both your budget and palate.

Near suburbs Ranelagh and Rathmines (about 2km from the city centre), predominantly student areas, are both lively spots and home to some great buzzing restaurants. They're also a good place to try if you can't get a table in town on a weekend night.

North of the Liffey

BUDGET

Ailang (Map pp72-4; ☎ 874 6766; 102 Parnell St; mains €6-15; ⏰ noon-2.30pm Mon-Fri, 5.30-11.30pm Mon-Thu, 5.30-midnight Fri-Sun, 12.30pm-midnight Sat & Sun) With elements of Chinese, Japanese and Thai cuisine, this new Korean restaurant on ethnically diverse Parnell St, has plenty to whet Western appetites. Tasty dishes like *padun* (a seafood pancake), cod and tofu hotpot or barbecued meats brought to your table DIY-style, with gas burner, skillet and spicy marinade make the food a talking piece. Although the bright and shiny décor may not be conducive to romantic first dates, the atmosphere at Ailang is strangely inviting. Steer clear of the dull wine list in favour of Ailang's own Hite beer.

Cobalt Café & Gallery (Map pp72-4; ☎ 873 0313; 16 North Great George's St; mains €4-7; ⏰ 10am-4.30pm Mon-Fri) This gorgeous, elegant café in a bright and airy Georgian drawingroom is a must if you're in the hood. Almost opposite the James Joyce Cultural Centre, the menu is simple but you'll be welcomed with hearty soups by a roaring fire in winter or fresh sandwiches in the garden on warmer days.

Epicurean Food Hall (Map pp80-1; Lower Liffey St; lunch €3-12; ⏰ 9.30am-5.30pm Mon-Sat) You'll be spoilt for choice in this newly refurbished arcade that has almost every imaginable type of food stall to whet the appetite. The quality varies, but good choices include Itsabagel, Taco Taco and Istanbul House.

Winding Stair Café (Map pp80-1; ☎ 873 3292; 40 Lower Ormond Quay; lunch €4-10; ⏰ 10.30am-6pm Mon-Sat) The Winding Stair is a beautifully dusty old bookshop with a café spread across the 2nd and 3rd floors. It's perfect for reading while you eat wholesome soups, savoury crepes or paninis. The noticeboard on the stairway is useful for local information of all kinds.

Panem (Map pp80-1; ☎ 872 8510; 21 Lower Ormond Quay; mains €2.60-5.80; 9am-5.30pm Mon-Sat) There isn't much space to sit in this tiny popular Italian café on the quays but you can take away hot filled foccacias, Torrisi coffee or daily pasta specials.

Ristorante Romano (Map pp80-1; ☎ 872 6868; 12 Capel St; mains €7-14; 12.30-3.30pm & 5.30-10pm Mon-Sat; ☒) If the overpowering pink interior and stark lighting don't put you off, your tastebuds will thank you for braving this eccentric restaurant. Delicious home-made pasta, cooked al dente and crisp pizzas from a wood-burning oven await, in big portions that won't hurt your pocket.

Soup Dragon (Map pp80-1; ☎ 872 3277; 168 Capel St; soups €4.25-9.50; 8am-5.30pm, Mon-Fri 11am-5pm Sat) Eat in or take away one of 12 tasty varieties of home-made soups, including shepherd's pie or spicy vegetable gumbo. Bowls come in three different sizes and prices include fresh bread and a piece of fruit. Kick start your day (or afternoon) with a healthy all-day breakfast selection; fresh smoothies (€3.75), generous bowls of yogurt, fruit and muesli (€4) or poached egg in a bagel (€3.20).

MID-RANGE

101 Talbot (Map pp72-4; ☎ 874 5011; 100-2 Talbot St; mains €12-19; 5-11pm Tue-Sat) 101 Talbot is a funky little restaurant with brightly painted walls, wooden floorboards and check tablecloths. The eclectic menu, which changes daily, is loosely based on Mediterranean and Middle Eastern cuisine with, as you'd expect, plenty of vegetarian dishes. The home-made pork, sage and apricot sausage with red onion relish starter (€5.50) is a particular favourite.

TOP END

Chapter One (Map pp72-4; ☎ 873 2266; 18-19 North Parnell Sq; mains €23-30; lunch Tue-Fri, dinner Tue-Sat) Savour classic French cuisine like *foie gras*, duck confit or rabbit cassoulet, to the tinkle of the grand piano, in the lovely vaulted basement of the Dublin Writer's Museum. This is one of the city's top 10 restaurants. Get there before 7pm for the three-course Pre-Theatre Special (€31).

Halo (Map pp80-1; ☎ 887 2400; Ormond Quay; mains €23-29; 12.30-2.30pm & 7-10.30pm) Befitting its title, food at Halo in the boutique hotel the Morrison, is simply divine. A cosmopolitan menu of spicy albacore tuna, barbary duck breast or lamb with couscous showcase chef Jean-Michel Poulot's versatile talents. The open plan room with its high ceilings and understated design attracts fashionistas, models and visiting celebs alike. You could make an afternoon of it and sample the three-course lunch menu for €29.

South of the Liffey

BUDGET

Temple Bar has a number of excellent cafés.

Bar Italia (Map pp80-1; ☎ 679 5128; 4 Essex Quay; lunch €6-9; 8am-6pm Mon-Fri, 9am-6pm Sat, noon-6pm Sun) This relatively new little café, with big windows and a terrace on the quays serves proper Italian risotto, a couple of daily pasta dishes and delicious panini with Italian fillings. The real McCoy.

Gruel (Map pp80-1; ☎ 670 7119; 68a Dame St; breakfast €4, lunch €3.50-8, brunch €5-12, supper €10; 7am-9.30pm Mon-Fri, 10.30am-4pm Sat & Sun) Run by the same people as the excellent Mermaid Café, Gruel offers more sophisticated food than its name suggests. This funky place, that wouldn't look amiss in downtown New York, sells good food that bursts with flavour: sandwiches to die for (slow roast organic meats or vegetables in a bap), zinging salads and a mix of risotto, baked fish or its trademark bangers and mash in the evening. The American-style weekend brunch shouldn't be missed.

Café Irie (Map pp80-1; ☎ 672 5090; 11 Upper Fownes St; mains €5.50-7; 9am-8.30pm) The dreadlocked waiter who serves you is about the only connection this hippyish little café has with Jamaica. There's a good choice of veggie combinations in Irie's choice of sandwich fillings – though we could probably live without the peanut butter and banana one.

Queen of Tarts (Map pp80-1; ☎ 670 7499; Cork Hill; from €3.50; 7am-6pm) Queen of Tarts is the mother of all bakery-cafés with its mouthwatering array of savoury tarts and filled foccacias, fruit crumbles, and sinful pastries. It's small, so get here early for lunch or take out to the quiet Chester Beatty garden, across the road.

Simon's Place (Map pp80-1; ☎ 679 7821; George's St Arcade, South Great George's St; mains from €4.50) Simon has been serving his unchanged menu of doorstep sandwiches and wholesome vegetarian soups to an adoring public for years. It's also a good place to mull over a coffee and watch life go by in the old-fashioned arcade.

Blazing Salads (Map pp80-1; ☎ 671 9552; 42 Drury St; mains €2.50-7) Organic breads (many special diet), Californian-style salads, smoothies and pizza slices can all be taken away from this delicious vegetarian deli.

Leo Burdock's (Map pp80-1; ☎ 454 0306; 2 Werburgh St) You'll see a queue at any hour of the day outside this Dublin institution. And there's a reason for it; thick-cut, real potato chips and crispy fish wrapped in paper to go. Sometimes you just have to do it.

Grafton St is the fast-food centre south of the Liffey. The area has office workers, students and tourists to feed and there are plenty of cafés and pubs to keep them happy at lunch-time.

Cornucopia (Map pp80-1; ☎ 677 7583; 19 Wicklow St; mains from €6) For those escaping the Irish cholesterol habit, Cornucopia is a popular wholefood café turning out healthy goodies. There's even a hot vegetarian breakfast as an alternative to muesli.

Listons (Map p88; ☎ 405 4779; 25 Camden St; lunch €3-8) Lunch-time queues out the door testify that Listons is undoubtedly the best deli in Dublin. Its sandwiches with fresh, delicious fillings, roasted vegetable quiches, rosemary potato cakes and sublime salads will have you coming back again and again. The only problem is there's too much to choose from. On fine days it's great to retreat to the solitude of the nearby Iveagh Gardens with your gourmet picnic.

Nude (Map pp80-1; ☎ 675 5577; 21 Suffolk St; wraps from €5) This ultra-cool place (owned by Bono's brother) just off Grafton St has been a huge hit since it opened, serving tasty wraps with all kinds of Asian fillings. You can eat in or take away, but be sure to try one of the freshly squeezed fruit juices.

The Powerscourt Townhouse shopping centre is stuffed with eating places and makes a great place for lunch.

Fresh (Map p88; ☎ 671 9552; top floor Powerscourt Townhouse shopping centre; lunch from €5-9) This long-standing vegetarian restaurant serves a variety of salads and filling, hot daily specials. Many dishes are dairy and gluten-free without compromising on taste. The baked potato, topped with organic cheese (€5.50) comes with two salads and is very reasonable and a hearty meal in itself.

Ba Mizu (Map p88; ☎ 674 6712, ground floor Powerscourt Townhouse shopping centre; mains €7-14) The laidback atmosphere of this new bar with its vaulted stone ceiling and leather sofas is conducive to a leisurely lunch of better-than-average bar food. The all-day menu is loosely Irish with favourites such as beef in Guinness stew and mimosa chicken with champ but also has good vegetarian pastas or dishes like *spanakopita* (spinach pancake) with mint and cucumber.

Lemon (Map pp80-1; ☎ 672 9044; 66 South William St; pancakes from €3.50) For proper pancakes of the thin crêpe variety, with any number of savoury or sweet fillings, Lemon will always please.

Dail Bía (Map p88; ☎ 670 6079; 46 Kildare St; mains form €6) The name means 'parliament food' in Irish, and it's appropriate: this basement café opposite the Dail has Irish-speaking staff and a bilingual menu, but you don't need to be an Irish speaker to enjoy its menu of salads, soup and sandwiches.

Busyfeet & Coco Café (Map p88; ☎ 671 9514; 41 South William St; lunch from €5-8) This hippyish little café is one of the only places in town to serve a really good *chai*, a marvellous alternative to the stronger Irish tea and a good noncaffeine alternative to coffee. Its Greek salad is as good as it gets. The young staff are extremely friendly and the outdoor tables are usually packed by mid-afternoon.

There are several pubs with good food close to Grafton St.

Stag's Head (Map pp80-1; ☎ 679 3701; 1 Dame Ct; lunch from €7) For a good pub lunch, we recommend the Stag's Head. Apart from being a popular drinking spot, this place turns out simple, well prepared, filling meals in elegant Victorian surroundings.

O'Neill's (Map pp80-1; ☎ 679 3671, 2 Suffolk St; lunch €8-10) O'Neill's is famed for its traditional carvery lunches where they pile 'em high with roast meat of the day and any number of vegetables. It's popular with local business people and with plenty of snugs and quiet corners, is a comfortable place to come if you're on your own.

Brazen Head (Map pp72-4; ☎ 679 5186; 20 Lower Bridge St; mains from €8-11) Claiming to be Ireland's oldest pub, dating from 1198, this famous place just west of the city centre, offers everything from sandwiches to a carvery lunch, and is always packed at lunch-time with tourists and local business people.

Steps of Rome (Map p88; ☎ 670 5632; 1 Chatham Ct; mains €6-15) You can get rustic pizza slices to take away (€2) or authentic pasta staples in this tiny kerbside café where real Italians meet. It's always packed and you can't book but service is smart so you'll usually get a table after a short wait.

Havana (Map p88; ☎ 476 0046; 3 Grantham St; tapas €3.50-7) Get into the swing of things Latin-style in this colourful little Cuban tapas bar. Some dishes are better than others but you can't go wrong with *patatas bravuras*, *gambas con ajio*, the chicken stew or mushrooms in garlic. A selection of Spanish beers and wines is available and the atmosphere is welcoming.

Govinda's (Map p88; ☎ 475 0309; 4 Aungier St; mains €5-9) You can smell the patchouli oil from 50m at this authentic beans-and-pulses vegetarian place. Its cheap, wholesome mix of salads and Indian-influenced hot daily specials are filling and tasty.

Nectar (☎ 491 0934; 53 Ranelagh; mains €5-11) Hot wraps, healthy daily specials and flavoursome fresh smoothies and juices are what you'll find in this modern little juice bar in the village centre.

MID-RANGE

Bad Ass Café (Map pp80-1; ☎ 671 2596; 9-11 Crown Alley; mains €9-14; 🕑 11.30am-late) This bustling pizza joint, south of Ha'penny Bridge, is a bright and cheerful warehouse-style place with reasonable pizzas, burgers and Cajun nosh. Sinéad O'Connor once worked here as a waitress.

Café Bardeli (Map pp80-1; ☎ 677 1646; 12-13 Sth Great George's St; mains €9-12; noon-midnight; 🕑 ⊠) Pizzas with imaginative toppings such as potato and rosemary or roasted pepper and goats cheese, with their crispy base, are probably the best you'll find this side of Naples...well, this side of the Liffey, at least. The home-made pasta menu is equally enticing and favourites such as spag bol or fettuccine amatriciana are also sold by the family-size bowl. Good, fresh food, at prices that won't break the bank in a buzzing atmosphere. What more could you want, hey?

Elephant & Castle (Map pp80-1; ☎ 679 3121; 18 Temple Bar; mains €8-15; 🕑 8am-11.30pm Mon-Fri, 11.30am-11.30pm Sat & Sun) If it's massive New York–style sandwiches or towering burgers with matchstick chips you're after, this bustling upmarket diner is just the ticket. Be prepared to queue though, especially at weekends, when Elephant & Castle heaves to the joints with the hassled parents of wandering toddlers, wealthy suburbanites and hungover 20-somethings, all in pursuit of a carb-feast and quiet corner to peruse the paper.

Odessa (Map pp80-1; ☎ 670 7634; 13 Dame Ct; mains €13-20) Just off Exchequer St, Odessa's loungy atmosphere with comfy sofas and retro standard lamps attracts the city's hipsters who flock in for its home-made burgers, steaks or daily fish specials. You might not escape the sofa after a few of Odessa's renowned cocktails, quaffed to a game of backgammon. Weekend brunch is extremely popular: you were warned.

Bistro (Map pp80-1; ☎ 671 5430; 4-5 Castle Market; mains €9-19) The real draw at this place is its outdoor seating in summer on a lively pedestrianised strip behind the George's St arcade. Its fish, pasta and pizza specials are sinfully rich but very tasty.

Juice (Map pp80-1; ☎ 475 7856; 73 South Great George's St; mains €8-16) A creative vegetarian restaurant, Juice puts an imaginative, California-type spin on all kinds of dishes. The real treat is the selection of fruit smoothies, a delicious and healthy alternative to soft drinks.

Monty's of Kathmandu (☎ 670 4911; 28 Eustace St; mains €13-21; 🕑 12.30-2.30pm & 6-11.30pm Mon-Sat, 6-11pm Sun) Ethnic food doesn't get much better than this. Award-winning Monty's trade is built on people who keep returning for typical Nepalese dishes like *gorkhali* (chicken cooked in chilli, yoghurt and ginger) or *kachela* (raw marinated meat). The Shiva beer complements these hearty, spicy dishes.

Yamamori (Map pp80-1; ☎ 475 5001; 71 Sth Great George's St; mains €8-17) This popular Asian restaurant with its long communal tables serves filling noodle and rice-based staples. Children are welcome and well catered for and service is smart, which is handy for a pre-cinema bite.

La Maison des Gourmets (Map pp80-1; ☎ 672 7258; 15 Castle Market; mains €5-15) The city's Francophiles all seem to amass at this tiny French café above a bakery – and for good reason. The menu is small but its *tartines* (open sandwiches) with daily toppings like roast aubergine and pesto, salad specials or plates of *charcuterie* are divine. It also has a fine range of pastries, baked goodies and herbal teas. You can get a traditional country breakfast of meats, cheeses and warm crusty bread for €9.50.

Gotham Café (Map p88; ☎ 679 5266; 8 South Anne St; mains €7.50-13) You won't find it easy to get a table at child-friendly Gotham at peak times because its massive selection of pizzas with unusual toppings are just too popular.

Avoca Handweavers (Map pp80-1; ☎ 677 4215; 11-13 Suffolk St; mains €8-15) This airy 1st-floor café was one of Dublin's best kept secrets (because of an absence of any obvious signs), until discovered by the Ladies Who Lunch. If you can battle your way past the designer shopping bags to a table, you'll relish the simply delicious, rustic delights of organic shepherd's pie, roast lamb with couscous, or sumptuous salads from the Avoca kitchen. There's also a take-away salad bar and hot counter in the basement.

El Bahia (Map pp80-1; ☎ 677 0213; 1st floor, 37 Wicklow St; mains €10-18) Dark and sultry, the intimate atmosphere at El Bahia, reputedly Ireland's only Moroccan restaurant, is like that of a desert harem. The food is equally exotic with a range of daily *tagines* (stews), couscous and *bastilles* (pastry stuffed with chicken or fish) to tempt you. The sweet Morroccan coffee brewed with five warming spices is delicious.

Il Primo (Map p88; ☎ 478 3373; 16 Montague St; mains €12-23) This classy restaurant, just off Harcourt St, serves upmarket Italian fare in a relaxed atmosphere. Décor is minimalist in the small upstairs eating room and tables may be a little too close together for some but the food is consistently good and there's an excellent wine list, with many choices available by the glass.

Aya (Map pp80-1; ☎ 677 1544; Clarendon St; mains €12-25) Attached to the swanky Brown Thomas department store, this relatively new Japanese restaurant is the best in the city centre. There's a revolving sushi bar where you can eat your fill for €23 Sunday to Tuesday between 5pm and 9pm (maximum 55 minutes) or, if you prefer, go á la carte from the great menu. There's a five-course early bird special (up to 7pm) nightly for €21.

Tiger Becs (Map p88; ☎ 677 8677; 36 Dawson St; mains €9-25) Below oriental superpub Samsara, Tiger Becs is a long, cavernous eating hall serving good Thai nosh to Dublin's fine young things. The starter crispy aromatic duck is delicious and a meal in itself. It's not cheap but this loud, buzzing place has oodles of atmosphere; a great place to start an evening on the town.

Imperial Chinese Restaurant (Map pp80-1; ☎ 677 2580; 12a Wicklow St; dim sum per dish from €3.50, mains €9-16) This long-established place is a favourite with the Chinese community and is noted for its lunch-time dim sum. These Chinese snacks are popular on Sunday, when the Imperial serves brunch Chinese-style in what is known as yum cha, or 'drink tea', the traditional accompaniment to dim sum.

Pizza Milano (Map p88; ☎ 670 7744; 38 Dawson St; main €7-15) Pizzas are pretty good in this large but stylish pizza emporium but what we really like are the on-site free child-minders, who entertain your little ones while you eat, on Sundays between noon and 4.30pm.

Rajdoot Tandoori (Map p88; ☎ 679 4274; 26-28 Clarendon St; mains €11-19) Visitors to India may remember Rajdoot as a popular brand of Indian motorcycle. In Dublin, however, the name is a byword for Indian cuisine at its very best, particularly the more aromatic flavours of North India.

The following places are all around St Stephen's Green and beyond.

Ely Wine Bar (Map p88; ☎ 676 8986; 22 Ely Pl; mains €11-18) Home-made burgers, bangers and mash or tasty pasta dishes are some of what you'll find in this intimate basement restaurant, just off Baggot Street. All dishes are prepared with organic and free-range produce from the owner's organic family farm in Co. Clare so you can rest assured of the quality. There's a large wine list to choose from, with over 70 sold by the glass. Its friendly, relaxed atmosphere makes it popular with female and lone diners.

Langkawi (Map p88; ☎ 668 2760; 46 Upper Baggot St; set lunch €15, mains €15-35) This upmarket Pacific Rim restaurant has a loyal clientele who return for its good food and relaxed atmosphere. *Nasi goreng* (spicy rice dish with prawn and satay chicken) is a popular choice.

French Paradox (☎ 660 4068; 53 Shelbourne Rd; mains €8-16) This bright and airy wine bar over an excellent wine shop of the same name serves fine authentic French dishes such as *cassoulet*, a variety of *foie gras*, cheese and *charcuterie* plates and large green salads. All there to complement the main attraction: a dazzling array of fine wines, mostly French unsurprisingly, sold by the bottle, glass or even 6.25cl taste! A little slice of Paris in Dublin 4.

Ocean (☎ 668 8862; Charlotte Quay Dock; mains €9-16) Popular with the local business fraternity, Ocean Bar, in the Grand Canal basin is a trendy, minimalist place with big windows overlooking the water (and U2's soon-to-be-demolished recording studio). There are plenty of outdoor seats too from which to savour half a dozen oysters, crab cakes or a variety of wraps.

Diep Noodle Bar (☎ 497 6550; Ranelagh; mains €6.50-16.50) Brand new Diep is a funky and welcome addition to Ranelagh's eateries. Top-notch Thai and Vietnamese dishes such as pad Thai, red snapper vermicelli or seafood rice noodles come to your table at lightening speed. Décor is sparse, modern and clean. It's packed at weekends but you'll get a table early or late without a booking.

Tribeca (☎ 497 1474; 65a Ranelagh; mains €8-15) Tribeca is a popular modern New York–style diner with burgers, omelettes and chicken wings to write home about. Get there early at weekends for the excellent brunch.

Mash (☎ 497 9463; Castlewood Ave, Rathmines; mains €6-20) This tiny eclectic place, opposite the Swan Centre, run by possibly the friendliest duo in Ireland, Bobby and Jerome, serves fresh, home-made dishes in a cosy atmosphere. The small menu consists of daily specials such as Thai chicken curry, roast red snapper, organic steaks or the popular range of Mash potato cakes, all made with TLC and served with a smile. Get there while the prices are still reasonable and you can get a table. Come back once and they'll remember your name.

TOP END

Mermaid Café (Map pp80-1; ☎ 670 8236; 22 Dame St; mains €18-31; 🕐 12.30-2.30pm & 6-11pm Mon-Sat, 12.30-3pm & 6-9pm Sun) The Mermaid is an American-style bistro with natural wood furniture and abstract canvasses on its panelled walls. It caters mainly to a hip *gourmand* crowd who appreciate inventive ingredient-led, organic food such as monkfish with buttered red chard or braised lamb shank with apricot couscous. Its informal atmosphere, pure food and friendly staff make it difficult to get a table without notice.

Eden (Map pp80-1; ☎ 670 5372, Meeting House Sq; mains €15-25; 🕐 noon-2.30pm & 6-10.30pm Mon-Fri, noon-3pm & 6-11pm Sat & Sun) Eden is the epitome of Temple Bar chic with its trendy waitstaff, minimalist surroundings, high ceiling, hanging plants and terrace onto Meeting House Square. But the food is the real star: Eleanor Walsh's unfussy modern Irish cuisine that uses organic seasonal produce, complemented by a carefully chosen wine list. Seating on the gas-heated terrace is at a premium on summer evenings, when classic films are projected onto the nearby Gallery of Photography.

Tea Rooms (Map pp80-1; ☎ 407 0813; 6-8 Wellington Quay; 2-course lunch €24, 2-course dinner €41.50, 3-course dinner €52.50; 🕐 12.30-2.30pm Mon-Fri, 6.30-10.30pm Mon-Sat, 12.30-3pm & 6.30-9.30pm Sun) Anthony Ely's ambitious menu in the Clarence Hotel's Tea Rooms features classic French cuisine – based equally on fish as meat – with an Irish twist. This is *haute cuisine*, stripped of pretension, leaving solid, well-prepared seasonal food which is still beautifully presented.

Merrion Row, leading southeast from St Stephen's Green, and its extension, Baggot St, have an eclectic selection of pubs and restaurants.

Bang (Map p88; ☎ 676 0898; 11 Merrion Row; mains €11-23) One of our favourite restaurants in Dublin, young twin restaurateurs Simon and Christian Stokes are onto a winner here. Chef Lorcan Cribbin (headhunted from London's famous Ivy) whips up a varied but consistently good menu that includes Thai baked sea bass, medallions of beef and melt-in-your-mouth roast scallops. But no matter how replete you are, you can't leave without trying the heavenly warm chocolate brownie, oozing with chocolate sauce. The atmosphere is young, vibrant and eternally stylish.

Restaurant Patrick Guilbaud (Map p88; ☎ 676 4192; 21 Upper Merrion St; set lunch €30, set 3-course dinner €65) With two Michelin stars on its résumé, this elegant restaurant is perhaps one of the best in Ireland, and head chef Guillaume Lebrun does his best to ensure that it stays that way. Next door to the

Merrion Hotel, Guilbaud's French *haute cuisine* is beautifully executed and served in delectable surroundings.

Thornton's (☎ 478 7000; Fitzwilliam Hotel; midweek 3-course lunch/dinner €40/65, mains €50) Kevin Thornton is probably the only chef in Dublin able to challenge Guilbaud's top-dog slot with two Michelin stars apiece, and he does so with a mouth-watering interpretation of new French cuisine. The service is faultless, if a little too formal in this *uber*trendy room overlooking the Green. Don't ask for ketchup.

DRINKING

Pubs are still the hub of virtually all social activity in the city, a meeting point for friends and strangers alike, and where Dubliners are at their friendly and convivial best (and, it must be said, sometimes their drunken and incoherent worst!). This thriving nightlife has made the city one of the most popular getaway destinations in Europe.

Dublin's 'party district' is undoubtedly Temple Bar, although its designation as the city's cultural quarter is somewhat of a misnomer, at least after sundown, when it turns into a northern Gomorrah with few rivals in Europe. The pubs and clubs are crammed, the music is loud, and the party goes on till the wee hours. If 'Ibiza in the rain' isn't to your taste, do not despair: there's still plenty to do outside the confines of Temple Bar's cobbled streets. In fact, most of the best old-fashioned pubs are outside the district.

Extended opening hours mean that pubs now close at midnight Monday to Wednesday (last drinks served at 11.30pm), 1am Thursday to Saturday (last drinks at 12.30am) and 11.30pm on Sunday (last drinks 11pm). However, many also avail of late licences, which means they can serve up to around 2.30am except on Sunday when bars stop serving at 1am.

For information on clubs and on pubs with live music, see Entertainment below.

Traditional Pubs

Dublin is full of old-style, traditional establishments. Here are some of the best.

Flowing Tide (Map pp118-19; ☎ 874 0842; 9 Lower Abbey St) Directly opposite the Abbey Theatre, this place attracts a great mix of theatregoers and northside locals. It's loud, full of chat and a great place to drink.

Patrick Conway's (Map pp118-19; ☎ 873 2687; 70 Parnell St) Although slightly out of the way, this place is a true gem of a pub. It has been operating since 1745, and no doubt new fathers have been stopping in here for a celebratory pint since the day the Rotunda Maternity Hospital opened across the road in 1757.

Palace Bar (Map pp118-19; ☎ 677 9290; 21 Fleet St) With its mirrors and wooden niches, Palace Bar is often said to be the perfect example of an old Dublin pub. It's within Temple Bar and is popular with journalists from the nearby *Irish Times*.

John Mulligan's (Map pp118-19; ☎ 677 5582; 8 Poolbeg St) Just off Fleet St, outside the eastern boundary of Temple Bar, John Mulligan's is another pub that has scarcely changed over the years. It featured as the local in the film *My Left Foot* and is also popular with journalists from the nearby newspaper offices. Mulligan's was established in 1782 and has long been reputed to have the best Guinness in Ireland as well as a wonderfully varied collection of regulars.

Stag's Head (Map pp118-19; ☎ 679 3701; 1 Dame Ct) At the intersection of Dame Ct and Dame Lane, just off Dame St, the Stag's Head was built in 1770 and remodelled in 1895. It's sufficiently picturesque to have featured in a postage stamp series of Irish pubs.

Long Hall (Map pp118-19; ☎ 475 1590; 51 South Great George's St) Luxuriating in full Victorian splendour, this is one of the city's most beautiful and best-loved pubs. Check out the ornate carvings in the woodwork behind the bar and the elegant chandeliers. The bartenders are experts at their craft, an increasingly rare sight in Dublin these days.

Kehoes (Map pp118-19; ☎ 677 8312; 9 South Anne St) This is one of the most atmospheric pubs in the city centre and a real favourite with all kinds of Dubliners. It has a beautiful Victorian bar, a wonderful snug and plenty of other little nooks and crannies. Upstairs drinks are served in what was once the publican's living room. And it looks it!

Neary's (Map pp118-19; ☎ 677 8596; 1 Chatham St) Neary's is a showy Victorian-era pub with a particularly fine frontage; it's popular with actors from the nearby Gaiety Theatre. The upstairs bar is one of the only spots in the city centre where you stand the chance of getting a seat on a Friday or Saturday night.

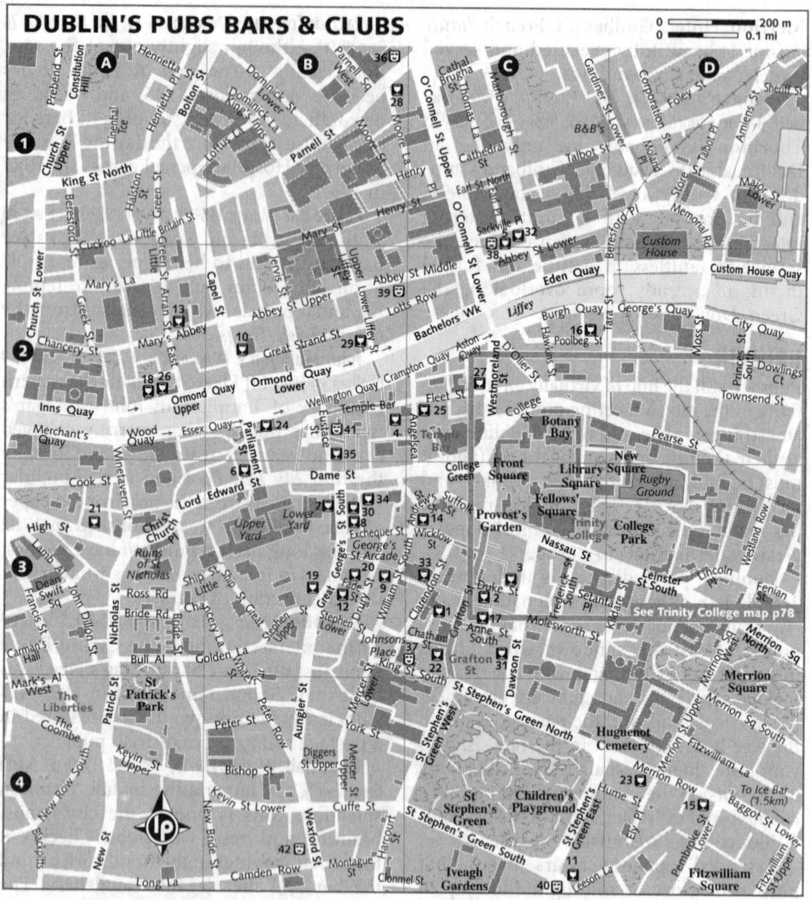

Grogan's Castle Lounge (Map pp118-19; ☎ 677 9320; 15 South William St) This place is known simply as Grogan's (after the original owner), and is a city-centre institution. It has long been a favourite haunt of Dublin's writers and painters as well as others from the bohemian, alternative set, most of whom seem to be waiting for the 'inevitable' moment when they are finally recognised as geniuses. An odd quirk of the pub is that drinks are marginally cheaper in the stone-floor bar than the carpeted lounge, even though they are served by the same bar!

James Toner's (Map pp118-19; ☎ 676 3090; 139 Lower Baggot St) Toner's, with its stone floor, is almost a country pub in the heart of the city and the shelves and drawers are reminders that it once doubled as a grocery store. Not that its suit-wearing business crowd would ever have shopped here...

Hartigan's (Map pp118-19; ☎ 676 2280; 100 Lower Leeson St) This is about as spartan a bar as you'll find in the city and is the daytime home to some serious drinkers, who appreciate the quiet, no-frills surroundings. In the evening it's popular with students from the medical faculty of University College Dublin.

Sackville Lounge (Sackville Pl) Just off O'Connell St, this tiny wood panelled bar dating from the 1880s, claims to be one of Dublin's smallest. Full of local traders and actors from the nearby Abbey and Peacock theatres, its relaxed, down-at-heel atmosphere makes it a great place for a drink and a chinwag.

DRINKING	pp117-20	
Bruxelles	1	C3
Davy Byrne's	2	C3
Duke	3	C3
Eamonn Doran's Imbibing Emporium	4	B2
Flowing Tide	5	C1
Front Lounge	6	B3
George	7	B3
Globe	8	B3
Grogan's Castle Lounge	9	B3
Gubu	10	B2
Hartigan's	11	C4
Hogan's	12	B3
Hughes' Bar	13	A2
International	14	C3
James Toner's	15	D4
John Mulligan's	16	C2
Kehoe's	17	C3
Lobo (Morrison Hotel)	18	A2
Long Hall	19	B3
Market Bar	20	B3
Molloy's	21	A3
Neary's	22	C3
O'Donoghue's	23	D4
Octagon Bar (Clarence Hotel)	24	B2
Oliver St John Gogarty	25	C2
Out on the Liffey	26	A2
Palace Bar	27	C2
Patrick Conway's	28	B1
Pravda	29	B2
Rí Rá	30	B3
SamSara	31	C3
Sean O'Casey's	32	C1
Spy	33	C3
Stag's Head	34	B3
Switch	35	B2
ENTERTAINMENT	**pp120-4**	
Ambassador	36	C1
Gaiety Theatre	37	C3
Sackville Lounge	38	C1
Spirit	39	B2
Sugar Club	40	C4
Temple Bar Music Centre	41	B2
Village	42	B4

Ryan's (☎ 677 6097; 28 Parkgate St; bus No 23, 25, 26 from city centre) Near Phoenix Park, this is one of only a handful of city pubs that has retained its Victorian decor virtually intact, complete with ornate bar and snugs and it vies with Mulligan's (see above) as purveyor of the finest pint of Guinness in Dublin. An institution among Dublin's public houses, this is truly worth the trip.

Live Music Pubs

The following places are excellent venues for catching some traditional Irish and contemporary music.

Sean O'Casey's (Map pp118-19; ☎ 874 8675; 105 Marlborough St) This place has a weekly menu of live rock and some Irish traditional music sessions.

For the best Irish traditional sessions in Dublin, two northside pubs are a must.

Hughes' Bar (Map pp118-19; ☎ 872 6540; 19 Chancery St) This pub is directly behind the Four Courts and has nightly, if impromptu, sessions which often result in a closed door – that is, they go on long past official closing time. The pub is also a popular lunch-time spot with barristers working nearby.

Cobblestones (Map pp72-4; ☎ 872 1799; North King St) This pub is on the main square in Smithfield, an old northside marketplace. There's a great atmosphere in the cosy upstairs bar where nightly music sessions, both traditional and up-and-coming folk and singer-songwriter acts, are superb.

Oliver St John Gogarty (Map pp118-19; ☎ 671 1822; 58-59 Fleet St) There's live traditional music nightly at this busy Temple Bar pub, catering to a mostly tourist crowd.

International (Map pp118-19; ☎ 677 9250; 23 Wicklow St) The International has live jazz and blues most nights.

Bruxelles (Map pp118-19; ☎ 677 5362; 7-8 Harry St) This place has weekly live rock music, perhaps the only link the now-trendy pub has to its heavy metal past.

O'Donoghue's (Map p88; ☎ 661 4303; 15 Merrion Row) This, the most famous traditional music bar in Dublin, is where world-famous folk group the Dubliners started off in the 1960s. On summer evenings a young, international crowd spills out into the courtyard beside the pub.

Comhaltas Ceoltóiri Éireann (☎ 280 0295; 35 Belgrave Sq, Monkstown) Serious aficionados of traditional music should make the trip towards Dun Laoghaire. The name (cole-tas kyohl-thori erin) means 'Fraternity of Traditional Musicians of Ireland'. It's here that you'll find the best Irish music and dancing in Dublin, with some of the country's top players. To get there, take bus No 7, 7A or 8 from Trinity College, get off before Monkstown village and follow the blue signpost. Alternatively, you can take the DART; it's a five-minute walk inland (westwards, following the signs) from Seapoint Station.

Mother Redcaps (Map pp72-4; ☎ 453 8306; Back Lane, Christchurch) A legendary, spit-on-the-floor, no-frills folk music venue, which reopened after a few year's respite, over a pub of the same name.

Trendy Bars

These modern bars are Dublin's current hot spots.

Dice Bar (Map pp72-4; ☎ 674 6710; 79 Queen St) Co-owned by singer Huey from band Fun Lovin' Criminals, the Dice Bar looks like something you'd find on New York's Lower

East Side. Its black and red painted interior, dripping candles and stressed seating, combined with rocking DJs most nights, make it a magnet for Dublin's beautiful beatnik crowds.

Ice Bar (Map p70; ☎ 665 4000; Four Seasons Hotel, Simmonscourt Rd) Not to be confused with the Dice Bar in a taxi; both bars are worlds apart. The Ice Bar is the latest place for young, single 20-somethings with infinite disposable incomes to be seen. Flash your convertible beemer car keys at the door for speedy access. The all-white chichi interior with central chrome and marble bar is softened by some lovely specially-commissioned wall hangings by Irish artists. Vodka based cocktails (€4.50 to €10.50) are the house specialty.

Voodoo Lounge (Map pp72-4; ☎ 873 6013; 37 Arran Quay) Run by the same crew as Dice Bar, the Voodoo Lounge, on the quays, just south of Smithfield, is a long, dark bar with decadent, gothic Louisiana-style décor. Music is loud and that's the way the young fun-lovin' crowd likes it.

Forum Bar (Map pp72-4; ☎ 878 7084; 144 Parnell St) A welcome addition to the scene, this bar is the first run by and catering (though not exclusively) to Dublin's thriving black community – and not before time. The place heaves on weekend nights (Thursday to Saturday) with young scenesters and bar staff, getting on down to the DJ's hip hop beats.

Market Bar (Map p88; ☎ 677 4835; Fade St) Newly opened, this fashionable watering hole is run by the same guys as The Globe around the corner. Little would you know this beautiful airy Victorian space was a sausage factory in a former life.

Pravda (Map pp118-19; ☎ 874 0076; 35 Lower Liffey St) Pravda, near the Ha'penny Bridge, is Russian in name only. It's a cavernous place designed with, you guessed, Russian-inspired murals and Soviet iconography. Packed with pre-clubbers, the bouncers can become heavy on the style policing at weekends.

Lobo (Map pp118-19; ☎ 878 299; Morrison Hotel, Lower Ormond Quay) Dublin's well-heeled denizens of cool; designers, media types and wannabees flock to Morrison's snazzy Lobo bar to schmooze over pricy cocktails and talk about property prices. If you do get past the door staff, you'll find a comfortable, modern lounge with the now ubiquitous standard lamp and leather sofa interior evident in many new bars.

Octagon Bar (Map pp118-19; ☎ 670 9000; Clarence Hotel, 6-8 Wellington Quay) Temple Bar's most chic watering hole is where you'll find Dublin's celebrities and their hangers-on. Drinks are more expensive than elsewhere – a flute of bilini will set you back €13 – but judging by the clientele that have passed the bouncer's strict entry test this is hardly a concern.

Globe (Map pp118-19; ☎ 671 1220; 11 South Great George's St) One of Dublin's first proper café-bars, the Globe, with its wooden floors and plain brick walls, is as much a daytime haunt for a good latte as a super-cool watering hole by night. Nightly DJs, a relaxed atmosphere and its friendly, mostly foreign staff keeps the place buzzing with a mix of hip young locals and clued-in visitors.

Hogan's (Map pp118-19; ☎ 677 5904; 35 South Great George's St) Once an old-style, traditional bar, Hogan's is now a gigantic boozer spread across two floors. A popular hangout for young professionals, it gets very full at the weekend with folks eager to take advantage of its late licence.

SamSara (Map pp118-19; ☎ 671 7723; 35-36 Dawson St) This huge Middle Eastern–themed drinking emporium packs young office types and pre-clubbers in at weekends when the bar runs late.

Thomas House (Map pp72-4; ☎ 671 6987; 86 Thomas St) Once a dingy 'old man's pub', Thomas House, down the road from the National College of Art & Design, was given a cheap lick of paint and, hey presto, the city's arty alternative crowd can't get in its doors quick enough. This place is a real dive, thankfully, and a great antidote to the increasing number of characterless 'superpubs' springing up over town. It rocks most nights as both well known and great obscure DJs spin discs on its two tiny floors.

ENTERTAINMENT

Dublin is undoubtedly one of Europe's most vibrant entertainment capitals, with a plethora of options to satisfy (nearly) every desire. It has theatres, cinemas, nightclubs, concert halls, stadiums, horse racing and dog tracks.

For entertainment information, pick up a copy of the weekly music review *Hot Press*, the *Event Guide*, a bimonthly freebie available at many locations, including bars, cafés and hostels; or the fortnightly magazine *In Dublin*. Thursday's *Irish Times* has a pull-out entertainment section called *The Ticket* which has comprehensive listings of clubs and gigs.

Cinemas

Ireland boasts the highest attendances in Europe of young cinemagoers. Consequently it's best to book in advance by credit card, or be prepared to queue for up to half an hour for tickets at night-time screenings. Dublin's cinemas are more heavily concentrated on the northern side of the Liffey. Admission prices are generally €5 for afternoon shows, rising to €7.50 in the evening.

Irish Film Centre (Map pp80-1; ☎ 679 5744; 6 Eustace St) The Irish Film Centre has a couple of screens and shows classics and art-house films. The complex also has a bar, a café and a bookshop. Weekly (€1.30) or annual (€14, €10 with concession) membership is required for some uncertified films which can only be screened as part of a 'club'.

Savoy (Dublin map: ☎ 874 6000; Upper O'Connell St) The Savoy is a traditional four-screen first-run cinema, and has late-night shows on weekends.

Screen (Around Temple Bar map; ☎ 671 4988; 2 Townsend St) Between Trinity College and O'Connell Bridge, the Screen shows new independent and smaller commercial films on its three screens.

UGC Multiplex (Dublin map: ☎ 872 8400; Parnell Centre, Parnell St) This seven-screen cinema has replaced many smaller cinemas and shows only commercial releases.

Clubs

A few years ago, Dublin was awash with billboards that showed a sweaty, packed dance club with the words 'Open Your Windows Tokyo, Dublin's Having a Party' across the top. Much of Dublin's success as a tourist destination comes from the fact that the city has developed a reputation for being one of the party hotspots of Europe, despite the fact that nightclubs here close earlier than in any other European capital!

The seemingly endless list of 'what's on' is constantly changing, so check out the listings in *In Dublin* and *Event Guide*; the listings here are by no means exhaustive. Most clubs open just after pubs close (11.30pm to midnight) and close at 2.30am or 3am. Admission to most costs between €5 and €8 Sunday to Thursday, rising to as much as €15 or €20 on Friday and Saturday. For gay and lesbian clubs, see the boxed text 'Gay & Lesbian Dublin' on p104.

Eamonn Doran's Imbibing Emporium (Map pp118-19; ☎ 679 9773; 3a Crown Alley; admission €5-8; 🕒 nightly) A large place with food, drink and live indie music, followed by DJs. Sunday night alternates between R&B and Hip Hop.

Parnell Mooney (Map pp72-4; ☎ 873 1544; 71 Parnell St; admission €7) This late night bar at the top of O'Connell St is only worth going to on Wednesday, when it hosts the fabulous Firehouse Skank, Dublin's only hard reggae and dub night.

PoD (Place of Dance; Map p88; ☎ 478 0225; 35 Harcourt St; admission €5-20; 🕒 Mon-Sat) Dublin's most renowned nightclub, this futuristic, metal-gothic cathedral of dance attracts a large weekend crowd of 20-somethings. To get past the notoriously difficult bouncers you'll really need to look the part. Saturday night is Access All Areas, where the crowd goes mad to house and techno music in the PoD, Chocolate Bar and Red Box. Admission is €5 cheaper if you get there before 11.30pm on Saturdays.

Red Box (Map p88; ☎ 478 0225; 35 Harcourt St; admission €5-20; 🕒 Mon-Sat) Located upstairs from the PoD, if you like your music hard and fast, this is one of the best places to come. The floor is enormous and the willing crowds really fill it up. Look out for the big name international DJs that play here regularly.

Rí Rá (Map pp118-19; ☎ 677 4835; Dame Ct; admission €5-11; 🕒 Mon-Sat) Rí Rá is one of the friendlier clubs in the city centre and is full nearly every night with a diverse crowd who come for the house-free, mostly funk music downstairs or more laid back lounge tunes and movies upstairs. Refreshingly, the bouncers here are friendly, funny and very fair. Thursday's Funk Off club is a veritable institution and Monday's '80s club Strictly Handbag is now in its fourth year.

Spirit (Map pp118-19; ☎ 877 9999; 57 Middle Abbey St; admission €5-20; 🕒 Thu-Sat) Dublin's newest dance club provides a whole night's multi-experience for hardcore clubbers under one roof. Spanning three floors, visiting and local DJs play pretty commercial house on one floor, soul and funk in the middle (complete with sound-proofed cinema) and downstairs – wait for it – a classical cellist plays in the nonsmoking chill out area, complete with on-site masseuses, tarot readers and body painters.

Spy (Map pp118-19; ☎ 679 0014; 59 Sth William St) In a beautiful Georgian building in the Powerscourt Townhouse centre, Spy attracts the city's fine young things in search of a good time. But there's a distinction: easy access clubs in the small vaulted basement are strictly for dancing and drinking while upstairs an exclusive door policy ensures that only minor celebrities and the rich and beautiful gain access.

Switch (Map pp118-19; ☎ 670 7655; 11 Eustace St; admission €7-15; ⏲ nightly) Located beneath a pretty cheesy bar, this is one of our favourite nightclubs in town: it's small, sweaty and seriously hip, with a terrific selection of different dance beats mixed by excellent local DJs, helped along by international guests.

Temple Bar Music Centre (Map pp118-19; ☎ 670 9202; Curved St) There's something going on every night at the no-frills, factory-like TBMC to suit lovers of indie, garage and funk sounds.

Temple Theatre (Map pp72-4; ☎ 874 5088; St George's Church, Hardwicke Pl; admission €12-20; ⏲ Fri & Sat) The sound of church bells has been replaced by the reverberations of loud house music at this stunning northside club, formerly a church. Big-name international DJs often play here. Amazingly admission is free before 10.30pm on Saturday and €20 thereafter.

Music Venues

Bookings can be made either directly at the venues or through **HMV** (Map p88; ☎ 679 5334, 24-hr credit card bookings ☎ 456 9569; 65 Grafton St) or through **Ticketmaster** (☎ 1890 925 100; www.ticketmaster.ie) but they charge a whopping 12.5% service charge *per ticket*, not per booking, on credit card bookings.

CLASSICAL MUSIC & OPERA VENUES

Classical music concerts and opera take place in a number of city-centre venues. There are also occasional performances in churches: check the press for details.

Bank of Ireland Arts Centre (Map pp80-1; ☎ 671 1488; Foster Pl) The arts centre hosts a regular midweek lunch-time recital beginning at 1.15pm (free) as well as an occasional evening programme of concerts. Call for details.

Gaiety Theatre (Map p88; ☎ 677 1717; www.gaietytheatre.com; King St South) This popular Dublin theatre hosts, among other things, a programme of classical concerts and opera.

Helix (Map p70; ☎ 700 7000; www.thehelix.ie; Collins Ave, Glasnevin) Based in Dublin City University, the stunning new Helix theatre hosts, among other things, an impressive array of international operatic and classical recitals and performances. Check the website for details. Bus Nos 11, 13, 13A or 19A stop at the Ballymun Rd entrance.

Hugh Lane Municipal Gallery of Modern Art (Map pp72-4; ☎ 874 1903; Charlemont House, Parnell Sq) From September to June the art gallery hosts up to 30 concerts of contemporary classical music at noon on Sunday.

National Concert Hall (Map p88; ☎ 417 0000; www.nch.ie; Earlsfort Tce) Ireland's premier orchestral hall hosts a variety of concerts year round, including a series of lunch-time concerts from 1.05pm to 2pm on Tuesday, June to August.

Royal Dublin Showground Concert Hall (Map p70; ☎ 668 0866; Ballsbridge) The huge hall of the RDS Showground hosts a rich programme of classical music and opera throughout the year.

ROCK & POP VENUES

Ambassador Theatre (Map pp118-19; ☎ 1890 925 100; O'Connell St) The Ambassador started life as a theatre and then a cinema. Not much has changed inside, making it a cool retro place to see visiting and local rock acts perform.

Gaiety (Map p88; ☎ 677 1717; www.gaietytheatre.com; Sth King St; ⏲ to 4am) This old Victorian theatre is an atmospheric place to come and listen to late night jazz, rock or blues on weekends.

Isaac Butt (Map pp72-4; ☎ 855 5884; Store St) Local garage, rock, metal and indie bands sweat it out most nights in this grungy venue opposite Busáras.

Olympia Theatre (Map pp80-1; ☎ 677 7744; Dame St) This pleasantly tatty place features everything from disco to country on Friday night. Midnight at the Olympia runs from midnight to 2am on Friday.

Point Depot (☎ 836 3633; East Link Bridge, North Wall Quay) This is the premier indoor venue for all rock and pop acts playing in Dublin. Artists such as Diana Ross, Prince and Jamiroquai have all played here. Originally constructed as a rail terminus in 1878, it has a capacity of around 6000.

Red Box (Map p88; ☎ 478 0166; Harcourt St) In the old Harcourt St station, this is one of the best venues for dance gigs, with top European dance bands and DJs strutting their stuff to a largely young crowd. Queues go all the way around the corner from about 10pm on Friday and Saturday nights.

Sugar Club (Map pp118-19; ☎ 678 7188; 8 Lower Leeson St) There's live jazz, cabaret and soul music at weekends in this comfortable new theatre-style venue on the corner of St Stephen's Green.

Temple Bar Music Centre (Map pp80-1; ☎ 670 0533; Curved St) The centre hosts all kinds of gigs from Irish traditional to drum-and-bass for a nonimage-conscious crowd.

Vicar Street (Map pp72-4; ☎ 454 5533; www.vicarstreet.com; 58-59 Thomas St) Smaller performances take place at this intimate venue near Christ Church Cathedral. It has a capacity of 1000 between its table-serviced group seating downstairs and theatre style balcony. It has a varied programme of performers, with a strong emphasis on folk and jazz.

Village (Map pp118-19; ☎ 475 8555; www.thevillagevenue.com; 26 Wexford St) Opened in March 2003 by the people who run Whelan's next door, this attractive new mid-sized venue hosts a range of acts from local singer-songwriters to visiting rock bands.

Whelan's (Map p88; ☎ 478 0766; 25 Wexford St; www.whelanslive.com) Whelan's is long established as the place to catch up-and-coming international rock acts and established local folk, country acts and singer-songwriters. Its intimate setting with ground and balcony levels make it a good place to see a gig.

Sport

Croke Park Stadium (☎ 855 8176; Clonliffe Rd; bus No 19 or 19A) Hurling and Gaelic football games are held from February to November here, at headquarters of the Gaelic Athletic Association, north of the Royal Canal in Drumcondra. Call ☎ 1550 112 215 (24 hours) for the latest details.

Harold's Cross Park (☎ 497 1081; 151 Harold's Cross Rd; bus No 16 or 16A) Greyhound racing takes place near Rathmines in this newly revamped venue.

Lansdowne Rd Stadium (☎ 668 9300; Ballsbridge) Rugby and international football matches take place here, near Ballsbridge. The rugby season is from September to April and the football season from August to May. The Landsdowne Rd DART station is a short walk from the stadium.

Leopardstown Race Course (☎ 289 3607; Foxrock) The Irish love of horse racing can be observed about 10km south of the city centre in Foxrock. Special buses depart the city centre on race days: ring the race course for details.

Shelbourne Stadium (☎ 668 3502; Bridge Town Rd, Ringsend; bus No 3 from D'Olier St) This is also a greyhound track. For current information on horse and greyhound meetings call ☎ 1550 112218 (24 hours).

Theatre

Dublin's theatre scene is small but busy. Bookings can usually be made by quoting a credit card number over the phone, and the tickets can then be collected just before the performance.

Abbey Theatre (Map pp72-4; ☎ 878 7222; www.abbeytheatre.ie; Lower Abbey St) The famous Abbey Theatre near the river is Ireland's national theatre. It puts on new Irish works as well as revivals of classic Irish works by writers such as WB Yeats, JM Synge, Sean O'Casey, Brendan Behan and Samuel Beckett. Tickets for evening performances can cost up to €25 except on Monday when they are cheaper. The smaller and less expensive **Peacock Theatre** (☎ 878 7222) is part of the same complex.

Andrew's Lane Theatre (Map pp118-19; ☎ 679 5720; 9-17 St Andrew's Lane) This is a well established fringe theatre.

Ark (Map pp118-19; ☎ 670 7788; 11a Eustace St) Has a 150-seater venue that stages shows for kids aged between five and 13.

Gaiety Theatre (Map p88; ☎ 677 1717, www.gaietytheatre.com; Sth King St) Opened in 1871, the theatre is used for modern plays, TV shows, musical comedies and revues.

Gate Theatre (Map pp72-4; ☎ 874 4045; www.gatetheatre.ie; 1 Cavendish Row) Also to the north of the Liffey, the Gate Theatre specialises in international classics and older Irish works with a touch of comedy by playwrights such as Oscar Wilde, George Bernard Shaw and Oliver Goldsmith, although newer plays are sometimes staged too. Prices vary according to what's on, but they're usually around €20.

Helix (Map p70; ☎ 700 7000; www.thehelix.ie; Collins Ave, Glasnevin) The Helix, Dublin City University's new theatre venue has already established its reputation as a serious theatre with its mix of both accessible and more challenging productions. Check the website for details. Bus Nos 11, 13, 13A or 19A stop at the Ballymun Rd entrance.

International Bar (Map pp80-1; ☎ 677 9250; 23 Wicklow St) This is one of several pubs that host theatrical performances.

Olympia Theatre (Map pp80-1; ☎ 677 7744; 72 Dame St) This theatre specialises in light plays and, at Christmas time, pantomime.

Players' Theatre (Map p78; ☎ 677 2941 ext 1239; Regent House, Trinity College) The Trinity College Players' Theatre hosts student productions throughout the academic year as well as the most prestigious plays from the Dublin Theatre Festival in October.

Project Arts Centre (Map pp80-1; ☎ 1850 260027; www.project.ie; 39 East Essex St) The centre puts on excellent productions of experimental plays by up-and-coming Irish and foreign writers.

Tivoli Theatre (Map pp72-4; ☎ 454 4472; 135-136 Francis St) Experimental and less-commercial performances take place here.

SHOPPING

If it's made in Ireland, you can probably buy it in Dublin. Popular purchases include fine Irish knitwear such as the renowned Aran sweaters; jewellery with a Celtic influence, including Claddagh rings; books on Irish topics; crystal from Waterford, Galway, Tyrone and Tipperary; Irish coats of arms; china from Beleek; Royal Tara chinaware; and linen from Donegal. If you're interested in **antiques**, Francis St, south of Tivoli Theatre in the Liberties area, is the place to go.

Citizens of non-EU countries can reclaim the VAT (sales tax) paid on purchases made at stores displaying a cashback sticker; ask for details. For information on bookshops, see p71.

Most department stores and shopping centres are open from 9am to 6pm Monday to Saturday (open to 8pm Thursday) and noon to 6pm Sunday.

Department Stores & Shopping Centres

Dublin's main shopping streets are on and around pedestrianised Grafton St and, on the northside, on and around Henry St, just off O'Connell St. Here you'll find the top department stores and shopping malls. Needless to say, Grafton St shops are posher and more expensive.

Arnott's (Map pp72-4; ☎ 805 0400; 12 Henry St) Occupying a huge block with entrances on Henry, Liffey and Abbey Sts, this formerly mediocre department store has been completely overhauled and is now probably Dublin's best. It stocks virtually everything you could possibly want to buy, from garden furniture to high fashion, and everything is relatively affordable.

Brown Thomas (Map pp80-1; ☎ 605 6666; 92 Grafton St) This is Dublin's most expensive department store, suitably stocked to cater for the city's more moneyed shoppers. You'll find every top label represented here.

Clery's & Co (Map pp72-4; ☎ 878 6000; O'Connell St) This graceful shop is a Dublin classic. Recently restored to its elegant best, it caters to the more conservative Dublin shopper.

ILAC Centre (Map pp72-4; ☎ 704 1460; off Henry St) The ILAC Centre, off Henry St near O'Connell St, is a little dilapidated but still has some interesting outlets with goods at affordable prices.

Jervis St Centre (Map pp72-4; ☎ 878 1323; Jervis St) Just north of Capel St Bridge, this is an ultramodern mall with dozens of outlets.

Powerscourt Townhouse shopping centre (Map p88; ☎ 679 4144; 59 South William St) The wonderful Powerscourt Townhouse shopping centre between South William St and Clarendon St, just to the west of Grafton St, is a big, modern shopping centre in a fine old building. There are some decent restaurants on all its floors and the Irish Design Centre sells the work of up-and-coming Irish fashion designers.

St Stephen's Green Shopping Centre (Map p88; ☎ 478 0888; St Stephen's Green) Inside this flash shopping centre you'll discover a diverse mixture of chain stores and individual shops.

Designer Clothes

Temple Bar and the area around Grafton St are the best places for all kinds of designer gear, both new and second-hand.

Costume (Map pp80-1; ☎ 679 5200; 10 Castle Market) This chic upmarket shop sells a range of women's European designer labels that include Sabina di Lorenzo and emerging Irish duo Nic & Suki.

Smock (Map pp80-1; ☎ 613 9000; Smock Alley Ct, West Essex St) This little designer shop sells quirky international womenswear from investment labels Easton Pearson, Veronique Branquinho and A.F. Vandevorft and a small range of interesting jewellery.

Tulle (Map p88; ☎ 679 9115; 29 George's St Arcade) European designers with attitude Matthew Williamson, Holly and Othtude are stocked in this small outlet for young females.

Secondhand Shops

Eager Beaver (Map pp80-1; ☎ 677 3342; 17 Crown Alley) Need a black suit for a wedding? A cricket jumper? A Victorian shirt? Don't want to spend a fortune? Then this is your place – it's a clothes hunter's paradise.

Harlequin (Map pp80-1; ☎ 671 0202; 13 Castle Market) This is a wonderful store with a great selection of second-hand jeans, shirts and suits.

Jenny Vander (Map pp80-1; ☎ 677 0406; George's St Arcade) A visit to Jenny Vander's is like walking into an exotic 1940s' boudoir: the selection of antique clothing, hats and jewellery is pretty wild. You won't find many bargains here though.

Irish Crafts & Souvenirs

Avoca Handweavers (Map pp80-1; ☎ 677 4215, 11-13 Suffolk St) Contemporary craft shop Avoca, with another branch in Co. Wicklow, is a treasure trove of interesting Irish and foreign products. The colourful shop is choc-a-bloc with woollen knits, ceramics, hand-crafted gadgets and a wonderful toy selection – and not a tweed cap in sight.

Claddagh Records (Map pp80-1; ☎ 677 0262; 2 Cecilia St) This shop sells a wide range of Irish traditional and folk music.

DesignYard (Map pp80-1; ☎ 677 8453; 12 East Essex St) This modern warehouse space showcases beautiful contemporary work by Irish and European jewellers, potters and craftspeople.

Dublin Woollen Company (Map pp80-1; ☎ 677 5014; 41 Lower Ormond Quay) Near the Ha'penny Bridge, this is one of the major wool outlets in Dublin. It has a large collection of sweaters, cardigans, scarves, rugs, shawls and other woollen goods and runs a tax-free shopping scheme.

Kilkenny Shop (Map pp80-1; ☎ 677 7066; 6 Nassau St) This shop has a wonderful selection of finely made Irish crafts, featuring clothing, glassware, pottery, jewellery, crystal and silver from some of Ireland's best designers.

Knobs & Knockers (Map pp80-1; ☎ 671 0288; 19 Nassau St) This is where you'll find a Dublin doorknocker to grace your front door.

Markets

George's St Arcade (Map pp80-1; between South Great George St & Drury St) This excellent covered market has some great second-handclothes shops, and stalls selling Mediterranean food, jewellery and records.

Meeting House Square Market (Map pp80-1; Meeting House Sq) This open-air food market in Temple Bar takes place every Saturday, but get there early for best pickings and to avoid the huge crowds. With a multitude of stalls selling top organic produce from around the country, you can also buy diverse snacks such as sushi, waffles, tapas, oysters and handmade cheeses.

Blackberry Fair (Lwr Rathmines Rd) You'll have to root through a lot of rubbish to find a gem in this charmingly rundown weekend market that stocks furniture, record and a few clothes stalls. It's cheap though.

Blackrock Market (Main St, Blackrock; 🕐 11am-5.30pm Sat & Sun) The long-running Blackrock Market in an old merchant house and yard in this seaside village has all manner of stalls selling everything from New Age crystals to futons.

GETTING THERE & AWAY

Air

Dublin is Ireland's major international gateway airport, with direct flights from Europe, North America and Asia. See p671 for details on flights and fares.

Airline offices in Dublin include:

Aer Lingus (☎ 886 6705 for departures & arrivals; ☎ 886 8888 for reservations; www.aerlingus.com) The only walk-in branch is at Dublin airport.
Aeroflot (☎ 844 6166; www.aeroflot.org) Dublin airport
Air Canada (☎ 1800 709 900; www.aircanada.ca)
Air France/cityjet (☎ 844 5633; www.airfrance.co.uk; www.onlinehelp@cityjet.com) Dublin airport
Alitalia (☎ 677 5171; www.alitalia.co.uk)
British Airways (☎ 1800 62 67 47; www.britishairways.com) Dublin airport
British Midland (☎ 407 3036; www.flybmi .co.uk) Dublin airport
Delta Air Lines (☎ 1800 768 080; www.delta.com) Dublin airport

Finnair (☎ 844 6565; www.finnair.com)
Iberia (☎ 407 3017; www.iberia.com)
Lufthansa Airlines (☎ 844 5544; www.lufthansa.com) Dublin airport
Qantas Airways (☎ 407 3278; www.qantas.com.au) Dublin airport
Scandinavian Airlines (SAS; ☎ 844 5888; www.scandinavian.net) Dublin airport
Swiss (☎ 1890 200515; www.swiss.com) Dublin airport

Boat

There are two direct services from Holyhead on the northwestern tip of Wales: one to Dublin port at North Wall and the other to Dun Laoghaire, the port on the southern side of Dublin Bay. There are also services from Liverpool.

You can also take advantage of bus/train and ferry combinations in the UK. See p674 for more information.

Bus

Busáras, at Store St, just north of the Custom House and the Liffey, is Bus Éireann's central bus station. Information on buses is available there from the **Travel Centre** (☎ 836 6111; www.buseireann.ie; 🕑 8.30am-7pm Mon-Sat, 9am-7pm Sun).

For information on fares, frequencies and durations to various destinations in the Republic and Northern Ireland, see p677.

Car & Motorcycle

RENTAL

A number of rental companies have desks at the airport, and other operators are based close to the airport and deliver cars for airport collection. Some of the main rental companies in Dublin are:

Avis City (☎ 605 7500; www.avis.com; 1 East Hanover St) Airport (☎ 844 5204)
Budget City (☎ 837 9802; www.budgetcarrental.ie; 151 Lower Drumcondra Rd)
Airport (☎ 844 5150)
Dan Dooley Car & Van Hire City (☎ 677 2723; www.dan-dooley.ie; 42-43 Westland Row)
Airport (☎ 844 5156)
Hertz City (☎ 660 2255; www.hertz.com; 149 Upper Leeson St) Airport (☎ 844 5466)
Murrays Europcar City (☎ 614 2800; www.europcar.com; Baggot St Bridge) Airport (☎ 844 4179)
Sixt City (☎ 862 2715; www.icr.ie; Old Airport Rd, Santry) Airport (☎ 844 4199)
Windsor Thrifty City (☎ 1800 515800; www.thrifty.ie; 125 Herberton Bridge, South Circular Rd) Airport (☎ 840 0800)

Train

For general information contact **Iarnród Éireann Travel Centre** (Map pp72-4; ☎ 836 6222; www.irishrail.ie; 35 Lower Abbey St; 🕑 9am-5pm Mon-Fri, 9am-1pm Sat). **Connolly Station** (☎ 836 3333), just north of the Liffey and the city centre, is the station for Belfast, Derry, Sligo and other points north. **Heuston Station** (Map pp72-4; ☎ 836 5421), just south of the Liffey and well west of the centre, is the station for Cork, Galway, Killarney, Limerick, Wexford, Waterford and other points west, south and southwest. See p679 for more information.

GETTING AROUND

To/From the Airport

Dublin airport (Map p70; ☎ 814 1111) is 13km north of the centre and can be reached by bus or taxi.

It has a **left-luggage office** (☎ 814 4633; €6 per item daily; 🕑 6am-11pm).

BUS SERVICES

The **Airlink Express Coach** (☎ 872 0000, 873 4222), operated by Dublin Bus, runs to/from Busáras (Dublin's central bus station) costing €5 for adults and €2 for children. It also runs to/from Heuston and Connolly train stations for the same price. Both journeys take about 30 to 40 minutes. Timetables are available at the airport or in the city.

From the airport to Busáras, bus No 747 departs every 10 minutes between 5.45am and 11.30pm Monday to Saturday (every 20 minutes between 7.15am and 11.30pm on Sunday). From Busáras, the service runs every 10 minutes between 6.30am and 10.45pm Monday to Saturday (every 20 minutes between 7.30am and 11.10pm on Sunday).

From the airport to Heuston Station, bus No 748 departs every 15 minutes from 6.50am to 9.30pm Monday to Saturday (at 7am, 7.45am and every 25 minutes thereafter until 12.25pm Sunday). From Heuston Station, buses run every 15 minutes between 7.10am and 10.20pm Monday to Saturday (7.50am, 8.40am and every 25 minutes until 10.50pm Sunday). From Connolly Station, buses also run every 15 minutes between 7.20am and 10.30pm

Monday to Saturday, and every 25 minutes between 8.55am and 11pm on Sunday (first departure at 8am).

Aircoach (☎ 844 7118; www.aircoach.ie) is a privately run service that operates luxury air-conditioned coaches between the airport and 18 locations throughout the city and as far south as Sandyford, usually to cater for residents of the city's biggest hotels, but they will pick up anyone. From the airport, coaches run between 4am and midnight daily, and they stop at over a dozen points throughout the city centre, usually close to the bigger hotels (check the website for exact locations). You will be charged a flat rate of €6 passenger (accompanied children free), irrespective of destination.

The alternative service is on the slower bus Nos 41 and 41A, which make a number of useful stops on the way, terminate on Eden Quay near O'Connell St and cost €1.70. The trip takes about an hour.

There are also direct buses between Dublin airport and Belfast.

TAXI SERVICES

Taxi passengers are subject to additional charges for baggage, extra passengers, bank holidays and 'unsociable hours'. However, a taxi usually costs about €20 between the airport and the centre, so between four people it's unlikely to be more expensive than the express bus. There's a supplementary charge of €2.50 from the airport to the city, but this charge doesn't apply from the city to the airport. Make sure the meter is switched on, as some Dublin Airport taxi drivers can be as unscrupulous as their brethren anywhere else in the world.

To/From the Ferry Terminals

Buses go to Busáras from the **Dublin Ferryport terminal** (Map p130; ☎ 855 2222; Alexandra Rd) after all ferry arrivals from Holyhead. Buses also run from Busáras to meet ferry departures. For the 9.45am ferry departure from Dublin, buses leave Busáras at 8.30am. For the 9.45pm departure, buses depart from Busáras at 8.30pm. For the 1am sailing to Liverpool, the bus departs from Busáras at 11.45pm. All buses cost €2.

To travel between Dun Laoghaire's **Carlisle terminal** (☎ 280 1905) and Dublin, take bus No 46A to St Stephen's Green, or bus No 7, 7A or 8 to Burgh Quay, or take the DART to Pearse station (for south Dublin) or Connolly Station (for north Dublin).

Between Connolly & Heuston Stations

The 90 Raillink Bus runs between the two stations every 10 to 15 minutes at peak per iods and costs €1.10. Connolly Station is a short walk north of Busáras; Heuston is by the Liffey, on the western side of town.

Car

As in most cities, having a car in Dublin is as much a millstone as a convenience, though it can be useful for day trips outside the city.

There are parking meters around central Dublin and a large number of (phenomenally expensive) open and sheltered car parks. Parking illegally is not advised, especially as Dublin has introduced a clamping system, with a €80 charge for removal. Free roadside parking is practically nonexistent. However, the gardaí warn visitors that it's safer to park in a supervised car park, since cars are often broken into even in broad daylight. Cars with foreign number plates, which may contain valuable personal effects, are a prime target. Rental cars are also targeted, but nowadays most have no external indication that they're owned by a rental company.

When you're booking accommodation check on parking facilities.

Avoid driving in the city centre if you can help it at peak times such as 7.30am to 9.30am or 5pm to 7pm (up to 9pm on Thursday when there's late shopping in town). Traffic is noticeably lighter in the mornings during school holidays.

Public Transport

BUS

Dublin Bus' information office (Bus Átha Cliath; ☎ 873 4222; www.dublinbus.ie; 59 Upper O'Connell St; 9am-5.30pm Mon-Fri, 9am-2pm Sat) has free single-route timetables. The central bus station, Busáras, is just north of the river, behind the Custom House, and has a left-luggage facility (€4 to €9 per day).

Buses run from around 6am (some start at 5.30am) to 11.30pm daily. Fares are calculated according to stages: one to three stages costs €0.80; four to seven costs €1.20; eight to 12 costs €1.40; and 13 to 23 costs €1.60. The city centre (Citizone) is within a 12-stage radius, so the maximum fare for travelling within the centre is €1.40.

You must tender exact change when boarding; if you give anything more you will be given a receipt for reimbursement, which you can only collect at the Dublin Bus main office.

One-day rambler passes cost €5 for the bus, or €8 for bus and rail. There are other bus passes for unlimited bus travel for three days (€9.50) and five days (€14.50). There are no discounts on these passes for students. Weekly bus passes cost €17.50 (students €14.50); weekly bus and rail passes cost €25 (plus €2.50 for an ID photo).

Nitelink late-night buses run from the College St, Westmoreland St and D'Olier St triangle. From Monday to Wednesday, there are usually only two departures, at 12.30am and 2am. From Thursday to Saturday, departures are at 12.30am, then every 20 minutes until 4.30am on the more popular routes and until 3.30am on the less frequented ones. Fares are €4 unless you're travelling to the far suburbs (places like Balbriggan in North County Dublin or Ashbourne in County Meath); then the fare is €6.

TRAIN

The **Dublin Area Rapid Transport** (DART; ☎ 836 6222) provides quick train access to the coast as far north as Howth and as far south as Bray. Pearse Station is convenient for central Dublin south of the Liffey, and Connolly Station for north of the Liffey. There are services every 10 to 20 minutes, sometimes even more frequently, from around 6.30am to midnight Monday to Saturday. Services are less frequent on Sunday. It takes about 30 minutes from Dublin to Bray to the south, or to Howth to the north. Dublin to Dun Laoghaire takes about 15 to 20 minutes. There are also Suburban Rail services north as far as Dundalk, inland to Mullingar and south past Bray to Arklow.

A one-way DART ticket from Dublin to Dun Laoghaire or Howth costs €1.70; to Bray it's €2.50. Within the DART region, a one-day, unlimited travel ticket costs €6.50 for an adult, €3 for a child or €11 for a family. A one-day ticket combining DART and Dublin Bus services costs €7.70 for an adult and €11.60 for a family (there is no child rate). A three-day pass allows you unlimited DART and bus travel for €15. A weekly rail and bus ticket costs €26 but requires an ID photo (€2.50).

Bicycles can't be taken on DART services, but they can be taken on the less frequent suburban train services, either in the guard's van or in a special compartment at the opposite end of the train from the engine. There's a €4 charge for transporting a bicycle up to 56km.

Heuston Station has left-luggage lockers of three sizes, costing €1.50/3/5 for 24 hours. At Connolly Station the facility costs €2.50.

Taxi

Taxis in Dublin are expensive with a €2.75 minimum charge and €0.15 for one-ninth of a mile (or 30 seconds) thereafter from 8am to 10pm (€0.20 per unit from 10pm to 8am and bank holidays). In addition there are a number of extra charges – €0.50 for each extra passenger, €0.50 for each piece of luggage and €1.50 for telephone bookings.

Taxis can be hailed on the street and are found at taxi ranks around the city, including on O'Connell St in north Dublin, College Green in front of Trinity College and St Stephen's Green at the end of Grafton St. There are numerous taxi companies that will dispatch taxis by radio. Phone **City Cabs** (☎ 872 2688) or **National Radio Cabs** (☎ 677 2222). Even with the addition of 2000 new taxi plates in 2002, queues at ranks can be frustratingly long late at night, and even calling one by phone is often met with a negative response. Phone the **Garda Carriage Office** (☎ 475 5888) for complaints about taxis and queries regarding lost property.

AROUND DUBLIN

There are a number of seaside suburbs round the curve of Dublin Bay. Dun Laoghaire to the south and Howth to the north are historic ports and popular day trips from the city. Connected to central Dublin by the convenient DART train service, they also make interesting alternatives to staying in the city. Malahide with its castle, the imposing Anglo-Irish mansion of Newbridge House, and the village of Swords are other Dublin-area attractions.

DUN LAOGHAIRE

Dun Laoghaire *(dun leary)*, only 13km southeast of central Dublin, is both a busy harbour with ferry connections to Britain and a popular resort. From 1821, when King George IV departed from here after a visit to Ireland, until Irish independence in 1922, the port was known as Kingstown. The fact that there are many B&Bs in Dun Laoghaire that are a bit cheaper than those in central Dublin, combined with the fast and frequent DART train connections, makes it an attractive alternative to town.

History

There was a coastal settlement on the site of Dun Laoghaire over 1000 years ago, but it was little more than a small fishing village until 1767, when the first pier was constructed. Dun Laoghaire grew more rapidly after that, and the Sandycove Martello Tower was erected in the early 19th century, as there was great fear of an invasion from Napoleonic France.

Construction of the harbour was proposed in 1815 to provide a refuge for ships unable to reach the safety of Dublin Harbour in inclement weather. Work began in 1817 but wasn't completed until 1842, at a cost of £1 million sterling, an astronomical figure in the mid-19th century.

Orientation & Information

Upper and Lower George's St, which runs parallel to the coast, is the main shopping street through Dun Laoghaire. The huge harbour is sheltered by the encircling arms of the East and West Piers. Sandycove with the James Joyce Museum and Forty Foot Pool is about 1km east of central Dun Laoghaire.

Just inside the terminal is a walk-in-only office of **Dublin Tourism** (🕑 10am-1pm & 2-6pm Mon-Sat). A bureau de change, also in the terminal, opens for ferry arrivals and departures.

There is a branch of the Bank of Ireland at 101 Upper George's St, which has an ATM. It opens 10am to 4pm Monday to Wednesday and Friday (to 5pm Thursday). The post office, next door at No 102, opens 9am to 6pm Monday to Friday and 9am to 5.30pm on Saturday.

For the police dial ☎ 999, or ☎ 666 5000 for Dun Laoghaire's Garda station, 34-35 Corrig Ave.

The Harbour

The 1290m East and 1548m West Piers, each ending at a lighthouse dating from the 1850s, have always been popular for walking (especially East Pier), bird-watching and fishing (particularly from the end of West Pier). You can ride a bicycle out along the piers (bottom level only). In the 19th century the practice of 'scorching' – riding out along the pier at breakneck speed – became so prevalent that bicycles were banned for some time.

The East Pier has an 1890s bandstand and a memorial to Captain Boyd and the crew of the Dun Laoghaire lifeboat who were drowned in a rescue attempt. Near the end of the pier is the 1852 anemometer, one of the first of these wind-speed measuring devices to be installed anywhere in the world.

The harbour has long been a popular yachting centre and the Royal Irish Yacht Club's building, dating from around 1850, was the first purpose-built yacht club in Ireland. The Royal St George Yacht Club's building dates from 1863 and that of the National Yacht Club from 1876. The world's first one-design sailing-boat class (a race in which all boats are the same type, so there's no need for handicaps) started life at Dun Laoghaire with a dinghy design known as Water Wag. A variety of specifically Dublin Bay one-design classes still race here, as do Mirrors and other popular small boats.

Around the Town

Nothing remains of the *dún* (fort) that gave Dun Laoghaire its name, as it was totally destroyed during the construction of the train line.

Sandycove

Approximately 1km south of Dun Laoghaire is Sandycove, with a pretty little beach and the Martello tower housing the James Joyce Museum. Sir Roger Casement, who attempted to organise a German-backed Irish freedom force during WWI, was born here in 1864. He was captured after being landed in County Kerry from a German U-boat and executed by the British as a traitor in 1916.

JAMES JOYCE MUSEUM

The Martello tower, which houses the **museum** (☎ 280 9265; Sandycove; adult/student/child €6/5/3.50; 🕑 10am-1pm & 2-5pm Mon-Sat, 2-6pm Sun

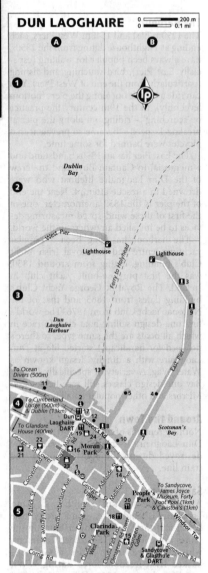

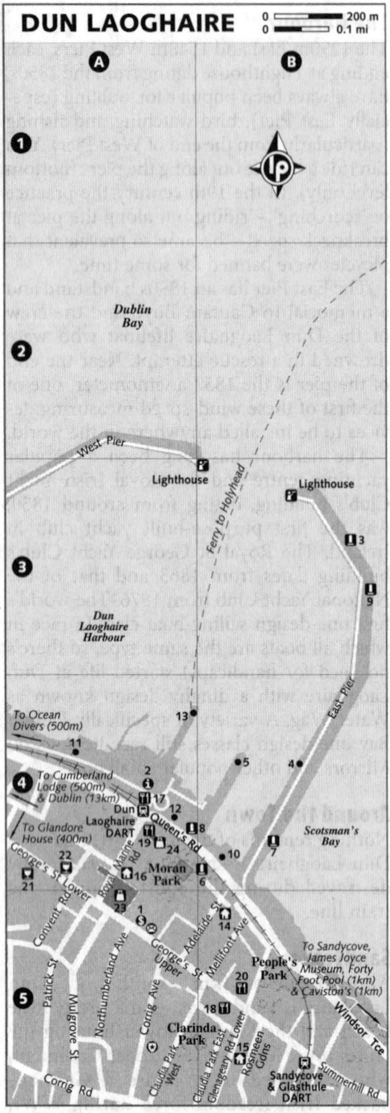

INFORMATION		
Bank of Ireland	1	A5
Dublin Tourism	2	A4
SIGHTS & ACTIVITIES		pp129-31
Anemometer	3	B3
Bandstand	4	B4
Carlisle (Mailboat) Pier	5	B4
Christ the King Sculpture	6	B4
Compass Pointer	7	B4
King George IV Monument	8	A4
Lifeboat Memorial	9	B3
National Yacht Club	10	B4
Royal Irish Yacht Club	11	A4
Royal St George Yacht Club	12	A4
St Michael's (Car Ferry) Pier	13	A4
SLEEPING		p131
Kingston Hotel	14	B5
Rosmeen House	15	B5
Royal Marine Hotel	16	A4
EATING		p131
Brasserie Na Mara	17	A4
Domates	18	B5
Forty Foot	19	A4
Mao Café Bar		(see 19)
Walter's	20	B5
DRINKING		
Dunphy's	21	A4
Weir's	22	A4
SHOPPING		
Dun Laoghaire Shopping Centre	23	A5
Pavilion Complex	24	A4
TRANSPORT		p132
Ferry Terminal		(see 2)

Apr-Oct; by arrangement only Nov-Mar), is where the action begins in James Joyce's epic novel *Ulysses*. The museum was opened in 1962 by Sylvia Beach, the Paris-based publisher who first dared to put *Ulysses* into print, and has photographs, letters, documents, various editions of Joyce's work and two death masks of Joyce on display. Note that it's possible to buy a combination ticket (€10/8/5.50) that also gives you access to the Dublin Writers' Museum, G.B. Shaw House or Malahide Castle.

A string of Martello towers was built around the coast of Ireland between 1804 and 1815 in case of invasion by Napoleon's forces. The granite tower stands 12m high with walls 2.5m thick and was copied from a tower at Cape Mortella in Corsica. Originally, the entrance to the tower led straight into what is now the 'upstairs'. Other tower sites included Dalkey Island, Killiney and Bray, south of Dun Laoghaire; and to the north, Howth and Ireland's Eye, the island off Howth. There are fine views from the tower. To the southeast you can see Dalkey Island with its signal tower and Killiney Hill with its obelisk. Howth Head is visible on the northern side of Dublin Bay. There's another Martello tower not far to the south near Bullock Harbour.

You can get to the tower by a 30-minute walk along the seafront from Dun Laoghaire Harbour, a 15-minute walk from Sandycove & Glasthule DART station or a five-minute walk from Sandycove Ave West, served by bus No 8, which runs from Dublin through Dun Laoghaire.

FORTY FOOT POOL

Below the Martello tower is the **Forty Foot Pool**, an open-air seawater bathing pool that took its name from the army regiment, the Fortieth Foot, that was stationed at the tower until the regiment was disbanded in 1904. At the close of the first chapter of *Ulysses*, Buck Mulligan heads off to the Forty Foot Pool for a morning swim. A morning wake-up here is still a Dun Laoghaire tradition, winter or summer. In fact, a winter dip isn't much braver than a summer one since the water temperature varies by only about 5°C. Basically, it's always bloody cold.

Originally nudist and for men only, pressure from female bathers eventually opened this public stretch of water to both sexes, despite strong opposition from the 'forty foot gentlemen'. They eventually compromised with the ruling that a 'togs must be worn' sign would now apply after 9am. Prior to that time nudity prevails and swimmers are still predominantly 'forty foot gentlemen'.

Activities

A series of walks in the area make up the signposted Dun Laoghaire Way. *The Heritage Map of Dun Laoghaire*, available from the tourist office and from bookshops, includes a map and notes on the seven separate walks.

Scuba divers head for the waters around Dalkey Island. **Ocean Divers** (☎ 280 1083; www.oceandivers.ie; West Pier) offers qualified divers a half-day's dive, full equipment and a boat for €50.

Sleeping

As a major ferry port, Dun Laoghaire has plenty of accommodation, especially B&Bs.

Rosmeen House (☎ 280 7613; 13 Rosmeen Gardens; s/d €45/65) This is the best of the B&Bs on Rosmeen Rd, a lovely Spanish villa with four elegant bedrooms that are supremely comfortable.

Glandore House (☎ 280 3143; www.glandorehouse.com; Glandore Park, Lower Mounttown Rd; s/d €58/116; ⊠) This Gothic house, dating from 1858, was once the residence of Kingstown landlord Lord De Vesci. This extremely comfortable guesthouse feels like a small hotel and has 12 en suite rooms. It's just west of the town centre.

Other B&Bs can be found on nearby Mellifont and Corrig avenues.

Kingston Hotel (☎ 280 1810; reserv@kingstonhotel.com; Adelaide St; s/d/t €100/130/150) A (long overdue) refurbishment has restored this fine hotel to its rightful position as one of Dun Laoghaire's best. The rooms are absolutely gorgeous and, for the money, better value than the town's top dog, the Royal Marine Hotel.

Gresham Royal Marine (☎ 280 1911; Royal Marine Rd; s/d €150/170) Built in 1865, this Victorian pile is easily the best hotel in town. Sea-facing rooms have incredible views of much of Dublin Bay, while the general facilities are top class.

Eating

Forty Foot (☎ 284 2982; Pavillion Complex; mains €14-25) The hip new Forty Foot, which takes its name from the famous bathing area in Sandycove, offers creative modern pasta, fish and meat dishes in a large, stylish lounge overlooking the harbour.

Mao Café Bar (☎ 214 8090; Pavilion Complex; mains €11-16) This upmarket 'fast food' joint as far from the golden arches as you can get. The menu is 'Asian fusion', with European spins on Chinese and Thai dishes, there's a buzzing atmosphere and the service is smart.

Brasserie Na Mara (☎ 280 6787; 1 Harbour Rd; mains from €27) Located in a beautiful airy Georgian room, next to the harbour, Brasserie Na Mara is an elegant choice if it's lavish seafood and slightly prim service you're after.

Domates (☎ 230 0611; 60 Upper George's St; mains €5-13) The delicious waft of spices will greet you as you enter Domates, Dun Laoghaire's brand new Turkish place. Koftes, falafel or the tasty *melemem* (famous Antolian Vegetable stew) are reasonably priced favourites. Vegetarians will do well here.

Walter's (☎ 280 7442; 68 Upper George's St; mains €14-22) This classy bar, with a vaguely nautical theme serves great food such as seared tuna, roast guinea fowl or a delicious Thai shellfish broth. You can also grab a decent soup or sandwich at the bar.

Caviston's Seafood Restaurant (☎ 280 9245; Glasthule Rd, Sandycove; mains €14-23) OK, so it's not strictly Dun Laoghaire but self-respecting crustacean lovers should make the 1km trip to Caviston's for a meal to remember. Local fish and seafood are cooked simply with imaginative ingredients that enhance rather than overpower their flavour.

Getting There & Away

See p674 for details of the ferries between Dun Laoghaire and Holyhead in Wales.

Bus Nos 7, 7A and 8 from next to Trinity College or 46A from the Savoy cinema cost €1.60 one way to Dun Laoghaire. The trip can take anywhere from 25 minutes to one hour depending on the traffic. The DART rail service takes you from Dublin to Dun Laoghaire in 15 to 20 minutes and also costs €1.70 one way.

DALKEY

About 1km south of Sandycove is Dalkey *(Deilginis)*, which has the remains of a number of old castles. On Castle St, the main street, two 16th-century castles face each other: Archibold's Castle and Goat Castle. Next to the latter is the ancient St Begnet's Church, dating from the 9th century. **Bulloch Castle** overlooking Bullock Harbour, north of town, was built by the monks of St Mary's Abbey in Dublin in the 12th century.

Goat Castle and St Begnet's Church have recently been converted into the **Dalkey Castle & Heritage Centre** (☎ 285 8366; Castle St; adult/student/child €4/3.50/2.50; ⏰ 9.30am-5pm Mon-Fri, 11am-5pm Sat & Sun, May-Oct, closed Mon-Fri Nov-Apr). Models, displays and exhibitions form a pretty interesting history of Dalkey and an insight into the area during medieval times.

Dalkey has several holy wells, including **St Begnet's Holy Well** (Dalkey Island) next to the ruins of another church dedicated to St Begnet on the nine-hectare Dalkey Island, a few hundred metres offshore from Coliemore Harbour. Reputed to cure rheumatism, the well is a popular destination for tourists and the faithful alike. To get there, you can rent a boat with a small outboard engine in Coliemore Harbour. To get one, simply show up (you can't book them in advance); they cost around €25 per hour.

To the south there are good views from the small park at Sorrento Point and from Killiney Hill. Dalkey Quarry is a popular site for rock climbers, and originally provided most of the granite for the gigantic piers at Dun Laoghaire Harbour. A number of rocky swimming pools are found along the Dalkey coast.

Dalkey is on the DART suburban train line, or, for a slower journey, you can catch bus No 8 from Burgh Quay in Dublin. Both cost €1.60.

About 1km further south from Dalkey is the affluent seaside suburb of **Killiney** with its wonderful curving sandy beach. It's home to some of Ireland's wealthiest businesspeople and a handful of celebrities – Bono, Enya and filmmaker Neil Jordan included. Though rarely on the market, a five-bedroom house on the ultra-desirable Sorrento Terrace overlooking Killiney Bay, sells for in the region of €5 million.

HOWTH

The bulbous Howth Peninsula forms the northern end of Dublin Bay. Howth (Binn Éadair) town is only 15km from central Dublin and is easily reached by DART train or by simply following the Clontarf Rd out around the northern bay shoreline. En route you pass Clontarf, site of the pivotal clash between Celtic and Viking forces at the Battle of Clontarf in 1014. Further along is North Bull Island, a wildlife sanctuary where many migratory birds pause in winter.

Howth is a popular excursion from Dublin and has developed as a residential suburb. It is a pretty little town built on steep streets running down to the waterfront. Although the harbour's role as a shipping port has long gone, Howth is now a major fishing centre and yachting harbour.

History

Howth's name (which rhymes with 'both') has Viking origins and comes from the Danish word 'hoved' (head). Howth Harbour dates from 1807 to 1809 and was at that time the main Dublin harbour for the packet boats from England. Howth Rd was built to ensure rapid transfer of incoming mail and dispatches from the harbour to the city. The replacement of sailing packets with steam packets in 1818 reduced the transit time from Holyhead to seven hours, but Howth's period of importance was short because, by 1813, the harbour was already showing signs of silting up. It was superseded by Dun Laoghaire in 1833. The most famous arrival to Howth was King George IV, who visited Ireland in 1821 and is chiefly remembered because he staggered off the boat in a highly inebriated state. He did manage to leave his footprint at the point where he stepped ashore on the West Pier.

In 1914 Robert Erskine Childers' yacht, Asgard, brought a cargo of 900 rifles into the port to arm the nationalists. During the Civil War, Childers was courtmartialled by his former comrades and executed by firing squad for illegal possession of a revolver. The Asgard is now on display at Kilmainham Jail in Dublin.

Around the Peninsula

The **Summit** (171m), to the southwest of the town, offers views across Dublin Bay to the Wicklow Mountains. From the Summit you can walk to the top of the Ben of Howth, which has a cairn said to mark a 2000-year-old Celtic royal **grave**. The 1814 **Baily Lighthouse** at the southeastern corner is on the site of an old stone fort and can be reached by a dramatic cliff-top walk. There was an earlier hill-top beacon here in 1670.

Ireland's Eye

A short distance offshore from Howth is **Ireland's Eye**, a rocky sea-bird sanctuary with the ruins of a 6th-century monastery. There's a Martello tower at the northwestern end of the island, where boats from Howth land, while the eastern end plummets into the sea in a spectacularly sheer rock face. As well as the sea birds overhead, you can see young birds on the ground during the nesting season. Seals can also be spotted around the island.

Doyle & Sons (☎ 831 4200) takes boats out to the island from the East Pier of Howth Harbour during the summer, usually on weekend afternoons. The cost is €8 return. Don't wear shorts if you're planning to visit the monastery ruins because they're surrounded by a thicket of stinging nettles. And bring your rubbish back with you – far too many island visitors don't.

Further north from Ireland's Eye is **Lambay Island,** an important sea-bird sanctuary that cannot be visited.

Sleeping

All of the B&Bs listed here are on Howth Hill, above the town. You can walk, but they are all served by bus No 31A from the port. The fare is €0.70.

Inisradharc (☎ 832 2306; Balkill Rd; s/d from €54/70) Inisradharc means 'Island View' and that's just what you get from the three lovely en suite rooms in this modernist 1950s B&B.

Highfield (☎ 832 3936; Thormanby Rd; s/d 40/65) This is a fine Victorian house set back from the road. Its three rooms are beautifully decorated with a mix of antiques and modern comforts.

King Sitric (☎ 832 5235; East Pier; s €89-121, d €126-198) Howth's most famous restaurant has added eight marvellous rooms to its premises right on the port. Each, named after a lighthouse, is extremely well decorated and has wonderful views of the port.

Eating

If you want to buy food and prepare it yourself, Howth has fine seafood that you can buy fresh from the string of **seafood shops** on West Pier.

Aqua (☎ 832 0690; West Pier; mains €24-32) Modern place with its minimalist interior serving variations on traditional seafood dishes. Carnivores also well served.

Abbey Tavern (☎ 839 0307; Abbey St; mains around €24, 3-course dinner €30) They serve better-than-average pub grub, with the emphasis on seafood and meat in this atmospheric 16th-century tavern. There's a bar menu all day.

King Sitric (☎ 832 5235; East Pier; mains €25-55, 5-course dinner €49) This place is rightfully praised for its fine seafood. Try the excellent crab, which is always fresh. The wine list is superb and has won a number of domestic and international awards.

Getting There & Away

The easiest and quickest way to get to Howth from Dublin is on the DART train, which whisks you there in just over 20 minutes for a fare of €1.60. For the same fare, bus Nos 31 and 31A from Lower Abbey St in the city centre run as far as the Summit, 5km to the southeast of Howth.

MALAHIDE

Malahide (Mullach Ide) is 13km north of Dublin on the coast beyond Howth. It has virtually been swallowed by Dublin's northwards expansion, although it still has its own pretty marina. The well kept 101 hectares of the Malahide Demesne, which contains Malahide Castle, is the town's principal attraction. Talbot Botanic Gardens are next to the castle and the extensive Fry Model Railway is in the castle grounds.

Malahide Castle

Despite the vicissitudes of Irish history, the Talbot family managed to keep **Malahide Castle** (☎ 846 2184; Malahide; adult/student/child/family €6/5/3.50/16.50; including the Fry Model Railway €10/8/5.50/28; 🕐 10am-5pm Mon-Sat, 11am-6pm Sun Apr-Oct, 11am-5pm Sat & Sun Nov-Mar) under its control from 1185 to 1976, apart from when Cromwell was in power (1649–60). It's now owned by Dublin County Council. The castle is the usual hotchpotch of additions and renovations. The oldest part is a three-storey, 12th-century tower house. The façade is flanked by circular towers, tacked on in 1765.

The castle is packed with furniture and paintings. Highlights include a 16th-century oak room with decorative carvings and the medieval Great Hall with family portraits, a minstrel's gallery and a painting of the Battle of the Boyne. Puck, the Talbot family ghost, is said to have last appeared in 1975.

The **parkland** (admission free; 🕐 10am-9pm Apr-Oct, 10am-5pm Nov-Mar) around the castle is a good place for a picnic.

Fry Model Railway

Ireland's biggest **model railway** (☎ 846 3779; Malahide Castle; adult/student/child/family €6/5/3.50/16.50, including Malahide Castle €10/8/5.50/28; 🕐 10am-1pm & 2-5pm Mon-Sat, 2-6pm Sun Apr-Sep, 2-5pm Sat, Sun & holidays only rest of year) at 240 sq metres, this model authentically displays much of Ireland's rail and public transport system, including the DART line and Irish Sea ferry services, in O-gauge (32mm track width). A separate room features model trains and other memorabilia. Unfortunately the operators suffer from the over-seriousness of some grown men with complicated toys; rather than let you simply look and admire, they herd you into the control room in groups for demonstrations.

Getting There & Away

Malahide is 13km north of Dublin. Bus No 42 (€1.50) from Talbot St takes about 45 minutes. The DART now stops in Malahide (€2.40), but be sure to get on the right train (it's marked at the front of the train) as the line splits at Howth Junction.

County Wicklow

CONTENTS

Welcome to the Garden of Ireland. County Wicklow's nickname is not simply due to the fact that, at 16km south of Dublin's city centre, the county is the capital's favourite place for weekend play, but mostly because Wicklow (Cill Mhantáin) is where you'll find the richest and most varied greenery anywhere in the country.

Wicklow's most imposing natural feature is its mountains, a gorse-and-bracken spine that cuts through the county from north to south. Here, geology and history have combined to conjure up one of the country's most beautiful landscapes, home to rugged mountaintops, deep wooded valleys, cascading waterfalls, still lakes, magnificent country homes and, at Glendalough, some of the best-preserved early Christian remains in Ireland.

Not surprisingly, Wicklow is a walker's paradise, and the country's most popular trail, the Wicklow Way, is the best way to explore the county. From Marlay Park in south Dublin, the Way runs 132km along disused military supply lines, old bog roads and nature trails over the eastern flanks of the mountains down to Clonegal, County Carlow (for more information see p657).

Away from the mountains, Wicklow offers plenty for those loath to put on sturdy hiking boots. The county is renowned for its beautiful gardens, which are best explored during the Wicklow Gardens Festival in May and June, when many gardens not usually open to the public welcome visitors. Most of Wicklow's main towns lie on the coast, where you'll also find pleasant seaside resorts and some fine beaches.

HIGHLIGHTS

- Visit one of the most evocative and beautifully situated early Christian remains in Ireland – glorious **Glendalough** (p141)
- Capture the true essence of St Kevin's spiritual journey at **Glendalough Cillíns** (p145)
- Explore the county on Ireland's most popular hiking trail, the **Wicklow Way** (p657)
- Immerse yourself in the art and atmosphere of magnificent **Russborough House** (p147)
- Admire the gorgeous Italianate gardens and impressive waterfall at **Powerscourt Estate** (p138)

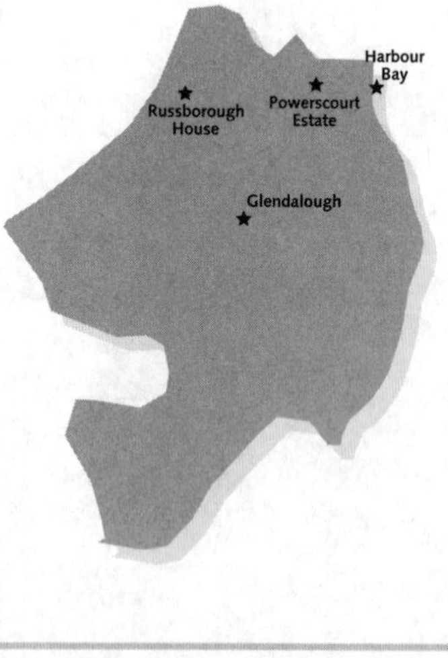

- POPULATION: 114,676
- AREA: 2025 SQ KM

NATIONAL PARKS

Wicklow Mountains National Park covers more than 20,000 hectares of mountainous blanket bogs and woodland. Eventually, virtually all of the higher ground stretching the length of the mountains will fall under the protection of the national park, which will cover over 30,000 hectares.

Within the boundaries of the protected area are two nature reserves, owned and managed by Dúchas, and legally protected by the Wildlife Act. The larger reserve, west of the Glendalough Visitor Centre, conserves the extensive heath and bog of the Glendalough Valley plus the Upper Lake and valley slopes on either side. The second reserve, Glendalough Wood Nature Reserve, conserves oak woods stretching from the Upper Lake as far as the Rathdrum road to the east.

Most of Ireland's native mammal species can be found within the confines of the park. Large herds of deer roam on the open hill areas, though these were introduced in the 20th century after the native red deer population became extinct during the first half of the 18th century. The uplands are the preserve of foxes, badgers and hares. Red squirrels are usually found in the pine woodlands – look out for them around the Upper Lake.

The bird population of the park is plentiful. Birds of prey abound, the most common being peregrine falcons, marlins, kestrels,

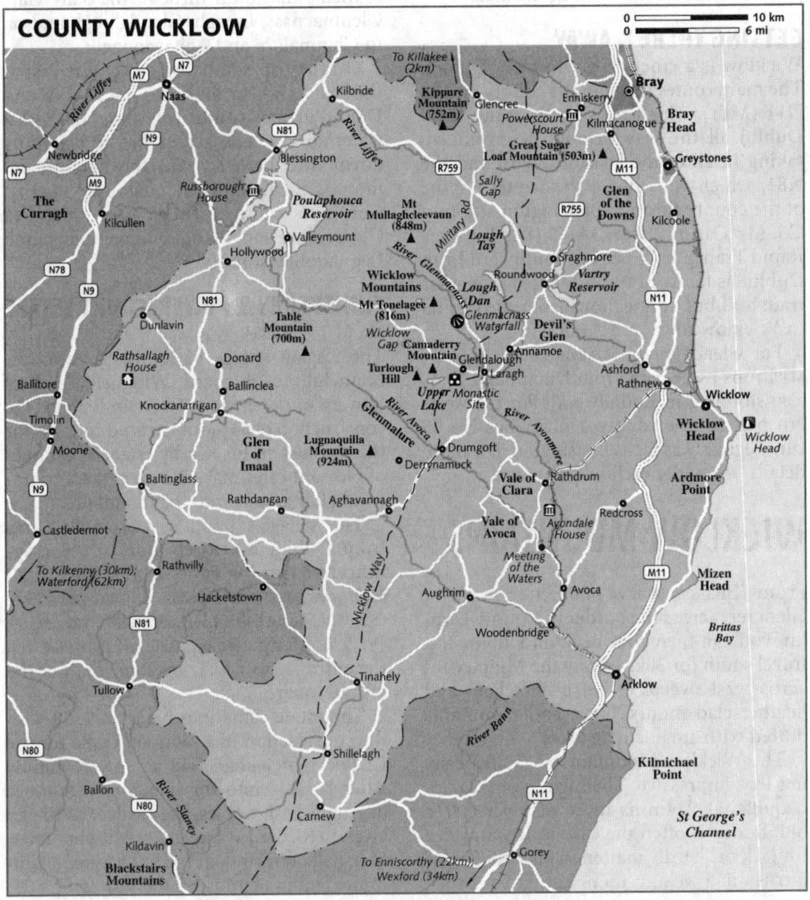

hawks and sparrowhawks. Hen harriers are a rarer sight, though they too live in the park. Moorland birds found in the area include meadow pipits and skylarks. Less common birds such as whinchats, ring ouzels and dippers can be spotted, as can red grouse, whose numbers are quickly disappearing in other parts of Ireland. For information, call in or contact the **Information Point** (☎ 0404-45425; Upper Lake, Glendalough; 🕑 10am-6pm May-Aug, weekends only Apr & Sep, closed rest of year), off the Green Rd that runs by the Upper Lake, about 2km from the Glendalough Visitor Centre. There's usually someone on hand to help, but if you find it closed the staff may be out running guided walks. *Exploring the Glendalough Valley* (Dúchas, €1.50) is a good booklet on the trails in the area.

GETTING THERE & AWAY

Wicklow is a cinch to get to from Dublin. The main routes through the county are the N11 (M11), which runs north–south from Dublin all the way through to Wexford, taking in all of the coastal towns; and the N81, which runs down the western spine of the county through Blessington and into County Carlow. The DART (Dublin Area Rapid Transport) line runs southward from Dublin as far as Bray, and there are regular train and bus connections from the capital to Wicklow town and Arklow.

For Glendalough, **St Kevin's Bus** (☎ 01-281 8119) runs twice daily from Dublin and Bray, also stopping in Roundwood. For the western parts of the county, Dublin Bus No 65 runs regularly as far as Blessington. For more details, see under each relevant section.

WICKLOW MOUNTAINS

From Killakee, a few kilometres north of Glencree, across the border in County Dublin, you can turn your back on Dublin and travel south for 30km along the Military Rd across vast sweeps of gorse-, bracken- and heather-clad moors, bogs, and mountains dotted with small corrie lakes.

The Wicklow Mountains are statistically not that impressive. The highest peak, Lugnaquilla, at 924m, is more of a very large hill, but as is often the case in Ireland, size (or lack of) hardly matters. This vast granite intrusion, a welling-up of hot igneous rock that solidified some 400 million years ago, was shaped during the Ice Ages into the schist-capped mountains visible today. The peaks are marvellously desolate and as raw as only nature can be. Between the mountains are a number of deep glacial valleys, most notably Glenmacnass, Glenmalure and Glendalough, while corrie lakes such as Lough Bray Upper and Lower – gouged out by ice at the head of the glaciers – complete the wild topography.

Beginning on Dublin's southern fringes, the narrow Military Rd winds its way through the remotest parts of the mountains, offering some extraordinary views of the surrounding countryside. The best place to join it is at Glencree (from Enniskerry). It then runs south through the Sally Gap, Glenmacnass, Laragh, Glendalough and on to Glenmalure and Aghavannagh.

On the trip south you can divert east at the Sally Gap to look at Loughs Tay and Dan. Further south you pass the great waterfall at Glenmacnass before dropping down into Laragh, with the magnificent monastic ruins of Glendalough nearby. Continue south through the valley of Glenmalure and, if you're fit enough, climb Lugnaquilla Mountain.

ENNISKERRY & POWERSCOURT ESTATE

☎ 01 / pop 2804

The elegant village of Enniskerry was the brainchild of Richard Wingfield, earl of Powerscourt, who in 1760 commissioned the construction of a row of terraced cottages for the workers on his nearby estate. A number of pleasant cafés make it a great place to unwind after a foray into the mountains.

The village's popularity as a day trip from Dublin is entirely due to the magnificent 64-sq-km **Powerscourt Estate** (☎ 204 6000; www.powerscourt.ie; house & gardens adult/child €8.50/5.10, house only €2.50/1.60, gardens only €6/3.50; 🕑 9.30am-5.30pm Feb-Oct, 9.30am-4.30pm Nov-Jan), the entrance to which is 500m south of the village square.

The estate came into being in 1300 with the construction of a Norman castle for the Le Poer (later anglicised as Power) family. After passing into the hands of a number of Anglo-Irish nobles, the castle was finally given to Richard Wingfield, newly appointed Marshall of Ireland, in 1603. It was to remain in the family's hands for the next 350 years.

In 1731 the German-born architect Richard Cassels (aka Castle) was commissioned to build a Palladian-style mansion around the core of the old castle. He completed his work in 1743, but an extra storey was added in 1787 and other alterations were made in the 19th century. The Wingfields left the house in the 1950s, after which it underwent extensive restorations; however, the day before it was to open to the public in 1974, a fire gutted the whole building. Today it is owned by the Slazenger family, but except for a small exhibition room and a cafeteria, the house remains off-limits to the public as the painstaking process of restoration continues.

Visitors need not despair, however, as the 20-hectare formal gardens are more than splendid enough to keep you occupied. Originally laid out in the 1740s, they were redesigned in the 19th century by Daniel Robinson, who had as much a fondness for the booze as he did for horticultural pursuits. Perhaps this influenced his largely informal style, which resulted in a magnificent blend of landscaped gardens, sweeping terraces, statuary, ornamental lakes, secret hollows, rambling walks and walled enclosures replete with over 200 types of trees and shrubs, all beneath the stunning natural backdrop of the Great Sugarloaf Mountain to the southeast. Tickets come with a map laying out 40-minute and hour-long tours of the gardens. Don't miss the exquisite Japanese Gardens or the Pepperpot Tower, modelled on a three-inch actual pepperpot owned by Lady Wingfield. Our own favourite, however, is the animal cemetery, final resting place of the Wingfield pets and even some of their favourite milking cows. Some of the epitaphs are astonishingly personal.

A 7km walk to a separate part of the estate takes you to the 130m **Powerscourt Waterfall** (☎ 204 6000; adult/child €4/3; ⌚ 9.30am-7pm, to dusk Oct-Jan). It's the highest waterfall in Britain and Ireland, and is most impressive after heavy rain. You can also get to the falls by road, following the signs from the estate. A nature trail has been laid out around the base of the waterfall, taking you past giant redwoods, ancient oaks, beech, birch and rowan trees. There are plenty of birds in the vicinity, including the chaffinch, cuckoo, chiffchaff, raven and willow warbler.

Sleeping

Lacken House Hostel (☎ 286 4036, 830 4555 for bookings; www.irelandyha.org; Knockree, Enniskerry; dm €11) The 58 beds are housed in an 18th-century farmhouse that is fairly spartan, but it's clean, comfortable and beautifully situated with wonderful views over Glencree. It's about 7km west of town and accommodation can be booked only through the An Óige head office in Dublin.

Corner House (☎ 286 0149; Main St; s/d €38/58; Ⓟ) This 200-year-old place in Enniskerry has three large doubles, and although none has an en suite (there are two bathrooms), each room has its own shower.

Powerscourt Arms (☎ 282 8903; fax 286 4909; Main St; s/d €50/90 with breakfast; Ⓟ) This busy hotel in Enniskerry village, facing the square, has 12 modern rooms. What they lack in traditional charm they more than make up for in comfort.

Summerhill House Hotel (☎ 286 7928; www.summerhillhousehotel.com; s/d €90/140; Ⓟ) Enniskerry's best hotel, about 700m south of town along the N11, is a fabulous country mansion set amid its own grounds. The rooms are exquisitely decorated and the breakfast (included in the price) is top-notch.

Eating

Buttercups (☎ 286 9669; snacks from €4.50; ⌚ 8am-8.30pm) Up the hill past the post office, this small deli and bread shop serves delicious takeaway food.

Powerscourt Terrace Café (☎ 204 6070; Powerscourt House; mains €8-12; ⌚ 10am-5pm) A cut above the usual café you find in a tourist attraction, this place serves good food (the quiche is lovely) in a marvellous setting, overlooking the terraced gardens of the Powerscourt Estate.

Poppies Country Cooking (☎ 282 8869; the Square; lunch €14; ⌚ 8.30am-6pm) On the main square, this is the best place to eat in Enniskerry. It offers solid lunches (including several vegetarian options) and great cakes in a rustic atmosphere.

Johnnie Fox's (☎ 295 5647; Glencullen; mains €12-17; ⌚ noon-10pm) Famous throughout the area for its excellent seafood and nightly trad music sessions, Johnnie Fox's draws in the tourists in their hundreds. Such popularity has rendered the atmosphere somewhat artificial, but there's nothing fake about the food and it's a lot of fun. The pub is 3km northwest of Enniskerry in Glencullen.

Wingfield's Bistro (☎ 204 2854; Church Hill; mains €15-22; 🕑 7-9pm Mon-Sat, 1-7.30pm Sun) This excellent restaurant has earned a reputation as one of the best in the area; the Wicklow rack of lamb comes highly recommended. All the breads are home-made and the service is relaxed and unpretentious.

Tours

Aran Tours (☎ 280 1899; www.wildcoachtours.com; adult/child €20/16) is a popular half-day tour to Powerscourt, and the price includes admission to the gardens and waterfall. There are several pick-up points throughout Dublin; check when booking for the one nearest you. It departs at 1.30pm and returns at 6pm.

Mary Gibbons Tours (☎ 283 9973; €35) has wonderful and insightful full-day tours of Powerscourt and Glendalough run by expert guides with an in-depth knowledge of their subject matter. They leave from the Dublin Tourism Centre at 2 Suffolk St at 10.15am, returning 4.30pm (see p75).

Getting There & Away

Enniskerry is 18km south of Dublin, just 3km west of the M11 along the R117. **Dublin Bus** (☎ 872 0000, 873 4222) No 44 (€1.65, every 20 minutes) takes about 1¼ hours to get to Enniskerry from Hawkins St in Dublin. Alternatively, you can take the Dart train to Bray (€1.70) and catch bus No 185 (€1.35, hourly) from the station.

Getting to Powerscourt House under your own steam is not a problem (it's 500m from the town), but getting to the waterfall is tricky. **Alpine Coaches** (☎ 286 2547) runs a shuttle service between the Dart station in Bray, the waterfall (€5 return) and the house (€3.60). From the station, there are pick-ups at 11.05am, 11.30am, 12.30pm and 1.30pm, July to August (11.05am, 12.30pm, 1.30pm and 3.30pm rest of the year). The last departure from Powerscourt House is at 5.30pm.

GLENCREE

☎ 01

Just south of the border with County Dublin and 10km west of Enniskerry is Glencree, a leafy hamlet set into the side of the valley of the same name, which opens east to give a magnificent view down to Great Sugar Loaf Mountain and the sea.

The valley floor is home to the Glencree Oak Project, an ambitious plan to reforest part of Glencree with the native oak vegetation, mostly broadleaf trees, that once covered most of the country but now covers only 1% of Ireland's landmass.

The village, such as it is, has a tiny shop and a hostel but no pub. There's a poignant **German cemetery** dedicated to 134 servicemen who died in Ireland during WWI and WWII. Just south of the village, the former military barracks are now a retreat house and reconciliation centre for people of different religions from the Republic and the North.

Sleeping

Stone House (☎ 286 4037; www.irelandyha.org; Knockree; dm €11; 🕑 8-10am & 5-10pm) Located in a lovely old stone house, this An Óige hostel is clean and neat, if a little bare. There are fabulous views of the surrounding countryside. It is very popular with walkers in summer, so be sure to book ahead.

SALLY GAP

The Sally Gap is one of the two main east–west passes across the Wicklow Mountains. From the turn-off on the lower road (R755) between Roundwood and Kilmacanogue near Bray, the narrow road (R759) passes above the dark waters of Loughs Tay and Dan and the Luggala Estate. It then heads up to the Sally Gap crossroads, where it cuts across the Military Rd and heads northwest for Kilbride and the N81, following the young River Liffey, still only a stream. Just north of the Sally Gap crossroads is Kippure Mountain (752m) with its TV transmitter. The surrounding bogs have dark lines cut into them by turfcutters.

ROUNDWOOD

☎ 01 / pop 440

At 238m above sea level, Roundwood is widely touted as Ireland's highest village, but you'd hardly notice. The village is essentially one long main street, which leads south to Glendalough and southern Wicklow. Turn-offs lead to Ashford to the east and the southern shore of Lough Dan to the west. Unfortunately, almost all Lough Dan's southern shoreline is private property and you can't get to the lake on this side. To the north is the turn-off to Bray.

Roundwood's pubs are usually packed with tired walkers on weekend afternoons. There are shops and a post office, and a

CONOR CAFFREY

St Patrick's Day Festival (p103), Dublin

RICHARD CUMMINS

Oscar Wilde statue (p90), Dublin

Long Room (p77), Trinity College, Dublin

HANNAH LEVY

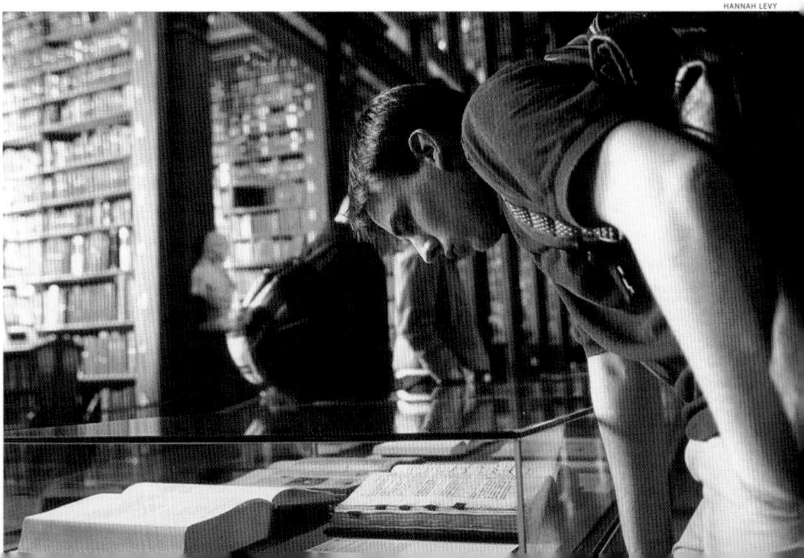

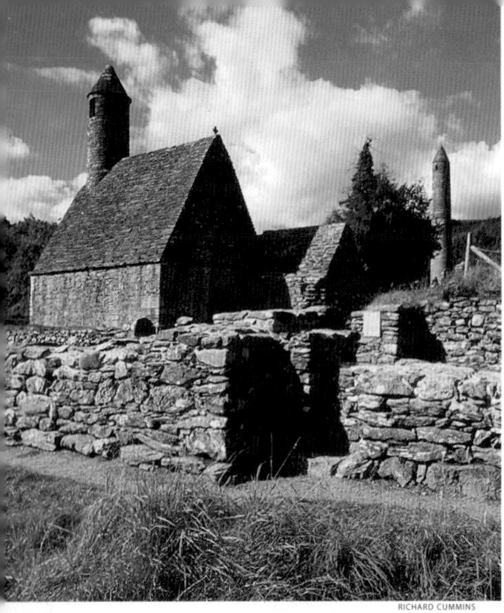

RICHARD CUMMINS

St Kevin's Kitchen (p143), Glendalough

EMMA MILL

Walking sign, **Wicklow Way** (p657)

Powerscourt Estate (p138), Enniskerry

GREG GAWLOWS

thriving market is held every Sunday afternoon, March to December, in the small hall on Main St. What the town doesn't have, however, is a bank or ATM; the nearest ATM is at the petrol station in Kilmacanogue, at the junction of the M11 and the R755. Glendalough, south of Roundwood, doesn't have ATMs either.

Northwest of the village you'll find some of the county's best scenery on the road to the Sally Gap, with a tremendous panorama over Lough Tay and the Luggala Estate.

Wicklow Web Centre (☎ 201 2988; Main St; €2/30min; 🕑 10am-6pm Mon-Sat) offers Internet access.

Sleeping & Eating

Roundwood Caravan & Camping Park (☎ 281 8163; dicksonn@indigo.ie; camp site €8-13; 🕑 Easter-Sep) Within 500m of the village, this place has top-notch facilities, including a daily bus to and from Dublin and Glendalough.

Ballinacor House (☎ 281 8168; ballinacor@eircom.net; s/d €25/50; 🕑 May-Sep) This is one of the friendliest and most comfortable B&Bs in the whole area, a place where guests are treated like friends of the family. It is popular with walkers and has fabulous views of the surrounding countryside. It is a couple of kilometres out of town on the road to Laragh.

Tochar House (☎ 281 8247; dm/s/d €20/35/65) In the middle of Main St, the house has fairly comfy rooms, even though they could use a makeover. The separate dorm – which is extremely popular with walkers and cyclists – has a bathroom, shower, and tea and coffee facilities, but is not available to single travellers, only to groups of two or more. It is directly behind the pub, so there's plenty of noise at weekends.

Roundwood Inn (☎ 281 8107; Main St; mains €16, bar food €8-11; 🕑 bar noon-9pm, restaurant 7.30-9.30pm Fri & Sat, 1-3pm Sun) This 17th-century German-owned house has a gorgeous bar with a snug and an open fire, in front of which you can sample bar food with a difference: on the menu are dishes like Hungarian goulash and Irish stew with a German twist. The more formal restaurant is the best in town, and has earned deserved praise for its hearty, delicious cuisine. The menu favours meat dishes, including season game, Wicklow rack of lamb, and a particularly good roast suckling pig. Reservations are required.

Getting There & Away

St Kevin's Bus (☎ 281 8119) passes through Roundwood (one way/return €7/12, 1¼ hours) on its twice-daily jaunt between Dublin and Glendalough; see p145 for more details.

GLENMACNASS

The most desolate section of the Military Rd runs through wild bogland between the Sally Gap crossroads and Laragh. Until you reach the top of Glenmacnass Valley, not a single building breaks the sense of isolation.

The highest mountain to the west is Mt Mullaghcleevaun (848m), and River Glenmacnass flows south and tumbles over the edge of the mountain plateau in a great foaming cascade. There's a car park near the top of the waterfall. Be careful when walking on rocks near **Glenmacnass Waterfall** as a few people have slipped to their deaths. There are fine walks up Mt Mullaghcleevaun or in the hills to the east of the car park.

WICKLOW GAP

Between Mt Tonelagee (816m) to the north and Table Mountain (700m) to the southwest, the Wicklow Gap is the second major pass over the mountains. The eastern end of the road begins just to the north of Glendalough and climbs through some lovely scenery northwestwards up along the Glendassan Valley. It passes the remains of some old lead and zinc workings before meeting a side road that leads south and up Turlough Hill, the location of Ireland's only pumped storage power station. You can walk up the hill for a look over the Upper Lake.

GLENDALOUGH

☎ 0404 / pop 278

Glendalough (Gleann dá Loch, 'Valley of the Two Lakes') is a magical place – an ancient monastic settlement tucked beside two dark lakes and overshadowed by the sheer walls of a deep valley. It's one of the most picturesque settings in Ireland and is the site of one of the most significant ancient monastic settlements in the country.

Huge popularity is the price of such beauty. Visit early or late in the day – or out of season – to avoid the coach-tour crowds and atmosphere-shattering school parties. Remember that a visit here is all about walking, so wear comfortable shoes.

History

In 498 a priest named Kevin arrived in the valley and set up home in what had been a Bronze Age tomb on the southern side of the Upper Lake. For seven years he slept on stones, wore animal skins, ate sparingly and had only birds and animals as companions. Word soon spread of Kevin's natural lifestyle, and he began attracting disciples unaware of the irony that they were flocking to hang out with a hermit who wanted to live as far from other people as possible.

Kevin's preferred isolationism notwithstanding, a settlement quickly grew and by the 9th century Glendalough rivalled Clonmacnoise (see p331) as Ireland's premier monastic city: thousands of students studied and lived in a thriving community that was spread over a considerable area. Inevitably, Glendalough's success made it a key target of Viking raiders, who sacked the monastery at least four times between 775 and 1071. The final blow came in 1398, when English forces from Dublin almost completely destroyed it. Efforts were made to rebuild and some life lingered on here as late as the 17th century, when, under renewed repression, the monastery finally died.

Orientation & Information

At the valley entrance, before the Glendalough Hotel, is **Glendalough Visitor Centre** (☎ 45325, 45352; adult/child & student €2.70/1.25; 🕐 9am-5.15pm Jun-Aug, 9.30am-5.15pm Sep–mid-Oct & mid-Mar–May, 9.30am-4.15pm mid-Oct–mid-Mar). It has a high-quality 20-minute audiovisual presentation on the Irish monasteries.

Coming from Laragh you first see the visitor centre, then the Glendalough Hotel, which is beside the entrance to the main group of ruins and the round tower. The Lower Lake is a small dark lake to the west, while further west up the valley is the much bigger and more impressive Upper Lake, with a large car park and more ruins nearby. Be sure to visit the Upper Lake and take one of the surrounding walks.

A model in the visitor centre should help you fix where everything is in relation to everything else.

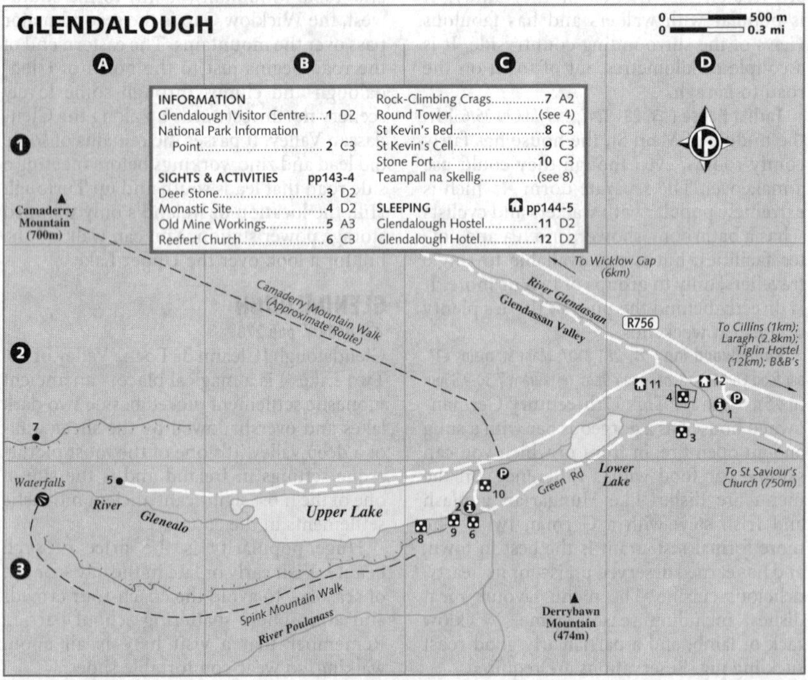

Sights

UPPER LAKE

The original site of St Kevin's settlement, **Teampall na Skellig**, is at the base of the cliffs towering over the southern side of the Upper Lake and accessible only by boat; unfortunately, there's no boat service to the site and you'll have to settle for looking at it across the lake. The terraced shelf has the reconstructed ruins of a church and early graveyard. Rough wattle huts once stood on the raised ground nearby. Scattered around are some early grave slabs and simple stone crosses.

Just east of here and 10m above the lake waters is the 2m-deep artificial cave called **St Kevin's Bed,** said to be where Kevin lived. The earliest human habitation of the cave was long before St Kevin's era – there's evidence that people lived in the valley for thousands of years before the monks arrived. In the green area just south of the car park is a large circular wall thought to be the remains of an early Christian *caher* or stone fort.

Follow the lakeshore path southwest of the car park until you come to the considerable remains of **Reefert Church** above the tiny River Poulanass. It's a small, plain, 11th-century Romanesque nave-and-chancel church with some reassembled arches and walls. Traditionally, Reefert (literally 'Royal Burial Place') was the burial site of the chiefs of the local O'Toole family. The surrounding graveyard contains a number of rough stone crosses and slabs, most made of shiny mica schist.

Climb the steps at the back of the churchyard and follow the path to the west and you'll find, at the top of a rise overlooking the lake, the scant remains of **St Kevin's Cell,** a small beehive hut.

LOWER LAKE

While the Upper Lake has the best scenery, the most fascinating buildings lie in the lower part of the valley east of the Lower Lake.

Just round the bend from the Glendalough Hotel is the stone arch of the **monastery gatehouse**, the only surviving example of a monastic entranceway in the country. Just inside the entrance is a large slab with an incised cross.

Beyond that lies a **graveyard**, which is still in use. The 10th-century **round tower** is 33m tall and 16m in circumference at the base. The upper storeys and conical roof were reconstructed in 1876. Near the tower, to the southeast, is the **Cathedral of St Peter and St Paul,** with a 10th-century nave. The chancel and sacristy date from the 12th century.

At the centre of the graveyard to the south of the round tower is the **Priest's House.** This odd building dates from 1170 but has been heavily reconstructed. It may have been the location of shrines of St Kevin. Later, during penal times, it became a burial site for local priests – hence the name. The 10th-century **St Mary's Church,** 140m southwest of the round tower, probably originally stood outside the walls of the monastery and belonged to local nuns. It has a lovely western doorway. A little to the east are the scant remains of **St Kieran's Church,** the smallest at Glendalough.

Glendalough's trademark is **St Kevin's Kitchen** or Church at the southern edge of the enclosure. This church, with a miniature round-tower-like belfry, protruding sacristy and steep stone roof, is a masterpiece. How it came to be known as a kitchen is a mystery as there's no indication that it was anything other than a church. The oldest parts of the building date from the 11th century – the structure has been remodelled since but it's still a classic early Irish church.

At the junction with Green Rd as you cross the river just south of these two churches is the **Deer Stone** in the middle of a group of rocks. Legend claims that, when St Kevin needed milk for two orphaned babies, a doe stood here waiting to be milked. The stone is actually a *bullaun* (a stone used as a mortar for grinding medicines or food). Many such stones are thought to be prehistoric and they were widely regarded as having supernatural properties: women who bathed their faces with water from the hollow were supposed to keep their looks forever. The early churchmen brought the stones into their monasteries, perhaps hoping to inherit some of the their powers.

The road east leads to **St Saviour's Church,** with its detailed Romanesque carvings. To the west, a nice woodland trail leads up the valley past the Lower Lake to the Upper Lake.

Activities

The easiest and most popular walk is the gentle hike along the northern shore of the Upper Lake to the lead and zinc mine workings, which date from 1800. The better route is along the lakeshore rather than on the road (which runs 30m in from the shore), a distance of about 2.5km, one way, from the Glendalough Visitor Centre. Continue on up the head of the valley if you wish.

Alternatively, you can walk up **Spink Mountain**, the steep ridge with vertical cliffs running along the southern flanks of the Upper Lake. You can go part of the way and turn back, or complete a circuit of the Upper Lake by following the top of the cliff, eventually coming down by the mine workings and going back along the northern shore. The circuit is about 6km long and takes about three hours.

The third option is a hike up Camaderry Mountain (700m), hidden behind the hills that flank the northern side of the valley. The walk starts on the road just 50m back towards Glendalough from the entrance to the Upper Lake car park. Head straight up the steep hill to the north and you come out on open mountains with sweeping views in all directions. You can then continue up Camaderry to the northwest or just follow the ridge west looking over the Upper Lake. To the top of Camaderry and back is about 7.5km and takes about four hours.

If you intend to go on a serious hike, make sure you take all the usual precautions, have the right equipment, tell someone where you're going and when you should be back. For Mountain Rescue call ☎ 999. For more detailed information on walking in the area, check *Hill Walker's Wicklow, New Irish Walk Guides: East* and *New Irish Walk Guides: South East*, all by David Herman. For walking partners check at the hostels or go on an organised walk with the **National Park Information Point** (☎ 45425) or the National Outdoor Training Centre (see following).

At the western end of the valley beyond Upper Lake and the mine workings are a couple of large crags popular with rock climbers. The Mountaineering Council of Ireland publishes a guide to the routes, which is available from **Joss Lynam** (☎ 01-288 4672).

National Outdoor Training Centre (☎ 40169; www.tiglin.com; Tiglin, Ashford; weekend courses €180-190; 🕑 9am-5pm Mon-Fri, 9am-1pm Sat), directly across from the Tiglin Hostel (see below) runs courses in outdoor pursuits like hill walking, mountaineering, rock climbing, canoeing and kayaking. Most courses are run during a weekend and all prices include accommodation, food, gear rental, in-course transportation and training. It's a terrific place, run by enthusiastic and knowledgeable instructors who are all experts in their chosen field.

Tours

The **Bus Éireann** (☎ 01-836 6111; www.buseireann.ie) Glendalough & Wicklow Panorama tour has plenty of takers, and while the guides are generally pretty good, they can often lack the personal touch that other companies make their selling point. It costs €30/19.50 per adult/child April to October, €25/16.25 November to March. Tours depart 10.30am and return 5.45pm April to October (10.30am and 4.30pm Wednesday and Sunday only, November to March).

Aran Tours (☎ 01-280 1899; www.wildcoachtours.com; adult/child €28/25; departs 9.30am & returns 5.30pm) Wild Wicklow Tour, which also includes a short Dublin City tour and a visit to Avoca and the Sally Gap, never fails to generate rave reviews for atmosphere and all-round fun, but so much craic has made a casualty of informative depth. It has a variety of pick-up points throughout Dublin; check the point nearest you when booking.

Irish Rover Tours (Tir na nÓg Tours ☎ 01-836 4684, 1800 226 242; www.tirnanogtours.com; 57 Lower Gardiner St, Dublin) has full-day tours of Wicklow including Glendalough, the Sally Gap, Lough Tay, Laragh, Rathdrum and Avoca. Tours cost €25/20 per adult/child and depart at 9am from Gardiner St and 9.30am from Dublin Tourism Centre Tuesday and from Thursday to Sunday.

Mary Gibbons Tours (☎ 283 9973) runs the most in-depth and informative tour to Glendalough and includes Powerscourt.

Sleeping

BUDGET

There are a couple of hostels in the area.

Glendalough Hostel (☎ 45342; www.irelandyha.org; the Lodge; dm €20.50 Jun-Oct, €18 Nov-May) Conveniently, this modern hostel is near the round tower, set amid the deeply wooded glacial area that makes up the Glendalough Valley.

Tiglin Hostel (☎ 49049, 01-830 1766 for bookings; www.irelandyha.org; Devil's Glen State Forest, Tiglin, Ashford; dm €13; 🕑 7-10am & 5-11pm) About 10km northeast of Laragh via Annamoe, this 50-bed An Óige hostel was built in 1870. It was originally a farmhouse frequented by the

SOMETHING SPECIAL

Glendalough Cillíns (☎ 45140, for bookings 45777, St Kevin's Parish Church, Glendalough; r €35) In 2001, in an effort to re-create something of the contemplative spirit of Kevin's early years in the valley, St Kevin's Parish Church opened six hermitages, or *cillíns*, for folks looking to take time out from the bustle of daily life and reflect on more spiritual matters. In keeping with more modern needs, however, there are a few more facilities than were present in Kevin's cave. Each hermitage is a bungalow consisting of a bedroom, a bathroom, a small kitchen area and an open fire supplemented by a storage heating facility. The whole venture is managed by the local parish, and while there is a strong spiritual emphasis here, it is not necessarily a Catholic one. Visitors of all denominations and creeds are welcome, so long as their intentions are reflective and meditative; backpackers looking for a cheap place to bed down are not. The hermitages are in a field next to St Kevin's Parish Church, about 1km east of Glendalough on the R756 to Laragh.

playwright JM Synge. You can book only through the An Óige head office in Dublin.

MID-RANGE

Most B&Bs are in or around Laragh, a village 3km east of Glendalough, or on the way there from Glendalough.

Valeview (☎/fax 45292; lisa.mc@oceanfree.net; Laragh; s/d €30/50; P ⊠) Just opposite Trinity Church, Valeview has beautifully maintained rooms, great views of the valley and serves a terrific breakfast.

Glendale (☎ 45410; www.glendale-glendaloug.com; Laragh East; s/d €40/60, cottage €240-580 per week; P) This is an immaculately modern and tidy B&B with large, comfortable rooms. Also available are five brand-new self-catering cottages that sleep six. Every cottage has all mod cons, from TV and video to a fully equipped kitchen complete with microwave, dishwasher and washer-dryer. The owners will also drop you off in Glendalough if you don't fancy the walk.

Laragh Mountain View Lodge (☎ 45282; fax 45204; Glenmacnass; s/d €35/70; P) It praises itself as 'heaven on earth', which it isn't, but it's a pretty nice place nevertheless. The house itself is a modern bungalow with comfortable, tidy rooms, but what makes this place worth checking out is the location, in the middle of gorgeous nowhere. It's about two miles north of Laragh, on the R115 to Glenmacnass.

Glendalough Hotel (☎ 45135; www.glendaloughhotel.com; s/d €97/150; P) Glendalough's best hotel is conveniently right next to the ruins, which ensures that there's no shortage of takers of its 44 luxurious bedrooms.

Eating

Laragh's the place for a bit of grub, as there's only one sit-down spot in Glendalough.

Wicklow Heather Restaurant (☎ 45157; Main St, Laragh; mains €12-15; 🕒 noon-8.30pm) This is about the best place for anything substantial. The trout (farmed locally) is excellent. During summer, villagers put out signs and serve tea and scones on the village green.

Lynham's of Laragh (☎ 45345; Laragh; mains €12-16; 🕒 noon-7pm) This hotel restaurant serves large portions of the standard hotel restaurant fare: chicken and chips, fish in batter, and lamb. It's nothing spectacular, but you won't go away feeling that you haven't eaten enough.

Glendalough Hotel (☎ 45135; 3-course lunch €19; 🕒 noon-6pm) The hotel's enormous restaurant serves a very good lunch. There's also a limited bar menu.

Getting There & Away

St Kevin's Bus (☎ 01-281 8119) runs to Glendalough (one way/return €9/15, 1½ hours) from outside the Royal College of Surgeons, St Stephen's Green West, Dublin, at 11.30am and 6pm Monday to Saturday (11.30am and 7pm on Sunday) year-round. From Glendalough, the service to Dublin runs at 7.15am and 4.15pm Monday to Friday, and 9.45am and 4.15pm Saturday and Sunday.

GLENMALURE

Deep in the mountains, near the southern end of the Military Rd, is Glenmalure, a sombre and majestic blind valley overlooked on its western side by Lugnaquilla Mountain and flanked farther up by classic scree slopes of loose boulders. After coming over the mountains into Glenmalure you turn northwest at the Drumgoft bridge. From there it's about 6km up the road beside the River Avonbeg to a car park where trails lead off in various directions.

For a long time, Glenmalure was a stronghold of clan resistance to the English. The most famous clan leader was Fiach MacHugh O'Byrne, who in 1580 defeated an army of 1000 English soldiers; over 800 men died in the battle and English control over Ireland was set back for decades. Fiach was captured in 1597 and his head impaled on the gates of Dublin Castle.

Sights & Activities

Near Drumgoft is Dwyer's or **Cullen's Rock**, which commemorates both the Glenmalure battle and Michael Dwyer, a 1798 Rising rebel who holed up here. Men were hanged from the rock during the Rising.

You can walk up Lugnaquilla Mountain or head up the blind Fraughan Rock Glen east of the car park. Alternatively, you can go straight up Glenmalure Valley passing the small, seasonal An Óige Glenmalure Hostel, after which the trail divides – heading northeast, the trail takes you over the hills to Glendalough, while going northwest brings you into the Glen of Imaal (p148).

The head of Glenmalure and parts of the neighbouring Glen of Imaal are off-limits – it's military land, well posted with warning signs.

Sleeping

These hostels make good bases for walking up Lugnaquilla.

Glenmalure Hostel (☎ 01-830 4555; www.irelandyha.org; Glenmalure, Greenane; dm €19; ⏰ Jun-Aug, Fri & Sat only Sep-May; ☒) No phone, no electricity (lighting is by gas), just a rustic two-storey cottage with 19 beds and running water, this place has a couple of heavyweight literary links: it was once owned by WB Yeats' *femme fatale*, Maud Gonne, and was also the setting for JM Synge's play, *Shadow of a Gunman*. It's an isolated place, but it is beautifully situated beneath Lugnaquilla.

Aghavannagh House (☎ 0402-36366; www.irelandyha.org; Aghavannagh) Formerly a military barracks built at the time of the 1798 Rising to defend the area from pesky partisans, it subsequently became a shooting lodge (used by Charles Stewart Parnell) before eventually being converted into a hostel. Structural wear and tear has resulted in the hostel's temporary closure, but we're assured that it will reopen in the summer of 2004; call the **An Óige head office** (☎ 01-830 4555) for details.

WESTERN WICKLOW

As you move further west into the county the landscape softens considerably, as the western slopes of the mountains were less deeply glaciated than the eastern ones. Here, on the border with Counties Carlow and Kildare, the wild terrain gives way to rich pastures; east of Blessington the countryside is dotted with private stud farms where some of the world's most expensive horses are trained in jealously guarded secrecy. It's not all gentle farmland, however. From the Sally Gap crossroads to Kilbride you pass the upper reaches of the River Liffey and some lovely wild scenery, while further south is the scenic Glen of Imaal.

Nature aside, most visitors to western Wicklow come to amble about Russborough House and the Poulaphouca Reservoir, also known as Blessington Lakes.

BLESSINGTON

☎ 045 / pop 3147

Little more than one long street lined with pubs, shops and 17th- and 18th-century town houses, there's not much to do in Blessington, but it does make a good base for exploring the surrounding area. The town is near the shores of the Poulaphouca Reservoir, created in 1940 to drive the turbines of the local power station to the east of town and to supply Dublin with water.

The **tourist office** (☎ 865 850; Blessington Craft Centre, Main St; ⏰ 10am-5pm Mon-Fri) is across the road from the Downshire House Hotel.

Sleeping & Eating

Baltyboys Hostel (☎ 867 266; www.irelandyha.org; Baltyboys, Blessington; dm €13; ⏰ Mar-Nov & weekends Dec-Feb) This converted schoolhouse overlooking Blessington Lakes has 18 bunks and not much else. If you're into fishing, you're in luck: the nearby lakes are jumping with finny creatures. The hostel is 5km from Blessington, but two buses daily (Dublin Bus No 65, departing Dublin at 6.05am and 5.40pm) stop directly in front of the hostel; otherwise you'll have to walk from Blessington. Take the road south to Poulaphouca and turn east at Burgage Cross towards Valleymount.

Haylands House (☎ 865 183; haylands@eircom.net; Dublin Rd; s/d €40/60) We highly recommend this comfortable B&B for its lovely rooms (all with en suite), warm welcome and excellent breakfast. It's only 500m out of town on the main Dublin road. As it's popular, book early if you can.

Downshire House Hotel (☎ 865 199; www.downshirehouse.com; Main St; s/d €84.50/150) Blessington's most prominent landmark is this family-run hotel, which has 25 simply furnished, tidy rooms.

Rathsallagh House & Country Club (☎ 403 112; www.rathsallaghhousehotel.com; Dunlavin; s/d €175/250, 5-course meal €60) Twenty kilometres south of Blessington, this fabulous country manor, converted from Queen Anne stables in 1798, is more than just a fancy hotel. Luxury is par for the course here – from the splendidly appointed rooms to the exquisite country house dining (the food here is some of the best you'll eat anywhere in Ireland) and the marvellous golf course that surrounds the estate. Even the breakfast is extraordinary: it has won the National Breakfast Award three times (is there anything Irish tourism doesn't have an award for?).

Old Schoolhouse (☎ 891 420; Old Kilbride Rd; lunch mains €8-10, dinner mains €13-18; 🕑 noon-10pm Tue-Sat, noon-9pm Sun) This good Italian restaurant just off Main St has a fairly standard lunch menu of salads and pizzas, but dinner offers a far more interesting choice of dishes, from pasta to grills.

Activities

Rathsallagh Golf Club (☎ 403 316; green fees hotel guest/visitor €50/60; 🕑 for nonhotel guests Mon-Thu only) is one of the best parkland courses in Ireland, stretching over 7200yd amid mature trees, small lakes and shallow streams.

Blessington Sports Centre (☎ 865 092; www.blessingtonsports.com; Burgage; 🕑 10am-6pm) is an outdoor adventure centre that runs a variety of activities on and around Blessington Lakes, from kayaking (adult/child €16/11 per hour) to orienteering (adult/child €10/6 per hour). All equipment and instruction is included in the rate.

Getting There & Away

Blessington is 35km southwest of Dublin on the N81. There are regular daily services by **Dublin Bus** (☎ 01-872 0000, 873 4222) No 65 from Eden Quay in Dublin (€3.20, 1½ hours, every 1½ hours). **Bus Éireann** (☎ 01-836 6111) express bus No 005 to and from Waterford stops in Blessington two or three times daily; from Dublin it's pick-up only, from Waterford drop-off only.

RUSSBOROUGH HOUSE

About 5km southwest of Blessington is one of Ireland's finest stately homes, built for Joseph Leeson (1705–83), later the first earl of Milltown and later still, Lord Russborough.

Built between 1741 and 1751, Russborough House is a magnificent **Palladian villa** (☎ 865 239; Blessington; adult/child/student €6/3/4.50; 🕑 10am-5pm Apr-Sep, 10.30am-5.30pm Sun & bank hols Oct, closed rest of year). It was designed by Richard Cassels, at the height of his fame and ability (although he did not live to see it completed), with the help of another Irish architect, Francis Bindon.

The house was taken by Irish forces during the 1798 Rising and then by government forces, who left only in 1801 after a furious Lord Russborough challenged the commander of the British forces, Lord Tyrawley, to a duel 'with blunderbusses and slugs in a sawpit'.

The house remained in Leeson family hands until 1931. In 1952 it was sold to Sir Alfred Beit, the eponymous nephew of the cofounder of the de Beers diamond mining company. Uncle Alfred was an obsessive art collector, and when he died his impressive haul – which includes works by Velázquez, Vermeer, Goya and Rubens – was passed on to his nephew, who brought it to Russborough House. Thus began the sorry saga of the Beit collection.

The house has been the victim of three major robberies, beginning in 1976 when 16 paintings were stolen for the IRA, all of which were eventually recovered. Ten years later, despite increased security, the notorious Dublin gangster, Martin Cahill, masterminded another robbery, but this time the clients were Loyalist paramilitaries. Only some works were recovered, and of those several were damaged beyond repair – a good thief does not a gentle curator make. Twice bitten, Beit decided to hand over the most valuable paintings to the National Gallery in 1988. In return for the gift, the National Gallery often lends paintings to the collection as temporary exhibits.

But the story doesn't end there. In June 2001 a pair of thieves drove a jeep through the front doors and walked out with two paintings worth nearly €4 million, including a Gainsborough that had already been stolen – and recovered – twice before. Thankfully, all of the paintings were found and the house – which is often criticised as being unsuitable as a gallery for works of such importance – has once more tightened its security measures.

The admission price includes a 45-minute tour of the house and all the important paintings. You can take an additional 30-minute **tour** (adult/child €3.50/free; 2.15pm Mon-Sat, hourly on Sun) of the bedrooms upstairs, which contain more silver and furniture.

GLEN OF IMAAL

About 7km southeast of Donard, the lovely Glen of Imaal is about the only scenery of consequence on the western flanks of the Wicklow Mountains. It's named after Mal, a brother of the 2nd-century king of Ireland, Cathal Mór. Unfortunately, the glen's northeastern slopes are mostly cordoned off as an army firing range and for manoeuvres. Look out for red danger signs.

The area's most famous son was Michael Dwyer, who led rebel forces during the 1798 Rising and held out for five years in the local hills and glens. On the southeastern side of the glen at Derrynamuck is a small whitewashed, thatched cottage where Dwyer and three friends were surrounded by 100 English soldiers. One of his companions, Samuel McAllister, ran out the front, drawing fire and meeting his death, while Dwyer escaped into the night. He was eventually deported in 1803 and jailed on Norfolk Island, off the eastern coast of Australia, but became chief constable of Liverpool, near Sydney, before he died in 1825. The cottage is now a small **folk museum** (☎ 01-647 3000; Derrynamuck; admission free; 2-6pm mid-Jun–Sep) located on the Knockanarrigan–Rathdangan road.

Ballinclea Hostel (☎ 404 657; www.irelandyha.org; Ballinclea; dm €13; Mar-Nov & weekends year-round) This lovely 40-bed hostel, a converted traditional cottage 5km southeast of Donard on the road to Knockanarrigan, makes the best base for exploring the Glen of Imaal and nearby Lugnaquilla.

BALTINGLASS

☎ 0508 / pop 1976

Baltinglass, on the banks of the River Slaney, is in the far west of County Wicklow. This small town grew up around the Cistercian **Abbey of Vallis Salutis**, founded in 1148 by Dermot MacMurrough as a satellite to Mellifont Monastery in County Louth. The ruined nave, with several simple Gothic arches and scant remnants of a cloister, lies 350m north of the town centre.

A stiff climb to the summit of Baltinglass Hill to the northeast brings you to **Rathcoran**, a large hill fort, and a Bronze Age cairn with several passage graves.

Getting There & Away

Bus Éireann buses pass through Baltinglass (one way/return €6.50/9.20, 1¼ hours) between Dublin and Waterford and vice versa; from Busáras, in Dublin, buses depart at 9am and 5.30pm Monday to Saturday, and at 11.30am, 4pm and 6pm on Sunday. From Baltinglass, departures are at 10.10am and 6.35pm Monday to Saturday, and 3.30pm and 7.23pm on Sunday. All buses stop in Main St.

THE COAST

The N11 (M11) from Dublin to Wexford passes to the west of Bray and then south through Wicklow. South of Kilmacanogue you see Great Sugar Loaf Mountain (503m) to the west and pass through a great glacial rift, the **Glen of the Downs**, carved out of an Ice Age lake by floodwaters. There's a forest walk up to a ruined teahouse on top of the ridge to the east.

If you're travelling further south, the coastal route through Greystones, Kilcoole and then along country lanes to Rathnew is preferable.

Worth seeing around Wicklow town are the Mt Usher Gardens near Ashford and the fine beaches of Brittas Bay, which stretch into County Wexford.

BRAY

☎ 01 / pop 26,215

Bray is a busy coastal town trying to shake off the dust of neglect that has settled on it in recent decades, reducing the once handsome resort to a run-down dormitory town with little to offer except a dirty beach and a promenade lined with decrepit B&Bs and tawdry amusement arcades. The glory of yesteryear – when Bray was known as the Irish Brighton – hasn't quite returned, but the modern town has seen vast improvements. The beach has been given a serious makeover, the promenade is being cleaned up and many of the town's buildings are being restored. Apart from the obvious attraction of the beach (and a lovely walk from there south to Greystones), Bray is now home to a fabulous new art centre, our favourite restaurant in Wicklow, and one of the best bars you'll find anywhere along the eastern seaboard.

Information

The **tourist office** (☎ 286 7128, 286 6796; 9.30am-1pm & 2-5pm Mon-Sat Jun-Sep, 2-4.30pm Oct-May) is in the courthouse (built in 1841) beside the Royal Hotel at the bottom of Main St.

Sights

Right above the tourist office, the **heritage centre** (☎ 286 7128; Old Courthouse; adult/student €3/1; 9am-5pm Mon-Fri & 10am-3pm Sat Jun-Aug, 9.30am-4.30pm Mon-Fri, 10am-3pm Sat, Sep-May) has a permanent exhibit titled 'From Strongbow to Steam', basically a look at Bray's history over the last 1000 years or so. Spread across two floors, the lower floor is designed to look like the banqueting hall of a medieval castle, while upstairs is largely devoted to the efforts of engineer William Dargan (1799–1867) to bring the railroad to Bray.

The brand-new **Mermaid Art Centre** (☎ 272 4030; Main St; admission free; 10am-6pm Mon-Sat) is home to an art gallery, a theatre and a cinema. The theatre puts on excellent gigs and modern, experimental-style plays, while the cinema shows art movies almost exclusively. Call to check prices. The art gallery has constantly changing exhibitions featuring the latest Irish and European works.

On the seafront in Bray is **National Sealife** (☎ 286 6939; www.sealife.co.uk; Strand Rd; adult/child €7/5; 9.30am-6pm Mon-Sat). The British-run aquarium has a fairly big selection of tanks stocked with 70 different sea and freshwater species.

Like Sandycove, Bray has a **Martello Tower** (not open to the public), which is now a private residence owned by U2's Bono.

About 3km south of Bray on the Greystones road are **Kilruddery House & Gardens** (☎ 286 3405; Kilruddery; adult/child €6/4 house & gardens, €4/2 gardens only; 1-5pm May, Jun & Sep). Kilruddery has been home to the Brabazon family (earls of Meath) since 1618 and has one of the oldest gardens in Ireland. The house was designed in Elizabethan style by Richard Morrisson and his son William in 1820, but was reduced to its present-day proportions by the 14th earl in 1953. Although the house itself is quite impressive, it is the orangery that truly captures the eye, full of light, plantlife and sculptures.

The centre of indoor movie production in Ireland is **Ardmore Studios** (Herbert Rd), host to practically every high-profile Irish film from *The Commitments* to *My Left Foot*.

Activities

One of the most beautiful coastal walks in Wicklow stretches from the southern end of Bray's promenade over Bray Head and down to Greystones, 7km further south. The path is pretty smooth and easy to follow, but you can make a detour and clamber up Bray Head (240m), through the pine trees all the way to the large cross, erected in 1950. The head is full of old smuggling caves and railway tunnels, including one that's 1.5km long. From the top, there are fine views of the Great Sugar Loaf Mountain. Back on the coastal path, you approach Greystones via a narrow footbridge over the railway, after which the path narrows until you hit the lovely harbour in Greystones. Here you should relax in **Byrne's** (Greystones Pier), better known as Dan's, which serves a gorgeous pint.

Sleeping

If Dublin is full (highly probable over summer weekends) there are many B&Bs along Bray's sea-facing Strand Rd, just minutes from the Dart station. At the northern end they tend to overlook car parks so it's worth continuing south towards Bray Head.

Westbourne (☎ 286 2362; fax 286 8530; Quinsboro Rd; s/d €60/100) This ultra-cool spot is our favourite place in town, a minimalist hotel with very clean rooms – even if they're a little on the small side.

Moytura (☎ 282 9827; braybandb@eircom.net; junction of Herbert & King Edward Rds; s/d €32/60; P) This elegant house provides three gorgeous en-suite rooms, a terrific breakfast and a friendly personal touch.

Mayfair Hotel (☎ 274 5914; www.mayfairhotel.net; 1 Florence Tce; s/d €50/100) This is a comfortable, friendly hotel with decent-sized rooms that are clean and neat.

Royal Hotel (☎ 286 2935, fax 286 7373; Main St; s/d €95/170; P) Bray's top spot may have

COUNTY WICKLOW

been the latest in modern chic in 1980, but these days it's just a large hotel with a leisure centre and fairly compact rooms.

Eating

Escape (☎ 286 6755; 1 Brennan's Tce; mains €12-18; ⏲ 4- 10.30pm) This is one of Ireland's best veg restaurants, a crowded, poky place with more atmosphere than a Parisian café full of existentialist philosophers. At a time when most other eateries are flying the minimalist flag, Escape's every corner is crammed with diners enjoying their delicious cuisine.

Escapade (☎ 276 4647; 8 Meath Rd; sandwiches €4-6; ⏲ noon-10pm Mon-Sat) This gorgeous café is relaxed, quiet and a great place to eat a sandwich and read a book. It's just around the corner from Escape, with whom it (nearly) shares a name and ethos, but not its owner.

Betelnut Café (☎ 272 4030; Mermaid Art Centre, Main St; snacks €3-6; ⏲ 8am-6pm Mon-Fri, 10am-6pm Sat, noon-6pm Sun & late on show nights) This pleasant spot in the new art centre is a good spot for a sandwich and a nice coffee.

> **SOMETHING SPECIAL**
>
> **Harbour Bar** (☎ 286 2274; Seapoint Rd) A strong contender for Ireland's best pub, this wonderful place is proof that tradition and modernism are not mutually exclusive concepts. The pub is divided in two: on the left is the traditional bar, a stone-floor sailor's tavern adorned with all kinds of mementos, from an ancient set of golf clubs to half a trombone. Here you can enjoy an excellent pint of Guinness in a quiet atmosphere of conviviality. Come 7pm, the doors open to the lounge, a large comfortable room where velvet curtains, assorted paintings, wall hangings (including a giant moose head donated by actor Peter O'Toole) and couches fit for slouching in, provide the décor. But it's the crowd that really makes this place worth going out of your way for. In keeping with its alternative, Bohemian ethos, everyone is welcome here, not least the area's gay and lesbian community, who have made Sundays their own with themed lounge parties that feature some excellent, laid-back mellow house music played by some terrific DJs. In summer, weekend barbecues are held in the courtyard at the front. You'll really struggle to find a better pub anywhere on your travels.

Barracuda (☎ 276 5686; Strand Rd; mains €16-24; ⏲ noon-9pm) This new restaurant above National Sealife serves up excellent steaks and fine-tasting seafood in minimalist surroundings; glass and metal are central themes.

Entertainment

Clancy's Bar (☎ 286 3191; Quinnsboro Rd) This is a real spit-and-sawdust kind of place, an old-fashioned pub that is perfect for a quiet pint and a chat.

Porter House (☎ 286 0668; Strand Rd) This popular pub claims to have Ireland's largest selection of beers from around the world. We won't argue with either the boast or its popularity, but the place lacks genuine atmosphere.

Getting There & Away

BUS

Dublin Bus No 45 (from Hawkins St) and No 84 (from Burgh Quay) serve Bray (one way €1.50, one hour).

St Kevin's Bus Service (☎ 281 8119) takes about an hour to get into Dublin (one way €2) and departs Bray Town Hall at 8am and 5pm, returning from Dublin at 11.30am and 6pm. From Dublin, buses leave from in front of the Royal College of Surgeons, St Stephen's Green West.

TRAIN

Bray train station (☎ 236 3333) is 500m east of Main St just before the seafront. The Dart (one way €1.80, 30 minutes) runs trains into Dublin and further north to Howth every five minutes at peak times and every 20 or 30 minutes at quiet times.

The station is also on the main line from Dublin to Wexford and Rosslare Harbour, with up to five trains daily in each direction Monday to Saturday, four on Sunday.

AVOCA HANDWEAVERS

The biggest and best local craft shop is **Avoca Handweavers** (☎ 01-286 7466; Main St). Set in a 19th-century arboretum in Kilmacanogue, 4km south of Bray on the N11, the showroom has a huge array of handmade crafts and garments. The splendid **café** (mains €10-14) serves excellent dishes, including beef and Guinness casserole, though vegetarians are very well catered for as well. Many of the recipes are available in the *Avoca Cookbook*, on sale for €24.99.

Bus No 145 from Bray sometimes stops in Kilmacanogue; check with the driver.

Activities

Towering above the village of Kilmacanogue, the Great Sugarloaf, at 501m, is not quite gigantic, neither is it the highest, but it is the county's most impressive mountain, its distinctive conical peak visible for miles around. The 7km, moderately difficult walk to the summit should take about three hours. Before you go, we recommend that you get the *Wicklow Trail Sheet No 4* (€1.50) from the tourist office in Bray.

Start your walk by taking the small road opposite St Mochonog's Church (named after the missionary who administered the last rites to St Kevin). Ignore the left turn and continue round the bend until you get to a small bridge on your right. To your right, you'll see the expanse of the Rocky Valley below, a defile eroded by water escaping from a glacial lake that developed during the last Ice Age about 10,000 years ago. Continue on the path until you reach a fork: the lower road to the right continues round the mountain, while the left turn will take you up to the summit. As you reach the top, the track starts to drop: turn left and scramble up the rocky gully to the top. Return by the same path and continue southwards until you reach a large grassy area. Cross it, keeping to your left until you reach a gate. With the fence on your right, go downhill until you reach a path of grass and stones. This path takes you around the southern side of the mountain, where you will eventually pass a small wood on your right. Immediately afterward you will see, on your left, a sports pitch known as the Quill. Beyond it is Kilmacanogue.

GREYSTONES TO WICKLOW

The resort of **Greystones**, 8km south of Bray, was once a charming fishing village, and the seafront around the little harbour is idyllic. In summer, the bay is dotted with dinghies and windsurfers. Sadly, the surrounding countryside is vanishing beneath housing developments.

About 10km south of Greystones on the N11 is Ashford, an unremarkable little town save for one attraction on its eastern outskirts that draws horticulturists from all over the world. The eight-hectare **Mt Usher Gardens** (☎ 0404-40116; www.mount-usher-gardens.com; adult/student & child €6/5; ⌚ 10.30am-6pm mid-Mar–Oct) are informally laid out around the River Vartry with rare plants from around the world. They were first designed in 1868 by Dublin textile magnate Edward Walpole, with succeeding generations of the Walpole family working to maintain and expand the grounds. There are guided tours of the gardens (for groups only) that cost €32.

Bus Éireann (☎ 01-836 6111) buses stop outside Ashford House (€5.50, 50 minutes, 10 daily) between 8am and 8.30pm on the Dublin–Rosslare Harbour route.

West of Ashford the road leads into the Wicklow Mountains through Devil's Glen (beginning 3km from Ashford), a beautiful wooded glen with a fine walking trail.

Tinakilly Country House & Restaurant (☎ 0404-69274; www.tinakilly.ie; Rathnew; s/d €125/250; 5-course meal €60) This absolutely gorgeous Victorian Italianate manor house is just outside Rathnew, on the road to Wicklow. The restaurant takes country-house cuisine to a high level of sophistication, using plenty of fresh produce to create imaginative dishes that are simply delicious. Breakfast is included.

WICKLOW TOWN

☎ 0404 / pop 7007

There's really not much to do in Wicklow town, save sit by the fine harbour on a nice day or admire the sweep of beach and bay to the north and the bulge of Wicklow Head to the south. Aside from one museum, Wicklow town offers little else to the visitor, but it's a good base from which to explore the surrounding area.

The **tourist office** (☎ 69117; www.wicklow.ie; Fitzwilliam Sq; ⌚ 9.30am-6pm Mon-Sat Jun-Sep, 9am-1pm & 2-5pm Mon-Sat Oct-May) is in the heart of town.

Sights

WICKLOW'S HISTORIC GAOL

Wicklow's infamous **gaol** (☎ 61599; www.wicklowshistoricgaol.com; Kilmantin Hill; adult/student/child incl tour €5.70/4.40/3.50; ⌚ 10am-6pm, last admission 5pm) was renowned for the brutality of its keepers who didn't hold with the theory of prison as a force of rehabilitation. You can get a fairly sanitised-but-fun version of the prisoners' experience – minus the smells, vicious beatings, shocking food and disease-ridden air – in the actual prison, now converted into a modern heritage centre. In an effort to draw more visitors, the centre is constantly adding new exhibits, which now include a treadmill, which prisoners would have to turn for hours on end as punishment. Actors play the roles of the various 'personalities' (read sadists) that ran the prison, making this a worthwhile tour for kids especially. On the 2nd floor, however, is a model of the HMS *Hercules*, a convict ship that was used to transport convicts to New South Wales under the captaincy of the genuinely psychotic Luckyn Betts: six months under his iron rule and you would wish you were dead. The top floor is devoted to the stories of the prisoners once they arrived in Australia. Tours are every 10 minutes except between 1pm and 2pm.

THE BLACK CASTLE

The few remaining fragments of the **Black Castle** are on the shore at the southern end of town, with pleasant views up and down the coast. The castle was built in 1169 by the Fitzgeralds from Wales after they were granted land in the area by the Anglo-Norman conqueror, Strongbow. It used to be linked to the mainland by a drawbridge, and rumour has it that an escape tunnel ran from the sea cave underneath up into the town. At low tide you can swim or snorkel into the cave.

WICKLOW HEAD

The walk along the cliffs to **Wicklow Head** offers great views of the Wicklow Mountains. A string of beaches – Silver Strand, Brittas Bay and Maheramore – start 16km south of Wicklow; with high dunes, safe bathing and powdery sand, the beaches attract droves of Dubliners in good weather.

Special Events

Wicklow Regatta Festival (☎ 69117) Ireland's longest established festival, is held every year for two weeks over July and August. The full programme of events includes swimming, rowing, sailing and raft races, singing competitions, concerts and a Festival Queen Ball.

Sleeping

Wicklow Bay Hostel (☎ 69213, 61174; www.wicklowbayhostel.com; Marine House; dm €14; P) With two large kitchens, spotless dorms and a friendly atmosphere, this is a great hostel that is popular with backpackers.

There's a clutch of B&Bs in and around Dunbur Hill and a few more uphill along St Patrick's Rd.

Bayview Hotel (☎ 67383; www.wicklowbayviewhotel.com; the Mall; s/d €45/60; P) This town-centre hotel has comfortable rooms, and live music in the bar at weekends.

Grand Hotel (☎ 67337; www.grandhotel.ie; Abbey St; s/d €85/125; P) This mock-Tudor hotel offers guests comfortable, pleasantly furnished rooms.

Eating

Bakery Restaurant (☎ 66770; Church St; mains €18-32; 6-10pm daily & 11.30am-3.30pm Sun) A mouth-watering menu that changes monthly offers all kinds of good dishes – from rich game meats to interesting vegetarian options. This is perhaps the best restaurant in town.

Hannah's Coffee Shop (☎ 66264; 57 Main St; mains €6-9; 10am-4pm Jun-Sep, 9am-5pm Mon-Sat Oct-May) Hannah's will sort you out for breakfast, light lunches or afternoon tea.

Rugantino's River Café (☎ 61900; Schooner House, South Quay; mains €15-19; 6-11pm daily, plus 1-4pm Sun) Fish and seafood, rarely less than top-notch, are the specialities at this popular waterside restaurant.

Getting There & Away

Up to two **Bus Éireann** (☎ 01-836 6111) buses leave daily from the Grand Hotel on Abbey St for Dublin (€6.25 one way, one hour) and for Rosslare Harbour. Three **trains** (☎ 01-836 6222) depart Dublin's Connolly station bound for Rosslare Harbour daily, stopping at Wicklow (one way/return €11/13.70, 1¼ hours). The station is 10 minutes' walk north of the town centre.

Getting Around

Wicklow Cabs (☎ 66888; Main St) usually sends a few cabs to meet the evening trains from Dublin. The fare to anywhere in town is €5.50. The same company organises tours to local beauty spots, nightclubs and pubs.

SOUTHERN WICKLOW

RATHDRUM

☎ 0404 / pop 2122

These days Rathdrum is little more than a few old houses and shops to the south of Glendalough and the Vale of Clara, the pleasant valley leading north to Laragh, but in the late 19th century it had a healthy flannel industry and a poorhouse. The railway and fine aqueduct were built in 1861.

There's a small **tourist office** (☎ 46262; 29 Main St; 9am-5.30pm Mon-Fri). It has leaflets and information on the town and surrounding area, including the Wicklow Way.

Avondale House

About 2km south of Rathdrum, set in a marvellous 209-hectare estate, is **Avondale House** (☎ 46111; adult/student & child €5/4.50; 11am-6pm May-Aug, Tue-Sun Mar-Apr & Sep-Oct, by appointment only rest of year). It was the birthplace and family residence of 'Ireland's uncrowned king', Charles Stewart Parnell (1846–91), one of the leading figures of Irish history. The house was designed by James Wyatt in 1779 and features a stunning vermilion-coloured library, purported to be Parnell's favourite room, and a beautiful dining room.

From 1880 to 1890, Avondale became synonymous with the fight for Irish home rule, which was brilliantly led by Parnell until his shocking fall from grace. Another parliamentarian, Captain O'Shea, in a messy divorce suit, named Parnell as co-respondent – Parnell was indeed having an affair with O'Shea's wife, Kitty. Although Parnell married Kitty as soon as the divorce was granted, he was deemed 'unfit to lead' by the ultraconservative church authorities and he retired in despair to Avondale.

Surrounding the house are 200 hectares of forest and parkland, where the first silvicultural experiments by the Irish Forestry Service (now called Coillte) were conceived, after the purchase of the house by the state in 1904. These plots, about half a hectare in size, are still visible today, flanking what many consider to be the best of Avondale's many walking trails, the Great Ride. You can visit the park during daylight hours year-round.

Sleeping

Old Presbytery Hostel (☎ 46930; www.hostels-ireland.com; the Fairgreen, Rathdrum; dm/d €13/28; P) This modern, centrally located IHH hostel has large, comfy dorms and eight doubles. A laundry and TV room round off the facilities. You can also camp in the grounds.

Most of Rathdrum's B&Bs are actually in the hamlet of Corballis, 1km along the road south to Avoca.

Avonbrae Guesthouse (☎/fax 46198; avonbrae@gofree.indigo.ie; Laragh Rd; s/d €42/65; P) The seven rooms at this charming guesthouse, about 500m northwest of Rathdrum on the road to Laragh, have fairly spartan furnishings, but they're neat and very comfortable.

Getting There & Away

The **Bus Éireann** (☎ 01-836 6111) twice daily Dublin–Wexford–Rosslare Harbour service stops at Rathdrum (once on Sunday) in each direction (one way/return €8.20/13, 1¾ hours). From Dublin, they depart at 9am and 5.30pm (2pm on Sunday). Three **trains** (☎ 01-836 6222) stop at Rathdrum daily in each direction between Dublin and Rosslare Harbour (€11.50/14, 1½ hours).

VALE OF AVOCA

The Rivers Avonbeg and Avonmore come together to form the River Avoca at the **Meeting of the Waters**, a lovely spot made famous by Thomas Moore's 1808 poem of the same name.

The Vale of Avoca is a charming, darkly wooded valley. Unfortunately there's some badly scarred landscape northwest of Avoca village, the legacy of centuries of copper mining. In the 18th century the valley was cut off from the outside world and had its own coinage, the *cronbane*.

The Meeting of the Waters is marked by a pub called the **Meetings** (☎ 0402-35226; mains €10-14), which serves food all day and has music on weekends year-round. There are *ceilidhs* (traditional music and dancing sessions) between 4pm and 6pm Sunday, April to October. Buses to Avoca from Dublin stop at the Meetings, or try walking from Avoca.

Avoca

☎ 0402 / pop 770

The tiny village of Avoca (Abhóca) is best known as the location for the fictional TV series, *Ballykissangel*, but since that show's demise, Avoca has withdrawn once more into pleasant obscurity. The **tourist office** (☎ 35022; Old Courthouse; 10am-5pm Mon-Sat) is in the library.

The main reason for visiting these days is to amble about **Avoca Handweavers** (☎ 35105; Old Mill, Main St; 9.30am-6pm), housed in Ireland's oldest working mill, which has been operational since 1723. All the company's much-admired line of tweeds, throws and

COUNTY WICKLOW

other fabrics are produced here, and you are free to wander in and out of the weaving sheds.

Sleeping

Sheepwalk House & Cottages (☎ 35189; www.sheepwalk.com; Arklow Rd; s/d in main house €47/70; cottages €250-500 per week) Built in 1727 for the earl of Wicklow, this is our favourite place to stay in Avoca (although it's 2km out of town). The main house is splendid, with beautifully appointed rooms, while the converted outbuildings – complete with beamed ceilings, fireplaces and flagstone floors – are a wonderful option for groups of four or six.

River Valley Park (☎ 41647; fax 41677; camp sites €14) This well-equipped campsite is about 1km south of the village of Redcross, 7km northeast of Avoca on the R754 country road.

Koliba (☎/fax 32737; koliba@eircom.net; Beech Rd; s/d €40/60; ⏲ Apr-Oct only) A thoroughly modern bungalow with comfortable, well-appointed rooms (all with en suite), it's 3km out of Avoca on the Arklow road.

Getting There & Away

Bus Éireann (☎ 01-836 6111) bus No 133 from Dublin departs at 9am and 5.30pm daily (2pm on Sunday) and serves Avoca (one way/return €8.60/14, two hours) via Bray, Wicklow and Rathdrum on its way to Arklow.

ARKLOW

☎ 0402 / pop 9963

A thriving commercial centre built around a once busy port, Arklow holds little interest for the visitor but it does make a good base for exploring the surrounding area. The town was best known as a shipbuilding centre: Sir Francis Chichester's *Gypsy Moth III* (now in Greenwich, England) was built in John Tyrell's boatyard, which opened in 1864 and shut its doors only in the mid-1990s, but these days Arklow earns most of its crust from light industry.

There is a white, sandy beach, but it lies between the docks and a gravel plant; you're better off heading 10km north to **Brittas Bay** or 7km south to the more sheltered **Clogga Beach**.

The **tourist office** (☎ 32484; www.arklow.ie; ⏲ 9.30am-1pm Mon-Sat, Jun-Sep) is in a Portakabin beside the courthouse.

The town's seafaring past is explored in the small **maritime museum** (☎ 32868; St Mary's Rd; €3.50; ⏲ 10am-1pm & 2-5pm Mon-Sat May-Sep), which features a model of the *Titanic*, some salvaged items from the *Lusitania* and an extraordinary model of a ship made from 10,000 matchsticks.

Sleeping & Eating

There are plenty of places to bed down in, especially on the southern side of town.

Valentia House (☎ 39200; www.geocities.com/valentiahouse; Coolgreany Rd; s/d €40/60) The rooms in this house are decorated in a typically comfortable, simple fashion.

Plattenstown House (☎/fax 37822; Coolgreany Rd; s/d €45/80; P ⊠) This is a gorgeous traditional farmhouse set in 50 acres of land about 5km south of town. Family antiques, great views and comfortable rooms make this place a terrific choice in the area.

Kitty's of Arklow (☎ 31669; Main St; early-bird's dinner €25, set dinner €35; ⏲ noon-5pm & 6-10.30pm) An Arklow institution, Kitty's serves the usual selection of bar food during the day, but the evening menu is more exciting and delicious. The sugar-spiced salmon is good.

New Riverwalk Restaurant (☎ 31657; Riverwalk La; mains from €14; ⏲ 5.30-10.30pm) This recent addition to Arklow's dining scene specialises in surf and turf – of the well-prepared kind. Imaginative, well-presented dishes have already earned it rave reviews from locals and visitors alike.

Getting There & Away

BUS

Bus Éireann's (☎ 01-836 6111) express bus No 2 (one way/return €10/14.50, 1½ hours) from Busáras in Dublin to Rosslare Harbour via Wicklow town serves Arklow 11 times daily (nine on Sunday), with departures from 7.30am (8.30am Sunday) to 8.30pm. Alternatively, for the same price, you can get the slower (but more scenic) bus No 133, which also serves Avoca (2¼ hours). All buses stop outside the Chocolate Shop.

TRAIN

From Dublin, Irish Rail's **southeastern suburban line** (☎ 01-836 6222) serves Arklow (one way/return €12/15, 1½ hours) twice a day Monday to Friday, and once on Saturday. Intercity trains to Gorey and Rosslare Harbour stop in Arklow three times daily.

Counties Wexford & Waterford

Being the warmest and driest counties in Ireland may be no great boast, but working-class Dubliners have long flocked to the sunshine and sandy beaches of Counties Waterford and Wexford. But both counties have a lot more to offer than a couple of days out by the sea. Attracted by the pleasant climate, easily navigable rivers, deep sheltered harbours and rich, fecund soil, the southeast corner of Ireland was usually the gateway and first stop for foreign invaders.

Waterford city and Wexford town are the birthplaces of Viking and Norman history in Ireland. Ferns, Lismore and Johnstown castle, once impregnable, are now home to the magnificent ruins of these faded empires. The fire of Cromwell's rage was also felt in the major towns of the region, long known for their rebellious streak. The rugged, unspoilt Ring Peninsula is home to a thriving Gealteacht (Irish speaking) community, and the little fishing villages of Hook Head are perfect bases for diving expeditions.

While the interior countryside lacks the rugged splendour of the island's west and southwest, Mt Leinster in Wexford and the Comeragh Mountains in Waterford are ideal for hill walking and climbing. Beyond family friendly Tramore town and beach the land starts to climb as you round rugged Helvick Head and enter the foothills of the elegant Knockmealdown Mountains near Dungarvan.

HIGHLIGHTS

- Walk, cycle or drive along the beautiful **Hook Peninsula** (p166) in County Wexford
- Learn about Wexford's rebel history at the **1798 Visitor Centre** (p170) in Enniscorthy
- Relax and enjoy the views in the picture-perfect coastal town of **Dunmore East** (p179) in County Waterford
- Explore the Irish-speaking area of **An Rinn** (p182)
- Stay at the secluded **Hanora's Cottage** (p184) in the undiscovered Nire Valley

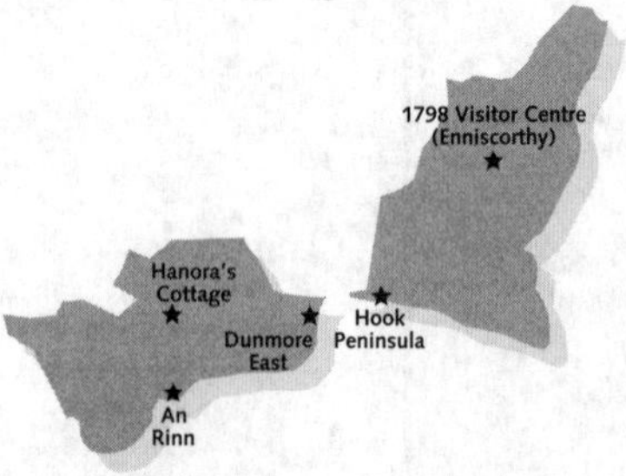

- POPULATION: 218,061
- AREA: 4201 SQ KM

COUNTY WEXFORD

Occupying the southeastern corner of Ireland, the flat, navigable County Wexford has always attracted European invaders and privateers. As they moved west they founded Ireland's first major towns on the wide, easy-flowing River Slaney, which cuts a swathe through the middle of the county. Only near its western borders with Kilkenny and Carlow, where the Blackstairs Mountains rise to 796m at their highest point, Mt Leinster, does Wexford at last make life difficult for any invading army. But even here there are some great winding roads and paths through these little-explored hills, particularly to the west of Enniscorthy and over the Scullogue Gap.

Wexford town is pleasant enough but only retains a few traces of its Viking past. To its north, a string of fine beaches runs along the coast towards County Wicklow. In the centre of County Wexford, Enniscorthy is an attractive town on the Slaney. Further west, the River Barrow runs through New Ross, a base for exploring the river's upper reaches.

On the southern coast is the village of Kilmore Quay with its thatched cottages and, further west, the flat and lonely Hook Peninsula, home to Europe's oldest lighthouse.

The Wexford Coastal Walk (Slí Charman) follows the county's coastline for 221km from Ballyhack to Kilmichael Point, and the Southeast Coastal Drive takes you from Wexford town right through to the Waterford border and beyond.

WEXFORD TOWN

☎ 053 / pop 15,862

Defiant West Gate and the narrow, meandering lanes off Main St are a few reminders that Wexford (Loch Garman) has a glorious Viking and Norman past. It was once a thriving port but over the centuries the slow-moving Slaney has deposited so much silt and mud in the estuary that the channel has become almost unusable. Now most commercial sea traffic goes through Waterford and all passenger traffic through Rosslare Harbour, 20km southeast.

The liveliest, and busiest, time to visit is during Wexford's world famous opera festival, in late October (see p159).

History

The Vikings named it Waesfjord (harbour of mud flats) and its handy location near the mouth of the Slaney encouraged landings as early as AD 850. The Normans captured the town in 1169, and traces of their fort can still be seen in the grounds of the Irish National Heritage Park northwest at Ferrycarrig.

Cromwell included Wexford in his Irish tour from 1649 to 1650. Around 1500 of the town's 2000 inhabitants were put to the sword, including all of the Franciscan friars – the standard treatment for towns that refused to surrender. Not surprisingly, after the massacre at Wexford surrender became increasingly popular. During the 1798 Rising, rebels made a determined, bloody stand in Wexford town before they were defeated.

Orientation

From Wexford Bridge at the northern end of the town, the quays lead southeast along the waterfront, with the tourist office in the small kink called The Crescent.

As well as the Chamber of Commerce building, which houses the tourist office, The Crescent is home to a statue of windswept Commodore John Barry. A local seaman born in 1745, he emigrated to America and founded the US navy during the American Revolution.

North and South Main St, a block inland, are where you'll find most of the shops and other commercial outlets.

Information

BOOKSHOPS

Book Centre (☎ 23543; 5 South Main St; ⌚ 9am-5.30pm Mon-Sat) Stocks books on Irish topics as well as a limited selection of foreign newspapers and magazines.

Readers' Paradise (☎ 71886; 3 Selskar St; ⌚ 9am-5.30pm Mon-Sat) A great spot for second-hand paperbacks.

INTERNET ACCESS

Westgate Computer Centre (☎ 46291; Westgate; €5/hr; ⌚ 9am-1pm & 2-5pm Mon-Fri) Next to the Westgate Heritage Centre.

LAUNDRY

Pádraig's Laundrette (☎ 24677; 4 Mary St; ⌚ 9.30am-6pm Mon-Fri, 9am-9pm Sat) Beside Kirwan hostel.

LEFT LUGGAGE

O'Hanrahan Station (☎ 22522; Redmond Pl) Has left luggage facilities for €1.25 per item per day.

MEDICAL SERVICES

Wexford General Hospital (☎ 42233) For emergencies go 2.5km west of the centre on the N25.

MONEY

There are two banks on North Main St near Common Quay St, and another on the corner of Common Quay St and Custom House Quay; all have ATMs.

POST

Main post office (☎ 45314; Anne St; 9am-5.30pm Mon-Fri, 9am-1pm Sat)

Sub-post office (☎ 45314; 113 North Main St; 9am-5.30pm Mon-Fri)

TOILETS

There are public toilets near the tourist office and near St Iberius' Church.

TOURIST INFORMATION

Tourist office (☎ 23111; Chamber of Commerce, Cresent Quay; 9.30am-1pm & 2-5pm Mon-Fri Nov-Mar, 9am-1pm & 2-6pm Mon-Sat Apr-Oct) Has a bureau de change, though rates are pretty bad.

Bull Ring

At the intersection of Common Quay St and North Main St is the **Bull Ring**, once a centre for bull-baiting. The town's butchers gained their guild charter by providing a bull each year for the sport. The **Lone Pikeman statue** commemorates the participants in the 1798 Rising.

There are usually market stalls beside the Bull Ring on Friday and Saturday mornings.

Westgate

Of the six original town gates only the 14th-century West Gate (not to be confused with the area around it, called Westgate) survives, at the northern end of town on Westgate opposite the end of Slaney St. It was originally a tollgate, and the recesses used by the toll collectors are still intact, as is the lockup used to incarcerate 'runagates' – those who tried to avoid paying. Some stretches of the town wall also remain intact, including a fine section near Cornmarket.

Beside the gate is the **Westgate Heritage Centre** (☎ 46506, 42611; Westgate; adult/child €1.90/1.25; 9.30am-5.30pm Mon-Sat, 2-6pm Sun Jul & Aug, 11am-5.30pm Mon-Fri, 2-6pm Sun May, Jun & Sep). Here, an audiovisual display tells the history of Wexford on the hour between 11am and 4pm (except 1pm).

Selskar Abbey

Founded by Alexander de la Roche in 1190 after a crusade to the Holy Land, it was **Selskar Abbey** that Henry II did penance for the bloody murder of his friend Thomas á Becket. Bascilla, the sister of Richard FitzGilbert de Clare (Strongbow), is supposed to have married Raymond le Gros, one of Henry II's brave lieutenants, in the abbey. Its present ruinous state is a result of Cromwell's visit in 1649.

The ruins should be unlocked when the Westgate Heritage Centre is open. At other times, a key is available from the guardian at 9 Abbey St.

St Iberius' Church

South of the Bull Ring, the existing **St Iberius' Church** (☎ 22936; North Main St; 10am-5pm Mon-Sat) was built in 1760 on the site of several previous churches (including one reputed to have been founded by St Patrick). The Renaissance-style frontage is worth a look, but the real treat is the Georgian interior with its finely crafted altar rails and set of 18th-century monuments in the gallery. Ring for a guided tour (€1.25).

Franciscan Friary

The **friary** (☎ 22758; cnr Francis & School Sts; 10am-5pm) houses a relic and wax effigy of St Adjutor, a boy martyr slain by his own father in ancient Rome. The original friary on this spot was established in 1230, but Cromwell's forces made a bonfire of it in 1649 and most of the present building is 19th century. Only two walls date from pre-Cromwellian times. Some parts, such as the tabernacle, are very modern, creating an architectural incongruity that's quite appealing.

Activities

Wexford Golf Club (☎ 42238; Mulgannon; 18 holes weekdays/weekends €30/35; 8am-dusk Mon-Sat, Sun members only) is well signposted off the R733, about 2km southwest of town. Even hackers will appreciate the views of Wexford and the harbour.

Tours

In July and August, **Bus Éireann** (☎ 22522) runs tours of the surrounding area. For guided walking tours in July and August, phone ☎ 46505 or **Thomas Molloy** (☎ 22663).

Festivals & Events

The **Wexford Festival Opera** (☎ 22400, box office ☎ 22144; www.wexfordopera.com; Theatre Royal, 27 High St), an 18-day extravaganza held in October, began in 1951 and has grown to be the country's premier opera event, presenting many rarely performed operas and shows to packed audiences. Fringe street theatre, poetry readings and exhibitions give the town a real fiesta atmosphere. Local bars even run an amateur song competition.

Tickets for the principal operas are hard to come by. Booking is essential and should be done at least three months in advance.

Sleeping

BUDGET

Ferrybank Camping & Caravan Park (☎ 42611; www.wexfordcorp.ie; Ferrybank; tent & 2 people €14; Easter-Sep;) Location and luxury, right across the river from the town centre, Ferrybank boasts a heated pool, laundry and children's play area.

Kirwan House (☎ 21208; kirwanhostel@eircom.net; 3 Mary St; dm/q/tr per person €13.50/13.50/18; P) Big, comfortable rooms and a tranquil garden add extra class to this lovely old Georgian building.

MID-RANGE

Westgate House (☎ 22167; westgate@wexmail.com; Westgate; s/d €35/50; P) With Selskar Abbey

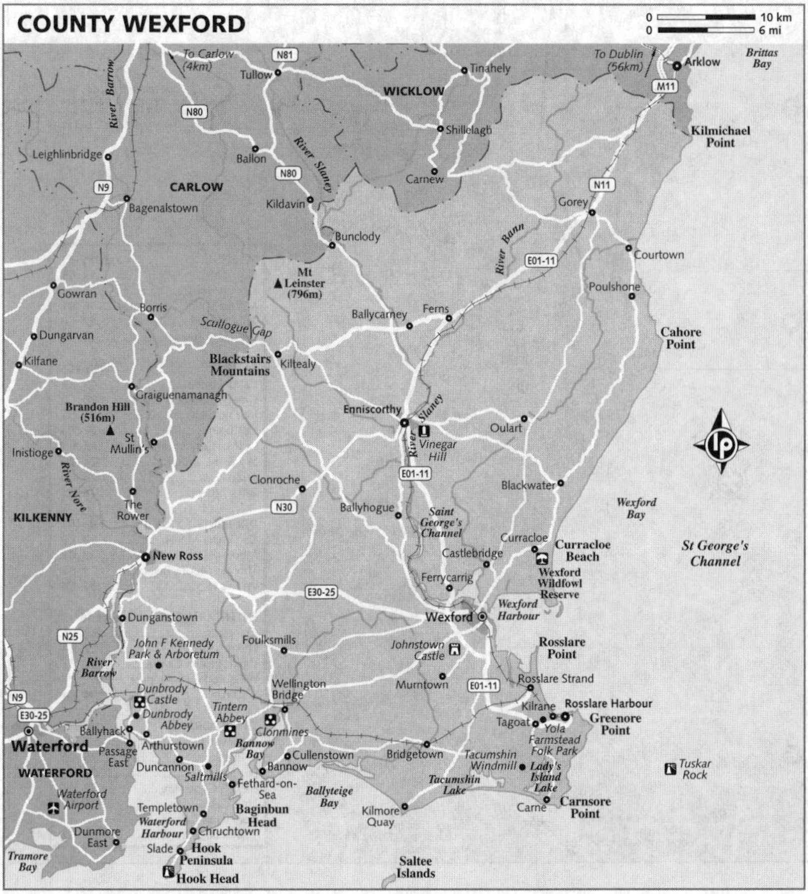

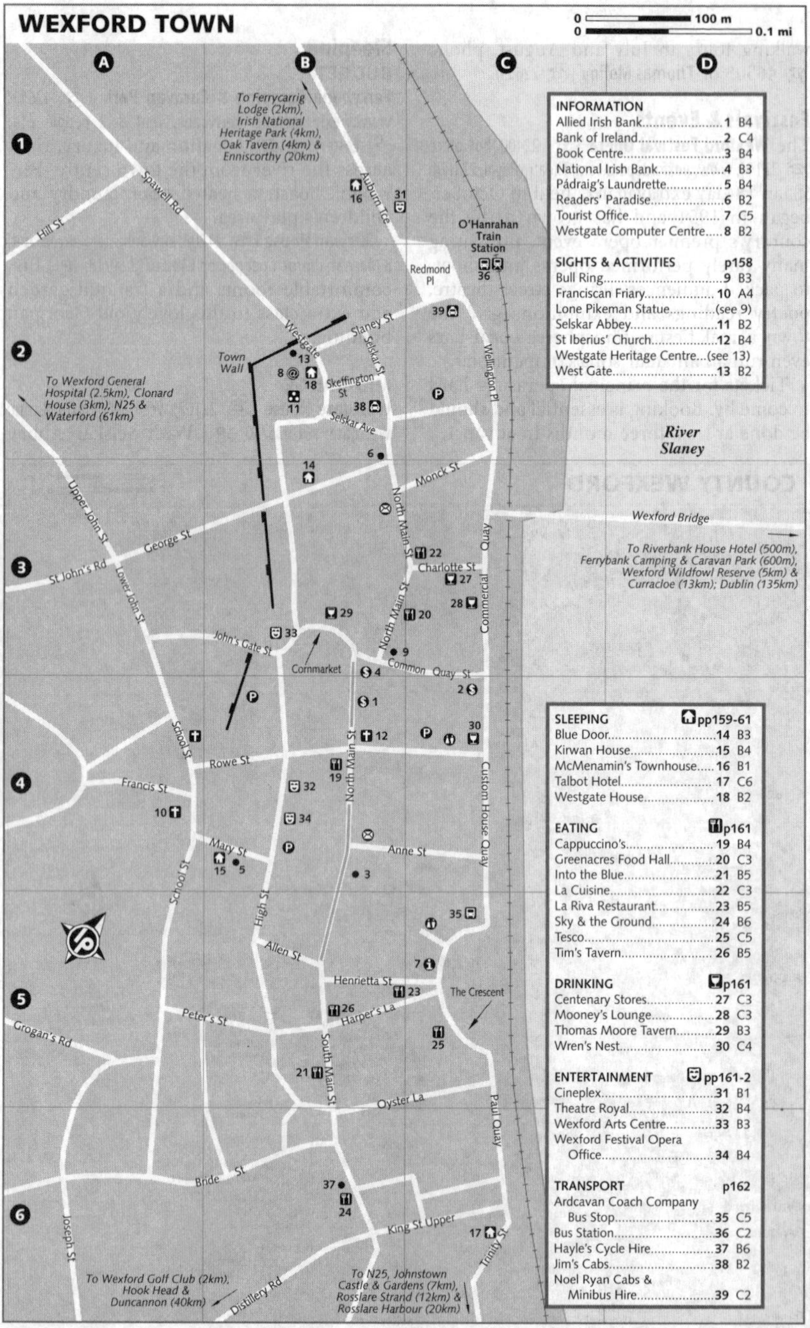

WEXFORD TOWN
0 100 m
0 0.1 mi
A
B
C
D
1
2
3
4
5
6
To Ferrycarrig Lodge (2km), Irish National Heritage Park (4km), Oak Tavern (4km) & Enniscorthy (20km)
To Wexford General Hospital (2.5km), Clonard House (3km), N25 & Waterford (61km)
To Riverbank House Hotel (500m), Ferrybank Camping & Caravan Park (600m), Wexford Wildfowl Reserve (5km) & Curracloe (13km); Dublin (135km)
To Wexford Golf Club (2km), Hook Head & Duncannon (40km)
To N25, Johnstown Castle & Gardens (7km), Rosslare Strand (12km) & Rosslare Harbour (20km)
O'Hanrahan Train Station
River Slaney
Wexford Bridge
Town Wall
Cornmarket
The Crescent
Redmond Pl
Hill St
Spawell Rd
Auburn Tce
Westgate
Slaney St
Selskar St
Skeffington St
Selskar Ave
Wellington Pl
Monck St
North Main St
Upper John St
George St
St John's Rd
Lower John St
Charlotte St
Commercial Quay
John's Gate St
Common Quay St
School St
Rowe St
Francis St
Custom House Quay
Mary St
Anne St
High St
Allen St
Henrietta St
Peter's St
Harper's La
Grogan's Rd
South Main St
Oyster La
Paul Quay
Bride St
King St Upper
Trinity St
Joseph St
Distillery Rd
INFORMATION
Allied Irish Bank 1 B4
Bank of Ireland 2 C4
Book Centre 3 B4
National Irish Bank 4 B3
Pádraig's Laundrette 5 B4
Readers' Paradise 6 B2
Tourist Office 7 C5
Westgate Computer Centre 8 B2
SIGHTS & ACTIVITIES p158
Bull Ring 9 B3
Franciscan Friary 10 A4
Lone Pikeman Statue (see 9)
Selskar Abbey 11 B2
St Iberius' Church 12 B4
Westgate Heritage Centre (see 13)
West Gate 13 B2
SLEEPING pp159-61
Blue Door 14 B3
Kirwan House 15 B4
McMenamin's Townhouse 16 B1
Talbot Hotel 17 C6
Westgate House 18 B2
EATING p161
Cappuccino's 19 B4
Greenacres Food Hall 20 C3
Into the Blue 21 B5
La Cuisine 22 C3
La Riva Restaurant 23 B5
Sky & the Ground 24 B6
Tesco 25 C5
Tim's Tavern 26 B5
DRINKING p161
Centenary Stores 27 C3
Mooney's Lounge 28 C3
Thomas Moore Tavern 29 B3
Wren's Nest 30 C4
ENTERTAINMENT pp161-2
Cineplex 31 B1
Theatre Royal 32 B4
Wexford Arts Centre 33 B3
Wexford Festival Opera Office 34 B4
TRANSPORT p162
Ardcavan Coach Company Bus Stop 35 C5
Bus Station 36 C2
Hayle's Cycle Hire 37 B6
Jim's Cabs 38 B2
Noel Ryan Cabs & Minibus Hire 39 C2

and West Gate right across the road you won't lack for a good view from this refurbished family guesthouse.

Clonard House (☎/fax 43141; clonardhouse@indigo.ie; Clonard Great; s/d €35/40; Ⓟ) A real gem, this 1780s farmhouse in a sylvan setting is 3km west of town off the N25 to Waterford. Ask for a bedroom with a four-poster bed.

Blue Door (☎ 21047; bluedoor@indigo.ie; 18 Lower George St; s/d €45/70) This 200-year-old town house serves smoked salmon and vegetarian alternatives.

Ferrycarrig Lodge (☎ 42605; ferrycarrig@wexford-accommodation.com; Ferrycarrig Rd; s/d €50/74; Ⓟ) On the banks of the Slaney 2km north of town and a 10-minute walk from the Heritage Park (see p162), Ferrycarrig has a great little pub attached.

McMenamin's Townhouse (☎ 46442; mcmem@indigo.ie; 3 Auburn Tce, Redmond Rd; s/d €45/70; Ⓟ) Always quiet and peaceful, this eight-bedroom Victorian house has tea/coffee making facilities in each room.

TOP END

Talbot Hotel (☎ 22566; sales@talbothotel.ie; Trinity St; s/d €100/150; Ⓟ) The bar at the Talbot is a favourite with locals, but the big, stylish bedrooms are the real attraction.

Riverbank House Hotel (☎ 23611; river@indigo.ie; Wexford Estuary; s/d €105/170; Ⓟ) The rooms here are all done in a Victorian style. Ask for one with a view of the river.

Eating

La Cuisine (☎ 24986; 80 North Main St; sandwiches €2.50-5; 🕒 9am-6pm Mon-Sat) Expect a lunchtime queue at this popular deli.

Cappuccino's (☎ 23669; 25 North Main St; breakfast €4-7.50; 🕒 8am-6pm Mon-Sat, 10am-6.30pm Sun) From heartstopper to healthy, from full Irish to bagel with cream cheese, this little eatery is perfect for breakfast.

Sky & the Ground (☎ 21273; 112-113 South Main St; mains €10-15; 🕒 12.30-4pm & 6.30-11pm) This pub is a great spot for lunch, where you get the same food as the restaurant on the 1st floor but at half the price (anyone for wild venison?).

Oak Tavern (☎ 20922; Enniscorthy Rd; mains 10-15; 🕒 noon-11pm) Near the gates to the Irish National Heritage Park (4km outside Wexford), this family-run tavern on the banks of the Slaney is renowned for its surf 'n' turf, salmon and steak. The big open fire is perfect in winter.

Tim's Tavern (☎ 23861; 51 South Main St; bar mains €9, restaurant mains €14-20; 🕒 12.30-4pm & 6-10pm) This cosy pub-restaurant has a large menu and award-winning food. The portions are huge and all the famous Irish dishes are represented, such as bacon and cabbage, Irish stew, and oysters and Guinness.

La Riva Restaurant (☎ 24330; The Crescent, entrance on Henrietta St; mains €18-22; 🕒 6-11pm) This 1st-floor bistro is casual about everything except the food. The menu is modern with French, Italian and Asian influences.

Into the Blue (☎ 22011; 80 South Main St; lunch €4-9, set dinner menu €24-28; 🕒 8am-5pm & 6-9.30pm Wed-Sat) Recommended by locals, this place is a deli and restaurant with sandwiches, salads and breakfasts, as well as set three-course dinners that include a bottle of wine.

There's a Tesco supermarket on The Crescent. You can put together a gourmet picnic at **Greenacres Food Hall** (☎ 22975; North Main St) where you'll find a great selection of cheese, meats, olives and wine.

Drinking

To say an Irish town has a lot of pubs is redundant, but Wexford really does have a vast selection and a few are top-quality watering holes.

Sky & the Ground (☎ 21273; 112-113 South Main St) A great place to eat and one of the most popular pubs in town, this family establishment has old-style décor and traditional music sessions almost every night.

Thomas Moore Tavern (☎ 24348; Cornmarket) Locals would call this an 'old man's pub', meaning it is a lovely place for a quiet drink and a good chat.

Wren's Nest (☎ 22359; Custom House Quay) This is the ideal place for a drink with a few friends.

Centenary Stores (☎ 24424; Charlotte St) One of the livelier, more youthful spots in town, this former warehouse is home to modern and traditional music from Wednesday to Sunday.

Mooney's Lounge (☎ 24483; Commercial Quay) A pub and club all in one, Mooney's is the place in Wexford for live rock music and late night dancing.

Entertainment

THEATRE & CINEMA

Wexford has a number of venues dedicated to the arts.

Theatre Royal (☎ 22144; 27 High St) The Royal stages drama and opera by local and touring companies.

Wexford Arts Centre (☎ 23764; Cornmarket; 🕓 10am-6pm Mon-Sat) In the 18th-century Market House and Assembly Room, this centre, which is also open during the evening for scheduled events, caters for exhibitions, theatre, dance, music and film.

Cineplex (☎ 22321; The Square, Redmond Rd) This multiscreen cinema is near the train station.

Getting There & Away

The N25 leads southeast from the quays and Trinity St to Rosslare Harbour. For Duncannon or Hook Head, turn west either at The Crescent along Harpers Lane or from Paul Quay along King St. For bus and train information to/from Wexford phone ☎ 33114 or 33162.

BUS

Bus Éireann (☎ 22522) buses leave from O'Hanrahan train station on Redmond Place and travel to Rosslare Harbour (€3.70, 30 minutes, every 45 minutes Monday to Saturday, 10 on Sunday), Dublin (€11, 2¼ hours, 10 Monday to Saturday, eight on Sunday), Killarney (€22, 5½ hours, four Monday to Saturday, two on Sunday), Waterford (€10.60, one hour, nine Monday to Saturday, three on Sunday), Enniscorthy (€4.70, 25 minutes, hourly Monday to Saturday, seven on Sunday) and Cork (€17, 3½ hours, five Monday to Saturday, three on Sunday). Tickets are available from **Station Café** (1a Redmond Sq) across from the station.

Ardcavan Coach Company (☎ 22561) operates daily services to/from Dublin (€10, 2¼ hours); buses leave from The Crescent at 8am.

TRAIN

O'Hanrahan Station (☎ 22522; Redmond Pl) is at the northern end of town.

Wexford is on the Dublin (€16.50/21 adult/child, three hours) to Rosslare Harbour (€6, 30 minutes) line (via Enniscorthy and Wicklow) and is serviced by three trains daily in each direction.

Getting Around

Parking discs (€1 per hour) for street parking can be bought in most newsagencies.

Taxi companies include **Noel Ryan Cabs & Minibus Hire** (☎ 24056; Station Café, 1a Redmond Sq) and **Jim's Cabs** (☎ 47108; Selskar St). Most fares around the centre are €4.

You can rent bikes at **Hayle's Cycle Hire** (☎ 22462; 108 South Main St) for €14 per day.

AROUND WEXFORD TOWN

Irish National Heritage Park

About 4km northwest of Wexford town on the N11 is the **Irish National Heritage Park** (☎ 053-20733; Ferrycarrig; adult/13-18 years/under 13 €7/4/3.50; 🕓 9.30am-6.30pm Mar-Nov, last admission 5pm), a brave and mostly successful attempt to squash all of Irish history into one outdoor theme park.

Take a deep breath and plunge into the 1½-hour guided tour that takes in re-creations of a Mesolithic camp site, a Neolithic farmstead, a dolmen, a *cist* (box-shaped) burial tomb, a stone circle, a *ráth* or ring fort, a monastery, a *crannóg* (lake settlement), a Viking shipyard, a motte and bailey (external ditch and wall around a settlement), a Norman castle, a round tower and a couple of other smaller displays. A replica Viking longship is anchored on the Slaney outside the park.

A taxi to the park from Wexford should cost about €6.

Johnstown Castle & Gardens

About 7km southwest of Wexford town on the way to Murntown, the former home of the once-mighty Fitzgerald and Esmonde families is a splendid 19th-century castellated house overlooking a small lake and surrounded by 20 hectares of thickly wooded gardens with ornamental lakes.

The **gardens** (adult/child €2/1; 🕓 9am-5.30pm) are open to the public, but the castle and its outbuildings now house an agricultural research centre, the headquarters of the Irish Environmental Protection Agency and the **Irish Agricultural Museum** (☎ 053-42888; adult/child €4/2.50; 🕓 9am-5pm Apr-Nov, 9am-5pm Mon-Fri Dec-Mar). The main attraction here is the collection of Irish country furniture. There's also a small Famine exhibition detailing life before, during and after the potato blight.

Wexford Wildfowl Reserve

Welcome to bird heaven. The North Slobs, a swathe of low-lying land reclaimed from the sea 5km northeast of Wexford town, are home to half the world's population of the Greenland white-fronted goose, some 10,000 birds in total.

Wexford Wildfowl Reserve (☎ 053-23129; North Slob; admission free, guided tours on request; 🕓 9am-6pm mid-Apr–Sep, 10am-5pm Oct–mid-Apr) was set up to protect the birds' feeding grounds. Alongside the usual visitor centre there's an observation tower and assorted hides.

Winter is also a good time to spot the brent goose from Arctic Canada, and throughout the year you'll see the mallard, pochard, godwit, mute and Bewick's swans, redshank, tern, coot, oystercatcher and many other species.

The reserve is on the Wexford to Dublin road; head north for 3.5km from Wexford until you see a signpost pointing to the right.

Curracloe Beach

Over 11km long, Curracloe is one of a string of magnificent beaches that line the coast north of Wexford town. If you're discreet you can pitch a tent in the sheltered dunes. The high-octane, Normandy landing opening scenes of the 1997 film *Saving Private Ryan* were filmed here. It's 13km northeast of Wexford off the Dublin road.

Curracloe House Equestrian Centre (☎ 053-37583; 🕓 9am-5pm) offers trail rides along the beach for €14 per hour year round.

Hotel Curracloe (☎ 053-37308; hotelcurracloe@eircom.net; s/d €60/100) is a small, family-run hotel. It's a good walk from the beach but it's worth it for the snug surroundings and great traditional sessions at the weekend.

ROSSLARE STRAND

☎ 053

If you don't like crowds or children avoid Rosslare Strand in the height of summer. The beaches are long and golden and the long shallow bay is perfect for windsurfing.

Boards, wetsuits and tuition are available from the **Rosslare Windsurfing Centre** (☎ 32101; 🕓 10am-6pm May-Sep). **Rosslare Sailboard Centre** (☎ 32566; 🕓 9.30am-6pm May-Sep) provides canoes and dinghies too. **Rosslare Golf Links** (☎ 32203; green fee weekdays/weekends €36/48) runs along the beach road. There are gentle walks north to Rosslare Point. It's about 8km northwest of Rosslare Harbour and 15km southeast of Wexford town.

Sleeping & Eating

Burrow Holiday Park (☎ 32190; burrowpk@iol.ie; tent sites €24-28) Just south of the village, this park has excellent facilities, including a laundry, games room and tennis courts. The fee takes no account of tent size or number of people.

Lyngfields B&B (☎ 32593; Tagoat; s/d €30/60; P) Simple but very comfortable en-suite rooms make this a good spot. Watch out for the signpost about 3km from Rosslare on the road to Tagoat.

Kelly's Resort Hotel (☎ 32114; fax 32222; s/d €75/140; P) With every sports and leisure facility in the book, this hotel is a big weekend hit with families. The three-course set menu costs €22 per person in the restaurant and there is a café for snacks.

Oyster Restaurant (☎ 32439; mains €12/20; 🕓 6-9pm Mon-Fri, 5-9pm Sat & Sun) This place, 100m from Kelly's, serves unambitious but top-quality roasts, steaks and fish dishes.

Getting There & Away

Only the 9.30am bus from Rosslare Harbour to Wexford and the 5.45pm from Wexford to Rosslare Harbour stop at Rosslare Strand, Monday to Saturday (€3.70, one hour). Trains on the main line from Dublin to Rosslare Harbour (single and return €16.50, 3¼ hours) via Wexford (€6, 30 minutes) stop at Rosslare Strand three times a day. Trains to Waterford leave twice daily.

ROSSLARE HARBOUR

☎ 053 / pop 900

Most visitors get out of busy, congested Rosslare (Ros Láir) Harbour as soon as possible. A busy port with connections to Wales and France, the harbour's surroundings are not particularly pretty or pedestrian-friendly and you might prefer to head straight on to Wexford. If you do need to stay there is plenty of accommodation in what is really a large village.

Orientation & Information

The ferry port is the main focus of the town. A road leading uphill from the harbour becomes the N25 and takes you to the B&Bs and hotels. A little further along this road is Kilrane where there are a few more B&Bs and a pub.

There is a **tourist office** (☎ 33232; 🕓 11am-2pm) on the N25 in Kilrane about 1.5km west of town and a **Bank of Ireland** (St Martin's Rd) with an ATM and bureau de change, just off the N25.

Yola Farmstead Folk Park

Just outside of Tagoat, on the N25, is a slightly twee but interesting 18th-century themed **folk park** (☎ 32610; Tagoat; adult/child €5.50/4; 9.30am-5pm May-Oct, 9.30am-4.30pm Mon-Fri Mar, Apr & Nov). It's basically a reconstructed village with thatched cottages, a working windmill (one of the few left in the country) and a tiny church, all intended to give visitors an impression of what life was like in rural Ireland (minus the hopeless poverty and the smells). There's the ubiquitous craft shop and a Heritage & Genealogy Centre where visitors can trace their roots.

Sleeping & Eating

Most people arriving in Rosslare Harbour head straight out again. With the exception of one or two nice B&Bs, there's not much here except big unattractive hotels and bad food. If you find yourself stuck or just too tired to go any further there are plenty of places to stay.

An Óige Rosslare Harbour Hostel (☎ 33399; www.irelandyha.org; Goulding St; dm €15.50) With a cute schoolhouse appearance, this place is up the hill from the ferry terminal; take the flight of steps on the left as you leave the harbour and cut down beside Hotel Rosslare. It opens early or late for ferry arrivals and departures.

Clifford House (☎ 33226; cliffordhouse@eircom.ie; St Martin's Rd; s/d €35/70) The pleasant gardens are the attraction here, with serene views from most rooms.

St Martin's B&B (☎ 33133; St Martin's Rd; s/d €35/70) The beautifully decorated rooms in this comfortable place are as good as most of the local hotels.

MacFadden's Bar & Restaurant (☎ 33590; Kilrane; mains €12-16; noon-9.15pm) Don't be thinking anything fancy about this place on the N25 about 2.5km from the harbour terminal. It serves good solid pub grub and meat and veg staples.

Getting There & Away

Buses and trains both depart from the Rosslare Europort station at the ferry terminal.

FORTH & BARGY IS YOLA TO ME

Keep your ears open for the faint remnants of a dialect called Yola, sometimes called 'Forth and Bargy', which still survives in southeastern County Wexford. Yola stands for 'ye olde language' and is a mixture of old French, English, Irish, Welsh and Flemish. Examples of the language would be to *curk*, meaning to sit on your thighs, or to be *hachee* or bad-tempered. A *chi o' whate* means a small amount of straw, while a *stouk* is a truculent woman. A few other useful words might be *kyne* (cow), *toan* (toes) and *hime* (home). There is a story told of a local Yola speaker who had never left the valley where she was born. In the late 1960s she was brought to the top of the valley so that she could take a peek at the world beyond. She took one look and turned to go home, muttering that she didn't like what she saw!

BOAT

Two ferry companies operate services to and from Rosslare Harbour and there's a convenient train and bus station by the ferry terminal.

Stena Line (☎ 33997) sails to Fishguard in Wales on the Lynx catamaran (foot passenger €30, car and driver €229, four daily between 8.30am and 11pm, 3½ hours). There are two crossings daily by the Superferry, which is €6 to €13 cheaper.

Irish Ferries (☎ 33158) sails to Pembroke in Wales (foot passenger €31, car plus driver €229, two daily, 3¾ hours). It also sails to Cherbourg in France and from April to September there are also sailings to Roscoff in France (foot passenger €120, car plus two adults €539, three to six a week, 16 to 24 hours). For more information see Sea, p674.

BUS

Bus Éireann (☎ 01-836 6111) has regular services to Wexford (€3.70, 30 minutes, six daily), Dublin (€14, three hours, 12 daily) and Waterford (€11.70, 1¼ hours, five Monday to Saturday, three Sunday).

CAR

Budget (☎ 33318), **Hertz** (☎ 23511) and **Murrays** (☎ 33634) share a desk in the ferry terminal.

TRAIN

Trains operate the Dublin and Waterford routes to Wexford (€4.45, 30 minutes, three daily), Dublin (€19.05, 3¼ hours, three daily), to Waterford (€12.50, 1¼ hours, two Monday to Saturday) and Rosslare Strand (€4.45, 10 minutes, five daily). For more information call ☎ 33114.

SOUTH OF ROSSLARE HARBOUR

Thank God for government cutbacks. About 9km south of Rosslare Harbour is Carnsore Point, where Ireland's first nuclear power station was to be built, had cost not killed it off. Carnsore Point was noted as the country's southeasternmost point on the map drawn by Ptolemy in the 2nd century. Offshore to the east is Tuskar Rock Lighthouse. The village of **Carne** has a few pretty, whitewashed, thatched cottages and a fine beach.

Locals and visitors alike pack **Lobster Pot** (☎ 053-31110; Carne; mains €5-9) out in the summer, but it's worth the squeeze to get at the super fresh seafood. The chowder is one of the best on this planet.

Heading back up the road takes you past Lady's Island Lake in the middle of which is **Our Lady's Island**, site of an early Augustinian priory (you can still see a tower and graveyard) and still a centre of devotion and pilgrimage. Turning west brings you to Tacumshin, where in 1840 Nicholas Moran built the **Tacumshin Windmill**, one of Ireland's few thatched windmills. The key can be picked up from the shop where you park but you may be charged to visit the windmill.

Bridgetown, 12km southwest of Wexford town, was the first part of Ireland to be colonised by the Anglo-Normans.

There's no public transport to this area.

KILMORE QUAY

☎ 053 / pop 400

Straight out of a postcard, peaceful Kilmore Quay is a small village on the eastern side of Ballyteige Bay noted for its lobsters and deep-sea fishing. The **Seafood Festival** in the second week of July involves all types of seafood tastings, music and dancing.

Lining the attractive main street up from the harbour are a fair number of pretty whitewashed thatched cottages. The harbour is the jumping-off point for the Saltee Islands (see p166), home to Ireland's largest bird sanctuary, clearly visible out to sea. In the harbour the Guillemot Lightship houses a small **maritime museum** (☎ 21572; adult/child €3/1.50; 🕑 noon-6pm May-Sep, Sat & Sun only Apr & Oct).

Activities

There are some wrecks and great marine life around Kilmore Quay and the nearby Saltee Islands for divers to explore. Contact **Quay House** (☎ 29988) or **Pier House Diving Centre** (☎ 29703) to hire gear.

To the northwest, a good sandy beach stretches towards Cullenstown and there are some signposted **walking trails** behind the dunes.

Sleeping & Eating

Kilturk Hostel (☎ 29883; fax 29522; 2km out of Kilmore Quay along the R739; d/tr €15/20) Renovated with all salvaged materials, this hostel was originally an old school. You can still stay in the headmaster's room, or in a classroom dormitory.

Quay House (☎ 29988; kilmore@esatclear.ie; s/d €35/70) Once the village post office, this roomy, whitewashed guesthouse is all country pine floors and bedroom furniture. The lounge and dining room are great places to meet fellow guests.

Haven (☎ 29979; Off Main St near Quay house; s/d €35/70) The spectacular sea views (from some rooms only) and Main St location make this place a great option.

Silver Fox Restaurant (☎ 29888; starters €5-9, mains €15-22; 🕑 noon-10pm Mon-Sat, 6-10pm Sun) Book in advance because chef-owner Nicky Cullen's seafood specialities attract big crowds. The deep-fried cheese is a fantastic starter.

Wooden House Restaurant & Bar (☎ 29804; mains €12-16) Traditional music and a great pint of stout add to the atmosphere of this pub-restaurant.

Kehoe Pub & Parlour (☎ 29830; mains €11-18; 🕑 food served 12.30-8.30pm Mon-Thu, 12.30-7.30pm Fri-Sun) In the family for six generations, Kehoe's has grown into one of the best pub dining experiences in Ireland. Of course seafood dominates and the roll mop herring salad is as delicious as it is unusual.

Getting There & Away

Public transport to Kilmore Quay is very limited. **Viking Buses** travel between Kilmore Quay and Wexford three times daily. **Bus Éireann** (☎ 01-836 6111) has a service on Wednesday and Saturday from Wexford. For details, ask at the post office.

SALTEE ISLANDS

The Saltee Islands are 4km offshore from Kilmore Quay and feature some of the oldest rocks in Europe, dating back 2000 million years or more. Findings also suggest that the islands were inhabited by the pre-Celts as long ago as 3500 to 2000 BC.

In more recent times the haunt of privateers and smugglers, the Saltees now constitute one of Europe's most important bird sanctuaries, home to over 375 recorded species, principally the gannet, guillemot, cormorant, kittiwake, puffin and the Manx shearwater. The best time to visit is the spring and early-summer nesting season; once the chicks can fly, the birds leave. By early August it's eerily quiet.

The Saltees – nicknamed the 'graveyard of a thousand ships' – were touched by the 1798 Rising: it was here that two of the Wexford rebel leaders, Bagenal Harvey and Dr John Colclough, were found hiding before they were both brought to Wexford, hanged and beheaded.

The Saltees were bought in 1943 by Michael Neale, who then crowned himself Prince Michael, the 'First Prince of the Saltees'. He even erected a throne and obelisk in his own honour on the Great Saltee.

To book a crossing to the Saltees try local boatmen such as **Dec Bates** (☎ 053-29684, 087 252 9736), **John Devereaux** (☎ 053-29637, 087 292 6469) or **Dick Hayes** (☎ 053-29704, 087 254 9111).

Boats leave from the harbour at Kilmore Quay most days in summer at about 10.30am and return at about 3pm, with more crossings according to numbers. Docking on the islands depends on the direction of the winds, and the operators will know the night before whether a landing is possible or not. It's a 30-minute crossing and the return fare is €18 if the boat is full, €70 if you're the only one. For more on the islands read *The Saltees, Islands of Birds and Legends* by Richard Roche & Oscar Merne (O'Brien Press).

HOOK PENINSULA & AROUND

☎ 051

The southwest of the county is dominated by the long, tapering finger of the Hook Peninsula, terminating at Hook Head. Cromwell's statement that Waterford town would fall 'by Hook or by Crooke' referred to the two possible landing points from which to take the area: here or at Crooke in County Waterford. In good weather, it's a fine journey out to the lighthouse at the tip of the head and back along the western side to Duncannon.

The area between Kilmore Quay and Bannow, just east of the peninsula, is littered with Norman ruins. There's a good reason for this. Just south of Bannow Bay is Baginbun Head where the Anglo-Normans made their first landings in Ireland. At **Bannow Bay** are the overgrown earthen ramparts built by the Normans when they first arrived. The stone Martello tower dates back to the early 19th century. The estuary here is rich in birdlife such as brent geese, redshank, wigeon and teal.

Travelling back to the R733 towards Hook Peninsula you'll pass through **Wellington Bridge** where the Irish chapter of the Hell's Angels meet over the June bank-holiday weekend. Talking of wild men who love hot metal, in this town are the ruins of a **Norman village** that was known as Clonmines. Unfortunately the ruins are on private land and access is prohibited, but you will get a good view of them just south of the bridge as you come east into town. The redbrick chimney in a paddock by the roadside on the north side of the bridge is the remains of a **silver mine**. It was in operation from the 16th to the 19th centuries and supplied the Irish mint.

On the way out to Hook is a 12th-century Cistercian abbey in a lovely rural setting near the village of Saltmills, **Tintern Abbey** (☎ 562 650; Saltmills; adult/child €2/1 incl guided tour; 🕒 9.30am-6pm Jun-Sep). It was founded by William Marshall, earl of Pembroke, after he nearly perished at sea, and was named after another abbey in Wales where its first monks came from. To get there turn off the R734 at Saltmills where the sign for the abbey points along the road you're on. Also here is a three-way sign for **Tintern Trails**, 3km of walks around the abbey estate and surrounding area.

Continuing south towards the head, **Fethard-on-Sea** is the largest village in the area and home to the ruins of a 9th-century church and a 15th-century castle. Due to instability you can't wander through the ruins. There is a small **tourist office** (☎ 397 502; Main St; 🕒 9.30am-5.30pm Mon-Fri Jul & Aug).

The journey out to **Hook Head** is lovely, the land extremely flat with few houses interrupting the open space. On a clear day you can see across to the Blackstairs

Mountains to the north. About 2km from the head, turning left at a T-junction brings you down to the village of **Slade**, where a ruined castle dominates the harbour.

Further south, Hook Head is crowned by Europe's, and possibly the world's, oldest **lighthouse** (☎ 397 055; guided tours adult/child €4.75/3.50; 9.30am-5.30pm Mar-Oct). It's said that monks lit a beacon on the head from the 5th century and that the first Viking invaders were so happy to have a guiding light that they left the monks alone. In the 12th century a more solid beacon was erected by Raymond le Gros; 800 years later it's largely the same structure you see today and was manned until 1996.

There are fine **walks** both sides of the head, a haunting and beautiful place in the evening. Be careful of the numerous blowholes on the western side of the peninsula. The rocks around the lighthouse are Carboniferous limestone, rich in fossil remains. If you search carefully, you may find 350-million-year-old shells and tiny disc-like pieces of crinoids, a type of starfish. Hook Head is also a good vantage point for **bird-watching**: over 200 species have been recorded passing through.

Coming back up the other side of the peninsula, about 5km from the lighthouse, is the enormous **Loftus Hall**, a privately owned, English-style mansion which looks desperately out of place here. The entire Hook Peninsula once formed part of the Loftus Estate.

Continue along the road towards Duncannon and you'll come across the ruins of a **medieval church** by the roadside. It's opposite the Templar's Inn (see Eating p168). Here there is a 13th-century cross with a lamb engraving. This was known as the Agnus Dei and was associated with the Knights Templar who were given land around here by Henry II in 1172.

The village of **Duncannon** is a small holiday resort with a wide, sandy Blue Flag beach and a good view over Waterford Harbour. To the west is **Duncannon Fort** (☎ 389 454; adult/child €4/2; 10am-5.30pm Jun-Sep). It's a star-shaped fortress built in 1586 on the site of an earlier Norman construction in defence from an attack by the Spanish Armada. The fort was used by the Irish army as a training base during WWI and, more recently, as a set for *The Count of Monte Cristo* starring Richard Harris and Guy Pearce. There is a small café on the premises.

About 4km north of Duncannon is Ballyhack, from where a ferry sails year round to Passage East in County Waterford (see Passage East p179). There's also a 15th-century **Knights Templar castle** (☎ 389 468; adult/child €1.50/0.75; 9.30am-6.30pm Jun-Sep).

Dunbrody Abbey is a beautiful ruin on the western side of Hook Head, near the village of Campile and about 9km north of Duncannon. It was built around 1170 by Cistercian monks from Buildwas in Shropshire, England. Most of the structure survives and there is also a hedge maze. Nearby are the ruins of **Dunbrody Castle** (☎ 388 603; adult/child €2/1; 10am-7pm Jul & Aug, 10am-6pm Apr-Jun & Sep). It has a craft shop and small museum that includes a huge doll's house. There's an additional charge to visit the maze (adult/child €4/2).

Scuba Diving

Hook Head is popular with divers. The best spots are out from the inlet under the lighthouse or from the rocks at the southwestern corner of the head. The underwater scenery is pleasant, with lots of caves, crevasses and gullies. It's a maximum of 15m deep. If it's too rough, try Churchtown, about 1km back from the point just before the road goes inland by the ruined church. Follow the path west to some gullies and coves. Otherwise, try the rocks south of Slade Harbour, a popular area.

The **Hook Sub-Aqua Club** (☎ 388 302; Slade; 9am-6pm) provides dive-site information and a full range of facilities, including a compressor and storage. **Wexford Diving Centre & Dive Charters** (☎ 053-39373; Riverstown Farm, Murrintown; 9am-6pm) has similar facilities and offers diving charters. Tanks can be filled at Hotel Naomh Seosamh in Fethard-on-Sea (see Sleeping, p168), and in summer local dive groups often meet here.

Sleeping

Most accommodation is in Fethard-on-Sea or Arthurstown, but there are a few B&Bs in more remote areas. Campers should stock up and head 12km south out to Hook Head, where there's free camping along the shore.

Fethard Camping & Caravan Park (☎ 397 123; Fethard-on-Sea; tent & 2 people €15) On the northern end of Fethard-on-Sea, this park has all the regular amenities plus some great views.

Ocean Isle & Caravan Park (☎/fax 397 148; Fethard-on-Sea; tent & 2 people €15.50) About 1km north of town this park boasts a shop and games room.

Arthurstown Hostel (☎ 389 411; Arthurstown; dm €12, d €34-40, q €52) In a 200-year-old building, this hostel has a great big kitchen where guests like to commune around the wooden table. It's 1km south of Ballyhack on the western side of the peninsula.

Glendine House (☎ 389 258; Duncannon Hill; s/d €55/80) The huge bedrooms make this B&B special, but the horses grazing in the front field are a nice bonus.

Hotel Naomh Seosamh (☎ 397 129; Fethard-on-Sea; s/d €35/70) Sitting near all the town's facilities right in the middle of main street, this small hotel is popular at the weekend.

Dunbrody Country House Hotel (☎ 389 600; www.dunbrodyhouse.com; Arthurstown; s €117-192, d €234-384 May-Oct, s €95-155, d €190-310 Nov-Apr) This luxurious 1830s country manor has period decorated rooms, a gourmet restaurant (see below), and stunning grounds for an after-dinner stroll.

Eating

Fethard-on-Sea's hotels and pubs are the peninsula's principal eating spots.

Village Kitchen (☎ 397 460; Fethard-on-Sea; snacks €3.50-9; ⏲ 10am-6pm) This is a small coffee shop with sandwiches and light meals.

Templar's Inn (☎ 397 162; Templetown; snacks €3-8) This popular inn specialises in seafood and gets very crowded at lunch-times, so get there early.

Sqigl Restaurant & Roches Bar (☎ 389 188; Quay Rd, Duncannon; mains €10-18; ⏲ 7-10.30pm Tue-Sat year round, noon-2.30pm & 7-9.30pm Sun Jul & Aug, noon-2.30pm Sun Sep-Jun) Local produce – mostly seafood and lamb – are the mainstay of the exquisite menu at this fabulous barnyard restaurant (pronounced squiggle) located behind the pub (which also serves some good pub grub).

Dunbrody Country House Hotel (☎ 389 600; Arthurstown; mains €19-27) This superb restaurant boasts award-winning chef Kevin Dundon and a hat-full of wonderful reviews.

Getting There & Away

Bus services are virtually nonexistent to this part of Wexford. On Monday and Thursday, **Bus Éireann** (☎ 01-836 6111) buses running from Wexford to Waterford will drop you in Fethard-on-Sea. They leave Wexford town at 2.50pm; return services leave Fethard-on-Sea (€10.60, 1¾ hours) at 11.26am. At least one bus daily runs from New Ross to Duncannon.

If you're travelling on to Waterford, it's well worth taking the 10-minute crossing on the Ballyhack to Passage East ferry. It'll save you a long drive northwards via New Ross. For details on fares and times see Passage East, p179.

NEW ROSS

☎ 051 / pop 6147

New Ross (Rhos Mhic Triúin), 34km west of Wexford town on the River Barrow, was developed as a port by the Normans in the 12th century. It was given its name to distinguish it from Old Ross, which was a large settlement to the east. Today it advertises itself as the 'Norman gateway to the Barrow Valley', but you'd have to look fairly hard to find any trace of its Norman past. It's not an especially pretty town, with large oil-storage tanks and old warehouses looming over the riverbanks, but the eastern bank is better than the western one, with some steep, narrow streets and St Mary's Church.

New Ross was the scene of fierce fighting during the 1798 Rising when a group of rebels under Bagenal Harvey and John Kelly tried to take the town. They were repelled by the defending garrison, leaving 3000 people dead and much of the town in ruins.

A **tourist office** (☎ 421 857; 22 The Quay; ⏲ 9am-1pm & 2-6pm Mon-Sat, 11am-4pm Sun Jun-Aug) operates from a refurbished grain-store building.

Sights

The roofless ruin on Church Lane is **St Mary's Church**, which was founded by Isabella of Leinster and her husband, William, in the 13th century. It's one of the largest medieval churches in Ireland. The church key is available from the caretaker across the road.

The **SS Dunbrody Emigrant Ship** (☎ 425 239; adult/child €6/4.50; ⏲ 9am-6pm Apr-Sep, noon-5pm Oct-Mar) is a full-scale reconstruction of SS *Dunbrody*, built in 1845 and used to ferry emigrants escaping the ravages of the Famine to the USA. On board is a visitor centre that features a short film detailing the history of the original ship as well as the construction of the new one. There's also a database of Irish emigration to America from 1820 to 1920. The plan is for the SS *Dunbrody* to make a return voyage to Boston, but this is on hold until funding can be found.

Sleeping & Eating

MacMurrough Farm Hostel (☎ 421 383; MacMurrough; dm €12-14, d €28-32) The family sheep and dogs give every visitor a loud welcome at this cosy hostel. It's 3km northeast of town and bikes are available for hire.

Riversdale House (☎ 422 515; fax 422 800; Lower William St; s/d €42/56; Apr-Nov) Rooms with a view. Only a five-minute walk from the centre, this place has pleasant gardens and a personal touch.

Clarion Brandon House Hotel (☎ 421 703; brandonhouse@eircom.ie; Roslare Rd; s/d €90/170) This hotel 2km south of New Ross has all the hallmarks of an upscale hotel: open log fires in the lobby, quality art on the walls and extensive gardens. The rooms are big enough for a small family.

Gallery Cruising Restaurant (☎ 21723; North Quay; mains €20-30; Easter-Oct) A great idea for a warm evening. Cruise slowly up the River Barrow, through rolling fields and peaceful farmlands, while enjoying a quality dinner and some good wine. They also do lunch and tea cruises.

Getting There & Away

Bus Éireann (☎ 053-22522) buses depart from Ryan Brothers on the quay and travel to Waterford (€5, 20 minutes, three daily), Rosslare Harbour (€10, one hour, seven daily, three Sunday) and Wexford (€8.20, 40 minutes, seven daily, three Sunday).

AROUND NEW ROSS

About 5km south of New Ross, **Dunganstown** was the birthplace of Patrick Kennedy, grandfather of John F Kennedy. Patrick left Ireland for the USA in 1858 and JFK visited the town during his presidency. The original Kennedy house no longer exists, but there's a small cottage belonging to the Ryan family, who are direct descendants, and a small plaque marks the spot. Nearby is **Kennedy Homestead** (☎ 051-388 264; Dunganstown; adult/child €4/2; 10am-5.30pm May-Sep). This visitor centre celebrates five generations of the Irish-American dynasty – no mention of Grandad Kennedy's bootlegging career or JFK's penchant for ladies that he wasn't married to.

About 2km to the south is the **John F Kennedy Park & Arboretum** (☎ 051-388 171; New Ross; adult/child €2.55/1.25; 10am-8pm May-Aug, 10am-6.30pm Apr & Sep, 10am-5pm Oct-Mar). It covers 252 hectares of woodlands and gardens with more than 4500 species of trees and shrubs. Funded by some prominent Irish-Americans, the park was opened by Eamon de Valera in 1968 in memory of the late US president. There is a small visitor centre, tearooms and a picnic area.

Slieve Coillte Hill, opposite the park entrance, offers a splendid view of the surrounding countryside and the Saltee Islands.

ENNISCORTHY

☎ 054 / pop 7640

Enniscorthy (Inis Coirthaidh) is an attractive hilly town on the banks of the Slaney in the heart of County Wexford, 20km north of Wexford town. For the Irish its name is forever linked to some of the fiercest fighting of the 1798 Rising when rebels captured the town and castle and set up camp nearby at Vinegar Hill. A visitor centre tells the bloody story brilliantly.

Information

The **tourist office** (☎ 34699; Castle Hill; 10am-1pm & 2-5.30pm Mon-Sat mid-Jun–Aug, 2-5.30pm Sun & bank hols Sep–mid-Jun) is located in the Castle and County Museum. Grab a free *Enniscorthy Town Trail* map.

There is a Bank of Ireland on Abbey Square. The main post office has a bureau de change and is at the bottom of Castle Hill on Abbey Square. Internet access is available from **Café del Mar** (☎ 38531; Castle Hill; €1.25/15min).

Enniscorthy Castle & Wexford County Museum

The Normans left Enniscorthy the gift of a strong **castle** (☎ 35926; Castle St; adult/child €3.80/0.65; 10am-1pm & 2-6pm Mon-Sat, 2-5.30pm Sun Jun-Sep, 2-5.30pm Oct-Nov & Feb-May, 2-5.30pm Sun Dec & Jan). A defiant stout building with drum towers at the corners, it dates back to 1205 and was a private residence until 1951. Queen Elizabeth I rewarded the poet Edmund Spenser for the many flattering things he said about her in his epic *The Faerie Queene* by awarding him the lease on the castle, but he sold it on to a local landlord, Edward Sinnott, whose grandson then sold it on to Sir Henry Wallop in 1580.

Like everything else in these parts, it was attacked by Cromwell in 1649, and during the 1798 Rising rebels took control of the town and used the castle as a prison. Today it houses the Wexford County Museum, a slightly chaotic but interesting mishmash of bits and pieces. The 1st floor mainly covers 20th-century history and includes artefacts from the 1916 Easter Rising, as well as the 1798 Rising. On the top floor, among cobwebs, chipped paint and inches of dust, you'll find exhibits on local sports, agriculture and maritime history.

1798 Visitor Centre

The castle was overtaken as the town's most important attraction in 1998 by the opening of this interpretative **visitor centre** (☎ 37596; Mill Park Rd; adult/child €5.10/3.20; 🕑 9.30am-6pm Mon-Sat, 11am-6pm Sun, last admission 5pm). It commemorates Wexford's abortive uprising against British rule in Ireland. Little is left to the imagination, with rich interactive displays and audiovisuals highlighting the circumstances and events surrounding the rebellion, as well as the fate of the rebels, most of whom were butchered with impunity by Crown forces. It's an excellent museum – it has been heralded as Ireland's best – and is well worth the admission cost. From Abbey Square walk along Mill Park Rd for about five minutes and then take the first right after the school.

St Aidan's Cathedral

Lovingly restored to its original glory (check out the star-spangled roof), this impressive Roman Catholic **cathedral** was built in 1846 and designed by Augustus Pugin, who had a passion for late-13th- and early-14th-century Gothic church architecture. The son of a French immigrant, he was also responsible for designing the Houses of Parliament in London.

Vinegar Hill

Every Irish schoolchild knows the name of **Vinegar Hill**, where bravery and butchery held equal sway for a fateful month in 1798. Just 2km southeast of the town, this was where a group of rebels set up camp after having captured the town. After 30 days on the hill, a bloody encounter forced them to withdraw. There is a memorial to the uprising and great views of the Slaney and surrounding countryside. To get there, follow the sign from Templeshannon on the eastern side of the river that says 'Vinegar Hill 2km' – *not* the sign that mentions the golf course and Country House as well. It should take you about 30 minutes.

Activities

Enniscorthy Golf Club (☎ 33191; New Ross Rd; green fee weekday/weekend €25/34) is 2.5km southwest of town.

Slaney Canoe Hire (☎ 34526; canoes per day €63.50) rents top-of-the-range, Canadian-made canoes. Just call ahead and they'll bring the canoe to a place on the riverbank that suits you.

One-hour guided walks of the town in English and French can be booked at **Castle-hill Crafts & Tours** (☎ 36800; fax 36628; Castle Hill; tour €3.80) next to Café del Mar. There must be a minimum of five people.

There's plenty of good **fishing** in the Slaney. Go to **Cullens** (☎ 33478; 14 Templeshannon) for tackle hire and permits.

Festivals & Events

Enniscorthy holds its **Strawberry Fair** in late June/early July when pubs extend their hours and strawberries and cream are laid on heavily. For exact dates and details phone ☎ 21688.

The **Blackstairs Blues Festival** (☎ 35364), over a weekend in September, attracts a number of international artists and appreciators.

Sleeping

Platform 1 (☎ 37766; plat@indigo.ie; Railway Sq; dm €12.70, s/tw €20/40) This clean, roomy and well run hostel is highly recommended. There is a pool room and TV lounge, and staff will help you find your way around town.

PJ Murphy's (☎ 33522; 9 Main St; s/d from €22.90/40.65) Rooms, located above the bar, are small but comfortable enough for the price.

Old Bridge House (☎ 34222; obhouse@indigo.ie; Slaney St; d €46) This small place is well situated overlooking the river, though rooms are basic.

Castle Hill House (☎ 37147; 2 Castle Hill; d €50) This is the pick of places to stay with nicely decorated rooms, a homely atmosphere and friendly, helpful hosts.

Lemongrove House (☎ 36115; Blackstoops; s/d €32/56) An elegant country house, it's 1km north of town on the N11. Rates usually drop a little in winter.

Treacy's Hotel (☎ 37798; info@treacyshotel.com; Templeshannon; s €44-57, d €89-100) Just over Enniscorthy Bridge from the town centre, rooms here are somewhat overpriced for what you get but it's friendly and offers good service.

Murphy Flood's Hotel (☎/fax 33413; Main St; s/d €44.50/76.25) Conveniently close to Market Square and room rates include breakfast.

Eating

De Olde Bridge (☎ 33917; 2 Templeshannon; snacks €2.50-3.80, meals €5.70-7.50; 🕒 8.30am-6pm) This is the place to go for sandwiches, pasta or curries.

Cozy Kitchen (☎ 36488; 11 Rafter St; meals €4.80-6.30; 🕒 9am-6pm Mon-Sat) This popular deli and restaurant serves healthy meals and vegetarian dishes.

Galo Chargrill Restaurant (☎ 38077; 19 Main St; mains €10-14; 🕒 noon-3pm & 6-11pm Tue-Sun) Great smells emanate from this place where you can also get pasta and vegetarian dishes.

Self-caterers could try Pettitt's Supermarket on Duffey Hill.

Entertainment

There are plenty of pubs in Enniscorthy. Most of those directed at a younger crowd are on the eastern side of the river, especially along Templeshannon.

Antique Tavern (☎ 33428; 14 Slaney St) This tiny, half-timbered tavern is a nice place for beer (but not for 'footpads, thimblemen or three-card tricksters').

White House (☎ 33096; Templeshannon) The small, inviting White House is in stumbling distance of the Platform 1 hostel. There's live music every weekend during summer and on Sundays only the rest of the year.

Tavern (☎ 33016; 5 Templeshannon) This cosy pub with an open fire is not as wild as the Old House next door.

Shopping

The Enniscorthy area has been well known as a centre of pottery since the 17th century. The tourist office has a free pottery trail guide.

Forestwood (☎ 051-424844; Clonroche) and **Carley's Bridge Potteries** (☎ 33512), which dates back to 1694, are both on the road to New Ross.

Getting There & Away

BUS

Bus Éireann (☎ 01-836 6111) buses stop on Templeshannon Quay on the eastern bank of the river outside the Bus Stop Shop. There are about nine buses daily (roughly every two hours) to Dublin (€10, two hours), Wexford (€4.70, one hour) and Rosslare Harbour (€7.50, one hour).

TRAIN

The **train station** (☎ 33488) is on the eastern bank of the river. The one line serves Dublin (€14.60, 2½ hours), Rosslare Harbour (€9, one hour) and Wexford (€6, 30 minutes) three times daily.

FERNS

☎ 054 / pop 1000

About 7km northeast of Enniscorthy, Ferns is a sleepy village with a glorious history. Once the administrative capital of Leinster and an important diocese for several hundred years, it was the base of the MacMurrough kings of Leinster, in particular Dermot MacMurrough, whose name is forever associated with bringing the Normans to Ireland. He died here in 1171 (see Of Norse & Normans p28). Places to stay are disappointing here and, as you really only need an hour or so to take in the sights, you'd be better off using nearby Enniscorthy as a base.

Ferns Castle

Dating back to around 1220, the remains of this **castle** (admission free; 🕒 year round) at the northwestern end of the village are thought to stand on the site of Dermot MacMurrough's old fortress. A couple of walls and part of the moat survive, with good views available from the top of the one complete tower. To the left of the door at the top is a murder hole through which oil or arrows could be dropped onto attackers below. Parliamentarians under Sir Charles Coote destroyed the castle and put most of the local population to death in 1649.

Other Sights

At the eastern end of the main street is **St Edan's Cathedral** which was built in the early Gothic style in 1817. The remains of a high cross near the entrance are said to mark the grave of Dermot MacMurrough. The **graveyard** here also marks the burial place of Father Redmond who supposedly saved the life of a young French student, one Napoleon Bonaparte.

Other antiquities include the remains of **St Mary's Abbey**, founded by Dermot MacMurrough in 1158, just southeast of the cathedral, and **Ferns Cathedral** just behind it. The latter was built by Normans in the 13th century but was burnt down in 1577 by a local chieftain.

At the top of the main street (the western end) is the modern **St Aidan's Cathedral** and a little further along you'll find the remains of Ferns Castle.

Getting There & Away

Ferns is on the **Bus Éireann** (☎ 01-836 6111) Dublin to Rosslare Harbour route via Wexford and Enniscorthy. Buses run nine times a day. Buses from Dublin to Waterford also stop in Ferns three times a day (€12, three hours).

MT LEINSTER

Bunclody, on the border with County Carlow 16km northwest of Ferns, is a good base from which to climb Mt Leinster. At 796m it's the highest mountain in the Blackstairs. If you want to drive to the top, take the Borris road out of Ferns for 8km, turn right at the sign for the South Leinster Scenic Drive, and continue to the radio mast at the top. The last few kilometres are on narrow, exposed roads with steep fall-offs, so drive slowly and watch out for sheep. If the weather is good you should be able to see parts of counties Waterford, Carlow, Kilkenny and Wicklow.

Mt Leinster is also home to some of Ireland's best hang-gliding. The **Mt Leinster Hang-Gliding Club** (☎ 01-455 6437) runs day courses for around €170. For guided walks in the Blackstairs Mountains you could contact **Brian Gilsenan** (☎ 054-77828).

COUNTY WATERFORD

Wedged into Ireland's southeastern corner, County Waterford combines the low farmland and sandy coastlines typical of County Wexford with the more rugged landscape common in County Cork. Long maligned, Waterford city has been rejuvenated in the last few years and the attractive coastal towns of Dunmore East, Tramore and Dungarvan have great character. It's well worth diverting away from the coast for a drive through the Nire Valley, which sits between the Comeragh and Monavullagh Mountains, and further west to the historical towns of Lismore and Cappoquin on the River Blackwater.

South of Dungarvan, in the county's southwest, the area between An Rinn and Ardmore is a Gaeltacht (Irish-speaking) area with its own road signs, special heritage and culture.

WATERFORD TOWN

☎ 051 / pop 44,155

Ireland's oldest city, Waterford (Port Láirge) is first and foremost a commercial city and port. The River Suir's estuary is deep enough to allow large modern ships right up to the city's quays and the port is still one of Ireland's busiest. The northern bank of the river is somewhat marred by this industrial development, but the city has received a facelift in recent years and is now a much more attractive place to stroll around.

Some parts of the city still feel almost medieval, with narrow alleyways leading off many of the larger streets. Reginald's Tower marks the city's Viking heart and there are some attractive Georgian houses and commercial buildings. The town's commercial centre is still a little blighted with fast-food restaurants, but a programme of pedestrianising streets and erecting public artworks has helped revamp the old city's faded image.

History

In the 8th century Vikings settled at a riverside site called Port Láirge, which they renamed Vadrafjord. Recent excavations suggest the city was founded in 914 and quickly became a booming trading post. In their efforts to consolidate their presence, the Vikings adopted a ferocity in dealing with the natives which made it the most powerful – and feared – settlement in the country. All the local tribes paid them a tribute, known in Irish as the Airgead Sróine (nose money): if you didn't pay it, they cut off your nose!

Waterford's strategic importance ensured that its fortunes were closely linked to those of the island as a whole. In 1170 an Irish-Viking army was defeated in battle by the newly arrived Anglo-Normans: 70 prominent citizens were thrown to their

Hook Head lighthouse (p167), Hook Peninsula

RICHARD CUMMINS

DOUG MCKINLAY

Rolling farmlands, **Hook Peninsula** (p166)

MANFRED GOTTSCHALK

Gaeltacht sign, **An Rinn** (p182)

RICHARD CUM

Harbourfront, **Cobh** (p200)

RICHARD CUMMINS

Standing stone, **Beara Peninsula** (p222)

Al-fresco dining, **Cobh** (p201)

RICHARD CUM

COUNTY WATERFORD

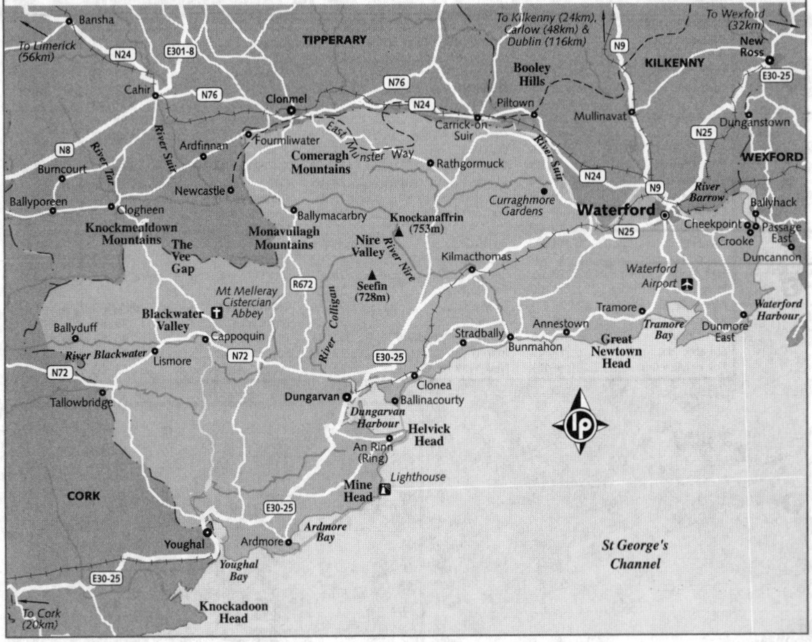

deaths off Baginbun Head. Later that year the city was besieged by Strongbow, who overcame a desperate defence.

In 1210 King John extended the original Viking city walls and Waterford became Ireland's most powerful city and an important trading centre. In the 15th century it resisted the forces of two pretenders to the English Crown, Lambert Simnel and Perkin Warbeck, thus earning the motto *Urbs intacta manet Waterfordia* (Waterford city remains unconquered).

The town defied Cromwell in 1649 but in 1650 his forces returned and the city finally surrendered. Although it escaped the customary slaughter, much damage was done and the population declined: Catholics were either exiled to the west or shipped as slaves to the Caribbean.

Orientation

Waterford lies on the tidal reach of the River Suir, 16km from the coast. The main shopping street runs directly south from the Suir, beginning as Barronstrand St and changing names as it runs south to become Michael St and John St before intersecting with Parnell St. This runs northeast back up to the river, becoming The Mall on the way. Most of the sights and shopping areas lie within this triangle.

Information

BOOKSHOPS

Book Centre (25 Barronstrand St) This excellent store has three floors and sells books (including some foreign papers and magazines) and records; there's also a café.

Gladstone's (12 Gladstone St) Sells second-hand paperbacks.

INTERNET ACCESS

Waterford e-Centre (☎ 878 448; 10 O'Connell St; €2/30 min; 🕒 11am-11pm) In Parnell Court, off Parnell St, you can send and receive email.

LAUNDRY

Duds 'n' Suds (6 Parnell St; 🕒 8.30am-8pm Mon-Sat) A laundrette with a rudimentary café.

LEFT LUGGAGE

Plunkett train station (☎ 873 401) You can leave luggage for €1.25 per item per 24 hours.

WATERFORD TOWN

INFORMATION
- Book Centre....1 C3
- Duds 'n' Suds....2 C6
- Gladstone's....3 C3
- Tourist Office....4 B4
- Waterford e-centre....5 B4

SIGHTS & ACTIVITIES pp175-6
- Beach Tower....6 B5
- Bishop's Palace....7 D4
- Blackfriars Abbey....8 C3
- Chamber of Commerce....9 C3
- Christ Church Cathedral....10 D3
- City Hall....11 D3
- French Church....12 D3
- Half Moon Tower....13 B5
- Holy Trinity Cathedral....14 C3
- Municipal Art Gallery....(see 11)
- Reginald's Tower....15 D3
- Rice Chapel....16 B6
- St Patrick's Church....17 C3
- Tower Museum....(see 15)
- Waterford Heritage Survey....18 C3
- Waterford Treasures....(see 4)

SLEEPING p177
- Beechwood....19 D3
- Corlea House....20 C4
- Derrynane House....21 D4
- Dooley's....22 B4
- Granville Hotel....23 C3
- Mayor's Walk House....24 B5
- O'Connell House....25 B4
- Portree Guesthouse....26 A4

EATING pp177-8
- Bia....27 C3
- Bodega....28 C4
- Café Luna....29 C4
- Dwyer's....30 A4
- Geoff's....31 C4
- Haricot's Wholefood....32 B4
- Johnny Fan's....33 D3
- New York Pie Co....34 C4
- Skippers....35 C3
- Suí Síos....36 C3
- Wine Vault....37 D3

DRINKING p178
- Katty Barry's....38 D4
- T&H Doolan....39 C3

ENTERTAINMENT p178
- Galley Theatre....40 A4
- Garter Lane Arts Centre....41 B4
- Theatre Royal....42 D3
- Waterford Cineplex....43 C3

SHOPPING
- City Square Shopping Centre....44 C3

TRANSPORT pp178-9
- BnB Cycles....45 B5
- Bus Station....46 B4
- Rapid Express Coaches Stop....47 D3
- Wright's Cycle Depot....48 D3

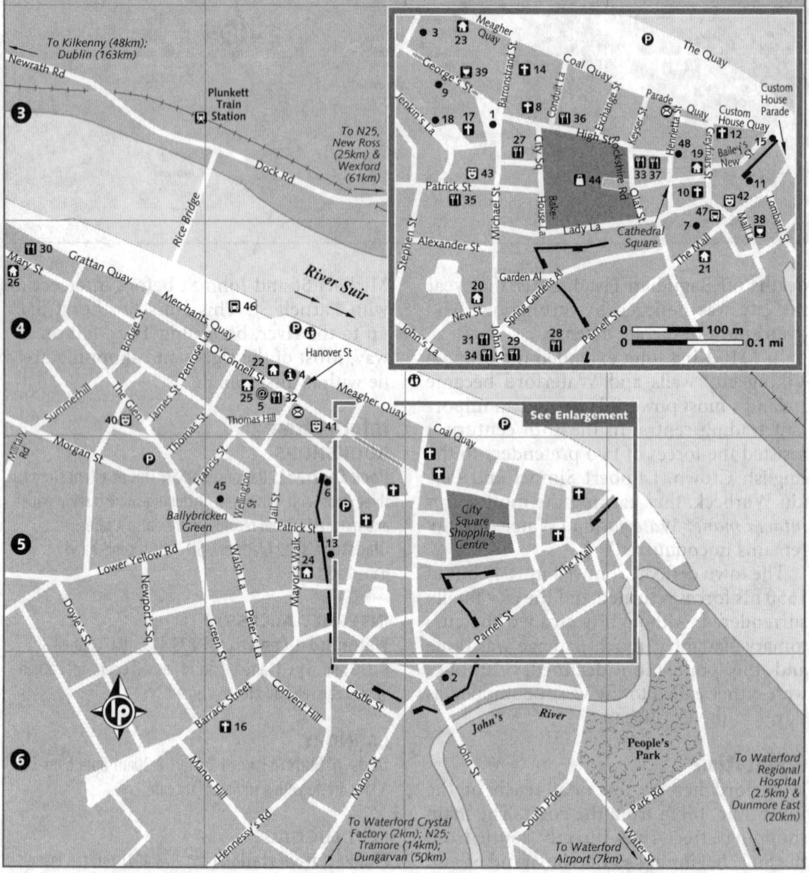

MONEY
There are ATMs throughout the town. There is a branch of **Allied Irish Banks** (☎ 874 824; Meagher Quay) by the clock tower.

MEDICAL SERVICES
Waterford Regional Hospital (☎ 873 321; Dunmore Rd) A little out of town. Just follow the Quays east and watch out for the signs leading you to the hospital.

POST
The main post office is on Parade Quay in the city centre but there's also a smaller post office on O'Connell St.

TOILETS
You'll find public toilets on Merchant's Quay, near the bus station, and others further down near the clock tower.

TOURIST OFFICES
Tourist office (☎ 875 788; fax 877 388; Merchants Quay; 9am-6pm Mon-Sat, 11am-5pm Sun Apr-Sep, 9am-1pm & 2-5pm Mon-Fri Oct-Mar) Located in The Granary and is one of the better ones in Ireland.

Waterford Crystal Factory

The pride of every middle-class living room, **Waterford Crystal** has grown to become one of the world's most famous luxury brands. Touring a factory might not sound like fun, but Waterford Crystal is special. The first Waterford glass factory was established at the western end of the riverside quays in 1783, but closed in 1851 as a result of punitive taxes imposed on the raw materials by the British government. The business wasn't revived until 1947, and the existing factory opened in 1971. Today, it employs 1600 people, among them highly skilled glass blowers, cutters and engravers who take from eight to 10 years to learn their craft. The glass is a heavy lead (over 30%) crystal made from red lead, silica sand and potash.

The **visitor centre** (☎ 373 311; Cork Rd; admission free; 8.30am-6pm Mar-Oct, 9am-3.15pm Nov-Jan) is 2km south of the centre. You can wander about on your own, but we recommend a **guided tour** (adult/child €6.50/free) every 15 minutes, which are led by guides with real insider knowledge of the factory's workings.

In summer buy a ticket in advance from the tourist office to avoid queues. Afterwards you can part with your cash in the Crystal Gallery and then have lunch in the café.

Reginald's Tower

The oldest complete building in Ireland and the first to use mortar, **Reginald's Tower**, at the northern end of the Mall, was built by the Normans in the 12th century on the site of a Viking wooden tower. With walls 3m to 4m thick, it was the city's key fortification. It also housed the wedding feast of Strongbow and Aoife, the marriage of Norman adventurer and Celtic princess.

Over the years the tower has served as a mint, an arsenal and a prison. Many of Waterford's royal visitors stayed in this 'safe house', including Richard II, Henry II and James II, who took a last look at Ireland from the tower before departing to exile in France.

The **tower museum** (☎ 873 501; The Quay; adult/child €1.90/1.25; 10am-5pm Mon-Fri, 2-6pm Sat-Sun Easter-Oct) has several exhibits, including artefacts connected to one of Waterford's most famous sons, Thomas Francis Meagher (1823–67). Meagher was a Young Ireland leader captured for his part in the 1848 Rising and shipped to a penal colony in Australia. From there he escaped to the USA, where he became governor of Montana.

Behind the tower, a section of the **old wall** is incorporated into Reginald's bar and restaurant. The two arches were sallyports, to let boats 'sally forth' onto the inlet, which used to flow right by the wall.

The Mall

This is a wide 18th-century street running back from the river and built on reclaimed land which, until 1735, was a tidal inlet running alongside the walls. At the river end of The Mall, the **City Hall** was built in 1788 by local architect John Roberts. A remarkable Waterford glass chandelier hangs in the council's meeting room (there's a replica in Philadelphia's Independence Hall in the USA). The City Hall houses Waterford's **Municipal Art Gallery** but access is only via sporadic **guided tours** (☎ 873 501, extension 489). It is also home to the music and dance performance called the Waterford Show.

Just up from City Hall, and also built by John Roberts, the **Theatre Royal** is Ireland's finest intact 18th-century theatre.

A little further away from the river again, the austere **Bishop's Palace** was begun in 1741 after a stretch of the wall was demolished. One of Ireland's finest town houses, it was designed by Richard Cassels (or Castle), who was also responsible for Powerscourt House in County Wicklow, Westport House in County Mayo, and Dublin's Leinster House and Rotunda Hospital. It now acts as the city engineering offices.

Waterford Treasures

Housed in The Granary, a superbly converted grain store, **Waterford Treasures** (☎ 304 500; adult/child €6/3.20; 🕙 9.30am-9pm Jun-Aug, 9.30am-6pm Sep & May, 10am-5pm Oct-Apr) is arguably Ireland's most hi-tech museum exhibition. Inside it's all sleek metal and glass plus a dash of evocative Celtic music and audiovisual displays. Luckily the exhibits live up to the wrapping. Dazzling gold Viking broaches, jewel encrusted Norman crosses, 18th-century church silver; the place overflows with the booty of a thousand years of urban history. Each floor is dedicated to a historic period.

Christ Church Cathedral

Behind City Hall is Europe's only neo-classical Georgian cathedral, **Christ Church Cathedral** (☎ 874 119; Cathedral Sq; admission by donation). It was designed by John Roberts and stands on the site of an 11th-century Viking church. When the medieval cathedral was demolished, a remarkable collection of 15th-century Italian priests' vestments was uncovered.

Don't miss the **tomb of James Rice**, seven times lord mayor of Waterford, who died in 1469 and is depicted in a state of decay with worms and frogs crawling out of his body. The cathedral also houses several **Bibles** written in Irish.

There is usually someone there to guide you around the place if you wish.

French Church

Sitting on Greyfrairs St you'll find the elegant ruins of a **French Church** given to Franciscan monks in 1240 by Hugh Purcell. In exchange he asked only that they pray for him once a day every day. It became a hospital after the dissolution of the monasteries and was then occupied by French Huguenot refugees between 1693 and 1815. You can pick up the church key across the road at 5 Greyfriars St.

Other Buildings

The ruins and square tower of the Dominican **Blackfriars Abbey** on Arundel Square date back to 1226. Nearby on Barronstrand St the Catholic **Holy Trinity Cathedral** was built between 1792 and 1796 by John Roberts, who also designed the Protestant Christ Church Cathedral. The sumptuous interior boasts a fine carved pulpit, painted pillars with Corinthian capitals and lovely Waterford crystal chandeliers.

Near Patrick St is the old city wall's **Half Moon Tower**. **St Patrick's Church** on Jenkin's Lane is an 18th-century Catholic chapel which managed to survive the savage suppression of Catholicism at that time. At the top of Jenkin's Lane is the **Beach Tower**, another remnant of the old city wall.

The **Chamber of Commerce** building on George's St was originally built as a town house by John Roberts and has a magnificent staircase.

Edmund Ignatius Rice, founder of the Christian Brothers, established his first school at Mt Sion on Barrack St, where the **Rice Chapel** is a delightful combination of red brick and stained glass, with Rice's tomb in pride of place awaiting the likely canonisation of its occupant. If you phone ☎ 874390 you can also arrange to see an audiovisual presentation on Rice's life and works.

Genealogical Centre

If you have ancestors from the Waterford area, the Genealogical Centre at the **Waterford Heritage Survey** (☎ 876 123; Jenkin's Lane; 🕙 9am-1.15pm & 1.45-5pm Mon-Fri May-Oct) may have all the details you need to complete the family tree.

Tours

A must-do for any visitor to Waterford is a one-hour **guided walking tour** (☎ 873 711, 851 043; €6; 🕙 11.45am & 1.45pm Mar-Oct). For some reason Waterford has gathered together a couple of guides truly blessed with the 'gift of the gab.' Audience participation is expected as you travel from the Granville Hotel on Meagher Quay through every nook and cranny of this tiny city. Against all the rules of physics, the guides squeeze 1000 years effortlessly into one wonderful hour.

Festivals & Events

Waterford's **Light Opera Festival** takes place in September and October. It's cheaper and more easily accessible than the more famous

Wexford Festival Opera but booking is still advisable. For more details contact the **Theatre Royal** (☎ 874402, The Mall).

Sleeping

The frequency of buses to Tramore (see p179) means you can stay there and commute into Waterford if you can't find anything here that takes your fancy. The only hostel in town is now closed to tourists.

MID-RANGE

For a city with such a huge amount of tourist traffic, Waterford is disappointingly lacking in good, central B&Bs. Wherever you stay in the centre, traffic noise can be a problem.

Mayor's Walk House (☎ 855 427; 12 Mayor's Walk; s/d €25/45) A big welcome and a huge breakfast set this place above the B&B pack. It's about 15 minutes from the centre of town.

Portree Guesthouse (☎ 874 574; Mary St; s/d €40/65) An attractive Georgian house in a quiet part of town, this B&B is one of the best in the centre.

Beechwood (☎ 876 677; 7 Cathedral Sq; s/d €40/75) Welcome to Mrs Ryan's house, where you'll soon feel like one of the family. A cosy little B&B gem on a quiet side street.

O'Connell House (☎ 874 175; 3 O'Connell St; s/d €28/56) A great location at a good price, this no-frills guest house is perfect for a one-night stay.

Derrynane House (☎ 875 179; 19 The Mall; s/d €25/50) It can get a little noisy, but the dining room windows here are a great place for a bit of people watching. It has spacious, functional rooms.

Corlea House (☎ 875 764; 2 New St; s/d €30/50) Nothing special about this place except that it's close to some good cafés and bars.

TOP END

There is one classy hotel in town, and an OK alternative.

Granville Hotel (☎ 305 555; stay@granville-hotel.ie; Meagher Quay; s/d €100/165; P) A real gem, this floodlit 18th-century building overlooking the river is one of Ireland's oldest hotels. Public rooms and bedrooms maintain a touch of Georgian elegance.

Dooley's (☎ 873 531; hotel@dooleys-hotel.ie; Merchant's Quay; s/d €85/155) The rooms are big and comfortable, but there's not much else special about this place.

Eating

BUDGET

New York Pie Co (☎ 304 204; 17 John St; mains €3-7; noon-3am Wed-Sat, 5pm-3am Sun) A huge selection of pies and hotdogs bring in the after-pub crowd.

Skippers (☎ 872 942; 46 Patrick St; snacks €2-6) This fish-and-chip shop has a burger menu too.

MID-RANGE

The city's cafés offer the best value eating in the city. The most interesting places are on Michael St and John St.

Bia (☎ 854 023; Arundel Lane; mains €5-7.50; 9am-3pm) The name simply means food in Irish and this young, colourful place has impressive breakfast and lunch menus. The chili wrap is a great between-meals snack.

Suí Síos (☎ 841 063; 54 High St; mains €5-10; 8.30am-6pm) 'Take a seat' says the name and you won't be disappointed at this pleasant little cafe. It serves healthy salads, sandwiches, breakfasts and great coffee.

Café Luna (☎ 843 439; 53 John St; mains €5-10; 10am-midnight Mon-Wed, 10am-3am Thu-Sun) This rather groovy place is popular with students drawn to the home-made soup and bread. It also serves great coffee.

Haricot's Wholefood (☎ 841 299; 11 O'Connell St; mains €8-10; 9am-8pm Mon-Sat, 9am-6pm Sun) Vegetarian dishes and a full licence make this place a winner with students eager to blow their grants.

Geoff's (☎ 874 787; 9 John St; mains €4-8; 10am-4pm) Geoff's is always full of people, which is a good sign. Panini, sandwiches and Mexican-influenced meals are the main fare here.

TOP END

A few new, innovative restaurants have livened up Waterford's dining scene.

Bodega (☎ 844 177; 54 John's St; mains €10-18; noon-2.30pm & 6.30-10pm Mon-Sat) The décor is all Spanish cantina, but the food at this wonderful new restaurant is pure country French. Half the Cronan family seem to be on hand at any one time to serve up dishes like escargot in puff pastry and fish pie with salad. The wine bar stays open until around 2am and locals love to gather here for a late-night chat.

Wine Vault (☎ 853 444; High St; mains €15-20; noon-10pm Mon-Sat) A choice of 350 different wine labels, a beautiful setting in the cellar of an Elizabethan town house, and a quality menu including escallop of beef with spinach on home-made bread with a warm potato salad; what is there to not like?

Johnny Fan's (☎ 879 535; High St; mains €18-22; ⏲ noon-10pm) This highly rated Chinese restaurant is run by the ever talkative Johnny Fan. The fish of the day dishes are very popular.

Dwyer's (☎ 877 478; 8 Mary St; mains €20-25; ⏲ 6-11pm Mon-Sat) An old police barracks is the setting for this French-style eatery. The menu changes every month or so; if the venison is on it's worth a try.

Drinking

Waterford's nightlife relies heavily on the presence of students from all over the country who attend the local technical college. Weekends are the big nights, when many pubs feature live music.

Katty Barry's (☎ 855 095) This small, dark and friendly place is rumoured to serve the best Guinness in the area.

T&H Doolan (☎ 872 764; 31 George's St) The venerable T&H Doolan incorporates a remnant of the 1000-year-old city wall. Sinead O'Connor played here before she hit the big time and there is still live music most nights.

Geoff's (☎ 874 787; 9 John St) One of the city's hippest bars, Geoff's is where John St becomes Michael St. Food is served from 10am to 4pm (see p177).

Entertainment

Most clubs stay open till around 4am and are concentrated around the intersection of Parnell St, John St and John's Lane.

THEATRE & CINEMAS

There are plenty of opportunities for exploring the arts in Waterford.

Garter Lane Arts Centre (☎ 855 038; 22a O'Connell St) This theatre, in an 18th-century building, stages films, exhibitions, poetry readings and plays.

Galley Theatre (☎ 871 111; The Glen) Located in The Forum, this place puts on plays most nights.

City Hall (☎ 875 788; The Mall; admission €8.90; ⏲ 8.45pm Thu-Sun May-Sep) The 1½-hour *Waterford Show* here combines music, dancing and wine in a programme about the city's history. Tickets can be booked at the tourist office, Waterford Crystal Factory or City Hall.

Waterford Cineplex (☎ 874 595; Patrick St) This five-screen complex shows first-run films.

Getting There & Away

AIR

Waterford Airport (☎ 875 589) is 7km south of the city at Killowen. **Euroceltic Airways** (reservations ☎ 875 020) has two daily flights to London's Luton airport from around €80 one way.

BUS

The **Bus Éireann** (☎ 879 000) station is on the waterfront at Merchant's Quay. There are plenty of buses daily to Dublin (€10, three hours), Cork (€13.30, 2¼ hours), Wexford (€10.60, 1½ hours), Killarney (€18.50, 4¼ hours) and Dungarvan (€8.20, 50 minutes).

Rapid Express Coaches (☎ 872 149; Parnell Court, Parnell St) runs a service between Waterford and Dublin (€8, eight daily, three hours) via Dungarvan and Carlow.

Suirway (☎ 382 209) buses go to Dunmore East (€2.80, 30 minutes, four daily Monday to Saturday) and Passage East (€2.50, 30 minutes, four daily Monday to Saturday). They depart from the waterfront next to the Bus Éireann station. Look for the red-and-white buses.

TRAIN

Plunkett train station (☎ 873 401) is on the northern side of the river. Trains run to Dublin (€21, three hours, five daily), Kilkenny (€10, 45 minutes, five daily), Limerick (€21, three hours, two daily) and Cork, via Limerick Junction (€22, three to five hours, four daily). You can leave luggage at the station for €1.25 per item per 24 hours.

Getting Around

There is no bus service to the airport. A **taxi** (☎ 877 773) will cost around €14.

Disc parking (€0.65 per hour) is in operation in the centre and there are paid car parks along the quays and at The Glen, just west of the centre.

There are taxi ranks at Plunkett train station and outside Penney's department store at City Square Shopping Centre.

Wright's Cycle Depot (☎ 874 411; Henrietta St; rental €14/60 per day/week) is a Raleigh Rent-a-Bike outlet. **BnB Cycles** (☎ 870 356; 22 Ballybricken

Green) also hires out bikes for around the same prices.

PASSAGE EAST

About 11km east of Waterford city on the coast road is Passage East, with its little harbour and thatched cottages at the foot of low hills. The Passage East to Ballyhack ferry makes a useful short cut between Counties Waterford and Wexford. The **ferry** (☎ 051-382 480) operates a continuous service throughout the day. Return tickets (pedestrian/cyclist/car €1.25/2.55/8.25) for the 10-minute crossing are valid for an unlimited time. The ferry operates from 7am to 10pm Monday to Saturday and 9.30am to 10pm Sunday from April to September, 7.20am to 8pm Monday to Saturday and 9.30am to 8pm Sunday October to March

Just south of the village is **Crooke**, with the remains of the Geneva Barracks nearby. Built in the 18th century as part of a settlement for Swiss refugees, the buildings were turned into barracks after the plan fell through. It was here that a young rebel of the 1798 Rising came to confess his sins to a priest who turned out to be an army officer in disguise. The lad was arrested and subsequently hanged, a story immortalised in the song *Croppy Boy*.

Suirway (☎ 051-382 422) runs buses here from Waterford; see p178 for details.

DUNMORE EAST

☎ 051 / pop 1500

Dunmore East (Dún Mór), a fishing village strung out along a coastline of red sandstone cliffs and discreet coves, is a really lovely spot. The main street is lined with thatched cottages and the larger buildings, such as the Haven Hotel, were once homes of wealthy merchant families who called the village home during the early 19th century.

The harbour is overlooked by an unusual **Doric lighthouse** built in 1823. At this time the town was a station for the steam packets which carried the mail between England and the south of Ireland.

There's a good view of Hook Head lighthouse across the water in County Wexford. The noisy birds nesting in the cliffs around the harbour are kittiwake. The most popular **beaches** are Counsellor's Beach, facing south and set among the cliffs, and Ladies Cove, in the village. As it's only 20km from Waterford city, it's a popular getaway for day-trippers so it gets very busy during summer and on weekends.

Activities

Dunmore East Adventure Centre (☎ 383 783) hires out equipment for windsurfing, canoeing, surfing and snorkelling. Short courses in most of these sports are also available. Half-day activities cost €30.

If you fancy a bit of **shark fishing** or exploring old wrecks off the coast contact **Dunmore East Angling Charters** (☎ 383 397, 087 268 2794).

Sleeping

Creaden View (☎ 383 339; Harbour Rd; s/d €45/80) Make sure you get a room with a view overlooking the bay at this excellent B&B.

Church Villa (☎ 383 390; churchvilla@eircom.net; s/d €29/50) One of a row of cottages near the Ship bar/restaurant (see below). Rooms are cosy and spotless and the breakfast is a treat.

Ocean View (☎ 383 695; s/d €30/60) This is next door to Church Villa and is very similar in design and standard.

Springfield B&B (☎ 383 448; s/d €40/56) Only 150m from the beach, this roomy place has a great conservatory for breakfast.

Eating & Drinking

Bay Café (☎ 383 900; Harbour Rd; mains €3-6; 🕒 9am-6pm) Everything is home-made here including the burgers, lasagne and pies.

Ship (☎ 383 141, 383 144; Harbour Rd; mains €18-22; 🕒 6-10pm daily Apr-Oct, 6-10pm Tue-Sat Nov-Mar, noon-2.30pm daily Jun-Aug) It doesn't look like much but this bar/restaurant serves up the best seafood for miles.

Strand Inn (☎ 383 174; Ladies Cove; mains €20-25; 🕒 12.30-2.30pm & 7-10pm) Overlooking Ladies Cove, this inn also specialises in seafood. The bar food is also top quality.

Power's Bar (☎ 383 318; Dock Rd) This is a nice, intimate place for a drink.

Getting There & Away

Suirway (☎ 382 422) runs buses here from Waterford; see p178 for details.

TRAMORE

☎ 051 / pop 6536

The name simple means 'big beach' in Irish and Tramore is the busiest of County Waterford's seaside resorts. About 14km south of Waterford, the delightful 5km beach is backed with 30m-high dunes at its eastern end. Tramore itself is fairly tacky, with amusement arcades and fast-food outlets running along the seafront and a monstrous water park plonked in the middle of town.

The **tourist office** (☎ 381 572; Railway Sq; 🕑 9.30am-5.30pm Mon-Sat Jun-Aug) is in the old train station that ran trains to Waterford city from 1853 to 1960. It has a brochure detailing two walks in and around town, and another detailing a 35km drive that takes in **megalithic tombs** (dolmens) and **standing stones** in the area.

Sights & Activities

Standing on the shore, the bay is hemmed in by **Great Newtown Head** to the southwest and **Brownstown Head** to the northeast, with their standing pillars and the **Iron Man**, a huge painted iron figure of an 18th-century sailor in white breeches and blue jacket with his arm pointing seawards as a warning to approaching ships. The pillars were erected by Lloyds of London in 1816 after 360 lives were lost when a boat mistook Tramore Bay for Waterford Harbour and was wrecked.

One of Tramore's biggest attractions is **Splashworld** (☎ 390 176; Railway Sq; adult/child €8.50/6.50; 🕑 9am-8pm Mon-Fri, 10am-7pm Sat & Sun, reduced hours Nov-Feb) indoor waterpark, 'where you can enjoy tropical temperatures all year round'.

Sleeping

Newtown Caravan & Camping Park (☎ 381 979; Dungarvan Coast Rd; sites per person €6-14; 🕑 Easter-Sep) About 2km outside of town, this family-run affair is the best of the local camp sites.

Cliff House (☎ 381 497; hilary@cliffhouse.ie; 14 Cliff Rd; s/d €32/64) A long walk to the centre of town is compensated for with stunning views over the water.

West Cliffe (☎ 381 365; 5 Newtown; s/d €35/70) This place also has nice views and is closer to the centre than Cliff House.

Turret House (☎ 386 342; Church Rd; s/d €40/80) Located on top of Gallwey's Hill, this stylish place boasts spacious bedrooms and a knockout breakfast.

Eating

Tramore might just have more fast food per square foot than anywhere on the planet. Good eateries are hard to come by and pub grub is often your best option.

Apple Brown Betty (☎ 391 680; snacks €3-6; 🕑 10am-7pm) A little gem of a place, this little shack on the beach beside the lifeguard station serves up surprisingly good seafood. Try the crepes for a snack.

Rocketts Seahorse Tavern (☎ 386 091; Main St; bar meals €9-12) This is an award-winning pub grub joint.

Getting There & Away

Bus Éireann (☎ 873 401) runs over 20 buses daily from Waterford to Tramore (€2, 30 minutes). Rapid Express buses also serve Tramore from Waterford. The bus stop is outside the tourist office near Splashworld.

DUNGARVAN

☎ 058 / pop 7175

Dungarvan (Dún Garbhán) is a picturesque port and market town with an attractive centre and lively waterfront. Surrounded by patchwork hills, it sits on the wide bay where the River Colligan meets the sea and derives its name from St Garvan who founded a monastery here in the 7th century. A castle was built here by the Anglo-Normans in the 12th century but many of the town's buildings date from the early 19th century when the duke of Devonshire began a programme of rebuilding.

Modern Dungarvan is now the administrative centre of Waterford. Abbeyside, in the northeast of town, was the birthplace of Ernest Walton, whose work on nuclear fission won the Nobel Prize for physics in 1951.

Dungarvan has some great restaurants and makes a convenient base for exploring western County Waterford, the Ring Peninsula and the mountainous north.

Orientation & Information

Dungarvan is easily navigated on foot. The town's main shopping area is the neatly laid out Grattan Square on the southern side of the river. Main St (also called O'Connell St) runs along one side of it. Parnell St, which comes off the square towards the harbour, is also called Lower Main St.

The very helpful **tourist office** (☎ 41741; tiodgar@indigo.ie; 🕑 9am-6pm Mon-Sat) is in the council building on TF Meagher St next to the post office. It has a free town trail and map.

The post office is on TF Meagher St and most of the banks are on Grattan Square.

Free, 15-minute Internet access is available at the **library** (☎ 41231) on The Quay but it's wise to book ahead.

Sights

A major renovation project has restored the walls of **King John's Castle** (☎ 48144; Dungarvan; adult/child €2/1; 🕓 10.30am-5pm Jun-Sep), originally erected in 1185. a nearby former British Army barracks building has been turned into a visitor centre with audio visual history and various exhibits concerning the castle and the barracks itself.

Dungarvan Museum (☎ 45960; St Augustine St; admission free; 🕓 10am-4.45pm Mon-Fri) is small but nicely presented and well worth a visit. It covers the town's maritime history with relics from shipwrecks. It also includes local Famine history, newspaper clippings and titbits from the last two centuries and focuses on local personalities and their achievements. Look for the pink and grey building with the coat of arms.

The solitary **Augustinian Abbey** on the other side of the bridge overlooks Dungarvan Harbour. It dates mainly from the 19th century but incorporates features from the original 13th-century building, including a well-preserved tower and nave. The original abbey was destroyed during the Cromwellian occupation of the town.

The **Old Market House** (☎ 48944; Lower Main St; admission free; 🕓 afternoons Tue-Sat) is home to an arts centre and hosts regular exhibitions.

As you leave Dungarvan on the R672 to travel west, you'll pass a **monument** to the greyhound Master McGrath, which won the Waterloo Cup three times in the 1860s.

Festival & Events

Over the early May bank-holiday weekend, 17 Dungarvan pubs and two hotels play host to the **Féile na nDéise**, a lively traditional music and dance festival that attracts around 200 musicians. For more information phone ☎ 42998.

Sleeping

Although there are a number of B&Bs on the other side of the bridge from the centre, they are a bit of a walk from the sites.

Dungarvan Holiday Hostel (☎ 44340; fax 36294; Youghal Rd; dm/d €11.50/26) Located in a former friary opposite the garda station on the N25, this place is not in an attractive part of town but is less than a 10-minute walk to the centre.

THE BARBER OF KILMACTHOMAS

In 1650 when Oliver Cromwell and his army prepared to take Waterford city, they were delayed by flooding of the River Mahon and were forced to camp outside the town of Kilmacthomas (between Waterford and Dungarvan). Ever conscious of his appearance, Cromwell ordered that the local barber be brought to him so that he could get a decent shave. The barber duly arrived and was preparing his razor when Cromwell warned him that a cut would cost the barber his life. Undeterred, he proceeded to shave his belligerent customer cleanly and without drawing blood.

Later, when recounting the story to the locals, the barber was asked whether Cromwell's threat had made him nervous. 'Well, look at it this way', he is said to have answered, 'I was holding the razor to his neck!' Apocryphal or not, the story guaranteed the barber a free pint in his local pub for the rest of his days.

Amron (☎ /fax 43337; Mitchell St; s €28-30, d €40-50) It's close to the centre and just a few minutes to the harbour.

Casey's Townhouse (☎ 44912; 8 Emmet Tce; s/d €35/55) The breakfasts are huge and delicious at this impressive guesthouse.

Alwin House (☎ 45994; alwin@cablesurf.com; 1 South Tce; s/d €38/60) This beautiful home has only three rooms, so it's always a quiet spot.

Lawlor's Hotel (☎ 41122; info@lawlors-hotel.ie; TF Meagher St; s €38-70, d €80-110) There's a real old-world feel to this tastefully decorated hotel just off Grattan Square.

Eating

An Bialann (☎ 42825; 31 Grattan Sq; lunch special €5.70; 🕓 9am-6pm) This popular place serves healthy home-cooked food.

JR's Hamburger Restaurant (☎ 42769; 71 O'Connell St; snacks €4-7.50; 🕓 noon-1am Mon-Thu, noon-3am Fri-Sun) Fast food is taken to a whole new level at this classy little eatery.

Mill (☎ 45488; Davitts Quay; mains €16-20; 🕓 5-9.45pm) Cajun and Louisiana cuisine might come as something of a shock in the middle of Waterford, but the quality here is always very good.

Tannery (☎ 45420; Quay St; mains €17-22; ⏲ noon-2.30pm & 6-10pm) This is the other top restaurant in town and is highly recommended by locals. Dishes are modern Irish with some French and Asian influences.

Entertainment

Anchor Bar (☎ 41249; The Quay) A little further along on the harbour front, this bar is open only in the evening and often features traditional music.

Bean A'Leanna (☎ 44882; 86 O'Connell St) This traditional pub has music sessions Thursday to Sunday and set dancing classes on Monday night.

Getting There & Away

Bus Éireann (☎ 051-873 401) buses pick up and drop off on Davitt's Quay on the way to and from Dublin (€11.40, 3½ hours, five Monday to Saturday, four Sunday), Waterford (€7.35, one hour, five Monday to Saturday, four Sunday) and Cork (€11.60, 1¾ hours, 10 Monday to Saturday, six Sunday).

RING PENINSULA

☎ 058

An Rinn, 12km south of Dungarvan on Helvick Head, is one of the most famous Gaeltacht areas in Ireland. It's rugged and unspoilt – the real Ireland. All the road signs are in Irish and the drive from Dungarvan is stunning. At the small harbour in Helvick Head is a **monument** to the crew of *Erin's Hope* who died when it sank near here in 1867. Nearby is an interesting house, sitting on rocks right over the water, that was once a monastery. You can look down on its roof from high spots in the town.

Colaiste na Rinne (☎ 46128), the 100-year-old Irish language college on the Helvick Head road, runs summer language courses for children (10 to 18 years old). It also runs *ceilidhs* (traditional music and dance) most nights during the summer.

Criostal na Rinne (☎ 42127; ⏲ 9am-6pm Mon-Fri & 10am-6pm Sun) is a crystal workshop and showroom in Helvick Head. You can have items inscribed.

Sleeping & Eating

Leaba & Bricfeasta B&B & Ceol na Mara Hostel (☎ 46425; An Rinn; dm/s/d €12/28/48; ⏲ Mar-Oct) Sitting high above the town, this combined B&B and hostel is always full of intrepid travellers from around the globe.

Helvick View (☎ 46297; Helvick Head Road; s/d €24/48) This B&B offers basic accommodation and stunning views of Dungarvan Bay and the surrounding countryside.

An Carn (☎/fax 46611; Rath na mBíninneach, An Rinn; s/d €40-70; ⏲ mid-Mar–mid-Dec) In a big old house on the hill, this B&B doubles as a nice restaurant from Thursday to Saturday.

Getting There & Away

The limited **Bus Éireann** (☎ 051-873 401) service runs from Waterford (€9.20) at 1.45pm on Saturday. This becomes a daily service during July and August.

ARDMORE

☎ 024 / pop 330

South of Helvick Head the coast road veers inland and, after 23km, brings you back to the sea at Ardmore, famous for its 12th-century round **tower**. It's claimed locally that St Declan set up shop here between AD 350 and 420, well before St Patrick arrived from Britain to convert the heathens. Now Ardmore is a popular seaside resort with a Blue Flag beach. Don't be put off by the ugly sprawl of caravan parks that spoil the coastal view to the east: this is a pleasant little place, as long as you like things nice and quiet.

Information

The **tourist office** (☎ 94444; Seafront; ⏲ 11am-4pm May-Sep) is in a white sandcastle-shaped building on the seafront and it has a bureau de change. A town walk leaflet is available here or from Dungarvan's tourist office.

St Declan's Church & Oratory

In a striking position on a hill above the town, the ruins of **St Declan's Church** and a fine slender round tower stand on the site of St Declan's original monastery. The 29m-high **tower** dates back to the 12th century.

The outer western gable wall of the 13th-century church features stone carvings retrieved from an older 9th-century church and placed here. They show the Archangel Michael weighing souls, the adoration of the Magi, Adam and Eve, and a clear depiction of the judgement of Solomon. Inside the church are two ogham stones (the earliest form of writing in Ireland), one of them with the longest inscription of any known ogham stone in Ireland. The site was leased to Sir Walter Raleigh in 1591 after the dissolution of the monasteries and, in 1642, the building was occupied by Royalist troops.

The smaller building in the compound is the 8th-century **St Declan's Oratory**, or Beannachán, which is said to be the final resting place of St Declan. The roof and upper parts of the walls were restored in the 18th century. The depression in the floor is due to worshippers removing earth from the gravesite – it was supposed to protect from disease.

St Declan's Well

Overlooking the sea, **St Declan's Well** is beyond the Cliff House Hotel to the south of town. Pilgrims once washed in it. Beside it are the ruins of Dysert Church. A fine 5km **cliff walk** leads from the well; a free map is available from the tourist office or from the Cliff House Hotel. On the way you'll pass the wreck of a crane ship that was blown ashore in 1987 on its way from Liverpool to Malta.

At the southern end of the beach is **St Declan's Stone**, said to have arrived from Wales across the sea borne by a glacial boulder. Crawling under it on St Declan's Day (24 July) is said to cure rheumatism and bring spiritual benefits.

St Declan's Way

This 94km **walk** mostly traces an old pilgrimage way from Ardmore to the Rock of Cashel in Tipperary. A map guide (€6), which also shows circular routes taking in parts of it, is available from the tourist office.

Sleeping & Eating

Ask at the tourist office about camping for free at Goat Island.

Byron Lodge (☎ 94157; Middle Rd; s/d €33/56; ⌚ Apr-Sep) A classy little thatched cottage on the top of the hill houses this super little B&B. Rooms are light-filled and a joy to come home to.

Ardmore Beach Hostel (☎ 94501; Main St; dm/d €14/34) Direct beach access is the big attraction at this hostel in an old stone house near the seafront.

Paddy Mac's (☎ 94166; Main St; bar food €5-9) Music every weekend and a good pub carvery brings regular crowds to this local favourite. They make a mean sandwich too.

Getting There & Away

There are three buses daily (one on Sunday) from Cork (€10.10, 1¾ hours) to Ardmore. There are two daily to Waterford (€10.30, two hours) via Dungarvan in July and August (otherwise it's a Friday and Saturday only service). Buses stop outside O'Reilly's pub on Main St.

NORTHERN COUNTY WATERFORD

Some of the most scenic parts of County Waterford are in the north around **Ballymacarbry** and in the **Nire Valley**, which runs between the Comeragh and Monavullagh Mountains. The hills form the easternmost extension of a great mass of red sandstone from the Devonian period, some 370 million years ago, which underlies most of Cork and Kerry's scenery. While not as rugged as the west of Ireland, the mountain scenery here has a stark beauty of its own and doesn't attract much tourist traffic. Take care driving through here as stock and wide tractors wander onto the roads.

Sights

Driving from Waterford to Ballymacarbry you can take in **Curraghmore Gardens** (☎ 051-387 102; Portlaw; admission to gardens & shell grotto by guided tour €4; ⌚ 2-5pm Thu), 14km northwest of Waterford city. The fine Georgian house dates from the 18th century but the estate has been home to the marquis of Waterford since the 12th century. You can visit the gardens but the house opens only to groups by prior arrangement.

Activities

The **East Munster Way** walking trail covers some 70km between Carrick-on-Suir in County Tipperary and the northern slopes of the Knockmealdown Mountains. Access to the route is at Fourmilewater, a few kilometres northwest of Ballymacarbry. For more details see p656.

For an excellent **guided walk** of the area covering archaeology, geology, flora and fauna, contact **Michael Desmond** (☎ 052-36238; hiking@indigo.ie). Six-hour walks take place on Saturdays and a reasonable degree of fitness is required.

Otherwise make sure you're around for the **Comeragh Mountain Walking Festival** (☎ 052-36239), which takes place on the second weekend in October. There are a number of guided walks varying in difficulty and length and all the local pubs have plenty of traditional music each night.

The lovely wooded valleys and heathery mountains are good for pony trekking. **Melody's Riding Stables** (☎ 052-36147; Ballymacarbry, behind Melody's pub; 2hrs/3hrs/day €25/35/70; 🕒 Easter-Oct) has wonderfully scenic trail rides including lunch.

From March to September the Rivers Nire and Suir provide great opportunities for **fishing**. Permits can be arranged through Hanora's Cottage (see boxed text below).

Sleeping

Powers the Pot (☎ 052-23085; fax 23893; Harney's Cross; tent & 2 people €14; 🕒 May-Oct) is a charming camp site, signposted off the road between Rathgormuck and Clonmel, about 5km east of Clonmel. There's a bar here with an open fire and meals are served.

Getting There & Away

There's a Tuesday-only bus service from Dungarvan at 2pm, and two buses from Clonmel on Friday at 1.20pm and 5.35pm.

CAPPOQUIN

☎ **058 / pop 1000**

The small market town of Cappoquin is overlooked by the Knockmealdown Mountains. The River Blackwater takes an abrupt turn southwards near the town and the Blackwater Valley to the west is picturesque. The valley is where traces of the earliest Irish peoples have been found; Mesolithic microliths (small stone blades) from around 9000 years ago have been discovered.

There's excellent coarse and game **fishing** locally, and **Glenshelane Park**, just outside the town, offers some lovely forest walks and picnic spots. Salmon-fishing permits are available from **Titelines** (☎ 54152) tackle shop in the main street.

The stunning **Mt Melleray Cistercian Abbey** (☎ 54404; admission free; 🕒 year round) is just over 6km to the north of town and is signposted from the centre. The abbey was founded in 1832 by a group of Irish monks who had been expelled from a monastery near Melleray in Brittany, France. A fully functioning monastery, Mt Melleray opens to visitors seeking quiet reflection and to those who wish to see something of the daily routine. There's no charge for a bed in the guesthouse, but it would be bad manners not to make a donation.

Cappoquin House (☎ 54004; adult/child €7/3.50; 🕒 Apr-Jul) is a Georgian mansion (built 1779) and gardens overlooking town and the River Blackwater. It's the private residence of the Keane family who've lived here for 200 years. The entrance to the house is in the centre of town; take the road for the monastery and look for a set of huge black iron gates just a few metres up on your left.

Getting There & Away

One bus a day (except Sunday) leaves Dungarvan for Cappoquin (€3.70) at 9.30pm and returns to Dungarvan at 7am (15 minutes). There are two buses a week from Waterford (€10.60, 1¼ hours) via Dungarvan leaving at 8.30am Friday and 5.30pm Sunday. There's also one bus a week leaving Cork (€10.60, 1¼ hours) at 4.30pm on Friday. Buses stop outside Morrissey's pub. For details contact **Waterford bus station** (☎ 051-873 401).

LISMORE

☎ **058 / pop 750**

Lismore is a small town beautifully situated on the River Blackwater at the foot of the Knockmealdown Mountains. The river rolls on east and then south to Youghal and the sea.

Although most of the buildings in the town date from the early 19th century, Lismore was the location of a great monastic

SOMETHING SPECIAL

Hanora's Cottage (☎ 052-36134; www.hanorascottage.com; Nire Valley, Ballymacarbry; s €60-90, d €120-180; dinner €40) Put simply, this is one of the best B&Bs in the country. The spacious rooms at this 19th-century ancestral home have all been beautifully decorated and even have hot tubs. There's also a larger spa tub in the conservatory, from which visitors can relax and take in the views of the surrounding mountains. There is an excellent gourmet restaurant too, and the packed lunches with their famous brown bread are unbeatable. Breakfast is included in the room rates. Take the main Dungarvan to Clonmel road (R672), head to Ballymacarbry then turn east off the N72 to Nire Church.

university first founded by St Cartach, or Carthage, in the 7th century. In the 8th century the monastery became a famous centre of learning under St Colman. From the 10th century on it was sacked many times by the Vikings but hung on as the religious capital of Deise (Deices). Until the 17th century, the remains of eight churches could still be seen.

Lady Louisa's Walk follows the banks of the Blackwater from the town centre for about 400m.

Information

The **tourist office** (☎ 54975; Main St; ⏰ 10am-4pm Apr-Oct) is in the Lismore Heritage Centre, in the old courthouse in the town centre. It has a bureau de change and stocks a free town walk map. Guided tours of the town take place at 11.30am and 3pm daily. Alternatively, for €1.40 you can buy *A Walking Tour of Lismore*, which describes all the local sights.

St Carthage's Cathedral

This striking **cathedral** was built in 1633 but stands on the site of another church built in the early 13th century. The spire and ceilings were added in the early 19th century. Inside are some noteworthy tombs, including a MacGrath family crypt dating from 1557, and the small chapel of St Colmcille.

Lismore Castle

From the Cappoquin road there are fine glimpses of majestic **Lismore Castle** overlooking the river. At night time it's lit up like a Christmas tree and looks stunning. The original castle was erected by Prince John, Lord of Ireland, in 1185. It was the local bishop's residence until 1589, when it was presented to Sir Walter Raleigh along with around 200 sq km of the surrounding countryside. He later sold it to the earl of Cork, Richard Boyle, whose 14th child, Robert Boyle (1627–91), was born here and is credited with being the first methodical modern scientist.

Lismore Castle passed to the duke of Devonshire in 1753, and the sixth duke of Devonshire built the current structure in the early 19th century. It does incorporate small sections of the earlier buildings, however. During rebuilding, the 15th-century *Book of Lismore* and the Lismore Crozier (both now in the National Museum in Dublin) were discovered. The book not only documents the lives of a number of Irish saints, but also holds an account of the voyages of Marco Polo. A more recent castle occupant was Adele Astaire, sister of the famous Fred.

The castle is closed to day-trippers but can be rented by seriously rich groups for functions. You can visit the three hectares of the dual-level **gardens** (☎ 54424; adult/child €4/2; ⏰ 1.45-4.45pm Easter-Sep). The lower level is a stunning flower garden while the upper level is a formal garden in an Elizabethan layout.

Lismore Heritage Centre

In the old courthouse is the **Lismore Heritage Centre** (☎ 54975; fax 53009; Main St; adult/child €4/3.30; ⏰ 9.30am-6pm Mon-Sat, noon-6pm Sun). Every half-hour there is an audiovisual presentation that takes you through local history, from the arrival of St Carthage in AD 636 to the present day. It also tells the story of the *Book of Lismore*, discovered in the castle in 1814.

Sleeping & Eating

There's no official camp site nearby but you could ask local farmers if you can camp in their fields.

Beechcroft (☎ 54273; Deerpark Rd; s/d €26/50) The lovely garden is the selling point at this comfortable place. It's in a high part of town and there are pleasant views of the surrounding countryside.

Madden's Bar (☎ 54148; East Main St; mains €5-10) Serving decent lunches in summer, this place has pictures of Fred Astaire on his visits to the town to see his sister when she lived at Lismore Castle.

Getting There & Away

One bus a day (except Sunday) leaves Dungarvan for Lismore via Cappoquin at 9.30pm and returns to Dungarvan at 6.55am (€4.70, 20 minutes). There are two buses a week from Waterford (€11.20, 1¼ hours) via Dungarvan leaving at 8.30am Friday and 5.30pm Sunday. Buses stop outside O'Dowd's pub on West St. For details contact **Waterford bus station** (☎ 051-873 401).

County Cork

CONTENTS

County Cork (Corcaigh) reflects Ireland in all its rich diversity; it's a sampler of everything that the nation has to offer, from lively regional city to seaside resort, sleepy country town to remote village, green pasture to rugged mountain, river to roaring sea. You'll find Irish culture rubbing shoulders with modern art and music, old Irish pubs alongside trendy cafés, and traditional cooking at the same table as modern Irish and international cuisine.

The least dramatic part of Cork is its northern area, where it shares with neighbouring Limerick and Tipperary a farmed landscape dotted with sleepy towns and villages. Cork's long southern coast mirrors this pastoral theme but offers also a fascinating trail of sea inlets, seaside resorts, historic towns, ancient monuments and medieval castles that leads the traveller enticingly towards the fabled world of the county's western shores. And it's here in the dwindling peninsulas of Mizen Head, Sheep's Head and The Beara that the seductive beauty of Atlantic Ireland captivates.

Cork's towns are not high-flyers by nature, but the capital, Cork, is gaining ground as a buzzing city, crammed with historic and cultural venues, and with a growing number of terrific restaurants to match Dublin's. The city's pub and club scene offers the very best of Irish music with contemporary sounds and club culture. Smaller towns, such as Clonakilty, Skibbereen and Bantry, have hung on to their individuality, easily absorbing tourism's pressures without losing touch with Ireland's old cherished values of cheerfulness, kindness and humour.

HIGHLIGHTS

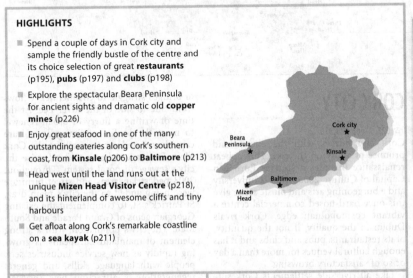

- Spend a couple of days in Cork city and sample the friendly bustle of the centre and its choice selection of great **restaurants** (p195), **pubs** (p197) and **clubs** (p198)
- Explore the spectacular Beara Peninsula for ancient sights and dramatic old **copper mines** (p226)
- Enjoy great seafood in one of the many outstanding eateries along Cork's southern coast, from **Kinsale** (p206) to **Baltimore** (p213)
- Head west until the land runs out at the unique **Mizen Head Visitor Centre** (p218), and its hinterland of awesome cliffs and tiny harbours
- Get afloat along Cork's remarkable coastline on a **sea kayak** (p211)

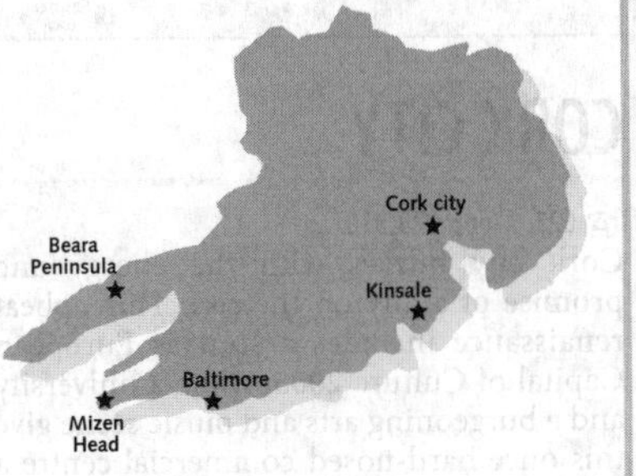

POPULATION: 448,181	AREA: 7457 SQ KM

COUNTY CORK

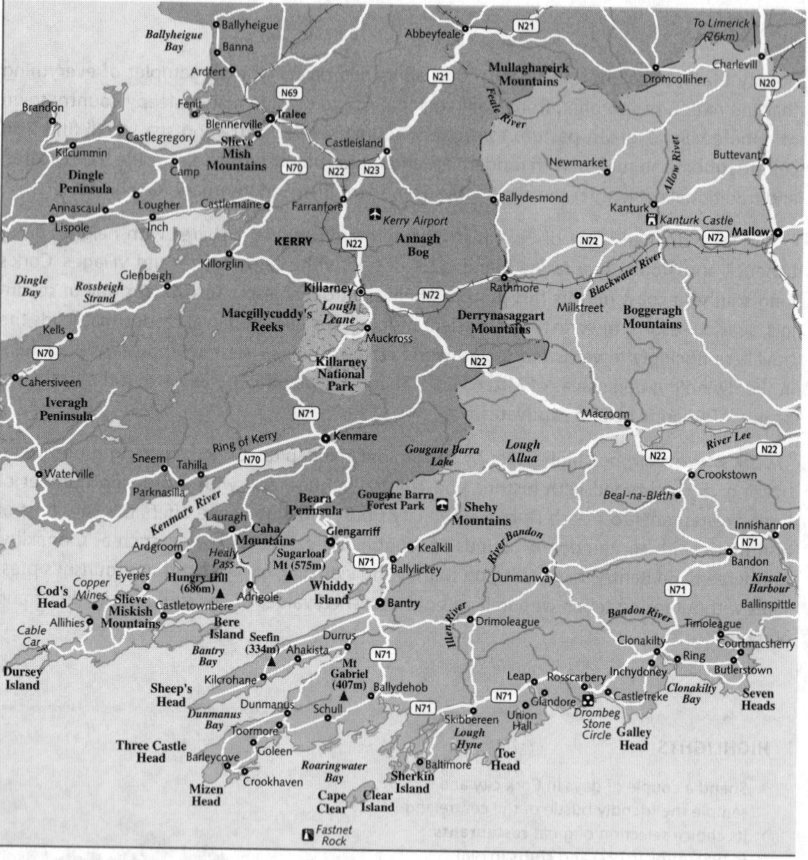

CORK CITY

☎ 021 / pop 123,338

Cork city buzzes with the energy and promise of a city on the rise. This upbeat renaissance includes a stint as European Capital of Culture 2005, while a university and a burgeoning arts and music scene give this once hard-nosed commercial centre a vibrant cosmopolitan edge. Cork rivals Dublin in the quality, if not the quantity, of its restaurants, pubs and clubs and it has enough cultural venues for more than a day or so of satisfactory browsing.

Like all riverside settlements Cork suffers from traffic congestion, as a handful of bridges struggle to channel heavy flows from side to side of the River Lee. At the time of writing a flurry of urban renewal to meet the profile of European culture capital was underway, not least the Cork Main Drainage Scheme to modernise the city's sewage disposal system. Throughout 2003 pedestrian areas and street furniture were being added to the city's main drag, St Patrick's St, to complement the existing Georgian gems of Grand Parade and South Mall. The city's population, with a strong element of mainland Europeans, is growing rapidly as new service industries seek people with language skills, and general regeneration is attracting new services, leisure and cultural interests.

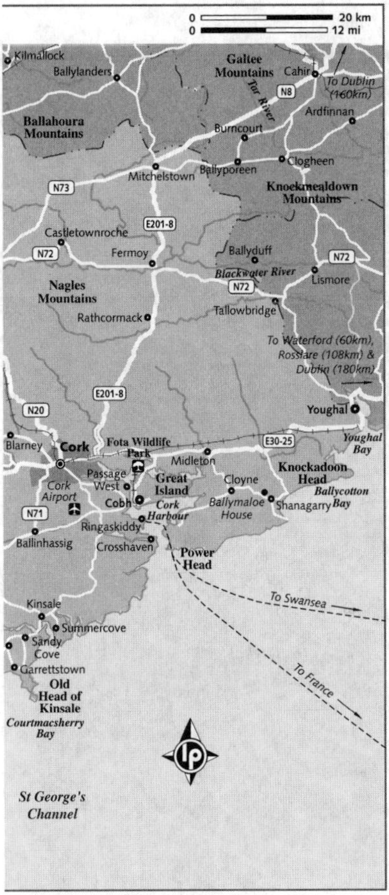

HISTORY

Cork has had a long, distinguished and often bruising history that is etched deeply with the triumphs and tragedies of Ireland's struggle to reassert nationhood.

The city's recorded history dates from the 6th to the 7th centuries when St Finnbarr founded a monastery on what may be the site of the present St Finbarr's Cathedral. By the 12th century the settlement that had developed became the chief city of the Kingdom of South Munster, having survived raids and some sporadic settlement by Norsemen. It was a short-lived Irish rule, however, and by 1185 Cork was under the English Crown. Thereafter it changed hands regularly during the relentless struggle between Irish and Crown forces. It survived Cromwellian assault only to fall to the forces of that merciless champion of Protestantism and commerce, William of Orange. During the 18th century Cork prospered, but a century later famine devastated county and city and bled Cork of its native people, either by death or emigration.

Cork's deep-seated Irishness ensured that the city played a key role in Ireland's struggle for independence. Thomas MacCurtain, a mayor of the city, was killed by the Black and Tans in 1920. His successor, Terence MacSwiney, died in London's Brixton prison after 75 days on hunger strike. The British were at their most brutally repressive in Cork and among general atrocities by the Black and Tans, much of the city centre, including St Patrick's St, the City Hall and the Public Library were burned down. Ever turbulent within its own political factions, Cork was also a regional focus of Ireland's self-destructive Civil War that followed independence in 1921.

ORIENTATION

The city centre is located, island-like, between two channels of the River Lee. The graceful curve of St Patrick's St runs from St Patrick's Bridge on the North Channel of the Lee, through the heart of the city's main shopping and commercial area to the Georgian Grand Parade that runs south to the river's South Channel. From midway down Grand Parade, Washington St (which becomes Lancaster Quay and Western Rd) leads southwest to the university, Killarney and West Cork. North and south of St Patrick's St lie the city's most entertaining quarters, webs of narrow streets, crammed with pubs and cafés, restaurants and all kinds of shops.

Across St Patrick's Bridge is an equally bustling area whose focus is the traffic-logged MacCurtain St, which has its own rewarding spread of pubs, restaurants and shops. East of MacCurtain St is Kent Train Station, budget B&Bs and the road to Youghal, Waterford and Rosslare. West of MacCurtain St is the distinctive Shandon area, set on high ground and with a village-like atmosphere, especially in the narrow lanes that cluster round its hill-top churches.

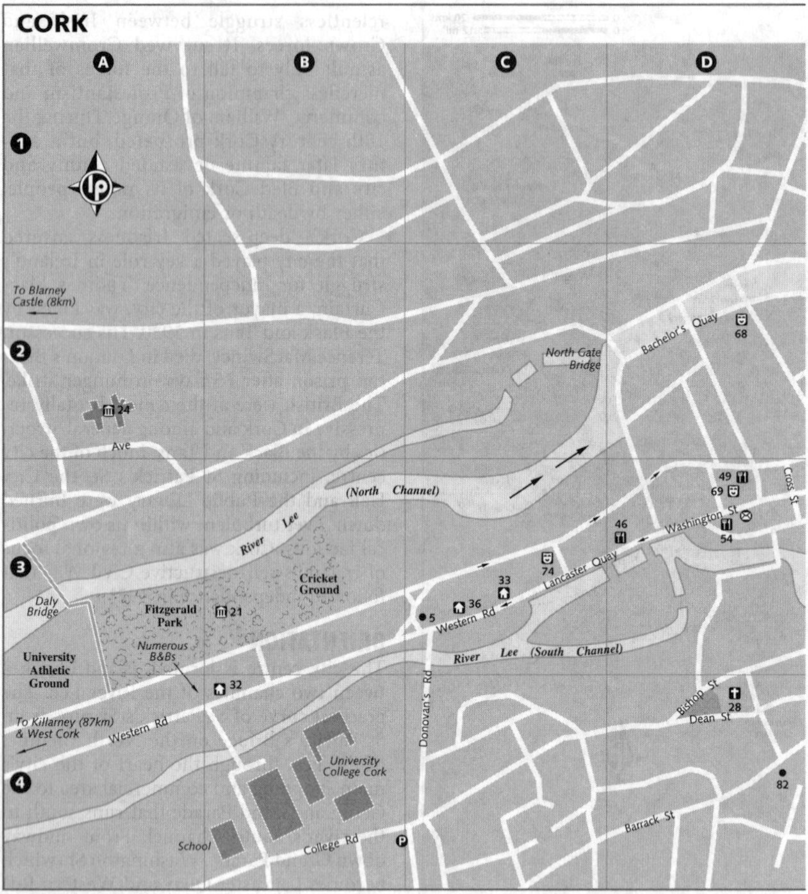

INFORMATION

BOOKSHOPS

Connoly's Bookshop (☎ 427 5366; Rory Gallagher Pl, Paul St) Great chat goes with masses of second-hand books.

Liam Ruiséal Teo (☎ 427 0981; 49-50 Oliver Plunkett St)

Mainly Murder (☎ 427 2413; 2a Paul St) Crime novels galore.

Shelf (☎ 431 2264; 12 George's Quay) There's a pleasant jumble of second-hand books in this little shop.

Vibes & Scribes (☎ 450 5370; 3 Bridge St) Good selection of second-hand books, records and CDs.

Waterstone's (☎ 427 6522; 69 St Patrick's St) A big spacious place that runs between St Patrick's and Paul Sts with entrances on both, this branch has the best travel section in the southwest.

EMERGENCY

City General Hospital (☎ 431 1656; 6 Infirmary Rd) About 1km southeast of the centre, just south of the river.

GAY & LESBIAN

L.Inc (☎ 480 8600; www.linc.ie; 11a White St; 🕑 10am-5pm Mon-Wed & Fri, 8-10pm Thu) Excellent resource centre for lesbians and bisexual women.

Gay Information Cork (☎ 427 1087; gayswitchcork@hotmail.com)

INTERNET ACCESS

Webworkhouse.com (☎ 427 3090; 8a Winthrop St; 🕑 24 hr) You can make low-cost international phone calls at this popular and busy centre. It costs anywhere between €1.25 and €5 per hour depending on the time of day.

Net House (☎ 422 2174; 128 Oliver Plunkett St; €5/hr)

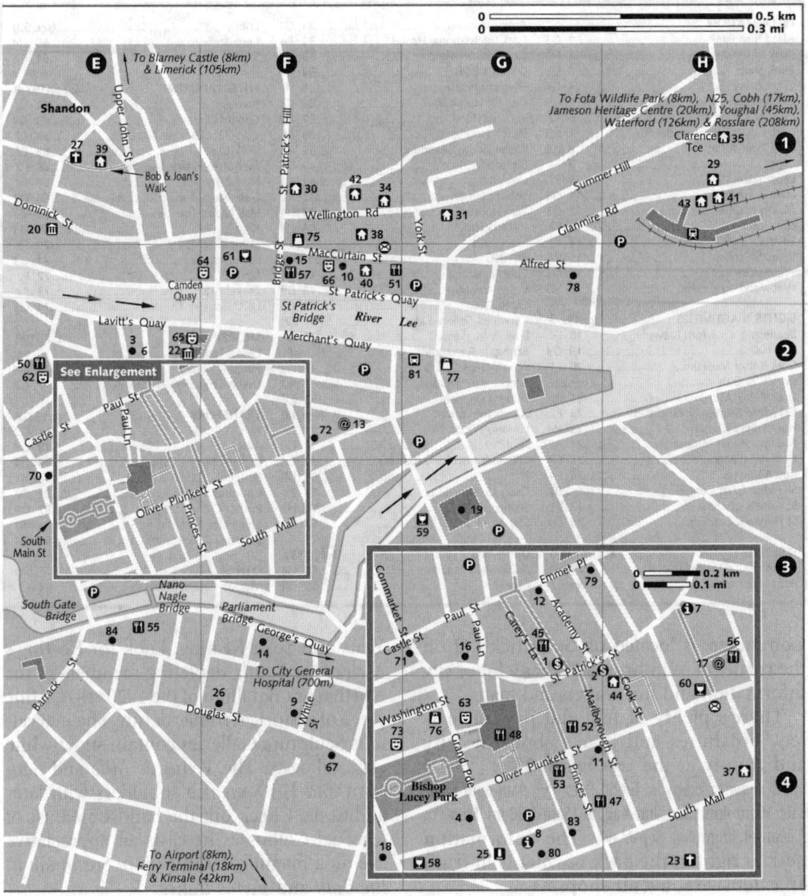

Cork City Library (☎ 427 7110; www.corkcitylibrary.ie; 57-61 Grand Pde; €1.25/30min)

LAUNDRY

Laundrette (14 MacCurtain St)

Clifton Laundrette (Western Rd) Opposite the gates of University College Cork (UCC).

LEFT LUGGAGE

You can't leave luggage at Kent station.

Cork Bus Station (☎ 450 8188; cnr Merchant's Quay & Parnell Pl; €2 per item for 24 hr; 7.45am-6pm Mon-Fri, 9am-6pm Sat)

LIBRARIES

Cork City Library (☎ 427 7110; www.corkcitylibrary.ie; 57-61 Grand Pde; 10am-5pm Mon-Sat)

MONEY

The Bank of Ireland and Allied Irish Bank, both on St Patrick's St, have ATMs and currency-exchange facilities. There are bureaux de change in the Cork Tourist Office and in Cork Bus Station.

POST

Main post office (☎ 485 1032; Oliver Plunkett St; 9am-5.30pm) There are also smaller post offices on MacCurtain St (in Spar shop) and Washington St.

TOURIST INFORMATION

Budget Car and Stena Line Ferries have desks in the tourist office.

From June to September the Cork City Information Booth, run by the Chamber of

INFORMATION
Allied Irish Bank.......1 G3
Bank of Ireland.......2 H3
Book Shop.......3 E2
City Library.......4 G4
Clifton Laundrette.......5 C3
Conolly's Book Shop.......6 E2
Cork City Information Booth.......7 H3
Cork Tourist Office.......8 G4
L.Inc.......9 F4
Laundrette.......10 F2
Liam Ruiséal Teo.......11 G4
Mainly Murder.......12 G3
Net House.......13 F2
Shelf.......14 F3
Vibes & Scribes.......15 F2
Waterstone's.......16 G3
Webworkhouse.com.......17 H3

SIGHTS & ACTIVITIES pp192-3
Beamish & Crawford Brewery.......18 F4
City Hall.......19 G3
Cork Butter Museum.......20 E1
Cork City Gaol.......(see 24)
Cork Public Museum.......21 B3
Crawford Municipal Art Gallery.......22 E2
Holy Trinity Church.......23 H4
National Radio Museum.......24 A2
Nationalist Monument.......25 G4
Red Abbey.......26 F4
Shandon Craft Centre.......(see 20)
St Anne's Church.......27 E1
St Finbarr's Cathedral.......28 D4

SLEEPING pp194-5
Aaran House Tourist Hostel.......29 H1
Acorn House.......30 F1
Auburn House.......31 G1
Cork International Hostel.......32 B4
Crawford House.......33 C3
D'Arcy's B&B.......34 F1
Emerson House.......35 H1
Garnish House.......36 C3
Imperial Hotel.......37 H4
Isaac's Hotel.......38 F1
Kinlay House Shandon.......39 E1
Metropole Hotel.......40 F2
Oaklands.......41 H1
Sheila's Hostel.......42 F1
Tara House.......43 H1
Victoria Hotel.......44 H4

EATING pp195-7
Café Mexicana.......45 G3
Café Paradiso.......46 D3
Clancy's.......47 G4
Crawford Gallery Café.......(see 22)
English Market.......48 G4
Farmgate Restaurant.......(see 48)
Fenn's Quay.......49 D3
Greene's Restaurant.......(see 38)
Hungry Elephant.......50 E2
Isaac's Restaurant.......(see 38)
Luciano's Pizza.......51 F2
Nash 19.......52 G4
O'Brien's Irish Sandwich Bar.......53 G4
Pi.......54 D3
Quay Co-op.......55 E3
Scoozi.......56 H3
Star Anise.......57 F2

DRINKING pp197
An Spailpín Fánach.......58 G4
Charlie's.......59 G3
Lobby.......(see 59)
Long Valley.......60 H4
Sin É.......61 F2

ENTERTAINMENT pp197-8
Bodega.......62 E2
Capitol Cineplex.......63 G4
Cork Arts Theatre.......64 F2
Cork Opera House.......65 E2
Everyman Palace Theatre.......66 F2
Fred Zeppelins.......67 F4
Gate Multiplex.......68 D2
Half Moon Theatre.......(see 65)
Kino.......69 D3
Other Place.......70 E3
Roundy.......71 G3
Scotts.......72 F2
Triskel Arts Centre.......73 F4
UCC Granary Theatre.......74 C3

SHOPPING p198
Living Tradition.......75 F1
Plugd Records.......76 G4
Union Chandlery & Hillwalkers.......77 G2

TRANSPORT pp198-9
Avis.......78 G2
Avis.......79 G3
Brittany Ferries Office.......80 G4
Budget.......(see 8)
Cork Bus Station.......81 G2
Rothar Cycles.......82 D4
Stena Line Ferries Office.......(see 8)
Swansea Cork Ferries Office.......83 G4

OTHER
Munster Literary Centre.......84 E3

Commerce, is located on St Patrick's St on the corner of Winthrop St. It has a lot of city information and free leaflets and maps.

There's plenty of free and pay-for leaflets, brochures and books about the city and county at the **Cork Tourist Office** (☎ 427 3251; www.corkkerry.ie; Grand Pde; ⏲ 9am-6pm Mon-Sat, 10am-4pm Sun Jun-Aug, 9.15am-5.30pm Mon-Fri, 9.30am-4.30pm Sat Sep-May). The information desk is right at the back of what is in truth an extensive souvenir shop.

DANGERS & ANNOYANCES

Cork cherishes its reputation as being a friendlier and less hard-skinned place than Dublin. But late at night and in the early hours there can be some ugly little scenes around central pubs and clubs. At these times it's also best not to linger at such places as the Fountain in Grand Parade.

SIGHTS

Crawford Municipal Art Gallery

Cork's public **gallery** (☎ 427 3377; Emmet Pl; admission free; ⏲ 10am-5pm Mon-Sat) is in the city's old Customs House of 1724. It became the Cork School of Art in 1884 and now houses a small but excellent permanent collection, featuring works by Irish artists such as Jack Yeats and Seán Keating. Look for Keating's *Men of the South*, depicting members of the North Cork Batallion of the 1920s IRA, a fine piece of historical romanticism. The marvellous Sculpture Galleries contain snow-white classical casts. The *Venus de Milo* and *Laocoon and His Sons* rub shoulders with later additions. Check out the handsome bust of Michael Collins as he casts an appreciative eye on a magnificent line up *of Susannah at the Bath* and *Venus Italica.*

St Finbarr's Cathedral

Cork's imposing Protestant **cathedral** (☎ 432 2993; cathedral@cork.anglican.org; Bishop St; donation of €2.50 appreciated; ⏲ 10am-5.30pm Mon-Sat Apr-Sep, 10am-12.45pm & 2-5pm Mon-Sat Oct-Mar) perches rather grandly on a shelf of land to the south of the centre. It dates from 1879 and may stand on the foundations of St Finbarr's monastery. It supplanted 11 other churches and cathedrals on the same site. The building's exterior is an entertaining merging of French Gothic and medieval whimsy, all lofty, spiky spires and rich sculpture. Of note inside are the Bishop's Throne, the marble floor mosaics in the sanctuary, the huge pulpit, the colourful chancel ceiling, and a wealth of restored stained glass. There are several quirky items such as a cannonball that was shot from Elizabeth Fort during the siege of Cork in 1690. The fort, of which little remains, dated from the late medieval period. The cannonball lodged in the original cathedral's spire and was not discovered until 1865 when the medieval building was demolished.

Shandon

Throw in a few art and craft galleries, antique shops, cafés and restaurants among **Shandon's** attractive little lanes and squares and the area could well emerge in a few years time as Cork's 'Latin' quarter. Shandon sits on a hilltop site overlooking the centre of the city and is dominated by the Italianate stepped tower of 18th-century **St Anne's Church** (☎ 450 5906; John Redmond St; admission free; 🕑 9.30am-5pm Mon-Sat). This is the home of the famous chiming bells and you may climb the tower and ring the **bells** (adult/child €4.60/3.90), for a price. The church also contains a small collection of 17th-century Bibles and other books including the letters of poet John Donne.

Nearby is the **Shandon Craft Centre** (O'Connell Sq) in what was once part of the Cork Butter Exchange with a few shops selling souvenirs. Next door is the **Cork Butter Museum** (☎ 430 0600; O'Connell Sq; adult/child €3.50/2.80; 🕑 10am-1pm & 2-5pm May-Sep, by arrangement only Oct-Apr). Exports from the Exchange went to Europe, India, South America and Australia.

Cork Public Museum

Located in a pleasant Georgian House in the delightful Fitzgerald Park, north of Western Rd, this **museum** (☎ 427 0679; Fitzgerald Park; admission free; 🕑 11am-1pm & 2.15-5pm Mon-Fri, to 6pm Jun-Aug, 3-5pm Sun) has a fine collection of artefacts that reflect Cork's history from the early Stone Age onwards. The collection includes items of needlepoint lace and Cork glass and silver.

Take bus No 8 to the main gates of UCC and follow the brown sign pointing to the museum.

Beamish & Crawford Brewery

Fronted by the Counting House, a building that takes first prize for eye-blinding architectural awfulness (mock Tudor, crow-stepped gables, classical pediment *and* pebbledash), this famous **brewery** (☎ 491 1100; South Main St; guided tour adult/child €4/3.60) runs enjoyable guided tours at 10.30am and noon every Thursday from May to September, and at 11am from October to April. The tour ends with a tasting.

Cork City Gaol

The **jail** (☎ 430 5022; Convent Ave, off Sunday's Well Rd; adult/child €5/3; 🕑 9.30am-5pm Mar-Oct, 10am-4pm Nov-Feb), west of the city, received its first prisoners in 1824 and its last in 1923. The 35-minute taped tour, which guides you around the restored and refurnished cells, is very moving. Upstairs is the **National Radio Museum** (adult/child €5/3) where, alongside collections of beautiful old radios, you can hear the story of Guglielmo Marconi's conquest of the airwaves. Take bus No 8 from the bus station to the stop outside UCC, then walk north across Fitzgerald Park and over Daly Bridge. Turn right up the hill along Sunday's Well Rd, left along Convent Ave and you'll see the brown signpost to the jail.

Red Abbey

At the time of writing this **medieval tower**, the oldest building in Cork, and all that's left of a 14th-century Augustinian priory, was scheduled for refurbishment. Its location in Red Abbey St, between Mary and Dunbar Sts, is fairly anonymous, but as far as history goes it gently stirs.

WALKING TOUR

RIVER TOUR WITH A TWIST
Distance of Trail: 1.3km
Duration: one hour

This tour starts at the eastern end of South Mall, across the river from the **City Hall** (**1**).

Walk west along the river until you reach **Holy Trinity Church** (**2**), designed by the Pain brothers in 1834 for Father Theobald Matthew, the 'Apostle of Temperance'. He led an effective, but short-lived, crusade against 'the demon drink', which resulted in a reduction in the production of whiskey by more than half in the early 1840s.

Continue alongside the river then turn left onto the single-arched **Parliament Bridge** (**3**), built by the British in 1806 to commemorate the union of the British and Irish Parliaments five years previously. Cross the

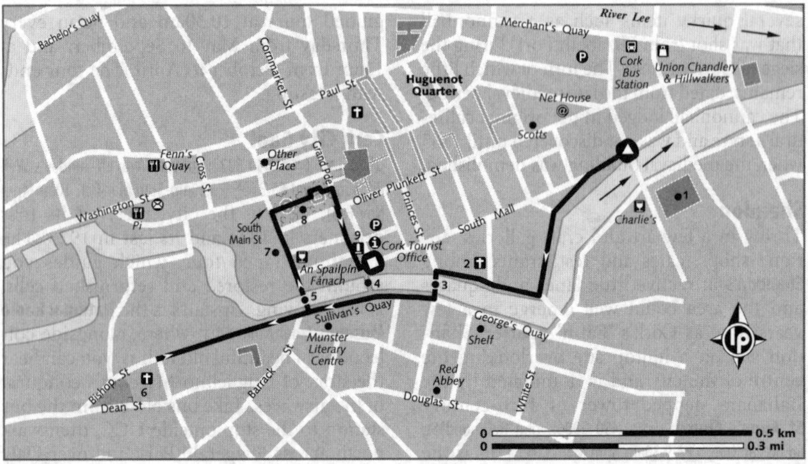

bridge and turn right along Sullivan's Quay. You pass **Nano Nagle Bridge** (**4**) and then **South Gate Bridge** (**5**) built in 1713, which marks the site of the medieval entrance to the city.

Continue straight ahead along French Quay and Bishop St to **St Finbarr's Cathedral** (**6**; p192).

Return from the Cathedral to South Gate Bridge. Turn left across the bridge and onto South Main St. Pass the **Beamish & Crawford Brewery** (**7**; p193) and then turn right into the pleasant little **Bishop Lucey Park** (**8**), a popular lunch-time spot with locals. Leave by the opposite gate onto Grand Parade and turn right to reach the ornate **Nationalist Monument** (**9**), erected in memory of the Irish patriots who died during the 1798 and 1867 Risings. The tourist office is just across the way.

TOURS

Between June and September, **Arrange Unlimited** (☎ 429 3873; arrange@iol.ie) organises walking tours on request.

Bus Éireann (☎ 450 8188; www.buseireann.ie/site/home) operates a three-hour open-top bus tour of Cork city and Blarney Castle from June to mid-September (adult/child €8/4), departing from the bus station at 10.30am and 2.45pm daily.

Between late May and September, **Guide Friday** (☎ 01-676 5377) runs open-top hop-on, hop-off daily bus tours around Cork city from Grand Parade opposite the tourist office. Tickets cost €11/3 per adult/child.

FESTIVALS & EVENTS

The **Cork International Jazz Festival** and the **International Film Festival** take place in October. Tickets sell out quickly. Programmes are available from **Cork Opera House** (☎ 427 0022; Emmet Pl). The **International Choral & Folk Dance Festival** runs from late April to early May in the City Hall and other venues.

The **Ulster/Munster Literary Festival** takes the form of writing workshops, readings, seminars and exhibitions during February and March in various towns all over County Cork. It attracts around 50 local and overseas writers. For details contact **Munster Literary Centre** (☎ 431 2955; www.munsterlit.ie; Tigh Litríochta, 26 Sullivan's Quay). The entrance is tucked away in a back street.

SLEEPING

Budget

Kinlay House Shandon (☎ 450 8966; kinlay.cork@usit.ie; Bob & Joan's Walk; dm €14-16, d €45, with bathroom €50; 💻) Light breakfast is included in the price at this excellent hostel where smart décor, a fun but sensible atmosphere and a sense of security are definite pluses. It has Internet access for €2 per 15 minutes.

Cork International Hostel (☎ 454 3289; 1 Western Rd; dm €12.50-16, d €42) In a handsome building near the university, this busy An Óige hostel has bright décor and cheerful staff who do a great job coping with the busy flow of young travellers and the occasional lively group.

Sheila's Hostel (☎ 450 5562; www.sheilashostel.ie; Belgrave Pl, Wellington Rd; dm €14-16, d €48; 💻) A big and busy place with lots of young travellers passing through, Sheila's is handy for MacCurtain St and only a few minutes from the centre. At the time of writing refurbishment was going on apace. Facilities are good and you can arrange bicycle and car hire.

Aaran House Tourist Hostel (☎ 455 1566; www.aaranhouse.com; Lower Glanmire Rd; dm €11-13, d €28) Set back far enough to cut out the traffic blare from Glanmire Rd, this down-to-earth hostel has friendly staff.

Close to the train station in Glanmire Rd there's a handful of fairly basic, but clean B&Bs, including **Tara House** (☎ 450 0294; 52 Glanmire Rd Lower; s/d €40/56) and the neighbouring **Oaklands** (☎ 450 0578) with similar prices.

Mid-Range

B&B prices in a few places in the centre of the city are rising alarmingly and some hotels are responding with price cuts that offer bigger rooms and better facilities. Glanmire Rd Lower near the train station has the cheapest places. Western Rd has a big choice of pricier options.

Garnish House (☎ 427 5111; garnish@iol.ie; Western Rd; s/d €35/60; P) An outstanding B&B of increasing fame, this place has comfy rooms and charming little touches everywhere. You get welcoming tea and treats on arrival and the breakfasts are delicious. The hallways and staircases are enhanced with impressive landscape photographs.

Crawford House (☎ 427 9000; crawford@indigo.ie; Western Rd; s/d €60/90; P) Top end B&B'ing complete with spacious rooms, Jacuzzis, stylish furnishings and a choice of buffet, continental or full Irish breakfast. This is contemporary hotel standard without the formal atmosphere.

Victoria Hotel (☎ 427 8788; www.thevictoriahotel.com; Patrick St; s/d €65/90) You won't get more central than this old established hotel that once saw Charles Stuart Parnell and James Joyce as guests. At the time of writing plans were afoot to reopen the St Patrick's St entrance and carry out general refurbishment. Don't expect a view, but the rooms are big and comfortable.

Auburn House (☎ 450 8555; auburnhouse@eircom.net; 3 Garfield Tce, Wellington Rd; s/d €40/66, with bathroom €52/72; P) The impeccably kept rooms in this neat B&B are small, but there's a nice welcome and an almost village-like feel to a place that's also very handy for the centre.

Emerson House (☎ 450 3647; 2 Clarence Tce, Summer Hill North; s/d €40/80; P) Tucked away on a quiet terrace near the top of busy Summer Hill is this exclusively gay and lesbian B&B that has a relaxing mood amidst elegant and comfy surroundings.

Acorn House (☎ 450 2474; www.acornhouse-cork.com; 14 St Patrick's Hill; s/d €60/75) A handsome Georgian terrace house, this listed building has attractive rooms with pleasant furnishings.

D'Arcy's B&B (☎ 450 4658; accommodation@darcysguesthouse.com; 7 Sidney Pl, Wellington Rd; s/d €40/80, with bathroom €50/90) This large terraced house still has a sense of spacious living from its heyday as a 19th-century merchant's home. High ceilings and big rooms go with lofty views over the city from the front rooms. There's engaging artwork on the walls and tasty breakfasts.

Top End

Metropole Hotel (☎ 450 8122; ryan@indigo.ie; MacCurtain St; s/d €115/140; P) At the time of writing a full refurbishment of this long-established hotel had just been completed. Now you can pad soundlessly around on lush carpets and feel comfortably corporate in the lavish rooms, swimming pool, health club and elegant bars and restaurant.

Isaac's Hotel (☎ 450 0011; www.isaacs.ie; 48 MacCurtain St; s/d €104/96; P) Rooms have pleasant furnishings and wooden floors at this long-established hotel on the north side of the river. The hotel's **Greene's Restaurant** does a three-course early bird menu from 6pm to 7pm for €20 against an outside backdrop of a rocky waterfall, courtesy of an electric pump; but impressive all the same for a city venue.

Imperial Hotel (☎ 427 4040; imperial@iol.ie; South Mall; s/d €98/196; P) The Imperial hangs on to its 190-year history and has been refurbished in the past few years to recapture its period luxury.

EATING

Budget

Nash 19 (☎ 427 0880; 19 Princes St; breakfast from €2, lunch from €6.50; 7.30am-4.30pm Mon-Sat) A terrific place to start the day, or to join the buzzing Cork crowd for full carvery lunch from noon onwards. There's a traditional and a cholesterol-conscious breakfast choice, while lunches are delicious, with ingredients sourced from the nearby English Market. Modern décor with quirky touches here and there enhance the happy mood and there are special needs and baby-changing facilities.

Quay Co-op (☎ 431 7026; 24 Sullivan's Quay; mains €6.70-8; 9am-9pm) Flying a cheerful flag for alternative Cork, this long-established favourite rattles out a great range of self-service veggie options, from big breakfasts to rib-sticking soups, casseroles, lasagnes and pizzas. It's all organic and caters for gluten-free, dairy-free and wheat-free needs. You can track down most of Cork's alternative and minority organisations and events on a big noticeboard downstairs. Next door is the **Quay Co-op Organic & Wholefood Shop** (☎ 431 7753; 9am-6.30pm) with a huge range for the self-caterer.

Crawford Gallery Café (☎ 427 4415; Emmet Pl; lunch mains €4-8; 10am-5pm Mon-Sat) Elegant, minimalist surroundings and exquisite food complement gallery grazing at the Crawford. There's a set lunch for €18.

Clancy's (☎ 427 6097; 15-16 Princes St; bar meals €5-11.50, restaurant mains €8-16; 8am-midnight Mon-Fri, 10.30am-midnight Sat, 12.30-4.30pm Sun) You can eat all day in this huge, cheerful bar that fairly buzzes most of the time between its two entrances from the streets to either side. The bar menu rings the changes from Italian to Mexican bites and the restaurant offers Irish to Italian dishes and a fixed price of €13 for two courses, €16.50 for three, up to 7.30pm.

Hungry Elephant (☎ 427 8243; 50 Cornmarket St; mains €8; 10am-7pm Mon-Sat) Eat easy-going in this cheerful vegetarian drop-in that offers salads and wraps and home-made cakes to go with the engaging hippy trail nostalgia. There's even a Moroccan-style *teteria* (tea) table with low seats.

Luciano's Pizza (☎ 455 8095; MacCurtain St; pizzas €5.50-10, mains €6-8.50; noon-late Mon-Sat, 1pm-late Sun) Standard range of pizzas for fuel feeders is available at this popular place that also does all-day dishes such as lasagne, and fish and chips.

O'Brien's Irish Sandwich Bar (☎ 427 9522; 58 Oliver Plunkett St; sandwiches €3-6; 8am-5.30pm Mon-Sat) This handy budget stop is right at the heart of the city centre and does a good selection of tasty fillings.

Mid-Range

Farmgate Restaurant (☎ 427 8134; English Market; mains €8.50-10; 8.30am-5pm) An unmissable Cork experience at the heart of the colourful English Market, the Farmgate, like its sister restaurant at Midleton (see p202) has mastered the magic art of producing delicious food without fuss and without bowing to fleeting fashion. Filling breakfasts, morning and afternoon tea and coffee, or lunch of bouncingly fresh salads, Irish lamb or shepherd's pie, draw a regular Cork clientele to the Farmgate's balcony which overlooks the bustle of the market below, source of the food on your plate. If you're lucky you may catch the eloquent pianist Donal Casey at the corner piano.

Café Mexicana (☎ 427 6433; 1 Carey's Lane; mains €13.50-17; noon-late) Authentic surroundings and great food make this long-established Cork eatery an enduring favourite. Cross your cultures with ease for an evening of mixed Mexican and Spanish with subtle French and Italian influences. There's a lively rising scale of nachos. Try the 'Dynamite' option – if you like it hot.

Isaac's Restaurant (☎ 450 3805; 48 MacCurtain St; lunch €9.65, dinner €7.50-15; 12.30-2.30pm & 6.30-10.30pm Mon-Sat, to 9pm Sun) Housed in a converted 18th-century warehouse, Isaac's captures a nostalgic Mediterranean ambience to go with its lively menu. The tapas plate adds to the tone and there's excellent vegetarian choices amidst the inventive meat and fish dishes.

Scoozi (☎ 427 5077; 3/4 Winthrop Ave; mains €10-12; 9am-11pm Mon-Sat, noon-10pm Sat) There's lots of exposed brickwork and burnished wood inside this hugely popular break-time café-restaurant tucked down a little lane between Winthrop St and Caroline St. Smart little tables and cosy alcoves add intimacy as a fast and friendly young staff keep dishing up breakfasts, pizzas, pastas, grills and salads and a fair selection of French and New World wines.

Top End

Café Paradiso (☎ 427 7939; 16 Lancaster Quay; lunch €8.50, dinner €18.50; 12.30-3pm & 6.30-10.30pm Tue-Sat) Top class vegetarian dishes that will seduce the most committed carnivore make this cheerful restaurant a busy place. It's small and lively, the charming staff create happy interaction and there's a Mediterranean ambience. Creativity maintains the standard of dishes – desserts are divine – and the wine list is terrific, reflecting a passion for the vine rather than just passing fancy.

Fenn's Quay (☎ 427 9527; 5 Fenns Quay; lunch €4.25-7.50, dinner €15.50-22; 🕑 10am-10pm Mon-Sat) Tucked away from the centre, this is one of Cork's finest eating places. Understated but cool and stylish surroundings with artwork enhance the excellent international menu that does not sacrifice Irish traditional attitudes. You can start the day with eggs Benedict or enjoy lunch of goat's cheese salad or smoked fish cakes with lemon butter spinach. Dinner is mainly meat of excellent quality, but fish dishes are also available. Book before 7.30pm for the early dinner (€20). There are vegetarian options and delicious desserts are gluten free. Thursday nights are jazz nights.

Star Anise (☎ 455 1635; 4 Bridge St; lunch €7.60-9.50, dinner €17-22; 🕑 noon-6pm Tue-Fri, 6-10pm Tue-Sat) Ultra-cool orange and blond wood surrounds make this small restaurant a Cork cosmopolitan experience. The international menu, with strong Mediterranean influences, makes the sun-beach ambience even more persuasive. From juice bar to pan-fried chicken schnitzel and pastas to seafood chowder, the choice is delectable.

Pi (☎ 422 2860; Courthouse Chambers, Washington St; pizzas €10-16, á la carte €16-24) A sharply modernist interior has won Pi recognition for its open landscape of cool beechwood and aluminium and glass fittings. The food's not bad either, although top end is a bit pricey. There's a modern European slant to most dishes. Menus are in several languages and there's a healthy wine list.

Self-Catering

If you're self-catering or want to put together a picnic, head straight for the **English Market** (9am-5.30pm Mon-Sat), off the western end of St Patrick's St (access from Grand Parade too). There's great local and imported produce here, such as cheeses, pâté, terrines, smoked fish, bread, olives and wine.

DRINKING

Cork's pub life has long been brimming and the choice rivals that of Dublin's, in quality if not quantity. Locally brewed Murphy's is the stout of choice here, or there's Beamish, which is often cheaper.

An Spailpín Fánach (☎ 427 7949; South Main St) The 'wandering labourer' really does hang on to its character with exposed brickwork, stone-flagged floors, tucked away corners and open fires glowing. There are good trad sessions every night except Saturday. It gets very busy and there's a fair request not to stand drinking at the fairly cramped bar after 8.30pm.

Lobby (☎ 431 9307; 1 Union Quay) Over the south river, the Lobby is one of Cork's most popular venues with trad and contemporary gigs every night. Next door is **Charlie's** (☎ 496 5272; 2 Union Quay) with equally good music.

Long Valley (☎ 427 2144; Winthrop St) A Cork institution that dates from the mid-19th century and is still going strong, the Long Valley has a landscape to fit its name, with trappings of character. It does great sandwiches to go with your pint. The main bar is hugely popular and busy, but the upstairs Hayloft is usually quieter.

Sin É (☎ 450 2266; Coburg St) Over the north river, this is a great old pub with traditional music Tuesday to Friday and Sunday nights from 9.30pm.

ENTERTAINMENT

For information about what's on in Cork pick up a copy of *Whazon?*, available from the tourist office, newsagencies, some clothes and record shops, hostels and a few B&Bs.

Theatre & Cinemas

Classical to contemporary performances and performers of international standard make Cork's cultural life as fine as any in Ireland.

Cork Opera House (☎ 427 0022; Emmet Pl) There's everything from opera to stand-up at Cork's leading venue, which has seen performances as varied as *Carmen*, *Flamenco Express* and the *Vagina Monologues*.

Cork Arts Theatre (☎ 450 8398; Knapps Sq) Some excellent experimental theatre is part of the mix at this north-of-the-river venue.

UCC Granary Theatre (☎ 490 4272, box office ☎ 490 4275; Mardyke St) The UCC's own drama group as well as guest companies stage a mix of plays throughout the university terms.

Everyman Palace Theatre (☎ 450 1673; 15 MacCurtain St) There's a range of musical and dramatic productions here most nights of the week.

Kino (☎ 427 1571; Washington St West) and the **Triskel Arts Centre** (☎ 427 2022; Tobin St) show art-house films. **Gate Multiplex** (☎ 427 9595; North Main St) and **Capitol Cineplex** (☎ 427 8777; Grand Pde) show mainstream films.

Nightclubs

Cork's club life really does rival Dublin's. With a vibrant university population to fuel the beat, Cork rocks just about every night of the week. Door charges range from free to €15 depending on who's gigging.

Bodega (☎ 427 2878; 46-49 Cornmarket St) A big bouncing venue located in what was once the old workhouse. There's a big mid-range (€8 to €15) food choice in the Café Bar Deli, with full-on music mix in the huge front bar or in the White and Green Rooms. Everything from open mic nights to Playstation tournaments and duelling DJs is on the cards.

Half Moon Theatre (☎ 427 0022) One of Cork's best for live acts and top DJs, the Half Moon (behind Cork Opera House) has featured acts such as Ruby Horse and Jerry Dammers. Saturday night's Planet Funk piles on some great raw talent bands.

Scotts (☎ 422 2779; Caroline St) This big luxe venue has a fine restaurant downstairs and an upstairs club that features mainstream disco music for the over 20s smart crowd.

Fred Zeppelins (Douglas St) Hard-edged action at this rock bar on the south side. There's a good mix of DJs and live gigs. Happy hours are 3pm to 8pm Monday to Thursday when all pints are €2.75.

Roundy (☎ 427 7682; 1 Castle St) DJs and live bands add to the cool trappings of this favourite meeting place.

Other Place (☎ 427 8470; 8 South Main St) A popular and long-established gay and lesbian club, the Other Place also hosts the Southern Gay Health Project, a bookstore and café. There's dancing at weekends.

COUNTY CORK

SHOPPING

Cork has the full range of national and international stores, plus some excellent specialist outlets. The little streets and lanes north of St Patrick's St are the most interesting. Try Paul's Lane or antiques.

Living Tradition (☎ 450 2564; 40 MacCurtain St; 🕑 9.30am-5.30pm Mon-Sat) If you like traditional music look in here. It sells a range of tapes, CDs and music publications.

Plugd Records (☎ 427 6300; 4 Washington St) A terrific music shop, stocking everything from techno to nu jazz beats; you'll also pick up on the very latest on the club scene here.

Union Chandlery & Hillwalkers (☎ 427 1643; 10 Clontarf St) has camping and trekking gear as well as a range of trekking guides.

GETTING THERE & AWAY

Air

Cork airport (☎ 431 3131) is 8km south of the city on the N27. Airlines servicing the airport are British Airways, Ryan Air, Aer Lingus, Aer Arann, British European, bmi baby, bmi British Midland, Brymon Airways, Keenair (see p671 for contact details). There are direct flights to Dublin, London, Birmingham, Manchester, Bristol, Exeter, Jersey, Paris, Prague, Rennes, Amsterdam and Malaga. Other overseas flights go via Dublin.

Boat

Regular ferries link Cork with the UK and France. **Brittany Ferries** (☎ 427 7801; 42 Grand Pde) runs to Roscoff at 3.30pm every Saturday from March to September. The crossing takes 14 hours. Prices on request only.

Swansea Cork Ferries (☎ 427 6000; 52 South Mall) operates four times a week. One-way fares are: €25 to €36 for a foot passenger, €95 to €165 for a car and driver and €8 for a bike depending on the month you travel. The crossing between Cork and Swansea takes 10 hours. There is also an office at the ferry terminal.

For more details see p674.

Bus

Bus Éireann (☎ 450 8188) operates from the bus station on the corner of Merchant's Quay and Parnell Place. You can get to most places from Cork, including Dublin (€20, 4¼ hours, six daily), Killarney (€11.90, two hours, 12 daily), Waterford (€13.30, 2¼ hours, 13 daily) and Kilkenny (€15.20, three hours, four daily).

Car

Budget (☎ 427 4755) has a desk at the tourist office as well as at the airport (☎ 431 4000). **Avis** (☎ 428 1111) is on Emmet Place, opposite the Crawford Municipal Art Gallery and at Alfred St at the east end of MacCurtain St.

Train

Kent Train Station (☎ 450 4777) is north of the River Lee on Glanmire Rd Lower.

There's a direct train connection to Dublin (€48.50, three hours, nine daily) and Limerick (€19.60, 1½ hours, eight daily). There's a service to Tralee (€22.90, 2¼ hours) via Killarney (€19.50, 1½ hours) five times a day. There's also a rather circuitous route to Waterford (€22.90, three to five hours) via Limerick Junction and Tipperary once a day.

An hourly service southeast to Cobh (€4.40 return, 24 minutes) stops at Fota (€3.30 return, 14 minutes) enabling you to take in the Fota Wildlife Park and Cobh Heritage Centre (see p200) on a round trip.

GETTING AROUND

To/From the Airport

The airport is 8km south of the city centre on the South City Link Rd. It takes about 20 minutes to get there by car. Taxis cost around €15. Bus Éireann No 226 runs between the airport and the bus station on Parnell Place and into the city centre (€3.40, 25 minutes).

To/From the Ferry Terminal

The ferry terminal is at Ringaskiddy, about 15 minutes by car southeast from the city centre along the N28. Bus Éireann runs a fairly frequent daily service to the terminal; the journey takes about 45 minutes and costs €4.40/2.80 per adult/child.

Bus

Most places you'll need to get to are within easy walking distance of the centre. If you're staying a long time it might be worth considering a weekly ticket. You'll need photo ID to obtain it.

Car

Streetside parking requires scratch card parking discs (€1.25 per hour) obtained from the tourist office and some newsagencies. Be warned, clamping of vehicles is sharpish once you're over time and it costs a hefty €160 to retrieve your vehicle. Visitors are probably best to head for one or another of the 10 or so signposted public car parks dotted round the central area. Charges are about €2 for one to four hours, €5 overnight.

Taxi

Try **Shandon Cabs** (☎ 450 2255) or **Cork Taxi Co-op** (☎ 427 2222).

Bicycle

For bicycle hire try **Rothar Cycles** (☎ 431 3133; 55 Barrack St; day/week €20/80). Rothar's offers a one-way pick-up service from other towns for €25 with €100 refundable deposit. You can join a once a week sociable cycle trip from Cork into the surrounding countryside, which is not that far away. Cyclists meet outside the opera house at 6.50pm on Thursdays from mid-April to mid-September. Afterwards there's a get-together in a local café. Contact Rothar Cycles for details.

AROUND CORK CITY

BLARNEY CASTLE

If you go to **Blarney Castle** (☎ 021-438 5252; Blarney; adult/child €4.45/1.25; 🕑 9am-6.30pm Mon-Sat, 9.30am-5.30pm Sun May & Sep, 9am-7pm Mon-Sat, 9.30am-5.30pm Sun Jun-Aug, 9am-6pm or sundown Mon-Sat, 9.30am-5pm or sundown Sun Oct-Ap) someone will soon talk you into kissing the **Blarney Stone**; but get there before the coach crowds. The custom of kissing the stone is a relatively modern invention but Blarney's association with the gift of the gab or, as an 18th-century French consul put it, 'the privilege of telling lies for seven years', goes back a long time. It was Queen Elizabeth I who is said to have invented the term, out of exasperation with Lord Blarney's ability to talk endlessly without ever actually agreeing to her demands.

Dating from 1446, the castle is a tower house built on solid limestone in wonderful grounds that are ideal for a picnic.

You have to bend over backwards to kiss the Blarney Stone. There's an interesting drop beneath your head, but there's a safety grill and an attendant. Go carefully up the long spiral staircases, however. They are narrow, steep and uneven. The castle has little interpretation material, but it's an atmospheric place. Getting there at opening time is one way to beat the crowds. Blarney is 8km northwest of Cork and buses run there regularly from Cork bus station (€3, 30 minutes). Last admission to the castle is 30 minutes before closing.

PASSAGE WEST

If you're travelling from west to east Cork and want to avoid going through Cork city use the **Ferry Link** (☎ 021-481 1223; pedestrian/car €0.75/3 one way; 🕑 7.05am-12.15am) which connects Passage West and Glenbrook with Carrigaloe. Bikes are free. The crossing takes five minutes.

FOTA WILDLIFE PARK

Fota Wildlife Park (☎ 021-481 2678; Carrigtwohill; adult/child €7/4.20; ⏲ 10am-5pm Mon-Sat, 11am-5pm Sun mid-March–Oct, 10am-3pm Mon-Sat, 11am-3pm Sun Nov–mid-Mar) is 10km east of Cork. It covers 70 acres and kids love the free-ranging giraffes, ostriches, monkeys, kangaroos and penguins. Look out for the glorious white-and-brown scimitar-horned oryx, believed to be extinct in the wild.

A wildlife tour train runs a circuit round the park every 15 minutes (one way/round trip €0.70/1.40). Gates are locked at 6pm in summer and at 4pm in winter.

You can take a stroll down to the graceful Regency-style **Fota House** (☎ 021-481 5543; Carrigtwo hill; adult/child €5/2; ⏲ 10am-6pm Mon-Sat, 11am-6pm Sun). The interiors have been stocked with 18th- and 19th-century furnishings and there are touch screens giving information as you self-guide. Last admission is at 5pm. Access is free to the nearby 150-year-old **arboretum**.

There's a car park inside the main entrance to Fota Wildlife Park (€2). You pay at a barrier on the way out.

A good bet is to take the hourly Cork to Fota train (€3.30 return, 14 minutes) which goes on to Cobh.

Close to the park is an excellent B&B, the friendly **Belvelly Court** (☎ 021-481 2214; Belvelly, Cobh; www.dragnet-systems.ie/dira/belvelly; s/d €43/66; ⏲ May-Oct). The bright and spotless rooms are in a separate annexe flanked by a big garden, in which the owners are likely to invite you to a merry barbecue.

COBH

☎ 021 / pop 6771

Picturesque Cobh (pronounced cove) was for many years the port of Cork and has always had a strong connection with Atlantic crossings. In 1838 the *Sirius* was the first steamship to cross the Atlantic, sailing from Cobh. The *Titanic* made its last stop here before its fateful Atlantic crossing in 1912, and when the *Lusitania* was sunk off the coast of Kinsale in 1915, it was here that many of the survivors were brought and the victims buried.

In 1849 a visit by Queen Victoria resulted in the town's leading citizens requesting successfully that Cobh be renamed Queenstown. The name lasted until 1921 when, not surprisingly, the local council reverted to the Irish Cobh. The world's first yacht club, the Royal Cork Yacht Club, was founded here in 1720, but now operates from Crosshaven on the other side of Cork Harbour.

There's a fair bit of industrial activity around Cobh, but the broad, glittering estuary with its grassy islands, and the town's tall, brightly coloured buildings clustered below the spectacular cathedral, lend the town a distinctive charm.

Cobh has become a popular stopover for visiting cruise liners whose clientele are whisked off in coaches to tourist hot spots.

Orientation

Cobh is on Great Island, which fills much of Cork Harbour, and is joined to the mainland by a causeway. It faces Haulbowline Island (once the base of the Irish Naval Service) and Spike Island (the greener of the islands; it houses a prison). The waterfront area comprises the broad Westbourne Place and West Beach from where steep streets climb inland. Several quays and piers project into the harbour and there's a delightful waterside park with seating, a bandstand and children's play area next to the tourist office.

Information

The old yacht club building now houses a small tourist office and **arts centre** (☎ 481 3301; ⏲ 9.30am-5.30pm Mon-Fri, 11.30am-5.30pm Sat & Sun Mar-Sep, 2.30-5.30pm daily Oct-Feb). At the time of writing there was some uncertainty about staffing levels and whether or not these hours would be strictly maintained.

At Atlantic Inn on West Beach there's an **Internet café** (☎ 481 1489) on West Beach; it costs €3 for 15 minutes.

A 1½-hour guided walk, the **Titanic Trail** (www.titanictrail.com; €7.50), lasting 1½ hours leaves at 11am and 3pm Monday to Saturday, May to September, from the Commodore Hotel or the Waters Edge Hotel (see p201). Phone for details. You get a free sampling of Guinness and a free coffee on the way. A 1¼-hour **Ghost Walk** (€7.50) leaves from Pillars Bar on Westbourne Place at 8.30pm Tuesday, Thursday and Saturday Easter to October. Ask at the tourist office for details on both these walks or ring ☎ 481 5211 or email info@titanic-trail.com.

Cobh, The Queenstown Story

Part of Cobh train station has been cleverly converted into a **heritage centre** (☎ 481 3591;

Old Railway Station; adult/child €5/2.50; ⌚ 10am-6pm, last admission 5pm May-Oct, 10am-5pm, last admission 4pm Nov-Apr; wheelchair access). It contains an impressive series of exhibitions about the mass emigrations that followed Ireland's Famine years. It also covers the era of the great liners and the tragedies of the *Titanic* and *Lusitania* and is a cut above many 'interpretive centres'. There's an adjoining café (see Queenstown Restaurant following) and a gift shop.

St Colman's Cathedral

The massive French Gothic **St Colman's** (☎ 481 3222; Cathedral Pl; admission by donation) stands on a hillside terrace and brings the flavour of a French harbour town to Cobh. It was begun in 1868 but was not completed until 1915. The grandiose nature of the cathedral reflects the sizable cash contribution that flowed from nostalgic Irish communities in Australia and the USA, as well as from local people. The cathedral's 47-bell carillon is the largest in Ireland; the biggest bell weighs 3440kg. A leaflet, with versions in several languages, explains the main features. Mass takes place at 8am and 10am Monday to Friday, 6pm Saturday, and 8am, 10am, noon and 7pm Sunday.

Cobh Museum

A small history **museum** (☎ 481 4240; High Rd; adult/child €2/0.70; ⌚ 11am-1pm & 2-6pm Mon-Sat, 3-6pm Sun Easter-Oct) is housed in the 19th-century Scottish Presbyterian church that overlooks the train station. There are model ships as well as paintings, photographs and some artefacts from 18th- and 19th-century Cobh.

Harbour Cruises

June to September, **Marine Transport Services** (☎ 481 1485) organises three one-hour harbour cruises each day costing €5/3 per adult/child. The tourist office has details.

Sleeping

Westbourne House (☎ 481 1391; 12 Westbourne Pl; s/d €20/40) The friendly owner of this sunny old house provides good value beyond the reasonable price. Don't expect lavishness, but the rooms are big and the yachting pictures everywhere go with the harbour views.

Ardeen (☎ 481 1803; 3 Harbour Hill; s/d €43/64) A good location, high up and overlooking the harbour, adds to the pleasant rooms in this attractive period house.

Water's Edge Hotel (☎ 481 5566; www.watersedgehotel.ie; s/d €85/150; P) Loads of bright décor, and an almost cruise-liner feel along the verandahs (from where you can view the real cruise liners) adds to the appeal of this smart but friendly family-run hotel that stands right where its name implies. There's a restaurant (see Jacob's Ladder below) and also on offer are attractive suites from €175, and special two-night deals with dinner.

Commodore Hotel (☎ 481 1277; commodorehotel@eircom.net; Westbourne Pl; s/d €85/125) Rates drop by up to 20% in the off-season at this classic seaside hotel that has all the mod cons, but hangs on to a pleasant retro appeal in its rooms and surroundings.

Eating & Drinking

Queenstown Restaurant (☎ 481 3591; lunch €3.50-5.70; ⌚ 10am-5pm) Coffee and tea and tasty lunches including salads and lasagnes are served up in Cobh's old train station in the same complex as Cobh Heritage Centre. You can eat on the platform in far better surroundings and with tastier food than in most real train stations.

Hong Kong Kitchen (☎ 481 4996; 7a West Beach; mains €6.30-10.50; ⌚ 5-11.30pm Mon-Thu, 5pm-midnight Fri-Sat, 1-10.30pm Sun, lunch 12.30-2.30pm Thu & Fri) A good location on the main street and friendly service in relaxed surroundings complements the above-average Chinese dishes that include good vegetarian options.

Jacob's Ladder (☎ 481 5566; www.watersedgehotel.ie; lunch €7-12.50, dinner €15-25; ⌚ 11.30am-9pm) This bright and upbeat restaurant at the Water's Edge Hotel has a genuine overview of the harbour. It is fairly pricey but has a wide range of meat, poultry and excellent fish dishes, all done with some creativity.

Mansworths Bar (☎ 481 1965; Midleton St, Top o' the Hill) This fine old pub is a local favourite and pulls one of the best pints of Guinness you're likely to get. There's music most weekends; otherwise the feast of Cobh maritime photos and artefacts will keep you entertained.

Getting There & Away

Cobh is 24km southeast of Cork, off the main N25 Cork to Rosslare road. Hourly trains connect Cobh with Cork (€4.40 return, 24 minutes). Alternatively, between June and September you can take a passenger cruiser which leaves Cobh for Passage West at 3.15pm and costs €8.

Getting Around

All of Cobh's sites are within easy walking distance. If you need a cab try **Harbour Cabs** (☎ 481 4444) or **Cove Cabs** (☎ 481 2299).

JAMESON HERITAGE CENTRE

☎ 021

This **distillery** (☎ 461 3594; adult/concession €5.70/2.50; ⏰ 10am-6pm) is about 20km east of Cork in Midleton. Whiskey has been distilled here since the early 19th century, and the old works were opened to the public after a new distillery was developed. Twenty-four million bottles of whiskey are produced at this new plant each year.

Guided tours (45 minutes) start with a film show and continue with a walkabout that reveals the whole whiskey making process. The tour ends in the bar, where two lucky volunteers get to compare assorted Irish whiskeys with scotch and bourbon. Everyone gets a free tipple and there's a café for snacks and lunches.

Between March and October there are regular daily tours between 10am and 6pm. During the rest of the year there are daily tours at 11.30am, 2.30pm and 4pm.

There are 18 buses a day (13 on Sunday) from Cork bus station (€4.70, 25 minutes).

There's a **tourist office** (☎ 461 3702; ⏰ 9.30am-5pm Mon, Tue & Thu-Sat mid-Apr–mid-Sep, 9.30am-5pm Sun Jul & Aug) by the entrance gate to the distillery.

For the best of Irish cuisine try the **Farmgate Restaurant** (☎ 463 2771; The Coolbawn; ⏰ coffee & snacks 10am-5pm Mon-Sat, lunch noon-4pm, dinner 6.30-9.45pm Thu-Sat), sister establishment to Cork's Farmgate in the English Market and with the same superb blend of traditional and modern Irish in its approach to food and to cooking. In the front is a shop selling local produce, including organic fruit and vegetables, cheeses and preserves. Behind is the café-restaurant where you'll eat as well as anywhere in Ireland.

About 12km southeast of Midleton on the R629 between Shanagarry and Cloyne is **Ballymaloe House** (☎ 465 2531; www.ballymaloe.ie; Shanagarry; s/d €131/212; P; wheelchair access). This guesthouse, restaurant and cookery school is of the highest standard. Rooms are elegant and furnished superbly. Guests can enjoy a lovely garden and woodland walks. Modern Irish cuisine at its best is offered at the restaurant with a five-course set menu for around €55 per person. The cookery school (www.cookingisfun.ie) offers half-day courses (from €95) in a variety of styles to 12-week certificate courses (€6635). They also run half-day to full-day gardening courses (€75 to €125).

YOUGHAL

☎ 024 / pop 6203

Youghal (Eochaill; pronounced yawl), at the mouth of the River Blackwater, has history coming out of its ears and is fast making the best of it. With the opening of a bypass in 2003 the once traffic-logged Main St has regained some semblance of calm. Youghal is a good base for exploring the surrounding area and there are even a couple of reasonable beaches nearby.

The town was granted to Sir Walter Raleigh during the Elizabethan Plantation of Munster, but Raleigh spent very little time in the house he built there, nor did he plant the first potatoes to be cultivated in northern Europe in his garden, as is often claimed.

Orientation & Information

The **Clock Gate** at the southern end of North Main St is Youghal's major landmark. **Youghal Visitor Centre** (☎ 20170; youghaltourism@eircom.net; Market Sq; ⏰ 9am-6.30pm Mon-Fri, 9.30am-5pm Sat & Sun Jul-Aug, 9am-5.30pm Mon-Fri, 9.30am-5pm Sat & Sun mid-Mar–Jun & Sep-Oct, 9am-5pm Mon-Fri Oct–mid-Mar) is in the attractive old market house on the waterfront. There is a **Heritage Centre** in the visitor centre that gives an excellent overview of the town.

The free leaflet *Youghal Town Trail* is available from here as is the excellent booklet *Youghal: Historic Walled Port* (€3.50).

Guided tours (adult/child €4.50/free, 1½ hours) of the town leave from the tourist information point at 10.30am Monday to Friday.

Sights

Heading from south to north, some of the town's sights are detailed here.

Fox's Lane Folk Museum (☎ 20170, 291 145; North Cross Lane; ⏰ 10am-1pm & 2-6pm Tue-Sat Jul & Aug), signposted down an alley between The Mall and South Main St, displays over 400 items and a Victorian kitchen.

The curious **Clock Gate** bridges Main St. In 1777 the present building, a combination of clock tower and jail, replaced the medieval Trinity Gate, a key part of the town's fortifications.

The red-brick **Red House**, on North Main St, was designed in 1706 by the Dutch architect Leuventhen with some Dutch Renaissance details including cornerstones on the central façade below a handsome pediment. A few doors further up the street are **Alms Houses** built to house ex-soldiers in 1610 by local lord Richard Boyle to whom Raleigh had sold his properties.

Across the road stands the 15th-century **Tynte's Castle**. Originally it had a defensive riverfront position but as the Blackwater silted up and changed course it was left high and dry.

Built in 1220, **St Mary's Collegiate Church** incorporates elements of an earlier Danish church dating back to the 11th century. Inside there's a monument to Richard Boyle, who bought Raleigh's Irish estates and became the first earl of Cork. It shows him with his wife and his 16 children. The churchyard is bounded by a fine stretch of the 13th-century town wall and one of the remaining turrets.

Beside the church, **Myrtle Grove** is an interesting house which retains some 16th-century features. The weather vane depicts the famous story of Raleigh, Elizabeth I, the puddle and the cloak.

Sleeping

Sonas Caravan Park (☎ 98960; sonas_camping@yahoo.co.uk; Ballymacoda; tent & 2 people €12.50; ⏰ May–mid-Sep) Beachside access and a generally relaxed and quiet atmosphere are top features of this pleasant site. It's about 15km south of Youghal, on the seashore. To get there, take the road off the N25 (west of town) to the village of Ballymacoda, then head west through the village.

Roseville (☎ 92571; rosevillebandb@eircom.net; New Catherine St; s/d €40/60; Ⓟ) This handsome old building has the mood of a country house at the heart of Youghal. Stylish rooms and a relaxed ambience are matched by the friendly welcome.

Aherne's (☎ 92424; www.ahernes.com; 163 North Main St; s/d €110/180; Ⓟ; wheelchair access) You get excellent value for the price at this charming place where rooms are individually decorated and there's a great sense of style and comfort.

Eating

Coffee Pot (☎ 92523; 77 North Main St; meals €5.50-15) This busy and basic coffee shop offers good-value sandwiches, burgers and mixed grills all day.

Casserole (☎ 20909; 3 South Main St; mains €12-26) You can choose from affordable pastas to pricey lobster at this uncluttered little restaurant with a mid-European feel. It's right by the Clock Gate.

Aherne's Seafood Bar & Restaurant (164 North Main St; bar food €3.75-13.50, dinner menu €42; ⏰ bar food noon-10pm, dinner 6.30-9.15pm) A terrific seafood menu offers everything from *moules mariniere* to a cracking seafood pie at Aherne's comfy bar. There are meat-eaters delights as well, but fish is the real feast.

Getting There & Away

There are frequent Bus Éireann buses to Cork (€8.20, 50 minutes, 13 daily) and Waterford (€12.50, 1½ hours, every hour).

WESTERN CORK

KINSALE

☎ 021 / pop 3035

Busy Kinsale (Cionn tSáile) has all the trappings of a picture-postcard seaside resort, plus plenty of heritage sights. There's a seductive Cornish-Breton feel to it with its sea haven of sheltered tidal inlet fringed by wooded slopes. Fishing boats, and yachts in summer, add to the ambience. Blessed by media visits from gourmet gossips such as Keith Floyd and Rick Stein, Kinsale has been labelled the gourmet centre of Ireland, but do not expect a huge number of restaurants, as the recurring claim that Kinsale eclipses Dublin and Cork in the culinary stakes reflects overblown marketing hype. For such a small place, however, there are certainly several outstanding seafood restaurants of international standard.

History

In September 1601 a Spanish fleet anchored at Kinsale was besieged by the English. The Irish army marched the length of the country to attack the English but were defeated in battle outside Kinsale on Christmas Eve. For the Catholics of Kinsale, the immediate consequence was that they were banned from the town. It was another 100 years before they were allowed to return. Historians now cite 1601 as the beginning of the end of Gaelic Ireland.

After 1601 the town developed as a shipbuilding port. In the early 18th century Alexander Selkirk left Kinsale Harbour on a voyage that left him stranded on a desert island, providing Daniel Defoe with the idea for Robinson Crusoe.

Orientation

Most of Kinsale can be covered quite easily on foot. Most of the hotels and restaurants are near the harbour, but there are a couple of restaurants out at Scilly, a peninsula to the southeast. A path continues from there to Summercove and Charles Fort. To the southwest, Duggan Bridge links Castlepark Marina and the scant ruins of James Fort to Pier Rd.

Information

On the harbourfront close to the bus stop is the **Tourist Office** (☎ 477 2234; cnr Pier Rd & Emmet Pl; 🕑 9.30am-1pm & 2.15-5.30pm Mon-Sat Mar-Oct, daily Jul & Aug). You may find its opening hours flexible on occasion, especially in the quieter months. It has a walking map detailing three walks in and around Kinsale lasting from one to two hours.

Kinsale Bookshop (☎ 477 4244; 8 Main St) has all you need for a good read. **Finishing Services** (☎ 477 3571; 71 Main St; €2.50/15min; 🕑 9am-7pm Mon-Fri, 10am-4pm Sat May-Sep, 9am-5.30pm Mon-Fri Oct-

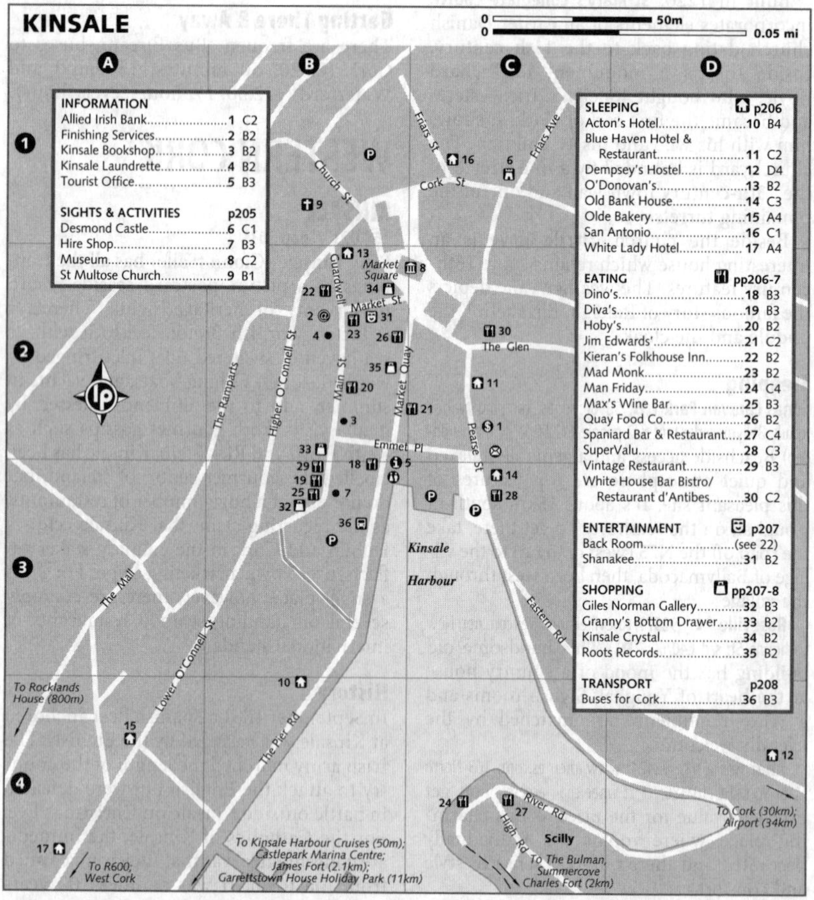

> **LUSITANIA**
>
> On 7 May 1915, the Cunard liner RMS *Lusitania*, on its way from New York to Liverpool, was torpedoed by a German U-boat about 19km south of the Old Head of Kinsale. She sank within 18 minutes with the loss of 1198 souls. Nine survivors and five bodies from the *Lusitania* were landed at Kinsale.
>
> There had been strong warnings of U-boat activity in the area, and there was much debate over the perceived foolhardiness of the *Lusitania's* master who seemed to have ignored official advice to steer well clear of land. It was claimed that the vessel was carrying armaments to Britain. This was always denied by the British, but was claimed as a justification for the sinking by the Germans. The tragedy brought America into WWI.

Apr) will get you hooked up to the Internet, and you can wash clothes at **Kinsale Laundrette** (☎ 477 2205; Main St; ⌚ 9am-6.30pm Mon-Fri).

There's an Allied Irish Bank with ATM on Pearse St and the post office is also on Pearse St. Toilets are next to the tourist office.

Check out www.kinsale.ie for information about Kinsale.

Museum

The small **museum** (☎ 477 7930; Market Sq; adult/child €2.75/1.25; ⌚ 10.30am-5.30pm Mon-Sat, 2.30-5.30pm Sun Apr-Oct) in the 17th-century courthouse has a number of displays, including exhibits relating to the 1915 sinking of the *Lusitania*.

Desmond Castle

This early-16th-century **tower house** (☎ 477 4855; Cork St; adult/child €2.50/1.20; ⌚ 10am-6pm mid-Apr–early Oct, closed Mon except public hol) was occupied by the Spanish in 1601. Since then it has served as a prison for French and American captives and as a workhouse during the Famine. In the care of Dúchas, it now houses a small museum on the history of wine. Last admission is 45 minutes before closing.

St Multose Church

St Multose is the patron saint of Kinsale and this **Church of Ireland church** (rectory ☎ 477 2220; Church St) is one of Ireland's oldest. It was built around 1190 by the Normans on the site of a 6th-century church. Apparently it was here that Prince Rupert proclaimed Charles II as king of England. Not much of the interior is original but the exterior is preserved beautifully and the graveyard has some interesting large family tombs. A guide is available for €1.50 at the entrance.

Charles Fort

In Summercove, 2km east of Kinsale, stand the huge ruins of 17th-century **Charles Fort** (☎ 477 2263; adult/child €3.50/1.25; ⌚ 10am-6pm mid-Mar–Oct, 10am-5pm Nov–mid-Mar; last admission 5.15pm). This is one of the best-preserved star-shaped forts in Europe. Now a Dúchas site, it was built in the 1670s and remained in use until 1921, when much of the fort was destroyed as the British withdrew. Most of the ruins you see inside date from the 18th and 19th centuries.

Activities

WALKING TOURS

One-hour guided walking tours are run by **Herlihy's Guided Tour** (☎ 477 2873; adult/child €4.50/1) and leave from outside the tourist office at 11.15am daily.

HARBOUR CRUISES

For **harbour cruises** to Charles Fort, James Cove and up the Bandon River phone **Kinsale Harbour Cruises** (☎ 477 3188, 087 227 2319). Boats leave seven times a day during summer, five times a day at the weekend the rest of the year, from Denis Quay on Pier Rd, at the southern end of town. It costs €8/4 per adult/child.

FISHING

Tackle can be hired at the **Hire Shop** (☎ 477 4884; 18 Main St) for €10 per day. Ask here about other fishing trips.

Castlepark Marina Centre (☎ 477 4959) organises deep-sea fishing (€55 with rod).

Festivals & Events

Kinsale's **Festival of Autumn Flavours**, held in early October, highlights the town's gourmet reputation in a big way. There are numerous events and activities such as tastings, meals, harbour cruises and general celebration of good food. Tickets to some events are available on the day, but it's wise to book ahead. For details of events and prices and how to book, check www.kinsale.ie.

Sleeping

BUDGET

Garrettstown House Holiday Park (☎/fax 477 8156; tent & 2 people €14; ⌚ May-Sep) This is the closest camp site to Kinsale and is in the grounds of an 18th-century estate. It's a peaceful place but gets quite lively with families in summer. The site is 1.3km southwest of Ballinspittle (11km southwest of Kinsale) on the R600.

Dempsey's Hostel (☎ 477 2124; Eastern Rd; dm/d €16/36) The only hostel accommodation in the immediate area, Dempsey's is an uphill walk from the centre and is located alongside a garage on the busy Cork road. It has all the necessary equipment (you can hire linen for €1.55) but could do with a brightening up inside.

MID-RANGE

Olde Bakery (☎ 477 3012; theoldebakery@oceanfree.net; 56 Lower O'Connell St; s/d €40/70; ☒) A short walk southwest of the centre is this very friendly little house that was once the British garrison bakery. Rooms are a reasonable size and terrific breakfasts around a big kitchen table get everyone chatting happily.

O'Donovan's (☎ 477 2428; odonovans_bb@iolfree.ie; Guardwell; s/d €35/60; ☒) Bright, fresh colours, simple, comfy rooms and a nice welcome, plus worthwhile advice on the town, make this central place deservedly popular.

San Antonio (☎ 477 2341; 1 Friar's St; s/d €40/60) Another reasonably priced winner in a fine old house a short way up from the harbour. It has comfy old-fashioned interiors that add a relaxing bonus to a stay in Kinsale.

TOP END

Rocklands House (☎ 477 2609; rocklandhouse@eircom.net; Compass Hill; s/d €80/90) Treat yourself to this top-of-the-range B&B, or to its self-catering cottage (enquire for terms). It's outside the town and high above the estuary among beautiful hillside gardens. Even the rooms that don't have great views of the estuary are lie-back-and-dream quality, and the service is impeccable.

Blue Haven Hotel & Restaurant (☎ 477 2209; bluhaven@iol.ie; 3 Pearse St; standard s/d €127/180, superior s/d €178/220) Look for off-season deals, although they're still fairly hefty, at this central hotel that adds all sorts of persuasive touches to its lavish rooms.

White Lady Hotel (☎ 477 2737; wlady@indigo.ie; Lower O'Connell St; s/d €80/100) At this modern upbeat hotel with comfortable rooms there's a good chance of reasonable off-season discounts. The restaurant, the busy bar and nightclub (see p207) add to the appeal for the gregarious.

Old Bank House (☎ 477 4075; www.oldbankhousekinsale.com; 11 Pearse St; r €170-215) Georgian elegance and style throughout gives a timeless quality to this top-of-the-range hotel where beautiful *objets d'art* and paintings grace the walls; luxurious public rooms add a country house ambience. Breakfasts are superb.

Acton's Hotel (☎ 477 2135; www.actonshotelkinsale.com; Pier Rd; s/d €139/196) This is a fairly pricey option compared to other top hotels, but rooms are well appointed and there's a good range of facilities, including a lush swimming pool and fitness club.

Eating

Kinsale's long history as a fishing port and its still busy fleet of vessels ensures that the town's restaurants have a high reputation for seafood. Meat eaters are not neglected, however, and you can also get cheap snacks and meals.

BUDGET

Diva's (☎ 477 3837; 40 Main St; snacks €3.70-5; ⌚ 9am-7pm Mon-Sat, 11am-6pm Sun) A charming little oasis of affordable, healthy food, Diva's has a gently alternative mood. Coffee refills are the norm. There's a tasty choice of panninis, including veggie options, with home-made cakes and brownies to follow.

Spaniard Bar & Restaurant (☎ 477 2436; Scilly; lunch €5-9.50; ⌚ noon-6pm) A good old seafarers' bar on Scilly. You can indulge in cracking crab claws or settle for a sandwich. During the early part of the winter there's a herring barbecue, and there's a restaurant during the summer months (mains €15 to €19.50).

Dino's (☎ 477 4561; Pier Rd; mains €7.75-10; ⌚ 8.30am-10.30pm) Kinsale's most convenient fuel stop, Dino's is near the car park, tourist office and bus stand. You hardly need to move. No-fuss food includes filling breakfasts (€5.50), fish and chips galore and an all-day four-courser (€17.50).

Mad Monk (☎ 477 4609; 1 Main St; meals €5.40-8.20; ⌚ 10am-10pm) No monkish stinting on food here with plenty of meat dishes, but with alternatives that include tasty chowder (€5.40), an even better fish pie (€8) and well-filled open baguettes (€6.50 to €8).

MID-RANGE

Jim Edwards' (☎ 477 2541; Market Quay; bar meals €4-14.90, restaurant meals €17-29.50; ⏲ bar 12.30-10pm, restaurant 6-10pm) Like so many places, this extremely popular eatery has bar food that is of restaurant standard. A steady Irish touch is nicely frothed with European influences. In the bar you may need to fight for attention amidst the clamour, but once served you'll want to stay all night. The restaurant does an excellent cold seafood platter, all wonderful shellfish and salmon, for €25.50.

White House Bar Bistro/Restaurant d'Antibes (☎ 477 2125; Pearse St; bar meals €4.40-10, restaurant meals €17.50-26; ⏲ bar noon-10pm, restaurant 6-10pm) There's fairly standard décor, but enjoyable food in this busy central pub/restaurant. It doesn't try too hard to fit the 'gourmet' bill, but settles for efficient service and an unfussy menu.

Kieran's Folkhouse Inn (☎ 477 2382; Guardwell; snacks €5.50-8.50, mains €9-12; ⏲ 12.30-10.30pm) A popular place done out in sunny colours, it has a pricier seafood bistro with a dash of Pacific rim cuisine. The bar menu has choices ranging from snacks and sandwiches to heftier meals.

TOP END

Vintage Restaurant (☎ 477 2502; 50 Main St; mains €29-31.50; ⏲ 6.30-10pm Tue-Sat) The Vintage is one of the real reasons that Kinsale deserves the gourmet label. There's real style here to match the prices. Unbeatable dishes range from oyster starters to mains of monkfish or sea bass, fish that demand a magic touch – and get it.

Bulman (☎ 477 2131; Summercove; bar meals €4-9.50, mains €14-24; ⏲ 12.30-9.30pm) This is seaside eating at its best. The Bulman is an escape from mainstream Kinsale to an unspoiled harbourside venue where informality is a style in its own right. Seafood really does excel here, with chowder or smoked salmon for lunch options, and with starters that add adventurous New World touches to sea bream and tiger prawns, among many choices.

Max's Wine Bar (☎ 477 3677; 48 Main St; lunch €4.50-9, dinner €16-20; ⏲ 12.30-2.45pm & 6.30-10.30pm Wed-Mon) There's definitely an Irish-French crossover touch in the surroundings and in the subtle cuisine of this charming place, where exposed stone walls and burnished wooden tables reinforce Kinsale's unquestionable Brittany coast feel.

Hoby's (☎ 477 2200; 5 Main St; mains €12.50-21; ⏲ 6-10.30pm) More excellent Irish-European cuisine at this very stylish place, where subtle colours and thoughtful seating make you feel that it's all just for you.

Man Friday (☎ 477 2260; cnr River & High Rds, Scilly; mains €19.50-23.50; ⏲ 6.45-10.15pm Mon-Sat) Out of town and on relaxing Scilly this popular restaurant has terrace seating with views across the harbour to Kinsale. Book ahead if you want a terrace table on balmy evenings. Cosy up inside otherwise. The menu has traditional leanings and while excellent fish dishes are the norm, there's steak, lamb, duck and vegetarian options.

SELF-CATERING

If you've overdosed on gourmet outings there's the SuperValu supermarket on Pearse St and Market Quay Food Co on Markey Quay for some luxuries.

Entertainment

Spaniard Bar & Restaurant (☎ 477 2436; Scilly) There's a regular all-year-round Wednesday night trad music session here at 9.30pm. There's also music throughout summer on Friday nights and Sunday afternoons.

Acton's Hotel (☎ 477 2135; Pier Rd) Stages a terrific Sunday lunch-time jazz session (12.30pm to 2.30pm) featuring the famous Cork City Jazz Band.

Shanakee (An Seanachai; ☎ 477 7077; 6 Market St) This big barn-like pub has trad music sessions on Tuesdays and there's a fairly stomping disco till late on Thursday, Friday and Saturday.

White Lady Hotel (☎ 477 2737; Lower O'Connell St) The nightclub has a breezy, youngish crowd at weekends and it runs '60s and '70s chart nights.

Back Room (☎ 477 2382; Guardwell; ⏲ 10pm-2.30am Thu-Sat) Attached to Kieran's Folkhouse Inn and featuring local DJs cranking out chart faves.

Shopping

Giles Norman Gallery (☎ 477 4373; 45 Main St) There's a big selection of powerful and evocative black-and-white imagery, mainly stunning landscapes, from a master of the *genre*. Prices, framed or unframed, start about €25 and rise into the hundreds.

Granny's Bottom Drawer (☎ 477 4839; 53 Main St) A great range of exquisite Irish linen, damask and nightwear is on offer at this cheerful shop.

Roots Records (☎ 477 4963; www.rootsrecords.ie; 1 Short Quay) There's absolutely everything from trad to reggae at this useful music shop.

Kinsale Crystal (☎ 477 4493; Market St) Exquisite work by an ex-Waterford craftsman who stands by the traditional 'deep-cutting, high-angle style' is available here. A napkin ring will cost you about €36, while large pieces cost in the mid-hundreds.

Getting There & Away

Bus Éireann (☎ 450 8188) buses connect Kinsale with Cork (€5.50, 45 minutes, 10 daily, five Sunday). The bus stops at the Esso garage on Pier Rd near the tourist office.

Getting Around

You can hire bikes, including tandems, for €10 per day from the **Hire Shop** (☎ 477 4884; 18 Main St). For a taxi try **Kinsale Cabs** (☎ 477 2642).

KINSALE TO CLONAKILTY

Following the quays west out of Kinsale, the main R600 road passes through Ballinspittle and sleepy creekside Timoleague where you'll find the ruins of a **Franciscan friary**. From here you can continue on the R600 to Clonakilty, but a more pleasant detour is along the R601 to picturesque **Courtmacsherry** on another tidal inlet on Courtmacsherry Bay.

CLONAKILTY

☎ 023 / pop 3437

You'll feel at home in cheerful Clonakilty. There's still a bustling market town mood about the place, and tourism is well catered for by a mix of good B&Bs and hotels and some choice restaurants. A strong thread of traditional and contemporary live music in cosy pubs keeps Clonakilty alive at night.

The bay is good for swimming, albeit in a bracing sort of way. The beach at nearby Inchydoney Island is also good, but watch for the dangerous riptide; when lifeguards are on duty a red flag indicates danger.

Michael Collins (see p210) was born near Clonakilty, a fact of which the community is very proud – witness the stalwart statue of Collins on the corner of Emmet Square.

History

Clonakilty received its first charter in 1292 but was refounded in the early 17th century by the first earl of Cork. He settled it with 100 English families and planned a Protestant town from which Catholics would be excluded. His plan failed: Clonakilty is now very Irish and very Catholic – the Presbyterian chapel has been turned into a post office.

From the mid-18th to mid-19th centuries over 10,000 people worked in the town's linen industry. The fire station stands on the site of the old linen market.

Orientation

Roads converge on Asna Square, dominated by a monument commemorating local men who died at the Battle of Big Cross during the 1798 Rising. Also in the square is the small Kilty Stone (stone of the wood), which gave Clonakilty its name. Inchydoney Island is about 4km from the centre.

Information

The **tourist office** (☎ 33226; Ashe St; ⏲ 9am-7pm daily Jul & Aug, 9am-5pm Mon, Tue & Thu-Sat Sep-Jun) has a good map of the town and its surrounds; the map is available for free from here and also from many hotels and B&Bs.

The Allied Irish Bank on the corner of Pearse and Bridge Sts has an ATM. The post office is in the old Presbyterian chapel on Bridge St. For Internet access the best bet is to join the local **library** (The Old Mill Library; ☎ 34275; Kent St; ⏲ 10.30am-6pm Tue-Sat). It costs €2.50 to join but you get 'free' use of Internet. The **Wash Basket** (☎ 34821) is a laundrette on Spiller's Lane. There are public toilets on the corner of Rossa and Kent Sts.

Sights

The impressive **Church of the Immaculate Conception** (cnr Bridge & Oliver Plunkett Sts) was built in the 1870s and has some handsome mosaic work.

West Cork Model Railway Village (☎ 33224; Inchydoney Rd; adult/child €6/4; ⏲ 11am-5pm Feb-Oct) features not only a working replica of the West Cork Railway as it was during WWII, but superb miniature models of the main towns in western Cork – Clonakilty, Dunmanway, Kinsale and Bandonas – as they were in the 1940s.

Sleeping

Desert House Caravan & Camping Park (☎ 33331; deserthouse@eircom.net; Coast Rd; tent & 2 people €8;

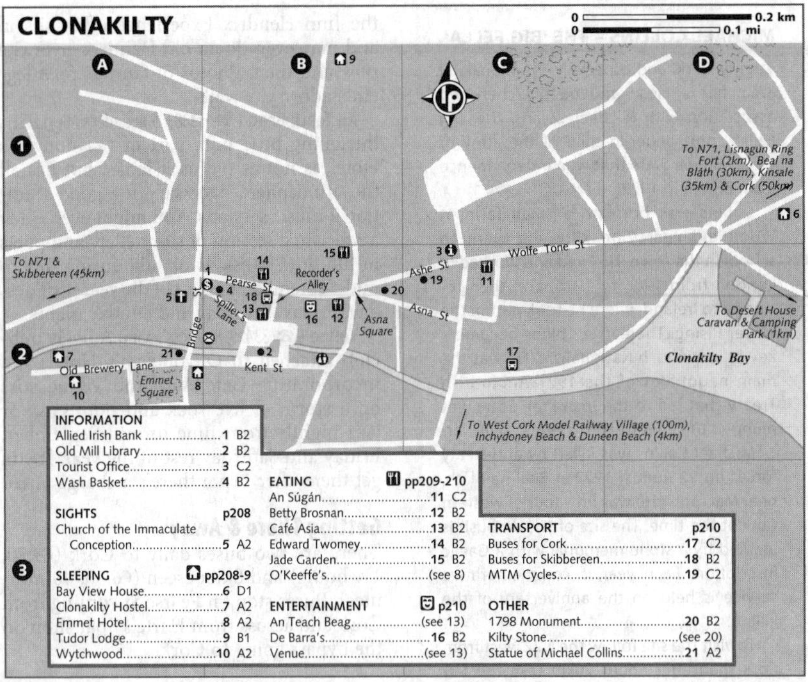

Easter & May-Sep) This attractive park is 1km east of town on the road to Ring. It's on a dairy farm overlooking the bay.

Clonakilty Hostel (☎ 33525; fax 35673; Old Brewery Lane; dm/d €12/30; wheelchair access) This well-maintained and quiet place is at the end of a cul-de-sac in one of the oldest parts of town off Emmet Square.

Wytchwood (☎ 33525; wytchost@iol.ie; Emmet Sq; s/d €40/60) Opposite the hostel, and run by the same people, this is an engaging house, rooted in Clonakilty's past. The furnishings and dark wood add to the reflective mood.

Tudor Lodge (☎ 33046; tudorlodge1@eircom.net; MacCurtain Hill; s/d €40/64) Sitting pleasantly above it all is this pleasant B&B where standards are kept up to scratch in fresh, bright rooms.

Bay View House (☎ 33539; Old Timoleague Rd; s/d €52/64) This fine modern house overlooking Clonakilty Bay offers impeccable B&B standards with frills, and serves great breakfasts.

Emmet Hotel (☎ 33394; www.emmethotel.com; Emmet Sq; s/d €55/110) Refurbishment of this old town hotel has retained its period charm, if you're looking for a relaxing ambience.

Eating

An Súgán (☎ 33498; 41 Wolfe Tone St; bar meals €5.50-10.50, mains €11-21.50; 12.30-10pm) Top choice in town, this family-run eatery exudes style. There's a choice of traditional main bar and restaurant or a more modern café-bar and outside courtyard. Meat and duck dishes are on offer but seafood is the great thing here, from exquisite crab cocktail to a great selection of prawns, salmon, scallops and monkfish in a filo pastry basket for €21.50.

Betty Brosnan (☎ 34011; 58 Pearse St; meals €5.50-10; 9am-6pm Mon-Sat) A great place for affordable yet satisfying snacks and dishes, this busy café offers a breakfast choice (€5 to €6.20) as well as tasty sandwiches (€2.50 to €5.75).

O'Keeffe's (☎ 33394; www.emmethotel.com; Emmet Sq; 2-course meals €28; 6.30-9.30pm) A good selection of standard Irish food in subtle sauces is on offer in the relaxing surroundings of Emmet Hotel's restaurant.

Café Asia (☎ 33419; Recorder's Alley; mains €6.50-17; 7-11pm Thu-Mon) Describing itself as a 'Fusion Food Bar' this is part of the Venue nightclub (see p210). Go for Celtic paella

MICHAEL COLLINS – THE 'BIG FELLA'

County Cork, and especially the Clonakilty area, has a close and deeply cherished association with Michael Collins, the 'Big Fella', commander-in-chief of the army of the Irish Free State that won independence from Britain in 1922.

Collins was born on a small farm at Woodfield near Clonakilty and went to school in the town. He lived and worked in London from 1906 to 1916, and then returned to Ireland where he took part in the Easter Rising. Thereafter Collins became a key figure in Irish Nationalism. He was the main negotiator of the 1921 Anglo-Irish Treaty that led to the Irish Free State, yet plunged the country into a brutal civil war.

Michael Collins was killed by anti-treaty forces on 22 August 1922 at Beal-na-Bláth, near Macroom. He was on a tour of western Cork at the time. The site of the ambush is marked by a stone memorial with a Gaelic inscription. Each year, a commemorative service is held on the anniversary of the killing.

To visit the site follow the N22 west from Cork then after about 20km take the left turn (R590) to Crookstown. From there turn right onto the R585 to Beal-na-Bláth. The ambush site is on the left after 4km.

A useful map and leaflet *In Search of Michael Collins* can be obtained at Clonakilty tourist office. It outlines the various key places in the district that were associated with Michael Collins.

(€18.60) or veggie enchiladas (€12) or 'fuse' with jungle curry (€12.70).

Jade Garden (☎ 34576; MacCurtain Hill; mains €6-10.50; 🕒 7-11pm) Enjoy tasty Chinese in an Irish setting at this popular central restaurant.

Clonakilty is famous for producing the best black pudding in Ireland. For a variety of products, starting at a minimum of €2.50, head for **Edward Twomey** (☎ 33733; 16 Pearse St).

Entertainment

De Barra's (☎ 33381; 55 Pearse St) Marvellous atmosphere and great surroundings make this pub popular, as does live music every night of the week, starting round about 9.30pm. On Friday nights Noel Redding of the Jimi Hendrix Experience often sits in and may even do an old Hendrix favourite now and then. Photos of famous rock legends adorn the walls.

An Teach Beag (☎ 33883; 5 Recorder's Alley) This intriguing little pub, part of O'Donovan's Hotel, is not as old as it looks, but has all the atmosphere necessary for good traditional music sessions. You might even catch a *scríocht*, a session of storytellers and poets in full flow. Music is nightly during July to mid-September; the rest of the year it's Tuesday, Friday, Saturday and Sunday nights.

Venue (☎ 33419; Recorder's Alley) A lively pub-club attached to O'Donovan's Hotel, and incorporating Café Asia, the Venue stirs up a storm of live rock and pop, salsa or jazz nightly from June to mid-September, Friday and Saturday rest of the year. If you get there after 11pm there's a charge of €5.

Getting There & Away

There are two buses daily to Cork (€9.20, 1¼ hours) and Skibbereen (€6.50, 40 minutes). Buses stop on Pearse St coming from Cork and across from Harte's Spar shop on the bypass going to Cork.

Getting Around

MTM Cycles (☎ 33584; 33 Ashe St) hires out bikes for €10/45 per day/week. A nice bike ride is to Duneen Beach, 13km south of town.

AROUND CLONAKILTY

Lisnagun Ring Fort

Of more than 30,000 ring forts scattered across Ireland, **Lisnagun** (Lios na gCon; adult/child €2.60/1.30; 🕒 9am-5pm Mon-Fri, 10am-5pm Sat & Sun) is the only one that has been reconstructed to give an impression of life in a 10th-century defended farmstead. It is complete with a souterrain and a central thatched hut.

To get there take the turning at the roundabout at the end of Strand Rd signposted to Bay View House B&B. Follow this road uphill for 2km until you reach a T-junction. Turn right and about 100m along you'll see cast iron farm gates on your right. Go through the gates and keep walking straight ahead until you come to a crossroads with a cowshed. Take the track to the left and walk downhill until you reach a minor road. Turn right and the fort is on the left, near the Clonakilty Agricultural College.

CLONAKILTY TO SKIBBEREEN

You can get from Clonakilty to Skibbereen along the main N71 via Roscarberry and Leap, but far more enjoyable is to detour via the R597 that winds southwest from just beyond the western end of the causeway at Rosscarberry, signposted Glandore and Coppinger's Court. This takes in the picturesque villages of Glandore and Union Hall, as well as some fine coastal scenery.

Drombeg Stone Circle

This atmospheric site was once thought to date from the 1st century AD or even earlier, but may be as late as the 5th century AD, representing a sophisticated Iron Age update of an earlier Bronze Age monument. There are 17 uprights comprising a circle of 9m in diameter. The setting, on an exposed hillside terrace, is superb; the land sweeps away to the south. Just beyond the circle are the remains of a hut and a fascinating Iron Age cooking pit, known as a *fulachta fiadh*. Experiments have shown that heated stones from the nearby hearth would bring water to the boil and would keep it hot for nearly three hours – enough to cook meat.

The circle is reached by turning off the R597, signposted Drombeg, about 4km west of Roscarberry. There's a car park here and be assured that access to the circle, along a surfaced path, is free.

Glandore & Union Hall

☎ 028

The pretty waterside villages of Glandore (Cuan Dor) and Union Hall burst into life in summer when fleets of yachts tack into the shelter of the Glandore Harbour inlet.

Union Hall, accessible from Glandore via a narrow road bridge over the estuary, was named after the 1800 Act of Union, which abolished the separate Irish parliament. Big fishing boats work from here.

ACTIVITIES

You can try a sea kayaking trip round the beautiful coast and sheltered inlets of the area with **Atlantic Sea Kayaking** (☎ 21058; Union Hall). It can also be contacted through Maria's Schoolhouse (see below).

SLEEPING & EATING

Meadow Camping Park (☎ 33280; the_meadow@oceanfree.net; Rosscarbery road, Glandore; small tent & 1 person €7, tent & family €18; ⏲ mid-Mar–Sep) This delightful park is 2km east of Glandore on the R597 to Rosscarbery. It's in a garden setting with lots of trees and flowers adding to the tranquillity.

Maria's Schoolhouse (☎ 33002; mariasschoolhouse@eircom.net; Cahergal, Union Hall; dm €12, d with bathroom €38-64) No longer owned by Maria but in safe hands, this outstanding hostel occupies a converted 19th-century schoolhouse of great character and in peaceful surroundings. Dinners on request cost €24 per person (vegetarians catered for) and the buffet breakfast costs €6.50. The hostel can organise sea-kayaking trips with Atlantic Sea Kayaking (see above). To get there turn right after crossing the causeway into Union Hall and continue through the village following the sign for Skibbereen. It's signposted at the edge of town about 1km from the centre.

Ardagh House & Restaurant (☎ 33571; Union Hall; s/d €28/56; mains €14-20; restaurant ⏲ daily Apr-Oct, Sat & Sun Nov-Mar) A friendly place by the harbour. The popular restaurant does plentiful helpings of straightforward fish and meat dishes.

GETTING THERE & AWAY

Although buses do not pass through these two villages, they do stop in nearby Leap (3km north) and most hostel and B&B owners will pick you up from here if you prearrange it.

SKIBBEREEN

☎ 028 / pop 2015

Skibbereen (Sciobairín) is a name to roll round the tongue. It's a typical market town, unvarnished, down-to-earth and warm hearted. Times were tough for Skibbereen during the Famine years and huge numbers of the local population died or emigrated. One result was a later resurgence of powerful nationalism, both locally and with strong support from emigrants. Today the town is a thriving commercial centre with a busy Friday **market** (⏲ 12.30-2.30pm) and a steady influx of tourists stopping off on their way to western Cork.

For three days in July, Skibbereen hosts a **traditional music festival** when the streets and pubs come alive with music day and night. For more information contact skibbereenfleadh@hotmail.com.

Orientation

The main landmark in town is a statue, which stands at the junction of three roads and is dedicated to the heroes of the many Irish rebellions against the British. From here Market St heads south past the post office to Lough Hyne and Baltimore. The main shopping street, Main St, leads to a junction with Ilen St, which heads west over the river to Ballydehob and Bantry. North St heads towards the main Cork road.

Information

The **tourist office** (☎ 21766; North St; 🕑 9.15am-1pm & 2.15-5.30pm Mon-Fri Oct-May, 9am-6pm Mon-Sat Jun-Sep, 9am-7pm Jul & Aug) is very helpful. There's an excellent pamphlet, the *Skibbereen Trail* (€1.75) which takes you on a historical walking tour of the town and is available from the tourist office, newsagencies and the Heritage Centre on Upper Bridge St.

There is an Allied Irish Bank with ATM on Bridge St. For Internet access head to the top floor of the **West Cork Arts Centre** (☎ 22090; North St; 🕑 10am-6pm Mon-Sat; €2.70/hr).

Heritage Centre

Built on the site of the town's old gasworks, the **heritage centre** (☎ 40900; Old Gasworks Bldg, Upper Bridge St; adult/child €4/2; 🕑 10am-6pm Tue-Sat, last admission 5.15pm) houses a haunting exhibition about the Famine and a smaller exhibition about nearby Lough Hyne, the first marine nature reserve in Ireland. It also has a genealogical centre and a great deal of information on local archaeological sites.

Abbeystrewery Cemetery

A visit here puts Irish history into harrowing perspective. It's 1km east of the centre on the N71 to Schull, and comprises mass graves of 8000 to 10,000 local people who died during the Famine.

Sleeping

Hideaway Camping & Caravan Park (☎ 33280, 22254; the_hideaway@oceanfree.net; R596; tent & 2 people €14; 🕑 late Apr–mid-Sep) This attractive park is 1km southeast of town on the road to Castletownsend. There's a marshland bird reserve nearby.

Russagh Mill Hostel & Adventure Centre (☎ 22451; tent & 2 people €7, dm €11, private rooms €30) This outdoor activity centre is 1.5km southeast of town on the R596 and occupies an atmospheric old corn mill where the mill machinery has been preserved. It's run by experienced mountaineers and canoeists and for about €15 you can sample some activities including a day's **kayaking**, or **climbing instruction** on the centre's climbing wall.

Bridge House (☎ 21273; Bridge St; s/d €30/60) Not to be missed if you're looking for a truly different experience, this main street house draws you in to fabulous Victorian tableaux, the creation of the charming owner who has filled every room with period memorabilia. Adding to the overall style is a distinctly un-Victorian spa bath in the bathroom.

Ilenroy House (☎ 22751; ilenroyhouse@oceanfree.net; 10 North St; s/d €45/60) There are excellent rooms and friendly service in this fine old town house that has managed to retain character in spite of modernisation.

Eldon Hotel (☎ 22000; www.eldon-hotel.com; Bridge St; s/d €65/130) There's a lot of history in this attractive old hotel, where the walls in the reception and bar are covered with photographs and memorabilia of Michael Collins, a friend of the hotel's owner of the time. Collins was in the hotel on the day he was shot at Beal na Bláth (see p210). You can muse on the past in comfy rooms.

Eating

Kalbo's Bistro (☎ 21515; 48 North St; snacks €4.50- 9, dinner mains €13-21; 🕑 11.30am-4.30pm & 6.30-9.30pm Mon-Sat, noon-2.30pm & 6.30-9.30pm Sun) This bustling place serves delicious soup, sandwiches, salads and a selection of main meals that includes a couple of vegetarian options.

Ty Ar Mor (☎ 22100; 46 Bridge St; lunch €9-15, dinner €35-47; 🕑 lunch from noon, dinner 6.30-9.15pm Jul-Aug, closed Mon & Tue winter, closed Oct–mid-Nov & mid-Feb–mid-Mar) An award-winning restaurant, this wonderful centre of Breton cuisine offers the finest fish, such as turbot, black sole and John Dory, as well as shellfish from the tank. Seafood is the main thing here, but lamb and steak also feature, all done with inimitable Breton flair. Check for opening times out of season. Upstairs is the **Thai @ Ty Ar Mor Noodle & Wine Bar** (mains €6-15) with Thai staff and traditional Thai décor.

Porch Bar/Gallagher's Restaurant (Bridge St; bar snacks €3.20-14.90, dinner mains €13.90-21.50; 🕑 lunch noon onwards, dinner 6.30-9pm) There's plenty of choice at the Eldon Hotel's adjoining bar and restaurant, from strongly traditional

COUNTY CORK

dishes to international cuisine, with local meat and poultry and a great fish menu.

Getting There & Away

Bus Éireann buses run four times daily (three on Saturday and Sunday) to Cork (€12.50, 1¾ hours), and three times daily (one only on Sunday) to Schull (€4.50, 30 minutes) from outside the Eldon Hotel on Main St.

BALTIMORE

☎ 028 / pop 260

An emphatically seagoing sort of place and just 13km down the River Ilen from Skibbereen, picturesque Baltimore has a population that swells enormously during the summer months as sailing folk, anglers, divers and visitors to Sherkin and Clear Islands flock in. There's not that much to shout about here but the natural surroundings speak eloquently for themselves, the village has a couple of fine restaurants, and the pubs are lively in summer and relaxing in winter. The harbour is dominated by the remains of the Dún na Sead (Fort of the Jewels), one of nine castles built in the area by the O'Driscoll clan. A white-painted landmark beacon (aka Lot's wife) stands on the western headland of the peninsula and makes for a pleasant walk, especially at sunset.

At the time of writing there was no tourist office at Baltimore, but there is an information board at the harbour.

Activities

There's some great **diving** to be had on the reefs around Fastnet Rock and a number of nearby shipwrecks. **Aquaventures Dive Centre** (☎ 20511; aquavent@aquaventures.ie; Lifeboat Rd) charges €60 for one dive with gear rental, €35 if you have your own wetsuit and fins, and €25 without rental.

Baltimore Sailing School (☎ 20141) provides sailing courses from May to September for both beginners and advanced sailors.

For **deep-sea fishing** trips phone **Nick Dent** (☎ 21709), or **Mossie O'Halloran** (☎ 20643) for angling and whale- and dolphin-watching trips.

Festivals & Events

Over the third weekend of May, Baltimore stages a seafood festival: jazz bands perform and mussels and prawns are on offer in the pubs.

Sleeping

Rolf's Holiday Hostel (☎ 20289; www.rolfsholidays.com; Baltimore Hill; dm €13-15, d €40) Excellent value in bright, clean rooms is just the start at this well-run place on the outside of town. There's a charming café and restaurant (see Café Art below) and the whole place is set in peaceful gardens. Self-catering units are also available. Rolf's is gay friendly.

Casey's of Baltimore (☎ 20197; www.caseysofbaltimore.com; Skibbereen Rd; s/d €103/155) Top-end price, but you can get reasonable discounts off-season and the rooms are wonderfully lavish and spacious; many overlook the sea and there's a delightful sense of peacefulness throughout.

Fastnet House (☎ 20515; fastnethouse@eircom.net; Main St; s/d €50/72) This early-19th-century house is just up from the main harbour and has an easy-going ambience in its uncluttered and simply decorated rooms.

Stone House (☎ 20511; aquavent@aquaventures.ie; Lifeboat Rd; s/d €55/72.50) This is also home of the Aquaventures Dive Centre (see above) and there's a friendly, outdoorsy spirit about the place.

Eating

Customs House Restaurant (☎ 20200; Main St; dinner €22-32; ⌚ 7-9.30pm Wed-Sat, closed Oct-Apr) A modest frontage belies the cool, contemporary interior of this fine restaurant which adds to the area's reputation for gourmet food. There's good value set dinners that feature subtle Italian and French preparations of local seafood and fish such as top-tasting red mullet and monkfish.

Chez Youen (☎ 20136; The Quay; dinner from €35; ⌚ 6-10pm, closed Nov & Feb) Terrific seafood is the rule in this Breton-inspired restaurant where the shellfish platter (€45) really offers the chance of sampling shellfish at its best. There's not much for the meat lover, but vegetarians are indulged.

Café Art (☎ 20289; Baltimore Hill; baguettes €4-5, mains €14-18; ⌚ 8.30am-9.30pm, closed Mon & Tue winter) You can also order tasty light pasta, salad or vegetarian meals (€5.50 to €11) at this relaxing place located at Rolf's Holiday Hostel. There's a light European touch to all the food and an excellent wine list has been developed for the in-house wine bar. The café stages painting exhibitions and current works grace the walls.

> **CAPE CLEAR ISLAND STORYTELLING FESTIVAL**
>
> The brainchild of an American expat writer who moved to the island in the early 1990s, the Cape Clear Island Storytelling Festival brings hundreds of people to Cape Clear from all over the world to celebrate writing and to exchange stories and experiences. Activities such as boat trips to Fastnet lighthouse, bird-watching, and archaeological and nature walks are part of the festival activities.
>
> The festival usually takes place over three days at the beginning of September. Enquire well ahead for prices and for prior booking of tickets and accommodation; the festival is becoming more popular each year and there's limited availability. For more information contact Christine Sawyer on ☎ 028-39116 or stories@indigo.ie. The website is http://indigo.ie/~stories.

Casey's of Baltimore (☎ 20197; mains €13.65-25; 🕑 12.30-2.30pm & 6.30-9.30pm) Even if you don't stay at Casey's you can call in for breakfast, sandwiches (€3.40 to €8.80) or dinner of a seafood platter (€24) if you want to really sample the local fish.

Declan McCarthy's Bar (☎ 20263; The Square; bar food €6-11, restaurant mains €12-20) A handy venue for bar food and evening meals, this harbourside bar dishes up traditional Irish food, including good seafood, without frills.

Getting There & Away

From Monday to Friday there's four buses a day to Baltimore from Skibbereen with an extra two services during July and August. There are four buses on Saturday from May to mid-September (€3, 20 minutes).

See p215 for the Schull–Clear Island–Baltimore ferry service.

CLEAR ISLAND

☎ 028 / pop 150

Clear Island (Oileán Cléire), also called Cape Clear Island, is an escapist heaven but you need time to spare to enjoy this rugged outlier, the second-most southerly point of Ireland after Fastnet Rock, 6km to the southwest. Clear Island is also an Irish-speaking (Gaeltacht) area, with one shop, a few B&Bs and three pubs. It's a place for walking, exploring archaeological ruins and bird-watching. Each year at the beginning of September the island hosts a week-long storytelling festival (see the boxed text opposite).

The island has its own website at www.oilean-chleire.ie/index.htm.

Orientation & Information

The island is 5km long and just over 1.5km wide at its broadest point. It narrows in the middle where an isthmus divides the northern and southern harbours. There's a **tourist information post** (☎ 39100; 🕑 4-6pm Jul & Aug) beyond the pier, next to the coffee shop. If it's closed the coffee shop has various leaflets.

You'll find public toilets down at the harbour.

Sights

The small **heritage centre** (🕑 2.30-5pm Jun-Aug) has exhibits on the island's history and culture. There are fine views looking north across the water to the Mizen Head Peninsula.

The ruins of **Dunamore Castle**, the stronghold of the O'Driscoll clan, can be seen perched on a rock on the northwestern side of the island (follow the track from the harbour).

Activities

BIRD-WATCHING

The white-fronted, two-storey **bird observatory** is by the harbour. Turn right at the end of the pier and it's 100m along. It's worth calling in to ask about any planned bird-watching trips.

Clear Island is famous for large movements of sea birds, including Manx shearwater, gannet, fulmar and kittiwake. The guillemot breeds on the island but other birds head to and fro on hunting trips from the rocky outposts of the western peninsulas. Tens of thousands of birds can pass hourly, especially early morning and at dusk.

For a guided bird-watching tour contact the adventure centre at Cape Clear Island Hostel (see below).

For trips to Fastnet or **bird-watching boat trips** phone ☎ 39153.

OUTDOOR ACTIVITIES

Cape Clear Island Hostel (☎ 39198) houses an adventure centre that arranges a number of outdoor activities, including kayaking, diving, fishing and whale- or dolphin-

COUNTY CORK

watching. For guided walks covering historical, archaeological or ecological aspects of the island phone ☎ 39157 (during summer).

Courses

Irish-language courses are run by Ciarán and Mary O'Driscoll from time to time. Ask at **Ciarán Danny Mike's** (☎ 39172) or phone ☎ 39153 for details.

If there's anything you need to know about **goat husbandry** contact the resident goat farmer on ☎ 39126. He makes ice cream and cheese, available for tastings, and runs day-/week-long courses on goat keeping.

Sleeping & Eating

Accommodation on the island is satisfyingly simple and unfancy. You are advised to book ahead, especially from May to September.

There is a **camp site** (☎ 39119; per person €3.80; Jun-Sep) and An Óige's **Cape Clear Island Hostel** (☎ 39198; fax 39144; South Harbour; dm €10.50-12; Jun-Oct), which is in a large white building at the south harbour.

There are a couple of similar B&Bs that are both friendly places in typical island houses: **Cluain Mara** (☎ 39153, 39172; www.capeclearisland.com; North Harbour; s/d €35/60) and **Ard Na Gaoithe** (☎ 39160; The Glen; s/d €28/56). Just ask directions.

Self-catering cottages are available. Ask at the coffee shop or Ciarán Danny Mike's.

In summer there's a chip van at the north harbour.

Other recommendations:

Siopa Beag (☎ 39145; North Harbour) This coffee shop and grocery store has a few supplies for self-caterers.

Chistin Cléire (☎ 39145; Easter-Oct) Near the pier; serves light meals.

Ciarán Danny Mike's (☎ 39172; meals €6.35-11.45) Generous bar meals.

Getting There & Away

The boat from **Baltimore** (☎ 39159; www.emara.com/capeclearferry) takes 45 minutes to cover the 11km journey and it's a stunning trip on a clear day. From Baltimore there are four boats a day during July and August and at least three a day the rest of the year; return fare is €11.50/6.50 per adult/child and there are special family rates. Bikes travel free of charge.

A **boat** (☎ 39153; www.westcorkcoastalcruises.com) leaves Baltimore for Schull and then Clear Island daily mid-June to mid-September at 10.30am and 2pm. One-way/return fare is €8/13.

GOUGANE BARRA FOREST PARK

This is the most picturesque part of inland Cork. The source of the River Lee is a mountain lake fed by numerous silver streams. St Finbarr, the founder and patron saint of Cork, came here in the 6th century and established a monastery. He had a hermitage on the island in **Gougane Barra Lake** (Lough an Ghugain), which is now approached by a short causeway. The small, modern chapel on the island has fine stained-glass representations of obscure Celtic saints.

A road runs through the park in a loop and you can walk the network of paths and nature trails that are indicated on a signboard map.

Getting There & Away

In July and August there's a Saturday-only bus service that leaves Macroom at 8am and passes by the Gougane Barra Forest Park.

Driving from Cork to Bantry along the N22 and R584 you'll see a signpost for the park after Ballingeary. Returning to the main road afterwards and continuing west, you'll pass over the Pass of Keimaneigh and emerge on the N71 at Ballylickey, midway between the Beara Peninsula and the Sheep's Head Peninsula.

MIZEN HEAD PENINSULA

From Skibbereen the road heads west through Ballydehob, the gateway to the Mizen, and then on to Schull. Beyond here the deeper Mizen draws you ever westwards, through Toormore and on across undulating, sparsely populated countryside to the village of Goleen.

Even here the Mizen is in no way finished. From Goleen ever-narrowing roads head further west to the spectacular Mizen Head itself and to the hidden corners of Barleycove Beach and Crookhaven. Without a decent map you may well reach the same crossroads several times.

Heading back from Goleen you can bear off north to join the scenic coast road that follows the edge of Dunmanus Bay for most of the way to Durrus. At Durrus, one road heads for Bantry while the other turns west to Sheep's Head Peninsula.

SCHULL

☎ 028 / pop 650

Schull (pronounced skull) is a small fishing village where a few vessels still keep the trade alive with some success. The harbour has the satisfying clutter of a working port and water sports also play their part in making Schull a busy tourist centre in summer. Out of season it's even more attractive in some ways, with a strong local community.

Orientation & Information

Schull's shops and hotels line a long main street that runs parallel with the harbour. Halfway along, a road to the left leads to the planetarium and hostel.

There is no tourist office, but a very useful booklet, *Schull: A Visitor's Guide* can be obtained from hotels and some shops. There's also a website www.schull.ie with information.

The Allied Irish Bank branch at the top of Main St has an ATM and bureau de change.

There's Internet access at the **Computer Store** (☎ 27801; Main St; €2/30min).

Fuchsia Books (☎ 28016; Main St) has a good general collection.

Schull Planetarium

In the grounds of Schull Community College, the Republic's only **planetarium** (☎ 28552; Colla Rd; adult/child €4.50/2.20; ⏲ 3.30-5pm Sun May & Sep, 3.30-5pm Tue & Sat, 7-9pm Thu Jun, 2-5pm Tue & Sat, 7-9pm Mon & Thu Jul & Aug) has an 8m dome and a video and slide show. There's a star show most days, starting about 30 minutes after opening time, which is included in the admission price.

The planetarium is at the Goleen end of the village on the Colla road, just past Schull Backpackers' Lodge. You can also reach it by walking along the Foreshore Path from the pier.

Activities

There are a number of **walks** in the area including a serious outing up **Mt Gabriel** from Schull, making a round trip of about 14km. The route is partly across open country that demands skilled map and compass work in misty conditions. The mountain was once mined for copper and there are Bronze Age remains as well as 19th-century mine shafts and chimneys. Less active people could try the short Foreshore Path from the pier out to Roaringwater Bay and the many nearby islands. The publication *Schull: A Visitor's Guide* has information on walking routes and there's also a small leaflet *Walks Around Schull*.

The helpful **Schull Watersports Centre** (☎ 28554; schullwatersports@oceanfree.net; The Pier; ⏲ 9.30am-6pm Mon-Sat) rents out sailing dinghies (€40 per half-day) and snorkelling gear (€8 per day). **Diving instruction** (☎ 28943) and trips are also available and the centre can arrange angling trips.

Sea Kayaking Schull (☎ 28681) organises trips (€30 for two hours). For a fishing trip contact **Rooster Deep Sea Angling** (☎ 086 824 0642). You can also go **horse riding** (☎ 37246) for €25 per hour.

Sleeping

Schull Backpackers' Lodge (☎ 28681; www.schullbackpackers.com; Colla Rd; dm €12-13, s €18, d €36-40) A quiet and wooded edge-of-town location adds to the charms of this pleasant timber lodge where rooms are neat as a pin and comfy. There's also limited camping space and you can hire bikes (€11 per day). Ask about diving trips at the hostel.

Adele's (☎ 28459; adeles@oceanfree.net; Main St; B&B s/d €27.50/55) There's good value at this friendly place that's attached to a bakery (see p217). Breakfasts are continental and the bread selection is delicious.

Schull Central (☎ 28227; Main St; s/d €35/58) Remarkably narrow hallways and stairs don't detract from this simple, well-kept central house, where the owners exude kindness.

Glencairn (☎ 28007; Ardmanagh Dr; s/d €35/58) Excellent value is the norm at this friendly place in a peaceful cul-de-sac only 100m from Main St. Rooms are comfy and breakfasts will set you up for the day.

At the time of writing the useful **East End Hotel** (☎ 28101; eastendhotel@eircom.net; Main St) was due for complete refurbishment and was due to reopen sometime in 2004. Phone for further information and prices.

Eating

You'll find that most places offer local produce such as Gubbeen cheese and oak-smoked bacon on their menus. For self-catering there are supermarkets on the main street.

Courtyard (☎ 28390; Main St; snacks & light meals €3.20-11.50) More than a shop, this delicatessen and its bar and coffee shop have rare character. The shop has a great selection of local and continental cheeses, olive oil, pasta and organically grown vegetables. Behind the deli is the **Courtyard Bar** where you can drink tea or coffee, as well as alcohol, and enjoy everything from toasties to Mediterranean beef stew.

Waterside Inn (☎ 28203; Main St; bar food €2.50-5, restaurant mains €21.50-27) Locals will stand by the claim that the chowder (€5) here is the best for a long way. Mains are seafood orientated too, with dishes such as pan-fried scallops doused in champagne, pernod and ginger.

Organic Oasis (☎ 27886; Main St) Buy tasty and healthy foodstuffs to takeaway, and browse the wide range of alternative remedies in this pleasant shop.

Adele's (☎ 28459; Main St; lunch €5-10) A strong commitment to locally sourced and organic ingredients makes Adele's a place for the taste buds.

Getting There & Away

There are three buses per day Monday to Saturday and one on Sunday that leave Skibbereen at 1.05pm and travel to Schull (€4.70, 30 minutes). Boats for Clear Island and Sherkin Island leave from the pier. See p215 for details of the Schull to Baltimore boat service.

Getting Around

Parking in Schull's main street is difficult in summer. There are car parks opposite the East End Hotel and at Pier Rd.

For bus and taxi services around the peninsula try phoning **Betty Johnson's Bus Hire** (☎ 28410, 087 265 6078).

Bikes can be hired from Schull Backpackers' Lodge (see p216) or from **Cotter's Yard** (☎ 28165, after hours & Sun ☎ 35185; Main St) for €11 per day.

WEST OF SCHULL TO MIZEN HEAD

☎ 028

If you are driving or cycling take the coastal route from Schull to Goleen. On a clear day there are some great views out to Clear Island and Fastnet lighthouse. The landscape becomes wilder around the hamlet of Toormore. From Goleen roads run out to Mizen Head and to the picturesque harbour village of Crookhaven.

Goleen

Tourism in the Goleen area has been handled well by the local community with the Mizen Head Visitor Centre being a token of their commitment and imagination.

Mizen Tourism/Telecottage (☎ 35255; mizentc@eircom.net; 🕓 10am-6pm) in Goleen at the eastern end of town opens year round. There's plenty of free information here on local sights and activities as well as a bureau de change and Internet access (€4.50 for 30 minutes).

Ewe Art Centre (☎ 35492; www.theewe.com; Goleen; 🕓 May-Aug) is a magical artists' hideaway with pretty gardens and stunning views. You can try your hand at pottery and other handicrafts such as puppet making, tiles and decorating and sculpture on one-week courses. One week's accommodation and three days' tuition costs €225 per person; accommodation only is €179. Nonresidential and shorter term courses are available also. Even if you don't go on a course you can enjoy a visit to the centre's excellent **gallery and sculpture garden** (adult/child €3.50/1.25) and there's a small shop with colourful work for sale. Look for a blue house tucked into the hillside. It's signposted to the right as you enter Goleen from Schull.

SLEEPING & EATING

Fortview House (☎ 35324; fortviewhousegoleen@eircom.net; Gurtyowen, Toormore; s/d €40/80; 🕓 Apr-Oct) Out on its own, in terms of location certainly, but more because of its outstanding quality, this lovely house has its bedrooms stylishly decked out in individual colour schemes, such as lavender and daffodil. The breakfast choice is gourmet standard. Head along the road that turns off the R592 for Durrus about 1km northeast of Goleen.

Heron's Cove (☎ 35225; www.heronscove.com; Goleen; s/d €35/70) A delightful location on the shores of the tidal inlet of Goleen Harbour makes this fine restaurant and B&B a top choice on the Mizen. Rooms have individual charm and several overlook the inlet and the soothing turn of the tide. The **restaurant** (mains €17-25.50; 🕓 7-9.30pm Apr-Oct, bookings only Nov-Mar) has an excellent menu with fresh fish and shellfish featuring strongly, but with lamb, duckling and meat dishes too, and a vegetarian option.

Green Kettle (☎ 35033; Main St; lunch & snacks €5-8, dinner €12-18) This pleasant café serves coffee, cream teas, snacks and toasted sandwiches during the day and more-substantial meals for dinner.

GETTING THERE & AWAY

Two buses go to Goleen from Skibbereen (€6.75, one hour) Monday to Saturday, via Schull, leaving Skibbereen at 4.05pm and 7.45pm; Sunday 11.30am and 1.05pm. In the other direction buses leave Goleen at 7.45am and 5.30pm; Sunday 1.50pm and 5.30pm. Buses go no further down the peninsula than Goleen.

Crookhaven

Keep on beyond Goleen and you'll find Crookhaven, a place that is probably more easily reached by boat. It stands on a spur of land that runs eastwards from the mainland and traps a narrow stretch of sea that's protected from southwesterly winds. In its heyday Crookhaven's natural harbour was an important anchorage. Mail from America was collected here and sailing ships and fishing vessels found ready shelter.

On the opposite shore the gaunt remains of quarry buildings, closed in 1939, remain embedded in the hillside, source of many tall tales by locals in response to curious questions from visitors. In summer there's a big yachting presence here and Crookhaven bustles with life. Off-season you can stop the world and get off.

Galley Cove House (☎ 35137; www.galleycovehouse.com; s/d €50/76) Terrific views out across the ocean and a cheerful welcome enhance the secluded location of this modern home on the way to Crookhaven.

Turning Point (☎ 35520; tess@crookhaven.ie; s/d €40/65; 🕑 Easter-Oct) You have to keep going even beyond Crookhaven for this delightful place that offers modern comfort in a remote location. There's even a guest sauna to complement the bright cheerful rooms and great welcome.

O'Sullivan's Bar (☎ 35319; light snacks €3-8; 🕑 10.30am-8.30pm) Located on the waterfront and a popular place in summer, this friendly bar serves up sandwiches, soup and chowder and very tasty traditional desserts year-round.

Crookhaven Inn (☎ 35309; mains €6.50-11; 🕑 Apr-Oct) Expect a lot of seagoing tales in this pleasant bar; it's next to the sailing club and fills up with yachtspeople in summer.

Brow Head

This is the most southerly point on the Irish mainland and well worth the walk there. As you leave Crookhaven you will notice a turn-off to the left marked 'Brow Head'. If travelling by car, park at the bottom of the hill and stretch your legs. The track is very rough and narrow and there's nowhere to pull over should you meet a tractor coming the other way. After about 1km the road ends. Continue on a walking track to Brow Head where you'll see an observation tower. This is the place from where Guglielmo Marconi transmitted his first message (to Cornwall) and received a reply.

Barleycove

This is western Cork's finest beach and there always seems to be space. It's a great place for youngsters and has long stretches of sand and a safe area where a stream flows down to the sea. Access to the beach is via a boardwalk and pontoon bridge to protect the surrounding wetlands. There is a car park at the edge of the beach on the south side of the causeway on the road to Crookhaven.

Mizen Head

For the full Mizen experience don't miss the **Mizen Head Visitor Centre** (☎ 35115; Mizen Head; adult/concession/under 12/under 5 €4.50/2.50/2.50/free; 🕑 10.30am-5pm mid-Mar–May & Oct, 10am-6pm Jun-Sep, 11am-4pm Sat & Sun Nov–mid-Mar). Apart from the thrill of standing at the most southwesterly point of Ireland, the walk down to the Head, and the fascinating displays in the signal station itself, make for a unique experience. There's a reception area and café alongside the arrival car park and here in Fastnet Hall, amidst striking sculptures, there are a number of displays on the ecology, geology and history of the immediate area. From reception it takes about 10 minutes to walk down to the **signal station** via protected walkways, steps and a spectacular arched bridge that spans a vast gulf in the cliffs; far below seals roll lazily in the dark water when the sea is calm.

Beyond the bridge, and at the far point of the outer rock island, is the Keeper's House and Engine Room of the Mizen Head Fog Signal Station, completed in 1909 and demanned and automated in 1993. It complements Fastnet lighthouse and gives extra protection to Atlantic-bound ships.

You can see how the keepers lived and how the signal station worked both before and after automation, but the real experience even among crowds on a busy day is the sense of so much Atlantic beneath vast, booming skies.

NORTHSIDE OF THE PENINSULA

Although the landscape is less dramatic on this side of the peninsula, it's well worth driving along the coast road as there are great views out to Sheep's Head Peninsula and beyond to the magnificent Beara Peninsula.

Durrus & Around

The coastal road on the northern side of the peninsula takes you past the ruins of another **medieval castle** at Dunmanus.

In Durrus (Dúras) you could drop into **Kilravock Garden** (☎ 027-61111; adult/child €5/3; 🕑 noon-5.30pm May-Sep) for a feast of exotic plants in a delightful setting. There's a Mediterranean section as well as beautiful shrubs and trees. It's advisable to check opening times by phone before a visit.

Dunbeacon Campsite (☎ 027-61246; camping@fishpublishing.com; tent & 2 adults €10; 🕑 Easter–mid-Oct) is about 5.5km southwest of Durrus on the R591 and is in a fine location overlooking Dunmanus Bay amid sheltering trees.

Blairs Cove House (☎ 027-61127; Durrus; blairscove@eircom.net; s/d €130/200) An exquisite courtyard is the focus of this beautiful Georgian house where rooms and self-catering apartments display immense elegance and style in décor and furnishings. The restaurant is in a high-ceilinged hall off the courtyard and offers a set dinner (€48) with a choice from meat and fish dishes that reflect superb international influences. The restaurant opens for dinner only, Tuesday to Saturday during March to October. Booking is advised.

BANTRY

☎ 027 / pop 3147

Bantry (Beanntrai) narrowly missed a big place in history during the late 18th century thanks to storms that prevented a French fleet landing to join the United Irishmen's rebellion. A local Englishman, Richard White, was rewarded with a peerage for trying to alert the British military in Cork. His grand home is open to the public and this, along with an exhibition devoted to the events of 1796, is now the town's main attraction.

Before Irish independence, Bantry Bay was a major anchorage for the British navy and, after WWII, foreign trawlers were regular visitors. The bay's deep waters were also exploited by Gulf Oil, which built an oil terminal on Whiddy Island, bringing unexpected prosperity.

Orientation & Information

The two main roads into Bantry converge on the large Wolfe Tone Square, where the central concourse has been transformed into a fine pedestrianised area complete with seats, fountains and statues of Wolfe Tone and the Brendan Voyagers (see p30).

The **tourist office** (☎ 63084; Wolfe Tone Sq; 🕑 9.30am-5pm Mon-Sat mid-Mar–Oct, Sun Jul & Aug) is in the old courthouse at the eastern end of Wolfe Tone Square. The post office is on Blackrock Rd and there's an Allied Irish Bank with ATM on New St. **Laundrette** (☎ 51403) is next to the tourist office but the entrance is on New St.

Internet access, photocopying and other printing services are available at **Fast.net** (☎ 51624; New St; €1/10min, €5/hr; 🕑 9am-6pm Mon-Fri, 10am-5pm Sat).

Bantry House & Gardens

The magnificent **Bantry House** (☎ 50047; www.bantryhouse.ie; Bantry Bay; admission €9.50, gardens & French Armada Centre only €4, accompanied children free; 🕑 9am-6pm) is superbly situated overlooking the bay and set within acres of gardens. It was bought in 1739 by Richard White who was made Lord Bantry by the English in 1797.

Parts of the house date back to the mid-18th century, but the fine sea-facing northern front was added in 1840. Despite its air of fading gentility, the interior is noted for its French and Flemish tapestries and the eclectic collection of art objects assembled by the second earl of Bantry during his overseas travels between 1820 and 1850.

But the gardens of Bantry House are its greatest glory. A vast lawn sweeps down towards the sea from the front of the house and the formal Italian garden has an enormous

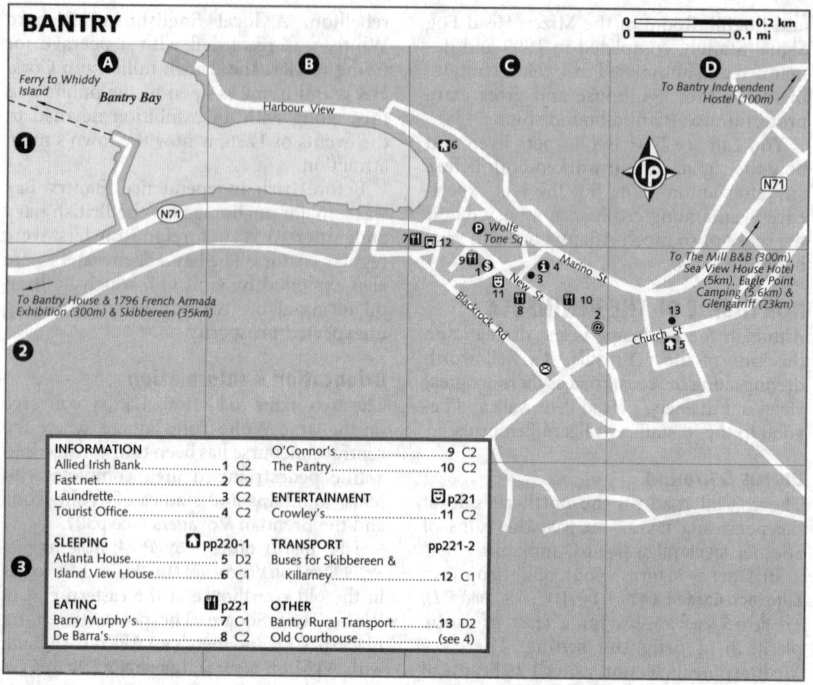

stairway offering spectacular views over the house and Bantry Bay.

The house is about 1km southwest of the centre on the N71.

It's possible to stay in one wing of the house (see p221).

1796 French Armada Exhibition Centre

Considering how Lord Bantry obtained his title it's appropriate that the grounds of Bantry House now harbour an exhibition recording the sorry saga of the attempted landing of the French Armada frigate *La Surveillante*. It was scuttled by the crew in 1796 and today lies 30m down in the bay. It was discovered in 1981 after sonar equipment was used in a salvage attempt of an exploded tanker. The exhibition includes a detailed history of the time, a display about the salvage mission and a few artefacts rescued from the frigate. The centre is located in the house's former stables.

Tours

George Plant Minibus Tours (☎ 50654, 086 239 8123) operates day trips to the Mizen Head Peninsula on Tuesday and Thursday (€10.15), the Beara Peninsula on Monday, Friday and Saturday (€12.70) and to Kenmare and Gougane Barra Forest Park on Wednesday (€15). Trips may depend on numbers wishing to take part.

Festivals & Events

In the second week of May, Bantry holds a **mussel fair** with various musical events and free mussels distributed around the pubs.

The week-long **West Cork Chamber Music Festival** is held at Bantry House at the end of June and beginning of July. The house closes to the public during this time, although the garden, craft shop and tearoom remain.

Sleeping

BUDGET

Eagle Point Camping (☎ 50630; www.eaglepointcamping.com; Glengarriff Rd; Ballylickey; tent & 2 people mid-Jun–Aug €19, other times €18; ⏲ late Apr–Sep) An enviable location at the end of a promontory about 6km north of Bantry makes this a popular site. There are pebbly beaches nearby.

Bantry Independent Hostel (☎ 51050; bantryhostel@eircom.net; Reenrour East; dm/d €11/24; ⌚ Apr-Sep) The décor may be a bit subdued at this good budget place but it's in a quiet location and there's a women-only dorm. Coming from the town centre along Marino St, take the left fork up Old Barrack Rd to the top of the hill.

Island View House (☎ 50257; Harbour View; s/d €25/46) Rooms are not en suite at this harbourfront house. There are no frills, and furnishings are old-fashioned, as is the very kindly welcome.

MID-RANGE

Mill (☎ 50278; Glengarriff Rd; www.themill.net; s/d €40/68) One of the best B&Bs in the west, this modern house on the immediate outskirts of town has great individuality. The delightful rooms are just part of it. There's even a little kitchen for guests and the spacious breakfast/dining room has a wonderful collection of Indonesian puppets and sunflower paintings to accompany terrific breakfasts. You can arrange bike hire here (see below). A laundry service is also available.

Atlanta House (☎ 50237; atlantaguesthouse@eircom.net; Church St; s/d €40/60) You won't get a more conveniently central place than this fine old town house, which has good-sized rooms and a reassuring sense of comfort and calm.

TOP END

Bantry House (☎ 50047; Bantry Bay; s/d €140/240) The place to luxuriate and dream away the hours in the east or west wing. Guests use the library as a sitting room and you can enhance the dream by playing croquet, lawn tennis or billiards.

Sea View House Hotel (☎ 50073; www.seaviewhousehotel.com; Ballylickey; s/d €85/130) There's everything you would expect from a luxury hotel such as Sea View – country house ambience and great comfort in the good-sized rooms and tastefully decorated public rooms. It's on the N71 5km northeast of Bantry. If you reach a sharp bend where the road to Macroom is signposted, you've passed it.

Eating

O'Connor's (☎ 50221; Wolfe Tone Sq; lunch €4.50-8.50, mains €18-23; ⌚ lunch 12.15-5pm, dinner 6-10pm; wheelchair access) Bantry seafood at its best and its most selective, makes O'Connor's an institution. You can pick from over a half dozen differently prepared mussel dishes.

De Barra's (☎ 51924; Wolfe Tone Sq; sandwiches & lunch dishes €3.30-6.85, dinner mains €16-23; ⌚ 8.30am-10pm) A long-established Bantry eatery that offers a range of breakfasts, from a hefty 'working' version (€6.50) to a veggie (€5). Lunch options include a big range of sandwiches as well as salads and grills. Evening meals are meaty but with a couple of good vegetarian options and some shellfish.

Pantry (☎ 52181; New St; snacks & light meals €3-8) One of Bantry's best cafés is located up a flight of stairs near Vickery's Inn. Alongside the usual salads, soups and sandwiches, you can get chicken curry or a veggie special.

Barry Murphy's (☎ 50900; The Quay; sandwiches & light meals €3.50-8) Down-to-earth pub grub is a good bet in this harbourfront bar.

Entertainment

There are a several cheerful bars around but one of the best for music is **Crowley's** (☎ 50029; The Square) where there's traditional music on Wednesday nights, ballads on Fridays and a *ceilidh* (traditional music) band on Sundays. In summer you may also catch set dancing.

Getting There & Away

Bus Éireann (☎ 450 8188) has six buses Monday to Saturday between Bantry and Cork (Parnell Place; €13, 2½ hours), and a service to Killarney (€11.70, 2¼ hours) via Glengarriff and Kenmare. The private **Berehaven bus** (☎ 70007) links Castletownbere with Bantry via Glengarriff. It leaves from the fire station in Wolfe Tone Square at noon and 5.50pm on Monday, and 3.45pm on Tuesday, Friday and Saturday.

Bantry Rural Transport (☎ 52727; 5 Church St) runs a useful series of circular routes to Durris, Goleen, Schull, Skibbereen, and outlying villages. There's a set price of €4/6 one way/return. Services run on set days only. Phone for details.

Getting Around

Bikes can be hired at the **Bicycle Shop** (☎ 52657; Glengarriff Rd) behind the Quik-Pik shop, from €12 per day. Hire can also be arranged at the **Mill** (☎ 50278; Glengarriff Rd; www.themill.net) but you pick up the bikes at the shop, which is just down the road.

SHEEP'S HEAD PENINSULA

The least visited of Cork's three peninsulas, Sheep's Head has a rare charm of its own. There are no substantial antiquities but a loop road runs close to the sea along most of its length; there are wonderful seascapes to appreciate and there's a chance to stretch your legs in solitude.

The second turning on the right after leaving Bantry southwards for Cork is the beginning of **Goat's Path Scenic Route**, a narrow surfaced road which runs along the northern side of the peninsula. The southern part of the road begins further along the main Cork road, just past the Esso garage. This road also follows part of the 88km **Sheep's Head Cycle Route** that traces the peninsula's coastline round to Durrus. The **Sheep's Head Way** is a walking route that also traces a circuit of the peninsula, but on roads, paths and tracks, where it can. A good link road, with terrific views, between the north and south coasts of Sheep's Head runs between Gortnakilly and Kilcrohane and over the western flank of Mt Seefin (see Walking below).

Ahakista (Atha an Chiste) consists of a couple of pubs and a few houses stretched out along the R591. An ancient stone circle is signposted at the southern end of Ahakista where the road bends to the left. Access is via a short pathway.

The peninsula's other village is Kilcrohane, 6km to the southwest beside a fine beach.

WALKING

An exhilarating walk to the summit of **Seefin** (334m) begins at the top of the Goat's Path Road, about 2km equidistant between Gortnakilly and Kilcrohane. There's ample car parking. At the roadside is an out-of-place imitation of Michelangelo's Pietá, erected by an American with local family roots; a case of sentimentality overcoming taste. On the other side of the road is an inscribed slate bench, again in rather unsympathetic style, but restful.

Seefin is not a huge challenge. It's only about 1km to the summit and should take under an hour to get there. But it is still open country, where mist can easily descend, so take a compass. There's a path, but it fades out in places. To get to the summit, follow the track that starts opposite the parking area on the south side of the Pietá. Keep to the occasionally fading path along the rocky spine of the hill and reach a depression. Follow a path up a short, easy gully to the right of a small cliff and then continue, again on the rocky spine of the broad ridge, to a trigonometry point on the summit.

Retracing your steps is not so obvious. From the trig point it's best to keep high along the broad ridge and not to drift too far to the left.

You can also walk part or all of the Sheep Head's Way, but you should use Ordnance Survey maps 85 and 88 and an up-to-date guidebook.

GETTING THERE & AWAY

Bantry Rural Transport (☎ 52727; 5 Main St) buses run a circular route on Tuesday and Thursday, leaving Bantry at 9.15am and 2.05pm and going via the Goat's Path Road to Kilcrohane and Durrus.

BEARA PENINSULA (RING OF BEARA)

The Beara Peninsula (Mor Choaird Bheara) is the most impressive of Cork's western outliers and is on a grander scale than the Mizen and Sheep's Head Peninsulas. It occupies parts of both Cork and Kerry and is a beautiful place of rock-studded mountains and green valleys, peppered with prehistoric stone circles, standing stones and old tombs.

There's exhilarating hillwalking that requires some skill and commitment, as well as proper clothing and navigational experience. But there are more amenable possibilities for simply enjoying the Beara's stunning beauty.

The 196km **Beara Way** is a signposted walk linking Glengarriff with Kenmare (in Kerry) via Castletownbere, Bere Island, Dursey Island and the north side of the peninsula. You can find maps and guidebooks to the Beara Way in most of the main tourist offices in the area. For more details see p655.

ORIENTATION & INFORMATION

A small northern part of the peninsula lies in Kerry but is dealt with here for the convenience of people travelling the Ring of Beara. Castletownbere in Cork or Kenmare in Kerry would make good bases for exploring the peninsula.

In theory you could drive the 137km around the coast in one day, but at the price of missing a great deal. In particular you would miss the spectacular **Healy Pass**, which cuts across the peninsula to join Adrigole in Cork with Lauragh in Kerry.

The following towns are described in a route that assumes you are starting out from Glengarriff and working your way round the peninsula clockwise to Kenmare. There are seasonal tourist offices in Castletownbere and Glengarriff in July and August.

GLENGARRIFF

☎ 027 / pop 871

Glengarriff (An Gleann Garbh) is an attractive village located between the tree-fringed coastal inlets of its natural harbour and the rough rock of the Caha Mountains behind. It's on the main Cork to Killarney road and thus draws the crowds in season, but there is still a satisfying back-country feel to the place. Glengarriff's sheltered position, deep into Bantry Bay, together with the warming influence of the sea, creates a micro climate that encourages lush and often exotic growth. The best place to explore this unique vegetation is Bamboo Park and Garinish Island (see below).

In the second half of the 19th century, Glengarriff became a popular retreat for prosperous Victorians, who sailed from England to Ireland then take the train to Bantry, from where a paddle steamer chugged over to Glengarriff. By 1850 the road to Kenmare had been blasted through the mountains and the link with Killarney was established.

A major attraction is the Italianate garden on nearby Garinish Island. There's pleasant walking in the Blue Pool Amenity Area, which lies on the coastal side of the village. From the shore here you might be lucky enough to see seals loitering on the large rocks in the bay.

Information

The **Fáilte Ireland tourist office** (☎ 63084; 9.30am-5pm Mon & Tue, Thu-Sat Jun–mid-Sep & Sun Jul & Aug) is in the main street. A useful alternative is the privately run **office** (10am-1pm & 2-6pm Mon-Sat Jun-Aug) beside the Blue Pool Ferries terminal in the main street. There's a small Allied Irish Bank on the main street but no ATM. The post office/Spar Shop in the main street has a bureau de change.

Bamboo Park

This fascinating **park** (☎ 63570; adult/child €5/1.25; 9am-7pm) flourishes because of the mild, wet and frost-free climatic conditions of Glengarriff. There are 12 hectares of exotic gardens and woodland including palm trees, bamboo and tree ferns. Lining the waterfront are 13 ivy covered stone pillars, the origin of which remains a mystery, even to locals.

Garinish Island

In the early 20th century the English architect Harold Peto created an Italianate **garden** (☎ 63040; adult/senior or child €3.50/1.25; 10am-4.30pm Mon-Sat, 1-6.30pm Sun Mar & Oct, 10am-5.30pm Mon-Sat, noon-6.30pm Sun Apr-Jun & Sep, 9.30am-6.30pm Mon-Sat, 11am-6.30pm Sun Jul & Aug) on Garinish (Ilnacullin) island. He planted exotic plants never before seen in Ireland, and they continue to flourish, the camellias, magnolias and rhododendrons especially providing a blaze of colour in a landscape usually dominated by greens and browns. There are panoramic views from the top of the 19th-century Martello tower, built to watch out for a possible Napoleonic invasion. The gardens are run by Dúchas and last admission is one hour before closing.

Three ferry companies serve the island about every 20 to 30 minutes, in accordance with opening times, from 9am to 5.30pm Monday to Saturday. **Harbour Queen Ferries** (☎ 63116) leave from a pier on the other side of the road from the Eccles Hotel, while the **Blue Pool Ferries** (☎ 63333) terminal is in the centre of the village, near the Quills Woollen Market. A smaller ferry, the *Lady Ellen*, leaves from Ellen's Rock, 1.6km along the Castletownbeare road. The crossing takes 10 minutes (adult return €7 to €10, child €4, children under six free) and you'll probably see colonies of seals basking on rocks on your way there.

Glengarriff Woods Nature Reserve

These 300-hectare oak and pine **woods** were owned by the White family of Bantry

House in the 18th century. The thick tree cover maintains humid conditions that allow ferns and mosses to flourish. Look out especially for tiny white flowers on red stems rising from rosettes of leaves: these are rare kidney saxifrage.

The woodlands and bogs are also home to the Kerry slug, the 'aristocrat of slugs', found only here and in parts of Kerry and the Iberian Peninsula. It's coffee-coloured with cream spots.

To get to the woods, leave Glengarriff on the N71 Kenmare road. The entrance is about 1km along on the left. A sign, just inside the gate, points across a footbridge to **Lady Bantry's Lookout**. It's a short, steep climb which brings you out on top of the world. There are other waymarked walks through the woods.

Activities

West Cork Sailing Centre (☎ 60132; www.westcorksailing.com; The Boathouse, Adrigole) is a well-equipped centre that offers everything from instructional courses to family sailing holidays, and powerboat training to kayak rental. A half-day sailing course costs €70 for one person or €116 for two in July and August and there's about a 25% reduction in low season.

Ocean Discovery Diving Centre (☎ 60290) in Adrigole charges €76.25 for two dives with full equipment hire.

For **deep-sea fishing** trips contact **Harbour Queen Ferries** (☎ 63116).

Sleeping

Dowlings Camping & Caravan Park (☎ 63154; Castletownbere Rd; tent & 2 people €15; Easter-Oct) About 1km west of Glengarriff on the Castletownbere road, this park is in an attractive woodland setting and has good amenities including a games room and a licensed bar that stages traditional music every night from July to August.

Murphy's Village Hostel (☎ 63555; murphyshostel@eircom.net; Main St; dm/d €12/32;) Right at the heart of Glengarriff, this cheerful and well-run hostel has bright rooms and the owners have a lot of information about the area. The Village Kitchen café is also here (see Eating below). Internet access is €2 for 15 minutes.

Maureen's B&B (☎ 63201; www.maureensglengarriff.com; Main St; s/d €35/60; P) Reasonable rooms here can be cheaper by €5 without breakfast. At the time of writing Maureen's was being extended to expand the craft shop at the front.

River Lodge B&B (☎ 63043; Castletownbere Rd; s/d €40/70; P) Just on the way out of Glengarriff on the road to Castletownbere is this welcoming house where rooms are a fine mix of elegance and comfort and even the loos have pretty stencilled decoration.

Casey's Hotel (☎ 63010; Main St; s/d €55/100; P) Long-established Casey's is proud of such historic past visitors as Eamon de Valera. It's a good place to stay although some rooms are a touch narrow and cramped. There is a restaurant and bar meals are also available.

Eating

Village Kitchen (☎ 63555; Main St) The cheerful café of Murphy's Village Hostel does a hefty breakfast (€7.50) including a vegetarian option, and a good range of sandwiches (€2.50 to €5). Treat yourself to a banana and chocolate muffin (€3.30).

Johnny Barry's (☎ 63315; Main St; bar food €3.20-9.90) You can go for traditional dishes such as Irish stew and bacon and cabbage or try local smoked salmon or a fish platter in this old Glengarriff pub.

Blue Loo (☎ 63167; Main St; snacks €3-8; 9am-6pm) There's a good range of coffee, tea and other hot drinks here, as well as tasty sandwiches and cold plates of ham, chicken or fresh and smoked salmon.

Rainbow Restaurant (☎ 63440; Main St; mains €10-20, kids meals €5) At the time of writing the restaurant was being refurbished but aimed to maintain its menu of local dishes with international options, and favourites such as Bantry Bay mussels with white wine.

Getting There & Away

A bus travels three times a day between Cork, Bantry and Glengarriff (€3, 25 minutes) then to Adrigole and Castletownbere. From May to September certain buses connect to Kenmare and Killarney. Coming from Bantry the bus stops outside the post office; going back to Bantry it stops by the phone boxes across the road. For details of the private Berehaven bus service to Cork see p221.

Getting Around

Jem Creations Art Gallery (☎ 63113), where the road divides for Castletownbere, rents out bicycles for €12/72 per day/week.

GLENGARRIFF TO CASTLETOWNBERE

Heading west from Glengarriff towards Castletownbere the landscape becomes very rugged and impressive. The geology of the area has created a series of sandstone mountains that have been heavily glaciated. The highest hills are those of the Sugarloaf and Hungry Hill. Exposed bands of rock create a series of short walls called benches that snake across the slopes and can make walking on these mountains quite challenging. It's advisable to use a map (Ordnance Survey Discovery series 84 and 85 cover the area) and compass if venturing onto the hills.

Hungry Hill Lodge (☎ 60228; www.hungryhilllodge.com; Adrigole; tent & 2 people €12, dm €13, d €30-40; mid-Mar–Dec; P) This well-situated and simple hostel is just beyond Adrigole village. It's in a great location for walking and cycling and you can hire bikes for €10 per day.

CASTLETOWNBERE & AROUND

☎ 027 / pop 391

Castletownbere (Baile Chais Bhéara) has one of Ireland's largest fishing fleets and the town retains the atmosphere and bustle of a working port. Rural industry has always been the main feature here, the town having developed originally out of the copper mining at Allihies. Tourism is not of first concern in Castletownbere, yet there's a refreshing appeal to the everyday bustle of the harbour areas and the often traffic-crammed main street.

Tourist information (☎ 70344) is available in July and August from a kiosk next to the fire station. Otherwise there are supermarkets, a post office with a limited bureau de change, an Allied Irish Bank branch with an ATM and a string of pubs. **O'Shea's Laundrette** (☎ 70966; Main St; 9am-6pm) charges €8 per load.

Sights

The impressive **Derreenataggart Stone Circle** of 10 stones is close to the roadside, about 2km from Castletownbere, and is reminiscent of the Drombeg Circle near Glandore. It is signposted at a turn off to the right at the western end of town. There are a number of standing stones in the area. On the R571 road running north from Castletown is **Call of the Sea** (☎ 70835; Beara North Rd; adult/child €4/2; 10am-5pm Mon-Fri, 1-5pm Sat & Sun), an interesting series of exhibitions about the area's mining, smuggling, naval history and fishing.

Dzogchen Beara Retreat Centre

This remote **Buddhist meditation and training centre** (☎ 73032; info@rigpa.ie; Garranes, Allihies) is about 8km southwest of Castletownbere in a fine position on top of Black Ball Head. The solitude and inspiring views set the mood. Accommodation is available in self-catering cottages or the hostel. Visitors are welcome to attend sessions and the retreat offers regular seminars and study groups. It's necessary to inquire first by phone or email.

Sleeping

Rodeen B&B (☎ 70158; www.welcome.to/rodeen; s/d €40/70; Mar-Oct) A delightful haven tucked away above the eastern approaches to the town, this lovely house with sea views is surrounded by gardens that are full of surprises, including Delphic columns. Rooms are comfy, bright and airy and there's stylish artwork everywhere. Evening meals are an option.

Harbour Lodge Budget Accommodation (☎ 71043; bearalodge@eircom.net; per person sharing from €13; P; wheelchair access) Adjacent to the church and just off Main St this large building, once a convent, has rooms rather than dorms, but has the style of a hostel. Rooms are reasonable.

Cametringane Hotel (☎ 70379; www.camehotel.com; The Harbour; s/d €55/90) This hotel is on the other side of the harbour from Main St and looks out over the town. At the time of writing it was undergoing refurbishment. Rooms are fresh and of good size and all have open views.

Eating

Cronin's Hideaway (☎ 70386; Main St; mains €5.50-13; takeaways 12.30pm-late, restaurant 5.30-9pm) There are straightforward filling meals at this cheerful place. Takeaways cost €1.50 to €4.

Murphy's Restaurant (☎ 70244; Main St; meals €6.50-14; 9am-9pm) Filling meals such as the mixed grill or seafood platter are the order in this busy place.

Getting There & Away

Bus Éireann (☎ 450 8188) buses run from Cork (€16, 2½ hours) twice daily via Bantry (€13,

2½ hours), Glengarriff (€6.50, 40 minutes) and Adrigole. **Private buses** (☎ 74003, 70007) also run between Cork and Castletown.

DURSEY ISLAND

☎ 027 / pop 60

At the end of the peninsula is Dursey Island, just 6.5km long by 1.5km wide and 250m offshore. Ireland's only **cable car** (adult/child €4/1 return; 9-11am, 2.30-5pm & 7-8pm Mon-Sat, 9-10am, noon-1pm, 4-4.30pm & 7-7.30pm Sun), swaying precariously 30m above Dursey Sound, is the only link with the mainland for the inhabitants and their cattle. The island is a wild bird and whale sanctuary, and dolphins can sometimes be seen swimming in the waters around it.

Note that livestock takes precedence over humans in the queue for the cable car. There's no accommodation on the island, but it's easy to find somewhere to camp. The **Beara Way** loops round the island for 11km, and the signal tower is an obvious destination for a shorter walk. Bikes are not allowed on the cable car.

ALLIHIES & THE COPPER MINES

Copper ore deposits were first identified on the far Beara in 1810. While mining quickly brought wealth to the Puxley family, who owned the land, it brought low wages and dangerous, unhealthy working conditions for the workforce, which at one time numbered 1300 men, women and children. Experienced Cornish miners were brought into the area, and the dramatic ruins of engine houses replicate those of Cornwall's coastal tin mines. As late as the 1930s, over 30,000 tonnes of pure copper were being exported annually, but by 1962 the last mine was closed.

In Allihies (Na hAilichí), a small tourist information kiosk, beside the church, opens in the peak season. Allihies is served by the privately run **O'Donoghue bus company** (☎ 027-70007).

NORTHSIDE OF THE BEARA

Heading north and east from Allihies, a 23km coastal road with hedges of fuchsia and rhododendron twists and turns all the way to **Eyeries**, a cluster of brightly coloured houses overlooking Coulagh Bay. The town is also home to Milleens cheese, a popular brand throughout Ireland.

The coast road eventually rejoins the main road at the small village of **Ardgroom** (Ard Dhór).

As you head east towards Lauragh look for signs pointing right to the Ardgroom **stone circle**, a beautifully located Bronze Age monument. At the end of a narrow approach lane there is rough parking. The circle is visible about 200m away and a path leads to it across bogland. There is no intrusion on crops or managed ground, but at the time of writing a notice on a nearby post proclaimed 'This walk has been closed due to the withdrawal of government funding for public access', which clearly places a price on 4000 years of history.

Although **Lauragh** (Laith Reach), northeast of Ardgroom, is actually in Kerry, it's included here for the convenience of people travelling the Ring of Beara. Lauragh is home to the century-old **Derreen Gardens** (☎ 064-83103; adult/child €4/2; 10am-6pm Apr-Sep), planted by the fifth Lord Lansdowne around the turn of the 20th century. An abundance of interesting plants thrive here, including spectacular New Zealand tree ferns and red cedars, normally found in rainforests.

From Lauragh, a serpentine road travels 11km south across **Healy Pass**, and down to Adrigole offering spectacular views of the rocky inland scenery. About 1km west of Lauragh along the R572, is a road to **Glanmore Lake**. The scenery along here is stunning. In the middle of the lake on a tiny island are the remains of an old hermitage. There are walking opportunities in the Glanmore Lake area, but access may be problematic. It's best to ask locally for advice on walking.

Sleeping

Glanmore Lake Hostel (☎ 064-83181; Glanmore Lake; dm €12; Easter-Sep) A timeless atmosphere and an engaging location at the wooded heart of Glanmore makes this remote An Óige hostel an appealing place. You can order continental breakfast (€5) or full Irish (€6.50). It's in Glanmore's old National Schoolhouse, 5.6km from Lauragh. Take the road for Glanmore Lake and just keep going.

Josie's Lakeview House & Restaurant (☎ 064-83155; Glanmore Lake; s/d €45/70) Another great location, but this time overlooking lake and mountain, this modern bungalow has smallish but cosy rooms. It has a restaurant (prices on request). It's 4.5km from Lauragh along the road to Glanmore Lake.

Getting There & Away

The bus service is very limited. Each Wednesday a **bus** (☎ 1890 528528) leaves Kenmare at 1.30pm and passes the hostel (€3, 45 minutes). Running between Killarney and Castletownbere, it operates only in July and August, and stops in Lauragh once daily, Monday to Saturday.

NORTHERN CORK

Northern Cork lacks the glamour and romance of the county's south and west coast regions, but there is a pleasant sense of escape from the mainstream and the area's towns and villages have a refreshing rural integrity. The area is popular for fishing and golf.

MALLOW & AROUND

pop 7109

Mallow (Mala) is a prosperous, picturesque town located in the Blackwater Valley that caters for fishing, golfing and horse racing. Nineteenth-century visitors to its spa christened it the 'Bath of Ireland', although these days the comparison would seem pretty far-fetched. Today it's a sugar manufacturing and agricultural centre. It makes for a useful stop on the way west from Dublin.

At Buttevant, 20km north of Mallow on the N20, are the ruins of a 13th-century **Franciscan abbey**. From Mallow to Killarney the landscape is fairly nondescript, although you might want to divert to see the well-preserved remains of 17th-century **Kanturk Castle.**

A haven of peace, **Ard Na Laoi** (☎/fax 022-22317; Bathview, Mallow; s/d €39/52; P) is a lovely house in garden surroundings and has big comfortable rooms. The hallway and reception rooms have remarkable tin ceilings, embossed and painted, an American custom introduced by the house's original owner.

Buses run hourly every day between Mallow and Cork (€7.20, 35 minutes) and trains run every two hours (€12, 25 minutes). For Kanturk you need your own transport.

County Kerry

CONTENTS

Kerry and its awesome mountains, corrugated coastline and misty islands fulfil the romantic dream of Ireland. It contains some of the country's wildest terrain and is the location of its highest mountain, the 1039m Carrantuohil, at the heart of the magnificent Macgillycuddy's Reeks on the Iveragh Peninsula. One result of all this beauty is an almost year-round influx of visitors to the county's main town of Killarney and a cavalcade of summertime tour buses around the Iveragh Peninsula's coastal road, the Ring of Kerry. But the rest of the county is big enough if you want to escape the crowds, and there are plenty of opportunities for walking, cycling and scenic driving.

Smaller than the Iveragh Peninsula, but no less stunning, is Dingle Peninsula, with its outflung Blasket Islands and its shapely peaks such as Mt Brandon, at 951m Ireland's second-highest mountain. The northern part of Kerry becomes flatter and far less dramatic as it stretches towards the River Shannon, the boundary between Kerry and County Clare.

Kerry's main town, Killarney, with its picturesque lakes, is the busy hub of all this high-profile tourism, and is never quiet because of it. The town has inescapable charm and the flow of international visitors through its busy streets adds to an already strong local identity. Smaller towns such as Kenmare, Tralee and Dingle have a terrific individual appeal and the county's outlying villages (always, it seems, among hills or by the sea) reward time spent lingering.

HIGHLIGHTS

- Walk or cycle in beautiful **Killarney National Park** (p235)
- Get off the main Ring of Kerry road and follow your nose – and a good map – by bike or car through the **Ballaghbeama Gap** (p239) or the **Ballaghisheon Pass** (p239)
- Take a boat trip to Skellig Michael and its astonishing 6th-century **monastery** (p243)
- Stop the world and get off in the timeless Mt Brandon area of **Cloghane** (p260)
- Linger in the superb **Blasket Centre museum** (p265) on the Dingle Peninsula, then visit the **Blaskets** (p266) themselves

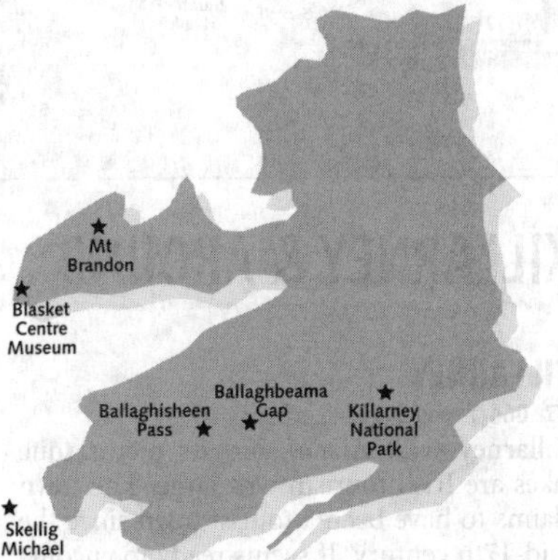

- POPULATION: 132,424
- AREA: 4746 SQ KM

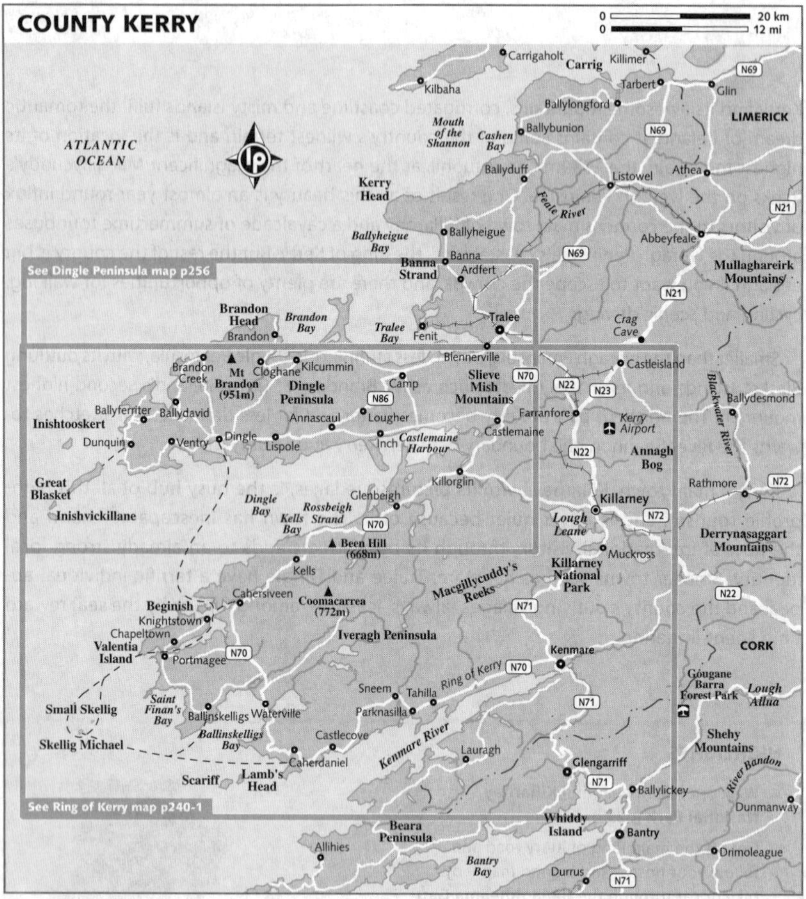

KILLARNEY & AROUND

KILLARNEY

☎ 064 / pop 9470

Killarney (Cill Airne) and its picturesque lakes are Irish tourism writ large. The town claims to have been a tourist town since the mid-17th century. It seems ready to encourage even more visitors by staging a 250-year anniversary of tourism in 2004–05. Killarney's very name is synonymous with souvenirs, jaunting cars, leprechauns and coach tours and there's more registered accommodation here than anywhere else outside Dublin. You'll find plenty of souvenir shops, but Killarney also boasts some excellent craft galleries and there's a range of attractive pubs and restaurants. The town has few individual attractions, but its setting and proximity to magnificent scenery is its great gift.

History

Killarney and its valley has been inhabited probably since the Neolithic period and was certainly an important Bronze Age settlement based on the copper ore that was mined at Ross Island. At that time Cashel in County Kilkenny was the power base of Ireland and Killarney was a subkingdom. It became a stronghold of the O'Donoghue clan. In the 7th century a monastery was founded by St Finian on Inisfallen Island

and Killarney became a focus for Christianity in the region.

It wasn't until the 18th century that the town was developed as a centre for tourism by Lord Kenmare. A century later it was being visited by royals and dignitaries from around Europe. Even Queen Victoria made her way here, though as an enthusiast for the Scottish Highlands, most of which she owned, it's not known what her opinion of Killarney was.

Orientation

The centre of Killarney is the T-junction where New St meets High and Main Sts. As it heads south, High St becomes Main St then swings around to the left into East Ave Rd where all the large hotels are. The national park is to the south, while the bus and train stations are to the east of the centre.

Information

BOOKSHOPS

Killarney Bookshop (☎ 34108; 32 Main St)

CULTURAL CENTRES

Irish Roots Services (☎ 33506; Tralee Rd; info@irishrootsservices.com) Can help you trace your Irish ancestors and relatives.

EMERGENCY

Killarney District Hospital (☎ 31076; St Margaret's Rd) Just northwest of the centre.

INTERNET ACCESS

Café Internet (☎ 30207; New St; €1/15 min)

Killarney Library (☎ 32655; Rock Rd) Free Internet access.

WEB-Talk (☎ 37033; 53 High St; €1/15min; 10am-9pm Mon-Sat, 2-8pm Sun) Also offers cheap phone calls abroad.

LAUNDRY

Park Laundry (☎ 35282; Park Rd; €10 per load; 9am-6.30pm Mon-Sat)

LEFT LUGGAGE

There's a **left-luggage office** (☎ 37509; 7.30am-6.30pm; €1.60 per bag per 12 hr) at the bus station. Ask at the coffee shop in the station.

LIBRARY

Killarney Library (☎ 32655; Rock Rd; 10am-5pm Wed, Fri & Sat, 10am-8pm Tue & Thu)

MONEY

Many banks have either a bureau de change or an ATM or sometimes both; there's a branch of **American Express** (☎ 35722) on East Avenue Rd.

POST

Killarney Post Office (☎ 31461; New St; 9am-5.30pm Mon-Sat, 9.30am-5.30pm Tue)

TOILETS

There are public toilets at the main car park, Beech Rd.

TOURIST INFORMATION

Killarney has a busy but efficient **tourist office** (☎ 31633; www.corkkerry.ie; Beech Rd; 9am-6pm Mon-Sat, 10am-6pm Sun Jun-Sep, 9.15am-5.30pm Mon-Sat rest of year). *Where Killarney* (€5) is a good monthly 'what's on' guide. You may find it in your B&B or hostel, in bookshops or at the tourist office.

St Mary's Cathedral

Built between 1842 and 1855, this cruciform **cathedral** (☎ 31014; Port Rd), at the western end of New St in Cathedral Place, was designed by the architect Augustus Pugin and is a superb example of neo-Gothic revival architecture.

In the 1840s the cathedral was used as a hospital, and during the Famine it acted as a refuge for the destitute – the huge tree on the front lawn marks the mass grave of those who died.

Museum of Irish Transport

This **museum** (☎ 32638; Scott's Gardens, East Ave Rd; adult/child €4/2; 10am-6pm Jun-Aug, 11am-5pm Sep-Oct) is a diverting place with a collection of shiny old cars, bicycles and assorted odds and ends that includes an 1844 Meteor Starley Tricycle found in a shop's unsold stock in 1961. Another exhibit is a 1910 Wolseley that was used by Countess Markievicz and WB Yeats.

Other Sights

At the northern end of High St is a **memorial** to Famine victims erected by the Republican Graves Association in 1972. With a determination that reflects the implacable hope of a united Ireland the inscription reads: 'This memorial will not be unveiled until Ireland is free.'

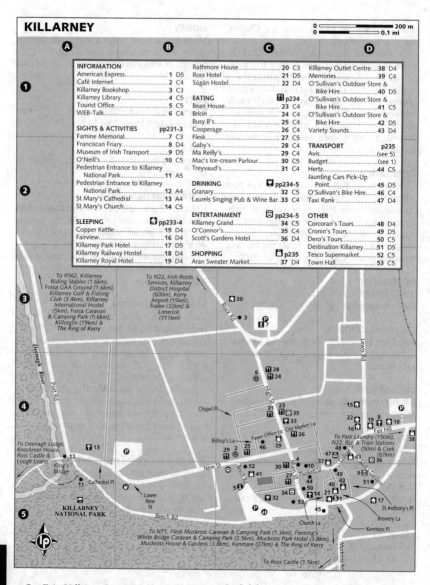

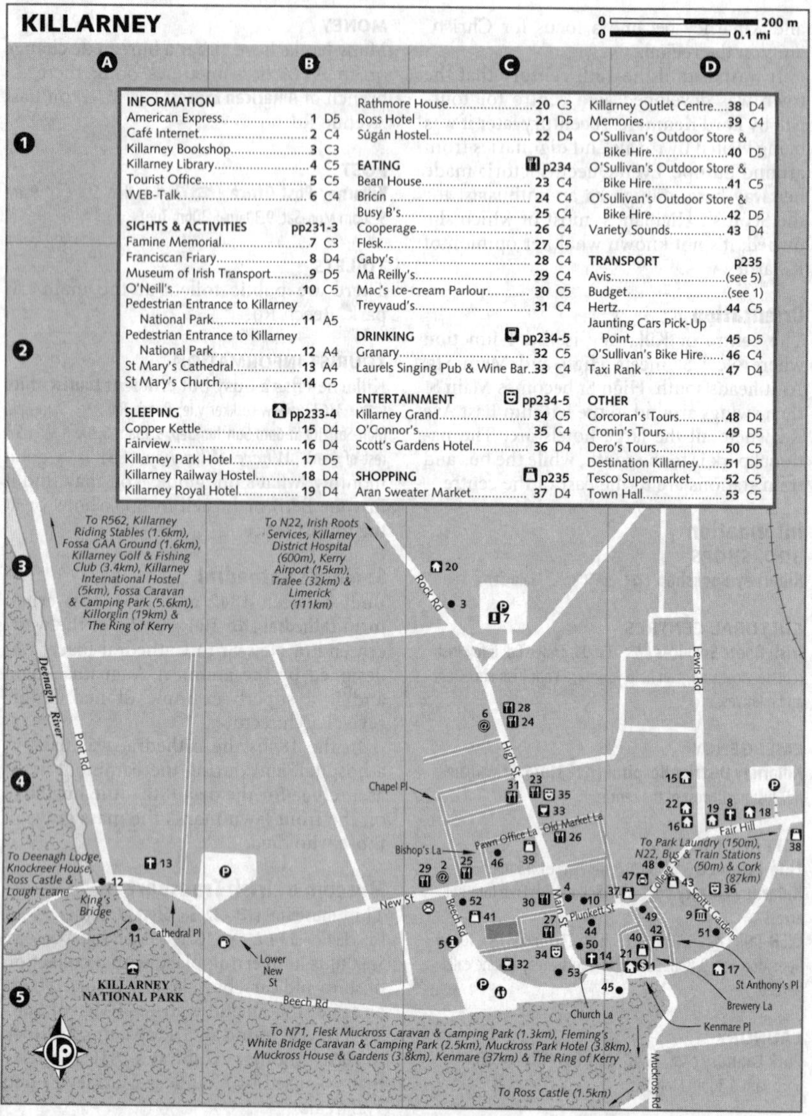

On Fair Hill is a **Franciscan friary**, built in the 1860s, displaying an ornate Flemish-style altarpiece and some impressive tile work. It has stained-glass work by Harry Clarke.

If you would like to watch some **Gaelic football** and you're in town during the football season, head for the Fossa GAA ground on the N72, 2km west of the centre.

Activities

You can **fish** for trout and salmon in the Rivers Flesk and Laune and in the lakes in Killarney National Park. The small lakes around the southern side of Killarney towards Kenmare also have trout, although there's no coarse fishing locally. Permits, licences, equipment and information can be purchased from **O'Neill's** (☎ 31970; 6 Plunkett St).

Killarney Riding Stables (☎ 31686; Ballydowney, Killarney; 1-/2-/3-hr rides €25/40/50) is 2km west of the centre on the R562. Four- and six-day rides for more experienced riders are also available.

Killarney Golf & Fishing Club (☎ 31034; www.killarney-golf.com) is 4km west of town on the N72. The course hugs Lough Leane and has great views of the mountains. Green fees are €70 per person; club hire is €21.

Sleeping

BUDGET

Some hostels arrange pick-ups from the bus and train stations. It's advisable to book ahead in the summer.

Killarney International Hostel (☎ 31240; anoige@killarney.iol.ie; Aghadoe House; dm €12-15, d €33-44; P) Occupying a splendid 18th-century manor house overlooking lakes and forests, this An Óige hostel is 5km west of the centre and off the N72 to Killorglin. A complimentary bus service runs to/from the bus and train stations from June to September and staff can arrange packed lunches, tours to the national park and bike hire (€10 per day).

Súgán Hostel (☎ 33104; Lewis Rd; dm/d €12/28) A hostel with a big heart and a trail's end atmosphere, the very down-to-earth Súgán is ably run by Pa Sugrue, who'll keep you right on how to have a good time in Killarney. You can even catch Pa performing on stage at O'Connor's in High St (see p234).

Killarney Railway Hostel (☎ 35299; railwayhostel@eircom.net; Fair Hill; dm/d €13.50/36) A handy position close to the train and bus stations and the centre of town makes this a useful stopover. It's also extremely well equipped and well run and has cheerful clean rooms and good kitchen facilities. Guests can take advantage of discounted tours of the Ring of Kerry (€15), Dingle Peninsula (€19) and Gap of Dunloe (€18), as well as lake cruises (€9 per hour) and bike hire (€10 per day).

Camping options include the following:

Flesk Muckross Caravan & Camping Park (☎ 31704; killarneylakes@eircom.net; Muckross Rd; small tent & 2 adults €16; mid-Apr–Oct) About 1.3km out of town on the N71 to Kenmare, the park is surrounded by woods and has great views of the mountains. There's a wide range of facilities, from a supermarket to bike rental.

Fossa Caravan & Camping Park (☎ 31497; www.camping_holidaysireland.com; Fossa; tent & 2 people €15; Apr-Oct) About 5.6km west of Killarney on the N72 Killorglin road, this site is a bit out of town. But it's in a fairly relaxing spot among trees and has views of the Macgillycuddy's Reeks.

Fleming's White Bridge Caravan & Camping Park (☎ 31590; www.killarneycamping.com; White Bridge, Ballycasheen Rd; tent & 2 people €17; mid-Mar–Oct) This small site on the banks of the River Flesk is about 2.5km from town. It's in a delightful location and is enhanced even more by flower beds and sheltering woods. To get there head south out of town along Muckross Rd and turn left at Woodlawn.

MID-RANGE

There are dozens, if not hundreds, of B&Bs and guesthouses in Killarney. It can be difficult, however, to find a room from June to August when it's often best to let the tourist office find one for you for a €1.50 fee. New Rd, Rock Rd and Muckross Rd are good places to start looking.

Rathmore House (☎ 32829; rathmorehouseklly@iol.ie; Rock Rd; s/d €38/68; P) There's a real Irish welcome at this long-established family-run place right at the entrance to town. Rooms are comfy and breakfasts are cheerful affairs.

Fairview (☎ 34164; www.fairviewkillarney.com; Lewis Rd; s/d €80/110; P; wheelchair access) More a small hotel than a guesthouse, the Fairview never ceases to keep ahead of things and lavish refurbishment has ensured high standards in the smart but comfy rooms. Breakfasts are delicious. There are substantial discounts in the low season.

Copper Kettle (☎ 34164; www.fairviewkillarney.com; Lewis Rd; s/d €70/90; P) Under the same management as the Fairview, this smaller place is just up the road and is all bright wood surrounds and pleasant rooms. You need to head a few metres down the road to the Fairview for a big breakfast. Good discounts are available in the low season and at quiet periods.

TOP END

Ross Hotel (☎ 31855; ross@kph.iol.ie; Kenmare Pl; s/d €100/130; P) There's a stylish old-fashioned feel to this long-established hotel where the modern and the classical sit easily together in comfortable rooms. Low-season discounts of about 20% are available.

Killarney Park Hotel (☎ 35555; www.killarneyparkhotel.ie; Kenmare Pl; s/d €220/360; P) Nicely detached from the tumult of busy Killarney, this hotel has beautiful surroundings and individually designed rooms. You can lounge stylishly in the elegant library or disport in the pool and spa.

Killarney Royal Hotel (☎ 31853; www.killarneyroyal.ie; College St; s/d €140/190; P) Spacious rooms with individuality in décor and furnishings make the Royal a spoil-yourself option at the heart of Killarney.

Eating

BUDGET

Bean House (☎ 37877; 8 High St; sandwiches & baguettes €2.60-4.70; 8.30am-6.30pm Mon-Sat, 10am-5pm Sun) This busy café maintains its great reputation for a big choice of coffees; there's at least a dozen. Tea buffs can choose from half a dozen choice blends. Breakfasts (€4) are available until noon.

Ma Reilly's (☎ 39220; 20 New St; meals €3.75-10.50; 9am-6pm daily, 9am-10pm Thu-Sun Jun-Sep) No-frills food at Ma's ensures a hefty breakfast (€5.90), filling sandwiches and traditional Irish mains. There's a tasty vegetarian stir-fry (€8.75) and kid's meals (under €5).

Busy B's (☎ 31972; 15 New St; snacks & meals €2.55-10; 11am-10.40pm) There's everything from sandwiches to spaghetti bolognese, veggie burgers to baked spuds at this useful eatery. There's even a low-calorie menu on which you can tally up points.

Mac's Ice-Cream Parlour (☎ 35213; 6 Main St) The ice cream sold here – around 30 flavours – is made on the premises and is delicious.

TOP END

Cooperage (☎ 37716; Old Market Lane; lunch €3.95-9.50, dinner mains €13.70-22; 12.30-3pm & 6-10pm Easter-Oct, closed Mon rest of year) Studio chic at this modern restaurant is echoed by restrained background jazz. The food matches the mood with while-away lunch dishes such as julienne of venison, *fusilli* Florentine or subtle sandwiches. Dinner mains are mainly meat and game but there's always a choice of fresh fish of the day.

Gaby's Seafood Restaurant (☎ 32519; 27 High St; mains €23-30; 6-10pm Mon-Sat) There's top seafood and top table service at this smart restaurant. Cosy up to the open fire in the reception bar before settling down to superbly prepared pan-seared turbot or grilled lobster. There's a set menu (€29). Dress smartly.

Treyvaud's (☎ 33062; 62 High St; mains €15-23.50; noon-10.30pm Tue-Sun) Just opened at the time of writing, Treyvaud's was already setting the pace for creative lunch choice and traditional Irish meat dishes with modern European flair. There are some fish dishes also and vegetarian cannelloni and pasta, all enjoyed in modish, uncluttered space.

Flesk (☎ 31128; 14 Main St; mains €14-22; 5.30-10.30pm) A popular place in busy Main St, the Flesk has an early-bird deal (5.30pm to 7pm) with €3 off all mains.

Brícín (☎ 34902; 26 High St; lunch around €7-10, dinner mains €15-22; 5.30-9.30pm Mon-Sat Apr-Nov) Countryside Kerry comes to town at this upstairs restaurant above a craft shop. There's an informal setting of individual eating areas and the food is a great mix of traditional Kerry cooking with international influences. At the time of writing Brícín was poised to open for lunch as well.

Entertainment

Many Killarney pubs have live music. At some it's traditional and often impromptu while at others it's a bit stagey.

O'Connor's (☎ 30200; 7 High St) A great venue for a mix of all things Irish. There's trad music, stand-up comedy (Pa Sugrue of Súgán Hostel does his thing here), readings and pub theatre. Entertainment starts at around 9.15pm each night.

Laurels Singing Pub & Wine Bar (☎ 31149; Main St) It's knees up Molly Brown style at this popular place that unashamedly caters for enthusiastic coach parties attempting traditional Irish dance. It's all good fun and you'll find something on here every night of the week. Doors open at 8.30pm and entertainment begins at 9.15pm.

Killarney Grand (☎ 31159; Main St; 8.30pm-late) This large bar is very popular. It has traditional music nightly from 9pm to 11pm, but the music can get a bit lost in the general hubbub. At 11pm, live bands take over and really grab the attention with a mix of everything contemporary. You're charged €6 admission after 11pm.

Scott's Gardens Hotel (☎ 31060; Scott's Gardens) Scott's has traditional music from Thursday to Sunday night and every night during July and August. Things get going at around 9pm.

Granary (☎ 20075; Beech Rd) There's something on every night at the Granary, a fairly bouncing place, where you can join in pub quizzes and karaoke or bop to bands and DJs. On Friday nights there's a late bar until 2.30am.

Shopping

Killarney has a good number of excellent shops that balance the shamrock-shifting, booze-badge, T-shirt tat emporiums.

Variety Sounds (☎ 35755; 7 College St) This music shop has a fairly eclectic selection but has a good range of traditional music, instruments, sheet music and learn-to-play books.

Aran Sweater Market (☎ 39756; Plunkett St) Aran sweaters galore wrap round you at this well-stocked place.

Killarney Outlet Centre (☎ 36744; Fair Hill) Big discounts on a range of clothing, including Nike sportswear, are available here.

Memories (☎ 34447; 74 High St) Head here for a selection of good quality Irish linen and lace.

O'Sullivan's Outdoor Store (☎ 31282) A general spread of activity gear. There are three branches in town (see Bicycle opposite).

Getting There & Away

AIR

Kerry Airport (☎ 066-64644) is at Farranfore, about 15km north of Killarney off the N22. There are direct Aer Lingus flights to Dublin, and Manx Airlines flights to Luton and Manchester. It's also possible to fly direct from Germany and from London Stansted to Kerry airport; call **Ryanair** (☎ 0818 303030) for details.

BUS

Bus Éireann (☎ 34777, 30011) operates from next to the train station, with regular links to Tralee (€5.80, 35 minutes, hourly), Cork (€11.90, two hours, 12 daily), Dublin (€19, six hours, four daily), Galway (€17, seven hours, four daily), Limerick (€12.40, 2¼ hours, four daily), Waterford (€18.50, 4½ hours, hourly) and Rosslare Harbour (€20.20, six to seven hours, two daily).

From late May to mid-September, the Ring of Kerry has its own service, departing Killarney at 8.30am and 1.30pm Monday to Saturday for Killorglin, Caherciveen, Waterville, Caherdaniel, Sneem and back to Killarney. There are also departures at 9.40am (July and August only) and 12.45pm on Sunday.

TRAIN

Killarney's **train station** (☎ 31067) is next to the bus station on Park Rd, just east of the centre. Five trains a day go to Cork (€22.90, 2¼ hours) and Tralee (€7, 45 minutes). Take the train to Mallow to change for Dublin, Waterford and Limerick.

Getting Around

TO/FROM THE AIRPORT

There's no bus service from the airport to town. A taxi will cost about €15.

CAR

The centre of Killarney can be thick with traffic at times. Disc parking costs €1 per hour. For car hire there's **Avis** ☎ 36655) at the tourist office on Beech Rd; **Budget** (☎ 34341) is in Kenmare St next to the Amex office and **Hertz** (☎ 34126) is on Plunkett St.

BICYCLE

Bicycles are ideal for exploring the scattered sights of the Killarney area, many of which are accessible only by bike or on foot. Several places hire bikes at €12/70 per day/week including pannier bags, tool kit and maps. There's **O'Sullivan's Bike Hire** (☎ 31282), with one shop on Bishop's Lane, another opposite the tourist office and a third on Brewery Lane.

JAUNTING CAR

If you're not on two wheels, Killarney's traditional transport is the horse-drawn **jaunting car** (☎ 33358), which comes with a driver known as a jarvey. The pick-up point is on Kenmare Place just past the town hall but they also congregate in the N71 car park opposite Muckross House and at the Gap of Dunloe. Trips cost €20 to €56, depending on distance; traps officially carry four people.

KILLARNEY NATIONAL PARK

Killarney's 10,236-hectare **national park** extends to the southwest of town, with two pedestrian entrances immediately opposite St Mary's Cathedral and others (for drivers) off the N71.

Enclosed within the park are beautiful Lough Leane (the Lower Lake or 'Lake of

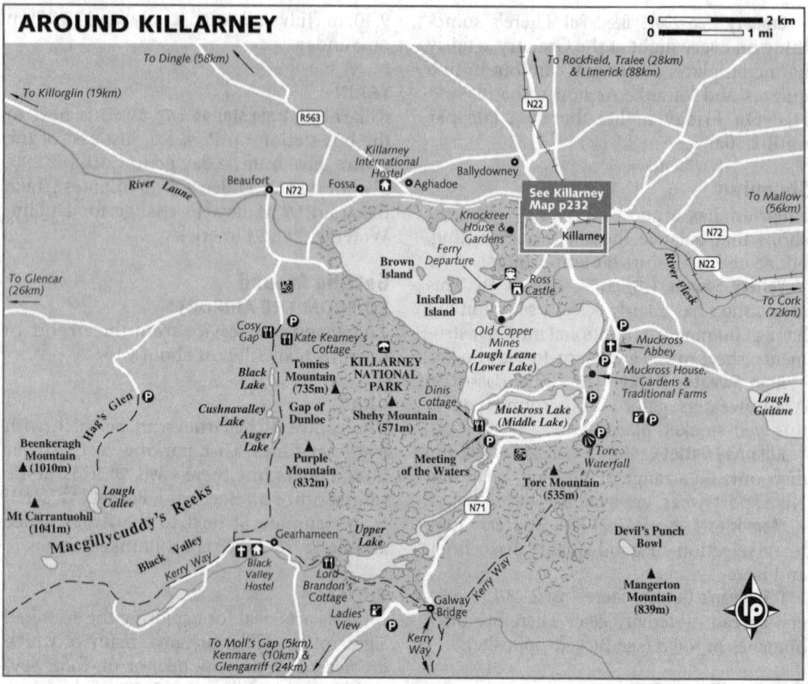

Learning'), Muckross Lake and the Upper Lake, as well as the Mangerton, Torc, Shehy and Purple Mountains. Areas of oak and yew woodland stretch for miles. This is wonderful walking and biking country, although there are also specific sights to see. A herd of red deer lives in the park and many species of bird can be spotted. In 1982 the park was designated a Unesco Biosphere Reserve.

An adventurous 55km cycle tour of the park (best undertaken on a dry day) is marked on the Around Killarney map.

Knockreer House & Gardens

Near the St Mary's Cathedral entrance to the park stands **Knockreer House**, surrounded by lovely **gardens**. The original 19th-century building burned down and the present incarnation dates from the 1950s. The house isn't open to the public, but you can walk around the gardens and there are great views across the valley and lakes to the mountains. To get to the house from the St Mary's Cathedral entrance, follow the path immediately to your right uphill for about 500m.

Ross Castle

Restored by Dúchas, **Ross Castle** (☎ 35851; Ross Rd; adult/child €5/2.50; 🕑 9am-6.30pm Jun-Aug, 9.30am-5.30pm Sep–mid-Oct & Mar-May, 9.30am-4.30pm mid-Oct–mid-Nov) dates back to the 14th century, when it was a residence of the O'Donoghues. It was the last place in Munster to succumb to Cromwell's forces commanded by Ludlow.

According to prophecy, the castle would be captured only from the water, so in 1652 Ludlow had floating batteries brought upriver from Castlemaine, then transported overland before being launched onto the lake. Seeing the prophecy about to be fulfilled, the defenders, having resisted the English siege from the land for months, surrendered promptly.

It's a 2.4km walk from the St Mary's Cathedral pedestrian park entrance to Ross Castle. If you're driving from Killarney, turn right opposite the Esso garage at the start of Muckross Rd, just past the roundabout. The castle is at the end of the road near the car park. There's a path leading through the woods from the castle to Muckross House.

Inisfallen Island

The first monastery on the island is said to have been founded by St Finian the Leper in the 7th century. The island's fame dates from the early 13th century when the Annals of Inisfallen were written here. The annals, now in the Bodleian Library, Oxford, England, remain a vital source of information on early Munster history. On the island, there are ruins of a 12th-century **oratory** with a carved Romanesque doorway, and of a later **monastery** built on the site.

You can hire boats from Ross Castle to row to the island. Alternatively, boatmen charge passengers around €8 each for the crossing. Some Gap of Dunloe boat and bus tours also stop at the island (see p238).

Muckross Estate

The core of Killarney National Park is the Muckross Estate, which was donated to the state by Arthur Bourn Vincent in 1932. **Muckross House** (☎ 31440; www.muckross-house.ie; adult/child €5.50/2.25; 9am-6pm year round) opens to the public and, unusually, you can walk around the rooms, with their faded 19th-century fittings, free of guided tours or overly intrusive custodians. You can inspect a variety of crafts, including bookbinding and stone cutting, in the basement.

The beautiful gardens slope down to the lake and include an arboretum. A block behind the house contains a restaurant and craft shop. Jaunting cars wait outside to run you around the park.

Immediately east of Muckross House are the **Muckross Traditional Farms** (☎ 35571; adult/child €5.50/2.25, combined ticket with Muckross House €8.25/3.75; 10am-7pm Jun-Sep, 1-6pm May, 1-6pm Sat, Sun & public hols 21 Mar–Apr & Oct). These are reproductions from Kerry farmhouses of the 1930s complete with chickens, pigs, cattle and horses. You can walk around the circuit or save your legs and use the 'vintage coach' that shuttles between the buildings.

Muckross House is 5km from town on the N71 Kenmare road. Vehicle access is about 1km beyond the Muckross Park Hotel. During the summer a tourist bus leaves for the house at 1.45pm from outside O'Connor's pub in Killarney, returning at 5.15pm (return €8). The house is also included in some day tours of Killarney.

If you're walking or cycling to Muckross there's a cycle track alongside the Kenmare road for most of the first 2km. A path then turns right into Killarney National Park. Following this path, after 1km you'll come to **Muckross Abbey**, which was founded in 1448 and burned by Cromwell's troops in 1652. WM Thackeray called it 'the prettiest little bijou of a ruined abbey ever seen'. Muckross House is another 1.5km from the abbey ruins.

From Muckross House, there's a 3.7km walking/cycle track round the northern shore of Muckross Lake to the **Meeting of the Waters**, the point where the three lakes meet; Lough Leane or Lower Lake, Muckross or Middle Lake, and Upper Lake. Nearby **Dinis Cottage** (☎ 31954) serves teas in a 200-year-old hunting lodge. The graffiti etched in the window underpins Killarney's claim to tourism longevity: the oldest dates back to 1816. From the Meeting of the Waters it's another 1.5km back onto the N71 Kenmare road.

A REEK BY ANY OTHER NAME

Macgillycuddy's Reeks is the name of the magnificent group of mountains to the west of Killarney, contained between the Gap of Dunloe in the east and the Caragh River in the west. The name Macgillycuddy derives from the Mac Gilla Muchudas, an ancient clan of the area. The word *reek* means pointed hill. As far as pronunciation goes, Macgillycuddy is a name to take a run at. The accent is on the first syllable; the pronunciation should be 'Mak'lcuddy', roughly speaking of course.

The highest peak of the Reeks is Carrantuohil (1039m), whose name is said to translate prosaically as 'reversed reaping hook', perhaps because of its curved outline. These are mountains of old red sandstone that were carved by minor glaciers into the elegant forms we see today. They're studded with awesome cliffs, the summits are buttressed by ridges of purplish rock and the cupped valleys between are filled with glittering lakes. Their world is as wild as their name.

Warning for Cyclists

If you're planning to cycle around Muckross Lake, note that you should do so only in an anticlockwise direction (from Muckross House towards the Meeting of the Waters and not vice versa). Nasty accidents involving broken limbs have occurred when two cyclists travelling at speed in opposite directions have collided on corners.

Gap of Dunloe

Geographically the **Gap of Dunloe** is outside the national park but, as most people start or end their visit to it in the park, details are included here. In high summer, the Gap is Killarney tourism at its full-blown worst. Every day cars and buses disgorge countless visitors at Kate Kearney's Cottage, who then proceed on a one-hour horse-and-trap ride through the Gap; no cars are allowed in summer. You could also walk through the Gap but it's not much fun in summer if you want to be alone. A trip there and back in a hackney carriage costs €54 for four.

The best way to see the Gap is to hire a bike from Killarney and cycle to Ross Castle, then take the boat across the lakes to Lord Brandon's Cottage and cycle through the Gap and back into town via the N72 and a path through the golf course (including bike hire about €22).

The boat ride alone justifies the trip. It lasts 1½ hours and passes through all three lakes, with lovely views of the surrounding mountains and of the Meeting of the Waters and Ladies' View, which was much enjoyed by Queen Victoria's ladies-in-waiting, who gave it its name. Lunches and teas are available at the 19th-century **Kate Kearney's Cottage** (☎ 44146; lunch mains €10-15) and **Lord Brandon's Cottage** (snacks €5-8).

WALKING

There are numerous low-level walking opportunities around Killarney and there are several useful walking guidebooks to the area, available through such outlets as the Killarney Bookshop (see p231). Hillwalking on Macgillycuddy's Reeks and their neighbouring Mangerton Mountains and Purple Mountains, east of the Gap of Dunloe, should never be undertaken without skilled use of map and compass. Weatherproof and waterproof footwear and clothing are essential at all times of year.

There are several ways up Carrantuohil. Some require reasonable hillwalking skills; others are serious rock-climbing routes. You can get a taste of the Reeks at close quarters by walking up the Hag's Glen, the beautiful approach valley that leads to the twin lakes of Callee and Gouragh below the north face of Carrantuohil.

The best approach is from a small car park at OS ref 836873 (Ordnance Survey Map Discovery Series No 78). It is reached from the N72 via Beaufort, to the west of Killarney. The car park is at a farm at the road's end; please pay the small fee if you come by car. From the car park the way lies alongside the Gaddagh River, which you need to ford in places. Great care is required if the river is in flood. It's just over 3km to the lakes.

The popular way to the summit of Carrantuohil from the lakes is via the Devil's Ladder, a badly eroded route up a steep gully southwest of the lakes. The ground is loose in places and in wet conditions the way becomes very muddy.

ORGANISED TOURS

Guided two-hour national-park **walks** (☎ 44339, 087 639 4362; www.kerrygems.ie/killarneywalks; adult/child €7/3.50) leave at 11am daily from the Shell petrol station on Lower New St in Killarney.

A number of Killarney companies run daily day trips by bus around the Ring of Kerry, the Gap of Dunloe and Dingle Peninsula, all costing about €20. Tours last from 10.30am until around 5.30pm. Half-day tours, taking in Aghadoe, Ross Castle, Muckross House and Torc Waterfall, also operate daily, as do bike tours and lake cruises. Some companies you might try are **O'Connor Tours** (☎ 32456; 7 High St), **Dero's Tours** (☎ 31251; 22 Main St), **Corcoran's** (☎ 36666; 8 College St) and **Cronin's Tours** (☎ 31521; College St). However, unless you're really pushed for time these are too rushed a way to do justice to the scenery.

Destination Killarney (☎ 32638; Scott's Gardens) and **Killarney Watercoach Cruises** (☎ 31068) operate hour-long lake cruises with commentary from Ross Castle five times a day (€7.50). A number of private boat owners offer lake trips for the same price from near Ross Castle but you won't find them around during winter.

KILLARNEY TO KENMARE

The N71 links Killarney to Kenmare, with spectacular lake and mountain scenery along the way. About 2km south of the entrance to Muckross House a path leads 200m to the pretty **Torc Waterfall**. After another 8km on the N71 you come to **Ladies' View**, with fine views along Upper Lake. There's another good viewpoint 5km further along at **Moll's Gap**.

RING OF KERRY

The Ring of Kerry, the 179km road circuit around the Iveragh Peninsula, is one of Ireland's premier tourist attractions. Although it can be 'done' in a day by car or bus, or three days by bike, the more time you take the more you'll enjoy it. The stretch of road between Waterville and Caherdaniel in the southwest of the peninsula is reason enough for coming here. The Ballaghbeama Gap cuts across the peninsula's central highlands with some spectacular views and remarkably little traffic: it's perfect for a long cycle, as is the longer Ballaghisheon Pass to Waterville. See p656 for details of the 214km Kerry Way, which starts and ends in Killarney. It is marked on the Ring of Kerry map on p240.

Tour buses approach the Ring in an anticlockwise direction. In high season it's hard to know which is more unpleasant – driving around behind them or travelling in the opposite direction and meeting them on blind corners. Things get much quieter at the western end of the Iveragh Peninsula, when you leave the Ring of Kerry for the Skellig Ring.

An 80km cycle tour via Lough Acoose and Moll's Gap is marked on the Ring of Kerry map (p240).

GETTING AROUND

From late May to mid-September Bus Éireann operates a Ring of Kerry bus service. Buses leave Killarney at 8.30am and 1.30pm Monday to Saturday, and 9.40am (July and August only) and 12.45pm Sunday. One bus a day leaves Killarney at 3pm Monday to Saturday the rest of the year. Buses stop at Killorglin, Glenbeigh, Kells, Caherciveen, Waterville, Caherdaniel and Sneem before returning to Killarney via Moll's Gap. For details ring **Killarney bus station** (☎ 064-30011).

KILLORGLIN

☎ 066 / pop 3521

Travelling anticlockwise from Killarney, the first town on the Ring is Killorglin (Cill Orglan), which is famed for its annual Puck Fair Festival. Although there's not a great deal to see here, it's a pleasant town with a nice setting on the River Laune – the eight-arched bridge over the river was built in 1885. On the Killarney side of the river there's a handsome statue of King Puck himself. Killorglin has a reasonable choice of sleeping and eating options and a few pubs with live music.

There's no tourist office at Killorglin.

Puck Fair Festival (Aonach an Phuic)

This lively three-day celebration takes place during the second weekend in August. It is based around the custom of installing a billy goat (a poc, or puck), the symbol of mountainous Kerry, on a pedestal in the town, its horns festooned with ribbons. Everyone takes advantage of the special licensing hours and pubs stay open, notionally, until 3am. Accommodation is hard to come by if you have not booked in advance.

Sleeping

West's Holiday Park (☎ 976 1240; enquiries@westcaravans.com; Killarney Rd; tent & 2 people €15; Easter-Oct) This is a small site that is family-oriented and lies amid tree-lined fields. It has a pool, tennis court and children's play area, and is just under 2km from the bridge in Killorglin on the road to Killarney.

River's Edge (☎ 976 1750; coffeya@tinet.ie; The Bridge; s/d €60/80; P) An unbeatable location right by the bridge over the River Laune on the village side makes this an attractive stop. Rooms are smart and bright.

Eating

If you're self-catering there's a useful supermarket with a help-yourself deli counter in The Square, Upper Bridge St.

Nick's Restaurant (☎ 976 1219; Lower Bridge St; mains €17.65-35; 6.30-10pm daily May-Sep, Wed-Sun rest of year) Experience luxurious eating in sophisticated surroundings at this famous restaurant, where you can choose the best Kerry beef and lamb as well as delicious fish dishes such as grilled plaice and Dover sole or a fantastic selection of cold shellfish.

Bunkers Bar & Coffee Shop (☎ 976 1381; Iveragh Rd; mains €7.50-16.50; 11am-10pm) This combined pub-restaurant-takeaway pays no dues to smart, trendy décor but deals with a big choice of food from steak to chicken Kiev.

Da Vinci (☎ 976 1055; Old School Rd; pasta & pizza €9-10; 6-11pm) There's good Italian eating in this pleasant, subtly lit restaurant.

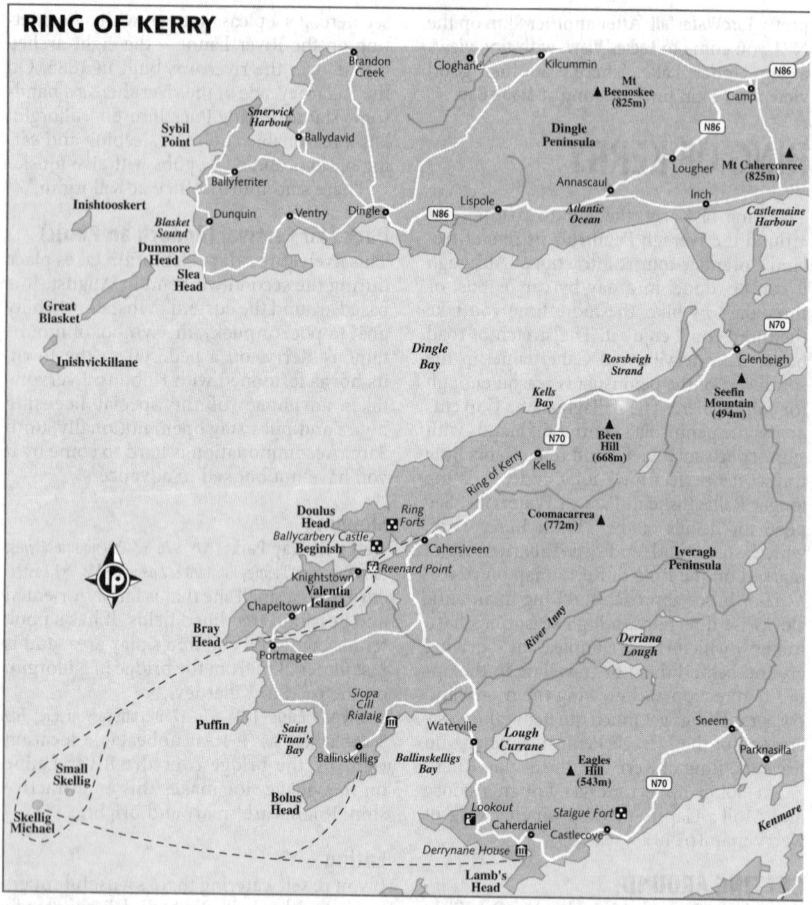

Entertainment

Clifford's Tavern (☎ 976 1539; Upper Bridge St) There's room to move in this spacious old pub, but things get fairly packed and smoky on Friday and Saturday nights when there are trad music sessions.

Laune Bar (Lower Bridge St) The décor's unprepossessing in this little street corner bar, but there's a good Thursday night music session.

KERRY BOG VILLAGE MUSEUM

On the N70 between Killorglin and Glenbeigh and worth a quick stop is the **Kerry Bog Village Museum** (☎ 066-976 9184; adult/child €4/3; 9am-7pm Mar-Oct, on request Nov-Feb). It re-creates the buildings of a 19th-century bog village, with the homes of the turfcutter, blacksmith, thatcher and labourer, and a dairy. Admission includes €0.55 off an Irish coffee at the Red Fox pub next door. Some Kerry Bog ponies are in a field behind the museum.

Red Fox (☎ 066-976 9288; Glenbeigh; meals €6-8) The parking area is bigger than the pub, always a sign that coach parties pile up on a good day, but there's reasonable nosh here, masquerading under names like 'turfcutter's delight', a steakburger by any other name.

CAHERCIVEEN

☎ 066 / pop 1300

You reach deep into the Iveragh Peninsula when you get to Caherciveen (Cathair Saidhthin). In 1815 there were reportedly

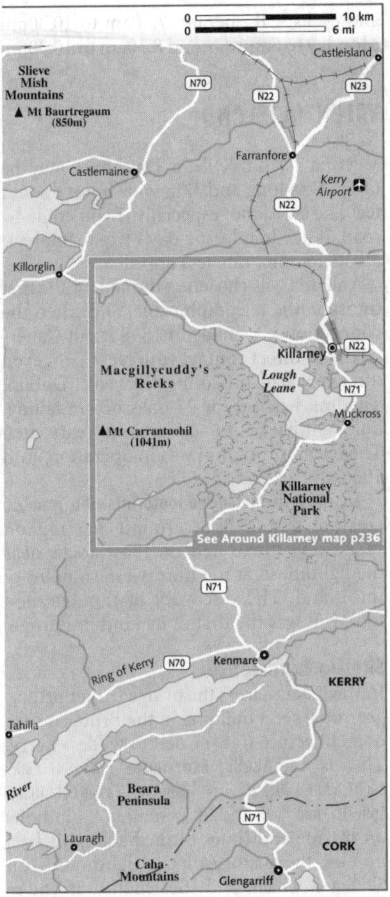

only five houses here. Now the village is a long straggling settlement with a refreshingly down-to-earth rural charm. Once a month there's a street market, overflowing with wonderful items, but the days on which it's held vary almost as much as the weather does.

Daniel O'Connell, 'The Great Liberator', was born near here. On the eastern outskirts, as you approach from Kells, there's a bridge over the Carhan River. The ruins of O'Connell's birthplace can be seen on the east bank. On the west bank is a delightful little amenity area complete with a handsome bust of the great man. There are paths along the river and various boards explain the area's wildlife.

The **tourist office** (☎ 947 2589; The Barracks; 9.30am-5pm Mon & Tue, Thu-Sun Jul & Aug) sells an *O'Connell Heritage Trail* leaflet (€2). The 6.5km trail takes about 2½ hours.

From June to September you can join a two-hour **guided walk** (☎ 947 3186; €7) to archaeological and historic sites that leaves from the UN Bar opposite the post office at 11am every morning.

For attractive local pottery try the **GT Pottery & Gallery** (☎ 947 2444; New St) near the western end of the village.

The Barracks

This **heritage centre** is superbly situated in what was once the **Royal Irish Constabulary (RIC) barracks** (☎ 947 2777; adult/child €4/2; 10am-6pm Mon-Sat, 1-6pm Sun May-Sep, 10am-5pm Mon-Fri Oct-Apr). The building was burned down in 1922 by anti-Treaty forces, but was later reconstructed. It's a theatrical pile, oddly out of place for its surroundings. The story goes that the plans for the building got mixed up with ones intended for a barracks in India. There's a definite North West Frontier look.

The exhibits feature information on Daniel O'Connell, the Fenian Rising and other subjects of local and national interest. To get there, coming from the Kells end of town, turn right at the junction of Bridge and Church Sts.

Ballycarbery Castle & Ring Forts

Continue past The Barracks and over the bridge for 2.4km to find the ruins of **Ballycarbery Castle**. Unfortunately, the castle is on private land and the only access is via the beach at the end of the road, and then only when the tide's out.

Along the same road are two stone **ring forts**. Leacanabuaile is the smaller one and dates from the 9th century. Cahergall, the larger, dates from the 10th century and has stairways on the inside walls, a beehive hut, or *clochan*, and the remains of a house. It's accessible by foot. If driving you should leave your car in the parking area next to a stone wall and walk up the pathway.

Special Events

The **Caherciveen Celtic International Music Festival** takes place over the bank holiday on the first weekend in August. Contact the Killarney **tourist office** (☎ 31633) for details.

Sleeping

Mannix Point Camping & Caravan Park (☎ 947 2806; www.campinginkerry.com; Mannix Point; tent per person €6.50; 🕑 mid-Mar–Sep) An invigorating place to stay, this nicely kept and superbly appointed site is a 15-minute walk west of town and is signposted off the N70.

Sive Hostel (☎ 947 2717; sivehostel@oceanfree.net; 15 East End; dm/d €12.50/15) This small, simple IHH property is at the eastern end of the long main street. It has well-kept, modest rooms. Boat trips to the Skellig Islands can be arranged here.

O'Shea's B&B (☎ 947 2402; Church St; s/d €35/50) There's excellent value at this very pleasant house that's set back from the main street just east of the church. You can get plenty of local information here.

Keating's Corner (☎ 947 2107; josephinekeating@eircom.com; s/d with shared bathrooms €30/52) Another good value stopover is this pleasant corner pub. Rooms ramble through several floors and there's a welcoming atmosphere.

Caherciveen Park Hotel (☎ 947 2543; fax 947 2893; Valentia Rd; s/d €35/60) A modern hotel on the western outskirts of town and popular with anglers, this place has decent, but ordinary, rooms. Breakfast is €10 and prices shoot up in summer and especially in August.

Eating

Helen Shine Coffee Shop (☎ 947 2056; Main St; snacks €3.20-5) A cheerful gem of a place. You can choose from a range of coffee options as well as tasty soups and sandwiches amid colourful surroundings.

Fertha (☎ 947 2023; 20 Main St; bar food €8-10) This spacious pub offers a range of steady dishes including roasts and poached salmon. The chowder (€4) is worthwhile. In summer there are music sessions on Thursday, Friday and Saturday nights.

Red Rose (☎ 947 2293; 24 Church St; lunch €3-8, dinner mains €9-19) Friendly service and a busy menu of lunch and dinner options with an international dash make this central place a worthwhile stop.

Getting There & Away

As well as the regular Ring of Kerry bus service, from April to October there is a **ferry service** (☎ 947 6141) to Knightstown on Valentia Island from Reenard Point, 5km west of Caherciveen. The 10-minute crossing costs €6 for a car and €4 for pedestrians and cyclists. It operates 7.30am to 10.30pm Monday to Saturday and 8.30am to 10.30pm Sunday.

VALENTIA ISLAND

☎ 066

Valentia Island (Oileán Dairbhre) may be only 11km long and 3km wide but it doesn't feel like an island, especially if you come by road. It needs at least a day's trip to appreciate its remote, timeless appeal.

Valentia was chosen as the site for the first transatlantic telegraph cable, and when the connection was made in 1858 it put Caherciveen in direct contact with New York even though it had no connection with Dublin. The link worked for 27 days before failing, but went back into action some years later. The telegraph station was in operation until 1966.

In 1992 the **fossilised footprints** of a marine creature dating back around 365 million years were discovered on some rocks near the lighthouse at the northwestern point of the island. The discovery of this tetrapod footprint was the first of its kind in Europe.

Skellig Experience

Immediately across the bridge from Portmagee you'll see a building in the Brutalist style of architecture transported to wildest Kerry. This is the **Skellig Experience** (☎ 947 6306; adult/child €4.40/2.20; 🕑 10am-6pm Easter-Oct, 10am-5pm Oct–mid-Nov) and it contains exhibitions on the life and times of the Skellig Michael monks, the history of the lighthouses on Skellig Michael, and the wildlife. If you're planning a trip to the Skelligs it's worth coming here for background information. If the weather's bad this may be as close as you get to the islands.

Getting There & Away

Most visitors reach Valentia Island via the bridge from Portmagee. From April to October, pedestrians, cyclists and motorists can also cross by ferry from Reenard Point near Caherciveen to the pier at Knightstown (see p242).

SKELLIG ISLANDS

The Skellig Islands (Oileáin na Scealaga) are spectacular in the truest meaning of the word and a boat trip to the islands, 12km out in the Atlantic Ocean, is one of the highlights of a trip to Ireland. The crossing can be rough, so brace yourself if you're a poor sailor. It's worth it. There are no toilets or shelter on Skellig Michael, the only island you may land on. Wear stout shoes and weatherproof clothing, including a waterproof for the often wave-spattered boat trip, and bring something to eat and drink.

Bird-Watching

The Skelligs are a bird paradise. Keep a sharp look out during the boat trip and you may spot diminutive storm petrels, also known as Mother Carey's Chickens, that dart above the water like swallows. Gannets, with savage beaks, imperious eyes and yellow caps, are unmistakable, not least because of their wing spans of 107cm. They dive like tridents into the sea to snatch fish from below the surface. Kittiwakes – small, dainty seabirds with black-tipped wings – are easy to see and hear around the covered walkway of Skellig Michael as you step off the boat. They winter at sea but then land in their thousands to breed between March and August. Further up the rock you'll see stubby-winged fulmars, with distinctive bony 'nostrils' from which they eject an evil-smelling green liquid if you get too close. Black-and-white guillemots and razorbills are also present. Look also for the delightful puffins with their multicoloured beaks and waddling gait. In May, puffins come ashore to lay a solitary egg at the end of a burrow and parent birds can be seen guarding their nests. Puffins stay only until the first week or two of August.

Skellig Michael

The 217m-high jagged rock of **Skellig Michael** (Archangel Michael's Rock), the larger of the two islands and a Unesco World Heritage site, looks like the last place on earth that anyone would try to land, let alone establish a community. Yet early-Christian monks survived here from the 6th until the 12th or 13th century. They were influenced by the Coptic Church founded by St Anthony in the deserts of Egypt and Libya, and their determined quest for ultimate solitude led them to this remote, Atlantic edge of Europe.

The monastic buildings are perched on a saddle in the rock, some 150m above sea level, and are reached by 600 steps cut into the rock face. The astounding 6th-century oratories and beehive cells vary in size, the largest cell having a floor space of 4.5m by 3.6m. The projecting stones on the outside have more than one possible explanation: steps to reach the top and release chimney stones, or maybe holding places for turf that covered the exterior.

Little is known about the life of the monastery, but there are records of Viking raids in AD 812 and 823. Monks were killed or taken away but the community recovered and carried on. Legend even says that one of these raiders, Olaf Tryggvesson, was converted by the monks and became Norway's first Christian ruler. In the 11th century a rectangular oratory was added to the site, but although it was expanded in the 12th century the monks abandoned the rock around this time, perhaps because of more than usually ferocious Atlantic storms.

After the introduction of the Gregorian calendar in 1582, Skellig Michael became a popular spot for weddings. Marriages were forbidden during Lent, but since Skellig used the old Julian calendar a trip over to the islands allowed those unable to wait for Easter to tie the knot.

In the 1820s two lighthouses were built on Skellig Michael, together with the road that runs around the base.

You're asked to do your picnicking on the way up to the monastery, or at Christ's Saddle just before the last flight of steps, rather than among the ruins. This is to keep sandwich-loving birds and their droppings away from the monument.

WARNING

A notice on the island warns of 'an element of danger' in visiting Skellig Michael. Although you need to be sensible anywhere on the rocks or stone steps, special care should be taken when getting off the boat at the island. Above all concentrate, be positive, and make sure your feet are firmly placed.

Small Skellig

Small Skellig is a bird sanctuary and no landing is permitted. While Skellig Michael looks like two triangles linked by a spur, Small Skellig is longer, lower and much craggier. From a distance it looks as if someone had battered it with a feather pillow that burst. Close up you realise you're looking at a colony of 20,000 pairs of breeding gannets, the second-largest breeding colony in the world. Most boats circle the island so you can see them. There may also be a chance of seeing basking seals.

Getting There & Away

Because of concerns for the fragility of Skellig Michael there are limits on how many people can visit on the same day. There are 19 boats licensed to carry no more than 12 passengers each, so there should never be more than 250 people there at any one time. Because of these limits it's wise to book ahead in July and August, always bearing in mind that if the weather's bad the boats may not sail. Trips usually start around Easter but high seas and bad weather can put them off until May.

Boats leave around 10am and return at 3pm. You can depart from either Portmagee (and even Caherciveen), Ballinskelligs or Derrynane. The boat owners try to restrict you to two hours on the island, which is the bare minimum, on a good day, to see the monastery, look at the birds and have a picnic. The crossing from Portmagee takes about 1½ hours and from Ballinskelligs it's about one hour (around €25 return from both places).

Some operators to try include **Owen Walsh** (☎ 066-947 6327, 947 6115), **Michael O'Sullivan** (☎ 066-947 4255), **Des Lavelle** (☎ 066-947 6124), **Sean and Sheila O'Shea** (☎ 066-947 5129) and **Patrick Casey** (☎ 066-947 2069). Most pubs and B&Bs in the area will point you in the right direction.

WATERVILLE

☎ 066 / pop 500

The popular beach resort of Waterville (An Coireán) is a triangle of pubs, restaurants and shops on a narrow bit of land between Ballinskelligs Bay and Lough Currane. Charlie Chaplin was probably the town's most famous visitor and there's an uncannily lifelike statue of him in his famous tramp's garb on the footpath above the beach.

Activities

Waterville Golf Links (☎ 947 4102) charges a hefty €130 per round, or €62 before 8am and off-season, but it is one of the most stunning links courses in the world and attracts serious golfers from all over.

There are lots of **angling** possibilities around Waterville. Lough Currane has free fishing for sea trout while the Inny River is a breeding ground for wild salmon and trout. Sea angling offers the chance of catching mackerel, pollack and shark. The **Tadhg O'Sullivan tackle shop** (☎ 947 4433; Main St) has information.

You can go quad-biking through the nearby mountain passes, bog swamps and forest trails with **Quad Safari** (☎ 947 4465; Upper Main St; www.actionadventurecentre.com).

Sleeping

Clifford's B&B (☎ 947 4283; cliffordbandb@eircom.net; Main St; s/d €43/60; P) This comfortable modern house is on the inland side of the main road at the southern end of town, but has clear views of the sea from the front upstairs rooms.

Bayview Hotel (☎ 947 4122; Main St; s/d €45/90; P) You keep bumping into Charlie Chaplin's statue every time you walk out the door of this hotel. The place has seen better days, but rooms are a good size and there's the chance of healthy discounts in the low season.

Butler Arms Hotel (☎ 947 4144; www.butlerarms.com; Main St; s/d €141/192; P) There are delightfully comfy rooms in the older part of this long-established hotel or smart modern ones in an extension. The public rooms add a stylish tone and you can reflect on the spirit of Charlie Chaplin, who often stayed here.

Smuggler's Inn (☎ 947 4330; thesmugglersinn@eircom.net; Cliff Rd; s/d €76/101; P) Standing in splendid isolation near the golf course and above a long, sandy beach, this pleasant guesthouse and restaurant has light and airy rooms with bright fittings. There are unquestionably spacious views from all points, but especially from sea-facing rooms and from the comfy sitting room.

Eating

Sheilin (☎ 947 4231; Top Cross; dinner mains €14-22; 🕑 6-10pm) Located uphill from the foreshore road, this is the place for good seafood, including lip-smacking Valentia scallops and freshwater fish such as rainbow trout.

Smuggler's Inn (☎ 947 4330; thesmugglersinn@eircom.net; Cliff Rd; bar food €4.50-14, dinner mains €19-29; 🕑 8.30am-9.30pm; P) Within sight and sound of the sea, especially through its floor-to-ceiling windows, it's no surprise that fish is a strong speciality at this restaurant. Shellfish feature strongly and the baked salmon is delicious, while there's a tasty vegetarian platter.

SKELLIG RING

The Skellig Ring, in a Gaeltacht or Irish-speaking area, is a scenic route that links Waterville with Portmagee via Ballinskelligs (Baile an Sceilg). It's signposted as you leave and is an enjoyable cycle route; however, there are lots of small unmarked roads, making it easy to get lost without a map, preferably an Ordnance Survey one.

Siopa Cill Rialaig Art Gallery

This splendid **gallery** (☎ 066-947 9324; cillrialaig@easatclear.ie; Ballinskelligs; 🕑 10.30am-7pm daily Easter-Sep, 11am-5pm Thu-Sat rest of year), en route to Ballinskelligs, contains work by local and international artists, writers and composers. It is the shop window of the Cill Rialaig Project, which provides an international retreat for creative people. Free accommodation and free studio space at the retreat are available to people who are invited to donate work to the gallery at the end of their stay. Standards are very high and the result is as fine a collection of pieces as you'd find in a top Dublin gallery. Those wishing to apply to the project need to send a CV with pictures of their work and details of any exhibitions.

The gallery is by the roadside on the R566 – the thatched roofs are unmissable. There's a café in the gallery. Sit outside on a spectacular bench.

Ballinskelligs Monastery & Bay

The sea and salty air are eating away at the atmospheric ruins of this **medieval building**, a monastic settlement that was probably associated with the monks of Skellig Michael after they left their rocky outpost during the 12th or 13th century. To reach it, and Ballinskelligs' fine little Blue Flag award beach, continue past the post office down to Ballinskelligs Bay and walk to the remains from there. At the western end of the **beach** are the last remnants of a 16th-century castle stronghold of the McCarthys. Turn left at the junction after the post office for the castle.

Sleeping & Eating

Ballinskelligs Hostel (☎ 066-947 9229; Prior House; dm/d €12/26; 🕑 Easter-Sep) The mural on the end wall goes well with the very Irish tone of this little place that's attached to the local shop. Turn right at the junction after passing the post office.

Ballinskelligs Inn (☎ 066-947 9104; www.ballinskelligsinn.com; per person €32; lunch €8, dinner €12-18; Ⓟ) The pub at this handy place draws a good local crowd. Rooms are clean and unfancy, and food is standard and traditional.

CAHERDANIEL

☎ 066 / pop 342

Caherdaniel is neatly wedged between the sea and the foothills of Eagle Hill and has a delightful atmosphere because of it. There's an important historic house to enhance the cluster of buildings, and a couple of sandy beaches by the harbour add to the appeal.

Derrynane National Historic Park

Having grown rich on smuggling with France and Spain, the O'Connells bought **Derrynane House** (☎ 947 5113; Derrynane; adult/child €3/1.50; 🕑 9am-6pm Mon-Sat, 11am-7pm Sun May-Sep, 1-5pm Tue-Sun Apr & Oct, 1-5pm Sat & Sun Nov-Mar; last admission 45 min before closing) and the surrounding parkland.

The house is largely furnished with items relating to Daniel O'Connell, the campaigner for Catholic emancipation. Most amazing of all is the restored triumphal chariot in which O'Connell rode around Dublin after his release from prison in 1844.

There is a walking track through the surrounding wetlands from where you can spot wild pheasants and other birds. The grounds also include a sandy beach and **Abbey Island**, which can usually be reached on foot across the sand. The **chapel**, which O'Connell added to Derrynane House in 1844, is a copy of the ruined one on Abbey Island.

Look out for an **ogham stone**, a stone with carved notches representing the simple alphabet, called Ogham, of the ancient Irish. The Derrynane stone has several missing letters but may represent the name of a local chieftain. It is on the left of the road leading down to the house.

Activities

Caherdaniel competes with Valentia Island as the **diving** base for the Iveragh Peninsula. Try **Activity Ireland** (☎ 947 5277; www.activity-ireland.com), which also organises a range of other outdoor activities. **Derrynane Sea Sports** (☎ 947 5266) organises canoeing, windsurfing and water-skiing and operates from the beach from June to August.

Sleeping & Eating

Glenbeg Caravan & Camping Park (☎ 947 5182; glenbeg@eircom.net; tent & 2 people €11; 🕒 mid-Apr–early Oct) Overlooking a sandy beach and with great views across to the Beara Peninsula, this site can't be beaten for a genuine seaside location. It's 2.5km east of Caherdaniel on the N70.

Travellers' Rest Hostel (☎ 947 5175; dm/d €12.50/32; P) Located right by the main road, opposite a garage, this is a charming little cottage-style hostel, with cosy rooms and a pleasant kitchen area. Call at the garage if there's nobody about.

Kerry Way B&B (☎ 947 5227; info@activity-ireland.com; s/d €35/50) Run by the same people as Activity Ireland, this pleasant old house has good-sized en-suite rooms and a friendly atmosphere.

Olde Forge (☎ 947 5140; theoldforge@eircom.net; s/d €35/60) If Caherdaniel is too busy for you this well-positioned place with its great views and peaceful ambience is the ultimate escape. It's 1.2km east of Caherdaniel on the N70.

Blind Piper (☎ 947 5126; bar food €5.20-17.70; 🕒 for food noon-10pm Jun-Sep, noon-8pm rest of year) Even in summer the Piper does not lose its local atmosphere. There's a garden and outside seating in which to savour the ambience.

STAIGUE FORT

This **fort** is a powerful evocation of late Iron Age Ireland. Its 5m-high circular wall is up to 4m thick and is surrounded by a large bank and ditch. Steps lead up to the interior wall and there are two small rooms in the walls. There was some reconstruction of the fort in the 19th century.

Staigue probably dates from the 3rd or 4th century. Despite having sweeping views down to the coast it can't be seen from the sea. It may have been a communal place of refuge, or a cultural and commercial centre, where people came to celebrate, exchange goods and stage ceremonies. The sophistication of the building suggests that it may have been in the control of a chieftain's family.

The fort is near the village of Castlecove, about 4km off the N70, and is reached by a potholed country lane which narrows as it climbs to the site. Traffic jams can occur. This is a Dúchas site and access should be free, but there may be a (non-Dúchas) demand of a €2 or so for 'access across private land'.

KENMARE

☎ 064 / pop 2665

Picturesque Kenmare (Neidín) carries its romantic reputation more stylishly than does Killarney and there is an elegance about its handsome central square and attractive buildings. It still gets very busy in summer all the same. The town stands where the delightfully named Finnihy, Roughty and Sheen Rivers empty into Kenmare River. For those with transport, Kenmare makes a pleasant alternative to Killarney as a base for visiting the Ring of Kerry and the Beara Peninsula.

Orientation & Information

In the 18th century Kenmare was laid out on an X-plan, with a triangular market square in the centre and Fair Green nestling in its upper V. To the south, Henry and Main Sts are the main shopping and eating/drinking thoroughfares, with Shelbourne St linking them at the southern end. Kenmare River stretches out to the southwest, and there are glorious views of the mountains.

Tourist office (☎ 41233; The Square; 🕒 9.30am-5pm Mon & Tue, Thu-Sun Jul & Aug) provides a free heritage-trail leaflet showing places of historic interest. The post office at the top of Henry St has some local walking maps and guides. It also has Internet access for €1 for 10 minutes. Kenmare has its own website at www.neidin.net.

The Allied Irish Bank, on the corner of Main and Henry Sts, has an ATM and bureau de change. You'll find public toilets opposite the Holy Cross Church in Old Killarney Rd. There's free parking around the square, but competition for spaces is fierce in summer.

Kenmare Heritage Centre

This **heritage centre** (☎ 41233; adult/child €2.70/1.30; 🕒 9.15am-7pm Mon-Sat Jul & Aug, 9.15am-5.30pm Mon-Sat Easter-Jun & Sep) is behind the tourist office. It recounts the history of the town from its founding as Neidín by William Petty-Fitzmaurice in 1670. Particularly interesting is the information about the Kenmare Poor Clare Convent (still standing behind Holy Cross Church), which was founded in 1862 and provided local women with work as needlepoint lace-makers. Samples of their work are on display here and more can be seen upstairs in **Kenmare Lace and Design Centre**. Also interesting in the heritage centre is the story of Margaret Anna Cusack (1829–99), the Nun of Kenmare and an early advocate of women's rights who was eventually hounded out of Kenmare as a political agitator, then renounced Catholicism in favour of Protestantism and died, embittered, in Leamington, England.

Other Sights

Southwest along Market St and Pound Lane is the fancifully named **Druid Circle**, with 15 stones ringing a boulder dolmen. The date is early Bronze Age. The context of this fine monument is rather marred by its suburban surroundings and the proximity of waste ground and a sewage treatment plant. There may be an admission fee demand of about €2 at busy times.

Holy Cross Church on Old Killarney Rd was built in 1864 and boasts a splendid wooden roof with 14 angel carvings. There are fine mosaics in the aisle arches and around the stained-glass window over the altar.

Activities

Kenmare Golf Club (☎ 41291; 18 holes €28, Sun €39, club hire €10) has its entrance on the R569 to Cork, about 100m from the top of Main St.

You can hire **snorkelling** and **diving** gear from **Kenmare Bay Diving** (☎ 42238) in nearby Bonane. A half-day beginner's course costs €60.

Seafari River Cruises (☎ 83171; adult/child €16/8) depart from Kenmare Pier around Kenmare Bay on whale, dolphin and seal watching trips. The company also rents out **sailing**, **canoeing** and **windsurfing** equipment. Reservations are advised.

Beach and mountain rides are offered by **Hazelwood Riding Stables** (☎ 41420), 3.2km southwest of Kenmare on the R571 to Lauragh, as well as lessons for children and beginners.

Kenmare is ringed with lovely scenery and short walks can be made along the river or into the hills. The Kerry Way passes through Kenmare (see p656).

Sleeping

BUDGET

Ring of Kerry Caravan & Camping Park (☎ 41648; info@kerrycamping.com; Kenmare; tent & 2 adults €17; Apr-Sep) Mountain and sea views enhance this lovely site in wooded country. It's located 5km west of town on the Sneem road.

Fáilte Hostel (☎ 42333; failtefinn@eircom.net; cnr Shelbourne & Henry Sts; dm €12, s & d €16-20; Apr-Oct; P) Excellent rooms and spick-and-span facilities characterise this pleasant hostel in a fine old building.

MID-RANGE

Hawthorn House (☎ 41035; www.hawthornehousekenmare.com; Shelbourne St; s/d €45/70; P) A marvellous place to stay, this stylish house has lovely rooms, each with great individuality and charming touches such as fresh flowers and fruit every day.

Rose Cottage (☎ 41330; The Square; www.kenmare.net/rosecottage; s/d €45/64; P) A picturesque building set back from Fair Green, this old house was where the original Poor Clare nuns stayed when they arrived in Kenmare in 1861. It has charming rooms and elegant furnishings.

Ard Na Mara (☎ 41399; Pier Rd; s/d €37/60; P) This 1950s lodge-style house is about a three-minute walk from the centre and stands high above the pier and estuary. The approach drive is very steep. Rooms are comfy and there's a long lounge with great views.

Whispering Pines (☎ 41194; wpines@indigo.ie; s/d €40/72; Mar–mid-Nov) In a quiet location, this attractive bungalow offers immaculate rooms, a cheerful welcome and marvellous breakfasts.

Ashberry Lodge (☎ 42720; www.ashberrylodge.com; Sneem Rd; s/d €50/65) Located about an eight-minute walk from the centre on the N70 to Sneem, this modern house is set back from the road and has pleasant rooms and views of the Caha Mountains. It's right on the Kerry Way walking route.

Wander Inn (☎ 42700; wanderinn@eircom.net; 2 Henry St; s/d €60/90) Rooms at this central place are modern and nicely decorated. There are good discounts in the low season and at quiet times.

Eating

Kenmare has a good range of eating places and there are some outstanding restaurants to merit the town's reputation for good food.

BUDGET

Purple Heather Bistro (☎ 41016; Henry St; lunch & snacks €3.40-12.95; 10.45am-7pm Mon-Sat) A terrific atmosphere and comfy traditional décor makes this popular place ideal for a relaxing chat. Enjoy a great range of tasty sandwiches, or Irish dishes with a dash of European cuisine. There are good vegetarian options and the home-made desserts are a final flourish.

Jam (☎ 42144; Henry St; sandwiches €3-4.90, meals €7.50; 🕑 8am-5pm Mon-Sat) A bustling, popular place, Jam does filling sandwiches, tasty salads and other dishes.

MID-RANGE

Mickey Ned's (☎ 40200; The Square; bar meals €3.55-10.30, dinner €14-19; 🕑 noon-9pm) From the outside you might think Mickey Ned's was just another old Irish bar complete with a Brendan Behan quote on the wall, but inside it's cool and contemporary, all stylish colours and subdued lighting, but spacious and with a great atmosphere. The owner was a famous captain of the Kerry football team that won the All-Ireland title in 1975; photographs on the walls tell it all.

An Leath Phingin (☎ 41559; 35 Main St; mains €13.90-19.50; 🕑 6-10pm) Irish by name it may be, but this excellent eatery is distinctly Italian cuisine at its best. The introductory reception area is Kerry; the upstairs restaurant is Italy. The food is grand, and ranges from pasta and lasagne to fennel- and bruschetta-flavoured sausages.

Horseshoe (☎ 41553; 3 Main St; mains €9-14; 🕑 noon-10.30pm Mon-Sat, Sat & Sun only Jan-Mar) Irish mood and style is persuasive at this charming place where even the chips are home-made. Tasty chowder, fish and meat dishes, good vegetarian options and no unnecessarily fancy touches are the thing here.

TOP END

Packies (☎ 41508; Henry St; mains €15.50-26; 🕑 6-9.30pm Tue-Sat) Treat yourself to this award-winning restaurant where a sure touch with flavours creates an unbeatable merging of traditional Irish with Mediterranean flair, underpinned with tried and tested methods. Seafood matters here, and there's a strong bias towards organic produce. There's chicken, lamb and tagliatelle choices and the setting is stylish but not over the top.

Mulcahy's Restaurant (☎ 42383; 16 Henry St; mains €18-24.50, set dinner €38; 🕑 6-10pm Wed-Mon) Mulcahy's brings world style in décor to Kenmare and the food's just as modernist, with sushi starters and Pacific Rim touches to the mains. Vegetarians are well catered for and the décor is trendsetting.

D'Arcy's (☎ 41589; Main St; dinner €15-27.50; 🕑 6-10pm May-Sep, phone for rest of year openings) Great contemporary is the mark of this popular place in a one-time bank. Meat and fish dishes are on equal offer. The poached turbot with fennel-smoked mussels does justice to a splendid fish, although it's pricey at €27.50.

Shopping

Kenmare has a fair mix of quality craft shops and souvenir centres. Most things are fairly pricey. At the time of writing the handsome Italianate market house in The Square was being refurbished and was due to house a number of shops.

Nostalgia (☎ 41389; 27 Henry St) Superb antique linen and lace can be bought here, but for a price that matches the high quality.

PF Kelly (☎ 42590; 18 Henry St) Fine modern jewellery is on sale here. The salt servers by the West Cork designer Marika O'Sullivan are stunning. It also takes commissions.

Soundz of Muzic (☎ 42268; 9 Henry St) Selection of Irish and contemporary music.

Kenmare Bookshop (☎ 41578; Shelbourne St) Wide range of books, including a strong Irish section with maps and guides.

Noel & Holland (☎ 42464; 3 Bridge St) This excellent second-hand bookshop sells some rare editions and also has a terrific range of paperbacks, all neatly collated.

Getting There & Away

As well as the main Ring of Kerry bus service, there's a bus to Killarney (€7.20, 45 minutes) where you can change for Tralee, and a twice-daily bus to Skibbereen (€12.20, 2½ hours) via Glengarriff and Bantry. Every Friday afternoon a bus goes to Lauragh, Ardgroom and Castletownbere. Buses stop outside Roughty Bar on Main St.

Getting Around

Finnegan's Cycle Centre (☎ 41083), opposite the Fáilte Hostel below Finnegan's Corner Hostel on Shelbourne St, is the Raleigh Rent-a-Bike dealer, with bikes costing €12/70 per day/week.

NORTHERN KERRY

The landscape of Northern Kerry is often dull compared with the glories of the Iveragh and Dingle Peninsulas, Killarney and Kenmare. There are fascinating places all the same and enough compelling history to reward a few days' exploration. The coastal area is popular with Irish holiday-makers.

TRALEE

☎ 066 / pop 21,100

Tralee's (Trá Lí) name may have a lilt to it, but this is a down-to-earth town with an authentic and appealing atmosphere of everyday Irish life. Do not expect the picturesque, but there are handsome Georgian buildings, an excellent museum and several other attractions.

Founded by the Normans in 1216, Tralee has a long history of rebellion. In the 16th century the last ruling earl of the Desmonds was captured and executed here. His head was sent to Elizabeth I, who spiked it on London Bridge. The Desmond castle once stood at the junction of Denny St and The Mall, but any trace of medieval Tralee that survived the Desmond Wars was razed during the Cromwellian period.

The Rose of Tralee festival is in the last week of August.

Orientation

Tralee is a fairly small town and you'll find most things you need along The Mall and its continuation, Castle St. Wide, elegant Denny St and Day Place are the oldest parts of town with buildings from the 18th century. Ashe St is home to the Courthouse, a solemn, fortress-like building. The tourist office is beyond the southern end of Denny St. The bus and train stations are a five-minute walk northeast of the town centre.

Information

The **tourist office** (☎ 712 1288; www.shannon-dev.ie; ⏲ 9am-7pm Mon-Sat, 9am-6pm Sun Jul-Aug, 9am-6pm Mon-Sat May, Jun, Sep & Oct, 9am-5pm Mon-Fri rest of year) is at the back of Ashe Memorial Hall.

On Castle St you'll find banks with ATMs and bureaux de change. The **post office** is on Edward St, which runs off Castle St. **Web Café** (☎ 719 4009; Church St; €4/hr, students €3.60; ⏲ 8.30am-10pm Mon-Sat, noon-7pm Sun) also does snacks.

O'Mahony's Booksellers (☎ 712 2266; Upper Castle St) has a good selection of local and general books. The **Walk Information Centre** (☎ 712 8733; swwi@iol.ie; 6 Church St; ⏲ 8.30am-6pm Mon-Sat) is the headquarters of South-West Walks Ireland and has a lot of useful maps and walking guides.

There's a left-luggage office at the train station costing €3 per item for 24 hours, and you'll find public toilets off Russell St.

Kerry the Kingdom Museum

Also in the Ashe Memorial Hall but entered around the corner from the tourist office is this **museum** (☎ 712 7777; Ivy Tce; adult/child €8/5; ⏲ 10am-6pm mid-Mar–Oct, 10am-5pm Nov & Dec). It has an excellent series of displays on Irish history with emphasis on Kerry. At the time

ROSE OF TRALEE

Every August Tralee comes into its own when it hosts the famous Rose of Tralee festival. Beauty contest or not, this is a time-honoured event that's been going for over 40 years. Broadcaster Terry Wogan used to compere proceedings in the 1960s and probably honed his later inimitable Eurovision Song Contest style in old Tralee.

The inspiration for the event is the famous 19th-century song by local toff and poet William Mulchinock in praise of local beauty and modest housemaid Mary O'Connor. Star-crossed lovers of classic style, William and Mary never married, because William fled for his life after a little local difficulty, of which he was innocent. After six years in exile in India he returned only to find Mary newly dead, a victim of the Famine. The song he is said to have written for his beloved is guaranteed to draw the odd tear from even the most hard-skinned of cynics.

Modern Rose contestants must be Irish by birth or ancestry, which is why many past winners have been American or Australian; the 2002 winner, Tamara Gervasoni, had an Irish mother and an Italian father. During the five days of the festival, the town's pubs, theatres and restaurants feature events and live music well into the evening.

The **Rose of Tralee Festival Office** (☎ 066-712 1322; info@roseoftralee.ie; www.roseoftralee.ie) is in Ashe Memorial Hall on Ivy Terrace.

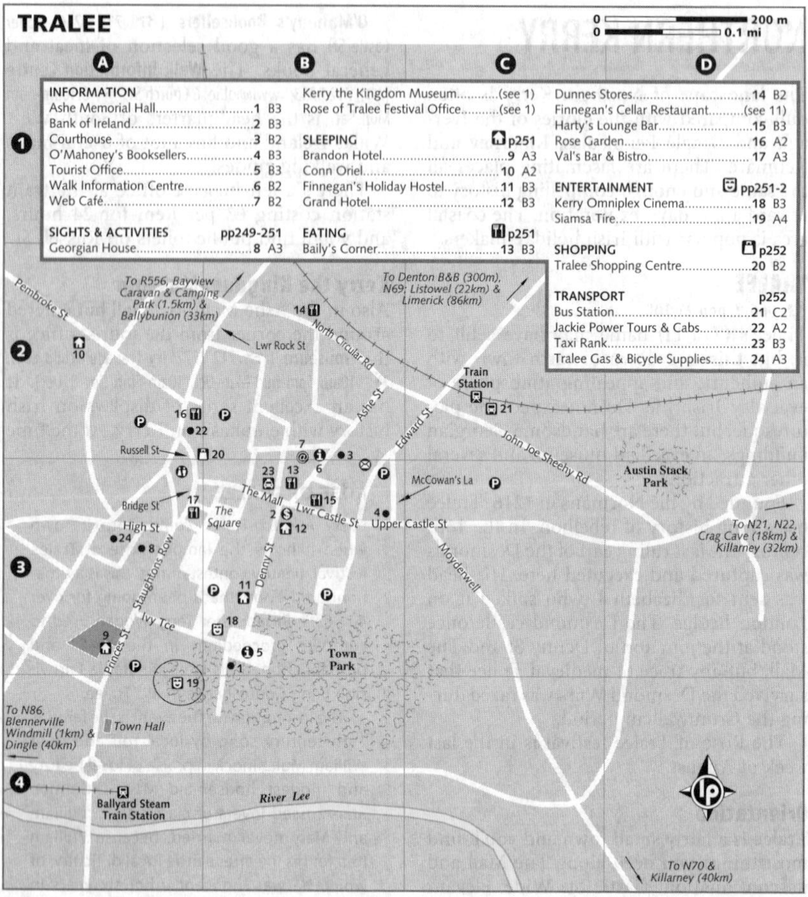

of writing there was also an **Antarctica Exhibition** celebrating the remarkable Tom Crean from Annascaul (see p262) who accompanied Shackleton on an epic journey in Antarctica. The exhibition was being extended and deserves to become permanent. Also here is the **Geraldine Experience**, a multimedia presentation that includes a ride around the re-creation of a walled town from 1450. Children love it and there's a commentary in eight languages.

Other Sights

The **Georgian House** was built by Justice Robert Day, a member of Tralee's upper class and a local political figure in the 1790s. He was the son of Maurice Day, who was the Knight of Kerry. Today the house is a **visitor centre** (☎ 712 6995; 3 Day Pl; adult/child €5/4.50; ⏲ noon-4pm May-Sep; ☎ 087 264 7195 for an appointment at other times). It re-creates a typical Georgian household. There's also a tearoom.

Between 1891 and 1953 a narrow-gauge **steam railway** connected Tralee with Dingle. The first short leg of the journey, from Tralee to Blennerville, was reopened and now operates from May to September. The train leaves **Ballyard station** (☎ 712 1064; adult/child €4/2; ⏲ on the hour 11am-5pm, 20 min duration).

Blennerville used to be the chief port of Tralee, though it has long since silted up. A flour **windmill** was built here in 1800 but fell into disuse by 1880. It has been restored and is the largest working mill in Ireland or Britain. The modern **visitor centre** (☎ 712 1064; adult/child €4/2; 🕑 10am-6pm Apr-Oct) houses an exhibition on the grain milling process and another on the thousands of emigrants who boarded 'coffin ships' for a new life in the USA from what was then Kerry's largest embarkation point. A 30-minute guided tour is included in the admission price. Blennerville Windmill is on the N86, 1km southwest of Tralee. One way to get there is by the steam railway.

Sleeping

Most B&Bs raise their prices by about €10 during the Rose of Tralee festival.

Bayview Caravan & Camping Park (☎ 712 6140; Killeen; tent & 2 people €13) This small park is in a pleasant tree-lined location and has good facilities. It's 1.5km north of the centre on the R556.

Finnegan's Holiday Hostel (☎ 712 7610; 17 Denny St; dm/d €15/40) Located in a fine old Georgian house, this hostel has a lot of character. Rooms are spacious and the cooking and lounge facilities are good.

Denton (☎ 712 7637; dentonbandb@eircom.net; Oakpark Rd; s/d €35/55; Ⓟ) This spick-and-span modern house on the Limerick road is good value and is only a short walk from the centre. There's a friendly welcome as well. Rooms are a reasonable size and immaculate; breakfasts are generous.

Conn Oriel (☎ 712 5359; www.connoriel.mainpage.com; 6 Pembroke Sq, Pembroke St; s/d €35/55; Ⓟ) Another fine choice only 200m from the centre, this modern house has bright woodwork and cheerful rooms.

Grand Hotel (☎ 712 1499; info@grandhoteltralee.com; Denny St; s/d €70/130) The Grand's prices are a trifle grand, but this is a comfy, pleasantly old-fashioned place that still hangs on to a nice period feel in its public rooms. Bedrooms are a good size.

Brandon Hotel (☎ 712 3333; www.brandonhotel.ie; Princes St; s/d €90/130; Ⓟ) If you want corporate big hotel anonymity, then the Brandon is the place. Pricey but with good facilities including a spa and leisure centre, the rooms are smart, with bright pinewood surrounds.

Eating

There are plenty of lunch-time places in Tralee and a couple of excellent restaurants and bar food places. For self-caterers there's **Dunnes Stores** (North Circular Rd).

Baily's Corner (☎ 712 6230; Ashe St; bar meals €4-6.50) A deservedly popular corner pub, Baily's has a cheerful bar menu offering tasty chowder, Irish stew and lasagne as well as sandwiches, all enjoyed in a lively atmosphere.

Harty's Lounge Bar (☎ 25385; Lower Castle St; bar meals €5-9) Something of a Tralee institution, this spacious and well-maintained bar has old-fashioned courtesy and timeless style. It does no-frills food such as Irish stew and mash, sandwiches and salads.

Rose Garden (☎ 712 9393; Lower Rock St; mains €9.90-15.90; 🕑 5pm-12.30am) A good quality Chinese place that offers a three-course dinner for €22. The Rose also has a takeaway counter next door, where prices are €3 to €5 less.

Finnegan's Cellar Restaurant (☎ 718 1400; 17 Denny St; mains €14.50-22.50; 🕑 6-11pm) Located downstairs from Finnegan's Holiday Hostel in the one-time servants' quarters, basement kitchen and wine cellar of a classic Tralee Georgian house, this atmospheric place is all exposed stone, gingham tablecloths and subdued lighting. It offers mainly meat, lamb and poultry with an international touch.

Val's Bar & Bistro (☎ 718 1289; Bridge St; mains €11.50-19.90; 🕑 6.30-10.30pm) Cool cosmo décor of dark wood and dark leather, chrome and subtle lighting makes this a favourite for Tralee's trend-tasters. The upstairs bistro does good seafood and a couple of excellent vegetarian options. Starters are imaginative, and there are meat and poultry dishes.

Entertainment

Castle St is thick with pubs, many of them with live entertainment of one kind or another.

Baily's Corner (☎ 712 6230; Ashe St) Baily's maintains its popularity with traditional sessions on Tuesday nights, while local musicians perform original material on Sunday, Monday, Wednesday and Thursday.

Harty's Lounge Bar (☎ 25385; Lower Castle St) If you want some quiet conversation, Harty's is the place. On Friday nights there's Irish music and you might even catch a poet performing now and then.

Val's Bar & Bistro (☎ 718 1289; Bridge St) Val's stages traditional music in trendy surroundings on Monday, Tuesday and Thursday nights.

Siamsa Tíre (☎ 712 3055; www.siamsatire.com; Ivy Tce; booking office 🕑 9am-6.30pm Mon-Sat) In a pleasant location in the town park, near the tourist office, Siamsa Tíre (shee-am-sah tee-reh), the National Folk Theatre of Ireland, re-creates aspects of Gaelic culture through song, dance, drama and mime. There are several shows weekly May to September at 8.30pm and cost €18/15 per adult/child.

Shopping

Tralee Shopping Centre (Russell St) has a maze of shops for the avid spender.

Getting There & Away

Bus Éireann station (☎ 712 3566) is next to the train station. Daily buses connect Tralee with Dublin (€20, hourly; change at Limerick) via Listowel (€5.50, 30 minutes, seven daily). Bus No 40 runs daily to Waterford (€20, 5½ hours) via Killarney (€6.50, 35 minutes) and Cork (€14, five hours).

From the **train station** (☎ 712 3522) there's a service five times a day to Cork (€25, 2¼ hours) via Killarney (€7.50, 45 minutes). Trains to Dublin depart four times a day (€51.50, four hours). Change at Limerick Junction for Limerick (€21.50).

Getting Around

There's a taxi rank on The Mall, or try **Tralee Radio Taxis** (☎ 712 5451) or **Jackie Power Tours & Cabs** (☎ 712 9444). **Tralee Gas & Bicycle Supplies** (☎ 712 2018; Strand St) rents bikes.

AROUND TRALEE

Crag Cave

Crag Cave (☎ 714 1244; Castleisland; adult/child €6.50/4; ⏲ 10am-6.30pm Jul & Aug, 10am-6pm mid-Mar–Jun & Sep-Nov) was discovered only in 1983 when problems with water pollution led to a search for the source of the local river. Although the cave entrance had been known for years, the system had never been explored until then. The 4km-long cave opened to the public in 1989; admission is by a 30-minute guided tour.

To get there, take the N21 to Castleisland from Tralee. The cave is signposted to the left – from here it's only 4km along a minor road. In July and August there's at least one bus a day Monday to Saturday between Tralee and Castlemaine, which stops in Castleisland.

Ardfert

☎ 066 / pop 861

Ardfert (Ard Fhearta) lies about 7km north-west of Tralee on the Ballyheigue road. Most of **Ardfert Cathedral** (☎ 713 4711; adult/child €2/0.80; ⏲ 9.30am-6.30pm May-Sep & Oct bank holiday weekend), which is owned by Dúchas, dates back to the 13th century. Additions were made in the 15th and 17th centuries. Set into one of the interior walls is an effigy, said to be of St Brendan the Navigator, who was educated in Ardfert and founded a monastery here. There are ruins of two other churches – 12th-century Templenahoe and 15th-century Templenagriffin – in the grounds, and there's a small visitor centre with an exhibition on the cathedral's history. The continuing work on shoring up the cathedral will take many years and access to the interior is by guided tour only.

Turning right in front of the cathedral and going 500m down the road brings you to the extensive remains of a **Franciscan friary**, dating from the 13th century but with 15th-century cloisters.

In July and August, Bus Éireann No 274 between Tralee and Ballyheigue stops in Ardfert at least once daily.

LISTOWEL

☎ 068 / pop 3569

Listowel (Lios Tuathail), home of the Kerry butter factory, is 15km south of Tarbert, from where a ferry crosses the Shannon Estuary to County Clare. It's an attractive and tidy Georgian town with a handsome central square, a large park and the scenic River Feale running along its southern side. Listowel does not have many attractions, but the town itself is a pleasurable place in which to linger or to use as a regional base.

Orientation & Information

The Square is the main focus and at its centre is St John's Theatre and Arts Centre, formerly St John's Church, which houses the **tourist office** (☎ 22590; ⏲ 10am-1pm & 2-6pm Mon-Sat Jun-Sep, 9.30am-1pm & 2-6pm Mon-Fri Oct-Apr). Church and William Sts, north from The Square, are where you'll find most pubs and restaurants, while a short walk down Bridge Rd to the south will take you to the river and Childers Park.

There's a Bank of Ireland with an ATM and bureau de change in the Square. The post office is at the northern end of William St. Ó Hannán's Book Shop is opposite where William St joins Main St. A number of titles by local writers are also available from the

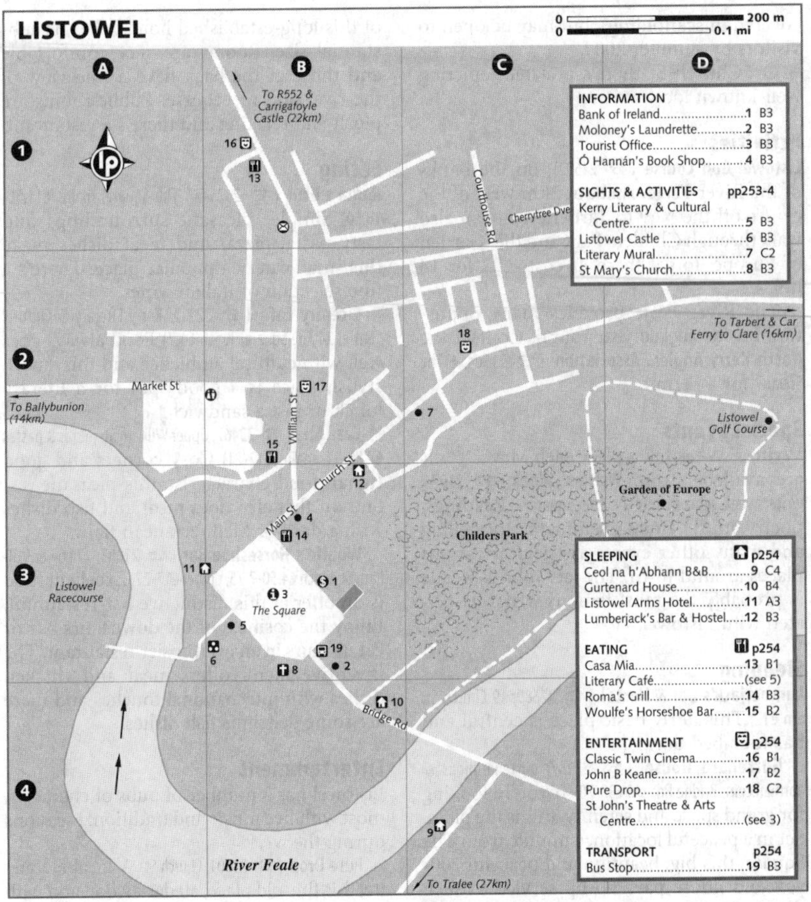

bookshop at the Kerry Literary & Cultural Centre (see below).

Moloney's Laundrette (☎ 21263; Bridge Rd) opens 9.30am to 6.30pm Monday to Saturday, and you'll find public toilets off Market St.

Sights

Listowel is home to the **Kerry Literary & Cultural Centre**. Inside is the **Writers' Exhibition** (☎ 22212; www.seanchai-klcc.com; 24 The Square; adult/child €5.20/3; 10am-6pm Apr-Sep). It consists of a visual presentation about historical and literary Northern Kerry and an exhibition on local writers. You get to listen to a *seanchaí* (shan-a-key; storyteller). Every Tuesday and Thursday in July and August the centre puts on a Seisiún-Cois na Feile – a **performance** (adult/child €7/4) of traditional song, music, dance and folklore.

St Mary's Church in The Square was built in 1829 in the neo-Gothic style. It has some lovely mosaic work over the altar and a vaulted roof with timber beams.

Listowel Castle, behind the Kerry Literary and Cultural Centre, was built in the 12th century and was once the stronghold of the Fitzmaurice family, the Anglo-Norman lords of Kerry. The Dúchas-owned castle was the last in Ireland to hold out against the Elizabethan attacks during the Desmond revolt. Now it's just a ruined tower and has been undergoing conservation work for some time (at the time of writing it was covered in scaffolding), but may be open to visitors by summer 2004.

On Church St there's a **mural** depicting well-known local writers.

Activities

Listowel Golf Course (☎ 21592), on the banks of the River Feale, is about 2km west of the centre off the N69 to Tarbert. You can also walk through Childers Park and the 'Garden of Europe' to get there. It costs €22 for 18 holes.

The River Feale provides many opportunities for **angling** year round. Contact the **North Kerry Anglers Association** (☎ 21504; 6 The Square) for a permit.

Special Events

Writers' Week takes place each May. Details are available from **Writers' Week** (☎ 21074; writersweek@eircom.net; 24 The Square). Readings, poetry, music, drama, seminars, storytelling and many other events are held at various places around town. The late John B Keane is probably the most famous writer associated with Listowel.

Sleeping

Lumberjack's Bar & Hostel (☎ 22689; 19 Church St; dm €12) This fairly basic place is central and has four-bed dorms.

Gurtenard House (☎ 21137; gurtenardhouse@hotmail.com; Bridge Rd; s/d €30/70) If you're looking for grand space and serenity, this is the place. Set in a peaceful location, a minute from The Square, this big, beautiful and peaceful 200-year-old house pays no lip service to such things as TVs in the bedroom. With such huge windows, who needs it?

Ceol na h'Abhann B&B (☎ 21345; knstack@eircom.net; Tralee Rd; s/d €50/60) A great location enhances the excellence of this picturesque, thatched-roof house on the banks of the River Feale. Elegant surroundings and impeccable rooms are backed up with a charming welcome. It's just across the bridge, downhill from the centre, on the N69 Tralee road.

Casa Mia (☎ 23467; Upper William St; s/d €50/70) Just on the edge of town beside the cinema, the rooms above this restaurant are a good size and have a hint of the Med about their fresh and colourful style.

Listowel Arms Hotel (☎ 21500; The Square; listowelhotel@ireland.com; s/d €65/110) Tucked away in a corner of The Square, the Georgian front of this long-established hotel belies its substantial size. Rooms are very comfortable and those at the back have a fine view of the river and racecourse. Public rooms are plush and relaxing and there's a restaurant.

Eating

Roma's Grill (☎ 23254; 1 The Square; mains €11.50-18.50) Simple, pleasant surroundings and tasty pasta, pizzas and meat dishes make this small eatery a popular place. There's a fine selection of Italian wines.

Literary Café (☎ 22212; Kerry Literary & Cultural Centre, 24 The Square; lunch €4-7) Food always goes well with cultural ambience and this smart, stylish place is a good spot for a literary lunch or just a sandwich.

Casa Mia (☎ 23467; Upper William St; pizzas & pastas €7.80-11, mains €12-21) Cosy corners and good Italian food characterise this pleasant restaurant that also does meat and fish dishes with a dash of Mediterranean flair.

Woulfe's Horseshoe Bar (☎ 21083; 17 Lower William St; lunch €4.50-7.75, dinner €17-22) Excellent food is on offer at this distinctive bar-restaurant. Enjoy the cosiness of the downstairs bar or eat upstairs in an even cosier restaurant. The inventive menu offers meat and chicken dishes with international touches and there are some delicious fish dishes.

Entertainment

Listowel has a number of pubs of character, most with live music and traditional sessions during the week.

Pure Drop (☎ 23001; Church St) A local favourite, this fine old place, all dark wood and with a long bar, has live music at the weekend.

John B Keane (37 William St) Owned by the late writer of the same name, this small, unassuming bar features pub theatre every Tuesday and Thursday at 9.15pm.

St John's Theatre & Arts Centre (☎ 22566; The Square) The centre hosts drama, music and dance events year round.

Getting There & Away

Buses run daily to Tralee (€5.50, 30 minutes, every two hours) and Limerick (€12.50, 1½ hours, four daily, one on Sunday). In July and August there are three buses daily to Ballybunion. Buses from Cork to the Cliffs of Moher and Galway also stop in Listowel three times a day (twice on Sunday). The bus stop is on the northern side of The Square.

AROUND LISTOWEL

Carrigafoyle Castle

A fine location above the Shannon Estuary adds to the romantic drama of this late medieval castle. Built in the channel between the mainland and Carrig Island, its name comes from Carragain Phoill (Rock of the Hole). It was probably built at the end of the 15th century by the O'Connors, who ruled most of northern Kerry. It was besieged by the English in 1580, was retaken by O'Connor but was finally destroyed by Cromwell's forces in 1649. You can climb the spiral staircase to the top for a good view of the estuary.

You really need a car to get here. The castle is 2km west of the village of Ballylongford (Bea Atha Longphuirb), which is rarely accessible by bus from Listowel.

Tarbert

pop 806

Tarbert is 16km north of Listowel on the N69. **Shannon Ferry Limited** (☎ 065-905 3124; one way/return bikes & foot passengers €3/5, cars €13/20, motorcyclists €7.50/10; 🕐 7.30am-9pm Mon-Sat, 9.30am-9.30pm Sun Apr-Sep, 7.30am-7.30pm Mon-Sat, 10.30am-7.30pm Sun Oct-Mar) runs a 20-minute car ferry between Tarbert and Killimer in County Clare. It's useful if you want to avoid travelling through congested Limerick city. The ferry dock is 2.2km west of Tarbert and is clearly signposted. You pay on board.

If you have a bit of time before you catch your ferry you should visit the **Tarbert Bridewell Jail & Courthouse** (☎ 065-36500; adult/child €5/2.50; 🕐 10am-6pm Apr-Oct). The exhibition features models and displays on the social and political conditions of the 19th century. From the jail you can take the **John F Leslie Woodland Walk**, a 3.8km walk along Tarbert Bay towards the mouth of the Shannon.

Bus Éireann No 13 runs to Tarbert from Tralee (€8, 55 minutes) via Listowel (15 minutes) once a day.

DINGLE PENINSULA

You step onto the Dingle Peninsula and things change. Kerry time becomes even slower and the world fills with shapely mountains and curving bays, long golden beaches and deep woods that lie like felt along the base of the rocky hills. There are still plenty of fellow visitors in summer, but you can find yourself happily alone on Dingle, where ring forts, beehive stone huts, burial chambers and standing stones punctuate a remarkable landscape.

Dingle is the main town. Ferries run from Dunquin to the now-unpopulated, and protected, Blasket Islands, off the tip of the peninsula. A touring route, the Slea Head Drive, heads west from Dingle to Slea Head, Dunquin, Ballyferriter, Brandon Creek and back to Dingle. You could drive it in a day but it's worth taking your time and staying overnight en route.

An unusual way to get around the peninsula is by horse-drawn caravan. This is only possible between March and September and prices start at about €350 per week. Ask at Dingle's tourist office for more details or phone David Slattery on ☎ 066-718 642.

ORGANISED TOURS

A number of Dingle-based companies operate tours of the peninsula for about €15 per person.

O'Connor's (☎ 087 248 8008) Bus tours of Slea Head depart from the tourist office in Dingle at 11am daily.

Moran's Slea Head Tours (☎ 066-915 1155, 087 275 3333; Moran's Garage) Buses leave from the pier in Dingle at 10am and 2pm daily.

Sciúird (☎ 066-51937; Fios Feasa) Sciúird has 2½-hour archaeological tours (€15 per person) departing from Dingle at 10.30am and 5pm daily, but only if the demand merits it in the winter months. These tours explore the many remarkable prehistoric sites and monastic ruins of the peninsula.

DINGLE

☎ 066 / pop 1629

The attractive port of Dingle (An Daingean) makes a good base for exploring the Dingle Peninsula. The town has a famous resident dolphin that has long boosted an already steady tourist trade. Dingle's still sizable fishing fleet gives the town a healthy down-to-earth edge and fishing quays lie happily side-by-side with water sports and tourism offices.

Information

The helpful, but busy in summer, **tourist office** (☎ 915 1188; The Pier; 🕐 9am-7pm Jun-Sep, 9.15am-1pm & 2.15-5pm Oct-May) has plenty of information on the entire peninsula.

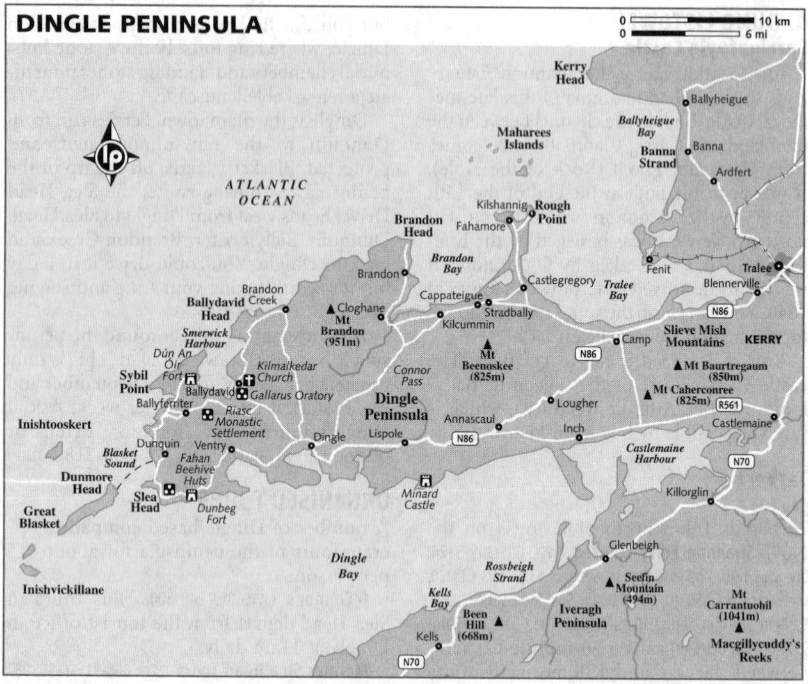

The banks on Main St have ATMs and bureaux de change. **Dingle Internet Café** (☎ 915 2478; Lower Main St; €2.60/30min, €5/hr; 🕒 10am-10pm May-Sep, 10am-6pm rest of year) also offers cheap rate international calls.

Fungie the Dolphin

In the winter of 1984 Dingle fishing crews began to notice a solitary bottlenose dolphin that followed their vessels, jumped about in the water and sometimes leapt over smaller boats. Fungie the dolphin is now an international celebrity. Legend has it that no-one thought of running trips until a visiting American offered to pay a boatman to take him out to see Fungie. Free enterprise leapt the Atlantic faster than Fungie ever could.

Now boats leave the pier daily year round for a one-hour dolphin-spotting trip; call **Dingle Boatmen's Association** (☎ 915 2626; adult/child €10/5). It's free if Fungie doesn't show, but he usually does. The association also runs a daily two-hour boat trip, leaving at 8am, for those who want to **swim with Fungie** (adult/child €10/5 plus €20 to hire wetsuit) but you need to book ahead. Wetsuits and snorkelling gear can also be hired from **Flannery's** (☎ 915 1967; Cooleen) and from **Dingle Marine & Leisure Centre** (☎ 915 1066; Strand St).

Dingle Oceanworld

Opposite Dingle Harbour, this **aquarium** (☎ 915 2111; Dingle Harbour; adult/child €8/5; 🕒 10am-8.30pm Jul & Aug, 10am-6pm May, Jun & Sep, 10am-5pm Oct-May) displays many of the types of local sea fish as they glide effortlessly in large tanks. There's a walk-through tunnel, a touch pool and a display of tropical fish and corals to add to what is a pricey experience. But if you want to see the kind of fish you eat in gourmet restaurants, now's your chance.

Other Sights

Next to St Mary's Church in Green St is the **Trinity Tree**, an unusual three-trunked tree, representing the Holy Trinity, which has been carved with biblical characters. It looks like something out of a fairy tale.

Every second weekend in August the **Dingle Races** bring crowds from far and wide. The racetrack is opposite Ballintaggart Hostel, about 1.6km east of town on the N86.

The **Dingle Regatta**, a race in the harbour in traditional Irish *currach* canoes, is held at the end of August.

Activities

Hidden Ireland Tours (www.hiddenirelandtours.com) provides organised **walking** tours of the Dingle Peninsula.

Snorkelling and **scuba diving** in Dingle Bay and around the Blasket Islands can be arranged at **Dingle Marina Diving Centre** (☎ 915 2422) on the waterfront, near the harbour.

Ask at the tourist office for details of **sea fishing** trips, or call ☎ 915 1163. **Dingle Marine & Leisure Centre** (☎ 915 1066; Strand St) hires out fishing tackle. A full day's fishing costs about €65.

Horse riding can be arranged through **Mountain Man** (☎ 915 2400; Strand St). **Long's Trekking Centre** (☎ 915 9034) in Ventry has guided horse rides of the area costing €19 per hour.

Sleeping

BUDGET

Ballintaggart Hostel (☎ 915 1454; www.dingleaccommodation.com; Racecourse Rd; tent site per person €6.50, dm/d €13/46; mid-Mar–Oct) A popular place, this old hunting lodge dates from 1703. It has excellent rooms and a great atmosphere. Out back there's a cobbled yard where there are giant soup urns, used when the building was a soup kitchen during the Famine years. The hostel is 1.6km east of Dingle on the N86. There's a free shuttle service to/from town, plus coin-operated Internet access.

Lovett's (☎ 915 1903; Cooleen; dm/d €12.50/32) This is a small place in a family home and rooms are quite small, but it's well kept and there's a friendly attitude. It's also handy for town, but in a quiet location.

Ocean View B&B (☎ 915 1659; 133 The Wood; s/d €25/80) Though this place has no en-suite rooms, it's very good value and rooms at the back have pleasant views of the harbour.

Sráid Eoin House (☎ 915 1409; sraideoinhouse@hotmail.com; John St; s & d €32; mid-May–mid-Sep) A quiet location and a quiet house, with comfortable rooms that have a home-like atmosphere. It's close enough to the centre but feels comfortably out of town.

MID-RANGE

Dingle has plenty of mid-range B&Bs, but quite a few charge a bit too much for what has become, in a few cases, a fairly indifferent service. There are, however, several 1st-class places.

Kirrary (☎ 915 1606; Avondale; collinskirrary@eircom.net; s/d €45/70) You'll get plenty of chat and info at this cheerful place. Rooms are a reasonable size and breakfasts are hefty. Bike hire is available, and the family runs the three-hour archaeological tours to Slea Head (see p255).

Holy Ground (☎ 915 1937; arches@eircom.net; s/d €40/70) There are neat, pleasant rooms at this modern house, which is just over the wall from Kirrary and run by members of the same family.

Captain's House (☎ 915 1531; homepage.eircom.net/-captigh/; The Mall; s/d €55/90; mid-Mar–mid-Nov) An enviable streamside garden and beautiful interior furnishings make this handsome house a great choice.

Pax House (☎ 915 1518; fax 915 1650; Upper John St; s & d €60) From its highly individual décor, all bold colours and bright paintings, to the outstanding views over the estuary – you can catch Fungie in action from the fabulous balcony – Pax House is an absolute treat. It's just under 1km from the centre of town.

Benner's Hotel (☎ 915 1638; www.dinglebenner.com; Lower Main St; s/d €127/202) Prices drop by 20% in spring and autumn and by nearly half in winter at this long-established hotel, where old-fashioned style and modern amenities make a fine combination.

Eating

Dingle rings the changes on eating out, from no-nonsense cafés to some of the best restaurants in Kerry. For self-catering there's a big supermarket in Holyground, next to Greany's restaurant. The garage just past the big roundabout on the eastern exit from town has a shop and sandwich bar.

BUDGET

Café Po'oka (☎ 915 9773; Upper Main St; snacks €3.20-7; 10am-6pm May-Oct, 10.30am-5pm Nov-Apr) The place to meet the whole gamut of locals, with a fair sprinkling of Dingle's creative crowd, this cheerful, no-frills café dishes up all-day breakfasts, soup, sandwiches, omelettes and salads and is strongly vegetarian oriented.

An Café Liteártha (☎ 915 2204; Dykegate Lane; snacks €3-5; 9am-6pm) Prices don't change much at this delightful place where you can

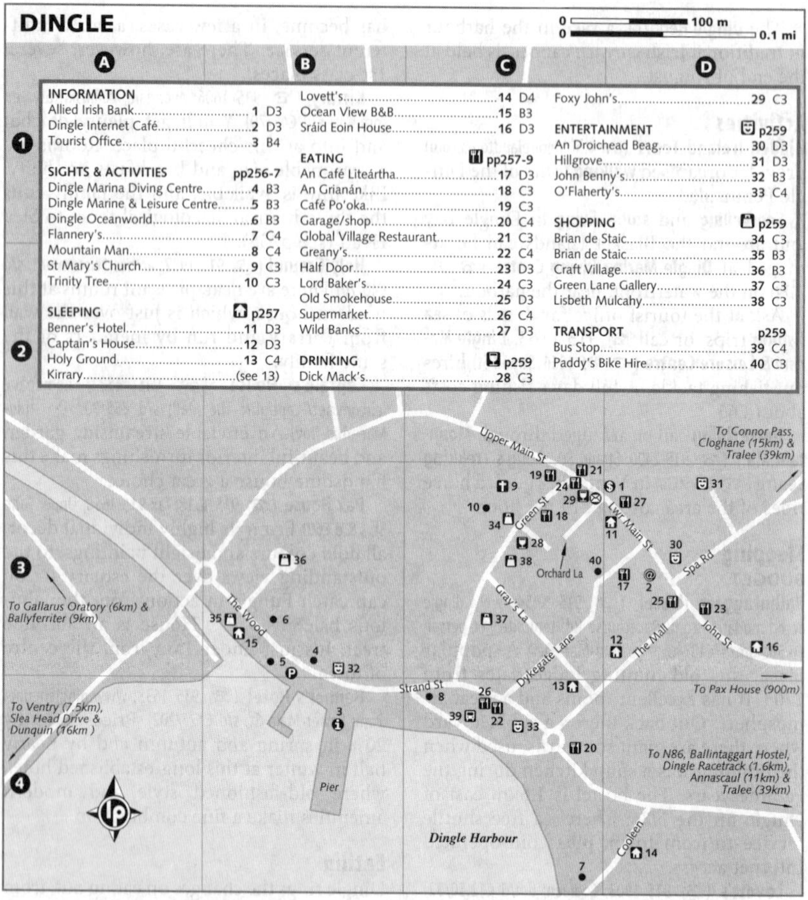

relax at the back of an excellent bookshop engulfed in the spirit of literary Dingle.

John Benny's (☎ 915 1215; Strand St; snacks €3-8, mains €8.25-10; 🕑 12.30-9.30pm) Benny's pub down on busy Strand St is a lively, popular place and a good bet for soup, chowder and sandwiches, or heftier dishes such as Irish stew or bacon and cabbage, as well as fish. There's good music here too (see opposite).

Greany's (☎ 915 0924; Holyground; lunch €5.60-13.50; 🕑 noon-9pm Fri-Wed) Good value, unpretentious meals, including chicken and mushroom pie, lasagne and a tasty range of vegetarian dishes, are on offer at this licensed restaurant complete with its exposed stone walls, modern décor and cheerful service.

An Grianán (☎ 915 1910; Green St; snacks €3-4) Wholefood and organic is the style at this shop where you can select fillings for tasty takeaway sandwiches.

MID-RANGE

Global Village Restaurant (☎ 915 2325; Main St; mains €13-20; 🕑 6-10pm) The owner-chef of this excellent restaurant is well travelled, and it shows in the mix of style, from modern European to Pacific Rim cuisine and adventurous dishes that include such specialities as roast skate in a tomato, saffron and cumin broth. Vegetarians are well catered for.

Wild Banks (☎ 915 2888; Lower Main St; mains €14.60-24; 🕑 6-9.30pm) There's imaginative modern Irish cuisine at this attractive res-

COUNTY KERRY

taurant that has a good choice of meat and fish dishes as well as such vegetarian delights as spinach and cheese roulade in filo pastry with tomato and red pepper sauce (€14.60).

Half Door (☎ 915 1600; John St; mains €23-35, set dinner €35; 6-10pm Mon-Sat) You'll pay for the privilege at this outstanding seafood restaurant where fish and shellfish are superbly presented. But spoil yourself and go for lobster, or Cromane mussels in a garlic and wine sauce, or the seafood platter, hot or cold. There are meat and duck dishes too and the surroundings are suitably cosy.

Old Smokehouse (☎ 915 1061; cnr Main St & The Mall; lunch €5.50-9.50, dinner €14.50-20; noon-10pm) An attractive riverside location and unfancy surroundings make this small restaurant a local favourite. Lunch can be hefty sandwiches or bangers and mash, while dinner offers traditional Irish meat and fish dishes with a vegetarian option.

Lord Baker's (☎ 915 1277; Lower Main St; bar menu €4-15.20, mains €15.90-24; 12.30-9.45pm Fri-Wed) A Dingle institution, established as a pub in 1890 by local worthy 'Lord Baker', this big bar-restaurant has an excellent choice of meat and fish dishes. The front bar has a cheerful turf fire and serves up great seafood with a couple of meat and poultry dishes thrown in. The restaurant dishes range from brill, monkfish and salmon to lobster, with Kerry lamb and steak as well.

Drinking

Foxy John's (☎ 915 1316; Main St) It's hardware counter to the right, drink to the left in this wonderful old pub, where even the characters on tap are persuasive.

Dick Mack's (☎ 915 1960; Green St) Celebrity status declares itself outside Dick Mack's with the names of famous patrons engraved on the pavement for the rest of us to walk over. Dolly Parton, Charlie Haughey, Robert Mitchum, Julia Roberts and the Hothouse Flowers are all there. Paul Simon merits a stone stool. Inside, the old shoe-repair section of the pub now makes leather belts.

Entertainment

John Benny's (☎ 915 1215; Strand St) Everything from lively trad and set dancing to blues and contemporary is on offer from 9.30pm Monday, Wednesday, Friday and Saturday at Benny's. There's good food here too (see opposite).

O'Flaherty's (☎ 915 1983; Strand St) Summer nights trad sessions are popular at this big spacious bar and sessions can spark up at any time of the year.

An Droichead Beag (Small Bridge Bar; ☎ 915 1723; Lower Main St) Traditional music kicks off at 9.30pm nightly at this pub by the bridge.

Hillgrove (☎ 915 1131; Off Spa Rd) There's a break from Dingle traditional at the Hillgrove, where weekend nights feature chart sounds. Don't expect a blitz.

Shopping

Brian de Staic (☎ 915 1298; www.iol.ie/brian-de-staic; The Wood) Exquisite modern Celtic work by this local jewellery designer reflects the whole gamut of tradition and culture. The company also has a shop on Green St.

Lisbeth Mulcahy (☎ 915 1688; Green St) An outstanding collection of scarves, rugs and wall hangings are created on a 150-year-old loom by this fine designer. Also sold here are superb ceramics by her husband, who has a workshop west of Dingle (see p264).

Green Lane Gallery (☎ 915 2018; Green St) There's a good choice of paintings and sculpture, many by local artists, at this little gallery.

Craft Village (The Wood) The Craft Village is a group of multiworkshops, in shades of lemon, lilac and purple poster paint, that turn out linen, pottery, woodwork, leatherwear and clothes.

Getting There & Away

Bus Éireann (☎ 712 3566) buses stop outside the car park behind the SuperValu store. There are five buses Monday to Saturday between Dingle and Tralee and three on Sunday (€8.60). At least five buses a day Monday to Saturday depart Killarney for Dingle via Tralee (€10.60).

Three buses run Monday and Thursday only between Dingle, Ventry, Ballferriter and Dunquin.

Getting Around

Dingle is easily navigated on foot. For a taxi call **Dingle Co-op Cabs** (☎ 915 1000), which can also give private tours of the peninsula.

There are several bike rental places, including **Paddy's Bike Hire** (☎ 915 2311; Dykegate St), which charges €8/40 per day/week, and **Foxy John's** (☎ 915 1316; Main St), charging €10/45 per day/week.

NORTHSIDE OF THE PENINSULA

☎ 066

There are two routes from Tralee to Dingle, though they both follow the same road out of Tralee past the Blennerville Windmill. Near the village of Camp a right fork heads off to the Connor Pass, while the N86 via Annascaul takes you to Dingle quicker. The Connor Pass route is much more beautiful and panoramic. At Kilcummin a road to the west heads to the relatively little-visited villages of Cloghane and Brandon and on to Brandon Point, with fine views of Brandon Bay.

Castlegregory

pop 870

A small, rather scattered village, Castlegregory (Caislean an Ghriare) once rivalled Tralee as a busy local centre. A sand-strewn road heads north from the village along a broad spit of land between Tralee Bay and Brandon Bay to Rough Point. It's an intriguing place, flat, breezy and with terrific views across the water to Mt Brandon. Caravans and bungalows pepper the grassy duneland and the flanking beaches are excellent venues for wind-sailing and surfing, although sets don't get too awesome. The Brandon Bay side is good for long boards and beginners, especially when there's a northerly swell. Wave-sailing is big here and there are major competitions staged at prime points with names such as Dumps and Mosies. Kite-surfing is also beginning to catch on.

Jamie Knox Watersports (☎ 713 9411; www.jamieknox.com; The Maharees) covers just about every aspect of surf-related sports. It's halfway along the peninsula.

Beyond Rough Point are the **Maharees Islands**. Illauntannig is the largest of these and is the site of a 6th-century monastery. Remains of the settlement include a stone cross, a church and beehive huts. Two small adjoining islands can be reached by foot from Illauntannig at low tide, but make sure you know exactly what the tide is doing. The islands are privately owned and were used to graze cows, but trips (taking about 10 minutes) can be arranged through Castle House, or Harbour House in conjunction with a **scuba diving** trip (for both see below). These waters have great underwater visibility and offer some of the best diving you're likely to get anywhere.

SLEEPING & EATING

Anchor Caravan Park (☎ 713 9157; www.caravanparksireland.net; Castlegregory; tent & 2 people €12; Easter-Sep) Wooded surroundings make this a sheltered place that has very good, well-kept facilities. The park is on the R560 just east of Castlegregory.

Castle House (☎ 713 9183; www.caisleanti.com; s/d €40/60; P) Located at the northern edge of Castlegregory at the start of the road along the Rough Point peninsula, this handsome house has fine, big rooms. You can pop out the back and down a track to the beach in minutes. Trips to the Maharees Islands can be arranged.

Harbour House (☎ 713 9292; dive@iol.ie; Scraggane Pier, near Kilshannig; s/d €42/64; P) This busy place is in a great position right at the end of the peninsula 5km north of Castlegregory, overlooking the Maharees Islands. It's a popular diving centre and has excellent facilities including an indoor pool and a state-of-the-art fitness room. It provides diving instruction (PADI) and takes divers to the waters around the Maharees.

Spillane's (☎ 713 9125; Maharees; bar meals €4.20-11.50, mains €10.50-21; 1-9.30pm) Very popular on weekends and high season (closed for food November to mid-March), Spillane's churns the food out without losing quality. The steaks are huge and the fish is excellent. This is where the wind-sailing crew blast out on 'chocolate milkshake'. It's good for you.

GETTING THERE & AWAY

A year-round bus service leaves Tralee for Castlegregory on Friday only at 8.55am and 2pm and returns at 10.35am only. In July and early August there are also two services daily on Wednesday, leaving Tralee at 10.20am and 4.15pm, and returning at 11.05am and 5pm. There's no bus service along the peninsula.

Cloghane

pop 267

Cloghane (An Clochán), on the southwestern edge of Brandon Bay, is a marvellous 'stop the world and get off' place. You'll leave with reluctance. There's a fine beach and a fascinating foreshore, and the road ends at far Brandon Point. There's terrific coastal and mountain walking and the best way up Mt Brandon starts from here (see p261).

Cloghane has an **information centre** (☎ 713 8277; 🕐 daily May-Sep, Sat & Sun rest of year) at the southern entrance to the village where you can buy the excellent *Cloghane and Brandon Walking Guide* (€3.80) with details of all the trails you'll see signposted. Those interested in the region's many archaeological sites should ask about guided walks or buy the equally excellent *Loch a'Dúin Archaeological and Nature Trail* (€3.80).

Immediately opposite the information centre, **St Brendan's Church** has a stained-glass window showing the Gallarus Oratory and Ardfert Cathedral.

CLIMBING MT BRANDON

At 951m, **Mt Brandon** (Cnoc Bhréannain) is Ireland's second-highest mountain. It's made up of a beautiful series of high summits that lie along the edge of a spectacular series of east-facing cliffs and steep ridges above a rocky lake-filled valley. An ascent of the mountain is a serious all-day trip. You should be well-equipped and experienced in the use of a map (Ordnance Survey Map No 70) and compass. Allow at least six to seven hours there and back.

A popular route from the west is the Saint's Rd, which starts officially at Kilmalkedar Church (see p263) but can be more easily started at OS ref 435095, 1km east of the hamlet of An Baile Breac, itself 4km northeast of Kilmalkedar. This is a straightforward 6km slog there and back and is fairly well marked, although you'll definitely need good compass work in mist.

The classic way up Mt Brandon starts from Faha road-end (OS ref 493120) above Cloghane. (You can drive or cycle there, although it's a steep option for bikes. If you walk this road section it adds a couple of hours onto the six-hour there-and-back climb from Faha.) To reach Faha take the turn left, signposted 'Mt Brandon', about 300m northeast of Cloghane and follow the narrow lane to a T-junction. Go left here until you reach a car parking area at the road-end (2km from Cloghane). From here the route there and back to the summit is a fairly tough 7km on foot.

Walk left up the track above the car park and follow the obvious path onto the open mountain and past a grotto. The rocky path is very clear. Occasional guide poles mark the way along a rising grassy ridge with a magnificent line of cliffs and ridges ahead. The path contours around rocky slopes and then descends into the glaciated wilderness at the valley head, from where it winds its way between great boulders and slabs. Far too many yellow painted arrows on the rocks point the way. Some guidance is sensible, but any more yellow paint and this beautiful wilderness will resemble a no-parking zone.

When the back wall is reached the path zigzags very steeply to the rim of the great cliffs. Turn left at the top and head for the summit of Mt Brandon, marked by a trig point, a wooden cross and the remains of Teampaillin Breanainn (St Brendan's Oratory). The views in clear weather from the summit are beyond words. The edge of the cliffs is sudden, so care should be taken at all times. You can continue along the edge of the cliffs to the subsidiary summits and to Brandon Peak 2km south, but this will add a couple of hours. Retracing your way down requires care and concentration on the initial steep zigzags. The rest of the way back to Faha is freewheeling.

CONNOR PASS & AROUND

At 456m, the **Connor (or Conor) Pass** is the highest in Ireland and offers spectacular views of Dingle Harbour to the south and Mt Brandon to the north. On a foggy day you'll see nothing but the road just in front of you. There's a car park near the summit. Take the path up behind it to see the peninsula spread out below you.

SLEEPING & EATING

Mount Brandon Hostel (☎ 713 8299; www.mountbrandonhostel.com; dm/d €16/36) Right at the heart of Cloghane, this smart little place has delightful rooms and a terrific four-person apartment (€350 per week June to September, €300 rest of year). There's also a café.

Benagh (☎ 713 8142; mcmorran@eircom.net; r €28; P) There's a very fair deal for singles at this friendly and superbly located house overlooking Brandon Bay. You can watch the mud banks melt into the tide then reappear six hours later. Guided walks can be arranged from here and the owners have great knowledge of local archaeology and ecology.

O'Connors Guesthouse (☎ 713 8113; oconnorsguesthouse@eircom.net; Cloghane; tent site per person €6, s/d €35/52; meals €13-17; P) A classic village pub and B&B, this place has fresh, bright rooms.

Camping is in a field behind the pub. You can get an evening meal between 7pm and 8pm although you should book.

Crutch's Hillville House Hotel (☎ 713 8118; macshome@iol.ie; Connor Pass Rd; s/d €50/100 incl breakfast; mains €17.50-23.50; Ⓟ) An experience in itself, this handsome old house stands in glorious isolation amid trees 6km from Cloghane on the road to Castlegregory. There's a cheerful welcome and a sense of gracious, but easy living amid bright and airy rooms. The restaurant offers good traditional Irish fare with subtle international touches.

GETTING THERE & AWAY

On Fridays only, bus No 273 leaves Tralee at 8.55am and 2pm for Cloghane (1¼ hours). Returning, it leaves at 10.05am and 3.10pm.

TRALEE TO DINGLE VIA ANNASCAUL

For drivers this route has little to recommend it other than being faster than the Connor Pass route. By bike it's less demanding. On foot the journey constitutes the first three days of the Dingle Way.

The main reason to pause in Annascaul (Abhainn an Scáil), also spelled Anascaul, is to visit the **South Pole Inn** (☎ 066-915 7388; Main St; bar meals €7.50-11; 🕑 noon-8pm Easter-Sep) by the river, on your way to or from Dingle. It commemorates villager Tom Crean (see below), who went to the South Pole with Robert Falcon Scott and Ernest Shackleton. You can study the memorabilia and read up on his expeditions while tucking into your lunch. The pub has traditional music on Wednesday, Friday, Saturday and Sunday nights.

KILLARNEY TO DINGLE VIA CASTLEMAINE

☎ 066

The quickest route between Killarney and Dingle is by way of Killorglin and Castlemaine. At Castlemaine (Caisleán na Mainge; birthplace of the Australian outlaw, the Wild Colonial Boy) the R561 heads west to Dingle, soon meeting the coast and passing Inch on the way to joining the main Tralee road to Dingle. Apart from the odd pub or two there's little provision for food, so bring your own.

At least three Bus Éireann buses between Tralee and Dingle stop at Lispole, Annascaul and Inch daily. Seven buses between Tralee and Killorglin stop at Castlemaine from Monday to Saturday, with four buses on Sunday.

Mt Caherconree

About 11km west of Castlemaine is the turn-off for **Mt Caherconree**, one of the higher mountains on the peninsula at 825m. The road ends at Camp on the northern side of the peninsula; about 4km along this road coming from the south is an Iron Age promontory fort that may have been built by Cúror MacDáine, king of Munster. Whichever direction you come, there are

TOM CREAN – ANTARCTIC HERO

County Kildare may boast the great polar explorer Ernest Shackleton as a native son, but Kerry has its own polar hero, Tom Crean, who was a key member of several early Antarctic expeditions.

Crean (1877–1938) came from Annascaul on the Dingle Peninsula. At age 15 he signed up with the British Navy and in later life was a member of three of the four British Antarctic expeditions in the vessels *Discovery* (1901–04), *Terra Nova* (1910–13) and *Endurance* (1914–16).

Both Scott and Shackleton saw Tom Crean as a crucial member of their expeditions and Shackleton's letters to Crean reflect immense warmth and liking for the Kerryman, whose physical and mental strengths were outstanding. When the *Endurance* was trapped and crushed in ice and the crew sailed in small boats to Elephant Island, Shackleton chose Crean as one of the small crew that continued on the epic 800-mile sea voyage from Elephant Island to South Georgia to bring help to their stranded companions.

Tom Crean also served throughout WWI and retired in 1920. Shackleton wanted Crean to accompany him on his final expedition on the *Quest* in 1921, but he declined. He had spent more time in Antarctica than either Scott or Shackleton. He opened his pub, The South Pole, at Annascaul, married and had three daughters. Crean's later life was quiet and unassuming, like the man himself, but his remarkable achievements have become recognised increasingly both at home and abroad. His name lives on in the title of the Crean Glacier on South Georgia and Mt Crean in Victoria Land.

stunning views from this narrow, exposed and high (even a little scary) road that demands concentration from drivers; stop driving if you want to admire the views.

Inch

The main attraction at Inch (Inse) is the 6km-long **sand spit** that runs into Dingle Bay – a location for the archetypal leprechaunish film *Ryan's Daughter* and the film of the more muscular *Playboy of the Western World*. The sand dunes once sheltered Stone Age and Iron Age settlements.

Cars are allowed on the beach, but be very careful because vehicles regularly get stuck in the wet sand. This is a hot surfing beach. It faces west and waves average 1m to 3m. **Sammy's Store** (☎ 915 8118), at the car park for the beach, has some tourist information, foodstuffs and refreshments.

Lispole

The road from Inch to tiny Lispole (Lios Póil) passes through Annascaul.

If you have time you might want to stop at the **Freshwater Experience** (☎ 915 1042; Lispole; adult/child €4/3; 9.30am-6pm Mon-Sat, noon-6pm Sun Jun-Aug, 9.30am-4.30pm Mon-Fri May & Sep). On the N86, this is a wildfowl and otter sanctuary with an archaeological park featuring models of an ancient ogham stone, a stone circle, a wedge tomb and a *crannóg* (artificial island). Youngsters will enjoy it.

Camping is possible in the field opposite Inch Beach (€6 for a tent and two people). Ask at Sammy's Store (see above).

Caherbla House (☎ 915 8120; caherbla@eircom.net; Inch; s/d €26/52; P) Located just along the road from Inch on the way to Castlemaine, this is another B&B that deserves an award for fair dealing with singles as well as doubles. It offers good value in a modern house with a nice, friendly welcome and views to go with it. It's also on the Dingle Way walking route.

Phoenix Vegetarian Restaurant & Accommodation (☎ 976 6284; www.kerryweb.ie/thepheonix; Shanahill East, Castlemaine; tent site per person €6 incl shower, dm €12.50, d with/without bathroom €50/40; breakfast €10, lunch €4-7.50, dinner mains €7.50-16.50; P ☒) The ultimate alternative is this creative place with its own organic garden and marvellous features. There's always something, or someone, of interest around and there's an international throughput of travellers to enhance the laid-back atmosphere. It's about 6km west of Castlemaine on the R561. The owners will pick you up from Castlemaine by prior arrangement. Things are strictly vegetarian, and vegans are catered for too. If you wish to eat at the café only, it's advisable to book.

WEST OF DINGLE

☎ 066

The area west of Dingle takes in the Slea Head Drive – a beautiful stretch of road – and has the greatest concentration of ancient sites in Kerry, if not in the whole of Ireland. To do the sites justice you should use one of the specialist guides on sale in the An Café Liteártha café/bookshop or the tourist office in Dingle town (see p255). The sites listed here are among the most interesting and easiest to find.

This part of the peninsula is a Gaeltacht, or Irish-speaking, area. The landscape is dramatic, and can be even more so in shifting mist, although full-on sea fog obliterates everything – just let all that bracing sea air wash over you. There are stunning views of the Blasket Islands from Slea Head. The sandy beach nearby, Coumenole, is lovely to walk along but, like most in the area, is treacherous for swimming.

Orientation

If you cross the bridge west of Dingle and take the first right, where there's a clutter of signs (mostly in Gaelic), you come to a Y-junction after 5km. To the right are Kilmalkedar Church and Brandon Creek, from where you could return to Dingle on a circular route. To the left are the Gallarus Oratory and the Riasc site, from which you can reach Ballyferriter and Dunquin. This road continues down the coast and back to Dingle. Continuing straight on after the bridge will take you to Slea Head and Dunbeg Fort.

Kilmalkedar Church

This 12th-century **church** was once part of a complex of religious buildings. The characteristic Romanesque doorway has a tympanum with a head on one side and a mythical beast on the other. There is an ogham stone, pierced by a hole, in the grounds as well as a very early sundial. About 50m away is a two-storey building known as **St Brendan's House**, which is believed to have been the residence of the medieval clergy. The road connecting these two ruins is the beginning of the **Saint's Rd**, the traditional approach to Mt Brandon (see p261). The church is 1.7km southeast of Murreagh village on the R559 to Dingle.

Gallarus Oratory

Simple but stunning, this superb dry-stone **oratory** is in perfect condition, apart from a slight sagging in the roof, and has withstood the assault of the elements for some 1200 years. Traces of mortar suggest that the interior and exterior walls may have been plastered. Shaped like an upturned boat, it has a doorway on the western side and a small round-headed window on the eastern side. Inside the doorway are two projecting stones with holes that once supported the door.

The oratory is signposted off the R559 about 3km northeast of Ballyferriter. It's 500m down the road on the left. Bus No 275 leaves Dingle at 9am and drops off at Gallarus 10 minutes later on Tuesday and Friday only. From Gallarus it picks up for Dingle at 1.25pm and 6.30pm. If you arrive by car, be warned that the Gallarus Visitor Centre is a private venture. It charges €2.50 per person, for parking, for the privilege of an audiovisual presentation and for then passing through its doors to walk up to the oratory. Access to the oratory is in fact free. The lane that runs inland from the main road leads in about 200m to a limited parking space from where a well-tended right-of-way leads to the oratory. Congestion from vehicles is an understandable problem, so if drivers can park sensibly somewhere else and then walk to the oratory, they'll feel even better.

Riasc Monastic Settlement

The remains of this 5th- or 6th-century **monastic settlement** are quietly impressive and rather haunting. Excavations have revealed, among other finds, the foundations of an oratory first built with wood and later stone, a kiln for drying corn and a cemetery. Most interesting is a pillar with beautiful Celtic designs. The ruins are signposted along a narrow lane off the R559, 1.5km east of Ballyferriter.

Ballyferriter

Continue towards Slea Head and you'll come to the small village of Ballyferriter (Baile an Fheirtearaigh), named after Piaras Ferriter, a poet and soldier who emerged as a local leader in the 1641 rebellion and was the last Kerry commander to submit to Cromwell's army.

There is the small **Dingle Peninsula Museum** (Músaem Chorca Dhuibhne; ☎ 915 6333; adult/child €2.50/1.50; ⏲ 9.30am-5pm Easter-Sep, by appointment rest of year). It has displays on the ecology and geology of the Dingle Peninsula.

Just as you enter Ballyferriter from the east, a side road signposted 'Cuan Ard na Caithne/Smethwick Harbour' will take you to a fine little beach about 1km from the main road.

Just north of Ballyferriter is **Dún an Óir Fort** (Fort of Gold), the scene of a hideous massacre during the 1580 Irish rebellion against English rule. The fort was held by Sir James Fitzmaurice, who commanded an international brigade of Italians, Spaniards and Basques. On 7 November, English troops under Lord Grey attacked the fort and within three days the defenders surrendered. 'Then putt I in certeyn bandes who streight fell to execution. There were 600 slayne,' said the poet Edmund Spenser, who was secretary to Lord Grey and patently not in lyrical mood at the time.

You can walk to the fort along the beach from Ballyferriter (1.5km). To reach it by road head west from Ballyferriter and after 1km turn right at a brown sign to Dún an Óir Ostán (Hotel). After a further 1.3km, take the right fork at a Y-junction and go straight on, ignoring side tracks, until you come to a T-junction in another 1.4km. Turn right for another 1.3km, then right again and in about 300m you'll see a signpost to the fort. You can drive down the track, which was lavishly surfaced in the 1980s to accommodate the limousine of the then President of Ireland, Charles Haughey, who officially opened the car park at the track's end. There's a handsome memorial sculpture by Cliodna Cussen here. The fort has been much eroded, but it's an atmospheric place.

Faoileán Pottery Studio (☎ 915 6294; Ballyferriter West) is about 1.5km west of Ballyferriter. You can buy an unfired pot here, paint it as you wish and collect it later after firing. Ask here about knowledgeable taxi tours of sights in the area.

One of the most interesting potteries on the peninsula is **Louis Mulcahy Pottery** (☎ 915 6229; Clogher, Ballyferriter; ⏲ 10am-5.30pm Mon-Sat,

11am-5.30pm Sun). Some pieces are as tall as the potter himself and have been sold or given to such people as Bill Clinton and the Pope. Purchases can be delivered overseas from the shop. The pottery is on the road just north of Dunquin.

Dunquin

If Ballyferriter is small, it does at least have a centre, unlike scattered Dunquin (Dún Chaion), from where you catch a boat to the Blasket Islands. It's on the Slea Head Drive.

The superb **Blasket Centre** (Ionad an Bhlascaoid Mhóir; ☎ 915 6444; Dunquin; adult/child €3.10/1.20; ⌚ 10am-7pm Jul & Aug, 10am-6pm Easter–Jun & Sep-Oct) is a brilliant example of how architecture and design can do justice to an awesome subject. This Dúchas- operated centre celebrates the lost lifestyle of the Blasket Islanders, and the Irish language and culture. The building cost €5 million to build, most of it provided by the EU. The interiors are stunning; features replicate with great subtlety and drama a sense of sea and sky and the captivating uniqueness of the Blaskets. There's a café with Blasket Island views, and a small bookshop. Last admission is 45 minutes before closing.

Slea Head & Dunmore Head

Slea Head offers some of the Dingle Peninsula's best views, good walks and fine beaches, and is thoroughly popular with coach parties.

Dunmore Head is the most westerly point on the Irish mainland and the site of the wreckage in 1588 of two Spanish Armada ships.

The road between Dunquin and Slea Head is dotted with **beehive huts**, **forts**, **inscribed stones** and **church sites**. The **Fahan huts** are accessible from two points and you'll see signs pointing the way from the road.

Prehistoric **Dunbeg Fort**, on a cliff-top promontory, has a sheer drop to the Atlantic and four outer walls of stone. Inside are the remains of a house and a beehive hut as well as an underground passage. The fort is 8km south of Dunquin on the R559. On the inland side of the road is a car park and the **Stone House Restaurant** (☎ 915 9970; lunch €3.80-8, dinner mains €14.50-17.50), a replica of the Gallarus Oratory style offering a pleasant choice of sandwiches or more substantial meat, chicken and fish dishes as well as vegetarian options.

To visit the sights mentioned above you'll be charged a steep €2; unavoidable during the summer when there are attended kiosks. Comfort yourself with the thought that the original occupants of the ancient sites would probably have charged as well.

Ventry

pop 460

The small village of Ventry (Ceann Trá) is next to a wide sandy bay. Between Ventry and Dunbeg Fort, on the R559, is the **Celtic & Prehistoric Museum** (☎ 915 9941; adult/child €4/2.70; ⌚ 10am-5pm Apr-Sep). It has a collection of fossils including a woolly mammoth skull with 3m tusks, and artefacts from the Bronze Age, Celtic and Viking periods. Phone for opening hours out of season.

Activities

Ceann Sibéal Golf Club (☎ 915 6255; Ballyferriter) is a wild and windy links course and costs €45 plus €15.50 club hire from June to September (€35 the rest of the year). It's signposted from the R559.

Irish language courses are available at **An Portán B&B** (☎ 915 6212; www.anportan.com), in Dunquin (see below), which offers course, accommodation and food packages. Courses for adults only cost from €30 per day with accommodation extra.

You could also try **Oidhreacht Chorca Dhuibhne** (☎ 915 6100) in Ballyferriter for language courses.

Sleeping

Free camping is possible near Ferriter's Cove but there are no facilities.

Oratory House Camping (Campaíl Teach An Aragail; ☎ 915 5143; www.dingleactivities.com; Gallarus; small tent & 2 people €11; ⌚ Easter–late Sep) Europe's most westerly camp site is 300m from the Gallarus Oratory on a fine airy site. It's a source of much local information on a mass of activities, walking especially.

Dunquin Hostel (☎ 915 6121; anoigedun@eircom.net; Dunquin; dm/d €11.50/30; ⌚ year round) This An Óige hostel has a terrific location, near the Blasket Centre, not too far from the ferry departure point for Great Blasket Island and with stunning views. Rooms are smart and there's a cheerful atmosphere.

An Portán B&B (☎ 915 6212; www.anportan.com; Dunquin; s/d €31.75/50.80; lunch from €12, dinner €15-25; restaurant ⌚ Easter-Sep) An Portán is a superbly

LITERARY ISLAND

Great Blasket Island has a remarkable literary tradition that is responsible for around 40 published titles. It says much for the inspirational beauty of the islands, but this rich seam of island writing received an initial stimulus in the 1930s when a visiting English scholar encouraged an islander to write down his memoirs. This roused the interest of other scholars who visited the island to learn more about the remote community. They in turn encouraged more islanders to write about their experiences and language. Lyrical stories of many islanders' lives survive and are available at the Blasket Centre in Dunquin or at An Café Liteártha or the tourist office in Dingle. Some of the many diaries and notes, still in manuscript form, can also be seen at the Blasket Centre.

One of the best books to come from Great Blasket is the English translation of Thomas O'Crohan's *The Islandman*. Maurice O'Sullivan's *Twenty Years A-Growing*, the translation of Peig Sayers' *An Old Woman's Reflections* and *Peig*, and Pádraig Tyers' *Blasket Memories* are well worth reading.

organised and well-appointed place, with pleasant rooms in a separate complex to the restaurant. Meals are a mix of traditional Irish and international flair and include such dishes as cajun cod in mango, salsa and lemon butter sauce. You can even take a one-week Irish language course here (see p265).

Ferriter's Cove (☎ 915 6295; Ballyferriter; s/d €35/53) Get well away from it all, apart from a neighbouring golf course, at this bright and airy B&B where wooden floors and large rooms go with the terrific airiness of the coastal location. To get there, follow the signs to the golf club and you'll see it on your left.

Ceann Trá Heights (☎ 915 9866; ventry@iol.ie; s/d €40/60) A delightful bungalow high above Ventry harbour. Rooms are comfy and breakfasts hearty. It makes a good base for exploring the area.

Getting There & Away

Year round, Monday and Thursday only, bus No 276 operates three times daily from Dingle to Dunquin via Ventry, Slea Head and Ballyferriter. For more details phone **Bus Éireann** (☎ 712 3566) in Tralee.

BLASKET ISLANDS

The Blasket Islands (Na Blascaodaí), 5km out into the Atlantic, are the most westerly islands in Europe. At 6km by 1.2km, Great Blasket (An Blascaod Mór) is the largest and most visited, and is mountainous enough for strenuous walks, including a good one detailed in Kevin Corcoran's *Kerry Walks*. All of the Blaskets were inhabited at one time or another and there is evidence of Great Blasket being inhabited during the Iron Age and early-Christian times. The last islanders left for the mainland in 1953 after the government and the remaining inhabitants agreed that it was no longer feasible to live in such remote and harsh conditions.

Two- and three-hour **cruises** (€25) around the islands can be booked through **Dingle tourist office** (☎ 066-915 1188).

There's no accommodation on the islands but camping is free. A **café** on Great Blasket Island serves snacks and campers can arrange to have cooked meals.

Getting There & Away

Weather permitting, boats operate April to October (adult/family €20/50 return, 20 minutes). Prices for individual children are flexible. Boats leave Dunquin every 30 minutes, 10am to 7pm. The last boat from Great Blasket leaves at 6pm.

Counties Limerick & Tipperary

CONTENTS

The names Limerick and Tipperary are as recognisably Irish as shamrock and Guinness. Yet both counties transcend such easy association. They are the heartland of Irish heritage and though they lack the dramatic coastal and mountain scenery of neighbouring Cork, Kerry and Clare, both have a wealth of intriguing historical sites, attractive towns and villages, gentle hills and dappled woods that offer a refreshing alternative to the misty-eyed romanticism of the far west.

County Limerick is a mainly agricultural region that lies south of the inner estuary of the River Shannon. Landlocked Tipperary continues the theme of well-tended farmland peppered with attractive country towns and villages, but the shapely heights of the Galtee Mountains add a touch of breezy wilderness to the overall appeal.

History fans and lovers of old buildings are the winners here. They'll relish the medievalism of Limerick and Tipperary, where sleepy towns and villages are transformed by the presence of awesome castles, prehistoric remains, ruined abbeys and churches, ancient town walls, and legends of a lost age. From Limerick city's mighty King John's Castle to the compelling religious ruins of Tipperary's Rock of Cashel there's an absorbing trail to follow. You can soak up the past at Adare and Kilmallock in Limerick county, and at Cahir and Fethard in Tipperary, among some of the finest medieval buildings in Europe.

For city lovers the only substantial urban centre is Limerick city, itself steeped in Ireland's history, yet with a satisfying urban buzz that's lifted even more by a student population and an impressively lively nightlife.

HIGHLIGHTS

- Visit the **Hunt Museum** (p270) in Limerick city for a blissful bout of culture
- Spend a night on the town in **Limerick** (p274) in a music pub or club after a meal in one of the more idiosyncratic restaurants
- Go heritage hunting among the medieval buildings of **Adare** (p276) in County Limerick, or **Fethard** (p288) in County Tipperary
- Escape to the woods and walks of the **Galtee Mountains** (p281)
- Wander round the **Rock of Cashel's** (p281) compelling religious buildings

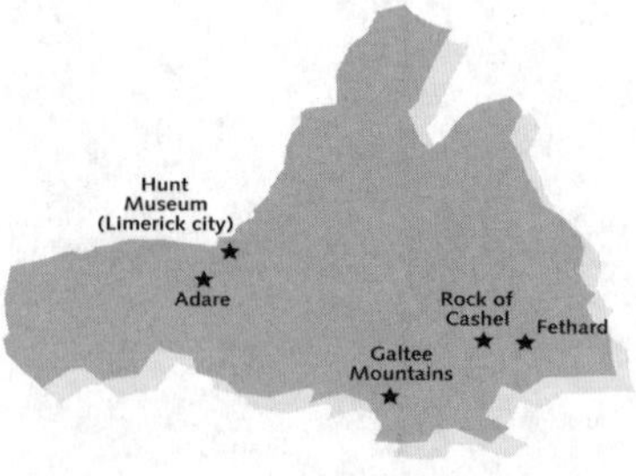

- POPULATION: 253,281
- AREA: 6989 SQ KM

GARETH MCCORMACK

Deserted cottage, **Great Blasket Island** (p266)

GARETH MCCORMACK

Mt Brandon (p261), Dingle Peninsula

Gap of Dunloe (p238), Killarney National Park

RICHARD CUMMINS

RICHARD CUMMINS

Church of the Most Holy Trinity (p277), Adare

Rock of Cashel (p281), Cashel

RICHARD CUMM

COUNTY LIMERICK

Most of Limerick is unspectacular low-lying farmland, except on the county's southern border where the western outliers of the Galtee Mountains slide out of Tipperary, and the Mullaghareirk and Ballyhoura Mountains escape from County Cork. Limerick city is brashly urban in contrast and has more than enough historic interest and attractions to satisfy even the most jaded traveller. About 10km south of the city lie the fascinating archaeological sites around Lough Gur and just a few kilometres southwest is the village of Adare, with its handsome old churches, castle ruins and rustic cottages.

LIMERICK CITY

☎ 061 / pop 54,058

Limerick (Luimneach) may be famous for lending its name to a cheerful verse form, but the city has also been unfairly branded over the years as a bit of a rough old place, characterised by the painful squalor so graphically portrayed by Frank McCourt in his novel *Angela's Ashes.* Hard times clung to Limerick for decades, but the city has revived in recent times. Its general bustle, many shops and services, and fine museums and galleries make Limerick a place to savour. The refurbishment of Georgian houses that match many of Dublin's finest, a thriving restaurant and pub culture and a fairly storming club scene have energised the city's already warm heart.

History

Viking adventurers established a settlement on an island in the Shannon in the 9th century. They fought with the native Irish for control of the site until Brian Ború's forces drove them out in 968 and established Limerick as the royal seat of the O'Brien kings. Brian Ború finally destroyed Viking power and presence in Ireland at the Battle of Clontarf in 1014. By the late 12th century invading Normans had supplanted the native Irish. The two remained divided and throughout the Middle Ages the repressed Irish clustered to the south of the Abbey River in Irishtown while the Anglo-Normans fortified themselves to the north, in Englishtown.

In 1690, Limerick acquired heroic status in the endless saga of Ireland's struggle against English occupation. After the Battle of the Boyne, the defeated Jacobite forces withdrew west behind the famously strong walls of Limerick town. Months of bombardment followed and eventually the Irish Jacobite leader Patrick Sarsfield sued for peace. The terms of the Treaty of Limerick were agreed and Sarsfield and 14,000 soldiers were allowed to leave the city for France. The treaty guaranteed religious freedom for Catholics, but the English reneged on it and enforced fierce anti-Catholic legislation, an act of betrayal that came to symbolise the injustice of British rule.

During the 18th century, the old walls of Limerick were demolished and a well-planned and prosperous Georgian town developed. Such prosperity had waned by the early 20th century. Now the city is meeting the challenges of the 21st century with optimism. Technological industries have supplanted traditional food processing and clothing manufacture, while tourism and service industries are encouraging a growing pride in modern Limerick.

Orientation

Limerick straddles the Shannon's broadening tidal stream, where the river swings west to join the Shannon estuary. The city has a clearly defined grid of main streets. The central thoroughfare runs roughly north to south and its name changes, from Rutland St in the north to Patrick St, O'Connell St, The Crescent and Quinlan St. It then exits south along O'Connell Avenue onto the Cork and Killarney roads. The main places of interest are clustered to the north, on King's Island (the oldest part of Limerick and once part of Englishtown), to the south around The Crescent and Pery Square (the city's noteworthy Georgian area), and along the riverbanks. The joint train and bus station lies southeast, off Parnell St.

Information

BOOKSHOP

O'Mahony's (☎ 418 155; 120 O'Connell St) Ireland's largest independent bookshop has occupied these premises for over 100 years.

INTERNET ACCESS

Surfers (☎ 440 122; 1 Upper William St; €1.25/15min, €1 for students; 🕑 9.30am-10pm Mon-Sat & noon-9pm Sun) Busy central Internet café.

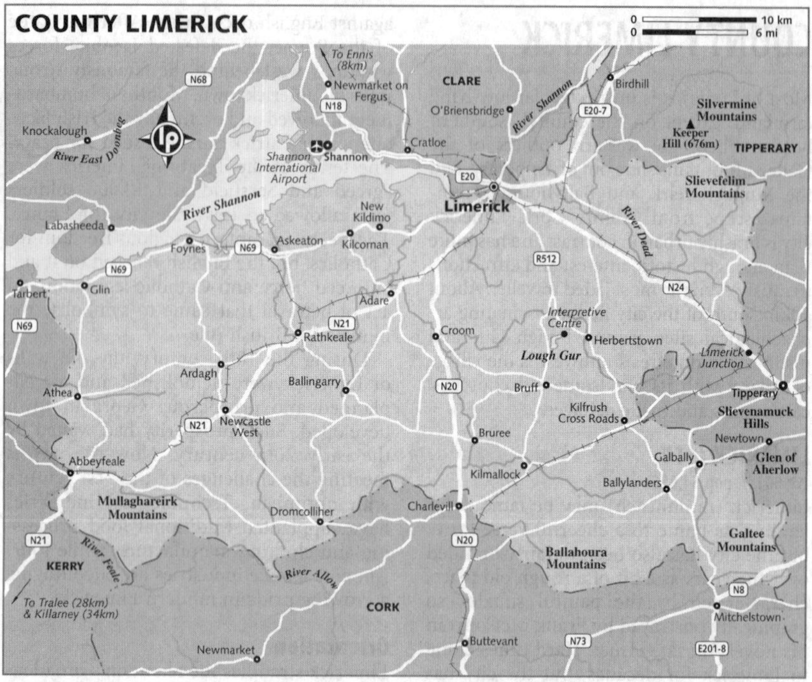

LAUNDRY

Superwash Launderette (☎ 414 027; 19 Ellen St; €10 per load)

LEFT LUGGAGE

Limerick Train Station (☎ 313 333; Colbert Station, Parnell St) has a left-luggage facility (€2.50 per item for 24 hours). It's open 8am to 6pm and 6.30pm to 8.30pm Monday to Friday and 8am to 6pm Saturday and Sunday.

MEDICAL SERVICES

Limerick Regional Hospital (☎ 482 219, 482 338; Dooradoyle)

MONEY

Allied Irish & Ulster Banks (O'Connell St) ATMs and bureaux de change. There's a handy ATM alongside the O'Connell St exit of the Arthur's Quay Shopping Centre.

POST

Limerick Main Post Office (☎ 316 777; Lower Cecil St)

TOILETS

Toilets can be found in Arthur's Quay Shopping Centre; admission €0.20.

TOURIST INFORMATION

Limerick Tourist Office (☎ 317 522; www.shannon-dev.ie/tourism; Arthur's Quay; 🕒 9am-6pm Mon-Fri, 9am-5.30pm Sat & Sun Jul-Aug, 9.30am-1pm & 2-5.30pm Mon-Sat May-Jun & Sep-Oct, 9.30am-1pm & 2-5.30pm Mon-Fri, 9.30am-1pm Sat Nov-Apr) There is a bureau de change inside the tourist office from mid-June to mid-September.

Dangers & Annoyances

History's rough handling of Limerick has left the modern city with a reputation for toughness and criminal violence. The latter should be seen in context, however. There is a 'gang' culture in the city, linked increasingly to drug supplying, but its violence seems to be internecine and does not impinge overtly on mainstream life, or on visitors. As with cities of any size if you are out on the streets late at night, be alert and keep a low profile.

Sights

HUNT MUSEUM

Housed in the Palladian Custom House on the banks of the Shannon, this splendid **museum** (☎ 312 833; Rutland St; adult/child €6/3; 🕒 10am-5pm Mon-Sat, 2-5pm Sun; wheelchair access) contains probably the finest collection of Bronze Age, Iron Age and medieval treasures outside Dublin. All items are from the private collection of the late John and Gertrude Hunt, antique dealers and consultants, who gifted their collection to the nation in the 1970s. Exhibits are displayed in a succession of elegant galleries. Look out for the tiny, but exquisite bronze horse by da Vinci, and for a Syracusan coin thought to have been one of the '30 pieces of silver' paid to Judas for his betrayal of Christ. Paintings by Renoir, Picasso and Jack B Yeats add to the feast. Guided tours are available. The museum has an in-house restaurant, DuCartes (see p274).

KING JOHN'S CASTLE

The massive curtain walls and towers of Limerick's showpiece **castle** (☎ 360 788; Nicholas St; adult/student/child €7/5.60/4.20; 🕑 10am-5.30pm Apr-Oct, 10.30am-4.30pm Nov-Mar; last admission 1hr before closing) are best viewed from the west bank of the River Shannon, although a wholly unsympathetic interpretive centre, which looks like the back of a football stand, now pokes its façade above the old battlements. The castle was built by King John of England between 1200 and 1212 on the site of an earlier fortification. It served as the military and administrative centre of the rich Shannon region.

Inside are enjoyable exhibitions and audiovisual commentaries about the castle's history. Remnants of medieval siege mines and countermines, excavated Viking house-sites, reconstructed Norman features and artefacts offer graphic evidence of Limerick's colourful past.

Across medieval Thomond Bridge, on the other side of the river, the **Treaty Stone** marks the spot on the riverbank where the Treaty of Limerick was signed. Before you cross the bridge look out for the 18th-century **Bishop's Palace** and the ancient **toll gate**.

GEORGIAN HOUSE & GARDEN/ASHES EXHIBITION

There is a charming eeriness about the lofty, echoing rooms of the restored **Georgian House** (☎ 314 130; 2 Pery Sq; adult/child €5/3; 🕑 10am-4pm Mon-Fri), one of Limerick's finest treasures. A few plaster models in period dress enhance the background of marble, stucco and wall decoration in the main rooms and the bare boards and dusty furnishings of the servants quarters. Brace yourself for some tortuous, but entertaining limericks on various wall plaques. The restored back garden leads to a coach house which contains a photographic memoir of Limerick and a small but evocative **Ashes Exhibition**, including a reconstruction of the childhood home of novelist Frank McCourt.

LIMERICK CITY GALLERY OF ART

A happily random mix of traditional paintings covers every inch of wall space in the **Limerick City Gallery of Art** (☎ 310 633; Carnegie Bldg, Pery Sq; admission free; 🕑 10am-6pm Mon-Fri, 10am-7pm Thu, 10am-1pm Sat, 2-5pm Sun). The gallery is beside the peaceful People's Park, at the heart of Georgian Limerick. The permanent collection features work by Sean Keating and Jack B Yeats. Notable paintings include Keating's *The Kelp Burners* and Harry Kernoff's *The Turf Girl*; both infuse their traditional subjects with great energy and joy. The gallery also stages changing exhibitions of some fairly adventurous contemporary work that can sometimes set Limerick tongues wagging.

ST MARY'S CATHEDRAL

Limerick's ancient **cathedral** (☎ 310 293; Bridge St; admission by €2 donation; 🕑 9am-1pm Jun-Sep,

LIMERICK & ANGELA'S ASHES

Rarely does a city become so overwhelmingly associated with one book as Limerick has with Frank McCourt's *Angela's Ashes*, published in 1996, for which McCourt won the prestigious Pulitzer Prize. The book is still popular and details the sometimes harrowing, sometimes humorous recollections of the McCourt family's desperate poverty in 1930s and 1940s Limerick.

McCourt's memories of Limerick have drawn some fire from fellow citizens, the inevitable price of fame and fortune. Some claim that his recollections were exaggerated and selective and Limerick's other famous son, the late actor Richard Harris, penned a passionate and colourful newspaper article in which he established Limerick as the real prizewinner. The city has been quick to capitalise on the novel and you can take a guided tour of the parts of Limerick associated with *Angela's Ashes* (see p272).

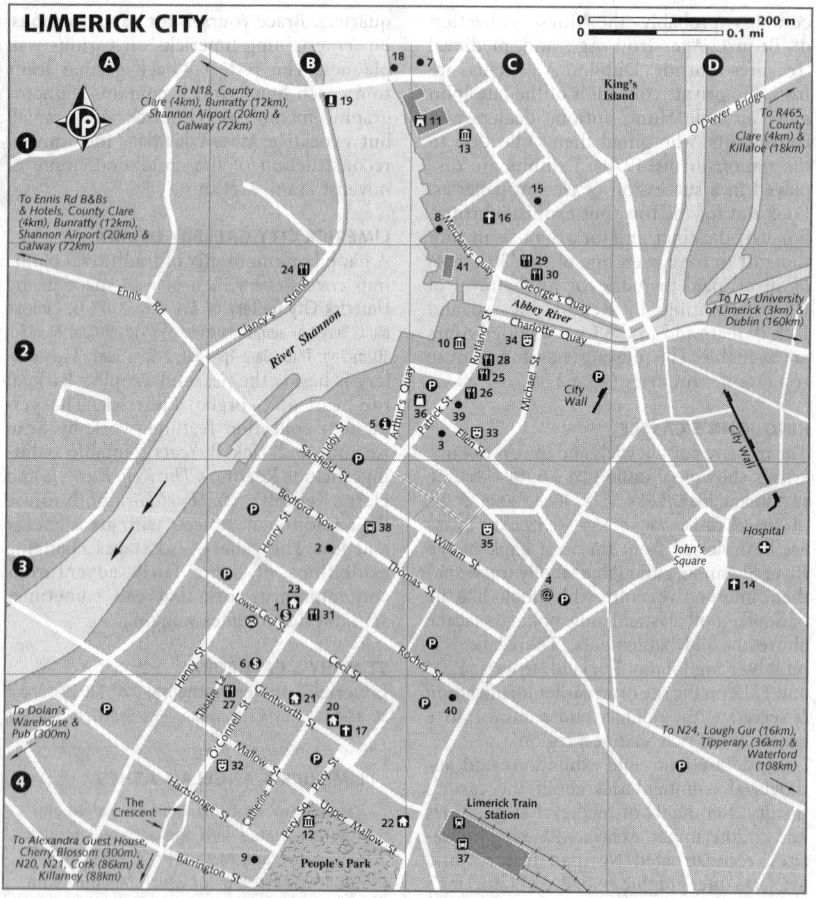

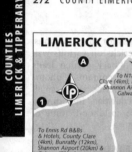

9am-5pm Oct-May) was founded in 1168 by Domhnall Mór O'Brien, king of Munster. Parts of the 12th-century Romanesque western doorway, the nave and aisles survive and there are splendid 15th-century black-oak misericords (support ledges for choristers), unique examples of their kind in Ireland.

LIMERICK MUSEUM

This small award-winning **museum** (☎ 417 826; Castle Lane; admission free; ⌚ 10am-1pm & 2.15-5pm Tue-Sat) is beside King John's Castle. Exhibits include Stone Age and Bronze Age artefacts, the civic sword, samples of Limerick silver and examples of Limerick's lace- and kid-glove manufacturing, as well as a collection of paintings.

Tours

A two-hour walking tour (2.30pm daily) of Limerick locations mentioned in Frank McCourt's *Angela's Ashes* (see the boxed text p271) starts and ends at the tourist office on Arthur's Quay. There is a historical walking tour of Limerick (departing at 11am and 2.30pm Monday to Friday). The start point is by arrangement. Both tours cost €8 per person. For information contact **St Mary's Action Centre** (☎ 318 106; www.iol.ie/~smidp/; 44 Nicholas St).

Sleeping

BUDGET

At the time of writing there were no hostels operating in Limerick city. The nearest

INFORMATION		
Allied Irish Bank	1	B3
O'Mahony's	2	B3
Superwash Launderette	3	C2
Surfers Internet Cafe	4	C3
Tourist Office	5	B2
Ulster Bank	6	B3
SIGHTS & ACTIVITIES	**pp270-2**	
Bishop's Palace	7	C1
Civic Centre	8	C1
Georgian House & Garden	9	B4
Hunt Museum	10	C2
King John's Castle	11	C1
Limerick City Gallery of Art	12	B4
Limerick Museum	13	C1
St John's Cathedral	14	D3
St Mary's Action Centre	15	C1
St Mary's Cathedral	16	C1
St Saviour's Dominican Church	17	B4
Toll gate	18	B1
Treaty Stone	19	B1
SLEEPING	**pp272-3**	
Glentworth Hotel	20	B4
Hanratty's Hotel	21	B4
Railway Hotel	22	B4
Royal George Hotel	23	B3
EATING	**pp273-4**	
Chimes	(see 32)	
Curragower Seafood Bar	24	B2
Danny's Coffee House	25	C2
DuCartes	(see 10)	
Fat Zoe's	26	C2
Freddy's Bistro	27	B4
Green Onion	28	C2
Locke Bar	29	C2
Moll Darby's	30	C2
Sails	(see 36)	
Wokking	31	B3
ENTERTAINMENT	**pp274-5**	
Belltable Arts Centre	32	B4
Cosmo Club (Vintage Club)	33	C2
Doc's	34	C2
Nancy Blake's	35	C3
SHOPPING		
Arthur's Quay Shopping Centre	36	C2
TRANSPORT	**p275**	
Bus Station	37	C4
Bus Stop	38	B3
Emerald Alpine	39	C2
McMahon's Cycle World	40	C4
OTHER		
Courthouse	41	C2

hostel to the city is **Jamaica Inn** (☎ 061-369 220; www.jamaicainn.ie; Mount Levers, Sixmilebridge, Clare; dm/d €15/32), 13km northwest of the city.

Cherry Blossom (☎ 469449; cherblos3@netscape.net; 3 Alexandra Tce, O'Connell Ave; s/d €16/25) This is a bright and cheerful place that is young-person oriented, but not exclusively. Rooms are pleasant and simple and the larger rooms are dormitory-style, with bunk beds. Light breakfast is included; full breakfast costs extra. Booking is advised.

MID-RANGE

Alexandra Terrace on O'Connell Ave, just south of the centre, has several B&Bs, all in the mid-price range. Ennis Rd, leading northwest towards Shannon also has a selection of mid-range B&Bs, although most are a kilometre or so from the centre.

Alexandra Guest House (☎ 318 472; info@alexandra.iol.ie; 6 Alexandra Tce, O'Connell Ave; s/d €20/60) There's an upbeat, caring attitude at this happily rambling house run by a member of the same family that operates the Cherry Blossom. Rooms are no-frills, but comfy. Light breakfast is included.

Hanratty's Hotel (☎ 410 999; hanratttyshotel@hotmail.com; 5 Glentworth St; s/d €55/88; P) Hanratty's is the oldest hotel in Limerick and hangs on to elements of period grace – witness the elaborate chandelier in the stairwell. Rooms are comfy, but some of the smaller ones feel a touch enclosed.

Woodfield House Hotel (☎ 453 022; Ennis Rd; www.woodfieldhousehotel.com; s/d €55/88; P) The spacious bars and restaurant of this out-of-town hotel, and its comfortable, relaxing bedrooms, manage to achieve a very pleasant country-house ambience in suburban Limerick.

Glen Eagles (☎ 455 521; 12 Vereker Gardens, Ennis Rd; s/d €42.50/60; Mar-Oct; P) Only 400m from the centre, Glen Eagles is in a peaceful cul-de-sac and has decent-sized, comfortable rooms for those who want peace and quiet.

Railway Hotel (☎ 413 653; sales@railwayhotel.ie; Parnell St; s/d €46/90; P) Right across from the bus and train station, this long-established, family-run hotel has a pleasant period feel to its sizable rooms. There is a bar and restaurant.

St Anthony's (☎ 452 607; 8 Coolraine Tce, Ennis Rd; s/d with shared bathroom €23/46, s/d with bathroom €50/100; Apr-Oct; P) An out-of-centre option, this pleasant house is set back from busy Ennis Rd and has quiet rooms. There are similar B&Bs in the same terrace.

Royal George Hotel (☎ 414 566; www.royalgeorge.com; O'Connell St; s/d €60/75; P) If you want to be at the heart of the city, the Royal George fits the bill; but if it's peace and quiet you're after, specify a room at the back. The hotel has a cellar bar and a nightclub (see An Sibin, p275) and its main bar believes in sharing its full-blast music with everyone.

TOP END

Glentworth Hotel (☎ 413 822; glentworthhotel@oceanfree.net; Glentworth St; s/d €80/140; P; wheelchair access) The smooth Georgian façade hides a smart designer interior of bright tiling, blonde wood and steel fittings. The comfortable rooms are equally stylish. There may be some late-night noise from the Catherine St side at weekends.

Eating

Limerick has a generally low-key eating scene, but there are a couple of outstanding restaurants.

BUDGET

Curragower Seafood Bar (☎ 321 788; Clancy's Strand; mains €4.50-9.50; 🕑 noon-late) You can get cracking on delicious crab claws or sup tasty chowder from the unfancy but authentic seafood menu of this great little bar on the west bank of the Shannon. There's a solid view of King John's Castle from the outside terrace; but half-close your eyes on a sunny day and you could be by the seaside.

Danny's Coffee House (☎ 400 694; 5 Rutland St; mains €5.50-8) Danny's dishes up tea and coffee in big mugs to go with its tasty menu and its wicked selection of pastries.

Chimes (☎ 319 866; Belltable Arts Centre, 69 O'Connell St; mains €6.30-7.30; 🕑 8.30am-5pm Mon-Fri) The Belltable's basement café sidesteps the cultural diet and offers fat sandwiches and artful pastas. Breakfast is €3.75.

Sails (☎ 416 622; 1st floor, Arthur's Quay Shopping Centre, Patrick St; meals €6-8) Choose from a straightforward menu that includes pasta, and fish and chips at the heart of the Limerick shopping experience. There's a deli counter for takeaways.

Wokking (☎ 312 444; 37 O'Connell St; meals €6-11.50) Takeaway and an eat-in counter are the options at this busy Chinese servery with its varied choice that includes a 'create your own' menu.

MID-RANGE

Locke Bar (☎ 413 733; George's Quay; lunch mains €8.50-9.50, dinner mains €16.95-26; 🕑 5-10.30pm) This popular riverside bar and restaurant has good helpings of Irish stew, chicken Kiev or fillet of cod for the lunch crowd. Evening meals mix in continental themes. There are comfy sofas indoors and tables on an outdoor terrace beside the river.

DuCartes (☎ 312 662; Hunt Museum, Rutland St; meals €8-11.50; 🕑 10am-5pm Mon-Sat, 2-5pm Sun) Cultural lunches at the museum's pleasant restaurant offer tasty soups and Mediterranean cheeses and salads as well as lamb and chicken dishes in tangy sauces. Window seats have a Shannon view.

Moll Darby's (☎ 411 511; George's Quay; pizza €10-14, mains €12-21; 🕑 5.30-11pm) Moll's, by the river, offers a dizzying international choice of appetisers, fish, game, poultry, vegetarian meals and tasty pizzas.

Fat Zoe's (☎ 314 717; Rutland St; pasta €8-13, pizza €15-19) Tasty Italian-based food, especially pizzas and pastas, is the main fare in this popular and cheerful eatery.

TOP END

Green Onion (☎ 400 710; Old Town Hall, Rutland St; mains €13.70-21.50; 🕑 noon-10pm Mon-Sat, noon-3pm & 6-10pm Sun) Limerick's trend-setting eatery is in the city's old town hall that has had its lofty interior transformed into a vibrant red and blue dreamspace by the accomplished Bogside Artists from Derry. The menu rings the modern-Irish changes from traditional meat, poultry and fish dishes to veggie tortillas and big open sandwiches. Try a dish of ultra-Irish colcannon: mashed potatoes with all sorts of tasty additions. There's an all-day menu and a great range of coffees for break time.

Freddy's Bistro (☎ 418 749; Theatre Lane; mains €19-26.50; 🕑 6.30-10pm Tue-Sat) A quiet location in a former coach house adds to the relaxing ambience of this consistently good restaurant. The menu combines the best of traditional and new cuisine in its subtly prepared steaks and imaginative sauces and garnishes, and there are vegetarian options.

Drinking & Entertainment

Limerick nightlife has lifted off in recent years and reflects the city's growing vibrancy. Courtesy of local acts or visiting headliners, you'll find everything from trad Irish to trash rock, chart, soul, reggae, drum and bass, jazz and classical, as well as theatre and stand-up comedy. Most clubs have strict door checks. The *Limerick Event Guide*, whose rather bland title translates happily into 'The LEG', can be found for free in pubs, eateries and hotels all over town, and is full of great info about the scene.

Dolan's Warehouse (☎ 314 483; www.dolans.ie; 3/4 Dock Rd; admission €9-15) Limerick's most eclectic venue promises an unbeatable gig list that in the past has featured everyone from Evan Dando, Justin Sullivan, Julia Turner and folk legends The Fureys, to punky Japanese garage rockers Mikabomb. Wednesday night is Dot Comedy Club night with cutting edge stand-ups. The Warehouse is grafted on to the atmospheric Dolan's Pub, where you're guaranteed authentic trad music sessions most nights, though it gets very crowded.

Belltable Arts Centre (☎ 319 866; www.belltable.ie; 69 O'Connell St) Less funk and more fettuccini than Dolan's, the Belltable is a class venue and a crucible for the arts in the mid-west. It covers everything in theatre, visual arts, music, cinema and comedy – you're as likely to catch Voltaire's *Candide* as brilliant satirist Pakie O'Callaghan. There's an art gallery too, and the Belltable's annual festival of fringe theatre, Unfringed (January and February), gets better every year.

Doc's (☎ 318 466; Michael St; ⏲ Wed-Sun nights) is a floor-burning venue located in Limerick's refurbished old Granary building. There's a funky indoor bar and plenty of outside space in a fountain-spoutin' courtyard that helps cool the close-quarters mostly-student crowd. Local and guest DJs keep things thumping and there's a good spread of chart sounds, trance, funk, soul and reggae.

University Concert Hall (☎ 331 549; University of Limerick) Permanent home of the Irish Chamber Orchestra, the UCH adds lustre to Limerick's cultural scene with visits from world-class performers and regular concerts, opera, drama and dance events.

Nancy Blake's (☎ 416 443; Upper Denmark St) They still spread sawdust on the floor in this great old pub, and there's a backyard bar that rocks at the weekend to regular music sessions.

Cosmo Club (☎ 414 144; Vintage Club, Ellen St) A friendly gay and lesbian weekend venue at Limerick's long-established pub, the Vintage Club. Friday nights are disco nights, starting at 9.30pm.

An Sibin (☎ 414 566; O'Connell St) The Royal George Hotel's basement bar has live Irish and contemporary music seven nights a week, although it's full-blast amps. The décor's a bit outdated.

Getting There & Away

AIR

Shannon Airport (☎ 712 000), in County Clare, handles domestic and international flights. A taxi from Limerick city to the airport costs €20.

BUS

Bus Éireann (☎ 313 333; Parnell St) services operate from the bus and train station, a short walk south of the centre. There are regular connections to Dublin (€14.50 one way, one hour 15 minutes), Tralee (€13.20, two hours), Cork (€13.20, one hour 50 minutes), Galway, Killarney, Rosslare, Donegal, Sligo, Shannon, Derry and most other centres. You can be dropped at the bus stop on O'Connell St.

TRAIN

There are regular trains to all the main towns: eight trains daily to Dublin (€36.50), two daily to Rosslare Harbour (€16.50), Cahir (€8.50) and Tipperary (€6), and one to Cork (€19.50). Other routes involve changing at Limerick Junction, 20km southeast of Limerick. Phone **Colbert station** (☎ 315 555) for details.

Getting Around

Regular buses connect Limerick bus and train station with Shannon Airport (€4.70 one way). The airport is 24km northwest of Limerick, about 30 minutes by car.

Limerick is small enough to get around easily on foot or by bike. To walk across town from St Mary's Cathedral to the train station takes about 15 minutes.

Taxis line up outside the tourist office, the bus and train station, and in Thomas St.

Scratch card parking discs (€1 per hour) are available from most newsagencies and corner shops. Multistorey car parks around the city centre are open from 7.45am to 7pm (€1.30 per hour, €6 overnight).

Bikes can be hired at **Emerald Alpine** (☎ 416 983; Patrick St) for €20/70 per day/week. **McMahons Cycle World** (☎ 415 202; 30 Roches St) is part of the national Raleigh Rent-a-Bike scheme and rents at €15/80 per day/week. Both businesses charge an extra €15.80 for retrieval or delivery at places outside Limerick, including Galway or Cork.

AROUND LIMERICK CITY

South of the city there's a clutch of outstanding historic sites that reward a day visit by car or a couple of days by bike. Only the larger villages are served by bus.

Lough Gur

The wider area around this small horseshoe-shaped lake abounds with fascinating archaeological sites. To get there, leave Limerick on the N24 road south to Waterford. Look for a sign to Lough Gur indicating a right turn at the roundabout outside town. This takes you onto the R512. In about 18km, you reach the superb **Grange Stone Circle**, known as The Lios, a 4000-year-old circular enclosure made up of 113 embanked uprights. It is the largest prehistoric circle of its kind in Ireland. There's roadside parking. Access to the site is free but you may face a notice demanding a 'donation of €2 towards the cost and maintenance of the fence erected by the landowner to preserve this circle'. It's your call.

Around 1km further south along the R512, at Holycross garage and post office, a left turn takes you towards Lough Gur, past a ruined 15th-century church and a **wedge tomb** on the other side of the road.

Another 2km leads to a car park by Lough Gur and the thatched replica of a Neolithic hut containing the **Lough Gur Interpretive Centre** (☎ 360 788; adult/child €4/2; 10am-6pm early May–late Sep; P). The centre has audiovisual presentations, and a small **museum** displaying a few Neolithic artefacts and a replica of the Lough Gur shield that's now in the National Museum in Dublin. The 700 BC shield is 72cm in diameter with six circles of raised bosses designed to weaken the impact of an enemy's sword.

There are short walks along the lake's edges that take you to burial mounds, standing stones, ancient enclosures and other points of interest. The whole area is ideal for picnics amid prehistory.

Kilmallock

☎ 063 / pop 2085

Kilmallock's scattering of outstanding medieval buildings reflects its past status during the Middle Ages as Ireland's third-largest town, after Dublin and Kilkenny. Today the village lies sleepily beside the River Lubach 26km south of Limerick, a world away from the city's urban racket. Kilmallock developed around a 7th-century abbey and from the 14th to the 17th centuries it was the seat of the earls of Desmond.

Coming into Kilmallock from Limerick, the first place you'll see (to your left) is a **medieval stone mansion** – one of 30 or so that housed the town's prosperous merchants and landowners. Further along, the street dodges round the four-storey **King's Castle**, a 15th-century tower house with a ground-floor archway, beneath which the pavement now runs. Across the road, a lane leads down to the tiny **Kilmallock Museum** (☎ 91300; Sheares St; admission free; 2-5pm). It houses a random collection of historical artefacts and a model of the town in 1597.

Beyond the museum and across the River Lubach are the impressive ruins of the 13th-century **Dominican priory**. Outstanding is the five-light west window of the choir.

Returning to the main street, head back towards Limerick, then turn left into Orr St, which runs down to the 13th-century **Collegiate Church**. This has a round tower, which probably belonged to an earlier, pre-Norman monastery on the site.

Further south along the main street turn left (on foot, the road is one-way against you) into Wolfe Tone St. On the right, just before the bridge, you'll see a plaque marking the house where the Irish poet Aindrias Mac Craith died in 1795. Across the road, one of the pretty, single-storey cottages (the fifth one from the bridge) preserves a 19th-century interior. Obtain the key from next door.

On the other side of the main street in Emmet St is **Blossom Gate**, the one surviving gate of the original medieval town wall.

Kilmallock has an excellent facility in its **Friars' Gate Theatre and Arts Centre** (☎ 98727; www.friarsgate.net; Main St), where you can also find tourism information about the village. The centre hosts art exhibitions and has a fine little theatre in which it stages plays, music events and recitals.

Deebert House (☎ 98106; www.deeberthouse.com; Kilmallock; s/d €40/60; Mar-Nov; P) There are big, relaxing rooms in this fine Georgian house that has a charming garden and attached restaurant. It's best reached from the southern exit to the village by turning off down the road signed Tipperary. Deebert House is on the corner at the next junction. Inquire about rates for the two self-catering apartments.

Two Bus Éireann buses run Monday to Saturday from Limerick to Kilmallock (€8.20, one hour).

ADARE & AROUND

☎ 061 / pop 2591

Picturesque ruins have made Adare a tourist honeypot and the wedding capital of the west of Ireland. This charming village on the River Maigue lies 16km southwest of Limerick on the busy N21 and the only thing that spoils it all is the torrent of cars and lorries that rattle through relentlessly. Yet, in spite of the cars, coaches and crowds, Adare's remarkable medieval buildings are a delight. The nuptial magic lies in the photo-backdrops and romance of handsome old churches. The main street is lined with thatched cottages that were created during the improving landlordship of the third earl of Dunraven in the 1820s. There's an interesting **heritage exhibition**, a pleasant **riverside walk**, which offers escape from the crowds, and some fine restaurants and cheerful pubs to enhance all that medievalism.

Information

In the Adare Heritage Centre is the helpful **tourist office** (☎ 396 255; Main St; 🕑 9am-7pm Mon-Fri & 9am-6pm Sat-Sun Jun-Sep, 9am-1pm & 2-6pm daily Oct, 9am-1pm & 2-6pm Mon-Sat May, 9am-1pm & 2-5pm Mon-Sat Feb-Apr & Nov-Dec). The office has plenty of brochures and maps about Adare.

The Allied Irish Bank (AIB) nearby has an ATM and bureau de change.

Sights

ADARE HERITAGE CENTRE

In the centre of the village is the **heritage centre** (☎ 396 666; Main St; adult/child €5/3.50; 🕑 9am-6pm Mon-Fri, 10am-5pm Sat & Sun May-Sep, 10am-5pm Mon-Fri Oct-Dec, 10.30am-4pm Mon-Fri, 10.30am-4.30pm Sat & Sun Jan-Feb, 9.30am-4.30pm Mon-Fri, 11am-5pm Sat & Sun Mar-Apr). The centre's audiovisual presentation and exhibits explain the history and the medieval context of Adare's old buildings in an entertaining way.

RELIGIOUS HOUSES

During the Tudor dissolution of the monasteries in 1539, Adare had three flourishing religious houses, the remains of which can still be seen. In the village itself, next to the heritage centre, the dramatic tower and southern wall of the **Church of the Most Holy Trinity** are the remains of a 13th-century Trinitarian monastery that was restored by the first earl of Dunraven and is now the Catholic church. There's a restored 14th-century **dovecote** down the side turning next to the church.

The ruins of a **Franciscan friary** founded by the earl of Kildare in 1464 stand in the middle of Adare Manor golf course beside the River Maigue. Public access is assured, but ask at the clubhouse for permission to visit, then follow a track leading away from the clubhouse car park for about 400m; watch out for flying golf balls. There's a handsome tower and a fine sedilia (row of seats for priests) in the southern wall of the chancel.

South of the village, on the N21, and close to the bridge over the River Maigue, is the Church of Ireland parish church, once the **Augustinian friary**, and founded in 1316. It was also known as the Black Abbey. The interior of the church is pleasantly cavernous, but the real joy is the atmospheric little cloister.

A pleasant **riverside path**, with occasional seats, starts from just outside the friary gates. Look for a narrow access gap and head off alongside the river. After about 250m turn left along the road to reach the centre of Adare, from where the main road leads noisily back to the friary entrance.

DESMOND CASTLE

Dating back to around 1200, this picturesque feudal ruin saw rough usage until it was finally wrecked by Cromwell's troops in 1657. By then it had already lost its strategic importance. Restoration work is endlessly 'in progress', but one day there may even be secure access. At present the castle can be viewed only from the always-busy main road or, more safely, from the riverside footpath or the grounds of the Augustinian friary.

CELTIC PARK & GARDENS

About 8km northwest of Adare there's an interesting collection of re-created 'Celtic' structures (plus a few originals) on the site of an original Celtic settlement, at **Celtic Park** (☎ 394 243; Kilcornan; adult/child €5/free; 🕑 9.30am-6pm Mar-Oct). There's also an extensive rose garden and tearoom.

LIMERICK'S LIMERICKS

The limerick is a type of comic verse with a simple metre and rhyming scheme that are both engaging and direct. The limerick is said to have originated in the works of the Fili na Maighe, the Gaelic poets of the River Maigue area. Two of the most famous 18th-century limerick composers were Sean O'Tuama and Andrias Mac Craith. They were close friends for years, but after falling out, began a series of 'duelling' limericks in which they satirised each other. There is information about the Maigue poets at the Adare Heritage Centre.

ORGANISED TOURS

June to September a guide leads a daily 30-minute **historical walking tour** (☎ 396 666; Adare Heritage Centre) of Adare, by prior arrangement.

Sleeping

Accommodation in Adare's big hotels is not cheap, but there are reasonable options to balance the high prices. An alternative is to stay in Limerick and then make a day visit.

Riversdale (☎ 396 751; Manor Court, Station Rd; s/d €35/60; mid-Mar–Nov) There's excellent value at this sparkling house, where good-sized rooms and hearty breakfasts set you up for the short stroll to the centre of village action. Station Rd has several other B&Bs.

Elm House (☎ 396 306; Clounanna Rd, Mondellihy; s/d €35/56) Peacefully located 1km north of the village is this friendly B&B with a cosy atmosphere. It has three rooms, one with en suite.

Curragh Lodge (☎ 396 329; curraghlodge@eircom.net; Askeaton Rd; s/d €25/56; P) This small, cheerful B&B is next to a handy little garage about 250m from the centre of Adare along the quiet Askeaton Rd.

Dunraven Arms (☎ 396 633; www.dunravenhotel.com; Main St; s/d €170/190) It's tough prices for singles at this enjoyable luxury-with-tradition hotel, where separate breakfast and service charges hike the bill even higher. The Dunraven hosts a lot of Adare's wedding receptions, so if you're budgeting on luxury rooms, get married there.

Eating

Blue Door (☎ 396 481; Main St; lunch mains €8-11, dinner mains €15-21.55; 11am-3pm & 6.30-10pm) This delightful thatched-cottage restaurant serves mouthwatering lunches and a tempting evening menu. There's even a tasty veggie option of walnut ravioli with blue cheese sauce among the delicious meat, chicken and fish dishes.

Wild Geese (☎ 396 451; Main St; mains €25; 12.30-2.30pm & 6.30-10pm Tue-Sat) A relaxing and stylish interior adds to the pleasure of this award-winning restaurant's imaginative menu. Offerings can include chargrilled tuna as well as choice meat and poultry dishes. For lunch there are terrific sandwiches and hot platters.

Seán Collins (☎ 396 400; Main St; mains €6.95) Cheer yourself up at this down-to-earth pub which, as well as bar meals, serves simple sandwiches for €3.50.

Pink Potato & Pizza Blue (☎ 396 723; Main St; snacks €2.65-5, pizzas €7.50-16) Next door to Seán Collins and run by the same owners, you won't beat this place for sandwiches, burgers, chicken and fries.

Dovecot (☎ 396 255; Adare Heritage Centre, Main St; mains €8-9) This bright and airy cafeteria is open the same hours as the heritage centre and does sandwiches for €4, lunch-time fare such as Irish stew, fish pie and shepherd's pie, and snacks during the rest of the day.

Drinking

Bill Chawke Lounge Bar (☎ 396 160; Main St) Comfy traditional is the mood here; there's trad music every Thursday night and a sing-along on Saturday nights.

Seán Collins (☎ 396 400; Main St) A great local atmosphere, plus Irish music on Tuesday and Sunday nights, is nicely spiced on Thursdays with one of the best karaoke nights around.

Getting There & Away

Twelve Dublin–Adare buses a day call at Limerick and then Adare (return to Limerick €5). Fourteen buses a day leave Adare for Tralee and Killarney. For times contact **Limerick bus station** (☎ 313 333) or pick up a timetable from the tourist office.

Getting Around

There's streetside parking, but the best bet is a free car park behind the heritage centre.

COUNTY TIPPERARY

Landlocked Tipperary occupies a fair chunk of Ireland's southern midlands and boasts the sort of fertile soil that farmers dream of. There's still an Anglo-Irish gloss to traditions here. Local fox hunts are in full cry during the winter season and the villages can look like something out of Middle England. The central area of the county is low-lying, but handsome hills spill over from adjoining counties, while in the south the highest tops of the Galtee Mountains give Tipperary an attractive context. The River Suir runs through it all and the county's major towns lie on the river's banks or on those of its tributaries. Tipperary town is not the county's main settlement. Clonmel and Carrick-on-Suir are larger.

TIPPERARY TOWN

☎ 062 / pop 4560

Tipperary (Tiobrad Árann) may have lent its melodic name to a famous music-hall song but this one-time Anglo-Norman settlement is a low-key, working town that has no pretensions to being anything else. It does have Irish charm, though, while the scenic backdrop of the nearby Slievenamuck Hills adds to Tipperary's attractions as a useful centre from which to enjoy the county's gentle landscapes and rich heritage sites.

The **tourist office** (☎ 51457; Excel Heritage Centre, Mitchell St; 9.30am-5.30pm Mon-Sat) is reached via St Michael's St, a side street leading off the north side of Main St. There's a useful car park alongside the Excel Heritage Centre. On either corner of the access street to the tourist office there are banks with ATMs and bureaux de change. The post office is on Davis St, off the north side of Main St.

Sights & Activities

The tourist office is part of the larger **Excel Heritage Centre** (☎ 80520; www.tipperary-excel.com; Mitchell St; adult/child €2.50/1.30; 9.30am-5.30pm Mon-Sat), a well-run and interesting facility that also houses a café, a local-history centre, theatre, cinema, art gallery and gift shop. The charge is for exhibitions.

Midway along Main St there's a **statue of Charles T Kickham** (1828–82), a local novelist (author of *Knocknagow*, a novel about rural life) and Young Irelander. He spent four years in London's Pentonville Prison in the 1860s. A lively cattle mart is held at the eastern end of Main St on Wednesday and Friday.

Sleeping & Eating

There's not a big choice in Tipperary, but standard B&Bs can be found on the N24 on either side of town and most pubs along Main St serve breakfast, tea and coffee, and lunch. Some do evening meals in summer.

Ach na Sheen (☎ 51298; gernoonan@eircom.net; Bansha Rd; s/d €45/68) Well-positioned on the immediate outskirts of town on the N24 Clonmel road, this friendly B&B, with a big, curved picture window, has good-sized comfy rooms and filling breakfasts.

Royal Hotel (☎ 33244; royalhtl@iol.ie; Bridge St; s/d €40/90) At the time of writing, the Royal had just come under new management. Rooms are a bit dated but are cosy. The hotel has a restaurant and there's bar entertainment at weekends.

Mary Hanna's (Excel Heritage Centre, Mitchell St; breakfast €5-7, paninis €6; 10am-5.30pm Mon-Sat, 10am-3pm Sun) The Excel Heritage Centre's useful in-house café offers snacks, but starts with a breakfast choice from standard to very big. There's a tasty vegetarian option.

Punjab Tandoori (☎ 80893; 7 St Michael's St; mains €9-12; 5-11pm) There's a big selection of tandoori and other dishes, including vegetarian, at this Indian restaurant just off Main St.

Sport

Tipperary Racecourse (☎ 51357; www.tipperaryraces.com; Limerick Rd) One of Ireland's leading tracks, it's 3km out of town and has regular meetings during the year. See the local press or phone the course for details. The course is within walking distance of Limerick Junction station. On race days there are minibus pick-ups from Tipperary town; phone for details.

Getting There & Away

Rafferty Travel (☎ 51555; Main St) does bookings for Bus Éireann and for Iarnród Éireann.

IT'S A LONG WAY...

No WWI movie would be complete without some British private singing:

It's a long way to Tipperary,
It's a long way to go.
It's a long way to Tipperary,
To the sweetest girl I know...

It was written in 1912 by Englishman Jack Judge, who had never set foot in Ireland. Judge was a fish seller by day and a music-hall performer by night. During a drinking session, he took on a friendly bet that he would write a song in 24 hours and perform it on stage at the local music hall the next evening. On his way home Judge heard someone giving directions and caught the phrase 'It's a long way to...' Next morning he hit on the name Tipperary for its melodic sound and its metre. Judge wrote the song that day and performed it on stage the same evening, winning both his bet and a later fortune from royalties.

COUNTY TIPPERARY

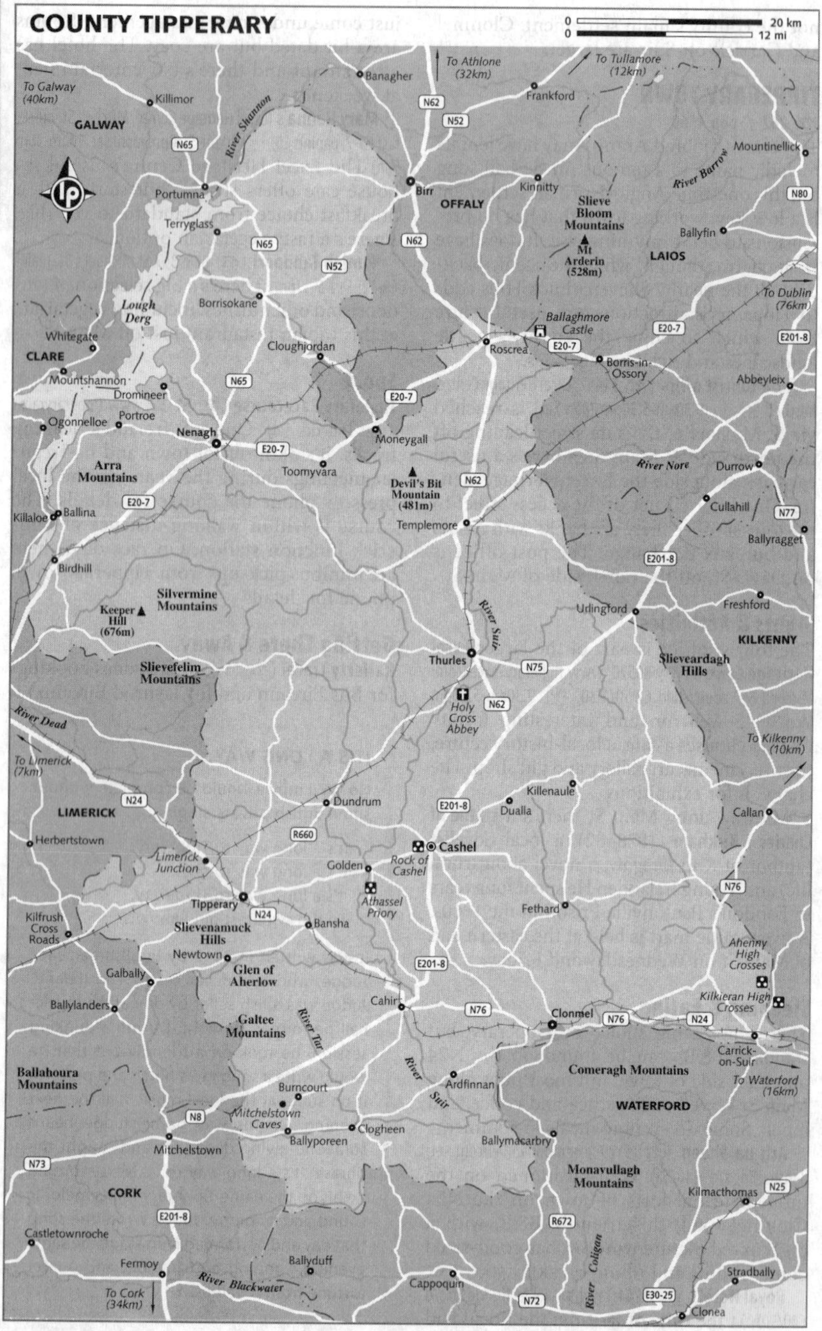

BUS

Most buses stop on Abbey St by the river, except for the Rosslare Harbour service, which stops outside the Supervalu supermarket on the link road. Bus Éireann runs up to 10 buses daily on the Limerick–Waterford express route. There's also one a day on weekdays in each direction between Tipperary and Shannon in County Clare. Monday to Saturday, **Kavanagh's** (☎ 51563) runs services to Dublin via Cahir and Cashel. Buses leave at 7.45am from outside the Marian Hall at the northern end of St Michael's St.

TRAIN

To get to the station, head south along Bridge St. Tipperary is on the Waterford–Limerick Junction line. There's one daily service to Cahir, Clonmel, Carrick-on-Suir, Waterford and Rosslare Harbour, and multiple connections to Cork, Kerry, Waterford, Rosslare Harbour and Dublin from **Limerick Junction** (☎ 51406), barely 3km from Tipperary along the Limerick road.

GLEN OF AHERLOW & GALTEE MOUNTAINS

South of Tipperary are the splendid Slievenamuck Hills and Galtee Mountains, separated by the broad chequered valley of the Glen of Aherlow. A scenic drive through the Glen of Aherlow is signposted from Tipperary town. Between Tipperary and Cahir is Bansha (An Bháinseach), at the eastern end of the glen. The village marks the start of a 20km trip west to Galbally, an easy bike ride that takes in the best of the county's landscapes. It's a rewarding area for quiet walking, and has a good choice of countryside accommodation.

Sleeping

Ballinacourty House Caravan & Camping Park (☎ 56000; www.ballinacourtyhse.com; Glen of Aherlow; tent & car €14; ⌚ mid-Apr–Sep) Against a great backdrop of the Galtees, this attractive site is 10km from Bansha on the R663 to Galbally. It has excellent facilities, as well as a fine garden, restaurant, wine bar and tennis court.

Ballydavid Wood (☎ 54148; Glen of Aherlow; adult/child €10.16/7.62) In the southeastern corner of the glen, this An Óige hostel is an old hunting lodge in a beautiful setting on the north slopes of the Galtees. It's 3km off Tipperary– Cahir road, from which it's signposted.

Bansha House (☎ 54194; www.tipp.ie/banshaas.htm; Bansha; s/d €45/90) Period elegance and high ceilings characterise this Georgian country house in spacious grounds. There's a grand feeling of being away from it all here. The house is signposted and is 250m along a lane at the western entrance to Bansha.

Getting There & Away

Bus Éireann express bus No 55 from Limerick to Waterford via Tipperary town stops at Bansha five times daily. Contact **Rafferty Travel** (☎ 51555) in Tipperary town.

CASHEL

☎ 062 / pop 2401

Cashel (Caiseal Mumhan) is a chart-topper in tourist Ireland. This prosperous, but unremarkable market town is transformed by the compelling Rock of Cashel and the clutch of dramatic religious buildings that crowns its breezy summit. The town is marred slightly by a traffic-clogged main street, part of the Dublin–Cork route, but there are fine restaurants and pubs. In any case, the rock and its ruins stand loftily apart from the traffic. An additional attraction in Cashel is the excellent Brú Ború traditional music centre (see p283).

Information

The town hall in Main St contains Cashel's **tourist office** (☎ 61333; ⌚ 9am-1pm & 2-6pm Mon-Sat May-Sep). The heritage centre (see p283) is in the same building and doubles as a very helpful information source, with better opening hours than the tourist office. The post office is at the bottom of Main St. The AIB and Bank of Ireland on Main St have ATMs and bureaux de change. There is a car park off Main St (€2 per day).

Rock of Cashel

The **Rock of Cashel** (☎ 61437; adult/child €5/2; ⌚ 9am-7.30pm mid-Jun–mid-Sep, 9.30am-5.30pm mid-Mar–mid-Jun, 9.30am-4.30pm mid-Sep–mid-Mar; final admission 45 min before closing) is one of Ireland's most spectacular archaeological sites. The 'rock' is a prominent green hill, banded with limestone outcrops. It rises from a grassy plain on the outskirts of the town and bristles with ancient fortifications – the word 'cashel' is an anglicised version of the

Irish word *caiseal*, meaning 'fortress'. Sturdy walls circle an enclosure that contains a complete round tower, a roofless abbey and the finest 12th-century Romanesque chapel in Ireland. For more than 1000 years, the Rock of Cashel was a symbol of power, the base of kings and churchmen who ruled over the region.

It's a five-minute stroll from the town centre to the rock. If driving use the car park at the foot of the rock (€2). There are a couple of parking spaces for disabled visitors at the top of the approach road to the ticket office. The rock is a major draw for coach parties and is at its busiest during July and August.

HISTORY

In the 4th century, the Rock of Cashel was chosen as a base by the Eóghanachta clan from Wales, who went on to conquer much of Munster and become kings of the region. For some 400 years it rivalled Tara as a centre of power in Ireland. The clan was associated with St Patrick, hence the rock's alternative name of St Patrick's Rock.

In the 10th century the Eóghanachta lost possession of the rock to the O'Brien, or Dál gCais, tribe under Brian Ború's leadership. In 1101, King Muircheartach O'Brien presented the rock to the Church, a move designed to curry favour with the powerful bishops and to end secular rivalry over possession of the rock with the Eóghanachta, by now known as the MacCarthys. Numerous buildings of all kinds must have occupied the rock over the years, but it is the ecclesiastical relics that survived even the depredations of the Cromwellian army in 1647.

HALL OF THE VICARS CHORAL

The entrance to the Rock of Cashel is through this 15th-century building, once home to the male choristers who sang in the cathedral. It houses the ticket office. The exhibits in the adjoining undercroft include some very rare silverware, Bronze Age axes and **St Patrick's Cross**, an impressive, although eroded, 12th-century crutched cross with a crucifixion scene on one face and animals on the other. A replica stands outside, in the castle courtyard. The kitchen and dining hall upstairs contain some period furniture, tapestries and paintings beneath a fine carved-oak roof and gallery. A 20-minute audiovisual presentation on the rock's history runs every half-hour. There are French, German and Italian showings as well as English.

THE CATHEDRAL

This 13th-century Gothic structure overshadows the other ruins. Entry is through a small porch facing the Hall of the Vicars Choral. The cathedral's western location is formed by the **Archbishop's Residence**, a 15th-century, four-storey castle which had its great hall built over the nave. Soaring above the centre of the cathedral is a huge, square tower with a turret on the southwestern corner.

Scattered throughout are monuments, panels from 16th-century altar tombs and coats of arms. If you have binoculars, look for the numerous stone heads on capitals and corbels high above the ground.

ROUND TOWER

On the northeastern corner of the cathedral is an 11th- or 12th-century round tower, the earliest building on the Rock of Cashel. It's 28m tall and the doorway is 3.5m above the ground – perhaps for structural rather than defensive reasons.

CORMAC'S CHAPEL

If the Rock of Cashel boasted only Cormac's Chapel, it would still be an outstanding place. This compelling building dates from 1127, and the medieval integrity of its trans-European architecture survives. It was probably the first Romanesque church in Ireland. The style of the square towers that flank it to either side may reflect Germanic influences, but there are haunting similarities in its steep stone roof to the 'boat-hull' shape of older Irish buildings, such as the Gallarus Oratory in County Clare and the beehive huts of the Dingle Peninsula.

The true Romanesque splendour is in the detail of the exquisite doorway arches, the grand chancel arch and ribbed barrel vault, and the outstanding carved vignettes that include a trefoil-tailed grotesque and a Norman-helmeted centaur firing an arrow at a rampaging lion. The chapel's interior is tantalisingly dark, but linger for a while and your eyes adjust. Inside the main door, on the left, is the sarcophagus said to house King Cormac, dating from between 1125 and 1150. Frescoes once covered the walls, but only vestigial elements of these survive.

The southern tower leads to a stone-roofed vault or croft above the nave (no access).

Hore Abbey

Cashel throws in another bonus for the heritage lover. This is the formidable ruin of 13th-century Hore Abbey, located in flat farmland just under 1km north of the rock. Originally Benedictine and settled by monks from Glastonbury in England at the end of the 12th century, it later became a Cistercian house, gifted to the order by a 13th-century archbishop who expelled the Benedictine monks after dreaming that they planned to murder him. The complex, although roofless, is still impressive and is pleasantly gloomy.

Brú Ború

Cashel's award-winning cultural centre, **Brú Ború** (☎ 61122; www.comhaltas.com; 9am-5pm daily Jun-Sep, 9am-5pm Mon-Fri Oct-May) offers an absorbing insight into the nation's heritage, especially into Irish traditional music, song and dance. When not on tour, the internationally known Brú Ború group performs here regularly. The centre occupies a modern building just along from the car park below the Rock of Cashel. It has a shop and café, but its main daytime attraction is **Sounds of History** (adult/child €5/3), an exhibition in a subterranean chamber where the story of Ireland and its music is told through imaginative audio displays. Part of the experience is an exhilarating screening of the Fleadh Ceol, Ireland's great annual traditional festival. If you want even more, the centre stages a traditional **show with dinner** (9-11.30pm Tue-Sat Jun-Sep; €40) in its theatre.

Other Sights

The **Cashel Heritage Centre** (☎ 61333; Town Hall, Main St; admission free; 9.30am-5.30pm daily mid-Mar–Oct, 9.30am-5.30pm Mon-Fri Oct–mid-Mar) is located in the town hall, alongside the tourist office. It has a small interpretive centre that features a model showing what Cashel looked like in the 1640s.

The **Cashel Folk Village** (Dominic St; adult/child €3.50/1; 9.30am-7.30pm) incorporates old buildings and shopfronts from around the town.

Sleeping

BUDGET

O'Brien's Holiday Hostel & Camping Park (☎ 61003; obriensholidayhostel@eircom.ie; Dundrum Rd; dm/s/d €15/25/50, camping €7) This IHH hostel, in a converted coach house northwest of town, is friendly, very well equipped and has high-standard rooms and a pleasant camp site. Terrific views of the nearby Rock of Cashel and Hore Abbey are unbeatable bonuses.

Cashel Holiday Hostel (☎ 62330; www.cashelhostel.com; 6 John St; dm €13, s €18-20, d €36-40) This is a worthwhile budget option in a quiet, three-storey Georgian terrace off Main St. It has a recreation room, kitchen and laundry. The décor is fresh and colourful and there's a friendly, relaxed atmosphere.

MID-RANGE

Dominic St, on the way from Main St to the Rock of Cashel, has several quiet B&Bs with views of the rock.

Rockside House (☎ 63813; fax 63813; Rock Villas; s/d €45/64) A terrific location right beside the rock, coupled with immaculate rooms and a warm welcome makes this B&B hard to beat.

Rockville House (☎ 61760; 10 Dominic St; s/d €39/52; P) Well-kept, brightly decorated rooms enhance this friendly place that is within a short distance of the rock.

Abbey House (☎ 61104; teachnamainstreach@eircom.net; 1 Dominic St; s/d €40/60) There's a cheerful mood at this bungalow opposite St Dominic's Friary. It lies midway between the rock and the town centre and is popular, so booking is advised.

Ashmore House (☎ 61286; ashmorehouse@eircom.net; 16 John St; s/d €45/68) This is Georgian Cashel at its most affordable, in a handsome old town house with big, high-ceilinged rooms. It's located in a quiet street, just up from the Cashel Holiday Hostel.

TOP END

Cashel Palace Hotel (☎ 62707; www.cashel-palace.ie; Main St; s/d €171/254) There are right-royal rates at the Cashel Palace, a handsome red-brick, late–Queen Anne house. It was built in 1732 for a Protestant archbishop. Its rooms are luxurious and some have views of the rock, but it costs extra for the privilege. Head off along the private footpath through the hotel's fine gardens – it takes you right to the rock.

Eating & Drinking

On the whole, Cashel beats no drums for dinner, but there are satisfactory eating places and one particularly good restaurant.

Chez Hans (☎ 61177; Dominic St; starters €5.50-11.50, mains €17.75-36; 6-10pm Tue-Sat) You'll go far to find a more enticing menu than the one at this stylish restaurant, located in a converted chapel. There's great subtlety in the often Mediterranean-influenced dishes. Tempting starters can include a risotto of wild mushrooms with duck *confit* and chorizo cream. Mains include a couple of delicious vegetarian dishes among the great choice of fish, meat and game.

Spearman's Bakery (☎ 61143; 97 Main St; sandwiches €3.20; 9am-5pm) Excellent home-cooking characterises this pleasant café, where you can supplement your sandwiches with tasty soup (€3.20) or break for coffee and scrumptious cakes.

Coffee Shop (☎ 61680; 7 Main St; meals under €7; 9am-5pm) Head for this busy café for tea and coffee, breakfast or a light lunch. It's just across from the tourist office and above the Bakehouse Bakery. A local speciality is the tasty Cashel blue-cheese quiche.

Hannigan's (☎ 61737; Ladyswell St; mains €9.50-19) Filling and unpretentious food in a cosy pub atmosphere is the hallmark of Hannigan's and it draws the locals, especially at lunch time. Get outside a bowl of Hannigan's Irish stew (€7.50) and you'll know you've been well fed. This pub also pulls a good pint and has traditional music sessions on Friday nights in summer.

Pasta Milano (☎ 62729; Ladyswell St; pizza €8.30-17.95, pasta €8.80-17.70; noon-midnight daily) Ignore the idiosyncratic décor of this Italian restaurant and concentrate on the great food that's served up with gusto. It has a 10% service charge.

Davern's (☎ 61121; 20 Main St) This local is popular for its good chat and its live music at the weekend.

Getting There & Away

Bus Éireann runs six express buses daily between Dublin and Cork via Cahir and Fermoy. Late June to August there are an extra four buses daily to Cahir, which has the closest train station. There's also one bus daily on the Cork–Athlone route via Thurles, Roscrea and Birr. Tickets are bought on the bus. The bus stop for Cork is outside the Bakehouse Bakery. The Dublin stop is opposite.

Kavanagh's (☎ 51563) has one bus daily to Dublin, leaving Cashel at 8.30am. From Dublin, it leaves George's Quay near Tara St Station at 6pm. It also does a twice-daily run between Cashel and Clonmel, departing from Cashel at noon and 6.35pm.

The nearest train stations are at Cahir and Thurles.

Getting Around

McInerney's (☎ 61225) on Main St hires out bicycles (€10 per day) as do the two hostels (see p283). Cahir and Fethard are both within cycling distance.

AROUND CASHEL

The atmospheric **Athassel Priory** sits on the western bank of the River Suir 8km southwest of Cashel. The original was founded in 1205 by the splendidly named William FitzAdelm de Burgo and it became one of the richest and most important monasteries in Ireland. What survives of the monastery includes its gatehouse and portcullis gateway, the cloister and extensive stretches of walled enclosure.

To get there take the N74 to the village of Golden, then head south for 2km to the priory.

CAHIR

☎ 052 / pop 2500

Cahir (An Cathair; pronounced care) is 15km south of Cashel, at the eastern tip of the Galtee Mountains and on the banks of the River Suir. This pleasant country town is enhanced by its riverside location and spectacular castle.

Orientation & Information

Buses stop in Castle St near a large car park (€0.60 for two hours) alongside the river and castle. East of Castle St is the centre of town, the sloping square. It is surrounded by shops, pubs and cafés and also has some parking.

At the **tourist office** (☎ 41453; 9am-6pm Mon-Sat Mar-Oct, 11am-5pm Nov-Feb), ask for the free leaflet showing walking routes around Cahir Park.

The AIB in Castle St has an ATM and bureau de change.

The post office is north of the square in Church St.

Internet access is available at the **Enterprise Centre** (☎ 42626; Market Yard; €1/5min) which is at the back of a courtyard off the upper side of the square.

There are toilets in the car park just below the tourist office.

Cahir Castle

Cahir's awesome **castle** (☎ 41011; Castle St; adult/child €2.75/1.25; ⌚ 9am-7.30pm mid-Jun–mid-Sep, 9.30am-5.30pm mid-Mar–mid-Jun & mid-Sep–mid-Oct, 9.30am-4.30pm mid-Oct–mid-Mar) is feudal fantasy in a big way. A river-island site, rocky foundations, massive walls, turrets and towers, defences and dungeons are all there. This castle is one of Ireland's largest. Founded by Conor O'Brien in 1142, it was passed to the Butler family in 1375. The castle was surrendered to Cromwell in 1650 without a struggle; its solidity may have discouraged the usual Cromwellian vandalism. Consequently the castle is remarkably intact. It was restored in the 1840s and again in the 1960s, when it came under state ownership.

There's a short audiovisual show on other local sites of historic interest. The buildings within the castle are sparsely furnished, although there are small exhibitions. The real rewards come from simply wandering through this remarkable survivor of Ireland's medieval past.

Swiss Cottage

A pleasant riverside path from behind the car park meanders 2km south to Cahir Park and the **Swiss Cottage** (☎ 41144; Cahir Park; adult/child €3/1.25; ⌚ 10am-6pm daily May-Sep, 10am-1pm & 2-5pm Tue-Sun Apr, 10am-1pm & 2-4.30pm Tue-Sun late Mar & Oct-Nov). Also run by Dúchas, the Swiss Cottage is an exquisite thatched cottage *orné*, surrounded by roses, lavender and honeysuckle. It is the best in Ireland, and was built in about 1810 as a retreat for Richard Butler, 12th Baron Caher, and his wife. The design was by the London architect John Nash, creator of the Royal Pavilion at Brighton and of London's Regent's Park. The cottage-orné style emerged during the late 18th and early 19th century in England in response to the prevailing taste for the picturesque. Thatched roofs, natural wood and carved weatherboarding were characteristics, and most were built as ornamental features on estates. There could be no more lavish example of Regency Picturesque than the Swiss Cottage. It is more of a sizable house than a cottage and has a basement kitchen and wine cellar, a ballroom and salon and upper-floor bedrooms with balconies. The 30-minute (compulsory) guided tours are thoroughly enjoyable.

Sleeping

Apple Caravan & Camping Park (☎ 41459; www.theapplefarm.com; Moorstown; adult/child including tent €4.50/2.50; ⌚ May-Sep) This quiet camp site on a fruit farm of mainly apple orchards is on the N24 between Cahir (6km) and Clonmel (9km). There's free use of a tennis court and racquets.

Lisakyle Hostel (☎ 41963; Church St; dm €12, d €36) An out-of-town location adds to the rustic appeal of this attractive IHH hostel, 2km south of Cahir on a back road to Ardfinnan past the Swiss Cottage. In Cahir, the house opposite the post office in Church St handles inquiries and arranges lifts to the hostel.

Kilcoran Farm Hostel (☎ 41906; Cahir; s/d €13/26) There's a marvellous outback atmosphere at this secluded hostel that lies near the Galtee Mountains, 6km west of Cahir. It's signposted off the N8 Mitchelstown road at the Top petrol station, from which it's another 1km. Turn right at the first junction on the road.

Rectory (☎ 41406; faheyr@eircom.net; Cashel Rd; s/d €35/55; ⌚ May-Sep) There are refreshingly big rooms and big bathrooms in this splendid Georgian house, tucked away off the busy main road about 1km from the centre. There's a big welcome too.

Ashling (☎ 41601; Cashel Rd; s/d €38.10/50.80; ☒) Close to the Rectory, this smaller place cannot match the latter's Georgian spaciousness but is every bit as welcoming and is set in pleasant gardens.

Kilcoran Lodge Hotel (☎ 41288; www.tipp.ie/kilcoran; Cork Rd; s/d €65/100; ♿) Well-placed above the main road, this pink-coloured, three-star hotel, 6km along the Cork road, has good-sized rooms. There's a corporate feel to it all, what with a pool and health club to work off the filling breakfasts. You can get reduced rates on B&B and evening meals for more than one night.

Eating

Coffee Pot Restaurant (☎ 41728; 2 Castle St; snacks €3.50/7; meals €9-12; ⌚ 8.30am-9.30pm) Often busy with coach parties, this handy café is above a souvenir shop. It offers breakfast all day.

Galtee Inn (☎ 41247; The Square; mains €7.95) A prominent location and reasonably priced lunches make this pub popular. The menu includes beef curry and bolognese as well as more traditional offerings.

La Serenata (☎ 45689; Church St; pizza & pasta €7-10.80) Lots of bare wood, exposed stone and brick walls give a fresh ambience to this Italian café-restaurant that does sandwiches (€5.20 to €6) and salads (€3.50 to €5.50).

Getting There & Away

BUS

Cahir is on several **Bus Éireann** (☎ 062-51555) express routes, including Dublin–Cork, Limerick–Waterford, Galway–Waterford, Kilkenny–Cork and Cork–Athlone. There are six buses daily to Cashel (€3.70, 15 minutes). Buses stop in the car park beside the tourist office.

Kavanagh's (☎ 062-51563) buses travel Monday to Saturday between Tipperary town, Cashel and Dublin via Cahir.

TRAIN

Monday to Saturday, the Cork–Rosslare Harbour train stops once a day at Cahir, while the Dublin–Clonmel train stops twice. Contact **Thurles train station** (☎ 0504-21733) for details.

MITCHELSTOWN CAVES

The Galtee Mountains are mainly sandstone, but along the southern side runs a narrow band of limestone, location of the **Mitchelstown Caves** (☎ 052-67246; Burncourt; adult/child €4.50/2.50; ⏰ 10am-6pm) near Burncourt, 16km southwest of Cahir and signposted on the N8 to Mitchelstown (Baile Mhistéala). Superior to Kilkenny's Dunmore Caves and yet less developed for tourists, these caves are among the most extensive in the country.

There are nearly 2km of passages and spectacular chambers full of textbook formations with names such as The Pipe Organ, Hanging Gardens of Babylon and Eagle's Wing. Limestone leaks, so if there's been heavy rain, bring a waterproof hooded jacket.

Call at English's farmhouse opposite the car park for tickets and a tour guide (a tour requires a minimum of two people).

Sleeping

Mountain Lodge Hostel (☎ 052-67277; Burncourt; adult/child €12/10; ⏰ Apr-Sep) This An Óige hostel, in an attractive one-time shooting lodge, lies 6km north of the caves and is a handy base for exploring the Galtee Mountains. It lies to the north of the main Mitchelstown–Cahir road.

Getting There & Away

Daily **Bus Éireann** (☎ 062-51555) express buses from Dublin to Cork or Athlone drop off at the gate to Mountain Lodge Hostel, from where it's a 2km walk.

CLONMEL

☎ 052 / pop 15,721

Clonmel (Cluain Meala, 'Meadows of Honey') is Tipperary's largest and busiest town. There's much more going on here than in neighbouring towns, but Clonmel is still essentially a fairly subdued rural centre. Laurence Sterne (1713–68), author of *A Sentimental Journey* and *Tristram Shandy*, was a native of the town; but the commercial cheerleader for Clonmel was Italian Charles Bianconi (1786–1875), who at the precocious age of 16 was sent to Ireland by his father in an attempt to break his youthful liaison with a woman. Bianconi later channelled all his frustrated passion into setting up a coach service between Clonmel and Cahir; his company quickly grew to become a nationwide passenger and mail carrier. For putting Clonmel on the map, Bianconi was twice elected mayor.

Orientation

Clonmel's centre lies on the northern bank of the River Suir. Set back from the quays and running parallel to the river, the main street runs east–west, starting off as Parnell St and becoming Mitchell St and O'Connell St before passing under West Gate, where it changes to Irishtown and Abbey Rd. Running north from off this long thoroughfare is Gladstone St, which has lots of shops and pubs.

Information

Clonmel Bookshop (☎ 80752; 52 O'Connell St) has a good selection of general books as well as books of local interest, while **Clonmel Library** (☎ 24545; Market Place; ⏰ 10am-5.30pm Mon-Tue, 10am-8.30pm Wed-Thu, 10am-5pm Fri & Sat) beats anywhere else in town for **Internet access** (€2/50min). The **AIB** (O'Connell St) has an ATM and bureau de change. To find the **post office** (Emmet St), turn north off Mitchell St. The **tourist office** (☎ 22960; www.clonmel.ie;

Sarsfield St; ⏲ 9.30am-6pm Mon-Sat May-Sep, 9.30am-5pm Mon-Fri Oct-Apr) offers lots of information and enthusiasm in equal measure. Ask for the *Clonmel Heritage Trail* leaflet.

Sights

In Nelson St, south of Parnell St, is the refurbished **County Courthouse** designed by Richard Morrison in 1802. It was here that the Young Irelanders of 1848, including Thomas Francis Meagher, were tried and sentenced to transportation to Australia.

West along Mitchell St (past the pistachio-coloured town hall with its statue commemorating the 1798 Rising) and south down Abbey St is the **Franciscan friary**. Inside, near the door, is a 1533 Butler tomb depicting a knight and his lady. There's some fine modern stained glass, especially in St Anthony's Chapel to the north.

On Mitchell St, at the junction with Sarsfield St, is the superb **Main Guard**, a Butler courthouse dating from 1674, based on a design by Christopher Wren. At the time of writing it was undergoing major restoration and is scheduled for reopening in 2004. Turn south down Bridge St and cross the river, following the road round until it opens out at **Lady Blessington's Bath**, a picturesque stretch of the river, excellent for picnicking.

A modern, custom-made building houses **Tipperary South Riding County Museum** (☎ 25399; The Borstal, Market Place; admission free; ⏲ 10am-5pm Mon-Fri, 10am-1pm & 2-5pm Sat). It has displays on the history of County Tipperary from Neolithic times to the present and hosts regular temporary exhibitions.

Sleeping

Power's the Pot Caravan & Camping Park (☎ 23085; fax 23893; Harney's Cross, Clonmel; tent, car & 2 people €15) This park has a Clonmel address even though it's 9km southeast in County Waterford on the northern slopes of the Comeragh Mountains. It's in a good location for exploring the Comeraghs. To get there, cross south over the river in Clonmel and then follow the road to Rathgormuck.

Amberville (☎ 21470; amberville@eircom.net; Glenconnor Rd; s/d €40/60 Ⓟ) North off Western Rd beside St Luke's Hospital, this pleasant B&B is about 500m from the centre. It has five homely rooms.

Also recommended among several B&Bs on Marlfield Rd, due west of Irishtown and Abbey Rd, are **Benuala** (☎ 22158; benuala@indigo.ie; Marlfield Rd; s/d €35/70; Ⓟ), which has comfortable rooms and does good breakfasts, and **Hillcourt** (☎ 21029; www.hillcourt.com; Marlfield Rd; s/d €35/53; Ⓟ), a pleasant bungalow with a garden for guests' use and a large reduction for children.

Clonmel Arms Hotel (☎ 21233; theclonmelarms@eircom.net; Sarsfield St; s/d €57/114; Ⓟ) Three-star quality is maintained at this long-established hotel that has a restaurant and popular bar.

Hearn's Hotel (☎ 21611; fax 21135; Parnell St; s/d €50/100; Ⓟ) The historical gloss on Charles Bianconi's former coach house is wearing a bit thin. Rooms are comfortable enough and have the usual TV and tea-making facilities, but at the time of writing the hotel was undergoing a much-needed refurbishment.

Eating

Angela's (☎ 26899; 14 Abbey St; meals €5.80-6.80; ⏲ 9am-5.30pm Mon-Fri, 9am-5pm Sat) This is the place for tasty and imaginative lunches with a strong organic bias. Specials can include Thai fishcakes or char-grilled Toulouse sausages on a mustard mash with onion gravy. There are vegetarian options too, filling bruschettas and warm wraps (€6.60 to €7.50) and great coffee, all in relaxing, unpretentious surroundings.

Catalpa (☎ 26821; Sarsfield St; pasta & pizza €6.30-9.20, mains €13-20; ⏲ 12.30-2pm & 6.30-11pm Wed-Fri, 6.30-11pm Tue, Sat & Sun) Right next to the handsome Main Guard building, Catalpa is a delightful, candlelit basement restaurant that serves traditional Italian food, plus a delectable selection of chicken, veal and steak dishes and a couple of seafood options.

The Clonmel Arms Hotel's plush **Paddock Bar** (lunch €8.50, mains €12-16; ⏲ 12.30-9.30pm) dishes up good-value pub meals, from smoked salmon to chicken curry.

Tierney's Pub (☎ 24467; 13 O'Connell St; snacks €8-15, mains €13-24) Award-winning Tierney's is dense with entertaining pub bric-a-brac. Its popular upstairs restaurant favours traditional dishes, but with a nod to *nouvelle cuisine*. Expect filling steaks, grills, fish dishes and vegetarian possibilities.

O'Gorman's (☎ 21380; 61/62 O'Connell St; lunch €4.25; ⏲ 9am-5pm) Popular with locals, O'Gorman's does breakfasts (€4.25 to €5.90) and sandwiches and paninis (€3.25 to €5), as well as lunch dishes such as lasagne and shepherd's pie. In the adjoining shop you can buy sandwiches to take away.

Mulcahy's (☎ 25054; 47 Gladstone St; carvery €5-8, ⏰ 8.30am-4pm; restaurant mains €14-20, ⏰ 5.30-9.30pm) This vast rambling, brightly decorated pub is a good place to lose yourself in. It has a self-service carvery and the restaurant, East Lane Café, rings the changes, from Irish beef to Moroccan ostrich.

Entertainment

Clonmel is the tops among Tipperary's country towns for pub and club music.

Gallery on Gladstone (Devane's; ☎ 28680; 13 Gladstone St; ⏰ 9.30pm-12.30am) Clonmel's most interesting line-ups are featured at the Gallery, which hosts the likes of Julia Turner as well as good local bands. There are live turns on Thursday and Sunday nights and DJs blast out chart mix on Friday and Saturday nights.

Mulcahy's (☎ 25054; 47 Gladstone St) Mulcahy's hosts Irish music in its bar on Wednesday, Friday and Saturday nights, while its Danno's nightclub, entered from Market St, whisks up a froth of chart and retro on Thursday to Sunday nights from 11pm to 2am.

The Clonmel Arms Hotel's **Paddock Bar** (☎ 21233; theclonmelarms@eircom.net; Sarsfield St; Ⓟ) has live music on Thursday, Friday and Sunday nights, while its Waterfront Bar trundles out '80s nostalgia on Friday nights, and a mix of DJs and live bands on Saturdays, from 11pm, for the 20-plus age group.

Lonergan's (☎ 21250; 35-36 O'Connell St) Monday nights see trad music sessions at this very traditional pub in the heart of Clonmel's main street.

South Tipperary Arts Centre (☎ 27877; Nelson St) There's an excellent programme of art exhibitions, plays and films at this focus of the arts in Tipperary.

Sport

North of town is the **Powerstown Park Racecourse** (☎ 21422; Powerstown Park, Clonmel). It holds 13 meetings a year; call for details of fixtures.

Getting There & Away

BUS

Bus Éireann (☎ 051-79000) has two buses daily to Cork (€13.20) up to six to Dublin (€11.50), and numerous services to Waterford, Limerick and Kilkenny. Tickets can be bought at **Rafferty Travel** (☎ 22622; 45 Gladstone St) or at the train station where the buses stop. **Kavanagh's** (☎ 062-51563) has twice-daily buses between Cashel and Clonmel.

TRAIN

The **train station** (☎ 21982) is on Prior Park Rd. Head north along Gladstone St, past the Oakville Shopping Centre and it's just after the Statoil service station. Clonmel is on the Cork–Rosslare Harbour line, with one train a day Monday to Saturday. The Dublin–Clonmel train runs twice a day Monday to Saturday via Limerick Junction.

AROUND CLONMEL

Directly south of Clonmel, over the border in County Waterford, are the Comeragh Mountains. There's a scenic route south to Ballymacarbry and the Nire Valley. For more details, see p183.

The **East Munster Way** (see p656) passes through Clonmel. Heading east towards Carrick-on-Suir, the way follows the old towpath along the River Suir for much of the way. At Sir Thomas Bridge it cuts south away from the river and into the Comeraghs and through Gurteen Wood to Harney's Crossroads. It rejoins the River Suir again at Kilsheelan Bridge, from where it follows the towpath all the way to Carrick-on-Suir. Going west from Clonmel, the way first leads south into the hills and then descends to Newcastle and the river once more. The route east is pleasant for a short there-and-back outing from Clonmel.

FETHARD

☎ **052 / pop 843**

Fethard (Fiodh Ard) is where keen medievalists will really get carried away. This quiet little place, 14km north of Clonmel on the River Clashawley, has a good slice of its old walls still intact, as well as a fair sprinkling of other ruins. The generous width of the main street alone signifies medieval survival and conjures up images of boisterous markets and the delightful randomness of historical 'town planning'.

Fethard has no official tourist office but you can get information and local leaflets from the helpful office of the **Tirry Community Centre** (☎ 31000; Barrack St). Ask for the useful walking-tour leaflet.

Sights

Fethard's **Holy Trinity Church and churchyard** (☎ 26643; Main St; admission free; open by appointment) make up a splendid little time warp. The church lies off Main St and is reached through a cast-iron gateway. The main part of the church dates from the 13th century, but its ancient walls have been rather blighted by being covered with mortar for weatherproofing. The handsome west tower was added later and has had its sturdy stonework uncovered. It looks more like a fortified tower house and has savage-looking finials on its corner turrets. The interior of the church has an aisled nave and a chancel of typical medieval style, but it is sparsely furnished. A ruined chapel and sacristy adjoin the south end of the church. It is the context of the entire churchyard that is the real winner. Old gravestones descend in ranks to a refurbished stretch of medieval wall complete with a guard tower and a parapet, from where you can look down on the gentle River Clashawley between its green banks.

To enter the church and churchyard you have to collect keys from Barmor's Shop a few doors along from the entrance gate. The notice on the gate refers you to 'Whyte's Shop', but that's no longer the case.

Close to the church in Main St is the 17th-century **town hall**, with some fine coats of arms mounted on the façade.

Fethard's main concentration of medieval remains (some of which have been incorporated into later buildings) are just south of the church at the end of Watergate St. Beside Castle Inn are the ruins of several fortified 17th-century **tower houses**. Just under the archway to the river bank and Watergate Bridge is a fine **sheila-na-gig** embedded in the wall to your left. You can stroll the river bank provided the resident geese are not in bullying mood. From here the backs of the Abbey St houses, although much added to and knocked about in places, once again display the pleasing irregularities of typical medieval building style.

East along Abbey St is the 14th-century **Augustinian friary**, now a Catholic church, with some fine, medieval stained glass and another brazen **sheila-na-gig** in its east wall.

SHAMELESS SHEILAS OR SYMBOLIC SHAMANESSES?

Sexually explicit stone images of women, known as *sheila-na-gig,* have long been a feature on the walls of church buildings and other old structures in Ireland. Theories about their origin are still debated. One suggestion is that they are a medieval concept brought to Ireland by the Normans and that they were placed on church walls as some kind of male-oriented warning against lust. Another suggestion is that they are ancient survivors of pre-Christian fertility symbolism that were simply incorporated into church buildings as recycled stonework. One English translation of the name is suggested as 'the old woman on her hunkers'. There are sheilas on display in the National Museum in Dublin. The village of Fethard once had four sheilas, but one was stolen from the wall of nearby Kiltinaban Church in 1990. In spite of a reward being offered for its return and Interpol being alerted, it has never been recovered.

Sleeping & Eating

Gateway (☎ 31701; Rocklow Rd; s/d €30/55) Tucked away at the edge of the village, alongside the ruined 15th-century North Gate, this little house is a pleasant stopover.

PJ Lonergan's (☎ 31447; Market Sq; lunch mains €8-9, salads €6-8; 🕑 12.30-2.30pm) Enjoy a relaxed lunch at this pleasant pub that as well as roast beef and lasagne offers a good selection of sandwiches (€3.50 to €4).

Getting There & Away

There's no public transport to Fethard but it would make a pleasant cycle ride from Cashel, 15km to the west.

CARRICK-ON-SUIR

☎ 051 / pop 5543

The market town of Carrick-on-Suir (Carraig na Siúire), 20km east of Clonmel boasted twice its present population during the late medieval period, when it was a centre of the brewing and wool industries. The modern town is fairly quiet and unassuming, although the traffic flow is relentless along the main street.

Carrick-on-Suir was rightly quick to honour local boy Sean Kelly, one of the world's greatest cyclists in the late 1980s. The town square bears his name, as does the sports centre.

From Carrick-on-Suir the **East Munster Way** winds west to Clonmel before heading south into Waterford. For more details see p656.

Orientation & Information

Few streets have signs on them, but you can orient yourself using the street map on Main St near the AIB.

Off Main St, through a cast-iron gate, an old church houses the **tourist office** (☎ 640 200; 9am-6pm daily May-Sep, 9am-5pm Mon-Sat Oct-Apr). Part of the tourist office is a small **heritage centre** (adult/child €3/2), which opens the same hours. It has a rather random display on local history.

Ormond Castle

Carrick-on-Suir was once the property of the Butlers, the earls of Ormond, who built the **castle** (☎ 640 787; Castle St; adult/child €3/1.50; 9.30am-6.30pm mid-Jun–early Sep) on the banks of the river in the 14th century. Anne Boleyn, the second of Henry VIII's six wives, may have been born here, though other castles also claim this distinction. The Elizabethan mansion next to the castle was built by the 10th earl of Ormond, Black Tom Butler, in anticipation of a visit by his cousin, Queen Elizabeth I, who rather thoughtlessly never turned up.

Some rooms in this Dúchas-owned edifice have fine 16th-century stuccowork, especially the Long Gallery with its depictions of Elizabeth and of the Butler coat of arms.

Sleeping & Eating

Carrick-on-Suir Caravan & Camping Park (☎ 640 461; Kilkenny Rd, Ballyrichard; tent & car €7.60, hikers & cyclists including tent €4.45 per person; Mar-Oct) This small park with 12 tent pitches is only a few minutes' walk from the centre. The excellent B&B **Fatima House** (☎ 640 298; www.fatimahouse.com; John St; s/d €35/60) has lovely rooms and there's a mellow mood throughout. It is about 500m west of the Greenside bus stop.

Carraig Hotel (☎ 641 455; www.carraighotel.com; Main St; s/d €57/114; bar snacks €3.50-8; mains €13.50-19.50) has bright, pleasant rooms of a comfortable standard.

There are few good eateries in town, though most of the Main St pubs offer reasonably priced lunches. The Carraig Hotel's **Weavers Restaurant** does seafood and steak dishes and tasty alternatives such as stuffed peppers. **Weir** (☎ 640 205; 3 Bridge St; snacks €4.75-8, mains €7.25-10.25) is a slightly pokey but reasonable café that serves breakfasts, snacks and hot lunches in gigantic portions.

Getting There & Away

BUS

Buses stop at Greenside, the park beside the N24 road. Follow New St north from Main St, then turn right.

Bus Éireann (☎ 879 000) has numerous buses to Carrick-on-Suir. Bus No 55 between Limerick (€13.20) and Waterford (€6) serves Tipperary town, Cahir, Clonmel and Carrick-on-Suir up to seven times daily, with connections to Galway and Rosslare Harbour. Bus No 7 from Clonmel to Dublin via Carrick-on-Suir and Kilkenny stops up to six times daily, with connections to Cork.

TRAIN

The station is north of Greenside, off Cregg Rd. There's one train a day Monday to Saturday on the Cork–Rosslare Harbour line via Limerick Junction and Waterford. Contact **Thurles train station** (☎ 0504-21733) for details.

ROSCREA

☎ **0505 / pop 5478**

The pleasant little town of Roscrea (Ros Cré) is a useful stopover on the journey between Dublin and Limerick.

Roscrea owes its beginnings to a 5th-century monk, St Crónán, who set up a way station for the travelling poor. Most of the historical structures are on or near the main street, Castle St.

Tourist information is available from Roscrea Castle, a Dúchas-run 13th-century property in the town centre. There are substantial remains of a gatehouse, walls and towers, and inside the courtyard stands austere **Damer House**, the Queen Anne–style residence of the Damer family, which houses the **Roscrea Heritage Centre** (☎ 21850; Castle St; adult/concession €3.10/1.20; 10am-6pm daily Apr-Oct, Sat & Sun only Nov-Mar). The centre contains several interesting exhibitions, including one on the medieval monasteries of the midlands and another on early-20th-century farming life. There's free parking in the main street.

Sleeping & Eating

Grant's Hotel (☎ 23300; fax 23209; Castle St; s/d €55/95) A classic country-town hotel and former coaching inn, this is the place to switch off and enjoy fully restored, elegant and comfortable surroundings. Grant's **Lemon Tree Restaurant** (lunch €8, dinner mains €18) has a good carvery and offers everything from ostrich and pheasant to salmon.

Quigley's Bakery (Roscrea Shopping Centre) does great sandwiches for about €2.

La Seranata (☎ 22431; The Mall; pizza & pasta €6.70-8.70; noon-10pm Mon-Sat, 1-9pm Sun) This cosy restaurant is just off Castle St beside the river and has lots of intimate little corners amid exposed stonework, artworks and bright surroundings.

Getting There & Away

Up to 13 **Bus Éireann** (☎ 01-836 6111) express buses stop at Roscrea between Dublin (two hours) and Limerick (one hour). There are daily buses to Sligo, Carrick-on-Shannon, Athlone, Thurles, Cahir, Cork and to Shannon.

Dublin–Limerick trains stop at Roscrea twice a day Monday to Saturday, and once on Sunday (☎ 21823 for details).

ROSCREA & AROUND

About 30km west of Roscrea along the N7 is the busy town of Nenagh with the ruins of **Nenagh Castle**. Nenagh is the gateway to the eastern shore of Lough Derg, a popular boating and fishing area.

About 9km northwest of Nenagh, on the R495, is the waterfront hamlet of Dromineer, a good place to sample lakeside life. There are plenty of visiting boats in summer and you can swim, fish, go cruising or rent a canoe. Inquire at **Shannon Sailing** (☎ 067-24499; www.shannonsailing.com).

The **Dromineer Bay Hotel** (☎ 067-24114; www.dromineerbay.com; s/d €65/120; P) is a busy and attractive lakeside place with bright rooms. Prices jump by about €10 at weekends and drop the same from October to March. The hotel's **Crow's Nest Bar** (mains €10.50-19) does hefty sandwiches (€3.25 to €6.75) and a kids menu (€5.50).

County Kilkenny

CONTENTS

The verdant farming county of Kilkenny is a pastoral wonderland of solid stone walls, scenic highways, medieval ruins, horse farms and contemporary restaurants. The Normans liked this part of Ireland and settled here in large numbers, leaving an indelible stamp on Kilkenny city, the county's well-preserved capital. County Kilkenny's most attractive areas are along the Rivers Nore and Barrow, on which there are some delightful villages, such as Inistioge and Graiguenamanagh. Jerpoint Abbey and Kells Priory are two of the country's finest medieval monastic settlements. Walking the stretch of the South Leinster Way that crosses southern Kilkenny offers an opportunity to see rural Ireland at its prettiest.

The past and present seem to coexist comfortably in Kilkenny's towns and countryside. Along the River Barrow, an old-timer steps into a rustic old grocery-pub and asks for fishing tackle and a pint of Guinness. Down the road a piece, a solitary boy whiles time away by whacking a ball at a barn with his hurling stick. Sheep graze amid graceful stone hulks left by 15th-century monks. In the city, young professionals slide into the sleek, vinyl booths of a trendy café. The traveller catches only brief glimpses of such real-life details, but long after the castles and ruins have blurred, the subtle spirit of Kilkenny stays with you.

Since medieval times, Kilkenny's history has been inextricably linked with the fortunes of one Anglo-Norman family, the Butlers, earls of Ormond. After arriving in 1171, they made the region their own, promoting first the Norman cause and then that of the English royal household. They were based in Kilkenny city.

HIGHLIGHTS

- Live it up in Kilkenny city's exuberant **bars and restaurants** (p301)
- Get outdoors along the scenic River Nore near **Bennettsbridge** (p303)
- Laze away a few days in charming **Inistioge** (p305) or **Graiguenamanagh** (p305)
- Get medieval at **Kilkenny Castle** (p297), **Kells Priory** (p304) and **Jerpoint Abbey** (p304)
- Laugh your head off at Kilkenny's **'Cat Laughs' Comedy Festival** (p299)

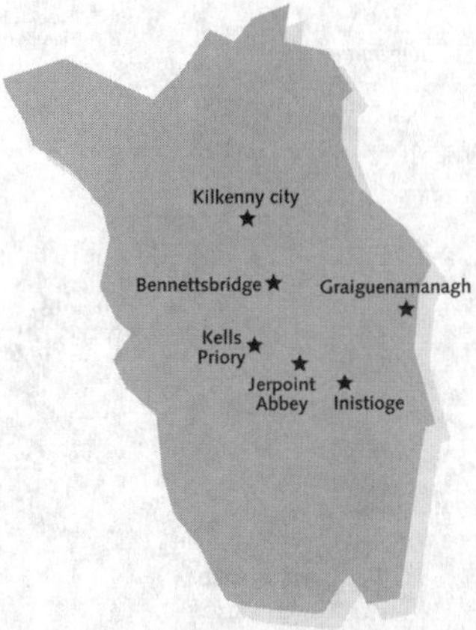

- POPULATION: 75,366
- AREA: 1274 SQ KM

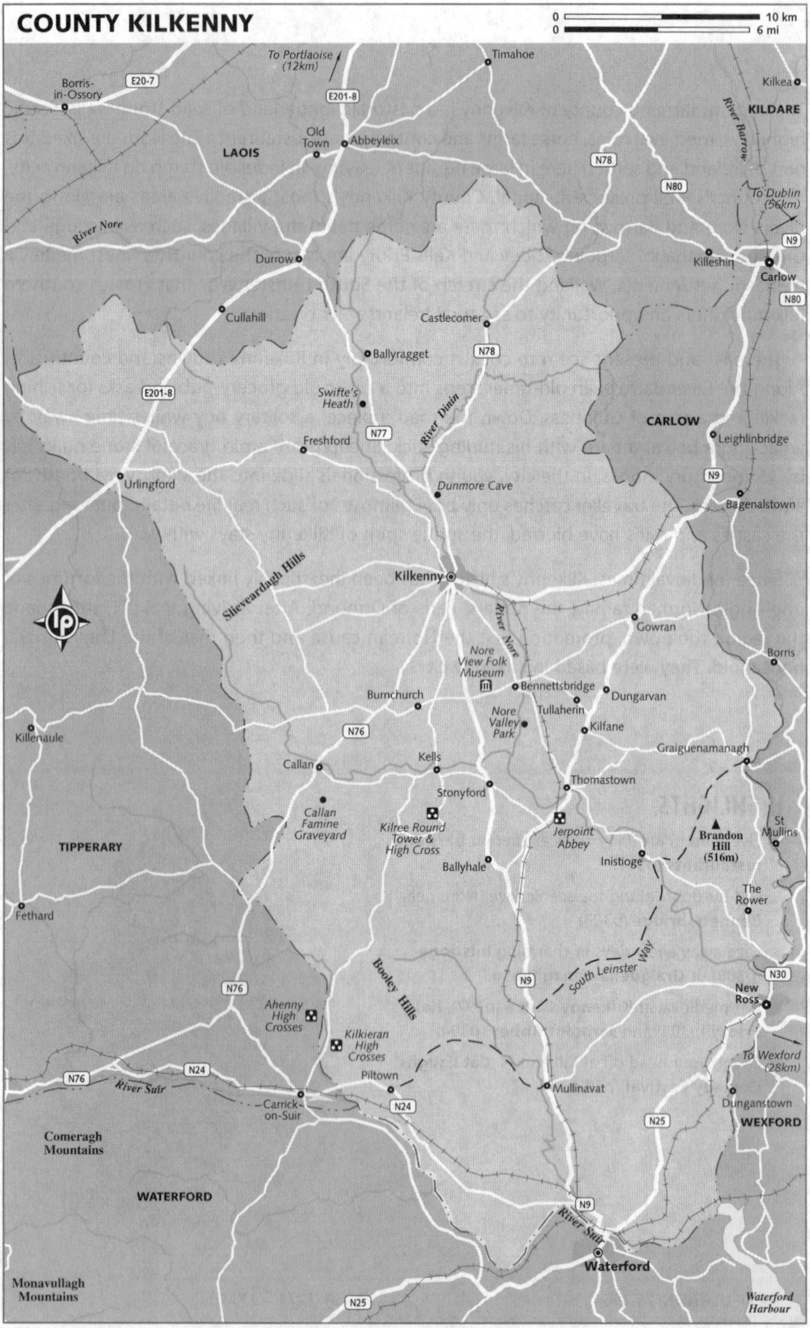
COUNTY KILKENNY
0 10 km
0 6 mi
To Portlaoise (12km)
Timahoe
Borris-in-Ossory
E20-7
E201-8
Kilkea
KILDARE
River Barrow
Old Town
Abbeyleix
LAOIS
N78
N80
To Dublin (56km)
River Nore
N9
Durrow
Killeshin
Carlow
N80
Cullahill
Castlecomer
Ballyragget
N78
E201-8
Swifte's Heath
River Dinin
CARLOW
N77
Leighlinbridge
Freshford
N9
Urlingford
Dunmore Cave
Bagenalstown
Slieveardagh Hills
Kilkenny
River Nore
Gowran
Nore View Folk Museum
Borris
Bennettsbridge
Dungarvan
Burnchurch
Tullaherin
Nore Valley Park
Killenaule
N76
Kilfane
Graiguenamanagh
Callan
Kells
Thomastown
Stonyford
Callan Famine Graveyard
Kilree Round Tower & High Cross
Jerpoint Abbey
Brandon Hill (516m)
St Mullins
TIPPERARY
Inistioge
Ballyhale
The Rower
Fethard
South Leinster Way
Booley Hills
N9
N30
N76
New Ross
Ahenny High Crosses
Kilkieran High Crosses
To Wexford (28km)
N76
N24
Piltown
River Suir
Mullinavat
Carrick-on-Suir
N24
Dunganstown
N25
WEXFORD
Comeragh Mountains
WATERFORD
N9
River Suir
Waterford
Monavullagh Mountains
N25
Waterford Harbour

KILKENNY CITY

☎ 056 / pop 8594

To simply call Kilkenny a 'medieval city', as many tourist brochures do, is rather misleading. There's no pile of dead bodies in the gutter, no-one's heaving slops out the window, and ruddy-faced fools and laughing strumpets no longer thrash the hay in ox carts behind the pub. Beer isn't served in wooden buckets, the common folk don't smell like barnyards and knights in shining armour don't shove the peasants out of their way as they clip-clop by on well-bred horses. Let's just establish that up front.

Kilkenny has, shall we say, aged gracefully. It rates among Ireland's most elegant cities. Although much of Kilkenny's architectural charm owes a huge debt to the Middle Ages, when the city was a powerful seat of political power, modern Kilkenny is a vibrant cultural centre, renowned throughout Ireland for its devotion to the arts. Its cobbled pedestrian passageways and old-fashioned shop fronts may look like the way to mysterious, time-warped quarters, but in reality they lead to hip bars, fashion boutiques and chic restaurants. Kilkenny is clearly in the modern world, but it didn't sell its soul to the devil to get here.

Presiding over the town is a splendid medieval cathedral, named after St Canice (Cainneach or Kenneth), who founded a monastery here in the 6th century; hence the city's Irish name, Cill Chainnigh. The town's other 'must-see' attraction is the mighty castle, which sits majestically on a sweep in the Nore.

Kilkenny is sometimes called the 'marble city' because of the local black limestone, seen to most striking effect in the cathedral. The people of Kilkenny call themselves 'Kilkenny Cats', recalling the traditional nursery rhyme about two cats who clawed each other to death.

HISTORY

In the 5th century, St Kieran is said to have visited Kilkenny and, on the site of the present Kilkenny Castle, challenged the chieftains of Ossory to accept the Christian faith. Subsequently, St Canice established his monastery here. Kilkenny consolidated its importance in the 13th century under William Marshall, the earl of Pembroke and son-in-law of the Anglo-Norman conqueror Strongbow. Kilkenny Castle was built to secure a crossing point on the Nore.

During the Middle Ages, Kilkenny was intermittently the unofficial capital of Ireland, with its own Anglo-Norman Parliament. In 1366 the Parliament passed the so-called Statutes of Kilkenny, a set of Draconian laws aimed at preventing the assimilation of the increasingly assertive Anglo-Normans into Irish society. Anglo-Normans were prohibited from marrying the native Irish, taking part in Irish sports, speaking or dressing like the Irish or playing any Irish music. Any breach of the law was to result in the confiscation of Anglo-Norman property and death to the native Irish. Although the laws remained theoretically in force for over 200 years, they were never enforced with any great effectiveness and did little to halt the absorption of the Anglo-Normans into Irish culture.

During the 1640s, Kilkenny sided with the Catholic royalists in the English Civil War. The 1641 Confederation of Kilkenny, an uneasy alliance of native Irish and Anglo-Normans, aimed to bring about the return of land and power to Catholics. After Charles I's execution, Cromwell besieged Kilkenny for five days, destroying much of the southern wall of the castle before Ormond surrendered. The defeat signalled a permanent end to Kilkenny's political influence over Irish affairs.

ORIENTATION

At the junction of several major highways, Kilkenny straddles the River Nore, which flows through much of the county. St Canice's Cathedral sits on the northern bank of the River Bregagh (a tributary of the Nore) to the north of the town centre outside the town walls. Kilkenny's main thoroughfare runs southeast from the cathedral, past St Canice's Place to Irishtown (where the common folk were once concentrated, outside the town walls) then over the bridge, eventually becoming Parliament St, which then splits into two. Kilkenny Castle, located on the banks of the River Nore, dominates the town's southern side.

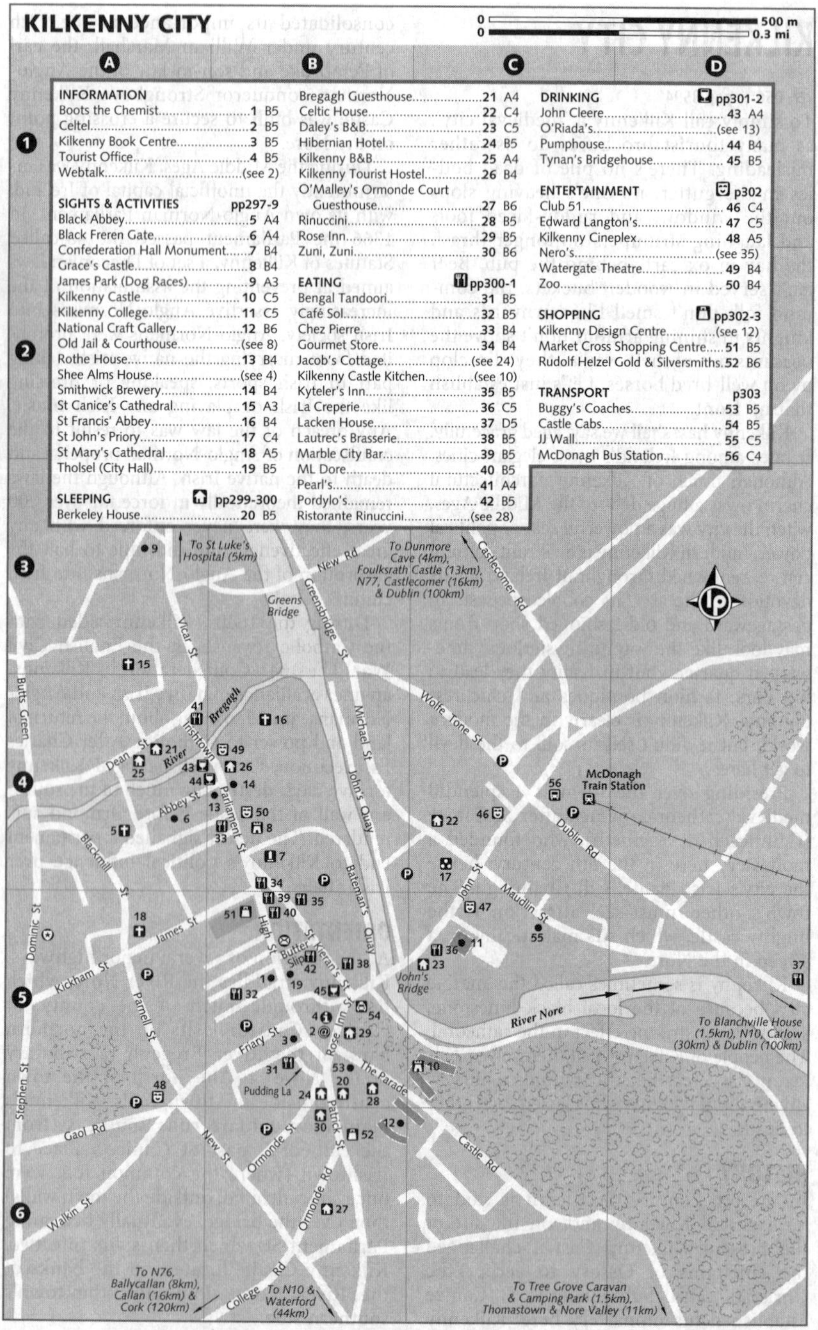
KILKENNY CITY
0 500 m
0 0.3 mi
A
B
C
D
1
2
3
4
5
6
INFORMATION
Boots the Chemist.........1 B5
Celtel.........2 B5
Kilkenny Book Centre.........3 B5
Tourist Office.........4 B5
Webtalk.........(see 2)
SIGHTS & ACTIVITIES pp297-9
Black Abbey.........5 A4
Black Freren Gate.........6 A4
Confederation Hall Monument.........7 B4
Grace's Castle.........8 B4
James Park (Dog Races).........9 A3
Kilkenny Castle.........10 C5
Kilkenny College.........11 C5
National Craft Gallery.........12 B6
Old Jail & Courthouse.........(see 8)
Rothe House.........13 B4
Shee Alms House.........(see 4)
Smithwick Brewery.........14 B4
St Canice's Cathedral.........15 A3
St Francis' Abbey.........16 B4
St John's Priory.........17 C4
St Mary's Cathedral.........18 A5
Tholsel (City Hall).........19 B5
SLEEPING pp299-300
Berkeley House.........20 B5
Bregagh Guesthouse.........21 A4
Celtic House.........22 C4
Daley's B&B.........23 C5
Hibernian Hotel.........24 B5
Kilkenny B&B.........25 A4
Kilkenny Tourist Hostel.........26 B4
O'Malley's Ormonde Court Guesthouse.........27 B6
Rinuccini.........28 B5
Rose Inn.........29 B5
Zuni, Zuni.........30 B6
EATING pp300-1
Bengal Tandoori.........31 B5
Café Sol.........32 B5
Chez Pierre.........33 B4
Gourmet Store.........34 B4
Jacob's Cottage.........(see 24)
Kilkenny Castle Kitchen.........(see 10)
Kyteler's Inn.........35 B5
La Creperie.........36 C5
Lacken House.........37 D5
Lautrec's Brasserie.........38 B5
Marble City Bar.........39 B5
ML Dore.........40 B5
Pearl's.........41 A4
Pordylo's.........42 B5
Ristorante Rinuccini.........(see 28)
DRINKING pp301-2
John Cleere.........43 A4
O'Riada's.........(see 13)
Pumphouse.........44 B4
Tynan's Bridgehouse.........45 B5
ENTERTAINMENT p302
Club 51.........46 C4
Edward Langton's.........47 C5
Kilkenny Cineplex.........48 A5
Nero's.........(see 35)
Watergate Theatre.........49 B4
Zoo.........50 B4
SHOPPING pp302-3
Kilkenny Design Centre.........(see 12)
Market Cross Shopping Centre.........51 B5
Rudolf Helzel Gold & Silversmiths.........52 B6
TRANSPORT p303
Buggy's Coaches.........53 B5
Castle Cabs.........54 B5
JJ Wall.........55 C5
McDonagh Bus Station.........56 C4
To St Luke's Hospital (5km)
To Dunmore Cave (4km), Foulksrath Castle (13km), N77, Castlecomer (16km) & Dublin (100km)
New Rd
Castlecomer Rd
Greens Bridge
Greensbridge St
Vicar St
Butts Green
Bregagh River
Irishtown
Dean St
Michael St
Wolfe Tone St
John's Quay
Abbey St
Parliament St
McDonagh Train Station
Dublin Rd
Blackmill St
Bateman's Quay
John St
Maudlin St
Dominic St
James St
High St
St Kieran's St
Butter Slip
Kickham St
John's Bridge
River Nore
Parnell St
Friary St
Rose Inn St
To Blanchville House (1.5km), N10, Carlow (30km) & Dublin (100km)
The Parade
Pudding La
Stephen St
Patrick St
Gaol Rd
New St
Ormonde St
Castle Rd
Ormonde Rd
Walkin St
To N76, Ballycallan (8km), Callan (16km) & Cork (120km)
College Rd
To N10 & Waterford (44km)
To Tree Grove Caravan & Camping Park (1.5km), Thomastown & Nore Valley (11km)

INFORMATION

Bookshop

Kilkenny Book Centre (☎ 776 2117; 10 High St) This, the largest bookshop in town, stocks a range of titles and maps on Ireland, as well as periodicals.

Emergency

Police station (☎ 999 or 22222; Dominic St)

Internet Access

Celtel (☎ 772 0303; 26 Rose Inn St; €3.50/30min; 🕒 10am-9pm Mon-Sat, 11am-8pm Sun)
Webtalk (☎ 775 0066; 25 Rose Inn St; €3.50/30min; 🕒 9am-9pm Mon-Sat, 2-8pm Sun)

Medical Services

Boots the Chemist (☎ 777 1222; 36-38 High St) Sells medicine and first-aid supplies.
St Luke's Hospital (☎ 775 1133; Freshford Rd)

Money

All of Ireland's big banks have branches, with ATMs, on High St.

Tourist Information

Tourist office (☎ 775 1500; Rose Inn St; www.southeastireland.com; 🕒 9am-5pm Mon-Sat Sep-Jun, 9am-6pm Mon-Sat & 11am-5pm Sun Jul-Aug) In the lovely stone Shee Alms House. The office sells excellent guides to the town and inexpensive walking maps of the county.

SIGHTS

Kilkenny Castle

On a lovely bend of the Nore is **Kilkenny Castle** (☎ 772 1450; adult/child €5/2; 🕒 10am-7pm daily Jun-Sep, 10.30am-12.45pm & 2-5pm Tue-Sat & 11am-12.45pm & 2-5pm Sun Oct-Mar, 10am-5pm daily Apr-May), one of Ireland's most magnificent fortresses. The first structure on this strategic site was a wooden tower built in 1172 by Richard de Clare, the Anglo-Norman conqueror of Ireland better known as Strongbow. In 1192 Strongbow's son-in-law, William Marshall, erected a stone castle with four towers, three of which still survive. The castle was bought by the powerful Butler family in 1391 and their descendants continued to live there until 1935. Maintaining such a structure became a big financial strain and most of the furnishings were sold at auction. The castle was handed over to the city in 1967 for the princely sum of £50 and is now administered by Dúchas.

Work continues to restore the castle to its Victorian splendour and many of the rooms have only recently been opened to the public. Most of the furnishings are not original to the castle, although a few items have been purchased back by Dúchas. What you do see are Victorian antiques that would evoke gasps from viewers of the *Antique Roadshow*.

The **Long Gallery** (the wing of the castle nearest the river), with its vividly painted ceiling mixing Celtic and Pre-Raphaelite motifs with portraits of the Butler family members over the centuries, is particularly splendid and forms the focus of the 40-minute guided tour.

The castle is also home to the **Butler Gallery** (☎ 776 1106; www.butlergallery.com; admission free), one of the country's most important art galleries outside Dublin. Small art exhibitions featuring the work of contemporary artists, are held throughout the year.

In the basement, the castle kitchen houses a popular summertime café.

About 20 hectares of **parkland** (admission free; 🕒 10am-8.30pm daily in summer) extend to the southeast, with a Celticcross-shaped rose garden, a fountain to the northern end and a children's playground to the south.

St Canice's Cathedral

Although **St Canice's Cathedral** (☎ 776 4971; stcanicecathedral@eircom.net; St Canice's Pl; admission €3; 🕒 9am-1pm & 2-6pm Mon-Sat & 2-6pm Sun Easter-Sep, 10am-1pm & 2-4pm Mon-Sat & 2-4pm Sun Oct-Easter) was built between 1202 and 1285, it has a much longer history. Legend has it that the first monastery was built here by St Canice, Kilkenny's patron saint, who moved here from Aghaboe, County Laois, in the 6th century. There are records of a wooden church on the site which was burned down in 1087.

St Canice's was built in early English Gothic style but then suffered a catalogue of catastrophes and resurrections. The first disaster, when the bell tower collapsed in 1332, is connected with the story of Kilkenny's legendary witch, Dame Alice Kyteler (see the boxed text on p298). In 1650, Cromwell's forces defaced and damaged the church, using it to stable their horses. Repairs began in 1661, but there was still much to be done a century later.

Outside the cathedral, a 30m-high **round tower** (adult/child €2/1.50) rises amid an odd array of ancient tombstones and is the oldest structure within the grounds. It was

COUNTY KILKENNY

built sometime between AD 700 and 1000 on the site of an earlier Christian cemetery. Apart from missing its crown, the round tower is in excellent condition, and you can admire a fine view from the top. It's a tight squeeze and you'll need both hands to climb the steep ladders. The approach to the cathedral on foot from Parliament St leads you over Irishtown Bridge and up St Canice's Steps, which date from 1614; the wall at the top contains fragmentary medieval carvings.

Inside, highly polished ancient **graveslabs** are set on the walls and the floor. On the northern wall opposite the entrance a slab inscribed in Norman French commemorates Jose de Keteller, who died in 1280; despite the difference in spelling he was probably the father of Alice Kyteler. The stone chair of St Kieran embedded in the wall dates from the 13th century. The fine 1596 monument to Honorina Grace at the western end of the southern aisle is made of beautiful local black limestone. In the southern transept, a handsome **black tomb** has effigies of Piers Butler, who died in 1539, and his wife, Margaret Fitzgerald. Tombs and monuments (listed on a board in the southern aisle) to other notable Butlers crowd this corner of the church.

THE WITCH OF KILKENNY

In the Middle Ages, Dame Alice Kyteler went through four husbands, all of whom died in suspicious circumstances. Having acquired some powerful enemies, she was charged with witchcraft in 1324. Witnesses claimed to have seen her sweeping dust to the door of her son, William Outlawe, while chanting: 'To the house of William, my son, lie all the wealth of Kilkenny town.' Worse still, she was supposed to have sacrificed cockerels and consorted with the devil. She was duly convicted, along with her sister, her son and her maid, Petronella. Dame Alice managed to escape to England but Petronella was burned at the stake outside Kilkenny's Tholsel (City Hall). The sister's fate is unknown. Alice's son escaped his sentence by offering to re-roof part of St Canice's Cathedral with lead tiles. Unfortunately, the new roof proved too heavy and collapsed in 1332, bringing the church tower down with it.

Dame Alice's former home at 27 St Kieran's St is now Kyteler's Inn, a restaurant and bar (see p301).

Black Abbey

The Dominican **Black Abbey** on Abbey St was founded in 1225 by William Marshall and takes its name from the monks' black habits. In 1543, six years after Henry VIII's dissolution of the monasteries, it was turned into a courthouse. Following Cromwell's visit in 1650, it remained a roofless ruin until restoration in 1866. Much of what survives dates from the 18th and 19th centuries, but pieces of more ancient archways are still evident within the newer stonework.

Rothe House

The best surviving example of a 16th-century merchant's house in Ireland is **Rothe House** (☎ 772 2893; Parliament St; adult/child €3/1; 🕑 10.30am-5pm Mon-Sat & 3-5pm Sun Apr-Oct, 1-5pm Mon-Sat & 3-5pm Sun Nov-Mar). The fine Tudor house was built around a series of courtyards and now houses a museum with a sparse collection of local artefacts from various periods displayed in its old timber-vaulted rooms. The more interesting objects are a well-used Viking sword found near here and a grinning head sculpted from a stone by a Celtic artist. The fine king-post roof of the 2nd floor is a meticulous and impressive reconstruction. A costume exhibit on the 1st floor is primarily good for mild laughs, with its cordon of strange, oddly shaped mannequins looking very clumsy in period attire.

In the 1640s, the wealthy Rothe family played a part in the Confederation of Kilkenny, and Peter Rothe, son of the original builder, had all his property confiscated. His sister was able to reclaim it, but just before the Battle of the Boyne (1690) the family supported James II and so lost the house permanently. In 1850 a Confederation banner was discovered in the house. It's now in the National Museum, Dublin.

Smithwick Brewery

Founded in 1710 on the site of a Franciscan monastery, the **Smithwick Brewery** (☎ 772 1014; Parliament St) is now owned by Guinness and brews Budweiser under licence as well as Smithwick's own brands. The brewery doesn't exactly encourage visitors; call to see which way the wind's blowing.

St Francis' Abbey, behind the brewery, was founded by William Marshall in 1232, but desecrated by Cromwell in 1650. The monks were reputed to be expert brewers.

National Craft Gallery

Recently opened, the **National Craft Gallery** (☎ 776 1804; www.ccoi.ie; Castle Yard; admission free; 10am-6pm Apr-Dec, closed Sun Jan-Mar) is funded by the Crafts Council of Ireland and showcases contemporary Irish crafts. Its high-quality exhibitions highlight the diversity and imagination of crafts in Ireland, with a special emphasis on ceramics.

Other Sights

Stretches of the old Norman city walls can still be traced, but **Black Freren Gate** on Abbey St is the only gate still standing, with the help of metal bracing to ensure the safety of those who pass through. Just north of the Tholsel is **Butter Slip**, a narrow alleyway built in 1616 to connect High St with Low Lane (now St Kieran's St) and once lined with the stalls of butter sellers.

Shee Alms House, on Rose Inn St, was built in 1582 by local benefactor Sir Richard Shee and his wife to provide help for the poor. It continued as a hospital until 1740 but now houses the tourist office. The **Tholsel**, or City Hall, on High St was built in 1761 on the spot where Dame Alice Kyteler's maid, Petronella, was burned at the stake in 1324 (see the boxed text opposite).

On the corner of Parliament St and the road leading down to Bateman's Quay, a **monument** beside the Bank of Ireland marks the site of the Confederation Hall, where the national Parliament met from 1642 to 1649. Nearby is **Grace's Castle**, originally built in 1210, but lost to the family and converted into a prison in 1568, and then in 1794 into a courthouse, which it remains today. Rebels from the 1798 Rising were executed here. People taking part in one of Tynan Tours (see following section) can enter to peek inside the cells.

Across the river stand the ruins of **St John's Priory**, which was founded in 1200 and was noted for its many beautiful windows until Cromwell's visit. Nearby, **Kilkenny College**, on John St, dates from 1666. Its students included Jonathan Swift and the philosopher George Berkeley, but it now houses Kilkenny's county hall.

TOURS

Central Kilkenny city is a small, walkable area, well-suited to comprehensive walking tours.

Tynan Tours (☎ 087 265 1745; www.tynantours.com; adult/student €6/5) conducts hour-long walking tours of the town six times daily (four on Sunday) March to October, starting from the tourist office. Three tours per day Tuesday to Saturday are scheduled for the rest of the year. Tours meander through the narrow lanes, steps and pedestrian passageways, while guides recount the intriguing stories these buildings might tell if they could talk.

FESTIVALS & EVENTS

Kilkenny is rightly known as the festival capital of Ireland, with several world-class festivals throughout the year that attract thousands of people. The following festivals are staged throughout the year:

Cat Laughs Comedy Festival (☎ 776 3416; (www.thecatlaughs.com; late May–early Jun) Cat Laughs is a much-acclaimed gathering of world-class comics.

Kilkenny Arts Festival (☎ 775 2175; kaw@iol.ie; late Aug) The city plays host to theatre, music, literature, visual arts, children's events and other outdoor activities for 10 activity-packed days. Accommodation at this time is like gold, and you're seriously advised to book far in advance.

Kilkenny International Air Rally (☎ 087 241 1955; www.kinair.ie; mid-Jun) This impressive air display takes place at Kilkenny airport.

Kilkenny Rhythm & Roots (☎ 777 1908; early May) Over 30 different venues participate in hosting Ireland's biggest music festival, with country and western, bluegrass and 'old-time' American roots music being strongly emphasised.

Pan Celtic Festival (☎ 775 1500; www.panceltic.com; late Apr) People from Scotland, Wales, Cornwall and Ireland congregate in Kilkenny to celebrate the old ways. Distinctive costumes, music, dance, and – what the heck – a golf tournament make a week of fun in and around the city.

Ultimate Frisbee Tournament (☎ 775 1500; iancud@hotmail.com; mid-Jun) This is an excellent weekend of booze, lunacy and ultimate Frisbee.

SLEEPING

If you're arriving in town with no room booked, the **tourist office** (☎ 775 1500; Rose Inn St; www.southeastireland.com) runs an efficient accommodation booking system costing €4. (It will also charge 10% of the cost of the accommodation, but this amount is deducted when you pay the hotel or B&B.)

Alternatively, you might be able to check into modest digs above many of the pubs along John St.

Budget

Foulksrath Castle (☎ 776 7674; mailbox@anoige.ie; Jenkinstown; dm €9-12) This An Óige hostel is beautifully sited in a 16th-century Norman castle 13km north of Kilkenny in Jenkinstown, near Ballyragget. For details of how to get there by bus, see p303.

Kilkenny Tourist Hostel (☎ 776 3541; kilkennyhostel@eircom.net; 35 Parliament St; dm €13-18) This IHH hostel is friendly, clean and central. It has a charming kitchen and sitting room and the information board keeps guests up to date on tours and nightlife.

Rose Inn (☎ 777 0061; 9 Rose Inn St; s/d €25/50) This pleasant little B&B opposite the tourist office is a serviceable cheapie. Its furnishings are dated but the place is central, cheerful, and quiet on the rear side of the building. If you're really looking to save money, inquire about dorm beds in the noisier front rooms.

Tree Grove Caravan & Camping Park (☎ 777 0302; New Ross Rd; tent & 2 people €11) This camping ground in a small park is 1.5km south of Kilkenny.

Nore Valley Caravan & Camping Park (☎ 772 7229; Annamult) This park is about 11km away, near Bennettsbridge (see p303 for details).

Mid-Range

Bregagh Guesthouse (☎ 772 2315; Dean St; s/d €40/80; P) This pleasant home near St Canice's Cathedral is very comfortably furnished with sturdy antiques.

Celtic House (☎ 776 2249; john376@gofree.indigo.ie; 18 Michael St; s/d €40/70) This beautifully decorated house just a short walk from the High St has modern, airy rooms, all with en suite. See if a room with a view of the castle is available.

Daley's B&B (☎ 776 2866; 82 John St; s €35-45, d €70-90; P) This old motor court is nothing fancy, but perfectly serviceable and very central.

Kilkenny B&B (☎ 776 4040; kilkennybandb@eircom.net; Dean St; s/d €45/90) You can't miss this place on Dean St; it's the only house painted royal blue with yellow railings. It's comfortable but the owners are sticklers on breakfast times: you must show up between 8.30am and 9.30am.

O'Malley's Ormonde Court Guesthouse (☎ 777 1003; omalleysguesthouse@eircom.net; Ormonde Rd; s/d €45/90; P) This friendly B&B, just two blocks from High St, offers very simple and clean rooms, all with en suite.

Top End

Berkeley House (☎ 776 4848; berkeleyhouse@eircom.net; 5 Lower Patrick St; s/d €59/108; P) This Georgian place, half a block from the High St, has a distinct air of faded glory, though it's pretty comfortable. Breakfast is included.

Hibernian Hotel (☎ 777 1888; www.kilkennyhibernianhotel.com; 1 Ormonde St; s/d €95/190) In a stolid Victorian building that once housed a bank, the Hibernian exudes grand hotel swank, with a stately bar.

Lacken House (☎ 776 1085; www.lackenhouse.ie; Dublin Rd; s/d €59/108; Apr-Oct; P) Just out of town, this beautiful 1847 Victorian guesthouse is highly rated. The standard rate includes a superb breakfast; for a real treat, throw in a five-course dinner in the award-winning restaurant for €99 inclusive (see opposite). More-expensive suites are also available.

Rinuccini (☎ 776 1575; www.rinuccini.com; 1 The Parade; s/d €50/100) Above a very popular restaurant, Ristorante Rinuccini (see opposite), this is a plush, modern guesthouse with gorgeous Italian furnishings. Continental breakfast is served in the bedrooms.

Zuni (☎ 772 3999; www.zuni.ie; 26 Patrick St; s/d €65/80 to €120/150) In a 1902 building that once served as a playhouse, Zuni has an ultramodern, minimalist design, with lots of clean lines, muted lighting and not a flower in sight. See also following section.

EATING

Cafés

Gourmet Store (☎ 777 1727; 56 High St; sandwiches €3; 9am-6pm Mon-Sat) This small deli has terrific takeaway sandwiches packed with fresh, mouthwatering ingredients.

La Creperie (☎ 341 6062; 80 John St; mains €3-5; 10am-6pm Mon-Sat, 11am-6pm Sun) On the north side, this café is a fast, inexpensive stop for sandwiches, sweet or savoury crepes, and strong coffees and espressos.

Chez Pierre (☎ 776 4655; 17 Parliament St; mains €3-8; 10am-5pm) This relaxed, unpretentious French café serves sandwiches, soups and sweets. The open-faced leek and Parma ham sandwich is a toothsome midday repast.

RICHARD CUMMINS

Stone carvings, **Jerpoint Abbey** (p304), near Thomastown

River Nore, near **Bennettsbridge** (p303)

RICHARD CUMMINS

RICHARD CUMMINS

Parliament St, **Kilkenny** (p295)

DOUG MCKINLAY

O'Connor's pub (p361), Doolin

RICHARD CUMMINS

Bunratty Castle (p345), Bunratty

Poulnabrone Dolmen (p365), Central Burren

EOIN CLARK

Kilkenny Castle Kitchen (☎ 772 1450; Kilkenny Castle; mains €4-10; ⌚ noon-5pm Jun-Aug) The castle's surprisingly humble café, looking very much the country kitchen, is a good place for lunch or delicious cakes; you don't have to pay the castle admission charge to eat here.

Café Sol (☎ 776 4987; William St; lunch €5-8, dinner mains €13-19; ⌚ 10am-5pm Mon-Sat, 6.30pm-close Wed-Sat) Bright, warm and cheery, with yellow walls and lots of windows, this place evokes a sunny Mediterranean escape from wet and windy Kilkenny. It's an excellent choice for sandwiches and simple lunches.

ML Dore (☎ 776 3374; 65 High St; mains €5-10; ⌚ 8am-9pm Mon-Sat, 9am-7pm Sun) ML Dore is funny, with its over-the-top kitsch décor with price stickers. It's also an old standby for traditional Irish grub, full breakfasts, fried plaice, a smattering of veg dishes, sandwiches and weak coffee.

Kilkenny Design Centre (☎ 772 2118; Castle Yard; mains €10; ⌚ 9am-5pm, closed Sun Jan-Mar) The café upstairs is excellent for snacks or lunch but attracts large coach parties.

Restaurants

Pearl's (☎ 772 3322; 10 Irishtown; mains €4-18; ⌚ noon-9pm) Pearl's serves excellent Chinese dishes in its stylish but relaxed dining room.

Bengal Tandoori (☎ 776 4722; Pudding Lane; mains €6-12, Sun brunch €14; ⌚ 12.30-2.30pm & 6-11pm Mon-Sat, 1-11pm Sun) Locals flock to this place for the all-you-can-eat Sunday brunch (1pm to 5pm). Otherwise, it has the usual selection of Indian dishes, with a particular emphasis on hotter Bengali dishes.

Marble City Bar (☎ 776 1143; 66 High St; lunch €4-8, dinner €7-11; ⌚ noon-10pm) At this stark, modern bar (run by the owners of Langton's) tasty and smart-looking roasts, pastas, cod and chips are a good notch above the usual bar food standards. Very nice for the price.

Kyteler's Inn (☎ 772 1064; 27 St Kieran's St; mains €9; ⌚ noon-10pm) Dame Kyteler's old house, built in 1224, is one of the tourist magnets in town and while the food at this pub is not great, it is very popular. For a real witchin' experience, sit in the solid stone-walled basement, which feels like a catacomb.

Edward Langton's (☎ 776 5133; 69 John St; mains €9-18; ⌚ noon-10pm Mon-Sat, noon-9pm Sun) Langton's is an enormous, snazzy pub with an award-winning restaurant. The varied crowd – well-dressed old-timers, belligerent hurling fans, trendy blondes gossiping at the bar – is as interesting as the food is good. Surf and turf dishes get creative, contemporary treatment here.

Lautrec's Brasserie (☎ 776 2720; 9 St Kieran's St; mains €10-20; ⌚ 6-10pm Sun-Thu, 6-11pm Fri-Sat) Small and romantically lit, Lautrec's eclectic offerings include Italian-Mediterranean and Cajun Gumbo.

Ristorante Rinuccini (lunch €8-13, dinner €13-20; ⌚ noon-2.30pm & 6-9pm) Beneath Rinuccini guesthouse (see opposite), this cellar restaurant is fairly upmarket and has delicious pasta dishes, all freshly prepared.

Jacob's Cottage (☎ 779 1220; 1 Ormonde St; lunch €7-13, dinner €16-24; ⌚ 12.30-3pm & 6.30-10pm) Part of the Hibernian Hotel, Jacob's isn't so much a cottage as a sleek and polished operation, where thoroughly competent staff put some fine, imaginative Irish cuisine on the table.

Zuni (☎ 772 3999; 26 Patrick St; lunch €8-14, dinner €18-26; ⌚ 12.30-2.30pm Tue-Fri, 6.30-10pm Tue-Sun) The menu at this busy, trendy restaurant has an impressive international range, with Thai chicken, spinach tagliatelle, lamb rump and even kangaroo all vying for a spot in your stomach. Everything is good.

Lacken House (☎ 776 1085; Dublin Rd; set 4-course €39, set 5-course €45; ⌚ 6-9pm) Widely regarded as the best local restaurant, Lacken House dishes out appetising original creations like pork with cider potato, and ostrich fillet with aubergine caviar.

Pordylo's (☎ 777 0660; Butter Slip; mains €13-24; ⌚ 6-10pm) Perhaps it's just another excuse to stroll down Butter Slip, Kilkenny's crooked, narrow stone walkway, but Pordylo's stands on its own merit as well. It's creative and cosy, with sea scallops and lime risotto, blackened meat and fish dishes served in its upstairs dining room.

DRINKING

Kilkenny's grog houses are not the most atmospheric, but rest assured, there's no shortage of them. The city has more than 65 licensed pubs, which amounts to roughly one drinking establishment for every 300 inhabitants. The following are all good:

Hibernian Bar (☎ 777 1888; Patrick St) Few things are as sublime as an afternoon drink in a plush red booth near the Hibernian's front windows. Sometimes a swank, early-20th-century hotel bar, with high ceilings and soothing dark-wood trim is just what you're looking for.

John Cleere (☎ 776 2573; 22 Parliament St) This pub is well known for its regular productions of plays and poetry readings. It's also becoming one of Kilkenny's best rock venues, with touring alternative acts frequently passing through. You might also catch a traditional Irish session here.

O'Riada's (27 Parliament St) This unpretentious old pub, whose only acknowledgment of the 20th century is electric light and a TV set (there's no recognition of the current century), fills up and gets pretty lively when there's a game on the tube. Most of the time it's just central Kilkenny's best local, favoured mostly by men.

Pumphouse (☎ 776 3924; 26 Parliament St) With live rock and pop groups many nights a week, this pub draws a 20-something crowd. Sometimes traditional céilidh musicians perform.

Tynan's Bridgehouse (☎ 772 1291; St John's Bridge) Conversation is generally audible in this grand old Georgian pub, which recently celebrated its 300th birthday. The building has settled a bit over the years, and its sloping ceilings and tilting walls will make you think you're drunk before you are. After a few pints everything sort of straightens itself out.

ENTERTAINMENT

For information on local events, check out the weekly *Kilkenny People* newspaper. The **Kilkenny Tourist Hostel** (☎ 776 3541; kilkennyhostel@eircom.net; 35 Parliament St) has an excellent notice board for events around town. A good website for finding out what's on is www.kilkennyexposed.com.

Theatre & Cinema

Watergate Theatre (☎ 776 1674; www.watergatekilkenny.com; Parliament St) This theatre hosts drama, comedy and musical performances.

John Cleere (☎ 776 2573; 22 Parliament St) Stages small productions.

Kilkenny Cineplex (☎ 772 3111; Fair Green, Gaol Rd) This is Kilkenny's only multiplex cinema, with four screens showing the latest releases.

About 15km south of Kilkenny, just outside the hamlet of Callan, is a disused **quarry** that has been turned into an amphitheatre with superb acoustics. It is planned to stage drama, pageants, music and choral recitals here but nothing yet has happened; contact the Kilkenny tourist office for the current schedule.

Nightclubs

Zoo (☎ 777 0555; 40 Parliament St; admission €8) In a basement a few doors up from the Kilkenny Tourist Hostel, this club has discos nearly every night, starting around 11pm. On occasion the Zoo also hosts touring independent rock bands. Some nights admission is free.

Nero's (☎ 772 1064; 25 St Kieran's St; admission €8; 🕑 11.30pm-3am Thu-Sun) Next door to Kyteler's Inn, Nero's is a big and popular dance club spread across two floors featuring the latest dance music.

Edward Langton's (☎ 776 5133; 69 John St; admission Tue/Sat €7/13) With resident DJs on Tuesday and Saturday nights, Langton's is the most popular club in town. It gets packed to the rafters.

Club 51 (O'Faollain's Pub; ☎ 776 1018; Patrick St; admission €8-10) Club 51 has live DJs nightly, starting around 10.30pm. This is one of Kilkenny's most interesting clubs, with three levels and the remains of an old church inside.

Morrison's Bar (☎ 777 1888; 1 Ormonde St; 🕑 5pm-1am) In the cellar of the Hibernian Hotel there's this stylish hideaway, with its atmospheric lighting and snazzy *belle époque* décor. DJs spin an eclectic mix for a local professional crowd.

Sport

James Park (☎ 772 1214; Freshford Rd; 🕑 8pm Wed & Fri) Kilkenny may be rather sophisticated, but its residents still get excited when a dog named Fast Eddie crosses the line first.

SHOPPING

Kilkenny has a reputation as one of Ireland's cultural and artistic centres. Yet, there's really not much of a gallery scene here, and overall Kilkenny is not much of a shopper's mecca.

Kilkenny Design Centre (☎ 776 1804; www.kilkennydesign.com; Castle Yard) Across The Parade from Kilkenny Castle are the elegant former castle stables (1760), which have been tastefully converted into the Kilkenny Design Centre. There's an outstanding collection of Irish goods and crafts for sale, with potters, knitters, and goldsmiths and silversmiths among the centre's many shopkeepers. Behind the shop, through the arched gateway, is Castle Yard, lined with the studios of various local craftspeople.

Rudolf Helzel Gold & Silversmiths (☎ 772 1497; 10 Patrick St) Attractive contemporary designs are on sale here.

GETTING THERE & AWAY

Bus

Bus Éireann (☎ 776 4933; www.buseireann.ie; cnr Dublin Rd & John St) operates out of McDonagh train station and provides at least five daily services to and from Dublin (one way/return €10/12, two hours). There are three buses daily (two on Sunday) to and from Cork city (€14/22, three hours). Two buses daily (except Sunday) also pass through Kilkenny en route from Dublin to Waterford. Bus Éireann also stops at the very central Tea Shop on St Patrick's St.

Daily buses to Waterford (€7/12) stop in Bennettsbridge and Thomastown.

Buggy's Coaches (☎ 444 1264) runs a service to Foulksrath Castle (and the An Óige hostel), Ballyragget, Dunmore Cave and Castlecomer. Buses (€2, 20 minutes) leave The Parade at 11.30am and 5.30pm Monday to Saturday; they leave from the hostel at 8.25am and 3pm.

Train

McDonagh train station (☎ 772 2024) is on Dublin Rd, northeast of the town centre via John St. Four trains daily (five on Friday) link Dublin (Heuston Station) with Waterford via Kilkenny (one way/return €16/21, two hours). For details of departure times phone ☎ 01-836 6222.

GETTING AROUND

JJ Wall (☎ 772 1236; 86 Maudlin St) rents out bikes at €15/85 per day/week. The circuit round Kells, Inistioge, Jerpoint Abbey and Kilfane makes a fine day's ride. There's no deposit, but you'll need to present photo identification.

Castle Cabs (☎ 776 1188; 1 Rose Inn St) has taxis available 24 hours a day. Its small fleet also includes an eight-seater cab, and it offers a left-luggage service (€2 per bag per day).

CENTRAL KILKENNY

The area south – and most notably southeast – of Kilkenny city is graced with comely country towns and eye-popping scenic roads overlooking the rich, green Barrow and Nore Valleys. It's best to nudge out to the riverside towns of Graiguenamanagh and Inistioge, where the scenery is tops. This is prime walking country, and the South Leinster Way cuts right through the area. You can also hop aboard a barge and laze away your days on the Barrow.

BENNETTSBRIDGE & AROUND

☎ 056 / pop 922

Bennettsbridge, on the Nore, has two of Ireland's most renowned potteries and an official camping ground. In a big mill by the river is **Nicholas Mosse Pottery** (☎ 972 7105; www.nicholasmosse.com; 🕒 10am-6pm Mon-Sat year round, 2-6pm Sun Jul & Aug). It turns out handmade spongewear – creamy-brown pottery covered with sponged patterns – and there's a café upstairs offering reasonably priced fare, including scones from €2.

In the centre of town, the **Bridge** (☎ 972 9156; www.bridgepottery.com; Chapel St; 🕒 1-6pm Tue-Fri, 11am-6pm Sat) is a nice little shop specialising in brightly coloured pottery and personalised plates.

Almost 2km north of Bennettsbridge on the R700 road to Kilkenny, **Stoneware Jackson Pottery** (☎ 972 7175; www.stonewarejackson.com; Ballyreddin; 🕒 10am-6pm Mon-Sat) produces groovy pots, jugs, tea sets and even lamps.

On the other side of the Nore is **Dyed in the Wool** (☎ 27684; www.dyedinthewool.ie; Bennettsbridge; 🕒 10am-6pm Mon-Fri, noon-6pm Sat & Sun). This knitwear factory sells its wares in some of Ireland's best design stores. Fetching chenille hats for the ladies are a forte.

About 2km west of Bennettsbridge, near the hamlet of Danesfort, is the **Nore View Folk Museum** (☎ 972 7749; Danesfort Rd; admission free; 🕒 10am-6pm Jun-Sep, 2.30-5.30pm Oct-May). It's a privately owned folk museum displaying local items of interest, including old farming tools and other bric-a-brac.

Nore Valley Camping & Caravan Park (☎ 972 7229; norevalleypark@eircom.net; Annamult; day admission adult/child €2.50/2; camping for hikers & cyclists €8 per person, camping with car €17; 🕒 9am-7pm Mon-Sat Mar-Oct). is an open farm aimed at kids and

COUNTY KILKENNY

campers. Kids can bottle-feed lambs and goats, cuddle rabbits, play in a fort and jump on a straw bounce. There is a tearoom and picnic area. If you're coming into Bennettsbridge from Kilkenny along the R700, turn right just before the bridge; the park is signposted.

Calabash Bistro (☎ 27850; Chapel St; starters €4-9, mains €19-25; ⏰ 6pm-close Thu-Mon) Opposite the bridge in town, Calabash is a stylish eatery that treats its guests to creative Irish cuisine, like fillet steak on chive potato cakes, and mustard-glazed duck breast.

KELLS & AROUND

Only 13km south of Kilkenny, Kells (not to be confused with Kells in County Meath) is a mere widening of the road, a hamlet with a fine stone bridge on a tributary of the Nore. However, in Kells Priory, the village has one of Ireland's most impressive and romantic monastic sites.

Kells Priory

This is the best sort of ruin, where visitors are free to explore as they like, whenever they like, with no tour guides, tours, ropes or restrictions. At dusk on a vaguely sunny day the old priory is simply beautiful. Most days, you stand a chance of exploring the site alone, with only the company of bleating sheep.

The earliest remains of this gorgeous monastic site date from the late 12th century, while the bulk of the present ruins dates from the 15th century. In a sea of rich farmland, a protective wall, carefully restored, connects seven dwelling towers. Inside the walls are the remains of an Augustinian abbey and the foundations of some chapels and houses. It's unusually well fortified for a monastery and the heavy curtain walls hint at a troubled history. Indeed, within a single century from 1250, the abbey was twice fought over and burned down by squabbling warlords.

There's no charge for visiting and no set opening hours. The ruins are 800m east of Kells on the Stonyford road.

Kilree Round Tower & High Cross

About 2km south of Kells (signposted from the priory car park) there's a 29m-high **round tower** and a simple early **high cross**, which is said to mark the grave of a 9th-century Irish high king, Niall Caille. He's supposed to have drowned in the King's River at Callan some time in the 840s while attempting to save a servant, and his body washed up near Kells. His final resting place lies beyond the church grounds because he wasn't a Christian.

Callan Famine Graveyard

About 10km west of Kilree, and signposted off the main road 2km south of Callan, is a **cemetery** where the local victims of the Great Famine are buried. It isn't much to look at, but the unmarked graves are a poignant reminder of the anonymity of starvation.

THOMASTOWN & AROUND

☎ 056 / pop 1704

Thomastown is a small market town nicely situated by the Nore. Unfortunately it's also on the main Dublin–Waterford road (N9) and the traffic can be horrific. Named after Welsh mercenary Thomas de Cantwell, Thomastown has some fragments of a medieval wall and the partly ruined 13th-century **Church of St Mary**. Down by the bridge, **Mullin's Castle** is the sole survivor of the 14 castles that were originally here.

At the edge of town, there's a craft shop at **Grennan Mill Craft School** (☎ 792 4557; Waterford road; ⏰ 9am-5pm Mon-Sat).

Jerpoint Abbey

About 1.5km southwest of Thomastown is **Jerpoint Abbey** (☎ 792 4623; Waterford road; admission €2.75; ⏰ 10am-6.30pm Jun-Sep, 10am-4pm Oct-May), one of Ireland's finest Cistercian ruins. It was established in the 12th century and has been partially restored. The fine tower and cloister are late 14th or early 15th century. Fragments of the cloister are particularly interesting, with a series of often amusing figures carved on the pillars. There are also stone carvings on the church walls and in the tombs of members of the Butler and Walshe families. Faint traces of a 15th- or 16th-century painting remain on the northern wall of the church. This chancel area also contains a tomb thought to be that of Felix O'Dullany, Jerpoint's first abbot and bishop of Ossory, who died in 1202.

According to local legend, St Nicholas (or Santa Claus) is buried near the abbey. While retreating in the Crusades, the knights of Jerpoint removed his body from Myra in modern-day Turkey and reburied him in the Church of St Nicholas to the west of the abbey. The grave is marked by a broken slab decorated with a carving of a monk.

A few kilometres from Jerpoint Abbey, in the town of Stonyford, and housed in an old stone-walled farm building is the nationally renowned **Jerpoint Glass Studio** (☎ 792 4350; Stonyford; ⏲ 9am-5pm Mon-Fri, 11am-5pm Sat & Sun). Many of the pieces produced here are extremely beautiful. You can watch glass-blowers at work 9am to 5pm Monday to Thursday and 9am to 2pm Friday.

Kilfane

The village of Kilfane, 3km north of Thomastown on the Dublin road, has a small, ruined **13th-century church** and **Norman tower**, 50m off the road and signposted. The church has a remarkable stone carving of Thomas de Cantwell called the Cantwell Fada or Long Cantwell. It depicts a tall, thin knight in detailed chain-mail armour brandishing a shield decorated with the Cantwell coat of arms.

Kilfane Glen & Waterfall (☎ 792 4558; admission €5; ⏲ 11am-6pm daily Jul & Aug, 2-6pm Sun Apr, Jun & Sep) is a pretty spot with wooded paths winding through its wild 6-hectare gardens, which date from the 1790s. An elaborately decorated thatched cottage is worth hiking to. The top part of the garden is replete with works by Irish artists. Kilfane Glen is 2km north of town along the N9.

Getting There & Away

Bus Éireann (☎ 64933) operates six buses daily (five on Sunday) between Dublin and Waterford with stops at Gowran and Thomastown. One service daily links Waterford with Longford via Thomastown and Kilkenny. Buses stop outside O'Keeffe's supermarket on Main St. From Kilkenny, the fare to Thomastown is €6/8 one way/return.

The train station is 1km west of town past Kavanagh's supermarket. Thomastown is on the main Dublin–Waterford line.

INISTIOGE

☎ 056 / pop 714

The little village of Inistioge (in-ish-teeg) is picture-perfect. It has a 10-arched stone bridge spanning the Nore, a tranquil square and antiquated shop signs. Somewhere so inviting could hardly hope to escape the Hollywood sleuths: Inistioge's film credits include *Widow's Peak* (1993), *Circle of Friends* (1994) and *Where the Sun Is King* (1996). With the South Leinster Way coursing through town, this is a good base for exploring the region on foot, by bike or motor vehicle.

Approximately 1km south, on Mt Alto, is **Woodstock Park**. The hike up is well worth the effort for the panorama of the valley below and the demesne itself. The 18th-century house was one of the finest in the county but was destroyed during the Civil War in 1922. The elevated garden and forest are now a state park with picnic areas and trails. For another fine walk, follow the riverbank and climb any of the surrounding hills.

Woodstock Arms B&B (☎ 795 8440; www.woodstockarms.com; Inistioge; s/d €40/60) The interior of this pub has been rather plainly remodelled, but on a warm day you'll want to have a pint on the front patio, overlooking the pretty square. This is also a B&B, with utilitarian but sparkly clean rooms, all with bathroom.

Motte Restaurant (☎ 795 8655; Plas Newydd Lodge; set dinner €33; ⏲ 7-9.30pm Tue-Sat) This beautiful country restaurant has a delightful contemporary Irish menu. It's very relaxed, and diners can linger over cordials and conversation till midnight.

Getting There & Away

Infrequent buses run between New Ross and Kilkenny, calling at Inistioge on the way.

GRAIGUENAMANAGH

☎ 059 / pop 1620

Graiguenamanagh (greg-na-mana) is a small market town on a lovely stretch of the River Barrow, 23km southeast of Kilkenny at the foot of Brandon Hill (516m). The town has a picturesque setting, with fishing boats on the river and a six-arch stone bridge that is illuminated at night. This is good walking country. 'Graigue', like Inistioge, is on the South Leinster Way. There's a lovely wooded walk, of about 1½ hours, to St Mullins, just a few kilometres downstream from town.

Dating back to 1204, **Duiske Abbey** (☎ 24238 ⏲ 10am-5pm Mon-Fri year round, 2-5pm Sat & Sun Jun-Aug) was once Ireland's largest Cistercian abbey. Today it has been completely restored and its pleasantly simple, whitewashed interior is in everyday use. Its name comes from the Irish Dubh Uisce (Black Water), a tributary of the Barrow. Inside the abbey, to the right of the main entrance, is the Knight of Duiske, a 14th-century, high-relief carving of a knight in chain mail who's reaching for his sword. On the floor nearby, a glass panel reveals some of the original 13th-century floor tiles, now 2m below the present floor level. In the grounds stand two early high crosses, brought here for protection in the last century. The smaller Ballyogan Cross has panels on the eastern side depicting the crucifixion, Adam and Eve, Abraham's sacrifice of Isaac, and David playing the harp. The western side shows the massacre of the innocents.

Around the corner, the **Abbey Centre** (🕑 10am-1pm & 2-5pm Mon-Fri) houses a small exhibition of Christian art, plus pictures of the abbey in its unrestored state.

Waterside (☎ 792 4246; info@waterside.iol.ie; s/d €59/108; mains €17-22) is a three-star hotel overlooking the River Barrow that also has a fine restaurant.

Anchor Bar (☎ 792 4207; Lower Main St; s/d €30/60), just a few paces from the river, does B&B and quite serviceable pub grub day and night.

For fishing tackle, canned vegetables and a pint of Guinness, head to McDoyle's or McRyan's, two old relics on Abbey St that admirably attempt to address a traveller's basic needs.

ST MULLINS

A tranquil spot just a few kilometres downstream from Graiguenamagh, St Mullins (on the County Carlow line) is good for a relaxing getaway, a picnic, or as rewarding destination on a long walk from Graigue. The river snakes through here in the shadow of Mt Juliet, and from it a trail winds up hill to the ruined hulk of an old monastery surrounded by the graves of 1798 rebels. A 9th-century Celtic cross, badly worn down over the centuries, still stands beside the monastery. Nearby, St Moling's Well is worthy of some spare change.

Mulvarra House (☎ 051-424936; www.mulvarra.com; s/d €38/74) is a B&B just up the hill from the river. It's modern and comfortable, a good base for exploring the area.

Helen Blanchfield (☎ 051-424745; The Green, St Mullins; weekly rooms €240; 🕑 Jun-Sep), adjacent to a pub, is just opposite the monastery and does weekly bookings in summer.

NORTHERN KILKENNY

There isn't much happening amid the rolling green hills of northern County Kilkenny. It's lovely driving country, though, and the picturesque towns of Ballyraggat and Castlecomer always tempt the traveller to pull over for a brief stroll. Dunmore Cave is the most frequently visited sight in these parts.

CASTLECOMER & AROUND

☎ 056 / pop 2319

An attractive town 18km north of Kilkenny, Castlecomer is on the River Dinin, which flows across the Castlecomer Plateau. The town became a centre for anthracite mining after the fuel was discovered nearby in 1636; the mines closed for good only in the mid-1960s. The anthracite was widely regarded as being Europe's best, containing very little sulphur and producing almost no smoke.

Castlecomer saw action in the 1798 Rising when the Fenian rebels, led by Father John Murphy, captured it en route from Wexford to the midlands. There's little to do here, but the tree-lined square and neat town houses are thoroughly eye-pleasing.

About 8km west of Castlecomer is Ballyragget, with an almost-intact square tower in the 16th-century **Butler Castle** (closed to the public).

Almost 2km south of Ballyragget is **Swifte's Heath**, home to Jonathan Swift during his school years in Kilkenny.

Foulksrath Castle (☎ 67674; mailbox@anoige.ie; Ballyragget; dm €10-12) Near Ballyragget, this busy An Óige hostel has a superb setting.

Avalon Inn (☎ 41302; The Square; s/d €33/66) In Castlecomer, this flower-covered pub/guesthouse on the square near the bridge is in the old mine offices.

Getting There & Away

The **Bus Éireann** (☎ 64933) bus stops outside Houlihan's in Castlecomer. **Buggy's Coaches** (☎ 41264) runs a service from Kilkenny to Castlecomer; four buses leave in each direction Monday to Saturday (€2, 25 minutes).

DUNMORE CAVE

About 10km north of Kilkenny on the Castlecomer road (N78) is **Dunmore Cave**

(☎ 056-67726; admission €2.50; 🕓 10am-5pm Mar-Oct, 10am-7pm in summer). It is a large cave divided into three parts, with many limestone formations. According to sources, marauding Vikings killed 1000 people at two ring forts near here in 928. When survivors hid in the caverns, the Vikings tried to smoke them out by lighting fires at the entrance. It's thought that they then dragged off the men as slaves and left the women and children to suffocate. Excavations in 1973 uncovered the skeletons of at least 44 people, mostly women and children. They also found coins dating from the 920s but none from a later date. One theory suggests that the coins were dropped by the Vikings (who often carried them in their armpits, secured with wax) while enthusiastically engaged in the slaughter. However, there are few marks of violence on the skeletons, lending weight to the theory that suffocation was the cause of death.

The cave is well lit and spacious. After a steep descent you enter imaginatively named caverns full of stalactites, stalagmites and columns, including the 7m Market Cross, Europe's largest freestanding stalagmite. It's damp and cold in the cave, so it's advisable to wear a sweater. The compulsory guided tours are worthwhile.

Buggy's Coaches (☎ 056-41264) runs four buses a day Monday to Saturday (return €4) from The Parade in Kilkenny, dropping you off 1km from the cave.

Central South

CONTENTS

Lush farmland, rolling hills, magnificent Georgian homes and vast tracts of bog make up the four midland counties of Kildare, Carlow, Laois and Offaly. Although the area may not have the immediate beauty or attractions of some of Ireland's more visited counties, scratch under the surface and you'll find a region shaped by its ancient pagan past, its monastic settlements, its planters and its waterways.

Whether you're a history buff, a horse fanatic or an avid golfer, there's plenty to see and do and above all a real opportunity to sample authentic rural Irish life, uncommercialised and unadorned for the tourist market. The unhurried pace of life combined with the gentle hills and patchwork of inland waterways make the Central South prime walking and cycling territory, and you can be guaranteed a genuine welcome wherever you go.

If you don't have much time, some of the region's main attractions are easy day trips from Dublin: the pristine National Stud in Kildare gives a fascinating insight into the horse-breeding industry; and the Palladian mansion, Castletown House, in Celbridge is one of Ireland's finest country houses. A little further afield is the restored Georgian town of Birr, home to the historic Rosse estate and observatory.

Other highlights include the mysterious Rock of Dunamaise, near Portlaoise; Browne's Hill Dolmen, just outside Carlow town; the elegant Moone High Cross in Kildare; and, most impressive of all, Clonmacnoise on the banks of the River Shannon, probably Ireland's most important monastic site.

HIGHLIGHTS

- Get an insight into the region's major money-spinning industry at the **Irish National Stud** (p315) in Kildare
- Explore historic **Birr Castle** (p327), built in the 17th century
- Ramble through the ruins at **Clonmacnoise** (p331), Ireland's most important monastic site
- Have a flutter on the horses at the **Curragh racecourse** (p314) and witness the thrill of the chase
- Spend a night or two luxuriating in the sumptuous surroundings of **Kilkea Castle** (p317)

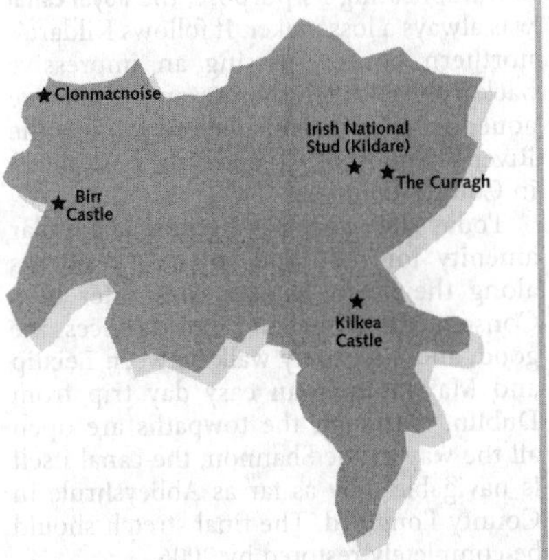

- POPULATION: 332,274
- AREA: 24,312 SQ KM

GRAND & ROYAL CANALS

In the 18th century the Grand and Royal Canals revolutionised goods and passenger transport in Ireland. However, their heyday was short-lived and the railways soon superseded them. Today they're popular for cruising and fishing and offer easy access to walking and cycling paths.

GRAND CANAL

The **Grand Canal** threads its way from Dublin to Robertstown in County Kildare, where one branch continues west through Tullamore before joining the River Shannon, while the other turns south to join the River Barrow at Athy. The canal opened in 1779 and carried passengers until 1852 when services went into decline. A trickle of commercial traffic survived until 1960.

The canal passes through relatively unpopulated countryside, and many finely crafted locks, cottages and picturesque villages line the journey. Near the village of Sallins, the graceful seven-arched **Leinster Aqueduct** carries the canal across the River Liffey, while further south sections of the River Barrow are particularly beautiful.

ROYAL CANAL

Fourteen years behind the Grand Canal and duplicating its purpose, the **Royal Canal** was always a loss maker. It follows Kildare's northern border, passing an impressive backdrop of stately homes and a massive aqueduct near Leixlip, before joining the River Shannon at Cloondara (or Clondra) in County Longford.

Today the canal has become a popular amenity for thousands of new residents along the north Kildare commuter belt. Consequently, bus and rail services are good, and a leisurely walk between Leixlip and Maynooth is an easy day trip from Dublin. Although the towpaths are open all the way to the Shannon, the canal itself is navigable only as far as Abbeyshrule in County Longford. The final stretch should be completely restored by 2006.

For detailed information on the section of the canal between Robertstown and Lullymore, see p314.

BARGES & BOATS

The canals offer a relaxing way to drift across the country and narrowboats can be hired at a number of locations. Two-/eight-berth boats range in price from about €500/900 in September to about €900/1600 in July and August.

Barrowline Cruisers (☎ 0502-25888; barrowline@eircom.net; Vicarstown, Co Laois)
Canal Ways (☎ 045-524 646; www.canalways.ie; Rathangan, Co Kildare)
Celtic Canal Cruisers (☎ 0506-21861; www.celticcanalcruisers.com; Tullamore, Co Offaly)
Valley Boats (☎ 059-972 4945; www.valleyboats.ie; Graiguenamanagh, Co Carlow)

WALKING THE TOWPATHS

Canal towpaths are ideal for leisurely walkers and there are numerous access points along both canals. Robertstown is a good starting point for long-distance walkers. The village is the hub of the Kildare Way and River Barrow towpath trails, the latter stretching all the way to St Mullins, 95km south in County Carlow. From there it's possible to connect with the South Leinster Way at Graiguenamanagh, or the southern end of the Wicklow Way at Clonegal, north of Mt Leinster.

A variety of leaflets detailing the paths can be picked up at regional tourist offices.

COUNTY KILDARE

Kildare (Cill Dara) is one of the most prosperous counties in Ireland, with rich, fertile soil, a growing population of commuters and some of the most lucrative thoroughbred stud farms in the world. The multimillion-pound bloodstock industry thrives in the county – partly because Irish law levies no taxes on stud fees (thanks to former prime minister and horse owner Charles J Haughey), and partly because Kildare town is twinned with another famous horse-breeding centre, Lexington-Fayette in Kentucky, USA.

Kildare's proximity to Dublin also makes it an increasingly appealing option for commuters, and many of the main towns are choked with traffic and overrun with ugly new housing developments. A new bypass system was being built at the time of writing and should help once finished,

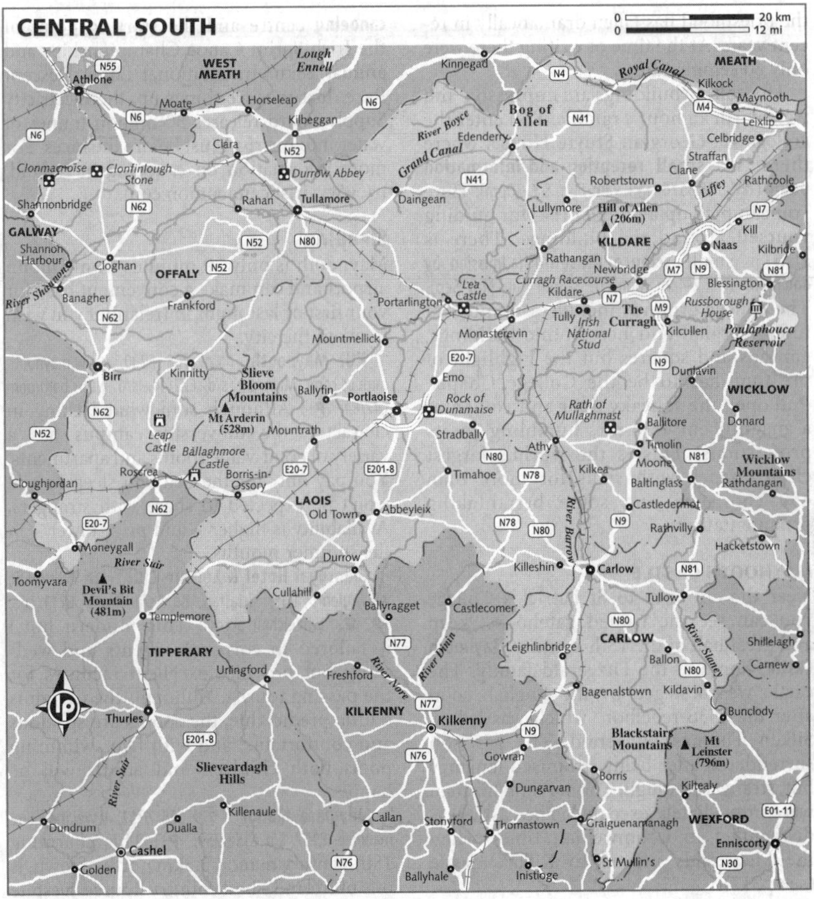

probably sometime in 2004. Geographically, the county has some of the best farmland in Ireland, as well as a vast swathe of bog to the northwest and the sweeping grasslands of the Curragh to the south.

MAYNOOTH & AROUND

☎ 01 / pop 10,845

The vibrant university town of Maynooth (Maigh Nuad) has a pretty tree-lined main street with stone-fronted houses and shops and easy access to the Royal Canal.

Orientation

Main St runs east–west, while Leinster St runs south to the canal and the train station (accessed via a couple of footbridges).

Information

You can access the Internet at **Tech Store** (☎ 629 1747; info@techstore.ie; Unit 5, Glenroyal Shopping Centre; €5/hr; noon-11pm).

Sights

ST PATRICK'S COLLEGE

St Patrick's College & Seminary (☎ 628 5222; Main St) has been turning out Catholic priests since 1795. Ironically, it was founded by the English in an attempt to steer Irish priests away from the dangerous ideals of revolution and republicanism being taught in France. The college joined the National University in 1910 and currently has about 5500 students. The seminary, however, has not fared so well and the number of young men studying for the priesthood has fallen dramatically in recent years. At the time of writing there were only 60 seminarians.

The college buildings are impressive and well worth an hour's ramble. You enter the college via Georgian Stoyte House, where there is a small **reception and information point** (☎ 708 3576; 9am-5pm & 6-10pm). Here you can pick up a booklet (€4) for guiding yourself around the buildings. There is also a small **science museum** (admission by donation; 2-4pm Mon-Fri, 3-5pm Sun May-Sep). The college grounds include a number of fine Georgian and neo-Gothic buildings, gardens and squares but the highlight of the tour has to be the College Chapel. Pull open the squeaky door and you enter a magnificent interior, humbling in its proportions. This is the world's largest choir chapel, with stalls for more than 450 choristers and some breathtaking ornamentation.

MAYNOOTH CASTLE

Near the entrance to St Patrick's College you can see the ruined gatehouse, keep and great hall of the 13th-century **Maynooth Castle**, home of the Fitzgerald family. The castle was besieged by the English soon after the 1536 rebellion, which was led by Silken Thomas Fitzgerald. The garrison surrendered after being promised leniency but, strangely enough, Thomas and his men were immediately executed. The castle was dismantled in Cromwellian times when the Fitzgeralds moved to Kilkea Castle (see p317).

LARCHILL ARCADIAN GARDENS

Once described in the Ordinance Survey of 1830 as 'the most fashionable garden in all of Ireland', **Larchill Arcadian Gardens** (☎ 628 7354; www.larchill.com; Kilcock; adult/child €7/5; noon-6pm Jun-Sep) are Europe's only example of a mid-18th-century Arcadian garden. A 40-minute walk takes you through the beautiful landscaped parklands, passing eccentric classical and Gothic follies, gazebos and a lake. There is also a large outside children's adventure playground, a maze and a model farm with rare breeds of animals.

Activities

The town of **Leixlip** on the River Liffey between Maynooth and Dublin is an important **canoeing** centre and the starting point of the Irish Sprint Canoe Championships and annual 28km International Liffey Descent Race. Just to spice things up, the Electricity Supply Board releases 30 million tonnes of water into the river just before the races. For more information on canoeing in Ireland, try www.irishcanoeunion.com.

Sleeping

Maynooth is only 30 minutes from Dublin airport and can make a convenient base for your first or last night in Ireland if you wish to avoid the city.

NUI Maynooth (☎ 708 6200; www.maynoothcampus.com; Main St; s/d €22/44, s/d with bathroom €42/84; P) Although somewhat lacking in character, the university campus has a variety of good-value rooms and apartments. You pay only for the bed you sleep in and won't be expected to share with strangers. Availability is higher – and price lower – in the summer months.

Glenroyal Hotel & Leisure Club (☎ 629 0909; www.glenroyal.ie; Straffan Rd; s/d from €111/162; P; wheelchair access) This modern hotel is tailored to corporate clients and weddings but provides excellent facilities for the passing tourist. Although the design is a little predictable, the rooms are spacious and comfortable, and with two swimming pools both children and adults will be happy.

Moyglare Manor (☎ 628 6351; www.moyglaremanor.ie; R157; s/d €158/259; P) This charming 18th-century manor, 3.5km north of town, is one of Ireland's best country houses. Despite the sumptuous decoration and period furniture, the atmosphere is incredibly relaxed and the excellent restaurant (set menu €50) is open to nonresidents.

Eating

Coffee Mill (☎ 601 6594; Mill St; lunch €4-6; 9am-5pm Mon-Sat) Tucked away in a basement, this is a great place for lunch or a snack and is deservedly popular with locals. It serves a good selection of deli-style lunches and interesting sandwiches and salads.

Stone Haven (☎ 629 1229; 1 Mill St; mains €12-15; 5-9.30pm Tue-Sun) Set in a 200-year-old building, the cut stone walls and warm alcoves give this place a great atmosphere. The menu isn't very adventurous but the food is good and the service friendly.

Getting There & Away

Bus Nos 66, 66X and 67A leave Wellington Quay in Dublin for Maynooth (€2, one hour, every 20 minutes).

Maynooth is linked to Dublin by the **Western Suburban railway line** (☎ 836 6222) and is on the main Dublin–Sligo line, with regular trains in each direction (single/return €2.70/5.20, 40 minutes, about every hour).

CELBRIDGE

☎ 01 / pop 14,251

Celbridge, 6.5km southeast of Maynooth, deserves a quick visit if only to see the magnificent Palladian Castletown House.

Sights

CASTLETOWN HOUSE

This huge Irish **mansion** (☎ 628 8252; castletown@ealga.ie; adult/child €3.50/1.25; 🕒 10am-6pm Mon-Fri, 1-6pm Sat & Sun Easter-Sep, 10am-5pm Mon-Fri, 1-5pm Sun Oct, 1-5pm Sun Nov, last admission an hr before closing) is one of Ireland's finest historic houses. It was built between 1722 and 1732 for William Conolly, a humble publican's son who became speaker of the Irish House of Commons and one of the richest and most influential men in Ireland.

A lengthy tree-lined avenue leads up to the imposing Palladian façade designed by Alessandro Galilei. His avant-garde design of a central block flanked by curved curtain walls soon became a model for many of Ireland's country houses. The interior has been completely restored and is magnificent. A visit will take about an hour.

There are two follies in the grounds commissioned by William Conolly's wife, Lady Louisa, to give employment to the poor during the famine. The **obelisk** can be seen from the Long Gallery at the back of the house, while the **Wonderful Barn**, four teetering domes scaled by a spiral staircase, is on private property just outside Leixlip.

Sleeping

Springfield (☎ 627 3248; fax 627 3123; on the R405, Celbridge; d from €165) This fabulous Georgian home is about 2km south of Celbridge village and has four stunning bedrooms. The whole place oozes a languid style, and the rambling garden includes an overgrown running track for the more energetic.

Getting There & Away

Bus Nos 67 and 67A go from Wellington Quay in Dublin to Celbridge (€3, about one hour, roughly every 40 minutes).

STRAFFAN

☎ 01 / pop 1306

For one wild weekend in September 2006, the world's golfing cognoscenti will descend on this tiny village just southwest of Celbridge. For the first time ever, the Ryder Cup, the biennial tournament that sees the best US golfers play the best of the Europeans, will be held in Ireland and hosted by the nearby **K Club** (Kildare Hotel & Country Club; ☎ 601 7200; www.kclub.ie), featured in Something Special below. Designed by Arnold Palmer, this is one of the best golf courses in Ireland and the home of the European Open since 1995. A second championship course was opened in 2003 and despite the added fairways and the stiff green fees (up to €265), you'd be well advised to book in advance.

Nearby, the **Straffan Steam Museum** (☎ 627 3155; www.steam-museum.ie; Straffan; adult/concession €4.50/3.50; 🕒 2-6pm Tue-Sun Jun-Aug, 2.30-5.30pm Sun only Apr, May & Sep) traces the history of steam power and the industrial revolution. The collection includes working steam engines from breweries, distilleries, factories and ships. Next door, the 18th-century **Lodge Park Walled Garden** (☎ 627 3155; garden@steam-museum.ie; admission €4; 🕒 2.30-5.30pm Tue-Fri & Sun Jun-Aug) has a beautiful rose garden, best seen in July and August.

Just down the road at the **Straffan Butterfly Farm** (☎ 627 1109; Ovidstown; adult/child €6/4; 🕒 noon-5.30pm late May–late Aug) you can wander through a tropical greenhouse full of enormous exotic

SOMETHING SPECIAL

Kildare Hotel & Country Club (☎ 601 7200; www.kclub.ie; Straffan; d €395-3810; P) This fabulous Georgian estate has been restored and converted into a golfer's paradise and one of the best hotels in Europe. Any self-respecting golf fanatic will at least have a drink at the bar. Set in 330 acres of gardens, the hotel is dedicated to lovers of undiluted luxury, with rich décor, service of the highest standard and two first-class restaurants (jacket and tie required).

butterflies fluttering about, or peer at the stick insects, bird-eating spiders and reptiles kept safely behind glass.

Bus Éireann's (☎ 836 6111) local bus Nos 120 and 123 pass through Straffan roughly every 30 minutes Monday to Friday, every hour Saturday and five times on Sunday. The journey takes 40 minutes and costs €3.20/5.20 for single/return.

BOG OF ALLEN

Stretching like a brown, dusty desert through Kildare, Laois and Offaly, the **Bog of Allen** is Ireland's best-known raised bog, once covering much of the midlands. Unfortunately, like most of Ireland's raised bogs, the huge expanse of peat is rapidly being reduced to potting compost and fuel. For details of the Bord na Móna Bog Rail Tour, see p331 and p57.

ALONG THE GRAND CANAL

Going west from Straffan you're heading well off the beaten track, but there are a few sites of interest as you follow the banks of the Grand Canal. Just past Clane it's worth making the short detour to tiny, tranquil **Robertstown.** This picturesque village has remained largely untouched and is dominated by the now dilapidated Grand Canal Hotel, built in 1801. It's a good place to start a canal walk (see p310).

Just south of Robertstown and at the centre of the Kildare flatlands, the **Hill of Allen** (206m) was a strategic spot through the centuries due to its commanding views in all directions. Today the site is marked by a folly and the ruins of some Iron Age fortifications said to mark the home of Fionn McCumhaill, the leader of the Fianna, a mythical band of warriors who feature in many tales of ancient Ireland.

Further west you'll find the ageing interpretive centre of **Peatland World** (☎ 860 133; R414, Lullymore; adult/student €7/5; 9.30am-6pm Mon-Fri year round, 2-6pm Sun Apr-Oct). The centre traces the social impact of peat production and its industrialisation and has some lacklustre displays on flora, fauna, prehistoric artefacts and experimental peat-based products. About 1km south is the **Lullymore Heritage & Discovery Park** (☎ 870 238; Lullymore; admission €7; 9am-5.15pm Mon-Fri, noon-5pm Sat & Sun Easter-Oct, 9am-4.30pm Mon-Fri Nov-Mar). It's a good place for children and has a variety of replica ancient dwellings, a miniature golf course, a road train and an adventure playground.

For information on hiring narrowboats on the canal, see p310.

NEWBRIDGE & THE CURRAGH

☎ 045 / pop 12,970

The unremarkable town of Newbridge (Droichead Nua) is well known for its silverware, and you can visit the **Newbridge Cutlery Visitor Centre** (☎ 431 301; www.newbridgecutlery.com). However, the town is infinitely more famous as the gateway to the Curragh, one of the country's largest pieces of unfenced fertile land and the centre of the Irish horse industry. In the past, the area was home to a large internment camp, but all that remains are the large military barracks, Curragh Camp, now used by the Irish army.

Today the Curragh is better known for its **racecourse** (☎ 441 205; www.curragh.ie), the oldest and most prestigious in the country. Even if you're not a horsey type, it's well worth experiencing the passion, atmosphere and general craic of a day at the races. On a good day it can verge on mass hysteria. If you miss the chance to have a flutter, you can still see some of the action if you get up early enough or pass by in the late evening as the horse trainers exercise their thoroughbred charges on the wide-open spaces that surround the racecourse.

The N7 runs through the Curragh between Newbridge and Kildare town. The No 126 Dublin–Kildare bus service stops in Newbridge and at Curragh Camp nine times daily (single/return €6.50/10.50). The Dublin–Kildare **train** (☎ 01-836 3333) runs from Heuston train station and stops in Newbridge (€11/12, 25 minutes, about every 35 minutes).

KILDARE TOWN

☎ 045 / pop 6893

Kildare is a small cathedral and market town now firmly part of the Dublin commuter belt. Its busy triangular square is surrounded by pubs and restaurants and is a pleasant place outside rush hour. Unfortunately the town is often choked with traffic and driving to or from Dublin during peak times is not a good idea. An extensive bypass is almost complete and should alleviate the problem when it opens, hopefully sometime in 2004.

Information

The **Tourist Office & Heritage Centre** (☎ 521 240; Market Sq; 🕑 9.30am-1pm & 2-5.30pm Mon-Sat, 2-6pm Sun May-Sep, 10am-1pm & 2-5pm Mon-Fri Oct-Apr) also features a **multimedia exhibition** (adult/child €3/1.50) upstairs, outlining the history of the town. Check out www.kildare.ie for information about the town.

Sights

ST BRIGID'S CATHEDRAL

The solid presence of the 13th-century **St Brigid's Cathedral** (☎ 521 229; Market Sq; admission by donation; 🕑 10am-1pm & 2-5pm Mon-Sat, 2-5pm Sun May-Oct) looms over Kildare Square. Look out for a fine stained-glass window inside, which depicts the three main saints of Ireland: Patrick, Brigid and Colmcille. The church also contains the restored tomb of Walter Wellesley, Bishop of Kildare, which disappeared soon after his death in 1539 and was only found again in 1971.

The 10th-century round tower in the grounds is Ireland's second highest at 32.9m. Its original conical roof has been replaced with an unusual Norman battlement, and provided the guardian is around, you can climb to the top for €3.20. Near the tower is a wishing stone – put your arm through the hole and touch your shoulder and your wish will supposedly be granted.

IRISH NATIONAL STUD & JAPANESE GARDENS

About 3km south of Kildare is the **Irish National Stud** (☎ 521 251; www.irish-national-stud.ie; Tully; adult/child €8.50/4.15; 🕑 9.30am-6pm mid-Feb–mid-Nov, last admission 5pm), founded by Colonel Hall Walker (of Johnnie Walker whiskey fame) in 1900. He was remarkably successful with his horses but his eccentric breeding technique relied heavily on astrology: the fate of a foal was decided by its horoscope and the roofs of the stallion boxes opened on auspicious occasions to reveal the heavens and duly influence the horses' fortunes. Today the immaculately kept centre is owned and managed by the Irish government and breeds high-quality stallions to mate with mares from all over the world.

There are guided tours of the stud on the hour every hour, with access to the intensive-care unit for newborn foals. If you visit in spring or early summer, you might even be able to watch a foal being born. Alternatively, the foaling unit shows a 10-minute video with all the action. Afterwards you're free to visit the small but interesting **Irish Horse Museum**, which examines the role horses have played in Irish life. You can also wander through the stables and paddocks and see the centre's most famous tenant, 22-year-old Indian Ridge, who has a straw allergy and is bedded on shredded paper. He covers 75 mares a season for €75,000 each. Not surprisingly, he's insured for over €15 million.

Next door, the delightful **Japanese Gardens** (☎ 522 963; admission included in Irish National Stud) are considered by experts to be the best of their kind in Europe. Created between 1906 and 1910, they trace the journey from birth to death through 20 landmarks, including the Tunnel of Ignorance, the Hill of Ambition

> **ST BRIGID**
>
> St Brigid is one of Ireland's best-known saints, hailed as an early feminist but also known for her compassion, generosity and beauty. She was a strong-willed character and when her father chose a suitor for her she refused to marry. According to legend she even pulled out her own eye to prove her resolve never to wed. After she had taken her vows, and was mistakenly ordained a bishop rather than nun, her beauty was miraculously restored.
>
> Brigid founded a monastery in Kildare in the 5th century and unusually it was shared by nuns and monks. Its most bizarre feature, however, was a perpetual fire tended by 20 virgins. The fire burned continuously until 1220 when the Bishop of Dublin stopped the tradition, citing it as 'unchristian'. The restored fire pit can be seen in the grounds of St Brigid's Cathedral where a fire is lit on 1 February, St Brigid's feast day.
>
> Brigid was a tireless traveller, and as word of her many miracles spread, her influence stretched across Europe. One legend claims that the medieval Knights of Chivalry chose St Brigid as their patron, and that it was they who first chose to call their wives 'brides'.
>
> Brigid is remembered by a simple reed cross first woven by her to explain the redemption to a dying chief. The cross, said to protect and bless a household, is still found in most rural homes.

and the Gateway to Eternity, beyond which lies not everlasting life but a Buddhist sand garden.

Also in the grounds is **St Fiacra's Garden** with a mixture of bog oak, gushing water, replica monastic cells and an underground crystal garden of dubious distinction. Both gardens are great for a relaxing stroll – provided it isn't raining – and if it is, the large visitor centre houses a café, shop and children's play area. A tour of the stud and gardens will take about two hours.

If you walk back to Kildare, look out for the ruins of the 12th-century **Black Abbey** on the left. Shortly afterwards a turn on the right leads to **St Brigid's Well** where five stones represent different aspects of Brigid's life.

Sleeping

Silken Thomas (☎ 522 232; fax 520 471; The Square; s/d €30/65; Ⓟ) This popular place is a good-value central option with a variety of new and newly refurbished rooms. It's nothing special but a very convenient place to put your head down for the night.

Curragh Lodge Hotel (☎ 522 144; fax 521 247; on the N7; s/d €60/102; Ⓟ) You'll find this conventional Irish hotel about 800m south of town on the main Dublin road. It's a child-friendly place with standard but comfortable rooms, a reliable restaurant and regular evening entertainment in the bar.

Martinstown House (☎ 441 269; www.martinstownhouse.com; The Curragh; s/d €115/180; mid-Jan–mid-Dec; Ⓟ) This beautiful 18th-century country manor is built in the 'strawberry hill' Gothic style and set in a 200-acre estate surrounded by trees. The house has a terrific, easy-going atmosphere and rooms elegant enough to be off limits to small children. The restaurant serves a very generous set dinner (€45) and you're welcome to serve yourself with second helpings.

Eating

Kristianna's Bistro (☎ 522 985; The Square; mains €12-17; closed Mon) This understated restaurant serves a good variety of simple modern bistro food in generous proportions. Seafood is the speciality of the house and well worth trying.

Silken Thomas (☎ 522 232; The Square; mains €12-20, carvery lunch €8) This popular pub is a Kildare institution and has a reasonable carvery lunch as well as a more refined restaurant. Bar food is served all day in a not-so-authentic old-world atmosphere of low ceilings, dim lights and open fires.

Getting There & Away

Bus Éireann serves Kildare from Dublin (single/return €8.20/13, one hour), with 14 buses a day Monday to Friday, 13 on Saturday and eight on Sunday. The 9.30am service stops outside the Irish National Stud and Japanese Gardens; on Sunday both the 10am and noon services stop here.

The **Arrow train** (☎ 836 3333) runs the 55km trip from Heuston in Dublin station (€11.80/12.50, 30 minutes, about every 35 minutes).

NAAS TO CARLOW

The 48km stretch of the N9 between Naas and Carlow town offers several interesting side trips.

Donnelly's Hollow

Dan Donnelly (1788–1820) is revered as Ireland's greatest bare-knuckle fighter of the 19th century. He's also the stuff of legend – his arms were so long, he could supposedly tie his shoelaces without having to bend down! This spot, 4km west of Kilcullen on the R413, was his favourite battleground, and the obelisk at the centre of the hollow details his glorious career. Back in Kilcullen, his mummified arm can be seen in the **Hideout** (☎ 045-482 121; Main St, Kilcullen), a famous and wildly eccentric pub.

Ballitore

pop 714

Ballitore was made famous by its Quaker residents of the 18th and 19th centuries. A small **Quaker Museum** (☎ 059-862 3344; Leadbetter House, Main St; admission by donation; noon-5pm Wed-Sat, 2-4pm Sun Jun-Sep, noon-5pm Tue-Sat Oct-May) documents the lives of the Quaker community and the ordinary people of Ballitore.

About 2km west is **Rath of Mullaghmast**, an Iron Age hill fort and standing stone where Daniel O'Connell, champion of Catholic emancipation, held one of his 'monster rallies' in 1843.

Moone

pop 372

Just south of Ballitore, the unassuming village of Moone is home to one of Ireland's most magnificent high crosses. The unusually tall and slender **Moone High Cross** is an 8th- or 9th-century masterpiece with numerous carved panels displaying biblical scenes. The cross can be found 1km west of Moone village in an early-Christian churchyard.

Moone High Cross Inn (☎ 0502-24112; fax 24992; Bolton Hill; s/d €45/75) This charming 18th-century inn, 1km south of Moone, has a few simple rooms decorated in country house style. The quirky bar downstairs serves good lunches (€6 to €10) and there is also a proper **restaurant** (mains €13-25; 🕑 6-8.45pm). The inn revolves around a Celtic theme, celebrating pagan festivals and hoarding healing stones, lucky charms and even a 'love' stone in the outside courtyards. It has regular trad sessions and a *seanachaí* (traditional story teller) on the third Saturday of the month.

Kilkea Castle

Built in the 12th century, **Kilkea Castle** (☎ 059-914 5156; www.kilkeacastle.ie; Castledermot; s/d from €196/258; 🅿; wheelchair access) is Ireland's oldest continuously inhabited castle and has a resident ghost, an air of romance and a long, bloody history. It was once the second home of the Maynooth Fitzgeralds, and the grounds are supposedly haunted by Gerald the Wizard Earl, who rises every seven years from the Rath of Mullaghmast to free Ireland from its enemies – a pretty good trick considering he was buried in London.

The castle was completely restored in the 19th century and is now an exclusive hotel and golf club. The exterior is highly impressive and among its oddities is an **Evil Eye Stone** set high up on a wall at the back of the castle. Thought to date from the 13th or 14th century, it depicts a wolf-headed man and a monster-headed woman erotically entwined. The interior decoration is a bit garish but service is excellent and the restaurant (set dinner €44.50) is open to nonresidents. Substantial reductions on rack rates are available at various times throughout the year.

The castle is 5km northwest of Castledermot on the Athy road.

FROM KILKEA TO THE ANTARCTIC

Sir Ernest Shackleton (1874–1922) may not have been the first man to reach the South Pole but he is widely recognised to be one of the greatest – and bravest – polar explorers of them all. In recent years Shackleton-mania seems to have hit the world with a tide of high-profile exhibitions, biographies, award-winning documentaries, an IMAX film and even a complete corporate training scheme based on his model for leadership.

Shackleton was born in Kilkea but financial hardships forced a family move to London at the age of 10. In 1901 he had his first polar adventure as a member of Robert Falcon Scott's first Antarctic expedition. Eight years later he led his own expedition to the pole but was forced to turn back only 97 nautical miles from his goal. Despite his failure, Shackleton's fame was established.

After Norwegian explorer Roald Amundsen reached the South Pole in 1911, Shackleton's objective became a crossing of the Antarctic icecap – a journey of more than 2000km. In August 1914, he set out with 27 men in his ship *The Endurance*. The following January, one day's sail from its destination on the Antarctic coast, the ship stuck 'like an almond in a piece of toffee' in an ice pack. For the next 10 months Shackleton and his men drifted with the floe before *The Endurance* was crushed and the men forced to abandon ship. They set up camp on the ice and for five months survived entirely on seals and penguins, before conditions finally improved enough to launch the salvaged lifeboats. After a nightmarish six-day journey they landed on Elephant Island.

With the mission to cross the continent now abandoned, and no hope of rescue, Shackleton embarked on what has been called the greatest small-boat journey in maritime history. Along with five of his men, they set off in one of the boats for South Georgia Island, nearly 1500km away. They arrived 16 days later and arranged for the rescue of the others. Despite the constant threat of starvation, mutiny and madness, Shackleton did it all without losing a single man. 'Not a life lost and we have been through Hell', he later wrote.

The expedition was a triumph of the human spirit over great adversities, and the magnificent example of his leadership under such terrible conditions assured his place in history. Shackleton died of natural causes on 5 January 1922, at the beginning of his fourth Antarctic expedition.

Castledermot

pop 1122

Castledermot was once home to a vast ecclesiastical settlement but all that remains of St Diarmuid's 9th-century **monastery** is a 20m round tower topped with a medieval battlement. Nearby are two 9th- or 10th-century granite high crosses and a 12th-century Romanesque doorway. The ruins are set back from the road on Main St. At the southern end of town, the remains of a 13th-century **Franciscan friary** can be seen by the road.

Doyle's Schoolhouse Inn (☎/fax 059-914 4282; Main St, Castledermot; s/d €40/70) is an intimate inn with elegant rooms decorated with Victorian and Georgian fixtures and fittings. The restaurant is consistently rated as one of Ireland's best, and the six-course dinner (set menu only €38) is a feast. Reservations are essential.

A circular community **bus service** (☎ 045-482 062, 1800 200 127) runs from Athy through Kilkea, Castledermot, Moone, Ballitore and back to Athy five times a day (single €3).

ATHY

☎ 059 / pop 6058

Strategically placed at the junction of the River Barrow and the Grand Canal, the Anglo Norman town of Athy (Áth Í; a-*thigh*) is a pleasant, unhurried place but ruined in parts by some modern eyesores. The town was founded in the 12th century and later became an important defence post. Many of the town's older buildings remain, including the impressive **White's Castle**, a tower built in 1417 to house the garrison.

Information

The **Tourist Office & Heritage Centre** (☎ 863 3075; Emily Sq; 9.30am-1pm & 2-5pm Mon-Sat, 2-5.30pm Sun Apr-Sep, 10am-1pm & 2-5pm Mon-Fri Oct-Mar) has information about the town. The **heritage centre** (adult/child €3/2) traces the history of Athy and has a fascinating exhibit on Antarctic explorer Sir Ernest Shackleton (see p317).

Access the Internet at **Omichimal** (☎ 863 3875; 16 Duke St; €4/hr; 10am-8pm Mon-Fri, 10am-10pm Sat, 2-8pm Sun).

Activities

Athy is a popular centre for coarse, salmon and trout **fishing**. For equipment and information, try **Griffin Hawe Hardware** (☎ 863 1221; griffinhawe@eircom.net; 22 Duke St; 9.30am-5pm Mon-Sat).

Sleeping & Eating

Coursetown House (☎ 863 1101; fax 863 2740; Stradbally Rd; s/d €44/75; P; wheelchair access) This 200-year-old farmhouse is dripping with character and charm and set in beautifully manicured gardens. Just 3km from town it's well worth seeking out for its excellent-value rooms and warm, relaxed atmosphere.

Tonlegee House (☎/fax 863 1473; www.tonlegeehouse.com; Kilkenny Rd; s/d €85/110; P) This elegant Georgian house, situated about 2km south of town, is one of the finest country homes in Ireland, with a restaurant to match. Despite the sumptuous décor, it's all very relaxed and children are welcome. The **restaurant** (mains €18-28) is open to non-residents.

J1 (☎ 863 3155; Emily Sq; mains €5-8) If you're stuck for somewhere for lunch you could try this small café with laminated 1980s-style menus – lasagne and curry a speciality – or the slightly better **Bistro** (☎ 863 3655; 4 Stanhope St; mains €7-10) for uninspired meat and fish dishes.

Getting There & Away

Bus Éireann (☎ 01-836 6111) has five buses a day that serve Athy (single/return €9/10, 1¼ hours from Dublin) on the Dublin–Cork route and vice versa. **JJ Kavanagh & Sons** (Kilkenny ☎ 056-883 1106; Dublin ☎ 01-679 1549) runs four buses a day (two on Sunday) between Dublin (from outside the Gresham Hotel on O'Connell St) and Clonmel, stopping in Athy (€4.50/8.50, 1¼ hours).

A circular community **bus service** (☎ 045-482 062, 1800 200 127) runs from Athy through Kilkea, Castledermot, Moone, Ballitore and back to Athy five times a day (single €3).

COUNTY CARLOW

Carlow (Ceatharlach), Ireland's second-smallest county, has the understated charm of small-town Ireland. The pace of life is unhurried, the locals are genuinely glad to see you and the undulating farmland has a beauty all of its own. Carlow's county town is an up-and-coming place, rising from its unexceptional past and just beginning to reinvent itself. Elsewhere around the county a string of quietly picturesque villages such as Rathvilly, Leighlinbridge and Borris have changed little in the past hundred years.

The scenic Blackstairs Mountains dominate the southeast of the county, while the Rivers Slaney and Barrow meander to the east and west. Browne's Hill Dolmen, the county's most interesting archaeological feature, is just outside Carlow town.

CARLOW TOWN

☎ 059 / pop 13,188

The winding streets and lanes of Carlow town have the general upbeat air of a place on the cusp of greater things to come. The county capital and student centre is experiencing something of a regeneration with buildings being renovated, trendy cafés and bars opening up and plenty of nightlife to choose from. The town also has its fair share of historic buildings, though little remains from its medieval foundation.

Orientation

Dublin St is the city's principal north–south axis, with Tullow St, the main shopping street, running off it at a right angle.

Information

The **tourist office** (☎ 913 1554; cnr Tullow & College Sts; ⏲ 9am-1pm & 2-5pm Mon-Fri year round, 10am-5.30pm Sat Jun-Aug) is a useful source of information. The beautifully restored building next door houses the County Carlow Museum (being renovated at the time of writing), which has

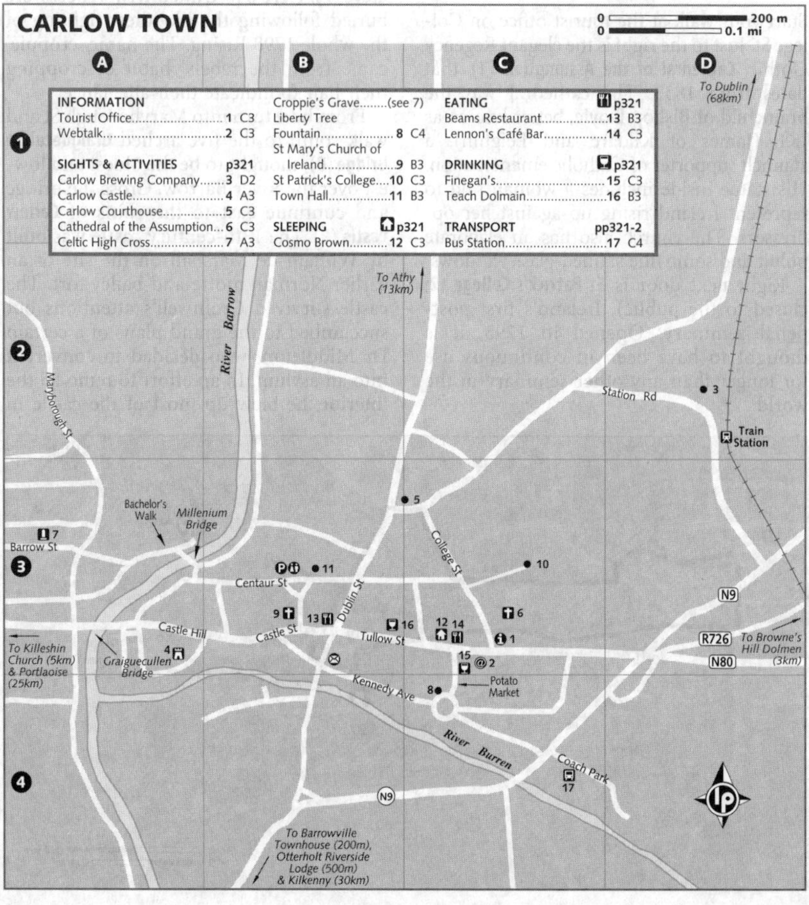

an interesting display on the town's history and heritage.

Access the Internet at **Webtalk** (☎ 913 9721; 44 Tullow St; €5/hr; ⏰ 9.30am-6pm Mon-Sat). The **post office** is on the corner of Kennedy Ave and Dublin St. Take a look at www.carlowtourism.com for information about the town and its surroundings.

Sights

WALKING TOUR

CARLOW TOWN WALK

Distance: 2.5km

Duration: one hour

Start your walk at the tourist office on College St. Just to the right is the elegant Regency Gothic **Cathedral of the Assumption** (**1**) that dates from 1833. The cathedral was the brainchild of Bishop Doyle, better known as JKL (James of Kildare and Leighin), a staunch supporter of Catholic emancipation. His statue inside includes a woman said to represent Ireland rising up against her oppressors. The church also has an elaborate pulpit and some fine stained-glass windows.

Right next door is **St Patrick's College** (**2**; closed to the public), Ireland's first post-penal seminary. Opened in 1793, it is thought to have been in continuous use for longer than any other seminary in the world.

Walking north and then left along College St, you'll come to the very impressive **Carlow Courthouse** (**3**), at the northern end of Dublin St. Designed by William Morrisson in 1830, this elegant building is modelled on the Parthenon in Athens and is considered to be one of the finest courthouses in the country. Carlow only got it through a mix-up in the plans – the building was originally intended for Cork.

Walk south down Dublin St and turn right into Centaur St and past the now dilapidated **Town Hall** (**4**), dating from 1884. When you reach the river, cross over on the newly opened **Millennium Bridge** (**5**) to Barrow St where you'll find the tall Celtic **high cross** (**6**) that marks the mass **Croppies' Grave** (**7**). Here 640 United Irish rebels were buried following the bloodiest fighting of the whole 1798 Rising. The name 'croppie' came from the rebels' habit of cropping their hair to indicate their allegiance.

From here turn into Maryborough St and walk south to the five-arched **Graiguecullen Bridge** (**8**), thought to be the oldest and lowest over the River Barrow. Cross the bridge and continue east to the ruins of **Carlow Castle** (**9**). The 13th-century castle was built by William de Marshall on the site of an earlier Norman motte-and-bailey fort. The castle survived Cromwell's attentions but succumbed to the grand plans of a certain Dr Middleton, who decided to convert it into an asylum. In an effort to remodel the interior, he blew up most of the castle in

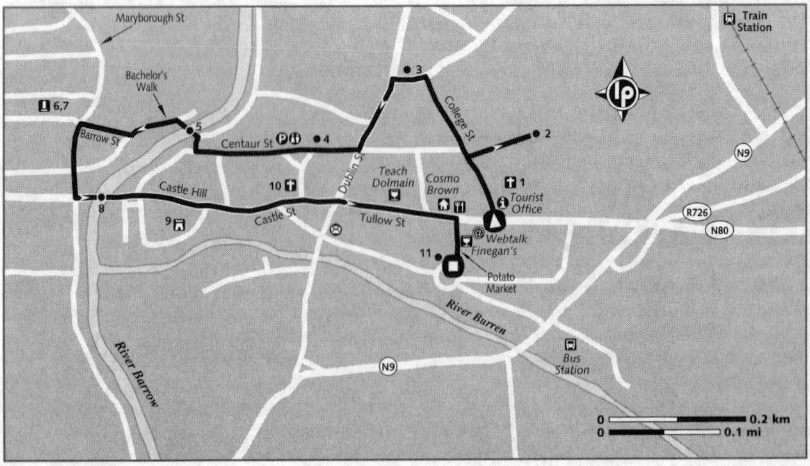

1814. All that is left is a single wall flanked by two towers.

Continue up Castle Hill and take the fork to your left onto Castle St. On your left you'll see **St Mary's Church (10)**, built in 1727 (the tower and spire were added in 1834). Inside there are a number of statues by Richard Morrison.

Walk on up Tullow St, the town's principal shopping thoroughfare, and take the second right into Potato Market. At the end of the lane is a small square. The bronze statue in the middle of the fountain is the **Liberty Tree (11)**, designed by John Behan to commemorate the 1798 Rising.

CARLOW BREWING COMPANY

If you're feeling more thirsty than energetic, you could visit the **Carlow Brewing Company** (☎ 913 4356; www.carlowbrewing.com; The Goods Store, Station Rd; admission €4.50; visits by prior arrangement only). This small microbrewery has been phenomenally successful since it opened in 1998, with its O'Hara Stout walking off with the first prize at the International Brewing Industry Awards just two years later. Tours include a glass of the prize-winning black stuff.

Activities

The Barrow is popular with canoeists, kayakers and rowers. **Adventure Canoeing Days** (☎ 087-252 9700) does guided river trips (€40) at weekends and rents canoes (€50 per day).

Festivals & Events

Every summer (usually in June) Carlow town celebrates **Éigse Arts Festival**, which showcases the work of Irish and international artists and performers. Ask at the tourist office for details.

Sleeping & Eating

Otterholt Riverside Lodge (☎ 913 0404; fax 913 5106; Kilkenny Rd; dm/s/d €14/20/36; P) This wonderful Independent Holiday Hostels of Ireland (IHH) hostel is just south of town in a large rambling house. It has one 10-bed dorm and a couple of private rooms, as well as a spacious garden by the river.

Barrowville Townhouse (☎ 914 3324; www.barrowvillehouse.com; Kilkenny Rd; s/d from €45/70; P) This attractive 18th-century town house has been meticulously restored and converted into a top-class B&B. The rooms are extremely comfortable and the atmosphere is relaxed and friendly. The breakfast spread, served overlooking the semi-formal garden, will fill you for the day.

Cosmo Brown (☎ 914 1384; Tullow St; s/d €80/130; wheelchair access) This brand new hotel on Carlow's main street has spacious modern rooms and a stylish attitude. Deep leather sofas, ambient light and hip music attract a trendy young crowd to the **bar** (mains €6-9; ⏰ food served noon-3pm & 5-7.30pm) and **restaurant** (mains €8-14; ⏰ noon-3pm & 5.30-8.30pm) downstairs.

Lennon's Café Bar (☎ 913 1575; 121 Tullow St; lunch €8.50; ⏰ 10am-5pm) Tantalise your taste buds with a gourmet lunch from Lennon's popular café, where delicious open sandwiches and mouthwatering hot lunches mean you might even have to queue for the pleasure.

Beams Restaurant (☎ 913 1824; 59 Dublin St; set dinner €37.50; ⏰ 7.30-9.30pm Tue-Sat) This is one of Carlow's best restaurants with a French chef serving up delectable modern Irish cuisine. Housed in an 18th-century coach house, it's an ambient spot and advertises itself as coeliac-friendly.

Drinking

Carlow has wall-to-wall pubs, several nightclubs and plenty of live music from dubious rock to traditional Irish. Just stroll along Tullow St and you're sure to find something to suit.

Finegan's (☎ 914 0458; Potato Market) If you fancy having a proper conversation without the twang of a banjo in your ear, then this popular pub in the middle of town is a good option.

Teach Dolmain (☎ 913 0911; 76 Tullow St) This is Carlow's happening, but slightly twee, trad pub with four bars, regular live music and its own DJ.

Getting There & Away

BUS

Bus Éireann (☎ 01-836 6111) operates buses to Dublin (single/return €9/10, 1½ hours, 10 services Monday to Saturday, five Sunday), Kilkenny (€6.40/7.30, 30 minutes, three daily except Sunday) and Waterford (€8.70/9.80, 1½ hours, 10 services Monday to Saturday, five Sunday).

JJ Kavanagh & Sons (☎ 914 3081; www.jjkavanagh.ie) has eight buses daily to Dublin (€13.30/18.90) and Waterford (€8.70/10.30). There is also a twice-daily bus service to Kilkenny

(€4.40/8.80, 45 minutes, Monday to Saturday). The twice-daily service to Portlaoise (€5.60/11.20, one hour, Monday to Saturday) also stops in Athy (€4.40/8.80, 30 minutes). There is also a service between Carlow and Newbridge (single €5.60, 1¾ hours) that stops in Kildare (€5.20, 1¼ hours) and the Curragh (€5.60, 1½ hours). This service runs Monday to Friday during college terms only (September to June).

Buses for both companies leave from the coach park located at the eastern end of Kennedy Ave.

TRAIN

The **train station** (☎ 913 1633) is on Station Rd to the northeast of town. Carlow is on the Dublin–Kilkenny–Waterford line with five trains daily in each direction (four Sunday). A day return to Dublin or Waterford will set you back €8.90.

AROUND CARLOW TOWN

Browne's Hill Dolmen

This 5000-year-old granite monster is Europe's largest **portal dolmen** and one of Ireland's most famous. The capstone alone weighs well over 100 tonnes and would have originally been covered with a mound of earth. The dolmen is 3km east of town on the R726 Hacketstown road; a path leads round the field to the dolmen. There's no public transport but you could walk.

Killeshin Church

Killeshin was once the site of an important monastery with one of the finest round towers in the country. However, the medieval masterpiece was destroyed early in the 18th century by a farmer worried that it might collapse and kill his cows. Ruins of a 12th-century church remain, including a beautiful doorway said to date from the 5th century. Look out for the wonderful old bearded face on the capstone. Killeshin Church is 5km west of Carlow on the R430, but there's no public transport. You could take a taxi. Try **Tips Cabs** (☎ 087-244 0621), which charges about €9 return, including a 20-minute wait.

BORRIS

☎ 059 / pop 877

This seemingly untouched Georgian village is well worth a visit for its beautiful mountain backdrop and traditional main street. The village is full of character with a graceful 16-arch railway viaduct at one end and the dramatic **Borris House** (☎ 977 3105; tours by appointment only) at the other. Residence of the MacMurrough Kavanaghs, descendants of the ancient kings of Leinster, the beautiful Tudor-style house is one of Ireland's finest stately homes. There are also plenty of friendly pubs well known for their music sessions. **O'Shea's** (☎ 977 3106), a genuine pub, hardware and grocery shop, still has its maze of tightly packed shelves, spare parts hanging from the ceiling and horse feed by the bar stools.

If you're feeling energetic, Borris is a starting point for the **Mt Leinster Scenic Drive** (which can also be walked) and is also on the South Leinster Way. Alternatively, there's a lovely 10km walk along the **River Barrow towpath** to picturesque Graiguenamanagh, just inside County Kilkenny.

Step House (☎ 977 3209; thestephouse@eircom.net; Main St; s/d €55/80; mid-Mar–mid-Dec; P), a Georgian home situated right in the centre of town, is a charming place to stay with comfortable rooms overlooking a large garden. Unfortunately, it's not suitable for children.

Lorum Old Rectory (☎ 977 5282; www.lorum.com; Kilgreaney; s/d from €80/120; mid-Jan–mid-Dec; P), halfway between Borris and Bagenalstown, is a historic manor house overlooked by the Blackstairs Mountains. It's a warm and welcoming place with great character,

> **SOMETHING SPECIAL**
>
> **Moongate** (☎ 977 3669; www.moongatesite.com; Tom Duff, Borris; d from €130, dinner €33; P) This eccentric guesthouse set in the lee of Mt Leinster is the perfect spot for a party or a weird and wonderful weekend. The whole place is a feast for the senses with lavish interiors decorated with an eclectic mix of salvaged materials, including chairs from the Scala cinema in Kings Cross, a door from Kabul, a wooden sculpture from a Filipino convent and, if you believe the owners, a light from the *Titanic*. The bedrooms are all individually themed (the Venetian Master is the best) and dinner is served communally at one long table. The only snag is that Moongate takes bookings for groups only (minimum of eight people).

wonderful organic cooking (a six-course dinner costs €38; closed for dinner Sunday) and peacocks roaming the croquet lawn.

Michael Kilbride (☎ 051-423 633) operates two buses daily (except Sunday) between Borris and Kilkenny, leaving at 8am and 2.15pm from Borris and noon and 5.30pm from Kilkenny (single/return €3.20/5.50, one hour).

MT LEINSTER

At 796m, **Mt Leinster** offers some of Ireland's finest hang-gliding. It's also worth the hike up for the panoramic views over Counties Carlow, Wexford and Wicklow. To get there from Borris, follow the Mt Leinster Scenic Drive signposts 13km towards Bunclody in County Wexford (see p172). It takes a good two hours on foot or 20 minutes by car.

SOUTH LEINSTER WAY

Southwest of Clonegal, on the northern slopes of Mt Leinster, is the tiny village of **Kildavin**, the starting point of the South Leinster Way. For details see p657.

COUNTY LAOIS

Little explored Laois (pronounced leash) is situated in the heart of Ireland and surrounded on all sides by counties that do not touch the coast. For most it's somewhere to whip through en route to Limerick or Cork, but for those willing to explore, it has some pleasant country towns, the unspoiled Slieve Bloom Mountains and a patchwork of rivers and walkways. For all you need to know about the county, check out www.laoistourism.ie.

PORTLAOISE

☎ 0502 / pop 3482

Portlaoise is an administrative and service centre for the county and there's very little to keep you here as a visitor. Its twin claims to fame are known locally as the 'nuts and bolts' – the large mental asylum and maximum-security prison. The town is mostly modern and the only building of note is the Richard Morrison courthouse on the corner of Main and Church Sts. However, the Slieve Bloom Mountains to the west and the impressive Rock of Dunamaise to the east (see p324) are well worth a visit.

Information

The **tourist office** (☎ 21178; James Fintan Lawlor Ave; 🕑 9.30am-2pm & 3-5.30pm Mon, Tue, Thu & Fri, 9.30am-1pm Wed May-Sep) is in the shopping-centre car park beside the bypass – to get there from Main St, cut through Lyster's Lane beside the Bank of Ireland.

Dunamaise Theatre Café (☎ 63356; Church St; €5/hr; 🕑 10am-5.30pm Mon-Sat) has Internet access.

Sleeping & Eating

Heritage Hotel (☎ 78588; www.theheritagehotel.com; Jessop St; s/d from €135/220; P) This giant complex is the town's newest and plushest hotel with understated décor and a good variety of rooms. There's a choice of several bars and two restaurants: **Spago's** (mains €12-18; 🕑 5.30-9.30pm), the Italian-style bistro, and the more refined **Fitzmaurice** (mains €16-22; 🕑 5.30-9.30pm).

Kitchen & Foodhall (☎ 62061; Hyand's Sq; mains €9; 🕑 9am-5.30pm; wheelchair access) This is a wonderful little place serving up delicious deli-style goodies and some great vegetarian options. The atmosphere is good, it's bright and cheery and it's child-friendly.

Entertainment

Dunamaise Theatre (☎ 63356; www.dunamaisetheatre.com; Church St) The county's purpose-built theatre and arts centre presents a varied programme of national and international performing and visual arts. If you're stuck in town overnight, it's worth checking out.

Getting There & Away

BUS

Portlaoise is on one of the busiest main roads in the country, at the junction of the N8 and N7. **Bus Éireann** (☎ 01-836 6111) runs 14 buses daily that pass through Portlaoise (single/return €10.20/16.50, 1½ hours) from Dublin on their way to Cashel, Cork, Limerick and Kerry. It is also on the Waterford–Kilkenny–Carlow–Athlone–Longford route.

JJ Kavanagh & Sons (☎ 056-883 1106) runs two buses daily to Carlow (single €6.50, one hour) and Kilkenny.

TRAIN

Just one hour from Dublin on the main line to Tipperary, Cork, Limerick and Tralee, Portlaoise is serviced by 12 daily trains from Dublin alone (single/return €16.80/17.50). The **train station** (☎ 21303; Railway St) is a five-minute walk north of the town centre.

HORSING AROUND

If you fancy seeing the countryside from a different perspective, you can hire your own traditional gypsy caravan through **Kilvahan Horse Drawn Caravans** (☎ 0502-27048; www.horsedrawncaravans.com; Kilvahan; per week €600-770). You'll spend your first night at the base in a beautiful Georgian house, and get some help choosing a horse and a route suitable to your experience – or lack of it! The caravans can accommodate up to four people.

ROCK OF DUNAMAISE

The **Rock of Dunamaise** is an arresting sight dramatically perched on a craggy limestone outcrop. It was first recorded on Ptolemy's map of AD 140 and suffered successive waves of Viking, Norman, Irish and English invasion and occupation. Cromwell's henchmen finally destroyed the site in 1650. The ruins are undergoing some badly needed restoration and, for now, require a good dose of imagination. For most a quick tour will suffice.

You enter the fort through a twin-towered gateway, which leads to the outer bailey and a fortified courtyard. The main sight is a badly shattered 12th- or 13th-century castle on the summit (best seen from the northern side) surrounded by a now dilapidated outer wall. The earth embankments 500m to the east of the rock are known as Cromwell's lines, although they're actually the remains of an Iron Age two-ringed fort.

The surrounding countryside is so flat that the views from the summit are spectacular on a clear day. If you're lucky you'll be able to see Timahoe round tower to the south, the Slieve Blooms to the north and the Wicklow Mountains to the east.

The rock is situated 6km east of Portlaoise along the Stradbally road. **JJ Kavanagh & Sons** (☎ 056-883 1106) runs two daily Portlaoise to Carlow buses that pass by the rock. Otherwise, **Portlaoise Taxi Service** (☎ 0502-62270) will take you out there for €9 return.

STRADBALLY

pop 230

The pretty village of Stradbally, 10km southeast of Portlaoise, is home to the newly renovated **Stradbally Steam Museum & Narrow Gauge Railway** (☎ 0502-25154; www.irishsteam.ie; Stradbally; 🕒 2-5pm Jun-Sep). The museum is a haven for steam enthusiasts with a collection of lovingly restored fire engines, steam tractors and steamrollers. During the August bank holiday weekend the museum hosts a three-day rally and the 40-hectare estate is taken over by steam-operated machinery and vintage cars.

The 1895 Guinness Brewery steam locomotive in the village is used six times annually for a day trip to Dublin. You can also take trips on the **narrow-gauge railway** (adult/child €3/1; 🕒 2.30-5pm Sun & Mon bank holiday weekends Easter-Oct).

JJ Kavanagh & Sons (☎ 056-883 1106) runs two buses a day Monday to Saturday from Portlaoise to Kilkenny via Stradbally (€2.90, 15 minutes). Stradbally is also on **Bus Éireann's** (☎ 01-836 6111) twice-daily (one on Sunday) Waterford–Longford service, which also passes through Kilkenny, Carlow, Portlaoise and Athlone.

EMO COURT

Giant sequoias line the avenue to the unusual, green-domed **Emo Court** (☎ 0502-26573; Emo; adult/child €2.75/1.25, grounds free; 🕒 noon-6.30pm mid-Jun–mid-Sep, last admission 5.45pm, grounds open during daylight hours year round). The impressive house was designed by James Gandon (architect of Dublin's Custom House) in 1790 and was originally the country seat of the first earl of Portarlington. After many years as a Jesuit novitiate, the house, with its elaborate central rotunda, has been impressively restored. The extensive grounds are littered with Greek statues and are ideal for a picnic or for a long walk through the woodlands to Emo Lake.

South of Emo village, off the main Portlaoise road, is the elegantly simple **St John's Church** (Coolbanagher; admission free; 🕒 10am-6pm). It's the only church designed and built by Gandon.

Emo is 13km northeast of Portlaoise, just off the main Portlaoise–Dublin road, and has daily buses in both directions.

PORTARLINGTON & AROUND

☎ 0502 / pop 4903

Portarlington (Cúil an tSúdaire) grew up under the influence of French Huguenot and German settlers and has some fine 18th-century buildings, many now terribly neglected. The 1851 **St Paul's Church** (admission free; 🕒 7am-7pm), on the site of the original

17th-century French church, was built for the Huguenots, some of whose tombstones stand in a corner of the churchyard.

About 4km east of town are the impressive ruins of **Lea Castle** on the banks of the River Barrow. The ivy-clad 13th-century ruin was the stronghold of Maurice Fitzgerald, second baron of Offaly. It consists of a fairly intact towered keep with two outer walls running down to the Barrow and a twin-towered gatehouse. Access is through a farmyard 500m to the north off the main Monasterevin road (R420).

Portarlington is on the main railway lines between Dublin and Galway, Limerick, Tralee and Cork, with hourly trains daily in both directions. For details, contact **Portlaoise train station** (☎ 0502-21303). There are no bus services.

MOUNTMELLICK

☎ 0502 / pop 2523

Mountmellick is a sleepy Georgian town 10km north of Portlaoise on the River Owenass. The town was renowned for its linen production in the 19th century and owes much of its history to its Quaker settlers. A looped heritage trail, beginning in the square, leads you through a tour of the town's most important landmarks. There's a display on Quaker life and Mountmellick work (white-on-white embroidery) at the new **heritage museum** (☎ 35315; Irishtown). At the time of writing, opening hours and admission prices had not been finalised.

Mountmellick is on **Bus Éireann's** (☎ 01-836 6111) twice-daily (one Sunday) Waterford–Longford route. There's also a twice-daily (one on Sunday) service to and from Dublin (single/return €10.90/16.30, two hours) via Newbridge and Kildare.

MOUNTRATH

☎ 0502 / pop 1899

Mountrath is a sleepy village that had its heyday in the 17th and 18th centuries when it prospered from the linen industry. Both St Patrick and St Brigid are supposed to have established religious houses here, although no trace of either remains.

Today, the local place of pilgrimage is the 6th-century monastery of St Fintan at Clonenagh, 3km east on the Portlaoise road. Its claim to fame is **St Fintan's Tree**, a large sycamore with a water-filled groove in one of its lower branches. Supposedly this never dries out, and the water is said to have healing properties, presumably paid for by the coins embedded in the trunk.

Ballyfin House, 8km north of Mountrath, is an architectural treasure and one of Ireland's finest 19th-century homes. The house was designed by Richard Morrison in 1850 and for many years was a private boarding school. It's currently undergoing extensive restoration work in order to reopen as an exclusive hotel.

You can stay at **Roundwood House** (☎ 32120; roundwood@eircom.net; Slieve Blooms Rd; s/d €95/140, coach house/forge/cottage per week €500/320/280; ⏲ Feb-Dec), one of the finest country houses in Ireland. This 18th-century Palladian mansion, 5km outside Mountrath, makes an excellent overnight stop. It's a wonderfully original place with a very relaxed, unceremonious atmosphere and superb service. The **restaurant** (set dinner €45; ⏲ 8pm sitting) serves delicious food and is open to nonresidents. Bookings are recommended. Self-catering accommodation is also available in the beautifully restored coach house, forge and cottage inside the grounds.

Mountrath is on the main **Bus Éireann** (☎ 01-836 6111) Dublin–Limerick route, with up to 14 buses daily in each direction.

SLIEVE BLOOM MOUNTAINS

One of the best reasons for visiting Laois is to explore the Slieve (shlee-ve) Bloom Mountains. Their name comes from the Celtic warrior Bladhma who used them as a refuge. Although not as spectacular as other Irish ranges, the Slieve Blooms are all the more attractive because of the relative absence of visitors. You'll get a real sense of being away from it all as you traipse through deserted moorland, pine forest and isolated valleys.

The highest point is Mt Arderin (528m), south of the Glendine Gap on the Offaly border, from where on a clear day it's possible to see the highest points of all four of the ancient provinces of Ireland. East is Lugnaquilla in Leinster, west is Nephin in Connaught, north is Slieve Donard in Ulster, and southwest is Carrantuohil in Munster.

If you're planning a walking tour, **Mountrath** (see above) to the south and **Kinnitty** (p330) to the north, are good bases. For leisurely walking, **Glenbarrow**, southwest of Rosenallis, has an interesting trail by the cascading River

Barrow. Other spots worth checking out are **Glendine Park**, near the Glendine Gap, and the **Cut mountain pass**. The road from Mountmellick to Birr via Clonaslee and Kinnitty is also well worth seeking out.

You can also pick up a *Laois Walks Pack*, which has information on more than 30 waymarked walks around the county, in the tourist office in Portlaoise.

The **Slieve Bloom Way** (p656) is a 77km signposted trail that does a complete circuit of the mountains, taking in most major points of interest. You can walk alone or join up with a guided group walk scheduled regularly throughout the year. Try www.slievebloom.ie for information on guided walks.

WESTERN LAOIS

South of the Slieve Bloom Mountains, **Borris-in-Ossory** on the N7 was a major coaching stop in the 18th century before the railways developed. It's on the Bus Éireann express Dublin–Limerick route, with 14 buses daily in each direction.

About 3km west of town is **Ballaghmore Castle** (☎ 0505-21453; www.castleballaghmore.com; Ballaghmore; adult/child €4.50/1.90; by appointment only). This square tower fortress from 1480 is soaked in atmosphere with heavy, creaking wooden doors, cold stone walls and a mysterious *sheila-na-gig* (female figure carved in stone with exaggerated genitalia). It's all faithfully restored and available to rent. If you'd just like to visit, accommodation is available at **Manor Guest House** (s/d €50/90) on the grounds and at the self-catering **Rose Cottage** (per week €380).

ABBEYLEIX

☎ 0502 / pop 2374

Abbeyleix (abbey-*leeks*), 14km south of Portlaoise, is a pretty tree-lined village with neat town houses and a lot of traffic. The town originally grew up around a 12th-century Cistercian monastery, but in the 18th century the local landowner, Viscount de Vesci, entirely remodelled the village and moved it to its present location. During the Famine, de Vesci proved a kinder landlord than many and the fountain obelisk in the square was erected as a thank you from his tenants.

Sights

De Vesci's mansion, **Abbeyleix House**, was designed by James Wyatt in 1773. It's 2km southwest of town on the Rathdowney road, but is not open to the public.

The old National School building at the northern end of town is now the interesting **Heritage House** (☎ 31653; on the N8; adult/child €4/2; 10am-5pm Mon-Sat, 1-5pm Sun Mar-Oct, 9am-5pm Mon-Fri Nov-Feb). The centre details the town's colourful history and contains some examples of the Turkish-influenced carpets woven in Abbeyleix from 1904 to 1913 – including carpets woven for the *Titanic*.

Sleeping & Eating

Preston House (☎/fax 31432; Main St; s/d €50/80) This ivy-clad town house has very comfortable accommodation in what were once the assembly rooms. The great country-style **café-restaurant** (10am-6pm Tue-Thu, 7-8.45pm Thu-Sat, 1-3pm Sun) is an excellent choice for a pit stop and has some wonderful vegetarian choices.

Abbeyleix Manor Hotel (☎ 30111; www.abbeyleixmanorhotel.com; d from €79; P) This is the town's newest hotel with an ugly motel-like exterior but incredibly good-value, spacious rooms. The décor is elegantly simple, and if you fancy a bit of local culture, **Malachi's Bar** on the ground floor has regular traditional music sessions.

Farran Farm Hostel (☎ 34008; www.farmhostel.com; Ballacolla; 6km from Abbeyleix on R435; dm €12.50; P) You can also stay at this beautiful independent hostel in a restored limestone grain loft.

Entertainment

Morrissey's (☎ 31233; Main St) This half-pub, half-shop and former travel agency and undertakers is a bit of a local legend and has been owned by the same family since 1775. In the half-light inside you can cradle a pint at the sloping counter while you soak up the atmosphere amid the ancient packets, the pew seats and the potbelly stove.

Getting There & Away

Abbeyleix is on the **Bus Éireann** (☎ 01-836 6111) route between Dublin (single/return €13.20/20.20, 1¾ hours) and Cork with six buses daily in each direction.

JJ Kavanagh & Sons (☎ 056-883 1106) runs a bus service twice a day Monday to Saturday between Portlaoise (€2.70, 20 minutes), Abbeyleix, Durrow and Urlingford (€3.80, 1¼ hours).

SOMETHING SPECIAL

Castle Durrow (☎ 0502-36555; www.castle durrow.com; d €180-260; Ⓟ) Even if you can't stay here, it's well worth nipping into this elegantly restored mansion for a coffee or light lunch (€10) on the terrace or a walk through the 30 acres of gardens and woodland. The whole castle has been refurbished in a contemporary style influenced by 18th-century grandeur. The bedrooms are individually decorated (Lady Hannah's room is particularly nice), many with sleigh beds or an oriental theme. Children are made very welcome and the family rooms are comfortable and well designed. The excellent **restaurant** (set menu €45; 6.30-9.30pm) is also open to nonresidents. It's worth calling ahead and enquiring about special offers that substantially reduce the rack rate quoted.

TIMAHOE

Tiny Timahoe is just a handful of houses around a grassy square. South of the village seven roads converge on a tilting 30m-tall **round tower**, all that remains of a 12th-century monastery. Look out for the beautifully worked Romanesque entrance.

Timahoe is 10km northeast of Abbeyleix on the R426. There is no public transport, but you could take a **taxi** (☎ 0502-30042; about €15) from Abbeyleix.

DURROW

pop 1161

Neat rows of houses surround Durrow's manicured green, with the imposing gateway to the 1716 **Castle Durrow**, a large Palladian villa, on the western side. The castle has been renovated and is now an upmarket hotel (see Something Special on p328).

Durrow is 10km south of Abbeyleix with three buses a day in each direction to Dublin and Cork.

COUNTY OFFALY

In Offaly the past is a very conspicuous feature of the present – the lowlands are dotted with monastic ruins, the towns are steeped in history and the county's pride and joy, the ecclesiastical city of Clonmacnoise, is one of Ireland's most famous sights.

Geographically, Offaly is dominated by the low-lying bogs that stretch across the county at regular intervals. Enormous brown expanses of peat such as the Bog of Allen and the Boora Bog, where peat is extracted on an industrial scale, are giant scars across the landscape, while Clara Bog is remarkably untouched and recognised internationally for its plant and animal life.

To the east the rugged and sometimes desolate Slieve Bloom Mountains (p325) provide excellent walking, while fishing and water sports are popular on the mighty River Shannon and the meandering Grand Canal. Access www.offaly.ie for information about County Offaly.

BIRR

☎ 0509 / pop 3573

Relax, recuperate and pile on the pounds – the restaurants are excellent, the accommodation options are consistently well above average and the town isn't bad either! Birr, in fact, is a little gem. If the magnificent castle and beautifully restored Georgian streets don't get you, then the vibrant nightlife and gastronomic delights will. It's an ideal base for exploring the area, or at least a worthwhile stopover.

History

Birr started life as a 6th-century monastic site founded by St Brendan. By 1208 the town had acquired an Anglo-Norman castle, home of the O'Carroll clan which reigned the surrounding territory. During the Plantation of 1620, the castle and estate were given to Sir Laurence Parsons, who changed the town's fate by carefully laying out streets, establishing a glass factory and issuing a decree that anyone who 'cast dunge rubbidge filth or sweepings in the forestreet' would be fined four pennies. The Parsons later became earls of Rosse and their castle home has remained in the family for 14 generations. The present earl and his wife still live on the estate.

Orientation

All the main roads converge on Emmet Square, where a statue of the duke of Cumberland (victor of the Battle of Culloden, Scotland) stood until 1925. In one corner, Dooly's Hotel, dating from 1747, was once a coaching inn on the busy route to the west.

CENTRAL SOUTH

Information

The **tourist office** (☎ 20110; Castle St; ⌚ 9.30am-5.30pm May–mid-Sep) is moving to Crotty's Church on Castle St once renovation is complete, although nobody knows when.

Ely O'Carroll Tourism (☎ 20923; www.elyocarroll.com; Brendan St; ⌚ 9am-5pm Mon-Fri) also provides tourist information.

The post office is in the northwestern corner of Emmet Square.

Sights

BIRR CASTLE

It's easy to spend half a day rambling through the grounds and gardens of **Birr Castle** (☎ 20336; www.birrcastle.com; adult/child €8/4.50; ⌚ 9am-6pm Mar–early Nov, 10am-4pm mid-Nov–Feb). The castle itself, however, is a private home and cannot be visited. The structure has a long history of attack and defence and was extensively remodelled over the years. Most of the present building dates from around 1620, with additional alterations made in the early 19th century. Extra fortifications were also added at this stage to placate a local Protestant woman, Mrs Legge, who was convinced the papists were about to rise up and kill the castle residents in their beds. Today the most heated fighting is seen in the jousting displays at the annual **National Country Fair** held in the grounds at the end of May.

The 50-hectare castle surroundings are famous for their magnificent gardens set around a large artificial lake. The restored **formal gardens** hold over 1000 species of shrubs and trees from all over the world, including a collection from the Himalayas and China. Here you'll also find the world's tallest box hedges, planted in the 1780s and now standing some 12m high.

The Parsons were known as a remarkable family of pioneering Irish scientists, and their work is documented in the **historic science centre** (admission incl in castle ticket; ⌚ 9am-6pm Mar–early Nov, 10am-4pm mid-Nov–Feb). The exhibits include a lunar heat machine invented by the fourth earl, early camera and darkroom equipment of Mary, Countess of Rosse, and in the Exhibition Pavilion, just north of the castle, the massive telescope built by William Parsons in 1845. The 'leviathan of Parsonstown', as it was known, was the largest telescope in the world for 75 years and attracted a wide variety of scientists and astronomers. It was used to map the moon's surface, and made innumerable discoveries, including the spiral galaxies. The telescope is fully operational and demonstrations are held three times daily.

The castle surrounds also house the **National Birds of Prey Centre** and its permanent aviaries.

OTHER SIGHTS & ACTIVITIES

Birr has no shortage of fine Georgian houses; just stroll down the tree-lined **Oxmantown Mall**, which connects Rosse Row and Emmet Square, or **John's Mall** to see some of the best examples. The tourist office hands out a free leaflet detailing a town trail that stops at the most important landmarks, including a statue of the third earl of Rosse, the megalithic **Birr Stone** – said to have marked the centre of Ireland – and **Old St Brendan's Church**, reputedly the site of St Brendan's 6th-century settlement. Alternatively, a beautiful **riverside walk** runs east along the River Camcor from Oxmantown Bridge to Elmgrove Bridge.

If you're feeling more energetic, the **Birr Outdoor Education Centre** (☎ 20029; Roscrea Rd) offers hill-walking, rock-climbing and abseiling in the nearby Slieve Blooms, as well as canoeing and kayaking on local rivers.

Sleeping

Spinner's Townhouse (☎ 21673; www.spinners-townhouse.com; Castle St; s/d €35/65; ⌚ Mar-Nov) This charming hotel is the best place in town and just a stone's throw from the castle gates. Its 14 rooms, all carefully decorated with locally made furniture and woven linen, are set round a fabulous courtyard garden that is great for reading and relaxing.

Maltings Guesthouse (☎/fax 21345; themaltingsbirr@eircom.net; Castle St; s/d €40/70; Ⓟ) Set in an old riverside malt storage building, this is another terrific option right by the castle. The tastefully decorated rooms are excellent value and there's a good restaurant downstairs.

Walcot B&B (☎ 21247; walcot@hotmail.com; Oxmantown Mall; s/d from €50/80) Great service and delightful rooms make this Georgian town house well worth a visit. It's located right in the centre of town but set back off the road; the four elegant rooms overlook a lovely private garden.

Stables Guesthouse (☎ 20263; cboyd@indigo.ie; Oxmantown Mall; d €80) Located on one of Birr's finest streets, this graceful Georgian town house is full of character. The rooms are spacious and luxuriously decorated and the service is friendly.

Croghan Lodge & Bothy (☎ 20023; www.birrcastle.com; Birr Castle surrounds; per week €380) These self-catering cottages in the castle surrounds are good options if you'd like to stay and explore the area for longer. They're fully restored and completely refitted with all modern conveniences.

Eating

You're spoilt for choice in Birr when you want a good meal, but finding a quick snack is much more difficult. Your best bet is to try one of the pubs mentioned below.

Spinner's Bistro (☎ 21673; www.spinners-townhouse.com; Castle St; mains €14-20) At Spinner's Townhouse, this is one the town's busiest restaurants, with a great reputation for good food and fine wine. The eclectic menu includes some good vegetarian options, and in warm weather diners spill out into the courtyard.

Stables (☎ 20263; cboyd@indigo.ie; Oxmantown Mall; mains €17-28; wheelchair access) Set in a converted stable yard at Stables Guesthouse, this fine restaurant is popular with diners from all over the county. Celebrated for its cuisine and its character, the staff are friendly and efficient and the ambience is relaxed.

County Arms Hotel (☎ 20791; countyarmshotel@eircom.net; Railway Rd; dinner €30; wheelchair access) This place is good for a quick bar lunch or a refined evening meal. The restaurant serves a popular mix of Irish and French cuisine and sources most of its vegetables from its own garden.

Riverbank (☎ 21528; Riverstown; mains €11-16) This wonderful restaurant is just south of town on the banks of the River Brosna. A favourite haunt for locals, it has earned plenty of rave reviews for its superb, freshly prepared dishes.

Thatch (☎ 20682; Crinkill; set dinner €30; 🕑 closed Mon) Only 2km southeast of Birr, this gorgeous thatched pub is a real find. The old-world atmosphere might not be to everyone's taste, but the food is excellent – chances are they'll have to roll you out of there.

Entertainment

Birr has a vibrant nightlife with music spilling out the doors of many of its pubs.

Craughwell's (☎ 21839; Castle St) Craughwell's is renowned for a fine traditional session on Friday night and impromptu sing-along sessions on Saturday.

Kelly's (☎ 20175; Green St) This is the locals' local, just off the square towards the castle. It's a good place for simple lunches and often has live music in the evenings.

Market House Tavern (☎ 20180; Market Sq) Birr's most modern bar is bright and cheerful but lacking in luxury. It's popular with the younger crowd.

Melba's Nite Club (☎ 20032; Emmet Sq) In the basement of Dooly's Hotel, this is the town's only nightclub and on a Saturday it gives a fine anthropological insight into the typical dancing and mating habits of rural Ireland.

Getting There & Away

Birr is on the Dublin–Portumna route, which also serves Tullamore and Maynooth. **Bus Éireann** (☎ 01-836 6111) has only one direct service from Dublin, which leaves at 4pm Monday to Friday (single/return €12.50/17, 2¼ hours). There are two other daily services via Roscrea (3¼ hours). For information, try the **bus station** (☎ 090-647 2651) in Athlone.

Kearn's Coaches (☎ 22244) runs daily services from Dublin and Tullamore through Birr to Portumna (in Galway). Buses from Dublin pass through Birr once daily Monday to Thursday, three times on Friday, four times on Saturday and twice on Sunday. From Portumna, buses serve Birr twice on Monday, once daily Tuesday to Friday, twice on Saturday and three times on Sunday on their route to Dublin (one way from Birr €7). All buses stop in Emmet Square and you can usually get up-to-date information from the newsagencies nearby.

LEAP CASTLE

One of the most haunted castles in Europe lies southeast of Birr between Kinnitty and Roscrea (in Tipperary). **Leap Castle** (☎ 0509-31115; seanfryan@oceanfree.net; admission €6; 🕑 10am-5pm) was originally an O'Carroll family residence, keeping guard over a crucial route between Munster and Leinster. The castle was the scene of many dreadful deeds and is famous for its eerie apparitions – its most renowned inhabitant is the 'smelly ghost', a spirit that apparently leaves a smell behind after sightings. Although the castle was

CENTRAL SOUTH

destroyed during the Civil War, it has been mostly renovated and hosts regular banquets with traditional Irish music sessions for groups.

There is no public transport to the castle but **Paddy Kavanagh** (☎ 090-647 4839; pkmail@eircom.net) runs tours (€25) from Athlone once a week.

KINNITTY

☎ 0509 / pop 504

Kinnitty is a pretty village and a good base or jumping-off point for the Slieve Bloom Mountains. Driving out of Kinnitty, the road across the mountains to Mountrath in County Laois, and a second route around the northern side of the hills to Mountmellick (also in County Laois), are particularly scenic.

Look out for the bizarre **stone pyramid** in the village graveyard behind the Church of Ireland. It's a scale replica of the pyramids of Egypt and was built as a tomb to a local family.

Sleeping

Kinnitty is well known for its superb castle hotel, but there's other, cheaper accommodation available.

Ardmore House (☎ 37009; ardmorehouse@eircom.net; The Walk; s/d €45/70) Brass beds, turf fires and home-made brown bread are the order of the day at this lovely Victorian stone farmhouse. It's set off the main road, about 200m east of Kinnitty.

Kinnitty Castle (☎ 37318; www.kinnittycastle.com; Kinnitty; s/d from €170/270) This former O'Carroll residence, 3km southeast of town, is one of Ireland's most renowned castles. Set on a vast estate, it is now a luxury hotel popular for celebrity weddings. The fine **restaurant** (mains €20-28) is open to nonresidents and there is traditional music in the Dungeon Bar every Friday and Saturday evening at 9pm.

BANAGHER & AROUND

☎ 0509 / pop 1793

The quiet riverside town of Banagher is fast becoming a popular stop for travellers on the Shannon thanks to its new marina, good angling and an easy-going attitude. It's a pleasant place with impressive fortifications on the west bank of the river and an intriguing literary history. In 1841 Anthony Trollope was a post office clerk in the village and in his spare time he managed to complete his first novel, *The Macdermots of Ballycloran.* Charlotte Brontë honeymooned and later lived here, and in another unusual twist, local boy George Frazer went on to become governor of Cuba – sealing the town's connection with the island forever.

Information

The **tourist office** (☎ 52155; Crank House, Main St; 9am-5pm Mon-Fri) provides information about Banagher and the surrounding region.

Sights

About 3km south of Banagher in Lusmagh is **Cloghan Castle** (☎ 51650; www.cloghancastleoffaly.com; Banagher; min €35 per group, tours by prior arrangement only), which has been in use for nearly 800 years. The castle has seen more than its fair share of bloodshed, beginning life as a McCoghlan stronghold and later becoming home to the mighty O'Carroll clan. Today the castle consists of a well-preserved Norman keep and an adjoining 19th-century house full of interesting antiques and armaments. The tour takes about an hour. There's no bus service, but the owners will collect people from Crank House Hostel by arrangement.

About 7km northeast of Banagher is **Cloghan**, where all six roads out of town lead into wide tracts of peat. Around 5km out on the road to Shannonbridge is the 16th-century **Clonony Castle**, a four-storey square tower enclosed by an overgrown castellated wall. Stories that Henry VIII's second wife, Anne Boleyn, was born here are unlikely to be true, but her cousins Elizabeth and Mary Boleyn are buried beside the ruins.

About 8km south of Banagher on the County Galway side of the border is the beautiful **Meelick Church**, one of the oldest still in use in Ireland.

Activities

You can hire canoes for trips on the River Shannon or Grand Canal from **Shannon Adventure Canoeing Holidays** (☎ 51411; Riverside Marina).

Sleeping & Eating

Crank House Hostel (☎ 51458; fax 51798; Main St; dm €11) This excellent IHH is the only hostel in the region and has a variety of two- and four-bed rooms. Crank House also contains

CENTRAL SOUTH

the tourist office and an exhibition room for local artists. At the back is **Heidi's Traditional Irish Coffee Shop** (mains €4-6; 9.30am-6pm), which serves snacks and light lunches.

Brosna Lodge Hotel (☎ 51350; www.brosnalodge.com; Main St; s/d €45/85; P) This conventional family-run hotel in the centre of town has recently been refurbished and offers good value for money. The **restaurant** (mains €9-16) is popular with locals and has access to a large garden in fine weather.

Vine House (☎ 51463; Main St; mains €8-12; 1-3pm & 7-10pm) Good food, good atmosphere and good conversation have earned this pub and restaurant a well-established reputation as one of the best eating places on the Shannon. It's a relaxed place and always busy during the summer with drop-in trade off the river.

Entertainment

JJ Hough's (☎ 51893; Main St) If you feel like stretching your vocal chords, this pretty, vine-draped 'singing pub' is a local institution legendary for its traditional sessions.

Getting There & Away

Kearn's Coaches (☎ 22244) includes Banagher on its daily Portumna–Dublin service. A **community bus service** (☎ 54956) runs from Banagher to Tullamore on Friday only at 10am and returns from Tullamore at 1.30pm (€6 single, 1¼ hours).

SHANNONBRIDGE

☎ 090 / pop 353

Shannonbridge gets its name from a narrow 16-span 18th-century bridge that crosses the river into County Roscommon. It's a sleepy little village with just one main street and two pubs. You can't miss the massive 19th-century **fortifications** on the western bank, where heavy artillery was placed to bombard Napoleon in case he was cheeky enough to try to invade by the river. The fort has now been converted into a fine **restaurant** (☎ 967 4973; mains €21-32; 4-9.30pm Wed-Sat, 12.30-2.30pm Sun).

Just south of Shannonbridge, you can take trips across the bog on the **Bord na Móna Bog Rail Tour** (☎ 967 4450; bogtrain@bnm.ie; adult/child €5.80/3.90; 10am-5pm Apr–early Oct). This 45-minute trip takes you through the Blackwater section of the Bog of Allen on a narrow-gauge line that used to transport peat. The diesel locomotive moves at around 10km/h – slow enough to take in the bog landscape and its special flora, which has remained unchanged for thousands of years. Trips leave on the hour from near the peat-fired power station, which is visible for miles around. Tickets are available from the coffee shop, though you should call ahead as tours can get fully booked with groups.

CLONMACNOISE

☎ 090 / pop 316

Superbly placed overlooking the River Shannon, **Clonmacnoise** (☎ 967 4195; adult/child €5/2; 9am-7pm Jun–early Sep, 10am-5pm mid Sep–May, last admission 45 min before closing) was one of Ireland's most important monastic cities. The site is enclosed in a walled field and contains numerous early churches, high crosses, round towers and graves in remarkably good condition. The surrounding area is marshy ground known as the Shannon Callows. These are home to many wild plants and are one of the last refuges of the seriously endangered corncrake (see p498).

History

Roughly translated, Clonmacnoise (Cluain Mhic Nóis) means 'Meadow of the Sons of Nós'. The marshy land would have been impassable for early traders, who instead chose to travel by water or on raised land. When St Ciarán founded a monastery here in AD 548 it was the most important crossroads in the country – the intersection of the River Shannon, the north–south artery, and the east–west glacial esker (ridge) known as Esker Riada (Highway of the Kings).

The giant ecclesiastical city had a humble beginning and Ciarán died just seven months after building his first church. Over the years Clonmacnoise grew to become an unrivalled bastion of Irish religion, literature and art and attracted a large lay population. Between the 7th and 12th centuries, while much of Europe languished in the Dark Ages, monks from all over Europe came to study and pray here, helping to earn Ireland the title of the 'land of saints and scholars'. Even the high kings of Connaught and Tara were brought here for burial.

The earliest monastic buildings of wood, clay and wattle have long since disappeared and most of what you can see today dates from the 10th to 12th centuries. The monks would have lived in small huts scattered in and around the monastery, which would probably have been surrounded by a ditch or rampart of earth.

The site was burned and pillaged on numerous occasions by both the Vikings and the Irish. After the 12th century it fell into decline, and by the 15th century it was home only to an impoverished bishop. In 1552 the English garrison from Athlone reduced the site to a ruin: 'Not a bell, large or small, or an image, or an altar, or a book, or a gem, or even glass in a window, was left which was not carried away.'

Among the treasures that survived the continued onslaught are the crozier of the abbots of Clonmacnoise in the National Museum, Dublin, and the 12th-century *Leabhar na hUidhre* (The Book of the Dun Cow), now in the Royal Irish Academy in Dublin.

Information

Dúchasprovides a museum, an on-site interpretive centre and a coffee shop. If you want to avoid the crowds it's a good idea to visit early or late. The **tourist office** (☎ 967 4134; ⏲ 10am-5pm Apr-Oct) can help with tourism information.

Museum

The three beehive-like structures near the entrance are a **museum** echoing the design of the early monastic dwellings. The centre's 20-minute audiovisual show is an excellent introduction to the site.

The exhibition area contains the original three principal high crosses (replicas have been placed in their original locations outside) and various artefacts uncovered during excavation, including silver pins, beaded glass and an ogham stone. It also contains the largest collection of early-Christian graveslabs in Europe. Many are in remarkable condition with inscriptions clearly visible, often starting with *oroit do* or *ar* (a prayer for).

High Crosses

The richly decorated sandstone **Cross of the Scriptures** is one of Ireland's finest high crosses with unique upwards-tilted arms. Its carved panels depict the crucifixion, the last judgement and the arrest of Jesus.

Only the shaft of the **North Cross**, which dates from around AD 800, remains. It is adorned by lions, convoluted spirals and a single figure, thought to be the Celtic god Cerrunnos, or Carnunas, who sits in a Buddha-like position. The richly decorated **South Cross** has mostly abstract carvings and, on the western face, the crucifixion.

Cathedral

The biggest building at Clonmacnoise, the **cathedral**, was originally built in AD 909 but was significantly altered and remodelled over the centuries. Its most interesting feature is the intricate 15th-century Gothic doorway with carvings of St Francis, St Patrick and St Dominic. A whisper carries

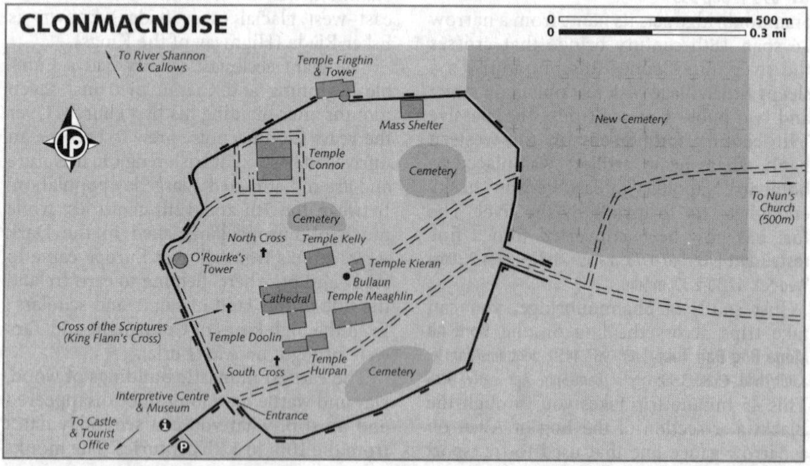

from one side of the door to the other, and this feature was supposedly used by lepers to confess their sins without infecting the priests.

The last high kings of Tara – Turlough Mór O'Connor (died 1156) and his son Ruairí, or Rory (died 1198) – are said to be buried near the altar.

Temples

The small churches are called temples, a derivation of the Irish word *teampall* (church). The little, roofed church is **Temple Connor**, still used by Church of Ireland parishioners on the last Sunday of the summer months. Walking towards the cathedral, you pass the scant foundations of **Temple Kelly** (1167) before reaching the tiny **Temple Kieran**, reputed to be the burial place of St Ciarán, the site's founder.

The floor level in Temple Kieran is lower than outside because local farmers have for centuries been taking clay from the church to place in the four corners of their fields, where it's said to protect crops and cattle. The floor has been covered in slabs, but even today handfuls of clay are removed from outside the church in the early spring.

Near the temple's southwestern corner is a *bullaun* (an ancient grinding stone), supposedly used for making medicines for the monastery's hospital. Today the rainwater that collects in it is supposed to cure warts.

Continuing round the compound you come to the 12th-century **Temple Meaghlin**, with its attractive windows, and the twin structures of **Temple Hurpan** and **Temple Doolin**.

Round Towers

Overlooking the River Shannon is the 20m-high **O'Rourke's Tower**. Lightning blew apart the top of the tower in 1135, but the remaining structure was used for another 400 years.

Temple Finghin and its round tower are on the northern boundary of the site, also overlooking the Shannon. The building dates from around 1160 to 1170 and has some fine Romanesque carvings. The tower roof is the only one in Ireland that has never been altered and has stones set in an unusual herringbone pattern. Most such towers were used by monks for protection when their monasteries were attacked, but this one was probably used as a bell tower as the doorway is at ground level.

Other Remains

Beyond the site's boundary wall, 500m east through the modern graveyard, is the secluded **Nun's Church**. From here the main site, including the towers, is invisible. The church has wonderful Romanesque arches and a tiny **sheila-na-gig**; it's well worth seeking out.

To the west of the site, on the ridge near the car park, is a motte with the oddly shaped ruins of a 13th-century **castle** built by John de Grey, bishop of Norwich, to watch over the Shannon.

Sleeping

Glebe Caravan & Camping Park (☎ 643 0277; Clonfanlough; sites €10; ⌚ Easter–mid-Oct) This caravan park, 5km east of Clonmacnoise, is on a beautiful eight-acre site. Amenities include a modern shower and toilet block, TV and games room, laundry, kitchen and playground.

Kajon House (☎ 967 4191; Creevagh; d from €55; ⌚ Feb-Nov; Ⓟ) The genial hosts, relaxed atmosphere and comfortable rooms are enough to recommend this small guesthouse. It's just 1.5km from the ruins on the road signposted to Tullamore.

Meadowview (☎ 967 4257; meadowviewaccom@eircom.net; Clonmacnoise; s/d from €30/48) This modern dormer bungalow is set back off the road about 1km from the entrance to the ruins. The rooms are bright and airy and there's a pleasant garden.

Getting There & Away

Clonmacnoise is 7km north of Shannonbridge and about 24km south of Athlone. **Bus Éireann** (☎ 01-836 6111) operates buses from Dublin to Athlone every hour (single/return €9.30/14, two hours), but after that things get more complicated. **Paddy Kavanagh** (☎ 087-240 7706) in Athlone runs a minibus to Clonmacnoise every Sunday. He departs Athlone Castle at 9.30am and returns at 2pm. The return trip costs €20. To visit both Clonmacnoise and the West Offaly Railway (see p331) costs €25.

There are river cruises to Clonmacnoise from Athlone in County Westmeath; see p461 for details.

A **taxi** (☎ 647 4400) from Athlone will cost roughly €35, including an hour waiting time.

TULLAMORE

☎ 0506 / pop 10,260

Tullamore (Tulach Mór), Offaly's county town, is growing fast and growing ugly. Despite a pleasant setting on the Grand Canal, it's a lacklustre place and worth a visit only for the magnificent Charleville Forest Castle. The town is famous for Tullamore Dew, claimed to be the easiest of Irish whiskies to drink. The whiskey has kept its original name but production has long since moved to Clonmel, County Tipperary.

Information

The **tourist office** (☎ 52617; Bury Quay; 9am-6pm Mon-Sat, noon-5pm Sun May-Aug, 9.30am-5pm Mon-Fri Sep-Apr) is at the Tullamore Dew Heritage Centre, while the post office is on O'Connor Square.

Sights

CHARLEVILLE FOREST CASTLE

Spires, turrets, clinging ivy and creaking trees combine to give this extraordinary structure something of an eerie Gothic fantasy feel. **Charleville Forest Castle** (☎ 23040; adult/student €5/3.50, children under 12 free; tours by appointment only Jun-Sep) was the family seat of the Burys, who in 1798 commissioned the design from Francis Johnston, one of Ireland's most famous architects. The interior is spectacular with stunning ceilings and one of the most striking Gothic revival galleries in Ireland. The kitchen block was built to resemble a country church, and nearby is an ornate stable yard. The extensive grounds are full of ancient oak trees and well worth exploring. The admission price includes a 30-minute tour of the castle.

The entrance to the castle is on Charleville Rd, south of town on the road to Limerick.

TULLAMORE DEW HERITAGE CENTRE

Located in a canalside warehouse, the **heritage centre** (☎ 25015; www.tullamore-dew.org; Bury Quay; adult/child €4.90/2.85; 9am-6pm Mon-Sat, noon-5pm Sun May-Sep, 10am-5pm Mon-Sat, noon-5pm Sun Oct-Apr) tells the story of Tullamore Dew whiskey and the importance of the distillery and the Grand Canal in the town's development. At the end of your visit, you get to sample a glass of the fine liquor.

Activities

For information on hiring narrowboats on the canal, see p310.

Sleeping & Eating

Moorhill Country House (☎ 21395; www.moorhill.ie; Clara Rd; s/d €68/100; P) This Victorian retreat is set amid chestnut trees and manicured lawns about 3km north of town on the N80. More a boutique hotel than a guesthouse, it is a charming place, newly renovated and eager to impress.

Bridge House Hotel (☎ 21704; www.bridgehouse.com; Bridge St; s/d €95/170; P) Tullamore's long-established hotel has recently undergone a massive face-lift and extended and upgraded its facilities to include a range of comfortable if fussy rooms. Its bars and **restaurants** (mains €10-15) are always busy and serve a familiar mix of grills and steaks.

Vista Bistro (☎ 51011; 1 Church St; mains €9-12) This is a young trendy bar-restaurant that thinks it's quite hip but somehow fails to hit the mark. Food is served all day with popular carvery lunches downstairs and a more formal seating area upstairs.

Also worth trying:

Senor Rico (☎ 52839; Patrick St; pizza & pasta €10-16)
Café Mezzo (☎ 29333; Patrick St; sandwiches €5)

Getting There & Away

BUS

Bus Éireann (☎ 21431) stops at the train station, south of town. From Tullamore there are eight buses daily each way on the route to Dublin (single/return €12.50/17, 1¾ hours), one daily to Portumna (€10.90/16.30, one hour), and two daily (one on Sunday) on the route between Waterford (€15.90/23.20, 3½ hours) and Longford (€12.50/17.10, 1½ hours).

Kearn's Coaches (☎ 0509-22244) runs services to Tullamore on its Dublin–Portumna route, with one bus daily Monday to Thursday, three on Friday, four on Saturday and two on Sunday (one way from Tullamore €6).

TRAIN

There are eight trains a day Monday to Saturday (five on Sunday) to Dublin (single/return €13.90/23.40, one hour) and Galway (€24/33.60, 2½ hours).

CENTRAL SOUTH

DURROW ABBEY

Founded by St Colmcille (also known as St Columba) in the 6th century, **Durrow Abbey** is most famous for producing the illustrated *Book of Durrow*, a Latin gospel. The 7th-century text is the earliest of the great manuscripts to have survived – quite a remarkable feat considering it was recovered from a farm where it was dipped in the cattle's drinking water to cure illnesses. It can be seen today at Trinity College in Dublin.

The rest of the monastery didn't fare so well and was badly damaged by Hugh de Lacy in 1186. He literally lost his head for it, though, when a local man took exception to his using the monastery stones to build a castle on the mound nearby.

Today a grand Georgian mansion and derelict 19th-century Protestant church overshadow the ruins of the abbey. The path north past the church leads to **St Colmcille's Well**, a place of pilgrimage marked by a small cairn of stones. West of the church is a 10th-century **high cross** with carvings depicting the sacrifice of Isaac, the last judgement and the crucifixion.

Durrow Abbey is 7km north of Tullamore down a long lane west off the N52 Kilbeggan road.

County Clare

Clare (An Clár) is topped and tailed by Galway and Kerry and is often compared unflatteringly with these stars of Irish tourism. Yet, in many ways Clare beats them hands down. There are few finer places in all of Ireland than the Burren of north Clare, with its dramatic limestone landscapes. The Burren is a haunting place where raw limestone is stitched together within a web of vividly coloured wild flowers and where the impact of the Atlantic's vast ocean and sky is exhilarating. Here you'll find the bare bones of ancient burial chambers, the curving walls of Iron Age castles, medieval tower houses, remote beaches and spectacular cliffs.

By contrast the eastern part of Clare is all mellow lakes and waterways. Only in the flat and featureless south is the spell broken, yet there is still much of interest in the lonely dwindling peninsula that runs southwest to the astounding Loop Head, or in the Shannon shoreline with its strange mix of medieval castles and its huge airport.

Many of Clare's towns and villages have avoided the commercialisation of other heavily visited places in Ireland. Ennis, Clare's county town, retains its charming narrow streets, while villages such as Ennistymon have many old pubs that host traditional music sessions on summer evenings. Two villages have become magnets for particular types of visitors. Doolin attracts music lovers and backpackers, while genteel Ballyvaughan is a weekend seaside retreat for those in search of serenity.

HIGHLIGHTS

- Enjoy some of Ireland's finest traditional musicians in the pubs of **Ennis** (p342) or **Doolin** (p361), or at Ennis' **Glor centre** (p342)
- Go walking or cycling around the Burren and visit such ancient sites as **Poulnabrone Dolmen** (p365)
- Get away from it all on the lonely **Loop Head peninsula** (p352) and around the remote villages of its south coast
- Explore the quieter Clare villages of **Corofin** (p366), **Kilfenora** (p366) and **Ennistymon** (p354)
- Go medieval at **Bunratty Castle** (p345) – good fun despite the kitsch

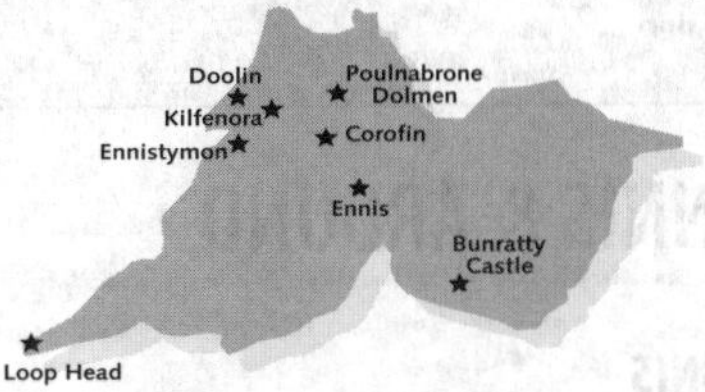

- POPULATION: 103,333
- AREA: 3147 SQ KM

COUNTY CLARE

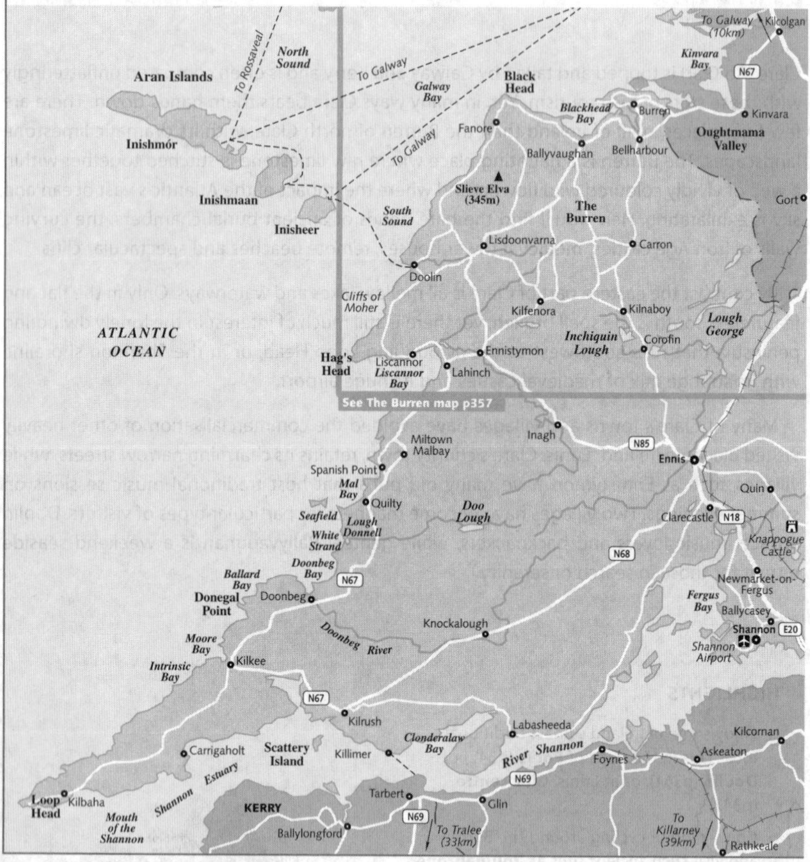

ENNIS & AROUND

ENNIS

☎ 065 / pop 18,977

Ennis (Inis), Clare's principal settlement, is a busy market centre and one of the Republic's larger towns. It lies on the banks of the River Fergus, which runs east, then south into the Shannon Estuary.

History

The town's medieval origins are seen in its narrow streets, and there are many old shops and pubs. The most important historical site is Ennis Friary, founded in the 13th century by the O'Briens, kings of Thomond, who also built a castle in Ennis in the 13th century. Much of the wooden town was destroyed by fire in 1249 and again in 1306, when it was razed by one of the O'Briens.

In the town centre, The Square, is a **Daniel O'Connell monument**. His election to the British parliament by a huge majority in 1828 forced Britain to lift its bar on Catholic MPs and led to the Act of Catholic Emancipation a year later. The 'Great Liberator' stands on an extremely high column, so far above the rest of us you would hardly know he was there.

Eamon de Valera was *teachta Dála* (TD; member of the Irish Parliament) for Clare from 1917 to 1959. There's a bronze **statue** of him near the courthouse.

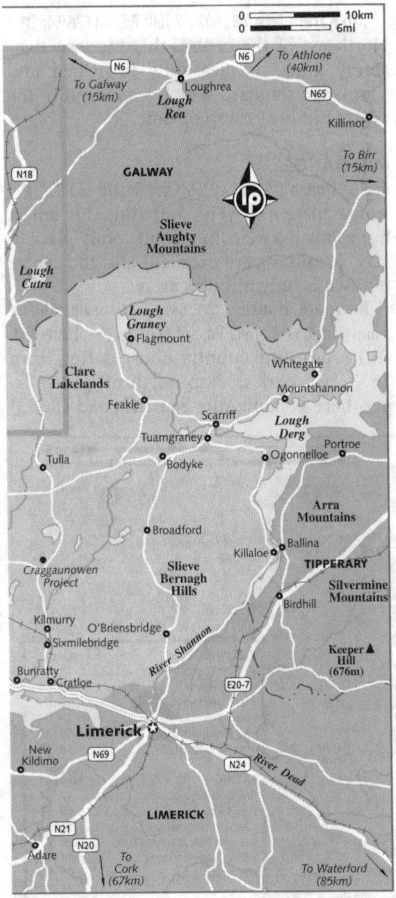

Orientation

The old town centre is on The Square, and the principal streets – O'Connell St, High St (becoming Parnell St), Bank Place and Abbey St – radiate from there. The large but fairly mundane **cathedral** (1843) is at the southern end of O'Connell St.

Information

The **tourist office** (☎ 682 8366; www.shannonheritage.com; Arthur's Row; 9.30am-6.30pm Jun-Sep, 9.30am-1pm & 2-5.30pm Mon-Sat Apr-May & Oct, 9.30am-1pm & 2-5.30pm Mon-Fri Nov-Mar) is very helpful and efficient.

A useful information source for young people is the **Youth Information Bureau** (☎ 682 4137; Carmody St; 9am-5.30pm Mon-Fri, 10am-3pm Sat). It's not a tourist information supplier, but has a general remit to advise young people, mainly on local matters. It has email, photocopying and other services.

You can change money at the Bank of Ireland (which also has an ATM) and Ulster Bank, both on The Square.

The post office is on Bank Place, northwest of O'Connell Square. **De Valera Library** (☎ 682 1616; Harmony Row; 10am-5.30pm Mon-Wed & Thu, 10am-8pm Tue-Fri & 10am-2pm Sat) offers one hour of free Internet access. There are also dedicated email screens for short-term use. **Edgecom Computing** (☎ 684 8642; 3 River Lane; €1.50/hr; 9am-11pm Mon-Sat, 11am-11pm Sun) is a friendly place with a café.

Ennis Bookshop (☎ 682 9000; 13 Abbey St) is good for maps and books of local interest.

White Knight Laundrette (☎ 682 3133; Old Barrack St; 9am-6pm Mon-Sat) is a useful and friendly place for catching up with laundry.

Ennis Friary

Just north of The Square is **Ennis Friary** (☎ 682 9100; Abbey St; adult/child €1.20/0.50; 10am-6pm Jun–mid-Sep, 10am-5pm Tue-Sun Apr-May & mid-Sep–Oct). It was founded by Donnchadh Cairbreach O'Brien, king of Thomond, some time between 1240 and 1249, though a lot of the present structure was completed in the 14th century. Partly restored, it has a graceful five-section window dating from the late 13th century and a McMahon tomb (1460) with alabaster panels depicting scenes from the Passion.

Being a Dúchas site, Ennis Friary offers the usual informative guided tours in season.

Clare Museum

In the same building as the tourist office is this absorbing **museum** (☎ 682 3382; Arthur's Row; adult/child €4/2; 9.30am-6.30pm Jun-Sep, 9.30am-1pm & 2-5.30pm Mon-Sat Apr-May & Oct, 9.30am-1pm & 2-5.30pm Mon-Fri Nov-Mar). The 'Riches of Clare' exhibition tells the story of Clare from 6000 years ago to the present day using original artefacts and audiovisual presentations. It also relates the development of the submarine by Clare-born JP Holland.

Festivals & Events

Fleadh Nua (☎ 684 2988 during week of event only, ☎ 086 8260 3000 rest of year; ceoltrad@eircom.net; May) is a lively traditional music festival with singing, dancing and workshops.

Sleeping

BUDGET

Abbey Tourist Hostel (☎ 682 2620; www.abbeytouristhostel.com; Harmony Row; dm €14-16, s/d €25/40) A well-run place, this old building stands alongside the River Fergus. Rooms are big and well equipped, and rates include a light breakfast. There's a kitchen and a laundry. The hostel minibus arranges pick-ups from Shannon Airport for four people or more (€5 each) and you can arrange day trips round the Burren and other locations.

Four Winds (☎ 682 9831; Clare Rd; s/d €45/64; mid-Mar–mid-Oct; P) This is a pleasant house with good-sized rooms. There's a fine back garden. The friendly and chatty owners accept credit cards.

Aín Karem (☎ 682 0024; 7 Tulla Rd; s/d €36/54; P) Northeast of the centre, this modern two-storey house is pleasantly furnished and rooms are standard size. It's a bit out of the centre but buses stop outside.

MID-RANGE

Ardlea House (☎ 682 0256; Clare Rd; s/d €60/80; P) Immaculate and very well run, this smart bungalow is a welcoming and comfy place to stay. Breakfasts are excellent and the centre of town is only minutes away.

Newpark House (☎ 682 1233; newparkhouse.ennis@eircom.net; Tulla Rd; s/d €60/80; Easter-Oct; P) A beautiful country house dating from 1650, Newpark is 2km north of Ennis. To get there go along the Scarriff road (R352)

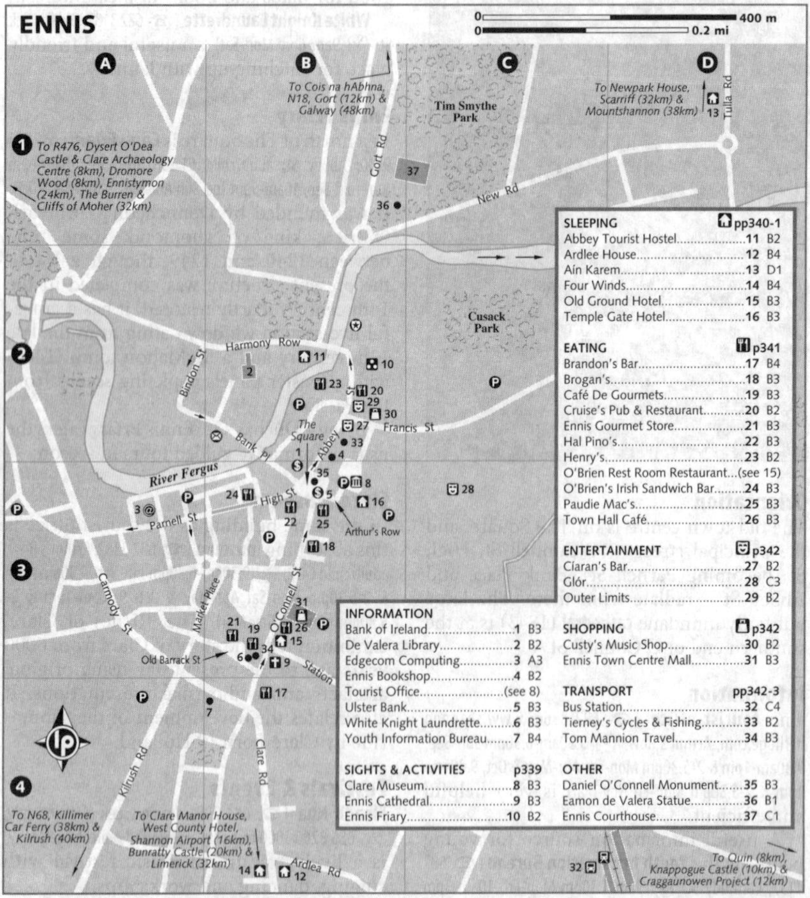

and turn right at the Roselevan Arms. Rooms are full of character and there are all sorts of fine furnishings. You can book a 6.30pm dinner for about €23.

West County Hotel (☎ 682 8421; www.lynchhotels.com; Clare Rd; s/d €60/75; P) About 10 minutes south of the town centre, this updated modern hotel has excellent rooms and all facilities are business standard. It handles a lot of conference business, but there's still a sense of individuality. Two rooms are equipped for wheelchair access. There's a swish leisure suite.

TOP END

Old Ground Hotel (☎ 682 8127; www.flynnhotels.com; O'Connell St; s/d €110/140; P) Rates drop by up to 30% during the off-season at this marvellous old hotel, an Ennis institution. The building dates from the 18th century. With its own walled gardens, bars and restaurant, rambling corridors and busy public rooms, it brings a great sense of ease.

Temple Gate Hotel (☎ 682 3300; www.templegatehotel.com; The Square; s/d €115/160; P) You won't get a more central location than at this modern hotel. There are good discounts at quiet times. It also offers short-break deals. Rooms are standard plush and they've made a good job of the mock gothic trimmings of the public rooms.

Eating

Ennis has a good mix of restaurants, cafés and bars that serve food. For self-catering, Dunne's on O'Connell St has everything you'd need.

BUDGET

Henry's (☎ 682 2848; Abbey St; lunch €4.50-8.50; 10.30am-6pm Mon-Sat) A cool, sunny café with a French feel, this is a great place for morning coffee and lunch by the river bank. There's a nice international touch to the simple food choices, from sandwiches to crisp salads.

Paudie Mac's (☎ 684 5965; The Square; lunch €4-8; 10am-3pm) Right in the heart of town, this smart cosmopolitan place draws a lively crowd for its tasty roasts and its create-your-own sandwich fillings.

O'Brien's Irish Sandwich Bar (☎ 682 2655; 5-6 Salthouse Lane; sandwiches €3-3.75) Takeaway culture and an all-day supply of sandwiches and wraps keeps this place busy.

Café de Gourmets (☎ 684 3314; 1 Old Barrack St; sandwiches €3.15-9, salads €7; 9am-7pm Mon-Sat) This small café-delicatessen has a cheerful approach to things and sets up tables outside in the summer. Just opposite is a sister shop **Ennis Gourmet Store** (☎ 684 3314; 1 Old Barrack St; 9am-7pm Mon-Sat) that sells a great range of cheeses, preserves and other treats as well as tasty sandwiches. It has some excellent wines.

Brandon's Bar (☎ 682 8133; O'Connell St; lunch mains €8-10; food served 12.30-4pm) Brandon's is a great old pub that dishes up Irish stew as well as baguettes.

MID-RANGE

Brogan's (☎ 682 9859; 24 O'Connell St; lunch mains €7.50-9, dinner mains €13-22; 10am-10pm) A big pub that stretches a long way back from the street, Brogan's can be a bit smoky in the back, but there's a non-smoking section by the entrance. Food is straightforward Irish with plenty of meat, lamb and chicken dishes.

Town Hall Café (☎ 682 8127; O'Connell St; lunch mains €4-12, dinner mains €14.75-22; 10am-10pm) Ennis' handsome old town hall has been converted into this stylish eatery where you can relax over coffee, or lunch on such treats as Cajun beef baguette, cottage pie or vegetarian lasagne amid artworks and elegant décor. Dinner offers a fine choice from a satisfyingly international menu.

TOP END

Cruise's Pub & Restaurant (☎ 684 1800; Abbey St; mains €13.65-20.25; food served 2-9.30pm) Rich with the mood of its 17th-century origins, this is a popular Ennis eatery, full of character and with good traditional food.

Hal Pino's (☎ 684 0022; 7 High St; mains €15-21.50; 5-10.30pm) From its smart and colourful exterior to the art-gallery ambience of its upstairs restaurant this is a stylish place. They use local produce, and everything is prepared with an emphasis on flavour. There's an early bird option (€15 to €19) between 5pm and 7pm, and a set dinner from €28.

O'Brien Room Restaurant (Old Ground Hotel; ☎ 682 8127; O'Connell St; mains €14-22, set dinner €32; 6.30-9pm) A strong emphasis on local produce prepared with a good mix of traditional and international touches makes this restaurant a sure bet for satisfying meals.

STRIKING A CHORD IN CLARE

Famous Clare names of Irish music include the piper Willie Clancy of Miltown Malbay; the fiddler Tommy Peoples, a Donegal man but associated closely with Clare's Kilfenora Céilí Band, one of the all time great bands; and Micho, Gus and Pakie Russell of Doolin. There are many more, still active today – among them great teachers as well as performers.

Modern Clare musicians who have gained worldwide acclaim include Sharon Shannon, an outstanding player of the button accordion, who comes from near the village of Corofin. Names to look out for currently include the Aran Island singer Lasairfhíona Ní Chonaola, who is closely associated with Clare and is a luminous performer of sean-nós, or 'old style' songs in Irish. The Ennis-based Céilí Bandits are exhilarating performers who even mix in the didgeridoo with great effect.

Most visitors love the merest echo of Irish music, but the famous pub *seisún* (music session) can often be something of a staged affair; the best are impromptu, the very best are the regular get-togethers of local musicians and singers. There's a legion of superb local musicians who can light up any evening in every corner of Clare, often in a remote village bar or local hall. You can also get closer to the culture by visiting specialist music shops such as Custy's in Ennis and Irish cultural centres such as Glór and Cois na hAbhna (see below).

Drinking & Entertainment

As the capital of a renowned music county, Ennis is not short of pubs with good music and other outlets for traditional culture as well as some contemporary clubs.

Brandon's Bar (☎ 682 8133; O'Connell St) is *the* place for terrific traditional music sessions on Monday nights, starting about 9.30pm. Anything up to 15 fiddlers let rip, plus the rest, as promising musicians sit in with seasoned performers and the place takes off. During the day Brandon's serves food (see p341). Brandon's also stages live music, from blues to glam rock, in its Boardwalk Club for late-night drinking and dancing.

Cruise's Pub & Restaurant (☎ 684 1800; Abbey St) Cruise's friendly bar is another good place for traditional music, with sessions nightly from 9.30pm.

Cíaran's Bar (☎ 684 0180; Francis St) This small, cosy place is popular with the local football crowd and has Irish music every night except Tuesday.

Outer Limits (☎ 682 8963; Abbey St) Attached to the Queen's Hotel this place is jam-packed into the early hours. Although the music is not exactly cutting edge Ibiza, there's a mix of chart and dance and '60s-onwards retro.

Glór (☎ 684 3103; www.glor.ie; Friar's Walk) Clare's flagship cultural centre, in a smart modern building, features the best of art, traditional music, theatre, dance and film. There's a big auditorium, a smaller studio, and exhibition space for mainly contemporary painting, sculpture, ceramics and photography. This is the place to catch the best traditional performers in a more formal setting. Films shown are right up-to-date.

Cois na hAbhna (☎ 682 0996; Gort Rd) It's hallowed ground at this centre of traditional music, housed in a custom-built pentagonal hall, 1.5km north of town along the N18. There's a music session held from 8.30pm to 11pm on Wednesday night, year round (€3) and on Saturday nights from 8.30pm to 10.30pm June to September (€3), with a full-blown *oíche ceilidh* (full session of music and dancing) one Saturday per month (€7). If you do go along, be assured – you'll be up and dancing before you know it. The centre has an outstanding music archive and a good selection of tapes, books and records for sale.

Shopping

On Saturday morning, there is a market at the Market Place. For general shopping, use the huge Ennis Town Centre mall, which contains Dunne's supermarket and can be entered halfway down O'Connell St.

Custy's Music Shop (☎ 682 1727; Francis St) is the place for a terrific stock of mainly Irish music, instruments and other musical items.

Getting There & Away

BUS

The **bus station** (☎ 682 4177; www.buseireann.ie/site/home) is beside the train station. Buses run from Ennis to Limerick (€7.50, 40 minutes) up to 16 times a day Monday to Saturday (15 on Sunday). There are 12 direct buses to Dublin (€14.50, four hours) Monday to

Saturday (10 on Sunday), 14 daily to Galway (€10.60, two hours), 12 to Cork (€15, three hours) and up to seven a day (four on Sunday) to Shannon Airport (€5, 30 minutes).

TRAIN

From **Ennis station** (☎ 684 0444), direct trains for Dublin (€28.50, three hours) via Limerick leave twice a day Monday to Saturday (once a day on Sunday). There are frequent trains between Dublin and Limerick, 37km southeast of Ennis; check with **Limerick train station** (☎ 061-313 333).

Getting Around

For a taxi call **Burren Taxis** (☎ 682 3456) or pick one up at the taxi stands at the train station and beside the Daniel O'Connell Monument.

Tierney's Cycles & Fishing (☎ 682 9433; 17 Abbey St) has well-maintained mountain bikes costing €20/80 per day/week, which includes a helmet, lock and repair kit. **Tom Mannion Travel** (☎ 682 4211; 71 O'Connell St) can fix you up with anything from a car to a motor home.

Parking is fairly good in Ennis. There's a big car park behind the tourist office in Friar's Walk and a useful one alongside the river just off Abbey St. It's pay and display and is about €1.50 per hour.

AROUND ENNIS

North of Ennis is the early Christian site of Dysert O'Dea; to the southeast are several fine castles.

Getting Around

Local and express buses cover most areas around Ennis, but their frequency varies; many buses run only May to September (some only July and August) and on certain days. Before making plans confirm times and destinations with **Ennis bus station** (☎ 065-682 4177).

You can pick up the express bus service between Galway and Limerick in Ennis (up to 14 times daily) to get to Clarecastle, Newmarket-on-Fergus and Bunratty, but many stops on the route are 'request only'. Bus No 334 also operates daily to Limerick via Clarecastle, Newmarket-on-Fergus and sometimes Bunratty. On weekdays an infrequent service goes northwest to Ennistymon, then south along the coast to Kilkee.

Dysert O'Dea

On the Corofin road (R476), 9km north of Ennis, is **Dysert O'Dea**, the site where St Tola founded a monastery in the 8th century. The church and high cross, the White Cross of St Tola, date from the 12th or 13th centuries. The cross depicts Daniel in the lions den on one side and a crucified Christ above a bishop carved in relief on the other. Look for carvings of animal and human heads in a semicircle on the southern doorway of the Romanesque church. There are also the remains of a 12m-high round tower.

In 1318 the O'Briens, who were kings of Thomond, and the Norman de Clares of Bunratty fought a pitched battle nearby, which the O'Briens won, thus postponing the Anglo-Norman conquest of Clare for some two centuries. The 15th-century O'Dea Castle nearby houses the **Clare Archaeology Centre** (☎ 065-683 7401; Corofin; adult/concession €4/2; 🕑 10am-6pm May-Sep). A 3km history trail around the castle passes some two dozen ancient monuments – from ring forts and high crosses to an ancient cooking site.

East of Dysert O'Dea off the N18 is **Dromore Wood** (☎ 065-683 7166; Ruan; admission free; visitor centre 🕑 10am-6pm mid-Jun–mid-Sep, wood 🕑 daylight hrs). This Dúchas nature reserve encompasses some 400 hectares as well as the ruins of the 17th-century O'Brien Castle, two ring forts and the site of Kilakee church.

GETTING THERE & AWAY

From mid-May to September, **Bus Éireann** (☎ 065-682 4177) runs one bus from Limerick (20 minutes), which leaves Ennis for Corofin and Ennistymon at 2.25pm Monday to Saturday and 12.25pm Sunday, passing Dysert O'Dea (€3) en route. The rest of the year, a bus departs Ennis on the same route at 3pm Monday to Saturday.

Quin

☎ 065 / pop 853

Quin (Chuinche), a tiny village 10km southeast of Ennis, was the site of the Great Clare Find of 1854, the most important discovery of prehistoric goldwork in Ireland. Sadly, only a few of the several hundred torcs, gorgets and other pieces, discovered by labourers working on the Limerick to Ennis railway, made it to the National Museum in

Dublin: most were sold and melted down. The source of this and much of ancient Ireland's gold may have been the Wicklow Mountains.

Abbey Tavern & Ardsolus Restaurant (☎ 682 5525; snacks €5-8, dinner mains €15-20) is at the centre of the village overlooking Quin Abbey. It's a friendly pub with a good local character. Bar meals are good value and the restaurant does traditional meat and fish dishes, with tasty stir-fries and herbed tagliatelle for vegetarians.

QUIN ABBEY

This is a **Franciscan friary** (☎ 684 4084; admission free; ⏲ 10.30am-6pm Mon-Fri, 11.30am-5pm Sat & Sun May-Oct) and was founded in 1433 using part of the walls of an older de Clare castle built in 1280. Despite many periods of persecution, Franciscan monks lived here until the 19th century. The last friar, Father Hogan, who died in 1820, is buried in one corner. The impressively named Fireballs McNamara, a notorious duellist and member of the region's ruling family, is also buried here. An elegant belfry rises above the main body of the abbey, and you can climb the narrow spiral staircase to look down on the fine cloister and surrounding countryside.

Beside the friary is the 13th-century Gothic **Church of St Finghin**.

Knappogue Castle

About 3km southeast of Quin is **Knappogue Castle** (☎ 061-368 103; adult/child €4/2.30; ⏲ 9.30am-4pm Apr-Oct). It was built in 1467 by the McNamaras, who held sway over a large part of Clare from the 5th to mid-15th centuries and built 42 castles in the region. Knappogue's huge walls are intact, and it has a fine collection of period furniture and fireplaces.

When Oliver Cromwell came to Ireland from England in 1649, he used Knappogue as a base while in the area, which is one of the reasons it was spared from destruction. The McNamara family regained the castle after the Restoration in 1660.

There's a small souvenir shop in the courtyard. Knappogue also hosts **medieval banquets** (☎ 061-360 788; adult/child under 9/child 9-12 €46/23/34.50); also see Medieval Banquets at Bunratty on p346. Knappogue, unlike Bunratty, lays on knives and forks.

Craggaunowen Project

For a sense of Irish history visit the **Craggaunowen Project** (☎ 061-367 178; adult/child/family of up to 6 children €6.70/4/16.80; ⏲ 10am-6pm May-Aug). Around 6km southeast of Quin, it includes re-created ancient farms, dwellings such as a *crannóg* (artificial island) and a ring fort, plus real artefacts including a 2000-year-old oak road, and other items such as Tim Severin's leather boat, the *Brendan*, in which he crossed the Atlantic in 1976–77. Craggaunowen Castle is a small, well-preserved McNamara fortified house. With lots of animals, some rare, this is a good place to bring kids.

The Craggaunowen Project also has a pleasant little café. Cullaun Lake nearby is a popular boating and picnic spot and there are forest trails.

EASTERN & SOUTHEASTERN CLARE

Eastern Clare has sweetly gentle countryside in contrast to the county's wild coast and the raw rocky beauty of the Burren. Clare's eastern boundary is formed by the River Shannon and long, narrow Lough Derg, which stretches some 48km from Portumna in County Galway, to just south of Killaloe. The road between the two towns swings west of the lake through picturesque hamlets such as Mountshannon. From the high ground there are panoramic views across the lake to the Silvermine Mountains in Tipperary.

Southeastern Clare is a fairly bland landscape of farms and small villages, with only the popular Bunratty Castle being a major draw. Some 24km west of Limerick is Shannon Airport.

SHANNON AIRPORT

☎ 061

Shannon, Ireland's second-largest airport, used to be a vital fuelling stop on the transatlantic air route, as piston-engine planes barely had enough range to make it across the ocean. If you fly into Shannon (Sionainn), the extensive runways and numerous departure gates will remind of its successful past. Large-scale redevelopment to upgrade is constantly progressing. During the Iraq conflict of 2003 there were protests against the use of Shannon as a refuelling stop for American military aircraft.

The world's first duty-free shop opened at Shannon in 1947; today, duty free is only available to those flying beyond the EU.

Information

The **tourist office** (☎ 471 664), in the arrivals hall, is open from 6am to 6pm daily; next door is the **Aer Rianta** (☎ 712 000) desk for airport and flight information.

The **Bank of Ireland** (☎ 471 100) is open from the first flight (about 6.30am) to 5.30pm. In Shannon Town Centre (an enclosed shopping mall in the fairly featureless town of Shannon) there are two banks (Ulster Bank and Allied Irish Bank) and a post office. There's an **Internet point** (€1.50/15 min) just left of the arrival gate.

Sleeping

There's accommodation 3km from the airport in Shannon, Ireland's only 'new town' – one that was built from scratch, in this case to serve the airport.

Moloney's B&B (☎ 364 185; 21 Coill Mhara St; s/d €30/50;) This is a good option if you need to stay in Shannon. Rooms are spick-and-span and there's a friendly welcome. It's quite hard to find. Coming from the airport you need to turn right off the main drag at the big roundabout by the town centre. Keep on past the centre and at a crossroads go left down a slip road. Continue left past a school and the Shannon Leisure Centre. At the next junction go right, and then take the first left.

Shannon Great Southern Hotel (☎ 471 122; r €150) This big modern hotel directly in front of the airport terminal is ideal if you're taking an early flight. There can be discounts at times.

Eating

Shannon Knights Inn (☎ 361 045; Shannon Town Centre; meals under €8) Bland but reasonably priced food is available at this large pub in the centre.

Café 2000 (☎ 361 992; Shannon Town Centre; lunch €7.55; 8am-5pm Mon-Fri, 9am-3.30pm Sat) Smack bang at the heart of Shannon's big shopping mall, this busy café offers decent lunches and tasty sandwiches.

Getting There & Around

AIR

For general inquiries, call the airport authority, **Aer Rianta** (☎ 712 000). Airlines with direct flights to Shannon include **Aer Lingus** (☎ 715 400), **Aeroflot** (☎ 472 299), **British Airways** (☎ 1800 626 747), **Delta Air Lines** (☎ 1800 768 080) and **Servisair** (☎ 472 344).

BUS

There are six **Bus Éireann** (airport ticket office ☎ 474 311) buses daily to Ennis (four on Sunday). The ticket office in the airport opens at 7am, the first bus leaves at 8am and the one-way fare is €4.40. There are also services to major centres including Limerick (€4.70, 40 minutes, eight daily, 10 on Sunday), Galway (€13, two hours, up to 12 daily, one on Sunday) and Dublin (€14.50, three hours, 15 daily Monday to Friday, 12 on Saturday, six on Sunday).

TAXI

A taxi to the centre of Limerick or Ennis costs about €26, with possible extra charges for luggage or 'unsociable hours'.

BUNRATTY

☎ 061

The castle at Bunratty (Bun Raite), which overlooks the Shannon Estuary, is in excellent condition and well worth a look, but it's a prime tourist attraction and is besieged by coach tours from April to September. With a folk park attached and Durty Nelly's 'auld Oirish' pub nearby, the area is as close as you'll get to a medieval Irish Disneyland. But it's fun; more so if you go early in the day.

There's a small **visitor information office** (☎ 364 321; 9am-5.30pm Mon-Fri all year, 9am-5.30pm Sat & Sun mid-May–Sep) in Bunratty Village Mills, opposite the castle. It has a bureau de change and beside it is an ATM.

Bunratty Castle & Folk Park

The Vikings built a fortified settlement at this spot, a former island surrounded by a moat. Then came the Normans, and Thomas de Clare built the first stone structure on the site in the 1270s.

There's a joint entry-fee option to both **Bunratty Castle & Folk Park** (☎ 361 511; adult/child/family €10/5.60/26.25 May-Sep, €8.40/5/23 Oct-Dec, €7.70/4.40/21 Jan-Apr, 9am-6.30pm Jun-Aug, 9.30am-5.30pm Sep-May). See p346 for Folk Park–only charges. The present castle is the fourth or fifth incarnation to occupy the location beside the River Ratty. It was built in the early 1400s by the energetic McNamara family, but fell shortly thereafter to the O'Briens, kings of Thomond, in whose possession it remained until the 17th century. Admiral Penn, father of William Penn, the Quaker founder of the US state of Pennsylvania and the city of Philadelphia, resided here for a short time.

A complete restoration was carried out in modern times, and today the castle's magnificent Great Hall holds a fine collection of 14th- to 18th-century furniture, paintings and wall hangings.

MEDIEVAL BANQUETS

The Great Hall hosts **medieval banquets** (☎ 360 788), replete with comely maidens playing the harp, court jesters cracking corny jokes, and food à la the Middle Ages (a pale imitation) served by wenches and washed down with mead, a kind of honey wine. You eat with your fingers. A seat at the banquet table costs €47.50/23.75/35.60 per adult/child under nine/child nine to 12, and they are heavily booked with coach parties. The whole thing is stage Irish but taken in spirit can be quite fun.

The banquets at Knappogue and Dunguaire castles (the latter in Galway) are generally smaller, quieter and often more pleasant. All run two banquets at 5.30pm and 8.45pm daily subject to demand. Bunratty's runs year round, Knappogue's from May to October and Dunguaire's from May to September.

BUNRATTY FOLK PARK

The **folk park** (adult/child €7/4.20 May-Sep, €6.25/3.80 Oct-Dec, €5.70/3.20 Jan-Apr) adjoins the castle. It is a reconstructed traditional Irish village with cottages, a forge and working blacksmith, weavers and buttermakers. There's a complete village street with post office, pub and small café, some of which are transplanted from the site of Shannon airport. Peat fires glow romantically in the hearths and there's a persuasive feel to it all.

The **Shannon Céilidh** (bookings ☎ 360 788; adult/child under 9/child 9-12 €40/20/30; 🕒 5.30-8.45pm daily May-Oct; open subject to demand Nov-Apr) is held in a barn in the folk park, serving up music, dancing, wine, Irish stew, apple pie and soda bread.

Sleeping

Bunratty's hotels tend to be expensive, but there are a couple of good-value B&Bs.

Rockfield House (☎ 364 391; Hill Rd; s/d €40/56; Ⓟ) High above the throng, this fine big house has excellent rooms, and you can even have the benefit of an electric blanket on chilly nights. Breakfasts are generous too.

Ashgrove House (☎ 369 332; www.ashgrovehouse.com; Low Rd; s/d €45/60; Ⓟ) Tucked well away from Bunratty centre this comfy and welcoming place has lots of little personal touches and you'll never go hungry.

Eating

Muses (☎ 364 082; Bunratty House Mews; mains €19.90-25.90; 🕒 6.30-9.30pm Tue-Sat) Definitely a classy alternative to all that mock-medieval tourism, Muses basement restaurant is in a lovely Georgian house, amid secluded grounds, and offers cuisine with a terrific international flair. To get there head up the lane past Fitzpatrick Bunratty Shamrock Hotel.

Durty Nelly's (☎ 364 861; beside Bunratty Castle; bar meals €5-12, restaurant mains €17.60) Nelly's churns out food with some style. Bar meals range from toasted sandwiches to poached salmon salad. The **Oyster Restaurant** (🕒 noon-10.30pm), downstairs, and **Loft** (🕒 6-10.30pm Mon-Sat) upstairs, do a roaring trade.

Blarney Woollen Mills (☎ 364 321; Bunratty Village Mills; mains €4.45-10.80 🕒 9am-6pm) Amid all the shopping extravaganza, this 1st-floor cafeteria-style restaurant serves a limited but generally tasty choice of dishes such as Irish stew and vegetable lasagne.

Drinking & Entertainment

Durty Nelly's (☎ 364 082; Bunratty House Mews) Nelly's manages the Irish hokum with some style and you feel that you're still in the world of the nearby Folk Park. Topped up with tourists in summer the local element still stands out and there's music every night, starting at 10pm. Durty Nelly's also serves food, see above.

Mac's Bar (☎ 361 511; Bunratty Folk Park) This engaging place is part of the Folk Park village. It has traditional music on Wednesday, Friday, Saturday and Sunday evenings June to September and on weekends the rest of the year. You can still get there when the rest of the park is closed.

Shopping

Avoca Cottage (☎ 364 029; Bunratty) Crammed full of tweeds, crafts and woollen clothes, plus Waterford crystal and Belleek pottery, this outlet is situated just across the river from Durty Nelly's. Prices tend to reflect the high-profile tourism of Bunratty.

Blarney Woollen Mills (☎ 364 321; Bunratty Village Mills) This store stocks every 'Irish gift' you might conceive of, including Irish jumpers (sweaters), Irish linen and Tipperary crystal, souvenirs, music tapes and CDs.

Getting There & Away

Up to eight **Bus Éireann** (☎ 065-682 4177) buses run directly from Limerick to Bunratty stopping outside the Fitzpatrick Bunratty Shamrock Hotel. Bunratty is also served by up to 17 daily buses (10 on Sunday) on the Shannon Airport to Limerick route. Contact **Limerick bus station** (☎ 313 333) for times.

Buses travelling south through Bunratty leave Ennis daily from 10.12am onwards. Contact **Ennis bus station** (☎ 065-682 4177) for more details.

KILLALOE & AROUND

☎ 061 / pop 1622

Killaloe (Cill Da Lúa) is picturesque Clare at its finest. It lies on the western banks of lower Loch Deirgeirt, the southern extension of Lough Derg, where the loch narrows at one of the principal crossings of the River Shannon. The village lies snugly against the Slieve Bernagh Hills that rise abruptly to the west. The Arra Mountains create a fine balance to the east and all of Lough Derg is at hand. The village is also on the 180km East Clare Way. A fine old 13-arch bridge spans the river linking Killaloe with Ballina in County Tipperary. Some of the better pubs and restaurants of the area are in Ballina. From Killaloe, the Shannon is navigable all the way north to Lough Key in County Sligo, and in summer the town is jammed with weekend sailors.

Orientation & Information

The narrow street running from the river on the Killaloe side is Bridge St, which turns right, becoming Main St. The **tourist office** (☎ 376 866; the Lock House, Bridge St; 🕑 10am-6pm May–mid-Sep) is beside Shannon Bridge in Killaloe. Below, in the same building, free Internet access is available at **Killaloe Library** (☎ 376 062; 🕑 10am-1.30pm & 2.30-5.30pm Mon-Tue & Thu, 10am-5.30pm & 6.30-8pm Wed & Fri, 10am-2pm Sat).

The AIB bank at the bottom of Church St has an ATM. There's parking on both sides of the river, although space can be limited in high summer and at weekends.

Sights and Activities

Killaloe Cathedral (St Flannan's Cathedral; ☎ 376 687; Limerick Rd) dates from the early 13th century and was built by the O'Brien family on top of an earlier 6th-century church. Inside there are some magnificent carvings on the Romanesque southern doorway. Next to the doorway is the shaft of a stone cross, known as Thorgrim's Stone. It dates from the early Christian period and is unusual in that it bears both the old Scandinavian runic and Irish ogham scripts. In the cathedral grounds is St Flannan's Oratory, of 12th-century Romanesque design.

Next to the tourist office is the **Killaloe Heritage Centre** (☎ 376 866; The Lock House, Bridge St; adult/child €2/1.50; 🕑 10am-6pm May-Sep). Its exhibits deal with local history and the cathedral.

For all your fishing needs go to **TJ's Angling Centre** (☎ 376 009; Main St, Ballina).

Sleeping

There are lots of B&Bs in the area, but it's a popular getaway spot so call ahead.

Lyons B&B (☎ 376 652; Church St, Killaloe; s/d €30/60) An immaculately kept house in central Church St, Lyons B&B has spotless rooms.

Kincora House (☎ 376 149; www.kincorahouse.com; Church St, Killaloe; s/d €40/70) A friendly, comfy place next door to Lyons B&B. **Waterman's Lodge** (☎ 376 333; www.watermanslodge.ie; Ballina; s/d €100/160; P; wheelchair access) In a great location on the Ballina side of the bridge, this colonial-style hotel faces downriver. Rooms have a satisfying country-house feel and there are handsome lounges and a restaurant.

Eating

Gooser's Bar & Eating House (☎ 376 792; Main St, Ballina; bar food €6-12, dinner mains €20-34.50; 🕑 10.30am-10.30pm) Only the masses of fellow foodies on busy weekends diminishes the Gooser's experience. It's a measure of the success of this farmhouse-style bar and restaurant that it does get crowded. Main meals are expensive but there's a terrific selection of fish, prepared with international flair, equally choice meat and lamb dishes and a discerning wine list. A three-course lunch costs you €25.

Simply Delicious (☎ 375 335; Main St, Ballina; lunch mains €6.30-7.65; ⏰ 8.30am-6pm) Down-to-earth and friendly, this is a great local favourite that offers tasty lunch dishes and sandwiches or salads. It's open for filling breakfasts, including a vegetarian option.

Molly's Bar & Restaurant (☎ 376 632; Main St, Ballina; mains €9.85-20; ⏰ food served noon-9pm) A riverside pub eatery, Molly's gets very busy. It offers strong Irish standards such as bacon and cabbage, but also does Greek salad and pastas, and filling baguettes (€6.45).

The restaurant at **Waterman's Lodge** (☎ 376 333; Ballina; P; wheelchair access) offers á la carte meals for €42.

Drinking & Entertainment

The pubs usually provide some kind of music during the week. As well as **Molly's** (see above) and **Gooser's** (see p347) there are a couple of others worth mentioning.

Crotty's Bar (☎ 376 965; Main St, Killaloe) Tucked away in a courtyard behind the Crotty grocery store, this plain local pub provides traditional music on some weekends.

Anchor Inn (☎ 376 108; Bridge St, Killaloe) The cheerful Anchor Inn stages traditional music sessions on Wednesday night, and there's a disco at weekends.

Getting There & Away

There are five **Bus Éireann** (☎ 313 333) buses a day Monday to Saturday from Limerick to Killaloe (€5, 45 minutes). The bus stop is outside the cathedral.

KILLALOE TO MOUNTSHANNON

The journey north, alongside Lough Derg, to Mountshannon, is pleasantly scenic. To get to Mountshannon from Killaloe take the Scarriff (An Scairbh) road.

About 1.5km north of Killaloe, **Beal Ború** is an earthen mound or fort said to have been Kincora, the palace of the famous Irish king Brian Ború, who defeated the Vikings at the Battle of Clontarf in 1014. Traces of Bronze Age settlement have been found. With its commanding view over Lough Derg, this was obviously a site of strategic importance.

About 4km north of Killaloe is the **University of Limerick Activity Centre** (☎ 061-376 622; www.ul.ie/~sports/activity.html; Two Mile Gate; wheelchair access). Here individuals and groups can learn kayaking, canoeing, sailing and windsurfing. There's an impressively high rigging frame on which to get to grips with rope work. A weekend training course costs €150/120 per adult/child.

About 4.5km north of Killaloe is Cragliath Hill, which has another fort, **Griananlaghna**, named after Brian Ború's great grandfather, King Lachtna.

Sleeping & Eating

Lough Derg Holiday Centre (☎ 061-376 777; www.loughderg.net; Scarriff Rd, Killaloe; tent & 2 adults €18.50; ⏰ mid-May–Sep) Located 5km north of Killaloe, near the loch shore, this is the place if you're into fishing and water sports. You can organise most of these activities from the site.

Lantern House (☎ 061-923 034; www.lanternhouse.com; Ogonnelloe, Killaloe; s/d €34/68; P ☒) Located about 9km north of Killaloe, and in a superb location overlooking Lough Derg, this modern house has high standards of service. There's a **restaurant** attached (mains €10-24; ⏰ 6-9pm) that offers distinctive modern Irish cuisine. Booking is advised.

Kincora Hall Hotel (☎ 061-376 000; www.kincorahall.com; Killaloe; s/d €110/180; P) This handsome hotel sits right on the lochside and has its own marina. There's a comfy away-from-it-all feel to everything; rooms are big and are stylishly done out and there's a plush library for relaxing in. The bar has an appealing menu of dishes such as chowder and stir-fry (€5.50 to €10.50) and the in-house **restaurant** (3-course dinner €35, mains €13.50-22.50) is noted for its tasty desserts.

MOUNTSHANNON & AROUND

☎ 061 / pop 312

The attractive village of Mountshannon (Baile Uí Bheoláin), on the southwestern shores of Lough Derg, was founded in 1742 by an enlightened landlord to house a largely Protestant community of flax workers.

The harbour is host to a fair number of angling boats and visiting yachts and cruisers in summer. It is the main centre for trips to Holy Island, one of Clare's finest early Christian settlements. There's great fishing here, mainly for brown trout, pike, perch and bream. Ask at B&Bs about boat hire and equipment.

Holy Island

Lying 2km offshore from Mountshannon, Holy Island (Inis Cealtra) is the site of a

monastic settlement thought to have been founded by St Cáimín in the 7th century. On the island you'll see a round tower that is over 27m tall (though missing its top storey). You'll also find four old chapels, a hermit's cell and some early Christian gravestones dating from the 7th to 13th centuries. One of the chapels has an elegant Romanesque arch. Inside the chapel is an inscription in old Irish, which translates as 'Pray for Tornog, who made this cross.'

The Vikings treated this monastery roughly in the 9th century, but under the subsequent protection of Brian Ború and others it flourished.

From Mountshannon you can take a cruise around the island with **Ireland Line Cruises** (☎ 375 011; Killaloe; adult/child €7/4.50; late Apr-Oct). Trips can also be arranged from Mountshannon through the **East Clare Heritage Centre** (☎ 921 351, 921 615; Tuamgraney), about 10km southwest on the R352.

Sleeping & Eating

Lakeside Caravan & Camping Park (☎ 927 225; www.lakesideireland.com; Mountshannon; tent & 2 adults €15; May-Oct) This spacious park has a fine lakeside location and hires out boats and equipment for **windsurfing**, **rowing** and **sailing**. From Mountshannon, head north along the Portumna road (R352) for 2km and take the first turning on the right.

Derg Lodge (☎ 927 180; fax 927 180; Whitegate Rd, Mountshannon; s/d €25/42; P) This pleasant four-room B&B is about 500m from the village. It hires boats for €25 per day, €50 with a gillie (boatperson).

Oak House (☎ 927 185; howemaureen@eircom.net; Mountshannon; s/d €40/60; P) Just 200m north of the village, this distinctive house is an angler's paradise. You can hire boats for €16 per day and there's plenty of fishing lore available. Rooms have a cosy lodge-like ambience and there's a lovely garden overlooking Lough Dearg.

Mountshannon Hotel (☎ 927 162; www.mountshannon-hotel.ie; Main St, Mountshannon; rooms per person €45) Rooms are a touch old-fashioned in this charming little hotel, but it has a pleasant atmosphere and there's a busy and popular bar and **restaurant** (lunch €9, dinner mains €13, 3-course meal €25).

Rob's An Cupán Caifé (☎ 927 275; Main St; dinner mains €11-15; 10.30am-9pm Wed-Mon May-Aug, 12.30-9pm Sep-Apr). This café-restaurant has a charmingly intimate atmosphere. It also does Irish, continental and vegetarian breakfasts (€7 to €9) and sandwiches (€3 to €4.50) and lunch dishes including salads and stir-fries (€7 to €8).

Getting There & Away

On weekdays, **Bus Éireann** (☎ 313 333) bus No 345 runs twice daily from Limerick to Killaloe and continues to Scarriff (8km southwest of Mountshannon). On Wednesday and Saturday only, bus No 346 from Limerick (departing at 1.15pm) to Whitegate via Scarriff runs to Mountshannon (1½ hours). Buses stop outside Keane's on the main street.

NORTH TO GALWAY

North of Mountshannon, the R352 follows Lough Derg to Portumna in Galway. Inland is an area known as the **Clare Lakelands**, based around Feakle, where numerous lakes offer good coarse fishing.

SOUTHWESTERN & WESTERN CLARE

Loop Head at the county's southwestern tip is a dwindling peninsula that thrusts into the Atlantic. In big storms, massive waves heave themselves onto the flat tops of the awesome cliffs that lie between Loop Head and Kilkee, and then drain back like waterfalls. North of the popular seaside resort of Kilkee, the road (N67) edges away from the coast, but there are some worthwhile detours to beaches where Spanish Armada ships were wrecked over 400 years ago. Kilkee, White Strand, Spanish Point and Lahinch all have good beaches.

North and northwest of Ennis are a number of small villages, including Corofin and Ennistymon. These are both at the southern limits of the outstanding Burren region, and nearby are Hag's Head (a superb walk with excellent views) and the Cliffs of Moher, one of Ireland's most spectacular natural features. From there the road dips downhill towards Doolin, a popular destination with backpackers and coach parties, and a centre of Irish music.

This region is great for cycling and two signposted routes are the Loop Head Cycleway and West Clare Cycleway.

GETTING THERE & AWAY

Boat

Shannon Ferry Limited (☎ 905 3124; www.shannonferries.com) runs a 20-minute car ferry from Killimer, across the Shannon Estuary, to Tarbert in County Kerry. You pay on board. See Tarbet on p255 for fares and times.

Bus

There are infrequent local bus services to the coastal towns and villages; some buses run from Limerick, while others are on express routes from Galway or Tralee. Services are more frequent May to September. Phone the **Ennis bus station** (☎ 065-682 4177) or **Limerick bus station** (☎ 061-313 333) for exact times and fares.

Bus Éireann (☎ 065-682 4177) express bus No 15 terminates in Ennis or Ennistymon. It runs through Doolin, Lisdoonvarna, Lahinch, Miltown Malbay, Kilkee and Kilrush. The Killarney to Galway bus No 50 stops in Ballyvaughan, Lisdoonvarna, Doolin, the Cliffs of Moher, Lahinch, Miltown Malbay, Doonbeg, Kilkee and Kilrush. Bus No 333 travels between Limerick, Ennis, Ennistymon, Lahinch, Milton Malbay, Quilty, Doonbeg, Kilkee and Kilrush.

Bus No 336 between Kilkee and Limerick travels via Kilrush and Ennis four times a day Monday to Saturday (three on Sunday) late June to August and twice a day rest of the year. Bus No 337 runs three times daily between Limerick and Lisdoonvarna, passing through Ennis, Ennistymon, Lahinch, Liscannor, the Cliffs of Moher and Doolin en route, from mid-May to September. The rest of the year it goes twice daily.

KILRUSH

☎ 065 / pop 2678

The attractive little town of Kilrush (Cill Rois) overlooks the Shannon Estuary and the hills of Kerry to the south. The main street, Frances St, runs directly to the harbour. It is more than 30m wide, reflecting Kilrush's origins as a port and market town. It has the western coast's biggest **marina** (www.kilrushcreekmarina.ie) located at Kilrush Creek.

Kilrush's tourist office (☎ 905 1577; Market Sq; 🕓 10am-1pm & 2-6pm Mon-Sat late May–Aug) is in the handsome old Market House. On Frances St you'll find an Allied Irish Bank (with an ATM) and the post office. The **Internet Bureau** (☎ 905 1061; Frances St; €2/10min) is at the very bottom of Frances St.

Sights

Situated in the old Market House of 1808 is the **Kilrush Heritage Centre** (☎ 905 1596; Market Sq; adult/child €2.70/1.50; 🕓 10am-6pm Mon-Fri, noon-4pm Sat & Sun Jun-Aug). It contains an exhibition on the history of the region and an audiovisual presentation on the Famine entitled 'Kilrush in Landlord Times'. There are interpretative panels scattered around the centre that outline historical Kilrush.

St Senan's Catholic church, on Toler St, contains eight detailed examples of stained glass, by well-known artisan Harry Clarke. East of town is **Kilrush Wood**, which has some fine old trees and a picnic area.

An exhibition on the history and wildlife of Scattery Island is housed in the Dúchas-run **Scattery Island Visitor Centre** (☎ 905 2144; Merchant's Quay; admission free; 🕓 10am-6pm mid-Jun–mid-Sep).

Vandeleur Walled Garden (☎ 905 1760; adult/child €2.50/1.25; 🕓 10am-6pm Apr-Oct, 10am-4pm Nov-Mar) is a remarkable 'lost' garden. It was the private domain of the wealthy Vandeleur family, merchants and landowners who engaged in harsh eviction and forced emigration of local people in the 19th century. The gardens lie within a large walled area and have been redesigned and planted with colourful and unusual plants. There are woodland trails around the area and the reception has a coffee shop.

Near the marina is **Kilrush Creek Adventure Centre** (☎ 905 2855; www.kcac.nav.to; Kilrush Creek; 🕓 10am-4.30pm). It offers a range of activities including archery, windsurfing, kayaking and sailing, power boating (nonresident multi-activity is €30/50 for a half/full day) plus accommodation (see Kilrush Creek Lodge on p351).

Weather permitting, you can do a two- to 2½-hour dolphin-watching trip on Shannon Estuary with **Scattery Island Ferries** (☎ 905 1327; Cappa, Kilrush; adult/child under 16 €14.50/7.50). Boats leave from Kilrush Marina.

Sleeping

Katie O'Connors Holiday Hostel (☎ 905 1133; cwglynn@eircom.net; Frances St; dm/d €12/27; 🕓 mid-Mar–Dec) This fine old main-street house dates from the 18th century, and was one of the town houses of the Vandeleur family (see Vandeleur Walled Garden on p350). It's located above T & M Interiors. It's an atmospheric place with pleasant rooms and there are nice touches, such as panels with historical details of Kilrush.

Kilrush Creek Lodge (☎ 905 2595; www.kilrushcreeklodge.ie; Kilrush Creek; s/d €50/80; P) At the time of writing this establishment had been newly refurbished and upgraded, reflected in its bright and colourful rooms. It's right next door to Kilrush Creek Adventure Centre.

Jemes/Dolphins Pass (☎ 905 1822; jemesbandb@esatclear.ie; Aylevarroo, Kilrush; s/d €35/56; Apr-Oct; P) Watch ruby-red sunsets flood the headlands, or spot dolphins from this bright and relaxed modern house overlooking Kilrush Creek, 3km west of town.

Eating

Kelly's Bar & Restaurant (☎ 905 1811; 26 Henry St; lunch €6.30-7.55, dinner mains €11.50-18.50; 12.30-9pm) This delightful pub-restaurant has polished dark woodwork and snug seating, with its handsome bar as the main focus. It does tasty sandwiches (€3.75 to €7.55) including a hefty double-decker, as well as pastas, stir-fries and traditional Irish dishes.

Coffey's (☎ 905 1104; Market Sq; sandwiches €3, pizzas €5-12; Tue-Sun) This cheerful and busy place on the main square serves breakfasts all day, decent sandwiches and pizzas, plus fish and chips from a takeaway section.

Drinking & Entertainment

Crotty's Pub (☎ 905 2470; Market Sq) Brimming with character, Crotty's has an old-fashioned high bar, tiled floors and a series of snugs decked out with traditional furnishings, including a kitchen complete with old range. You can enjoy music on Tuesday, Thursday and Saturday nights.

As well as being a good place to eat, **Kelly's Bar & Restaurant** (☎ 905 1811; 26 Henry St) is great for just a drink and has occasional music sessions.

Getting There & Around

For information on buses to and from Kilrush, see Getting There & Away on p350.

You can hire bikes at **Gleeson's Cycles** (☎ 905 1127; Henry St; €20/80 per day/week, deposit €40).

SCATTERY ISLAND

This uninhabited, windswept, treeless island, 2.5km southwest of Cappa pier, is the site of a Christian settlement founded by St Senan in the 6th century. Its 36m-high **round tower** is one of the tallest and best preserved in Ireland, and the entrance is at ground level instead of the usual position high above the foundation. There are remains of five **medieval churches**, including a 9th-century cathedral.

Getting There & Away

The harbour at Cappa village near Kilrush is where you catch the boat to Scattery Island. To get there turn left at the bottom of Frances St in Kilrush and follow the road for 2km.

During the summer, **Scattery Island Ferries** (☎ 065-905 1237) runs boats from Kilrush Creek Marina to the island (return adult/child under 16 €8/6, 20 minutes). There's no strict timetable as the trips are subject to demand and weather conditions. You can buy tickets at the small kiosk on Merchant's Quay. It's wise to book ahead.

KILKEE

☎ **065 / pop 1261**

During the summer, Kilkee's wide semicircular bay is thronged with day-trippers and holiday-makers, mainly from Clare and Limerick. Kilkee (Cill Chaoi) first became popular in Victorian times when rich Limerick families built seaside retreats here. Today, Kilkee is well supplied with guesthouses, amusement arcades and takeaways. Its exhilarating beach and good-natured atmosphere make it an enjoyable stop.

Information

The seasonal **tourist office** (☎ 905 6112; O'Connell St; 10am-1pm & 2-6pm Jun–mid-Sep) is just up to the left from the seafront. On O'Curry St, the main street, the Bank of Ireland has an ATM. The post office is on Circular Rd, off the western end of O'Curry St.

Sights & Activities

Many visitors come for the fine sheltered **beach** and the **Pollock Holes**, natural swimming pools in the Duggerna Rocks to the south of the beach. **St George's Head** to the north has good cliff walks and scenery, while south of the bay the **Duggerna Rocks** form an unusual natural amphitheatre. Further south is a huge **sea cave**. These sights can be reached by driving to Kilkee's West End area and following the coastal path.

Kilkee is a well-known **diving** centre. There are shore dives from the Duggerna Rocks fringing the western side of the bay, or boat dives on the Black Rocks further out. Experience and local knowledge or guidance is strongly advised. Right at the tip of the Duggerna Rocks is the small inlet of Myles Creek, out from which there's excellent underwater scenery. **Kilkee Diving & Watersports Centre** (☎ 905 6707; kilkee@iol.ie; George's Head, Kilkee) by the harbour has tanks and other equipment for hire and runs PADI courses.

Sleeping

There are plenty of guesthouses in Kilkee, though during the high season they are usually a little more expensive than in other areas. At busy times you may have to take whatever the tourist office can get you. There are a couple of budget options.

Bayview (☎ 905 6058; bayview3@eircom.net; O'Connell St; s/d €40/64) A very central guesthouse with lots of little personal touches, Bayview has good views out to the bay from its front rooms. There's a substantial reduction for children.

Harbour Lodge (☎ 905 6090; 6 Marine Pde; s/d €42.50/30; Apr-Oct; P) A cheerful welcome sets the tone for this homely place overlooking the harbour. Rooms are cosy and there's an excellent breakfast choice.

Kilkee Thalassotherapy Centre & Guest House (☎ 905 6742; www.kilkeethalasso.com; Grattan St; s/d €45/90; P) If you really want to get to grips with all that buzzing sea air and seaweed, this very smart and stylish place can offer everything from a seaweed bath (€16) body scrub (€34) or detox body wrap (€80) among its several treatments. The guesthouse is part of the complex and rooms are equally as stylish as the rest of the place.

Green Acres Caravan & Camping Park (☎ 905 7011; Doonaha, Kilkee; family tent €14; early Apr-Sep) This is a small, peaceful park beside the Shannon 6km south of Kilkee on the R487.

Kilkee Hostel (☎ 905 6209; O'Curry St; dm €13; Mar-Oct) This well-run place is only 50m from the seafront and is right at the heart of the village. There's a well-equipped kitchen, a laundry room and a small coffee shop.

Stella Maris Hotel (☎ 905 6455; info@stellamarishotel.com; O'Connell St; s/d €45/110; P) At the time of writing this long-established hotel was undergoing major refurbishment, the aim being to retain its traditional character but with total modernisation.

Eating

Old Bistro (☎ 905 6898; O'Curry St; mains €17-23) A bold black, yellow and red frontage draws you in to this popular and welcoming eatery that features fresh local seafood as well as meat and vegetarian choices.

Pantry (☎ 905 6576; O'Curry St; lunch mains €5.70-6.95, dinner mains €10.75-13.25) There are plenty of fast-food outlets, but this busy café stands out for its delicious home-made food and reasonable prices.

Entertainment

Myle's Creek (☎ 905 6670; O'Curry St) The Abyss Club is only part of this complex of bars and a restaurant. It's not the glossiest of places, but there's music every night from June to August and at weekends the rest of the year. In summer especially it sees a good spread of Ireland's established and up-and-coming rock groups.

Mary O'Mara's (☎ 905 6286; O'Curry St) For a more traditional music scene this is the place to be on Wednesday and Friday nights in July and August.

Getting There & Away

For information on buses to and from Kilkee, see Getting There & Away p350.

KILKEE TO LOOP HEAD

The land from Kilkee south to Loop Head is unrelentingly flat and rather nondescript, but the coastal cliff scenery is spectacular and there is a rewarding sense of escaping the mainstream. It's good cycling country and there are coastal walks.

Kilbaha

At the end of the R487, 7km east of Loop Head, is Kilbaha. Its tiny church, about 500m inland from the village towards Loop Head, contains an unusual relic of more repressive times. The **Little Ark** is a small, mobile, wooden altar used by Catholics in the 1850s. In order for the priest to celebrate mass, the altar was wheeled below the high-tide mark, where it was outside the jurisdiction of the local Protestant landlord. A stained-glass window above the church

COUNTY CLARE

door depicts the ark in use. Father Michael Meehan, the courageous local priest who had the ark built, is buried in the church.

Carrigaholt

☎ 065 / pop 100

On 15 September 1588, seven tattered ships of the Spanish Armada took shelter off Carrigaholt (Carraig an Chabaltaigh), a tiny village inside the mouth of the Shannon Estuary. One, probably the *Annunciada*, was torched and abandoned, sinking somewhere out in the estuary. Today Carrigaholt has a safe beach and the substantial remains of a 15th-century McMahon castle with a square keep overlooking the water.

To view resident bottlenose dolphins (there are about 120 pods in the Shannon Estuary), head for **Dolphinwatch** (☎ 905 8156, 088 258 4711; www.dolphinwatch.ie; Carrigaholt; adult/child €17/9). Opposite the post office, Dolphinwatch runs two-hour trips in the estuary from April to October.

There's no need for city-slick décor at **Long Dock** (☎ 905 8106; West St; snacks €4.45-11, mains €7.55-20; food served 11am-9pm). This cosy pub-cum-restaurant has won national awards for its food and its music. Stone walls and floors, and a welcoming fire are only the start. Fresh fish is the thing here; there are tasty meat and chicken dishes, but all that sea air demands fish.

Morrissey's Village Pub (☎ 905 8041; West St) hasn't changed much in a long time and is all the better for it. Get your feet ready for music and dancing Tuesday, Friday, Saturday and Sunday in summer and Tuesday and Saturday in winter.

Loop Head

On a clear day, Loop Head (Ceann Léime), Clare's southernmost point, has magnificent views south to the Dingle Peninsula crowned by Mt Brandon (953m), and north to the Aran Islands and Galway Bay. There are bracing walks in the area and a long hike running along the cliffs to Kilkee. When the winds blow, or *blast* as they often do, take care near the abrupt edge of the cliffs.

CÚCHULAINN'S LEAP

The 'Loop' in Loop Head is a corruption of the word 'leap'. Legend has it that the Celtic warrior Cúchulainn was being chased all over Ireland by the formidable Mal. Cornered on this headland, he leapt onto a sea stack and, when she tried to follow him, Mal fell to her death. The sea turned crimson and her body washed ashore at various points along the coast, giving Hag's Head and Malbay their names. Some say the headland resembles a seated woman looking out over the Atlantic. West of the lighthouse you'll find the sea stack in question; the gap is known as Cúchulainn's Leap.

KILKEE TO ENNISTYMON

North of Kilkee, there's a growing sense that you're heading into Ireland's fabled 'West'. The N67 runs inland for some 32km until it reaches Quilty. Take the occasional lane to the west and search out unfrequented places such as **White Strand**, north of Doonbeg. **Ballard Bay** is 8km north of Doonbeg, where an old telegraph tower looks over some fine cliffs. **Donegal Point** has the remains of a promontory fort. There's good **fishing** all along the coast, and safe **beaches** at Seafield, Lough Donnell and Quilty.

Getting There & Away

From May to September Bus Éireann's express Killarney to Galway bus No 50 stops three times a day (twice on Sunday) at Doonbeg, Miltown Malbay and Lahinch. From Monday to Saturday the rest of the year, bus No 333 connects Doonbeg, Quilty, Spanish Point, Miltown Malbay and Lahinch. Contact **Ennis bus station** (☎ 065-682 4177) for times and fares.

Doonbeg

☎ 065 / pop 596

Doonbeg (An Dún Beag) is a tiny seaside village about halfway between Kilkee and Quilty. Near the mouth of the River Doonbeg, another Armada ship, the *San Esteban*, was wrecked on 20 September 1588. The survivors were later executed at Spanish Point. **White Strand** (Trá Ban) is a quiet beach, 2km long and backed by dunes. There are two **ruined castles**: Doonmore is on White Strand, while Doonbeg is in the village by the river.

SLEEPING & EATING

For campers there's often a spot on the side roads around Doonbeg that makes a good pitch, with glorious sunsets as a bonus.

COUNTY CLARE

An Tinteán (☎ 905 5036; www.antintean.com; Main St; s/d €50/70; P) There's always a great welcome at this central house where rooms have individuality and where there's always a good flow of conversation and information. One room has an en suite that is wheelchair accessible.

San Esteban (☎ 905 5105; www.anicebandb.com; Rhynagonnaught; s/d €70/100; P) An out-of-the-way location makes this delightful house a winner for its sea views and its comfy rooms. To get there you need to escape from the main road at the northern end of the village. There are substantial off-season reductions available.

Olde Kitchen Restaurant (Igoe Inn; ☎ 905 5039, Main St; mains €11-16; 7-9pm) There's good seafood here and there's music in the bar on Monday and Saturday nights during July and August.

Miltown Malbay

☎ 065 / pop 1517

Like Kilkee, Miltown Malbay was a resort favoured by well-to-do Victorians, though the town isn't actually on the sea: the beach is 2km south at Spanish Point. Miltown Malbay has a thriving music scene and every year hosts a **Willie Clancy Irish Music Festival** (☎ 708 4148) as a tribute to a native son and one of Ireland's greatest pipers. The festival is usually the first week in July, when the town is overrun with wandering minstrels, the pubs are packed, and Guinness is consumed by the bucket load. There are workshops and classes underpinning the whole event and there's much music in the surrounding villages.

Old-fashioned style and service at **Ocean View Restaurant** (☎ 708 4649; Main St; mains €10.25-15.95; 11am-10pm) backs up solid traditional food. They do good Irish breakfasts (€4.35). Next door is O'Loughlin's Bar, which has traditional music and sing-along nights.

O'Friel's Bar (☎ 708 4275; The Square) The name over the door is 'Lynch', but who's complaining? It's a genuine old-style place, once home to Willie Clancy himself and where there are traditional sessions on Saturday and Sunday nights.

Lahinch

☎ 065 / pop 550

Lahinch (Leacht Uí Chonchubhair) is unashamedly resort land – full of fast-food joints and amusement arcades, but lively enough, and with a world-class golf course. The town sits on protected Liscannor Bay and has a fine beach, which draws big crowds in summer.

The tourist office, **Lahinch Fáilte** (☎ 708 2082; www.lahinchfailte.com; The Dell; 9am-8pm May-Oct, 9am-5pm Nov-Apr), is off the northern end of Main St. There are no banks, but you can change money at the post office and there's an ATM outside the tourist office.

The **surfing** can be good at any time of year. **Lahinch Surf Shop** (☎ 708 1543; www.lahinchsurfshop.com; Old Promenade) has gear and can put you in touch with surf instructors. **Lahinch Seaworld Leisure Centre** (☎ 708 1900; The Promenade; adult/child €5/3.50; 10am-8pm) has a collection of fish species from the surrounding seas on show in tanks, and the complex has a 25m pool for the human species to play in.

SLEEPING & EATING

Lahinch Caravan & Camping Park (☎ 708 1424; tent & 2 adults €14; May-Sep) A pleasant and fairly quiet place that's close to the beach and only 200m south of the village, this site has good amenities.

Lahinch Hostel (☎ 708 1040; lahinchok@eircom; Church St; dm/d €17/45) This excellent hostel is very well run and has clean, bright rooms. It's close to the beachfront and has laundry facilities.

Atlantic Hotel (☎ 708 1049; atlantichotel@eircom.net; s/d €72.50/113; P) It's resort chic at this fine old hotel right in the main street. The updated rooms are cosy and there's still a pleasant air of bygone times in the reception rooms and bars. Bar food (€3.50 to €9) is inventive and features some good seafood choices with additional and pricier meat and chicken dishes. The restaurant does a three-course dinner, with good choice, for €29.

Mrs O'Brien's Kitchen (☎ 708 1020; Main St; mains €8.95-13.50) You won't beat Mrs O'Brien's for good, straightforward food and cheerful service. Pizzas, chicken wings, chowder and a salad platter are among the choices and you can start the day with a really big breakfast special (€8).

ENNISTYMON

☎ 065 / pop 920

Don't be fooled by the fairly unexceptional main street of Ennistymon (Inis Díomáin), 3km inland from Lahinch. Step under the archway just down from the bridge, at the

COUNTY CLARE

south end of Main Street, and you'll find the town's fabulous glory, the **Cascades**, the stepped falls of the River Inagh. After heavy rain the falls roar, beer-brown and foaming, and you risk getting drenched on windy days in the flying drizzle.

There are no other attractions to match the river, but Ennistymon is a pleasant town with a couple of excellent pubs and good sleeping options.

The **library** (☎ 707 1245; 10am-1.30pm & 2.30-5.30pm Mon, Tue & Thu, 10am-5.30pm Wed & Fri, 10am-2pm Sat), just down from the square, offers free Internet access. The Bank of Ireland, in Parliament St, has a bureau de change and an ATM.

PASSIONATE POET & FAMOUS FATHERS

Ennistymon has more than its fair share of cultural associations. The Welsh poet Dylan Thomas lived at what is now the Falls Hotel (see below) when the house was the family home of his wife Cáitlín McNamara. There's plenty of Thomas memorabilia, and a Dylan Thomas Bar, at the hotel. At the other end of the scale are the cast of Ireland's groundbreaking TV comedy *Father Ted*, who spent a lot of time in the local area while filming the series. They also stayed at the Falls and were patrons of Eugene's marvellous bar (see below).

Sleeping & Eating

Station House (☎ 707 1149; cahilka@indigo.ie; Ennis Rd; s/d €27/66; P) There's excellent value on offer at this big modern house about 500m south of the centre. Rooms are a good size and it's in a quiet location.

Falls Hotel (☎ 707 1004; falls@iol.ie; s/d €65/85; P) This handsome Georgian house, built on the ruins of an O'Brien castle, is a real treat. The view of the Cascades from the entrance steps is stunning and there are walks around the 20 hectares of wooded gardens (see boxed text on this page for famous associations). Rooms are big and comfortable and there's a restaurant. One room is fully equipped for wheelchair use.

Fitzpatrick's Coffee House (☎ 707 1600; Parliament St; lunch mains €7-9) Hearty breakfasts (€4.90) are also available at this breezy and busy little café, where you can get lunch of roast beef or Irish stew as well as sandwiches and salads. There's a supermarket next door if you are self-catering.

Byrne's Restaurant (☎ 707 1080; Main St; mains €15-25; 6.30-9.30pm Mon-Sat) Handsome views of the Cascades enhance the bright, contemporary surroundings of this fine restaurant, where modern Irish cuisine – cod wrapped in Parma ham, for example – is the style. There's a three-course early bird offer for €23 from 6.30 to 7.15pm Monday to Friday.

Entertainment

Eugene's (☎ 707 1777; Main St) An experience not to be missed, Eugene's is a true talkers' pub. It's intimate, cosy and has a trademark collection of visiting cards covering its walls, alongside photographs of famous writers and musicians; not to forget the Father Ted crew (see boxed text above). There's also a stunning collection of whiskey (Irish) and whisky (Scottish). Chat is the main pastime but music happens now and then.

Cooley's House (☎ 707 1712; Main St) Another great talking pub, but with traditional music most nights in summer and on Wednesday in winter.

Getting There & Away

Bus Éireann's (☎ 065-682 4177) No 15 bus from Limerick runs four times a day Monday to Saturday and once on Sunday stopping at Ennistymon (€10.20, 30 minutes) in front of Aherne's on Church St. Contact the bus stations in **Ennis** (☎ 065-682 4177) or **Limerick** (☎ 061-313333) for details.

LISCANNOR & AROUND

☎ 065 / pop 352

This small seaside village overlooks Liscannor Bay where the road (R478) heads north to the Cliffs of Moher and Doolin. Liscannor (Lios Ceannúir) has given its name to a type of local stone, slate-like and with a rippled surface, which is used for floors, walls and even roofs.

John Philip Holland (1840–1914), the inventor of the submarine, was born in Liscannor. He emigrated to the USA in 1873, and wishfully hoped that his invention would be used to sink British warships.

Sleeping & Eating

Moher Lodge Farmhouse (☎ 708 1269; fax 708 1589; moherlodge@eircom.net; Liscannor; s/d €40/66;

COUNTY CLARE

(🕑 Apr-Oct; **P**) There's Irish hospitality at its finest at this big bungalow in a great position overlooking open countryside and the sea. It's 3km northwest of Liscannor, close to the Cliffs of Moher.

Sea Haven (☎ 708 1385; fax 708 1474; Liscannor; s/d €42.50/30) This exceptionally neat-as-a-pin bungalow is on high ground south of town.

Vaughan's Anchor Inn (☎ 708 1548; www.vaughansanchorinn.com; Main St; lunch mains €8.80-12.45, dinner mains €18-23; 🕑 noon-9.30pm) Noted for its excellent seafood, Vaughan's is a busy place. You can settle for tasty lunch sandwiches or a vegetarian dish, but there's also fresh salmon and scallops in the evening.

Getting There & Away

From May to September, **Bus Éireann's** (☎ 065-682 4177) Killarney to Galway express bus No 50 stops at Liscannor. Bus No 337 between Limerick and Lisdoonvarna stops daily year round. Contact the **Ennis bus station** (☎ 682 4177) or **Limerick bus station** (☎ 061-313 333) for times and fares.

Hag's Head

Hag's Head forms the southern end of the Cliffs of Moher and is an excellent place from which to view the cliffs.

To get to the head from Liscannor, go just over 5km towards the Cliffs of Moher until, about 500m past the Moher Lodge Farmhouse; there's a rough track rising steeply to the left. You can drive this track a short distance to the brow of the hill, where it's best to park. There's a maze of tracks leading off across rough ground. To reach the head you need to pick your way to the west. In clear weather the signal tower on the head is a guide. There's a huge sea arch at the tip of Hag's Head and another visible to the north. The signal tower was erected in case Napoleon tried to attack on the western coast. The tower is built on the site of an ancient promontory fort called Mothair, which has given its name to the famous cliffs to the north.

CLIFFS OF MOHER

One of Ireland's most famous sights, the **Cliffs of Moher** (Aillte an Mothair, or Ailltreacha Mothair) rise to a height of 203m. They are entirely vertical and the cliff edge is abrupt. Where access is permitted there's a protecting wall. On a clear day the views are tremendous. The Aran Islands stand etched on the waters of Galway Bay, and beyond lie the hills of Connemara in western Galway.

Be warned, however, this is a honey-pot destination besieged by visitors and tour coaches and its ease of access, right beside the main road, has turned it into something of a 'sightseeing circus'. Don't expect to be alone with the elements. It was once possible to enjoy less-crowded sections of the cliff top, but for some years now, access to either side of the Cliffs of Moher has been blocked by enough wire and obstacles to stop an army. An ambitious plan for a massively expensive reception and interpretive centre beside the car park seems to have stalled. Some say that's no bad thing.

Just north of the arrival point at the cliff edge is **O'Brien's Tower** (adult/child €1.50/0.80; 🕑 9am-7pm Mar-Oct) built by the eccentric local landlord Cornelius O'Brien (1801–57) to impress lady visitors. You can climb up and use the telescope. The **sea stack** – covered with seabirds and their guano – just below the tower is called Breanan Mór and is itself over 70m high.

Information

There's a bureau de change, a small café and a gift shop full of souvenirs at the **visitor centre** (☎ 065-708 1171; 🕑 9am-8pm Jul & Aug, 9am-7pm Jun, 9am-6.30pm May & Sep, 9.30am-6pm Apr, 9.30am-5pm Oct-Mar). The car park costs an exorbitant €3.

Getting There & Away

Bus Éireann's Limerick to Lisdoonvarna bus No 337 stops daily at the Cliffs of Moher, as does the express bus from Galway to Kilrush. Contact **Ennis bus station** (☎ 065-682 4177). Also see Organised Tours p376.

THE BURREN

The Burren region, contained between Corofin in northern Clare and Kinvara in County Galway, and stretching west to the Atlantic coast, is Clare's greatest glory, a compelling landscape, shaped beneath ancient seas, and then forced high and dry during some great geological upheaval.

Boireann is the Irish for 'rocky country', a plain, but graphic description of The Burren's acres of gleaming limestone karst pavements. The pavements, known as 'clints', lie like huge, scattered bones across the swooping hills. Between the seams of rock lie narrow fissures, known as 'grykes'. Their humid, sheltered conditions support exquisite wild flowers in spring, lending the Burren its other great charm: brilliant, if ephemeral, colour amid so much arid beauty. The Burren's real attraction is its natural beauty, but there are also fascinating villages, especially along the coastal fringe and in the south Burren. These include Doolin, on the west coast, and the lovely Ballyvaughan, on the remote north coast facing across Galway Bay. The Burren's coastline is a paradise of rocky foreshores, occasional beaches and splendid limestone cliffs, while inland lies a haunting landscape of rocky hills peppered with ancient burial chambers and medieval ruins.

Large areas of the Burren, about 40,000 hectares in all, have been designated as Special Areas of Conservation. Apart from being against the law, it makes ecological sense not to remove plants or to damage walls, ancient monuments, or the landscape itself. Visitors are also asked to resist the temptation of erecting 'sham' replicas of dolmens and other monuments, however small.

INFORMATION

The nearest information point is the **Cliffs of Moher Visitor Centre** (☎ 065-708 1171), but don't expect too much in-depth information. There is a wealth of literature about the Burren and it's best to trawl the bookshops of Ennis and any local heritage centres for publications such as Charles Nelson's *Wild Plants of The Burren and the Aran Islands* (€12.79). The Tír Eolas series of foldout maps, *A Rambler's Guide & Map* (€5) shows antiquities and other points of interest. The Burren *Journey* books by George Cunningham are excellent for local lore, but you may have to search for them.

ARCHAEOLOGY

The Burren's bare limestone hills were once lightly wooded and covered in soil. Towards the end of the Stone Age, about 6000 years ago, previously nomadic hunter-gatherers began to develop a settled lifestyle

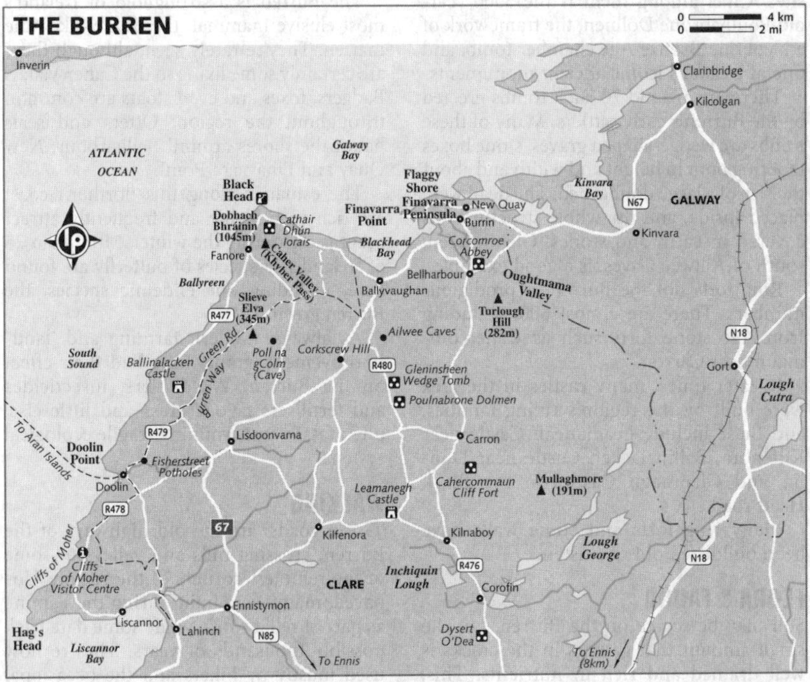

GEOLOGY OF THE BURREN

The Burren is the most extensive limestone region, or karst (after the original Karst in Slovenia), in Ireland or Britain. It consists almost entirely of limestone, except for a cap of mud and shale that sits on the higher regions.

During the Carboniferous period 350 million years ago, this whole area was the bottom of a warm and shallow sea. The remains of coral and shells fell to the sea bed, and coastal rivers dumped sand and silt on top of these lime deposits. Time and pressure turned the layers to stone, with limestone below and shale and sandstone above.

Massive shifts in the earth's crust some 270 million years ago buckled the edges of Europe and forced the sea bed above sea level, at the same time bending and fracturing the stone sheets to form long, deep cracks.

During numerous ice ages, glaciers scoured the hills, rounding the edges and sometimes polishing the rock to a shiny finish. The glaciers also dumped a thin layer of rock and soil over the region. Huge boulders were carried by the ice, incongruous aliens on a sea of flat rock. Seen all over the Burren, these 'glacial erratics' are often a visibly different type of rock.

of farming as well as hunting. They cleared the woodlands and used the hills for grazing. Over the centuries, much soil was eroded and the limestone bones of the country became increasingly exposed.

Despite its apparent harshness, the Burren supported quite large numbers of people in ancient times and has over 2500 historic sites. Chief among them is the 5000-year-old Poulnabrone Dolmen, the framework of a Neolithic/Bronze Age chamber tomb, and one of Ireland's iconic ancient monuments.

There are around 70 such tombs erected by the Burren's early settlers. Many of these tombs are wedge-shaped graves, stone boxes tapering both in height and width and about the size of a large double bed. The dead were placed inside, and the whole structure was covered in earth and stones. Gleninsheen, south of Aillwee Caves, is a good example.

Ring forts dot the Burren in prodigious numbers. There are almost 500, including Iron Age stone forts such as Cahercommaun near Carron.

In later times, many castles in the area were built by the region's ruling families, and these include Leamanegh Castle near Kilfenora, Ballinalacken Castle near Doolin and Gleninagh Castle on the Black Head road.

Many ring forts and stone walls have been bulldozed out of existence.

FLORA & FAUNA

Soil may be scarce on the Burren, but the small amount that gathers in the cracks is well drained and rich in nutrients. This, together with the soft Atlantic climate, supports an extraordinary mix of Mediterranean, Arctic and Alpine plants. Of Ireland's native wild flowers, 75% are found here, including a number of beautiful orchids, the creamy-white burnet rose, the little starry flowers of mossy saxifrage, and the magenta bloody cranesbill.

The Burren is a stronghold of Ireland's most elusive mammal, the weasel-like pine marten. They're rarely seen, although there are certainly some living in the Caher Valley. Badgers, foxes and even stoats are common throughout the region. Otters and seals haunt the shores around Bellharbour, New Quay and Finavarra Point.

The estuaries along this northern coast are rich in bird life and frequently attract brent geese during the winter. More than 28 of Ireland's 33 species of butterfly are found here, including one endemic species, the Burren green.

As always, modern farming and 'land-improvement' grants have had their effect on the Burren. Weedkillers, insecticides and fertilisers favour grass and little else, often fatally undermining fragile ecological systems.

WALKING

'Green roads' are the old highways of the Burren, crossing hills and valleys to some of the remotest corners of the region. Unpaved, many were built during the Famine as part of relief work, while some date back possibly thousands of years. They're now used mostly by hikers and the occasional farmer. Some are signposted, but there is an element of footpath blockage and neglect these days in spite of much publicity being given to walking and to 'official' walking routes.

The Burren Way (see p655) runs down through the Burren from Ballyvaughan to Doolin and then inland along mainly paved lanes, since cliff access around the Cliffs of Moher has been restricted.

Guided nature, history, archaeology and **wilderness walks** (€15 per half day) are available through **Burren Hill Walks** (☎ 065-707 7168) based at Corkscrew Hill in Ballyvaughan, or **Southwest Walks Ireland** (☎ 066-712 8733) in Tralee, County Kerry.

GETTING THERE & AWAY

For precise times and other details of buses to the Burren area, ring the **Ennis bus station** (☎ 065-682 4177), **Limerick bus station** (☎ 061-313 333) or **Galway bus station** (☎ 091-562 000).

Various buses pass through the Burren. From Limerick bus No 337 runs three times daily (once on Sunday) from late May to September, once daily the rest of the year. It connects with Ennis, Ennistymon, Lahinch, Liscannor, the Cliffs of Moher, Doolin and Lisdoonvarna. Express bus No 50 connects Galway with Ballyvaughan, Lisdoonvarna, Lahinch, Kilkee and Tralee. It runs three times daily (once on Sunday) from late May to late September. Bus No 423 runs from Galway to Kinvara, Ballyvaughan, Black Head, Fanore, Lisdoonvarna and Doolin. It runs three times daily (once on Sunday) from late May to late September. The rest of the year it runs once a day, Monday to Saturday. Also see Tours on p376.

GETTING AROUND

The best way to see the Burren is on foot (see Walking, p358) or by cycling; good mountain bikes are available in Doolin from **Aille River Hostel** (☎ 065-707 4260), or from **Burke's Garage** (☎ 065-707 4022) in Lisdoonvarna.

DOOLIN

☎ 065 / pop 200

Doolin, or Fisherstreet as it is also known, stretches for several kilometres along the road. Despite its remoteness and its treeless, often windswept surroundings, it has some of the best music pubs in the west, a couple of decent restaurants and cafés, and plenty of good hostels and guesthouses. It's also an excellent base for the Burren, which lies just to the north. There are ferries to the Aran Islands (see Getting There & Away, p361).

Doolin is extremely popular among backpackers and music lovers, and at night the pubs are filled with a cosmopolitan crowd. The downside is that Doolin is on the conventional coach trip trail and the 'backpacker' tour bus trail. Never the twain shall meet, but it all adds to the fun, if you like company and occasional theatricals. In the high season it can be difficult to get a bed, and you should definitely book ahead.

Orientation & Information

Doolin is made up of three parts. Coming from the north along the R479 you first reach Doolin Catholic church on the left, then after less than 1km the upper village, known as Roadford, with a shop, restaurant and cafés, hostels and two pubs. Then there's a slightly bigger gap before reaching Fisherstreet, the lower village, which has the popular Paddy's Doolin Hostel, more shops and O'Connor's pub. It's another 1.5km to the harbour and the ferry to the Aran Islands.

There are no banks in Doolin, but a mobile bank visits on Thursday. You can change money and travellers cheques in Fisherstreet at Paddy's Doolin Hostel. The nearest ATM is in Ennistymon.

Activities

The Doolin area is popular with cavers. The **Fisherstreet Potholes** are nearby, and **Poll na gColm**, 5km northeast of Lisdoonvarna, is Ireland's longest cave, with over 12km of mapped passageways. See www.cavingireland.org for more details.

The rocks to the north of Doolin Harbour are honeycombed with an unusual system of undersea caves called the **Green Holes of Doolin**. They're the longest known undersea caves in temperate waters. Nondivers can look, with care, into Hell, a large gash in the rocks, north of the harbour and about 50m from the sea. The gash is about 6m wide, and the heaving water at the bottom leads to a maze of submarine passages.

To explore the caves mentioned here, experience of caving, and use of full equipment, is essential.

Sleeping

BUDGET

Sleeping places in Doolin are generally of a good standard and the choice is wide.

Rainbow Hostel (☎ 707 4415; rainbowhostel@eircom.net; Roadford, Doolin; dm €11-12, d €28) Another good choice, this smart and friendly place is in a good location, near McGann's pub in the upper village.

Aille River Hostel (☎ 707 4260; ailleriver@esatclear.ie; Roadford, Doolin; camping per person €6, dm/d €11.50/26; mid-Mar–Dec) In a picturesque spot by the river in the upper village this converted 17th-century farmhouse is a great choice. It has turf fires, hot showers, free laundry and good company. There's Internet access for €1.50 per 15 minutes.

O'Connors Riverside Camping & Caravan Park (☎ 707 4314; joan@oconnorsdoolin.com; Roadford, Doolin; tent & 2 adults €12; May-Sep) Handily located in the upper village, beside the Aille River, this is a small, friendly site with immaculate facilities.

Paddy's Doolin Hostel (☎ 707 4006; doolinhostel@tinet.ie; Fisherstreet, Doolin; dm €12-13 d €35) Better known as Paddy Moloney's, this is a busy place and a great gathering point for backpackers.

Nagles Doolin Caravan & Camping Park (☎ 707 4458; ken@doolincamping.com; tent & 2 adults €12; Apr-Sep) With full-on views of the cliffs of Moher, and Doolin only a short distance away, this pleasant site is a good choice. It's open to the elements, so pin those pegs down.

MID-RANGE

Rainbow's End (☎ 707 4900; rainbowhostel@eircom.net; Roadford; s/d €40/60) Lots of exposed wood and light and airy rooms make this friendly family-run place a good choice. It's run by the owners of Rainbow Hostel.

Doonmacfelim House (☎ 707 4503; www.kingsway.ie/doonmacfelim; Roadford, Doolin; s/d €55/68; P) Doolin has lots of big detached guesthouses and this is a good one. Rooms are nicely done out and breakfasts are hearty. There's a bit of history as well; prehistoric artefacts were found on the surrounding property.

Island View House (☎ 707 4346; www.islandviewdoolin.com; Doolin; s/d €42.50/60; Apr-Oct; P) A good escape from main-street Doolin is this charming bungalow, 3km along the Cliffs of Moher road from the village. There are pleasant little treats and rooms are comfy. There are reduced rates for children.

Killilagh House (☎ 707 4392; killilaghhouse@esatclear.ie; Roadford, Doolin; s/d €50/70; P) Opposite the Doolin Café, this is a friendly place with clean, bright bedrooms and a comfortable lounge.

Atlantic View House (☎ 707 4189; Pier Rd, Doolin; s/d €50/70) Owned by the same people who operate the ferries, Atlantic View is the closest B&B to the harbour, but is a five-minute walk from the main village. It's fairly palatial for a B&B, with bright, decorative rooms, most with panoramic views of the cliffs and ocean.

TOP END

Aran View House (☎ 707 4061; www.aranview.com; Coast Rd, Doolin; s €65-85, d €100-140; May-Sep; P) Just outside the village on its northern edge is this handsome Georgian hotel. Rooms are spacious as expected with a Georgian building and there are great views seaward.

Eating

Doolin Café (☎ 707 4795; Roadford, Doolin; mains €15-21.50; 10am-10pm) There's a great atmosphere at this friendly café-restaurant where you can get hefty breakfasts from 10am onwards, as well as lunch and evening meals. The menu covers everything from fish to tasty vegetarian dishes.

Flagship Restaurant (☎ 707 4688; Ballyvoe, Lisdoonvarna Rd, Doolin; mains €7.90-11; 10am-6pm Easter-Sep) is attached to the excellent Doolin Craft Gallery (see Shopping, p361) and located 400m along the Lisdoonvarna road (turn just before Doolin Church at the northern approach to the village). It serves delicious home-cooked snacks and light meals. Treat yourself to Guinness cake or Kerry apple cake. Hilary Clinton probably did when she once dined (and shopped) here.

Bruach na hAille (☎ 707 4120; Roadford, Doolin; mains €11.35-19; 10am-9pm mid-Mar–Oct) A good merging of traditional cottage-style restaurant with international cuisine and French flair. It does breakfast as well, from full Irish (€9) to vegetarian (€8) and lunch dishes (€8 to €9).

O'Connor's (☎ 707 4168; Fisherstreet, Doolin; sandwiches €3, mains €8.50-15) Music and Irish pub grub are the things here, but don't expect a special experience. There's a big, busy coach trade and the bar surroundings are fairly standard.

McGann's (☎ 707 4133; Roadford, Doolin; mains €10-15) It's standard pub grub again at McGann's where there's usually a crowd and things get smoky and musical.

For self-catering there's the fairly well-stocked **Doolin Deli**, just down from O'Connor's pub on the road to the pier.

Drinking & Entertainment

Doolin is renowned for Irish music, and you can hear it almost every night in summer, in the company of a lot of other people, and at the weekend in winter.

O'Connor's (☎ 707 4168; Fisherstreet, Doolin) This favourite packs them in and has a great atmosphere when the traditional music, singing and drinking are all in full swing. Pub grub is also available.

McGann's (☎ 707 4133; Roadford, Doolin) McGann's has all the classic touches of a full-on Irish music pub with the action often spilling out onto the street. Food is also served here.

MacDiarmada's (☎ 707 4700; Roadford, Doolin) Also known as MacDermott's, this pub sees more of a local crowd with a younger set beering up at weekends. Music sessions are up to Doolin standards.

Aran View House (☎ 707 4061; Coast Rd, Doolin) The bar at this hotel provides a pleasant escape from the tumult in the village.

Shopping

Doolin Craft Gallery (☎ 707 4309; Ballyvoe, Lisdoonvarna Rd, Doolin; 🕑 9am-7pm Easter-Oct, 10am-6pm Tue-Sat rest of year) Ex-Dublin-based craftspeople run this gallery and shop attached to the Flagship Restaurant (see p360). In the shop there's a great selection of clothing, linen, lace, ceramics and crystal. The gallery specialises in fine jewellery and batik.

Doolin's **Traditional Music Shop**, next to the Doolin Deli and just down from O'Connor's Pub, has a good selection of traditional music tapes and CDs.

Getting There & Away

BOAT

Doolin is the ferry departure point to the Aran Islands (see p383). These are operated daily, Easter to September, by **Doolin Ferries** (☎ 707 4455; www.doolinferries.com; The Pier, Doolin). When the pier kiosk is closed contact the **Atlantic View House** (☎ 707 4189).

It takes around 25 minutes to cover the 8km to Inisheer, the smallest and closest of the three Aran Islands (return €25). There are around seven sailings daily from June to August, beginning at 10am. The last ferry returns from Inisheer at 5.30pm.

From June to August the first ferry to Inishmór, the largest island, leaves Doolin Harbour at 10am and the last ferry from Inishmór departs at 4pm (return €32, 50 minutes).

From June to August the first ferry to Inishmaan leaves at 10am and the last ferry back to Doolin leaves at 4.30pm (return €28, 40 minutes).

BUS

Buses stop outside the post office in Roadford, Paddy's Doolin Hostel in Fisherstreet, and the Rainbow Hostel near McGann's pub. There are buses between Doolin and Ennis, Limerick, Galway and Dublin. For contact details, see Getting There & Away p359.

Getting Around

The **Aille River Hostel** (☎ 707 4260; Roadford, Doolin) hires out bikes for €10 per day.

LISDOONVARNA

☎ 065 / pop 909

Lisdoonvarna (Lios Dún Bhearna), often just called 'Lisdoon', is well known for its mineral springs. For centuries people have been visiting the local spa to grit their teeth and swallow its waters, or to bathe in them. The town was once a centre for *basadóiri* (matchmakers) who for a fee would fix a person up with a mate. Most of the mainly male hopefuls, would hit town in September, feet shuffling, cap in hand, after the hay was in. Today, true matchmaking is unlikely, but the **Lisdoonvarna Matchmaking Festival** (www.matchmakerireland.com) held throughout September/early October, is a great excuse for daftness, drinking, merrymaking, music and of course moneymaking.

Orientation & Information

Lisdoonvarna is essentially a one-street town with a square in the centre from where you turn west for Doolin and the coast. The town has plenty of shops, pubs, B&Bs and smart hotels with some fine restaurants, but no bank or ATM. You can, however, change money at the post office on Main St to the north.

There's Internet access at the **Internet Café** (☎ 707 5005; Main St; €1.50/10min; ⏲ 9am-5pm Mon-Sat).

Spa Wells Health Centre

At the southern end of town is Ireland's only working **spa** (☎ 707 4023; Main St; sulphur bath €25; ⏲ 10am-6pm Jun-Sep). It has a sulphur spring, a Victorian pump house, massage room, sauna and mineral baths, all in an agreeable, wooded setting. The iron, sulphur, magnesium and iodine in the water are supposed to be good for rheumatic and glandular complaints. You can drink the water, but it's not a vintage-wine tasting experience. Modern treatments include wax bath, aromatherapy and reflexology.

Burren Smokehouse Visitor Centre

You can learn about the ancient Irish tradition of oak-smoking salmon from a video at the **visitor centre** (☎ 707 4432; www.burrensmokehouse.ie; Doolin Rd; admission free; ⏲ 9am-7pm). Smoked salmon in all its guises is on sale, with free samples. Tourist information is also available. The centre is just west of Lisdoonvarna on the Doolin road (N67).

Sleeping & Eating

Sheedy's Country House Hotel & Restaurant (☎ 707 4026; www.sheedys.com; Liscannor Rd; s/d €100/140; bar meals €4.50-14, dinner mains €18.50-25; ⏲ Mar-Oct; P) This is a top choice anywhere. Sheedy's is in a fine location in attractive grounds (look for the imaginative vegetable and herb plots). There is a sense of gracious living in this handsome house where rooms are individually and stylishly designed and the public areas are full of character. The bar menu has a terrific seafood choice and the restaurant offers modern Irish cuisine at its best with an excellent wine list. Sheedy's runs one-day cookery courses during the early and late season. It has good information on walking locally and can arrange guides.

Carrigann Hotel (☎ 707 4036; www.gateway-to-the-burren.com; Doolin Rd; s/d €75/110; bar meals €3.20-16.50, dinner mains €14-19.50; P) A relaxing atmosphere and bright, comfy rooms make this a good out-of-centre choice. The hotel offers weekend walking packages, with guide supplied. Its restaurant has a wide range of meat and fish dishes with an international theme.

O'Loughlin's (☎ 707 4038; Main St; s/d €30/50; ⏲ Apr-Oct) O'Loughlin's is an unpretentious, friendly B&B with an apparent maze of rooms that are plain, but good value.

Royal Spa Hotel (☎ 707 4288; Main St; bar meals €6.75-14.80) There's a good choice of bar food, ranging from pizzas to vegetarian lasagne in this pleasant main-street bar.

Irish Arms (☎ 707 4207; Main St; meals €9-11.50) This pub flies the flag for Ireland and the Glasgow Celtic football club. The food is good, solid pub fare.

Getting There & Around

For bus services, see Getting There & Away p359. **Burke's Garage** (☎ 707 4022), just off the square, has bikes for hire for €10/50 per day/week.

FANORE

☎ 065 / pop 150

Fanore (Fan Óir), 5km south of Black Head, is less a village and more a stretch of coast, with a shop, a pub, and a few houses scattered along the main road (R477). It has a fine sandy beach with an extensive backdrop of dunes. It's the only **safe beach** between Lahinch and Ballyvaughan. There's extensive parking and there are toilets open in summer.

There's a shop, **Siopa Fan Óir** (☎ 707 6131; Fanore; ⏲ 9am-9pm summer, 9am-7pm winter), just across from O'Donohue's pub. There's also a small grocery store/post office/newsagent/fishing-tackle shop next to the Admiral's Rest Seafood Restaurant (see below).

Sights & Activities

Just behind Fanore Beach, a road goes inland, by a church and up the Caher River Valley, or **Khyber Pass**. The first few kilometres are very pleasant. After about 4km you reach a junction with the Burren Way. There's limited parking if you're driving, but you can walk either way along the Burren Way.

The **Burren Riding Centre** (☎ 707 6140; burrenriding@eircom.net; Fanore) offers a five-hour outing for €25. There are shorter trips. It's best to book ahead.

John McNamara at the **Admiral's Rest Seafood Restaurant** (☎ 707 6105; jdmn@iol.ie; Fanore), the home of the Burren Conservation Trust, organises Burren wildlife weekends at various times. The trust also does historical research of some of the offshore islands. It has a **nature reserve** about 5km south of Fanore in the Caher River Valley.

Sleeping & Eating

Rocky View Farmhouse (☎ 707 6103; www.rockyviewfarmhouse.com; s/d €30/56; P) A charming place at the heart of the coastal Burren this detached house reflects the special ambience of the area in its fresh, airy rooms. Organic food is available and vegetarian and vegan diets are catered for. Here too is the Harebell Centre, devoted to holistic and healing workshops.

Admiral's Rest Seafood Restaurant (☎ 707 6105; jdmn@iol.ie; Fanore; s/d €25/50; dinner €6.35-27.75) This restaurant-cum-B&B is at the southern end of Fanore. It's an appealing place without anything fancy but with a great atmosphere and plenty of local information and good conversation. Rooms are clean and tidy and the restaurant uses only wild fish and fresh lobster, the latter being its speciality. If you stay a week or more you get a free boat ride on Galway Bay.

O'Donohue's (☎ 707 6119; Fanore; snacks €3.50) This pub, 4km south of the beach, offers soup and sandwiches. It has music on Saturday nights and hosts some of the sessions for the Lisdoonvarna Matchmaking Festival in September. There are no other bars along this stretch of coast.

Siopa Fan Óir Tea Room is next to the shop and craft gallery of the same name.

Getting There & Away

For information on bus services, see Getting There & Away, p359.

BLACK HEAD & CATHAIR DHÚN IORAIS

Black Head, Clare's northwesternmost point, is a wild and exhilarating headland of limestone that descends steeply to the sea. The main road curves around Black Head just above the sea and there is an automatic lighthouse at the head's northern tip. There's good shore **angling** for pollock, wrasse, mackerel – and sea bass if you're lucky – from the rocky platforms near sea level. Even in apparently calm conditions, great care should be taken when near sea level.

An exhilarating outing is the climb up Black Head to the Iron Age ring fort of Cathair Dhún Iorais. There's no path, so it's essential to take a map *(Ordnance Survey Discovery Series No 51)* and compass. The ground is very rocky in places, so strong footwear is essential. Be prepared for wet, windy and potentially cold conditions, even in summer. It's a steep one kilometre to the fort.

Start from just above the lighthouse on the northern tip of Black Head. There's limited parking on the inland side of the road. Head due south up the rocky hillside from the road, negotiating between rock shelves, to reach an old green track. Cross the track and continue directly to where things level off and Cathair Dhún Iorais stands amid a sea of limestone pavements. It's not the most dramatic of ring forts, but the setting is magnificent. The views to Galway and Connemara are breathtaking in clear weather.

From the fort you can bear southeast to skirt the limestone cliffs that run in an unbroken wall to the west. This takes you onto the broad shoulder that leads south, in 1.3km, to the summit of Dobhach Bhráinín, at 1045m one of the highest points in the Burren. Again, skilled use of map and compass is essential in case of sudden mist, when careless descent from Dobhach Bhráinin may land you above the cliffs. It's best to return to the fort and descend the way you came.

BALLYVAUGHAN & AROUND

☎ 065 / pop 2603

All the charm of the Burren is distilled into its favoured location, Ballyvaughan (Baile Uí Bheacháin), where the hard land of the hills gives way to a quiet leafy corner of Galway Bay. It makes for a persuasive base for visiting the northern part of the Burren. You'll be reluctant to leave.

The centre of the village is at the junction of the N67 and the coastal R477. Going south and inland on the N67 brings you to the centre of the Burren, Aillwee Caves, Poulnabrone Dolmen and Lisdoonvarna. Turning west leads you to the magnificent coast road (R477), Black Head and south towards Doolin. Going northeast on the N67, you reach Kinvara and County Galway.

Just west of the junction, on the R477, is the quay and Monk's Bar. The quay was built in 1829 at a time when boats traded with the Aran Islands and Galway, exporting grain and bacon and bringing in turf – a scarce commodity in the Burren.

A few metres past the harbour, a signposted track leads to a seashore bird hide from where there is a good view of tidal shallows. If driving, you'll find a car park and another access path to the bird hide a few metres further on.

Information

Linnane's Village Stores (☎ 707 7077; Ballyvaughan) in Ballyvaughan has an excellent **tourist information centre** (🕑 9am-5pm Mon-Sat). There are no banks in Ballyvaughan, but you can change money in the post office and withdraw cash if you have an AIB card. The nearest ATM is at Ennistymon.

Corkscrew Hill

About 6km south of Ballyvaughan on the Lisdoonvarna road is a series of severe bends up Corkscrew Hill (180m). The road was built as part of a Famine-relief scheme in the 1840s. From the top there are spectacular views of the northern Burren and Galway Bay, with Aillwee Mountain and the caves on the right and Cappanawalla Hill on the left, and with the partially restored 16th-century Newtown Castle, erstwhile residence of the O'Lochlains, at its base. From here, the route to Lisdoonvarna is through boggy, fairly characterless countryside.

Kayaking

River Ocean Kayaking (☎ 707 7043; www.riverocean.com; 2 Muckinish West, Ballyvaughan) offers half- to two-day kayaking trips and short courses for €25 (introductory) and €45 (advanced).

Sleeping

There are no hostels in Ballyvaughan; the closest is Johnston's Independent Hostel in Kinvara, County Galway (see p400).

Rusheen Lodge (☎ 707 7092; www.rusheenlodge.com; Lisdoonvarna Rd; s/d €65/90; P) Outstanding is the only word for this beautifully appointed house that outclasses many top hotels elsewhere with its tasteful luxury. It's about 750m south of the village, on the N67.

Hyland's Burren Hotel (☎ 707 7037; fax 707 7131; Main St; s/d €85/130; P) An appealing place, this central hotel has fine, spacious rooms and manages to retain a local feel alongside its corporate image. There's a bar and restaurant. Ask for the hotel's *Walks* leaflet.

Stonepark House (☎ 707 7056; Bishops Quarter; s/d with shared bathroom €27/40, d with bathroom €46; P) Stonepark is a small B&B in a peaceful location just over 2km along the Kinvara road. Things are pleasantly old fashioned and the welcome is kind and gentle.

Eating

Tea Junction (☎ 707 7289; Main St; lunch €3-4.80; 🕑 9am-5pm mid-Mar–Oct, Wed-Sun Nov–mid-Mar) It's all tasty soups, sandwiches and baguettes at this delightful place that also does breakfasts (€3.50 to €5.50), including a filling vegetarian option.

O'Brien's (☎ 707 7003; Main St; mains €9-11.50; 🕑 12.30-8.30pm) A few doors down from Hyland's Hotel, this is a relaxed, informal pub and restaurant. Seafood is a specialty and tasty baguettes are a good stopgap during the day.

Monk's Bar (☎ 707 7059; The Old Pier; mains €11-14.90; 🕑 noon-8pm) Famed for its delicious shellfish, Monk's is a cheerful, spacious and comfortable place. The harbour's just across the road to put you in the mood for oysters, mussels or crab claws. There's meat and vegetarian specials too.

Entertainment

O'Brien's (☎ 707 7003; Main St) is the place for a bit of Ballyvaughan bopping at the Thursday to Sunday night discos. There is also a restaurant (see above).

Monk's Bar (☎ 707 7059; The Old Pier) runs traditional music sessions Saturday night all year and Tuesday and Saturday night June to August. Food is also available (see above).

Ólólainn (Main St) is a tiny place (o-*loch*-lain) on the left as you head down to the pier. It is the place for a timeless moment or two in old-fashioned snugs.

Getting There & Away

For information on bus services see Getting There & Away on p359. The Spar supermarket is the Bus Éireann agent.

Getting Around

There are bikes for hire for €11 per day at John Connolle's, opposite the post office and filling station.

CENTRAL BURREN

The road through the heart of the Burren, the R480, runs south from Ballyvaughan to Leamanegh Castle, where it joins the R476, which runs southeast to Corofin, and northwest to Kilfenora. Travelling south from Ballyvaughan (on the N67), turn east before Corkscrew Hill at the Aillwee Caves sign. The road goes past Gleninsheen Wedge Tomb, Poulnabrone Dolmen and into some harsh, but inspiring scenery.

Aillwee Caves

A good place to spend a rainy afternoon or to take children is the extensive limestone **Aillwee Caves** (☎ 065-707 7036; www.aillwee.ie; Ballyvaughan; adult/child/family €7.50/4.50/€21; 10am-5.30pm Mar-Oct). The main passage penetrates for 600m into the mountain, widening into larger caverns, one with its own waterfall. The caves were carved out by water some two million years ago. Near the entrance are the remains of a brown bear, extinct in Ireland for over 10,000 years. You can only go into the cave as part of a guided tour. There are six tours daily (phone for times); the last tour departs at 5.30pm in summer. Try to visit early in the day before the crowds arrive.

Gleninsheen Wedge Tomb

One of Ireland's most famous prehistoric grave sites, **Gleninsheen** lies beside the R480 just south of Aillwee Caves. It's thought to date from 4000 to 5000 years ago. A magnificent gold torc (a crescent of beaten gold that hung round the neck) was found nearby in 1930 by a young boy called Paddy Dolan, who was hunting rabbits. Dating from around 700 BC, the torc is reckoned to be one of the finest pieces of prehistoric Irish craftwork and is now on display at the National Museum in Dublin. The gate giving access to the Gleninsheen tomb is a masterpiece of exclusion. A heavy padlock and a notice declaring 'Beware of the Bull', overlaid by another declaring 'Trespassers Prosecuted' glare dourly at the visitor – post-Stone Age, of course. Just inside the gate is a handsome memorial to Paddy Dolan, complete with gold-coloured torc inlay.

Poulnabrone Dolmen

Poulnabrone Dolmen, or Portal Tomb, is one of Ireland's most photographed ancient monuments – a trademark tourist icon. The dolmen, a large slab perched on stone uprights, stands amid a swathe of rocky pavements, for all the world like some surreal bird of prey about to take off. The capstone weighs five tonnes. The site is 8km south of Aillwee and is visible from the R480. A path leads to it from the roadside.

Poulnabrone was built over 5000 years ago. It was excavated in 1986, and the remains of 16 people were found as well as pieces of pottery and jewellery. Radiocarbon dating suggests that they were buried between 3800 and 3200 BC. When the dead were originally entombed here, the whole structure was partially covered in a mound of earth, which has since worn away.

Carron & Cahercommaun Cliff Fort

The tiny village of Carron (Carran on some maps; An Carn in Gaelic), a few kilometres east of the R480, is a delightfully remote spot. It was the birthplace of Michael Cusack, founder of the Gaelic Athletic Association. Signposted at the T-junction near the church is the remote **Burren Perfumery & Floral Centre** (☎ 065-708 9102; Carron; admission free; 9am-5pm Jun-Sep, 9am-5pm Jan-May & Oct-Dec). It uses wild flowers of the Burren to produce its scents, and it's the only handicraft perfumery in Ireland. There's a free audiovisual presentation on the flora of the Burren.

Below Carron lies one of the finest *turloughs* in Ireland. It's known as the Carron Polje. Polje is a Yugoslav term used universally for these shallow depressions that flood in winter and dry out in summer, when the lush grass that flourishes on the surface is used for grazing.

About 3km south of Carron and perched on the edge of an inland cliff is the great stone fort of Cahercommaun. It was inhabited in the 8th and 9th centuries by people who hunted deer and grew a small amount of grain. There are the remains of a souterrain leading from the fort to the outer cliff face. To get there, go south from Carron and take a left turn for Kilnaboy. After 1.5km a path on the left leads up to the fort.

Clare's Rock Hostel (☎ 065-708 9129; www.claresrock.com; Carron; P ☒) is an imposing building in grey exposed stone. It has big spacious rooms and excellent facilities. If you stay you can hire bikes for €10 per day. From April to October, **Cassidy's Croide na Boirne Pub** (☎ 065-708 9109; Carron; bar mains €3.95-8.25) serves up a good range of tasty dishes all with witty names and descriptions, several reflecting the pub's previous incarnation as a British RIC station, and then as a Garda barracks. Parts of the old furnishings are incorporated into the bar and there are traditional music sessions every Saturday with music and set dancing on Friday and Saturday nights.

KILFENORA

☎ 065 / pop 372

Kilfenora (Cill Fhionnúrach) lies on the southern fringes of the Burren, 8km south-east of Lisdoonvarna. It's a small place, in keeping with its diminutive 12th-century cathedral. There are several high crosses in its churchyard.

Burren Centre

The **Burren Centre** (☎ 708 8030; www.theburrencentre.ie; Main St; adult/child/family €5.50/3/15; 9.30am-6pm Jun-Aug, 10am-5pm Mar-Jun & Sep-Oct) has a series of entertaining and informative displays on every aspect of the Burren past and present. There's a tea room and a shop that sells local products.

Kilfenora Cathedral

The pope is, incidentally, the bishop of the diocese of Kilfenora and Killaloe; in the past the ruined 12th-century **cathedral** was an important place of pilgrimage. St Fachan (or Fachtna) founded the monastery here in the 6th century, and it later became the seat of Kilfenora diocese, the smallest in the country.

The cathedral is the smallest you're ever likely to see. Only the ruined structure and nave of the more recent Protestant church are actually part of the cathedral. The chancel has two primitive carved figures on top of two tombs.

High Crosses

Kilfenora is best known for its high crosses, three in the churchyard and a large 12th-century example in the field about 100m to the west.

The most interesting one is the 800-year-old **Doorty Cross**, standing prominently to the west of the church's front door. It was lying broken in two until the 1950s, when it was re-erected. A panel in the churchyard does an excellent job of explaining the carvings that adorn the crosses.

Sleeping & Eating

Mrs Mary Murphy (☎ 708 8040; Main St; s/d €30/50; mid-Feb–Nov) Located right on the main street, this family home is a welcoming place with unfussy rooms.

Carraigliath (☎ 708 8075; eimeorhowlwy@eircom.net; Kilfenora; s/d €25/50) This big detached house is just along the R476 Lisdoonvarna road from Kilfenora centre. There's a friendly welcome here and you may well hear the strains of excellent Irish music; most of the family play instruments.

Linnane's (☎ 708 8157; Main St; bar meals €3-8.50) You can get sandwiches at Linnane's, but there's rib-sticking soup and other Irish standards too in a bar that makes no concessions to modernism.

Vaughan's Pub (☎ 708 8004; Main St; mains €8-11.50; 10am-9pm) Bar meals cover a good range of seafood and meat dishes here and local produce is a strong feature. Classic Irish dishes such as beef and Guinness stew are backed by alternatives such as lasagne and vegetarian quiche.

Entertainment

Vaughan's Pub (☎ 708 8004; Main St) Vaughan's has a big reputation in Irish music circles. There's music in the bar every night during the summer and on several nights the rest of the year. The adjacent barn is the scene of terrific set-dancing sessions on Thursday and Sunday nights.

Linnane's (☎ 708 8157; Main St) Linnane's gears up for a big night of Irish music on Wednesdays in summer and at weekends most of the year.

Getting There & Away

Bus Éireann (☎ 065-682 4177) service No 333 leaves Ennis at 3pm Tuesday to Thursday and Saturday and stops at Kilfenora. Bus No 337 leaves Ennis at 2.25pm Monday to Saturday mid-May to September. Check with the **Ennis bus station** (☎ 065-682 4177) for times.

COROFIN & AROUND

☎ 065 / pop 200

Corofin (Cora Finne), also spelled Corrofin, is a quiet, friendly village on the southern fringes of the Burren. The surrounding area features a number of *turloughs*. There are several O'Brien castles in the area, two being on the shores of nearby Inchiquin Lough.

Corofin is home to the interesting **Clare Heritage Centre** (☎ 683 7955; clareheritage@eircom.net;

Church St; adult/concession €4/2; 10am-6pm mid-May–Oct). It has a display covering the period around the Potato Famine. Over 250,000 people lived in Clare before the Famine; today the county's population stands at about 91,000 – a drop of some 64%. In a separate building nearby, the **Genealogical Centre** (683 7955; 9am-5.30pm Mon-Fri) has facilities for people researching their Clare ancestry.

About 4km northwest of Corofin, on the road to Leamanegh Castle and Kilfenora (R476), look for the small town of **Kilnaboy**. The ruined church here is well worth seeking out for the *sheila-na-gig* (female figure carved in stone with exaggerated genitalia) over the doorway.

Sleeping & Eating

Lakefield Lodge (683 7675; mcleary.ennis@eircom.net; Ennis Rd; s/d €40/54; mid-Mar–Oct) A very well-run place just before the southern edge of the village. There are comfy rooms and a great welcome at this pleasant bungalow. Credit cards are accepted.

Shamrock and Heather (683 7061; Station Rd; bmkearney@eircom.net; s/d €37.50/50; Apr-Oct) Another welcoming place just a few minutes from the village centre, rooms are immaculate and of adequate size at this small bungalow.

Restaurant Le Catelinais (683 7425; mains €17.50-23.50; 5.30pm onwards Tue-Thu) Being tucked away in Corofin enhances the experience at this serene little restaurant, where the relaxing mood is matched by a fine merging of modern Irish and international cuisine.

Bofey Quinn's (683 7321; Main St; bar snacks €2.55-7.55, dinner €7.50-16; noon-9.30pm, pizzas to 11pm) Busy Bofey's does a wide range of seafood and meat and poultry dishes, as well as pastas and pizzas. Both bar and restaurant are friendly places without fancy trappings. There are good traditional music sessions round the big table on Thursday night and at other times.

Getting There & Away

Bus Éireann (065-682 4177) bus No 333 leaves Ennis at 3pm for Corofin, Monday and Friday only. Bus No 337 leaves Ennis at 2.25pm Monday to Saturday mid-May to September. Check with the **Ennis bus station** (065-682 4177) for times.

NORTHERN BURREN

There's low farmland stretching south from County Galway until it meets the bluff limestone hills of the Burren, which begins west of Kinvara and Doorus in County Galway. Here the road forks, going inland to Carron or along the coast to Ballyvaughan.

From Oranmore in County Galway to Ballyvaughan, the coastline wriggles along small inlets and peninsulas; some, such as Finavarra Point and New Quay, are worth a detour.

Inland near Bellharbour is the largely intact Corcomroe Abbey, while the three ancient churches of Oughtmama lie up a quiet side valley. Galway Bay forms the backdrop to some outstanding scenery: bare stone hills shining in the sun, with small hamlets and rich patches of green wherever there's soil.

Getting There & Away

June to mid-September, **Bus Éireann** (065-682 4177) bus No 50 between Galway and Cork passes through Kinvara and Ballyvaughan up to five times daily. Bus No 423 between Galway and Doolin also stops in those two places; there are up to three buses daily, May to September, and one bus a day Monday to Saturday the rest of the year. Check the details with the **bus station** at **Galway** (091-562 000) or **Ennis** (065-682 4177).

New Quay & the Flaggy Shore

New Quay (Ceibh Nua), on the **Finavarra Peninsula**, is about 1km off the main Kinvara to Ballyvaughan road (N67) and is reached by turning off the N67 at Ballyvelaghan Lough 3km north of Bellharbour.

It's worth stopping at the shoreside **Linnane's Bar** (065-707 8120; New Quay; mains €8.50-20) for its fresh seafood. For centuries this area was famous for its oysters; shellfish are still processed here and you can buy them from the little processing works behind the pub.

The **Flaggy Shore**, west of New Quay, is a particularly fine stretch of coastline where limestone terraces step down to the restless sea. About 500m west of Linnane's, at a crossroads, is **Russells Ceramics** (065-707 8185; Newquay), which specialises in *raku* work (Japanese lead-glazed earthenware).

The pottery shop has a range of other arts and craft work for sale.

Turn right at the crossroads for the Flaggy Shore. The road hugs the shoreline going west, then curves south past **Lough Muirí**, where you're likely to see a number of wading birds, as well as swans. There are said to be otters in the area. At a T-junction just past the lough a right turn leads to a Martello Tower on Finavarra Point.

Bellharbour

Bellharbour (Beulaclugga) is no more than a crossroads with some thatched holiday cottages and a pub, about 8km east of Ballyvaughan. There's a pleasant **walk** along an old green road that begins behind the modern Church of St Patrick, 1km north up the hill from the Y-junction at Bellharbour, and threads north along Abbey Hill.

Inland from here are the ruins of Corcomroe Abbey, the valley and churches of Oughtmama, and the interior road that takes you through the heart of the Burren.

Corcomroe Abbey

The beautiful and atmospheric **Corcomroe**, a former Cistercian abbey 1.5km inland from Bellharbour, lies in a small, tranquil valley surrounded by low hills. It is a marvellous place, one of the finest relics of its kind. It was founded in 1194 by Donal Mór O'Brien. His grandson, Conor na Siudaine O'Brien (died 1267), king of Thomond, is said to occupy the tomb in the northern wall, and there's a crude carving of him below an effigy of a bishop armed with a crosier, the pastoral staff, in the symbolic shape of a shepherd's crook, that was carried by a bishop or abbot. The surviving vaulting in the presbytery and transepts is very fine and there are some striking Romanesque carvings scattered throughout the abbey.

THE LEGEND OF CORCOMROE

In 1317, the Battle of Corcomroe was fought very near Corcomroe Abbey between two O'Brien clans trying to win control of Clare. Legend has it that one of the chieftains, Donough, was passing by Lough Rask on his way to battle when he saw a witch washing a pile of bleeding limbs in the water. The witch told Donough that her name was Bronach Boirne and that the corpses would be those of his soldiers if he insisted on going into battle. To make matters worse, Donough's own head was in the pile.

Donough's men tried to capture the elusive witch, but she flew up in the air and rained curses on them. To reassure his men, Donough told them that Bronach was the lover of his arch rival, Dermot O'Brien, and her warnings merely a ploy to frighten them off. Unfortunately for Donough, by that night he and most of his army were lying dead in the abbey.

OUGHTMAMA VALLEY

Oughtmama is a lonely, deserted valley hiding some small, ancient churches. To get there turn inland at Bellharbour, then go left at the Y-junction. In just under 1km you reach a house amid trees, on the right at Shanvally. A rough track leads inland from just beyond the house for about 1.5km to the churches. If you have a car, roadside parking is very limited, but there is a large roadside area about 400m before Shanvally, back towards the Y-junction, and with views of Corcomroe. The churches at Oughtmama were built in the 12th century by monks in search of solitude. It's a hardy walk up **Turlough Hill** behind the chapels, but the views are tremendous. Near the summit are the remains of a hill fort.

County Galway

CONTENTS

County Galway

For many travellers, County Galway evokes the age-old allure of Ireland's west. Remote beaches can seem like the ends of the earth, and the country's famous bleak weather and diffuse light draws out the landscape's palate of rusty browns and moody greens and blues. Islands just a few miles off the coast feel like they are centuries away. A spell, having originated in the region's mythology and song, takes root in fertile imaginations and claims travellers' hearts.

Connemara, largely a Gaeltacht region, is a patchwork of bogs, windswept hills and jagged beaches that affords superb hiking, biking and driving opportunities. To get away from it all and explore prehistoric forts, the Aran Islands and Inishbofin are easy ferry rides away.

While the rural parts are clearly what make County Galway one of Ireland's most magnetic destinations, its culturally dynamic city is what separates Galway from other, equally scenic counties. Galway city is a rare confluence of healthy elements: it's arty, romantic, youthful and eccentric.

HIGHLIGHTS

- Indulge in Galway City's dynamic **nightlife** (p380)
- Ride horseback on the white sands of **Connemara** (p393)
- Marvel at the stark beauty of **Inishmaan** (p388)
- Explore the ancient ring forts of **Dún Aengus** (p383) on Inishmór
- Tuck into a medieval banquet at **Dunguaire Castle** (p399)

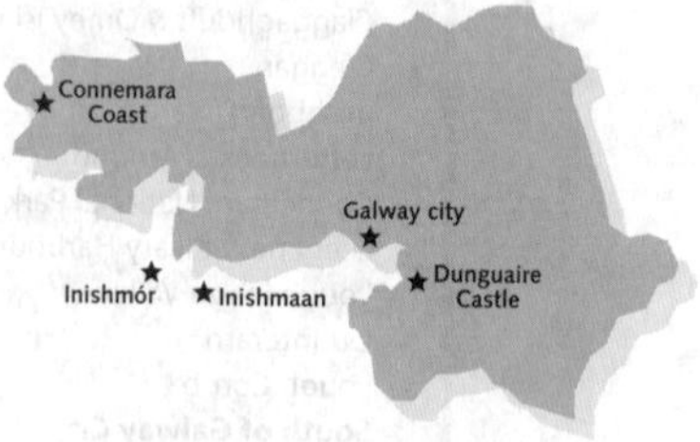

- POPULATION: 208,801
- AREA: 3760 SQ KM

GALWAY CITY

☎ 091 / pop 65,774

It isn't difficult to understand why so many people fall in love with Galway. The city offers little in terms of sightseeing opportunities, but more than compensates with atmosphere, panache and entertainment. Galway has long been a magnate for musicians, artists, thespians, intellectuals, young people and wayfarers. A curved, cobbled High St, lined with stone shop fronts, bohemian cafés and enticing pubs, is closed to auto traffic much of the time and generally swarms with a festive crowd. Buskers and performance artists – many of them genuinely entertaining – break the pedestrian flow year round. The River Corrib roils furiously beneath Galway's stone bridges, and one can work up a pleasant thirst strolling its banks and the picturesque canals that carve up the west side of town.

Of course, Galway's real appeal is its nightlife. Pubs and clubs come in all shapes and sizes. Your basic time-worn local, where the Guinness flows freely and the music is traditional and not amplified, will satisfy anyone who simply fancies a pint and some jovial company. But Galway is perhaps best known for its multilevel 'superpubs', with room after room of loud-talking, hard-drinking college students and party-mad tourists. Of late, Galway's after-dark scene is enhanced by a growing number of sleek lounges and dance clubs that reflect Ireland's increasingly cosmopolitan tastes. Theatre is another traditional strength.

That Dubliners can reach Galway in three hours helps augment the crowds every weekend, and the city's summer festivals – particularly Galway Race Week in July – draw multitudes of visitors. Advance accommodation booking is often necessary during these times.

Galway is an ideal stop before exploring Connemara and the Aran Islands.

HISTORY

Galway grew from a small fishing village in the Claddagh area at the mouth of the River Corrib to become an important walled town when the Anglo-Normans, under Richard de Burgo (also spelled de Burgh or Burke), captured territory from the local O'Flahertys in 1232. The Irish word for 'outsiders' or 'foreigners' is *gaill*, which may be the origin of the city's name in Irish, Gaillimh. The town walls were built by the Anglo-Normans from around 1270.

Galway became something of an outpost in Ireland's 'wild west'. In 1396, Richard II granted a charter to the city, effectively transferring power from the de Burgos to 14 merchant families or 'tribes' – hence the informal sobriquet 'City of the Tribes', by which Galway is still known. These powerful families were mostly English or Norman in origin, and clashes with the leading Irish families of Connemara were frequent. At one time the city's western gate bore the prayer and warning: 'From the fury of the O'Flahertys, good Lord deliver us.' To ensure the ferocity was kept outside, the city fathers warned in the early 16th century that no uninvited 'O' or 'Mac' should show his face on Galway's streets.

English power throughout the region waxed and waned, but the city maintained its independent status under the ruling merchant families, who were mostly loyal to the English Crown. Galway's relative isolation encouraged a huge trade in wine, spices, fish and salt with Portugal and Spain. At one point the city rivalled Bristol and London in the volume of goods passing through its docks.

For a long while Galway prospered. A massive fire in 1473 destroyed much of the town but created space for a new street layout, and many solid stone buildings were erected in the 15th and 16th centuries.

It's said that Christopher Columbus tarried in Galway to hear Mass and pray at the Collegiate Church of St Nicholas of Myra. This Galway side trip supposedly occurred either because one of the crew was a Galway man or because Columbus wished to investigate tales of St Brendan's earlier voyage to the Americas from here.

Galway's faithful support of the English Crown led to its downfall with the arrival of Cromwell. The city was besieged in 1651 and fell in April 1652. Cromwell's forces under Charles Coote wreaked their usual havoc, and Galway's long period of decline began. In 1691 the city chose the wrong side again, and William of Orange's forces added to the destruction. The important trade with Spain was almost at an end and, with Dublin

COUNTY GALWAY

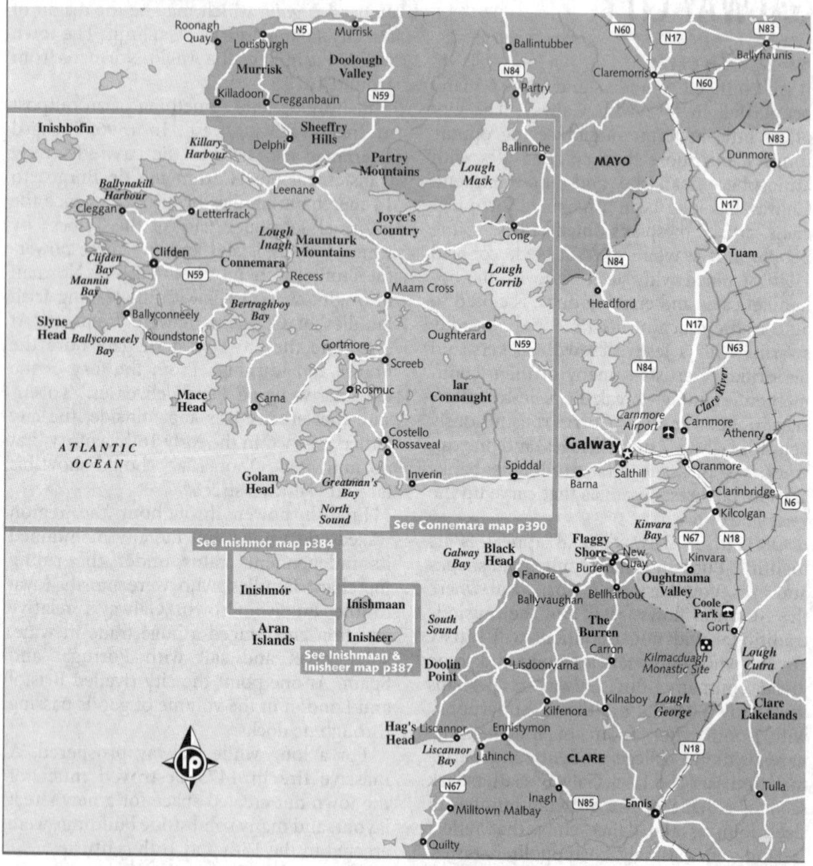

and Waterford taking most of the sea traffic, Galway stagnated until its revival in modern times.

ORIENTATION

Galway's tightly packed town centre lies on both sides of the River Corrib, which connects Lough Corrib with the sea, though Eyre Square and most of the main shopping areas are on the river's eastern bank. There are three main bridges; the northernmost, Salmon Weir Bridge, looks over a salmon trap and is overshadowed by Galway Cathedral.

From Eyre Square, the meandering main shopping street starts as Williamsgate St, becomes William St and then Shop St, before splitting into Mainguard St and High St. Just east of Eyre Square is the combined bus and train station, north of which is the tourist office.

South and east of Wolfe Tone Bridge is the historic, but totally redeveloped, district of Claddagh; to the west is the faded beach resort of Salthill.

INFORMATION

Bookshops

Charlie Byrne's (☎ 561 766; The Cornstore, Middle St) A huge collection of second-hand and discounted books.

Eason's (☎ 562 284; Shop St) Superstore with a large, general interest selection and Galway's biggest periodicals rack.

Kenny's Bookstore & Gallery (☎ 562 739; High St) The best shop in town for Irish literature and nonfiction,

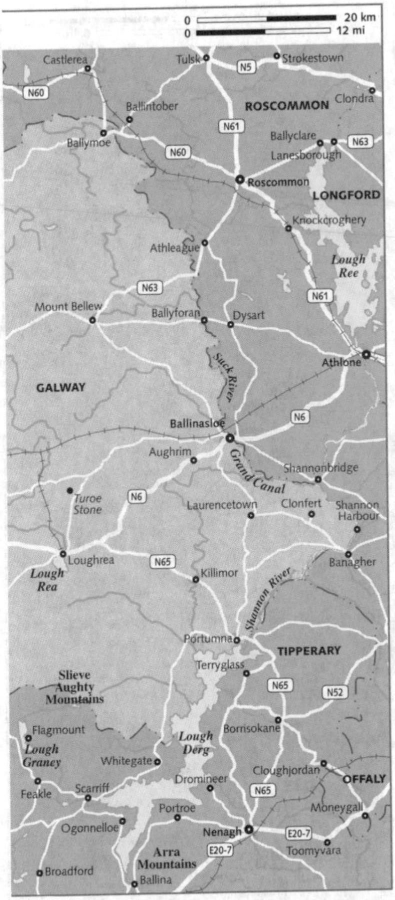

Kenny's is also one of the leading antiquarian bookshops in the country. The shop features old maps, prints and an art gallery.

Internet Access

The following Internet cafés charge around €6 for one hour.

Celtel e.centre (☎ 566 620; Kinlay House hostel, Merchant's Rd)
Galway e-centre (Shop St)
net@ccess (☎ 569 772; Old Malt shopping arcade, High St)

Laundry

Wash and fold service runs about €7 per load at **Laundrette** (☎ 584 524; 4 Sea Rd) and **Bubbles Laundrette** (☎ 563 434; 19 Mary St).

Money

Irish banks all have branches with ATMs in the city centre. The banks open 10am to 4pm Monday to Friday (to 5pm Thursday). The post office and tourist office change money.

Bank of Ireland (2 branches on Eyre Sq)
Allied Irish Bank (Lynch's Castle, Shop St)

Post

The post office on Eglinton St opens 9am to 5.30pm Monday to Saturday.

Telephone

Pay phones are located on the main pedestrian mall and on the southern side of Eyre Square. Eircom callcards are sold in convenience stores and supermarkets.

Tourist Information

Ireland West Tourism (☎ 563 081; Forster St, north of Eyre Sq; 9am-6pm daily Easter-Sep, 9am-6pm Mon-Fri, 9am-noon Sat Oct-Easter) This is a large information centre that can help set up accommodation locally, as well as bus tours and ferry trips outside the city. A row of telephones is available for free calls to local car rental agencies. The centre can be very busy in high season and there may be delays of an hour or more in making accommodation bookings.

Travel Agencies

Anyone, not just students, can arrange plans throughout Ireland and/or abroad at **usit NOW** (☎ 565 177; www.usitnow.ie; 16 Mary St).

SIGHTS

Eyre Square

The square is the focal point of the eastern part of the city centre, though it shows no great imagination in its design and layout. The eastern side of the square is taken up almost entirely by the Great Southern Hotel, a large, grey, limestone pile. In the centre of the square is **Kennedy Park**, named after US President John F Kennedy who visited Galway in 1963; a stone tablet in the square marks the occasion.

On the western side of the square is **Browne's Doorway** (1627), a fragment from the home of one of the city's merchant rulers. Behind Browne's Doorway is a curious, rusted, metal sculpture supposed to evoke the sails of a *húicéir* (hooker), a traditional Galway vessel. It was designed by Eamon

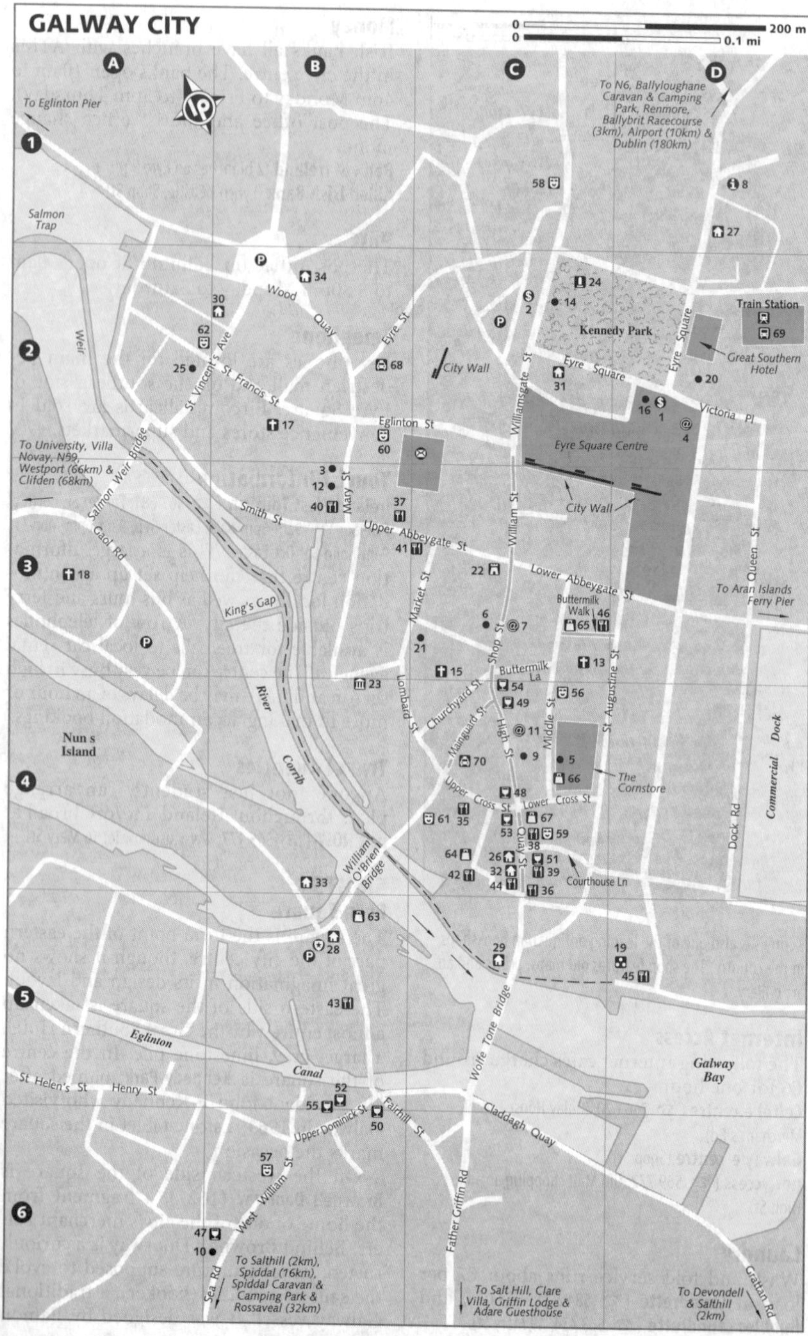
GALWAY CITY
0
200 m
0
0.1 mi
A
B
C
D
1
2
3
4
5
6
To Eglinton Pier
To N6, Ballyloughane Caravan & Camping Park, Renmore, Ballybrit Racecourse (3km), Airport (10km) & Dublin (180km)
Salmon Trap
Weir
Wood Quay
St Vincent's Ave
St Francis St
Eyre St
City Wall
Williamsgate St
Kennedy Park
Eyre Square
Train Station
Great Southern Hotel
Victoria Pl
Eglinton St
Eyre Square Centre
City Wall
To University, Villa Novay, N59, Westport (66km) & Clifden (68km)
Salmon Weir Bridge
Gaol Rd
Mary St
Smith St
Upper Abbeygate St
Lower Abbeygate St
William St
Queen St
To Aran Islands Ferry Pier
King's Gap
Market St
Buttermilk Walk
Shop St
Buttermilk La
Lombard St
Churchyard St
River Corrib
Nun s Island
Mainguard St
High St
Middle St
St Augustine St
The Cornstore
Commercial Dock
Dock Rd
Upper Cross St
Lower Cross St
Quay St
Courthouse Ln
William O'Brien Bridge
Wolfe Tone Bridge
Galway Bay
Eglinton Canal
St Helen's St
Henry St
Upper Dominick St
Fairhill St
Claddagh Quay
West William St
Father Griffin Rd
Sea Rd
Grattan Rd
To Salthill (2km), Spiddal (16km), Spiddal Caravan & Camping Park & Rossaveal (32km)
To Salt Hill, Clare Villa, Griffin Lodge & Adare Guesthouse
To Devondell & Salthill (2km)

INFORMATION
- Allied Irish Bank (see 22)
- Bank of Ireland 1 D2
- Bank of Ireland 2 C2
- Bubbles Laundrette 3 B3
- Celtel e.centre 4 D2
- Charlie Byrne's 5 C4
- Eason's 6 C3
- Galway e-centre 7 C3
- Ireland West Tourism 8 D1
- Kenny's Bookstore & Gallery 9 C4
- Laundrette 10 B6
- net@ccess 11 C4
- usit NOW 12 B3

SIGHTS & ACTIVITIES pp373-6
- Augustinian Church 13 C3
- Browne's Doorway 14 C2
- Collegiate Church of St Nicholas of Myra 15 C3
- Eyre Square Centre Entrance 16 D2
- Franciscan Abbey 17 B2
- Galway Cathedral 18 A3
- Galway City Museum 19 D5
- Island Ferries Ticket Office 20 D2
- Lynch Memorial Window 21 C3
- Lynch's Castle 22 C3
- Nora Barnacle House 23 B4
- Pádraic O'Conaire's Statue 24 C2
- Spanish Arch (see 19)
- Town Hall 25 A2

SLEEPING pp377-8
- Barnacle's Quay Street House 26 C4
- Eyre Square Hotel 27 D1
- Galway Arms Inn 28 B5
- Jury's Galway Inn 29 C5
- Salmon Weir Hostel 30 B2
- Skeffington Arms Hotel 31 C2
- Spanish Arch Hotel 32 C4
- St Martin's B&B 33 B4
- Woodquay Hostel 34 B2

EATING pp378-9
- Busker Brownes 35 C4
- Café du Journal 36 C4
- Couch Potatas 37 B3
- Druid Lane Restaurant 38 C4
- Fat Freddy's 39 C4
- Home Plate Organics 40 B3
- Java's 41 C3
- Kirwan's Lane Creative Cuisine 42 C4
- Left Bank Café 43 B5
- McDonagh's 44 C4
- Nimmo's 45 D5
- Tulsi 46 C3

DRINKING pp379-80
- Crane Bar 47 B6
- Front Door 48 C4
- King's Head 49 C4
- Monroe's Tavern 50 B6
- Quays 51 C4
- Roísín Dubh 52 B5
- Séhán Ua Neáchtain 53 C4
- Taafe's Bar 54 C4
- Taylor's Bar 55 B5

ENTERTAINMENT p380
- An Taibhdhearc na Gaillimhe (Galway Theatre) 56 C4
- Blue Note 57 B6
- cuba 58 C1
- Druid Theatre 59 C4
- GPO 60 B2
- Karma (see 31)
- Living Room 61 C4
- Town Hall Theatre 62 A2

SHOPPING p380
- Bridge Mills 63 B5
- Design Concourse Ireland 64 C4
- Mulligan Records 65 C3
- River Deep Mountain High 66 C4
- Thomas Dillon's Claddagh Gold 67 C4

TRANSPORT pp380-1
- Abbey Cabs 68 B2
- Bus Nestor (see 8)
- Bus Station 69 D2
- City Link (see 8)
- Galway Taxis 70 C4
- Michael Nee Coaches (see 8)
- Taxi Rank (see 2)

O'Doherty and erected during the city's quincentennial in 1984.

To the north of the square is a **statue** of the Galway-born writer Pádraic O'Conaire (1883–1928), a well-known hell-raiser.

Collegiate Church of St Nicholas of Myra

This **Protestant church** (☎ 564 648; Market St; donation €3; 🕒 9am-5.45pm Mon-Sat, 1-5pm Sun Apr-Sep, 10am-4pm Mon-Sat, 1-5pm Sun Oct-Mar), easily Galway's most important monument, is Ireland's largest medieval parish church still in use. It's a beauty, with a curious pyramidal spire and some awfully intriguing lore.

The structure dates to 1320, and although it has been rebuilt and enlarged over the centuries, much of the original form has been retained. After Cromwell's victory, the church suffered the usual indignity of being used as a stable. Much harm was done – look for the damaged stonework – but at least it survived; 14 other Galway churches were razed to the ground. The church has numerous finely worked stone tombs and memorials. The two church bells date from 1590 and 1630.

Parts of the floor are paved with gravestones from the 16th to 18th centuries, and the Lynch Aisle holds the tombs of the powerful Lynch family. A large block tomb in one corner is said to be the grave of James Lynch, a mayor of Galway in the late 15th century who condemned his son, Walter, to death for killing a young Spanish visitor. As the tale goes, none of the townsfolk would act as executioner and the mayor was so dedicated to upholding justice that he personally acted as hangman, after which he went into seclusion. Outside on Market St, north of the church, is a stone plaque on the **Lynch Memorial Window**, complete with skull and crossbones beneath it, which relates this legend and claims to be the spot where the gallows stood.

At the end of the southern transept is the empty frame that is said to have once held an icon of the Virgin Mary. It was supposedly whisked off to Gyor in western Hungary in the 17th century by an Irish bishop sent packing by Cromwell.

Nora Barnacle House

Nora Barnacle (1884–1951), companion and, later, wife to James Joyce, lived in this nondescript little **house** (☎ 564 743; 8 Bowling Green; admission €2; 🕒 10am-5pm mid-May–mid-Sep, or by arrangement) for several years. The great author visited his future wife here on many occasions, beginning in 1909 and again several times during the summer of 1912. The humble abode is now a museum dedicated to the couple.

Lynch's Castle

Parts of the old stone town house called **Lynch's Castle** (cnr Shop & Upper Abbeygate Sts), which in some circles is considered the finest town castle in Ireland, date back to the 14th century. Most of the surviving structure dates from around 1600. The Lynch family was the most powerful of the 14 ruling Galway 'tribes', and members of the family held the position of mayor no less than 80 times between 1480 and 1650.

Lynch's Castle has numerous fine stone features on its façade, including the coats of arms of Henry VII, the Lynches and the Fitzgeralds of Kildare, as well as gargoyles, which are unusual in Ireland. The castle is now a branch of the Allied Irish Bank, and you can enter the foyer to peer into an old fireplace, read some rather uninspired historical notes about the castle and, in a fully modernised compartment, withdraw money from the ATM.

Spanish Arch

A 1651 drawing of Galway clearly shows its extensive city walls. But since the visits of Cromwell in 1652 and William of Orange in 1691, and the subsequent centuries of neglect, the walls have almost completely disappeared.

Near the river, east of Wolfe Tone Bridge, the **Spanish Arch** (1584) appears to have been an extension of the walls through which ships unloaded their goods – often wine and brandy from Spain. (If such walls are of interest, another surviving portion has been fully incorporated into the design of a modern shopping mall, Eyre Square Centre.)

The small, rundown **Galway City Museum** (☎ 567 641; Spanish Pde; adult/child €2/1; ⏰ 11am-1pm & 2-5pm Wed-Sun) is by the arch. There are lots of exhibits but there's no cohesive narrative to them.

Galway Cathedral

From the Spanish Arch, a pleasant riverside path runs upriver and across the Salmon Weir Bridge to the second **church** (☎ 563 577; Gaol Rd; donation €3; ⏰ 8am-6pm) in town dedicated to St Nicholas. The cathedral's full name is a mouthful: the Catholic Cathedral of Our Lady Assumed into Heaven and St Nicholas. It's a huge, imposing structure, dedicated by the late Cardinal Richard Cushing of Boston in 1965. The exterior design isn't to everyone's taste, but the interior, with its high, curved arches and central dome, has a certain, simple, solid elegance.

Salmon Weir

Salmon Weir Bridge crosses the River Corrib just east of the cathedral. Upstream is the great weir where the waters of the Corrib cascade down one of their final descents before reaching the sea in Galway Bay. The **weir** controls the water levels above it, and when the salmon are running you can often see shoals of them waiting in the clear waters before making the rush upstream.

The earliest records of Galway include references to the de Burgo family owning the fisheries on the town's weirs. Today they're owned by the Central Fisheries Board. The salmon and sea trout seasons are usually February to September, but most fish pass through the weir during May and June. To obtain fishing permits and to book a time you must write to the manager at **Galway Fisheries** (☎ 562 388; Nun's Island, Galway) several months ahead of your visit.

TOURS

If you're short on time and travelling without wheels of your own, a bus tour could be the easiest way to see nearby scenery like Connemara, the Burren or the Cliffs of Moher. You can book tours with the following companies at the tourist office in Galway or near the Salthill Promenade. Similarly, a boat trip from Galway will get you right into the heart of Lough Corrib.

Corrib Princess (☎ 592 447; www.corribprincess.ie; Woodquay; adult/family €10/25; ⏰ May-Oct) runs 1½-hour cruises on the River Corrib and Lough Corrib. The boat depart from Woodquay, just beyond Salmon Weir Bridge.

Lally Coaches (☎ 562 905; www.lallytours.com; Spiddal; adult/student €25/20) offers bus tours of Connemara or the Burren and Cliffs of Moher.

O'Neachtain Tours (☎ 553 188; naugtour@iol.ie; Spiddal; adult/student €25/20) runs daily, year-round coach tours to Connemara or the Burren and Cliffs of Moher.

FESTIVALS & EVENTS

Galway and the surrounding communities host a number of festivals throughout the year. To enhance the fun, licensing laws are usually suspended during the events, permitting pubs to remain open 24 hours a day (many restaurants also stay open). Also see p399 for the Galway Hookers races and for events related to the Oyster Festival.

The following are the highlights of Galway's calendar:

Cúirt Poetry & Literature Festival (☎ 565 886; Apr) A well-established event that takes place in Galway and grows in importance each year.

Galway Arts Festival (☎ 566 6577; www.galwayartsfestival.ie; mid-Jul) During this two-week extravaganza of theatre, music, art and comedy, the city parties round-the-clock. For good measure, one of Ireland's biggest film festivals takes place at the same time.

Galway International Oyster Festival (☎ 527 282; oysters@iol.ie; last week of Sep) Oyster-slurping is accompanied by lots of partying.

Galway Race Week (☎ 753 870; late Jul/early Aug) Horse races in Ballybrit, 3km east of the city, are the centerpiece of this week-long, round-the-clock bacchanalia.

SLEEPING

To fully take advantage of Galway's easy living, try to get a room in the city itself, rather than in nearby Salthill (which involves a 20-minute walk to the centre). There are many B&Bs west of the Corrib, within a few minutes' stroll along pretty streets to the heart of town. At busy times, B&B owners, who seem to know one another, are generally willing to refer you to someone else when their own rooms are booked. July and August are particularly busy times, but most weekends can involve some calling around if you've not booked ahead.

Budget

Galway has several hostels. The following are central and open year round except for a few days over Christmas.

Woodquay Hostel (☎ 562 618; 23-24 Wood Quay; dm €15-20) This independent hostel, just north of the city centre, keeps a spotless kitchen and the modern showers are equally clean. There's a 4am curfew.

Kinlay House (☎ 565 244; www.kinlayhouse.ie; Merchant's Rd; dm €15-21, s/d €45/52) Modern and brightly lit Kinlay House is a convenient base. It's just half a block off Eyre Square and has clean, spacious rooms. Guests can book bus tours at the reception desk, and coaches pick up and drop off in front of the building. Only drawback: no lift to 4th-floor reception.

Barnacle's Quay Street House (☎ 568 644; www.barnacles.ie; 10 Quay St; dm €12-21, s/d €46/52) In a repurposed 16th-century town house, this hostel is at the heart of the action on the pedestrian mall. It is surrounded by all the pubs, restaurants and cafés you came to Galway for. Rooms are modernised (with no hint of the building's medieval history) and a kitchen is available for self-catering.

Salmon Weir Hostel (☎ 561 133; 3 St Vincent's Ave; dm €10-15, r €35) This clean, medium-sized hostel has a 3am curfew for late-night revellers. All rooms have shared bathroom.

Ballyloughane Caravan & Camping Park (☎ 755 338; fax 752 029; Ballyloughane Beach, Renmore; car & small tent €10; 🕑 Apr-Sep) This peaceful, secure camp site is off the Dublin road (N6), 5km from Galway. Its beachside location gives it good views across the bay.

See p391 for another camping option near Galway.

Mid-Range

The annoying tendency to charge per person rates in hotels and B&Bs means there are no really sweet deals for couples.

St Martin's B&B (☎ 568 286; 2 Nun's Island Rd; s/d €35/70) St Martin's is in an ideal spot, with back window views overlooking the William O'Brien Bridge and a simple garden that reaches the banks of the Corrib. It's in a well-kept, older town house, and the home cooking, comfortable rooms, friendliness of the owners, and central location put it above everything else.

Griffin Lodge (☎ 589 440; griffinlodge@tinet.ie; 3 Father Griffin Pl; s/d €30/60; Ⓟ) This B&B, in a large old house, only five minute's walk from the centre, has eight tidy en-suite guestrooms.

Devondell (☎ 528 306; www.devondell.com; 47 Devon Park, Lower Salthill; s/d €38/76; Ⓟ) It's not central, but this B&B makes up for it with excellent breakfasts, and tea and scones in the afternoon.

Clare Villa (☎ 522 520; clarevilla@yahoo.com; 38 Threadneedle Rd; r €30-60; 🕑 Feb-Oct) There are six clean, comfy rooms, all with showers, at this modern B&B near the beach.

Galway Arms Inn (☎ 565 444; cnr Lower Dominick & Mill Sts; d €65-85) Above a pub facing the William O'Brien Bridge, this nondescript inn has 11 simple but neat rooms. It's no beauty, but very central. Breakfast is included.

Villa Nova (☎ 524 849; 40 Lower Newcastle Rd; s/d €35/70; Ⓟ) In a quiet recess along the main

CLADDAGH

If you ever go across the sea to Ireland
Then maybe at the closing of your day
You will sit and watch the moon rise over Claddagh
And see the sun go down on Galway Bay

– *Arthur Cohalan, 'Galway Bay'*

A romantic icon in the hearts and songs of Irish-Americans for generations, Claddagh village was once Galway's main commercial fishing centre – up to 3000 people and 300 boats were based here at one stage. Strictly speaking, the district begins at the southern end of Wolfe Tone Bridge. Among the boats were the traditional Galway sailing vessels with pitched black hulls and rust-coloured sails known as *púcáin* and *gleoitoige*, today collectively called Galway hookers.

Claddagh used to have its own costume and dialect, as well as its own king. Although the traditional Claddagh of thatched roofs, Irish speakers and fishing boats disappeared in the 1930s, you'll still see many people wearing Claddagh rings. The rings depict a crowned heart nestling between two outstretched hands; it signifies friendship (the hands), loyalty (the crown) and love (the heart). If the heart points towards the hand, the wearer is taken or married; towards the fingertip means that he or she is looking for a partner. It has been the wedding ring used throughout much of Connaught since the mid-18th century.

road towards the University, Villa Nova is a friendly B&B. All its four rooms are en suite.

Top End

Adare Guesthouse (☎ 582 638; adare@iol.ie; 9 Father Griffin Pl; s/d €55/90; P) The Adare is in a large house overlooking a children's playground. It's convenient, tidy, furnished almost completely in pine, and just a five-minute walk from the centre.

Eyre Square Hotel (☎ 69633; eyresquarehotel@eircom.net; Eyre Sq; r €179) This large, fully refurbished hotel offers enticing extras for stylin' tourists, like hair dryers and trouser presses.

Jury's Galway Inn (☎ 566 444; jurysinngalway@jurysdoyle.com; Quay St; r €106) Overlooking the Corrib and Wolfe Tone Bridge, this is a completely modern, full-service hotel. Rooms can accommodate a family of four at no additional charge.

Skeffington Arms Hotel (☎ 563 173; www.skeffington.ie; Eyre Sq; r €130) Overlooking the square, the Skeff has 23 spacious and slightly pompous rooms. This is a modern, full-service hotel in a classic old building with an attractive pub. Breakfast is included.

Spanish Arch Hotel (☎ 569 600; www.spanisharchhotel.ie; Quay St; r €150) On the main drag, this 20-room hotel fusses over its guests with antiques and designer opulence.

EATING

Restaurants

Home Plate Organics (☎ 561 475; 13 Mary St; breakfast & lunch €4-7, dinner €7-10; 🕑 8.30am-9.30pm Mon-Sat) Home Plate is smart and homey and serves up high-quality, hearty meals in heaping quantities. It's the best deal in town, whether you crave roasted meat, a ciabatta sandwich or one of a variety of vegetarian omelettes.

Nimmo's (☎ 561 114; Long Walk; mains €12-23; 🕑 6-10pm Wed-Sat, 1-4pm & 6-10pm Sun) Hidden behind the Spanish Arch, Nimmo's is romantic and dimly lit for a special evening out. The menu is creative, with a strong seafood bias. A quality splurge.

McDonagh's (☎ 565 001; 22 Quay St; mains €4-7; 🕑 noon-3pm & 5-10pm Mon-Sat) McDonagh's is Galway's best chipper, and its sturdy, galley-like eating room is always crowded. Cod, plaice and haddock, lathered in a tasty batter, are churned nonstop out of the fryer.

Kirwan's Lane Creative Cuisine (☎ 568 266; Kirwan's Lane; mains €15-25; 🕑 noon-2pm & 6-10pm Mon-Sat) A stylish, somewhat formal restaurant with devoted followers, Kirwan's Lane spruces up Irish cuisine with international ingredients. Reservations advised.

Druid Lane Restaurant (☎ 563 015; 9 Quay St; mains €15-21; 🕑 5pm-late Tue-Sat) An intimate, tastefully decorated restaurant, Druid Lane serves imaginative, modern Irish dishes. Pastas, roasts and seafood anchor the menu, and the wine list is extensive.

Tulsi (☎ 564 831; 3 Buttermilk Walk; mains €12-19; 🕓 noon-2pm Mon-Fri, 6-11pm daily) Perhaps a bit overpriced, Tulsi is nevertheless the best choice for a curry in Galway.

Couch Potatas (☎ 561 664; 40 Upper Abbeygate St; mains €7; 🕓 noon-10pm) The specialty here is baked potatoes, tastily endowed with heaping portions of chicken strips, bologna sauce, chilli con carne, or curry. One potato, served with a tossed salad, will fill you up.

Fat Freddy's (☎ 567 279; Quay St; mains €7-11; 🕓 noon-10pm) With its chequered tablecloths and candles in wine bottles, Freddy's is fun because it draws a lively crowd day and night. The food is bland, but a sufficient base for boozing.

Cafés

Busker Brownes (☎ 563 377; Upper Cross St; breakfast €2-8, lunch €6-9; 🕓 10.30am-11.30pm Mon-Thu, 10.30-12.30am Fri-Sat, 12.30-11.30pm Sun) A café-bar that successfully weds medieval stonework with suave lounge décor, Busker Brownes does daytime meals. With tables beside the front windows, this is a nice spot for coffee and the morning paper.

Café du Journal (☎ 568 426; Quay St; mains €2-8; 🕓 10am-6pm winter, 10am-10pm summer) Arty deep-thinkers and French expats congregate here for zesty sandwiches, strong coffee and animated conversation.

Java's (Upper Abbeygate St; sandwiches €5; 🕓 11am-4am Mon-Sat, 2pm-3am Sun) Java's, a small room with an open fire going on cold days, is a good spot to head for an afternoon coffee, or to revive yourself with a sweet snack when it's long past midnight.

Left Bank Café (☎ 567 791; 49 Lower Dominick St; mains €3-7; 🕓 9am-7pm) Equal parts homey and bohemian, Left Bank dishes out a good Irish breakfast, sandwiches, a smattering of cooked meals and so-so coffee.

DRINKING

Visitors will notice that Galway has two, somewhat separate hubs for entertainment, divided by the river. The greatest concentration of pubs and clubs, around the pedestrian drag, is slightly more touristy but certainly worth a thorough investigation. Among the superpubs and sleek lounges are some graceful old watering holes. The west side, while not necessarily quieter, has a local feel and attracts a slightly hipper crowd. Either way, you can't go wrong, and the river is no obstacle to taking in pubs and clubs from either side.

Séhán Ua Neáchtain (☎ 568 820; 17 Upper Cross St) Known simply as Neáchtains, this dusty old pub has a truly fabulous atmosphere and attracts an eccentric, mixed crowd. Now and then someone will sing at the piano, to be barely heard above the din of amiable conversation.

Front Door (☎ 563 757; High St) This is Galway's best pub for an afternoon pint, thanks to its easy-going regulars and a row of front windows casting a most pleasing light.

Róisín Dubh (☎ 586 540; Upper Dominick St) Appearing like a reliable local boozer, Róisín Dubh is better known as *the* place to see new rock and roll talents before they get too big for such intimate venues. On occasion it's also good for traditional music.

Crane Bar (☎ 587 419; 2 Sea Rd) The Crane is an atmospheric old pub, west of the Corrib, that's good for a quiet pint even though a top-notch *ceilidh* (traditional music session) session is usually on.

Taylor's Bar (☎ 587 239; Upper Dominick St) A down-to-earth, arty crowd has claimed this unassuming old boozer. At its best, when casual *ceilidh* sessions take place round a table in the unadorned back room, Taylor's can feel like a private party. A pleasant beer garden is open in summer.

Quays (☎ 568 347; Quay St) One of Galway's most famous pubs, the Quays is another enormous tavern with an endless series of atmospheric rooms and passageways. There are some great vantage points from which to watch the upbeat crowd or the live music (traditional to pop) that's on most nights.

King's Head (☎ 566 630; 15 High St) The King's Head is a superpub fashioned from a 17th-century stone house. Beyond its narrow frontage it opens up way back to a small stage. Rock bands play most nights, and a popular jazz session takes place Sunday morning.

Taaffe's Bar (☎ 564 066; 19 Shop St) Taaffe's is well-loved for its nightly Irish music sessions, which begin at 5pm. The pub itself is nothing to marvel at, having been stripped of some of its charm when remodelled.

Monroe's Tavern (☎ 583 397; Upper Dominick St) A reliable spot for traditional music and ballads, Monroe's is the only pub in the city to offer set dancing (Tuesday).

ENTERTAINMENT

The free *Galway Advertiser* includes listings of what's on in the city. It's available every Thursday at the tourist office and newsstands around town, and copies get snatched up fast.

Nightclubs

Clubs generally get cranking around 11pm and don't wind down till around 2am. Admission prices vary according to the nightly programme.

Blue Note (☎ 589 116; 3 West William St) DJs spin every night in this slightly grungy club, and an interesting, mixed crowd generally makes the scene. There's usually no cover charge.

cuba (☎ 565 991; www.cuba.ie; Eyre Sq) Exuding Latin swank and attracting exuberant crowds, cuba has three cavernous floors with soulful DJs and live bands, often going simultaneously. The club also bills comedy acts and swing orchestras. Check the website or local papers to see what's on. During the day, good food is served from the ground-floor bar.

GPO (☎ 563 073; Eglinton St) Trendy 20-somethings flock here for 1980s, funk and hip-hop dance grooves. Cheap drinks are no deterrent either.

Karma (☎ 563 173; Eyre Sq) Downstairs in the Skeffington Arms Hotel, this dance club attracts a young, smartly dressed professional crowd.

Living Room (Bridge St) A young, well-heeled crowd is attracted to the Living Room's retro décor, nightly DJs and, in the early evening, televised sporting events.

Theatre

An Taibhdhearc na Gaillimhe (☎ 562 024; Middle St) Perhaps not of much interest to non-Irish speakers, this Galway Theatre stages plays in Irish.

Druid Theatre (☎ 568 617; Chapel Lane) The long-established Druid is famed for its experimental works by young Irish playwrights.

Town Hall Theatre (☎ 569 777; Courthouse Sq) On the corner of St Vincent's Ave, this theatre tends to feature Broadway or West End shows and visiting singers.

SHOPPING

When the weather is good, Galway's **Farmer's Market** can be an exuberant festival in its own right. Organic farmers and hippy crafts vendors line up along Churchyard St every Saturday morning.

There are a few general purpose shopping centres: the big **Eyre Square Centre**, southeast of Eyre Square; **Bridge Mills**, in an old mill building by the river at the western end of William O'Brien Bridge; and the **Cornstore** on Middle St.

Specialty stores are more Galway's style. Following are a few standout shops in the city centre:

Design Concourse Ireland (☎ 566 927; Kirwan's Lane) The Design Concourse Ireland is worth perusing if you're interested in familiarising yourself with contemporary Irish design in jewellery, tableware, greeting cards and high fashion in Donegal tweed.

Mulligan Records (☎ 564 961; 5 Middle St) Drop into this record store for Irish music and folk music from around the world; it does mail order.

O'Maille (☎ 562 696; 16 High St) If it's cold and damp out, nothing will suit you better than Irish woollens. This is the best shop in town for such things as tweed caps, Aran sweaters, and traditional long-sleeved undershirts just like grampaw used to wear.

River Deep Mountain High (☎ 563 938; Middle St) This is one of the better places for outdoor clothing and equipment.

Thomas Dillon's Claddagh Gold (☎ 566 365; 1 Quay St) The memento of choice for many visitors to Galway is a Claddagh ring in silver or gold. Before making your purchase you can learn a bit about the tradition of these rings here and see some vintage examples in Dillon's back-room 'museum'. See the boxed text on p378 for further details.

GETTING THERE & AWAY

Bus

From the **bus station** (☎ 562 000), just off Eyre Square, there are frequent Bus Éireann services to all major cities in the Republic and the North. The one-way fare to Dublin (3¾ hours) is €13.

A lot of private companies are also represented.

Bus Nestor (☎ 797 484; busnestor@eircom.net) runs five to eight daily services to Dublin via Dublin airport. Buses leave from outside the tourist office every couple of hours or so between 6.30am and 5.25pm.

Hourly buses to Dublin and Dublin airport, run by **City Link** (☎ 564 163; info@citylink.ie; Dublin/airport fare €10/15), depart from the tourist office several times daily.

Michael Nee Coaches (☎ 095-51082) runs two or three daily services to towns throughout Connemara. Buses depart from Forster St in Galway, just across from the tourist office.

Train

From the **train station** (☎ 564 222), just off Eyre Square, there are up to five trains daily to/from Dublin's Euston Station (one way from €20, three hours). Connections with other train routes can be made at Athlone (one hour).

GETTING AROUND

To/From the Airport

A bus runs daily Monday to Saturday between the airport and Galway bus station (€3.15). It leaves the airport at 1.25pm, and leaves the bus station at 12.50pm. A taxi to/from the airport costs about €15.

Bicycle

Most hostels, including Kinlay House and Salmon Weir Hostel, hire bikes. At **Europa Bicycles** (☎ 563 355), on Earl's Island opposite Galway Cathedral, bikes cost €10 for 24 hours.

Bus

You can walk to almost everything in Galway and even out to Salthill, but there are regular buses from Eyre Square. Bus No 1 runs from Eyre Square to Salthill and sometimes to Blackrock; bus No 2 goes from Knocknacarra and Blackrock through Eyre Square to Renmore; bus No 3 runs between Eyre Square and Castlepark; and bus No 4 goes to Newcastle.

Car

Drivers will need parking discs to park on the street; these are available from the tourist office and from newsagencies. The car park just over William O'Brien Bridge is next to the garda station, so it should be safe.

Taxi

Taxi ranks are located on Eyre Square, on Bridge St, and next to the bus/train station. You can also catch a cab by dropping by a taxi office. Try **Abbey Cabs** (☎ 569 469; Eyre St) or **Galway Taxis** (☎ 561 111; Mainguard St).

ARAN ISLANDS

☎ 091

The Aran Islands can be an unforgettable highlight of your trip to Ireland, or an extraordinary disappointment. It all depends on what you're after, which islands you go to and what time of year you visit. These stark, rocky outcrops are not always what visitors expect them to be. At their best, they are atmospheric, dramatic, slightly subdued and far from the modern world. Intense landscapes of small fields separated by a most impressive web of stone walls are conducive to long, contemplative walks. When the islands succeed in lulling the visitor to their ancient tempo, time spent following these dense stone mazes creeps by very slowly and it's strangely satisfying. However, the islands aren't well suited to large numbers of tourists, and a maddening crowd does show up in July and August.

Inishmaan and Inisheer are sublime any time of year, but especially in the early spring, when erratic weather draws out the islands' subtle colours and keeps the number of visitors down.

Inishmór, the largest island and most easily accessible from Galway, features one of Ireland's most important and impressive archaeological sites. There's generally more fun to be had on Inishmór, with tourists cruising its dusty roads on bikes and making merry in its pubs and restaurants. But Inishmór is the least appealing island in many ways. It is less beautiful, and Kilronan, its largest town, suffers from crass commercialism.

The islands are really an extension of the limestone escarpment that forms the Burren, and they look it. The outer periphery of the islands resembles cracked grey pavement that gives way, as the islands rise, to shallow topsoil on which buttercups, daisies and spring gentian naturally take root. The small pastures, so solidly fenced in, are covered with a very soft grass that would be irresistibly tempting for an afternoon nap if it weren't for random heaps of cow dung scattered about. The western edges of Inishmaan and Inishmór are dramatic, perfectly vertical cliffs, jutting 50m to 100m above a tumultuous surf.

The ancient forts on the islands – most notably Dún Aengus on Inishmór and Dún Chonchúir on Inishmaan – are some of the oldest archaeological remains in Ireland, and exploring them freely is a rare delight. The islands also have a few *clocháns* (dry stone beehive hut), resembling igloos made of stone, in which early Christian monks retreated.

Services are limited on the islands. There are no ATMs and restaurants tend to stay shut during the winter. Be sure to seek advice on such matters when you book accommodation and plan accordingly.

HISTORY

Almost nothing is known about the people who built the massive Iron Age stone structures on Inishmór and Inishmaan. These sites are commonly referred to as 'forts', but are actually believed to have served as pagan religious centres. In folklore, the forts are said to have been built by the Firbolgs, a Celtic tribe who invaded Ireland from Europe in prehistoric times.

It is believed that people came to the islands to farm, which would have presented a major challenge. The topsoil was rarely more than a foot deep, if that, and it was laden with stones. As a matter of necessity the early settlers began building the 1600km of stone walls we see today, which put extracted stones to good use (the stone walls keep precious dirt from blowing off to sea and help regulate livestock grazing habits). These early islanders augmented their soil by hauling seaweed and sand up from the shore. People also fished the surrounding waters on long *currach* (rowing boat made of a framework of laths covered with tarred canvas) which still remain as a symbol of the Aran Islands.

Christianity reached the islands remarkably quickly, and some of the earliest monastic settlements were founded by St Enda (Éanna) in the 5th century. Any remains you see today are later, from the 8th century onwards. Enda appears to have been an Irish chief who converted to Christianity and spent some time studying in Rome before seeking out a suitably remote spot for his monastery. Many great monks studied under him, including Colmcille (or Columba), who went on to found the monastery on Iona in Scotland.

From the 14th century, control of the islands was disputed by two Gaelic families, the O'Briens and the O'Flahertys. The English took over during the reign of Elizabeth I, and in Cromwell's times a garrison was stationed here.

As Galway's importance waned, so too did that of the islands. They became a quiet and windy backwater. Isolation permitted the islanders to maintain a traditional lifestyle well into the 20th century. Irish is still very much the local tongue, and until the 1930s people wore traditional Aran dress: bright-red skirts and black shawls for women, baggy woollen trousers and waistcoats with colourful belts (or *crios*) for men. The classic cream Aran sweater knitted in complex patterns originated here. These days some older women on Inishmaan still wear shawls and skirts.

BOOKS & MAPS

The elemental nature of life on the islands has always attracted writers and artists. The dramatist JM Synge (1871–1909) spent a lot of time on the islands, and his play *Riders to the Sea* (1905) is set on Inishmaan. His book *The Aran Islands* (1907) is the classic account of life here and is readily available in Penguin paperback.

The American Robert Flaherty came to the islands in 1934 to film *Man of Aran*, a dramatic account of daily life. It became a classic and there are regular screenings of it in Kilronan on Inishmór.

The islands have produced their own talent, particularly the writer Liam O'Flaherty (1896–1984) from Inishmór. O'Flaherty, who wandered around North and South America before returning to Ireland in 1921 and fighting in the Civil War, wrote several outstanding novels, including *Famine*.

The mapmaker Tim Robinson has written a wonderful, though not easily accessible, two-volume account of his explorations on Aran called *Stones of Aran: Pilgrimage* and *Stones of Aran: Labyrinthe*. His *The Aran Islands: A Map and Guide* is superb.

Two other excellent publications in paperback are *The Book of Aran*, edited by Anne Korf and published by Tír Eolas, consisting of articles by 17 specialists covering diverse aspects of the islands' culture, and *Aran Reader* (Lilliput Press), edited by Breandán and Ruairí O hEither, with essays by various scholars on the islands' history, geography and culture.

GETTING THERE & AWAY

Air

All three islands have landing strips, in case you are short on time or susceptible to seasickness. The mainland departure point is Connemara regional airport at Minna, near Inverin (Indreabhán), about 35km west of Galway. A connecting bus from outside the Galway tourist office costs €3 one way. The flights take just 10 minutes.

Aer Arann (☎ 593 034; www.aerarannislands.ie) offers return flights to any of the islands five times daily (hourly in summer) and costs €44/37/25 for adults/students/children.

Boat

There's at least one boat a day heading out to the Aran Islands. Around Galway's Eyre Square there are several Island Ferries offices that'll help you set everything up in one go. Galway's tourist office will do the same. Ferries from Doolin were suspended at the time of writing because the ferry launch in County Clare was condemned.

Island Ferries (☎ 568 903, 091-572 273; www.aranislandferries.com) is the biggest ferry line, and the only one to operate daily year round. Boats leave from Rossaveal, about 40km west of Galway, which makes for a quick crossing (about 40 minutes). Return fares are €19/15/10 per adult/student/child. The return Galway–Rossaveal bus trip costs €5/2.50 per adult/child and leaves Galway's Kilroy House Hostel 1½ hours before the ferry's scheduled departure. If you have a car you can leave it free in the car park near the Island Ferries' Rossaveal office.

GETTING AROUND

The islands of Inisheer and Inishmaan are small enough to explore on foot, but to see larger Inishmór, bikes are the way to go. You can also arrange transport on Inishmór with any of the small tour vans or pony traps (see p386).

Island Ferries (see above) runs inter-island services. Connections may require a trip back to Rossaveal from October to Easter.

INISHMÓR

☎ 099 / pop 1281

The vast majority of visitors to the Aran Islands don't make it beyond Inishmór (Árainn). Understandably, the attraction is ancient Dún Aengus, the spectacular stone crescent at the edge of the island's seacliffs. Tourism has had an impact on this island though, as should be abundantly clear once you disembark from the ferry in Kilronan. An armada of tour vans will be lined up to greet you, offering a ride round the sights (not a bad idea if you're just doing a quick day trip), and in summer the little town's narrow streets gridlock just before and after the arrival of a ferry. The best way around town is aboard a hired bicycle or in a small pony trap. After climbing the hill west of Kilronan, the island's main settlement, the landscape is dominated by stone walls and boulders, scattered buildings and the odd patch of deep-green grass and potato plants.

Orientation

Inishmór is 14.5km long and a maximum 4km wide, running northwest to southeast. All ferries and boats arrive and depart from Kilronan (Cill Rónáin) on the southeastern side of the island. The airstrip is 2km further southeast of town. One principal road runs the length of the island, with many smaller lanes and paths of packed dirt and stone leading off it.

Information

The **tourist office** (☎ 61263; 🕑 11am-1pm & 2-5pm Mon-Fri, 10am-1pm & 2-5pm Sat & Sun), on the waterfront west of the ferry pier in Kilronan, can help with accommodation and planning your visit, and can also change money. The **Bank of Ireland** (🕑 10am-12.30pm & 1.30-3pm Wed), north of the village centre, has no ATM.

Sights

Inishmór has three impressive stone forts, believed to be around 2000 years old. Chief among them, two-thirds of the way down the island from Kilronan and perched on the edge of the sheer southern cliff, is one of the most amazing archaeological sites in the country, **Dún Aengus** (Dún Aonghasa; ☎ 61008; adult/child €1.20/0.50; 🕑 10am-6pm). It has a remarkable chevaux de frise, a defensive forest of sharp stone spikes around the exterior of the fort to help stop any would-be raiders. If you

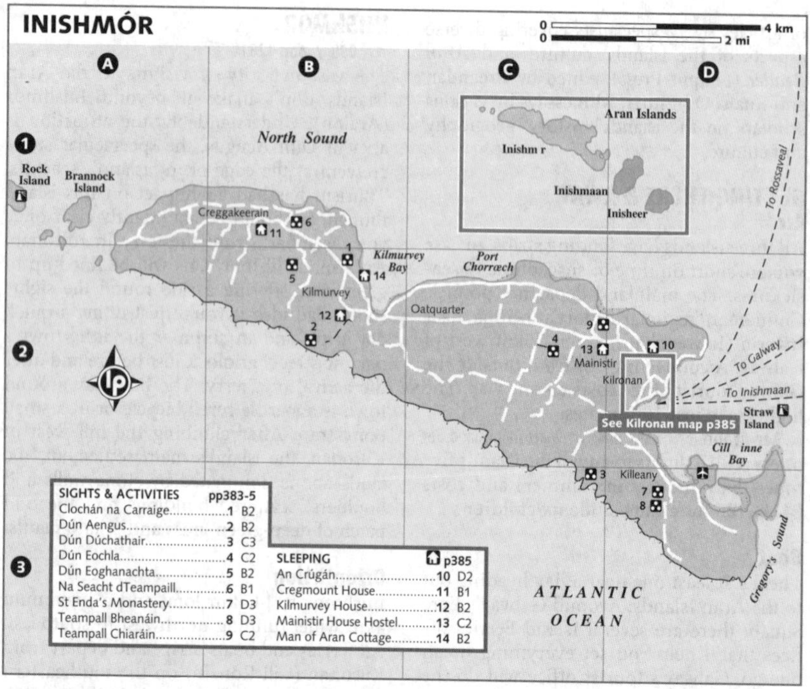

go at a quieter time, such as late evening, when there are fewer visitors, you won't forget the sight and sound of the powerful swells pounding the cliff face. There are no guard rails and the winds can be strong, so be careful; tourists have been blown off and killed on the rock shelf below. Of course, that won't keep people from creeping on hands and knees to the precipice for a peek over the edge.

Along the road between Kilronan and Dún Aengus is the smaller **Dún Eochla**, a perfectly circular fort. Directly south of Kilronan and dramatically perched on a promontory is **Dún Dúchathair**, surrounded on three sides by cliffs.

The ruins of numerous stone churches trace the island's monastic history. The small **Teampall Chiaráin** (Church of St Kieran), with a high cross in the churchyard, is near Kilronan. To the southeast, near Cill Éinne Bay, is the early-Christian **Teampall Bheanáin** (Church of St Benen). Past Kilmurvey is the perfect **Clochán na Carraige**, an early-Christian stone hut that stands 2.5m tall, and the ruins of various small early-Christian remains known rather inaccurately as the **Na Seacht dTeampaill** (Seven Churches), consisting of a couple of ruined churches, monastic houses and some fragments of a high cross from the 8th or 9th century. To the south is **Dún Eoghanachta**, another circular fort. Near the airstrip are the sunken remains of a church said to be the site of **St Enda's Monastery** in the 5th century.

There's a fine beach at **Kilmurvey**, west of Kilronan, and it's pleasant to stay here away from the bustle of Kilronan. Before the beach, in the sheltered little bay of **Port Chorrúch**, up to 50 grey seals make their home, sunning and feeding in the shallows.

To have a more informed appreciation of the island, stop in at **Ionad Árann** (Aran Heritage Centre; ☎ 61355; www.visitaranislands.com; Kilronan; adult/child €5.50/4; 🕑 11am-1pm & 2-5pm Mon-Fri, 10am-1pm & 2-5pm Sat & Sun). Just off the main road leading out of Kilronan, the centre offers a useful introduction to the geology, wildlife, history and culture of the three islands. The admission fee includes a viewing of Robert Flaherty's 1934 film *Man of Aran*, screened three times daily. The centre also has a coffee shop.

Sleeping

The **tourist office** (☎ 61263) can help book rooms, and a number of places to stay are near enough from the pier to check out before deciding.

HOSTELS

An Aharla Hostel (☎ 61305; Kilronan; dm €10) In a laid-back former farmhouse, quietly positioned in a grove of trees (a rarity on these islands), An Aharla has two four-bed dorms. Conveniently, Joe Watty's Bar is just paces away.

Artist's Lodge Hostel (☎ 61456; Kilronan; dm €10) This small, modern property has good ocean views and a complimentary light breakfast, but doesn't really have an 'artistic' vibe.

Kilronan Hostel (☎ 61255; www.kilronanhostel.com; Kilronan; dm €15) This clean, friendly hostel is a short walk from the pier. The floors have been insulated, so although the hostel is above Tí Joe Mac's pub, you hear very little noise. Breakfast is included, and guests can hire bikes for the day (€10).

Mainistir House Hostel (☎ 61169; fax 61351; Mainistir; dm €12, s/d €20/32, family €50) This appealing 60-bed hostel, on the main road north of Kilronan, is a fun place for young travellers, and for families as well. It has a large kitchen, and bicycles for hire. Breakfast, bed linen and free pick-up are included in the rates.

B&BS

St Brendan's House B&B (☎ 61149; stbrendansaran@eircom.net; Kilronan; s/d €25/50) A cheerful old house with views of the Kilronan harbour. It's a little rough around the edges, but the hospitality makes up for it. Guests can get lower rates if taking shared bathroom or passing on breakfast.

Claí Bán (☎ 61111; Kilronan; d €45-60) At the end of a quiet lane, welcoming Claí Bán has clean, modern facilities and good views of the bay from its dining area.

Cregmount House (☎ 61139; Creggakeerain; s €25-40, d €50-80; Apr-Oct; ⊠) At the northwestern end of the island, 9km from Kilronan, Cregmount House is a pleasant, three-room B&B with views across Galway Bay.

Dormer House (☎ 61125; Kilronan; d €50-64) Dormer House is a large, clean B&B, centrally located, with 12 rooms, some en suite, some with shared bathroom.

Kilmurvey House (☎ 61218; www.kilmurveyhouse.com; Kilmurvey; s/d €40/80; Apr-Sep) B&B here is in a lovely, old stone mansion on the path leading to Dún Aengus and close to a Blue Flag beach.

Man of Aran Cottage (☎ 61301; Kilmurvey; s/d €40/70) This cosy, thatched B&B overlooking Kilmurvey Bay was built for the 1930s film. Age has worn some of its ersatz sheen. It serves great food and rents out bikes.

An Crúgán (☎ 61150; www.ancrugan.com; Kilronan; s/d €50/64; Mar-Oct; P) Located off the main road north of Kilronan, An Crúgán has six well-appointed rooms, and bikes for hire.

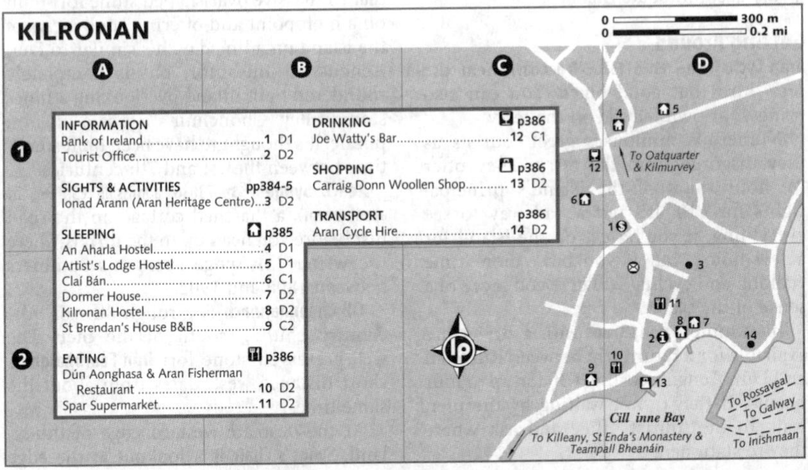

Eating

There's not much going on, in terms of fine eating, on Inishmór. There's a Spar supermarket in Kilronan.

Dún Aonghasa/Aran Fisherman Restaurant (☎ 61104; Kilronan; mains €7-20; 🕑 12.30-4pm & 5-9pm) A general-purpose restaurant with an extensive menu that will please the entire family. Fish features prominently, but there are also pizzas and sandwiches on offer.

Mainistir House Hostel (☎ 61169; fax 61351; buffet €12; 🕑 8pm-close summer, 7pm-close winter) Mainistir House serves great-value organic, largely vegetarian buffet dinners; book ahead.

Man of Aran Cottage (☎ 61301; Kilmurvey; sandwiches from €2.50, set dinner €20; 🕑 11.30am-7.30pm Apr-Sep) This idyllic place serves fresh fish and flavourful organic vegetables and herbs, which the owners grow in their garden. It offers light lunches during the day, and full dinners in the evening.

Drinking

Joe Watty's Bar (Kilronan) The best pub on the island is Joe Watty's, where a traditional session is on most nights. It's just north of Kilronan. Pub food is served.

Shopping

A hand-knitted Aran sweater is top of many people's shopping lists when visiting the islands. In Kilronan, **Carraig Donn Woollen Shop** (☎ 61123; Kilronan), near the old pier, will gladly accommodate this need.

Getting Around

Aran Cycle Hire (☎ 61132; €10 per day), near the pier, hires out good bikes. You can also bring your own bicycle on the ferry.

Numerous minibuses greet tourists as they disgorge from the ferry. They offer 2½-hour tours of the island's principal sights for €10. It's not a bad way to see everything, if you're just on the island for a few hours, but if you have more time walking and cycling will give you more of a sense of the place.

In summer, **pony traps** with a driver are available for a return trip between Kilronan and Dún Aengus, costing €30 for up to four people. If they're not waiting by the pier, walk to the tourist office and ask where they're stationed.

INISHMAAN

☎ 099 / pop 200

This is a sweet spot. The cows here groan with what must be the pure pleasure of grazing in such a peaceful place – or maybe they just need to be milked? Early Christian monks, seeking solitude but not wishing to compromise their refined sense of natural beauty, were drawn to Inishmaan (Inis Meáin), as was the author JM Synge, who spent five summers here over a century ago. The virtues they found in this island largely survive today: endless, snaking stone walls up to 2m high; docile farm animals; warm-hearted Irish speakers; impressive old forts; startling cliffs; and a welcomed respite from the fast-paced modern world. To their credit, the islanders here are mildly indifferent to the prospect of attracting tourist euros, so visitor facilities are limited.

Inishmaan is about 5km long by 3km wide. Walking is a fine way to get around.

Orientation & Information

Most of Inishmaan's buildings are spread out along the road that runs east–west across the centre of the island. The principal boat landing is on the eastern side of the island, while the airstrip is in the northeastern corner. In An Córa, the helpful **Inishmaan Island Co-operative** (☎ 73010), northwest of the pier and post office, dispenses tourist information.

Sights

The chief archaeological site is **Dún Conchúir**, a massive oval-shaped stone fort built on a high point and offering good views of the island on a fine day. It's similar to Dún Aengus on Inishmór, but is completely round and built inland overlooking a limestone valley. Chonchúir's age is a bit of a puzzle: it's thought to have been built sometime between the 1st and 7th centuries.

Teach Synge (☎ 73036; admission €3; 🕑 by appointment), a thatched cottage on the road just before you head up to the fort, is where the writer JM Synge spent his summers between 1898 and 1902.

Cill Cheannannach is a rough 8th- or 9th-century church, south of the pier. The well-preserved stone fort **Dún Fearbhaigh**, a short distance west, dates from about the same time.

At the desolate western edge of the island, **Synge's Chair** is a lookout at the edge of a sheer limestone cliff with the pounding surf from Gregory's Sound booming below. In a well-chosen spot the cliff ledge is often sheltered from the wind, so do like Synge did and find a comfortable seat to take it all in.

On the walk out to Synge's Chair a sign points the way to a **clochán**, hidden behind a house and shed. It's a small, domed monk dwelling that vaguely resembles a beehive. Needless to say, stark little huts such as this one did not represent the 'easy life'. Crazy monks!

In the east of the island, about 500m north of the boat landing stage, is **Trá Leitreach**, a safe, sheltered beach.

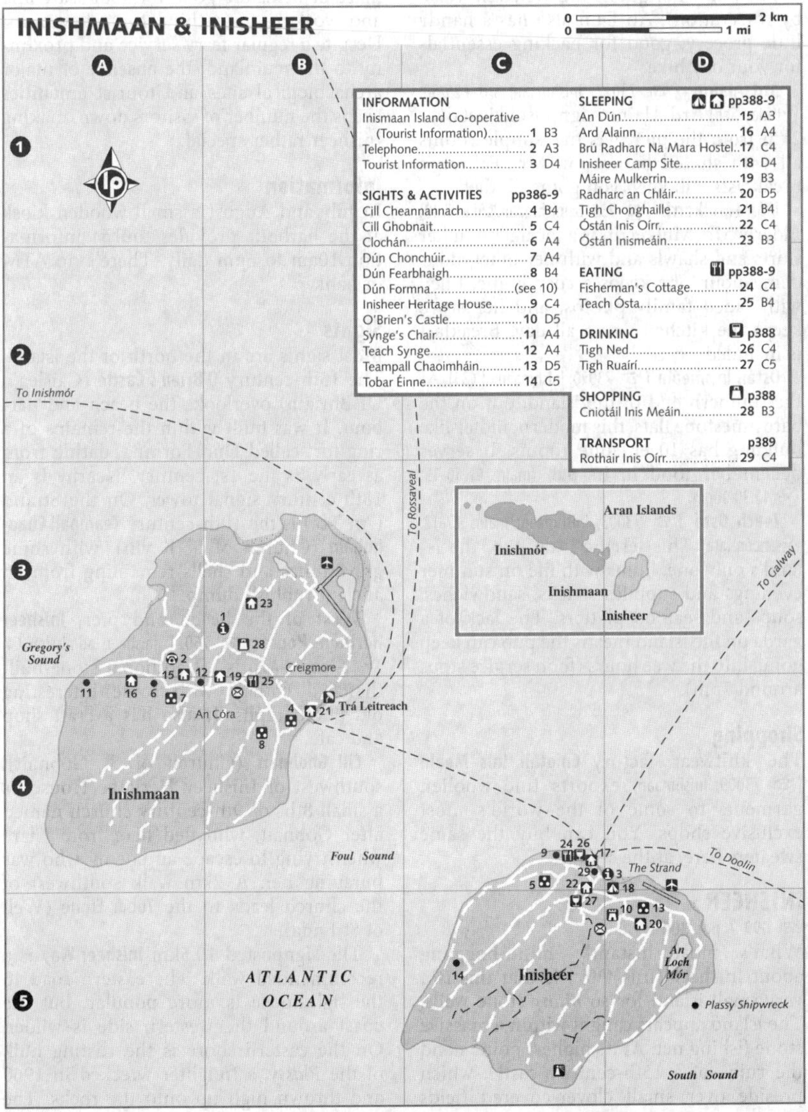

COUNTY GALWAY

Sleeping & Eating

Most B&Bs serve evening meals, mostly using organically grown food, costing around €20.

An Dún (☎ 73047; Inishmaan; s/d €38/64; ☒) Opposite the entrance to Dún Chonchúir, modern An Dún has comfortable en-suite rooms and a sauna. It serves very hearty set dinners and nonguests are welcome (€20; by reservation). An Dún also has a handy little grocery, good for packing essentials for your day hike.

Ard Alainn (☎ 73027; Inishmaan; s/d €25/50; ⏲ May-Sep) Ard Alainn, signposted just over 2km from the pier, has five simple rooms all with shared bathroom. Mrs Faherty's breakfasts will keep you going all day.

Máire Mulkerrin (☎ 73016; Inishmaan; s/d €20/40) Elderly Mrs Mulkerrin is a local icon in her skirts and shawls and with her quiet, dour demeanour. She keeps a cosy home, filled with faded family photos, and her stove keeps the kitchen warm all day. Breakfast is included.

Óstán Inismeáin (☎ 73020; Inishmaan; d €35) At the southern end of the island, out on the bare limestone flats, this modern, motel-like building has 10 en-suite rooms. It serves decent bar food in its **pub** (mains €7.50-15; ⏲ 12.30-10pm).

Teach Ósta (☎ 73003; Inishmaan; mains €7-12; ⏲ noon-late) This terrific little pub, the island's only one, hums with life on summer evenings and supplies snacks, sandwiches, soups and seafood platters. The lack of a garda on the island means the pub can keep going into the wee hours (food service stops around 7pm).

Shopping

The knitwear factory **Cniotáil Inis Meáin** (☎ 73009; Inishmaan) exports fine woollen garments to some of the world's most exclusive shops. You can buy the same sweaters here, at the source.

INISHEER

☎ 099 / pop 300

What's most instantly mind-boggling about Inisheer (Inis Oírr) is that this is a *very* small island for so *many* stone walls. The island appears caught within a massive stone fishing net. At its highest point stand the ruins of a 15th-century castle, which preside over small clover-covered fields and a small village. There's a small sandy beach next to the pier.

Only 8km off the coast from Doolin in County Clare, Inisheer is the smallest of the three Aran Islands. There isn't much to do here, although at night the pubs sometimes get cranking and are known to stay open far past midnight. Days spent wandering the maze of fields are good for soul-searching and working up a thirst for a few pints. Despite a regular ferry service and proximity to the mainland, the absence of major archaeological sites and tourist amenities keeps the number of visitors down, making Inisheer rather special.

Information

In July and August a small wooden kiosk at the harbour provides tourist information 10am to 6pm daily. There's no ATM or bank.

Sights

Most sights are in the north of the island. The 15th-century **O'Brien's Castle** (Caislea'n Uí Bhriain) overlooks the beach and harbour. It was built within the remains of a ring fort called Dún Formna, dating from as early as the 1st century. Nearby is an 18th-century signal tower. On the Strand (An Trá) is the 10th-century **Teampall Chaoimháin** (Church of St Kevin), with some gravestones and shells remaining from an ancient rubbish dump.

West of the beach and pier, **Inisheer Heritage House** (☎ 75021; Inisheer; admission €1; ⏲ 2-4pm Jul-Aug) is a traditional stone-built thatched cottage with some interesting old photographs. It also has a craft shop and café.

Cill Ghobnait (Church of St Gobnait), southwest of Inisheer Heritage House, is a small 8th- or 9th-century church named after Gobnait, who fled here from Clare when trying to escape an enemy who was pursuing her. A 2km walk southwest of the church leads to the **Tobar Éinne** (Well of St Enda).

The signposted 10.5km **Inisheer Way** is a recommended walk. The eastern road to the lighthouse is more popular, but the coast around the western side is wilder. On the eastern shore is the rusting hulk of the *Plassy*, a freighter wrecked in 1960 and thrown high up onto the rocks. The uninhabited lighthouse (1857) on the island's southern tip, with its neat enclosure, is off limits.

Sleeping & Eating

Inisheer Camp Site (☎ 75008; Inisheer; tent sites €5; ⌚ May-Sep) This is a basic camp site overlooking the windswept Strand, and it has showers.

Brú Radharc Na Mara Hostel (☎ 75024; maire.searraigh@oceanfree.net; Inisheer; dm €12, B&B €30; ⌚ Mar-Oct) This spotless Independent Holiday Hostels of Ireland (IHH) hostel near the pier has ocean views, kitchen facilities and bikes for hire. It's next to a pub. The owners of the hostel also run the adjacent B&B, with basic en-suite rooms.

Radharc an Chláir (☎ 75019; Inisheer; s/d €25/50; ⊠) This pleasant B&B near O'Brien's Castle has bike hire and serves evening meals (€20).

Óstán Inis Oírr (☎ 75020; Inisheer; s/d €33/63; ⌚ Apr-Sep) This modern hotel, just up from the Strand, has homely en-suite rooms, and serves hearty meals in its bar and **restaurant** (mains €6-12; ⌚ 9am-9pm).

Fisherman's Cottage (☎ 75073; Inisheer; mains €12-20; ⌚ Apr-Oct) Cosy Fisherman's Cottage, near the pier, specialises in tasty, fresh seafood and organically grown vegetables.

Drinking

Tigh Ned (☎ 75004; Inisheer) A mixed crowd comes to this welcoming, unpretentious place for its lively, traditional music.

Tigh Ruairí (☎ 75020; Inisheer) Rory Conneely's atmospheric and friendly old hostelry presents live music sessions.

Getting Around

Bikes are available for hire from **Rothair Inis Oírr** (☎ 75033; Inisheer; per day €8). The IHH hostel also hires out bicycles.

CONNEMARA

The name really sells the place. It would suit an epic poem and a fierce-eyed redhead equally well, and Connemara (Conamara), by turns wonderfully wild and eerily desolate, lives up to expectations. Immediately northwest of Galway city, it's a stunning patchwork of rusty bogs, lonely valleys, pale grey mountains and small black lakes that shimmer when the sun shines. At its heart are the Maumturk Mountains and the grey, quartzite peaks of the Twelve Bens, which offer some tremendous hill walking. The coastal road west of Spiddal (R336) skirts a tortuous series of small bays and inlets, and connects a succession of Gaeltacht (Irish-speaking) villages and seaside resorts.

Connemara offers a host of appealing choices for the multitudes who holiday here. Clifden, the region's largest resort, is sloppy and lacks soul, but the nearby coast is gorgeous. Roundstone is a sweet, sweet spot if you avoid the summer crowds. The area around Letterfrack has remote sandy beaches and twisting scenic roads that are great for cycling and hiking. The drive through Roundstone Bog is otherworldly and bumpy. The northernmost town of Leenane, on Killary Harbour, is charming, sleepy and uneventful. The Loch Corrib is good for a boat ride and especially for fishing. Inishbofin is a dream. A cursory bus tour from Galway hardly does Connemara justice. A two- or three-day driving trip is rushing it. Four or five days would satisfy. Connemara's true devotees, who number in the thousands, easily while away a month or two here every year.

Heading west from Galway you have two options: the coast road (R336) through Salthill, Barna and Spiddal, or the inland route (N59) through Oughterard, which leads directly to the heart of Connemara. The journey from Maam Cross northwest to Leenane (R336) or northeast to Cong (R345) takes you through Joyce country, a stunning mountainous region. The trip north along Lough Inagh Valley past the Twelve Bens and around Kylemore Lake is difficult to surpass.

One of the most important Gaeltacht areas in the country begins just west of Galway city around Barna and stretches westwards through Spiddal and Inverin, and along much of the coast as far as Cashel. Ireland's national Irish-language radio station, Radio na Gaeltachta, is based at Costello. The Irish-language weekly newspaper, *Foinse* (Source), is published in Spiddal.

If you intend any detailed exploration, the excellent *Connemara: Introduction and Gazeteer,* by Tim Robinson, is a must. *Connemara: A Hill Walker's Guide,* by Robinson and Joss Lynam, is also invaluable.

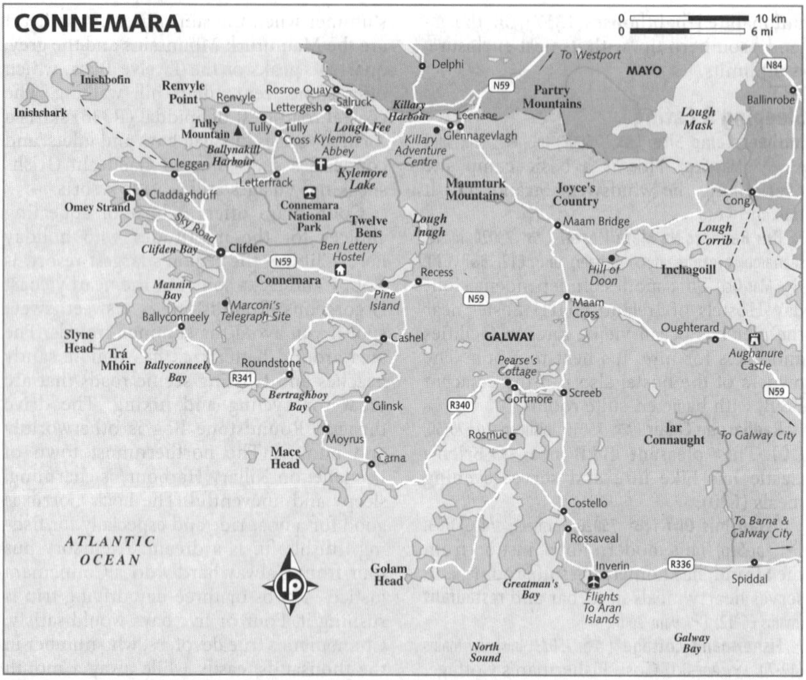

GETTING THERE & AWAY

Visitors can get almost anywhere by bus. Driving is a real pleasure in Connemara, though you'll need to be careful on the narrow roads lined with stone walls just waiting to scrape the sides of your car. Many road signs in this area are in Irish only, so note the Irish place names (in parentheses) as you read the following text.

Bus Éireann (☎ 091-562000; www.buseireann.ie) is the Republic's principle bus line and serves most of Connemara, with many buses originating in Galway. Check with the bus station there for times and fares. Services can be sporadic, and many buses operate May to September only or July and August only. Some drivers will stop in between towns if arranged at the beginning of the trip.

Michael Nee Coaches (☎ 095-51082) is an independent line that specifically serves Connemara, with daily buses beginning in Galway and connections within the area. The Galway stop is just opposite the tourist office. Connemara towns served include Maam Cross, Recess, Cashel, Clifden, Letterfrack, Tullycross and Cleggan. If you're going somewhere in between towns (a hostel in the countryside) you might be able to arrange a drop-off with the driver.

SPIDDAL TO MACE HEAD

If you elect to drive along the coast into Connemara, you'll pass through many little towns, some worth stopping in and some merely deserving a toot on the horn. Many anglers come here specifically for fishing the nearby lakes and sea. Just 17km west of Galway, Spiddal (An Spidéal) is an attractive little settlement with a couple of good pubs in case you're already thirsty. Some houses here are among the finest in Ireland, partly because of grants from the Irish government to encourage people to continue living in the area and to speak Gaelic. At the Galway city end of the village is the Irish-language **Connaught College** (Coláiste Chonnacht; ☎ 553 383; Spiddal), founded in 1910.

A few kilometres west of Spiddal, the scenery starts to become more dramatic, with parched fields delineated by low stonewalls rolling to a ragged shore. **Carraroe** (An Cheathrú Rua) is famous for its fine beaches, including the Coral Strand, which is composed entirely of shell and coral fragments. Equally well known is University College Galway's **Irish Language Centre** (Áras Mháirtín Uí Chadhain; ☎ 091-595 101; treasanimhaoil@eircom.net; An Cheathrú Rua). It offers four-week courses for all levels in the Irish language, and can arrange accommodation. Contact the centre to discuss prices.

Lettermore, **Gorumna** and **Lettermullen** islands are low and bleak, with a handful of farmers eking out an existence from tiny, rocky fields. Fish farming is big business in these parts, and there are salmon cages floating in some of the bays.

Near Gortmore, along the R340, is **Pearse's Cottage** (Teach an Phiarsaigh; ☎ 091-574 292; Hwy R340; adult/child €1.20/0.50; 🕒 10am-6pm daily Easter & mid-Jun–mid-Sep, 10am-5pm Sat & Sun spring & autumn). Pádraig Pearse (1879–1916) lead the Easter Rising with James Connolly in 1916. After the revolt he was executed by the British. Pearse wrote some of his short stories and plays in this cottage.

Continuing along the R340 brings you to **Carna**, a small fishing village from which there are nice walks out to **Mweenish Island** or north to Moyrus and out to **Mace Head**. It's a lovely journey from here heading north on the R340.

Sleeping & Eating

The following special places are worth hitting the brakes for if you aren't planning to make Roundstone or beyond by nightfall. Many have multiday and fishing packages.

Spiddal Caravan & Camping Park (☎ 091-553 372; fax 553 976; Spiddal; car & tent €11, cyclists/hikers €4.50; 🕒 mid-Mar–Oct) This riverside camp site is on the R336, 18km west of Galway and about 1.5km west of Spiddal village. It's also signposted in Irish as 'Pairc Saoire an Spidéil'. Its modern facilities include a toilet block, laundry and free showers.

Ballynahinch Castle Hotel (☎ 095-31006; www.ballynahinch-castle.com; Recess; s/d €106/133) This gorgeous hotel, southwest of Recess, is quite a treat. B&B and fishing packages are available. It's well worth a visit just for a drink in the bar and a stroll on the grounds.

Cashel House Hotel (☎ 095-31001; www.cashel-house-hotel.com; Cashel; s/d €125/250) At the head of Cashel Bay, this 32-room hotel, surrounded by 17 hectares of woodland and gardens, also has a stable of Connemara ponies; riding lessons are available.

Col Mar-House (☎ 091-553 247; Salahoona, Spiddal; s/d €40/60) This relaxed B&B, 1.5km west of Spiddal, is a country home surrounded by woods and gardens.

Zetland Country House Hotel (☎ 095-31111; www.zetland.com; Cashel Bay; s/d €105/210) This secluded, 19th-century manor has panoramic views and is in a tranquil setting overlooking Cashel Bay. Facilities include an excellent seafood restaurant and a tennis court.

ROUNDSTONE

☎ 095 / pop 424

Surely Roundstone (Cloch na Rón), a small fishing village with a narrow main street coursing through tidy rowhouses, shops and tempting pubs, is the most idyllic hamlet in Connemara. The harbour, in a dark recess along Bertraghboy Bay, is home to lobster boats and traditional *currachs* with their tarred canvas bottoms stretched over wicker frames. The people of Roundstone seem to enjoy the good life and are friendly to strangers. They have fine beaches and hillwalking within easy reach, and they eat and drink well. Roundstone's pleasures are well known, however, and in the summer the road through town gets clogged with artery-clenching traffic.

Just south of the centre is a **craft complex**, in Michael Killeen Park, with various small factory shops selling everything from teapots to sweaters. One of the more interesting shops is **Malachy Kearns** (☎ 35808; 🕒 9am-9pm daily Jul-Sep, 9am-6pm Mon-Sat Oct-Jun), a maker of the *bodhrán* (hand-held goatskin drum). The shop also sells tin whistles, harps and inexpensive booklets filled with Irish ballads.

Looming above the staunch stone pier is **Mt Errisbeg** (298m), the only significant hill along this section of coastline. The pleasant walk from Roundstone to the top takes about two hours. Follow the small road past O'Dowd's pub in the centre of the village. From the summit there are wonderful views across the bay to the distant humps of the Twelve Bens.

South of town, off the road to Ballyconneely (R341), are the magnificent **white beaches** of Gurteen (or Gorteen) Bay and Dog's Bay.

Sleeping

Gurteen Beach Caravan & Camping Park (☎ 35882; Roundstone; per person €10) This peaceful camp site is in a great spot 2km west of town near the beach, and has full facilities.

Eldon's Hotel (☎ 35933; eldonshotel@eircom.net; Main St; s/d €60/120; 🕑 Mar-Oct) This smartly refurbished B&B, which feels like a family-run hotel, is a class act. Service is friendly, guestrooms are elegant, and Eldon's has a reading room, a small cosy bar and a superb restaurant.

Roundstone House Hotel (☎ 35864; Main St; s/d €50/100) This is a friendly 13-room place. It has good views over the bay and in summer it serves an excellent evening meal.

St Joseph's (☎ 35865; www.connemara.net/stjosephs; Main St; s/d €40/65) Mrs Lowry's excellent, central B&B offers a warm welcome and good views over the harbour.

Eating & Drinking

Beola Restaurant (☎ 35871; Main St; mains €15-28, bar menu €7-18; 🕑 6-9pm Apr-Oct) Supremely fresh seafood prepared with a deft hand is the specialty in this stylish restaurant. The service is warm, and imaginative dishes like roast fillet of monkfish on basil mash with red wine sauce are elegantly arranged on the plate. The kitchen also provides for the Eldon Hotel's adjacent bar, with a more casual but equally delectable menu. Reservations recommended.

O'Dowd's (☎ 35809; Main St; mains €9-21; 🕑 noon-9pm) O'Dowd's, a well-worn and very comfortable old pub, dishes up tasty food in its cosy bar and in the restaurant. It has an extensive menu of pasta, fish, meat and vegetarian dishes, and views over the harbour.

ROUNDSTONE TO CLIFDEN

Some 12km west of Roundstone is **Ballyconneely**. If you detour south off the R341 from there towards the Connemara Golf Club, you pass the ruins of **Bunowen Castle** before reaching the shore at **Trá Mhóir** (great beach), a lovely expanse of white sand. Back on the R341, as it curves north toward Clifden, you'll pass the fine beach at **Mannin Bay**.

An alternate route is via the **bog road**, R341, which connects with the N59 east of Clifden. The old road is a bumpy ride, but passes through the eerily beautiful Roundstone Bog, a rust-collared wilderness. Locals who believe the bog is haunted won't drive this road at night (though, in truth, the roughness of the road is reason enough to avoid it after dark). In summer, you might see men manually cutting turf (blanket bogs cannot be cut mechanically). It takes about 10 to 15 minutes driving through the bog, and it's fast moving once you reach the N59.

ALCOCK & BROWN

Derrygimlagh Bog, 6km south of Clifden, is where the aviator Captain John Alcock and his navigator Lieutenant Arthur Brown landed after their historic transatlantic flight.

On 14 and 15 June 1919 Alcock and Brown flew a Vickers Vimy over 2000km from Newfoundland in Canada to Ireland, landing in the bog near Clifden. Along the way the pilots experienced a death spiral and a nose dive, each time pulling out within tasting distance of the salty sea. At four separate intervals Brown had to crawl out onto the wings to de-ice the engines. The men warmed themselves, midflight, by draining a bottle of whiskey. Their destination had been Galway city, but both pilots survived their crash landing in Derrygimlagh without injury. This first successful nonstop flight across the Atlantic took about 16 hours.

A stone 'wing' monument to Alcock and Brown was erected beside the R341, about 6km south of Clifden. From the wing a walking trail leads to the site of the landing. As an added bonus, a former Marconi wireless station stands near the landing site.

CLIFDEN

☎ 095 / pop 1925

Clifden (An Clochán), the capital of Connemara, is beautifully set at the head of narrow Clifden Bay, where the River Owenglin tumbles into the sea. Its Victorian houses and needle-sharp church spires appear inviting as one approaches the town on the coast highway, and the surrounding countryside promises leisurely walks through woods and along The Sky Road towering above the shore. But Clifden has succumbed to a sloppy brand of tourism and the town has a careless, ragged and vaguely jaded feel to it. Its numerous hotels and easy transit access (it's about 80km from Galway city) make it a useful stop, and certainly it is convenient for travellers intent on enjoying the sea and the Twelve Bens.

Information

The **tourist office** (☎ 21163; ⏰ 10am-5pm daily Jul-Aug, 10am-5pm Mon-Sat Sep-Jun) is on Galway Rd, while the post office is on Main St. For Internet access try **Two Dog Internet Café** (☎ 221 86; Church Hill; €7/hr) and wash those dirty clothes at **Shamrock Washeteria** (Market Sq). There are banks with ATMs around Market Square.

Activities

Heading directly west from Clifden, the **Sky Road** takes you on a loop out to a town known as Kingston and back to Clifden through some rugged, stunningly beautiful coastal scenery. The round trip of about 12km can easily be walked or cycled. To take advantage of Clifden's multitude of superb walking and cycling possibilities get a copy of Map 31 in the *OS Discovery Series*.

The **Connemara Walking Centre** (☎ 21379; walkwest@indigo.ie; Market St) runs guided walking trips exploring local sites of historical, geographical and natural interest. A day's walk costs €20; longer walks are available. The centre also sells maps.

Errislannan Riding Centre (☎ 21134; info@connemara-tourism.org; Ballyconneely Rd), about 3.5km south on the R341, has Connemara ponies for hire for riding along the beach and up into the hills. Lessons are available. Rates depend on type and length of ride you want to take.

Sleeping

HOSTELS

Brookside Hostel (☎ 21812; brooksidehostel@eircom.net; Fairgreen; dm €12-15; ⏰ Mar-Oct; Ⓟ) The River Owenglin trickles past this IHH hostel in a quiet spot off the bottom of Market St.

Clifden Town Hostel (☎ 21076; seancth@eircom.net; Market St; dm €12, r from €17; Ⓟ) A friendly establishment, this central IHH property has 34 beds in bright spick-and-span rooms.

B&BS & HOTELS

Ben View House (☎ 21256; www.house4rent.ie/BenView; Bridge St; s/d €35/70) This 19th-century town house is a family run B&B and retains a lot of homey, comfy and antiquated charm. It's very central.

Central B&B (☎ 21430; Main St; s/d €30/60) Above a pub, this B&B has slightly shabby hallways, but the rooms are nice enough and have private bathroom.

Foyle's (☎ 21801; www.foyleshotel.com; Main St; s/d €70/140; ⏰ Jun-Aug) Clifden's oldest hotel, Foyle's has 28 en-suite rooms with all mod cons. It has a lovely patio garden and a lively pub.

Kingstown House (☎ 21470; fax 21530; Bridge St; s/d €30/60) Kingstown House is a large, hospitable guesthouse in the town centre; there are eight rooms, most with private bathroom.

Mallmore House (☎ 21460; malmore@indigo.ie; Ballyconneely Rd; s/d €32/64; ⏰ Mar-Oct; Ⓟ) This restored Georgian manor house is a top choice for Clifden. It's set in 14 hectares of woodland about 2km from town, and is elegantly furnished. The super breakfasts include pancakes and smoked salmon.

Eating & Drinking

D'Arcy Inn (☎ 21146; Main St; mains €8-15; ⏰ 10.30am-late) Sandwiches and seafood are the staples in this friendly old pub. Live music and poetry readings give the joint added pep some nights.

EJ Kings (☎ 21330; Market Sq; mains €12-21; ⏰ 10.30am-9pm) A busy old pub with zero atmosphere, EJ Kings serves soups, salads and traditional food like Irish stew. It's OK for family dining.

Fogerty's (☎ 21427; Market St; mains €16-23; ⏰ 5.30-10pm Thu-Tue) Fogerty's, in a thatched stone house, ladles out traditional Irish and seafood dishes in its warm, traditional environs.

Lowry's Bar (☎ 21347; Market St) The traditional pleasures of Lowry's extend from the age-old look of the place and the *ceilidh* sessions that cheer things up most nights. Pub food is served.

Mitchell's Restaurant (☎ 21867; Market St; lunch €7-12, mains €16-25; ⏰ noon-10pm Mar-Oct) Mitchell's is a tad over impressed with itself, which is too bad as it's otherwise a small and homey spot for a quality seafood dish or Irish stew.

Upstairs Downstairs (Main St; sandwiches €3; ⏰ 9am-6pm Mon-Fri, 10am-6pm Sat, 10am-5pm Sun) A tasty sandwich and strong coffee at this bright and friendly spot is easily the best deal in town.

Getting There & Away

Buses stop on Market St near the library. For Bus Éireann information phone the **bus station** (☎ 091-562 000) in Galway.

Michael Nee Coaches (☎ 51082) runs between Clifden (from the square) and Galway three times daily, June to September. During the same period there are two buses daily to Cleggan (twice weekly from October to May), from where the ferry sails to Inishbofin.

Getting Around

A one-way traffic system operates in the town centre. Walking will get you around town. **John Mannion & Son** (☎ 21160; Bridge St) is a Raleigh agent and hires out bicycles for €10 per day.

CLAGGAGHDUFF & OMEY ISLAND

The deeply indented coastline north of Clifden brings you to the tiny village of **Claddaghduff** (An Cladach Dubh), which is signposted off the road to Cleggan. Turning west here down by the Catholic church you come out on **Omey Strand**, and at low tide you can drive or walk across the sand to **Omey Island**, a low islet of rock, grass and sand with a few houses for the island's population of 20. During the summer, horse races are held on Omey Strand.

CLEGGAN

☎ 095 / pop 303

Cleggan (An Cloiggean) is a small fishing village, 16km northwest of Clifden, which visitors pass through en route to Inishbofin island. This is a good headquarters for horse riding on sandy beaches, and many pony-loving families choose to stay a week here in an old farmhouse cottage.

To really experience the wild west, visit **Cleggan Riding Centre** (☎ 44746; Cleggan), which can set up a variety of horseback adventures, including a three-hour trek to Omey Island, via the sandy causeway. Prices depend on what sort of trek you decide to take.

Sleeping

Cleggan Farm Holiday Cottages (☎ 44648; Cleggan; clegganfarmhols@eircom.net; cottages per week €300-400; Ⓟ) Six stone farmhouses, which sleep between two and 10 people, ooze rustic charm without being precious. Prices are much lower during autumn and winter, but restrictions include a Saturday-to-Saturday time frame and extra charge for use of power and heat. Great for family holidays but contact well in advance.

Getting There & Away

See p393 and p390 for information on buses. Cleggan is the departure point for boats to Inishbofin Island. Boats also leave here for Inishturk Island (see p413).

INISHBOFIN

☎ 095 / pop 177

A typical story from a traveller who has been to Inishbofin goes like this: 'I hired a bike and wheeled around all day and I wondered where the heck all the people were. At night I went to the pub, and the entire town was there.'

Indeed, the sleepy island does tend to come alive after dark, and stays up late and sleeps in late – there are no cops on the island to enforce closing times. To be sure, that's not all there is to Inishbofin. It's a haven of tranquillity, and walking or biking its narrow, deserted lanes is a great way to take in green pastures, sandy beaches, farm animals and seals.

Inishbofin is just 9km out in the Atlantic from Cleggan. It's compact – 6km long by 3km wide – and the highest point is a mere 86m above sea level. Just off the northern beach is **Lough Bó Finne**, from which the island gets its name. Bó finne means 'white cow'.

St Colman exiled himself to Inishbofin in AD 664, after he fell out with the church over its adoption of a new calendar. He set up a monastery, supposedly northeast of the harbour, where the more recent ruins of a small 13th-century **church** still stand. Grace O'Malley, the famous pirate queen who was based on Clare Island, used Inishbofin as a base in the 16th century. Cromwell's forces captured Inishbofin in 1652 and built a star-shaped prison for priests and clerics. Many died or were killed; one bishop was reputedly chained to Bishop's Rock near the harbour and drowned as the tide came in.

Information

Inishbofin's small post office has a grocery shop as well as a currency-exchange facility. Pubs and hotels will usually change travellers cheques.

Sleeping & Eating

You can pitch a tent on most unfenced ground, but not on or near the beaches.

Inishbofin Island Hostel (☎ 45855; www.inishbofin-hostel.ie; dm €10, r €15; 🕑 Apr-Oct) A fine IHH hostel, 500m up from the harbour, it offers panoramic views and camping (€5 per person).

Doonmore Hotel (☎ 45804; www.doonmorehotel.com; s/d €40/80; ⏲ Apr-Oct) Close to the harbour, Doonmore has comfortable, unpretentious rooms in both its modern extension and the original building. Dinner in its nonsmoking dining room, where seafood is the specialty, costs around €25.

Day's Hotel (☎ 45809; s/d €40/60; ⏲ Apr-Oct) This modest, comfortable hotel has turf fires and a dining room looking out over the harbour. The food (mains €14 to €20) is creative, with excellent fresh fish.

Day's Bar (☎ 45829) Adjoining Day's Hotel, this welcoming bar supplies ample pub grub and a lively atmosphere. Traditional *ceilidh* sessions are held several nights a week.

Getting There & Away

Ferry trips from Cleggan to Inishbofin take 30 to 45 minutes. Sometimes dolphins follow the ferries. A nondescript kiosk on the Cleggan pier dispenses information.

King's Ferries (☎ 44642, 21520; www.inishbofinkingferries.com) runs the *Island Discovery* and *The Queen* at 11.30am and 6.45pm daily, April to October, with additional sailings in July and August. The trip takes 30 minutes and costs €15 return.

Inishbofin Ferries (☎ 45903, 45806, 45831; www.inishbofinferry.com) operates the *Galway Bay* twice daily April to October, and three times daily June to August. The fare is €15 return. This line also runs the older *Dún Aengus* mail boat (11.30am Monday to Saturday year round).

Getting Around

Inishbofin Cycle Hire (☎ 45833), at the pier, hires out bicycles for €10 per day.

LETTERFRACK & AROUND

☎ 095 / pop 150

Letterfrack (Leitir Fraic), founded by Quakers in the mid-19th century, is a good base for exploring Connemara National Park, Renvyle Point and Kylemore Abbey. The village is barely more than a crossroads with a few pubs and B&Bs, but the setting is wooded and very pretty. Letterfrack is 15km northeast of Clifden on the N59.

There's some fine scenery along the coast north of Letterfrack, especially from Tully Cross east to Lettergesh and Salruck. **Glassillaun Beach** is a breathtaking expanse of pure white sand. There are other fine beaches at **Gurteen** and at **Lettergesh**, where the beach horse-racing sequences for John Ford's 1952 film *The Quiet Man* were shot.

There are fine **walks** all along the coast and around Renvyle Point to Derryinver Bay. There's an excellent hill walk, which takes four to five hours each way, from the post office at Lettergesh up Binn Chuanna and Maolchnoc and then down to Lough Fee. A 4km walk from Letterfrack to the peak of Tully Mountain takes 30 minutes and affords wonderful ocean views.

On Glassillaun Beach, to the northeast, is **Scuba Dive West** (☎ 43922; www.scubadivewest.com; Letterfrack), offering courses and diving on the surrounding coast and islands. A full day with instructor and equipment costs €99/139 for shore/boat diving.

Kylemore Abbey & Lake

Just a few kilometres east of Letterfrack, towards the northern end of the scenic Lough Inagh Valley, stands **Kylemore Abbey** (☎ 41146; adult/child €7/4; ⏲ 9am-5.30pm). The castle-like, 19th-century neo-Gothic mansion was built for a wealthy English businessman, Mitchell Henry, after he had spent his honeymoon in Connemara and had fallen in love with the region. During WWI, a group of Benedictine nuns left Ypres in Belgium and eventually set up in Kylemore, turning the place into an abbey.

Today, the nuns run an exclusive convent boarding school here and some sections of the abbey are open to the public. There's also a craft shop and tearoom. The building is impressive, and the setting overlooking Kylemore Lake is beautiful, but the abbey interior is a fairly limited showpiece of stuffy furniture and the like. Without paying admission, you can take a walk around the lake and surrounding woods.

Sleeping & Eating

Renvyle Beach Caravan & Camping (☎ 43462; Renvyle; tent site per person €8; ⏲ Easter-Sep) This camp site, 1.5km west of Tully Cross, is in a beautiful location with direct access to the sandy beach.

Connemara Caravan & Camping Park (☎ 43406; Lettergesh; tent site per person €8; ⏲ May-Sep) Near the opening to Killary Harbour, this camping ground has modern conveniences plus the chance to see dolphins from the beach.

Old Monastery Hostel (☎ 41132; oldmon@indigo.ie; Letterfrack; dm €12-16; P ⊠) This rustic stone house, built in the 1840s, is in the woods 400m up a dirt road from the Letterfrack crossroads. It's an atmospheric setting, if you're up for the bohemian life. Upkeep and restoration of the old building is ongoing, but it's being done gracefully, with attractive rough edges kept intact. Rooms are very basic. Camping (€9 per person) is permitted, bikes can be hired (€10 per day) and most evenings there's a vegetarian buffet (€10). Afterwards, guests can retreat to a faded parlour, lit by candles and a fireplace. Connemara National Park is literally just a few paces away.

Renvyle House Hotel (☎ 43511; www.renvyle.com; Renvyle; s/d €88/150) This 56-room converted country house was once owned by the poet Oliver St John Gogarty and is the best place in the area to have a drink or snack or relax after a walk along the peninsula.

Pangur Ban (☎ 41243; Letterfrack; mains €15-21; 🕒 6-9pm) Worth a splurge, this thatched cottage restaurant, 100m west of the Letterfrack crossroads, serves terrific roasts and a venison stew cooked in Guinness.

Getting There & Away

Bus Éireann (☎ 091-562 000) bus No 420 runs year round between Galway and Clifden, calling at Salruck, Lettergesh, Tully Church, Kylemore, Letterfrack, Cleggan and Claddaghduff en route.

CONNEMARA NATIONAL PARK

Connemara National Park (☎ 095-41054; Letterfrack; adult/child €2.75/1.25; 🕒 10am-6.30pm Jun, 9.30am-6.30pm Jul-Aug, 10am-5.30pm Apr-May & Sep-Oct), managed by Dúchas, covers 2000 hectares of bog, mountain and heath southeast of Letterfrack. The headquarters and visitor centre are housed in old buildings just south of the crossroads in Letterfrack.

The centre gives an insight into the park's flora, fauna and geology, as well as showing maps and various trails. Bog biology and the video *Man and the Landscape* are interesting, so wandering around is not a waste of time. It has an indoor eating area and rudimentary kitchen facilities for walkers.

The park encloses a number of the **Twelve Bens**, including Bencullagh, Benbrack and Benbaun. The heart of the park is **Gleann Mór** (Big Glen), through which flows the River Polladirk. There's fine walking up the glen and over the surrounding mountains. There are two- to three-hour guided **nature walks** on Monday, Wednesday and Friday in July and August, leaving the centre at 10.30am. Bring good boots and rainwear. There are also short, self-guided walks and, if the Bens look too daunting, you can hike up **Diamond Hill** nearby.

LEENANE & KILLARY HARBOUR

☎ 095

The small and sleepy village of Leenane (also spelled Leenaun) makes a convenient, scenic stopover for travellers heading north to County Mayo. Leenane's name in Irish, An Líonán, means 'ravine', referring to the way the sea edges its way into narrow Killary Harbour.

The village boasts both a cinematic and literary connection. It was the location for *The Field* (1989), based on John B Keane's poignant play about a tenant farmer's ill-fated plans to pass on a rented piece of land to his son. The dance and pub scenes were filmed in the village and the church scene at nearby Aasleagh. The village's name made it onto the literary map with the success in London and New York of Martin McDonagh's play *The Beauty Queen of Leenane*.

There's no bank or ATM, but the post office changes foreign currency.

Mussel rafts dot long, narrow Killary Harbour, which looks like a fjord but may not actually have been glaciated. It's 16km long and over 45m deep in the centre, and has a superb anchorage. **Mt Mweelrea** (819m) towers over its northern shores.

Activities

The well-run **Killary Adventure Centre** (☎ 095-43411; www.killary.com; Leenane; 🕒 10am-5pm), 3km west of Leenane on the N59, offers activities in just about every adventure (and other) sport you can think of, including canoeing, sea kayaking, sailing, rock climbing and archery, to name just a few. Helicopter rides to the summit of Mweelrea are particularly exciting. Prices range fairly widely depending on the activity.

From Nancy's Point, about 2km west of Leenane, **Sea Cruise Connemara** (☎ 091-566 736; www.sea-cruiseconnemara.com; adult/child €17/8; 4 cruises daily Apr-Oct) offers 1½-hour cruises of Killary Harbour aboard the catamaran *Connemara Lady*.

There are several excellent walks from Leenane, including one to **Aasleagh Waterfall** (Eas Liath), about 3km away on the north-eastern side of Killary Harbour. Also from Leenane, the road runs west for about 2km along the southern shore. Where the highway veers inland, walkers can continue on an old road along the shore to Rosroe Quay.

Sleeping

Killary House (☎ 42254; www.connemara.com/killaryhouse; Leenane; s/d €30/60; P) In a converted farmhouse just a short walk from Leenane, its front rooms have views of the bay, while the rear ones look up to the hills behind.

Killary Adventure Centre (☎ 43411; www.killary.com; dm €14-30, lodge s/d €45/90; P) The adventure centre has clean, darn near sterile dorm rooms, as well as a restaurant and bar with a great view of Killary Harbour.

Killary Harbour Hostel (☎ 43417; Rosroe; dm €10-13; Jun-Sep; P) Set in wonderful scenery, this An Óige property is 13km northeast of Tully Cross on Rosroe Quay, 8km off the N59. The Austrian philosopher Ludwig Wittgenstein (1889–1951) stayed here for seven months in 1948. Some food and supplies are available at the hostel, but the nearest shop is 5km away in Lettergesh, so stock up in advance. There's a fine hike from the hostel along an old road by the fjord to Leenane.

Eating

Blackberry Cafe (☎ 42240; Leenane; mains €15-21; Apr-Sep) Mostly serving fresh seafood, this is a surprisingly stylish restaurant given the location.

Gaynor's (Leenane; mains €2-7) Offering sandwiches and light meals, Gaynor's is a traditional Irish pub where the farmers and other locals come for a quiet drink and to catch up on each other's news.

Village Grill (☎ 42253; Leenane; mains €3-15; 10am-10pm Apr-Sep) The Village Grill is a good choice for fish and chips, sandwiches and snacks.

LOUGH INAGH VALLEY

☎ 091

The journey north along the Lough Inagh Valley is one of the most scenic in the country. There are two fine approaches up valleys from the south, starting on either side of Recess, and the long sweep of Derryclare and Inagh Loughs accompanies you for most of the way. On the western side are the brooding **Twelve Bens**, while just beyond the valley on the northern side is the picturesque drive beside Kylemore Lake.

Towards the northern end of the valley, a track leads off the road west up a blind valley, which is also well worth exploring.

Sleeping

Ben Lettery Hostel (☎ 51136; Ballinafad, Recess; dm €8.50-13; Easter-Sep; P) You'll wake up to the sound of sheep bleating at this spotless An Óige hostel. On the main Clifden road, in the heart of the Connemara wilderness, it is an excellent base to explore the Twelve Bens and Lough Inagh Valley. It's a friendly place, with a tidy and homey kitchen and living room. The hostel is 8km west of Recess and 13km east of Clifden.

Lough Inagh Lodge (☎ 34706; www.commerce.ie/inagh; Recess; s/d €110/220; P) About 7km north of Recess on the R344 is the atmospheric, Victorian Lough Inagh Lodge, an upmarket country-house hotel. It's a worthwhile place to stop for a light meal, particularly in good weather. The location is magnificent and there's a path in front of the lodge down to the lake.

OUGHTERARD

☎ 091 / pop 2364

The small town of Oughterard (Uachtar Árd), 27km along the main road from Galway to Clifden, calls itself the 'Gateway to Connemara'. And sure enough, immediately west of town, the countryside opens up to sweeping panoramas of lakes, mountains and bogs that get more spectacular the further west you travel. Oughterard itself is a pleasant little town and one of Ireland's principal angling centres. It has a number of so-so lodgings, pubs and restaurants. Most travellers are just passing through, as this is along the fast route to the coast.

The focus of the anglers' attention is Lough Corrib (see p398), just north of town. Nearby attractions include Aughanure Castle to the southeast and the lovely drive along the Glann Rd by Lough Corrib to a vantage point overlooking the Hill of Doon.

Information

In addition to heaps of tourism brochures and assistance in booking tours and accommodation, the **tourist office** (☎ 552 808; www.oughterardtourism.com; Main St; 🕑 9.30am-5.30pm Mon-Fri, 10am-2pm Sat) offers Internet access at €4.70 per hour. The **Bank of Ireland** (Main St) has an ATM and bureau de change and the post office is on Main St, just east of Market Square.

Aughanure Castle

Built in the 16th century, this bleak **fortress** (☎ 552 214; Oughterard; adult/child €2.75/1.25; 🕑 10am-6pm daily Jun–early Sep, 10am-6pm Sat & Sun early Sep–Oct) was home to the Fighting O'Flahertys. The clan controlled the region for hundreds of years after they fought off the Normans. The six-storey tower house stands on a rocky outcrop overlooking Lough Corrib and has been extensively restored. Surrounding the castle are the remains of an unusual double bawn or perimeter fortification. Underneath the castle, the lake washes through a number of natural caverns and caves.

Aughanure Castle is 3km east of Oughterard, off the main Galway road (N59).

Sleeping

Canrawer House Hostel (☎ 552 388; Station Rd; dm €10-15; Ⓟ) This modern, purpose-built hostel is at the Clifden end of town, just over 1km south along the Galway road. It has a large, airy kitchen and, if you've ever wanted to learn to fish, the owner will take you on an organised trip. You can also hire a bicycle here (€15/70 per day/week).

Currarevagh House (☎ 552 312; www.currarevagh.com; Oughterard; s/d €97/194; 🕑 Apr-Oct; Ⓟ) It's difficult to think of a more romantic place than this 19th-century mansion on the shore of Lough Corrib, just outside Oughterard. It's renowned for its exquisite evening meals and quality accommodation.

Fairybridge Cottage (☎ 552 855; g53@familyhomes.ie; Tonwee, Oughterard; s/d €23/46; Ⓟ) This compound of kitschy thatched cottages is a fantasy land for little girls and nostalgic leprechauns. It's genuinely cosy and in a pretty spot, up a country road near the lake (take the high road about 1.5km from town). Families with children should stay in the self-catering family hut.

Jolly Lodger (☎ 552 682; Main St; s/d €25/50) Although modernised, this two-storey, greystone town house retains many of its original features. It's a B&B with excellent breakfasts.

Waterfall Lodge (☎ 552 168; www.waterfalllodge.net; Glann Rd; s/d €35/70; ☒ Ⓟ) This tastefully furnished Victorian home stands amid wooded gardens beside a babbling brook. It's a B&B, with delicious breakfast choices (not just Irish) and all rooms are en suite.

Eating & Drinking

Boat Inn (☎ 552 196; Market Sq; mains €5-16) Head to the Boat Inn for a wide choice of sandwiches, fish, steaks and pizzas.

Le Blason (☎ 557 111; Main St; mains €18-25; 🕑 7-10pm Tue-Sun) The elegant Le Blason, on the river near the bridge, combines French cuisine with the finest Irish produce. The chicken *vol au vent* is particularly good. Save room for the *crème brûlée*.

Power's Bar (☎ 557 047; Market Sq) This intimate, thatched old boozer serves a good pint and has live music on weekends.

Getting There & Away

Bus Éireann has coaches going from Galway to Oughterard every three or four hours. If driving from Galway, take Newcastle Rd (N59).

LOUGH CORRIB

The Republic's largest lake, Lough Corrib is over 48km long and covers some 200 sq km. It virtually cuts off western Galway from the rest of the country and encompasses over 360 islands. On the largest one, Inchagoill, there's a monastic settlement that visitors can get to from Oughterard or Cong.

Lough Corrib is world famous for its salmon, sea trout and brown trout, and the area attracts legions of anglers from all over the world in season. The highlight of the **fishing** year is the mayfly season, when zillions of the small lacy bugs hatch over a few days (usually in May) and drive the fish and anglers into a frenzy. The hooks are baited with live flies, which join their cousins dancing on the surface of the lake. The main run of salmon doesn't begin until June. The owner of **Canrawer House Hostel** (☎ 552 388; Station Rd, Oughterard) is a good contact for information and boat hire. You can buy fishing supplies from **Thomas Tuck** (☎ 552 335; Main St, Oughterard; 🕑 9am-6.30pm Mon-Sat).

Inchagoill Island

The largest island on Lough Corrib and some 7km northwest of Oughterard, Inchagoill is a lonely place hiding many ancient remains. Most fascinating is an obelisk called **Lia Luguaedon Mac Menueh** (Stone of Luguaedon, Son of Menueh) marking a burial site. It stands about 75cm tall, near the Saints' Church, and some people claim that the Latin writing on the stone is the oldest Christian inscription in Europe – apart from those in the catacombs in Rome.

Teampall Phádraig (St Patrick's Church) is a small oratory of a very early design with some later additions. The prettiest church is the Romanesque **Teampall na Naoimh** (Saints' Church), probably built in the 9th or 10th century. There are carvings around the arched doorway.

The island can be reached by boat from Oughterard (or Cong in County Mayo). **Corrib Cruises** (☎ 092-46029; www.corribcruises.com) sails from Oughterard to Inchagoill Island (adult/child €13/6) and on to Cong (€20) from April to October. Departures are at 11am, 2.45pm and 5pm.

SOUTH OF GALWAY CITY

There are many sites south of the city worth a gander, whether you're passing through en route to or from the Burren in County Clare or taking a day trip from Galway. The tranquil monastic settlement and round tower at Kilmacduagh is worth making a special effort to visit, and the quaint coastal town of Kinvara is a good place to stay overnight if you're looking to slow things down a bit.

CLARINBRIDGE & KILCOLGAN

☎ 091 / pop 2081

Some 16km south of Galway, Clarinbridge (Droichead an Chláirin) and Kilcolgan (Cill Choglán) are the focus of Galway's famous Clarinbridge Oyster Festival, held during the second weekend of September and precursor to the Galway International Oyster Festival. Oysters are at their best in the summer, beginning in May. Clarinbridge is also good for rummaging the antique stores along the highway.

Paddy Burke's Oyster Inn (☎ 796 107; Clarinbridge; 6 oysters €10, mains €10-22; ⏲ 12.30-10pm) This old-fashioned, thatched inn by the bridge is famous for its long association with the oyster festival and for its seafood.

Moran's Oyster Cottage (☎ 976 113; The Weir, Kilcolgan; 6 oysters €12, mains €13-18; ⏲ noon-10pm Mon-Sat, 10am-10pm Sun) Signposted near the post office just north of Kilcolgan, this wonderful thatched pub and restaurant overlooks narrow Dunbulcaun Bay, where the famous Galway oysters are reared. During the festival, the world oyster-opening championships are held here.

Getting There & Away

Clarinbridge is on the main Galway–Gort–Ennis–Limerick road (N18) and is served by numerous Bus Éireann buses from Galway. Kilcolgan is also on the N18; Moran's Oyster Cottage is about 1.5km to the west.

KINVARA

☎ 091 / pop 430

The quiet village of Kinvara (Cinn Mhara) is a delight. It's tucked away on the south-eastern corner of Galway Bay, with a small stone harbour that's home to a number of Galway hookers (traditional sailing boats). The village is endowed with a castle and several sanguine taverns.

Dunguaire Castle

This **castle** (☎ 637 108; Kinvara; adult/child €4/2; ⏲ 9.30am-5.30pm Apr-Sep) was erected around 1520 by the O'Hynes and is in excellent condition after extensive restoration. The castle is thought to be built on the site of the 6th-century royal palace of Guaire Aidhne, the king of Connaught. Its owners have included Oliver St John Gogarty (1878–1957), poet, writer, surgeon, Irish Free State senator and known to many as the wildest wit in Dublin.

A medieval banquet is held here. The banquets are an intimate affair, with music, storytelling, and a hearty meat and mead dinner costing €38, with sittings at 5.30pm and 8.45pm May to September.

Just south of Dunguaire is a bare **stone arch**, the only remains of an older castle.

Special Events

Fleadh na gCuach (Cuckoo Festival; late May) A music festival

Cruinniú na mBáid (Gathering of the Boats; second weekend in Aug) A celebration of Galway's traditional hooker boats

Sleeping & Eating

Johnston's Independent Hostel (☎ 637 164; Main St, Kinvara; dm €12; ⌚ Jul-Aug) Johnston's is a quaint, medium-sized hostel (24 beds) up the hill from the harbour. Showers and laundry cost extra.

Doorus House (☎ 637 512; www.irelandyha.org; Doorus, Kinvara; dm €13; P) This lovely An Óige hostel is 6km northwest of Kinvara, signposted off the main road to Ballyvaughan (N67). It's in an old mansion once owned by Count Floribund de Basterot, who entertained here such notables as WB Yeats, Lady Augusta Gregory, Douglas Hyde and Guy de Maupassant. Rooms are basic and spotless. It's a good base for exploring the Burren.

Burren View (☎ 637 142; burrenviewdorrus@eircom.net; Doorus, Kinvara; s/d €35/70; ⌚ Easter-Oct) About 6km northwest of Kinvara, it's in a scenic spot on a peninsula with views of Galway Bay and the Burren. You can swim at the nearby Blue Flag beach.

Clareview House (☎ 637 170; www.clareview hse.com; Kinvara; s/d €30/60; ⌚ Mar-Oct; P) Clareview is a large, modern farmhouse about 3km east of Kinvara on the R347. Its five rooms are all en suite and dinner is available.

Keough's (☎ 637 145; Main St, Kinvara; mains €8-12; ⌚ 10am-10pm) This friendly local, where you'll sometimes hear Irish spoken, serves up a fresh battered cod that'll get the job done.

Getting There & Away

Late May to late September, Bus Éireann's Galway–Killarney bus No 50 stops in Kinvara three to four times daily Monday to Saturday, and twice on Sunday. Bus No 423, linking Galway with towns in County Clare, stops in Kinvara. For more details contact **Galway bus station** (☎ 091-562 000).

GORT & AROUND

☎ 091 / pop 1795

Gort's a real honest-to-gosh working town, but there's not much to hold the common traveller's interest. Head out to the surrounding countryside to gawk at some well-known literary sights, including two of special interest to fans of poet WB Yeats.

A 16th-century Norman tower known as **Thoor Ballylee** (☎ 631 436; Peterswell; adult/child €4/2; ⌚ 10am-6pm May-Sep) was the summer home of WB Yeats from 1922. It was the inspiration for one of Yeats' best-known works, The Tower. The restored tower contains his furnishings and fittings and you can see an audiovisual presentation on the poet's life. From Gort take the Loughrea road (N66) for about 3km, then follow the sign.

About 3km north of Gort is **Coole Park** (☎ 631 804; exhibits €2.50; ⌚ 10am-5pm Easter-Sep). It was the home of Lady Augusta Gregory, co-founder of the Abbey Theatre and a patron of Yeats. An exhibit focuses on the literary importance of the house and the flora and fauna of the surrounding nature reserve. The main attraction on the grounds is the **autograph tree**, on which many of Lady Gregory's esteemed literary guests carved their initials.

About 5km southwest of Gort is the extensive monastic site of **Kilmacduagh**. Beside a small lake is a well-preserved round tower, the remains of a small, 14th-century cathedral (Teampall Mór MacDuagh), an oratory dedicated to St John the Baptist, and various other little chapels. The original monastery is thought to have been founded by St Colman MacDuagh at the beginning of the 7th century. St MacDuagh founded the monastery under the patronage of King Guaire Aidhne of Connaught, who gave his name to Dunguaire Castle in Kinvara. Such was the monastery's importance that it became the focus for a new diocese in the 12th century. The 34m-high round tower leans some 60cm from the perpendicular and the doorway is 8m above ground level. There are fine views over the Burren from here and you can visit any time.

There are regular buses from Galway to Gort, but you'll need a car or bike to get to the sights.

EASTERN GALWAY

Separated from the wild, bleak landscape of Connemara and the county's western coast by Lough Corrib, this region is markedly different. Eastern Galway is relatively flat, and its underlying limestone has given it a well-drained, fertile soil. This is the largest section of the county, but it lacks areas of significant interest.

GETTING THERE & AWAY

Bus Éireann (☎ 091-562 000) express buses from Galway serve Ballinasloe and Loughrea; local bus No 427 connects Galway, Ballinasloe and Loughrea with Portumna.

BALLINASLOE

☎ 0509 / pop 5977

The biggest town in eastern Galway, Ballinasloe (Béal Átha na Sluaighe) is on the main Dublin–Galway road (N6). The town is pleasant enough, but there's no real reason to stay, except possibly over the eight days at the start of October when the **Ballinasloe Horse Fair** attracts horse buyers and sellers and merrymakers.

Historically, Ballinasloe was a strategic crossing point over the River Suck. In the early 12th century, Turlough O'Connor, king of Connaught, built a castle to guard the river crossing, and this became the nucleus of the town's development.

Around 6km southwest of town on the N6, Aughrim was the site of a crucial victory by William of Orange over the Catholic forces of James II in 1691. It was the bloodiest battle ever fought on Irish soil. The **Battle of Aughrim Visitor Centre** (☎ 73939; Aughrim; adult/child €4/3; 10am-6pm Tue-Sat Jun-Aug) helps put it into perspective within the framework of the 'War of the Two Kings'. Signposts from the interpretive centre indicate the actual battle site.

Hyne's Hostel (☎ 73734; Ballinasloe; dm €12-15), close to the centre, is an IHH property. It only has 12 beds, so book ahead in summer or when the horse fair is on. It rents out bikes and can arrange pick-up.

CLONFERT CATHEDRAL

Around 21km southeast of Ballinasloe, off the R256, is the tiny 12th-century cathedral at Clonfert. It's on the site of a monastery said to have been founded in 563 by St Brendan the Navigator, which was ravaged by Vikings in AD 844 and 1179. The remarkable six-arched Romanesque doorway, with its human and animal heads, dates from the 1160s, but much of the limestone carvings were badly restored in the 19th century.

LOUGHREA & AROUND

☎ 091 / pop 4001

Loughrea (Baile Locha Riach) is a large, busy market town 26km southeast of Galway. It gets its name from the little lake at the southern end of town. Not to be confused with St Brendan's Church on Church St, which is now a library, **St Brendan's Catholic Cathedral** (☎ 841 212; Barrack St; admission free; 11.30am-1pm & 2-5.30pm Mon-Fri), dating from 1903, is renowned for its Celtic-revival stained glass, furnishings and marble columns. Loughrea has Ireland's only functioning medieval **moat**, which runs from the lake at Fair Green near the cathedral to the River Loughrea north of town.

Near Bullaun, 7km north of Loughrea, is the remarkable **Turoe Stone**, a phallic standing stone covered in delicate La Tène-style relief carvings. It dates from between 300 BC and AD 100. There are similarly carved stones in Brittany, associated with La Tène Celts (late Iron Age). The stone wasn't set here originally, but was found at an Iron Age fort a few kilometres away.

TRAVELLING LIKE TRAVELLERS

You can still travel the west of Ireland the old-fashioned way – in a horse-drawn Travellers' caravan. Into the West is a tour company (based at Cartron House Farm in eastern Galway) that can set you up with a tubular wooden trailer of the type the Travelling people once used. These caravans accommodate up to five people and have been updated slightly and include modest furnishings, beds, and a washbasin. You'll also get a mild-mannered draught horse, advice on how to manage your trip, and a detailed itinerary. Basically, the entire kit and caboodle is yours for one week (starting on Wednesday or Saturday). You'll travel a few hours each day, and you'll have your choice of family farms to stop at for the night. Contact **Cartron House Farm** (outside Ireland ☎ 509 45211, within Ireland 0509-5211; www.galway-southeast-tourism.ie/intothewest-caravans.htm; Ballinakill, Kylebrack, Loughrea; per week €560-740) for more information.

PORTUMNA

☎ 0509 / pop 1928

In the southeast corner of the county, the lakeside town of Portumna is an attractive village and a popular base for boating and fishing on **Lough Derg**. Dúchas-run **Portumna Castle** (☎ 41658; Castle Ave; adult/child €2/1; 10am-6pm Apr-Oct) was built in 1618 by Richard de Burgo (or Burke) and boasts an elaborate, geometrically laid-out garden.

Counties Mayo & Sligo

CONTENTS

Largely rural Mayo and Sligo have never had it easy. Both counties have suffered the devastating iniquities of famine, mass emigration and an unyielding landscape that has little agricultural value. Even today, they suffer a chronic shortage of population and an inadequate economic infrastructure that struggles to keep up with the rest of the country. These are very real problems, but for the visitor, things aren't so bleak. Both Mayo and Sligo are blessed with stunning scenery, rendered all the more beautiful by their isolation and remoteness. This is particularly true of the islands off Mayo's coast and the mountains north of Sligo town.

Mayo remains largely undiscovered, but Sligo is better known to travellers thanks largely to the evocative poetry of WB Yeats and the paintings of his brother Jack, who were obsessed with the county's natural beauty and cultural folklore, even if their views of the county were somewhat skewed by their penchant for romanticism and the fact that as adults they didn't visit the county nearly as often as the tourist offices would have you believe. However, the qualities of landscape and sense of place that inspired the Yeats boys belong equally to both counties. If you want to get off the well-worn tourist trail, you can get good-and-lost here. The distinct advantage to visiting counties ignored by the mass of other visitors is not just reflected in the lower prices, but in a sense of space and the presence of tradition that doesn't need artificial authentication, so often seen in other parts of the country.

HIGHLIGHTS

- Explore ruggedly remote **Achill Island** (p414) off the coast of western Mayo
- Cycle or drive from Louisburgh to Leenane (County Galway) through the wildly beautiful **Doolough Valley** (p411)
- Visit **Céide Fields** (p418) in northern Mayo, one of the most extensive Stone Age excavations in Europe
- Wander along the Hollow – the long, wide sandy beach at **Enniscrone** (p431)
- Take in the panoramic but spooky **Carrowkeel Passage Tomb Cemetery** (p430) in the Bricklieve Mountains

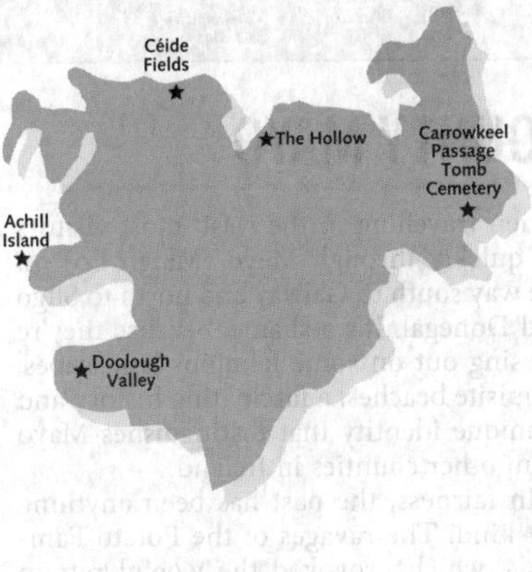

- POPULATION: 175,600
- AREA: 7195 SQ KM

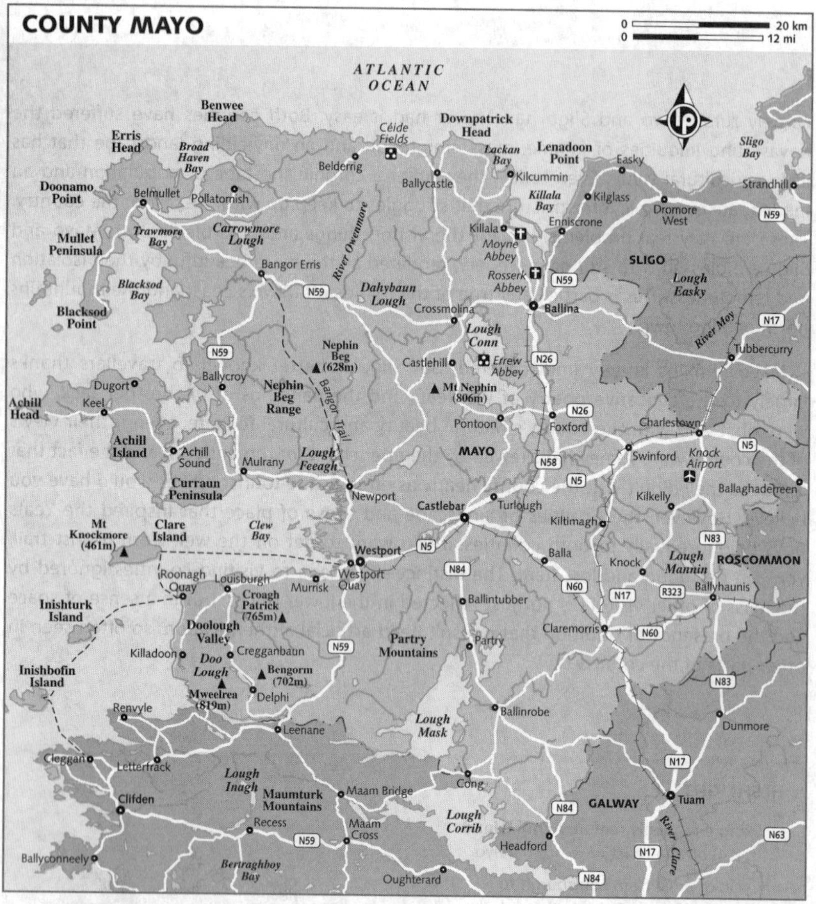

COUNTY MAYO

When travelling in the west, most visitors go quickly through Mayo (Maigh Eo) on the way south to Galway and north to Sligo and Donegal. It's a shame, because they're missing out on some fabulous landscapes, exquisite beaches, a fascinating history and a unique identity that distinguishes Mayo from other counties in Ireland.

In fairness, the past has been anything but kind. The ravages of the Potato Famine – which provoked the woeful refrain 'County Mayo, Mayo, God help us!' – were harshest here, and the emigration that it provoked still plagues the county to this day. The modernisation of its infrastructure and the creation of employment opportunities are a slow, on-going process, but they are making a difference and Mayo's future is looking brighter than its past ever did. If you want to get an intimate peek at a more traditional, introspective Ireland, where the landscape remains largely untouched and the people are unaffected by the trappings of a fast and prosperous lifestyle, we urge you to visit before it's too late.

CONG

☎ 094 / pop 500

It's a pretty village, there are some important monastic ruins, but let's be honest:

the main reason folks trundle into Cong is to visit the village made famous by Hollywood in 1951 as the postcard representation of rural Ireland. We're talking of course of *The Quiet Man,* filmed here over 10 weeks by John Ford and starring John Wayne and Maureen O'Hara. Cong (Cung, from the Irish for 'narrow strip of land') has made a big deal of its links with the film, and there are plenty of reminders scattered throughout of that momentous summer.

Cong is just east of the border with County Galway and lies on the narrow isthmus between Lough Corrib, 1km to the south, and Lough Mask, 5km north.

Information

The **tourist office** (☎ 954 6542; Abbey St; 🕒 10am-6pm Apr-May & Sep-Nov, 9.30am-7pm Jul-Aug, closed rest of year) is in the old courthouse building opposite Cong Abbey. Get a copy of the *Heritage Trail* brochure to explore the town and discover the fascinating history of the 1123 Cong Cross, now in the National Museum in Dublin. The local booklets *The Glory of Cong* and *Cong: Walks, Sights, Stories* have more information. A self-guided tour using *The Quiet Man* map takes in locations from the film, while real fanatics may want to equip themselves with a copy of Lisa Collins' *Complete Guide to the Quiet Man Locations* (€2.99).

There are no banks but you can change money at the post office on Main St.

Cong Abbey

Founded by Turlough Mór O'Connor, high king of Ireland and king of Connaught in 1120, this ruined Augustinian abbey occupies the site of an earlier 6th-century church. It has a carved doorway on the northern side, and fine windows and decorated medieval stonework in the **Chapter House**. West of the abbey on a small island in the nearby river stands the **Monk's Fishing House**, where a bell was rung every time a fish was caught. The concrete 1960s-style Catholic church, beside the abbey, is an eyesore built with utter disregard for its surroundings. The small **O'Duffy's Cross**, at the junction of Main and Abbey Sts, is the reconstructed remains of a 14th-century high cross.

Quiet Man Heritage Cottage

Just west of the tourist office is the **Quiet Man Heritage Cottage** (☎ 954 6089; Circular Rd; adult/child €3.75/2; 🕒 10am-5pm Mar-Oct). In a life-imitating-art exercise so twisted it begs a map, it attempts to re-create the exact set John Ford used to film many of the interior shots of *The Quiet Man* in Hollywood. Of course, original cottages such as this one – and their interiors – were his inspiration but, hey, they want real Hollywood. The cottage also contains the **Cong Archaeological and Historical Exhibition**, which rather ambitiously attempts to trace the story of Cong and its surrounds from 7000 BC to the 19th century in a very small space.

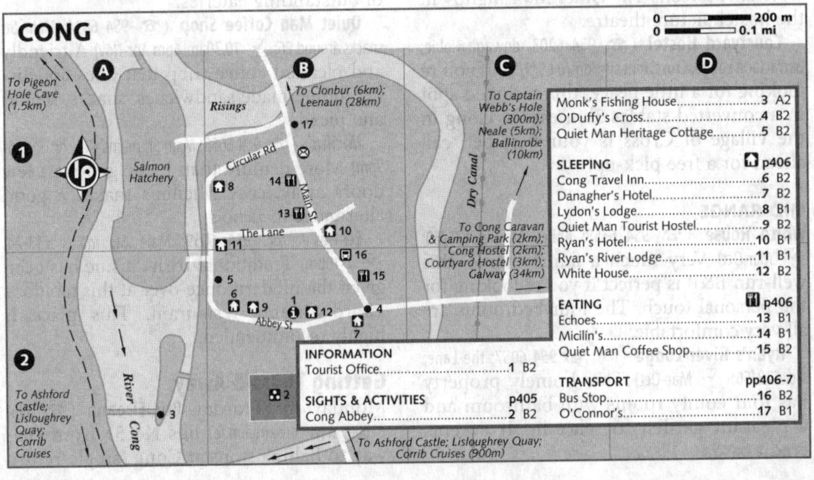

Cruises

A well-established operator, **Corrib Cruises** (☎ 954 6029; www.corribcruises.com; Cong; 🕒 11.15am & 3pm Apr-Nov) offers 1½-hour boat tours from Lisloughrey Pier at Ashford Castle to Inchagoill Island (€15) and then on to Oughterard (€20) in County Galway.

Sleeping

BUDGET

Cong Caravan & Camping Park (☎ 954 6089; fax 954 6448; Quay Rd, Lisloughrey; tent site & 2 people/caravan €9/17) This pleasant camp site 2km east of town off the Galway road (R346) and close to the shore of Lough Corrib is like a self-contained village. There are plenty of amenities, including a laundry, a shop and boat and bike rental.

There is no shortage of good-quality hostel accommodation; one proprietor owns three hostels in the vicinity.

Cong Travel Inn (☎ 954 6310; congtravelinn@eircom.net; Abbey St; s/d €17/34) This hostel provides excellent-value, modern, clean rooms with shower, tea and coffee facilities, plus a separate, self-catering communal kitchen.

Quiet Man Tourist Hostel (☎ 954 6089; Abbey St; dm/d €10/30) Opposite the abbey cemetery, this is a clean and comfortable modern hostel.

Cong Hostel (☎ 954 6089; www.irelandyha.org; Quay Rd, Lisloughrey; dm/d €10/30) A large congenial hostel affiliated with both An Óige and Independent Holiday Hostels of Ireland (IHH) is next to the camp site, it offers the benefits of modern facilities and proximity to Lough Corrib. It screens *The Quiet Man* nightly in the hostel picture theatre.

Courtyard Hostel (☎ 954 6203; dowagh@iol.ie; Garracloon Lodge, Cross; tent site/dm/d €5/9/28) If you're looking for a little peace, this secluded spot in a converted stables 3km east of Cong in the village of Cross is your best bet; call ahead for a free pick-up.

MID-RANGE

White House (☎ 954 6358; Abbey St; s/d €35/60; 🕒 Mar-Oct) Very much a family home, this well-run B&B is perfect if you're looking for the personal touch. The four bedrooms are all very comfortable.

Ryan's River Lodge (☎ /fax 954 6057; the Lane; s/d €28/56; 🕒 Mar-Oct) This homely property has four comfy rooms with bathroom and a pleasant garden to relax in. It accepts credit cards.

> **SOMETHING SPECIAL**
>
> **Ashford Castle** (☎ 954 6003; www.ashford.ie; Ashford; r €370; gardens adult/concession €5/2.50; 🕒 grounds to nonresidents 9am-5pm) Once owned by the Guinness family, this Victorian castle is now one of the top luxury hotels in the world, a fairy-tale place where everything and everyone is given the royal treatment. There are plenty of activities to keep guests entertained, from horse riding to golf. Ford and his actors stayed here during the filming of *The Quiet Man* (the film is shown 24 hours a day on a hotel TV channel) and nonresidents can wander about the 350 acres of parkland surrounding the castle (for a fee). This place is simply magnificent.

Lydon's Lodge (☎ 954 6053; fax 46523; Circular Rd; s/d €50/100; 🕒 Mar-Oct) This handsome two-storey lodge offers comfortable rooms in rustic surroundings.

Ryan's Hotel (☎ 954 6243; fax 954 6634; Main St; s/d €45/90; 🕒 Feb-Dec) Ryan's has a charming, old-world interior and an enviable riverside location.

Danagher's Hotel (☎ 954 6028; Abbey St; s/d €50/80) Near the town's main junction, this is an old-style, 11-room hotel with comfortable rooms.

Eating

For such a small town, Cong has a couple of outstanding eateries.

Quiet Man Coffee Shop (☎ 954 6034; Main St; snacks around €6; 🕒 10.30am-6pm Apr-Nov) A friendly and pleasant coffee shop that does appetising, home-made sandwiches, snacks, scones and pies.

Micilín's (☎ 954 6655; Main St; mains €11-20; 🕒 6-9pm) More demure than its neighbour a few doors away, cosy Micilín's makes a good alternative to Echoes.

Echoes (☎ 954 6059; Main St; mains €13-24; 🕒 7-10pm) Traditional Irish cuisine has been given the modern once-over at this fabulous award-winning restaurant. This place is highly recommended.

Getting There & Away

Monday to Saturday **Bus Éireann** (☎ 096-71800; www.buseireann.ie) bus No 51 from Galway to Ballina stops at Cong (single/return

€8.20/11) and at Ashford Castle gates in the early afternoon.

If you're travelling by car or bike further into County Mayo, eschew the main N84 to Castlebar and take the longer, but much more attractive, route west to Leenaun (starting with the R345) and north to Westport via Delphi.

Getting Around

There are enough interesting sites close to Cong to make a bike worth having. They can be hired from **O'Connor's** (☎ 954 6008; Main St; daily/weekly €20/80). O'Connor's is the combined Esso station, Spar supermarket and craft shop next to the Rising of the Waters pub.

AROUND CONG

There's a surprising amount to see and do around Cong, including a collection of caves, a stone circle and a curious folly. The limestone strata of the Cong area accounts for the numerous caves, for the failure of the canal and for the local phenomenon known as 'the rising of the waters', where water from Lough Mask to the north percolates through the limestone and emerges from the ground at Cong before flowing down to Lough Corrib.

Caves

The Cong area is peppered with caves, many of them only a short walk from the village.

Pigeon Hole is about 1.5km west of Cong and can be reached by road or by the walking track from across the river. Stone steps lead down into the cave, which is sometimes very wet. From the Pigeon Hole, take the R345 west towards Clonbur, passing the Giant's Grave turn-off, and go onto a lane that turns south about 5km from Cong. A stream flows into the extensive **Ballymaglancy Cave**, which is off the road to the right. The cave has stalactites and stalagmites.

Two other caves are northeast of Cong, near the road to Cross (R346). **Captain Webb's Hole** is just outside Cong, a short distance beyond the dry canal and behind the school grounds. It's actually a deep, water-filled hole in the ground where, two centuries ago, a local villain is said to have hurled a succession of local women. Another 200m

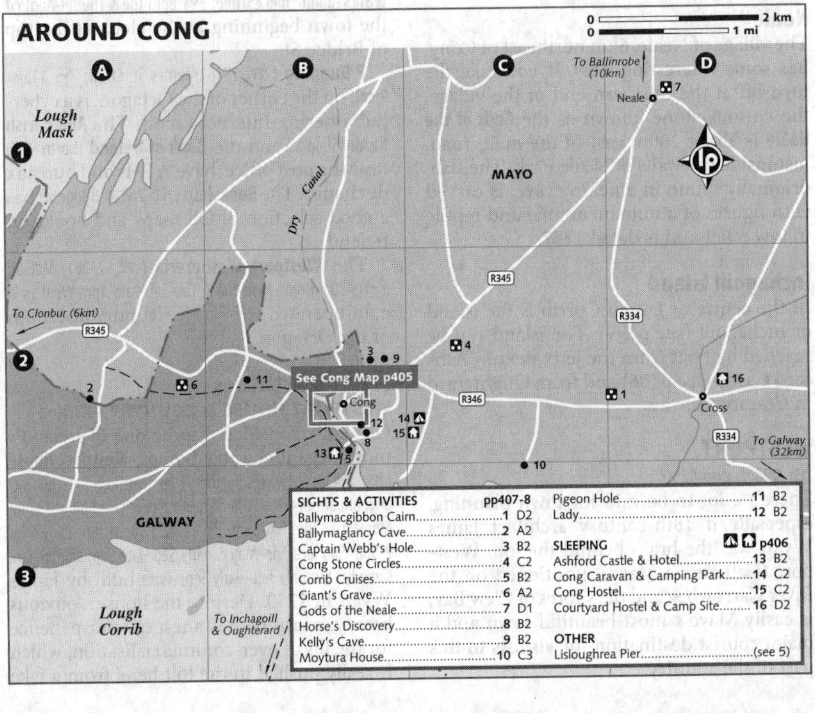

from Cong, a wide path leads to **Kelly's Cave**, which is usually locked up; the key is kept at the Quiet Man Coffee Shop (a small deposit may be required). The **Lady** and **Horse's Discovery** are two other caves beside a road to the castle.

Circles & Graves

The stone slabs of the megalithic burial chamber known as the **Giant's Grave** can be visited easily between the Pigeon Hole and Ballymaglancy Cave. A path leads into the forest south of the R345 road to Clonbur, about 2km from Cong. About 100m from the road take the turn-off to the left; the grave is off that path to the right.

There are several stone circles in the area, including the excellent **Cong Stone Circles** about 1.5km northeast of Cong just east off the Neale road (R345). About 3.5km east of Cong, north off the Cross road (R346), is **Ballymacgibbon Cairn**, supposedly the site of a legendary Celtic battle. **Moytura House**, near the shores of Lough Corrib, takes its name from this battle and was a childhood home of Oscar Wilde.

Neale

The village of Neale, 6km northeast of Cong, has some interesting sites. If you take the turn-off at the northern end of the village, the curious stone known as the **Gods of the Neale** is about 200m east of the main road, just inside the walls of Neale Park. The slab, originally found in a nearby cave, is carved with figures of a human, animal and reptile in low relief and is dated 1757.

Inchagoill Island

In the centre of Lough Corrib is the island of Inchagoill (see p399). The island can be reached by boat from the jetty next to Ashford Castle (see p406) and from Oughterard in County Galway.

WESTPORT

☎ 098 / pop 4250

There's a lot to be said for town planning, especially if 18th-century architect James Wyatt was the brain behind the job. Westport (Cathair na Mairt), positioned on the River Carrowbeg and the shores of Clew Bay, is easily Mayo's most beautiful town and a major tourist destination for visitors to this part of the country.

The original settlement of Westport was built around an O'Malley castle, but it disappeared beneath the confident demolish-and-build spree that was the Georgian era. The new town, designed by Wyatt with a little help from Georgian superstar Richard Castle, saw the creation of an octagonal square, handsome buildings and a tree-lined mall running alongside the Carrowbeg that to this day is one of Ireland's most pleasant streets. Museums and other attractions may be in short supply, but Westport is mostly about atmosphere – and neatness: in 2001 it was named Ireland's tidiest town and the tourist board has designated it a Heritage Town.

Orientation & Information

Westport consists of two parts: the town proper and Westport Quay on the bay, just outside town on the road to Louisburgh (R335). The **tourist office** (☎ 25711; www.irelandwest.ie; James St; ⌚ 9am-6pm Mon-Sat & 10am-6pm Sun Jul-Aug, 9am-5.45pm Mon-Sat Apr-Jun & Sep, 9am-12.45pm & 2-5pm Mon-Fri rest of year) is the best of its kind in the county. There are **guided walks** (adult/child €5/free; ⌚ 8pm Tue & Thu Jul-Aug) of the town beginning at the clock at the top of Bridge St.

P Dunning (☎ 25161; James St; €8/hr; ⌚ 11am-9pm), on the corner of the Octagon, is a cyber-pub offering Internet access. The **Allied Irish Bank** (Shop St) and the **Bank of Ireland** (North Mall) near the post office, have ATMs and bureaux de change. The **Bookshop** (☎ 26816; Bridge St) has a good selection of OS maps and books on Ireland.

The **Westport Washeteria** (☎ 25261; Mill St; ⌚ 9.30am-6pm Mon-Tue & Thu-Sat, 9am-1pm Wed) is a coin-operated self-service laundry just south of the Octagon.

Sights & Activities

WESTPORT HOUSE & COUNTRY PARK

Generally considered to be one of Ireland's most elegant country homes, **Westport House** (☎ 25430; www.westporthouse.ie; Quay Rd; adult/child incl animal park €24/15, 20% discount if purchased before 11am Mon-Fri & 1pm Sat-Sun; ⌚ 1.30-5.30pm Jun–early Sep, 2-5pm Sun late Apr–May & early Sep–late Sep; animal park same hrs but only Jun–early Sep) was built by James Wyatt in 1730. Despite the house's obvious beauty, a visit here is a test of your patience for the ills of over-commercialisation, which is really pushed to the hilt here, from a fake

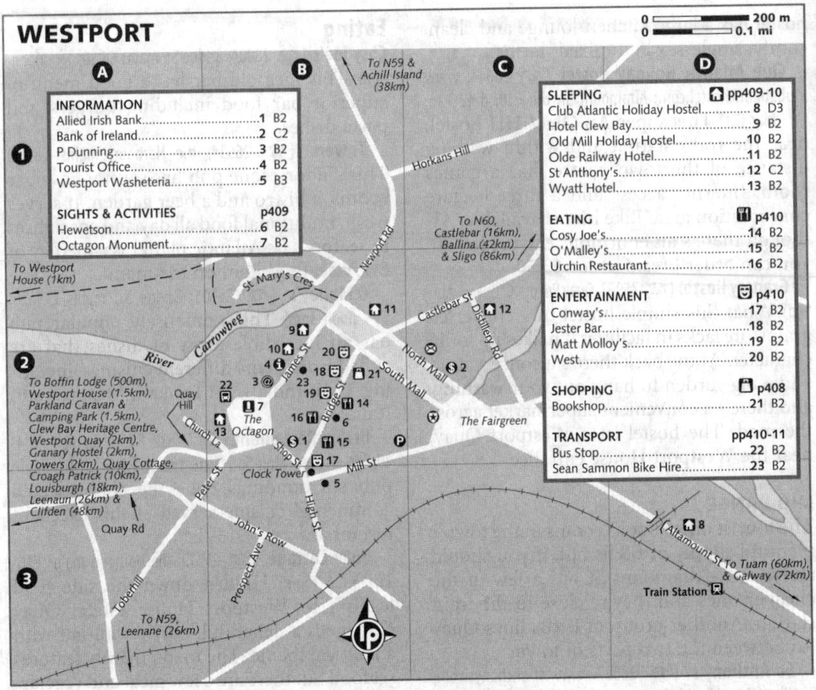

'dungeon' to tacky souvenirs for sale in the 'Gifte Shoppe'. Consider a visit only if your itinerary doesn't include an Irish stately home elsewhere.

To reach Westport House, head out of town west on Quay Rd towards Croagh Patrick and Louisburgh. After about 1km, just before you get to Westport Quay, there's a road to the right that leads to the entrance to the grounds.

OCTAGON MONUMENT

This memorial was erected in 1845 in honour of eminently forgettable George Clendening, a local banker who died before the Famine. Until 1922, his statue stood upon the podium, but it was decapitated during the Civil War, after which it was removed altogether. In 1990 a Roman-looking statue of St Patrick complete with serpent-entwined staff replaced the unfortunate capitalist.

CLEW BAY HERITAGE CENTRE

This **heritage centre** (☎ 26852; the Quay; adult/child €2.50/1.20; ⏰ 10am-5pm Mon-Fri & 3-5pm Sun Jul & Aug, 10am-5pm Mon-Fri Jun & Sep, 10am-2pm Mon-Fri Apr, May & Oct) is down on the pier in Westport Quay. It has an interesting collection of local artefacts and documents, including the spinning wheel presented by the people of Ballina to Maud Gonne, Yeats' unwilling muse – see Lissadell House (p433). The centre provides a genealogical service too.

FISHING

For information about fishing, inquire at **Hewetson** (☎ 26018; Bridge St).

Sleeping

BUDGET

Parkland Caravan & Camping Park (☎ 27766; camping@westporthouse.ie; Westport House, Quay Rd; tent & 2 people with/without car €25/22; ⏰ mid-May–early Sep) Part of the Westport House estate, this large camp site is scenically sited in woodland between the river and Clew Bay.

Old Mill Holiday Hostel (☎ 27045; oldmill@iol.ie; Barrack Yard, James St; dm/d €14/30; ⏰ closed Christmas) Our preferred hostel option in town is this charming converted mill next door to the tourist office; go through the arch. The Independent Holiday Hostels of Ireland (IHH) hostel has a large kitchen-lounge and clean, comfy, single-sex and mixed dorms.

Club Atlantic Holiday Hostel (☎ 26644; www.clubatlantichostel.com; Altamount St; dm €10, d €26-36; ⏲ Mar-Oct) This super An Óige/IHH hostel, near the train station and within walking distance of the town centre, has a games room, Internet access and a three-hectare conservation area. Bike hire is available. Although there's an enormous eat-in kitchen, you can order breakfast for €3.50.

Granary Hostel (☎ 25903; Quay Rd; dm €10; ⏲ Apr-Sep) What this simple hostel in a converted grainstore lacks in facilities it makes up for in character. At the back there's a conservatory and a big garden to hang out your washing, and there's a convenient supermarket across the road. The hostel is in Westport Quay, near the Westport House entrance.

MID-RANGE

The tourist office books rooms in the town's plentiful supply of B&Bs but, if you should arrive late, Altamount St has a few of the cheaper ones and they're close to the train station. Another group of B&Bs lines Quay Rd between the two parts of town.

St Anthony's (☎ 28887; www.st-anthonys.com; Distillery Rd; s/d with bathroom €40/80) This elegant home surrounded by a gorgeous garden is just west of North Mall. Two of the six rooms even have Jacuzzis.

Boffin Lodge (☎ 26092; www.boffinlodge.com; Quay Rd; s/d €50/90) About 500m west of town and close to the harbour is this lovely home with really comfortable bedrooms and very friendly service.

TOP END

Hotel Clew Bay (☎ 25438; www.clewbayhotel.com; James St; s/d €70/140) A recent refurbishment has brought new elegance to this Westport institution that simply oozes old-world charm.

Wyatt Hotel (☎ 25027; www.wyatthotel.com; the Octagon; s/d €70/140) Formerly the Grand Central, this elegant hotel features large, comfortable rooms that are thoroughly modern in appearance.

Olde Railway Hotel (☎ 25166; fax 25090; the Mall; s €65-90) 'One of the prettiest, comfortablist inns in Ireland', declared English novelist William Thackeray when he stayed here in 1834. This 15-room Victorian showcase hotel is indeed both of those, and it is a marvellous place for afternoon tea.

Eating

Cosy Joe's (☎ 28004; Bridge St; mains €6.50; ⏲ noon-3pm) This nice old bar has a good menu of superior bar food including burgers and pasta dishes.

Towers (☎ 26534; the Harbour; mains €8-14) This Tudor-esque pub has several cosy bar rooms, a bistro and a beer garden. It serves fresh, traditional food all day and specialises in seafood. Its Atlantic platter is a medley of every seafood item on the menu.

O'Malley's (☎ 25101; Bridge St; mains €11-20; ⏲ noon-3pm) This immensely popular pub has an incredible array of dishes that are culled from many different cuisines, including Thai, Indian, Sri Lankan, Mexican and Italian.

Urchin Restaurant (☎ 27532; Bridge St; mains €14-19; ⏲ 6-10pm Mon-Sat) The traditional, old-style pub surroundings belie the sophisticated continental cuisine served at this excellent restaurant.

Quay Cottage (☎ 26412; the Harbour; mains €16-25; ⏲ 6-10pm) Hidden down the side road leading to Westport House estate, Quay Cottage is a delightful, cosy restaurant with a nautical theme. The menu mainly features seafood but there are a few meat and vegetarian dishes.

Entertainment

Matt Molloy's (☎ 26655; Bridge St) This is a great old pub with wooden floors, a warm fire in the back and bric-a-brac everywhere. It's owned by Matt Molloy of the Chieftains and can get overcrowded when Irish music sessions are on. Sometimes there's an admission charge to hear well-known performers.

Conway's (☎ 26145; Bridge St) With its dark-wood walls, smoke-stained ceiling and friendly banter, Conway's exudes old-world charm by the bucket-load. The back room, like Molloy's, can get packed on traditional music nights.

West (☎ 28984; Bridge St) A trendy bar, despite the fact that it has done its utmost to ruin its old-style charm.

Jester Bar (☎ 29255; Bridge St) This new addition to the scene attracts the cool young things nightly.

Getting There & Away

Bus Éireann (☎ 096-71800) travels to Achill (adult/child €3/2, 30 minutes, two daily),

Ballina (€9.20/6, 1½ hours, four daily), Cork (€22/14.50, six hours, seven daily), Dublin (€15/10, seven daily, four hours), Galway (€11.20/7.50, two hours, eight daily) and Sligo (€14/9, two hours, two daily). Buses depart from and arrive at the Octagon. There are limited services on Sunday; phone for confirmation.

The **train station** (☎ 25253) is on Altamount St within easy walking distance of the town centre. There are three daily connections (four on Sunday) to Dublin (adult/child €25/12.50, 3½ hours) via Athlone.

Getting Around

For a cab call **Moran's Executive Taxis** (☎ 25539). **Sean Sammon Bike Hire** (☎ 25020; James St) hires out bikes for €12 per day, or you can hire one from the **Club Atlantic Holiday Hostel** (☎ 26644; Altamount St), which also provides a trilingual pamphlet with seven suggested itineraries.

AROUND WESTPORT

Croagh Patrick

Croagh Patrick (also known as 'the Reek') towers to the southwest of Westport. From the top of this mountain St Patrick performed his snake-expulsion act – Ireland has been free of venomous serpents ever since. Climbing the 765m holy mountain is an act of penance for thousands of pilgrims on the last Sunday of July (Reek Sunday). The truly contrite make the trek along Tóchar Phádraig (Patrick's Causeway), the original 40km route from Ballintubber Abbey, and ascend the mountain barefoot.

The trail for less contrite folk begins beside Campbell's pub in the village of **Murrisk** (Muraisc), west of Westport. There's a sign (between the pub and the car park) pointing the way, and there's no mistaking the route. At the start of the path is an **information centre** (☎ 098-64114; 🕒 11am-5pm). If the weather is clear, the 1½- to two-hour climb to the small church at the top gives fine views year-round.

Opposite the car park is the **National Famine Memorial**, a metal sculpture of a three-masted sailing ship covered in skeletons, commemorating the Famine (1845–49). Following the path down past the memorial brings you to the remains of **Murrisk Abbey**, founded by the O'Malleys in 1547.

Louisburgh & Around

☎ 098 / pop 500

The first marquess of Sligo, Lord Altamont (John Browne to you and I), had a relative who fought at the Battle of Louisburgh in Nova Scotia in 1758. The relative was killed, and Lord Altamont decided that the best tribute to his fallen hero was to design and build an entire town in his memory. The result is Louisburgh (Cluain Cearbán), founded in 1795 on a simple four-street system known as the Cross.

Here you can visit the **Granuaile Visitors Centre** (☎ 66341; Church St; adult/child €3.50/2; 🕒 11am-5pm Mon-Sat Jun-Sep). The centre, in a disused church, is dedicated to the life and times of Grace O'Malley (Grainne ni Mhaille, 1530–1603), the pirate queen and the most famous of the O'Malley clan. See the boxed text (p413). It also includes an exhibition on the Famine and the terrible privations it caused.

There are some excellent **beaches** in the vicinity: Old Head Beach and the Silver Strand are particularly sandy and safe, and are suitable for **surfing** and other water sports.

Old Head Forest Caravan & Camping Park (☎ 087-648 6885; fax 053-20041; Old Head, Louisburgh; large tent/hikers & cyclists €10.20/6.50; 🕒 Jun-Sep) This medium-sized camping park is about 4km from Louisburgh, just off the main road to Westport, and a short walk from the Blue Flag beach, where there is a pier and a slipway with a lifeguard on duty.

Bus Éireann (☎ 096-71800) bus No 450 links Westport and Louisburgh (single/return €2.80/4.50, 35 minutes, five daily Monday to Saturday) via Murrisk.

Killadoon

Killadoon is a small village of scattered houses on the coast. It's reached by a narrow coastal road heading south from Louisburgh or by turning west off the R335 at Cregganbaun. Its main attractions are the panoramic ocean views and long sandy beaches.

Bus Éireann (☎ 096-71800) bus No 450 from Westport and Louisburgh continues to Killadoon up to five times daily. The trip takes about 10 minutes.

Doolough Valley

There are two roads connecting Westport and Leenane (County Galway), but the one nearest the coast (the R335) via Louisburgh and Delphi travels through the stunning Doolough Valley. It's wildly beautiful, not least because of the lonely expanse of **Doo Lough** (Dark Lake) with the **Mweelrea Mountains** behind. At the southern end of the lake **Bengorm** rises to 702m. The landscape changes from baize-green and sparkling wet stone to a forbidding grey as shadows envelop everything when cloud-banks spread in from the Atlantic.

During the Potato Famine, the valley was the scene of tragedy when some 600 men, women and children walked from Louisburgh to Delphi Lodge hoping that the landlord would offer them food. Help was flatly refused and, on the return journey, around 400 perished through hunger and exposure. There's a memorial to the unfortunate souls along the road.

DELPHI

☎ 095

The second Marquess of Sligo, a friend of Byron, gave the unlikely name of Delphi to his fishing lodge on the border of Galway and Mayo. He had travelled in central Greece and returned home convinced that his starkly beautiful territory strongly resembled the area around Delphi. The closest settlement of size is Leenane in Galway.

Delphi Lodge (☎ 42222; www.delphilodge.ie; Leenane; s/d €120/180) Today, this remote Georgian lodge caters mostly for well-to-do anglers who fish in the peaceful local waters; permits (€50 per day) are available.

Delphi Mountain Lodge & Spa (☎ 42987, 42208; www.delphiescape.com; Leenane; s/d with meals & activities from €150/240) Beautifully remote and remarkably well-equipped, this wonderful lodge offers high-quality accommodation and a choice of 25 outdoor activities, as well as a comprehensive health-spa programme.

CLARE ISLAND

☎ 098 / pop 150

Clare Island, at the mouth of Clew Bay, is 5km from the nearest mainland point, Roonagh Quay. **Bay View Hotel** (☎ 26307), near the harbour, has tourist information.

The mountainous island rises up to **Mt Knockmore** (461m), which is the highest point and dominates the landscape. The island has the ruins of the Cistercian **Clare Island Abbey** (c.1460) and **Granuaile's Castle**, both associated with the piratical Grace O'Malley. The tower castle was her stronghold, although it was altered considerably when the coastguard took it over in 1831. Grace is said to be buried in the small abbey, which contains a stone inscribed with her family motto: 'Invincible on land and sea.'

The island has safe, sandy beaches and is a perfect place for **walking** and **climbing** on a clear day. It is also one of the dwindling number of places where you can find **choughs**, which look like blackbirds but have red beaks.

Sleeping & Eating

Cois Abhainn (☎ 26216; s/d €25/50; ⊠) In the remote southwestern corner of the island about 5km from the harbour, this is a secluded B&B with sensational views. Call ahead and a pick-up will be arranged.

Bay View Hotel (☎ 26307; clareislhotel@hotmail.com; s/d €33/60; 🕑 Jun-Sep) The island's main hotel is set back from the harbour and is a favourite with anglers, divers and other water-bound folk.

If you're just going for the day to the harbour it's best to take your own food, though pub grub is available at the Bay View Hotel, and B&Bs do evening meals for guests and nonguests (from €15.25).

Getting There & Away

Clare Island Ferries (☎ 26307, 087-241 4653) and **O'Malley's Ferries** (☎ 25045, 086-877 7390) make the 25-minute trip from Roonagh Quay, 8km west of Louisburgh (adult/child €15/5 return). There are eight sailings daily in July and August, and from three to five daily in May, June and September; for the October to April schedule call the operators.

INISHTURK ISLAND

☎ 098 / pop 98

Inishturk Island lies about 12km off Mayo's western coast. Evidence of pre-Christian life has been found, but it's believed that the ancestors of many of today's inhabitants were driven here in Cromwell's time. The island doesn't receive many tourists, despite the two **sandy beaches** on its eastern side, wonderful **flora and fauna**, and a rugged, hilly landscape ideal for **walking**.

B&B is available at **Ocean View House** (☎ 45520), 500m northeast of the harbour, and **Teach Abhainn** (☎ 45110), a working farm about 1.5km west the harbour. Rooms at both start at €20 per person. They also share a love of organic cuisine, and dinner (around €20) is available at both.

Helen and John Heanue operate a **ferry** (☎ 45541, 086-202 9670; Roonagh) from Roonagh Quay (adult/under-12 return €20/10, 11am and 6.30pm). There is also a Tuesday and Thursday service to Cleggan in County Galway; call for details of departure times.

NEWPORT

☎ 098 / pop 520

The small 18th-century town of Newport (Baile Uí Fhiacháin), on the River Newport about 12km north of Westport, is a popular base for **fishing** in the nearby loughs and Clew Bay.

The **tourist office** (☎ 41822; Main St; 10am-5pm Mon-Fri Jun-Sep) is opposite the Angler's Rest pub. The post office and bureau de change are on the other side of the river. There are no banks.

From 1892 to 1936, the Great Western Railway ran a line from Westport to Achill Sound. The seven-arch viaduct over the town has been pedestrianised and offers an interesting **walk** with views of the river (the viaduct is particularly beautiful at night, when it is lit up). Newport is also at one end of the Bangor Trail (see p417).

Sleeping & Eating

Debille House (☎ 41145; fax 41777; Main St; s/d €33/55; Jun-Sep) A stately three-storey town house in the middle of town with comfortable and elegant rooms plus a lovely garden.

Newport House (☎ 41222; www.newporthouse.ie; Main St; s/d with breakfast €136/224, dinner €40; Mar-Sep) This magnificent red-ivy-clad Georgian mansion is one of the top country hotels in Ireland and is a perennial award-winner. Every room in the hotel is beautifully appointed, but Newport House is especially known for its dining; the menu offers the best of contemporary Irish cuisine and a wine list that will make you drool. The bar is also worth checking out, even if you're not a guest.

Village Bakery (☎ 42949; Main St; lunch €5-9) The bakery, below Debille House, sells wonderful fresh cakes, pies and tarts, as well as quiches and hot soups at lunch-time.

PIRATE QUEEN OF CONNAUGHT

The life of Grace O'Malley (Gráinne Ní Mháille or Granuaile, 1530–1603) reads like an unlikely work of adventure fiction for overactive teenagers. Twice widowed and twice imprisoned for acts of piracy, she was a fearsome presence in the troubled landscape of 16th-century Ireland, when traditional chieftains were locked in battle with the English for control of the country. Her unorthodox life was the stuff of legend and mythology, and there are literally hundreds of stories testifying to her unequalled courage, skill and dogged determination to protect her clan against virtually everyone else – from rival chieftains to the armies of Queen Elizabeth I.

When she was 15 she married Donall O'Flaherty and when he died fighting a rival chieftain she asserted her rights as head of the unified clan, only for the O'Flaherty's to reject her claim on the basis that she was a woman and could not therefore lead a family. Unperturbed but eager to earn money, she and 200 of her clan took to sea and the legend of the pirate queen began. She was a terrific sailor and a fearsome commander, and she used her skills to literally terrorise merchant ships into paying her a duty for safe passage to port (usually Galway); if they didn't, she would order her men to board and loot to their hearts' content.

In 1566 she married Richard an-Iarrain (Iron Dick Burke) so as to gain full control of Clew Bay. As they were married under Brehon Law, which allowed for a divorce within the first year of marriage, she divorced him exactly a year later, but only after she had gained control of his family castle (Carrigahowley, now called Rockfleet Castle, near Newport). She did still love him, though, and despite the divorce they remained together until his death 17 years later. In the meantime, she went about her business, disrupted only by a couple of spells in prison.

Her activities frustrated the English so much that in 1593 she was ordered to London, whereupon Queen Elizabeth granted her a pardon and offered her a title: she declined, saying that she was already Queen of Connaught, and that was that. She died peacefully on her beloved Clare Island in 1603.

Getting There & Away

A **Bus Éireann** (☎ 096-71800) service links Achill Island and Westport via Newport once a day, Monday to Saturday, year-round. In July and August, bus No 66 from Achill Sound to Belfast stops at Newport and goes on through Ballina, Sligo and Enniskillen. The bus stop is outside Debille House.

NEWPORT TO ACHILL ISLAND

Burrishoole Abbey

Founded in 1486 by the Dominicans, what remains of the abbey is a solid tower and the eastern window of the cloisters. It's beside the river that drains Lough Furnace into the sea. About 2.5km northwest of Newport on the Newport–Achill road, a sign points the way, and it's 1km down to the left.

Rockfleet Castle

Formerly known as Carrigahowley, this 15th-century tower house has a strong association with Grace O'Malley (see the boxed text on p413). To get here, turn south at the sign about 5km west of Newport on the Achill road.

Mulrany & Curraun Peninsula

The village of Mulrany (An Mhala Raithní, also called Mallaranny or Mulranny) stands on the isthmus between Clew Bay – with its (supposed) 365 islands – and Bellacagher Bay and boasts a lovely, wide Blue Flag **beach**. To get to it, either take the footpath opposite the defunct Mulrany Bay Hotel, a huge cream-and-chocolate pile on the N59, or the one starting beside the Top service station.

Sleeping

Traenlaur Lodge (☎ 098-41358; www.irelandyha.org; Lough Feeagh, Newport; dm €13; Jun-Sep, Sat & Sun only rest of year) A gorgeous An Óige hostel in a former fishing lodge with its own small harbour on Lough Feeagh. It is 8km from Newport and signposted on the road to Achill. It's a great place to relax especially if you're walking the Western Way or Bangor Trail, which meet here.

Achill seems the obvious destination if you're travelling from Newport, but the wild Curraun Peninsula, joined to Achill Island by a bridge, has a B&B where you can get away from it all.

Teach Mweewillin (☎ 098-45134; fax 45225; Curraun, Achill; s/d €30/50; May-Sep; ⊠) The B&B sits on a hillside in the remote southwestern corner of the peninsula with views across to Achill Island. Evening meals (€10) are provided on request.

ACHILL ISLAND

☎ 098 / pop 2900

Achill (An Caol), Ireland's largest off-shore island, manages to cram dramatic cliff scenery, undulating stretches of moorland and wild mountains into 147 sq km. It's a pretty bleak place most of the year, but come the summer the rows of white holiday cottages fill up with vacationers from the mainland. The interest in the island is a relatively recent thing, though: for most of the last century Achill was a tough and largely forgotten place, mostly because there's virtually nothing to do here: farming is limited and jobs were scarce.

In recent years the Dublin government has remembered that Achill is in fact part of its territorial remit and has made efforts to encourage the island's only vibrant industry: seasonal tourism.

Achill is joined to the mainland (the Curraun Peninsula) by a bridge, and the village of Keel is the island's main centre of activity.

Information

The helpful, locally run **tourist office** (☎ 47353; www.achilltourism.com; Cashel; 9am-6pm Mon-Fri Jul-Aug, 9am-5pm Sep-Jun) is in a portable cabin beside the Esso service station in Cashel. The **Fáilte Ireland** (☎ 45384; www.ireland.ie; Cashel; 9am-5.45pm) office is in a cabin at the other side of the same service station.

Most villages have a post office and O'Malley's Spar supermarket in Keel doubles as a post office and changes money. There are no banks on the island but mobile banks visit the various villages (the tourist office's *A Visitor's Guide* has the times) and there's a Bank of Ireland ATM at the craft shop beside Sweeney's supermarket.

Slievemore Deserted Village

The now-renowned deserted village at the foot of Slievemore Mountain is a poignant reminder of the devastating effects of the Famine. Until the mid-19th century, the village was divided between permanent inhabitants and transhumance farmers (known here as 'booleying'), but as the Potato Famine took a grip of the west and

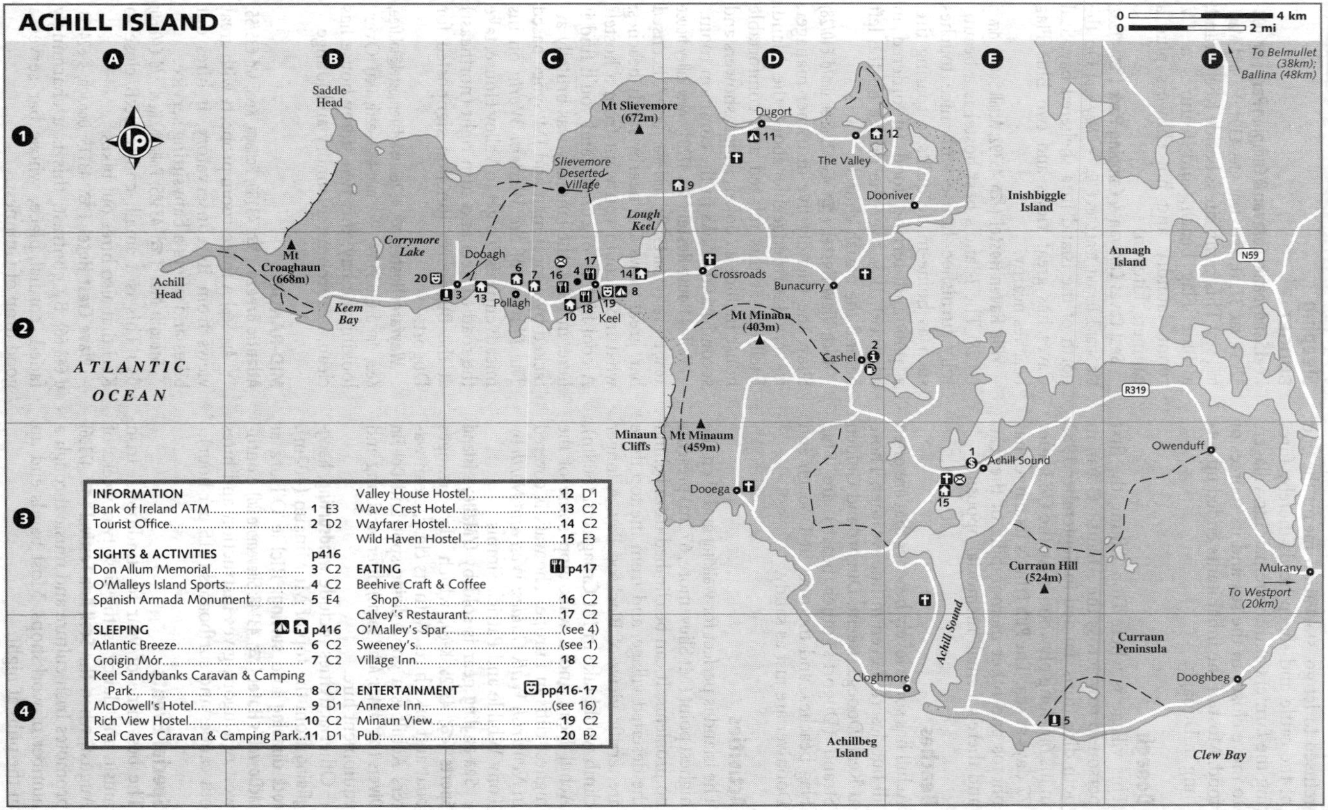
ACHILL ISLAND
0 4 km
0 2 mi
To Belmullet (38km); Ballina (48km)
Saddle Head
Mt Slievemore (672m)
Dugort
The Valley
Dooniver
Inishbiggle Island
Annagh Island
N59
Slievemore Deserted Village
Lough Keel
Corrymore Lake
Dooagh
Mt Croaghaun (668m)
Achill Head
Keem Bay
Pollagh
Keel
Crossroads
Bunacurry
Mt Minaun (403m)
Cashel
R319
ATLANTIC OCEAN
Minaun Cliffs
Mt Minaum (459m)
Achill Sound
Owenduff
Dooega
Curraun Hill (524m)
Mulrany
To Westport (20km)
Curraun Peninsula
Dooghbeg
Cloghmore
Achillbeg Island
Clew Bay
INFORMATION
Bank of Ireland ATM 1 E3
Tourist Office 2 D2
SIGHTS & ACTIVITIES p416
Don Allum Memorial 3 C2
O'Malleys Island Sports 4 C2
Spanish Armada Monument 5 E4
SLEEPING p416
Atlantic Breeze 6 C2
Groigin Mór 7 C2
Keel Sandybanks Caravan & Camping Park 8 C2
McDowell's Hotel 9 D1
Rich View Hostel 10 C2
Seal Caves Caravan & Camping Park 11 D1
Valley House Hostel 12 D1
Wave Crest Hotel 13 C2
Wayfarer Hostel 14 C2
Wild Haven Hostel 15 E3
EATING p417
Beehive Craft & Coffee Shop 16 C2
Calvey's Restaurant 17 C2
O'Malley's Spar (see 4)
Sweeney's (see 1)
Village Inn 18 C2
ENTERTAINMENT pp416-17
Annexe Inn (see 16)
Minaun View 19 C2
Pub 20 B2

refused to let go, starvation meant the end of the cattle and sheep herds thereby forcing the farmers and the remaining villagers to move closer to the sea and its sources of food. Most of the inhabitants ended up settling in Dooagh.

Dooagh

This village is where Don Allum, the first person to row across the Atlantic Ocean in both directions, landed in September 1982 in his 6m-long plywood boat, the *QE3*, after 77 days at sea. The **Pub** (that's its name) has photos and other memorabilia of the feat, and there's a small memorial opposite.

Beaches

Achill has some lovely beaches that are often all but deserted even in fine weather. Those at Keel, Dooega, Keem, Dugort and Golden Strand (Dugort's other beach) are Blue Flag beaches, and the ones at Dooagh and Dooniver are just as sandy.

Activities

The island is perfect for **walking** and even the highest point (Mt Slievemore, 672m) presents no problems. It can be climbed from behind the deserted village, and from the top there are terrific views of Blacksod Bay. A longer climb would take in Mt Croaghaun (668m), Achill Head and a walk atop some of the highest cliffs in Europe. The walk is covered in *New Irish Walk Guides: West and North* by Tony Whilde and Patrick Simms.

Sea-angling gear is sold by **O'Malley's Island Sports** (☎ 43125; Keel), which also arranges boat and bike hire. With its clear, clean waters Achill is a good **diving** spot and **Dol-Fin Divers** (☎ 45473; Achill Sound) offers training and equipment hire.

Other activities include **windsurfing**, **hang-gliding** from the top of Mt Minaun (403m), **rock climbing** and **surfing**. Richie O'Hara at **McDowell's Hotel** (☎ 43148; Slievemore Rd), southwest of Dugort, gives instruction and hires out canoes and surfboards (€15 per hour).

Special Events

The best time of year for traditional Irish music and dance is the first two weeks of August, when the **Scoil Acla Festival** (☎ 47306) promotes Irish culture and music through a number of workshops. Most bands end up in the pubs at night.

Sleeping

BUDGET

Keel Sandybanks Caravan & Camping Park (☎ 094-32054; fax 32351; Keel; tent sites €10; ⏰ mid-May–mid-Sep) This camp site is beside Keel Strand, a Blue Flag beach, and features a TV room, laundry and hot showers plus a campers' kitchen.

Seal Caves Caravan & Camping Park (☎ 43262; the Strand, Dugort; tent sites €10; ⏰ May-Sep) On the north of the island in a sheltered bay, Seal Caves has great views and two Blue Flag beaches nearby.

Wild Haven Hostel (☎ 45392; Achill Sound; dm/d €11/28) The island's best hostel is a beautifully furnished house with nice touches such as home-made quilts, a roaring fire, a pub and terrific food (if ordered in advance). It is over the bridge on the left behind the parish church.

Rich View Hostel (☎ 43462; Keel; dm/d €10/28) Shay, the friendly live-in owner-manager, is very knowledgeable about the island. Facilities at this relaxed and comfortable house include a cooker, fridge, showers and second-hand books in the common room.

Valley House Hostel (☎ 47204; www.valley-house.com; the Valley; dm €9; ⏰ mid-Mar–Oct) A licensed bar, great views and nearby sandy beaches: what more could you want from a hostel? A cool history of course, and you'll find it here: in 1894, the landlady was brutally attacked by a local man and JM Synge based *The Playboy of the Western World* on his misadventures. To get to Valley House, take the road to Keel and turn right (northeast) at the Bunacurry junction signposted for Dugort.

Wayfarer Hostel (☎ 43266; wayfarerhostel@iol.free; Keel; dm/d €10.50/24; ⏰ mid-Mar–early Oct) Overlooking the bay, this two-storey house has clean, neat rooms, a laundry and lounge.

MID-RANGE

Atlantic Breeze (☎ 43189; Pollagh, Keel; s/d €35/55; ⏰ Apr-Sep) A three-room property with great views from its conservatory, it hires out bikes and offers a babysitting service.

Groigin Mór (☎ 43385; Pollagh, Keel; s/d €40/60; ☒) This is a small, comfy B&B close to Keel that also hires out bikes.

Wave Crest Hotel (☎ 43115; Dooagh; s €24-33, d €48-66) By contrast, this is a charmingly faded, cordial place, whose bar serves a good drop of Guinness.

Eating

Calvey's Restaurant (☎ 43158; Keel; mains €6-18; 🕓 6-10pm Mon-Sat) Calvey's serves up fresh local seafood, and meat from its own attached butchery.

Village Inn (☎ 43214; Keel; mains €7-17) You can enjoy soup and sandwiches in the small front bar with its open fire, or dine in the adjoining restaurant.

Beehive Craft & Coffee Shop (☎ 43134; Keel; snacks around €7; 🕓 10.30am-6pm Easter-Oct) A combined craft shop and café, the Beehive specialises in home-made soups served with brown scones and a mouth-watering selection of baked goodies.

If you're camping or hostelling, stock up at **Sweeney's** supermarket, just across the bridge as you enter Achill, or at **O'Malley's Spar** supermarket in Keel. Nearly all the hotels serve lunch or dinner to nonguests.

Entertainment

From May to September most pubs and hotels have music.

Annexe Inn (☎ 43268; Keel) The Annexe is the best for traditional music, with sessions most nights in July and August, and weekends the rest of the year.

Minaun View (Keel) You'd expect to hear rebel or folk songs at this friendly Republican pub, but the music of choice is country.

Getting There & Around

A **Bus Éireann** (☎ 096-71800) bus runs across the island from Dooagh, taking in Keel, Dugort, Dooega and Achill Sound before crossing to Mulrany, Newport, Westport and finally Ballina, Monday to Saturday year-round. Check the schedule with the tourist office as it changes daily. In July and August bus No 66 runs from Dooagh to Keel, Achill Sound, Westport, Sligo, Enniskillen and eventually Belfast. It leaves Dooagh at 7.30am and Achill Sound 20 minutes later. Coming from Westport, the bus leaves at 5.45pm.

Bikes can be hired from a number of places around the island including **O'Malley's Island Sports** (☎ 43125; Keel).

BANGOR ERRIS

☎ 097 / pop 250

The main reason for visiting this village is to begin or end the 48km **Bangor Trail**, which connects Bangor (Bain Gear), as it's called, and Newport. This extraordinary walk takes you through the bleakest, most remote landscape found anywhere in Ireland. A useful guide is *County Mayo: The Bangor Trail* (€8.50) by Joe McDermott and Robert Chapman, available in Keohane's Bookshop in Ballina and elsewhere. Unfortunately, you'll need more than one of the 1:50,000 OS maps to cover the trail.

Hillcrest House (☎ 83494; Main St; s & d without/with bathroom €27/30) Mrs Cosgrove greets you with afternoon tea when you arrive at this carefully tended, well-appointed bungalow B&B.

Kitty's Tavern (Kiltane Tavern; ☎ 83034; Main St; mains from €8) Opposite Hillcrest House, Kitty's serves pub food all day and has fresh and smoked local wild salmon for sale.

For bus transport information see p418.

MULLET PENINSULA

☎ 097

Unspoilt and virtually ignored by most visitors, this bleak, sparsely populated peninsula juts 30km out into the Atlantic where it is exposed to the worst of its ravages. On kinder days, however, it is well worth making the effort to check it out, as the eastern, more sheltered, side is home to some of Ireland's most pristine beaches. The peninsula is Irish speaking and Belmullet is the main settlement.

Information

In Belmullet, **Erris Tourist Information Centre** (☎ 81500; Barrack St; 🕓 9.30am-4.30pm Mon-Fri Easter-Sep) is quite helpful. **Ulster Bank** (Banc Uladh; Main St) and **Bank of Ireland** (Carter Sq), by the roundabout, both have ATMs. The **post office** (Main St) is opposite the **Údarás na Gaeltachta** (Gaeltacht Authority; ☎ 82382) and library, which has a small exhibition on the peninsula.

Belmullet

Belmullet (Béal an Mhuirthead), a functional, laid-back town, was founded in 1825 by the local landlord William Carter who built it to an unimaginative plan – one main street with side roads at right angles. Carter also designed a canal joining Broad Haven Bay with Trawmore and Blacksod Bay to the south, and a bridge now crosses the narrow channel.

Blacksod Point & Around

The road south from Belmullet loops round the tip of the peninsula to rejoin itself at

Aghleam. Near the point are the remains of an old **church**, and the view across the bay takes in the spot where *La Rata Santa Maria Encoronada*, part of the 1588 Spanish Armada, came in and was later burned by its captain. It sank beneath the waters of Blacksod Bay where it remains today.

The road to Blacksod Point passes **Elly Bay** on the eastern coast, which has a pleasant beach and is a favourite haunt of birdwatchers. Further south it passes stunning **Mullaghroe Beach**. In the early years of the 20th century, a whaling station operated at Ardelly Point, just north of the beach.

Doonamo Point

Built on a spit of land and defended by water on three sides, this typical promontory fort is the main point of interest north of Belmullet. There are other forts further north at Doonaneanir and Portnafrankach near Erris Head, but this one is the most accessible.

Sleeping & Eating

The usual run of bungalow B&Bs lines the main road approaching Belmullet.

Chez Nous (☎ 82167; Church Rd; s/d €42/60; 🕑 Mar-Dec) This pleasant home has three well-appointed rooms, all with shower.

Western Strands Hotel (☎ 81096; Main St; s/d €38/62) The rooms are fairly basic but neat at this central hotel.

Square Meal Restaurant (☎ 20984; Carter Sq; mains €6-13; 🕑 9am-6pm Mon-Sat & 11am-4pm Sun) This smoothly polished restaurant lives up to its name serving substantial, honest food on pinewood tables.

Getting There & Around

Monday to Saturday a Bus Éireann bus runs once daily (twice daily in July and August) from Ballina to Bangor Erris (one hour) and Belmullet (1½ hours), then south to Blacksod Point. Contact Ballina **bus station** (☎ 096-71800) for the schedule.

McNulty's Coaches (☎ 81086; Chapel St), with an office down past the post office in Belmullet, runs a service departing Belmullet at 8.30am daily Monday to Wednesday and Friday, returning from Castlebar at 5.30pm on the same days. The 1¾-hour trip costs €9/13 single/return.

In Belmullet, you can hire bikes from **Walsh's Garage** (☎ 82260; Chapel St) opposite the McNulty's Coaches office.

POLLATOMISH

☎ 097 / pop 150

Pollatomish (Poll an Tómais), also spelled Pullathomas, is a lovely little village some 16km east of Belmullet, signposted on the road to Ballycastle (R314). There's a pleasant sandy **beach** nearby and walks up to **Benwee Head** from where there are terrific views.

Kilcommon Lodge Hostel (☎ 84621; kilcommonlodge@eircom.net; Pollatomish; dm/d €9.50/24) This small, 20-bed IHH property is a delight, with clean dorms, evening meals and a peat fire in the common room. Be careful of the 9am to 5pm lockout and the midnight curfew.

BALLYCASTLE & AROUND

☎ 096 / pop 200

The Ballycastle (Baile an Chaisil) area boasts some of the oldest, most extensive Stone Age excavations in Europe, and some beautiful coastal scenery. The pretty village consists of one sloping street. Tourist information is available from the craft shop at the Ballycastle Resource Centre on Main St.

Céide Fields

It's difficult to over-emphasise the singular importance of Céide Fields (Achaidh Chéide) to archaeologists. For the rest of us, this extensive museum is an evocative and interesting glimpse into the past of 5500 years ago. In the 1930s, a local man, Patrick Caulfield, was digging in the bog when he noticed that there were a lot of piled-up stones buried beneath it. About 40 years later, his son Seamus, who had become an archaeologist on the basis of his father's discovery, began extensive exploration of the area. What he, and later others, uncovered was the world's most extensive Stone Age monument, consisting of stone walled fields, houses and megalithic tombs. It seems incredible to believe, but five millennia ago, a thriving farming community lived here, growing wheat and barley, and grazing sheep and cattle. Over time, soil erosion or the wet climate gradually diminished the soil's fertility, which contributed to the growth of the bog.

You'll find lots of displays and plenty of other Stone Age titbits at the wonderful, award-winning **Interpretive Centre** (☎ 43325; Ballycastle; adult/child €3.10/1.20; 🕑 10am-6pm Jun-Sep, 10am-5pm mid-Mar–May & Oct-Nov, for groups by appointment only rest of year). Run by Dúchas in a modern glass pyramid overlooking the site, it incorporates an exhibition court and audiovisual room detailing aspects of the site's architecture, botany and geology. There's also a tearoom and, across the road, a panoramic viewing platform.

Céide Fields is 8km west of Ballycastle on the main R314 road.

Downpatrick Head

Northeast of Ballycastle, Downpatrick Head has a fenced-off blowhole that occasionally shoots up plumes of water. The rock stack just off the shore is called **Dun Briste**.

Sleeping & Eating

Céide House (☎ 43105; Main St; s/d €26/52) This pub offers inexpensive accommodation in the middle of the village, though the music may at times be loud.

Suantraí (☎ 43040; Killala Rd; s/d €32/48; 🕑 late Jun–late Aug) Its ample breakfasts and scenic location make this a good choice.

Mary's Cottage Kitchen (☎ 43361; Main St; mains €5-9; 🕑 9am-5.30pm Mon-Sat) At the lower end of Main St, this greystone cottage bakery serves tasty sandwiches, light meals and ambrosial apple and rhubarb pies.

Getting There & Away

Bus Éireann (☎ 71800) bus No 445 runs between Ballina and Ballycastle twice a day, Monday to Saturday, stopping outside Katie Mac's pub.

KILLALA & AROUND

☎ 096 / pop 710

Though the town itself is rather nondescript, Killala (Cill Alaidh or Cill Ála) has a scenic setting on Killala Bay and important historical connections.

It's claimed that St Patrick founded Killala, and the Church of Ireland cathedral is supposedly built on the site of the first Christian church, where St Patrick installed Muiredach as the town's first bishop. The 25m round tower is evidence of the role the town played in early Church history; it was struck by lightning in 1800 and the cap is a later reconstruction.

Rathfran Abbey

The Dominicans came here in 1274 and built a friary, but only some ruins remain. In 1590 the friary was closed down and burned by the English, but the monks stayed in the community until the 18th century.

Take the R314 road that heads north out of Killala and, after 5km and crossing the River Cloonaghmore, turn right. After another 2km turn right at the crossroads.

Moyne Abbey

Established by the Franciscans around the same time as Rosserk, this abbey was also burned down by Richard Bingham in the 16th century. Perhaps he did a better job on this one, as it is in worse condition than its neighbour.

After leaving Rosserk Abbey go back to the main road and continue north for another 3km until you can see the abbey on the right across a field. After returning across the field, continue northwest for 1.5km until the main R314 is reached. Turn right for Killala or left for Ballina.

Breastagh Ogham Stone

The stone is 2.5m high, but the ogham script is not easy to read. It's in a field by the left

YEAR OF THE FRENCH

Flush with revolutionary fervour and eager to hurt the English in their own backyard, on 22 August 1798 more than 1000 French troops commanded by General Humbert landed in Killala Bay. It was hoped (or rather promised by the Irish patriot Wolfe Tone while visiting Paris) that their arrival would inspire the Irish peasantry to rise up against the English. At first, everything went according to plan and there were dramatic successes, with Killala, Ballina and Castlebar falling to the Franco-Irish armies. It all went pear-shaped on 8 September when an English army led by Cornwallis – the same general who surrendered to the American general George Washington at Yorktown in 1781 – met the French and defeated them at Ballinamuck in County Longford. An eminently readable account of that year is Thomas Flanagan's *The Year of the French* (1989). Alternatively, a first-hand account of Humbert's landing was written by Bishop Joseph Stock, who was temporarily imprisoned by the French; his *Narrative* (1798) is available in some bookshops in Ballina and Castlebar.

side of the R314 just past the crossroads with the turning for Rathfran Abbey (not the earlier crossroads, which has a sign for both the stone and the abbey). Cross the ditch just where the sign points to the stone.

Kilcummin & Lackan Bay

Kilcummin, at the head of Killala Bay, is where General Humbert's army landed in 1798. A right turn off the main R314 is signposted for Kilcummin. On the R314 just after the turning to Lackan Bay a sculpture of a French revolutionary soldier helping a prostrate Irish peasant marks the place where the first French soldier died on Irish soil. Lackan Bay itself is wonderfully sandy and ideal for young children.

Getting There & Away

The Ballina–Ballycastle bus, which runs once or twice a day Monday to Saturday, stops outside McGregor's newsagency. Ring **Bus Éireann** (☎ 71800) for details.

BALLINA & AROUND

☎ 096 / pop 8200

The largest town in the county, unattractive Ballina (Béal an Átha; balli-*nagh*) is renowned for its fishing and is a good base for exploring northern Mayo and the North Mayo Sculpture Trail. The **tourist office** (☎ 70848; Cathedral Rd; 🕑 10am-5.30pm Mon-Sat), beside St Muredach's Cathedral across the River Moy from the centre, can give you information on interesting walks near the town.

Several banks line Pearse St, including the Ulster Bank and Bank of Ireland, both with ATMs and bureaux de change. The post office is at the top of O'Rahilly St, the southern extension of Pearse St.

Rosserk Abbey

Close to the River Rosserk, a tributary of the Moy, this Franciscan abbey dates from the mid-15th century. It's remarkably well preserved, and there's an interesting carved piscina (a perforated stone basin for carrying away the water used in rinsing the chalices) in the chancel. Like Rathfran Abbey near Killala, Rosserk was burned down by Richard Bingham, the English governor of Connaught, in the 16th century.

To get there, leave Ballina on the R314 for Killala and after 6.5km turn right at the sign and take the first left at the next crossroads. Continue for another 1km, then turn right at the next sign for the abbey.

North Mayo Sculpture Trail

This trail of 15 outdoor sculptures essentially follows the ,R314 from Ballina (*Point A; Guest Space* by Peter Hynes) to Blacksod Point (*Point O; Deirble's Twist* by Michael Bulfin). The project was inspired by the discoveries at Céide Fields and was inaugurated in 1993 to mark 5000 years of Mayo history. Leading sculptors from eight countries were commissioned to create works of art reflecting the beauty and wilderness of the northern Mayo countryside.

The North Mayo Sculpture Trail (Tír Sáile) is a 60-page book detailing each sculpture with notes on the location, artist, sculpture, history, flora and fauna. It's available from tourist offices and bookshops. It's about 90km and is walkable.

Fishing

The **River Moy** is one of the most prolific salmon rivers in Europe and a leaflet listing the fisheries and contacts for permits is available from the tourist office. You can see the scaly critters jumping in the Ridge (salmon pool), with otters and grey seals in famished pursuit. The season runs from February to September, but the best fishing is June to August.

Lough Conn, southwest of Ballina, is an important brown trout fishery, and there's no shortage of places with boats and *ghillies* (guides) available round the lake. Pontoon is a good base for trout fishing in both Lough Conn and **Lough Cullin** to the south, and again there are plenty of places hiring boats and dispensing advice. The daily rate for hiring a motor boat is around €60.

For licences, permits and supplies contact **Ridge Pool Tackle Shop** (☎ 72656; Cathedral Rd, Ballina).

Special Events

The two-week **Ballina Street Festival** (☎ 70905), one of the best outdoor parties in the country, takes place in early July. Heritage Day is when shop fronts – and Ballina townsfolk – take on a 19th-century look during the festival.

Sleeping & Eating

Belleek Caravan & Camping Park (☎ 71533; lenahan@indigo.ie; Ballina; large tent €13; hikers, cyclists & motorcyclists €5; mid-Mar–mid-Sep) This well-equipped park with 16 tent sites is 2.5km from Ballina, 300m off the Killala road.

Greenhill (☎ 22767; greenhillbandb@eircom.net; Cathedral Close; s/d €40/60) Smack in the town centre, this five-room house (four with en suite) is a comfortable place to bed down in.

Murphy Bros (☎ 22702; Clare St; bar food €8-19, restaurant mains €13-22; 12.30-2.30pm & 5-9pm) Salmon – poached, grilled, baked or smoked – is the speciality of Ballina and you can try it at this excellent old pub-restaurant, north of the tourist office.

Padraic's (☎ 22383; Tone St; mains €6-13; 9am-5.30pm) If you're suffering withdrawal symptoms from the 'full Irish' then Padraic's can satisfy – its breakfasts include black and white pudding, and waffles.

Entertainment

Ballina counts some 60 pubs, and many have traditional music sessions on Wednesday and Friday evenings. Among the best are the following.

An Bolg Buí (The Yellow Belly; ☎ 22561; Tolan St) By the bridge, this dark, intimate, wood-panelled pub has traditional and folk music every Wednesday night.

Garden Inn (☎ 70969; Garden St) One of the best places for traditional music, the Garden Inn welcomes all-comers to take part in the sessions.

Broken Jug (☎ 73097; O'Rahilly St) High, solid wooden doors lead into this cavernous pub, furbished in stone and wood, where young people come to drink and dance at its nightclub.

Getting There & Away

Bus Éireann runs services from the **bus station** (☎ 71800; Kevin Barry St) to Achill Island (adult/child €8.80/6, two to three hours, six daily), Sligo (€10.60/7, 1½ hours, nine daily) and Dublin (€14/9, 3¾ hours, seven daily). The bus station is southwest of the centre.

There are trains to Dublin (€25/12.50, 3¾ hours, three daily) from the **train station** (☎ 71818; Station Rd), which is at the southern extension of Kevin Barry St. Ballina is on a branch of the main Westport–Dublin line, which means you'll have to change at Manulla Junction, 6km south of Castlebar.

CROSSMOLINA & AROUND

☎ 096 / pop 350

The small undistinguished town of Crossmolina (Crois Mhaoiliona), 13km west of Ballina, sits near the northern shores of Lough Conn. There's a small seasonal tourist office off the main street, and a Bank of Ireland (no ATM) opposite Hiney's pub.

Errew Abbey

The abbey, beside Lough Conn, is the remains of a house for Augustinian monks built around 1250 on the site of an earlier 7th-century church. As with other abbeys in Mayo, the monks wisely chose to live close to where they could fish, and the location of Errew Abbey is particularly picturesque.

To get there, take the Castlebar road south, and 1km past the heritage centre turn left at the sign and keep going for another 5km. The entrance is next to a farm.

Activities

Crossmolina serves as a quiet retreat for anyone wishing to fish in **Lough Conn** or explore the lakes and scenery around **Mt Nephin** (806m). The mountain takes under two hours to climb and is described, along with other walks in Mayo, in *New Irish Walk*

GETTING IN TOUCH WITH YOUR NAME

If your family name is Barrett, Brennan, Dogherty, Doyle, Durkan, Foy, Gallagher, Gaughan, Harkin, Henry, Kelly, Lavelle, Loftus, McHale, McNulty or McNicholas, there's a more than strong chance that your people originally hailed from North Mayo. The **North Mayo Family History Research & Heritage Centre** (☎ 31809; Castlebar Rd; adult/child museum €3.80/1.25, garden €5.10/1.25, combined ticket €7.60/1.25; 9am-4pm Mon-Fri & 2-6pm Sat & Sun Jun & Sep, 9am-4pm Mon-Fri Oct-May, Jul & Aug) can provide a thorough exploration of your roots, beginning with an initial assessment (€75); if this looks promising your full family record is researched (around €300, minus the assessment fee). Attached is a fairly interesting museum with a collection of old farm machinery and domestic implements. The centre is 3km south of Crossmolina towards Castlehill.

Guides: West and North (Gill & Macmillan) by Tony Whilde and Patrick Simms.

Sleeping & Eating

Lake View House (☎ 31296; Ballina Rd; s/d €39/53; ⌚ Apr-Oct) About 500m east of the town centre, this aptly named B&B has six spick-and-span rooms, and bikes available for hire.

Enniscoe House (☎ 31112; www.enniscoe.com; Castlehill; s/d €100/172, dinner €40) This magnificent 18th-century mansion is the epitome of country home elegance. Surrounded by a Victorian walled garden, you can really live it up here.

Hiney's (☎ 31202; Main St; meals around €9) Though you wouldn't know it from the tacky doorway with the thatched cover, Hiney's is a great old pub where food, served all day, comes in huge helpings.

Tea Room (Main St; snacks around €2.50; ⌚ 9am-6pm Mon-Sat) Customers from the attached supermarket drop into this inexpensive tearoom for refreshment before lugging their shopping home.

Getting There & Away

There are regular **Bus Éireann** (☎ 71800) buses to Ballina and Castlebar. The bus stop is outside Hiney's.

CASTLEBAR & AROUND

☎ 094 / pop 7650

Mayo's county town is a busy enough place, but Castlebar (Caisleán an Bharraigh) is frankly not worth spending too much time in. Modernity has done its tourist appeal few favours and there's virtually nothing here to evoke its past.

Its place in Irish history was cemented in 1798, when General Humbert's army of French revolutionary soldiers and dispossessed Irish peasants encountered the numerically stronger British forces under the command of General Lake. The defeat of the British and their ignominious cavalry retreat became known as the Castlebar Races.

The large, attractive village green, known as the Mall, was once the cricket ground of the Lucan family, which owns a significant amount of property in the area. The notorious Lord Lucan disappeared after the murder of his children's nanny in London in 1974, and hasn't been heard of since.

Orientation & Information

The main thoroughfare changes its name from Ellison St to Main St to Thomas St as you head north. The Mall is to the east.

The **tourist office** (☎ 21207; Linenhall St; ⌚ 9.30am-1pm & 2-5.30pm) is west (left) off the northern end of Main St, by the bridge.

The **Allied Irish Bank** (Main St) and **Bank of Ireland** (Ellison St) have ATMs and bureaux de change. **Una's Laundrette** (☎ 24100; New Antrim St) is round the corner from the tourist office.

Sights

TURLOUGH ROUND TOWER

The 9th-century tower stands next to a ruined 18th-century church and a graveyard that is still in use. The tower is about 5km northeast of Castlebar on the N5 road.

MICHAEL DAVITT MEMORIAL MUSEUM

The **museum** (☎ 31022; Straide; adult/child €3.10/1.20; ⌚ 10am-6pm) houses a small collection of material relating to the life of Michael Davitt (1846–1906), a Fenian and founding member of the Irish National Land League, who is buried in the nearby churchyard. There's also a short video about the man.

Take the N5 east and turn left (northeast) onto the N58 to Straide (Strade on some maps). It's 16km from Castlebar.

BALLINTUBBER ABBEY

The only church in Ireland that was founded by an Irish king and is still in use, **Ballintubber Abbey** (☎ 30934; Ballintubber; admission free; ⌚ 9am-midnight) was set up in 1216 next to the site of an earlier church founded by St Patrick after he came down from Croagh Patrick. It's one of the most impressive church buildings in Ireland and well worth a visit.

Features of the church include the 15th-century western doorway and 13th-century windows on the right side of the nave. The nave roof was erected in 1965 and is an Irish-oak reproduction of the timber one burned down by Cromwell's soldiers in 1653.

Take the N84 south towards Galway and after about 13km turn left at the Campus service station; the abbey is 2km along this road.

Sleeping & Eating

If you have to stay over, there's plenty of accommodations in town; the tourist office will help locate one if you're stuck.

Rose Garden (☎ 21162; rosegdn@eircom.net; the Mall; s/d €35/50) Ideally positioned, this comfortable house has decent bedrooms and friendly service.

Daly's Hotel (☎ 21961; fax 22783; the Mall; s/d €40/80, bar food €7-15) Castlebar's oldest hotel has plenty of charm, expansive rooms and a warm, pleasant bar that serves up decent meals.

Café Rua (☎ 23376; New Antrim St; mains €7-10; 9.30am-6pm Tue-Sat) This friendly spot has a sophisticated menu with a range of appetising dishes including the very Irish champ, made with mashed potatoes and onions.

Gavin's Bakery (☎ 24300; Main St; sandwiches around €6) This bakery is good for sandwiches and cakes but also offers cooked breakfasts and soups.

Getting There & Away

Bus Éireann (☎ 096-71800) travels to Westport (adult/child €3.70/2.40, 20 minutes, five daily), Dublin (€15/10, 4½ hours, five daily) and Sligo (€13.20/8.50, 1½ hours, three daily). Services on Sunday are less frequent. Buses stop outside Flannelly's pub in Market St.

McNulty's Coaches (☎ 097-81086), based in Belmullet, runs a service from Castlebar to Belmullet at 5.30pm Monday to Wednesday and Friday, returning the next day at 8.15am.

The Westport–Dublin train stops at Castlebar (€22, 3¼ hours) up to four times daily. The station is just out of town on the N84 towards Ballinrobe.

KNOCK

☎ 094 / pop 440

Catholic Ireland's answer to Lourdes and Fatima was once an unremarkable little village at the junction of the N17 and the R323, but that all changed at the end of the 19th century thanks to an apparition and a succession of Vatican-approved miracles. Pilgrims come to Knock (Cnoc Mhuire) in ever-increasing numbers, but be warned: religion is big business here and the village is crammed with hawkers looking to cash in on the fervent, almost medieval piety of the pilgrims.

Such aggressive commercialism will strike many visitors as tasteless and unspeakably tacky – what do wall thermometers and shake-up snow domes have to do with honest piety? However, despite the vulgar incongruities, it is important to remember that this is now one of the world's most sacred Catholic shrines, as important to the faithful as the Wailing Wall in Jerusalem is to Jews, Mecca to Muslims or the Ganges to Hindus.

The Knock Marian Shrine consists of several churches and shrines, including the modern basilica and the Church of the Apparition. North of the latter are shops, restaurants and the **tourist office** (☎ 88193; 10am-6pm May-Sep). There's a **Bank of Ireland** (10.15am-12.15pm Mon & Thu May-Oct, Mon only rest of year) nearby with an ATM.

Church of the Apparition

On 21 August 1879, two young Knock women claimed they saw Mary, Joseph and St John the Evangelist standing in light against the southern gable of the parish church. A total of 13 other witnesses agreed with them, and a Church investigation quickly confirmed it as a bona fide miracle. Other miracles followed as the sick and disabled claimed amazing recoveries after visiting the church. Another Church commission upheld Knock's status in 1936. Today, the Knock industry continues, and dutiful worshippers are always found praying at the chapel built to enclose the scene of the apparition. Above the altar is a sculptural representation of what people saw. Near the church is the modern **Basilica of Our Lady, Queen of Ireland**, which can accommodate 12,000 people.

Knock Folk Museum

In a building near the basilica is this small **museum** (☎ 88100; adult/concession €4/2.75; 10am-6pm May-Oct). It's one of the better museums of its type and serves as an ideal introduction to the Knock phenomenon. There's plenty of attractively presented material on the apparition and subsequent Church commissions of inquiry, including photographs of the crutches left behind by grateful pilgrims. The museum also houses an extensive collection of craft tools, costumes and various artefacts relating to rural life in the west of Ireland.

Sleeping

Knock Caravan & Camping Park (☎ 88100; fax 88295; Claremorris Rd; tent site €10; Mar-Oct) This fully serviced, sheltered camp site is only a five-minute walk south of the shrine.

Aisling House (☎ 88558; Ballyhaunis Rd; s without/with bathroom €27.50/30) Mrs Coyne makes guests welcome at this roomy B&B, which is close to the shrine.

Knock International Hotel (☎ 88466; Main St; s/d €35/70) Though a humbler establishment than its name might suggest, this modest 10-room hotel is clean and comfortable.

Getting There & Away

Knock Airport (☎ 67222; www.knockairport.com), 15km north by the N17 near Charlestown, has daily scheduled flights to Dublin (Aer Lingus and Aer Arann), London Stansted (Ryanair), Manchester and Birmingham (British Airways).

Bus Éireann (☎ 096-71800) bus No 21 connects Knock with Westport, Castlebar, Athlone and Dublin three times daily (once on Sunday). There are also direct connections with Sligo, Ballina, Galway and Cork.

COUNTY SLIGO

Tiny County Sligo (Sligeach) provides a rich variety of scenery, the largest number of prehistoric sites in Ireland and a pretty strong association with the Nobel laureate, poet and dramatist William Butler Yeats (1865–1939), whose mother was born into a well-to-do Sligo family. Much of his writing is infused with the wild landscapes, bitter history and rich folklore of Sligo. The tourist authorities have made a big deal of his link with the county, carefully ignoring the fact that Yeats was born in Dublin, educated in London, and was an infrequent visitor to the county past his childhood – and then

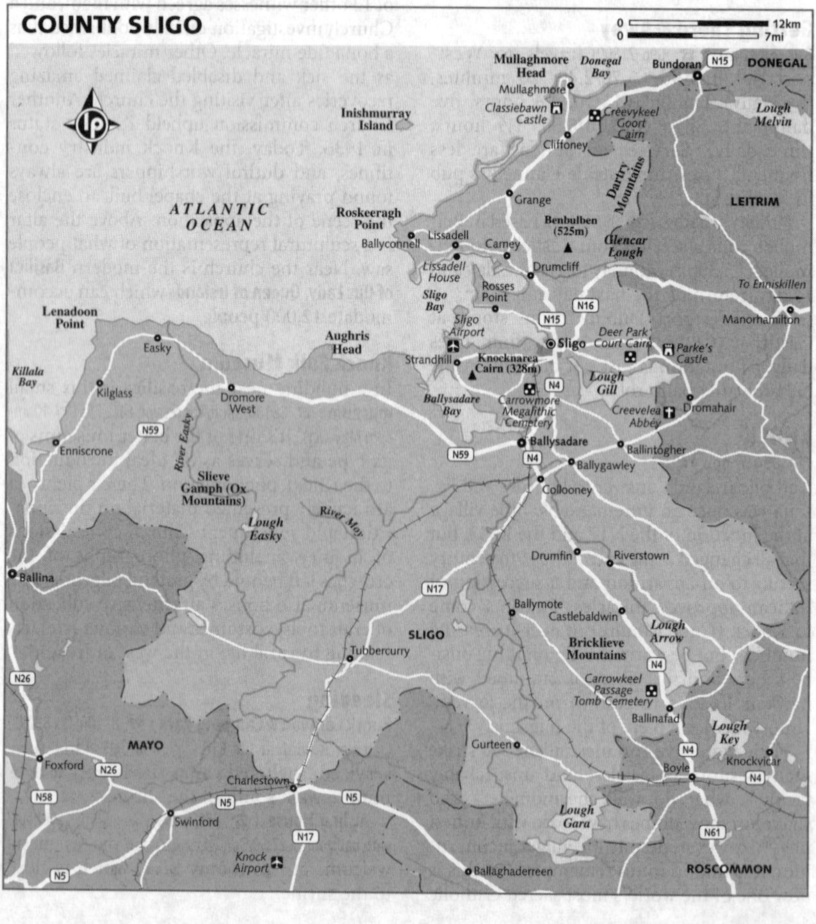

only as a guest of the Gore-Booths at Lissadell House.

SLIGO TOWN

☎ 071 / pop 17,800

Sligo town is a busy port and commercial centre on the banks of the River Garavogue as it flows into Sligo Bay, with the twin mountains of Knocknarea and Benbulben looming in the distance. The loveliest parts of town are on the river.

Information

The **North-West Regional Tourism office** (☎ 916 1201; Temple St; 9am-6pm Mon-Fri & 10am-6pm Sat & Sun Jun-Sep, 9am-5pm Mon-Fri Oct-May) is south of the centre.

Ulster Bank, the Bank of Ireland and the Allied Irish Bank, all with ATMs and bureaux de change, have branches on Stephen St. The post office is on Wine St.

You can check email at the **Cygo Internet Cafe** (☎ 914 0082; 19 O'Connell St; €2/15min; 10am-10pm Mon-Thu & 10am-7pm Fri-Sat). It's at the back of the arch.

You can leave your laundry at **Pam's Laundrette** (☎ 914 4861; Johnston Ct; 9am-7pm Mon-Sat), off O'Connell St.

Keohane's Bookshop (☎ 42597; Castle St) has maps and books by and about Yeats. The **Winding Stair Bookshop** (☎ 914 1244; Lower Knox St) is named after one of Yeats' works, and has Irish-interest books and a café.

Sights

SLIGO COUNTY MUSEUM

Although there is other material, the main appeal is the Yeats room at the **museum** (☎ 914 2212; Stephen St; admission free; 10.30am-12.30pm & 2.30-4.30pm Mon-Sat Jun-Sep, 10.30am-12.30pm Mon-Sat Apr, May & Oct). Here there are photographs, letters and newspaper cuttings connected with the poet WB Yeats, and drawings by Jack B Yeats, his brother. The room across the hall contains an apron dress worn by Countess Constance Markievicz (a member of the Gore-Booth family) while interned in Britain after the 1916 Rising.

MODEL ARTS & NILAND GALLERY

Sligo's most important **gallery** (☎ 914 1405; www.modelart.ie; the Mall; admission free; 10am-5.30pm Tue-Sat & 1-5pm Sun) is housed in this impressive 19th-century building. The fabulous collection includes works by Charles Lamb, Sean Keating and a couple of members of the Yeats family; WB's brother Jack B, one of Ireland's most important modern artists (who said he never painted anything without putting a thought of Sligo into it?), and the poet's daughter Anne. The gallery also plays host to a constantly changing schedule of travelling exhibitions, readings and music recitals.

SLIGO ABBEY

The town's founder, Maurice FitzGerald, established the **abbey** (☎ 914 6406; Abbey St; adult/child €2/1; 10am-6pm mid-Mar–Oct, 9.30am-4.30pm Fri-Sun Nov–mid-Mar) around 1250 for the Dominicans, but it burned down in the 15th century and was rebuilt. It was put to the torch once again in 1641, and a set of Dúchas-managed ruins are all that remain. The oldest parts of the abbey are the choir, the 15th-century eastern window and the altar.

COURTHOUSE

The Victorian architecture of the courthouse on Teeling St is very unusual for Ireland, and it stands out as a reminder of the other power that once ruled this land. The exterior is extravagantly Gothic and modelled on the Law Courts in London. Inside, the building still functions as a working courthouse, and on a busy day the foyer takes the overspill from the small public gallery.

YEATS BUILDING

On the corner of Lower Knox and O'Connell Sts, near Hyde Bridge, the Yeats Building is the centre for the **Yeats International Summer School** (☎ 914 2693), a two-week international gathering of scholars at the start of August each year. The rest of the year it houses the **Sligo Art Gallery** (☎ 914 5847; Lower Knox St; admission free; 10am-5pm Mon-Sat), with travelling exhibitions and paintings often up for sale.

Festivals

The 10-day **Sligo Arts Festival** (☎ 916 9802) takes place from late May to early June.

Sleeping

BUDGET

Gateway Caravan & Camping Park (☎ 914 5618; gateway@oceanfree.net; Ballinode; tent, 2 people & car €14.50, 2 hikers or cyclists €7; mid-Jan–mid-Dec) A medium-sized, fully equipped camp site about 1.5km northeast of Sligo on the Sligo–Belfast road (N16). Free showers, a

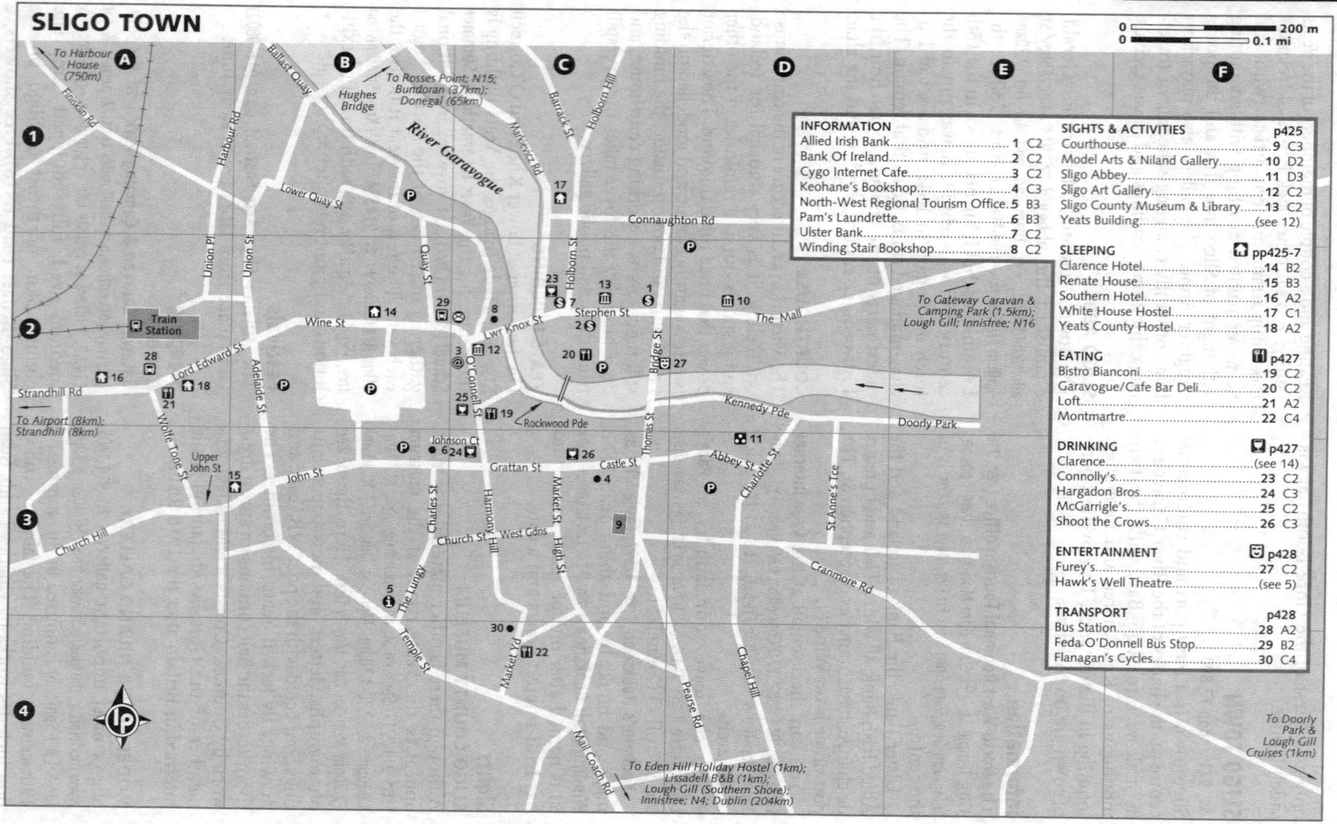
SLIGO TOWN
0 200 m
0 0.1 mi
INFORMATION
Allied Irish Bank 1 C2
Bank Of Ireland 2 C2
Cygo Internet Cafe 3 C2
Keohane's Bookshop 4 C3
North-West Regional Tourism Office 5 B3
Pam's Laundrette 6 B3
Ulster Bank 7 C2
Winding Stair Bookshop 8 C2
SIGHTS & ACTIVITIES p425
Courthouse 9 C3
Model Arts & Niland Gallery 10 D2
Sligo Abbey 11 D3
Sligo Art Gallery 12 C2
Sligo County Museum & Library 13 C2
Yeats Building (see 12)
SLEEPING pp425-7
Clarence Hotel 14 B2
Renate House 15 B3
Southern Hotel 16 A2
White House Hostel 17 C1
Yeats County Hostel 18 A2
EATING p427
Bistro Bianconi 19 C2
Garavogue/Cafe Bar Deli 20 C2
Loft 21 A2
Montmartre 22 C4
DRINKING p427
Clarence (see 14)
Connolly's 23 C2
Hargadon Bros 24 C3
McGarrigle's 25 C2
Shoot the Crows 26 C3
ENTERTAINMENT p428
Furey's 27 C2
Hawk's Well Theatre (see 5)
TRANSPORT p428
Bus Station 28 A2
Feda O'Donnell Bus Stop 29 B2
Flanagan's Cycles 30 C4
To Harbour House (750m)
To Rosses Point; N15; Bundoran (37km); Donegal (65km)
Hughes Bridge
River Garavogue
To Gateway Caravan & Camping Park (1.5km); Lough Gill; Innisfree; N16
To Airport (8km); Strandhill (8km)
To Eden Hill Holiday Hostel (1km); Lissadell B&B (1km); Lough Gill (Southern Shore); Innisfree; N4; Dublin (204km)
To Doorly Park & Lough Gill Cruises (1km)
Train Station
Finisklin Rd
Ballast Quay
Markievicz Rd
Barrack St
Holborn Hill
Harbour Rd
Lower Quay St
Connaughton Rd
Union Pl
Union St
Quay St
Holborn St
Stephen St
Wine St
Lwr Knox St
The Mall
Lord Edward St
O'Connell St
Bridge St
Strandhill Rd
Adelaide St
Rockwood Pde
Kennedy Pde
Doorly Park
Wolfe Tone St
Upper John St
Johnson Ct
Thomas St
Grattan St
Castle St
Abbey St
Charlotte St
St Anne's Tce
John St
Charles St
Harmony Hill
Market St
Church St
West Gdns
High St
Church Hill
Cranmore Rd
The Lungy
Temple St
Market Yd
Pearse Rd
Chapel Hill
Mail Coach Rd

campers' kitchen, a TV games room and a toddlers' playroom are on the premises. Local buses stop outside the park.

Sligo's hostels are pretty popular, so we advise you to book ahead if you can.

White House Hostel (☎ 914 5160; fax 914 4456; Markievicz Rd; dm €10) Friendly, easy-going and very popular with young backpackers, this centrally located hostel gets two thumbs up for its all-round atmosphere. The dorms are clean and neat. Breakfast is included in the price.

Yeats County Hostel (☎ 914 6876; 12 Lord Edward St; dm €10) It's close to the train station, which is the only real bonus to staying at this slightly faded IHO hostel. New management is in the process of dusting out the corners, so things are looking brighter.

Harbour House (☎ 917 1547; harbourhouse@eircom.net; Finisklin Rd; dm €16-20, d €18-25) Comfy beds are but one reason to stay at this modern, well-equipped IHH hostel about 1km northwest of the centre. A good choice, especially if you're keen on a little bit of budget comfort.

Eden Hill Holiday Hostel (☎ 914 3204; edenhill@eircom.net; Pearse Rd; dm/d €12.50/35) A converted Victorian home, this IHH/IHO-affiliated hostel is the quietest of the lot, probably because it's 1.2km southeast of town on the Dublin road. The 48 beds are run-of-the-mill: nothing special, but not bad either.

MID-RANGE & TOP END

The most central B&B is Renate House; other B&Bs line the various approach roads into town.

Renate House (☎ 916 2014; fax 916 9093; 9 Upper John St; s/d €39/56) This clean, three-storey B&B has a prime central position close to all amenities. There are six rooms, four en suite.

Lissadell (☎ 916 1937; Mail Coach Rd; s/d €42.50/64; P ⊠) This small, three-room B&B is pretty comfortable and is about a 10-minute walk southeast of town on the N16 Dublin road.

Clarence Hotel (☎ 914 2211; fax 914 5823; Wine St; s/d €55/110) This small hotel is one of Sligo's best, even though the rooms are decorated in standard business-hotel style.

Southern Hotel (☎ 62101; www.sligosouthernhotel.com; Strandhill Rd; s/d €92/140) Beside the bus and train stations, this stately hotel has comfortable rooms and an open fire in the lobby to greet its guests.

Eating

Loft (☎ 914 6770; 17-19 Lord Edward St; mains €10-17) One of the better eateries around, the Loft is opposite the train station and uses the railway as the theme for its décor. The menu is mostly made up of Mexican dishes, fish and burgers, with a small selection of vegetarian dishes.

Garavogue/Cafe Bar Deli (☎ 914 0100; 15-16 Stephen St; bar food €8-9, restaurant mains €9-14; lunch noon-3pm, bar food 3-6pm, restaurant 6-11pm) A marvellous pasta-and-pizza restaurant, this branch of the popular Cafe Bar Deli (also in Dublin and Cork) has recently opened on the top floor of the equally popular Garavogue Bar, where superior bar food is available daily. It's right on the river, behind Stephen St.

Bistro Bianconi (☎ 41744; 44 O'Connell St; mains €14-19; 12.30-2.30pm & 5.30-10pm Jun-Aug, dinner only rest of year) This friendly Italian bistro serves fresh pasta, and pizzas from its wood-fired oven.

Montmartre (☎ 916 9901; Market Yard; mains €15-25; 5-11pm Tue-Sun) Fancy French cuisine is on the menu at this wonderful new restaurant just off High St.

Drinking

Sligo has plenty of bars and other night-time activities to keep you entertained, but the town has a bit of a reputation for wildness. Booze and boredom are a bad combo, none more so than on a weekend night when trouble can quickly brew out of nothing.

Hargadon Bros (☎ 917 0933; 4 O'Connell St) No place in Sligo can beat this one for atmosphere. While it doesn't have music, its dark wood interior is like a stage set, with snugs, nooks, crannies and 19th-century bar fixtures. It is, however, in the process of being sold: we just hope that the new owners know a good thing when they buy one.

McGarrigle's (☎ 914 1667; O'Connell St) Cavernous McGarrigle's has dimly lit snugs downstairs and a good 'alternative music' bar upstairs.

Connolly's (☎ 914 3340; Markiewicz Rd) This gorgeous traditional pub is one of the better spots in town for a great pint and a chat.

Shoot the Crows (Castle St) This long, dark, narrow drinking establishment attracts a young, alternative clientele and has traditional music on Tuesday and Thursday nights.

Entertainment

Furey's (☎ 914 3825; Bridge St) Owned by Irish traditional band Dervish, this old-style bar has some superb traditional music three or four nights of the week.

Clarence (☎ 914 2211; Wine St; 🕑 11pm-2am Thu-Sat) Sligo's best nightclub (below the hotel) was undergoing renovation at the time of writing, and a state-of-the-art, modern new venue is promised. If the atmosphere is anything like it used to be, then it is definitely worth checking out.

Hawk's Well Theatre (☎ 61526; www.hawkswell.com; Temple St) This well regarded theatre, attached to the tourist office, presents a varied programme of concerts, dance and serious drama, and is always worth checking out. From June to August there's a programme of lunchtime theatre (€8) that also includes lunch.

Getting There & Away

AIR

From **Sligo Airport** (☎ 916 8280; Strandhill Rd) there are direct Aer Arann flights to Dublin twice daily from €40.

BUS

Bus Éireann (☎ 916 0066) buses run from the terminal below the train station, west of the centre on Lord Edward St. Destinations include: Ballina (adult/child €10.60/7, 1½ hours, nine daily), Castlebar (€13.20/8.50, 1½ hours, three daily), Dublin (€14/9, four hours, four daily) and Westport (€14/9, two hours, twice daily). Services are less frequent on Sunday on some routes.

Feda O'Donnell (☎ 074-954 8114, 091-761 656) runs a service between Crolly (in County Donegal) and Galway via Donegal and Sligo up to three times daily. The buses arrive and depart from in front of Henry Lyon's Store on the corner of Wine and Quay Sts.

TRAIN

Trains leave the **station** (☎ 916 9888) for Dublin (€25, 3¼ hours, three daily) via Boyle, Carrick-on-Shannon and Mullingar.

Getting Around

There's a bus service (€2.50) from the airport into town, while a **taxi** costs about €14. **Ace Cabs** (☎ 914 4444) and **Feehily's Taxis** (☎ 914 3000) offer a 24-hour service. Bike hire is available from **Flanagan's Cycles** (☎ 914 4477; Market Yard) for €15/60 per day/week.

AROUND SLIGO TOWN

Rosses Point

☎ 071 / pop 300

The scene of a battle between two Irish warlords in 1257, Rosses Point (An Ros) is a picturesque seaside resort with a lovely Blue Flag beach. It's easily reached on a Sligo town bus.

SLEEPING & EATING

B&Bs aren't difficult to find, although they can fill up quickly in season.

Greenlands Caravan & Camping Park (☎ 917 7113; tent sites €9; 🕑 Easter–mid-Sep) Greenlands, on the point next to the golf course, has 69 tent sites and access to two safe beaches.

Kilvarnet House (☎ 917 7202; s/d €45/60; 🕑 Mar-Oct) A friendly B&B with four rooms and all mod cons. To get there follow the road up beside the post office.

Yeats Country Hotel (☎ 917 7211; www.yeatscountryhotel.com; s/d €60/120; ♿) This sprawling three-star hotel on the point mostly attracts golfers and families. It has spacious bedrooms and a leisure centre for guests.

Moorings Restaurant (☎ 917 7112; mains €12-20; 🕑 noon-3pm & 6-11pm) Close to the Yeats Country Hotel and with views of the bay, Moorings specialises in fresh seafood served in elegant surroundings.

GOLF

One of Ireland's most challenging and renowned links courses, **County Sligo Golf Course** (☎ 917 7134) attracts golfers from all over Europe. Its position on the peninsula is simply stunning. Green fees are €60 Monday to Friday and €75 Saturday and Sunday.

Carrowmore Megalithic Cemetery

Carrowmore's **megalithic cemetery** (☎ 916 1534; adult/concession €1.90/0.70; 🕑 10am-6pm Apr-Oct) has over 60 stone circles and passage tombs, making it one of the largest Stone Age cemeteries in Europe, pre-dating Newgrange by some 700 years. Over the years, many of the stones have been removed – a survey in 1839 noted 23 more sites than now exist – and a complicating factor is that some of the best stones are on private land. The dolmens were the actual tombs and were probably covered with stones and

RICHARD CUMMINS

Wildflowers, **Connemara** (p389)

GARETH MCCORMACK

Lobster boats, **Roundstone** (p391)

Ancient stone marking, **Inishmaan** (p386)

EOIN CLARKE

GARETH MCCORMACK

Glencar Lough (p432), north of Sligo town

Keem Beach (p416), Achill Island

RICHARD CUMMI

earth, so it requires some imagination to picture what this 2.5km-wide area might once have looked like. The site is now managed by Dúchas.

To get there, leave town by Church Hill and carry on south for 5km; the site is clearly signposted.

Knocknarea Cairn

About 2km northwest of Carrowmore is the hilltop cairn grave of Knocknarea. Around 1000 years younger than Carrowmore, the huge cairn (328m) is supposed to be the grave of the legendary Queen Maeve (Queen Mab in Welsh and English folk tales). The 40,000 tonnes of stone have never been excavated, despite speculation that a tomb on the scale of the one at Newgrange in County Meath lies buried below.

Leave Sligo, as for Carrowmore, and a sign shows the way to Knocknarea. If you're leaving from the Carrowmore cemetery, continue down the road and turn right at the junction with a church. At the next crossroads (signposted Mescan Meadhbha Chambered Cairn) turn left, and leave your vehicle at the car park. From there it's a 30-minute walk to the summit and panoramic views.

Deer Park Court Cairn

Dating from around 3000 BC, the impressive court tomb (also called Magheraghanrush Court Cairn) stands on a wooded limestone hill with fine views of Lough Gill. The court area is in the centre of the tomb, with two burial chambers opening off at either end.

Take the N16 east from Sligo and turn off on the R286 for Parke's Castle. Almost immediately after joining this road turn left at the Y-junction onto a minor road signposted for Manorhamilton. Continue for about 3km, park in the car park, then follow the trail through the trees.

Strandhill

☎ 071 / pop 650

The long, sandy beach at Strandhill (An Leathras), 8km west of Sligo off the R292 airport road, is something of a **surfing** mecca, and at low tide you can walk across to Coney Island. The story goes that New York's Coney Island was named by a man from Rosses Point. There's also a golf course.

Strandhill Caravan & Camping Park (☎ 916 8111; tent site & 2 people €11; 🕑 mid-Apr–Sep) This camp site has 100 sites and is ideally positioned beside the beach; needless to say, it's popular with surfers.

Beach House (☎ 916 8140; Strandhill; s/d €40/60) Pretty much as the name says, this beachfront B&B has three en-suite rooms.

Ocean View Hotel (☎ 68115; fax 68009; Main St; s €45-68, d €90-136) This homely, mock-tudor, three-star hotel is on the main road in the shadow of Knocknarea Cairn. The rooms are pleasant and modern.

Getting There & Away

Bus Éireann (☎ 916 0066) buses run to Strandhill and Rosses Point, but there's no public transport to other places of interest in the area. A bicycle hired in Sligo would be the best way to get around. While it's possible to walk to both Carrowmore and Knocknarea from town, it's a long day's return trek.

SOUTH OF SLIGO TOWN

Collooney

☎ 071 / pop 200

Collooney (Cúil Mhuine) is about 15km south of Sligo on the N4. The **Teeling Monument**, at the village's northern end, commemorates the daring of Bartholomew Teeling. He was marching with Humbert's French-Irish army when it encountered stiff resistance from an English gunner. Teeling charged up to the gunner and killed him, thus allowing the army to march to eventual defeat at the Battle of Ballinamuck in Longford in September 1798. Although the French were treated as prisoners of war, Teeling and 500 other Irishmen were executed.

Now a three-star hotel, **Markree Castle** (☎ 916 7800; www.markreecastle.ie; Collooney; s/d €104/179), signposted off the main road on the left after leaving the village, has remained in the Cooper family since Cromwell's time. When Charles Kingsley stayed here in the 19th century he wrote that he cried over the misery inflicted on the local peasantry – at the same time exalting in the excitement of fishing for salmon in the estate's river. And it's said that Mrs Alexander wrote the hymn *All Things Bright and Beautiful* after her stay here.

Ballymote

☎ 071 / pop 250

Near this small town, 11km south of Collooney and off the tourist trail, is ivy-covered **Ballymote Castle**, on the Tubbercurry road. The early-14th-century castle, contested among Irish chiefs before succumbing to the English in 1577, is now crumbling into obscurity. From here O'Donnell marched to disaster at the Battle of Kinsale in 1601.

The **Protestant church** is worth a glance, if only to read the plaque saying that the clock was paid for by the tenants of Ballymote Estate as a mark of respect for Sir Robert Gore-Booth of Lissadell. Unlike many similar tributes this one was genuine: Robert Gore-Booth mortgaged Lissadell House during the Famine to raise money for food for the starving. Constance Markievicz, his daughter, received a minute-long ovation from the local peasants here after her release from a British jail in June 1917.

Temple House (☎ 918 3329; www.templehouse.ie; Ballymote; s/d €65/120, dinner €30; Apr-Nov) This magnificent country surrounded by 1200 acres of farmland and gardens – as well as a 12th-century Knights Templar castle – is one of the best places in the whole county. The exquisite dinner, served at 7.30pm sharp, features a mouth-watering array of organic products. Highly recommended.

There are also several unpretentious pubs to choose from.

Carrowkeel Passage Tomb Cemetery

Situated on a hilltop in the Bricklieve Mountains overlooking Lough Arrow, this place is uplifting, with panoramic views on a clear day, and also a little spooky, given the 14 cairns, various dolmens and scattered remnants of other graves. The place has been dated to the late Stone Age (3000 to 2000 BC).

The site, west off the N4 road, is closer to Boyle in County Roscommon than Sligo town. If you're coming from the latter, turn right at the sign in the village of Castlebaldwin, then left at the fork as indicated. The site is about 2km uphill from the gateway. You can take an Athlone bus from Sligo and ask to be dropped off at Castlebaldwin.

Coopershill House (☎ 071-9165108; www.coopershill.com; Riverstown; tw €198; Apr-Oct) A handsome retreat for anyone wanting to relax in a Georgian family mansion. There are facilities for boating and fishing, as well as an Irish meal with good wine and open log fires. Riverstown, close to the Carrowkeel Passage Tomb Cemetery, is halfway between Sligo and Boyle.

Lough Arrow

The 8km-long Lough Arrow close to the Leitrim border is a fly-fisherperson's dream, as the lake is packed with brown trout, pike and some salmon (the season runs May to September). Windsurfing and sailing are allowed on the lake.

Arrow Lodge (☎ 079-66298; www.arrowlodge.com; Kilmactranny; s €41, pack lunch €12; Feb-Nov) A restored Victorian lodge in a woodland setting by the lake, it offers B&B in four rooms and caters almost exclusively for anglers. Boat rental and guided services are available.

Tubbercurry

☎ 071 / pop 400

Quiet, off the beaten track Tubbercurry (Tobar an Choire), also spelled Tobercurry, comes alive around mid-July, when the week-long **South Sligo Summer School** (☎ 918 5010) of music and dance takes place. On the second Wednesday in August, the town's big **fair day** is held. Nearly all the pubs have music.

Killoran's (☎ 918 5679; Main St; mains €7-15; 8am-10pm Mon-Sat & 11am-8pm Sun) The first place to call in at is Killoran's, a multipurpose spot that serves as a restaurant, pub, tourist office, takeaway, travel agent and off-licence all under one roof.

Easky & Enniscrone

☎ 096 / pop 500

The main route west to Mayo is pleasant enough, but there's little to detain the visitor. Easky (Eascaigh) has the ruins of a 15th-century castle, and the **surfing**, possible year-round, is highly regarded. For details contact the **Easky Surfing & Information Centre** (☎ /fax 49020; 10am-6pm Mon-Fri), on the main street.

Atlantic 'n' Riverside Caravan & Camping Park (☎ 49001; Easky; tent site & 2 people €10.20; Apr-mid-Sep) Right on the River Easky, this well-equipped park is behind the information centre. Register at the post office. Bookings are not taken for July and August.

SOMETHING SPECIAL

If the thought of immersing yourself in hot sea-water and seaweed doesn't appeal, you haven't visited the **Kilcullen Seaweed Baths** (☎ 36238; Enniscrone; baths €17; ⏰ 10am-10pm May-Sep; noon-8pm Mon-Fri & 10am-8pm Sat & Sun Oct-Apr). Seaweed baths have been part of Irish homeopathy for thousands of years and have long been considered a cure for rheumatism and arthritis. We don't affirm to know the truth about this claim one way or the other, but we can assure you that after one session you'll feel utterly relaxed and moisturised. Basically, this is the natural version of the bath doused with expensive, store-bought bath oils, and all the better for it, as seaweed contains a massive concentration of iodine, one of the richest natural elements and a key presence in most moisturising creams.

At Enniscrone (Innis Crabhann) further west, the sandy, 5km-long, Blue Flag beach known as the Hollow is one of the best in Ireland.

SLEEPING

Atlantic Caravan & Camping Park (☎ 36132; fax 36980; Enniscrone; tent sites €10; ⏰ Apr-Oct) The camp site is wonderfully located next to the Hollow beach and has 50 tent sites.

Getting There & Away

Bus Éireann's (☎ 071-916 0066) Dublin–Sligo express bus No 23 and Galway–Derry express bus No 64 stop outside Quigley's in Collooney. Saturday only, Sligo–Castlerea bus No 460 stops at Collooney, Ballymote and Tubbercurry. Local bus No 475 runs from Sligo to Collooney, Monday to Saturday. From Easky and Enniscrone buses run four times daily (once on Sunday) to Sligo and Ballina, and three times daily (once Sunday) to Donegal.

The Dublin–Sligo train stops at Collooney and Ballymote three times daily (four Friday). Call **Sligo station** (☎ 071-916 9888) for times.

LOUGH GILL

A return trip of 48km would take in most of this lough southeast of Sligo as well as Parke's Castle, which, though in County Leitrim, is included in this section. There are many legends associated with Lough Gill; one that can be tested easily is the story that a silver bell from the abbey in Sligo was thrown into the lough and only those free from sin can hear its pealing. No, you didn't hear it (but neither did we!).

Dooney Rock

There are good views of the lough and its islands from the top of Dooney Rock. Yeats immortalises the rock in *The Fiddler of Dooney*.

Leave Sligo heading south on the N4 and after 500m turn left at the sign to Lough Gill. Another left at the T-junction brings you onto the R287 and the Dooney Rock viewpoint.

Innisfree Island

If Yeats hadn't written 'The Lake Isle of Innisfree', this tiny island (Inis Fraoigh) near the southeastern shore wouldn't attract so many visitors, and it would probably have kept the air of tranquillity that so moved the poet:

> I will arise and go now, and go to Innisfree,
> And a small cabin build there, of clay and wattles made;
> Nine bean rows will I have there, a hive for the honey bee,
> And live alone in the bee-loud glade.

From the Dooney Rock car park turn left at the crossroads and after 3km turn left again for another 3km. A small road leads down to the lake.

Creevelea Abbey (County Leitrim)

The ruinous Creevelea Abbey was the last Franciscan friary founded in Ireland before the orders were suppressed. The columns in the cloister have some interesting carvings of St Francis, one displaying his stigmata and another one showing him in a pulpit with birds perched on a tree. The abbey was burned in 1590 by Richard Bingham, but restored by the monks before they were again ejected by Oliver Cromwell. They returned yet again and thatched the church roof, remaining until the end of the 17th century.

From Innisfree, return to the R287 and continue east until you see the sign for the abbey in the village of **Dromahair**.

Parke's Castle (County Leitrim)

The placid setting of **Parke's Castle** (☎ 071-64149; Fivemile Bourne; adult/concession €2.75/1.25; 🕓 10am-6pm mid-Mar–Oct), with swans drifting by on Lough Gill, belies the fact that the early Plantation architecture was created out of an unwelcome English landlord's insecurity and fear. The carefully restored, three-storey castle forms part of one of the five sides of the bawn, which also has two rounded turrets at its corners. Try to join one of the guided tours after viewing the 20-minute video *Stone by Stone*, which gives a general introduction to the area's antiquities.

From Creevelea Abbey, continue east along the R287, turn left towards Dromahair and continue northwards. To return to Sligo from Parke's Castle turn west onto the R286.

Getting There & Away

CAR & BICYCLE

Leave Sligo east via the Mall past the hospital, then turn right off the N16 onto the R286, which leads to the northern shore of Lough Gill and round to Innisfree. The southern route is less interesting until you reach Dooney Rock.

BOAT

Wild Rose Water Bus (☎ 071-64266, 087 259 8869; adult/child 2-hr trip €15/7.50, 1-hr trip €8/4) offers live recitals of Yeats' poetry accompanying music to cruises on Lough Gill that run hourly between Doorly Park (2.30pm and 5.30pm) in Sligo and Parke's Castle (12.30pm to 6.30pm June to September and on Sundays April, May and October). Doorly Park is a 30-minute walk east of Sligo town; you can also get the bus (every 20 minutes), which departs from Gilmartin's in town.

NORTH OF SLIGO TOWN

Drumcliff & Benbulben

WB Yeats died in 1939 in Menton, France, but his wishes were: 'If I die here, bury me up there on the mountain, and then after a year or so, dig me up and bring me privately to Sligo'. True to his wishes, his body was interred in the churchyard at Drumcliff in 1948 – where his great-grandfather had been rector – although it was hardly a private affair, as the photographs in the Sligo County Museum make clear.

Yeats' grave is on the left near the Protestant church, and alongside Yeats is buried Georgie Hyde-Lee, whom he married in 1917, when she was 23 and he was 52. The beautiful epitaph is from his poem *Under Ben Bulben:*

> Cast a cold eye
> On life, on death.
> Horseman, pass by!

In the 6th century, St Colmcille had chosen the same location for the foundation of a monastery. You can still see the remains of the **round tower**, damaged by lightning in 1936, on the main road near the churchyard. In the churchyard is an 11th-century **high cross**, whose eastern face depicts Christ in Glory, Daniel in the lions' den, Adam and Eve, and Cain's murder of Abel; on the western side, you can make out the presentation in the temple and the crucifixion.

Outside the churchyard is **Drumcliff Visitors Centre** (☎ 071-914 4956; adult/child €2.5/1.90; 🕓 9am-5pm Mon-Sat & 1-5pm Sun). It has a 15-minute, interactive audiovisual presentation on Yeats, St Colmcille and Drumcliff. The admission fee includes entry to the church.

To get there take the 8.45am bus from Sligo (arriving 9am) because the next one is at 4.15pm, which means you'll miss the two daily return buses that pass through Drumcliff at 12.45pm and 4.53pm (though there is a 3pm bus from Sligo to Drumcliff on Saturday only).

The limestone plateau of **Benbulben** (525m), the most westerly of the Dartry Mountains, is about 2km northeast of Drumcliff and dominates the surrounding landscape.

Glencar Lough

As well as **fishing**, the attraction of the lake is the beautiful **waterfall** signposted from the car park. Yeats refers to this picturesque spot in *The Stolen Child.* The surrounding countryside is best enjoyed by walking east along the road and taking the steep trail that heads north to the valley. From Drumcliff it's less than 5km to the lake, and there's also a bus service from Sligo. Ring **Bus Éireann** (☎ 071-60066) for details.

Lissadell House

Hidden in woodland lies **Lissadell House** (☎ 071-916 3150; Drumcliff; adult/concession €4/2; ⏲ 10.30am-1pm & 2-5pm Mon-Sat Jun–mid-Sep), built by Sir Robert Gore-Booth in 1830 to 1835 in the Greek Revival style. It's not a particularly attractive building; it's hard, box-like shape and granite colour give it the appearance of a posh bunker, but inside it is anything but.

Sir Robert took to calling himself 'Count Markiewicz', an affectation that passed onto his granddaughter Constance Gore-Booth (1868–1927), who befriended the young Yeats. Despite her titled pretensions, she was a committed activist to the cause of Irish independence, and even earned a death sentence (later commuted) for her part in the Easter Rising. In 1918 she became the first woman elected to the British House of Commons but – like most Irish rebels – refused to take her seat. Her sister Eva was an ardent suffragette and poet, and the sisters' friendship with Yeats was commemorated by him in the poem *In Memory of Eva Gore-Booth and Con Markievicz,* inscribed on a sign at the entrance to the house.

> The light of evening, Lissadell,
> Great windows, open to the south,
> Two girls in silk kimonos...

Truth is that Yeats visited Lissadell no more than four times in his whole life, but still managed to write about the interior: 'Great sitting room as high as a church and all things in good taste'.

Lissadell has an informative, 45-minute guided tour. However, the house was sold privately in August 2003 and as yet it is unclear what will happen once the new owners settle in. Check before visiting. To get there, follow the N15 north from Sligo and turn west at Drumcliff, just past Yeats Tavern.

Mullaghmore

If you turn left at Cliffony, off the N15, the main road to Mullaghmore (An Mullach Mór) first passes **Streedagh Beach**, a grand crescent of sand that was the final resting place for many of the 1300 sailors who perished when three ships from the Spanish Armada were wrecked nearby.

The **beach** at Mullaghmore is also delightfully wide and safe. It was in this bay that the IRA assassinated Lord Mountbatten and members of his family in 1979. On the way to the Mullaghmore headland you pass **Classiebawn Castle**, built for Lord Palmerston in 1856 and later the home of Lord Mountbatten. The castle isn't open to the public, but the neo-Gothic pile can be viewed from the N15 and the R279 as you approach Mullaghmore.

Inishmurray Island

If access were easier to arrange, a visit to this uninhabited island would be a must. It contains the remains of **three churches**, **beehive cells** and **open-air altars**. The old monastery is surrounded by a stone wall with five separate entrances to the central area, which contains the churches and altars. The monastery was founded in the early 6th century by St Molaise, and a wooden statue of the saint that once stood in the main church is now in the National Museum in Dublin.

The monks on Inishmurray assembled some fascinating pagan relics. There's a collection of cursing stones: those who wanted to lay a curse did the Stations of the Cross in reverse, turning over the stones as they went along. There were also separate burial grounds for men and women, and a strong belief that if a body was placed in the wrong ground it would move itself during the night.

Only 6km separates Inishmurray from the mainland, but there's no regular boat service and the lack of a harbour makes landing subject to the weather. Trips can be arranged for about €12 return through **Lomax Boats** (☎ 071-916 6124; Mullaghmore) or **Joe McGowan** (☎ 071-916 6267; Streedagh Point).

Creevykeel Goort Cairn

North of Cliffony on the N15 is a well-preserved, stone court tomb. Constructed around 2500 BC it has a wide, high front tapering away to a narrow end with an open central area. The unroofed court stands outside the front entrance. At some later stage, chambers were added to the western side of the cairn.

Sleeping & Eating

Celtic Farm Hostel (☎ 071-916 3337; Grange; dm/d €11/26; ⊠) About 1km north of Grange, this 14-bed hostel is a useful base for exploring northern Sligo and offers a free pick-up.

Benbulben Farm (☎ 071-916 3211; fax 917 3009; Barnaribbon, Drumcliff; s/d €30/60; 🕑 Apr-Sep) The biggest drawcard of this farmhouse B&B, 2km north of Drumcliff, is its elevated setting on the slopes of Benbulben.

Yeats Tavern (☎ 071-916 3117; Drumcliff; mains €8-17; 🕑 noon-9pm) The huge car park is indicative of the popularity of this pub on the main N15 road about 100m from Yeats' grave. The extensive menu falls into three main categories: seafood, steak and poultry.

Getting There & Away

There are regular **Bus Éireann** (☎ 071-916 0066) buses between Sligo, Drumcliff, Grange and Cliffony, as most buses to Donegal and Derry go along the N15. In Drumcliff the bus stop is near the church, in Grange it's outside Rooney's newsagency, and in Cliffony it's O'Donnell's Bar. The first bus leaves Sligo at 8.45am; the last bus from Cliffony is at 4.35pm.

Central North

CONTENTS

Central North

Someone once described Ireland as a dull picture with a wonderful frame. Indeed, most visitors are attracted by the frame – the coast – and rarely venture inland to explore the picture. There is good reason for this, at least in part: the six counties of the central north (Cavan, Monaghan, Roscommon, Leitrim, Longford and Westmeath) have long been considered Ireland's less appealing counties, with comparatively little to distract the visitor. But while they may never lure the same hordes as the west or south, the scarcity of tour buses, lengthy queues and packed hotels, and the genuinely unspoiled landscape, make the region all the more attractive. For others the so-called big houses, relics of the 17th century Plantation years which are dotted around the border counties and the mansions of the landed gentry, such as Strokestown House, provide a living reminder of Ireland's colonial history. Fishing in the great lakes of Counties Monaghan and Cavan, cruising at a leisurely pace down the Shannon–Erne Waterway and cycling the accessible flatlands, make up part of central north's special allure. Here you'll come across a real taste of rural Ireland, unpolished and typically welcoming.

Cavan, Monaghan and Donegal border Northern Ireland and, together with the six counties there, make up the province of Ulster. It's a definition that may not be immediately noticeable, though, as all border crossing points between the Republic and the North are now open.

HIGHLIGHTS

- Kick back and relax on a leisurely cruise down the **Shannon–Erne Waterway** (p456)
- Follow in the footsteps of the famous with an overnight stop in Glaslough's **Castle Leslie** (p447)
- Admire the grandeur of **Strokestown Park House and gardens** (p449)
- Revitalise mind and body at a yoga weekend in the **Jampa Ling Buddhist Centre** (p443)
- Slake your thirst with a creamy pint in Ireland's oldest bar, **Sean's** (p462)

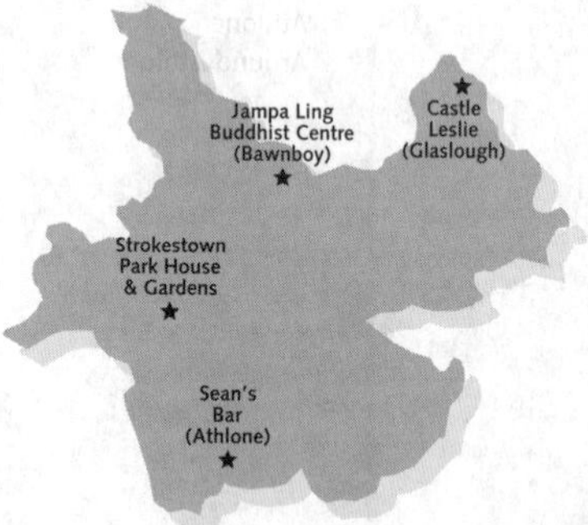

- POPULATION: 292,050
- AREA: 8555 SQ KM

COUNTY CAVAN

The low, undulating county of Cavan (An Cabhán) is a barely two-hour drive from Dublin and lies just south of the border with Northern Ireland. Cavan is dominated by lakes (it's said there is one for every day of the year), bogs and drumlins, which are small, round hills deposited and shaped by retreating glaciers during the last Ice Age. In the far northwest of the county, the wild and barren Cuilcagh Mountains are the source of the River Shannon, at over 300km long the mightiest river in Ireland or Britain.

Cavan is famous for its potholed roads, which are often twisty and badly signposted. The roads seem to go over the drumlins, whereas in neighbouring Monaghan they go round them.

There are some unexpected gastronomic rewards to be found in delis and on menus in Cavan, as it's home to some award-winning internationally recognised farmhouse cheeses: Corleggy, a hard pasteurised goat's cheese from Belturbet, and Boilie, the soft feta-like cream cheese from Lough Ramor, near Virginia, which is handrolled into balls and stored in oil.

Cavan is in many ways a hard place, with a no-nonsense attitude to life that is born out of the inclement weather, difficult economic circumstances and a people who have long been the butt of Irish humour as the most miserly in the country.

HISTORY

Archaeological evidence suggests that Cavan was inhabited as far back as Neolithic times. Magh Sleacht, a plain in the northwest of the county near the border village of Ballyconnell, was one of the most important druidic centres in the country in the 5th century, when St Patrick was winning the pagan Irish over to Christianity. The principal Celtic deity was Crom Cruaich, whose significance swiftly diminished as the Christian teachings of Patrick spread. In the 12th century, the Anglo-Normans made a concerted effort to get a foothold in Cavan, but the landscape proved difficult to penetrate and the region remained under the control of the Gaelic O'Reilly clan for many years.

The O'Reilly's grip on power began to slip in the 16th century. The English 'shired' the county into baronies, dividing these among clan members loyal to the English Crown. The end came when the O'Reillys joined with the other Ulster lords – the O'Donnells and the O'Neills – in the Nine Years' War (1594–1603) against the English and were defeated.

As part of the Plantation of Ulster, Cavan was divided up among English and Scottish settlers.

In the 1640s, with Charles I in trouble in England, the Confederate Rebellion led by Owen Roe O'Neill, who was based at Cavan, took place in opposition to Plantation. O'Neill, a returned exile, had one major victory over the English at the Battle of Benburb in County Tyrone in 1646. Only with the end of the English Civil War and the arrival of Cromwell in 1649 were the English again able to take control over Ireland. Owen Roe O'Neill died in suspicious circumstances in 1649 – poisoning was suspected – in Clough Oughter Castle near the town of Cavan (see p441).

The Irish population of Cavan generally remained in poverty and the Potato Famine led to massive emigration. After the War of Independence in 1922, the Ulster counties of Cavan, Monaghan and Donegal were incorporated into the South. With the border so close, republicanism is strong in Cavan: Sinn Féin, the political voice of militant republicanism, has achieved consistent success at the polls here.

FISHING

Anglers from all over Europe converge on Cavan in season to fish the many lakes along the county's southern and western borders. The fishing is excellent; it's primarily coarse fishing but there's also some game angling for brown trout in Lough Sheelin.

Some lakes, such as Lough Sheelin, are recovering after years of serious pollution from the numerous pig farms in the area. Most lakes are well signposted, with the types of fish available also marked. Some local villages and guesthouses depend heavily on anglers, many of whom return every year. For more information, contact **North West Tourism** (☎ 049-433 1942) or the **Northern Regional Fisheries Board** (☎ 049-37174), both in Cavan town.

CENTRAL NORTH

CENTRAL NORTH

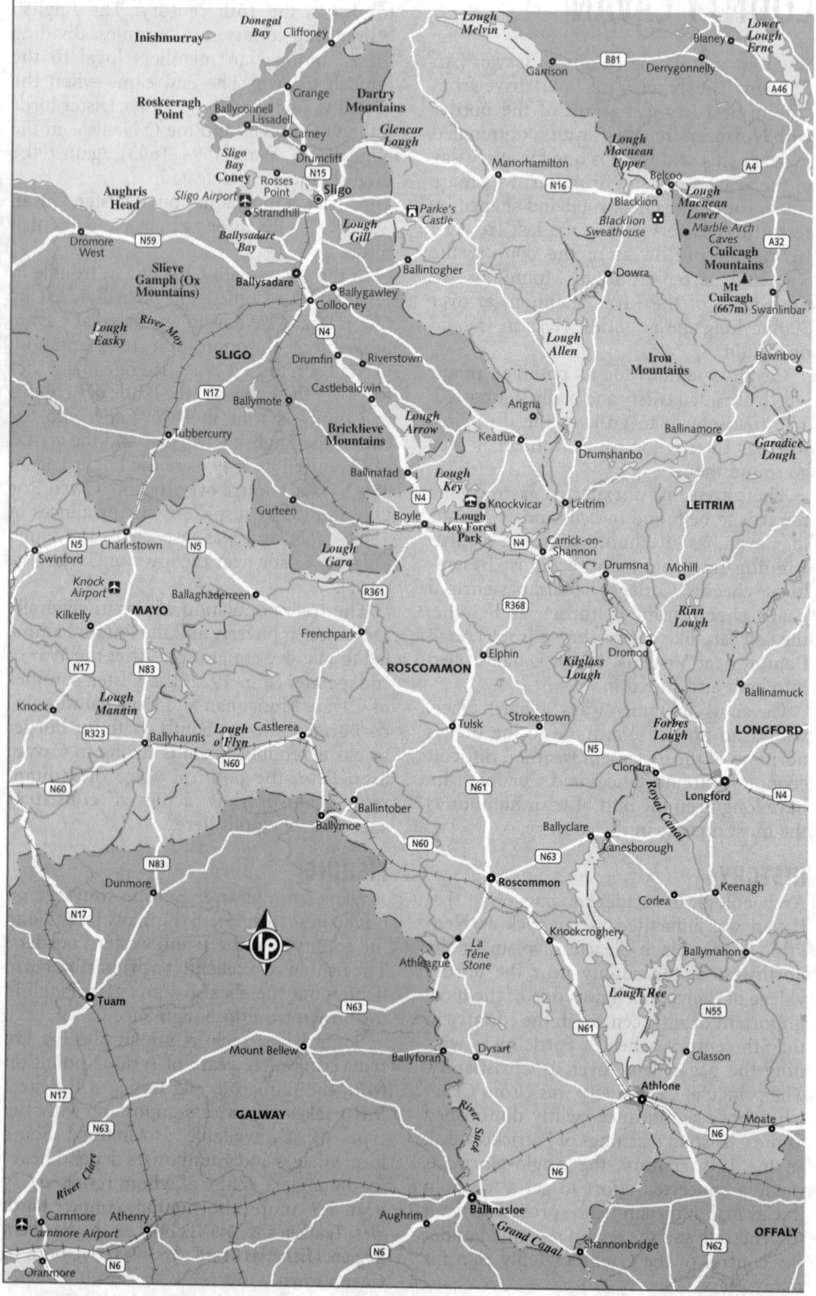

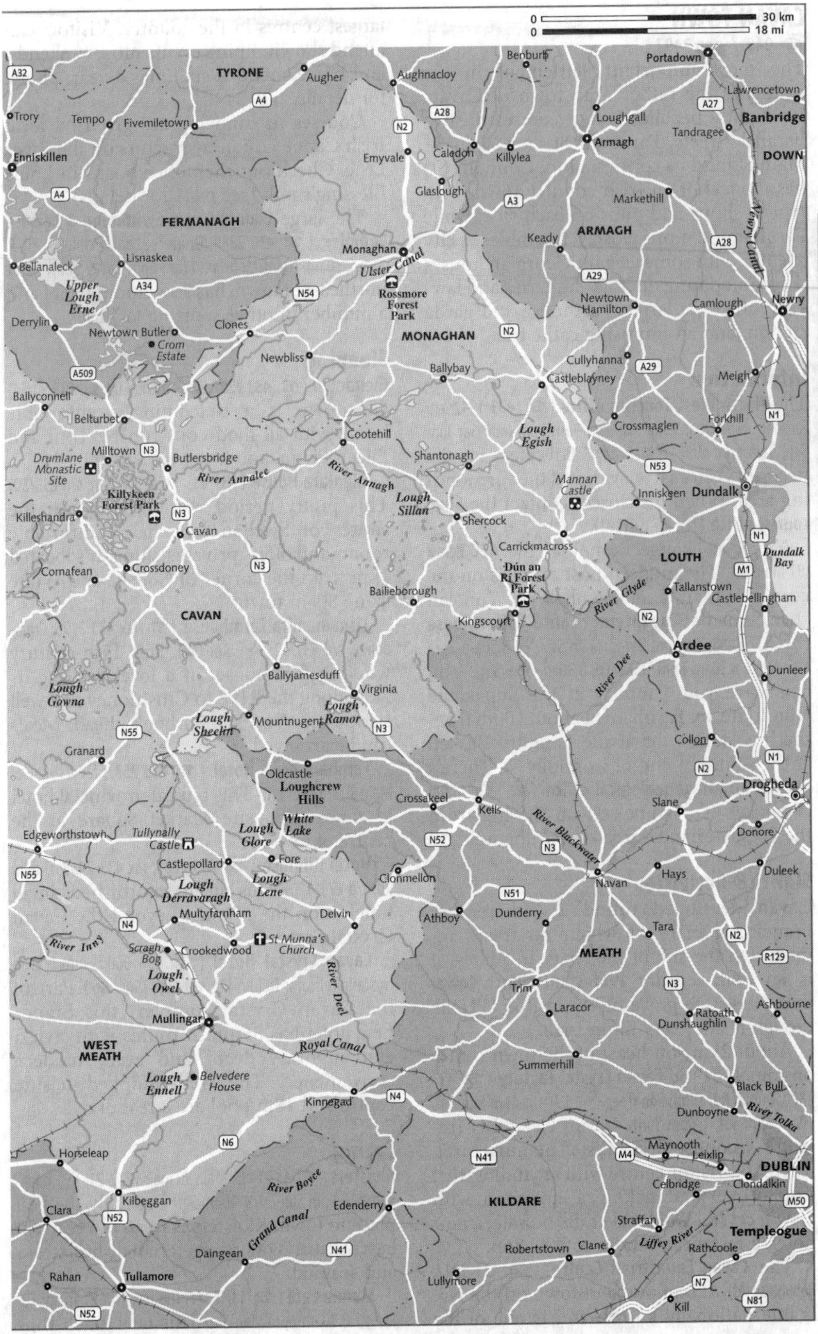
0 30 km
0 18 mi
TYRONE
FERMANAGH
MONAGHAN
ARMAGH
DOWN
CAVAN
LOUTH
MEATH
WEST MEATH
KILDARE
DUBLIN
Augher
Aughnacloy
Benburb
Portadown
Lawrencetown
Banbridge
Loughgall
Armagh
Tandragee
Trory
Tempo
Fivemiletown
Enniskillen
Emyvale
Caledon
Killylea
Glaslough
Markethill
Newry Canal
Monaghan
Keady
Ulster Canal
Bellanaleck
Lisnaskea
Upper Lough Erne
Rossmore Forest Park
Newtown Hamilton
Camlough
Newry
Derrylin
Newtown Butler
Crom Estate
Clones
Newbliss
Ballybay
Cullyhanna
Castleblayney
Meigh
Ballyconnell
Belturbet
Cootehill
Lough Egish
Crossmaglen
Forkhill
Milltown
Drumlane Monastic Site
Butlersbridge
River Annalee
River Annagh
Shantonagh
Lough Sillan
Mannan Castle
Inniskeen
Dundalk
Killykeen Forest Park
Killeshandra
Cavan
Shercock
Carrickmacross
Dundalk Bay
Cornafean
Crossdoney
Dún an Rí Forest Park
Bailieborough
Kingscourt
River Glyde
Tallanstown
Castlebellingham
Ardee
River Dee
Dunleer
Ballyjamesduff
Virginia
Lough Gowna
Lough Sheelin
Mountnugent
Lough Ramor
Granard
Collon
Oldcastle
Loughcrew Hills
Drogheda
Crossakeel
Kells
Slane
White Lake
Lough Glore
River Blackwater
Donore
Edgeworthstown
Tullynally Castle
Castlepollard
Fore
Lough Lene
Clonmellon
Navan
Hays
Duleek
Lough Derravaragh
Multyfarnham
Delvin
Athboy
Dunderry
Tara
River Inny
Scragh Bog
Crookedwood
St Munna's Church
River Deel
Lough Owel
Trim
Laracor
Ashbourne
Mullingar
Ratoath
Dunshaughlin
Royal Canal
Summerhill
Lough Ennell
Belvedere House
Kinnegad
Black Bull
Dunboyne
River Tolka
Maynooth
Leixlip
Horseleap
River Boyne
Celbridge
Clondalkin
Kilbeggan
Clara
Edenderry
Grand Canal
Straffan
Templeogue
Liffey River
Daingean
Robertstown
Clane
Rathcoole
Rahan
Tullamore
Lullymore
Kill
A32
A4
A28
N2
A3
A34
N54
A29
A509
N3
N1
N53
M1
N55
N52
N51
N4
R129
N6
N41
M4
M50
N7
N81
A27

CAVAN TOWN

☎ 049 / pop 3497

The most important settlement in the county is the rather drab town of Cavan. Its slightly peculiar layout centres on two parallel streets, Farnham St and Main St. Main St (and its continuation, Connolly St) has the feel of an Irish country town, with typical shops and pubs on each side, while Farnham St more closely resembles a city avenue, with some elegant Georgian houses accommodating doctors' surgeries and lawyers' offices, a large courthouse and garda station, and an imposing cathedral.

Information

The **North West Tourism office** (☎ 433 1942; cnr Farnham & Thomas Ashe Sts; 🕑 9am-5pm Mon-Sat Jun-Sep, 9am-5pm Mon-Fri Mar-May & Oct) caters for the needs of visitors to Cavan and the surrounding area. When it's closed, contact the **Sligo tourist office** (☎ 071-61201).

You can change money at the **ACC Bank** (91 Main St). The modern post office is on the corner of Main and Townhall Sts. You can check email at **Ego Internet Café & Coffee House** (☎ 437 3488; Convent Bldgs, Main St; 🕑 8.30am-7pm Mon-Wed, 8.30am-8pm Thu & Fri, 8.30am-6pm Sat). You can leave your laundry at the Supaklene laundrette, on Farnham St about 100m from the bus station, or at the Laundry Basket, at the southern end of Connolly St. There's also a small **genealogical office** (☎ 436 1094; Cana House). It's signposted up the hill from the Presbyterian church on Farnham St.

Sights & Activities

Cavan developed round a 13th-century Franciscan friary of which no traces remain. On the site of the friary in Abbey St is an 18th-century **Protestant church tower** that marks the grave of Owen Roe O'Neill, though it's not very impressive.

About 2km southeast of the town centre on the N3 is the **Cavan Crystal Factory** (☎ 433 1800; Dublin Rd; admission free; 🕑 9.30am-6pm Mon-Fri, 10am-5pm Sat, 1-6pm Sun). Cavan Crystal is Ireland's second-oldest crystal manufacturer. There is a visitor centre with an audiovisual display of crystal making, a showroom with Cavan crystal and local crafts on sale, a new hotel, a restaurant and a coffee shop.

The **Cavan Equestrian Centre** (☎ 433 2017; Ballyhaise Rd), 1.5km north of town off the N3, is internationally known and is one of the largest centres in the country. Visitors can attend showjumping events most weekends, and horse auctions six times a year; phone for details.

Courses in canoeing are given by local Irish Canoe Union instructors on the River Erne. Check out the notice board in Louis Blessing's pub (see p441 for details).

The large **County Cavan Swimming & Leisure Complex** (☎ 436 2888; Drumalee; adult/child €4.80/3; 🕑 7.30am-10pm Mon-Fri, 11am-6pm Sat & Sun), just northeast of town, has a swimming pool and a number of other sporting facilities.

Sleeping

Glendown (☎ 433 2257; 33 Cathedral Rd; s/d €38.50/54) Glendown is a welcoming, comfortable home with all mod cons run by Tom and Eileen Flynn, and it's gay-friendly.

Glenlara House (☎ 433 1136; Swellan; s/d €35/50) This pretty period manor house on the shores of Swellan lake has comfortable rooms and offers private fishing. It's located 1km from the corner of College and Wolfe Tone Sts in town.

Lisnamandra Farmhouse (☎/fax 433 7196; Crossdoney; s/d €37/52; 🕑 Apr-Oct) This 17th-century working farmhouse, in a lovely setting, is 7km along the R198 to Crossdoney and well signposted. You should book ahead. Meals can be arranged.

Farnham Arms Hotel (☎ 433 2577; fax 436 2606; Main St; s/d €70/110) This typical provincial hotel is almost opposite Market Square in the centre of town.

Hotel Kilmore (☎ 433 2288; fax 433 2458; Dublin Rd; s/d €71/120) This nicely refurbished, small hotel is on the N3 just beyond the Cavan Crystal Factory.

Cavan Crystal Hotel (☎ 436 0600; info@cavancrystalhotel.com; Dublin Rd; s/d €69/150; 🚭) Part of the Cavan Crystal complex, this brand-new hotel has 85 plush rooms with stylish contemporary décor and every modern convenience. The well-equipped leisure centre and 18m pool are a real draw.

Eating

Kloisters (☎ 437 1485; Main St; mains €12-21; 🕑 noon-3pm & 6-9pm Sun-Fri, 4-10pm Sat) Probably the best place in town, Kloisters is in an old convent basement and offers vegetarian dishes, steaks and seafood.

Manna Café (☎ 437 7777; Thomas Ashe St; mains €3-8; 🕑 8.30am-6pm Mon-Sat) This new lunch-time spot, near the tourist office, is a rustic place with home-made salads, hot specials and outdoor seating.

Ego Internet Café & Coffee House (☎ 437 3488; Convent Bldgs, Main St; 🕑 8.30am-7pm Mon-Wed, 8.30am-8pm Thu & Fri, 8.30am-6pm Sat) Check your email over a hot pitta sandwich, home-made dessert or good coffee in this friendly place in the middle of town.

Melbourne Bakery (☎ 436 1266; Main St; mains €6-9; 🕑 9am-5.30pm Mon-Fri) Halfway up Main St is this old-world canteen with Formica table tops and cream buns galore.

Farnham Arms Hotel (☎ 433 2577; fax 436 2606; Main St; mains €7-11; 🕑 ☒) The comfortable lounge here serves reliable carvery lunches, while the **Imperial bar** (☎ 437 3027) serves a good range of hot snacks and sandwiches in airy surroundings.

Side Door (☎ 433 1819; Drumalee Cross; mains €11-22, 3-course dinner €14; 🕑 5.30-10.30pm Mon-Thu, 6-11pm Sat, 5-10pm Sun) Seafood is the house speciality in this colourful little restaurant above the Orchard bar. The pizzas and pasta are good too.

Mustang Sally, a bar in the same building as Kloisters, serves decent bar food all day.

Drinking

McGinnity's Corner Bar (☎ 433 1236; College St) McGinnity's has won a regional 'pub of the year' title and sometimes has music at weekends.

Imperial (☎ 437 3027; Main St) This cavernous, trendy bar with stylish mosaic décor has music at weekends.

Black Horse Inn (☎ 433 2140; Main St) Near the post office, this is a popular place with young locals and has pool tables.

Louis Blessing's (☎ 433 1138; 92 Main St) This is a great, authentic pub and grocery, happily untouched for years, in a small courtyard off Main St.

An Síbín (Speakeasy; ☎ 433 1064; cnr Townhall & Main Sts) The most popular pub these days among Cavan's young things is the renovated Speakeasy, with wooden floors and real fires. It has live Irish music on Wednesday nights.

Getting There & Around

Buses arrive at and depart from the small **bus station** (☎ 433 1353; Farnham St; 🕑 7.30am-8.15pm).

Cavan is on the Dublin–Donegal, Galway–Belfast and Athlone–Belfast bus routes. On weekdays there are hourly buses to Dublin (one way €10, two hours), two buses to Belfast (€17, three hours), one to Galway (€17, 3¾ hours) and four to Donegal (€13.20, 2¼ hours). Bus Éireann also has services running from Cavan through the county to Bawnboy, Ballyconnell, Belturbet, Virginia, Kells, Dunshaughlin, Navan, Cootehill and many other small towns.

Taxis can be ordered on ☎ 433 1172 or ☎ 433 2876.

AROUND CAVAN TOWN

Killykeen Forest Park

On the shores of Lough Oughter, 12km northwest of Cavan, is **Killykeen Forest Park** (☎ 433 2541; killkeen@coillte.ie; car/pedestrians & cyclists €5/free). Lough Oughter has a tortuous outline, and the park has some fine walks, nature trails and fishing spots among its 243 hectares of trees and inlets. Many of the low wooded islands in the lake are likely to have been *crannógs* (fortified, artificial islands). Within the park to the north is the inaccessible **Clough Oughter Castle**, built in the 13th century by the O'Reillys on an island in the lake, and the place where the rebel leader Owen Roe O'Neill died in 1649. The best way to get near it is from the southeast, along a narrow road running north from the village of Garthrattan.

On the shores of Lough Oughter there are self-catering **chalets** (☎ 433 2541; 4/6 people for 3 nights €290/375).

You can rent Canadian-style canoes and other boats for a paddle on Lough Oughter or the Erne waterways, and there's coarse fishing, tennis and horse riding within the park.

Butlersbridge

About 6km north of Cavan is the pretty hamlet of Butlersbridge on the Annalee River. It's a tiny but pleasant place to stop for a riverside picnic.

Fortview House (☎ 433 8185; Cloverhill; s/d €36/60) This friendly, modern working farm has six rooms, three with en suite. It has a children's play area and full angling facilities. Take the N54 for 2km in the direction of Clones.

Derragarra Inn (☎/fax 433 1003; Butlersbridge; mains €8-20) An attractive ivy-clad, thatched pub by the River Annalee, it has good bar food available all day, a reasonably priced tourist menu and peat fires. The beer garden and live music draw crowds at weekends.

Belturbet & Around

☎ 049 / pop 1304

On the River Erne, 16km northwest of Cavan on the N3, Belturbet is an old-fashioned inland town that exudes a bleak charm. It is predominantly an angling centre with cruises available. **Emerald Star** (☎ 952 2933) has several cruisers for hire year round on the Shannon–Erne Waterway (p456) between Belturbet and Belleek. A four-berth boat costs from €910 per week in the low season.

Olde Post Inn (☎ 047-55555; fax 55111; Cloverhill; s/d €38/76; mains €18-25, 5-course dinner €40; 🕑 6.30-9.30pm Tue-Sat, 12.30-3pm & 6.30-8.30pm Sun) Situated 4km from Belturbet, this charming 200-year-old stone building originally housed the village post office. It has nine comfortable rooms and an excellent restaurant with modern Irish cuisine on offer.

Bus Éireann (☎ 433 1353) stops here (€3.60, 2¼ hours) four times daily (three times on Sunday) in each direction on the route between Cavan and Donegal. The bus stop is outside O'Reilly's Garage. You can rent bicycles – and seek advice about cycling routes – from **Padraig Fitzpatrick's** (☎ 952 2866) on Bridge St. Bike hire costs €15 per day.

Lough Sheelin

About 24km south of Cavan, Lough Sheelin is noted for its game angling, especially in May and June. The two main accommodation centres – at opposite ends of the 6km-long lough – are the villages of Finnea, just over the border in County Westmeath, and Mountnugent. There are several places in Mountnugent where you can stay and hire boats for fishing.

Ross House (☎/fax 854 0218; Mountnugent; s/d €45/70) This beautiful period farmhouse in mature grounds on the lake's edge has a sauna, Jacuzzi, tennis, horse riding and boat hire to entice you. Evening meals are by arrangement.

Crover House Hotel (☎ 854 0206; fax 854 0356; Mountnugent; €75/120) Recently refurbished, this family-run hotel with top facilities on the lakeshore has private gardens and boats for hire.

WESTERN CAVAN

Sometimes known as the Panhandle because of its long, narrow shape, western Cavan is dominated by the starkly beautiful, but little-visited, Cuilcagh Mountains. To the southwest, Magh Sleacht, which is the area around Kilnavert and Killycluggin, is supposed to have been a druidic centre dedicated to the deity Crom Cruaich. In the far northwestern corner of the county, the road runs parallel to the Northern Irish border before dividing. The left fork heads west to Dowra and Blacklion, a desolate area with some interesting ancient sites. The right fork heads north to Swanlinbar and the border.

Getting There & Away

There are few buses serving this remote part of the county. The express Donegal–Dublin buses pass through Ballyconnell, Bawnboy and Swanlinbar four times daily. Swanlinbar is also on the Athlone–Derry route, which runs once a day Monday to Saturday. The Galway–Belfast bus goes via Sligo and stops in Blacklion once daily. Contact **Bus Éireann** (☎ 433 1353) in Cavan for more information.

Ballyconnell

☎ 049 / pop 1064

Ballyconnell, 29km northwest of Cavan and 7km west of Belturbet, is the gateway to the Cavan Panhandle. There's nothing much for a visitor in the village itself, but it's a good base from which to explore. Ballyconnell has lots of B&Bs, most of them situated on the Cavan road into town.

Sandville House (☎ 952 6297; sandville@eircom.net; dm/d €12/48) The county's only hostel, this IHH property is 3km southeast of Ballyconnell, signposted off the Belturbet road (R200), in a peaceful, rural two-hectare setting. It also has an area to pitch tents; phone in advance if arriving in winter. The Dublin–Donegal bus stops at the Slieve Russell Hotel in Ballyconnell on request, and if you call the hostel beforehand they can arrange to pick you up.

An Crannog (☎ 952 6545; Cranaghan; s/d €40/60; ⊠; wheelchair access) This large modern bungalow has very comfy rooms and a pleasant garden. It's next door to the Slieve Russell Hotel.

Slieve Russell Hotel (☎ 952 6444; fax 952 6046; Cranaghan; slieve-russell@quinn-hotels.com; s/d €130/230; 🖳) About 2km southeast of Ballyconnell, this grandiose hotel is something of a legend. Built by a local millionaire, it features marble, fountains, restaurants, bars, nightclubs, a pool and an 18-hole golf course.

SOMETHING SPECIAL

Jampa Ling Buddhist Centre (☎ 952 3448; www.jampaling.org; Owendoon House, Bawnboy; dm/s/d €32/39/68) Those in search of enlightenment or time out, casual travellers and the plain curious have been coming to Jampa Ling (Place of Loving Kindness) since it opened over a decade ago. The centre, in a lovely pastoral setting, has two dorms and three doubles (the price includes full board) or self-catering accommodation (adult/child €16/8), surrounded by a walled garden, a lake and almost six hectares of woodland. As a Buddhist retreat centre it primarily offers courses (from about €45 per day) in Galupa Buddhism, philosophy and meditation, though you don't have to take part in a course to stay. One of the unique things about Jampa Ling is that a Panchen Lama, a revered senior figure in Tibetan Buddhism, is resident there year round and visitors may avail themselves of his wisdom over a cup of *chai*! The centre occasionally hosts weekends on everything from yoga to medicinal and culinary herbs and visitors can stay as long as they like. This is truly a special place.

Kilcorby Log Cabins (☎ 952 2869; fax 952 2698; kilcorby@utvinternet.com; 3-bedroom cabin 3/7 nights €330/526) Anglers in particular may wish to hire one of these fully equipped cabins on Lough Oughter, in a secluded spot 4km south of Ballyconnell on the Cavan road. Boats can be hired on a daily basis (€50).

Pólo D (☎ 952 6228; 3-course dinner €35; 10am-3pm Tue-Sat, 7-9.30pm Wed-Sat) This restaurant at the northern end of the main street is in an old-world cottage. Sandwiches, salads and light snacks are served for lunch, while the more substantial evening meals include crispy duck and grilled salmon.

Blacklion

☎ 071

About 5km south of Blacklion are the remains of a cashel (ring fort) with three large, circular embankments. Inside is a sweathouse, a stone hut that served as a type of Turkish bath or sauna, which was used mostly in the 19th century. Between Dowra and Blacklion there are the remains of several of these curiosities.

MacNean House & Bistro (☎ 985 3022, 985 3404; Main St; s/d €40/70; restaurant 7-9.30pm Wed-Sun, noon-2.30pm Sun) This is one of the few B&Bs in or around Blacklion and it also provides a much-praised set dinner in the evening (€55) cooked by award-winning TV chef Neven Maguire.

The Galway–Belfast and Sligo–Belfast buses stop in Blacklion twice daily, except in summer, when the latter bus originates in Westport and stops in Blacklion once daily. The bus stop is in front of Maguire's pub.

The Cavan & Ulster Ways

Blacklion is at the end of the 26km Cavan Way (p656), and is also on the northeastern section of the Ulster Way (p657).

EASTERN CAVAN

Heading east from Cavan town you move into the heart of drumlin (rounded hill formed by retreating glaciers) country. The history of foreign settlement has left its mark on the fabric and layout of the main towns, many of which centred around the estates of the 17th century plantations.

Getting There & Away

Four or five daily **Bus Éireann** (☎ 049-433 1353) express buses on the Dublin–Donegal route pass through Virginia (€10, 1¾ hours, three on Sunday), and there are also daily buses on the hour each hour between Cavan and Dublin. Cootehill (€5.50, 35 minutes) is on a Cavan–Dundalk route, and there are buses on Monday, Wednesday and Friday. One bus a day on weekdays during the school year (September to June) runs from Cootehill to Monaghan (€5.50, 30 minutes). A Cavan–Dundalk bus passes through Kingscourt (€8.20, one hour) on Tuesday and Thursday. There's also a Kingscourt–Navan–Dublin (€10, 1¾ hours) service, which has two buses a day Monday to Saturday and one on Sunday.

Virginia

☎ 049 / pop 2364

On the shores of Lough Ramor in the south-eastern corner of the county, the origins of the sleepy town of Virginia (Achadh Lir) go back to the Plantation of Ulster in the early 17th century. Like the US state first settled in 1607, it was named after Elizabeth I, the Virgin Queen. As in the rest of Cavan, the accent can be quite difficult to decipher; locals pronounce the town name *ver*-ginee.

Lisduff House (☎ 046-45054; Lisduff; s/d €35/56; wheelchair access) This large 18th-century working farm, located 4.5km from Virginia on the N3 to Kells, overlooks Lough Crew. It's a family-friendly place with a nice garden and five double rooms.

Park Hotel (☎ 854 7235; virginiapark@eircom.net; Virginia Park; s/d €65/130) An 18th-century former hunting lodge overlooking a small lake, it has 40 rooms, a nine-hole golf course, walking trails and pleasure gardens. The restaurant serves good evening meals (dinner €30) and bar snacks during the day.

Kingscourt

☎ 042 / pop 2019

In the far east of County Cavan, Kingscourt (Dún an Rí) is a fairly drab village, though **St Mary's Catholic Church** has some superb 1940s stained-glass windows by the artist Evie Hone. The church has views of the surrounding region, and just to the northwest is 225-hectare **Dún an Rí Forest Park** (☎ 966 7320; car/pedestrian €5/free; Apr-Oct), with wooded walks, picnic spots and a famous wishing well.

Cabra Castle (☎ 966 7030; fax 966 7039; s/d €139/214) About 3km out of Kingscourt on the Carrickmacross road, is this plush 15th-century castle with 80 rooms in 36 hectares of parkland and its own nine-hole golf course. It's worth trying for lunch or the set dinner (€39).

COUNTY MONAGHAN

Few visitors ever pass through Monaghan (Muineachán), a landscape of neat round hills crisscrossed by unkempt hedgerows and scattered farms. The hills are drumlins, deposited by the glaciers of the last Ice Age in a belt stretching from Clew Bay in County Galway across the country to County Down. It's pleasant but never spectacular scenery. Walkers and cyclists may enjoy the peaceful country lanes if the weather is cooperative. Monaghan has fewer lakes than neighbouring Cavan, though the fishing is still good.

Patrick Kavanagh (1905–67), one of Ireland's most respected poets, was born in this county, in Inniskeen. *The Great Hunger*, a long poem that he wrote in 1942, and *Tarry Flynn*, a novel written in 1948, evoke the atmosphere and frequently grim reality of life for the poor farming community.

The barren terrain has restricted the development of large-scale mechanised farming but, despite this, Monaghan's farming cooperatives are among the most active and forward-looking in the country. Monaghan is noted for its lace, and this eye-straining craft continues in Clones and Carrickmacross, the centres of the industry since the early 19th century.

HISTORY

The earliest traces of humans in this region date back to before the Bronze Age. None of the sites here measures up to the magnificent monuments of County Meath, though the Tullyrain Ring Fort close to Shantonagh in the south of the county is worth a look, as are Mannor Castle near Carrickmacross and the *crannóg* in Convent Lake in Monaghan. Like Cavan, County Monaghan is lacking in religious remains despite its proximity to Armagh, the principal seat of St Patrick in the 5th century. The round tower and high cross in Clones in the west of the county are among the scant remains from this period of Irish history.

Unlike Cavan and much of Ulster, Monaghan was largely left alone during the Ulster Plantation. The transfer of Monaghan land to English hands came later – after the Cromwellian wars – and much of it was granted to soldiers and adventurers or bought by them from local chieftains (under pressure and often for a fraction of its true value). These new settlers levelled the forests and built numerous new towns and villages, each with their own Protestant church. The planning and architecture exemplified their tidy, no-frills approach to life. Disapproving of Irish pastoral farming methods, they introduced arable farming, and the linen industry later became very profitable.

Monaghan's historical ties with Ulster were severed by the partition of Ireland in 1922 and, though republicanism is quite strong, it's not as visible as you might expect. A number of towns have Sinn Féin bookshops and advice centres.

MONAGHAN TOWN

☎ 047 / pop 5737

The county town of Monaghan is 141km northwest of Dublin and just 8km south of the border with Northern Ireland. Though it has a population of less than 6000, it's the only town of any size in the county. Its design and buildings reflect the influence of the British newcomers of the 17th and 18th centuries and of the money generated by the linen industry in the 18th and 19th centuries; many of the town's important buildings are quite elegant limestone edifices. Other than the county museum, though, there isn't much to keep a visitor here beyond a day.

Nothing remains of the ruling MacMahon's 1462 friary or their earlier forts, but in Convent Lake, just behind St Louis Convent, there is a small, overgrown *crannóg* that served as the headquarters for the family around the 14th century.

After the turbulent wars of the 16th and 17th centuries, the town was settled by Scottish Calvinists, who built a castle using the rubble of the old friary, some fragments of which can be seen near the Diamond. The 19th-century profits from the linen trade transformed the town and brought many sturdy new buildings.

Orientation & Information

The principal streets of Monaghan form a roughly continuous arc, broken up by the town's three main squares – Church Square, the Diamond (the Ulster name for town squares) and Old Cross Square – where most of the sights and important buildings can be found. To the west of this arc at the top of Park St are Market Square and the **tourist office** (☎ 81122; Market House, Market St; 🕑 9am-5pm Mon-Fri, 9am-1pm Sat Apr-Oct, 9am-6pm Mon-Fri, 9am-1pm Sat Jun-Aug).

The post office is on Mill St, which runs between Hill St and North Rd. There are two small lakes: Peter's Lake to the north of the Diamond and Convent Lake at the southwestern corner of town. A one-way traffic system operates through the centre of town.

Sights

Just northwest of the tourist office at the start of Hill St is the excellent **Monaghan County Museum & Gallery** (☎ 82928; 1-2 Hill St; admission free; 🕑 10am-1pm & 2-5pm Tue-Fri, 11am-1pm & 2-5pm Sat), one of the best regional museums in Ireland. Taking up two Victorian houses, it includes exhibits from the Stone Age to modern times, including local medieval *crannóg* artefacts, and has displays on lacemaking, the linen industries, the abandoned Ulster Canal and, of course, the border with the North. The museum's prized possession, though, is the **Cross of Clogher**, a bronze 13th- or 14th-century altar cross.

Local and national artists have occasional exhibits in the art gallery wing.

At the top of Dawson St is Church Square, the first of the three squares, with an 1857 **obelisk** for one Colonel Dawson, who was killed in the Crimean War. Overlooking the square is a fine Doric 1830 **courthouse**, the former **Hibernian Bank** (1875) and the Gothic **St Patrick's Church**.

In the centre of town, the Diamond is the town's original marketplace, with a Victorian sandstone fountain presented to the town in 1875 in honour of the baron of Rossmore, a member of the area's former leading family. This spot was once occupied by the **Market Cross** (and sundial), which was moved to Old Cross Square at the end of Dublin St to accommodate the baron's memorial.

South of the Ulster Canal on the Dublin road, the imposing **St Macartan's Catholic Cathedral** with its slender spire was designed by JJ McCarthy (responsible for the College Chapel in Maynooth, County Kildare) and is said to be his finest building, though some feel it has been marred by the later addition of incongruous Carrara-marble statues.

Sleeping & Eating

Glendrum House (☎ 82347; Drumbear; s/d €35/55) There are five comfortable rooms in this gay-friendly, modern home, a 10-minute walk from the town centre (on the R188).

Lakeside Hotel (☎ 83599; fax 82291; Lakeside, North Rd; s/d €60/120) This recently refurbished Georgian hotel beside Peter's Lake is a five-minute walk from town on the Derry road.

Four Seasons Hotel (☎ 81888; fax 83131; Coolshannagh; s/d €97/144; 🖳) Unconnected to the Four Seasons international chain, this large, modern hotel has good facilities, including a sauna and gym. It's less than 1km from town on the N2.

Mediterraneo (☎ 82335; 58 Dublin St; mains €11-20; 🕑 6.30-9.30pm Wed-Sun) This small, colourful bistro offers a good selection of fish as well as decent Italian staples.

Andy's Bar & Restaurant (☎ 82277; 12 Market St; lunch €8, set dinner €28; 🕑 noon-3pm daily, 6-10pm Tue-Sat, 4-9pm Sun) You'll have to loosen your belt a notch or two after a slap-up meal in award-winning Andy's Bar – a dark, old-fashioned place, full of locals. There's nothing to rave about on the pub nosh menu of roasts and breaded fish, but the food is well prepared, comes in humungous portions and is served with a smile.

Paramount (☎ 77333; 30 Market St; mains €16-22; ⏲ 6.30-10pm Wed-Mon) This classy, minimalist restaurant over Cooper's pub serves excellent seafood and steak. There's a three-course dinner for €35.

Drinking & Entertainment

Sherry's (☎ 81805; 24 Dublin St) Walking into Sherry's, one of Monaghan's oldest bars, is like stepping back into a spinster's parlour of the 1950s. The old tiled floor, beauty board and dusty memorabilia probably haven't been touched in decades – and that's just the way the few locals there like it.

An Poc Fada (☎ 72395; North Rd) A lively, traditional Irish bar that becomes packed in the late evening, especially on Wednesdays and Sundays for the live rock music. Its name means Long Puck, an ancient hurling game still played around the Cooley Mountains in County Louth.

Traynor's (☎ 82957; 30 Park St) Head here for traditional Irish music on Thursday nights.

Market House (☎ 71114; www.themarkethouse.ie; Market St) A brand-new arts venue hosts a mix of traditional, classical and jazz music, as well as poetry readings and drama.

Getting There & Around

From the **bus station** (☎ 82377) on North Rd beside the former train station, there are numerous daily intercity services within the Republic and into the North. These include 11 daily (six on Sunday) to Dublin (one way €10, two hours); five to Derry (€11.70, two hours) via Omagh; and five (four on Sunday) to Belfast (€10, two hours) and Armagh (€5.50, 40 minutes). There are also many daily local services to the nearby towns of Castleblayney, Ballybay, Carrickmacross and Ardee.

McConnon's (☎ 82020) private bus company runs two buses daily (one at weekends) from Church Square (outside Ronaghan's chemist) to O'Connell St in Dublin (€8), serving Castleblayney, Carrickmacross and Slane en route.

The closest place to hire a bike is the local Raleigh dealer, **Paddy McQuaid** (☎ 88108; day/week €20/80), in Emyvale, about 12km north of Monaghan. He can deliver bikes to Monaghan town if necessary.

ROSSMORE FOREST PARK

Rossmore Forest Park (☎ 047-4331046; car/pedestrian €5/free Jul & Aug), 3km southwest of Monaghan on the Newbliss road (R189), was originally the home of the Rossmores, but only the entrance stairway and the buttresses to their castle's walls remain. Besides forest walks and pleasant picnic areas, the park has Californian sequoias, some of the tallest trees in Ireland. Other points of interest include the Rossmores' pet cemetery as well as Iron Age wedge and court tombs. A gold collar (or lunula) from 1800 BC was found here in the 1930s and taken to the National Museum in Dublin. Fishing in the lakes here is popular.

GLASLOUGH

☎ 047 / pop 730

Glaslough, 9km northeast of Monaghan, is a quaint little village of cut-stone cottages set beside its namesake, Glaslough (Green Lake). The one-street village is neatly laid out, spotless and (unsurprisingly) has previously won the Tidy Towns competition. It's a more atmospheric place in which to base yourself than Monaghan town. To get there from Monaghan, take the N2 Derry road north, turn east onto the N12 for about 2km, then turn north onto the R185.

Beside the village is the 500-hectare demesne of **Castle Leslie**, a magnificent 19th-century Italianate mansion overlooking the lake. **Greystones Equestrian Centre** (☎ 88100; Castle Leslie) has some fine hacks in the demesne, where there are 40km of trails (€25 per hour). Don't leave the village without stopping at **J & W Wright** (☎ 88106; ⏲ Thu & Sun), a bar and grocery shop with old-fashioned petrol pumps outside. It's perfectly intact and untouched since the 1950s.

CLONES & AROUND

☎ 047 / pop 1728

The border town of Clones (Cluain Eois), 19km southwest of Monaghan, was the site of an important 6th-century monastery that later became an Augustinian abbey. The bus stop, post office and banks, including a Bank of Ireland branch, are in the central Diamond. The town is the birthplace and home of the Clones Cyclone, former world

SOMETHING SPECIAL

Castle Leslie (☎ 88109; www.castleleslie.com; s €132-177, d €214-304; 🕐 Sat & Sun only Jan & Feb, min 2-night stay weekends; under 12s not allowed) Trade has stepped firmly up a notch since Sir Paul McCartney's media-focused wedding to Heather Mills here in 2002. The secret arrangement was comically blurted out to the press by innocent eccentric Sir John Leslie, fourth baronet to the estate. At 86, Sir John is no stranger to the media himself: his passion for dancing to house music has taken him to raves in Ibiza and beyond and has been the subject of TV documentaries. But Castle Leslie, in all its crumbling glory, has always been a mecca for rock stars, actors and other Bohemians (Mick Jagger infamously spent an extended period *in situ*).

Its 14 atmospheric rooms each have a unique character and history to tell – and Sir John will be only too pleased to fill you in. The gorgeous Red Room, used by WB Yeats, contains the first bath plumbed in Ireland – a huge copper tub – and in Uncle Norman's Room, guests claim to have been levitated in the Gothic four-poster bed from Brede House (reputedly the most haunted house in England). Room rates depend on whether you choose a garden or lake view.

Candlelit dinner (from €47) at the castle is a sumptuous, communal affair (also open to nonresidents), with many gourmet and themed nights arranged. Residents can also fish on the estate's beautiful lake (boat hire €30 per day).

featherweight champion Barry McGuigan who, after retirement, returned to the limelight for a short-lived reincarnation as a country-and-western singer. Clones is also the setting for Monaghan-born Patrick McCabe's dark novel the *Butcher Boy*.

Sights

Along with the scant remains of the **abbey** founded by St Tiernach on Abbey St, there is a truncated 22m-high **round tower** in the old cemetery south of town; the layout suggests it may be an early-9th-century example. There's also a fine **high cross** on the Diamond, with beautiful carvings depicting Adam and Eve, Daniel in the lion's den and, on the other side, the marriage at Cana and the miracle of the loaves and fishes. Overlooking it is the Protestant **St Tiernach's Church**.

Sleeping & Eating

There's a dearth of B&Bs in Clones.

Glynch House (☎/fax 54045; Newbliss; s/d €45/80) Martha O'Grady's Georgian home makes a lavish stopover, 7km from Clones on the Newbliss road (R183).

Lennard Arms Hotel (☎ 51075; The Diamond, Clones; s/d €50/100) A plain, homespun country hotel, it offers simple comfort in its newly refurbished rooms. Bar snacks and more substantial fare are available all day.

Hilton Park (☎ 56007; fax 56033; www.hiltonpark.ie; Clones; s/d €140/220) For a real treat and to forget the 21st century, try the Hilton Park, 5km south along the L46 towards Scotshouse. This country pile with six rooms has its own estate and 18-hole golf course, and serves top-class food in regal surroundings. Many of the ingredients are grown on the estate's organic farm. Dinner costs €45. There's also self-catering accommodation available in the gate lodge, which sleeps four (from €600 per week); the price includes a round of golf.

Getting There & Around

Bus Éireann (☎ 82377) runs buses from Clones through Monaghan and on to Castleblayney, Carrickmacross, Slane and Dublin three times a day Monday to Saturday. Buses stop in the Diamond. **Ulsterbus** (☎ 048-6632 2633) has a number of daily buses on a route that takes in Enniskillen, Clones, Monaghan and Belfast. **McConnon's** (☎ 82020) runs a daily bus between Clones, Monaghan, Castleblayney, Carrickmacross, Slane and Dublin.

You can rent bikes in Clones at **Canal Stores** (☎ 52125; Cara St).

CARRICKMACROSS & AROUND

☎ 042 / pop 1970

Carrickmacross (Carraig Mhachaire Rois), Monaghan's second-most-important town, was once a stronghold of the MacMahon clan. It owes its origins to the third earl of Essex, who was a favourite of Elizabeth I and built a castle here in the 1630s. The site is now occupied by the Convent of St Louis. An extensive lace industry helped the early English and Scottish Planters to develop this little town, which consists of one wide street with some lovely Georgian houses and an old Protestant church. An hour or two's visit should suffice, though, as decent eating and sleeping options in the town are slim.

Sights & Activities

On Market Square is the **Carrickmacross Lace Gallery** (☎ 62506; 🕑 9.30am-1pm Mon & Tue, Thu & Fri Oct-May, 9.30am-noon Mon, Tue, Thu & Fri Nov-Apr). Run by the local lace cooperative, it has some fine displays and lace for sale. Main St is replete with shops, pubs and some quite elegant Georgian houses, a testimony to the town's wealthier past.

There's fishing in many of the lakes around Carrickmacross, including Loughs Capragh, Spring, Monalty and Fea. Contact Jimmy McMahon at the **Carrick Sports Centre** (☎ 966 1714) for information on where to fish. Lough Fea has an adjacent 1827 mansion and a demesne with oak parkland. The open **Dún an Rí Forest Park** (☎ 966 7320) has trails and picnic spots and is 5km southwest along the R179 Kingscourt road.

There are a few accommodation options outside the town.

Shanmullagh House (☎ 966 3038; Shanmullagh; s/d €40/60) This new bungalow in landscaped gardens has five spacious rooms; it's on the Dundalk road (R178) 3km from town. Shanmullagh House is signposted on the right.

Getting There & Away

Eleven **Bus Éireann** (☎ 047-82377) buses daily (six on Sunday) to and from Dublin (€10, 1¼ hours) pass through Carrickmacross. There are at least six daily on the Letterkenny–Dublin route, one on the Coleraine–Dublin route and two between Clones and Dublin. **Collins** (☎ 966 1631), a private bus company, offers two departures daily (one on Sunday) to Dublin (one way €6). **McConnon's** (☎ 047-82020) service includes Carrickmacross on its Dublin–Monaghan–Clones route, which also passes through Castleblayney, with two buses a day on weekdays.

The bus stop is outside O'Hanlon's shop on Main St.

INNISKEEN

☎ 042

The village of Inniskeen (Inis Caoin), birthplace of the poet Patrick Kavanagh, is 10km northeast of Carrickmacross. Kavanagh is buried in the local graveyard, where his cross reads: 'And pray for him who walked apart on the hills loving life's miracles.'

Housed in the village's plain chapel is the **Patrick Kavanagh Rural & Literary Resource Centre** (☎ 937 8560; adult/child €4/2, literary tour €7/5; 🕑 11am-4.30pm Tue-Fri, 2-6pm Sat & Sun Jun-Sep). It focuses on the acclaimed poet's life and work as well as local and folk history. A local actor leads groups on a literary tour of the area, including Brennan's pub, Kavanagh's local watering hole. Nearby, the forlorn skeletal ruin of a **round tower** is all that is left of the 6th-century **St Daig Monastery**.

COUNTY ROSCOMMON

County Roscommon (Ros Comáin) is more a transit route than a destination in itself. But besides the sleepy county town, there are places well worth visiting. Strokestown has one of the better-presented mansions in the country as well as the important Famine Museum. Just south of the Sligo boundary, the town of Boyle is also worth a stop, especially for the unique King House Interpretive Centre, as is the Arigna Mining Experience, a stone's throw from the pretty village of Keadue in the north of the county.

Much of Roscommon's western border follows the River Suck. A few kilometres east of the river from Ballyforan, is Dysart (Thomas St on some maps), the ancestral stomping grounds of the illustrious Fallon clan. The remains of their castle are near the town, as is a recently renovated church, parts of which date from the 12th century, in the middle of an ancient cemetery. Roscommon's eastern border is formed by a number of loughs, including the large Lough Ree (or Rea), and the River Shannon, which flows between them. Naturally, fishing is a major draw.

STROKESTOWN & AROUND

☎ 071 / pop 1003

Strokestown (Béal na mBuillí), on the N5 between the towns of Longford and Tulsk, is about 18km northwest of Roscommon town. It owes its existence to the Mahon family, owners of Roscommon's second-most-important estate. Its incredibly wide main street was designed by one of the early Mahons, who took it upon himself to create Europe's widest street!

Strokestown Park House

At the end of Strokestown's main avenue are three Gothic arches, beyond which is the impressive stately home, **Strokestown Park House** (☎ 963 3013; www.strokestownpark.ie; house & museum adult/child €8.50/4; house, museum & gardens €12/5.20; 45-min house tour €5/2; gardens only €5.70/1.90; 🕑 10.30am-5.30pm Mar-Oct). The house is the seat of a 12,000-hectare estate granted to Nicholas Mahon by Charles II after the Restoration as a reward for supporting the House of Stuart in the English Civil War.

Completed in 1697, the original house was not considered imposing enough for Nicholas' grandson, Thomas, who commissioned Richard Cassels to build him a grand house in the Palladian style, as was the current taste. The only part of the original house to survive Cassels' designs is the still room in the basement. Apart from some alterations made in the mid-19th century, the house has remained unchanged since Cassels' day. The actual estate, however, decreased along with the family's fortunes, and when they eventually sold up to the local garage owner in 1979 it had been whittled down to 120 hectares. However, as the estate was never sold at auction, virtually all of the contents were kept intact. It was opened to the public in 1987.

In 1914 Olive Pakenham-Mahon married the heir to the Rockingham estate in Boyle, thus uniting the county's two biggest demesnes. The union lasted only a couple of months as Pakenham was killed in the early days of WWI. His widow maintained the estate until its sale.

David Thomson's novel *Woodbrook* is perfect to read after your visit and is available here. There are paintings by Woodbrook's Phoebe Kirkwood adorning the walls of an upstairs bedroom.

Even children will enjoy the tour of the house, which provides an intriguing glimpse into the Anglo-Irish Ascendancy and takes in a schoolroom and a child's bedroom, complete with 19th-century toys and fun-house mirrors.

The lovely walled garden is best seen in summer in full bloom but there's also a recently opened Georgian fruit and vegetable garden with its organic produce on sale.

In the old stable yards is the **Irish Famine Museum** (☎ 963 3013). The museum is an absolute must for anyone seeking to understand the devastating effects of the potato blight on Ireland in the 1840s. In a marked departure from the traditional silence about the disaster, the museum outlines in vivid detail the horrors of starvation and the irresponsibility of the government, which was too wrapped up in a laissez-faire economic policy to intervene. In the mid-1840s, Major Denis Mahon (landlord of Strokestown at the time) and his land agent simply evicted the hundreds of starving peasants who could no longer contribute to the estate's coffers, and chartered ships to transport them away from Ireland. These overcrowded 'coffin ships', which carried emigrants to the USA and elsewhere, resulted in more suffering and deaths.

Cruachan Aí Visitor Centre

In Tulsk village, 10km northwest of Strokestown on the N5, is the fascinating **Cruachan Aí Visitor Centre** (☎ 963 9268; adult/child €4.95/2.75; 🕑 10am-6pm daily 1 May–30 Sep, 9am-5pm Mon-Sat rest of year) which explores the important Celtic royal sites of local Rathcroghan and Carnfree, one of the largest sites of its kind in Europe. Surrounding the village are some 60 unmarked national monuments, burial and ceremonial sites of the kings of Connaught, which have remained largely undisturbed for the past 3000 years. On visiting, you really can sense that the area is steeped in ancient history and, partly because this heritage site remains so untouched, it truly is a mystical place. According to the legend of Táin Bó Cúailnge (see p533), Cruachan or Rathcroghan was the site of Queen Medb (Maeve) and her consort Cúchulainn's palace. The Oweynagat Cave (Cave of the Cats), believed to be the entrance to the 'Otherworld' is also sited here. There's an audiovisual display in the visitor centre and a map of the sites in the car park. Though the surrounding land is privately owned, you can walk freely around the sites with the help of directions from the centre.

BOYLE & AROUND

☎ 071 / pop 2222

Boyle (Mainistir na Búille) is a garrison town in the northwest of the county at the foot of the Curlew Mountains and on the River Boyle between Loughs Key and Gara. Its attractions, including the fine Boyle Abbey, the renovated King House Interpretive Centre and the impressive Drumanone

Dolmen just outside town, should keep a visitor busy for at least a day. It's well worth stopping off in the last week of July for the 10-day Boyle Arts Festival which features an impressive programme of music, theatre and art, with many events taking place in King House. Maureen O'Sullivan, the American film actress and mother of Mia Farrow, was born in a house on Main St opposite the Bank of Ireland building in 1911.

History

Boyle grew up around the King family estate at Rockingham, Roscommon's largest and most powerful demesne. Up to the early 1600s, there was little more than a settlement here. Connaught kings and chieftains such as the MacDermotts and the O'Conors had engaged in a long-running battle to gain control over the area. In 1603, however, Staffordshire-born John King was granted land in Roscommon with a view to 'reducing the Irish to obedience' through the enforcement of the penal laws.

Over the next 150 years, his descendants proceeded to make their name and fortune, and by 1768 Edward King was made earl of Kingston. In 1730 the stately King House was built, but in 1780 the family moved to the grander Rockingham House, built in what is now Lough Key Forest Park. The majority of the estate was disbanded in the 19th century, leaving just the house, which was destroyed by fire in 1957.

Information

The **tourist office** (☎ 966 2145; cnr Military Rd & Main St; 🕓 10am-5pm Mon-Fri Jun–mid-Sep) is in King House. When it's closed, your call will be diverted to the Galway tourist office, or you can seek assistance from the friendly staff at the **Una Bhán Centre** (☎ 966 3033) also in King House, who can book local accommodation for a €4 fee. Alternatively, check the tourism information board in front of the clock tower in The Crescent, the central square.

There's a National Irish Bank branch with an ATM on the corner of Bridge and Patrick Sts and a Bank of Ireland at the eastern end of Main St. The post office is on Carrick Rd, south of the river.

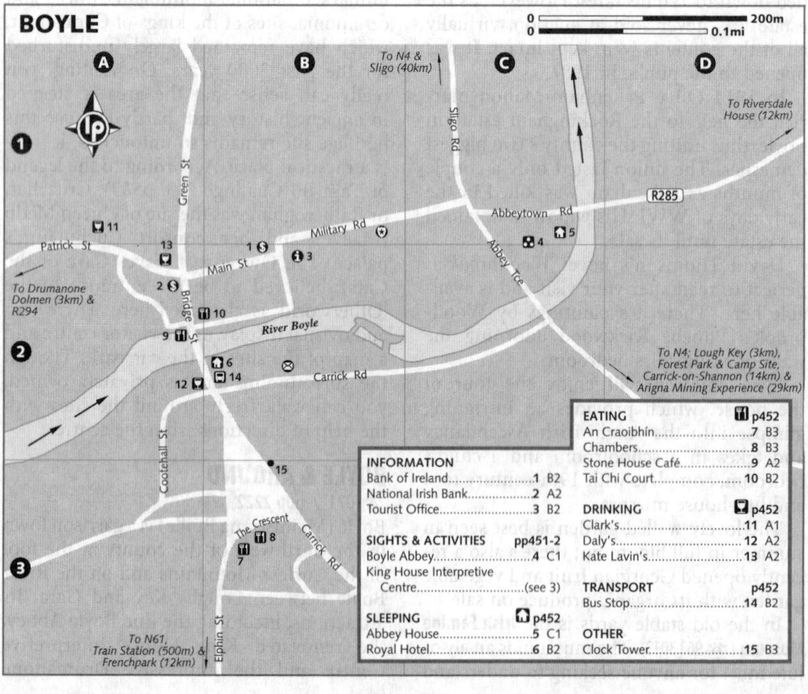

Sights & Activities

BOYLE ABBEY

Beside the N4, to the east of the town centre, is **Boyle Abbey** (☎ 966 2604; adult/concession €2/1; ⏰ 10am-6pm end Apr–end Oct), one of Ireland's finest Cistercian abbeys. It has remains dating back to the 12th century, when it was founded by monks from Mellifont in County Louth. In 1659 military forces occupied the abbey and turned it into a fort.

The interesting 13th-century nave in the northern part of the abbey has Gothic arches on one side that are narrower than the Romanesque arches on the other. The capitals are also distinctive. On the southern side of the abbey, once the refectory area, there is a fine stone chimney built after the monks left and the abbey became a fortified home. Edward King, whose death by drowning in 1637 inspired English poet John Milton to compose his elegy, *Lycidas*, is buried here.

Guided tours of abbey are available on the hour until 5pm.

KING HOUSE INTERPRETIVE CENTRE

The **King House Interpretive Centre** (☎ 966 3242; kinghouseboyle@hotmail.com; Main St; adult/student €4/2.50; ⏰ 10am-6pm Apr-Sep) is certainly one of the most inspired in the country. In a lovely mansion built by Henry King in 1730, it served as a military barracks for the fearsome Connaught Rangers (Wellington called them the 'Devil's Own') from 1788 until Irish independence in 1922, after which it sat derelict until the county council renovated it (1989–95) at a cost of €3.8 million. It contains audiovisual exhibits detailing the turbulent history of the Connaught kings, the chieftains, the town of Boyle and the King family, including a rather grim tale of tenant eviction during the Famine.

Kids will especially enjoy King House. It's very much a hands-on museum where they can try on ancient Irish cloaks, brooches and leather shoes, write with a quill and even 'build' a vaulted ceiling – King House has four floors of them – from specially designed blocks. A tour of King House is an excellent precursor to one of the Famine Museum in Strokestown.

DRUMANONE DOLMEN

This superb dolmen, one of the largest in Ireland, measures 4.5m by 3.3m and was constructed before 2000 BC. To get there, follow Patrick St west out of town for 2km, then bear left at the junction sign for Lough Gara for another 1km, passing under a railway arch. A sign indicates the path across the railway line.

LOUGH KEY FOREST PARK

The 290-hectare **Lough Key Forest Park** (☎ 966 2363; car/pedestrian €5/free Apr-Sep), on the N4 3km east of Boyle, was part of the Rockingham estate, owned by the King family from the late 18th century until it was sold to the Land Commission in 1957. Rockingham House, designed by John Nash, was destroyed by a fire in the same year; all that remains are some stables and outbuildings and a tunnel leading from what was the house to the lake. It's a great spot to have a picnic and children will enjoy the wishing chair, bog gardens, fairy bridge and viewing tower over the lake. There are several marked walking trails and deer roam about in summer.

Lough Key is at the northern limit for cruising on the Shannon. Fishing is a popular pursuit; record-breaking pike have been caught here. The ruins of a 12th-century abbey can be seen on tiny Trinity Island. On Castle Island, a 19th-century castle stands on the site of 16th-century MacDermott Castle.

About 6km from the park, on the N4 towards Carrick-on-Shannon, is **Woodbrook**, the demesne that is the setting for David Thomson's wonderful novel on the Anglo-Irish gentry. It is not open to the public.

DOUGLAS HYDE INTERPRETIVE CENTRE

Frenchpark, some 12km southwest of Boyle on the R361, is home to the **Douglas Hyde Interpretive Centre** (☎ 094-987 0016; admission free; ⏰ 2-5pm Tue-Fri, 2-6pm Sat & Sun May-Sep). It's housed in the former Protestant church where Hyde's father was rector. Hyde (1860–1949) was one of the founding members of the Gaelic League in 1893 and was later elected the first president of the Republic in 1937. This Renaissance man published many works of prose and poetry under the pen name An Craoibhín Aoibhinn (Delightful Little Branch), and he is buried in the churchyard; the centre is also known as the Gairdín an Craoibhín (Garden of the Little Branch).

ARIGNA MINING EXPERIENCE

Set in the hills above Lough Allen, the most northerly of the Shannon's three great lakes, the recently opened **Arigna Mining Experience** (☎ 964 6466; www.arignaminingexperience.ie; Derreenavoggy; adult/child €8/3.95; ⏲ 10am-6pm Apr-Sep) offers breathtaking views of the valley. More importantly, the museum documents the gruelling working conditions of the miners who worked in this, the first and last place in Ireland where coal was mined. Excavation was carried out in Arigna over 400 years until the last mine closed in 1990, creating considerable unemployment in the area. An interesting 30-minute guided tour, given informally by ex-miners, takes you 400m down the shaft where you can see the narrow paths, held up by timber pillars, through which miners crawled and hacked for up to 16 hours a day. A statue of Our Lady at the entrance marks where miners prayed for safety before entering. Your office job will never have seemed more attractive after a visit! Wear sturdy shoes for the tour, as it can be wet and muddy underfoot.

ARIGNA MINERS WAY AND HISTORICAL TRAIL

Covering 118km of North Roscommon, east Sligo and mid-Leitrim, these well-signposted tracks and hill passes of various lengths cover the routes originally taken by miners on their way to work. A guide with detailed maps is available from local tourist offices or the **Arigna Miners Way office** (☎ 964 6702).

Sleeping & Eating

Lough Key Forest Caravan & Camping Park (☎ 966 2212; single/family tent €5/12) There's a recreation room, laundrette and children's play area in this nicely located camp site.

Abbey House (☎ 966 2385; Abbeytown Rd; s/d €36/60; ⏲ Mar-Oct) This large, friendly Georgian house right in the grounds of Boyle Abbey has a lovely mature garden with a stream. Rooms are modest but spacious.

Riversdale House (☎ 966 7012; Knockvicar; d €64; ⏲ May-Oct) This rambling Georgian farmhouse on a 21-hectare estate is the former home of film star Maureen O'Sullivan. It has five spacious rooms with en suites and residents can fish or hire boats (€20 per day) on Lough Key in its grounds. It's located 12km northeast of Boyle on the R285. There's also a geothermal-heated, fully equipped log cabin on the lake's edge that sleeps six (€400 to €650 per week).

Royal Hotel (☎ 966 2016; fax 64949; Bridge St; s/d €55/100) In the town centre, this 18th-century hotel offers 16 plain but comfortable rooms. Its restaurant, with a Chinese menu, offers lunch and set evening meals (€25 to €36).

Chambers (☎ 966 3614; The Crescent; mains €14-24; ⏲ 6-10pm Tue-Sun) This is probably the best place to eat in town. Its varied menu, with a meat emphasis, includes a good selection of fish. Most produce is sourced locally and specials such as wild boar and ostrich feature at weekends.

An Craoibhín (☎ 966 2704; The Crescent; mains €4-7) This small but popular pub is good for a hearty pub lunch.

Stone House Café (Bridge St; lunch €3-5; ⏲ 9am-6pm Mon-Sat) A cosy place on the river with seats overlooking the water, this was a gate lodge to the now closed Frybrook House. It sells sandwiches, baked potatoes and desserts.

Tai Chi Court (☎ 966 3123; Bridge St; mains €8-15; ⏲ 5.30-11.30pm) Locals recommend this Chinese restaurant overlooking the river.

Drinking

Clark's (☎ 966 2064; Patrick St) This newly renovated pub has live music on Saturday and set dancing on Tuesday nights in winter only.

Kate Lavin's (☎ 966 2855; Patrick St) Don't pass Boyle without stopping in this authentic old-world pub with its preserved interior and traditional music most nights.

Daly's (☎ 966 2085; Bridge St) In the centre of town is this friendly old pub with open fires and good Guinness.

Getting There & Around

From almost outside the Royal Hotel (and opposite Daly's pub) on Bridge St, the **Bus Éireann** (☎ 60066) express bus leaves four times daily for Sligo (one way €8.60, 50 minutes) and three to Dublin (€14, three hours). Boyle **train station** (☎ 966 2027) is on Elphin Rd; from there trains go three times daily between Sligo (€8, 40 minutes) and Dublin (€19, 2½ hours) via Mullingar.

You can order a taxi on ☎ 966 3344 or ☎ 966 2119.

ROSCOMMON TOWN

☎ 090 / pop 1630

The small county town of Roscommon (Ros Comáin), sitting at the crossroads of several major highways, has a few sights of interest that make it worth a stopover.

The town gets its name from *ros* (wooded headland) and St Coman, who founded a monastery here in the 8th century. Roscommon's football fraternity was dancing in its boots when a steady stream of Brazilians began arriving during the 1990s to work in Roscommon's meat factories, giving this somewhat sleepy town a cosmopolitan boost. Now, not only has the county's football chances improved but samba soccer, Latin dance classes, a regular radio show and mass in Portuguese have become as familiar as bingo on the local scene.

Information

The local **tourist office** (☎ 662 6342; www.irelandwest.ie; John Harrison Hall, The Square; 9am-5.45pm Mon-Sat May-Sep & Sun Jul & Aug, 9am-5.45pm Mon-Fri, 9am-12.45pm Sat Oct-Apr) is next door to the post office, and there is a Bank of Ireland opposite Gleeson's Guesthouse in The Square.

Sights & Activities

The Norman **Roscommon Castle** built in 1269 was almost immediately destroyed by Irish forces and rebuilt in 1280. The mullioned windows were added in the 16th century. Though none of the interior remains, the massive walls and round bastions give it an impressive look, standing alone in a field at the northern end of town, off Castle St.

At the southern end of town off Circular Rd are the remains of a 13th-century **Dominican priory**, the most notable feature of which is an effigy of the founder, Felim O'Conor, carved around 1300. It's set in the north wall near where the altar once stood. There's also a rare depiction of eight *gallóglí* (mercenary soldiers) in costume of the day, dating from the 15th century.

Roscommon County Museum (☎ 662 6342; The Square; adult/child €2/1; 11am-1pm & 2-5pm Wed-Sun), in John Harrison Hall, a former Presbyterian church with an unusual window shaped as a Star of David supposedly representing the Trinity. It contains some vaguely interesting pieces, including an in-scribed slab from St Coman's monastery and a medieval *sheila-na-gig* (carved female figure with exaggerated genitalia) from Rahara.

The Square's Bank of Ireland used to be the **courthouse**. Opposite is the enormous **old jail**, where executions were carried out by 'Lady Betty' in the mid-18th century. She herself had been condemned to death after confessing to the murder of a lodger in her house – who turned out to be her own son. She escaped death by offering to take over as executioner. Despite planning objections, all but the façade and front block were demolished a decade ago to make way for a dismal shopping arcade.

Ask at the tourist office for a map of the **Suck Valley Way**, a 75km walking trail along the River Suck. The river offers some of the best mixed fishing in Ireland, with rudd, tench, pike and perch in abundance. En route you may pass **La Téne Stone** in Castlestrange, 7km southwest of town on the R366, an Iron Age spiral-inscribed stone, one of only two in the country from this period.

Sleeping & Eating

Gleeson's Guesthouse (☎ 662 6954; fax 662 7425; The Square; s/d from €40/100) This listed 19th-century house on the Square has 23 comfortable rooms with pine furnishings, decorated in Mediterranean colours. The service is extremely friendly. **The Manse** (mains €13-23, 4-course dinner €25) in the guesthouse, serves a hearty homespun menu based primarily on beef, duck and fish.

Tatler's Hotel (☎ 662 5460; Main St; s/d €40/70) This hotel over a busy pub on the main street has 11 surprisingly nice rooms with subtle furnishings and decent bathrooms. Rooms to the back, off Main St, are quietest. Tatler's Bar packs them in at lunch-time (€6 to €8) for its humungous carvery lunches and chunky sandwiches.

Abbey Hotel (☎ 662 6250; fax 662 6021; Abbeytown; s/d €85/150;) This 18th-century manor at the start of the Galway road is the poshest place in town. Try to get one of the five rooms in the old house, most of which have big four-poster beds and antique furniture. Those in the new wing are large and comfortable, but dull. The new fitness centre and pool will keep the health-conscious happy.

Drinking & Entertainment

Down the Hatch (☎ 662 7100; Church St) This is a small lively pub for the over-30s.

Central Bar (☎ 662 6219; The Square) A good mixed-age pub, full of locals, gets busy at the weekend.

JJ Harlow's (☎ 662 7505; The Square) Converted from a family drapery, this old-style bar with snugs attracts a young crowd at the weekend.

Roscommon Arts Centre (☎ 662 5824; Circular Rd) The newly opened arts centre, with its top-notch black-box auditorium, has so far provided an impressive programme of independent cinema and touring comedy, theatre and music.

Getting There & Around

Bus Éireann (☎ 071-60066) express buses between Westport (€13.50, 2¼ hours) and Dublin (€15, three hours) stop in Roscommon three times daily (once on Sunday). Buses stop in front of Regan's Guesthouse on the Square. Roscommon is also served by train three times daily (four on Friday) on the line from Dublin (€33, two hours) to Westport (€13, 1½ hours). The train station is in Abbeytown, just west of the town centre, near the Galway road.

You can order a taxi on ☎ 662 6096.

CENTRAL NORTH

COUNTY LEITRIM

Leitrim (Liatroim) stretches 80km from the border with Longford in the southeast to Donegal Bay in the northwest, with a short coastline of about 5km around Tulloghan. Lough Allen splits the county almost in two. With some of the worst soil fertility in the country, Leitrim was severely underpopulated for much of the last century and allegedly has more pubs per capita than anywhere else in Ireland! Southern Leitrim's main interest is its lush scenery of lakes and drumlins. A walking or cycling tour of the area is enjoyable, particularly if you like less tourist-populated areas. At the time of writing plans were afoot to promote Leitrim's green tourism potential by developing eco-friendly accommodation, organic restaurants and alternative living centres, a directory of which should be available at tourist offices by summer 2004.

CARRICK-ON-SHANNON

☎ 071 / pop 2664

Carrick-on-Shannon (known simply as Carrick, or in Irish as Cora Droma Rúisc) straddles the border with County Roscommon and is the main town in County Leitrim, marking the upper limit of navigation on the River Shannon. It is beautifully positioned over the river, and is a major centre for boating. In 1994 the last stretch of the Shannon–Erne Waterway was completed with the reopening of the Ballyconnell–Ballinamore Canal, linking 382km of navigable canals and loughs that begin in Limerick and end in Belleek on Upper Lough Erne. The canal has literally put Carrick-on-Shannon on the tourist map, and is one of the main reasons for visiting the town (see p456). Aquatic pursuits aside, Carrick is a thriving provincial town with some fine examples of early 19th-century architecture in the town centre. Among them, **Hatley Manor**, home of the St George family, the **Old Courthouse**, now seat of the County Council, whose underground tunnel led convicts from the dock to the now demolished jail, and the newly refurbished **Market Yard** are all on St George's Terrace – close to the Clock Tower.

Information

The **tourist office** (☎ 962 0170; www.leitrimtourism.com; Old Barrel Store, The Marina; 🕑 9am-6pm Mon-Sat Apr-Oct) has a signposted walking tour (a booklet is available here), which takes in all the buildings and places of interest in town.

There's an Allied Irish Bank branch at the top of Main St. The post office is on Bridge St opposite Flynn's Corner House bar.

Sights & Activities

COSTELLO CHAPEL

At the top of Bridge St, next to Flynn's Corner House, is the sombre little **Costello Chapel** – reputedly the smallest chapel in Europe. It measures only 5m by 3.6m and was built in 1879 by the distraught Edward Costello after the death of his wife. He had her embalmed and buried in a decorative coffin under a heavy slab of glass, on the left side of the chapel. Costello himself was interred on the other side in 1891. If the door is locked, ask at the tourist office for it to be opened.

BOATING & FISHING

Carrick Craft (☎ 01-278 1666) hires out motorised fishing boats (€60/100 per half/full day) and two- to eight-berth cruisers from €493 to €1206 per week. Daily cruises on the Shannon are available through **Moon River** (☎ 962 1777; The Quay). The 110-seater boat also doubles as a floating nightclub of sorts on Saturday night. The 1½-hour cruise leaves at 2.30pm and 4.30pm and costs €12/6 per adult/child. Contact the tourist office or check the information board on the quay for details.

The annual regatta run by **Carrick Rowing Club** (☎ 962 0532) takes place on the first Sunday in August and draws a big crowd. For information on fishing, contact the **Carrick-on-Shannon Angling Association** (☎ 962 0489; Gortmor House, Lismakeegan).

Sleeping

Camping is free on the Roscommon side of the riverbank, though there are no facilities. Tokens for the showers at the nearby Marina can be purchased from the Marina office.

An Oiche Hostel (☎ 962 1848; Bridge St; dm €20) This small new hostel has four dorms (no private rooms) that are comfortable if a little pricey.

Carrick is well supplied with B&Bs.

Hollywell (☎ 962 1124; hollywell@esatbiz.com; Liberty Hill; s/d from €50/86) This beautiful Georgian country house overlooking the river (on the Roscommon side), has four spacious antique-filled rooms and delicious breakfasts. It's undoubtedly the best place to stay in town.

Aisleigh (☎ 962 0313; Dublin Rd; s/d €40/55) This large modern home, 1km from town, has full facilities including a sauna and fishing tackle hire.

Glencarne Country House (☎ 966 7013; Sligo Rd; s/d €40/70) The welcoming Mrs Harrington runs this spacious Georgian farmhouse with five rooms on mature grounds 7km from town.

Bush Hotel (☎ 962 0014; Main St; s/d €65/125) This centrally located, family-run old hotel has lots of character and buzzes with activity.

Eating

Wheats (☎ 965 0525; Market Yard; snacks €3-5; ⏲ 8am-6pm Mon-Sat) Wheats has healthy home-made breads, salads and wraps to take away.

Coffey's Pastry Case (☎ 962 0929; Bridge St; mains €4-7; ⏲ 8.30am-7pm Mon-Sat, 9.30-7pm Sun) On the corner near the bridge is this cheap, self-service coffee shop-cum-bakery that looks like a 1970s TV sitcom set.

Oarsman Bar & Boathouse Restaurant (☎ 962 1139; Bridge St; mains €7-11) Upmarket pub grub and seafood are served all day at this cavernous watering hole.

Cryan's Pub (☎ 962 0409; Bridge St; mains €8-12; ⏲ 8am-9pm daily) An old-fashioned kitsch restaurant with tasselled lamps and banquettes, Cryan's serves lashings of all things traditional fr[...] to sirloin steak and th[...] – sherry trifle. Dinners [...] proud.

Fusion Brasserie (☎ [...] mains €17-24; ⏲ 9am-10pm [...] Tue-Sun Oct-Apr) The newes[...] [...]own, Fusion is a fully licensed [...]tro in an old market building serving paninis by day and good modern Irish and European dishes. There are plenty of fish and vegetarian options and an inspired children's menu that goes further than the usual chicken nuggets and chips.

Drinking & Entertainment

Flynn's Corner House (☎ 962 1139; cnr Main & Bridge Sts) Flynn's is a great, old-school traditional pub with a good drop of Guinness and live music on Friday night. Savour this authentic pub before it's modernised.

Moon River (☎ 962 1777; The Quay; admission €10) Dancers with sea legs can try this floating nightclub on a 110-seater cruiser departing from The Quay at 11.30pm on Saturday nights.

Gaiety Cinema (☎ 962 1869; Bridge St; ⏲ 8pm; adult/child €5/4) This no-frills one-screen cinema runs current releases and hosts regular film society screenings and occasional festivals. Call for details.

Getting There & Away

The bus stop is outside Coffey's Pastry Case on the corner near the bridge and tourist office. The **Bus Éireann** (☎ 071-60066) main express bus between Dublin (one way €14, 2¾ hours) and Sligo (one way €10, one hour) stops there four times daily in each direction (five on Sunday). There are also buses to Boyle, Longford and Athlone.

The **train station** (☎ 962 0036) is a 15-minute walk from the bridge on the Roscommon side of the river. Turn right over the bridge, then left at the service station. Carrick has three trains daily to Dublin (one way €19, three hours) and Sligo (one way €12, 50 minutes), with an additional one on Friday.

AROUND CARRICK-ON-SHANNON

Turlough O'Carolan Country

There are three places to visit in the area that are connected with the famous blind poet, composer and harpist Turlough O'Carolan (1670–1738). He spent most of his time in

...here his patron, Mrs MacDermott-...esided; a sculpture on the main street ... the town commemorates the association. To reach Mohill from Carrick-on-Shannon, follow the N4 to Dublin then turn east onto the R201 shortly after passing Drumsna.

O'Carolan is buried in **Kilronan church**, which preserves a 12th-century doorway, just over the border in County Roscommon. To reach the church, take the R280 north from Carrick-on-Shannon and at the village of Leitrim turn west on the R284 to Keadue (Keadew on some maps). In Keadue turn west on the R284 to Sligo.

Shannon–Erne Waterway

The Shannon–Erne Waterway stretches from the River Shannon beside the village of Leitrim, 4km north of Carrick-on-Shannon, through northwestern County Cavan to the southern shore of Upper Lough Erne, just over the Northern Ireland border in County Fermanagh.

The 382km-long waterway is a series of rivers and lakes linked by canals. The original canal, the Ballyconnell–Ballinamore Canal, was completed in 1860, but soon fell into disuse with the coming of the railway. The canal was reopened in 1994 and, with its 34 stone bridges and 16 locks, is now busy with boats. The waterway is jointly operated by Dúchas in the Republic and the Department of Agriculture in Northern Ireland.

Before you sail, rental companies give full instructions on how to manoeuvre a boat through the different locks. Make sure you take with you a chart of the waterway showing depths and locations of locks; the following companies provide this or it's available in bookshops. Prices vary according to season.

Carrick Craft (☎ 071-962 0236; fax 21336; The Marina, Carrick-on-Shannon) You can hire 2-/4-/6-/8-berth boats from €229/300/562/646 for three nights or €493/583/1049/1206 for one week, respectively.

Emerald Star (☎ 071-962 0234; info@emerald-star.com; The Marina, Carrick-on-Shannon) Hire 4-/6-/10-berth boats from €910/1140/2170 per week.

Leitrim Way

The Leitrim Way begins in Drumshanbo and ends in Manorhamilton, a distance of 48km. For more detailed information get a copy of *Way-Marked Trails of Ireland*, by Michael Fewer, from the tourist office.

COUNTY LONGFORD

The history of County Longford (An Longfort) dates back to prehistoric times. St Patrick visited here and for centuries it was the centre of power of the O'Farrell family, who arrived in the 11th century. During the 1798 Rising, the British army under Lord Cornwallis defeated a combined Irish and French army at Ballinamuck, 16km north of Longford. The Potato Famine of the 1840s and 1850s saw massive emigration; many Longford migrants went to Argentina, where one of their descendants, Edel Miro O'Farrell, became president in 1914.

Longford, the county town, is solidly agrarian and prosperous but of little interest to the tourist; many people pass through travelling between Dublin and Mayo or Sligo. **Carrigglas Manor** (☎ 043-48135; www.carrigglas.demon.co.uk; 40-min house tour €10/7.50; museum & garden only €5/2.50; 🕒 11am-5pm Sun-Fri 1 Jun–12 Aug), 5km northeast, has been the home of the Lefroy family since 1810. You can tour the castellated Gothic manor and visit a Victorian costume and lace museum in the Palladian yard buildings, designed by James Gandon, or stroll in the peaceful 18th-century pleasure gardens.

The 150km **Royal Canal** from Dublin passes through the county to meet the River Shannon near Clondra (or Cloondara) west of Longford. The canal's towpath provides an interesting walking route through the county.

The most popular attraction for most who visit County Longford specifically, however, is the fishing around Lough Ree and Lanesborough.

Discreetly hidden 15km southwest of Longford on a broad stretch of bogland is **Corlea Trackway Visitor Centre** (☎ 043-22386; Keenagh; adult/child €3.10/1.20; 🕒 10am-6pm Apr-Sep). This is well worth an afternoon's excursion. Here you'll find 1km of Europe's widest timber track way, dating from 148 BC that was discovered in Corlea bog in 1984. Now 18m of the track is on view and an interesting 45-minute tour details the bog's unique flora and fauna as well as the how the track was discoved and the methods used to preserve it.

COUNTY WESTMEATH

Characterised by lakes and rich pasture land, Westmeath (An Iarmhí) is noted more for its beef than its scenic splendour or historic sites. An exception to the generally monotonous landscape is the area north of Athlone known as Goldsmith country, while the other interesting places in Westmeath are mostly in the vicinity of Mullingar.

MULLINGAR

☎ 044 / pop 8733

Mullingar (An Muileann gCearr) is a prosperous market town – with a well-used commuter train service each morning and evening to and from Dublin – and much of the surrounding area is rich countryside. There are some fine fishing loughs in the vicinity and a preserved bog that delights naturalists. The town itself is one of the few places outside Dublin that James Joyce visited.

The Royal Canal, linking Dublin with the River Shannon via Mullingar, was constructed in the 1790s as a rival to the Grand Canal. It never managed to compete successfully and, by the 1880s, passenger business had ceased. There was a slight revival during WWII with a turf trade to Dublin, but it finally closed in 1955. Restoration work west of Mullingar is almost complete, with walkways now open; information on these is available from the tourist office.

Information

Midlands-East Tourism (☎ 48650; www.ecoast-midlands.travel.ie; cnr Mount & Pearse Sts; 🕑 9am-6pm Mon-Fri, 10am-1pm & 2-6pm Sat Jun-Sep, 9.30am-1pm & 2-5.30pm Mon-Fri Oct-May) is in Market House.

There are several banks on the main street, which changes name five times, including an ACC Bank branch at the start of Oliver Plunkett St. The post office is to the west on Dominick St. There's a laundrette on Oliver Plunkett St, near the roundabout.

Sights & Activities

Mullingar is known for its pewterware, and you can watch artisans turning the silvery-grey metal into cups, bowls and *objets d'art* at the **Mullingar Bronze & Pewter Visitor Centre**

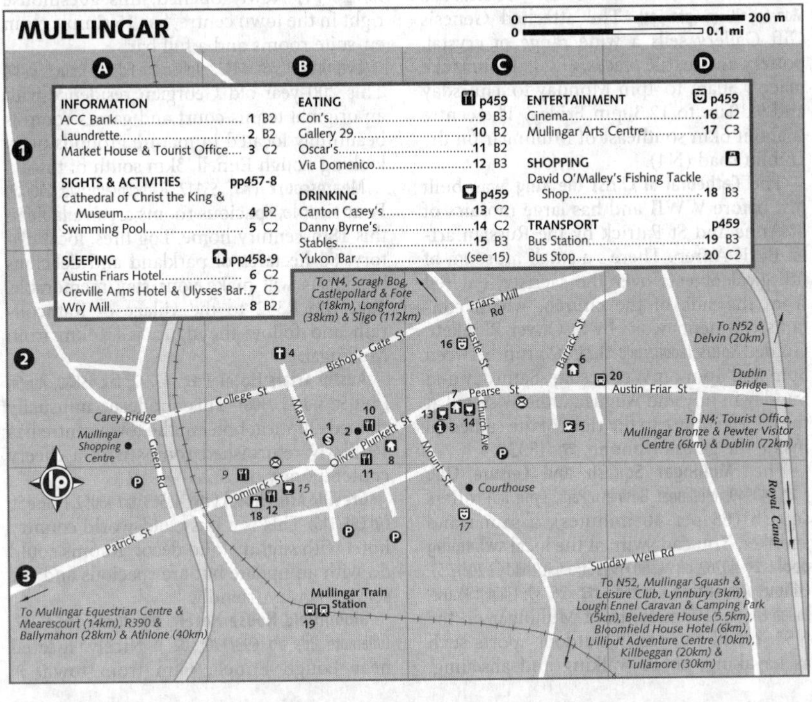

THE JOYCE CONNECTION

James Joyce came to Mullingar in his late teens in 1900 and 1901 to visit his father, John Joyce, a civil servant who had been sent to the town to compile a new electoral register. John Joyce worked in the courthouse on Mount St, and the Joyces stayed at Levington Park House near Lough Owel.

Parts of *Stephen Hero*, an early version (1904) of what would be published as *A Portrait of the Artist as a Young Man*, are set in Mullingar. The Greville Arms Hotel is mentioned, as are the *Westmeath Examiner* office, the Royal Canal and the Columb Barracks on Green Rd.

In *Ulysses*, Leopold Bloom's daughter, Millie, is working in a photographer's shop in Mullingar. This is now Fagan's newsagent and sub-post office on Pearse St near the junction with Castle St, but at the time of Joyce's visits it was owned by a photographer called Phil Shaw. Mullingar also gets a few brief mentions in *Finnegans Wake*.

(☎ 44948; Great Down, The Downs; 🕒 9.30am-6pm Mon-Fri, 10am-6pm Sat). The attached Genesis Gift Gallery sells a wide range of crystal, pottery and textile pieces. Guided tours take place 9.30am to 4pm Monday to Thursday and 9.30am to 12.30pm Friday. The centre is about 6km southeast of Mullingar on the Dublin road (N4).

The **Cathedral of Christ the King** was built just before WWII and has large mosaics of St Anne and St Patrick by the Russian artist Boris Anrep. There's a small museum of liturgical objects over the sacristy, entered from the side of the church, which contains vestments worn by St Oliver Plunkett. Guided **tours** (adult/child €1.25/0.65) run between 3pm and 4pm on Wednesday, Saturday and Sunday in July and August. Otherwise call at the church house to the right of the cathedral inside the gates or phone ☎ 48338.

The **Mullingar Squash and Leisure Club** (☎ 40949; Mullingar Business Park, Lynn Rd) offers squash (€5 per 40 minutes), a sauna and snooker. You can swim at the local **swimming pool** (☎ 40262; off Austin Friars St; adult/child €3.20/1.25). **Lilliput Adventure Centre** (☎ 26789; Lilliput House, Lough Ennell), 10km south of Mullingar on the N52, offers courses in outdoor sports such as kayaking, gorge walking and abseiling. A day's mixed-activity package including a night's dorm accommodation costs €45. **Mullingar Equestrian Centre** (☎ 48331; Athlone Rd), southwest of Mullingar on the Athlone road (R390), offers riding packages for €25 per hour.

Festivals

The **Mullingar Festival** (☎ 44044) is held in the second week of July. It's a low-key affair, the highlight of which is the election of the queen and the bachelor of the festival.

Sleeping

There's a camp site south of town.

Lough Ennell Caravan & Camping Park (☎ 48101; Tudenham; 2-person tent €15, hikers & cyclists €6.50; 🕒 Apr-Sep) This camp site with all mod cons is nicely set in eight hectares of woodland on the shore of Lough Ennell, 5km south of town on the N52 to Tullamore.

Most B&Bs are on the approach roads from Dublin and Sligo. It's worth checking out one of the many Georgian houses for an atmospheric slumber.

Wry Mill (☎ 49544; 9 Oliver Plunkett St; s/d €37.50/70; 💻 P) Newly opened, this guesthouse right in the town centre, has 15 simple clean en-suite rooms and a full bar.

Lynnbury (☎ 48432; Tullamore Rd; s/d from €50/80) This 200-year-old Georgian residence with an original tennis court and games room is beautifully located in mature grounds overlooking Lough Ennell, 3km south of town.

Mearescourt (☎ 55112; Rathconrath; s/d €50/80) Four simple, spacious rooms are available in this 18th-century home. Log fires, local history, 80 hectares of parkland and delicious breakfasts will make your stay memorable. Take the R392 to the village of Rathconrath and follow the signs; it's 14km from Mullingar.

Austin Friars Hotel (☎ 45777; fax 45880; Austin Friars St; s/d €59/106) This modern, unusually shaped elliptical hotel in the town centre has 19 newly refurbished rooms with a cheery contemporary décor.

Greville Arms Hotel (☎ 48563; fax 48052; Pearse St; s/d €65/115) This is a busy, old-world country hotel with slightly loud décor. Rooms could do with an update but are spacious and the service is very friendly.

Bloomfield House Hotel (☎ 40894; fax 43767; Tullamore Rd; s/d €93/170; ♿) Nicely located near Lough Ennell, 6km from town, is this rambling, old-fashioned hotel with a leisure centre.

Eating

Via Domenico (☎ 49480; 15 Dominick St; mains €4-8; ⌚ 9am-6pm Tue-Sat, 6.30-8.30pm Tue-Fri, 10.30am-2pm Sun) Ignore the checked tablecloths and unflattering lighting in this new patisserie-cum-café: the food is where it's at. Lasagne, chargrilled salmon and Greek salad are all simply superb. Or sink your teeth into a mouth-watering profiterole or feather-light pavlova.

Con's (☎ 40925; 24 Dominick St; mains €6-9; ⌚ noon-3pm) If you're hungry, try the superb carvery lunches or hearty sandwiches in this bustling pub.

Gallery 29 (☎ 49449; 16 Oliver Plunkett St; lunch mains €3-9, dinner mains €14-22; ⌚ 9am-6pm Tue-Thu, 7.15-9.30pm Fri & Sat) This funky little café with wooden floors, and wildflowers on tables, doubles as a gallery space for artworks gathered on the owner's travels. By day it serves delicious paninis, crepes and home-made desserts and at night there's a small imaginative menu that uses local produce with world influences. Vegetarians are well catered for.

Oscar's (☎ 44909; 21 Oliver Plunkett St; mains €12-19; ⌚ 6-9.30pm) This colourful eatery with an Italian propensity offers unusual pizza toppings like Clonakilty black pudding or chilli mango.

Drinking & Entertainment

Stables (☎ 40251; 11 Dominick St) A small, popular venue, the Stables hosts DJs on Friday nights and good live music on Saturdays. **Yukon Bar**, at the front of the Stables, is a peculiar, grungy place popular with young people; apparently the fortune teller, in attendence from 4pm to closing on weekdays, is a real draw.

Danny Byrne's (☎ 43792; 27 Pearse St) This renovated pub with dark mock-antique interior is strangely cosy and has live music on Sunday and Thursday. It pulls a young crowd.

Canton Casey's (☎ 42758; Pearse St) Canton Casey's is a museum-quality old-style pub with outdoor benches in Market House's courtyard.

Mullingar Arts Centre (☎ 47777; mgarartscentre@eircom.net; Lower Mount St) This centre runs a regular programme of music, drama and art exhibitions. Phone for details.

Sport

For some horse racing, **Kilbeggan Races** (☎ 0506-32176), in Kilbeggan, 20km south-west of town, runs popular evening meetings from May to September.

Getting There & Away

Bus Éireann (☎ 01-836 6111) runs one daily bus from Galway (€14.50, three hours) to Dundalk (€10.60, 2¼ hours); hourly from Dublin (€10.60, 1½ hours) six to Ballina (€14, 2¾ hours); four daily to Sligo (€12.40, 2½ hours) coming from Dublin; and six a day Monday to Saturday from Dublin to Longford (€12.40, one hour). All stop at Austin Friars St and the train station.

Trains (☎ 48274) stop at Mullingar three or four times daily in each direction on the line from Dublin (€14, one hour) to Sligo (€16.50, two hours).

AROUND MULLINGAR

Belvedere House & Gardens

The aptly titled **Belvedere** (Beautiful View; ☎ 49060; Mullingar; adult/child €6/3.80; ⌚ 9.30am-6pm Mon-Fri, 10.30am-7pm Sat & Sun May-Aug, 10.30am-6pm daily Sep & Oct, 10.30am-4.30pm daily Nov-Apr) overlooks Lough Ennell. It was the scene of a tale that finds its way into Joyce's *Ulysses*. Belvedere House was built in about 1740 for the recently remarried Lord Belfield, first earl of Belvedere, who soon accused his young wife of adultery with his younger brother Arthur and imprisoned her here. She remained under house arrest for 31 years. When the earl's death finally released her, she was dressed in the fashion of three decades earlier. She died still protesting her innocence. Belvedere also sued his brother and had him jailed in London for the rest of his life.

Not far from the house, the **Jealous Wall** was deliberately built by the cantankerous Lord Belfield as a ready-made 'ruin' to block a view of the neighbouring house of a second brother, George, with whom he also fell out.

It's worth wandering around the modestly sized house, pleasure gardens and visitor centre with its dramatised film on Belfield's life. An interesting audiovisual display in the recently restored house depicts life in an 18th-century household, and an interactive display details the work of the house's famous architect, Richard Cassels.

Belvedere House is 5.5km south of Mullingar on the N52 to Tullamore, just before Lough Ennell Caravan and Camping Park.

Locke's Distillery

Some 20km southwest of Mullingar on the N52 to Tullamore past Belvedere House, is **Locke's Distillery** (☎ 0506-32134; Kilbeggan; adult/concession/under 12s €5/4/free; 9am-6pm Apr-Oct, 10am-4pm Nov-Mar). There is a 50-minute tour of the distillery, bonded warehouse and cooper's room. The distillery still has a **working mill wheel**. Lunch and snacks are served at the adjoining coffee shop, whiskey at the bar.

Crookedwood & Around

Crookedwood, about 5km northeast of Mullingar off the R394, is a small village on the shores of Lough Derravaragh. The lough is associated with the tragic legend of the children of Lir, who were transformed into swans by a jealous stepmother. Two ecclesiastical sites near Crookedwood are worth a visit. About 3km to the west is the **Multyfarnham Franciscan friary**. In the present church, the remains of a 15th-century church still stand, and there are outdoor Stations of the Cross set beside a stream.

East of Crookedwood, a small road leads 2km to the ruins of **St Munna's Church**. It dates from the 15th century, replacing a 7th-century church founded by St Munna. This fortified church has a lovely location. Keys to the church are available from the nearby bungalow.

TULLYNALLY CASTLE GARDENS

The seat of the Pakenham family and the earldom of Longford is the impressive Gothic revival **Tullynally Castle** (☎ 044-61159; Castlepollard; adult/concession €5.50/2.25; 2-6pm mid-May–Aug). It is still home to the Pakenham family. The castle recently closed to visitors, but you can still roam the 12 hectares of gardens and parkland including a Chinese and a Tibetan garden and wonderful stretch of yews. To get there, take the N4 northwest out of Mullingar then follow the R394 northeast to Castlepollard. From there the castle and gardens are signposted 2km to the northwest.

Fishing

Trout fishing is popular in the loughs around Mullingar, including Loughs Owel, Derravaragh, Glore, Lene and Sheelin and White, Mt Dalton and Pallas Lakes, as well as Lough Ennell – where in 1894 an 11.9kg trout was landed, still the largest trout ever caught in Ireland. The fishing season runs from 1 March or 1 May (depending on the lake) to 12 October, and all the lakes except Lough Lene are controlled by the **Shannon Regional Fisheries Board** (☎ 48769).

For further information contact **Midlands-East Tourism** (☎ 48650) or the helpful **David O'Malley's** (☎ 48300; 33 Dominick St), both in Mullingar. O'Malley's can provide boats on Loughs Owel or Ennell, plus ghillies and permits. For Lough Derravaragh contact **Mr Newman** (☎ 71206); for Lough Owel, **Mrs Doolan** (☎ 42085); for Lough Sheelin, **Mr Reilly** (☎ 043-81124); and for Lough Ennell, **Mrs Hope** (☎ 40807) or **Mr Roache** (☎ 40314).

Swimming is possible in Loughs Lene, Ennell and Owel, but Derravaragh is very deep and has no shallows.

Fore Valley

Just outside the small village of Fore, in the northeast of the county near the shores of Lough Lene, is a group of early Christian sites that date back to AD 630, when St Fechin founded a monastery here. There are no visible remains of this early settlement, but three later buildings still standing in the valley plain are closely associated with a legend that 'seven wonders' occurred here. The Fore Valley is a great area to explore by bicycle or on foot.

THE SEVEN WONDERS OF FORE

The oldest of the three buildings is **St Fechin's Church**, which may well mark the site of the original monastery. The chancel and baptismal font inside are early 13th century, and over the unusually large entrance there is a huge lintel stone carved with a Greek cross. It was supposed to have been put into place through the divine power of St Fechin's prayers and, as such, counts as one of the seven wonders.

A path runs up from the church to the attractive little **anchorite cell**, which dates back to the 15th century and is another of the seven wonders. The Seven Wonders pub in the village holds the key to this hermit's cell.

Down on the plain, on the other side of the road, there are extensive remains of a 13th-century **Benedictine priory**, built on what was once bog (another wonder). In the next

Carlingford (p532), Cooley Peninsula

EOIN CLARKE

EOIN CLARKE

High crosses (p528), Monasterboice

Overleaf:
Marble Arch (p488), near Dunfanaghy

GARETH MCCORMACK

Burial mound, **Knowth** (p507)

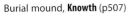

RICHARD CUMMINS

century it was turned into a fortification, hence the castle-like square towers, each of which formed a separate residence, and loophole windows. The western tower is in a dangerous state – keep clear. Two other wonders are a mill without a race and water that flows uphill. The mill site is marked, and legend has it that St Fechin caused water to flow uphill, towards the mill, by throwing his crosier against a rock near Lough Lene, about 1.5km away.

The last two wonders are water that will not boil and a tree with only three branches that will not burn. Both are associated with St Fechin's well, which can be seen on the way to the priory from the road.

To get to the Fore Valley from Mullingar take the N4 northwest out of town and then follow the R394 northeast to Castlepollard. From there the road to Fore is signposted.

ATHLONE

☎ 090 / pop 7479

The county town of Athlone (Baile Átha Luain) has historical importance, due mainly to its strategic position midway on the River Shannon. An attractive market town, it suffered for many years from heavy traffic congestion on its bridge, but has improved dramatically since a much-needed bypass was built in the late 1990s. Though predominantly a garrison town, Athlone is fast gaining a reputation as the culinary hub of the midlands with a plethora of reputable eateries emerging in its so-called 'Left Bank' quarter, behind the castle. Many of its tourist attractions are in the surrounding hinterland, but the town is still a pleasant enough place. A visit to the castle is worth considering, and there are fishing and boat trips along the river to Lough Ree or to the Clonmacnoise monastic site in County Offaly.

Orientation & Information

Athlone is in the far southwest of County Westmeath on the border with Roscommon. It's on the main Dublin–Galway road (N6), and the River Shannon flows northwards through town into Lough Ree. The landmarks here are Athlone Castle and Sts Peter and Paul Cathedral, prominently located on the western bank of the river by the Town Bridge and overlooking Market Square. The castle houses the tourist office, a museum and a heritage centre.

The **tourist office** (☎ 649 4630; Athlone Castle; 🕑 9.30am-5.30pm Mon-Fri Apr-Oct), closed during the off-peak season, is well-supported by the **information office** (☎ 647 3173; Jolly Mariner Marina, Coosan; 🕑 9am-5pm) run by the local chamber of commerce, and located north of the centre on the eastern bank of the Shannon beyond the railway bridge.

The Bank of Ireland is at the start of Northgate St, just up from Custume Place. The post office is on Barrack St beside the cathedral.

Sights & Activities

ATHLONE CASTLE & MUSEUM

The Normans probably had an encampment by the ford over the river before they built a **castle** here in 1210. In 1690 the castle held out for James II, but the following year the bridge came under Protestant attack again, and this time the Jacobite city fell to the troops under William of Orange's Dutch commander, Ginkel. Major alterations to the castle took place between the 17th and 19th centuries, and the ramp that forms the present entrance is a relatively recent addition. The oldest surviving part is the central keep, where the museum is now housed.

Athlone Museum (☎ 649 2912; adult/child/family €5/1.50/11.50; 🕑 10am-4.30pm May-Oct) has two floors: upstairs is the folk collection, and downstairs there are artefacts from prehistoric times. There's also an old gramophone that belonged to John McCormack (1884–1945), a native of Athlone and arguably one of the greatest tenors of all time. The admission price includes a visit to the **heritage centre**, which has an audiovisual presentation on the town's history and flora and fauna.

FISHING

Just below the Church St end of Town Bridge on the eastern bank of the river opposite the castle, the **Strand Tackle Shop** (☎ 647 9277; The Strand) is the place to go for information. Permits are required for certain areas and are available at the shop.

RIVER CRUISES

Several companies offer cruises from Athlone between May and September.

Viking Tours (☎ 647 3383; www.vikingtoursireland.com; 7 St Mary's Pl) offers daily cruises north to Lough Ree. The boats usually depart from

The Strand at 2.30pm and 4.30pm (€8/6 per adult/child); a timetable is available from the tourist office. The company also offers a cruise on its Viking ship south to Clonmacnoise (adult/child €14/9, 1½ hours), an important early monastic site in County Offaly. It departs from The Strand at 10am several days a week, depending on numbers; phone for a schedule.

MV Ross (☎ 647 2892; Jolly Mariner Marina, Coosan) You can make a group booking or join an existing group on a 1½-hour cruise (€10/5 per adult/child) on Lough Ree; phone for details.

Sleeping

Lough Ree Lodge (☎ 647 6738; Dublin Rd; dm/s/d €15/25/40; May-Sep;) The closest thing to a hostel in town, the Lough Ree Lodge normally houses students during term-time. It has a simple, clean, basic décor, a large kitchen and a TV lounge. There's a shuttle bus service into town (1km).

Bastion B&B (☎ 649 4954; bastion@iol.ie; 4-6 Bastion St; s €35-45, d €55) A great place to stay in town, over a funky surf and craft shop run by the same brothers, is this friendly, kooky house full of plants, paintings and curios. It has five simple rooms, a games lounge and serves a buffet breakfast of fresh fruit, cheeses and croissants.

Shannonside (☎ 649 4773; shannonside@eircom.net; West Lodge Rd; s/d €45/64) This is a newly revamped period house with 10 very comfortable, nicely decorated rooms about 1km from the town centre, with facilities for anglers.

Eating

Some of Athlone's best eateries are located in the small Bohemian area behind the castle, around Bastion St.

A Slice of Life (☎ 649 3970; Bastion St; mains €3-7; 8.30am-6pm Mon-Sat) This small delicatessen and café serves really tasty, filling hot specials or pizza slices and sandwiches at bargain basement prices.

Hugo's (☎ 649 8576; 6-8 Bastion St; mains €14-19; 5-10pm Mon-Sat) Hugo's has already earned great reviews and a reputation for its good home cooking and laid-back atmosphere. The menu is simple but prepared with care: traditional chicken, fish and meat dishes with at least three vegetarian choices.

Left Bank Bistro (☎ 649 444; Fry Pl; mains €18-27; noon-5pm & 6-10.30pm Tue-Sat) This stylish place is an airy, sophisticated bistro with large windows at the bottom end of Bastion St and probably the town's best restaurant. It's extremely popular with businesspeople at lunch-time. Always a good sign, the menu is short, with daily specials, and there's a separate fish and seafood menu.

Olive Grove (☎ 647 6946; Bridge St; Custume Pl; mains €15-22; noon-3pm & 6.30-9.30pm Tue-Sun) This colourful, informal place by the river serves Greek and Mediterranean cuisine that is light, healthy and extremely tasty. Here you might find falafel with minty tabbouleh or wild mushroom risotto; vegetarians will do well.

Le Chateau (☎ 649 4517; Peter's Port; mains €15-24; 12.30-10pm) There's a cosy old-world atmosphere about Le Chateau, housed in a former church behind the castle, and that extends to the menu. Chicken Kiev, sirloin steak or rack of lamb are traditional staples but if they're what you're after, you'll find no place better. There's a three-course early-bird menu (€23) for pre-6.30pm diners.

Drinking & Entertainment

Sean's Bar (☎ 649 2358; Main St) is something of a legend and, dating from 1600, claims to be Ireland's oldest pub. Though the old bus seats have gone, the interior is suitably down-at-heel with log fires, uneven floors and a rickety piano. You can catch live music most nights in summer from the riverside beer garden where, as they say, the 'craic is mighty'.

Palace Bar (☎ 649 2229; Barrack St) This cavernous bar beside the church has occasional folk and traditional music sessions in the upstairs loft venue.

Dean Crowe Theatre (☎ 649 2129; deancrowetheatre@eircom.net; Chapel St) This sizable, newly refurbished theatre has wonderful acoustics, and runs a broad programme of theatrical and musical events year round; call for details.

Getting There & Around

The **bus depot** (☎ 647 3322) is beside the train station, and express buses stop there on many routes from the east to the west coast. There are 15 buses daily to Dublin (one way €10.50, two hours) and Galway (€11, 1¼ hours); three daily (one on Sunday) to Westport (€13, 2¾ hours) in County Mayo; and three daily (four on Friday, one on Sunday) to Mullingar (€8.60, one hour).

From **Athlone train station** (☎ 647 3300), there are eight trains daily to Dublin (€16, 1½ hours); three daily (two on Sunday) to Westport (€16, 2¼ hours); and five daily (four on Sunday) to Galway (€13, 1¼ hours). The train station is on the eastern bank on Southern Station Rd. To get there, follow Northgate St up from Custume Place. Its extension, Coosan Point Rd, joins Southern Station Rd near St Vincent's Hospital.

You can order a taxi on ☎ 647 4400.

AROUND ATHLONE

Lough Ree

Just north of Athlone is Lough Ree, one of the three main lakes formed by the River Shannon. It's celebrated for the early monastic ruins on its many islands and for some excellent trout fishing. The lough is also home to many migratory birds that come here to nest, particularly swans, plovers, and curlews. Sailing is popular and the Lough Ree Yacht Club, established in about 1720, is one of the world's oldest yacht clubs.

Glasson

☎ 090

The pretty village of Glasson (Village of the Roses), 8km from Athlone on the N55, is well worth a visit. A stone's throw from Lough Ree and its amenities, it has a couple of very good restaurants, lively pubs and, in what looks like a garden shed, probably the smallest garda station in the country!

SLEEPING & EATING

Glasson has some good, friendly places to stay.

Lake Breeze Lodge (☎ 648 5204; Ballykeeran; s/d €35/60) This friendly, comfortable bungalow with gardens close to the lake is on the N55 road 2km from Glasson.

Grogan's (☎ 648 5158; mains €6-16) In the village centre, this pub is the real thing: an authentic old man's bar and lounge with peat fires and a great traditional atmosphere. It also serves good seafood and hearty pub grub all day.

Glasson Village Restaurant (☎ 648 5001; mains €19-24, 3-course dinner €34; 🕐 6-9.30pm Tue-Sat, 12.30-2.30pm Sun) People travel for miles to get a table in this restaurant at the northern end of the village. In a beautiful stone cottage that originally housed a garda barracks, it specialises in seafood and local produce. There's also a rustic five-bedroom outhouse to rent

SOMETHING SPECIAL

Wineport Restaurant (☎ 648 5466; www.wineport.ie; s/d €150/200; mains €24-29, 2-course dinner €30; 🕐 5-10pm Wed-Sat, 12.30-9pm Sun) This outstanding restaurant in a lovely cedar lodge on the lake's edge, showcases chef Feargal O'Donnell's award-winning modern Irish cuisine and carefully chosen wines. The atmosphere is surprisingly relaxed and it's a family-friendly place with a decent children's menu. Try the surprise seven-course menu (€89) which gives you a chance to sample some more unusual dishes with different matching wines.

The restaurant recently added 10 beautiful contemporary bedrooms, each with a decked balcony over the lake and fitted to an extremely high standard with Egyptian cotton duvets, flat screen TVs, Bose stereos, walnut furniture and gorgeous sandstone bathrooms. Each room is named after a wine or champagne and you get to sample the tipple of your chosen room when you arrive.

Boat hire can be arranged for a day's jaunt around the lake or a trip across to Glassan golf course.

(from €110 per person) in the grounds and the price includes a round of golf and dinner at the restaurant.

GETTING THERE & AWAY

Bus Éireann (☎ 647 3322) bus No 466 from Athlone to Longford has two services Monday to Saturday, stopping outside Grogan's pub.

Goldsmith Country

From Athlone, the N55 northeast to County Longford runs close to the eastern side of Lough Ree and through Goldsmith country, so called because of the area's associations with the 18th-century poet, playwright and novelist Oliver Goldsmith. The gentle landscape is ideal for cycling. The *Lough Ree Trail: A Signposted Tour*, by Gearoid O'Brien, published by Midlands-East Tourism, is available from the tourist offices in Athlone and Mullingar. This tour takes in places associated with Oliver Goldsmith. The whole tour, through Glasson, around the shores of Lough Ree and extending into County Longford, is 32km.

County Donegal

CONTENTS

'Up here, it's different.' Donegal's motto is a wonderfully succinct understatement, a mere hint of how unlike the rest of Ireland it really is. Ireland's second-largest county (after Cork) is indeed a place apart, separated from the rest of the Republic by the extended finger of County Fermanagh's northwestern border, but even before the twins of history and politics conspired to isolate it, Donegal was a place like no other on the island.

What strikes the visitor first is that Donegal is a county of extremes, where only superlatives do justice to description. While other parts of Ireland are remote, Donegal is, in huge swathes, sullen and saturnine, existing in profound isolation from the rest of the world. When describing the weather, words like 'bad' or 'good' are meaningless adjectives: in winter, the wind and rain can feel like a malevolent fury, but come the summer, the shining sun outdoes itself, warming everything in its glow so as to make you question the geographical fact that you're further north than Newfoundland.

Donegal's beauty, however, is neither fickle nor changeable. No other county in Ireland can boast such unspoilt splendour, and while the rugged delight of Donegal's interior should on no account be missed, it is the coastline – the longest of any county in Ireland – that is the major draw. Precipitous cliffs, windswept peninsulas and golden beaches to rival any in Europe separate the coastal resorts that, despite a couple of tawdry exceptions, are perfect destinations for a relaxing seaside holiday.

HIGHLIGHTS

- Hike in and around the **Glen Gesh Pass** (p477), a little bit of alpine magic in Ireland
- Walk up Mt Errigal and drink in the views of the **Poisoned Glen** (p483)
- Walk or cycle around **Horn Head** (p487) to watch the birdlife and explore the beautiful coastline
- Explore the **Rossguill Peninsula** (p492) via the scenic Atlantic Drive
- Spend a night in the **Old Glen Bar in Glen** (p493), near Carrigart

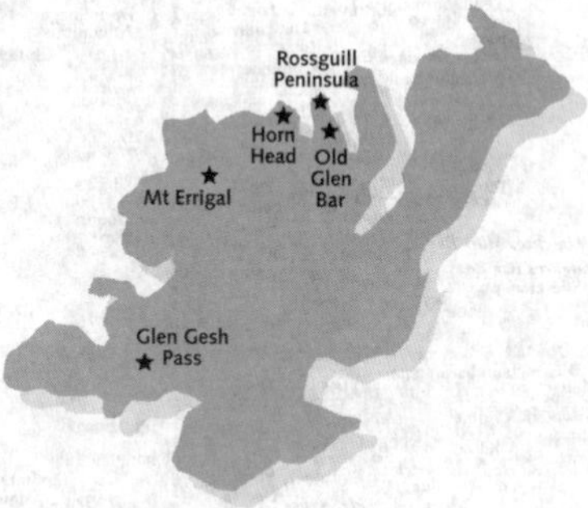

- POPULATION: 137,575
- AREA: 3001 SQ KM

HISTORY

The earliest evidence of human habitation dates back at least 9000 years, and the county is dotted with pre-Christian tombs and other prehistoric titbits. The arrival of the Celts and their fort-building endeavours provide the origins of the county's Irish name, Dun na nGall, or 'Fort of the Foreigner'. Christianity features prominently in the county's history, largely through the efforts of local boy St Colmcille, who not only spread the good word throughout the area but exported it across the sea to Scotland too.

Until the early 17th century, most of the county was roughly divided between two clans, the O'Donnells and the O'Neills, but the Plantation of Ulster that followed their defeat and flight from Ireland reduced the county to a subservient misery whose effects are felt to this day. The partition of Ireland in 1921 compounded Donegal's isolation, as it was cut off from Derry, which it served as a natural hinterland. Despite major efforts by the government to offer incentives to industry- and job-creating schemes, Donegal remains largely underdeveloped.

CLIMATE

Despite its northerly location, Donegal's thermometers rarely drop below zero, and in summer the temperature can top 25°C, although it generally hovers around the 18 to 19°C mark. This is largely due to

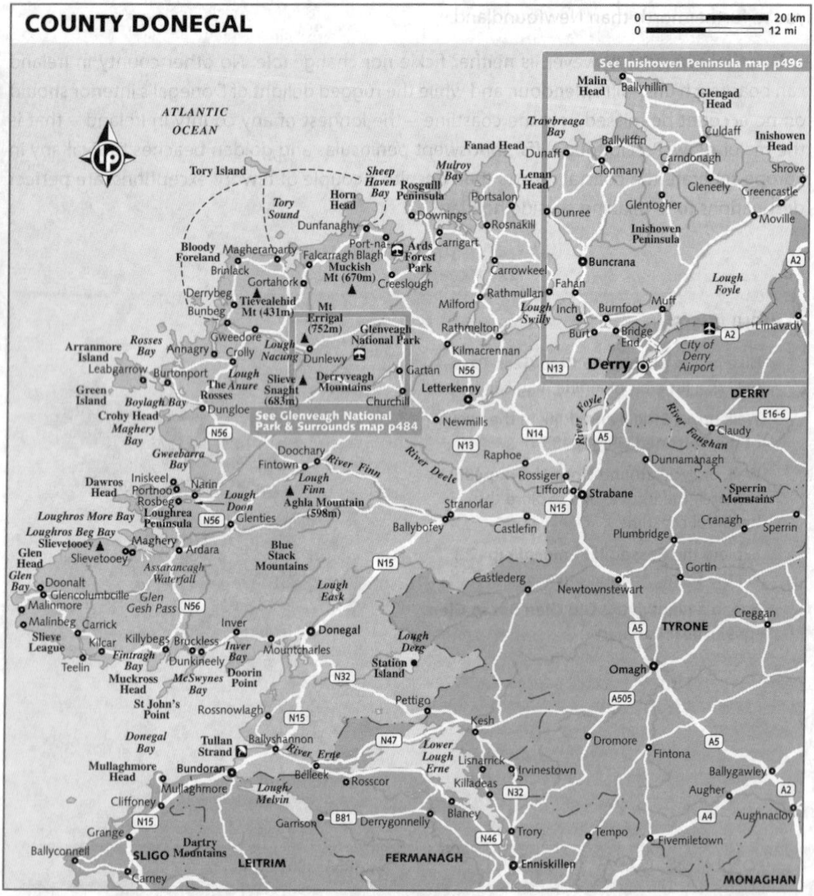

the moderating effect of the Atlantic Gulf Stream, which caresses the county's extra-long coastline. But when the winter winds and heavy rain are ripping through your semiprotective parka, it doesn't really matter that the 'official' temperature is a balmy 4°C – it can feel arctic. Conversely, when the summer gauge shows that it's less than 20°C, you'll soon find yourself stripping down to your swim trunks and diving into the sea because it's just too damn hot.

LANGUAGE

Roughly one-third of the county lies in the Gaeltacht, where Irish is the lingua franca and road signs challenge the reader to perform linguistic gymnastics to get the right pronunciation. Donegal Irish has a markedly different pronunciation from that spoken elsewhere, and even native speakers from, say, Kerry often have difficulty understanding the local vernacular. Before you panic and rush out to do a crash course in Irish, however, be assured that virtually everyone speaks English and, more importantly, will do so without hesitation. It would behove you, though, to familiarise yourself with the Irish place names; although we use English transliterations, their Irish names are included in brackets.

GETTING THERE & AWAY

Isolation is the leitmotif of Donegal's existence, especially in terms of transportation. There is no rail service to the county and the bus is your main option if you don't have your own car; details of the various services are listed in each destination section.

Donegal Airport (☎ 074-954 8284; www.aerarann.com; Carrick Finn) has flights to and from Dublin (return from €69) twice daily. It's in the townland of Carrick Finn (Charraig Fhion) about 3km northeast of Annagry along the northwestern coast, which makes it somewhat inconvenient for travellers going to the south of the county. There is no public transportation to the airport, so you'll have to rely on your own steam; there are car rental desks in the terminal.

GETTING AROUND

Although you can get around County Donegal by bus, it's a time-consuming endeavour, especially in winter. The **Lough Swilly** (in Letterkenny ☎ 074-912 2863, in Derry ☎ 028-7126 2017) private bus company has a six-day Runabout unlimited travel pass costing €30/15/22 for adults/children/students, but it's only valid during July and August.

This is very much walking and cycling country. Highly recommended companions for walkers are New Irish Walks: West and North by Tony Whilde & Patrick Simms (Gill & Macmillan), and Hill Walkers' Donegal by David Herman (Shanksmare Publications), which have details of all the walks mentioned in this chapter. Both are available in the Four Masters Bookshop in Donegal town (see p468) or at bigger booksellers throughout Ireland.

When driving, be prepared for switchback roads, directions only in Irish, signs hidden behind vegetation, signs pointing the wrong way, signs with misleading mileages or no signs at all. Most of all, prepare yourself for the lunatic boy-racers that seem to plague Donegal's roads: it's not uncommon to find yourself blinded at night by the oncoming beams of a souped-up Escort doing 140km/h – just for the thrill of it.

DONEGAL TOWN

☎ 074 / pop 3723

If you're coming from the south, chances are you'll arrive in Donegal town, the principal gateway to the rest of the county. It's not a particularly interesting spot, but it's pleasant enough to spend a day in. The town hugs the innermost edge of Donegal Bay, into which flows the River Eske. The focal point is the triangular Diamond, which is lined with souvenir shops.

Although the town dates back to the Vikings, who built a fort here in the 9th century, it owes its growth to the powerful O'Donnell family, who controlled this part of the country from the 15th to 17th centuries.

INFORMATION

The **tourist office** (☎ 972 1148; www.irelandnorthwest.ie; the Quay; 🕓 9am-6pm Mon-Sat, noon-4pm Sun Jul & Aug, 9am-5pm Mon-Sat Sep-Jun) is south of the Diamond by the Eske.

A great way of getting an overview of the town and area is by taking one of the 1½-hour boat tours run by **Donegal Bay Waterbus** (☎ 972 3666; Donegal Pier; adult/concession €10/5). Most of the major points of interest are included in the tour, which runs up to five times daily during the summer and at least once a day the rest of the year, depending on the weather. Call to check departure times.

On the Diamond, the Bank of Ireland, Allied Irish Bank and Ulster Bank all have ATMs and bureaux de change. The post office is on Tirchonaill St, north of the Diamond. The **Blueberry Cybercafe** (☎ 972 2933; the Diamond; €7/hr; 🕑 9am-7pm Mon-Sat), above the Blueberry Tearoom, offers Internet access. It's an honour system: you fill in a chit with your times and pay downstairs.

Four Masters Bookshop (☎ 972 1526; the Diamond) is a good spot for books, maps and travel guides, and also doubles as a gift shop.

DONEGAL CASTLE

Dúchas-operated **Donegal Castle** (☎ 972 2405; Castle St; adult/concession €3.80/1.50; 🕑 10am-6pm mid-Mar–Oct) is built on a rocky outcrop over the Eske, and what remains of this restored castle is impressive. Built by the O'Donnells in 1474, it served as the seat of their formidable power until 1607, when the English decided to be rid of pesky Irish chieftains once and for all. Rory O'Donnell knew he was beaten, but he wasn't going to make it easy, so he burnt his castle down to the ground before escaping with Hugh O'Neill to France in what became known as the Flight of the Earls. Their defeat paved the way for the Plantation of Ulster by thousands of newly arrived Scots and English

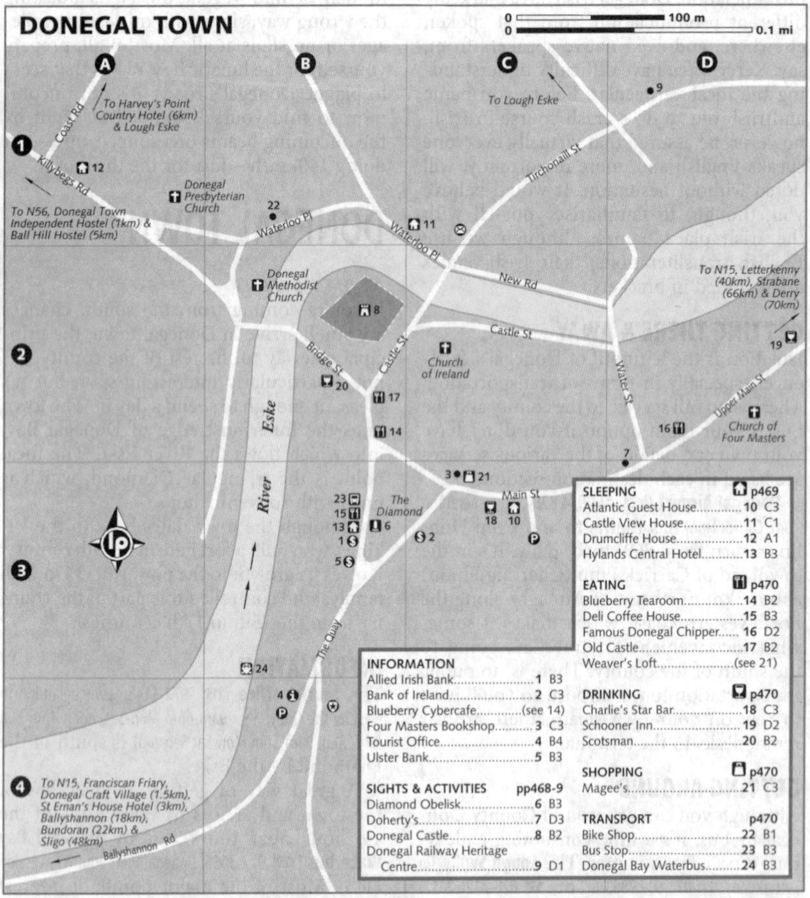

Protestants, thereby creating the divisions that still afflict the island today.

The castle was rebuilt in the Jacobean style in 1623 by Sir Basil Brooke, who then furnished it with plenty of Persian rugs and French tapestries. Information panels chronicle the history of the castle from its construction to its ownership by Brooke. Brooke is also responsible for the adjacent three-storey Jacobean house.

THE DIAMOND OBELISK

In 1474 Red Hugh O'Donnell and his wife, Nuala O'Brien, founded a **Franciscan friary** by the shore south of town. It was accidentally blown up in 1601 by Rory O'Donnell while laying siege to an English garrison, and little of it remains. What makes it famous is that four of its friars, fearing that the arrival of the English meant the end of Celtic culture, chronicled the whole of known Celtic history and mythology from 40 years before the Flood to AD 1618 in The Annals of the Four Masters, still one of the most important sources of early Irish history. The **obelisk** (1937) in the Diamond commemorates the work, copies of which are displayed in the National Library in Dublin.

DONEGAL RAILWAY HERITAGE CENTRE

The **heritage centre** (☎ 972 2655; Tirchonaill St; adult/concession €1.50/1; ⏲ 10am-5.30pm Mon-Sat, 2-5pm Sun Jun-Sep, 10am-4pm Mon-Fri Oct-May), in the former train station northeast of the town centre, tells the history of the steam railway that ran from Ballyshannon to Derry until 1959.

FISHING

Permits are required for fishing in many of the local rivers. A permit (€10) for the Eske, along with licences for salmon and sea trout, is available from **Doherty's** (☎ 972 1119; Main St; ⏲ 9am-6pm Thu-Tue).

FESTIVALS & EVENTS

The three-day **Donegal Town Summer Festival** in late June/early July features a variety of activities including singing, dancing and storytelling, with arts and crafts thrown in for good measure. The tourist office has details.

SLEEPING

Accommodation in town is plentiful, with dozens of B&Bs scattered throughout the centre and environs. You should have no problems finding a room; the tourist office will assist with any query. There are also some excellent choices at nearby Lough Eske; see p470 for details.

Budget

Donegal Town Independent Hostel (☎ 972 2805; Killybegs Rd, Doonan; dm/d €11.50/27; Ⓟ) This clean, friendly IHH/IHO hostel is in a big white building 1km northwest of town off the Killybegs road (N56). It's far enough out to be quiet, but within walking distance of town.

Ball Hill Hostel (☎ 972 1174; www.irelandyha.org; Ball Hill; dm €13.50; ⏲ Apr-Sep, weekends only Oct-Mar; Ⓟ) Formerly a coastguard station, this 66-bed An Óige hostel has a stunning setting on the shores of Donegal Bay about 5km southwest of town. To get here, follow the Killybegs road (N56) and look for the signs on the left. Stock up on food before you arrive.

Mid-Range

Castle View House (☎ 972 2100; Waterloo Pl; s/d €24/48; Ⓟ) Bathrooms are shared in this simple but clean two-storey B&B overlooking the castle's Jacobean house.

Atlantic Guest House (☎ 972 1187; Main St; s/d €22.50/45) This elegant town house near the Diamond has 16 pleasantly furnished rooms, five of which are en suite (these rooms are €30 per person).

Drumcliffe House (☎ 972 1200; Killybegs Rd; s/d €25/50; ⊠ Ⓟ) The relaxed atmosphere, fine furnishings and friendly service make this B&B a good choice. All rooms are en suite, and one has a four-poster bed. It was totally refurbished in 2003.

Top End

Hylands Central Hotel (☎ 972 1027; fax 972 2295; the Diamond; s/d €60/110; Ⓟ) The town's most modern hotel, the Central is a large hotel with its own gym, pool, Jacuzzi and solarium. The rooms are spotless.

St Ernan's House Hotel (☎ 972 1065; www.sainternans.com; R267; s/d €150/270; dinner €26-50; ⏲ mid-Apr–Oct) This magnificent country hotel (built by a nephew of Wellington in 1836) is set on its own wooded island about 3km south of Donegal town, signposted off the road to Laghey. Each of the gorgeous 12 rooms has wonderful views of the sea. The owners put a premium on peace and tranquillity, so children under six are not catered for.

EATING

There are at least half a dozen places to eat within 100m or so of the Diamond.

Deli Coffee House (☎ 972 1014; the Diamond; mains €3-6; ⏲ 9am-6pm) Heart-stopping Irish breakfasts and more artery-friendly sandwiches are on offer; this could be your only option on a Sunday morning.

Weaver's Loft (☎ 972 2660; Magee's, the Diamond; mains around €6; ⏲ 9am-6pm Mon-Sat) A pleasant self-service café on the 1st floor of Magee's department store in the middle of town.

Old Castle (☎ 972 1062; Castle St; mains €9-16; ⏲ noon-3pm) A grey stone pub that serves superior pub fare.

Blueberry Tearoom (☎ 972 2933; the Diamond; mains €5-8; ⏲ 9am-7pm Mon-Sat) Fresh, substantial sandwiches and excellent pies and cakes make this a local favourite.

Famous Donegal Chipper (☎ 972 1428; Upper Main St; fish & chips €6.50; ⏲ 12.30-11.30pm) They're not kidding: this place is well-known throughout the area for its fabulous fish and chips.

DRINKING

Numerous music pubs can be found on Main and Upper Main Sts, within a stone's throw of the Diamond. Check the Thursday edition of the *Donegal Democrat* for details of what's going on around town.

Schooner Inn (☎ 972 1671; Upper Main St) This classic Irish pub presents traditional and modern music at the weekend.

Scotsman (Bridge St) The Scotsman attracts a friendly local crowd ready to sing or strum at the drop of a pint.

Charlie's Star Bar (☎ 972 1158; Main St) Quiet during the week, it livens up at the weekend when a young crowd comes to enjoy the live, contemporary music.

SHOPPING

Magee's (☎ 972 2660; the Diamond; ⏲ 9.30am-6pm Mon-Sat) Magee's is Donegal's most celebrated fabric shop and is virtually eponymous with Donegal tweed. You can even buy tweed rolls straight from the attached garment factory.

Donegal Craft Village (☎ 972 2228; Ballyshannon Rd; ⏲ 9am-6pm Mon-Sat, 11am-6pm Sun) This complex of small art and craft workshops about 1.5km south of town is worth visiting. Pottery, crystal, batik, garments and jewellery are all made on the premises.

GETTING THERE & AWAY

Frequent **Bus Éireann** (☎ 972 1101; www.buseireann.ie) buses connect Donegal with Derry, Enniskillen and Belfast in the North; Sligo, Galway and Killybegs to the west; Limerick and Cork in the south; and Dublin in the southeast. The bus stop is outside the Abbey Hotel on the western side of the Diamond.

Private coaches operated by **Feda O'Donnell** (☎ 974 8114; www.fedaodonnell.com) run to Galway (single/return €15/22, 3½ hours, twice daily, three on Friday and Sunday) via Ballyshannon, Bundoran and Sligo. Departures are from the tourist office. Fares within Donegal range from €5.50 to €8, depending on where you're headed.

McGeehan Coaches (☎ 954 6150; www.mcgeehancoaches.com) runs buses to Dublin (single/return €16.50/23, four hours, two daily, three Sunday) from in front of the garda barracks across from the tourist office.

GETTING AROUND

The **Bike Shop** (☎ 972 2515; Waterloo Pl) is a good bet for cycle hire (€10/60 per day/week). The owner is friendly and knowledgeable and will help you plan a cycling itinerary.

AROUND DONEGAL TOWN

LOUGH ESKE

This lovely spot northeast of Donegal town isn't the fishing hole it once was (its name means 'Lake of the Fish'), but it's terrific for **cycling** or **walking** over the majestic Blue Stack Mountains, from which there are great views.

Sleeping & Eating

Ardeevin Guest House (☎ 074-972 1790; Lough Eske; s/d €50/70) This is a wonderful B&B about 4km north of town off the Letterkenny road (N15). Each of the clean, modern rooms has views of the Blue Stack Mountains and Lough Eske. Take the second left after the Skoda car dealership and follow the signs for Lough Eske and the B&B.

Harvey's Point Country Hotel (☎ 074-972 2208; www.harveyspoint.com; Harvey's Point; s €70-110, d €140-220; Ⓟ) This luxury 20-room hotel has an alpine feel to it, with the rooms scattered about a number of chalets. It is 6km north of

Donegal town. It also does a four-course dinner for €47. In fact the French-inspired cuisine at this hotel restaurant has been praised by foodies for quite a while: we concur, even if the place is a little stiff due to the required dress code. Reservations are a must.

Ardnamona House (☎ 074-972 2650; www.ardnamona.com; Ardnamona; s/d €80/120) This Victorian house is one of our favourite spots in the whole county. The five rooms are all magnificent, with some really classy touches such as free-standing 19th-century baths. The house also has a 2km-stretch of lakefront and exquisite formal gardens dating from the 1880s.

Getting There & Away

From the Diamond leave Donegal on the N56 to Killybegs. About 300m past the bridge, turn right following the signs to Harvey's Point Country Hotel. The ring road eventually joins the N15 to the northeast of Donegal, so it makes a convenient cycling trip. If you hire a bike from the Bike Shop in Donegal, you'll be given a photocopied map.

ROSSNOWLAGH

☎ 071 / pop 50

If you want a beach holiday away from it all, Rossnowlagh (Ross Neamblach), southwest of Donegal town, is the place. The sandy Blue Flag beach is stunning, extends for nearly 5km and is a great **surfing** spot. Deep in the adjacent forest is a Franciscan friary, which houses the **Donegal Historical Society Museum** (☎ 985 1342; admission free; 10am-5pm Mon-Sat). The place itself is of limited interest, but the gardens and surrounding woodland are lovely for a stroll.

Nestled in the hillside, **Ard-na-Mara** (☎ 985 1141; Rossnowlagh; s/d €46/75; Jan-Nov;) has fabulous views of the bay and six en-suite rooms. Be sure to opt for one of the four rooms with sea views.

The top spot in the area is the marvellous **Sand House Hotel** (☎ 985 1777; www.sandhouse-hotel.ie; Rossnowlagh; s €85-145, d €170-290; Feb-Dec), right on the beach. A former fishing lodge, it is now a perennial favourite with Irish holidaymakers.

BALLYSHANNON

☎ 072 / pop 2273

This busy, hilly town is set above the River Erne with a small adjunct of shops and houses south of the river connected by a bridge. Ballyshannon (Béal Átha Seanaidh, which means 'the ford entrance of the hill slope') is preferable to Bundoran as a base for exploring the coastline before heading up to Donegal.

Orientation & Information

The centre of Ballyshannon, north of the river, has two main streets converging below the distinctive clock tower of Gallogley Jewellers: Main St runs to the northwest and Market St to the northeast. There's an Allied Irish Bank with an ATM and a post office on Castle St.

PILGRIMAGE TO LOUGH DERG

One of Ireland's most significant centres of pilgrimage is **Station Island** in the middle of Lough Derg, east of Donegal town. It is believed that St Patrick himself fasted while staying on the island, and today some 30,000 pilgrims turn up every year from June to mid-August to do the same thing. The pilgrimage starts with a 24-hour vigil; one meal (of dry bread and black tea) a day is permitted; and everyone is expected to complete the Stations of the Cross in bare feet on the first day, having fasted from the preceding midnight. Anyone over 14 years is allowed on the island, but be warned that you must be a genuine pilgrim to participate. Further information is available from the **Priory** (☎ 071-986 1518; www.loughderg.org; St Patrick's Purgatory, Pettigo).

The pilgrims reach the island by boat from St Patrick's Purgatory, about 7km north of Pettigo, but outside the pilgrim season there's no regular service to the island. Pettigo and the lake are extremely remote, at the end of a road across the moors. During the pilgrim season (1 June to 15 August), a special Bus Éireann service (No 31) leaves Dublin's Busáras (€17) at 9am Monday to Saturday (10am Sunday), arriving at Lough Derg just over 4½ hours later. During the same period bus No 68 leaves Galway at 9am, stopping at Sligo and Ballyshannon – but not Donegal – before reaching Lough Derg at 1.35pm. The first boat leaves at 11am, the last at 3pm and costs €20, including lunch.

Allingham's Grave

The poet William Allingham (1824–89) was born in Ballyshannon and is buried in the graveyard beside **St Anne's Church**. It's signposted second left up Main St after Dorrian's Imperial hotel. The AIB bank on Castle St has a window on which Allingham scribbled his first attempts at verse when he was a kid and his dad was the local bank manager.

Donegal Parian China Visitor Centre

Parian china is lighter and more translucent than bone china. All the pieces manufactured by Donegal Parian China are on display (and for sale) at the **visitor centre** (☎ 985 1826; Ballyshannon; admission free; ⌚ 9am-6pm Mon-Fri year-round & 9am-6pm Sat May-Sep, 10am-6pm Sun Jun-Sep), about 1.5km southwest of Ballyshannon on the Bundoran road (N15). Prices range from around €8 for small pieces to €500 for a full dinner set. Free guided tours, a tearoom, a bureau de change and a mailing service are available.

Abbey Mills

Abbey Mills (☎ 985 8966; Abbeylands; admission free; ⌚ 11am-7pm Jun-Sep, 2.30-7pm Sun Oct-May) is a heritage centre with an audiovisual display, craft shop and café in the restored mills of Abbey Assaroe, founded in the late 12th century by Cistercian monks from Boyle in County Roscommon. To get there, turn left off Main St onto Bridge St, past the Thatch Pub, and take the road to Rossnowlagh (R231). After about 2km, signs indicate Abbey Mills on the left. There are fine views of the Erne Estuary and Donegal Bay.

Festivals & Events

BALLYSHANNON FOLK & TRADITIONAL MUSIC FESTIVAL

This excellent celebration of music takes place during the first weekend in August, and is probably the best time to visit the town. For information on the line-up and schedule of gigs, check out the website at www.ballyshannonfolkfestival.com.

Sleeping & Eating

Duffy's Hostel (☎ 985 1535; Donegal Rd; dm/d €10/23; ⌚ Mar–mid-Oct) Duffy's is a small, 12-bed hostel about 1km up Market St from the bus station. It can be a bit cramped, but there's a conservatory, garden and an attached second-hand bookshop.

Rockville House (☎ 985 1106; Belleek Rd; s/d €35/55) This is an elegant 17th-century house about 500m from the centre overlooking the River Erne. The rooms are very comfortable and nicely appointed.

Dorrian's Imperial (☎ 985 1147; fax 985 1001; Main St; s/d €65/130) This grand hotel with its 26 rooms, leisure centre and elegant décor is the best in town.

Devine's Bar (☎ 985 2981; Market St; mains €7-14) This pub has won awards for its freshly prepared food.

Kitchen Bake (Main St; snacks around €6; ⌚ 9am-6pm) At the Kitchen Bake, above a bakery and health-food shop at the junction of Main and Market Sts, you'll find delicious daytime snacks, fresh bread and cakes.

Drinking

Two deservedly popular pubs we recommend are **Finn McCool's** (☎ 985 2677; Main St) and the **Thatch Pub** (Bridge St), just off the top of Main St as you turn towards Rossnowlagh.

Getting There & Away

There are regular daily **Bus Éireann** (☎ 074-21309) buses to Bundoran, Derry, Sligo, Galway, Donegal and Dublin (via Enniskillen, Cavan and Navan). The bus station is between the bridge and the Gallogley Jewellers clock tower.

Feda O'Donnell (☎ 074-974 8114) buses depart from outside the Olde Distillery pub, which is opposite the bus station, for Donegal, Letterkenny, Dunfanaghy, Gweedore and Crolly twice daily, four Friday. For Sligo and Galway they leave from in front of Maggie's Bar, south of the river near the roundabout, twice daily, three Friday and Sunday.

BUNDORAN

☎ 071 / pop 1665

Bundoran (Bun Dobhráin) may be one of Ireland's most popular seaside resorts, but its success has ruined the town, frankly, and today it is little more than a tacky resort plagued by amusement arcades, greasy spoon diners and appalling souvenir stands. It is, however, one of Europe's premier surfing spots, which has made it a mecca for surfers. If you're a confirmed landlubber, though, there are far better places to visit.

The **tourist office** (☎ 984 1350; Main St; ⌚ 10am-5pm Mon-Fri mid-Mar–Sep, 10am-5pm Sat Oct–mid-Mar) is in a kiosk opposite the Holyrood

Hotel. The post office is about 120m south of the tourist office; the Allied Irish Bank on Main St has an ATM and bureau de change.

Activities

SURFING

The breaks of Tullan Strand, just north of the town centre, are big enough to offer some of the best surfing in Europe. Bundoran's Tullan Strand hosts the annual Irish National Surfing Championships, which are usually held sometime in April. For more information, check out the Irish Surfing Association website (www.isa.ie).

The **Donegal Adventure Centre** (☎ 984 2418; www.donegal-holidays.com; Dinglei Cush) rents gear and specialises in surf tuition but also offers a range of other programmes, from kayaking to gorge-walking.

If you're looking to just rent some gear, try **Fitzgerald's Surfworld** (☎ 984 1223; Main St).

HORSE-RIDING

Homefield Equestrian Trails (☎ 984 1288; www.homefieldhouse.com; Bayview Ave; adult/child per hr €16/13) is an excellent adventure centre and hostel that, amongst other activities, organises riding sessions along the beach and instructional courses.

Sleeping & Eating

There are plenty of accommodation and dining options scattered about town, although few stand out.

Homefield Hostel (☎ 984 1288; www.homefieldhouse.com; Bayview Ave; dm/d €16/32; P) The six-bed dorms and private rooms at the Homefield Equestrian Trails are uniformly excellent, and the rate includes breakfast. Bike hire is also available.

Gillaroo Lodge (☎ 984 2357; www.iol.ie/~gillaroo; West End; s/d €42/60; P) A favourite with anglers, this two-storey lodge is close to the beach and has plenty of fishy facilities, including boat and engine hire (€50 per day), permits and even a tackle storage. A packed lunch is available for €5 to €7.

Grand Central Hotel (☎ 984 2722; fax 984 2656; Main St; mains around €14; s/d €70/140) This modern hotel in the heart of town has traditionally decorated, pleasant rooms. The restaurant, featuring the usual array of dishes from fish to meat, is a local favourite, mostly due to the large portions.

There are plenty of quickie meal options around town, but two restaurants are worth checking out.

La Sabbia Wine & Oyster Bar (Homefield Equestrian Trails; ☎ 984 1288; Bayview Ave; mains €12-19; ⏲ 6-10pm) Pastas, salads, meat and fish dishes are all excellent at this popular Italian restaurant that drags Bundoran's gourmet status up a few notches.

Le Chateaubrianne (☎ 984 2160; Sligo Rd; set lunch/dinner €22/32) One of the best restaurants in town, the cooking combines French and modern Irish cuisine using fresh local seafood and game; it also has some imaginative vegetarian dishes.

Getting There & Away

Bus Éireann (☎ 074-912 1309) buses stop on Main St outside Pebbles shop. There are direct daily services to Dublin, Derry, Sligo, Galway and Westport. **Ulsterbus** (☎ 028-9033 3000) has three services daily (one on Sunday) to Belfast and Enniskillen. **Feda O'Donnell** (☎ 074-974 8114) buses from Crolly to Galway stop in Bundoran outside the Holyrood Hotel twice daily, three Friday and Sunday.

SOUTHWESTERN DONEGAL

MOUNTCHARLES TO BRUCKLESS

Apart from some pubs and cafés in Mountcharles and Dunkineely, there are few places to eat, so stock up before leaving Donegal or Killybegs.

Mountcharles

☎ 074 / pop 120

The hillside village of Mountcharles (Moin Séarlas), the first settlement along the coastal road (N56) west of Donegal town, is best known as the birthplace of Séamus MacManus, poet and *seanachaí* (storyteller) who practised the ancient art around the green village pump in the 1940s and 1950s. About 2km south of the village is a safe, sandy **beach.**

Mrs Harvey operates **Clybawn** (☎ 973 5076; Station Rd; s/d €25/50; ⏲ Apr-Sep), a comfortable B&B near the church, with good views of the bay. Rooms with bathroom are €27 per person.

The road west to Bruckless passes through the village of **Inver**, which has its own small beach.

Dunkineely

☎ 074 / pop 799

A little further west at Dunkineely (Dún Cionnfhaolaidh or Dún Cionnaola), a minor road runs down the promontory to the beach at **St John's Point**. There's no sand, but there are good coastal views, and the waters around the point are a prime **diving** site.

Blue Moon Hostel (☎ 973 7264; Main St; tent/dm €5/10) is an unremarkable-looking IHO hostel. It is surprisingly comfy, and offers a range of services, including two kitchens, a washer/dryer and plenty of information on local goings-on such as deep-sea diving and sea-angling. You can also camp on the grounds.

Bruckless

☎ 074 / pop 200

Bruckless (An Bhroclais) is about 2km west of Dunkineely. **Horse riding** and **pony trekking** are available at **Deane's Equestrian Centre** (☎ 973 7160; Darney, Bruckless).

Gallagher's Farm Hostel (☎ 973 7057; tent/dm €6/11) is a clean, attractive IHH hostel, with 18 beds in converted farm outbuildings. It is halfway between Dunkineely and Bruckless. Campers have separate kitchen facilities from hostellers. The hostel supplies guests with a list of walks in the area.

The ivy-clad Georgian **Bruckless House** (☎ 973 7071; bruc@bruckless.com; r €90-100; ⌚ Apr-Sep) is a luxury B&B with all the trimmings and even a traditional cobbled farmyard. Absolutely gorgeous.

Getting There & Away

Bus Éireann (☎ 972 1101) bus No 494 leaves Donegal for Killybegs (€3, 35 minutes) four times daily Monday to Saturday, stopping near the Village Tavern in Mountcharles, the Inver post office, Bruckless and Dunkineely Furniture Centre in Dunkineely.

KILLYBEGS

☎ 074 / pop 2426

Killybegs (Ceala Beaga), whose name translates as 'the little churches', is Ireland's most important fishing port, and some travellers may be put off by the smell created by the large fishmeal processing plant on the eastern outskirts. The town is also noted for its handmade carpets.

The Bank of Ireland, just up from the harbour on Main St, has an ATM and bureau de change. The post office is opposite the harbour.

Sights & Activities

A right turn in town up the steep hill brings you to St Catherine's Church, which contains the **tomb of Niall Mór MacSweeney**, who was head of the MacSweeney clan, one of Donegal's ruling families before the Flight of the Earls in 1607. The tombstone is carved with Celtic-style patterns and the figure of a *gallowglass*. *Gallowglasses* were Scottish mercenaries who first came to the north and west of Ireland in the late 13th century. At first they were only hired by the big chiefs, but by the late 15th century their descendants were being employed around the country as personal bodyguards and constables.

Several operators offer **fishing** expeditions with the opportunity to catch pollock, cod and whiting. **Brian McGilloway** (☎ 973 2444, 087-220 0982; trip per person with/without rod & tackle €50/60) runs fishing trips. To hire the boat for the day costs €350 and it fits between eight and 10 people. The **Harbour Store** (☎ 973 1569; the Harbour), by the wharf, sells fishing gear.

The wild, secluded **Fintragh Bay**, about 3km west, is fun to explore and the water is clean and safe for swimming.

Festivals & Events

The town hosts a huge **Sea Angling Open Boat Competition** (☎ 973 1901) in mid-July.

Sleeping

If you decide to stay in Killybegs and don't like the smell of fish, pick a guesthouse along Fintra Rd on the western outskirts.

Credo House (☎ 973 1364; credohouse@eircom.net; Benroe; s/d €35/70; ⌚ Apr-Sep) A lovely house overlooking the ocean on the Bruckless road, Credo's rooms are extremely well appointed (the room rate includes bathroom). The breakfast is terrific.

Oileán Roe House (☎ 973 1192; Fintra Rd; s/d €35/50; ⌚ mid-Mar–Sep) This is a clean, friendly, two-storey home about 1km from town. It accepts credit cards.

Bay View Hotel (☎ 973 1950; www.bayviewhotel@iol.ie; Main St; s/d €90/120; P) The Bay View is a large, modern, 40-room hotel that dominates the harbour in the centre of Killybegs.

Eating

Sail Inn (☎ 973 1130; Main St; pub grub €3-8, mains €13-21) The Sail Inn has an intimate upstairs restaurant for evening dining, or you can eat snacks or full meals in the colourful downstairs bar where traditional music sessions are held.

Kitty Kelly's (☎ 973 1925; Kilcar Rd; mains €8-14; 6-10pm Easter-Sep) The restaurant here, 5km west of Killybegs, serves fabulous seafood as well as pasta and traditional Irish dishes in a purple-painted, converted farmhouse. Reservations are recommended.

Getting There & Away

Bus Éireann (☎ 912 1309) bus No 494 from Donegal to Killybegs runs three times daily (four times in July and August) Monday to Saturday. Bus No 490 heads west to Kilcar and Glencolumbcille once daily Monday to Friday (twice Saturday). In July and August an extra bus runs daily Monday to Saturday, and buses continue to Malinmore twice daily, Monday to Saturday. The bus stop is outside Hegarty's shop.

McGeehan Coaches (☎ 954 6150) runs a daily service from Glencolumbcille to Dublin leaving from the Street News store by the harbour. Extra buses are laid on in summer.

KILCAR & AROUND

☎ 074 / pop 661

Kilcar (Cill Chártha) and neighbouring Carrick (An Charraig) are good bases for exploring the Slieve League cliffs and the magnificent indented coastline of southwestern Donegal. Kilcar is an important centre for the manufacture of Donegal tweed. Just outside Kilcar is a small, sandy beach.

Tourist information is available from the community centre, **Aísleann Cill Cartha** (☎ 973 8376; Main St; 9am-5.30pm Mon-Fri), which also has an Internet connection (€5 per hour). There are no banks in Kilcar or Carrick. The post office is off Main St past O'Gara's pub.

Studio Donegal

Beside the community centre is the **Studio Donegal** (☎ 973 8194; Kilcar; admission free; 10am-5.30pm Mon, 9am-5.30pm Tue-Thu, 9.30am-5pm Fri), a small tweed factory offering free guided tours. In its shop you can buy tweed by the metre for about €15; you're unlikely to get better prices than this elsewhere in Donegal.

Slieve League

Carrick, 5km northwest of Kilcar, is where you turn off for Teelin and the Bunglass viewing point for **Slieve League**, the highest cliffs in Europe dropping some 600m into the sea. To drive to the cliff edge, be sure to take the turn-off signposted Bunglass from the Killybegs to Glencolumbcille road (R263) at Carrick, and continue beyond the narrow track signposted Slieve League to the one that's signposted Bunglass.

Walks

There are a number of local walks that take in many prehistoric sites. Three walks that start in Kilcar are collectively known as the **Kilcar Way**. From Teelin, experienced walkers can spend a day walking north via Bunglass and the somewhat terrifying, cliff-top **One Man's Path** to Malinbeg, near Glencolumbcille. It shouldn't be attempted in windy conditions or if bad weather is likely to impede visibility.

Festivals & Events

On the first weekend in August, Kilcar, like Killybegs, hosts an **International Sea Angling Festival**, followed almost immediately by the week-long **Kilcar Street Festival**. Contact the community centre for details.

Sleeping

Dún Ulún House (☎ 973 8137; Coast Rd; tent per person €4, dm €12-18, s/d €25/50) Dún Ulún House, at the western end of the village, is an agreeable, friendly establishment. The camp site is across the road ensconced in the tiered hillside (with great views); a shower and toilet block is nearby.

Derrylahan Hostel (☎ 973 8079; derrylahan@eircom.net; Derrylahan, Kilcar; dm/d €10/28) The equally friendly IHH hostel is some 3km west of the village on a working farm. There's a small library, Internet access, plentiful cooking facilities and a group house accommodating 20 people. If you phone from Kilcar or Carrick, Shaun, the owner, will organise a lift to the hostel for you.

Eating

Piper's Rest (☎ 973 8205; Main St; mains €6-14) A lovely thatched pub that serves soup, sandwiches and seafood. Evenings are devoted to traditional music, and Irish is the spoken language.

Restaurant Teach Barnaí (☎ 973 8160; Main St; mains €12-25; ⏲ dinner 6-10pm & also noon-3pm Sun) One of Donegal's best restaurants, the seafood here is given a continental spin.

Getting There & Away

Bus Éireann (☎ 912 1309) bus No 490 connects Kilcar and Carrick with Killybegs and Glencolumbcille once daily Monday to Friday (twice daily Saturday). In July and August an extra bus runs daily Monday to Saturday. **McGeehan Coaches** (☎ 954 6150) runs a daily service from Glencolumbcille to Dublin stopping at Carrick and Kilcar. There are extra buses in summer.

GLENCOLUMBCILLE

☎ 074 / pop 714

The sheer beauty of Glencolumbcille (Gleann Cholm Cille, 'Glen of Columba's Church') is in stark contrast to the desolate landscapes that precede it as you travel westward from Killybegs and Kilcar. The dark turf bog gives way to a lush green valley that has been inhabited since 3000 BC and you'll find plenty of Stone Age remains throughout the collection of tiny settlements. It is believed that the 6th-century St Colmcille (or Columba) founded a monastery here (hence the valley's name) and incorporated Stone Age standing stones called turas into Christian usage by inscribing them with a cross.

At midnight on Colmcille's Feast Day (June 9) penitents begin a walkabout of the *turas* and the remains of Colmcille's church before attending Mass at 3am in the local church.

Information

The **Lace House** (☎ 973 0116; Cashel; ⏲ 10am-6pm Mon-Sat, 1-5pm Sun Apr, Jun & Sep–mid-Nov, 9.30am-9pm Mon-Sat, noon-6pm Sun Jul & Aug) craft shop dispenses information. There are no banks but the post office has a bureau de change.

Folk Village Museum & Heritage Centre

This **centre** (☎ 973 0017; Doonalt; adult/child €2.50/1.90; ⏲ 10am-6pm Mon-Sat, noon-6pm Sun Easter-Sep), 3km west of the village by the beach, was established by Father James McDyer in 1967 (when he also introduced electricity to the area). It comprises several replicated thatched cottages as lived in by people in the 18th and 19th centuries, with genuine period fittings. Admission includes a tour of the site's buildings. The *shebeen* (illicit drinking place) sells unusual local wines (made from things such as seaweed and fuchsias) alongside marmalade and fudge. The old National School is also open to visitors, and there's a short nature trail up the hill behind.

Malinmore Adventure Centre

Overlooking Malin Bay, this **adventure centre** (☎ 973 0123; Malinmore, Glencolumbcille) offers scuba diving, canoeing, snorkelling, fishing, orienteering, boat trips and other activities. Accommodation packages are available.

Beaches

There are two sandy beaches in **Doonalt**, west of Columbcille. Another beach can be found at the end of the road to Malinbeg, where steps descend to a lovely sheltered cove.

Courses

Oideas Gael (☎ 973 0248; www.oideas-gael.com; ⏲ mid-Mar–Oct), at the Foras Cultúir Uladh (Ulster Cultural Foundation) 1km west of the village centre, offers a range of adult courses in the Irish language (beginners welcome) and in traditional culture, from Donegal dancing and marine painting to bodhrán (hand-held goatskin drum) playing and tapestry weaving. Weekend/week-long courses per person with accommodation cost €90/180.

Sleeping

Dooey Hostel (☎ 973 0130; fax 973 0339; tent/dm/d €5/10/22) This friendly, isolated place is the flagship property of the IHO, and is built into the hillside about 1.5km beyond the village. It offers a range of accommodation, including a group house for 20 people with superb views out over Glen Bay. The hostel has six kitchens and, rather surprising for somewhere so remote, it offers wheelchair access. If you're driving, take the turn beside the Glenhead Tavern; if walking or cycling, take a short cut up the track beside the Folk Village.

Malinbeg Hostel (☎ 973 0006; Malinbeg, Glencolumbcille; dm/d €10/28) This is a purpose-built hostel with all the mod cons including en-suite rooms. If you call ahead the owners will pick you up.

Corner House (☎ 973 0021; Cashel, Glencolumbcille; s/d €33/50) Each bedroom has its own shower at this cosy B&B.

Glencolumbcille Hotel (Óstán Ghleann Cholmcille; ☎ 973 0003; fax 973 0222; s/d €55/80) You can't fail to spot this yellow-painted, old-world hotel with its 40 brightly furnished, en-suite rooms. To get there continue past the Folk Village Museum towards Malinbeg.

Eating

Lace House Restaurant (☎ 973 0444; Cashel, Glencolumbcille; mains €5.65-6.25; 9.30am-9pm) As well as fresh fish and chips, and other standard fare, the restaurant, above the shop of the same name, serves delicious home-made soups and desserts.

An Chistin (☎ 973 0213; Glencolumbcille; mains €6.25; 12.30-9.30pm Mon-Fri, 9.30am-9.30pm Sat & Sun) One of the best places to eat is this pleasant café at the Ulster Cultural Foundation. It specialises in seafood but also serves good sandwiches, cakes and pastries.

Shopping

Glencolumbcille Woollen Market (☎ 973 9377) This store is an outlet for Rossan knitwear, manufactured locally, and has a large array of Donegal tweed jackets, caps and ties alongside lamb's-wool scarves and shawls. Also available are Aran sweaters and hand-woven rugs. It's 3km southwest of Cashel on the R263.

Lace House (☎ 973 0116; Cashel, Glencolumbcille) As well as dispensing tourist information, the Lace House sells Rossan knitted garments, jackets and rugs.

Getting There & Away

Bus Éireann (☎ 912 1309) bus No 490 leaves for Killybegs daily with an extra service on Saturday and in July and August.

McGeehan Coaches (☎ 954 6150) leave from outside Biddy's Pub for Donegal and Dublin (€20 return, five hours, twice daily each way). There is an extra service from Dublin to Glencolumcille on Friday. McGeehan also runs to Ardara, Dungloe and Glenties.

MAGHERY & THE GLEN GESH PASS

☎ 074 / pop 640

A tiny picturesque village on the northern edge of the peninsula at the edge of Loughros Beg Bay, Maghery shouldn't detain you for too long, but it's the best place to stop before continuing northeast to Ardara (see below). If you follow the strand that fronts the village westward, you'll get to a rocky promontory full of caves. During Cromwell's 17th-century Irish Destruction Tour, 100 villagers sought refuge from the army but were discovered and massacred except one.

About 1.5km east of Maghery is **Assarancagh Waterfall**, beyond which is the beginning of a 10km marked trail to the **Glen Gesh Pass** (Glean Géis, 'glen of the swans'), one of the most beautiful spots in Europe. It's almost alpine in appearance; cascading mountains and lush valleys dotted with isolated farmhouses and small lakes. If you're driving, you can get to the pass directly from Glencolumbcille by following the road signs for Ardara.

ARDARA & AROUND

☎ 074 / pop 1020

A small heritage town set in aspic, scenically positioned Ardara (Árd an Rátha) is an important manufacturing centre for knitwear and hand-woven tweed.

Tourist information and Internet access (€1.25 for 10 minutes) are available from the Ardara Heritage Centre (see below). On the Diamond there's an Ulster Bank with an ATM; the post office is opposite.

Sights & Activities

ARDARA HERITAGE CENTRE

Ardara Heritage Centre (☎ 954 1704; the Diamond; admission free; 10am-6pm Mon-Sat, 2-6pm Sun Easter-Sep) tells the story of Donegal's role in the weaving industry and gives you the chance to watch a hand-loom weaver. An audiovisual presentation upstairs describes the surrounding area, and there is also a small café.

Festivals & Events

The **Ardara Weavers Fair** has its origins in the 18th century but went into decline early in the 20th century. It was revived and now takes place over the first weekend in June.

Sleeping & Eating

Drumbarron Hostel (☎ 954 1200; the Diamond; dm/d €10/22) A Georgian-style two-storey house with comfortable bunk beds, free hot showers and a large kitchen.

Greenhaven (☎ 954 1129; Portnoo Rd; s/d from €20/40) This is a wonderful B&B with six

COUNTY DONEGAL

comfy rooms and, best of all, a very friendly atmosphere.

Drumbarron House (☎ 954 1200; the Diamond; s/d €25/48) If you fancy home-made bread and scones for breakfast, then try this delightful, welcoming place just across from the hostel.

Green Gate (☎ 954 1546; Ardvally, Ardara; s/d €40/60) This fabulously rustic B&B consists of three traditional cottages with all the mod cons, and has great all-day breakfasts, an extensive library and sweeping views down to the bay.

Nancy's Bar (☎ 954 1187; Front St; mains €8-12) A white-washed pub with a row of mugs over the bar, this small bar has superb seafood and the best chowder we've tasted in a long, long while.

Entertainment

Corner House (☎ 954 1736; the Diamond) This bar has live traditional music at the weekend (nightly from June to September) and invites any visiting musicians to join in.

Nancy's Bar (☎ 954 1187; Front St) Besides the superb food, Nancy's is also the best – and most authentic – place for a quiet drink, except for summer evenings, when live traditional music is usually played.

Shopping

Not unexpectedly, several shops specialise in locally made knitwear, and prices are competitive. You could try **Kennedy's** (☎ 954 1106; Front St), up the hill from the Diamond, or **Francis O'Donnell** (☎ 954 1688; Ardconnell), a weaver fully versed with his profession's rich history – and plenty of stories to illustrate it.

Getting There & Away

In July and August, **Bus Éireann** (☎ 912 1309) bus No 492 from Killybegs stops twice daily Monday to Saturday, in each direction, outside O'Donnell's in Ardara. The rest of the year, these buses run on Tuesday, Thursday and Friday only. June to mid-September **McGeehan Coaches** (☎ 954 6150) runs a service from the post office to Dublin twice daily. The Glencolumbcille to Dublin bus via Glenties stops in Ardara twice daily (once Sunday).

Getting Around

Don Byrne's of Ardara (☎ 954 1156; Main St), east of the centre, is part of the Raleigh Rent-a-Bike scheme.

DAWROS HEAD

The landscape of this peninsula north of Ardara consists of numerous tiny lakes surrounded by gentle, rolling hills, and makes good walking territory. The twin resort towns of **Narin** and **Portnoo** are packed every summer with holidaymakers from the North and the magnificent Blue Flag beach at Narin is a particularly big crowd puller. At low tide you can walk out to **Iniskeel Island** where St Connell, a cousin of St Colmcille, founded a monastery in the 6th century, but no trace of it remains.

Signposts off the road from Narin to Rosbeg lead 3km to Lough Doon, in the centre of which sits 2000-year-old **Doon Fort**, a fortified oval settlement. To reach it, you need to hire a rowing boat (€5 per hour).

In 1588 the *Duquesa Santa Ana*, part of the Spanish Armada, ran aground off **Tramore Beach**. The survivors temporarily occupied O'Boyle's Island in Kiltoorish Lake, but then marched south through Ardara to Killybegs, where they set sail again in the *Girona*. The *Girona* met a similar fate that year off the Antrim coast in Northern Ireland, with the loss of over 1000 crew.

Sleeping

The remote **Tramore Beach Caravan & Camping Park** (☎ 074-955 1491; fax 955 1492; Rosbeg; small/large tents €9/10) has 24 tent sites among the sand dunes. Take the road from Ardara to Narin then turn left, following the signposts to Tramore Beach.

Narin and Portnoo have B&Bs that generally open April to September. **Roaninish** (☎ 074-954 5207; Narin; s/d €40/58; Jun-Aug; ⊠) is a small B&B with four pleasant rooms (with shower), close to the beach.

Getting There & Away

From Monday to Saturday in July and August **Bus Éireann** (☎ 074-912 1309) bus No 492 runs between Killybegs and Portnoo (€6 one way, twice daily each way).

GLENTIES

☎ 074 / pop 1400

A perennial performer in the Irish Tidy Towns competition, Glenties (Na Gleannta) is a pleasant town with an exquisite setting at the foot of two valleys with a southern backdrop laid on by the Blue Stack Mountains. It's a popular **fishing** destination and there are several pleasant **walks** in the area.

A **summer school** takes place in August in honour of Patrick MacGill (1891–1963), the 'navvy poet' who was sold by his parents at a hiring fair for servants, later escaped and eventually ended up writing for the English Daily Express. His best-known work is Children of the Dead End, something of an autobiography. Glenties is also linked with playwright Brian Friel, who spent most of his summers here; his play (and later film version), Dancing at Lughnasa, is set in the town.

On the main street there's a Bank of Ireland with an ATM and bureau de change, and a post office.

St Connell's Museum & Heritage Centre (☎ 955 1227; Main St; adult/child €2.50/0.60; ⏲ 10am-1pm & 2-5pm Mon-Fri Apr-Sep), beside the old courthouse at the western end of town, has a small collection of local artefacts and some old prison cells.

Also worth checking out is the modern **church** at the Ardara end of town; designed by Liam MacCormack (creator of the church in Creeslough, see Muckish Mountain on p487) it features a huge sloping roof and is testimony that traditionalism and modernity can live quite well side by side.

Sleeping & Eating

Campbell's Holiday Hostel (☎ 955 1491; campbellshostel@eircom.net; Glenties; dm/d €12/28; ⏲ Apr-Oct; 🅿) Clean and spacious, this IHH hostel has comfortable dorms, a couple of kitchens, a laundry room and a bureau de change. It's on the left behind the museum as you enter from Ardara on the N56.

Avalon (☎ 955 1292; Glen Rd; s/d €35/50; ☒) Scenically positioned about 500m from the centre, Avalon has four bedrooms (three with shower).

Highlands Hotel (☎ 955 1111; fax 955 1564; Main St; s/d €40/75; mains €10-18) This relaxed, 20-room hotel dominates the western end of Main St. It serves excellent food in substantial proportions using fresh produce; the menu includes a few vegetarian choices.

Entertainment

Paddy's Bar (☎ 955 1158; Main St) Paddy's is a lively old pub whose walls reverberate to the sound of traditional music several nights a week.

Limelight (☎ 955 1118; Main St) Clubbers from around Donegal flock to the county's largest nightclub, attached to Molloy's Bar, on Friday and Saturday night. The music is predictably charty but the kids love it.

Getting There & Away

From Monday to Saturday in July and August **Bus Éireann** (☎ 074-912 1309) bus No 492 between Killybegs and Portnoo stops in Glenties (twice daily each way). The rest of the year, the bus runs Tuesday, Thursday and Friday only.

McGeehan Coaches (☎ 954 6150) runs a service from Dungloe to Dublin via Glenties (€12/18 one way/return, 4¼ hours, twice daily).

INLAND TO THE FINN VALLEY

This part of Donegal is not well travelled – a blessing if you want to get away on your own for some fishing, hill walking or cycling. The **River Finn** is a good salmon river, especially if there has been heavy rain before the middle of June.

There's good **hill walking** on the Blue Stack Mountains and along the Ulster Way, but you need to be equipped with maps and provisions. Finn Farm Hostel (see Sleeping & Eating, p480) dispenses maps and advice and will even arrange a pick-up at the beginning or end of a walk. A long, one-day trek could start from the hostel and end at Campbell's Holiday Hostel in Glenties or Glenleighan Hostel near Fintown.

The main town is **Ballybofey** (Bealach Féich; pronounced bally-*boh*-fay), linked to adjoining **Stranorlar** by an arched bridge over the Finn. There's a small locally run **tourist office** (☎ 074-913 1840; Main St; ⏲ 9am-5pm Mon-Fri) in the Ballybofey Balor Theatre. In Ballybofey's Protestant church is the grave of Isaac Butt (1813–79), founder of the Irish Home Rule movement. Fishing gear is available from Mr G's Discount Store, Main St.

Fintown (Baile na Finne), 30km northwest on the hillside overlooking Lough Finn, is a much smaller settlement: just a cluster of houses, a shop, post office, garage and pubs lining the main road. Nevertheless, a renovated part of the narrow-gauge **Fintown Railway** (☎ 074-954 6280; Fintown; adult/child €2.50/1.25; ⏲ 11am-5pm Mon-Fri, 11am-6pm Sat & Sun Jul-Sep, 1-4pm Mon-Fri, 1-5pm Sat Jun) between Fintown and Glenties runs scenic excursions alongside Lough Finn on 5km of track.

Sleeping & Eating

Finn Farm Hostel (☎ 074-913 2261; Cappry, Ballybofey; tents/dm/d €6/11/26) is an IHH/IHO hostel on a working farm. It is also a centre for a community work scheme aimed at reviving dying musical traditions, so if you stay you'll be able to hear the musicians practising. It also offers horse-riding lessons and organised walks. Finn Farm is about 2km from Ballybofey; the turning is signposted simply 'Hostel' off the N15 Donegal road.

Caife na Locha (Fintown; meals around €8) is a small place, run by a women's cooperative. It serves light meals and opens the same hours as the Fintown Railway.

Getting There & Away

Bus Éireann (☎ 074-912 1309) express bus No 64 between Galway and Derry via Sligo, Donegal and Letterkenny stops up to six times daily in Ballybofey. Local buses connect Ballybofey with Killybegs and Letterkenny.

McGeehan Coaches (☎ 074-954 6150) runs a Glencolumbcille to Letterkenny bus Monday to Saturday that stops in front of the Fintown post office at 1.25pm (at 5.55pm heading for Glenties, Ardara, Killybegs, Kilcar and Glencolumbcille). There's also a McGeehan Coaches bus from Fintown to Ballybofey at 1.25pm Monday to Saturday, mid-July to August. It stops in Ballybofey en route to Fintown, Killybegs and Glencolumbcille at 5pm.

The **Feda O'Donnell** (☎ 074-974 8114) bus from Crolly to Galway stops in Ballybofey (€16, three hours, twice daily, three Friday and Sunday).

NORTHWESTERN DONEGAL

There are few places in Ireland that are more savagely beautiful than northwestern Donegal. Humans have been unable to tame the landscape, which varies from wild and bleak to the breathtakingly spectacular. The stretch of land between Dungloe and Crolly is a bleak, rocky Gaeltacht known as the Rosses (Na Rossa) containing numerous tiny lakes and a coastline of clean, sandy beaches. Further west, between Bunbeg and Dunfanaghy, the scenery is softer but more stunning – to many visitors, this is the epitome of what unspoilt Ireland should look like. Offshore, the islands of Arranmore and Tory are both beautiful and fascinating to those eager for a glimpse of a more traditional way of life.

Surprisingly, the numbers of tourists are relatively few and mostly from the North, although in recent years the coastline has been the victim of a bungalow blight, as developers have sought to take advantage of – many would say mar – the area's natural beauty.

DUNGLOE & AROUND

☎ 074 / pop 1870

Dungloe (An Clochán Liath), the capital of the Rosses, is the area's busiest town, especially in summer, even though there's nothing to do here except use the town as a base.

The **tourist office** (☎ 952 1297; 🕑 10am-2pm & 3-6pm Mon-Sat, 11am-5pm Sun Jun-Sep) is off Main St behind the Bridge Inn. The Bank of Ireland on Main St has an ATM and bureau de change. The post office is on Quay Rd off Main St past the Midway Bar.

Fishing for salmon and trout is popular and you can get tackle and permits from **Bonner's** (☎ 21163; Main St). The nearest good beach is 6km southwest of town at **Maghery Bay**.

Festivals & Events

In late July/early August, Dungloe hosts the 10-day **Mary from Dungloe Festival**, named after a 1968 hit by the Emmet Spiceland Band. Basically it's a minor version of the more famous Rose of Tralee festival; thousands pack the town for all kinds of raucous fun culminating in a pageant where this year's 'Mary' is selected. The host is usually local boy Daniel O'Donnell, the crooner heart-throb for pensioners throughout England and Ireland. It's fun and chaotic; if you're looking for some quiet time, steer well clear. For more information, contact **Anne Marie Doherty** (☎ 952 1254; www.maryfromdungloe.info).

Sleeping & Eating

Greene's Holiday Hostel (☎ 952 1943; greenesholidayhostel@eircom.net; Carnmore Rd; dm/d €11/28; Ⓟ) A modern IHH hostel, Greene's has 20 comfortable beds, a laundry and also rents bikes for €8 per day.

Crohy Head Hostel (☎ 952 1950; Crohy Head; dm €13; 🕑 Jun-Sep) An isolated house atop scenic Crohy Head (An Cruach) 8km southwest of Dungloe, this 36-bed An Óige hostel has panoramic views over Boylagh Bay. You'll have to bring your own provisions.

Atlantic Guesthouse (☎ 952 1061; www.atlantichousedungloe.com; Main St; s/d €35/70) Smack in the middle of town, this is a decent guesthouse with 10 en-suite rooms. The service is extremely friendly.

For eating there's very little choice beyond pub food and greasy spoon cafés.

Riverside Bistro (☎ 952 1062; Main St; mains €14-20; 🕒 12.30-3pm & 6-10pm) Probably the best place to eat in town, the Riverside is a busy, old-world, candle-lit restaurant serving tasty, wholesome Irish cuisine.

Getting There & Away

Dungloe is served by several private companies but not Bus Éireann.

McGeehan Coaches (☎ 954 6150) runs a service from Dungloe to Dublin (single/return €16.50/24, 4½ hours, two daily, three Sunday) via Glenties and Donegal.

Lough Swilly (☎ 912 2863) runs a Dungloe to Derry service (single/return €18/25, three hours, three daily Monday to Friday, one Saturday) via Burtonport, Crolly, Bloody Foreland, Falcarragh and Letterkenny.

Feda O'Donnell (☎ 974 8114) runs twice weekly from Annagry (Anagaire) to Killybegs via Burtonport, Dungloe (€5, 1¼ hours, 8.10am on Monday and 2.40pm on Sunday), Glenties and Ardara. In the other direction it runs twice on Friday only, stopping in Dungloe at 8.15am and 10pm.

BURTONPORT

☎ 074 / pop 380

The otherwise ordinary port village of Burtonport (Ailt an Chorráin, meaning 'curved ravine') is the embarkation point for Arranmore. Back in 1974 the Atlantis commune was established here by one Jenny James, who practised a form of primal therapy. Her followers became known as 'the Screamers'. Eventually the commune relocated to the Colombian jungle and another group arrived to take its place. The Silver Sisters chose to live a Victorian lifestyle, complete with Victorian dress, and soon bizarre stories were circulating about them. They, too, moved on, allowing Burtonport to sink back into anonymity.

For **fishing** trips contact **Donal O'Sullivan** (☎ 954 2077) at the cabin by the pier.

Cois Na Mara (☎ 954 2079; timothydoherty@hotmail.com; Main St; dm €14; 🕒 Mar-Oct) is a small, 12-bed hostel in the middle of town and is a friendly, easy-going place.

Lobster Pot (☎ 954 2012; Main St; mains €10-20) is a pub with a difference; it is probably the best place in the whole area to sample local seafood. The 'Titanic' shellfish and fish platter (€38) is massive and absolutely delicious.

Feda O'Donnell (☎ 974 8114) runs buses to Burtonport from Dungloe; see Getting There & Away above.

ARRANMORE

☎ 074 / pop 900

The small island of Arranmore (Árainn Mhór), 9km by 5km, has some spectacular cliff scenery, sea caves and sandy beaches. It has been inhabited since the Early Iron Age (800 BC), and a prehistoric triangular fort can be seen on the southern side. The western and northern parts are wild and rugged, with few houses to disturb the sense of isolation. The **Arranmore Way** circles the island (allow three to four hours) and off the southwestern tip is **Green Island**, a bird sanctuary. You'll hear mostly Irish spoken here, although most islanders are bilingual.

Sleeping & Eating

A few minutes' walk from the ferry, **Arranmore Hostel** (☎ 952 0015; fax 952 0014; Leabgarrow; dm/d €13/26; wheelchair access) is a modern, 30-bed hostel. Bed linen is included in the price.

Bonner's Ferryboat Restaurant (☎ 952 0532; Leabgarrow; s/d €22/44; mains around €10) is a short walk from the ferry pier. It is a comfortable B&B with an inexpensive café that serves up basic but tasty dishes.

Entertainment

The island's pubs enjoy a 24-hour licence to cater for the local fishing community; they regularly provide traditional music sessions.

Getting There & Away

The **Arranmore Ferry** (☎ 952 0532) plies the 1.5km from Burtonport to Leabgarrow (return adult/child €9/5, 25 minutes, seven Sunday, eight Monday to Saturday July and August, three Sunday, five Monday to Saturday September to June).

GWEEDORE & AROUND

☎ 074 / pop 1300

Not so long ago, there was virtually nowhere on the Irish mainland as remote as the Irish-speaking district of Gweedore (Gaoth Dobhair). Not anymore. The tiny villages along the rugged coastline between the white, sandy beaches have expanded and grown thanks to the haphazard efforts of developers who have built on virtually every available bit of land. Consequently, Derrybeg (Doirí Beaga) and Bunbeg (Bun Beag) virtually run into each other along the R257, while a few kilometres east on the R258, Gweedore, has been stretched out so as to lose its village feel.

Inland, however, it's a different story. Here, habitations are few and far between, and the only feature breaking up the bleak landscape is the presence of dozens of small fishing lakes.

On the main road in Bunbeg there's an Allied Irish Bank with an ATM and bureau de change, while Derrybeg has a post office. Ferries depart from Bunbeg for Tory Island (see p484).

Walks

One of the most beautiful walks in the area is the **Tullagobegley Walk** (Siúlóid Tullagobegley), a historical trample over **Tievealehid** (Taobh an Leithid; 431m), which was used for centuries by locals carrying corpses to the 13th-century graveyard in Falcarragh before there was one in Gweedore. The 5½-hour walk begins at Lough Nacung (Loch na Cuinge), just east of Gweedore off the main N56. The views from the top of Tievealehid are spectacular: to the north you can see the islands, to the south Dunlewy and Mt Errigal. The path brings you past some 19th-century silvermines to Keeldrum, a small townland on the outskirts of Gortahork, before finishing up at the Tullagobegley graveyard in Falcarragh.

This walk is not waymarked and is generally known only to locals, so we strongly advise that you carry with you an OS Sheet 1 of the area.

Sleeping & Eating

Backpackers Ireland Seaside Hostel (☎ 953 2244; Magheragallon, Derrybeg; dm/d €10/30; ⌚ mid-Mar–Oct) This isolated IHO hostel near the beach has bikes for hire.

Screag an Iolair Hostel (☎ 954 8593; Tor, Crolly; dm/d €15/28; ⌚ Mar-Oct) Surrounded by a rugged, rocky landscape, this beautifully remote, friendly hostel is in a farmyard in the hills above Crolly, southwest of Gweedore on the N56. It has a large selection of second-hand books and offers a free pick-up service if you don't fancy the 5km walk from the main road.

Óstán Radharc na Mara (Seaview Hotel; ☎ 953 1159; fax 953 2238; Bunbeg; s/d €50/100) On the main road, this modern but traditionally furnished hotel has 40 spacious en-suite rooms. Fine bar food is available in **Tábhairne Hughie Tim** (mains around €8; ⌚ 3-9.30pm) or you can dine á la carte in the more formal **Gola Bistro** (mains €11-20; ⌚ 6-10pm).

Entertainment

Leo's Tavern (☎ 954 8143; Meenaleck, Crolly), one of the most famous pubs in Donegal, is owned by Leo and Baba Brennan, parents of Máire, Ciaran and Pól, who were the core of the group Clannad. Another sibling, Enya, needs no introduction to fans of contemporary Irish music. The pub is adorned with various mementos of the successful kids. It is in the townland of Meenaleck, about 3km south of Gweedore on the road to Crolly; it's well signposted.

Getting There & Away

Feda O'Donnell (☎ 954 8114) runs a service twice daily (three Friday and Sunday) from Gweedore to Letterkenny, Donegal, Sligo and Galway.

DUNLEWY & AROUND

☎ 074 / pop 700

The village of Dunlewy (Dún Lúiche) sits at the foot of Mt Errigal beside Lough Dunlewy.

Ionad Cois Locha (Dunlewy Lakeside Centre)

The **lakeside centre** (☎ 953 1699; Dunlewy; admission to house & grounds or boat trip adult/child €4.50/2.75, combined ticket €7.50/5; ⌚ 10.30am-6pm Mon-Sat, 11am-7pm Sun Easter-Oct) reconstructs the home of Manus Ferry, the last of the local weavers, who died in 1975. Visitors can watch the stages of weaving in operation, then go outside to see assorted farm animals, walk along the lake shore, take a boat ride with a storyteller on board to fill them in on local history, geology and folklore, or go pony trekking. In summer there are traditional music concerts. There's an excellent café with a turf fire and craft shop.

Mt Errigal & the Poisoned Glen

Donegal's highest peak, **Mt Errigal** (752m) is both impressive and beautiful, but you don't have to be a mountaineer to scale its summit. The climber's danger, however, is the unpredictable weather, especially on misty, damp days when the mountain is shrouded in cloud and visibility is substantially reduced.

There are two paths to the summit: the easier tourist route, which covers 5km and takes roughly two hours to complete; and the more difficult 3.3km walk along the northwestern ridge, which involves scrambling over scree for about 2½ hours. Details of both routes are available at the Dunlewy Lakeside Centre.

There are plenty of tales as to how **Poisoned Glen** came to be so called. Legend has it that the ancient one-eyed giant king of Tory, Balor, was killed here by his exiled grandson, Lughaidh, whereupon the poison from his eye split the rock and poisoned the glen. The truth, however, is just a little more prosaic. Originally it was called An Gleann Neamhe (the Heavenly Glen) because its beauty inspired locals to think of it as heaven, but when an English cartographer was mapping the area, he inadvertently marked it as An Gleann Neimhe – the Poisoned Glen.

It's possible to walk through the glen, although some of the ground is rough and boggy. From the lakeside centre a return walk along the glen is about 12km and takes from two to three hours.

Sleeping

Backpackers Ireland Lakeside Hostel (☎ 074-953 2133; Dunlewy; dm €10; ⏲ mid-Mar–Oct) Sister hostel to the one just outside Derrybeg (see p482), it has pretty much the same facilities including bike hire.

Errigal Hostel (☎ 074-953 1180; www.irelandyha.org; Dunlewy; dm €14) Just 2km north of Dunlewy at the base of Mt Errigal, the An Óige hostel has 46 comfortable beds. There is no kitchen, however.

GLENVEAGH NATIONAL PARK

The lake-filled valley of **Glenveagh National Park** (Pairc Naísúnta Ghleann Bheatha; park admission adult/concession €2.50/1.20; ⏲ 10am-6.30pm mid-Mar–early Nov; last admission 1½ hrs before closing) is one of the most beautiful parts of the county. It's a 16,500-sq-km protected area that is overlooked by the Derryveagh Mountains and is home to plenty of wildlife, including the golden eagle, which was hunted to extinction in the area during the 19th century but was reintroduced in 2000.

Yet such serenity had a heavy price. The land was once farmed by 244 tenants who were forcibly evicted by landowner John George Adair in the winter of 1861 because their presence obstructed his view of the valley. Adair put the final touches on his paradise in 1870–73 by building Glenveagh Castle, while his wife Adelia introduced two things that define the national park's appearance: the herd of red deer and the rhododendrons. Green fingers and a love of animals notwithstanding, the Adair name wasn't a popular one in the area for a long time thereafter. Even today, in a land were feuds and resentments have real staying power, mention of Adair is often met with dripping scorn.

In 1929 the property was acquired by Kingsley Porter, Professor of Art at Harvard University, but he disappeared mysteriously in 1933 (presumed drowned), and six years later the estate was bought by Henry McIlhenny, once described by Andy Warhol as 'the only person in Philadelphia with glamour'. In 1975 he sold the whole kit and caboodle to the Irish government and it is now administered by Dúchas (a government department).

The park's features include a nature trail through woods of Scots pine and oak to a stretch of blanket bog, a viewing point that's a short walk behind the castle, and several lakes, the largest of which is Lough Beagh.

The cleverly designed **Glenveagh Visitor Centre** (☎ 074-913 7090; Churchill) has a 20-minute audiovisual display on the ecology of the park and the infamous Adair. There's also an imaginative toy-theatre representation of the story. The restaurant serves hot food and snacks, and the reception sells the necessary midge repellent, as vital in summer as walking boots and waterproofs are in winter.

The park opens year-round; camping is not allowed.

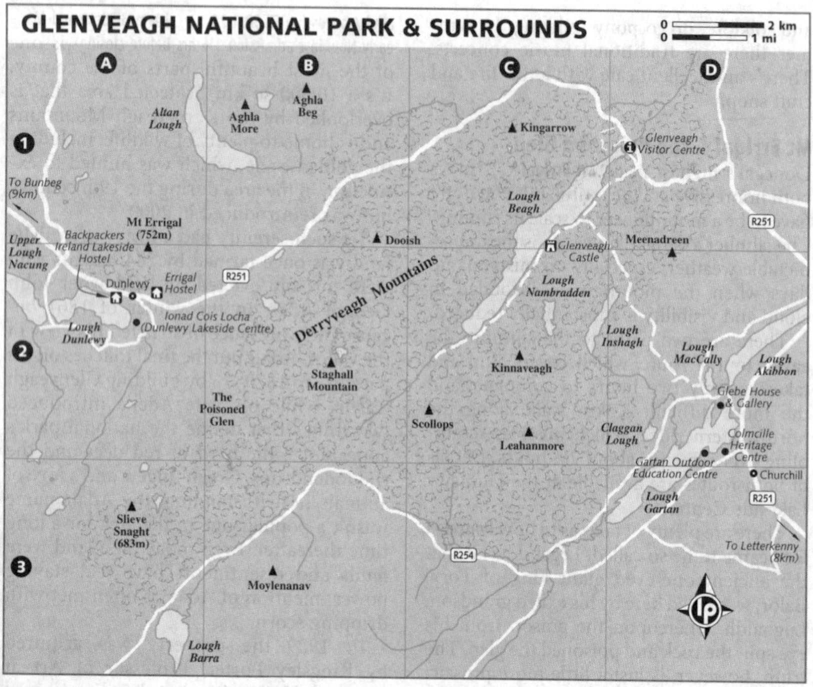

COUNTY DONEGAL

Glenveagh Castle

The **castle** (adult/child €2.50/1.20; 10am-6.30pm mid-Apr–Sep, 10am-6.30pm Sat-Thu Oct–early Nov) was modelled in miniature on Scotland's Balmoral Castle. Henry McIlhenny made it a comfortable home with lots of reminders of the deer hunting once so important to upper-class life.

A guided tour takes in a series of rooms that look as if McIlhenny just left them. Some of the nicer ones, including the tartan-draped music room and the guest room for female visitors, are in the round tower. The drawing room has a splendid 300-year-old Adams-style fireplace bought by McIlhenny from the Ards estate near Dunfanaghy.

On a dry day the gardens are spectacular. They were nurtured for decades and include a variety of features: a terrace, an Italian garden, a walled kitchen garden, and the Belgian Walk built by Belgian soldiers who stayed here during WWI.

The last guided tours of the castle leave about 45 minutes before closing time. Admission is on top of the national park admission charge. Free minibuses run from the visitor centre to the castle roughly every 15 minutes.

BLOODY FORELAND

Bloody Foreland (Cnoc Fola) gets its name from the red colour of the rocks at sunset, and the road to it is wonderfully remote, scenic and ideal for cycling.

Foreland Heights (☎ 074-913 1785; Bloody Foreland, Gweedore; s/d €40/70; Apr-Sep) is a small, old-fashioned, 12-room hotel. The main thing going for it is its location at the head of the foreland with magnificent views of the cliffs and ocean.

TORY ISLAND

☎ 074 / pop 180

There have been people living on remote, treeless, weather-beaten Tory Island (Oileán Thóraigh) for over 5000 years, but most Donegal locals – never mind outsiders – have never actually visited. Only 11km north of the mainland, Tory is worth a visit as it is one of the last places in Ireland that holds on to, rather than simply paying lip service to, traditional Irish culture. The island has its own dialect of Irish and even has a king (see the boxed text below), but it is best known for its unique art form, known as naïve art, first brought to the attention of the world by English painter Derek Hill.

Life on Tory has never been easy, and in 1974, after an eight-week storm that lashed the island mercilessly, the government made plans to evacuate the island permanently. Thankfully, this did not happen, due in part to the efforts of Fr Diarmuid Ó Peícín, who spearheaded an international campaign to raise funds, which were used to create a proper ferry service, establish a dependable electrical supply and update many of the island's facilities. The demise of the fishing industry has brought its own share of problems, namely unemployment, but the community has doggedly persevered and continues to thrive.

The island has just one pebbly beach and two recognisable villages: West Town (An Baile Thiar), containing most of the island's facilities, and East Town (An Baile Thoir). In recent years, construction has led to the naming of two other 'villages': Middletown and New Town.

Sights & Activities

St Colmcille is said to have founded a monastery here in the 6th century. The only remains of this monastic era are near West Town: the **Tau Cross**, a small undecorated T-shaped cross on the pier, and a **round tower**, with a circumference of nearly 16m, built of rounded beach-stones and rough granite, with a round-headed doorway some distance above the ground.

The island is a wondrous place for **bird-watching**: over 100 species of sea bird inhabit the island, and among the cliffs in the northeast you can see colonies of puffin. The southwest is topographically quite different: very flat but with some dangerous offshore rocks.

The Tory **school of primitive painters**, whose work is also known as naïve art and generally depicts island life, has been exhibited around Europe. The most accomplished was James Dixon, who started painting in his 60s, when he was inspired by (or rather thought he could do better than) the English artist Derek Hill (see Glebe House & Gallery, p491). He died in 1970. You can see and buy their work in the Dixon Gallery near the harbour.

Sleeping & Eating

The two villages have a number of B&Bs.

Grace Duffy's (☎ 913 5136; East Town; s/d €28/50; dinner €12; ⏲ May-Oct; ⊠) This welcoming B&B has three comfy bedrooms available (two with showers) and uses organically grown food.

Óstán Thóraigh (☎ 913 5920; fax 913 5613; West Town; s/d €50/80; mains €8; ⏲ Apr-Dec) Óstán Thóraigh is a modern, 14-room hotel where you can get good pub food or full meals.

Caife an Chreagáin (☎ 913 5856; West Town; meals around €10) This small café serves mainly snacks and light meals.

Entertainment

Club Soisialta Thóraigh (Tory Social Club; ☎ 916 5121; West Town) The island's most important social centre, the club regularly presents *ceilidhs* (traditional music and dancing sessions).

Óstán Thóraigh (☎ 913 5920; West Town) Besides serving good food, the pub at this hotel is a relaxed place for a drink and hosts regular traditional music sessions.

IRELAND'S ONLY MONARCH

With an earring and a blue fisherman's cap, Patsy-Dan Rogers doesn't look much like a royal, but he is the official King of Tory. He lives in an ordinary house, runs a pub and is a painter of some renown – hardly the qualities that one associates with a monarch. Yet it is these qualities, coupled with his friendliness and the warmth and wisdom of his speech, that make him so popular.

If the truth be told, he is more of a mayor than a king, as he was elected to the post in 1995 – but as the job is unsalaried he is supported in part by contributions from the islanders. His paintings are regularly exhibited and sold in galleries throughout Ireland and the UK, but he doesn't ignore his royal duties and usually greets visitors getting off the ferry. He is always ready to answer a question or tell a story – and he has plenty of them. The world's current monarchical crop could learn a thing or two from Tory's king, at least in how to earn the respect of one's subjects!

Getting There & Away

Donegal Coastal Cruises (Turasmara Teo; ☎ 953 1340) operates a boat service from Bunbeg (adult/child/student return €20/10/16, daily June to September, Monday to Friday October to May) and Magheraroarty (adult/child/student return €20/10/16, two daily June to September, with an extra trip daily July and August), which is reached by turning off the N56 at the western end of Gortahork near Falcarragh. The road is signposted Coastal Route/Bloody Foreland.

There's also a seasonal service from Port-na-Blagh, 2km east of Dunfanaghy (adult/child/student return €20/10/16, Wednesday July and August).

Be sure to call ahead, as weather and tides can affect sailings.

Getting Around

Bike hire is available from **Rothair ar Clós** (☎ 916 5614) in West Town.

FALCARRAGH & AROUND

☎ 074 / pop 1620

Falcarragh (An Fál Carrach) is a rather unremarkable resort village, but there's a good beach nearby. Together with neighbouring Gortahork (Gort an Choirce), it has a significant Irish-speaking community. The Bank of Ireland at the eastern end of Main St has an ATM and bureau de change, and the post office is at Main St's western end.

Sights & Activities

You can reach the **beach** (4km away) by following signs marked An Trá from either end of Main St. The beach is superb for walking, but swimming is unsafe because of the currents.

The grey bulk of **Muckish Mountain** (670m) is a distinctive landmark that dominates the coast between Dunfanaghy and the Bloody Foreland. From the top, on a fine day, there are sweeping panoramic views to Malin Head and Tory Island. It can be climbed from southeast of Falcarragh by way of the inland road through Muckish Gap.

Sleeping & Eating

Ferndale (☎ 916 5506; Falcarragh; s/d €32/50; ⏲ May-Sep) Set in a carefully manicured garden only 200m northwest of the centre, Ferndale has four comfy bedrooms, one of which has its own shower.

Cuan-na-Mara (☎ 913 5327; Ballyness, Falcarragh; s/d €35/54; ⏲ Jun-Sep; ⊠) Ballyness Bay and Tory Island are visible from this four-room, rural B&B, about 1km from town.

Óstán Loch Altan (☎ 913 5267; fax 916 5241; Gortahork; s/d €50/90; mains €14-21) This is the best hotel in the locality, with comfortable rooms. The restaurant serves up pretty good fare too, of the steak, salmon and lamb variety.

Maggie Dan's (☎ 916 5630; An Phanc, Gortahork; pizzas €5-9; ⏲ 6pm-midnight) A little bit of bohemia in the countryside, this is one of the best spots to relax and enjoy a truly tasty pizza. Highly recommended.

Entertainment

Falcarragh (and Gortahork) has a number of pubs that come alive at night especially in summer. The **Shamrock Lodge** (☎ 913 5192; Main St) is popular with younger people, but our favourite is **Teach Ruairi** (☎ 913 5428; Beltany, Gortahork), a beautiful traditional bar about 1km west of Gortahork, signposted off the Gweedore road. There is live traditional music most nights, and the atmosphere is as authentic as can be.

Getting There & Away

The **Feda O'Donnell** (☎ 954 8114) bus from Crolly stops in front of the phone box on Main St, Falcarragh twice daily Monday to Saturday (three Friday and Sunday). From Falcarragh it travels on to Letterkenny (€4, one hour) and Galway (€20, five hours).

The **John McGinley** (☎ 913 5201) bus leaves for Dublin at 7.25am daily (single/return €12/20, five hours) with extra trips Monday, Thursday, Friday and Sunday. The **Lough Swilly** (☎ 912 2863) Dungloe to Derry bus stops in Falcarragh twice daily Monday to Friday, three times on Saturday (single/return €6/9, 2½ hours).

DUNFANAGHY & AROUND

☎ 074 / pop 850

Easily the most attractive village along this stretch of coast, Dunfanaghy is unassumingly elegant, thanks to its partly Presbyterian heritage which sets it apart from other villages in the area. Even today, the village is roughly 50% Protestant, and their numbers inflate during the holidays when Northerners descend on the place for sun and seaside fun.

Dunfanaghy is blessed with the fabulous **Killyhoey Beach**, a wide, sandy, virtually empty beach that leads right into the heart of the village. **Marble Hill Beach**, about 3km east of town in Port-na-Blagh, is more secluded and is very popular, and is usually crammed in summer.

The Allied Irish Bank opposite the Carrig Rua Hotel has no ATM, but you'll find one in Ramsey's Shop, and the **post office** (Main St; 9am-1pm & 2-5.30pm Mon-Sat) has a bureau de change.

Dunfanaghy Workhouse

After the passage of the Poor Law in 1838, workhouses were set up around Ireland to accommodate and employ the destitute in conditions deliberately intended to be uncomfortable. Men, women, children and the sick were separated from one other, and their lives were rigorously governed, with hard work the order of the day. Dunfanaghy's workhouse opened in 1845, just before the onset of the Famine, which caused the number of residents to multiply. By 1847 it was expanded to accommodate some 600 people, double the number originally planned.

The workhouse, west of the centre up past the post office, is now a small **heritage centre** (913 6540; Main St; adult/concession €3/1.25; 10am-5pm Mon-Sat, noon-5pm Sun mid-Mar–Sep), which tells the history of the Famine in a series of audiovisual presentations in different rooms.

Dunfanaghy Gallery

Just up the road from the heritage centre, **Dunfanaghy Gallery** (913 6224; Main St; admission free; 10am-7pm Mon-Sat) started life as a fever hospital. Nowadays it houses art and crafts.

Horn Head

Horn Head (Corrán Binne) has some of Donegal's most spectacular coastal scenery and plenty of birdlife. The towering, dramatic headland has quartzite cliffs over 180m high, but the route can be perilous at times.

An alternative route is to go by bike or car from the Falcarragh end of Dunfanaghy. The road circles the headland and offers tremendous views on a fine day: Tory, Inishbofin, Inishdooey and tiny Inishbeg islands to the west; Sheep Haven Bay and the Rosguill Peninsula to the east; Malin Head to the northeast; and even the coast of Scotland.

Ards Forest Park

The **park** (admission free; 10.30am-4pm Sat & Sun Easter-Jun & Sep, 10.30am-9pm Jul & Aug), about 3km southeast of Dunfanaghy off the N56, is a wildfowl sanctuary and has marked nature trails varying in length from about 2km to 13km. It covers the northern shore of the Ards Peninsula and there are walks to its clean beaches. In 1930 the southern part of the peninsula was taken over by Capuchin monks; the grounds of their friary buildings are open to the public.

Doe Castle

Doe Castle (Caisléan na dTuath; Creeslough) was once the stronghold of the Scottish MacSweeney family, who were employed by the O'Donnells. Built in the early 16th century, it was constantly fought over by the MacSweeney brothers. Early in the 17th century it passed into English hands and was repaired and inhabited until well into the 19th century. The curious slab that rests against the tower near the entrance is thought to be the tomb of one of the MacSweeneys. The castle is picturesquely sited on a low promontory with water on three sides and a moat hewn out of the rock on the landward side. The best view is from the Carrigart to Creeslough road. At the time of writing it wasn't open to the public, but an ongoing restoration was to be completed by the end of summer 2003.

The castle is 16km from Dunfanaghy on the Carrigart road and is clearly signposted.

Muckish Mountain

The distinctive shape of Muckish Mountain (670m) – when it's not shrouded in the cloud and mist that locals call *smir* – is an eye-catching landmark and also a good climb. You can get to it via the nondescript village of **Creeslough,** 11km south of Dunfanaghy on the N56 Letterkenny road and home to our candidate for most beautiful **modern church** in Ireland. Designed by Liam McCormack, its shape is intended to mirror that of the mountain behind it. To get to Muckish, take a right about 2km northwest of the village and continue for about 6km, where a rough track begins the ascent.

Activities

WALKING

You could easily spend a day walking this area. For an exhilarating walk, take the road from Dunfanaghy to Horn Head (the right-hand fork at the top of the village) and continue until you get to the bridge. Immediately after crossing go through the gate on your left and continue along the track until you reach the dunes. A well-beaten path will lead you to the magnificent **Tramore Beach**, which is usually totally empty. Turn left and follow the beach to the end, where you can find a way up onto a path that leads north to **Pollaguill Bay**. From the bay you can continue to the cairn at the end of the bay and follow the coastline for a stupendous view of the 20m **Marble Arch**, carved out by the sea.

A shorter walk begins at Marble Hill Beach in Port-na-Blagh. Take the path on the left side of the beach past the cottage and work your way about 500m through the brush and along the top of the cliff until you reach **Harry's Hole**, a small crevice in the cliff that is popular with daredevil kids, who dive 10m into the water below. The surrounding rocks are a terrific place to hang out on, especially if you want to get away from the throng on the beach.

Finally, you can walk the entire length of **Killyhoey Beach** by crossing onto the golf course at Port-na-Blagh; behind the 9th green a path leads you onto the beach from where you can walk right into the village.

GOLF

You can play at **Dunfanaghy Golf Club** (☎ 913 6335; green fee weekday/weekends €25/30), a gorgeous 18-hole links course just outside the village on the Port-na-Blagh road. The views from the 9th and 10th tee-boxes are simply spectacular.

HORSE RIDING

This is a terrific way of exploring the expansive beaches and surrounding countryside. It can be arranged through **Arnold's Hotel** (see Sleeping below), which also offers **birdwatching**, **painting** and **photography** holidays.

SEA-ANGLING

Richard Bowyer (☎ 913 6640; Port-na-Blagh) and **Pat Robinson** (☎ 913 5062; Port-na-Blagh) organise sea-angling trips from the small pier in Port-na-Blagh between Easter and September.

WINDSURFING

Windsurfing lessons and gear rental are available through **Marble Hill Windsurfing** (☎ 913 6231; the Cottage, Marble Hill, Port-na-Blagh; 🕓 10am-7pm Mon-Sat, 11am-7pm Sun Jul & Aug). An eight-hour course costs €120, while two-hour Pico lessons are available for €40.

Sleeping

Corcreggan Mill Cottage Hostel (☎ 913 6409; millhostel@corcreggan.com; Dunfanaghy; tent €6, dm €11-14, d €28-32) The dorms at this beautiful IHH hostel 4km southwest of Dunfanaghy on the Falcarragh road (N56) are in a 200-year-old former kiln house, but it's the private rooms that are really special: they're in a converted, mahogany railway car that has been fixed into the old loading bay. It's close to Tramore Beach and there's also a pretty decent Chinese restaurant (see Jade Garden below) on the premises as well as three kitchens. Buses stop outside.

Whins (☎/fax 916 3481; Kill, Dunfanaghy; s/d €38/56) With lovely rooms and a gorgeous garden, this is one of the better options in town, about 750m south of the village overlooking the golf course and the beach. It also accepts credit cards.

Rosman House (☎/fax 913 6273; Figart, Dunfanaghy; s/d €46/60; ⊠) The six bedrooms in this modern, clean B&B on a working farm are all en suite and have great views. Credit cards are accepted here.

Carrig Rua Hotel (☎ 913 6133; fax 913 6277; Main St; s/d €55/110) A hotel with a tradition of good service and friendliness. Relaxed and easygoing, the rooms are neat without being spectacular. The room rate includes breakfast. Good food is available in the Highwayman Bar (mains €8-11), or in the more formal **Sheep Haven Room Restaurant** (mains €13-19, 🕓 6-9pm).

Arnold's Hotel (☎ 913 6208; fax 913 6352; Main St; s/d €60/120; 🕓 mid-Mar–Nov) Arnold's is a big, 32-room hotel overlooking Sheep Haven Bay.

Eating

Muck 'n' Muffin (☎ 913 6780; Main Sq; sandwiches €5-6; 🕓 10am-5pm Mon-Sat, 11am-5pm Sun) The perfect place for a quick informal lunch, this café upstairs from a craft shop serves a fabulous open prawn sandwich and a terrific chicken fajita.

Jade Garden (☎ 913 6900; Corcreggan Mill; 3-course early dinner €12.50; 🕓 4-11pm Tue-Sun) This new restaurant on the Corcreggan Hill Cottage Hostel premises serves up superior quality Chinese cuisine – nothing too out there, but altogether good food.

Mill (☎ 913 6985; Figart, Dunfanaghy; dinner €34; 🕑 7-9pm Tue-Sun) If you're looking for a special meal this highly recommended restaurant, at the edge of Dunfanaghy on the Falcarragh road, is hard to beat. Leave some room for dessert. Reservations are necessary.

Cove (☎ 913 6300; Port-na-Blagh; 4-course dinner €35; 🕑 6-10pm Wed-Mon & 1-4pm Sun) Dunfanaghy's newest culinary success features a mix of fish and meat dishes done to near perfection.

Getting There & Away

Feda O'Donnell (☎ 954 8114) buses from Crolly to Galway stop in the square Dunfanaghy twice daily Monday to Saturday, three Friday and Sunday.

John McGinley (☎ 913 5201) buses between Falcarragh and Dublin stop in Dunfanaghy; see p486 for details. The **Lough Swilly** (☎ 912 2863) Dungloe to Derry bus stops in Dunfanaghy three times daily Monday to Saturday (single/return €7/10, 1½ hours).

LETTERKENNY & AROUND

LETTERKENNY

☎ 074 / pop 7900

Letterkenny (Leitir Ceanainn) grew considerably after Derry, 34km northeast, was cut off from its hinterland by the partition of Ireland, and is now Donegal's largest town. There's not a great deal to detain a tourist, although it makes a pleasant enough stop en route to or from Derry. It's not a bad spot to base yourself in, especially if you're reliant on public transportation to explore the surrounding area.

Orientation & Information

Main St, said to be the longest high street in Ireland, runs from Dunnes Stores at one end to the courthouse at the other and divides into Upper and Lower Main Sts. At the top of Upper Main St there is a Y-junction: High Rd veers left, while Port Rd goes right and down to the bus station and the road out to Derry and Dublin.

The **Northwest Tourist Office** (☎ 912 1160; Derry Rd; 🕑 9am-5pm Mon-Sat, noon-3pm Sun Jun-Aug, 9am-5pm Mon-Fri Sep-May), run by Fáilte Ireland (Irish Tourist Board), has great information but is inconveniently located about 1.5km north of town and can only be accessed via the southbound lane; you could walk there from the roundabout where the buses stop. Alternatively, the local chamber of commerce has a good website at www.destinationletterkenny.com.

Along Main St are branches of the Allied Irish Bank, Bank of Ireland and Ulster Bank, all with ATMs. The post office is on Upper Main St almost opposite the Central Bar.

You can surf the Internet on the lower floor of **Four Lanterns** (☎ 912 0440; Lower Main St; €2/15min), a fast-food outlet.

Sights & Activities

The Gothic-style **St Eunan's Cathedral** (1901) sits west of the centre on Sentry Hill Rd (take Church Lane up from Main St) and contains stained-glass windows and much intricate Celtic carving.

The small, modern **Donegal County Museum** (☎ 912 4613; High Rd; admission free; 🕑 11am-12.30pm & 1-4.30pm Tue-Fri, 1-4.30pm Sat), on the left past the leisure centre, has a collection of local archaeological finds, including some interesting Iron Age stone axe heads and early Christian material. Downstairs there are temporary displays and some telling photos about the realities of life in 19th-century rural Ireland to counterbalance the rather rosy version on display upstairs.

There are some **salmon and trout** rivers and lakes surrounding Letterkenny. The Letterkenny Anglers Association opens to visitors; membership and permits are available from **Brian McCormick's Sports & Leisure** (☎ 912 7833; 56 Upper Main St).

Festivals & Events

The **Letterkenny Arts Festival** (☎ 912 7856) is a four-day international festival of music and dance held at the end of August. It features a variety of music, from Celtic rock to folk and jazz, and includes a crafts day and competitions.

Sleeping

Port Hostel (☎ 912 5315; fax 912 4768; Port Rd; dm/d €11/25) This secluded IHO hostel is at the end of a lane behind the An Grianán Theatre.

Arch Hostel (☎ 915 7255; Upper Corkey, Pluck; dm €11; ⌚ Jul-Aug) Admittedly six beds in a converted stable loft doesn't sound like much, but this remote IHO hostel, 10km east of Letterkenny off the Derry road, is lovely and secluded; call ahead to arrange pick-up.

Oakland (☎ 912 5529; 8 Oakland Pk; s/d €28/44; ⌚ Feb-Dec) A lovely white house in a quiet cul-de-sac about five minutes' walk from the bus station.

Castle Grove House Hotel (☎ 915 1118; fax 915 1384; Ramelton Rd; s €70-90) An elegant Georgian house about 5km out of town toward Ramelton, Castle Grove is a luxurious spot set in its own grounds. Breakfast is included.

Holiday Inn (☎ 912 4369; www.holiday-inn.com/letterkenny; Derry Rd; s/d €110/220) The doyen of business hotels, this brand new edition is pretty snazzy; the rooms are all extremely comfy and there's the ubiquitous fitness centre.

COUNTY DONEGAL

Eating

Yellow Pepper (☎ 912 4133; 36 Lower Main St; dinner mains €8-17; ⌚ 9am-10pm) Terrific sandwiches and a mouth-watering selection of seafood dishes are but the highlights at this excellent eatery.

Pat's Pizza (☎ 912 1761; Upper Main St; pizzas €6-10) It's nothing fancy to look at, but the pizzas are all uniformly excellent.

Bakersville (☎ 912 1887; Church La; snacks around €5) Delicious bread, scones, cakes and sandwiches are available from this bakery just off Main St, which has a small eating area and does good coffee.

Entertainment

Cottage Bar (☎ 912 1338; 49 Upper Main St) Locals flock to this emerald-green, character-laden pub with its low ceiling, buzzy atmosphere, open fire, bric-a-brac and Thursday night music sessions.

Central Bar (☎ 912 4088; 58 Upper Main St) With its dark, wood-panelled walls and brass rails, this is one of the better pubs for music; it has a separate nightclub at the weekend.

An Grianán Theatre (☎ 912 0777; Port Rd) An Grianán Theatre is both a community theatre and major arts venue for the northwest, presenting national and international drama, comedy and music. It also has a good café and bar.

Getting There & Away

Letterkenny is a major bus transport hub for northwestern Ireland, with a number of bus companies stopping here. The **bus station** (☎ 912 2863) is by the roundabout at the junction of Ramelton Rd and the Derry road.

Bus Éireann (☎ 912 1309) express bus No 32 runs from Dublin four times daily (three on Sunday) to Letterkenny via Omagh and Monaghan. The Derry to Galway bus No 64 stops at Letterkenny three times daily (twice on Sunday) before continuing to Donegal, Bundoran, Sligo, Knock and Galway. The Derry to Cork express bus No 52, via Letterkenny, Sligo, Galway and Limerick, runs twice daily (once on Sunday). The daily service (bus No 69) from Derry to Westport via Donegal, Sligo and Ballina also stops in Letterkenny.

John McGinley (☎ 913 5201) buses run twice daily Sunday to Thursday (three times Friday, once Saturday) from Annagry to Dublin through Letterkenny and Monaghan.

Lough Swilly (☎ 912 2863) runs services regularly from Derry to Dungloe, via Letterkenny and Dunfanaghy, as well as direct to Letterkenny (single/return €8/11, two hours).

Feda O'Donnell (☎ 954 8114) runs a bus from Crolly to Galway twice daily through Letterkenny and continues to Donegal, Bundoran, Sligo and Galway.

McGeehan Coaches (☎ 954 6150) runs a Letterkenny to Glencolumbcille service daily except Sunday.

Getting Around

A taxi can be ordered from **O'Donnell Cabs** (☎ 912 2444). There's a taxi stand on Main St opposite the square. In summer, you can hire bikes (€13/55 per day/week) from **Church Street Cycles** (☎ 912 6204), near the cathedral.

AROUND LETTERKENNY

Newmills Corn & Flax Mills

In the village of Newmills, 6km southwest of Letterkenny, the restored Dúchas-run **mills** (☎ 074-912 5115; Newmills; adult/concession €2.50/1.20; ⌚ 10am-6.30pm, last tour 5.45pm, mid-Jun–late Sep) feature one of Ireland's largest water mills and a couple of buildings that are 400 years old. The visitor centre explains the role of corn and flax and how they were milled. There's a riverside walk to a two-room, 19th-century flax-worker's cottage and a village forge.

Colmcille Heritage Centre

The patriarch of Irish monasticism, Colmcille (or Columba), was born in Gartan, 17km northwest of Letterkenny. The **heritage centre** (☎ 074-913 7306; Gartan; adult/concession €2/1.50; ⌚ 10.30am-6.30pm Mon-Sat, 1pm-6.30pm Sun, Easter & early May–late Sep), on the shore of Lough Gartan, is his Hall of Fame, with a lavish display on the production of illuminated manuscripts.

Gartan clay is associated with the birth of Colmcille. The story is that Colmcille's mother, on the run from pagans, haemorrhaged during childbirth and her blood changed the soil's colour from brown to pure white. Ever since, the clay has been regarded as a charm. The clay is found only on townland belonging to the O'Friel family, whose oldest son is the only one allowed to dig it up. Ask nicely and the staff may produce some from under the counter.

On the way to the heritage centre you'll also see signs to the ruins of **Colmcille's Abbey** and to the hillside location of the **saint's birthplace**, marked by a cross erected by Cornelia Adair in 1911 (there are great views of the lake from the latter).

To get to the heritage centre, leave Letterkenny on the R250 road to Glenties and Ardara. A few kilometres out of town, turn right on the R251 to the village of Churchill and follow the signs. Alternatively, from Kilmacrennan on the N56 turn west and follow the signs.

Gartan Outdoor Education Centre

The **centre** (☎ 074-913 7032; Gartan, Churchill), 18km northwest of Letterkenny, is set in its own 35-hectare estate on the shores of Lough Gartan. It conducts a variety of courses in summer, such as rock climbing, sea canoeing, windsurfing and hill climbing. Courses are run for both adults and children, groups and individuals, and full details are available on request. Including hostel accommodation, weekend multi-skill courses for adults cost from €125.

Glebe House & Gallery

The early-19th-century **Glebe House** (☎ 074-913 7071; Churchill; adult/concession €2.50/1.20; ⌚ 11am-6.30pm Easter, Sat-Thu only mid-May–Sep), on the shore of Lough Gartan, was once a rectory, then a hotel, and was bought by the artist Derek Hill in 1953 for IR£1000. Hill was born in England in 1916 and worked in Germany before travelling to Russia. He visited Armenia with the intrepid explorer Freya Stark and became interested in Islamic art.

Dúchas-operated Glebe House is worth visiting for its works of art alone, and a fascinating guided tour of the house takes about an hour. Landseer, Pasmore, Hokusai, Picasso, Augustus John, Jack B Yeats and Kokoschka are all represented. The kitchen is full of paintings by the Tory Island artists, including a bird's-eye view of West Town by James Dixon (see p484). The kitchen is done up in a wonderfully folksy style and there's some original William Morris wallpaper in several rooms. Don't miss the unusual bathroom with the forwards-flushing toilet. The gardens are also wonderful.

Doon Well & Rock of Doon

During penal times it was believed that wells had curative properties, and some people still believe this to be true of **Doon Well** (Tobar a' Duin), judging from the bits of cloth left hanging on the nearby bushes. There are good views from the top of the **Rock of Doon** (Carraig a' Doon), which is where the O'Donnell kings were crowned.

To get here the most straightforward route is to take the signposted turn-off from the N56 just north of Kilmacrennan (the well and rock are about 1.5km north of the village).

Lifford & Around

☎ 074 / pop 1460

Right on the border and across the River Foyle from Strabane in County Tyrone, the small town of Lifford (Leifear) is usually bypassed by motorists entering from the North. Indeed, there's not much going on in the one-time judicial capital of Donegal (a position now held by Letterkenny, 22km northwest), but there are a couple of attractions to distract you on your journey.

The fine 18th-century courthouse has been converted into a **heritage centre** (☎ 914 1733; Lifford; adult/concession €4/2; ⌚ 9am-5pm Mon & Wed, 9am-8pm Tue & Thu, 9am-6pm Fri, 12.30-8pm Sun) looking at both the historic role of Donegal's Gaelic chieftains and at some of the cases tried in the court and their verdicts. The basement cells where prisoners were kept are a chilling reminder of a penal code that didn't care much for the rights or comforts of the reluctant lodgers.

At Rossiger, 3km north of Lifford off the N14, **Cavanacor House** (☎ 914 1143; Rossiger; adult/concession €3.50/2; 🕑 noon-6pm Tue-Sat, 2-6pm Sun Easter-Sep) is an attractive 17th-century building, once inhabited by Magdalen Tasker, the great-great-great-grandmother of James Knox Polk, 11th president of the USA from 1845 to 1849. King James II is said to have dined beneath a sycamore in the front garden during the siege of Derry in 1689. Three rooms in the house are open to visitors, although the gallery at the back housing the paintings and sculptures created by its current owners is probably more interesting. Painting and pottery workshops take place year-round and the tearoom serves home baking.

GETTING THERE & AWAY

Bus Éireann's (☎ 912 1309) express bus No 32 from Dublin to Letterkenny stops in Lifford up to four times daily. Local buses connect Lifford with Letterkenny, Ballybofey and Strabane.

NORTHEASTERN DONEGAL

ROSGUILL PENINSULA

☎ 074

The sprawling village of **Carrigart** (Carraig Airt) marks the entrance to one of the most beautiful peninsulas in Donegal. The best way to explore Rossguill's scenic splendour is by driving, cycling – or even walking – the 15km Atlantic Drive, signposted to your left as you come into Carrigart from the south. There are plenty of pubs in the village to cure the thirst and a nice, secluded beach at **Trá na Rossan.** On no account should you swim in Boveeghter or Mulroy Bay – both are unsafe. The summer crowds don't linger here, though, preferring instead to travel 4km northward to the fishing village of **Downings**.

There's plenty of social life at night in Downings' pubs, which are often packed with holidaymakers from the North staying at Casey's Caravan Park, while nearby Rosapenna Golf Club is a favourite with golfers.

Golf

The superb links of **Rosapenna Golf Club** (☎ 915 5301; Downings; green fee hotel resident/nonresident €30/50) designed by St Andrew's Old Tom Morris in 1891 and remodelled by Harry Vardon in 1906, is one of the outstanding seaside courses in Ireland. The scenery is spectacular as is the layout, which can challenge even the lowest handicapper. See also the Rosapenna Hotel below.

Sleeping

Casey's Caravan Park (☎ 915 5376; rosapenna@eircom.net; Downings; tent small/large €13/15; 🕑 Apr-Sep) Extremely popular and always busy, this large camp site is next to a Blue Flag beach and within 200m of shops, restaurants and pubs. It usually fills up with caravans so be sure to book first.

Trá na Rosann Hostel (☎ 915 5374; www.irelandyha.org; Downings; dm €12; 🕑 Easter-Sep) Knockout views and a terrific atmosphere are this former hunting lodge's – now an An Óige hostel – biggest draws. The one drawback is that it's 6km east of Downings and you'll have to hitch if you don't have your own wheels.

Mevagh House (☎ 915 5693; fax 915 5512; Milford Rd, Carrigart; s/d €32/50) Next to the Esso service station on the edge of the village, Mevagh has large, clean, bright rooms.

An Crossog (☎/fax 915 5498; Downings; s/d €32/52) An Crossog has four comfy rooms (three with showers) and hires out bikes; it also accepts credit cards.

Beach Hotel (☎ 915 5303; fax 915 5907; Downings; s/d €39/78; 🕑 Apr-Oct) Close to the beach in Downings, this family-run hotel has 20 pleasant rooms, most of which are en suite.

Rosapenna Hotel & Golf Club (☎ 915 5301; www.rosapenna.ie; Downings; s/d €90/180; Mar-Oct) The fanciest hotel in the area, it is only worth staying here if you're looking to play the course as guests can benefit from a whole array of special offers.

Eating

Carrigart is best for food.

North Star (☎ 915 4990; Carrigart; mains €10-16) This busy bar has surprisingly modern décor and serves good pub grub in plentiful proportions.

Weavers Restaurant & Wine Bar (☎ 915 5204; Carrigart; mains €9-15; 🕑 6.30-9.30pm) This would

SOMETHING SPECIAL

Old Glen Bar & Restaurant (☎ 915 5130; Glen, Carrigart; mains €14-21; ⏲ 6-11pm) There's nothing short of wonderful about the whole experience of this pub and restaurant in the middle of the tiny hamlet of Glen. To get there (alas, you'll need your own wheels) you travel through some extraordinarily beautiful scenery, and once there, you won't want to leave. The pub is classic Irish countryside, entirely authentic and serving a sensational pint. At the back of the pub, though, modernity rules and does so in elegant style; the new restaurant serves up a fabulous menu of fish, seafood and meat in a thoroughly contemporary setting. Glen is signposted off the R245 between Creeslough and Carrigart, about 6km south of the latter.

constitute a fancy spot in town, and the menu, though unremarkable, serves up some interesting dishes from a range of cuisines.

Getting There & Around

A local bus connects Carrigart and Downings, but it's of limited use for visitors. You really do need your own transport for this area.

FANAD PENINSULA

The second-most northern point in Donegal, Fanad Head is immediately west of Rossguill but is accessible via Milford, about 25km northeast of Letterkenny. On its western side, **Carrowkeel** (Kerrykeel on some maps) has an attractive location overlooking Mulroy Bay and nearby is the early 19th-century **Knockalla Fort**, built to warn of any approaching French ships. The **Kildooney More portal tomb** is also worth a visit. The small villages of Milford and Rosnakill have little for visitors, but Portsalon does have a beautiful beach and excellent golf course.

The **Lough Swilly** (☎ 074-912 2863) bus leaves Letterkenny twice daily for Milford (single/return €3.50/4.75, one hour). From Milford it takes a further 10 minutes to Carrowkeel and 35 minutes to Portsalon on the eastern side, handy for the Knockalla camp site (see under Portsalon & Fanad Head p494).

The eastern side of the peninsula is more interesting, and both Rathmelton (also spelled Ramelton) and Rathmullan make good bases for a quiet break. Accommodation is relatively limited, so it's wise to book ahead.

Rathmelton

☎ **074 / pop 1900**

On the eastern side, the first town you come to is the slightly faded (but still handsome) heritage town of Rathmelton (Ráth Mealtain). It was founded in the early 17th century by William Stewart, and boasts some fine Georgian houses and stone warehouses. When the railway was routed to Letterkenny instead of Rathmelton, a hush descended on the town.

The National Irish Bank, on the Mall by the River Lennon, has a bureau de change but no ATM. The post office is off the Mall on Castle St.

The **Donegal Ancestry Family Research Centre** (☎ 915 1266; the Quay; admission free; ⏲ 9am-4.30pm Mon-Thu, 9am-4pm Fri) houses an exhibition on the history of Ramelton and also does genealogical research. Coming from Letterkenny turn right at the river and follow it round for about 400m. The ruined **Tullyaughnish Church**, on the hill, is also worth a visit because of the Romanesque carvings in the eastern wall, which were taken from a far older church on nearby Aughnish Island, on the River Lennon.

SLEEPING & EATING

Rathmelton has a number of accommodation and restaurant options.

Lennon Lodge Hostel (☎ 915 1227; Market Sq; dm €14) A hostel with hotel-like facilities, this place has hot showers, central heating, kitchen, laundry, a large common room and TVs in every room. There's also live music in the attached bar Thursday to Sunday nights.

Crammond House (☎ 915 1055; crammondhouse@ramelton.net; Market Sq; s without/with bathroom €23/26.50; ⏲ Apr-Oct) This is an elegant Georgian terraced house at the northern end of Rathmelton.

Meadowell (☎ 915 1125; meadowwell@ramelton.net; Burnside Rd; s/d €30/45; ⏲ Mar-Oct; ⊠) A whitewashed bungalow off the Letterkenny to Rathmullan road, Meadowell is a clean B&B about 500m from the town centre.

Mirabeau Steak House (☎ 915 1138; the Mall; mains €9-18; ⏲ 6-10pm) The Mirabeau, in a

COUNTY DONEGAL

two-storey Georgian house in the town centre facing the river, is Rathmelton's most upmarket restaurant. The cuisine is French with an emphasis on steak and seafood.

Bridge Bar (☎ 915 1833; Bridgend; mains €13-18; 🕑 6-11pm) On the other side of the river, the Bridge Bar is a lovely old pub with a 1st-floor seafood restaurant whose menu includes such dishes as roasted swordfish.

GETTING THERE & AWAY

Lough Swilly (☎ 912 2863) buses connect Rathmelton with Letterkenny (single/return €2.85/3.75, 30 minutes, three times daily Monday to Saturday).

Rathmullan

☎ 074 / pop 820

Like Rathmelton, quiet Rathmullan (Ráth Maoláin) is a sleepy place that's only now catching up with the modern world, although in the 16th to 18th centuries it was the scene of momentous events.

In 1587, Hugh O'Donnell, the 15-year-old heir to the powerful O'Donnell clan, was tricked into boarding a ship at Rathmullan and taken to Dublin as prisoner. He escaped four years later on Christmas Eve and, after unsuccessful attempts at revenge, died in Spain, aged only 30. In 1607, despairing of fighting the English, Hugh O'Neill, the earl of Tyrone, and Rory O'Donnell, the earl of Tyrconnel, boarded a ship in Rathmullan harbour and left Ireland for good. This decisive act, known as the Flight of the Earls, marked the effective end of Gaelic Ireland and the rule of Irish chieftains. In the aftermath of the earls' departure, large-scale confiscation of their estates took place, preparing for the Plantation of Ulster with settlers from Britain.

Wolfe Tone (see p30) was captured in Rathmullan following the 1798 Rising.

The sandy area near the pier outside the heritage centre is the only clean part of the town's beach, but there's a strong smell of fish from the quayside warehouse.

RATHMULLAN HERITAGE CENTRE

This small **heritage centre** (☎ 915 8229; Rathmullan Pier; adult/child €2.50/1.25; 🕑 10am-1pm & 2-5pm Thu-Sat, noon-5pm Sun Easter-Sep) focuses on the Flight of the Earls and will mainly appeal to those with a deep interest in Irish history. It's housed in an early-19th-century fort built by the British when fearing Napoleon's intentions. In lieu of a tourist office, the heritage centre can help with inquiries about local accommodation, sights in the surrounding area and so on.

RATHMULLAN PRIORY

This Carmelite **friary** was founded around 1508 by the MacSweeneys, and it was still in use in 1595 when an English commander, George Bingham, raided the place and took off with the communion plate and priestly vestments. The earls left Ireland forever from just outside the priory. Although a ruin, it looks so well preserved because of Bishop Knox's renovation in 1618; he wanted to use it as his own residence.

SLEEPING & EATING

Rathmullan has three hotels, all quite different in appearance and style.

Pier Hotel (☎ 915 8115; s/d €23/46) This 10-room hotel was originally a 19th-century coaching inn and is very much a family establishment. The room rate includes breakfast.

Rathmullan House (☎ 915 8188; www.rathmullanhouse.com; s/d €105/210; 🏊) About 2km north of town on the shores of Lough Swilly, this genteel country house, with an indoor heated swimming pool and sauna, is set in a beautifully wooded garden.

Fort Royal (☎ 915 8100; www.fortroyalhotel.com; s/d €115/170; 🕑 Apr-Oct) A superb 15-room hotel by the lake where the service is meticulous and friendly. It has its own private beach and golf course.

Dinner at all three of these hotels costs around €35.

An Bonnan Bùi (☎ 915 8453; mains €10-17; 🕑 6-11pm Thu-Mon) Near the Pier Hotel, An Bonnan Bùi's imaginative menu mixes Italian with Portuguese, Brazilian and Middle Eastern dishes.

GETTING THERE & AWAY

The **Lough Swilly** (☎ 912 2863) bus from Letterkenny arrives in Rathmullan (single/return €2.80/3.50, 45 minutes, twice daily) en route to Milford, Carrowkeel and Portsalon (morning bus only).

Portsalon & Fanad Head

The appeal of tiny Portsalon (Port an tSalainn), once a popular holiday resort, lies

COUNTY DONEGAL

in its long, golden, sandy Blue Flag beach that's safe for swimming.

Portsalon Golf Club (☎ 915 9459; Portsalon; green fees weekday/weekend €30/35) is a marvellously scenic 18-hole links course.

Knockalla Caravan & Camping Park (☎ 074-915 9108; Portsalon; tents €11; mid-Mar–mid-Sep) is close to the beach at Portsalon. It has a kitchen, laundry, shop, games room and outdoor play area for kids.

It's another 8km to the rocky promontory of Fanad Head, the best part of which is the scenic drive there. The lighthouse here overlooks Lough Swilly.

INISHOWEN PENINSULA

The Inishowen (Inis Eoghain) Peninsula, with Lough Foyle to the east and Lough Swilly to the west, reaches out into the Atlantic and extends to Ireland's northernmost point: Malin Head. The landscape is typically Donegal: rugged, desolate and mountainous. Ancient sites abound, but there are also some wonderful beaches and plenty of places where travellers can go off alone. Tourist offices in Donegal, Letterkenny and Derry have free leaflets about walks in the Inishowen area, complete with maps.

The peninsula is a European Special Area of Conservation and home to over 100 species of migrating and indigenous birds.

The towns in the next section are part of a route that follows the road west of Derry up the coast of Lough Foyle to Moville and then northwest to Malin Head, before heading down the western side to Buncrana. If you're coming from Donegal, the peninsula can be approached from the south west by turning off for Buncrana on the N13 road from Letterkenny to Derry. Leaving from Derry, though, the first village in the Republic is Muff. A scenic drive, the **Inis Eoghain 100**, is clearly signposted round the peninsula.

Muff to Moville

The tiny village of Muff (Mugh), only 8km north of Derry, has pubs offering food and music and a fair share of Northern visitors. Northeast of Muff along the coast there are larger pubs catering to the same market. **Horse riding** is available at **Lenamore Stables** (☎ 077-84022; Muff).

North of Muff at **Quigley's Point** (Rinn Mic Coigus) there are good views across Lough Foyle to County Derry.

Lough Swilly (☎ 912 2863) runs up to nine buses daily from Derry to Carndonagh via Muff (single/return €1.95/2.50, 15 minutes), with almost as many buses to Shrove that also pass through Muff. There's no Sunday service on either route.

Moville & Around

☎ 077 / pop 2270

Now a sleepy seaside town, Moville (Bun an Phobail) was once a busy port where emigrants set sail for America. The **coastal walkway** from Moville to Greencastle takes in the stretch of coast where the steamers used to moor. There's **fishing** off the pier for mackerel, mullet and coalfish.

Main St has several banks with ATMs and the post office.

COOLEY CROSS & SKULL HOUSE

By the gate of the Cooley gravehouse is a 3m-high **cross**, unusual because of the ringhole in its head through which the hands of negotiating parties are said to have clasped to seal an agreement. In the graveyard the small **Skull House** still contains some old bones. It may be associated with St Finian, the monk who accused Colmcille of plagiarising one of his manuscripts in the 6th century. He lived in a monastery here that was founded by St Patrick and survived into the 12th century.

Approaching Moville from the south, look out for a turning on the left (if you pass a church, you've gone too far) that has a sign on the corner for the Cooley Pitch & Putt. The graveyard is just over 1km up this road on the right.

FESTIVALS & EVENTS

The **Foyle Oyster Festival** (☎ 918 2042; Main St) is held in late September.

SLEEPING & EATING

There are several B&Bs in and around Moville.

Barron's Café (☎ 918 2472; Main St; s/d €24/48) Barron's is a central, friendly, renovated B&B where the rooms are all en suite. It also serves good, traditional food including an all-day breakfast (€5.50).

Bridget McGroarty (☎ 918 2091; Main St; s/d €23/40; Mar-Sep) A small, cosy place with three rooms and a shared bathroom.

McNamara's Hotel (☎ 918 2010; fax 918 2564; Main St; s/d €45/90; mains €7-14; wheelchair access) Off

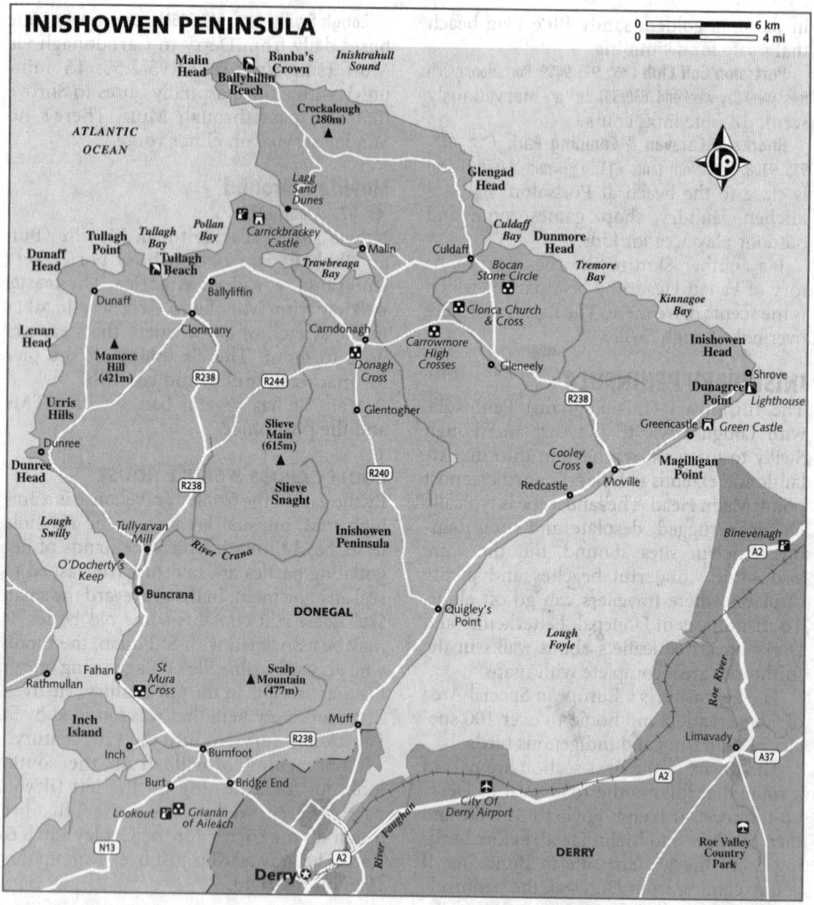

the bottom of Main St, behind Barron's Café, McNamara's is a family-run, 60-room establishment with lots of old-world character. It has a good restaurant.

GETTING THERE & AWAY

Lough Swilly (☎ 912 2863) runs four buses daily Monday to Saturday to Moville (single/return €6.50/8.25, 45 minutes) from Derry.

Greencastle

☎ 074 / pop 740

The popular fishing and holiday village of Greencastle (An Cáisleán Nua), north of Moville, gets its name from the castle built in 1305 by Richard de Burgo – known as the Red Earl of Ulster because of his florid complexion. The Green Castle functioned as a supply base for English armies in Scotland and for this reason was attacked by the Scots under Robert Bruce in the 1320s. In 1555 the castle was demolished, and little of it survives.

Inishowen Maritime Museum & Planetarium (☎ 938 1363; museum adult/child €2.50/1.25, planetarium adult/child €2.50/1.25; 🕑 10am-6pm Mon-Sat, noon-6pm Sun Jun-Sep), by the harbour in a former coastguard station, houses an interesting collection of exhibits on the history of local sailing and fishing boats and the Spanish Armada; there's also a fascinating, state-of-the-art planetarium.

Kealy's Seafood Bar (☎ 938 1010; mains €11-27; 🕑 12.30-3pm & 6.30-10pm Jun-Aug, Thu-Sun only rest of year) is just near the harbour. Its rather simple exterior belies the fact that it houses a top restaurant serving excellent, fresh, locally caught seafood.

Five **Lough Swilly** (☎ 912 2863) buses travel daily, Monday to Saturday, between Derry and Shrove, passing through Greencastle (single/return €8.25/12.35, one hour).

Inishowen Head

A right turn outside Greencastle leads to Shrove; a sign indicating Inishowen Head is 1km along this road. It's possible to drive or cycle part of the way, but it's also an easy walk to the headland, from where you can see (on a clear day) the Antrim coast as far as the Giant's Causeway. A more demanding walk continues to the sandy beach of **Kinnagoe Bay**. At Shrove, where the road left goes to the headland, a right turn goes to Dunagree Point and back to Greencastle, but this loop has little to recommend it.

Culdaff & Around

☎ 074 / pop 840

Several ancient sites surround the sleepy, secluded, resort village of Culdaff (Cúil Dabhcha), which can be visited from the main Moville to Carndonagh road (R238).

CLONCA CHURCH & CROSS

The carved lintel over the door of this **17th-century building** is thought to come from an earlier church. In the northeastern corner, the rather interesting tombstone was erected by one Magnus MacOrristin and has a sword and hurling stick carved on it. The remains of the **cross** show the miracle of the loaves and fishes on the eastern face and geometric designs on the sides.

Look for the turn-off to Culdaff, on the right if coming from Moville, on the left after about 6km if coming from Carndonagh. The Clonca Church and Cross are 1.5km on the right behind some farm buildings.

BOCAN STONE CIRCLE

There are better stone circles in Ireland than this one, which has only a few of some 30 original stones left, but the surrounding views help to conjure up the kind of significance the place must have held some 3000 years ago.

From Clonca Church, continue along the road until you reach a T-junction with a modern church and a cemetery facing you. Turn right here and after about 500m turn left (no sign). The **stone circle** is inside the first heather-covered field on the left.

CARROWMORE HIGH CROSSES

Like the Bocan Stone Circle, these **high crosses** may prove a little disappointing to some. One is basically a decorated slab showing Christ and an angel, while on the other side of the road there is a taller cross with stumpy arms.

From Bocan Stone Circle and Clonca Church, retrace the route back to the main Carndonagh to Moville road and turn left, then almost immediately right.

ACTIVITIES

Culdaff has a beach that's good for **swimming** and **windsurfing** and, from Bunagee Pier, **sea angling** and **diving** are popular.

SLEEPING & EATING

Pines Hostel (☎ 937 9060; Culdaff; dm €9.45) This modern, clean, purpose-built hostel, close to town on the Bunagee road, has 18 beds. Bed linen is included in the price and there are bikes for hire.

McGrory's Bar (☎ 937 9104; mcgr@eir.com.ie; Culdaff; s €38-55, d €76-110) This is the place to stay if you want to be near the action. It offers comfortable accommodation and also serves good, local seafood and traditional Irish food. As well, McGrory's hosts regular traditional music sessions on Thursday and Friday from 10pm that continue well into the night, while the attached Mac's Backroom Bar often attracts big-name musicians.

Malin Head

At the top of Inishowen Peninsula is Malin Head (Cionn Mhálanna), a familiar name to listeners of radio shipping forecasts throughout the island. The northernmost point of Malin Head – and of Ireland – is rocky **Banba's Crown** (Fíorcheann Éireann). Malin Head is one of the few places in Ireland where you can still hear the call of the endangered corncrake in summer. Other birds to look out for are choughs, snow bunting and puffins. The tower on the cliffs was built in 1805 by the British admiralty and later used as a Lloyds signal station. The ugly concrete huts were used by the Irish army in WWII as lookout posts. To

COUNTY DONEGAL

THE CORNCRAKE CRISIS

Once, nights in the Irish countryside were regularly punctuated by the distinctive 'crek, crek' cry of the lovelorn male corncrake. However, due to modern intensive farming practices, in 1988 an all-Ireland survey found only 903 birds still calling and, by the mid-1990s, this number had fallen to just 130. Today the corncrake is a protected bird high on the list of Irish endangered species and survives only in northern Donegal, the Shannon Callows, Mayo and small areas of the western coast.

The corncrake, a dowdy, secretive bird, winters in southeastern Africa before arriving in Ireland to breed in April. Like so many endangered species, it has habits that render it peculiarly vulnerable to modern life. It nests on small platforms of vegetation on the ground, in fields and undergrowth. After laying their eggs in long grass, females stay with their chicks even as a mowing tractor's blades descend on them. Even if they realise the danger, long centuries of programming make them reluctant to rush for the safety of open ground.

The Irish Wildbird Conservancy (IWC) offers grants to farmers who delay mowing until August, when the nesting season is over, or cut the grass in 'corncrake-friendly' fashion. There's a 24-hour **Corncrake Hotline** (☎ 074-916 5126) and you'll see notices in shop windows inviting people to ring in if they hear a corncrake. An IWC officer then visits the site and decides if a nest is in need of protection.

These efforts seem to have had some positive effect. In recent years bird-watchers have reported a rise in the number of singing males and there are around 200 breeding pairs. However, there's a very long way to go before the bird is removed from the endangered-species list.

COUNTY DONEGAL

the west from the car park a short path leads to **Hell's Hole**, a chasm where the incoming waters crash against the rocky formations. To the east a longer headland walk leads to the **Wee House of Malin**, a hermit's cave in the cliff face.

The pretty Plantation village of **Malin** (Málainn), on Trawbreaga Bay 14km south of Malin Head, is centred on a triangular village green. A circular walk from the green takes in Knockamany Bens, a local hill with terrific views, as well as Lagg Presbyterian Church, the oldest church still in use on the peninsula. Children will love the massive sand dunes at Five Fingers Strand near the church.

SLEEPING & EATING

There are two IHO/IHH hostels.

Malin Head Hostel (☎ 074-937 0309; dm/d €12/30) A clean and friendly 14-bed hostel whose facilities include free hot showers and an organic garden where you can buy cheap fruit and vegetables. There's also aromatherapy and reflexology treatment and bike rental. Local buses stop here.

Sandrock Holiday Hostel (☎ 074-937 0289; sandrockhostel@eircom.net; Port Ronan Pier, Malin Head; dm €10; wheelchair access) On the western side of the headland beside the ocean, Sandrock is another well-run place with 20 beds, free pick-up, and bike hire.

Malin Hotel (☎ 074-937 0645; fax 937 0770; Malin; s/d €44/88; mains €9-15; 🕑 restaurant 6-10pm) This lovely traditional hotel beside the green in Malin village serves good food in its restaurant, including fresh, local seafood, and offers entertainment at the weekend.

Cottage (☎ 074-937 0257; meals around €6; 🕑 11am-6pm Jun-Aug) Just west of Banba's Crown, above Ballyhillin Beach, this thatched tearoom serves tea and tasty snacks, and on Friday evenings hosts traditional music sessions.

GETTING THERE & AWAY

The best way to approach Malin Head is by the R238/242 from Carndonagh, rather than up the eastern side from Culdaff. **Lough Swilly** (☎ 074-912 2863) operates a bus that runs on Monday, Wednesday and Friday at 11am between Derry and Malin Head via Carndonagh (adult/child €3.75/2.50, 15 minutes); on the same days a bus leaves Carndonagh at 3pm for Malin Head. There are three buses from Derry to Malin Head on Saturday.

Carndonagh

☎ 074 / pop 1850

Carndonagh (Cardomhnach), surrounded by hills on three sides, is a busy commercial centre serving the local farming community.

The helpful, locally run **Inishowen tourism office** (☎ 937 4933; www.visitinishowen.com; Chapel St; 9.30am-5.30pm Mon-Fri Sep-May, 9.30am-7pm Mon-Fri, 10am-6pm Sat & noon-6pm Sun Jun-Aug), southwest of the Diamond, also sells fishing licences for all of Donegal. There are three banks on the Diamond and the Allied Irish Bank has an ATM; the post office is off the Diamond near the top of Bridge St.

Once an important ecclesiastical centre, Carndonagh has several early Christian stone monuments. At the Ballyliffin end of town, the finely shaped, 7th-century **Donagh Cross** stands erect against the wall of an Anglican church. Either side of the cross are two small pillars, one said to show a man with a sword and shield, possibly Goliath, the other David and his harp. In the graveyard there's a pillar with a carved marigold on a stem and nearby a crucifixion scene.

SLEEPING & EATING

Foden House (☎ 937 4172; Foden, Carndonagh; s/d €26/53) This converted 200-year-old farmhouse off the Moville road about 2km out of Carndonough is a wonderful B&B and working farm with fabulous views of the surrounding countryside.

Arch Inn (☎ 937 3209; the Diamond; snacks around €5) In the main square, the Arch Inn does good soup and sandwiches during the day and hosts a traditional music session on Sunday evening.

Corncrake Restaurant (☎ 937 4534; Malin Rd; mains €16-20; 6-10pm Wed-Sun Apr-Nov) Acknowledged by foodies as one of the best restaurants in Ireland, the Corncrake serves traditional Irish food using fresh ingredients and home-grown herbs in an intimate setting. It doesn't accept credit cards; reservations are recommended.

If you're off to Malin Head for the day or going on to the camp site at Clonmany, stock up with provisions at the Centra supermarket in Malin Rd.

GETTING THERE & AWAY

A **Lough Swilly** (☎ 074-912 2863) bus leaves Buncrana for Carndonagh (adult/child €8/5.30, 45 minutes) three times daily except Tuesday, Wednesday (once daily) and Sunday (no service). On weekdays they return from Carndonagh three times daily. Lough Swilly also runs a bus between Derry and Malin Head via Carndonagh once daily Monday, Wednesday and Friday (three times on Saturday).

Ballyliffin & Clonmany

☎ 074 / pop 750

The small, seaside resort of Ballyliffin (Baile Lifin) attracts more Irish than overseas visitors, many of whom come to play golf on either of the two championship 18-hole courses. There's plenty of accommodation in the area. Both villages have post offices but no banks.

About 1km north of Ballyliffin is the lovely, sandy expanse of **Pollan Strand**, but, unfortunately, the crashing breakers make it unsafe for swimming. A walk along the dunes to the north of this beach brings you to **Doagh Island** (now part of the mainland), where the battered ruins of 16th-century **Carrickbrackey Castle** (also spelt Carrickabraghy) face the ocean. Also on the island is the **Doagh Visitor Centre** (☎ 937 6493; Doagh Island, Inishowen; adult/child €4/2; 10am-5.30pm Easter-Oct), a reconstructed village of thatched cottages with an emphasis on the story of the Famine. Tea and scones are included in the admission fee.

The other beach is at **Tullagh Strand**. It's great for an exhilarating walk and, although swimming is possible, the current can be strong and it isn't recommended when the tide is going out. From Clonmany there are walks to **Butler's Glen** and **Dunaff Head**.

GOLF

With two championship courses, **Ballyliffin Golf Club** (☎ 937 6119; Ballyliffin; green fees weekday/weekend Old Links €45/50, Glashedy €60/70) is probably the best place to play golf in Donegal. The scenery is so beautiful that it can distract even the most concentrated golfer.

SLEEPING & EATING

Tullagh Bay Camping & Caravan Park (☎ 937 8997; Tullagh Bay; tents €13; May-Sep) About 5km from Clonmany, this park is ideal for beach-goers as it's just behind Tullagh Strand.

B&Bs line the 2km stretch of road between Ballyliffin and Clonmany.

Ard Donn House (☎ 937 6156; Ballyliffin; s/d €32/55) About 500m from the centre of Ballyliffin, this homely B&B uses organic farm produce and has five en-suite bedrooms.

Strand Hotel (☎ 937 6017; fax 937 6486; Ballyliffin; s/d €50/80; food served 12.30-10pm) This 12-room hotel is small enough to retain a friendly atmosphere and a personal touch. The pub grub is of the standard variety, but there's an emphasis on fish and seafood.

GETTING THERE & AWAY

Lough Swilly (☎ 912 2863) buses run between Clonmany and Carndonagh; see the Carndonagh section on p499 for details – buses leave/reach Clonmany 20 minutes before/after Carndonagh.

Buncrana

☎ 074 / pop 3420

Pubs, fast-food joints and shops line Buncrana's main street, which, during winter, quietly awaits the summer hordes that throng here from across the border, especially Derry. Inishowen's main town is the only serious rival to Bundoran as a major resort town, but unlike the southwestern resort, Buncrana remembers that there's life beyond tourism. A 5km-long sandy beach along the shores of Lough Swilly is the town's main attraction, but there are a couple of worthwhile sights to distract you from working on your tan.

Ulster Bank (Upper Main St), **Allied Irish Bank** (Lower Main St) and **Bank of Ireland** (Lower Main St) all have ATMs and bureaux de change. The post office is on Upper Main St. You can leave your laundry at **Valu Clean** (☎ 936 2570; Lower Main St).

SIGHTS

The community-run **Tullyarvan Mill** (☎ 936 1613; Carndonagh Rd; admission free; 🕑 10am-5pm May-Sep) is a combined textile exhibition, craft shop and café about 1km north of town on the River Crana. It is well worth a visit. The attractively presented exhibition is devoted to the restoration of the mill, local history, and flora and fauna. The place is also worth visiting for its classical and lively traditional music evenings that take place regularly in summer. To find it, head north out of town on the R238 and follow the signs.

At the northern end of the seafront the early-18th-century, six-arched Castle Bridge leads to **O'Docherty's Keep**, a tower house built by the O'Dochertys, the local chiefs, in 1430. It was burned by the English and then rebuilt for their own use. **Buncrana Castle** nearby was built in 1718 by John Vaughan, who also constructed the bridge; Wolfe Tone was imprisoned here following the unsuccessful French invasion in 1798.

SLEEPING & EATING

There's no shortage of B&Bs around town, but they can fill up quickly during August.

Town Clock Guest House (☎ 936 2146; 6 Upper Main St; s/d €25/50; mains around €5; 🕑 food served 8.15am-8pm Mon-Thu, to 9pm Fri & Sat, 10.30am-9pm Sun) This central B&B offers clean and spacious rooms (price includes bathroom). Breakfast is in the downstairs café, which serves a range of dishes from lasagne to burgers. At lunchtime during the week it gets packed with hungry school children.

Lake of Shadows Hotel (☎ 936 1902; www.lakeofshadows.com; Grianán Park; s/d €48/70) A Victorian lakefront hotel where old-world character combines well with modern facilities. To get here from Main St head down Church St towards the bay.

Ubiquitous Chip (☎ 936 2530; 47 Upper Main St; mains €13-20) The best eatery in terms of choice is this terrific little restaurant and bar complete with jukebox. It provides friendly service and top-quality food, including seafood and vegetarian options, while the bar has a fine selection of beers and wines.

ENTERTAINMENT

Not surprisingly, most entertainment is found in the town's pubs along Main St.

Atlantic Bar (☎ 932 0880; Upper Main St) Dating from 1792, the Atlantic is Buncrana's oldest pub and can be relied on for live music at the weekend.

Óflaitbeartais (O'Flaherty's; ☎ 936 1305; Upper Main St) This large, popular local has a big TV screen for sports and frequently hosts traditional music sessions.

GETTING THERE & AROUND

From Buncrana, **Lough Swilly** (☎ 912 2863) buses run daily to Derry and Carndonagh. Taxis are available from **Town Clock Taxis** (☎ 63322).

South of Buncrana

FAHAN

A monastery was founded in Fahan by St Colmcille in the 6th century, and among its ruins is the beautifully carved, 7th-century **St Mura Cross** stone slab in the graveyard beside the church. Each face is decorated

COUNTY DONEGAL

with a cross, and the barely discernible Greek inscription is the only one known from this early Christian period.

GRIANÁN OF AILEÁCH

This impressive stone fort atop Grianán Hill in Burt, 18km south of Buncrana and signposted off the N13, offers panoramic views of the surrounding countryside: Loughs Swilly and Foyle, Inch Island and distant Derry. The walls are 4m thick and enclose an area 23m in diameter. The fort may have existed at least 2000 years ago, but the site itself has pagan associations that go back to pre-Celtic times. Between the 5th and 12th centuries it was the seat of the O'Neills before being demolished by Murtogh O'Brien, king of Munster. You might wonder how a fort demolished 800 years ago could look so complete – well, between 1874 and 1878 an amateur archaeologist from Derry reconstructed the fort, and this is mostly what you see today.

The attractive, circular **Burt Church** at the foot of the hill was modelled on the fort by Derry architect Liam McCormack and built in 1967.

The 19th-century church of Christchurch at Burt, on the N13 about 300m south of the turn-off to the fort, houses the **Grianán of Aileách Visitor Centre** (☎ 074-936 8512; Burt; adult/child €2.50/1.20; 🕙 10am-6pm Jun-Aug, noon-6pm Sep-May). It has displays on the hill fort and on the church's history. There's a life-size model of Muirchertach na gCochall Craicinn, a 10th-century ancestor of the O'Neills and king of Aileách from 938 to 943. In 942 he went on an extended tour of Ireland, recorded in verse by Cormacan Eigean. There are also models of members of Christchurch's Victorian congregation and information about the local flora and fauna.

The **restaurant** (mains €7-11; 🕙 10am-10pm Mon-Sat, to 9pm Sun) here has a lot of character – the bar counter is created out of a Boer War memorial slab, for example – and serves snacks and light meals during the day, with an á la carte menu in the evening with plenty of choices, including several vegetarian options.

INCH ISLAND

Few tourists make it to tranquil Inch Island, accessible from the mainland by a causeway, but it does have plenty of **birdlife** in its western wetlands, two small **beaches** and the remains of an old **fort**. **Inch Island Stables** (☎ 074-936 0335) organises **horse-riding** lessons and trips around the island.

Counties Meath & Louth

CONTENTS

Heading north from Dublin along the coast takes you through Counties Meath and Louth before crossing the border into Northern Ireland. This low, coastal landscape is a contrast to the hilly country south of the capital, rising only slightly inland to the plain known in folklore as Murtheimne – the setting for much of the great Iron Age saga, Táin Bó Cúailnge (Cattle Raid of Cooley). The epic's dramatic climax occurred on Louth's beautiful Cooley Peninsula, and many places there owe their names to the legendary heroes and battles of that time. Meath and Louth are home to some of the most remarkable legacies of the ancient Irish people – the tombs of Newgrange and Loughcrew – as well as the fine monasteries at Monasterboice, Mellifont and Kells, built by early Irish Christians.

It would be wrong, however, to assume that the verdant, settled farmland of these two counties is firmly rooted in the past. The rapid, unplanned growth of Dublin is turning parts of these two counties into commuter zones for the capital. Older farming traditions have been forced to come to terms with a newer, more urban outlook, which seeks to capitalise on opportunities in tourism and industry. Louth has two major industrial towns, Dundalk and Drogheda, and even in the smaller towns and villages old ways of life are starting to pass, and the whole area is in danger of being swamped by Dubliners with a seemingly never-ending appetite for new housing.

HIGHLIGHTS

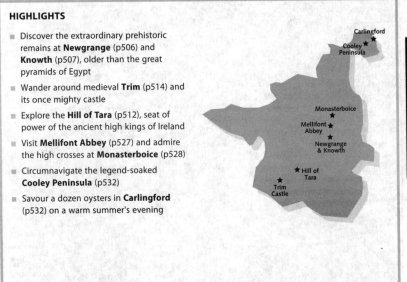

- Discover the extraordinary prehistoric remains at **Newgrange** (p506) and **Knowth** (p507), older than the great pyramids of Egypt
- Wander around medieval **Trim** (p514) and its once mighty castle
- Explore the **Hill of Tara** (p512), seat of power of the ancient high kings of Ireland
- Visit **Mellifont Abbey** (p527) and admire the high crosses at **Monasterboice** (p528)
- Circumnavigate the legend-soaked **Cooley Peninsula** (p532)
- Savour a dozen oysters in **Carlingford** (p532) on a warm summer's evening

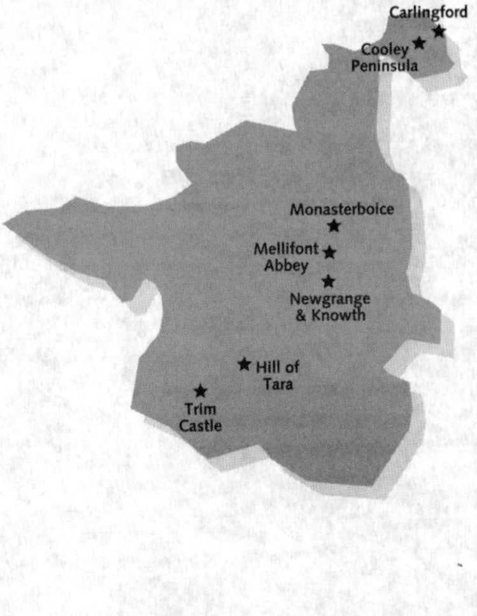

POPULATION: 235,738	AREA: 2849 SQ KM

COUNTY MEATH

A farm in Meath is worth two in any other county, so goes the old saying. Meath (An Mhí), Dublin's immediate neighbour to the north and northwest, has long been one of Ireland's leading agricultural counties, a plain of extremely rich soil stretching north to the lakes of Cavan and Monaghan and west before running into the bleak Bog of Allen. Among the huge fields are the solid houses of Meath's former settlers and today's prosperous farmers – many of whom are even wealthier since EU farming policies started offering subsidies for letting land lie fallow. This same fecund earth has always attracted settlers from the earliest times, and Meath's principal attractions are its ancient sites in the Boyne Valley and among the isolated hills of Tara and Slane. Also be sure to visit Butterstream Gardens in Trim, which are some of the finest in Ireland.

The towns of Meath have experienced rapid growth in the last five years. Dubliners searching for affordable housing have led to the establishment of housing estates on the outskirts of Navan, Trim and Kells. But worse affected are places such as Ashbourne, Dunshaughlin and Dunboyne on the southern fringe, where traffic jams and standing-only commuter trains have suddenly replaced tractors and empty buses.

COUNTIES MEATH & LOUTH

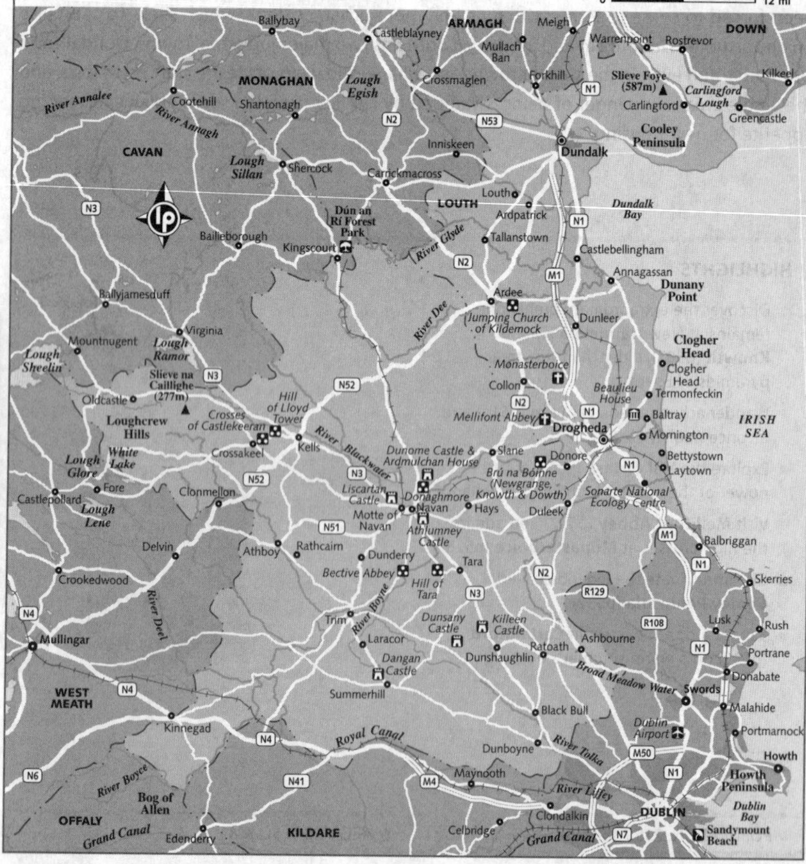

HISTORY

Meath's rich soil, laid down during the last Ice Age, attracted settlers as early as 8000 BC. They worked their way up the banks of the River Boyne transforming the landscape from forest to farmland. Brú na Bóinne, an extensive prehistoric necropolis dating from around 3000 BC when the pyramids where still but a dream, lies on a meandering section of the Boyne between Drogheda and Slane. There's a group of smaller passage graves in the Loughcrew Hills near Oldcastle. For a thousand years the Hill of Tara was the seat of power for Irish high kings (*ard ríthe*; pronounced *ard* ree-huh), until the arrival of St Patrick in the 5th century. Later, Kells became one of the most important and creative monastic settlements in Ireland and lent its name to the famed *Book of Kells*, a 9th-century illuminated manuscript now displayed in Trinity College, Dublin.

THE COAST

Meath's mere 10km of coastline includes a number of small resorts with wide expanses of sand dunes and safe beaches popular with Dubliners and people from Drogheda and Dundalk. From the Elizabethan **Maiden Watchtower**, in Mornington at the mouth of the Boyne, there are fine views of Drogheda, 5km to the west, and the Boyne Estuary.

Laytown is a busy little seaside town with golf, tennis and good windsurfing. It hosts a wild annual **festival of horse racing** on the beach in mid-August. Outside Laytown, on the road to Julianstown (the R150), is **Sonairte National Ecology Centre** (☎ 041-982 7572; The Ninch; adult/student/child €3.20/1.90/1.30; 🕑 9am-5pm Mon-Fri, 11am-5pm Sat, 11am-6pm Sun), beside the River Nanny. It has an organic garden, a nature trail, an adventure playground and exhibits displaying the use of wind, water and solar power. In the gift shop you can buy wine made from its own organically grown grapes.

Barely 1km north of Laytown is **Bettystown**, whose claim to fame is that the magnificent 8th-century Tara Brooch was found in a box on the beach here in 1850. The only link between the brooch and Tara is that the magnificent ornamentation and preciousness of its materials seem to indicate a wealthy, if not royal, association with the high kings, who were based in Tara. It's now on display in the National Museum in Dublin. There is a long strand on the edge of the village, which is very popular in summer, affording long walks and, if you can overcome the pollution, some pretty good swimming.

Sleeping

Tara Guesthouse (☎/fax 041-982 7239; beachfront, Laytown; s/d €30/60) It's all about the wonderful ocean views at this comfortable guesthouse right on the sand. Breakfast is extra, and they also serve a good, hearty dinner (€20).

Neptune Beach (☎ 041-982 7107; fax 982 7412; Bettystown Beach; s/d €75/150) The classy option in Bettystown, this little hotel has spacious rooms right on the seafront.

Eating

There are a handful of greasy-spoon diners and fish and chip shops in Bettystown, but there's only one place where you can get really good food.

Bacchus at the Coastguard (☎ 041-982 8251; Bayview, Bettystown; mains from €12, 3-course early-bird dinner €27; 🕑 6-11pm Tue-Sat, noon-7pm Sun) As you might expect, seafood is the speciality here and the place has a big reputation. You have to book at the weekend. Hours for the early-bird dinner are 6pm to 7.30pm.

Getting There & Away

Bus Éireann (☎ 041-983 5023; www.buseireann.ie) runs at least four buses daily along the coast, stopping at Laytown and Bettystown. From here to Drogheda costs single/return €2.50/4.50, and to Dublin €8.20/11.

The coast is served by regular **trains** (☎ 01-836 6222) on the Dublin to Belfast line: eight a day Monday to Thursday and Saturday, nine on Friday and four on Sunday. Dublin to Laytown costs single/return €9/13 and takes 20 minutes. Belfast to Laytown is €23/33 and takes a bit over 1½ hours.

BRÚ NA BÓINNE

A thousand years older than Stonehenge, the extensive Neolithic necropolis known as Brú na Bóinne (the Boyne Palace) is, quite simply, one of the most extraordinary sites in Europe, a powerful and evocative testament to the mind-boggling achievements of prehistoric humans.

This necropolis was built to house the VIP corpses. Its tombs were the largest artificial structures in Ireland until the construction of the Anglo-Norman castles four thousand years later. The area consists of many different sites, the three principal ones being Newgrange, Knowth and Dowth.

Over the centuries the tombs decayed, were covered by grass and trees and were plundered by everybody from Vikings to Victorian treasure hunters, whose carved initials can be seen on the great stones of Newgrange. The countryside around them is littered with countless other ancient mounds (or tumuli) and standing stones.

The entire complex, including the three main passage tombs (of which only Newgrange and Knowth are accessible) can only be visited as part of a tour run by the **Brú na Bóinne Visitor Centre** (☎ 041-988 0300; www.heritageireland.ie; Donore; visitor centre only adult/senior/student €2.50/1.90/1.20, visitor centre, Newgrange & Knowth €8.80/6.30/4.10; 🕒 9am-7pm Jun–mid-Sep, 9am-6.30pm mid-Sep–end Sep, 9.30am-5.30pm Oct & Mar-Apr, 9.30am-5pm Nov-Feb), located south of the River Boyne and 2km west of Donore. This high-quality interpretative centre provoked enormous controversy when it opened in 1997, largely because it was deemed an unwelcome and artificial interference in a unique natural setting. Whatever the case may be, the centre has turned out to be a fairly remarkable place, with an extraordinary series of interactive exhibits on the passage tombs and prehistoric Ireland in general.

You should allow plenty of time to visit this unique centre. If you're only planning on taking the guided tour of the interpretative centre, give yourself about an hour. If you plan a visit to Newgrange or Knowth, allow at least two hours. If, however, you want to visit all three in one go, you should plan at least half a day. In summer, particularly at the weekend, and during school holidays, the place gets very crowded, and you will not be guaranteed a visit to either of the passage tombs; call ahead to book a tour and avoid disappointment. In summer, the best time to visit is mid-week and/or early in the morning.

Newgrange

From the surface **Newgrange** (visitor centre & Newgrange adult/senior/student €5/3.80/2.50, visitor centre, Newgrange & Knowth €8.80/6.30/4.10) is a somewhat disappointing flattened, grass-covered mound about 80m in diameter and 13m high. Underneath lies the finest Stone Age passage tomb in Ireland and one of the most remarkable prehistoric sites in Europe. It dates from around 3200 BC, predating the great pyramids of Egypt by some six centuries. The purpose for which it was constructed remains uncertain. It may have been a burial place for kings or a centre for ritual – although the alignment with the sun at the time of the winter solstice also suggests it was designed to act as a calendar.

The name derives from 'new granary' (the tomb did in fact serve as a repository for wheat and grain at one stage), although a belief more popular in the area is that it comes from the Irish for 'Cave of Gráinne', a reference to a Celtic myth taught to every Irish schoolchild. The story of The Pursuit of Diarmuid and Gráinne tells of the illicit love between the wife of Fionn McCumhaill (or Finn McCool), leader of the Fianna, and one of his most trusted lieutenants. When Diarmuid was fatally wounded, his body was brought to Newgrange by the god Aengus in a vain attempt to save him, and the despairing Gráinne followed him into the cave, where she remained long after he died. This suspiciously Arthurian legend (for Diarmuid and Gráinne read Lancelot and Guinevere) is undoubtedly untrue, but it's still a pretty good story. Newgrange also plays another role in Celtic mythology, serving as the site where the hero Cúchulainn was conceived.

Over the centuries, Newgrange, like Dowth and Knowth, deteriorated and was even quarried at one stage. There was a standing stone on the summit until the 17th century. The site was extensively restored in 1962 and again in 1975.

A superbly carved kerbstone with double and triple spirals guards the tomb's main entrance. The front facade has been reconstructed so that tourists don't have to clamber in over it. Above the entrance is a slit or roof box, which lets light in. Another beautifully decorated kerbstone stands at the exact opposite side of the mound. Some experts say that a ring of standing stones encircled the mound, forming a Great Circle about 100m in diameter, but only 12 of these stones remain – with traces of some others below ground level.

Holding the whole structure together are the 97 boulders of the kerb ring, designed to stop the mound from collapsing outwards. Eleven of these are decorated with motifs similar to those on the main entrance stone, although only three have extensive carvings.

The white quartzite was originally obtained from Wicklow, 80km to the south, and there is also some granite from the Mourne Mountains in Northern Ireland. Over 200,000 tonnes of earth and stone also went into the mound.

You can walk down the narrow 19m passage, lined with 43 stone uprights, some of them engraved, which leads into the tomb chamber, about one-third of the way into the colossal mound. The chamber has three recesses, and in these are large basin stones that held cremated human bones. Along with the remains would have been funeral offerings of beads and pendants, but these must have been stolen long before the archaeologists arrived.

Above, the massive stones support a 6m-high corbel-vaulted roof. A complex drainage system means that not a drop of water has penetrated the interior in 40 centuries.

At 8.20am during the winter solstice (19 to 23 December), the rising sun's rays shine through the slit above the entrance, creep slowly down the long passage and illuminate the tomb chamber for 17 minutes. There is little doubt that witnessing this is one of the country's most memorable, even mystical, experiences. However, places for the annual event are booked up for at least 15 years, and the waiting list is now closed. For the legions of daily visitors there is a simulated winter sunrise for every group taken into the mound.

Knowth

The burial mound of Knowth (Cnóbha; visitor centre & Knowth adult/student/child €3.80/2.50/1.50, visitor centre, Knowth & Newgrange €8.80/6.30/4.10; 🕓 May-Oct), northwest of Newgrange, was built around the same time and seems set to surpass its better-known neighbour, both in the extent and the importance of the discoveries made here. It has the greatest collection of passage-grave art ever uncovered in Western Europe. Under excavation since 1962, it recently opened to the public at last.

Modern excavations at Knowth soon cleared a 34m passage to the central chamber, much longer than the one at Newgrange. In 1968 a second 40m passage was unearthed on the opposite side of the mound. Although the chambers are separate, they're close enough for archaeologists to hear each other at work. Also in the mound are the remains of six early-Christian souterrains (underground chambers) built into the side. Some 300 carved slabs and 17 satellite graves surround the main mound.

Human activity at Knowth continued for thousands of years after its construction, which accounts for the site's complexity. The Beaker folk, so called because they buried their dead with drinking vessels, occupied the site in the Bronze Age (c 1800 BC), as did the Celts in the Iron Age around 500 BC. Remnants of bronze and iron workings from these periods have been discovered. Around AD 800 to 900 it was turned into a *ráth* (earthen ring fort), a stronghold of the very powerful Uí Néill (O'Neill) clan. In 965, it was the seat of Cormac MacMaelmithic, later Ireland's high king for nine years. The Normans built a motte and bailey here in the 12th century. In about 1400 the site was finally abandoned. Further excavations are likely to continue at least for the next decade, and one of the thrills of visiting Knowth is being allowed to watch them at work.

Dowth

The circular mound at Dowth (Dubhadh, meaning 'dark') is similar in size to Newgrange – about 63m in diameter – but is slightly taller at 14m high. It has suffered badly at the hands of everyone from road

NEWGRANGE FARM

One for the kids. Situated a few hundred metres down the hill to the west of Newgrange tomb is a 135-hectare **working farm** (☎ 041-982 4119; Newgrange; adult/family €5/14; 🕓 10am-5.30pm Mon-Fri, 2-5.30pm Sun, Easter-Sep, also 2-5.30pm Sat Jul & Aug). The truly hands-on, family-run farm allows visitors to feed the ducks and the lambs and tour the exotic bird aviaries. Charming Farmer Bill keeps things interesting and demonstrations of threshing, sheepdog work and shoeing a horse are absorbing. Sunday at 3pm is a very special time when the 'sheep derby' is run. Finding jockeys small enough wasn't easy, so teddy bears are tied to the animals' backs. Visiting children are made owners of individual sheep for the race. A unique place full of fun and fascination.

builders and treasure hunters to amateur archaeologists, who scooped out the centre of the tumulus in the 19th century. For a time, Dowth even had a teahouse ignobly perched on its summit. Relatively untouched by modern archaeologists, Dowth shows what Newgrange and Knowth looked like for most of their history. Because it's unsafe, Dowth is closed to visitors, though the mound can be viewed from the road. Excavations began in 1998 and will continue for years to come.

There are two entrance passages leading to separate chambers (both sealed), and a 24m early-Christian souterrain at either end which connects up with the western passage. This 8m-long passage leads into a small cruciform chamber, in which a recess acts as an entrance to an additional series of small compartments, a feature unique to Dowth. To the southwest is the entrance to a shorter passage and smaller chamber.

North of the tumulus are the ruins of **Dowth Castle** and **Dowth House**.

Sleeping

There are a couple of really beautiful B&Bs in the area.

Glebe House (☎ 041-983 6101; fax 041-984 3469; Dowth; s/d €45/90) This old country house, near the Dowth burial mound and 7km west of Drogheda, has gorgeous rooms with open, log-burning fireplaces. The breakfast is bountiful and included in the price.

Mattock House (☎/fax 041-982 4592; off N51, Newgrange; s/d €35/50) About 2km east of Slane, near the Newgrange mound, is this classic Irish farmhouse. Large, comfortable rooms and a breakfast that struggles to fit on the plate are the order of the day.

Tours

Brú na Bóinne is one of the most popular tourist attractions in Ireland, and there is a plethora of organised tours transporting busloads of eager tourists to the interpretative centre.

The best of them all, as far as we've discovered, is the tour run by **Mary Gibbons** (☎ 01-283 9973; tour & admission fees €35). Tours depart from Northside Star Hotel Amiens St at 9am, Buswells Hotel Molesworth St 10am, Dublin Tourism Centre Suffolk St 10.15am, Royal Dublin Hotel O'Connell St 10.30am Monday to Wednesday and Friday and take in the whole of the Boyne Valley, including Newgrange and the Hill of Tara (p512). Eamonn P Kelly, the Keeper of Irish Antiquities at the National Museum in Dublin, described it as 'the authentic tour of Ireland's history'. The expert guides offer a fascinating insight into Celtic and pre-Celtic life in Ireland.

Bus Éireann (☎ 01-836 6111; www.buseireann.ie; adult €24.20-30, student €20-28, child €12.10-19.50) runs Newgrange and the Boyne Valley tours departing from Busáras in Dublin. The tours are cheaper from October to December. They depart 9.30am and return 5.45pm Thursday to Saturday in April, Monday to Thursday and weekends May to September, and 10am to 4.15pm Thursday to Saturday October to December.

Irish Rover Tours (☎ 01-836 4684; www.irishrover.ie; adult/student/child €25/23/13) depart 57 Lower Gardiner St 9am and Dublin Tourism Centre at 9.30am. It does a Meath tour that includes the Boyne Valley, Monasterboice, Trim Castle and the Hill of Tara.

Getting There & Away

Newgrange, Knowth and Dowth are all well signposted. Newgrange lies just north of the River Boyne, about 13km southwest of Drogheda and 5km southeast of Slane; Dowth is between Newgrange and Drogheda; while Knowth is about 1km northwest of Newgrange or almost 4km by road.

From Drogheda, Bus Éireann (from Drogheda: single €1.45, 20 minutes, six daily 10.15am-4pm; from Dublin: return €12.70, 1½ hours, one daily) runs a service that drops you off at the gates of the interpretative centre. Visitors are bussed from the centre to the sites.

SLANE

☎ 041 / pop 1339

Built as a manorial village for an important castle, Slane (Baile Shláine) is a charming little hamlet that has 18th-century stone houses and cottages and mature trees. Just southwest of the centre is the massive grey gate to the privately owned Slane Castle. Four identical houses face each other at the junction of the main roads. Local lore has it that they were built for four sisters who had taken an intense dislike to one another and kept watch from their individual residences.

Orientation & Information

Slane is perched on a hillside overlooking the River Boyne, at the junction of the N2 and N51, some 15km west of Drogheda. At the bottom of the hill to the south, the Boyne glides by under a narrow bridge. The hairpin turn on the northern side of the bridge is considered to be one of the most dangerous in the country as there is a steep hill preceding it; fatal accidents occur there on an all-too-regular basis. If you are driving, be extra careful.

The helpful, community-run **tourist office** (☎ 988 4055; info@meathtourism.ie; Main St; ⏲ 9.30am-5pm Mon, Thu & Sat) is directly opposite the Conyngham Arms Hotel.

The Hill of Slane

Just above the village, about 1km to the north, is the Hill of Slane. Tradition holds that St Patrick lit a paschal (Easter) fire here in 433 – just a year after his arrival in Ireland – to proclaim Christianity throughout the land. This act was in direct contravention of a decree issued by Laoghaire, the pagan high king of Ireland, that no flame should be lit within sight of the Hill of Tara. The king was furious but was restrained by his druids, who warned that 'the man who had kindled the flame would surpass kings and princes'. Laoghaire set out to meet Patrick and question him, and all but one of the king's attendants – a man called Erc – greeted him with scorn.

During the encounter, Patrick killed one of the king's guards and summoned an earthquake to subdue the rest. He then plucked a shamrock and used its three leaves to explain the paradox of the Trinity – the union of the Father, the Son and the Holy Spirit in one Godhead. The king made peace and, while he refused to be converted, allowed Patrick to continue his missionary work. Erc was baptised and later named as the first bishop of Slane. On Holy Saturday the local parish priest still lights a fire on the hill.

The Hill of Slane originally had a church associated with St Erc and, later, a round tower and monastery, but only an outline of the foundations remains. Later a motte and bailey was constructed and is still visible on the western side of the hill. A ruined church, tower and other buildings once formed part of an early-16th-century Franciscan friary. On a clear day, from the top of the tower, which is always open, you can see the Hill of Tara and the Boyne Valley, as well (it's said) as seven Irish counties.

St Erc is believed to have become a hermit in old age, and the ruins of a small Gothic **church** (⏲ 15 Aug only) mark the spot where he is thought to have spent his last days, around 512 to 514. It's on the northern riverbank, behind the Protestant church on the Navan road, and lies within the private Conyngham estate.

Slane Castle

The private residence of Lord Henry Conyngham, earl of Mountcharles, **Slane Castle** (☎ 041-988 4400; www.slanecastle.ie; admission €7; ⏲ noon-5pm Mon-Thu May-Sep) is west of the centre along the Navan road and is best known in Ireland as the setting for major outdoor rock concerts in its natural amphitheatre.

Built in 1785 in Gothic Revival style by James Wyatt, the building was altered later by Francis Johnson for George IV's visit to Lady Conyngham. She was allegedly his mistress, and it's said the road between Dublin and Slane was built especially straight and smooth to speed up the randy king's journeys.

Unfortunately, much of the castle, including some valuable furnishings, was destroyed by fire in 1991, whereupon it was discovered that the earl – a Lloyd's name – was under-insured. Money was finally raised for restoration and the castle only recently reopened to the public for tours.

Ledwidge Museum

Just about 1.5km northeast of Slane on the Drogheda road is the **Ledwidge Museum** (☎ 982 4544; Janesville; admission €2.60; ⏲ 9am-1pm & 2-7pm Apr-Sep, 9am-1pm & 2-4.30pm Mon-Fri Oct-Mar). This stone labourer's cottage was the birthplace of Francis Ledwidge, a poet who died on the battlefield of Ypres in Belgium in 1917 just short of his 30th birthday.

Sleeping

Slane Farm Hostel (☎/fax 988 4985; paddymacken@eircom.net; Harlinstown House, R163 Navan road; dm/d €14/34) Just 1km from the castle gates are the stables of Harlinstown House, built by the Marquis of Conyngham in the 18th century for his stable man. They have been converted by the current owners (who reside in the house itself) into this wonderful hostel that has earned rave reviews from our readers.

Boyne View (☎ 982 4121; Slane Village; s/d €35/55) Scenically located down by the river near the bridge, this elegant Georgian town house has three rooms, two en suite.

Conyngham Arms Hotel (☎ 982 4155; fax 982 4205; Slane; d €115-135) This 19th-century hotel maintains that village-inn feel and look. The four-poster bed in each room is a real treat.

Eating

Boyle's Licensed Tea Rooms (☎ 982 4195; Main St; snacks from €3; 🕑 10am-5pm) This marvellous tea shop and café lies behind an equally beautiful shop front with gold lettering. The menu – written in 12 languages – is strictly of the tea-and-scones type, but people come here for the ambience, which is straight out of the 1940s.

Conyngham Arms Hotel (☎ 982 4155; Slane; mains €10; 🕑 noon-8pm) Using mostly local meat and veg, this place serves traditional, home-made food. The roast chicken with stuffing and the bacon and cabbage are excellent.

Getting There & Away

Bus Éireann (☎ 01-836 6111) buses for Dublin (single/return €7.40/10.80, 45 minutes, five daily) stop in front of the sweet shop on the main Derry road, and at Conlon's Shop near the crossroads for buses to Drogheda (single €1.60, 35 minutes) and Navan (single €1.20, 30 minutes) both of which run six a day Monday to Saturday and five on Sunday.

SLANE TO NAVAN

The 14km journey on the N51 southwest from Slane to Navan follows the Boyne Valley past a number of manor houses, ruined castles, round towers and churches; they're only of moderate interest compared to the fine sites elsewhere in County Meath, though.

Dunmoe Castle lies down a badly signposted cul-de-sac to the south, 4km before reaching Navan. This D'Arcy family castle is a 16th-century ruin with good views of the countryside and of the impressive red-brick **Ardmulchan House** (closed to the public), on the opposite side of the River Boyne. Cromwell is supposed to have fired at the castle from the riverbank in 1649, and local legend holds that a tunnel used to run from the castle vaults under the river. Near Dunmoe Castle is a small overgrown chapel and graveyard, with a crypt containing members of the D'Arcy family. Ardmulchan House, though somewhat dilapidated, is still used as a private residence.

You can't miss the fine 30m round tower and 13th-century church of **Donaghmore**, on the right 2km nearer Navan. The site has a profusion of modern gravestones, but the 10th-century tower with its Crucifixion scene above the door is interesting, and there are carved faces near the windows and the remains of the church wall.

NAVAN

☎ 046 / pop 3415

The county town of Navan (An Uaimh) at the confluence of the Boyne and Blackwater Rivers is disfigured by the busy N3 Dublin to Cavan and N51 Drogheda to Westmeath roads, which cut off the rivers from the town. Navan was the birthplace of Sir Francis Beaufort of the British Navy, who in 1805 devised the internationally accepted scale for wind strengths. The town has Europe's largest lead and zinc mine, Tara, 3km along the Kells road. Frankly, there is little here of any great interest.

Orientation & Information

Market Square is the town hub, with Ludlow, Watergate and Trimgate Sts leading from it in the directions of the former town gates.

The local **tourist office** (☎ 902 1581; Railway St; 🕑 9.30am-12.30pm & 1.30-5pm Mon-Sat) is in the town library about 500m southwest of Market Square.

There's a map and information point in the town hall car park at the northern end of Watergate St.

The modern **post office** (Kennedy Rd) is past the big shopping centre on Kennedy Rd, which runs off Trimgate St, and there's an Allied Irish Bank branch (with ATM) on the corner of these two streets. **Hi Way** (☎ 902 1910; Brew's Hill) is a pretty good bookshop, with plenty of titles on local history and folklore.

Sleeping

If you decide to stay in Navan there are several good B&Bs and one fine country house.

Athumley Manor (☎ 907 1388; pboylan@eircom.net; Athumley, Duleek road R153; s/d €35/55) The best B&B in town at large, this comfortable home has well-appointed, tastefully decorated rooms.

Killyon House (☎ 907 1224; fax 907 2766; Dublin road; s/d €45/70) This guesthouse may be modern, but the use of antiques and stylish design ensures that it has a lot of charm.

Mountainstown House (☎ 905 4154; Castletown, Navan; d €90-144) This restored Queen Anne house has been in the Pollock family for over 200 years. The old manor is surrounded by hundreds of acres of rolling grass with horses, poultry and even peacocks running about. The rooms are all designed in period fashion and always seem to be full of sunlight.

Eating

Loft (☎ 907 1755; 26 Trimgate St; mains from €12, early-bird dinner €14; 6-11pm Mon-Sat, 12.30-11pm Sun) Known for its fun, relaxed ambiance, this is one of the best places around. The menu promises 'funky food, art and music' every night.

Mountainstown House (☎ 905 4154; Castletown, Navan; meals €32; 7-11pm) This place is worth a visit just for the spectacularly ornamental dining room, but the top quality food won't disappoint. Try the game dishes.

Ryan's Pub (☎ 902 1154; 22 Trimgate St; bar food from €4; noon-8pm) This lovely old pub serves great pub grub, including brown bread with smoked salmon.

Chekhov's Coffee Shop (☎ 907 4422; 17 Trimgate St; mains from €5; 10am-6pm Mon-Sat & noon-5pm Sun) We don't quite get the Russian reference, but no matter; this is a wonderfully cosy place.

Entertainment

O'Flaherty's (☎ 902 2810; cnr Railway St & Brews Hill) A popular, modern, comfortably furnished pub.

Lantern (☎ 902 3535; 32 Watergate St) Delivering foot-tapping Irish music every Wednesday night.

Getting There & Away

Bus Éireann (☎ 01-836 6111) runs buses almost hourly on the Dublin–Cavan–Donegal route, which stop in Navan and also serve Kells (to Dublin: single/return €7.50/10, 50 minutes; to Kells: €3.20/5.20, 15 minutes). Navan is also on the Dundalk to Galway route (to Dundalk: €7.90/12.10, 1¼ hours; to Galway: €15.50/23, 3¼ hours), with one bus daily stopping also at Drogheda (€3.75/5.60, 35 minutes). All buses stop in front of the Mercy Convent on Railway St and in Market Square.

Getting Around

You can order a taxi from **Navan Cabs** (☎ 902 3053), and ranks are on Market Square and in front of the shopping centre on Kennedy Rd. **Clarke's Sports** (☎ 902 1130; 39 Trimgate St; rental per day €14, plus deposit €70), in the back of the Navan Indoor Market, rents bikes by the day. You'd have to negotiate a weekly rate.

AROUND NAVAN

There are some nice **walks** in the area, particularly the one following the towpath that runs along the old River Boyne canal towards Slane and Drogheda. On the southern bank, you can easily go out about 7km as far as Stackallen and the Boyne bridge, passing Ardmulchan House and, on the opposite bank, the ruins of Dunmoe Castle (see opposite for details). Going beyond the bridge towards Slane is trickier as the path is rough and in some places switches to the opposite side of the bank, with no bridge for you to cross over.

Just west of town is the **Motte of Navan**, a scrub-covered mound that tradition holds to be the burial site of Odhbha (oh-bah), the wife of a Celtic prince who had abandoned her for Tea (*tay*-ah), the lady who gave her name to Tara. Odhbha followed her husband to Navan and died of a broken heart. In reality, the 16m-high mound was probably formed naturally – a deposit of gravel from the Ice Age – and was then adapted by the Normans as a motte and bailey.

About 2km southeast of town are the impressive remains of **Athlumney Castle**, built by the Dowdall family in the 16th century with additions made a hundred years later. This relatively intact castle was said to have been set alight in 1690 by Sir Lancelot Dowdall, after James' defeat at the Battle of the Boyne. Dowdall vowed that the conqueror, William of Orange, would never shelter in or confiscate his home. He watched the blaze from the opposite bank of the river before leaving for France and then Italy. As you enter the estate, take a right toward the Loreto Convent, where you can pick up the keys to the castle. In the convent yard is another **motte**; at one time it had a wooden tower on it.

Close to the Kells road (N3), 5km northwest of Navan, is the large ruin of a castle that once belonged to the Talbot family. **Liscartan Castle** is made up of two 15th-century square towers joined by a hall-like room.

TARA

The **Hill of Tara** (Teamhair) has occupied a special place in Irish legend and folklore for millennia, although it's not known exactly when people first settled on this gently sloping hill with its commanding views over the plains of Meath. One of the many mounds on the hill was found to be a Stone Age passage grave from about 2500 BC, and during the Bronze Age people of high rank and status were certainly being buried here.

Much of the pagan significance of Tara seems to have derived from its associations with the goddess Maeve (or Medbh) and the mythical powers of the druids or priest-rulers who reigned over part of the country from here. By the 3rd century, Tara was the seat of the most powerful rulers in Ireland (Cormac MacArt was the most powerful of them all), a place where the high king and his royal court had their ceremonial residence, feasted and watched over the realm. While Tara's kings may have been more powerful than the others, they would by no means have held sway over all Ireland as there were countless other *rí tuaithe* (petty kings) controlling many smaller areas. Celtic titles were not hereditary, either, so it was not uncommon for the ultimate prize of high king to be won on the battlefield.

Tara's remains are not visually impressive. Only mounds and depressions in the grass mark where the Iron Age hill fort and surrounding ring forts once stood, but it remains an evocative, somewhat moving place, especially on a warm summer's evening.

As the focus of Irish political influence and a centre of pagan worship, Tara was targeted by the early Christians. A great pagan *feis* (festival) is thought to have been held around what is now Halloween. On Tara – if not on the Hill of Slane – St Patrick supposedly used the shamrock and its three leaves to explain the Christian Trinity to King Laoghaire in the 5th century. Hence the adoption of the shamrock as the Irish national symbol.

After the 6th century, once Christianity had taken hold and Tara's pagan significance had waned, the high kings began to desert Tara. The kings of Leinster continued to be based here until the 11th century, however.

In August 1843, Tara saw one of the greatest crowds ever to gather in Ireland. Daniel O'Connell, the 'Liberator' and leader of the opposition to union with Great Britain, held one of his 'monster rallies' at Tara, and up to 750,000 people came to hear him speak.

Tara Visitor Centre

The former Protestant church (with a window by well-known artist Evie Hone) houses the impressive **Tara Visitor Centre** (☎ 046-902 5903; Navan; adult €1.90, student & child €0.70; ⏰ 9.30am-6.30pm mid-Jun–mid-Sep, 10am-5pm May–mid-Jun & mid-Sep–Oct, last admission 45 min before closing), where a 20-minute audiovisual presentation on the site called *Tara: Meeting Place of Heroes* is shown. During summer the tour from here is a must, as the anecdotes really bring the mounds and relics to life (see Tours, p513).

Ráth of the Synods

The names applied to Tara's various humps and mounds were adopted from ancient texts, and mythology and religion intertwine with the historical facts. The Protestant church grounds and graveyard spill onto the remains of the Ráth of the Synods, a triple-ringed fort supposedly where some of St Patrick's early meetings (or synods) took place. Excavations of the enclosure suggest that it was used between AD 200 and 400 for burials, rituals and living quarters. Originally the ring fort would have contained wooden houses surrounded by timber palisades.

During a digging session in the graveyard in 1810, a boy found a pair of gold torcs (necklaces of twisted gold bands), now in the National Museum in Dublin. Later excavations brought a surprise when Roman glass, shards of pottery and seals were discovered, showing links with the Roman Empire, even though the Romans never extended their power into Ireland.

The poor state of the enclosure is due in part to a group of British 'Israelites' who in the 1890s dug the place up looking for the Ark of the Covenant, much to the consternation of the local people. The Israelites' leader claimed to see a mysterious pillar on the enclosure, but unfortunately it was invisible to everyone else. After they failed to uncover anything, the invisible pillar moved to the other side of the road but, before the adventurers had time to start work there, the locals chased them away.

The Royal Enclosure

To the south of the church, the Royal Enclosure (Ráth na Ríogh) is a large, oval Iron Age hill fort, 315m in diameter and surrounded by a bank and ditch cut through solid rock under the soil. Inside the Royal Enclosure are smaller sites.

MOUND OF THE HOSTAGES

This bump (Dumha na nGiall) in the northern corner of the enclosure is the most ancient known part of Tara and the most visible of the remains. Supposedly a prison cell for hostages of the 3rd-century king Cormac MacArt, it is in fact a small Stone Age passage grave dating from around 1800 BC and later used by Bronze Age people. The passage contains some carved stonework, but it's closed to the public.

The mound produced a treasure trove of artefacts, including some ancient Mediterranean beads of amber and faïence (glazed pottery). More than 35 Bronze Age burials were found here, as well as a mass of cremated remains from the Stone Age.

CORMAC'S HOUSE & THE ROYAL SEAT

Two other earthworks found inside the enclosure are Cormac's House (Teach Cormaic) and the Royal Seat (Forradh). Although they look similar, the Royal Seat is a ring fort with a house site in the centre, while Cormac's House is a barrow, or burial mound, in the side of the circular bank. Cormac's House commands the best views of the surrounding lowlands of the Boyne and Blackwater Valleys.

Atop Cormac's House is the phallic **Stone of Destiny** (Lia Fáil), originally located near the Mound of the Hostages and representing the joining of the gods of the earth and the heavens. It's said to be the inauguration stone of the high kings of Tara. The would-be king stood on top of it and, if the stone let out three roars, he was crowned. The mass grave of 37 men who died in a skirmish on Tara during the 1798 Rising is next to the stone.

Enclosure of King Laoghaire

South of the Royal Enclosure is the Enclosure of King Laoghaire (Ráth Laoghaire), a large but worn ring fort where the king – a contemporary of St Patrick – is supposedly buried dressed in his armour and standing upright.

Banquet Hall

North of the churchyard is Tara's most unusual feature, the Banquet Hall, or Teach Miodhchuarta (House of Meadcircling; mead, which was a popular tipple, is fermented from honey). This rectangular earthwork measures 230m by 27m along a north–south axis. Tradition holds that it was built to cater for thousands of guests during feasts. Much of this information about the hall comes from the 12th-century *Book of Leinster* and the *Yellow Book of Lecan*, which even includes drawings of it.

Opinions vary as to the site's real purpose. Its orientation suggests that it was a sunken entrance to Tara, leading directly to the Royal Enclosure. More recent research has uncovered graves within the compound, and it's possible that the banks are in fact the burial sites of some of the kings of Tara.

Gráinne's Fort

Gráinne's Fort (Ráth Gráinne) and the northern and southern Sloping Trenches (Claoin Fhearta) off to the northwest are burial mounds. Gráinne was the same daughter of King Cormac who was betrothed to Fionn McCumhaill (Finn McCool) but eloped with Diarmuid ÓDuibhne, one of the king's warriors, on her wedding night and became the subject of the epic *The Pursuit of Diarmuid and Gráinne*. See p506 for more about the legend.

Tours

Mary Gibbons (☎ 01-283 9973) has an excellent Boyne Valley tour that includes the Hill of Tara as well as Brú na Bóinne. See p508 for prices and departure times.

Bus Éireann (☎ 01-836 6111) tours to Newgrange and the Boyne Valley sometimes include a visit to Tara. See p508 for prices and departure times.

Getting There & Away

Tara is 10km southeast of Navan just off the N3 Dublin to Cavan road. **Bus Éireann** (☎ 01-836 6111) buses linking Dublin and Navan pass within 1km of the site (from Dublin: single €7.40, 40 minutes, hourly Monday to Saturday and four on Sunday). Ask the driver to drop you off at the Tara Cross and then follow the signs.

AROUND TARA

About 5km south of Tara on the Dunshaughlin to Kilmessan road is **Dunsany Castle** (☎ 046-902 5198; Dunsany; downstairs €6.35, downstairs & upstairs bedrooms €10.20; 🕑 9am-1pm Mon-Fri May-Aug & Oct-Nov, by arrangement only weekends). It's the residence of the lords of Dunsany, former owners of the lands around Trim Castle. The Dunsanys are related to the Plunkett family, the most-famous Plunkett being St Oliver, who was executed and whose head is kept in a church in Drogheda (see p523).

There's an impressive private art collection and many other treasures related to important figures in Irish history, such as Oliver Plunkett and Patrick Sarsfield, leader of the Irish Jacobite forces at the siege of Limerick in 1691. A number of upstairs bedrooms have been restored and are now included in an expanded tour (though the charge to visit these is extra). Maintenance and restoration is ongoing (as it would be in a castle built in 1180!) and different rooms are open to visitors at different times.

Housed in the old kitchen and in part of the old domestic quarters is a **boutique** (🕑 10am-5pm) that proudly sells the Dunsany Home Collection, featuring locally made table linen and accessories, as well as various articles for the home designed by Lord Dunsany himself, who is something of a well-known artist and designer.

About 1.5km northeast of Dunsany is the ruined **Killeen Castle** the seat of another line of the Plunkett family. The 1801 mansion was constructed around a castle built by Hugh de Lacy, lord of Meath, originally dating from 1180. It comprises a neo-Gothic structure between two 12th-century towers. It is closed to the public.

According to local lore, the surrounding lands were divided at one point among the two Plunkett branches by a race. Starting at the castles, the wives had to run towards each other and a fence was placed where they met. Luckily for the Killeen womenfolk, their castle was on higher ground and they made considerable gains as they ran downhill towards their Dunsany counterparts.

TRIM

☎ 046 / pop 1460

Trim (Baile Átha Troim, Town at the Ford of the Elder Trees) is a lovely sleepy little town on the River Boyne with a glorious past evident in several interesting ruins. The medieval town was a busy jumble of streets and once had five gates. At one stage, there were no fewer than seven monasteries in the immediate area. In the past, few visitors have paused to inspect the impressive ruins of Trim Castle, Ireland's largest Anglo-Norman structure, which many will recognise as having served as a 'castle double' for York Castle in Mel Gibson's 1996 film *Braveheart*. The interesting historical coincidence is that Queen Isabella's real lover, Roger de Mortimer, the earl of March, actually lived in the castle between 1316–20.

According to local history, Elizabeth I considered Trim as a possible site for Trinity College, which eventually ended up in Dublin. The Duke of Wellington went to school for a time in Talbot Castle/St Mary's Abbey, which served as a Protestant school in the 18th century. There's a local (and unlikely) belief that he was born in a stable south of the town, which probably arose from the duke's observation that being born in a stable didn't make one a horse, and thus his birth in Ireland didn't make him Irish! A **Wellington column** stands at the junction of Patrick and Emmet Sts. After defeating Napoleon at the Battle of Waterloo, the Iron Duke went on to become prime minister of Great Britain and in 1829 passed the Catholic Emancipation Act, which repealed the last of the repressive penal laws.

Trim was home to the county jail, giving rise to the ditty: 'Kells for brogues, Navan for rogues and Trim for hanging people'.

Information

Among the brochures for sale in the **tourist office** (☎ 943 7111; Mill St; 🕑 9.30am-5.30pm Mon-Sat, noon-5.30pm Sun May-Sep, 9am-5pm Mon-Sat Oct-Apr) is the handy little *Trim Tourist Trail* (€3) walking-tour booklet.

The **post office** (cnr Emmet & Market Sts; 🕑 9.30am-6pm Mon-Fri & 9.30am-1pm Sat) is right beside a branch of the **Allied Irish Bank**.

Trim Heritage Centre

Immediately next to the tourist office in Mill St is the informative **Trim Heritage Centre** (☎ 943 7227; Mill St; adult/concession €3.20/2.20; 🕑 10am-5pm Mon-Wed & Fri-Sat, noon 5.30pm Sun Apr-Sep), which has an exhibit known as *The Power and the Glory* outlining the

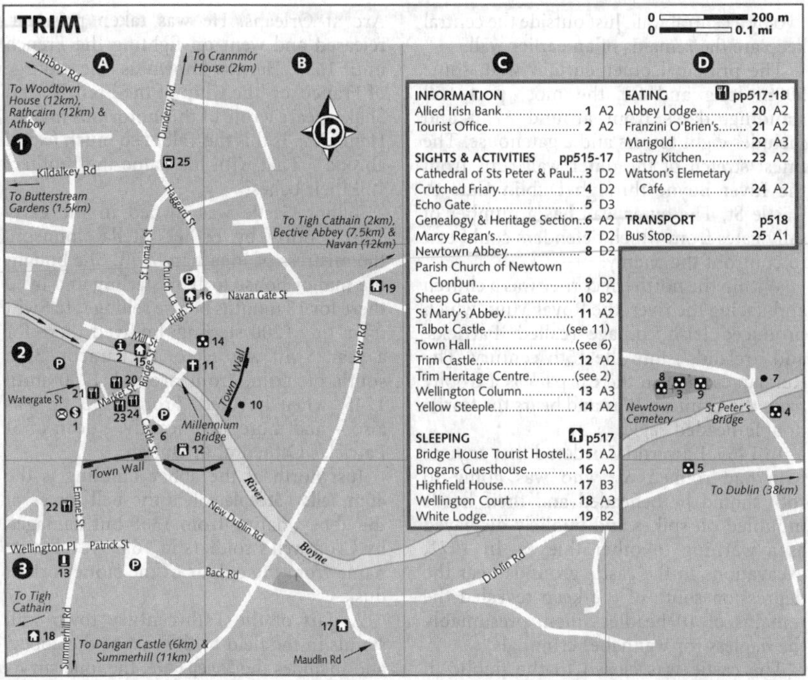

medieval history of Trim in audiovisuals. The 20-minute film is shown six times daily and focuses on delights like the medieval plague of rats.

The **genealogy & heritage section** (☎ 943 6633; Castle St; initial consultation €19, personalised family tree €89; 🕑 9am-5pm Mon-Thu, 9am-2pm Fri) of the Heritage Centre is in the town hall. Here, under the expert guidance of local historian Noel French (who also penned the *Trim Tourist Trail* booklet), there's an extensive genealogical database for people trying to trace Meath ancestors.

Trim Castle

Where now the glories of Babylon? Proof of Trim's medieval importance, Hugh de Lacy founded **Trim Castle** (☎ 943 8619; adult/student €3.20/1.20, castle grounds not incl keep €1.20/0.50; 🕑 10am-6pm May-Oct) in 1173, but Rory O'Connor, said to have been the last high king of Ireland, destroyed this motte and bailey within a year. De Lacy did not live to see the castle's replacement, and the building you see today was begun around 1200. It has hardly been modified since then.

Although King John visited Trim in 1210 to bring the de Lacy family into line – hence the building's alternative name of King John's Castle – he never actually slept in the castle. On the eve of his arrival, Walter de Lacy locked it up tight and left town, forcing the king to camp in the nearby meadow.

Throughout Anglo-Norman times the castle occupied a strategic position on the western edge of the Pale, the area where the Anglo-Normans ruled supreme; beyond Trim was the volatile country where Irish chieftains and lords vied and fought with their Norman rivals for position, power and terrain.

Trim was conquered by Silken Thomas in 1536 and again in 1647 by Catholic Confederate forces, opponents of the English Parliamentarians. In 1649 it was taken by Cromwellian forces, and the castle, town walls and Yellow Steeple were badly damaged.

The grassy two-hectare enclosure is dominated by a massive stone keep, 25m tall and mounted on a Norman motte. Inside are three lofty levels, the lowest one divided in two by a central wall. Just outside the central keep are the remains of an earlier wall.

The principal outer curtain wall, some 500m long and for the most part still standing, dates from around 1250 and includes eight towers and a gatehouse. The finest stretch of the outer wall runs from the River Boyne through Dublin Gate to Castle St. The outer wall has a number of sally gates from which defenders could exit to confront the enemy.

Within the northern corner was a church and, facing the river, the Royal Mint, which produced Irish coinage (called 'Patricks' and 'Irelands') into the 15th century. The Russian cannon in the car park is a trophy from the Crimean War and bears the tsarist double-headed eagle.

In 1465, Edward IV ordered that anyone who had robbed or 'who was going to rob' should be beheaded and their heads mounted on spikes and publicly displayed as a warning to other thieves. In 1971, excavations in the castle grounds near the depression south of the keep revealed the remains of 10 headless men, presumably the hapless (or wannabe) criminals.

The castle was closed to the public in 1995, but reopened in 2000 under the care of Dúchas, the Heritage Service. You can now visit the restored keep (by guided tour only) and/or the rest of the castle grounds.

Talbot Castle/St Mary's Abbey

Across the river from the castle are the ruins of the 12th-century Augustinian St Mary's Abbey, rebuilt after a fire in 1368 and once home to a wooden statue of Our Lady of Trim, which was revered by the faithful for its miraculous powers. Cromwell's soldiers set fire to the statue in front of their injured commander, General Croot, a rather poignant slap in the face of Catholic belief. Just in case the locals didn't get the symbolism of the gesture, they destroyed the abbey as well. An artists' rendition of the statue is by the roadside in front of the ruins.

Part of the abbey was converted in 1415 into a fine manor house by Sir John Talbot, then viceroy of Ireland; it came to be known as Talbot Castle. The Talbot coat of arms can be seen on the northern wall. Talbot went to war in France, where in 1429 he was defeated by none other than Joan of Arc at Orleans. He was taken prisoner, released and went on fighting the French until 1453. He was known as 'the scourge of France' or 'the whip of the French', and Shakespeare wrote of this notorious man in Henry VI: 'Is this the Talbot so much feared abroad / That with his name the mothers still their babes?'

Talbot Castle was owned in the early 18th century by Esther 'Stella' Johnson, the mistress of Jonathan Swift. She bought the manor house for £65 sterling and lived there for 18 months before selling it to Swift for a tidy £200 sterling; he lived there for a year. Swift was rector of Laracor, 3km south of Trim, from around 1700 until 1745, when he died. From 1713 he was also – and more significantly – dean of St Patrick's Cathedral in Dublin.

Just north of the abbey building is the 40m **Yellow Steeple**, once the bell tower of the abbey, dating from 1368 but damaged by Cromwell's soldiers in 1649. It takes its name from the colour of the stonework at dusk.

A part of the 14th-century town wall stands in the field to the east of the abbey, and includes the **Sheep Gate**, the lone survivor of the town's original five gates. It used to be closed daily between 9pm and 4am, and a toll was charged for sheep entering to be sold at market.

Newtown

pop 382

About 1.5km east of town on Lackanash Rd, Newtown Cemetery contains an interesting group of ruins. What had been the **parish church** of Newtown Clonbun contains the late-16th-century tomb of Sir Luke Dillon, chief baron of the Exchequer during the reign of Elizabeth I, and his wife Lady Jane Bathe. The effigies are known locally as 'the jealous man and woman', perhaps because of the sword lying between them.

Rainwater that collects between the two figures is claimed to cure warts. Place a pin in the puddle and then jab your wart. When the pin becomes covered in rust your warts will vanish. Some say you should leave a pin on the statue as payment for the cure.

The other ruins here are Newtown's **Cathedral of Sts Peter and Paul**, and the 18th-century **Newtown Abbey** (Abbey of the Canons Regular of St Victor of Paris). The cathedral was founded in 1206 and burned down two centuries later. Parts of the cathedral wall were flattened by a storm in January 1839, which also damaged sections of the Trim Castle wall. The abbey wall throws a superb echo back to **Echo Gate** across the river.

Southeast of these ruins and just over the river is the **Crutched Friary**. There are ruins of a keep and traces of a watchtower and other buildings from a hospital set up after the crusades by the Knights of St John of Jerusalem, who wore a red crutch, or cross, on their cassocks. **St Peter's Bridge** beside the friary is said to be the second-oldest bridge in Ireland. **Marcy Regan's** (Lackanash Rd, Newtown Trim), the small pub beside the bridge, claims to be Ireland's second-oldest pub.

Sleeping

HOSTELS

Bridge House Tourist Hostel (☎ 943 1848; silversue@eircom.net, Bridge St; dm/d €15/36) Travellers from all corners of the globe chill out in Bridge House's stylish TV room built out of an old cellar. The large, comfortable doubles are the best option.

B&BS

Brogans Guesthouse (☎ 943 1237; brogangh@iol.ie; High St; s/d €40/64) Brogans has an old-world flavour and an adjoining bar and beer-garden that serves a decent lunch and often has live music.

White Lodge (☎ 943 6549; whitelodgetrim@eircom.net; New Rd; s/d €45/60) The owners of this cosy B&B have managed to design it so every room seems to be full of light all day long. It's 500m east of the centre at the northern end of New Rd.

Crannmór House (☎ 943 1635; www.crannmor.com; Dunderry Rd; s/d €45/60) Five acres of rolling farmland surround this converted farmhouse about 2km along the road to Dunderry.

Woodtown House (☎ 943 5022; Athboy; s/d €40/60) It's well worth the 12km trip on the R154 north out of Trim to stay at this very special country house. The perfectly restored 18th-century interiors compete with the beautiful, tree-filled grounds for your attention. You can get a high-quality dinner (€25) in the elegant dining room.

Tigh Cathain (☎ 943 1996; mariekeane@esatclear.ie; Longwood Rd; s/d €35/55) This is a family-run country house B&B surrounded by open fields, only 2km west out of Trim.

SOMETHING SPECIAL

'The most imaginative garden in Ireland' is how *House & Gardens* magazine described the multi-award-winning **Butterstream Gardens** (☎ 943 6017; Kildalkey Rd; admission €5; 🕑 11am-6pm Apr-Sep) on the western outskirts of Trim. Surprisingly it's still something of a hidden treasure often overlooked by visitors to Ireland. Designed and planted solely by the owner, Butterstream comprises a series of carefully integrated 'rooms' each with their own character and style. You will find a stream garden, obelisk garden, pool garden, kitchen garden and hot-coloured garden all side by side. Ideal for a gentle afternoon stroll, this place is a feast for the eyes and nose alike.

HOTELS

Highfield House (☎ 943 6386; highfieldhouseaccom@eircom.net; Maudlins Rd; s €45-75) Set on a hill south of town, this elegant 18th-century country house has great views of the town, Trim Castle, and the Boyne. The seven bedrooms have all been restored to their former elegance; it's like waking up in the gilded age.

Wellington Court (☎ 943 1516; wellingtoncourt@eircom.net; Summerhill Rd; s/d €55/90) Trim's fanciest hotel is well-equipped and modern, but it's still small enough to have a family feel to it.

Eating

There's no shortage of somewhere to get a bite in town, with plenty of pubs doing standard pub grub. There are also a couple of pretty good cafés.

Marigold (☎ 943 6544; Emmet St; mains €7; 🕑 5.30-11.30pm Sun-Thu, 5.30pm-12.30am Fri & Sat) Takeaways or sit down, if you want half-decent Chinese food in Trim, this is the place.

Pastry Kitchen (☎ 943 8902; Market St; snacks around €3; 🕑 7.30am-5.30pm Mon-Sat, 10am-2pm Sun) A great early morning spot, this place serves sandwiches and limited hot plates.

Abbey Lodge (☎ 943 1285; Market St; dishes €4.50-13; 🕑 noon-6pm) This nice pub does pretty good grub, from toasted sandwiches to more substantial dishes.

Watson's Elementary Café (Market St; mains €5; 🕑 9am-5pm Mon-Sat) A quality greasy spoon, Watson's big breakfast is a heart-stopping pile of meat and eggs.

Franzini O'Brien's (☎ 943 1002; French Lane; mains €12-20; 🕑 6.30-9.30pm Tue-Sat, 5-8.30pm Sun) This fancy café-bar, off Market St, has raised the standards of cuisine in Trim. The menu changes regularly and always includes noodle, meat, and pasta dishes.

Getting There & Away

Bus Éireann (☎ 01-836 6111) runs a very regular service between Dublin and Trim (single/return €7.50/10.20, one hour, every 15 minutes). All buses stop in front of Tobin's newsagent at the northern end of Haggard St.

AROUND TRIM

Some 7.5km northeast of Trim on the way to Navan is **Bective Abbey**, founded in 1147 and the first Cistercian offspring of magnificent Mellifont Abbey in Louth. The remains seen today are 13th- and 15th-century additions and consist of the chapter house, church, ambulatory and cloister. After the suppression of the monasteries in 1543, it was used as a fortified house, and the tower was built.

In 1186, Hugh de Lacy, lord of Meath, began demolishing the abbey at Durrow in County Offaly in order to build a castle. A workman, known both as O'Miadaigh and O'Kearney, was offended by this desecration, lopped off de Lacy's head and fled. Although de Lacy's body was interred in Bective Abbey, his head went to St Thomas Abbey in Dublin. A dispute broke out over who should possess all the bodily remains, and it required the intervention of the pope to, well, pontificate on the matter, with a ruling in favour of St Thomas Abbey.

Some 12km northwest of Trim on the road to Athboy is **Rathcairn**, the smallest Gaeltacht (Irish-speaking) district in Ireland. Rathcairn's population is descended from a group of Connemara Irish speakers, who were settled on an estate here as part of a social experiment in the 1930s.

Six kilometres south of Trim on the road to Summerhill stands **Dangan Castle**, built by the Wellesley family and the boyhood home of the duke of Wellington. The castle is also supposed to have been the birthplace of Don Ambrosio O'Higgins (1720–1801), the Spanish viceroy of Peru and Chile at the end of the 18th century. His son Bernardo O'Higgins went on to become the liberator of Chile, and Santiago's main thoroughfare is named after him (he was also the founder of Argentina's navy, and Buenos Aires has a number of statues in his honour). The mansion's current state is the result of the efforts of Roger O'Conor, its last owner, who set it alight on a number of occasions between 1808 and 1809 for the insurance money.

KELLS

☎ 046 / pop 2619

Most visitors to Ireland pay homage to the magnificent *Book of Kells* in Dublin's Trinity College, but few make it out to its place of origin. Frankly, they're not missing all that much as Kells is a little on the dreary side, but there are some interesting high crosses and a 1000-year-old round tower – the best remnants of the monastic site established here in the 6th century.

Orientation & Information

The N3 from Dublin to Cavan almost bypasses the town. Turning south at Cross St brings you down to Farrell St, where you'll find most of the pubs and shops (including Maguire's, a newsagent and grocery with disposable mousetraps among other useful items!). The **tourist office** (☎ 924 9336; Headfort Pl; 🕑 10am-5.30pm Mon-Sat & 1.30-5.30pm Sun May-Sep, 1-5pm Tue-Sat & 1.30-5pm Sun Oct-Apr) is in the heritage centre (see below) behind the town hall. Kells Hostel is also helpful with queries. There's also a **Bank of Ireland** (John St) and a **post office** (Farrell St).

Kells Heritage Centre

Spread across two detail-packed floors, the town's **heritage centre** (☎ 924 9336; Headfort Pl; adult/concession €4/2.50; 🕑 same hrs as tourist office) has a 12-minute audiovisual on the monastic era which sets the tone for the exhibits. On the ground floor is a replica of the Market Cross (the real one is outside), while upstairs is a rather beautiful copy of the area's most-famous object, the *Book of Kells*. Two touchscreens allow you to leaf interactively through the entire book, giving you a proper sense of the book's awesome beauty. Surrounding the book are various 6th- to 12th-century relics and artefacts as well as a scale model of the town around the 6th century.

Round Tower & High Crosses

The **Protestant Church of St Columba** (admission free; 🕑 10am-1pm & 2-5pm Mon-Sat, services only Sun), west of the town centre, stands in the

THE MAGNIFICENT BOOK OF KELLS

After establishing monasteries at Derry, Durrow and, in 559, Kells, St Colmcille (also known as St Columba) went into exile on the remote Scottish island of Iona. In 807, monks from the Iona monastery arrived in Kells after 68 of their brethren were killed in a Viking raid. It's thought that they brought both the remains of their revered saint and an illuminated manuscript of the Gospels with them, bound in vellum and enclosed in a gold case. This extraordinary work of art consequently came to be known as the *Book of Kells*.

It was stolen two centuries later, but the thief was only after its gold case, and the manuscript was later found buried in a bog. Kells proved to be no safer than Scotland for the monks, however, as Viking raids soon spread to Ireland. Kells was plundered on no less than five different occasions between the 9th and 11th centuries. A century later, the Columbans moved their headquarters to Derry and the monastery was abandoned.

grounds of the old monastic settlement. A square belfry dating from the 15th century stands beside the church. Above the doorway is an inscription detailing the addition of the neo-Gothic spire in 1783 by the earl of Bective from a design by Thomas Cooley, the architect of Dublin's City Hall.

The churchyard has a 30m-high, 10th-century round tower on the southern side. It's now without its conical roof but is known to date back at least as far as 1076, when Muircheartach Maelsechnaill, the high king of Tara, was murdered in its confined apartments.

Inside the churchyard are four 9th-century high crosses in various states of repair. The West Cross, at the far end of the compound from the entrance, is the stump of a decorated shaft with scenes of the baptism of Jesus, the Fall of Adam and Eve, and the judgement of Solomon on the eastern face, and Noah's ark on the western face. All that is left of the North Cross is the bowl-shaped base stone.

Near the tower is the best preserved of the crosses, the Cross of Patrick and Columba, with its semilegible inscription 'Patrici et Columbae Crux' on the eastern face of the base. Above it are scenes of Daniel in the lions' den, the fiery furnace, the Fall of Adam and Eve and a hunting scene. On the opposite side of the cross are the Last Judgement, the Crucifixion, and riders with a chariot and a dog on the base. The council has plans to move this cross into the new heritage centre when completed to protect it from the elements.

The other surviving cross is the unfinished East Cross. On the eastern side is a carving of the Crucifixion and a group of four figures on the right arm. The three blank, raised panels below these were prepared for carving, but the sculptor apparently never got round to the task.

St Colmcille's House

From the churchyard exit on Church St, **St Colmcille's House** (admission free; 10am-5pm Sat & Sun Jun-Sep) is left up the hill, among the row of houses on the right side of Church Lane. It is usually open in the summer; otherwise, pick up the keys from **Mrs Carpenter** (☎ 924 1778; 1 Lower Church View), at the brown-coloured house as you ascend the hill.

This squat, solid structure is a survivor from the old monastic settlement. Its name is a misnomer, as it was built in the 10th century and St Colmcille was alive in the 6th century. Although its use is unclear, experts have suggested that it was used as a scriptorium, a place where monks illuminated books. The original entrance to the 1000-year-old building was over 2m above ground level. Inside, a very long ladder leads to a low attic room under the roof line.

Market Cross

Until recently the Market Cross had stood for centuries in Cross St in the town centre, marking the furthest extent of the 10th-century monastery. It's said that it was moved here by Jonathan Swift, and in 1798 the British garrison executed rebels by hanging them from the crosspiece, one on each arm so the cross wouldn't fall over. Alas, in 1996 the cross met its ignoble fate – in a crass, modern manner. A motorist took a tight turn, reversed and toppled the 1000-year-old thing. It has now been repaired and has been placed outside the heritage centre; originally it was intended to go inside, but local objections to having to pay to see their monument forced a change of plans. Oddly, you can pay to see a replica, but you'll have to walk by the real thing to do so!

On the eastern side of the Market Cross are Abraham's sacrifice of Isaac, Cain and Abel, the Fall of Adam and Eve, guards at the tomb of Jesus and a wonderfully executed procession of horsemen. On the western face, the Crucifixion is the only discernible image. On the northern side is a panel of Jacob wrestling with the angel.

Sleeping

Kells Hostel (☎ 924 9995; hostels@iol.ie; The Carrick, Cavan Rd; dm/d/tent €13/32/8) This IHH hostel on the Cavan road is 200m uphill from the bus stop. A new renovation has enlarged the kitchen and added a laundry and pool table. You may have to check-in at Monaghan's Inn next door.

White Gables (☎ 924 0322; whitegables@tinet.ie; Headfort Pl; s/d €40/60) The best B&B in town, this place is all crisp linen and fresh flowers. The owner is a cordon bleu chef, so the breakfasts are fantastic.

Headfort Arms Hotel (☎ 924 0063; fax 924 0587; John St; s/d €65/125) Nothing fancy, this place offers 18 rooms, all well-appointed and very neat. It also has a nightclub and restaurant attached.

Boltown House (☎ 924 3605; boltown@iolfree.ie; off Oldcastle Rd; s/d €60/100) About 7km outside of town, this is a large farmhouse with cosy rooms and excellent food, including home-made scones.

Eating

Penny's Place (☎ 924 1130; Market St; sandwiches from €5; ⏰ 9am-6pm Mon-Sat) Brown bread without equal is the speciality at this excellent café with home-made food.

Ground Floor (☎ 924 9688; Bective Sq; mains €15-20; ⏰ 5.30-11pm Mon-Sat & 5.30-10pm Sun) This classy little eatery is renowned for its huge healthy portions and killer desserts.

Monaghan's (☎ 924 9995; The Carrick, Cavan Rd; lunch/dinner €7/10; ⏰ noon-8pm) This pub next to the hostel is something of a local institution. It serves a traditionally hearty lunch and dinner.

Vanilla Pod (☎ 924 0084; John St; mains €10-15; ⏰ 5.30-10pm Mon-Fri, 5.30-11pm Sat-Sun) One of the newer arrivals in Kells dining, Vanilla Pod is a cut above the competition. The healthy menu offers dishes from every corner of the globe with only the freshest ingredients, and the atmosphere is relaxed and a little funky.

SOMETHING SPECIAL

Lennoxbrook (☎ 924 5902; 5km north of Kells on N3; d €66) Live like a country squire for a night. Pauline Mullan is the fifth generation of her family to live in this wonderful, 200-year-old farmhouse outside Kells. She'll treat you as one of the family and give you the run of this beautifully designed and restored house. The four bedrooms are all decorated in a luxurious but restrained fashion, with patterned wallpapers and period furniture. Dinner (€20) in the elegant dining room is a must.

Entertainment

O'Shaughnessy's (☎ 924 1110; Market St) This pub features lots of rustic timber and is always choc full of chattering locals.

Blackwater Inn (☎ 924 0386; Farrell St) Another favourite with regular Irish music sessions.

Monaghan's (☎ 924 9995; The Carrick, Cavan Rd) Monaghan's is favoured by a younger crowd; it often has music at the weekend.

Getting There & Away

Bus Éireann (☎ 01-836 6111) runs buses from Dublin to Kells and Cavan (single/return €9.20/14.50, one hour, almost hourly from 7am to 10pm). Buses stop in front of the church on John St and near the hostel (this is a request stop only); times are posted at the stop. There are also regular services running to Navan (single/return €3.20/5.20, 15 minutes) and Drogheda (€6.20/10, 1½ hours, 12 daily).

AROUND KELLS

Hill of Lloyd Tower

The 30m **tower** (☎ 47840; adult/child €1.90/1.30; ⏰ by appointment) on the Hill of Lloyd is visible from behind the hostel in Kells, and it's easy to see why it became known as the 'inland lighthouse'. Built in 1791 by the earl of Bective in memory of his father, it has been renovated and if it's open you can climb to the top, or picnic in the surrounding park. The tower is 3km northwest of Kells, off the Crossakeel road.

Crosses of Castlekeeran

About 2km further down the Crossakeel road, signposted to the right, are the Crosses of Castlekeeran. Access is through a farmyard. Three plainly carved, early-9th-century crosses, one in the river, are surrounded by an overgrown cemetery, while at the ruined church in the centre are some early grave slabs and an ogham stone.

LOUGHCREW CAIRNS

Northwest of Kells and near Oldcastle, the Loughcrew Hills – of which Slieve (or Sliabh) na Caillighe (279m) is the highest peak – give marvellous views east and south to the plains of Meath and north into the lake country of Cavan. On the summit of three of the hills – Slieve na Caillighe, Carnbane East (194m) and Carnbane West (206m) – are the remains of 30 Stone Age passage graves built around 3000 BC but used up to the Iron Age. In some cases, a large mound is surrounded by numerous, smaller satellite graves. As at Newgrange, larger stones in some of the graves are decorated with spiral patterns. Archaeologists have unearthed bone fragments and ashes, stone balls and beads. Some of the graves look like large piles of stones, while others are less obvious, the cairn having been removed.

To get there from Kells, head northwest on the R163. About 5km from Oldcastle you'll see a sign for Sliabh na Caillighe. Turn right, and at the first house on the right collect the keys to the cairn entrances from Basil Balfe (but ring ☎ 049-41256 first).

If anybody is there to collect it, a deposit of €6.50 (hikers can leave their backpacks as collateral!) is required, and a leaflet about the sites is available. A torch (flashlight) is useful on dull days. Coming from the east, the first group of hills – Patrickstown Cairns – is of little interest; the most interesting and intact remains are on the next two, Carnbane East and Carnbane West.

Carnbane East

Carnbane East has a cluster of sites; Cairn T is the biggest at about 35m in diameter and has numerous carved stones. One of its outlying kerbstones is called the Hag's Chair and is covered in gouged holes, circles and other markings. You need the gate key to enter the passageway and a torch to see anything in detail. It takes about half an hour to climb Carnbane East from the car park. From the summit on a reasonably clear day, you should be able to see the Hill of Tara to the southeast, while the view north is into Cavan, with Lough Ramor to the northeast and Lough Sheelin and Oldcastle to the northwest.

Carnbane West

From the same car park, it takes about an hour to reach the summit of Carnbane West, where Cairn D and L are both some 60m in diameter. Cairn D has been disturbed in an unsuccessful search for a central chamber. Cairn L, northeast of Cairn D, is also in poor condition, though you can enter the passage and chamber, where there are numerous carved stones and a curved basin stone where human ashes were placed.

COUNTY LOUTH

'The Wee County' it is commonly called, and while Louth is Ireland's smallest county, it has plenty to offer. Louth is also home to the two principal towns of Ireland's northeastern region – Drogheda and Dundalk.

Drogheda is by far the more pleasant of the two, with a bustling town centre and some pretty interesting attractions; it also makes a good base for exploring the Boyne Valley, with its prehistoric sites to the west and the monastic relics to the north. The border town of Dundalk has little to offer the casual visitor save its position as the gateway to the lonely but scenic Cooley Peninsula.

HISTORY

As part of the ancient kingdom of Oriel, Louth is the setting for perhaps the most epic of all Irish mythological tales, the Táin Bó Cúailnge (Cattle Raid of Cooley), which includes a starring role for Ireland's greatest mythological hero, Cúchulainn (see the boxed text, p533). *The Táin* by Thomas Kinsella is a modern version of this compelling and bloody tale.

Louth is home to a number of monastic ruins dating from the 5th and 6th centuries; the monastery at Monasterboice and the later Cistercian abbey at Mellifont, both near Drogheda, are Louth's most interesting archaeological sites.

The arrival of the Normans in the 12th century ushered in a period of great change and upheaval; attracted by the fertile plains of the Boyne, the Anglo-Norman gentry set about subduing the local population and building mighty houses and castles. The Norman invaders were responsible for the development of Dundalk, and for the two towns, on opposite banks of the Boyne, which united in 1412 to become what is now Drogheda.

DROGHEDA

☎ 041 / pop 28,308

The historic town of Drogheda hugs a bend on the River Boyne, 5km from the sea. For years it was a compact settlement, with a small village-like adjunct to the south of the river around Millmount. But in recent years a project of urban renewal and a rapid population increase of Dublin commuters has brought new life to the place. The future looks bright for Drogheda, and continuing efforts to clean the Boyne (which was filthy around here) are going a long way towards making the town a very attractive spot.

Once fortified, Drogheda still has one town gate in fine condition, together with some interesting old buildings and the curious hump of Millmount, south of the river. The embalmed head of the Catholic martyr St Oliver Plunkett is housed in St Peter's Roman Catholic Church.

The town's name comes from Droichead Átha (Bridge of the Ford), after the bridge built by the Normans to link the two earlier Viking settlements.

History

There was probably a rough settlement here before the 10th century, but Drogheda really began to take shape around 910, when the Danes built defences to guard a strategic crossing point on the River Boyne. In the 12th century, the Normans built a bridge and expanded the two settlements forming on either side of the river. They also built a

GREAT PROTECTOR TURNS DESTRUCTOR

To Englishmen he is the first democrat of England, the leader of a revolution, the enemy of tyranny. But in Ireland the name Oliver Cromwell (1599–1658) is used to scare children at bedtime. It's synonymous with cruelty and destruction for his ruthless suppression of the whole nation when he invaded in 1649.

Cromwell didn't much like the Irish. He saw them as treacherous infidels, a dirty race of Roman Catholics who had sided with King Charles I during the Civil War. When 'God's own Englishman' landed his 17,000 troops at Dublin in August 1649, he immediately set out for Drogheda, a strategic fort town and bastion of royalist support. It was his first engagement in Ireland, and he was determined to 'make an example' of the town so as to discourage further resistance.

When Cromwell arrived at the walls of Drogheda, he was met with the resistance of 2500 men. After a week of planning, he called on the town to surrender. The head of the town garrison refused. Cromwell let fly with artillery, mostly heavy cannon, and after two days the walls were breached.

A pretty straightforward military engagement, it might seem. Had Cromwell simply held the town and put a military governor in command, the taking of Drogheda would have joined an already long list of failed attempts to resist English rule. Instead, Cromwell ordered that everyone who had resisted his troops should be rounded up and executed. Over a period of a few hours, an estimated 3000 were massacred, including priests, women and children. The governor of the town, Sir Arthur Ashton, was beaten to death with his own wooden leg. In one particularly gruesome episode, about 100 terrified locals hid in the tower of St Peter's Church of Ireland; Cromwell's soldiers simply burnt it down, killing everyone inside.

Of the survivors, many were captured and sold into slavery in the Caribbean; the genetic presence of red hair on some Barbadians is commonly attributed to the sexual intermingling of African and Irish slaves.

According to historians, only 64 of Cromwell's men were killed in the sack of Drogheda. To this day, Cromwell's name provokes loathing and hatred in Ireland, nowhere more so than in Drogheda. Hardly surprising really.

large defensive motte-and-bailey castle on the southern side at Millmount.

By the 15th century, Drogheda was one of Ireland's four major walled towns. Many Irish Parliament sessions were held here, and Poyning's Law, the most famous piece of legislation from Irish medieval times, was passed here in 1494. It diminished prospects of home rule or independence for Ireland by granting the English Crown the right to veto any measures the Irish proposed to enact.

In 1465, the Irish Parliament conferred on Drogheda the right to a university, but the plan foundered in 1468, when the earl of Desmond was executed for treason. During the period of the Pale, when only a small portion of the country around Dublin (known as 'The Pale') was fully controlled by the English, Drogheda was a frontier town. Further north were the fractious Ulster folk, definitely 'beyond the Pale'.

In 1649, the town was the scene of Cromwell's most notorious Irish slaughter (see the boxed text, p522). Drogheda also plumped for the wrong side at the Battle of the Boyne in 1690, but surrendered the day after James II was defeated.

It took many years for the town to recover from these events, but in the 19th century a number of Catholic churches were built. The massive railway viaduct and the string of quayside buildings hint at the town's brief Victorian industrial boom, when it was a centre for cotton and linen manufacture and brewing.

Orientation & Information

Drogheda sits astride the River Boyne with the principal shopping area on the northern bank along West and Laurence Sts. The area south of the river is residential, dull and dominated by the mysterious Millmount mound. The main road to Belfast skirts round the town to the west.

The **tourist office** (☎ 983 7070; Bus Station, Donore Rd; 🕑 9.30am-5.30pm Mon-Sat, noon-5pm Sun) is at the bus station on the southern side of the river. There is a second office in the Millmount Museum. The main **post office** (West St) is next to the Westcourt Hotel. Most of the main banks are also on West St.

There's terrible traffic congestion in the city centre and disc parking is in operation throughout the town. Discs can be bought in newsagents and other shops; they cost £0.30 for an hour's parking.

The **Wise Owl Bookshop** (☎ 984 2847; The Mall; 🕑 9am-5pm Mon-Sat) has a good range of books.

St Peter's Roman Catholic Church

The remains (a shrivelled little head) of the martyr St Oliver Plunkett (1629–81) are kept in this impressive **building** (West Street), which is actually two churches in one: the first, designed by Francis Johnston in the classical style and built in 1791, and the newer addition, built in the Gothic style visible today. Plunkett's head – from which the rest of him was separated following his hanging in 1681 – is in a glittering brass-and-glass case in the north transept, surrounded by flowers, candles and the attentions of the devout.

St Laurence's Gate

Astride Laurence St, the eastwards extension of the town's main street, is St Laurence's Gate, the finest surviving portion of the city walls and one of only two surviving gates from the original 11.

The 13th-century gate was named after St Laurence's Priory, which once stood outside the gate; no traces of it now remain. The gate consists of two lofty towers, a connecting curtain wall and the entrance to the portcullis. This imposing pile of stone is not in fact a gate but a barbican, a fortified structure used to defend the gate, which was further behind it. When the walls were completed in the 13th century, they ran for 3km round the town, enclosing 52 hectares.

Millmount Museum & Tower

Across the river from town, in a village-like enclave amid a sea of dull suburbia, is Millmount, an artificial hill overlooking the town. Although it may have been a prehistoric burial mound along the lines of nearby Newgrange, it has never been excavated. There is a tale that it was the burial place of Amergin, a warrior-poet who arrived in Ireland from Spain around 1500 BC. Throughout Irish history, poets have held a special place in society and have been both venerated and feared.

The Normans constructed a motte-and-bailey fort on top of this convenient command post overlooking the bridge. It

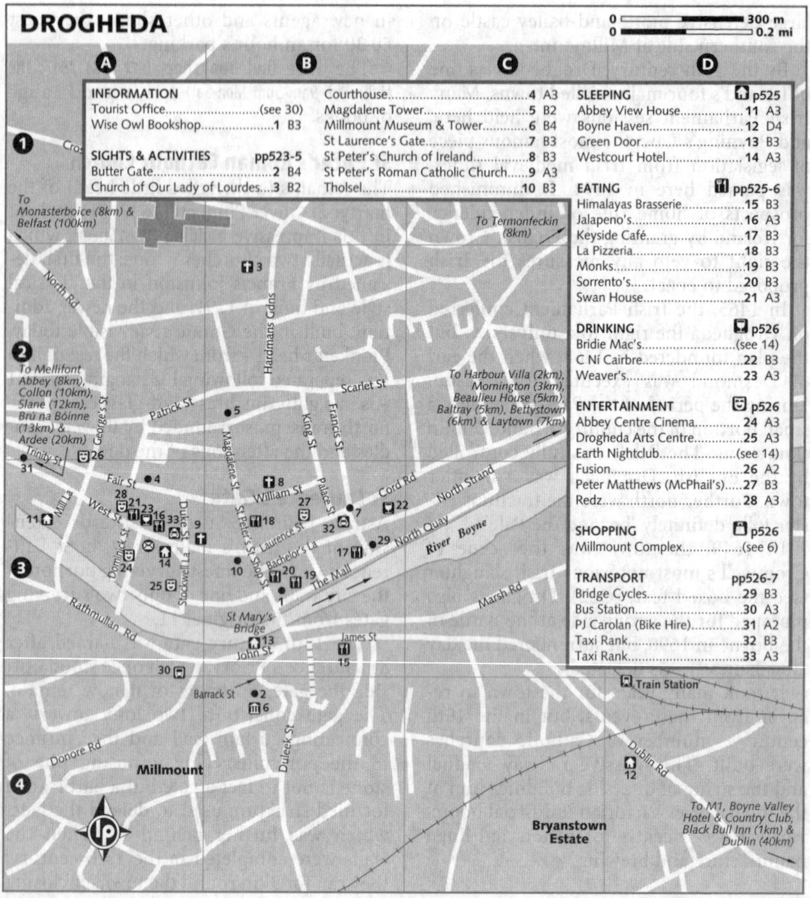

was followed by a castle, which in turn was replaced by a Martello tower in 1808.

It was at Millmount that the defenders of Drogheda, led by the governor, Sir Arthur Ashton, made their last stand before surrendering to Cromwell (see the boxed text, p522). Later, an 18th-century English barracks was built round the base, and today this has been converted to house craft shops, museums and a restaurant, though the courtyard retains the flavour of its former life.

The tower played a dramatic role in the 1922 Civil War, and the **Millmount Museum & Tower** (☎ 983 3097; Millmount; adult/student museum €3/2.50, tower €2.50/2, combined ticket €4.50/3; 10am-6pm Mon-Sat, 2.30-5.30pm Sun) has a colourful (and somewhat romanticised) painting of its bombardment. The top of the tower offers a fine view over the centre of Drogheda, on the opposite side of the river.

A section of the army barracks is now the Millmount Museum, with interesting displays about the town and its history. Displays include three wonderful late-18th-century guild banners, perhaps the last in the country. There is also a room devoted to Cromwell's siege of Drogheda and the Battle of the Boyne. The pretty, cobbled basement is full of gadgets and kitchen utensils from bygone times, including a cast-iron pressure cooker and an early model of a sofa bed. There's also an excellent example of a coracle. Across the courtyard, the **Governor's House** opens for temporary exhibitions.

You can drive up to the hilltop or climb Pitcher Hill via the steps from St Mary's Bridge.

The 13th-century **Butter Gate**, just northwest of Millmount, is the only genuine town gate to survive. This tower, with its arched passageway, predates the remains of St Laurence's Gate by about a century.

Other Buildings

Tholsel (cnr West & Shop Sts), an 18th-century limestone town hall, is now occupied by the Bank of Ireland. Off Hardmans Gardens is the rather charming and more recent **Church of Our Lady of Lourdes**.

North of the centre is **St Peter's Church of Ireland** (William St). This contains the tombstone of Oliver Goldsmith's uncle Isaac, as well as another on the wall depicting two skeletal figures in shrouds, dubiously linked to the Black Death. This is the church whose spire was burned by Cromwell's men, resulting in the death of 100 people seeking sanctuary inside. Today's church (1748) is the second replacement of the original destroyed by Cromwell. It stands in an attractive close approached through lovely wrought-iron gates. Note the old 'Blue School' of 1844 on one side.

The modest 19th-century **Courthouse** (Fair St) is being renovated and is home to the sword and mace presented to the town council by William of Orange after the Battle of the Boyne.

Topping the hill behind the main part of town is the **Magdalene Tower**, dating from the 14th century, the belltower of a Dominican friary founded in 1224. Here, England's King Richard II, accompanied by a great army, accepted the submission of the Gaelic chiefs with suitable ceremony in 1395; but peace lasted only a few months and his return to Ireland led to his overthrow in 1399. The earl of Desmond was beheaded here in 1468 because of his treasonous connections with the Gaelic Irish. The tower is reputed to be haunted by a nun.

Tours

Historical Drogheda Walking Tours (☎ 984 5684; adult/student €2/1.50; ⏰ 10.20am & 2.20pm Tue-Sat) leave from in front of the bus station. The tour takes about 1¼ hours. If you want a self-guided tour then pick up the *Drogheda Heritage Route* map at either of the tourist offices. They also have a leaflet entitled *The Oriel Trail*, which outlines a 150km tour through the county beginning in town.

Sleeping

HOSTELS

Green Door (☎ 983 4422; greendoorhostel@hotmail.com; 47 John St; dm/d/tr €13.50/42/53) Conveniently located 150m from the bus station, this friendly hostel has a small public area but large, clean dorms and private rooms.

B&BS

It's advisable to book ahead between May and October.

Abbey View House (☎ 983 1470; Mill Lane; s/d €35/50) Scenically located on the banks of the Boyne, the big rooms and relaxed atmosphere at this place attract travellers from all over the world.

Harbour Villa (☎ 983 7441; Mornington Rd; s/d €35/70) This place is 2km along the river towards the sea on the Mornington road. It overlooks the estuary and has small but pleasant rooms.

Boyne Haven (☎/fax 983 6700; Dublin Rd; s/d €55/95) Definitely an upscale B&B, with loads of space and a great breakfast, this excellent establishment is on the Dublin road.

HOTELS

Westcourt Hotel (☎ 983 0965; www.westcourt.ie; West St; s/d €65/120) Right in the town centre, it's worth asking about the special weekend bargain break rate at this more upmarket hotel. Rooms are clean and comfortable, but not very exciting.

Boyne Valley Hotel & Country Club (☎ 983 7737; www.boyne-valley-hotel.ie; Stameen, Dublin Rd; d €120-140; 🏊) It was beer that built this 19th-century mansion and long-time home of a Drogheda brewing family. It sits on 16 beautiful acres with a swimming pool and small golf course. The huge rooms have views of the river.

Eating

While things are slowly improving, Drogheda dining is nothing to write home about. The focus is still simply on eating, rather than eating well.

RESTAURANTS

Sorrento's (☎ 984 5734; 41 Shop St; mains €8-15; ⏰ 6.30-11pm Tue-Sun) This relatively new

Italian restaurant is a welcome addition to the scene. Simple, quality pasta and meat dishes are the order of the day. Try the *arancini*, a delicious rice and cheese starter.

Himalayas Brasserie (☎ 983 1423; 35 James St; mains €9-13; ⏰ 12.30-11pm) Northern Indian cuisine is the speciality at this good-value restaurant right in the middle of town.

CAFÉS & PUBS

Monks (☎ 984 5630; 1 North Quay; mains around €6; ⏰ 8.30am-6pm Mon-Sat, 10am-5pm Sun) At the southern end of Shop St, on the corner of North Quay, this lovely espresso bar and café is a local institution. The sandwiches are inventive, the coffees good and, strangely for Ireland, it is *mostly* smoke free.

Keyside Café (☎ 984 4878; The Mall; snacks around €5; ⏰ 9am-6pm Mon-Sat, 10am-4pm Sun) This is another good café, with an emphasis on modern Irish cuisine.

Jalapeno's (☎ 983 8342; Unit 1, West St; mains €6-8; ⏰ 9am-6pm Mon-Sat) This pleasant café serves really good sandwiches and brews an excellent cup of coffee. A great spot for a healthy breakfast.

La Pizzeria (☎ 983 4208; 15 St Peter's St; mains €8-9; ⏰ 10am-11pm Mon-Tue & Thu-Sun) You might need a reservation at this busy, Italian-owned joint featuring pizzas and pasta dishes.

Swan House (☎ 983 7506; Unit 3, West St; mains €8; ⏰ 5.30-11pm) This popular Chinese restaurant also offers takeaways; chicken, beef, and seafood are all well represented on the menu.

Black Bull Inn (☎ 983 7139; Dublin Rd; mains €10-17; ⏰ noon-10pm) About 1km along the Dublin road this pub was once winner of the regional Pub of the Year title and it still gets the local vote. Chinese-style duck is a speciality. It has music at the weekend.

Drinking

C Ní Cairbre (Carberry's; ☎ 984 7569; North Strand) This traditional, old pub is the town's best and most-popular watering hole, though you might need infrared glasses because it is so dark inside! There are Irish music sessions on Tuesday night and Sunday afternoon. In theory it opens from 7.30pm; in reality, opening hours vary depending on how the night is going. It gets busy on weekend nights and Sunday afternoon.

Weavers (☎ 983 2816; 82-3 West St) Weavers always has a youngish crowd and there's live music on Wednesday night and DJs at the weekend.

Bridie Mac's (☎ 983 0965; West St) Attached to the Westcourt Hotel, happy hour (5pm to 8pm) is always a cocktail-fuelled laugh at Bridie Mac's. This place also offers a wide range of musical possibilities on Thursday, Friday and Saturday.

Fusion (☎ 983 5166; 12 George's St) The beer garden is a big pull here, as is the fairly animated disco from Thursday to Sunday nights with a mix of '60s, rock, funk and dance music.

Entertainment

Peter Matthews (McPhail's; ☎ 984 3168; Laurence St) This is Drogheda's alternative to the older bars, attracting a younger crowd who prefer indie and dance music to the more traditional kind. Live rock, blues and jazz most nights.

Earth (☎ 984 5561; Stockwell St; admission €6, Sat €10) A planetary theme is played out in the décor of this popular nightclub downstairs in the Westcourt Hotel. Three bars and a huge dance floor keep the punters happy.

Redz (☎ 983 5331; 79 West St) A small, chilled-out bar at the front hides a big club out back at this new nightspot. DJs and live bands play on different nights.

Abbey Centre Cinema (☎ 983 0188; Abbey Shopping Centre) This two-screen cinema is at the back of the shopping centre, off West St.

Drogheda Arts Centre (☎ 983 3946; Stockwell Lane) Theatrical and musical events are staged in the municipal building.

Shopping

The **Millmount complex** (Millmount) has a number of craft studios where you can buy all sorts of *objets d'art*. There's a **jewellery studio** (☎ 984 1960), **ceramic potter** (☎ 984 6065), **decorative glassworks** (☎ 984 5018) and studio where you can buy **hand-painted silks** (☎ 984 1245). Call to arrange a viewing of the work; some of it is of extremely high quality.

Getting There & Away

BUS

Drogheda is only 48km north of Dublin, on the main N1 route to Belfast. The **Bus Éireann station** (☎ 983 5023; cnr John St & Donore Rd) is just south of the river. This is one of the busiest bus routes in the country, and regular buses serve Drogheda from Dublin (single/return €7.20/9.50, one hour, daily every half-hour between 7.30am and 4pm, every 15 minutes between 4pm and 7pm, and every half-hour thereafter until 11pm). Drogheda to Dundalk is another popular route (single/return €6.50/9, 30 minutes, hourly from 6.45am to 11.45pm daily).

There is also a daily Dundalk to Galway bus (single/return €17/23, 4¾ hours) departing Drogheda at 11.10am Monday to Thursday and Saturday, and 4.30pm Friday and Sunday, which stops at Athlone, from where you can make connections for Limerick, Sligo and Donegal.

Cheaper is **Capital Coaches** (☎ 042-934 0025), which has a daily Dundalk to Dublin service through Drogheda (single €6).

TRAIN

The **train station** (☎ 983 8749) is just south of the river and east of the town centre, off the Dublin road. Drogheda is on the main Belfast to Dublin line and there are five or six express trains (and many more slower ones) daily each way, with five on Sunday (€10.20, 30 minutes to Dublin; €22, 1½ hours to Belfast). This is the best line in Ireland, with excellent on-board service.

The train crosses the river just downstream from Drogheda on Sir John McNeill's mid-19th-century Boyne Viaduct, a fine piece of engineering that dominates the seaward view.

Getting Around

Drogheda itself is infinitely walkable, and many of the surrounding region's interesting sites are within easy cycling distance. **PJ Carolan** (☎ 983 8242; 77 Trinity St; day rental €15) offers good bikes. **Bridge Cycles** (☎ 983 3742; North Quay; day rental €14), near the bridge, also rents bikes.

There's a taxi rank on Duke St, just off West St, and another on Laurence St near St Laurence's Gate.

AROUND DROGHEDA

Drogheda makes an excellent base for exploring the Boyne Valley sites to the west – see the Brú Na Bóinne section on p505, for more details. In Louth itself, Mellifont and Monasterboice are two famous and picturesque monastic sites a few kilometres north of Drogheda. Travelling to or from Northern Ireland there's a coastal route, the faster and duller N1 main road route, and a more circuitous inland route via Collon and Ardee, which can include Mellifont and Monasterboice.

Beaulieu House

About 5km east of Drogheda on the Baltray road is Beaulieu House, built between 1660 and 1666. The land, which had belonged to the Plunkett family since Anglo-Norman times, was confiscated under Cromwell. This lovely red-brick mansion, with distinctive steep roof and tall chimneys, is thought to have been designed by Sir Christopher Wren (architect of St Paul's Cathedral in London).

In 800 years the estate has been in the possession of only two families, first the Plunketts and then the ancestors of Lord Tichbourne. There's an impressive art collection, but it's a private residence, not open to the public.

Mellifont Abbey

Ireland's first Cistercian monastery, **Mellifont Abbey** (☎ 041-982 6459; off the R168, Tullyallen; adult/student €2/1; 9.30am-6.30pm mid-Jun–mid-Sep, 10am-5pm May–mid-Jun & mid-Sep–Oct) is 8km northwest of Drogheda beside the River Mattock. The name comes from the Latin *mellifons* (honey fountain). In its prime, Mellifont was the Cistercians' most magnificent and important centre in the country but, while the remains are well worth seeing, they don't really do justice to the site's former significance.

In 1142 St Malachy, bishop of Down, brought in a new troop of monks from Clairvaux in France to combat the corruption and lax behaviour of the Irish monastic orders. These strait-laced new monks were deliberately established at this remote location, far from any distracting influences. The French and Irish monks failed to get on, and the visitors soon returned to the Continent. However, within 10 years nine more Cistercian monasteries were established and Mellifont was eventually the mother house for 21 lesser monasteries. At one point as many as 400 monks lived here.

Mellifont not only brought fresh ideas to the Irish religious scene, it also heralded a new style of architecture. For the first time in Ireland, monasteries were built with the formal layout and structure that was being used on the Continent. Only fragments of the original settlement remain, but the plan of the extensive monastery can easily be traced. Like many other Cistercian monasteries, the buildings clustered round an open cloister, or courtyard.

To the northern side of the cloister are the remains of a principally 13th-century cross-shaped church. To the south, the chapter house, probably used as a meeting hall by the monks, has been partially floored with medieval glazed tiles, originally found in the church. Here also would have been the refectory, or dining area, kitchen and warming room – the only place where the austere monks could enjoy the warmth of a fire. The eastern range would once have held the monks' sleeping quarters.

Mellifont's most recognisable building, and one of the finest pieces of Cistercian architecture in Ireland, is the lavabo, an octagonal washing house for the monks. It was built in the 13th century and used lead pipes to bring water from the river. A number of other buildings would have surrounded this main part of the abbey.

After the dissolution of the monasteries, a fortified Tudor manor house was built on the site in 1556 by Edward Moore, using materials scavenged from the demolition of many of the buildings. In 1603, this house was the scene of a poignant and crucial turning point in Irish history. After the disastrous Battle of Kinsale, the vanquished Hugh O'Neill, last of the great Irish chieftains, was given shelter here by Sir Garret Moore until he surrendered to the English Lord Deputy Mountjoy. After his surrender, O'Neill was pardoned but, despairing of his position, fled to the Continent in 1607 with other old-Irish leaders in the Flight of the Earls. In 1727 the site was abandoned altogether.

The visitor centre next to the site describes monastic life in detail. A back road connects Mellifont with Monasterboice. There is no public transportation to the abbey.

Monasterboice

Just off the N1 road to Belfast, about 10km north of Drogheda, is **Monasterboice** (Mainistir Bhuithe; off N1; admission free; sunrise-sunset), an intriguing monastic site containing a cemetery, two ancient church ruins, one of the finest and tallest round towers in Ireland and two of the best high crosses. The site can be reached directly from Mellifont via a winding route along narrow country lanes.

Down a leafy country lane and set in sweeping farmland, Monasterboice has a special atmosphere, particularly at quiet times. The original monastic settlement at Monasterboice is said to have been founded by St Buithe, a follower of St Patrick, in the 4th or 5th century, although the site probably had pre-Christian significance. St Buithe's name somehow got converted to Boyne, and the river is named after him. It's said that he made a direct ascent to heaven via a ladder lowered from above. An invading Viking force took over the settlement in 968, only to be comprehensively expelled by Donal, the Irish high king of Tara, who killed at least 300 of the Vikings in the process.

There's a small gift shop outside the compound. There are no set hours but come early or late in the day to avoid the crowds.

HIGH CROSSES

The high crosses of Monasterboice are superb examples of Celtic art. The crosses had an important didactic use, bringing the gospels alive for the uneducated – cartoons of the Scriptures, if you like. Like Greek statues, they were probably brightly painted, but all traces of colour have long disappeared.

Muiredach's Cross, the one nearest to the entrance, dates from the early 10th century. The inscription at the foot reads '*Or do Muiredach Lasndernad i Chros*' (A prayer for Muiredach for whom the cross was made). Muiredach was abbot here until 922.

The subjects of the carvings have not been positively identified. On the eastern face, from the bottom up, are thought to be: the Fall of Adam and Eve and the murder of Abel, David and Goliath, Moses bringing forth water from the rock to the waiting Israelites and the three wise men bearing gifts to Mary and Jesus. The Last Judgement is at the centre of the cross with the risen dead waiting for their verdict, and further up is St Paul in the desert.

The western face relates more to the New Testament, and from the bottom depicts the arrest of Christ, Doubting Thomas, Christ giving a key to St Peter, the Crucifixion in the centre, and Moses praying with Aaron and Hur. The cross is capped by a representation of a gabled-roof church.

The West Cross is near the round tower and stands 6.5m high, making it one of the tallest high crosses in Ireland. It's much more weathered, especially at the base, and only a dozen or so of its 50 panels are still legible.

The more distinguishable ones on the eastern face include David killing a lion and bear, the sacrifice of Isaac, David with Goliath's head, and David kneeling before Samuel. The western face shows the resurrection, the crowning with thorns, the Crucifixion, the baptism of Christ, Peter cutting off the servant's ear in the garden of Gethsemane, and the kiss of Judas.

A third, simpler cross in the northeastern corner of the compound is believed to have been smashed by Cromwell's forces and has only a few, straightforward carvings. Photographers should note that this cross makes a great evening silhouette picture, with the round tower in the background.

The **round tower**, minus its cap, stands in a corner of the complex. It's still over 30m tall but is closed to the public. In 1097, records suggest, the tower interior went up in flames, destroying many valuable manuscripts and other treasures. The church ruins are from a later era and of less interest.

ARDEE

☎ 041 / pop 3568

How many towns can claim to have two castles in their main street? The sleepy market town of Ardee (Baile Átha Fhirdhia) on the narrow River Dee is 10km north of Collon on the N2. Its long, tidy main street – divided into Bridge, Market and Irish Sts – is dominated by Ardee Castle to the south and Hatch's Castle to the north.

History

For a small town, Ardee has a colourful history. It takes its name from Áth Fhír Diadh (Fear Diadh's Ford), inspired by the well-known tale of the combat between Cúchulainn and his half-brother Fear Diadh, or Ferdia, as recorded by the ancient tale of the Táin Bó Cúailnge. After an almighty duel, Cúchulainn fatally wounded his beloved Ferdia with the *gae bolga*, a weapon given to him by the demi-god Lug. Cúchulainn's grief was such that he never fully recovered. It is one of the most tragic and beautiful stories of the Cooley cycle.

In the 12th century, the area was turned into a barony and the town remained in English hands until taken by the O'Neills in the 17th century. James II had his headquarters here for two months in 1689, prior to the Battle of the Boyne.

Sights & Activities

A square tower dating from the 13th century, **Ardee Castle** (☎ 685 3805; adult/child €1.30/0.60; 9am-5pm Mon-Sat Jun-Oct) was an important outpost on the edge of the English Pale. It later became a courthouse and now houses a museum on the town's history, as well as a coffee shop and craft units. The smaller **Hatch's Castle** also dates from this time and it remained, from Cromwellian times until 1940, in the hands of the Hatch family. It's still a private residence.

The riverbank can be explored around the ford, where there's a well-tended **riverside walk** that has an impressive new bronze sculpture of Cúchulainn and Ferdia.

Sleeping & Eating

Carraig Mor (☎ 685 3513; info@carraigmor.com; Blakestown; s/d €36/55) This family-run place is pretty fancy and located just 2km south of Ardee on the main Dublin to Donegal road. The five rooms, four en suite, are very well decorated.

Gables House & Restaurant (☎/fax 685 3789; Dundalk Rd; s/d €35/55; mains €15-22, set dinner €35) Everything you need in one luxurious setting, and the mahogany furniture, velvet curtains and oil paintings by local artists make this place a little special. The restaurant, serving French cuisine, is all white linen and silver cutlery.

Red House (☎ 685 3523; redhouse@eircom.net; Dundalk Rd; s/d €55/70) For a real treat, try this elegant Georgian residence, which stands in its own demesne. Take the Dundalk road past Gables Restaurant and it's about 500m along on the left. Dinner costs another €35.

Smarmore Castle (☎ 685 7167; fax 685 7650; Smarmore, Ardee; d €140) Fit for a minor king, this 14th-century castle has been converted into a lovely hotel 4km south of Ardee.

AROUND ARDEE

Jumping Church of Kildemock

About 3km southeast of town are the remains of the area's oddly named landmark, the Jumping Church of Kildemock. On a thunderous night in February 1715, a storm caused a wall of St Catherine's Church to shift inwards from its foundations. However, rather than settle for this straightforward explanation, locals decided the church had miraculously jumped to exclude the remains of an excommunicated member of the flock who had been buried within its walls. Thus was born the Jumping Church.

Louth

North of Tallanstown (but the turn-off is just south of town), the county's namesake is an insignificant little place with some mildly interesting remains. **St Mochta's** is a small 11th- or 12th-century church with an enclosure and stone roof. St Mochta, a British follower of St Patrick, founded a monastery here in the early 6th century. Nearby is the church of a 15th-century Dominican friary, sometimes called Louth Abbey.

Ardpatrick

To the east of Louth village are Ardpatrick and Ardpatrick House, home of Oliver Plunkett. There's a mound here where he is supposed to have illegally ordained priests. It was also a good vantage point to spot any advancing English soldiers.

THE COAST ROAD

While the most visually rewarding route between Drogheda and Dundalk is the minor inland road via Mellifont and Collon, the coastal route is also scenic. The latter heads off north under the railway viaduct, passes Baltray with its championship golf course, and continues on quiet country roads to Termonfeckin.

Termonfeckin

A 6th-century monastery was founded in Termonfeckin (Tearmann Féichín) by St Féichín of Cong, County Mayo. All that remains are some gravestones and a 10th-century **high cross**, on the left as you enter the churchyard.

There's also a 15th-century **castle** (⌚ 10am-6pm), or tower house, in a good state of preservation; it has two small corbel-vaulted alcoves and an anticlockwise spiral staircase (most go clockwise). From the village, follow the road to Seapoint Golf Club, take the first left, then the first right. You need to get the key from across the road.

Clogherhead

About 2km further north is the busy seaside and fishing centre of Clogherhead (Ceann Chlochair), with a good, shallow Blue Flag beach. Around the town there are enjoyable walks along the coast (partially marred by vistas of caravan parks) or out to **Port Oriel**, an attractive little harbour with views of the Cooley Peninsula and the Mourne Mountains further north. During the summer, Port Oriel is home to a fleet of trawlers and smaller fishing boats.

On the southern side of the headland is **Red Man's Cave**. At low tide a reddish fungus becomes visible, covering the cave walls. According to folklore, a group of people fleeing from Cromwell hid in the cave. A barking dog revealed the hide-out and the people were slaughtered, their blood splashing on the walls, where it remains to this day. The cave is hard to find, so it's sensible to ask a local for directions, but even if you don't find it the walk is satisfying enough.

Castlebellingham

North of Annagassan, the coast road joins the busy main N1 at Castlebellingham, only 12km south of Dundalk. The village grew up around its 18th-century mansion, which is something of a disappointment after the imposing castellated entrance. The mansion is on the site of an earlier castle burned down by James II's troops; the owner, Thomas Bellingham, worked as a guide to William of Orange during his visit to Ireland between 1689 and 1690. The building is now a major hotel: **Bellingham Castle** (☎ 042-937 2176; bellinghamcastle@eircom.net; Castlebellingham; s/d €70/115).

Buried in the local graveyard is Dr Thomas Guither, a 17th-century physician supposed to have reintroduced frogs to Ireland by releasing imported frog spawn into a pond in Trinity College, Dublin. Frogs, along with snakes and toads, had supposedly received their marching orders from St Patrick a thousand years earlier.

DUNDALK

☎ 042 / pop 27,399

Halfway between Dublin and Belfast, Louth's charmless county town of Dundalk takes its name from Dún Dealgan, a prehistoric fort which was reputedly the home of the hero Cúchulainn (see the boxed text on p533). Some people use it as a base to explore Louth and the North, but the town itself does not really have much to keep you long. It's not pretty, it doesn't have many historic sights, and the dining and accommodation are average at best.

The town grew under the protection of a local estate controlled by the de Verdon family, who were granted lands here by King John in 1185. In the Middle Ages, Dundalk was at the northern limits of the English-controlled Pale, strategically located on one of the main highways heading north.

Dundalk is only 13km from the border and widely regarded as a republican stronghold. Indeed, a residential area of the town has been nicknamed 'Little Belfast' for the numbers of Northerners who have settled here, including, most recently, members of the so-called 'Real IRA', a splinter republican group that is opposed to the peace treaty. This group admitted responsibility for the 1998 Omagh bomb, which killed 29 people.

Orientation & Information

Northbound traffic sweeps round to the east of the town centre. The main commercial streets are Clanbrassil and Park Sts. The **tourist office** (☎ 933 5484; Jocelyn St; 🕑 9.30am-5pm Mon-Fri, 9.30am-1pm & 2-5.30pm Sat Jun–mid-Sep, 9.30am-1pm & 2-5.30pm Mon-Fri mid-Sep–May) is next to Louth County Museum. There are also boards and maps with tourist information dotted around town. The main post office is on Clanbrassil St.

Sights

The **Courthouse** (cnr Crowe & Clanbrassil Sts) is a fine neo-Gothic building with large Doric pillars which was designed by Richard Morrison, who also designed the courthouse in Carlow. In the front square is the stone **Maid of Éireann**, commemorating the Fenian Rising of 1798.

St Nicholas' Church (Church St), also known as the Green Church, is the burial site of Agnes Burns, elder sister of Robert, the Scottish poet. She married the local rector, and the monument was erected by the townspeople to honour them both. The 15th-century tower to the right of the church entrance is the oldest structure on the site.

The richly decorated **St Patrick's Cathedral** was modelled on King's College Chapel in Cambridge, England. In front of it is the **Kelly Monument** (Jocelyn St), in memory of a local captain drowned at sea in 1858. Also here is the interesting **Louth County Museum** (☎ 932 7056; Jocelyn St; adult/concession €3.80/2.50; 🕑 10.30am-5.30pm Mon-Sat, 2-6pm Sun, closed Mon Oct-Apr) with displays depicting the growth of industry in Louth since 1750. Different floors in the museum are dedicated to the town's early history and archaeology and to the Norman period. Another floor deals with the growth of industry in the area from the 1750s right up to the 1960s and the cult classic Heinkel Bubble Car, which was manufactured in the area.

At the eastern end of Jocelyn St is the Seatown area of Dundalk with its **castle** (really a friary tower) and a derelict, sail-less **windmill**, the tallest in Ireland. If you arrive in Dundalk by train you pass the 1820 **garda station** (police station; St Dominick's Pl) on the way into town. Its first prisoner is believed to have been its architect, who misappropriated funds and was arrested for nonpayment of bills.

Sleeping

Townhouse (☎ 932 9898; thetownhouse@eircom.net; 5 Roden Pl; s/d €40/65) From the outside, this place looks like a top-notch guesthouse, but inside the rooms are slightly disappointing. It is across the street from St Patrick's Cathedral.

Ballymascanlon House Hotel (☎ 937 1124; fax 937 1598; Carlingford Rd; s/d €90/140; ♿) This is a manor-house hotel with a swimming pool, squash courts, a superb 18-hole golf course and other sporting facilities. In the grounds of the hotel, up by the 5th green of the golf course (there's a signposted trail for non-golfers), is the fine Giant's Load Proleek Dolmen and Gallery Grave. It's 6km north of Dundalk on the way to Carlingford.

Eating

Dundalk has plenty of cheap eateries, but not many quality spots.

Café Metz (☎ 933 9106; Williamson's Mall; mains €12-15; 🕑 6-11pm Mon-Sat) A very trendy place, with orange walls, wooden floors and Venetian blinds. The food is excellent, and the menu features such diverse treats as roast Barbary duck, salmon in filo pastry and a fabulous chowder.

La Cantina (☎ 933 4175; 7 Park St; mains €9-14; 🕔 6-10.30pm Mon-Sat) They only do dinner at this stylish Italian eatery, but it's arguably the best dinner in town. Try the veal; it's the best in the city.

Jade Gardens (☎ 933 0378; 24 Park St; mains €12-20; 🕔 noon-11pm) This is an excellent Chinese restaurant and the décor is unusually subdued, with low lighting, a black marble floor and an aquarium.

Drinking & Entertainment

Several good pubs are found on and around Park St.

Toal's Bar (☎ 933 2759; 7 Crowe St) This is one of the nicer pubs in town, with plenty of character...and characters.

Phoenix (☎ 935 2925; 15 Park St) This bar has an old frontage but has been renovated inside; it is a friendly, locals' kind of place with a terrific atmosphere.

McManus's (☎ 933 1632; 17 Seatown) This is very much a locals' local, and as such, is quiet and pleasant.

Spirit Store (☎ 935 2697; George's Quay) This wonderful little bar about 3km out of town by the harbour was originally your typical harbour saloon, but it has been taken over, painted in bright colours and turned into one of the hippest joints in the area. There's live music throughout the week.

Getting There & Away

BUS

Bus Éireann (☎ 041-982 8251) runs an almost hourly service to Dublin (single/return €10/13.50, 1½ hours) and a less-frequent one to Belfast. The **bus station** (☎ 933 4075; Long Walk) is near the shopping centre. There are plenty of local buses and daily connections to centres nationwide. **Capital Coaches** (☎ 934 0025) also runs buses to Dublin (single €7).

TRAIN

Clarke Train Station (☎ 933 5521), a few hundred metres west of Park St on Carrickmacross Rd, has trains daily on the Dublin to Belfast line (to Dublin: single €14.60, one hour, 10 daily).

Getting Around

The **Cycle Centre** (☎ 933 7159; 44 Dublin St; day rental €11), opposite the Dundalk Shopping Centre south of the town centre, rents out bikes.

Local taxi companies include **A-1 Cabs** (☎ 932 6666; 9 Crowe St) and **Five Star Cabs** (☎ 933 6000; 74 Clanbrassil St).

COOLEY PENINSULA

East of Dundalk, the lonely moorlands of the Cooley Peninsula are the setting for a large part of Ireland's most famous fable, the Táin Bó Cúailnge (The Cattle Raid of Cooley); see the boxed text on p533. The low mountains are really a part of Northern Ireland's Mourne Mountains, but are cut off from them physically by the flooded valley of Carlingford Lough and politically by the border, which runs up the centre of the lough. The peninsula is a world of its own and has strong republican traditions.

Carlingford

☎ 042 / pop 1329

Near Carlingford (Cairlinn), the Cooley Peninsula's mountains and views display themselves to dramatic effect. This pretty village, with its cluster of narrow streets and whitewashed houses, nestles on Carlingford Lough, beneath Slieve Foye (587m). After visiting in 1914, the Reverend Laurence Murray wrote of its 'medieval suggestiveness'; that suggestiveness survives today in the street plan and the crumbling walls and towers dotted around the village. Hard though it is to believe, not much of this was appreciated until the late 1980s, when the villagers got together to show what can be done to revive a dying community. The story of their efforts is vividly told in the heritage centre.

The Mourne Mountains are just a few kilometres north across the lough.

INFORMATION

The **tourist office** (☎ 937 3033; waterfront; 🕔 10am-5.30pm Mon-Sat, 11am-5.30pm Sun Apr-Sep, 11am-5pm Mon-Fri Oct-Mar) is right next to the bus stop on the waterfront.

HOLY TRINITY HERITAGE CENTRE

The **heritage centre** (☎ 937 3454; Churchyard Rd; adult/concession €1.25/0.65; 🕔 10am-12.30pm & 2-4.30pm Mon-Fri, noon-4.30pm Sat & Sun) is in the former Holy

THE TÁIN BÓ CÚAILNGE (CATTLE RAID OF COOLEY)

This remarkable tale of greed and war is one of the oldest stories in any European language and the closest thing Ireland has produced to the Greek epics. The story goes that Queen Maeve (Medbh), the powerful ruler of Connaught, was jealous because she couldn't match the white bull owned by her husband, Ailill. She heard tales of the finest bull in Ireland, the brown bull of Cooley, and became determined to rectify the situation.

Maeve gathered her armies and headed for Ulster, where she conspired with her druids to place the Ulster armies under a spell. A deep sleep descended on them, leaving the province undefended. The only obstacle remaining was the boy warrior Cúchulainn, who tackled Maeve's soldiers as they tried to ford the river at Ardee in County Louth. Cúchulainn killed many of them and halted their advance. Maeve eventually persuaded Cúchulainn's half-brother and close friend, Ferdia, to take him on, but he was defeated after a momentous battle and died in Cúchulainn's arms.

The struggle continued across Louth and onto the Cooley Peninsula, where many place names echo the ensuing action. Sex rears its head regularly in the *Táin*, for Maeve was more interested in her chief warrior, Fergus, than in her husband. At various spots in the saga, they sneak off to make love, and in one instance Ailill steals the sword of the distracted Fergus, to shame him and show how careless he is.

While Maeve's soldiers were being despatched in all sorts of ways by Cúchulainn, Maeve had managed to capture the brown bull and spirit it away to Connaught. The wounded Cúchulainn defeated her armies, but the bull was gone. In the end, the brown bull killed Ailill's white bull and thundered around Ireland leaving bits of his victim all over the place. Finally, spent with rage, he died near Ulster at a place called Druim Tarb (Ridge of the Bull). Cúchulainn and Ulster then made peace with Maeve, and thus the saga ended.

Trinity Church. The information boards are encased within closable doors so that the centre can double as a concert hall outside visiting hours. A fine mural shows what the village looked like in its heyday, when the Mint and Taafe's Castle were right on the waterfront. A short video describes the village history and explains what has been done to give it new life in recent years.

KING JOHN'S CASTLE

Carlingford was first settled by the Vikings, and in the Middle Ages became an English stronghold under the protection of the castle, which was built on a pinnacle in the 11th to 12th centuries to control the entrance to the lough. On the western side, the entrance gateway was constructed to allow only one horse and rider through at a time. King John's name stuck to a remarkable number of places in Ireland, given that he spent little time in or near any of them! In 1210 he spent a couple of days here en route to a nine-day battle with Hugh de Lacy at Carrickfergus Castle in Antrim. It's suggested that the first few pages of the Magna Carta, the world's first constitutional bill of rights, were drafted while he was here.

OTHER SIGHTS

Near the disused station is **Taafe's Castle**, a 16th-century tower house which stood on the waterfront until the land in front was reclaimed to build the short-lived train line. The **Mint**, in front of the hostel near the square, is of a similar age. Although Edward IV is thought to have granted a charter to a mint in 1467, no coins were produced here. The building has some interesting Celtic carvings round the windows. Near it is the **Tholsel**, the only surviving gate to the original town, although much altered in the 19th century when its defensive edge was softened in the interests of letting traffic through.

West of the village centre are the remains of a **Dominican friary**, built around 1305 and used as a storehouse by oyster fishermen after 1539.

Carlingford is the birthplace of Thomas D'Arcy McGee (1825–68), one of Canada's founding fathers. A bust commemorating him stands opposite Taafe's Castle.

THE TÁIN TRAIL

Carlingford is the starting point for the 40km Táin Trail, making a circuit of the Cooley Peninsula, through the Cooley Mountains. The route is a mixture of surfaced roads, forest tracks and green paths. For more information contact the local tourist office or the office in Dundalk (☎ 933 5484).

CRUISES

Carlingford Pleasure Cruises (☎ 937 3239; adult/child €6/3) runs one-hour cruises between May and September; there's no set time as departure depends on the tides.

FESTIVALS & EVENTS

In mid-August the pubs are packed from morning to midnight when the village is overrun by 20,000 visitors to the **Oyster Festival**, with funfairs, live bands and buskers alongside the official oyster-opening competitions and tastings.

Almost every weekend from June to September, Carlingford goes event-crazy – there are summer schools, medieval festivals, leprechaun hunts and homecoming festivals.

SLEEPING

Carlingford is a nicer place to stay than Dundalk and it has the bulk of the accommodation on the peninsula, but options are limited and the village gets busy in summer, especially at the weekend.

Ghan House (☎ /fax 937 3682; Main Rd; s/d €68/115) Just 2km outside the village on the Dundalk road, this lodging is the best of the lot, a wonderfully atmospheric house with beautifully appointed and comfortable rooms. The breakfast is excellent.

Carlingford Adventure Centre & Holiday Hostel (☎ 937 3100, fax 937 3651; Tholsel St; dm/d €15/36) A new floor of double rooms has been added to this IHH hostel just off the main street. The adventure centre exists to teach rock climbing, orienteering, hill walking and windsurfing to groups, so it's a good idea to check whether any large and potentially noisy gaggles of school kids will be staying at the same time as you.

Shalom (☎ 937 3151; kevinwoods@eircom.net; Ghan Rd; s/d €38.50/52) This stylishly decorated B&B is along the road towards the pier.

McKevitt's Village Hotel (☎ /fax 937 3116; Market Sq; s/d €45/85) The lovely hotel bar here draws lots of locals. The restaurant is also popular.

EATING

There are plenty of places with superior seafood on the menu.

Carlingford Arms (☎ 937 3418; Newry St; mains €7-12; ⏲ noon-9pm) Serves hefty helpings of pub food; two people could manage perfectly well with one serving of fish and chips.

Kingfisher Bistro (☎ 937 3151; Ghan Rd; mains €11; ⏲ 12.30-10.30pm Mon-Sat) Oysters and a pint of Guinness are a match made in heaven. This is an excellent restaurant that, not surprisingly, keeps the focus on seafood.

Jordan's Restaurant (☎ 937 3223; Newry St; mains from €11; ⏲ 6.30-11pm Mon-Sat) This is a cosy place overlooking the water and it serves surprisingly sophisticated food. The menu ranges from oysters to unusual Irish dishes such as *crubeens* (pigs' trotters). There's a set dinner but for à la carte count on around €40 per person with drinks. It's a good idea to make reservations in summer.

Magee's Bistro (☎ 937 3106; Tholsel St; mains café/restaurant from €5/10) There are two restaurants in one here; a cheaper café-type place and an excellent restaurant, serving delicious seafood (the oysters are superb).

DRINKING & ENTERTAINMENT

There are several good pubs in the village.

Carlingford Arms (☎ 937 3418; Newry St) The most popular pub in town, this is a fairly nice place with plenty of room for all of the summer visitors.

Central Bar (☎ 937 3444; Newry St) Opposite the Carlingford Arms, the Central has Irish music at the weekend.

GETTING THERE & AWAY

Bus Éireann (☎ 933 4075) runs buses to Dundalk (single/return €4.70/7.50, 50 minutes, six a day Monday to Saturday) and Newry (€3.50/6, 20 minutes, five a day Monday to Saturday). There are no Sunday services.

Belfast

CONTENTS

Imposing Victorian architecture, modern art on the waterfront, foot-stomping music in packed-out pubs and the UK's second-biggest arts festival – Belfast is a city that confounds expectations. Massive investment in recent years combined with the optimism engendered by the peace process have transformed Belfast into something of a boom town. First-time visitors soon cast aside their outdated preconceptions and immerse themselves in a city that is rapidly rebuilding and reinventing itself.

The city is compact and easy to get around, with most points of interest within easy walking distance of each other. There is a vibrant nightlife, much of it geared to the student population, and plenty of good places to eat – a colourful new wave of stylish bars and restaurants has emerged to complement the splendid Victorian pubs that have been a mainstay of the capital's social life for decades.

Classic Belfast experiences include the Victorian delights of City Hall and the Crown Liquor Saloon; a climb to the top of Cave Hill for a view over the city; a hike along the Lagan Towpath for lunch at a riverside pub; the 21st-century attractions of Laganside's waterfront artworks and the shiny new Odyssey Complex; and taking a thought-provoking tour around the powerful murals of West Belfast.

There are, of course, still plenty of reminders of the Troubles, and the passions that have torn Northern Ireland apart over the decades still run deep. But despite occasional setbacks, there is an atmosphere of determined optimism that will hopefully propel Belfast towards a peaceful future.

HIGHLIGHTS

- Enjoy the craic in Belfast's **traditional pubs** (p559)
- Check out the **murals** (p550) in West Belfast for an insight into the history of the Troubles
- Gastronomic delight along the **Golden Mile** (p558)
- Pack a picnic and hike up **Cave Hill** (p550) for the panoramic views.
- Step back in time at the **Ulster Folk and Transport Museums** (p566)

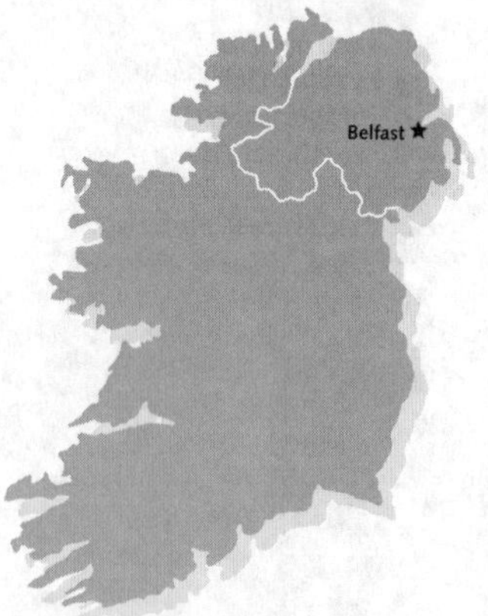

- POPULATION: 277,390
- AREA: 115 SQ KM

HISTORY

Belfast is a relatively young city, with few reminders of its pre-19th-century history. The city's name comes from Beál Feirste (Mouth of the Sandbank), a reference to the shallow ford at the mouth of the River Farset (now channelled through a culvert) where it flowed into the River Lagan. In 1177 the Norman John de Courcy built a castle here and a small settlement grew up around it. Both were destroyed 20 years later, and the town did not begin to develop in earnest until 1611 when Baron Arthur Chichester built a castle and promoted the growth of the settlement.

The early 17th-century Plantation of Ulster brought in the first waves of Scottish and English settlers, followed in the late 17th century by an influx of Huguenots (French Protestants) fleeing persecution in France, who laid the foundations of a thriving linen industry. More Scottish and English settlers arrived and other industries such as rope-making, tobacco, engineering and shipbuilding developed.

During the 18th and 19th centuries Belfast was the one city in Ireland that felt the full force of the Industrial Revolution. Sturdy rows of brick terraced houses were built for the factory and shipyard workers, and a town of around 20,000 people in 1800 grew steadily into a city of 400,000 by the start of WWI, by which time Belfast had nearly overtaken Dublin in size.

The partition of Ireland after WWI gave Belfast a new role as the capital of Northern Ireland. It also marked the end of the city's industrial growth, although decline didn't really set in until after WWII. With the outbreak of the Troubles in 1969, the city saw more than its fair share of violence and bloodshed, and shocking news images of terrorist bombings, murders and security forces brutality made Belfast a household name around the world. The mayhem reached its peak in the 1970s but continued through the 1980s until the 1994 cease-fire. Violence continues to rumble on, but at a much lower level, consisting mostly of infighting between paramilitary factions.

The cease-fire and the 1998 Good Friday Agreement raised hopes for the future, and Belfast has seen a huge injection of money, especially from the EU. Massive swathes of the city centre have been redeveloped, unemployment is low, house prices are rising faster than in any other UK city and tourism is beginning to take off.

ORIENTATION

Belfast sits at the head of Belfast Lough, straddling the lower reaches of the River Lagan and hemmed in to the west by the steep slopes of Black Mountain and Cave Hill. The city centre lies on the west bank of the Lagan, with the imposing City Hall in Donegall Square as a convenient central landmark. The principal shopping district is north of the square along Donegall Place and Royal Ave. North again, the once run-down area around Donegall St and St Anne's Cathedral forms the bohemian Cathedral Quarter.

South of Donegall Square, the so-called Golden Mile stretches for 1km along Great Victoria St, Shaftesbury Square and Botanic Avenue to Queen's University and the leafy suburbs of South Belfast. This area has dozens of restaurants and bars and most of the city's mid-range accommodation. Northwest of Donegall Square, Divis St leads across the Westlink Motorway to the Falls Rd and West Belfast. East of the river rise the huge yellow cranes of the Harland & Wolff shipyards in East Belfast.

The Europa Bus Centre and Great Victoria St Station are behind the Europa Hotel on Great Victoria St, 300m southwest of City Hall. The Laganside Bus Centre is near the Albert Memorial Clock Tower, 600m northeast of City Hall; the ferry terminals on Donegal Quay are 400m north of the clock tower. Central Station is 800m east of City Hall on East Bridge St.

Maps

The Belfast Welcome Centre provides a free map of the city centre. The *Collins Belfast Streetfinder Atlas* (£2.99) is more detailed and includes a full index of street names. Most detailed of all, but in the form of an unwieldy folded sheet, is the Ordnance Survey of Northern Ireland's 1:12,000 *Belfast Street Map* (£4.99).

INFORMATION

Bookshops

Bookfinders (☎ 9032 8269; 47 University Rd, South Belfast; 🕓 10am-5.30pm Mon-Sat) A second-hand bookshop and book-finding service with a gallery and café at the back.

BELFAST

INFORMATION		
Belfast Central Library	1	D2
Belfast Welcome Centre	2	D4
Bord Fáilte	3	D3
British Airways	4	D3
Eason	5	E3
Friends Café	6	D2
Globe Drycleaning & Laundrette	7	D6
I-Browse	8	D5
ITxp	9	E7
Mater Hospital	10	C1
Mike's Laundrette	11	E8
QUB Student's Union	(see 12)	
Queen's University Travel Centre	12	C7
Stationery Office Bookshop	13	E3
Thomas Cook	14	D3
Trailfinders	15	D4
usit Now	16	D3
Waterstones Bookshop	17	D3
Waterstones Bookshop	(see 15)	

SIGHTS & ACTIVITIES	pp542-52	
Albert Memorial Clock Tower	18	E3
Bank of Ireland Building	19	D2
Bigfish Sculpture	20	E2
Bookshop at Queens	21	C7
Clarendon Building	22	F1
Clifton House	23	C1
Commercial Building	24	E3
Crescent Church	25	D6
Custom House	26	E2
Former Methodist Church	(see 47)	
Harbour Commissioner's Office	27	E1
Lagan Lookout Visitor Centre	28	E2
Linen Hall Library	29	D4
Lord Kelvin Statue	30	C7
Methodist Church	31	C6
Moravian Church	32	C6
Northern Bank Building	33	E3
Northern Bank Building	34	E3
Ormeau Baths Gallery	35	D5
Palm House	36	D7
Pearl Assurance Building	37	D4
Robinson & Cleaver Building	38	D4
Royal Courts of Justice	39	E4
Scottish Provident Building	40	D4
Sinclair Seamen's Church	41	E1
Sinclair Store	42	D2
St Anne's Cathedral	43	D2
St George's Market	44	E4
Tropical Ravine	45	D8
Ulster Bank	46	E3
Ulster Bank	47	D4
Ulster Museum	48	D8
Union Theological College	49	D7
W5	50	F2
Whistle Laundrette	51	B8

SLEEPING	pp554-6	
Ark	52	D7
Arnie's Backpackers	53	C7
Belfast International Youth Hostel	54	C6
Benedicts	55	D6
Botanic Lodge Guesthouse	56	D7
Camera Guesthouse	57	B8
Crescent Town House	58	D6
Days Inn	59	D5
Dukes Hotel	60	D7
Eglantine Guesthouse	61	B8
Europa Hotel	62	D4
Helga Lodge	63	D6
Jury's Inn	64	D4
Linen House	65	D2
Madison's	66	D6
Malone Lodge Hotel	67	C8
Marine Guesthouse	68	B8
McCausland Hotel	69	E3
Pearl Court Guesthouse	70	C8
QUB Common Room	71	C7
TENsq	72	D4
Travelodge	73	D4
Wellington Park Hotel	74	C8

EATING	pp556-9	
Altos	75	D3
Ann's Pantry	76	D3
Apartment	77	D4
Archana	78	D5
Ba Soba	79	E2
Beatrice Kennedy's	80	C7
Bookfinders Cafe	81	C7
Café Paul Rankin	82	D3
Café Renoir	83	D3
Café Zinc	84	D8

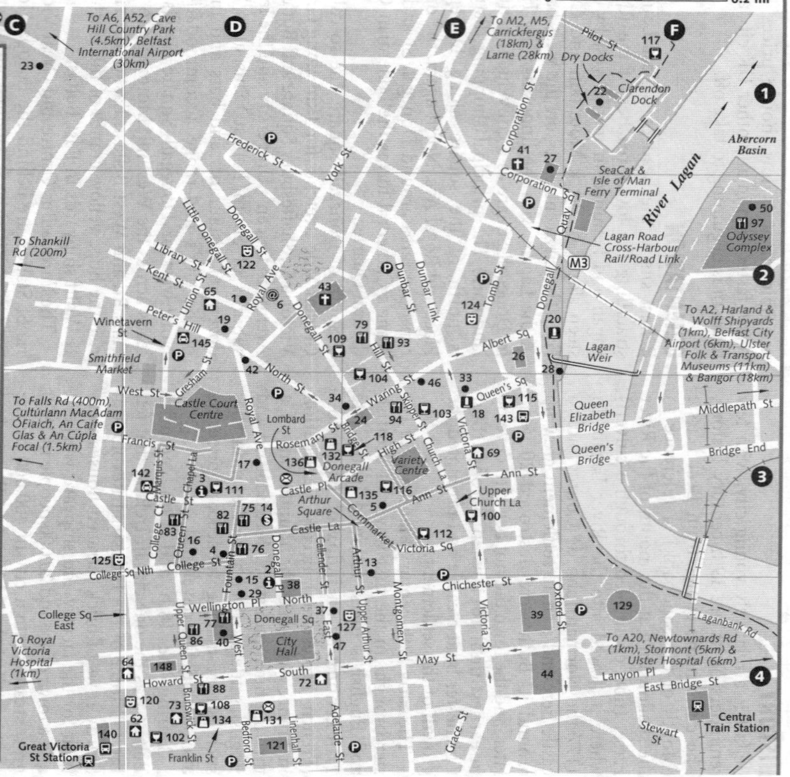

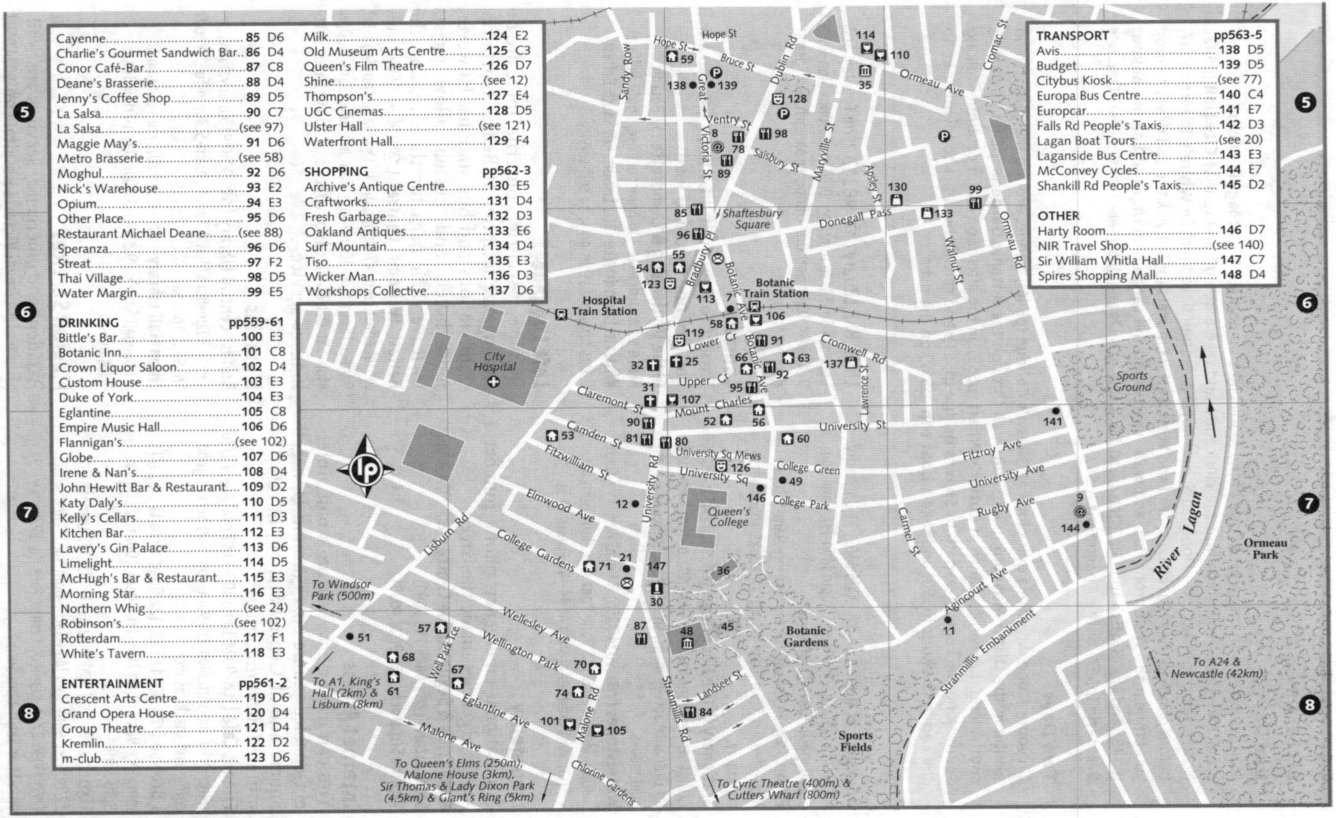
Cayenne.....85 D6
Charlie's Gourmet Sandwich Bar..86 D4
Conor Café-Bar.....87 C8
Deane's Brasserie.....88 D4
Jenny's Coffee Shop.....89 D5
La Salsa.....90 C7
La Salsa.....(see 97)
Maggie May's.....91 D6
Metro Brasserie.....(see 58)
Moghul.....92 D6
Nick's Warehouse.....93 E2
Opium.....94 E3
Other Place.....95 D6
Restaurant Michael Deane.....(see 88)
Speranza.....96 D6
Streat.....97 F2
Thai Village.....98 D5
Water Margin.....99 E5
DRINKING pp559-61
Bittle's Bar.....100 E3
Botanic Inn.....101 C8
Crown Liquor Saloon.....102 D4
Custom House.....103 E3
Duke of York.....104 E3
Eglantine.....105 C8
Empire Music Hall.....106 D6
Flannigan's.....(see 102)
Globe.....107 D6
Irene & Nan's.....108 D4
John Hewitt Bar & Restaurant.....109 D2
Katy Daly's.....110 D5
Kelly's Cellars.....111 D3
Kitchen Bar.....112 E3
Lavery's Gin Palace.....113 D6
Limelight.....114 D5
McHugh's Bar & Restaurant.....115 E3
Morning Star.....116 E3
Northern Whig.....(see 24)
Robinson's.....(see 102)
Rotterdam.....117 F1
White's Tavern.....118 E3
ENTERTAINMENT pp561-2
Crescent Arts Centre.....119 D6
Grand Opera House.....120 D4
Group Theatre.....121 D4
Kremlin.....122 D2
m-club.....123 D6
Milk.....124 E2
Old Museum Arts Centre.....125 C3
Queen's Film Theatre.....126 D7
Shine.....(see 12)
Thompson's.....127 E4
UGC Cinemas.....128 D5
Ulster Hall.....(see 121)
Waterfront Hall.....129 F4
SHOPPING pp562-3
Archive's Antique Centre.....130 E5
Craftworks.....131 D4
Fresh Garbage.....132 D3
Oakland Antiques.....133 E6
Surf Mountain.....134 D4
Tiso.....135 E3
Wicker Man.....136 D3
Workshops Collective.....137 D6
TRANSPORT pp563-5
Avis.....138 D5
Budget.....139 D5
Citybus Kiosk.....(see 77)
Europa Bus Centre.....140 C4
Europcar.....141 E7
Falls Rd People's Taxis.....142 D3
Lagan Boat Tours.....(see 20)
Laganside Bus Centre.....143 E3
McConvey Cycles.....144 E7
Shankill Rd People's Taxis.....145 D2
OTHER
Harty Room.....146 D7
NIR Travel Shop.....(see 140)
Sir William Whitla Hall.....147 C7
Spires Shopping Mall.....148 D4
5
6
7
8
Hope St
Bruce St
Dublin Rd
Great Victoria St
Ventry St
Salisbury St
Maryville St
Apsley St
Ormeau Ave
Cromac St
Sandy Row
Shaftesbury Square
Donegall Pass
Walnut St
Ormeau Rd
Bradbury Pl
Botanic Ave
Hospital Train Station
Botanic Train Station
City Hospital
Lower Cr
Upper Cr
Cromwell Rd
Lawrence St
Claremont St
Mount Charles
University St
Camden St
Fitzwilliam St
University Sq Mews
University Sq
College Green
College Park
Queen's College
University Rd
Elmwood Ave
Lisburn Rd
College Gardens
Fitzroy Ave
University Ave
Rugby Ave
Carmel St
Agincourt Ave
Stranmillis Embankment
Sports Ground
River Lagan
Ormeau Park
Botanic Gardens
Sports Fields
Landseer St
Stranmillis Rd
Wellesley Ave
Wellington Park
Well Park Tce
Malone Rd
Eglantine Ave
Malone Ave
Chlorine Gardens
To Windsor Park (500m)
To A1, King's Hall (2km) & Lisburn (8km)
To Queen's Elms (250m), Malone House (3km), Sir Thomas & Lady Dixon Park (4.5km) & Giant's Ring (5km)
To Lyric Theatre (400m) & Cutters Wharf (800m)
To A24 & Newcastle (42km)

BELFAST

BELFAST IN...

One Day

Start your day with breakfast in one of the many cafés on Botanic Ave - **Maggie May's** (p558) will do nicely - then stroll north into the city centre and take a free guided tour of **City Hall** (p542). Nose around the shops on Donegall St and Royal Ave, then have lunch in **White's Tavern** (p557) before phoning for a black taxi tour of the **West Belfast murals** (p550). Ask the taxi driver to drop you off near the Waterfront Hall, and walk north along the Lagan waterfront to **Lagan Lookout** (p545) and the **Bigfish** (p545) , then head back towards Donegall Square for dinner at **Deane's Brasserie** (p557) or the **Apartment** (p557).

Two Days

On your second day take a quick look at **Queen's College** (p546), wander around the Early Ireland exhibit in the **Ulster Museum** (p546) and stroll through the **Botanic Gardens** (p546), then walk south along the river for lunch at **Cutter's Wharf** (p559). In the afternoon either continue walking south along the Lagan Towpath to **Shaw's Bridge** (p551); and catch a bus back to town) or go to the **Lagan Lookout** (p550) and take a **boat trip** (p552) on the river.

Bookshop at Queen's (☎ 9066 6302; 91 University Rd, South Belfast; 🕑 9am-5.30pm Mon-Fri, 9am-5pm Sat) Opposite Queen's University.
Eason (☎ 9032 8566; 16 Ann St; 🕑 9am-5.30pm Mon-Wed, Fri & Sat, 9am-9pm Thu) Books, magazines, stationery.
Stationery Office Bookshop (☎ 9023 8451; 16 Arthur St; 🕑 9am-5pm Mon-Fri, 10am-4pm Sat) Good for Ordnance Survey maps, street plans and Lonely Planet guidebooks.
Waterstones (☎ 9024 7355; 8 Royal Ave; 🕑 9am-5.30pm Mon-Wed & Fri, 9am-9pm Thu, 9am-6pm Sat, 1-5pm Sun) Another branch at 44–46 Fountain St.

Emergency

For national emergency phone numbers, see Emergencies inside the cover.
Rape Crisis & Sexual Abuse Centre (☎ 9024 9696)
Samaritans (☎ 0845 790 9090)
Victim Support (☎ 9024 4039)

Internet Access

You can use British Telecom's blue, Internet-enabled phone boxes around Donegall Square and at Central Station, for £0.10 a minute (£0.50 minimum).
Friends Café (☎ 9024 1096; 109-113 Royal Ave; £1/30 min; 🕑 8am-5pm Mon-Fri, 9am-3pm Sat) Serves good coffee and snacks as well.
i-Browse (☎ 9024 6505; 122 Great Victoria St; £1/15 min; 🕑 9am-10pm Mon-Fri, 10am-10pm Sat, 11am-8pm Sun)
ITxp South Belfast (☎ 9022 8111; 175-177 Ormeau Rd; £2/hr; 🕑 9am-9pm Mon-Sat, 1-6pm Sun); West Belfast (☎ 9096 2222; Kennedy Centre, Falls Rd; £2/hr; 🕑 9am-9pm Mon-Sat, 1-6pm Sun)
Linen Hall Library (☎ 9032 1707; cnr Fountain St & Donegall Sq; £1/30 min; 🕑 9.30am-5.30pm Mon-Fri, 9.30am-4.30pm Sat) One computer on each floor; ask at desk before using.

Laundry

Expect to pay around £4 to £5 total to wash and dry one machine-load.
Globe Drycleaning & Laundrette (37 Botanic Ave)
Mike's Laundrette (46 Agincourt Ave, South Belfast)
Whistle Laundrette (160 Lisburn Rd, South Belfast) Offers service washes only; no self-service.

Left Luggage

Because of security concerns, there are no left-luggage facilities at Belfast's airports, train stations and bus stations. However, most hotels and hostels allow guests to leave their bags for the day, and the **Belfast Welcome Centre** (☎ 9024 6609; www.gotobelfast.com; 47 Donegall Pl; 🕑 9am-7pm Mon-Fri, 9am-5.15pm Sat, 10am-4pm Sun Jun-Sep, 9am-5.30pm Mon-Sat Oct-May) also offers a daytime left-luggage service.

Libraries

Belfast Central Library (☎ 9050 9150; Royal Ave; 🕑 9.30am-8pm Mon & Thu, 9.30am-5.30pm Tue, Wed & Fri, 9am-1pm Sat)
Linen Hall Library (☎ 9032 1707; cnr Fountain St & Donegall Sq; 🕑 9.30am-5.30pm Mon-Fri, 9.30am-4.30pm Sat)

Medical Services

Accident and emergency services are available at the **Royal Victoria Hospital** (☎ 9024 0503;

Grosvenor Rd), west of the city centre; at the **Mater Hospital** (☎ 9074 1211; Crumlin Rd), near the junction of Antrim Rd and Clifton St; at the **Ulster Hospital** (☎ 9048 4511; Upper Newtownards Rd, Dundonald), near Stormont Castle; and at **City Hospital** (☎ 9032 9241; Lisburn Rd).

For advice on medical and dental emergencies, call the Health Information Service on ☎ 0800 665 544.

Money

Most banks open 9.30am to 4.30pm Monday to Friday; some open late on Thursday, and on Saturday mornings. There are plenty of ATMs around town.

There are currency exchange facilities at the **Belfast Welcome Centre** (☎ 9024 6609; www.gotobelfast.com; 47 Donegall Pl; 9am-7pm Mon-Fri, 9am-5.15pm Sat, 10am-4pm Sun Jun-Sep, 9am-5.30pm Mon-Sat Oct-May), the post offices on Castle Place and Shaftesbury Square, and the following branches of Thomas Cook:

Thomas Cook City centre (☎ 9088 3900; 11 Donegall Pl; 9am-5.30pm Mon-Wed, Fri & Sat, 10am-5.30pm Thu); Belfast international airport (☎ 9442 2536; 5.30am-9.30pm Mon-Fri, 5.30am-midnight Sat & Sun) Times vary slightly in winter and during the summer peak to reflect flight activity.

Post

Main Post Office (Castle Pl; 9am-5.30pm Mon-Fri, 9am-7pm Sat)

Branch Post Office (16-22 Bedford St; 9am-5.30pm Mon-Fri, 9am-12.30pm Sat)

Branch Post Office (1-5 Botanic Ave; 9am-5.30pm Mon-Fri, 9am-12.30pm Sat)

Branch Post Office (cnr University Rd & College Gardens, South Belfast; 9am-5.30pm Mon-Fri, 9am-12.30pm Sat)

Tourist Information

Belfast Welcome Centre (☎ 9024 6609; www.gotobelfast.com; 47 Donegall Pl; 9am-7pm Mon-Fri, 9am-5.15pm Sat, 10am-4pm Sun Jun-Sep, 9am-5.30pm Mon-Sat Oct-May) Provides information about the whole of Northern Ireland, and books accommodation anywhere in Ireland and Britain. Services include left luggage (not overnight), currency exchange and Internet access.

Fáilte Ireland (Irish Tourist Board; ☎ 9032 7888; www.ireland.travel.ie; 53 Castle St; 9am-5pm Mon-Fri year round, 9am-12.30pm Sat Jun-Aug) Can book accommodation in the Republic of Ireland.

Tourist information desks Belfast city airport (☎ 9045 7745; 5.30am-10pm); Belfast international airport (☎ 9442 2888; 24 hr)

Travel Agencies

Queen's University Travel Centre (☎ 9024 1830; Student's Union Bldg, University Rd, South Belfast; 10am-5pm Mon-Fri)

Thomas Cook (☎ 9088 3900; 11 Donegall Pl; 9am-5.30pm Mon-Wed, Fri & Sat, 10am-5.30pm Thu)

Trailfinders (☎ 9027 1888; 44 Fountain St; 9am-5.30pm Mon-Wed & Fri, 9am-9pm Thu, 9am-6pm Sat, 1-5pm Sun) Upstairs in Waterstones bookshop.

usit NOW (☎ 9032 4073; 13b Fountain Centre, College St; 9.30am-5pm Mon-Fri, 9.30am-12.30pm Sat)

DANGERS & ANNOYANCES

Even at the height of the Troubles Belfast wasn't a particularly dangerous city for tourists, and today you're less at risk from crime here than you are in London. You should, however, keep away from the so-called 'interface areas' – near the Peace Lines in West Belfast, Crumlin Rd and the Short Strand (just east of Queen's Bridge) – after dark; if in doubt about any area, ask at your hotel or hostel.

One irritating legacy of the Troubles is the absence of left-luggage facilities at bus and train stations. You will also notice a much more obtrusive security presence than elsewhere in the UK and Ireland, in the form of armoured police Land Rovers, fortified police stations, and security doors on some shops (mostly outside the city centre) where you have to press the buzzer to be allowed in. There are doormen on many city centre shops.

If you want to take photos of fortified police stations, army posts or other military or quasi-military paraphernalia, ask first to be on the safe side. In the Protestant and Catholic strongholds of West Belfast it's best not to photograph people without permission: always ask first and be prepared to accept a refusal. Taking pictures of murals is fine.

You're unlikely to get into furious political or religious arguments in Belfast pubs because both topics are usually avoided with outsiders. In staunchly single-minded pubs of either persuasion, outsiders are often studiously avoided.

One thing you will find difficult to avoid in Belfast pubs is the eye-watering popularity of smoking in Belfast's pubs. While some restaurants have nonsmoking areas, you will almost always catch a whiff of tobacco fumes.

SIGHTS

City Centre

CITY HALL

The Industrial Revolution transformed Belfast in the 19th century, and its rapid rise to muck-and-brass prosperity is manifested in the extravagance of **City Hall** (☎ 9027 0456; Donegall Sq; admission free; guided tours at 11am, 2pm & 3pm Mon-Fri, 2.30pm Sat Jun-Sep, 11am & 2.30pm Mon-Fri, 2.30pm Sat Oct-May). Built in classical Renaissance style in fine, white Portland stone, it was completed in 1906 and paid for from profits of the gas supply company. Controlled by unionists throughout most of its existence, City Hall received its first ever Sinn Féin lord mayor in June 2002.

The hall is fronted by a statue of a rather dour 'we are not amused' **Queen Victoria**. The bronze figures on either side of her symbolise the textile and shipbuilding industries, while the child at the back represents education. At the northeastern corner of the grounds is a statue of **Sir Edward Harland**, the Yorkshire-born marine engineer who founded the Harland & Wolff shipyards, and served as mayor of Belfast in 1885–86. To his south stands a memorial to the victims of the *Titanic*. The **Marquess of Dufferin** (1826–1902), whose career included postings as ambassador to Turkey, Russia, Paris and Rome, governor-general of Canada and viceroy to India, has an ornate, temple-like memorial flanked by an Indian and a Turkish warrior, on the western side of the City Hall.

The highlights of the free **guided tour** of City Hall include the sumptuous, wedding-cake Italian marble and colourful stained glass of the entrance hall and rotunda, an opportunity to sit on the mayor's throne in the council chamber, and the idiosyncratic portraits of past lord mayors. Each lord mayor is allowed to choose his or her own artist, and the variations in personal style are intriguing.

LINEN HALL LIBRARY

Opposite City Hall, on Donegall Square North, is the **Linen Hall Library** (☎ 9032 1707; www.linenhall.com; 17 Donegall Sq North; admission free; 🕐 9.30am-5.30pm Mon-Fri, 9.30am-4pm Sat; wheelchair access). Established in 1788 to 'improve the mind and excite a spirit of general inquiry', the library was moved from its original home in the White Linen Hall (whose site is now occupied by City Hall) to the present building a century later. Thomas Russell, the first librarian, was a founding member of the United Irishmen and a close friend of Wolfe Tone – a reminder that this movement for independence from Britain had its origins in Belfast. Russell was hanged in 1803 after Robert Emmet's abortive rebellion.

The library houses some 260,000 books, more than half of which are part of its important Irish and local-studies collection. The political collection consists of pretty much everything that has been written (some 135,000 publications) about Northern Irish politics since 1966. Recent refurbishment has seen the creation of a new reading room and complete access for visitors with disabilities. The library also has a small café and all the daily newspapers.

OTHER DONEGALL SQUARE BUILDINGS

On Donegall Square West is the ornate **Scottish Provident Building** (1897–1902). It's decorated with a veritable riot of fascinating statuary, including several allusions to the industries that assured Victorian Belfast's prosperity, as well as sphinxes, dolphins and lions' heads. The building was the work of the architectural partnership of Young & MacKenzie, who counterbalanced it in 1902 with the red sandstone **Pearl Assurance Building** on Donegall Square East. Also on the east side of the square is the Classical Greek portico of the former **Methodist Church** (1847), now occupied by the Ulster Bank.

On the north side of square is the equally fine **Robinson & Cleaver Building** (1888), once the Royal Irish Linen Warehouse and later home to Belfast's finest department store. There are 50 busts adorning the façade, representing patrons of the Royal Irish Linen company – look out for Queen Victoria and the Maharajah of Cooch Behar, both former customers.

CROWN LIQUOR SALOON

There are not too many historical monuments that you can enjoy while savouring a pint of beer, but the National Trust's **Crown Liquor Saloon** (☎ 9027 9901; 46 Great Victoria St; admission free; 🕐 11.30am-midnight Mon-Sat, 12.30-10pm Sun) is one. Belfast's most famous bar was refurbished by Patrick Flanagan in the late

19th century and displays Victorian decorative flamboyance at its best (your man was looking to pull in a posh clientele from the new-fangled train station and Grand Opera House across the street).

The exterior (1885) is decorated with ornate and colourful tiles, and a mosaic of a crown on the floor outside the entrance, while the interior (1898) sports a mass of stained and cut glass, marble, ceramics, mirrors and mahogany, all atmospherically lit by genuine gas mantles. A long, highly decorated bar dominates one side of the pub, while on the other is a row of ornate wooden snugs. The snugs come equipped with gunmetal plates (from the Crimean War) for striking matches, and bell-pushes that once allowed drinkers to order top-ups without leaving their seats (alas, no more).

Above the Crown is **Flannigan's** (☎ 9027 9901), another interesting bar with *Titanic* and other maritime memorabilia.

GRAND OPERA HOUSE

One of Belfast's great Victorian landmarks is the **Grand Opera House** (☎ 9024 1919; www.goh.co.uk; Great Victoria St), across the road from the Crown Liquor Saloon. Opened in 1895, and completely refurbished in the 1970s, it suffered grievously at the hands of the IRA, having sustained severe bomb damage in 1991 and 1993. It has been suggested that as the Europa Hotel next door was the home of the media during the Troubles, the IRA brought the bombs to them so they wouldn't have to leave the bar.

The interior has been restored to over-the-top Victorian pomp, with swirling wood and plasterwork, purple satin in abundance, and carved elephant heads in the auditorium.

THE ENTRIES

The oldest part of Belfast, around High St, suffered considerable damage during WWII bombing. The narrow alleyways running off High St and Ann St, known as the Entries, were once bustling commercial and residential centres: **Pottinger's Entry** had 34 houses in 1822.

Joy's Entry is named after Francis Joy, who founded the *Belfast News Letter* in 1737, the first daily newspaper in the British Isles (and still in business). One of his grandsons, Henry Joy McCracken, was executed for supporting the 1798 United Irishmen's revolt.

The United Irishmen were founded in 1791 by Wolfe Tone in Peggy Barclay's tavern in **Crown Entry**, and used to meet in **Kelly's Cellars** (1720) on Bank St, off Royal Ave. **White's Tavern** (1630), on **Wine Cellar Entry**, is the oldest pub in the city and is still a popular lunch-time meeting spot.

RED HAND OF ULSTER

You'll see the Red Hand of Ulster in many places: on the official Northern Irish flag, in the Ulster coat of arms, above the entrance to the Linen Hall Library on Donegall Square, and laid out in red flowers in the garden of Mt Stewart in County Down. The story goes that the chief of a war party approaching the Ulster coast announced that the land would belong to the first man to lay his right hand upon it. One particularly competitive chap lopped off his own hand and flung it to the shore, claiming Ulster as his own. The O'Neill clan later adopted the Red Hand as their emblem and it went on to become the symbol of the Irish province of Ulster.

QUEEN'S SQUARE

At the east end of High St is Belfast's very own leaning tower, the **Albert Memorial Clock Tower**. Erected in 1867 in honour of Queen Victoria's dear departed husband, it is not so dramatically out of kilter as the famous tower in Pisa but does, nevertheless, tilt noticeably to the south – as the locals say, 'Old Albert not only has the time, he also has the inclination.' Recent restoration work has stabilised its foundations and left its Scrabo sandstone masonry sparkling white.

Many of the buildings around the clock tower are the work of Sir Charles Lanyon, Belfast's pre-eminent Victorian architect. The white stone building immediately north of the clock tower was completed in 1852 by Lanyon as a head office for the **Northern Bank**.

South of the tower on Victoria St is the **McCausland Hotel** (1868), formerly two seed warehouses – look for the friezes of exotic birds, plants and nut-munching squirrels on the left half of the façade.

Cathedral Quarter

The district north of the centre around St Anne's Cathderal, bounded roughly by Donegall St, Waring St, Dunbar St and York St, has been promoted in recent years as Belfast's Left Bank, a bohemian district of restored red-brick warehouses and cobbled lanes lined with artists' studios, design offices, and new bars and restaurants. It is home to the annual **Cathedral Quarter Arts Festival** (see p554).

Built in imposing Hiberno-Romanesque style, **St Anne's Cathedral** (☎ 9033 2328; Donegall St; admission by donation; ⏰ 10am-4pm Mon-Fri) was started in 1899 but did not reach its final form until 1981. As you enter you'll see the black and white marble floor is laid out in a maze pattern – the black route leads to a dead end, the white to the sanctuary and salvation. The 10 pillars of the nave are topped by carvings symbolising aspects of Belfast life; look out for the Freemasons' pillar (the central one on the right, or south side). In the south aisle is the tomb of unionist hero Sir Edward Carson (1854–1935). The stunning mosaic of *The Creation* in the baptistry contains 150,000 pieces of coloured glass; it and the mosaic above the west door are the result of seven years' work by sisters Gertrude and Margaret Martin.

A 10-minute walk northwest from the cathedral along Donegall St and Clifton St leads to **Clifton House** (2a Hopewell Ave, Carlisle Circus), built in 1774 by Robert Joy (Henry Joy McCracken's uncle) as a poorhouse, and the finest surviving 18th-century building in Belfast. It now houses a nursing home.

Walk south from the cathedral along Donegall St and you'll see the elegant Georgian **Commercial Building** (1822) ahead, easily identified by the prominent name of the Northern Whig Printing Company, with a modern bar on the ground floor. Opposite is the **Northern Bank Building**, the oldest public building in the city, which started life as the single-storey Exchange in 1769, became the Assembly Rooms with the addition of an upper storey in 1777, and was remodelled in Italianate style in 1845 by Charles Lanyon to become a bank.

Turn left along Waring St to find the most flamboyant legacy of Belfast's Victorian era, the grandiose **Ulster Bank** (1860) building. Currently closed to the public, this Italianate extravaganza has iron railings decorated with the Red Hand of Ulster and Irish wolfhounds, soaring columns and sculpted figures depicting Britannia, Justice and Commerce.

To the west of the cathedral, at the junction of Royal Ave and North St, is the **Bank of Ireland Building** (1929), a fine example of Art Deco architecture. The former **Sinclair Store** (1935), diagonally opposite the bank, is also in Deco style.

Laganside

The ambitious **Laganside Project** to redevelop and regenerate the centre of Belfast saw the building of the Waterfront Hall, British Telecom's Riverside Tower and the Belfast Hilton in the 1990s. Projects completed since then include several clusters of riverside apartments and the restoration of listed buildings such as McHugh's bar on Queen's Square, the ornate Victorian warehouses now housing the McCausland Hotel on Victoria St, and the Albert Memorial Clock Tower. Future plans include the redevelopment of Victoria Square and Custom House Square.

CLARENDON DOCK

Near the ferry terminal on Donegall Quay is the Italianate **Harbour Commissioner's Office** (1854). The striking marble and stained-glass interior features art and sculpture inspired by Belfast's maritime history. The captain's table built for the *Titanic* survives here – completed behind schedule, it never made it on board. Guided tours of the office are available during the Belfast Summer in the City festival (see p553). It's also open during European Heritage Weekend, which usually takes place in October or November.

Sinclair Seamen's Church (☎ 9086 8568; Corporation Sq; admission free; ⏰ 2-4.30pm Wed, 11.30am-7pm Sun), next to the Harbour Commissioner's Office, was built by Charles Lanyon in 1857–58 and was intended to meet the spiritual needs of visiting sailors. Part church, part maritime museum, it has a pulpit in the shape of a ship's prow, an organ that sports port and starboard lights, and the ship's bell from HMS *Hood*.

North of the Harbour Commissioner's Office is the restored **Clarendon Dock**. Leading off it are the dry docks where Belfast's shipbuilding industry was born – No 1 Dry Dock (1796–1800) is Ireland's oldest, and remained in use until the 1960s; No 2 (1826) is still used occasionally. Between the two sits the pretty little **Clarendon Building**, now home to the offices of the Laganside Corporation.

CUSTOM HOUSE SQUARE

South along the river is the elegant **Custom House**, built by Lanyon in Italianate style between 1854 and 1857; the writer Anthony Trollope once worked in the post office here. On the waterfront side the pediment carries sculpted portrayals of Britannia, Neptune and Mercury. There are plans to redevelop Custom House Square and Queen's Square as a pedestrian area linking the city centre to the riverbank, due for completion by the end of 2004.

Looking across the River Lagan from the Custom House, East Belfast is dominated by the huge yellow cranes of the Harland & Wolff shipyards. The modern Queen Elizabeth Bridge crosses the Lagan just to the south, but immediately south again is **Queen's Bridge** (1843) with its ornate lamps, Sir Charles Lanyon's first important contribution to Belfast's cityscape.

LAGAN WEIR & LOOKOUT

Across the street from the Custom House is *Bigfish* (1999), the most prominent of the many modern artworks that grace the riverbank between Clarendon Dock and Ormeau Bridge. The giant ceramic salmon is covered with tiles depicting the history of Belfast.

It sits beside **Lagan Weir**, the first stage of the Laganside Project, completed in 1994. Years of neglect and industrial decline had turned the River Lagan, the original lifeblood of the city, into an open sewer flanked by smelly, unsightly mudflats. The weir, along with a programme of dredging and aeration, has improved the water quality so much that salmon, eels and sea trout now migrate up the river.

The **Lagan Lookout Visitor Centre** (☎ 9031 5444; 1 Donegall Quay; adult/child £1.50/0.75; 🕑 11am-5pm Mon-Fri, noon-5pm Sat, 2-5pm Sun Apr-Sep, 11am-3.30pm Tue-Fri, 1-4.30pm Sat, 2-4.30pm Sun Oct-Mar) offers a state-of-the-art explanation of how the weir works and why it was needed, with interactive computers to bring things to life. The centre also has displays on the progress of the entire Laganside Project.

For details of the boat tours that depart from here, see p552.

ODYSSEY COMPLEX

Opened in 2001, the **Odyssey Complex** is a huge sporting and entertainment centre on the eastern side of the river across from Clarendon Dock. The complex features a hands-on science centre – W5 – a 10,000-seater sports arena (home to the Belfast Giants ice-hockey team), a multiplex cinema with an IMAX screen, a video games centre and a dozen restaurants, cafés and bars.

Also known as whowhatwherewhenwhy, **W5** (☎ 9046 7700; www.w5online.co.uk; adult/child/family £5.50/3.50/14; 🕑 10am-6pm Mon-Sat, noon-6pm Sun) is an interactive science centre aimed at children of all ages. Kids can compose their own tunes by biffing the 'air harp' with a foam rubber bat, try to beat a lie detector, create cloud rings and fire tornadoes, and design and build their own robots and racing cars.

The Odyssey Complex is a five-minute walk across the weir from the Lagan Lookout. The Airbus No 600 from the Europa Bus Centre to Belfast city airport stops at the complex (£0.70, 10 minutes, departing every 30 minutes Monday to Saturday, every 40 minutes Sunday), travelling via Ormeau Ave (outside the Holiday Inn), Chichester St and Laganside Bus Centre.

LANYON PLACE

A five-minute walk south from the Lagan Lookout leads to **Lanyon Place**, the Laganside Project's flagship site, dominated by the 2235-seat **Waterfront Hall** (☎ 9033 4400; www.waterfront.co.uk; Lanyon Pl). Across Oxford St lies the neoclassical **Royal Courts of Justice** (1933), bombed by the IRA in 1990 but now emerging from behind the massive security screens that once concealed them.

South of the courts is the elegant Victorian **St George's Market** (☎ 9043 5704; cnr Oxford & May Sts; admission free; 🕑 7am-3pm Fri, 8am-2pm Sat), built in 1896 for the sale of fruit, butter, eggs and poultry, and the oldest continually operating market in Ireland. Restored in 1999, it now sells fresh flowers, fruit, vegetables, meat and fish, plus general household and second-hand goods on Friday, and hosts a farmers' market on Saturday. The Ha'penny Fair, with antiques and collectables, arts and crafts, is held on the first Sunday of the month.

South of the Centre

The Golden Mile – a 1km strip of pubs and restaurants – stretches south from the city centre to the University district, and is the focus for much of Belfast's nightlife. The Mile is not confined to one street, but takes in Great Victoria St and Bedford St/Dublin St, which converge on Shaftesbury Square and Bradbury Place, then continues along Botanic Ave and University Rd.

Citybus Nos 69, 70 and 71 run from Donegall Square East along Bradbury Place and University Rd to Queen's University.

ORMEAU BATHS GALLERY

Housed in a 19th-century public bathhouse, the **Ormeau Baths Gallery** (☎ 9032 1402; www.obgonline.net; 18a Ormeau Ave; admission free; 🕒 10am-6pm Tue-Sat) is Northern Ireland's principal exhibition space for contemporary visual art. The gallery stages changing exhibitions of work by Irish and international artists, and has hosted controversial showings of works by Gilbert and George, and Yoko Ono. The gallery is a few blocks south of Donegall Square.

QUEEN'S UNIVERSITY

If you think that Charles Lanyon's **Queen's College** (1849), a Tudor Revival building in red brick and honey-coloured sandstone, has something of an Oxbridge air about it, that may be because he based the design of the central tower on the 15th-century Founder's Tower at Oxford's Magdalen College. Northern Ireland's most prestigious university was founded by Queen Victoria in 1845, one of three Queen's colleges (the others were in Cork and Galway) created to provide a nondenominational alternative to the Anglican Church's Trinity College in Dublin. In 1908 the college became the Queen's University of Belfast, and today its campus spreads across some 250 buildings. Queen's has around 17,500 students and enjoys a particularly strong reputation in medicine, engineering and law.

Just inside the main entrance is a small **visitor centre** (☎ 9033 5252; www.qub.ac.uk/vcentre; University Rd; admission free; 🕒 10am-4pm Mon-Sat May-Sep, 10am-4pm Mon-Fri Oct-Apr) with exhibitions and a souvenir shop. You can arrange a guided tour by phoning in advance.

The university quarter is an attractive district of quiet, tree-lined streets. **University Square** (1848–53), on the northern side of the campus, is one of the most beautiful terraced streets in Ireland. Opposite its eastern end is the grand, neo-Renaissance **Union Theological College** (1853), originally the Presbyterian College and yet another Lanyon design. It housed the Northern Ireland Parliament from the partition of Ireland until 1932, when the Parliament Buildings at Stormont were opened.

BOTANIC GARDENS

The green oasis of Belfast's **Botanic Gardens** (☎ 9032 4902; Stranmillis Rd; admission free; 🕒 8am-sunset) is a short stroll away from the university. Just inside the Stranmillis Rd gate is a statue of Belfast-born **Lord Kelvin**, who invented the Kelvin scale that measures temperatures from absolute zero (-273°C or 0°K).

The gardens' centrepiece is Charles Lanyon's beautiful **Palm House** (1839-52; admission free; 🕒 10am-noon & 1-5pm Mon-Fri, 2-5pm Sat, Sun & bank holidays, closes 4pm Oct-Mar) with its bird-cage dome, a masterpiece in cast-iron and curvilinear glass. Nearby is the unique **Tropical Ravine** (🕒 same hr as Palm House), a huge red-brick greenhouse designed by the garden's curator Charles McKimm and completed in 1889. Inside, a raised walkway overlooks a jungle of tropical ferns, orchids, lilies and banana plants growing in a sunken glen.

ULSTER MUSEUM

If the weather washes out a walk in the Botanics, head instead for the nearby **Ulster Museum** (☎ 9038 3000; www.ulstermuseum.org.uk; Stranmillis Rd; admission free; 🕒 10am-5pm Mon-Fri, 1-5pm Sat, 2-5pm Sun). Don't miss the **Early Ireland** gallery, a series of tableaux explaining Irish prehistory combined with a spectacular collection of prehistoric stone and bronze artefacts that help provide a cultural context for Northern Ireland's many archaeological sites. The exhibits are beautifully displayed – the Malone Hoard, a clutch of 16 polished, Neolithic stone axes discovered only a few kilometres from the museum, looks more like a modern sculpture than a museum exhibit.

Other highlights include the **Industrial History** gallery, based around Belfast's 19th-century linen industry, and the **Treasures of the Armada**, a display of artefacts and jewellery recovered from the 1588 wreck of the *Girona* and other Spanish Armada vessels, including a ruby-encrusted golden salamander.

The centrepiece of the Egyptian collection is the **mummy of Princess Takabuti**. She was unwrapped in Belfast in 1835, the first mummy ever to be displayed outside Egypt; more recently, her bleached hair has led the locals to dub her 'Belfast's oldest bleached blonde'.

West Belfast

Though scarred by three decades of civil unrest, the former battleground of West Belfast is one of the most compelling places to visit in Northern Ireland. Recent history hangs heavy in the air, but the old Victorian slums and most of the 1960s tower blocks have been replaced by greatly improved public housing, and there is a noticeable feeling of optimism and hope for the future.

The main attractions are the powerful murals that chart the history of the conflict as well as the political passions of the moment, and for visitors from mainland Britain there is a grim fascination to be found in wandering through the former 'war zone' in their own backyard.

West Belfast grew up around the linen mills that propelled the city into late 19th-century prosperity. It was an area of low-cost, working-class housing and even in the Victorian era was divided along religious lines. The advent of the Troubles in 1968 solidified the sectarian divide, and since 1970 the ironically named 'Peace Line' has separated the Loyalist and Protestant Shankill district from the republican and Catholic Falls.

Despite its reputation the area is safe to visit, though it's probably best avoided after dark.

FALLS RD

Although the signs of past conflict are inescapable, the Falls today is an unexpectedly lively, colourful and optimistic place. Local people are friendly and welcoming, and community ventures such as Conway Mill, the Cultúrlann centre and black taxi tours are drawing increasing numbers of tourists into the area.

You can walk along the Falls Rd from the city centre to Milltown Cemtery in an hour or so. To reach the Falls Rd from Donegall Square go north along Donegall Place and turn left on Castle St. Keep straight ahead along Divis St.

As you cross the busy Westlink dual carriageway, the first indication that this is no ordinary suburb you are entering is the army observation post atop the infamous **Divis Tower**. The security forces took over the top two floors of the tower block in the 1970s, and still use the post to monitor

'PEOPLE'S TAXIS'

The black taxis that cruise along the Falls and Shankill Rds in West Belfast have more in common with Turkey's 'dolmuş' minibuses than the black cabs of London. These are shared taxis that operate along fixed routes, departing only when full, then dropping off and picking up passengers as they go, more like buses than traditional taxis.

Indeed, the 'People's Taxis', as they became known, were introduced in the 1970s to replace local bus services that had been disrupted or cancelled as a result of street riots at the height of the Troubles. The drivers' associations that run the taxis are community-based ventures that provided much-needed employment during difficult times, and often gave jobs to ex-internees and prisoners who could not find work elsewhere.

About 30 years on, the black taxis are an accepted part of Belfast's public transport infrastructure. There are even plans to build a black taxi 'bus station' on Castle St. However, those on the unionist side allege that the Falls Rd taxis channel funds to the IRA, while republicans make similar claims about the Shankill taxis and Loyalist paramilitaries.

Falls Rd taxis (with green licence discs) depart from the corner of King and Castle Sts. During the day a sign in the windscreen shows their route; after 5.30pm the first person in the queue dictates the destination. You can hail a taxi anywhere; when you want to get out, knock on the window, then pay the driver from the footpath.

Shankill taxis (with orange licence discs) depart from North St. You can hail them at bus stops; when you want to get out, say 'next stop' to the driver, and pay before you get out. Fares on both services range from around £0.70 to £1 per person.

people's movements. When you get closer you'll see posters and graffiti calling for the 'Demilitarisation of the Divis'.

As you pass the Divis Tower, look to the right along the side street opposite and you'll see the beginning of the so-called **Peace Line**, the 6m-high wall of corrugated steel, concrete and chainlink that has divided the Protestant and Catholic communities of West Belfast for 30 years. Begun in 1970 as a 'temporary measure', it has now outlasted the Berlin Wall, and zig-zaggs for some 4km from the Westlink to the lower slopes of Black Mountain. These days the gates in the wall remain open during the day, but most are still closed from 5pm to 8am. There are now around 20 such barriers in Belfast, the most recent having been built in the Short Strand area of East Belfast in 2002.

Next, you pass the **Solidarity Wall**, a collection of murals expressing republican sympathies with, among others, the Palestinians, the Kurds and the Basques. Conway St, on the right at the Celtic Bar, leads to **Conway Mill** (☎ 9024 7276; 5-7 Conway St; admission free; 🕑 10am-4pm Mon-Fri), a 19th-century flax mill that now houses more than 20 small shops and studios

SECTARIAN PLOTS

Cemeteries always reveal something about the health and wealth of a city. In Belfast's case they also tell us something about the politics.

The sprawling **City Cemetery** on the Falls Rd, West Belfast, was opened in 1869 because the Famine had already filled up the other graveyards. Today it covers 99 acres and Travellers, Jews, Protestants and Catholics are all buried here – albeit in their own sections. Much of it is overgrown and you'll find rare varieties of roses here, planted in the past and left to their own devices while elsewhere they would have died out.

There's humour here, in epitaphs such as 'Beam me up Lord', 'I wish I was fishing' and 'I told you I was sick', but there's also concealed sectarianism. When part of the cemetery was allocated to Roman Catholics, a 3m-high wall was erected to divide the Protestant and Catholic plots. However, this wall, like the dead it was to separate, was built underground. The only evidence of it is a mown-grass divide running straight through the old part of the cemetery. Presumably there are Protestant worms on one side and Catholic worms on the other.

Headstone inscriptions from before the 1921 partition of Ireland show that it was not unusual to be both Protestant and an Irish patriot. Indeed, many Ulster folk saw themselves as Irish rather than British. There are men buried here who fought for the British army all over the Empire, yet their memorials have Irish references. One describes an occupant as a loyal Irish patriot and also a Grandmaster of the Orange Order.

One famous grave is that of William James Pirrie (1847–1924), who signed the contract for the *Titanic* with the White Star Line on behalf of Harland & Wolff. There's also a memorial to his nephew, who designed the ship, but was drowned when it sank. Pirrie himself was ill at the time of the liner's maiden voyage, stayed at home and survived.

Milltown Cemetery, further out along the Falls Rd, lies beneath the omnipresent gaze of a large fortified police barracks. Here you'll find the republican dead, many of whom died very young, victims of the UVF, the IRA, the RUC and the British Army. It was here that, in March 1988, a Loyalist gunman killed three mourners and injured 50 at the funeral of the three IRA members shot dead by the SAS in Gibraltar.

Two large green areas without headstones stand out, seemingly unused. These are the mass graves of victims of the 1918 flu epidemic, which killed 86,000 people. No-one dares reuse this land in case any disturbance releases the virus. There is however one memorial here marking the grave of a bishop. It was his request to be buried here because when people prayed for him they'd also be praying for those around him.

There are graves of republicans of every generation, killed during the civil war of the 1920s, IRA campaigns of the 1940s and the later Troubles. As in life, schisms in the republican paramilitaries are represented in this cemetery. There's an official IRA plot, an Irish National Liberation Association plot and the Provisional IRA plot, which contains the graves of the 10 hunger strikers who died in 1981, including Bobby Sands.

making and selling arts, crafts and furniture, and an exhibition on the mill's history.

On the corner with Sevastopol St is the red-brick **Sinn Féin headquarters**, with its famous mural of a smiling Bobby Sands, the hunger striker who was elected as MP for West Belfast just a few weeks before he died in 1981. The text reads, in Sands' own words, 'Our revenge will be the laughter of our children'. A few blocks further on, on the right between Waterford St and Springfield Rd, look out for the **Ruby Emerald Take-Away** at 105 Falls Rd – it was on the pavement outside this shop (known as Clinton's Hot Food from 1996 to 2003) that the historic handshake between Sinn Féin leader Gerry Adams and US president Bill Clinton took place in November 1995.

Beyond the new artwork railings of the **Royal Victoria Hospital**, which has a well-earned reputation for expertise in the treatment of gunshot wounds, is the Irish language and cultural centre **Cultúrlann MacAdam ÓFiaich** (☎ 9023 9303; 216 Falls Rd; 🕑 9am-5.30pm Mon-Fri, 10am-5.30pm Sat). Housed in a red-brick, former Presbyterian church, it's a cosy and welcoming place with a tourist information desk, a shop selling a wide selection of books on Ireland, crafts, and Irish music tapes and CDs, and an excellent café (see p559). The centre also stages music and poetry events.

All along the Falls Rd you'll see republican murals, as well as memorials in honour of people who have died during the conflict. At Islandbawn St on the right, the **Plastic Bullet Mural** commemorates the 17 people, including eight children, who were killed by plastic baton rounds (now banned) fired by the security services. Two streets on, on the right, is Beechmount Ave, with a huge **'Free Ireland' mural**. Look at the street name – a hand-painted sign reads **RPG Avenue**. RPG stands for rocket-propelled grenade, and the street earned its nickname because it offered a line of sight for IRA rocket attacks on the security forces base in nearby Springfield Rd.

Another 15 minutes of walking will take you past the **City Cemetery** and Falls Park to **Milltown Cemetery** (see Sectarian Plots, p548) where the 1981 hunger strikers are buried. You'll see lots of green Hs attached to lamp posts (in memory of the H-blocks at the Maze prison where the hunger strikers were incarcerated); at Hugo St, opposite the City Cemetery, there's a large mural entitled 'St James's Support the Hunger Strikers'.

Return by the same route or catch a bus or taxi back to the city centre. There's a bus stop across the road from the Milltown Cemetery entrance.

SHANKILL RD

Although the Protestant Shankill district (from the Irish *sean chill,* meaning 'old church') has received less media and tourist attention than the Falls, it also contains many interesting murals. The people here are just as friendly, but the Shankill has a rather foreboding atmosphere that contrasts with the more outgoing feel of the Falls Rd. Loyalist communities seem to have more difficulty in presenting their side of the story than the republicans, who have a far more polished approach to propaganda and PR.

Whereas the Falls Rd murals are often artistic and rich in symbolic imagery, the Shankill ones are generally more militaristic and defiant in tone. The Loyalist battle cry of 'No Surrender!' is everywhere, along with red, white and blue painted kerbstones, paramilitary insignia and images of King Billy.

To reach Shankill Rd on foot, walk north from City Hall along Donegall Place and Royal Ave, then turn left on Peter's Hill and keep straight on across the Westlink dual carriageway.

Beyond Shankill Rd, about 500m up Glencairn Rd, is **Fernhill House: The People's Museum** (☎ 9071 5599; Glencairn Rd; adult/child £2/1; 🕑 10am-4pm). A re-creation of a 1930s Shankill house, the museum has exhibitions detailing the history of the Shankill district, the Home Rule crisis, the two World Wars and the Orange Order. To get there, take bus No 63 from Wellington Place, at the northwest corner of Donegall Square.

GETTING THERE & AWAY

The easiest way to see West Belfast is on a black taxi tour (see p547 and p553). The cabs visit the more spectacular murals as well as the Peace Line (where you can write a message on the wall) and other significant sites, while the driver provides a colourful commentary on the history of the area.

There's nothing to stop you visiting under your own steam, either walking or using the shared black taxis along the Falls or Shankill

Rds (see The People's Taxis, p547). Alternatively, bus Nos 12 to 15 or 532 to 540 from Queen St will take you along the Falls Rd; bus Nos 39, 63 and 73 from Wellington Place go along Shankill Rd.

The Suburbs

CAVE HILL COUNTRY PARK

The best way to get a feel for Belfast's natural setting is to view it from above. In the absence of a private aircraft, head for **Cave Hill** (368m), which looms over the northern fringes of the city. The view from its summit takes in the whole sprawl of the city, the docks and the creeping fingers of urbanisation along the shores of Belfast Lough. On a clear day you can even spot Scotland lurking on the horizon.

The hill was originally called Ben Madigan, after a 9th-century Ulster king, Matudhain. Its distinctive, craggy profile, seen from the south, has been known to locals

MURALS OF BELFAST

Loyalist Murals

The mural tradition in the Loyalist camp dates from 1908, when images of King Billy appeared in protest against home rule for Ireland. From the mid-1980s, however, with the signing of the Anglo-Irish Agreement, the dominant image became that of armed paramilitaries posing with weapons.

Loyalist imagery is dominated by 'King Billy' (William III, Protestant victor over the Catholic James II at the Battle of the Boyne in 1690), usually shown on a prancing white horse; the Red Hand of Ulster, sometimes shown as a clenched fist (the symbol of the UFF); and references to the WWI Battle of the Somme in 1916 (in which many Ulster soldiers died; seen as a symbol of Ulster's loyalty to the British crown, in contrast to the republican Easter Rising of 1916).

Common mottoes include 'No Surrender', which originates in the Great Siege of Derry in 1689 (see p599); 'Quis Separabit' (Who Shall Divide Us?), the motto of the UDA; and the defiant 'We will maintain our faith and our nationality'.

The main areas for Loyalist murals are Shankill and Crumlin Rds, around Newtownards Rd in East Belast, and on Sandy Row and Donegall Pass south of the city centre.

Republican Murals

The first republican murals did not appear until 1981, when the republican hunger strike at the Maze prison saw the emergence of dozens of murals in support of the hunger strikers.

After 1981, republican muralists broadened their scope to cover wider political issues, Irish legends and historical events. The mural off the Falls Rd commemorating the 150th anniversary of the Potato Famine is particularly powerful; another is the mural celebrating women, children and workers on Ormeau Rd. In addition, republican murals often related directly to current political issues, such as elections, or other political campaigns, such as opposition to plastic bullets.

Following the republican cease-fire of August 1994, the 'armed struggle' images virtually ceased, and new murals appeared stating republican demands: prisoner releases, British army withdrawal, disbandment of the RUC, and so on. After the Good Friday Agreement of 1998, the murals came to demand police reform and the protection of nationalists from sectarian attacks.

Common images seen in republican murals around the Falls Rd include the phoenix rising from the flames (symbolising Ireland reborn from the flames of the 1916 Easter Rising), the face of hunger striker Bobby Sands, and scenes and figures from Irish mythology. Common mottoes include 'Free Ireland', 'Brits Out' and the Irish 'Caisc 1916' (Easter 1916) and 'Tíocfaídh Ár Lá' (Our Day Will Come, a republican slogan).

The main areas for republican murals are the Falls Rd, Beechmount Ave, Donegall Rd, Shaw's Rd and the Ballymurphy district in West Belfast, New Lodge Rd in North Belfast, and Ormeau Rd in South Belfast.

If you're interested in Northern Ireland's mural tradition, look out for the books *Drawing Support: Murals in the North of Ireland* and *Drawing Support 2: Murals of War and Peace* by Bill Rolston, and the Mural Directory website (www.cain.ulst.ac.uk/murals). See also p606.

for two centuries as 'Napoleon's Nose' – it supposedly bears some resemblance to Bonaparte's hooter, but you might take some convincing. On the summit is an Iron Age ring fort known as McArt's Fort where members of the United Irishmen, including Wolfe Tone, looked down over the city in 1795 and pledged to fight for Irish independence.

You can climb to the summit from **Cave Hill Country Park** (☎ 9077 6925; Antrim Rd; admission free; 🕑 7.30am-dusk), which spreads across the hill's eastern slopes. There are several waymarked walks in addition to the summit trail, and an adventure playground for kids aged three to 14 years.

To get there, take Citybus Nos 45 to 51 from Donegall Square West to Belfast Castle or Belfast Zoo.

BELFAST CASTLE

Built in 1870 for the third Marquess of Donegall, in the Scottish Baronial style made fashionable by Queen Victoria's recently built Balmoral, the multiturreted pomp of **Belfast Castle** (☎ 9077 6925; www.belfastcastle.co.uk; Antrim Rd; admission free; 🕑 9am-10pm Mon-Sat, 9am-5.30pm Sun) commands the eastern slopes of Cave Hill. It was presented to the City of Belfast in 1934.

Extensive renovation between 1978 and 1988 left the interior comfortably modern rather than intriguingly antique, and the castle is now a popular venue for wedding receptions. Upstairs is the **Cave Hill Visitor Centre** (admission free; 🕑 same hr as castle) with displays on the folklore, history, archaeology and natural history of the park. Downstairs is the Cellar Restaurant and a small **antiques shop** (🕑 noon-10pm Mon-Sat, noon-5pm Sun).

Legend has it that the castle's residents will experience good fortune only as long as a white cat lives there, a tale commemorated in the formal gardens by nine portrayals of cats in mosaic, painting, sculpture and garden furniture.

BELFAST ZOO

Belfast Zoo (☎ 9077 6277; Antrim Rd; adult/child £6.40/3.20 Apr-Sep, £5.40/2.70 Oct-May, children under 4 & senior citizens free; 🕑 10am-5pm Apr-Sep, 10am-2.30pm Oct-May; wheelchair access) is one of the most appealing zoos in Britain and Ireland, with spacious enclosures set on an attractive, sloping site; the sea lion and penguin pool with its underwater viewing is particularly good. Some of the more unusual animals include tamarins, spectacled bears and red pandas, but the biggest attractions are 'Jack' the white tiger, the ultra-cute meerkats and the colony of ring-tailed lemurs. Visitors with disabilities get free admission.

LAGAN TOWPATH

Part of Belfast's Laganside redevelopment project has been the restoration of the Lagan Towpath along the west bank of the River Lagan. You can now walk or cycle for 20km along the winding riverbank from central Belfast to Lisburn.

A shorter walk (10km) that you can easily do in half a day starts from Shaw's Bridge on the southern edge of the city. Take bus Nos 70 or 71 from Donegall Square East to the stop just before the Malone Roundabout (where Malone Rd becomes Upper Malone Rd). Bear left at the roundabout (signposted Outer Ring A55) and in five minutes or so you will reach the River Lagan at Shaw's Bridge.

Turn left and follow the cycle/walkway downstream on the left bank of the river (waymarked with red No '9' signs). After 30 minutes you will arrive at the most attractive part of the walk – **Lagan Meadows**, a tree-fringed loop in the river to the right of the path, and a good place for a picnic on a summer's day. Another half-hour will bring you to **Cutters Wharf** (☎ 9080 5100; Lockview Rd, Stranmillis; mains £6-11), a great place for a lunch break. From the pub it's another hour's walk to Lagan Weir in the city centre.

MALONE HOUSE

Malone House (☎ 9068 1246; Upper Malone Rd; admission free; 🕑 9am-5pm Mon-Sat) is a late-Georgian mansion in the grounds of Barnett Demesne. Built in the 1820s for local merchant William Legge, the house is now used mainly for social functions and conferences, with art exhibitions staged in the Higgin Gallery. The surrounding gardens are planted with azaleas and rhododendrons, with paths leading down to the Lagan Towpath (see the boxed text above).

The house is about 5km south of the centre; take bus No 70 or 71 to Dub Lane, Upper Malone Rd.

SIR THOMAS & LADY DIXON PARK

Sir Thomas & Lady Dixon Park (Upper Malone Rd; admission free; dawn-dusk year round) consists of rolling meadows, woodland, riverside fields and formal gardens. The main draw is its spectacular **Rose Garden**, which contains more than 20,000 blooms. Among other displays, a spiral-shaped garden traces the development of the rose from early shrub roses up to modern hybrids; the roses are in bloom from late July. The park also contains a walled garden, a Japanese-style garden, a children's playground and a café.

The park is 1.5km south of Malone House.

GIANT'S RING

This huge **prehistoric earthwork** (admission free; 24hr), nearly 200m in diameter, is a circular Neolithic ritual complex with a dolmen (known as the Druid's Altar) in the centre. Prehistoric rings were commonly believed to be the home of fairies and consequently treated with respect, but this one was commandeered in the 19th century as a racetrack, the 4m-high embankment serving as a natural grandstand. The site is 6.5km south of Belfast city centre, off Milltown Rd near Shaw's Bridge.

STORMONT

The dazzling white neoclassical façade of **Parliament House** at Stormont is one of Belfast's most iconic buildings. For 40 years, from its completion in 1932 until the introduction of direct rule in 1972, it was the seat of the parliament of Northern Ireland. More recently, from November 1999 to October 2002, it hosted the devolved Northern Ireland Assembly. In the North, 'Stormont' carries the same connotation as 'Westminster' does in Britain and 'Washington' in the USA – the seat of power.

The building occupies a dramatic position at the end of a rising, 1.5km-long avenue and is fronted by a defiant statue of the arch-unionist Sir Edward Carson. Parliament House is not open to the public, but you are free to walk in the extensive grounds, and you can take a virtual tour at www.ni-assembly.gov.uk. Nearby 19th-century **Stormont Castle** is, like Hillsborough in County Down, an official residence of the Secretary of State for Northern Ireland.

Stormont is 8km east of the city centre, off the A20 Newtonards road. Take bus Nos 16, 17 or 20 from Donegall Square West.

TOURS

You can find full details of organised tours at the Belfast Welcome Centre. If you want to hire a personal guide, call the Welcome Centre or contact the **Northern Ireland Tour Guide Association** (☎ 9042 6019; www.bluebadgeireland.org; half-day tours £55-85).

Boat Tours

Lagan Boat Company (☎ 9033 0844; www.laganboatcompany.com; adult/child £5/4) has two 1¼-hour boat tours.

River Lagan Tour (2pm & 3.30pm Mon, 12.30pm, 2pm & 3.30pm Tue-Thu May-Sep, 12.30pm & 2pm Sat & Sun Apr & Oct) heads upstream to Stranmillis, departing from the Lagan Lookout.

Titanic Tour (12.30pm, 2pm & 3.30pm Fri-Sun May-Sep) explores the docks and shipyards downstream of the weir, departing from Donegall Quay near the *Bigfish* sculpture and picking up passengers at the Odyssey Complex. You can book through the **Belfast Welcome Centre** (☎ 9024 6609); call to confirm times.

Bus Tours

Belfast International Youth Hostel (☎ 9032 4733; www.minicoachni.co.uk; 22 Donegall Rd; admission £8 10.30am daily, 12.30pm Mon-Fri) has been recommended by many readers for its two-hour minibus tour that takes in the city centre, Belfast Castle and the Falls and Shankill Rds. Tours depart from the hostel.

The following **Citybus Tours** (☎ 9045 8484; www.translink.co.uk/belfasttours.asp) leave from outside the main post office on Castle Place from May to September, last 1½ hours and cost £5/4 per adult/child; a reduced timetable operates from October to May.

Belfast City Tour (11am Thu-Tue) Takes in the city centre, Queen's University, Botanic Gardens and Stormont.

Living History Tour (2.30pm Mon-Sat) Covers the shipyards, City Hall, Odyssey Complex, Waterfront Hall and the Falls and Shankill Rds.

Titanic Tour (11am Wed & 2.30pm Sun) Includes a walking tour of the original Harland & Wolff drawing offices.

Cycling Tours

Irish Cycle Tours (☎ 90642222; www.irishcycletours.com; admission £12 6.30pm Mon-Fri, 10am & 2pm Sat & Sun

May-Sep) Two-hour tours of the city centre, South Belfast and the Lagan Towpath, departing from the McCausland Hotel (see p554). The cost includes bike and helmet rental.

Taxi Tours

Black taxi tours of West Belfast's murals – known locally as the 'bombs and bullets' tours – are being offered by an increasing number of taxi companies and local cabbies. These can vary in quality and content, but in general they're an intimate and entertaining way to see the sights and can be customised to suit your own interests. They also offer historical taxi tours of the city centre. For a one-hour tour expect to pay £20 total for one or two people, and £8 per person for three to six.

The two most recommended companies are: **Black Taxi Tours** (☎ 0800 052 3914, 0786 012 7207; www.belfasttours.com) and **Original Belfast Black Taxi Tours** (☎ 0800 032 2003, 0790 538 1997). Call and they will pick you up anywhere in the city centre; the front gate of City Hall is the traditional pick-up spot.

Walking Tours

Bailey's Historical Pub Tours (☎ 9268 3665; admission £6; 🕓 7pm Thu, 4pm Sat May-Sep) has a two-hour tour taking in six of the city's historic pubs, departing from Flannigan's on Great Victoria St, above the Crown Liquor Saloon.

The following three tours all depart from the Belfast Welcome Centre from June to September:

Belfast City Centre Walk (☎ 9049 1469; admission £4; 🕓 2pm Fri) offers a 1½-hour walking tour that explores the architecture and history of the Victorian city centre and Laganside.

Blackstaff Way (☎ 9029 2631; admission £2; 🕓 11am Sat) is a fascinating one-hour tour through the heart of the city along the route of the Blackstaff River, which was channelled underground in 1881.

Old Town: 1660-1685 (☎ 9024 6609; admission £4; 🕓 2pm Sat) is a 1½-hour tour following the line of the old town walls of Belfast and it describes the origins of the city.

SPECIAL EVENTS

The Belfast City Council organises **Summer in the City** (☎ 9027 0222; www.belfastcity.gov.uk/events), a programme of events from May to September covering everything from classical and traditional music concerts to community events and the Lord Mayor's Show. Several buildings are opened to the public for guided tours.

March

Belfast Film Festival (☎ 9032 5913; www.belfastfilmfestival.org) A new (since 2000) week-long celebration of Irish and international film-making held in late March.

St Patrick's Carnival (☎ 9031 3440) A celebration of Ireland's national saint marked by various community festivals and culminating in a grand city centre carnival on 17 March.

May

Belfast Marathon (☎ 9027 0345; www.belfastcity.gov.uk/marathon) First Monday in May. Runners from across the globe come to compete but it's also a people's event, with a Walk and Fun Run as well.

HARLAND & WOLFF SHIPYARDS

In March 2003 the 22,000-tonne ro-ro ferry *Anvil Point* – ship No 1742 – sailed off down Victoria Channel, and closed a chapter in Belfast's history. She was the last ship to be built from the keel up in the city's famous Harland & Wolff shipyards, whose slips once gave birth to such world-famous ocean liners as the *Titanic* (1911) and the *Canberra* (1960).

The shipyard was founded in 1861, when the Yorkshire engineer Edward Harland and the German marine draughtsman Gustav Wolff became partners. By a strange twist of fate, the shipping line that gave Messrs Harland and Wolff their first order – ship Nos 1, 2 and 3 – was J Bibby & Sons of Liverpool. Bibby Line is now a member of the AWSR shipping consortium that placed the final two orders, ship Nos 1741 and 1742. Priced out of the shipbuilding market by Chinese and Korean competition, H&W has not closed down, but now concentrates on ship repair and completion.

The shipyard is not open to the public, but you can view it from the water by taking a boat trip (see p552). The giant yellow cranes known as Samson and Goliath dominate Belfast's eastern skyline. The larger of the two is more than 100m high and 140m long, straddling a 550m-long dock capable of handling ships of up to 200,000 tonnes.

Cathedral Quarter Arts Festival (☎ 9023 2403; www.cqaf.com) Twelve days of drama, music, poetry, street theatre and art exhibitions in and around the Cathedral Quarter. Held in early May.

August

Féile an Phobail (☎ 9031 3440; www.feilebelfast.com) Said to be the largest community festival in Ireland, the Féile takes place in West Belfast over 10 days in early August. Events include an opening carnival parade, street parties, theatre performances, concerts and historical tours of the City and Milltown cemeteries.

October

Belfast Festival at Queen's (☎ 9066 7687; www.belfastfestival.com) The UK's second-largest arts festival held in and around Queen's University during three weeks in late October and early November.

Halloween Carnival (☎ 9027 0222; www.belfastcity.gov.uk/events) Held from 27 to 31 October, with special events across the city, including a carnival parade, ghost tours and fireworks.

December

Christmas Festivities (☎ 9027 0222; www.belfastcity.gov.uk/events) A range of events from late November to 31 December, including carol singing, lamplight processions, a street carnival and a huge outdoor ice rink at the Odyssey Complex.

SLEEPING

From backpacker hostels to the Belfast Hilton, the city's range of places to stay has continued to expand in recent years. The traditional accommodation scene – red-brick B&Bs in the leafy suburbs of South Belfast and city centre business hotels – has been lent a splash of colour in the form of stylish hotel-restaurant-nightclub combos (such as Benedicts and Madisons) and elegant but expensive boutique hotels set in refurbished historic buildings (eg, TENsq and the McCausland Hotel).

Most of Belfast's budget and mid-range accommodation is south of the centre, in the university district around Botanic Ave, University Rd and Malone Rd. This area is also crammed with good-value restaurants and pubs, and is mostly within a 20-minute walk of City Hall. You can expect to pay around £7 to £10 for a hostel dorm, £40 to £50 for a double room in a good B&B or guesthouse, and £60 to £80 for a double in a luxurious mid-range hotel. The top end and more expensive mid-range places attract a business clientele during the week, and usually offer lower rates at weekends (Friday to Sunday nights).

Book ahead in the summer or during busy festival periods. The Belfast Welcome Centre will make reservations for a fee of £2.

City Centre

BUDGET

Linen House (Paddy's Backpackers; ☎ 9058 6400; www.belfasthostel.com; 18-20 Kent St; dm £6.50-9, s/d £15/24; P ⊠ 💻) This independent hostel is housed in a former linen factory in the Cathedral Quarter, about a 15-minute walk from the ferry terminal. It comes well recommended by readers, though it lacks the cosy personal feel of Arnie's and the Ark (see p555), and has two big kitchens, a laundry and a basement games room.

Belfast International Youth Hostel (☎ 9031 5435; www.hini.org.uk; 22-32 Donegall Rd; dm £8.50-9.50, s/d £17/26; P ⊠ 💻) Belfast's modern Hostelling International Northern Ireland (HINI) hostel is conveniently sited on the Golden Mile, which means it can be a bit noisy at night when the pubs and clubs empty. There's a kitchen, laundry, and café, free linen and free car parking. Take bus Nos 69 to 71 from Donegall Square East to Bradbury Place.

MID-RANGE

Jury's Inn (☎ 9053 3500; www.jurysdoyle.com; Fisherwick Pl, Great Victoria St; r £73-85; ⊠) Jury's bland modernity is more than made up for by its top location (only three minutes from City Hall) and excellent value – fixed room rates apply for anything up to three adults, or two adults and two kids. Breakfast costs £6.95 extra.

Two more chain hotels with flat-rate rooms that can be recommended on price and location rather than character are:

Travelodge (☎ 9033 3555; www.travelodge.co.uk; 15 Brunswick St; r £43-60; ⊠)

Days Inn (☎ 9024 2494; www.daysinn.com; 40 Hope St; r £70-80; P ⊠)

TOP END

McCausland Hotel (☎ 9022 0200; www.mccauslandhotel.com; 34-38 Victoria St; s £110-190, d £150-190; ⊠) This elegant hotel occupies two beautifully restored Italianate warehouses built for rival firms in the 1850s. Many period features have been retained and the rooms, though equipped with all mod cons, have a pleasantly sepia-tinted feel.

TENsq (☎ 9024 1001; mail@ten-sq.com; 10 Donegall Sq South; d £160-200; Ⓟ) The designer name says it all – 'ten square' is a former bank building to the south of City Hall that has been given a luxurious feng-shui makeover with dark lacquered wood, cream carpets and low-slung futon-style beds.

Europa Hotel (☎ 9032 7000; www.hastingshotels.com; Great Victoria St; s £110-160, d £160-180; Ⓟ ⊠) Belfast's most famous landmark has shaken off its 1970s reputation as the world's most bombed hotel and is now better known as the place where Bill Clinton stayed in 1995 and 1998. The monumental, almost Stalinist façade conceals a fully renovated and very comfortable business hotel.

South Belfast

BUDGET

Arnie's Backpackers (☎ 9024 2867; 63 Fitzwilliam St; dm £7-8.50; ⊠) This long-established hostel is set in a quiet terraced house in the university area with plenty of lively bars and restaurants nearby. It has basic laundry and cooking facilities and is a bit on the cramped side, but is friendly and fun.

Ark (☎ 9032 9626; info@arkhostel.com; 18 University St; dm £8.50-9.50; s/d £20/32; ⊠ 💻) The Ark is a cosy, compact hostel in a pleasant terraced house in a quiet street, with comfortable dorms, a small sitting room, kitchen and laundry facilities. This is a good place to look for temporary work, and long-term accommodation is available.

Queen's Elms (☎ 9038 1608; qehor@qub.ac.uk; 78 Malone Rd; s £8.75-12.80, tw £22; ⊠) Available from late June to early September, this modern university hall of residence in leafy South Belfast offers standard student rooms with 24-hour reception. Rates include bed linen but not towels, and there are cooking and laundry facilities. Take bus No 70 or 71 from Donegall Square East.

Botanic Lodge Guesthouse (☎ /fax 9032 7682; 87 Botanic Ave; s/d £25/40; ⊠) The Botanic is one of the university district's best B&B bargains, a handsome red-brick house where all rooms have TV and a basin, but most bathrooms are shared; the two en-suite doubles cost £45.

Eglantine Guesthouse (☎ 9066 7585; 21 Eglantine Ave; s/d £25/40; ⊠) The family-run Eglantine is an elegant red-brick terrace on a quiet, leafy back street about a 15-minute walk from the bustle of Botanic Ave. All eight rooms have shared bathrooms.

MID-RANGE

To get to places on or near Botanic Ave, take bus No 83, 84 or 86 from Howard Place; for places on or near University and Malone Rds take bus Nos 69 to 71 from Donegall Square East.

Benedicts (☎ 9059 1999; www.benedictshotel.co.uk; 7-21 Bradbury Pl; s £50-60, d £60-70; ⊠) Set bang in the middle of the Golden Mile, Benedicts is a modern, style-conscious hotel at the heart of Belfast's nightlife. The rooms are above a huge Gothic bar and restaurant (where you also have breakfast), so don't expect peace and quiet till after 1am.

Crescent Town House (☎ 9032 3349; www.crescenttownhouse.com; 13 Lower Cres; s £50-80, d £70-100; ⊠) The Crescent is another stylish hotel, an elegant Victorian town house with a slightly country-house feel. The **Metro Brasserie** (☎ 9032 3349) is downstairs.

Helga Lodge (☎ 9032 4820; fax 9032 0653; 7-13 Cromwell Rd; s £25-35, d £46-66; ⊠) This is a large (25 rooms) and comfortable guesthouse with a great location just off Botanic Ave. Most rooms have a shared bathroom; eight are en suite with TV and phone.

Madison's (☎ 9050 9800; www.madisonshotel.com; 59-63 Botanic Ave; s £50-70, d £65-80; ⊠) Madison's successfully rolls a hotel, bar-restaurant and nightclub into one sharply styled package, pulling in a mixed crowd of tourists, business people and clubbers who just don't want to go home. There are two suites for guests with disabilities.

QUB Common Room (☎ 9066 5938; qubcr@compuserve.com; 1 College Gardens; s/d £37.50/52) The Queen's University Common Room, across the street from the main campus, offers excellent B&B accommodation year round. Most rooms are en suite; those with shared facilities are slightly cheaper.

Pearl Court Guesthouse (☎ 9066 6145; pearlcourtgh@hotmail.com; 11 Malone Rd; s £25-35, d £44-52; ⊠) Expect big bedrooms and big breakfasts at this elegantly old-fashioned B&B in a 200-year-old terrace south of Queen's University. Six of the 10 rooms are en suite.

Marine Guesthouse (☎ 9066 2828; marine30@utvinternet.com; 30 Eglantine Ave; s/d £40/50; Ⓟ ⊠) The family-friendly Marine is a large, detached red-brick villa set on a quiet, leafy side street, offering homely B&B in eight spacious en-suite rooms.

Camera Guesthouse (☎ 9066 0026; pauldrumm@hotmail.com; 44 Wellington Park; s £24-38, d £45-55; ⊠)

The Camera is a cosy, Victorian B&B that serves organic produce only for breakfast, set in yet another of South Belfast's peaceful, tree-lined terraces.

TOP END

Wellington Park Hotel (☎ 9038 1111; www.mooneyhotelgroup.com; 21 Malone Rd; s £95-105, d £110-130; P ⊠; wheelchair access) Next to the popular 'Welly Park' student pub, the 'Welly Park' hotel has been given a modern makeover and has several wheelchair-accessible rooms.

Malone Lodge Hotel (☎ 9038 8000; www.malonelodgehotel.com; 60 Eglantine Ave; s £59-95, d £79-115; P ⊠) The centrepiece of a Victorian terrace, the Malone Lodge has pulled in many plaudits for its luxurious but homely rooms, good food and pleasant, helpful staff.

Dukes Hotel (☎ 9023 6666; info@dukes-hotel-belfast.co.uk; 65-67 University St; s/d £85/110; ⊠) Red-brick Victorian look and Addams Family–style corner tower belie the fact that this is a thoroughly modern place – the Chinese owners have had the feng shui experts in so your room should be brimming with positive energy.

West Belfast

BUDGET

Farset International (☎ 9089 9833; www.farsetinternational.com; 446 Springfield Rd; s/d £30/40; P ⊠) Farset is a new, community-run venture in West Belfast, best described as a posh hostel. The attractive modern complex is set in its own grounds overlooking a small lake, and has 38 en-suite rooms with TV. Rates don't include breakfast; you can eat in the restaurant or use the self-catering kitchen.

East Belfast

BUDGET

Dundonald Touring Caravan Park (☎ 9080 9100; 111 Old Dundonald Rd, Dundonald; camp/caravan sites £7.50/14; ⏲ Apr-Sep) This small site (22 pitches) in a park next to the Dundonald Icebowl is the nearest camping ground to Belfast, 7km east of the centre.

North Belfast

TOP END

The following two hotels are the nearest to Belfast international and Belfast city airports, respectively:

Fitzwilliam International Hotel (☎ 9442 2033; www.fitzwilliaminternational.com; Belfast international airport, Aldergrove; s £119-159, d £127-167; P ⊠) Immediately opposite the terminal at Belfast international airport, the 106-room Fitzwilliam has a business centre, conference facilities and free courtesy transport to the city centre.

Park Avenue Hotel (☎ 9065 6520; www.parkavenuehotel.co.uk; 158 Holywood Rd; s £45-63, d £60-79; P) The classy 56-room Park Avenue is 3km south of Belfast city airport and 3km east of the city centre.

EATING

Belfast has a burgeoning restaurant scene that includes a couple of the best eating places in all Ireland. Prevented from eating out for many years, Belfastians are rapidly catching up with European dining habits, with new cafés, bistros and restaurants opening up every week.

City Centre

The main shopping area north of Donegall Square becomes a silent maze of deserted streets and steel shutters after 7pm, but during the day the many pubs, cafés and restaurants do a roaring trade.

BUDGET

Café Paul Rankin (☎ 9031 5090; 27-29 Fountain St; snacks £1.50-4; ⏲ 7.30am-6pm Mon-Wed & Fri-Sat, 7.30am-9pm Thu) Owned by Northern Ireland's top celebrity chef, this café serves quality coffee, cakes, focaccia, soups, pastas and salads, with comfy benches and sofas for lounging on.

Café Renoir (☎ 9032 5592; 5 Queen St; mains £3-5; ⏲ 9am-5pm Mon-Sat) Renoir tempts in hungry shoppers with decent coffee, home-baked bread and a range of filling vegetarian and wholefood dishes.

Ann's Pantry (☎ 9024 9090; 29-31 Queen's Arcade; snacks £1-3; ⏲ 9am-5.30pm Mon-Sat) A tiny bakery set incongruously at the end of an arcade of jewellery shops, Ann's serves superb home-made soups, pies, cakes and mix-your-own sandwiches to take away or sit (OK, squeeze) in.

Charlie's Gourmet Sandwich Bar (☎ 9024 6097; 48 Upper Queen St) Another good place for cheap, healthy and filling sandwiches.

MID-RANGE

Deane's Brasserie (☎ 9056 0000; 34-40 Howard St; mains £6-11; ⏲ noon-2.30pm & 5.30-11pm Mon-Sat)

The street-level brasserie beneath Restaurant Michael Deane (see Something Special below) is a big, bustling testimonial to the pulling power of fine food, packed to the gills day and night with diners enjoying the 'lite' version of the Michelin-starred eatery upstairs.

Apartment (☎ 9050 9777; 2 Donegall Sq West; mains £6-8; food served noon-9pm Mon-Sat, noon-6pm Sun) The hottest spot on Donegall Square – sit in a big brown leather sofa and gaze out at City Hall, or in at all the beautiful people, while tucking into a menu of lightly prepared Mediterranean and Asian fusion cuisine.

White's Tavern (☎ 9024 3080; 2-12 Wine Cellar Entry; mains £4-7; food served noon-6pm Mon-Sat) Historic White's, on a cobbled alley between Rosemary and High Sts, has an upstairs dining room decked out in warm brick, wood and copper, serving down-to-earth pub food such as baked potatoes, fish dishes, Irish stew, and sausage and champ. It's also a good place for a pint.

Morning Star (☎ 9023 5986; 17 Pottinger's Entry; mains £4-8; food served noon-9pm Mon-Sat) This former coaching inn is famed for its eat-all-you-can lunch buffet (£3.95). The upstairs restaurant features traditional Irish beef (big 24oz steaks cost £14), mussels, oysters and eels, as well as more unusual things like Irish-farmed ostrich. You can also kick back with a drink or two.

Altos (☎ 9032 3087; Anderson McCauley Bldg, Fountain St; mains £5-8; 10am-5pm Mon-Wed, 10am-8pm Thu, 10am-6pm Fri & Sat) Altos is an arty, high-ceilinged bistro with giant modern art canvases on the walls. The menu is Mediterranean-Asian-Irish fusion, with the likes of crispy chilli beef and focaccia with roast vegies and pesto; breakfast is served till 11.15am.

SOMETHING SPECIAL

Restaurant Michael Deane (☎ 9033 1134; 34-40 Howard St; 2-/6-course dinner £29/55, vegetarian 2-course dinner £21; 12.15-2pm Fri, 7-9.30pm Wed-Sat) Chef Michael Deane heads the kitchen in Belfast's only Michelin-starred restaurant, where he takes the best of Irish and British produce – beef, game, lamb, seafood, even black pudding – and gives it the gourmet treatment. The restaurant (upstairs from Deane's Brasserie) is a romantic, regency boudoir of marble, mirrors, taffeta and crisp, carpet-length table linen, frequented by local and international celebrities – past patrons include rock band U2, TV foodie Loyd Grossman and Belfast-born actor James Nesbitt.

Cathedral Quarter & Around

John Hewitt Bar & Restaurant (☎ 9023 3768; 51 Donegall St; mains £6; food served noon-3pm Mon-Sat, noon-6pm Fri) Named for the Belfast poet and socialist, this is a modern pub with a traditional atmosphere and a well-earned reputation for excellent food and as an atmospheric place for a drink.

Nick's Warehouse (☎ 9043 9690; 35-39 Hill St; mains £9-13; food served noon-3pm Mon-Fri, 6-9.30pm Tue-Sat) A Cathedral Quarter pioneer (opened in 1989), Nick's is an enormous red-brick and blonde-wood wine bar and restaurant buzzing with happy drinkers and diners. The menu is strong on inventive seafood and vegie dishes, and the wine list is excellent.

Ba Soba (☎ 9058 6868; 38 Hill St; mains £5-8; noon-2.30pm Mon, noon-11pm Tue-Sat) Bright and breezy Ba Soba is an Asian noodle bar, dishing up fragrant, steaming bowls of Japanese *ramen* (noodle broth), prawn tempura, Thai warm salad, Malaysian curry and a host of other oriental dishes.

Opium (☎ 9023 2448; 3 Skipper St; mains £8-13; noon-9pm) Oriental-themed and very, very red, Opium is the latest addition to the quarter's designer bar-restaurants, with a menu of succulent Chinese, Thai, Malay and Indonesian classics, including a six-dish dim sum spread for £16.

McHugh's Bar & Restaurant (☎ 9050 9999; 29-31 Queen's Sq; lunch £5-7, dinner £7.50-11.50; noon-10.30pm Mon-Sat, noon-9pm Sun) This restored pub is a highlight of the Laganside redevelopment project, and boasts one of the city's best bar-restaurants, serving traditional pub grub downstairs and fancier dishes in the restaurant upstairs. The house speciality is oriental stir-fries cooked in a flaming wok. McHugh's is also popular as a watering hole.

Odyssey Complex

There are a dozen or so eating places in the Odyssey Complex.

Streat (☎ 9045 0807; Odyssey Pavilion; sandwiches £2.50; 10am-8pm) One of a city-wide chain, the Streat is a comfortable, modern café serving good coffee, sandwiches and snacks with an Irish twist – where else would you find a champ bar? – and makes a good spot for a pre-cinema cappuccino.

La Salsa (☎ 9046 0066; Odyssey Pavilion; mains £9-12; 🕒 5pm-late) A big restaurant with stylish mock-Aztec décor, La Salsa serves Belfast's best Tex-Mex food – authentic nachos, home-made salsa and guacamole, and succulent, properly marinated fajitas. There's another branch at the university.

Golden Mile North

Jenny's Coffee Shop (☎ 9024 9282; 81 Dublin Rd; mains £3-5; 🕒 9am-5.30pm Mon-Sat) Jenny's is a pleasant little café–sandwich bar serving tasty and filling student nosh.

Archana (☎ 9032 3713; 53 Dublin Rd; mains £5.50-10; 🕒 noon-2pm & 5pm-midnight Mon-Sat, 5-11pm Sun) A cosy and unpretentious Indian restaurant, Archana offers a good range of vegetarian dishes from its separate 'Little India' menu. The *thali* – a platter of three curries with naan bread, pakora and dessert – is good value at £10/8 for the meat/vegie version.

Thai Village (☎ 9024 9269; 50 Dublin Rd; mains £8-10; 🕒 noon-2.30pm & 6.30-11pm Mon-Sat, 5.30-11pm Sun) This candle-lit nook serves tasty, and very nearly authentic (spot the bottled chilli sauce and supermarket mushrooms), Thai food, including an excellent selection of vegetarian and vegan dishes.

Speranza (☎ 9023 0213; 16-19 Shaftesbury Sq; mains £8-10; 🕒 5-11.30pm Mon-Sat, 3-10pm Sun) A local institution – it's been around for more than 20 years – Speranza is a big, buzzing Italian restaurant that complements the traditional pizzas and pastas with more sophisticated dishes. They don't take reservations – join the queue for a pager, then head upstairs for a drink and they'll buzz you when your table's ready.

Cayenne (☎ 9033 1532; 7 Ascot House, Shaftesbury Sq; mains £9.50-14.50; 🕒 noon-2.15pm Mon-Fri, 6-10.15pm Mon-Thu, 6-11.15pm Fri & Sat) Behind an anonymous frosted-glass façade lurks an award-winning restaurant clad in conceptual art, and serving quality Irish produce prepared with an Asian or Mediterranean twist. Cayenne is owned and operated by TV celebrity chef, Paul Rankin.

Water Margin (☎ 9032 6888; 159-161 Donegall Pass; mains £8.50-12.50; 🕒 noon-11pm) You can worship at the altar of Cantonese cuisine in this stylishly converted church, a five-minute walk west of Shaftesbury Square. Expect authentic Chinese food and friendly, professional service.

Golden Mile South

Moghul (☎ 9032 6677; 62a Botanic Ave; mains £6-8; 🕒 noon-2pm & 5-11pm Mon-Thu, 5pm-midnight Fri & Sat, 5-11pm Sun) The Moghul is a traditional Indian restaurant aiming at the student market, with good-value specials like the weekday lunch *thali* (£3 for two curries, rice and naan bread) and Friday's all-you-can-eat buffet (£5.50).

Metro Brasserie (☎ 9032 3349; 13 Lower Cres; mains £13-17; 🕒 noon-3pm & 6-9.30pm Mon-Sat, 6-10pm Fri & Sat) The Metro (in the Crescent Town House) is a bright and lively wine bar and brasserie with low ceilings, wood floors and wrought-iron railings, with a menu offering French and Asian flavours. The 'early bird' menu, served 6pm to 7pm, offers a two-/three-course dinner for £11.50/13.95.

Maggie May's (☎ 9032 2662; 50 Botanic Ave; mains £3-5; 🕒 8am-10.30pm Mon-Sat, 10am-10.30pm Sun) Maggie May's is a homely little café with wooden booths and colourful murals of old Belfast. The huge Ulster fry (£3.95) makes it breakfast nirvana for local students.

Other Place (☎ 9020 7200; 79 Botanic Ave; mains £6-7; 🕒 8am-11pm). This is another student favourite where you can linger over the Sunday papers amid red brick, orange pine and antique *objets*, or damp down a rising hangover with big plates of lasagne, cajun pitta or home-made hamburger.

University

La Salsa (☎ 9024 4588; 23 University Rd; mains £9-12; 🕒 5-11pm Mon-Sat, 5-10pm Sun) This is the original branch of the best Mexican in town.

Beatrice Kennedy's (☎ 9020 2290; 44 University Rd; mains £11-14; 🕒 5-10.30pm Tue-Sat, 12.30-2.30pm & 5-8.30pm Sun) This is where Queen's students take their parents for a posh dinner – an old-world décor of bare floorboards, crisp white linen and bent-wood chairs, and a simple menu of superb home cooking, including home-made bread and ice cream. From 5pm to 7pm you can get a two-course dinner for £10.

Bookfinders Cafe (☎ 9032 8269; 47 University Rd; mains £4; 🕒 10am-5.30pm Mon-Sat) Tucked away at the back of the bookshop, this is the sort of smoky, bohemian café where you would expect to find poetry readings...and, during the Belfast Festival, you do. It's famed for its excellent soup of the day and a range of vegetarian dishes.

Conor Café-Bar (☎ 9066 3266; 11a Stranmillis Rd; dinner mains £6.50-12.50; ⏲ 9.30am-11pm, dinner from 5pm) Set in the airy, glass-roofed former studio of William Conor, a Belfast artist, this is a relaxing place for a drink or a meal after a visit to the Botanic Gardens or Ulster Museum. The menu is 'poshed-up pub grub' such as fish and chips with mushy peas, or sausage and mash.

Café Zinc (☎ 9068 2266; 12 Stranmillis Rd; mains £4-9; ⏲ food served 10am-2.30pm Mon-Sat, 5-9pm Mon-Wed, 5-10pm Thu & Fri, brunch 10am-7pm Sun) Brushed steel, blonde wood and sharp styling complement Café Zinc's good-value bistro menu offering everything from bar snacks and sandwiches to steaks and hearty vegie dishes.

West Belfast

An Caife Glas (☎ 9023 9303; Cultúrlann MacAdam ÓFiaich, 216 Falls Rd; snacks £1.50-4; ⏲ 9am-5pm) If you're exploring West Belfast, drop in to the café in the Irish language and arts centre (see p549) for some good home-cooked food – the menu includes stews, soups, pizzas, cakes, scones and fresh pastries.

An Cúpla Focal (☎ 9023 2608; 145-147 Falls Rd; mains £6-10; ⏲ 10am-9.45pm Mon-Thu, 10am-10.45pm Fri-Sun) A community venture that employs people who speak or are learning the Irish language – the name means 'a few words of Irish' – An Cúpla Focal offers good food and good craic, with cosy open fires in winter.

Lagan Towpath

Cutters Wharf (☎ 9080 5100; Lockview Rd, Stranmillis; mains £6-11; ⏲ food served noon-9pm) One of the few bar-restaurants in Belfast with a waterside setting, Cutters Wharf has a terrace overlooking the River Lagan where you can enjoy excellent bar meals – sausage and champ with onion gravy, roast vegetable fettucini – while watching sculls and eights from the nearby rowing club messing about on the river. The colourful, California-themed restaurant upstairs also enjoys river views.

DRINKING

Bars are to Belfast what art galleries are to Florence – a distillation of the city's culture and one of the main reasons for visiting. The pub scene is lively and friendly, with the older traditional pubs complemented – and increasingly threatened – by a rising tide of stylish designer bars.

Standard opening hours are 11am or 11.30am to 11pm Monday to Saturday, though pubs with an entertainment licence stay open to 1am or 1.30am, and 12.30pm to 11pm Sunday; some pubs remain closed all day Sunday.

The worst thing about drinking in Belfast is getting past the bouncers on the door – the huge number of security staff employed in the city means that polite, well-trained doormen are a rarity. Some of the flashier bars have a dress code, usually no trainers, no jeans and no baseball caps (so that the security cameras can get a clear shot of your face!). A few even specify 'No political tattoos'.

City Centre

Crown Liquor Saloon (☎ 9024 9476; 46 Great Victoria St) Belfast's most famous bar has a wonderfully ornate Victorian interior. Despite being a tourist attraction, it fills up with crowds of locals at lunch-time and in the early evening.

Robinson's (☎ 9024 7447; 38-40 Great Victoria St) Next door to the Crown, this is a theme pub spread over four floors with music – from traditional music in **Fibber Magee's** to the latest DJs in the **Mezzanine** club – most nights. In the basement is **BT1**, a wine bar aimed at Belfast's young professionals.

Irene & Nan's (☎ 9023 9123; 12 Brunswick St) Named after two pensioners from a nearby pub who fancied themselves as glamour queens, I & N's typifies the new breed of Belfast bar, dripping with designer chic and tempting your taste buds with an in-bar bistro. It's a laid-back place with a 1950s retro theme, good food and good cocktails.

Morning Star (☎ 9023 5986; 17 Pottinger's Entry) One of several traditional pubs hidden away in the pedestrian alleys off High St, the Morning Star dates back to at least 1810 when it was mentioned in the *Belfast News Letter* as a terminal for the Dublin to Belfast stage coach. It has a big sweeping horseshoe bar, and cosy snugs for privacy. The food's not bad as well.

White's Tavern (☎ 9024 3080; 1-4 Wine Cellar Entry) White's claims to be Belfast's oldest tavern (unlike a public house, a tavern provided food and lodging), established in 1630. In those days the River Blackstaff had not been hidden underground and sailing ships would have been moored next to White's – the murals opposite the pub show life here in the 18th century. There's live music most nights, with traditional sessions Monday and Tuesday, and you can get a decent feed here too.

Kelly's Cellars (☎ 9032 4835; 1 Bank St) Kelly's is Belfast's oldest pub (1720), and was a meeting place for Henry Joy McCracken and the United Irishmen when they were planning the 1798 Rising. The story goes that McCracken hid behind the bar when British soldiers came for him. The pub features folk and blues bands on Friday and Saturday nights.

Kitchen Bar (☎ 9023 4901; 16 Victoria Sq) Formerly a lodging house for respectable young ladies, the Kitchen is a great spot for real ales, home-cooked food and traditional music sessions. In the days of the Empire Theatre next door a large number of the artists used to drink here and would leave behind one of their publicity photographs. There's a mass of them on the wall – somewhere there's meant to be one of Charlie Chaplin.

McHugh's Bar & Restaurant (☎ 9050 9999; 29-31 Queen's Sq) Built in the 1700s and restored at a cost of £2 million in 1998, this is the oldest surviving building in Belfast. McHugh's is now a very popular bar-restaurant with live music (mostly rock and cover bands) on Friday and Saturday nights and traditional music on Wednesday.

Bittle's Bar (☎ 9031 1088; 103 Victoria St) Bittle's occupies Belfast's only 'flat iron' building, a 19th-century triangular red-brick building decorated with gilded shamrocks. The wedge-shaped interior is covered in paintings of Ireland's literary heroes by local artist Joe O'Kane. Pride of place on the back wall is taken by a large canvas depicting Yeats, Joyce, Behan and Beckett at the bar with glasses of Guinness, and Wilde pulling the pints on the other side.

Cathedral Quarter & Around

John Hewitt Bar & Restaurant (☎ 9023 3768; 51 Donegall St) The John Hewitt is one of those treasured bars that have no TV and no gaming machines; the only noise here is the murmur of conversation. The bar has gained a reputation for its music sessions – jazz on Friday, folk several nights a week – and is also a venue during the annual Cathedral Quarter Arts Festival.

Northern Whig (☎ 9050 9888; 2 Bridge St) A stylish new bar set in an elegant Georgian printing works, the Whig's airy interior is dominated by three huge Socialist-Realist statues rescued from Prague in the early 1990s. Its relaxing sofas and armchairs in fashionable chocolate and café-au-lait colours encourage serious afternoon loafing, though the pace hots up considerably after 5pm on Friday and Saturday.

Duke of York (☎ 9024 1062; 11 Commercial Ct) Hidden away down an alleyway in the heart of the city's former newspaper district, the snug, traditional Duke was a hang-out for print workers and journalists and still pulls in a few hacks. One claim to fame is that the Sinn Féin leader, Gerry Adams, worked behind the bar here during his student days.

Rotterdam (☎ 9074 6021; 54 Pilot St) Those three little words that mean so much – cramped, smoky and dark. The Rotterdam is a purist's pub, unrepentantly old-fashioned, wonderfully atmospheric, and famed for the quality of its live music sessions. Jazz, folk, rock or blues plays most nights, and in summer the tables – and the gigs – spill outdoors.

Golden Mile & University

Limelight & Katy Daly's (☎ 9032 5942; 17-19 Ormeau Ave) This combined pub and club is a popular venue for live rock bands, and is recommended locally as the best place for a good old-fashioned piss-up in the company of good music.

Lavery's Gin Palace (☎ 9087 1106; 14 Bradbury Pl) Managed by the same family since 1918, Lavery's is a vast, multilevel, packed-to-the-gills boozing emporium, crammed with drinkers young and old, from students to tourists, businessmen to bikers. There's acoustic music in the Back Bar on Wednesday, while the 1st-floor bar has a DJ every night and the top floor hosts the **Heaven** nightclub from 10pm on Saturday (bit of an underage crowd, though).

Empire Music Hall (☎ 9024 9276; 42 Botanic Ave) A converted late-Victorian church with three floors of entertainment, the Empire is a legendary live music venue, preaching jazz on Tuesday, Irish music Wednesday, blues Thursday and live bands – tribute bands are a favourite – Friday and Saturday.

Globe (☎ 9050 9848; 36 University Rd) This popular student pub seems to be the karaoke capital of Belfast, with sing-it-yourself sessions almost every night; the pseudo-1970s décor goes well with the wild retro sessions on Wednesday nights. During the afternoons, sport is the order of the day with football or rugby blaring on half a dozen giant screens.

Eglantine (☎ 9038 1994; 32 Malone Rd) The 'Eg' is a local institution, and widely reckoned to be the best of Belfast's student pubs. It serves good beer and good food, and there are DJs spinning most nights except Tuesday, which is quiz night. Expect to see the odd stag and hen party stagger through at weekends.

Botanic Inn (☎ 9050 9740; 23-27 Malone Rd) The 'Bot' is the second pillar of Malone Rd's unholy trinity of student pubs, along with the 'Eg' and the 'Welly Park' (Wellington Park). The latter has sadly been renovated into airport-departure-lounge anonymity, but the Bot is still a wild place, with dancing in the upstairs Record Club Wednesday to Saturday, live music in the downstairs bar Monday to Wednesday, and big screen sport when there's a match on.

ENTERTAINMENT

The Belfast Welcome Centre issues *Whatabout?*, a free monthly guide to Belfast events. The Thursday issue of the *Belfast Telegraph* has a Nightlife section with club listings, and the Metro section in Friday's *Irish News* covers everything from music to art exhibitions and special events. *art.ie* is another free monthly that covers the arts scene throughout the whole of Northern Ireland.

The *Big List* (www.thebiglist.co.uk) is a weekly freesheet, published on Wednesday, that covers pubs, clubs and music events in Northern Ireland, although the emphasis is heavily on Belfast. The *Belfast Beat* is a free monthly guide listing what's on where each day of the week. The website www.wheretotonight.com is another useful guide to events and venues.

Cinemas

Queen's Film Theatre (☎ 0800 328 2811; www.qftbelfast.info; 20 University Sq) The QFT is a two-screen art-house cinema close to the university, and a major venue for the Belfast Film Festival.

UGC Cinemas (☎ 0870 155 5176; www.ugccinemas.co.uk; 14 Dublin Rd) The UGC is a convenient city-centre 10-screen multiplex.

Warner Village Cinemas (☎ 0870 240 6020; www.warnervillage.co.uk; Odyssey Pavilion) Belfast's biggest multiplex, with 12 screens and stadium seats throughout, is part of the Odyssey Complex.

Gay & Lesbian Venues

Belfast's compact but tentatively expanding gay scene is concentrated in the Cathedral Quarter.

Kremlin (☎ 9080 9700; www.kremlin-belfast.com; 96 Donegall St; admission £4-9; 🕒 4pm-1am Mon, 4pm-3am Tue-Thu, noon-4am Fri & Sat, noon-3am Sun) Gay-owned and operated, the Soviet-kitsch-themed Kremlin is the heart and soul of Northern Ireland's gay scene. A statue of Lenin guides you into Tsar, the pre-club bar, from where the Long Bar leads into the main clubbing zone, Red Square. There's something going on seven nights a week, but Revolution@Red Square on Saturday is the flagship club night.

Milk (☎ 9027 8876; www.clubmilk.com; Tomb St) Monday's Forbidden Fruit hardcore club night at Milk presents an extravaganza of drag and cabaret acts hosted by the Kremlin's outrageous Baroness Titti von Tramp.

Gay-friendly pubs include the **Custom House** (☎ 9032 5491; 22-28 Skipper St) and the **John Hewitt** (☎ 9023 3768; 51 Donegall St).

Live Music

Waterfront Hall (☎ 9033 4400; www.waterfront.co.uk; Lanyon Pl) The impressive 2235-seat Waterfront is Belfast's flagship concert venue, hosting local, national and international performers from pop stars to symphony orchestras.

Odyssey Arena (☎ 9073 9074; www.odysseyarena.com; 2 Queen's Quay) The home stadium for the Belfast Giants ice hockey team is also the venue for big entertainment events like rock and pop concerts, stage shows and indoor sports.

Ulster Hall (☎ 9032 9685; www.ulsterhall.co.uk; Bedford St) The 1862 Ulster Hall is a popular venue for a range of events including rock concerts, lunch-time organ recitals, boxing bouts and performances by the excellent Ulster Orchestra.

Crescent Arts Centre (☎ 9024 2338; www.crescentarts.org; 2-4 University Rd) The Crescent hosts some excellent concerts, from New York jazz to top-rate Irish music, and there's a regular Saturday night club (9pm to late, BYO drinks) offering a wide range of music. The Crescent also stages a 10-day literary festival called Between the Lines each March, and a dance festival, City Dance, in June.

Queen's University (☎ 9033 5337; www.music.qub.ac.uk; University Rd) The university's School of Music stages free lunch-time recitals on Thursday and regular evening concerts in the beautiful, hammer beam–roofed **Harty Room** (School of Music, University Sq), and occasional performances in the larger **Sir William Whitla Hall** (University Rd).

King's Hall (☎ 9066 5225; www.kingshall.co.uk; Lisburn Rd) Northern Ireland's biggest exhibition and conference centre hosts a range of music shows, trade fairs and sporting events. It's accessible by any bus along Lisburn Rd or by train to Balmoral Station.

Nightclubs

Club hours are generally 9pm to 3am, with no admittance after 1am.

Milk (☎ 9027 8876; www.clubmilk.com; Tomb St; admission £3-10; 🕑 daily) Set in a converted red-brick warehouse, Milk is one of Belfast's hottest and most sophisticated clubs (dress code: no effort, no entry), where you can dance every night of the week. Monday is gay night, Tuesday is student night (free admission before 11pm), funky house on Friday and club classics on Sunday.

m-club (☎ 9023 3131; Manhattan Bar, 23-25 Bradbury Pl; admission £8; 🕑 Mon & Thu-Sat) Belfast's biggest club, m-club offers a wild student night on Thursday (admission £4) and pulls in a slightly older crowd with Friday's '70s Disco Sensation and Saturday's commercial dance. Monday is 'rehab night' with £2 admission and drinks promos.

Thompson's (☎ 9032 3762; www.clubthompsons.com; 3 Patterson's Pl, Arthur St; admission £3-5; 🕑 Tue-Sun) The best night at Thompson's is Friday's Groovilicious, with DJs laying down everything from funky techno to breakbeat to classic acid house, while Faith on Sundays plays club classics late into the night for those who don't want the weekend to end.

Shine (☎ 0870 241 0126; www.shine.net; Mandela Hall, Queen's Students Union, University Rd; admission £10-12; 🕑 Sat) In Shine, the students union can boast one of the city's best club nights – many visiting clubbers have recommended it – with resident and guest DJs pumping out harder, heavier dance music than most of Belfast's other clubs. Student or photo ID required.

Sport

Rugby, soccer, Gaelic football and hockey are played through the winter, cricket and hurling through the summer. International rugby and soccer matches take place at **Windsor Park** (☎ 9024 4198; off Lisburn Rd), south of the centre; bus Nos 58 and 59 go that way. You can see Gaelic football and hurling at **Roger Casement Park** (☎ 9070 5868; Andersonstown Rd) in West Belfast. Take bus No 14, 15 or 90.

The Belfast Giants ice hockey team draws big crowds at the **Odyssey Arena** (☎ 9073 9074; www.odysseyarena.com; 2 Queen's Quay) at the Odyssey Complex. The season is September to March.

The **Sports Council** (☎ 9038 1222; www.sportni.net) provides information on a range of sporting events.

Theatre

Grand Opera House (☎ 9024 1919; www.goh.co.uk; 2-4 Great Victoria St; 🕑 box office 8.30am-6pm Mon-Sat, 8.30am-9pm Thu) This grand old venue plays host to a mixture of opera, popular musicals, and comedy shows. The box office is across the street on the corner of Howard St.

Lyric Theatre (☎ 9038 1081; www.lyrictheatre.co.uk; 55 Ridgeway St; 🕑 box office 10am-7pm Mon-Sat) Located on the riverside south of the Botanic Gardens, the Lyric stages serious drama and is a major venue for the Belfast Festival at Queen's (see p554). Hollywood star Liam Neeson first trod the boards here.

Group Theatre (☎ 9032 9685; Bedford St; 🕑 box office noon-3pm Mon-Fri) This theatre, located above the foyer in the Ulster Hall (p561), stages work by local companies from September to June.

Old Museum Arts Centre (☎ 9023 3332; 7 College Sq North; 🕑 box office 9.30am-5.30pm Mon-Sat, 9.30am-7pm before a performance) The Old Museum stages an exciting programme of drama and comedy, with occasional prose and poetry readings and dance performances.

SHOPPING

For general shopping you'll find all the usual high street chains and department stores in the compact central shopping area north of City Hall. Items particular to Northern Ireland that you may like to look out for include fine Belleek china, linen (antique and new) and Tyrone crystal.

Wicker Man (☎ 9024 3550; 14 Donegall Arcade; 🕑 9am-5.30pm Mon-Sat, 9am-9pm Thu, 1-5pm Sun) This shop sells a wide range of contemporary Irish crafts and gifts, including silver jewellery, glassware and knitwear.

Craftworks (☎ 9024 4465; 40 Bedford St; 🕑 9.30am-5.30pm Mon-Sat, 9.30am-8.30pm Thu) Craftworks specialises in top-quality crafts from all over Ulster. You'll find beautifully made designer knitwear, linen shirts, leather-wear, ceramics, *bodhráns* (traditional goatskin drums), textiles and jewellery.

Workshops Collective (☎ 9020 0707; 1a Lawrence St; 🕑 10am-5.30pm Mon-Fri, 11am-4pm Sat) You can buy paintings, sculpture, furniture and crafts direct from the artist at this collection of arts and crafts studios housed in an old mews courtyard near the university.

Other good places to shop for Irish crafts and traditional Irish music include **Cultúrlann MacAdam ÓFiaich** (☎ 9023 9303; 216 Falls Rd; 🕑 9am-5.30pm Mon-Fri, 10am-5.30pm Sat) and **Conway Mill** (☎ 9024 7276; 5-7 Conway St; admission free; 🕑 10am-4pm Mon-Fri).

Fresh Garbage (☎ 9024 2350; 24 Rosemary St; 🕑 10.30am-5.30pm Mon-Sat, 10.30am-8pm Thu) Easily recognised by the glumfest of goths hovering outside the door, this place has been around for 20 years but remains a cult favourite for hippie and goth clothes and Celtic jewellery.

Oakland Antiques (☎ 9023 0176; 135 Donegall Pass; 🕑 10am-5.30pm Mon-Sat) Donegall Pass, east of Shaftesbury Square, has half a dozen antiques shops. Oakland is the biggest, with a huge collection of Georgian, Victorian and Edwardian furniture, silver, porcelain and clocks.

Archive's Antique Centre (☎ 9023 2383; 88 Donegall Pass; 🕑 10.30am-5.30pm Mon-Fri, 10am-6pm Sat) This is a warren of curios and collectables spread over three floors, with Irish silver, brass, pub memorabilia, militaria, books and light fittings.

Tiso (☎ 9023 1230; 12-14 Cornmarket; 🕑 9.30am-5.30pm Mon, Tue, Fri & Sat, 10am-5.30pm Wed, 9am-8pm Thu) Make tracks to Tiso for hiking, climbing and camping equipment and outdoor clothing.

Surf Mountain (☎ 9024 8877; 12 Brunswick St; 🕑 9am-5.30pm Mon-Sat) Yo dude – come and join the goatee-stroking, nad-scratching crew checking out Surf Mountain's skate and snowboard gear.

GETTING THERE & AWAY

Air

There are direct flights from London, Birmingham, Bristol, Dublin, Edinburgh, Glasgow, Leeds/Bradford, Manchester and Southampton to the convenient **Belfast city airport** (☎ 9093 9093; www.belfastcityairport.com; Airport Rd). Most flights from the Republic, Britain, Amsterdam, Brussels and New York land at **Belfast international airport** (☎ 9448 4848; www.bial.co.uk; Aldergrove), 30km northwest of the city. For details of flights and fares, see p671.

Airline offices in Belfast:

Aer Lingus (☎ 0845 973 7747; 46-48 Castle St)
British Airways (☎ 0845 722 2111; 1 Fountain Centre, College St)

Boat

The giant catamaran car ferries operated by **Steam Packet/SeaCat** (☎ 0870 552 3523; www.seacat.co.uk) and serving the Isle of Man, Troon (Scotland), Heysham and Liverpool (England) dock at Donegall Quay, a short distance from the city centre. Car ferries to and from Scotland dock at Larne, 30km north of Belfast (see p628).

Norse Merchant Ferries (☎ 0870 600 4321; www.norsemerchant.com) between Belfast and Liverpool dock at the Victoria terminal, 5km northeast of town. Take the M2 motorway north and turn right at junction No 1.

For more information on ferry routes and prices, see p674.

Bus

Belfast has two bus stations. The main Europa Bus Centre is behind the Europa Hotel and next door to Great Victoria St Station, accessed via the Great Northern Mall beside the hotel. It's the main terminus for buses to Derry, Dublin and destinations in the west and south of Northern Ireland. The smaller **Laganside Bus Centre** (Oxford St), near the river, is mainly for buses to County Antrim, eastern Down and the Cookstown area.

There are **information desks** (🕑 7.45am-6.30pm Mon-Fri, 8am-6pm Sat) at both bus stations, where you can pick up regional bus timetables, and you can contact **Translink** (☎ 9066 6630; www.translink.co.uk) for timetable and fares information. Students are eligible for 15% reductions on Ulsterbus fares of more than £1.15 on production of their ISIC card.

Typical one-way fares from Belfast:

Service	Fare	Duration (hours)	Frequency
Armagh	£5.90	1¼	hourly Mon-Fri, six daily Sat, one Sun
Ballycastle	£6.50	2¾	four daily Mon-Fri, two Sat
Bangor	£2.60	¾	half-hourly Mon-Sat, eight daily Sun
Derry	£9.00	1¾	hourly Mon-Sat, six daily Sun
Dublin	£13	3	seven daily Mon-Sat, six Sun
Downpatrick	£4.10	1	at least hourly Mon-Sat, five daily Sun
Enniskillen	£8.20	1	eight daily Mon-Sat, two Sun
Newcastle	£5.30	1¼	13 daily Mon-Fri, nine Sat, six Sun

Eurolines (☎ 9033 7002) runs a daily coach service between Belfast and London (single/return £46/62; 14½ hours) via the Stranraer ferry, Dumfries, Carlisle, Preston, Manchester and Birmingham. The ticket office is in the Europa Bus Centre.

For information on bus fares, durations and frequencies in Ireland, see p677.

Train

Trains to Dublin and all destinations in Northern Ireland depart from Belfast's **Central Station** (East Bridge St), east of the city centre. Trains for Portadown, Lisburn, Bangor, Larne Harbour and Derry depart from **Great Victoria St Station** (Great Northern Mall), next to the Europa Bus Centre.

For information on fares and timetables, contact **Translink** (☎ 9066 6630; www.translink.co.uk). The **NIR Travel Shop** (☎ 9023 0671; Great Victoria St Station; 🕑 9am-5pm Mon-Fri, 9am-12.30pm Sat) books ferries, Dublin Rail Breaks and Scotland Rail Breaks (for Glasgow and Edinburgh).

Typical train fares from Belfast include:

Service	Fare	Duration (hours)	Frequency
Bangor	£3.10	½	half-hourly
Derry	£8.20	2¼	eight daily
Dublin	£22	2	eight daily
Larne Harbour	£3.90	1	hourly
Newry	£6.30	¾	seven daily
Portrush	£6.80	1¾	eight daily

On Sunday you can buy a Sunday Day Tracker ticket (£4), which allows unlimited travel on all scheduled train services within Northern Ireland.

For more information on the train network in Ireland, see p679.

GETTING AROUND

Belfast has that rare thing – an integrated public transport system, with buses linking both airports to the central train and bus stations and to the ferries.

To/From the Airports

Belfast international airport is 30km northwest of the city. The AirBus (No 300) service connects it with the Europa Bus Centre (single/return £6/9, 30 minutes, every 30 minutes) between 6am and 10.30pm. A taxi costs about £25.

The more convenient Belfast city airport is only 6km northeast of the centre. There's a shuttle bus from the terminal to nearby Sydenham Halt train station, where you can catch a train to Central Station (£1.10, 10 minutes, every 30 minutes), Botanic Station in the popular university area, or Great Victoria St (15 minutes). The AirLink Bus (No 600) links the terminal with the Europa Bus Centre (single/return £2.50/5, 20 minutes, every 40 minutes) between 6.30am and 10pm. The taxi fare to the city centre is about £7.

For details of the Airporter bus linking both airports to Derry, see p611.

Bicycle

National Cycle Network route No 9 runs through central Belfast, mostly following the western bank of the River Lagan. The Belfast Welcome Centre provides a free leaflet called *Belfast by Bike*.

McConvey Cycles (☎ 9033 0322; 183 Ormeau Rd; 🕑 9am-6pm Mon-Sat, closes 8pm Thu) rents out bicycles for £10/40 per day/week, or £20 from any time Friday to Monday morning.

To/From the Ferry Terminals

You can walk from Donegall Quay to City Hall in about 15 minutes. Alternatively, Laganside Bus Centre is only a five-minute walk away, where you can catch the Centrelink bus (No 100) to Central Station, the Europa Bus Centre and Donegall Square.

BELFAST

Trains for Larne Harbour depart from Great Victoria St Station (see p629).

Bus

Citybus (☎ 9066 6630; www.translink.co.uk) operates the bus network in Belfast. An increasing number of buses (including the Centrelink service) are low-floor, 'kneeling' buses with space for one wheelchair.

Buy your ticket from the driver (change given); fares range from £0.70 to £1.40 depending on distance. The driver can also sell you a One Day Travelcard (£3.20), giving unlimited bus travel within the City Zone from 9.30am Monday to Friday or all day on Saturday and Sunday.

Most city bus services depart from various stops on and around Donegall Square, at City Hall. You can pick up a free bus map from the **Citybus kiosk** (🕑 8am-5.30pm Mon-Fri) at the northwest corner of the square. It also sells Smartlink Travel Cards giving unlimited bus travel (within the city) for one week/one month for £12/45.

The Centrelink bus (No 100) is a circular service linking Donegall Square with the Europa and Laganside bus stations, and Central and Great Victoria St Stations. Holders of a valid rail or bus ticket can use the service free of charge; otherwise the flat fare is £0.70.

Car & Motorcycle

A car can be more of a hindrance than a help in Belfast, as parking is restricted in the city centre. For on-street parking between 8am and 6pm Monday to Saturday you'll need to buy a ticket from a machine; the cost is £0.25 per 15 minutes and there's a maximum stay of one hour. For longer periods, head for one of the many multistorey car parks that are dotted around the city centre.

Car rental agencies in Belfast:

Avis City (☎ 9024 0404; www.avisworld.com; 69-71 Great Victoria St); Belfast city airport (☎ 9045 2017); Belfast international airport (☎ 9442 2333)

Budget City (☎ 9023 0700; www.budget-ireland.co.uk; 96-102 Great Victoria St); Belfast city airport (☎ 9045 1111)

Europcar City (☎ 9031 3500; www.europcar.com; 159-161 University St); Belfast city airport (☎ 9045 0904); Belfast international airport (☎ 9442 3444)

Hertz Belfast city airport (☎ 9073 2451; www.hertz.co.uk); Belfast international airport (☎ 9442 2533)

There are a couple of local car hire companies, but their rates are not significantly better than Avis or Europcar.

Taxi

For information on the black cabs that ply the Falls and Shankill Rds, see People's Taxis, p547. Regular black taxis have yellow plates back and front (£2.50 minimum fare) and can be hailed on the street.

Minicabs are cheaper but you have to order one by phone. Companies to call include **Fona Cabs** (☎ 9023 3333), **Value Cabs** (☎ 9080 9080) and **Sure Cabs** (☎ 9076 6666).

Train

There are local trains every 20 or 30 minutes connecting Great Victoria St and Central Stations via City Hospital and Botanic Stations. There's a flat fare of £0.90 for journeys between any of these stops.

AROUND BELFAST

LISBURN & AROUND

The southwestern fringes of Belfast extend as far as the town of Lisburn (Lios na gCearrbhach), 12km southwest of the city centre. Similar to Belfast, Lisburn grew rich on the proceedsx of the linen industry in the 18th and 19th centuries. This history is celebrated in the excellent **Irish Linen Centre & Lisburn Museum** (☎ 9266 3377; Market Sq; admission free; 🕑 9.30am-5pm Mon-Sat), which is housed in the fine 17th-century Market House.

The museum on the ground floor has displays on the cultural and historic heritage of the region, while upstairs the award-winning 'Flax to Fabric' exhibition details the fascinating history of the linen industry in Northern Ireland – on the eve of WWI Ulster was the largest linen-producing region in the world, employing some 75,000 people.

There are plenty of audiovisual and hands-on exhibits – you can watch weavers working on Jacquard looms and even try your hand at spinning flax.

Lisburn Tourist Information Centre (☎ 9266 0038; Lisburn Sq; 🕑 9.30am-5pm Mon-Sat) is on the town's newly renovated main square.

Bus Nos 24, 523 and 532 run from Belfast's Europa Bus Centre to Lisburn (£2, 40 minutes, hourly). A slightly quicker option is to catch the train (£2.20, 30 minutes) from either Belfast Central or Great Victoria St Stations.

ULSTER FOLK & TRANSPORT MUSEUMS

Two of Northern Ireland's finest **museums** (☎ 9042 8428; www.magni.org.uk; Cultra, Holywood; each museum adult/child £4.50/2.50, combined ticket for both museums £6/3; 🕑 10am-6pm Mon-Sat, 11am-6pm Sun Jul-Sep, 10am-5pm Mon-Fri, 10am-6pm Sat, 11am-6pm Sun Mar-Jun, 10am-4pm Mon-Fri, 10am-5pm Sat, 11am-5pm Sun Oct-Feb) are located near each other on either side of the A2 road north-east of Belfast.

On the southern side of the road is the **Folk Museum**, where farmhouses, forges, churches and mills – even a complete village – have been carefully reconstructed, with plenty of human and animal extras combining to give a strong impression of Irish life over the past few hundred years. From industrial times, there are red-brick terraces from 19th-century Belfast and Dromore. During the summer, activities such as thatching and ploughing are demonstrated and you'll find characters dressed in period costume practising all kinds of crafts.

On the opposite side of the road is the **Transport Museum**, a sort of automotive zoo, with displays of steam locomotives, rolling stock, motorcycles, trams, buses, cars and bicycles. The flight section includes one of

AROUND BELFAST

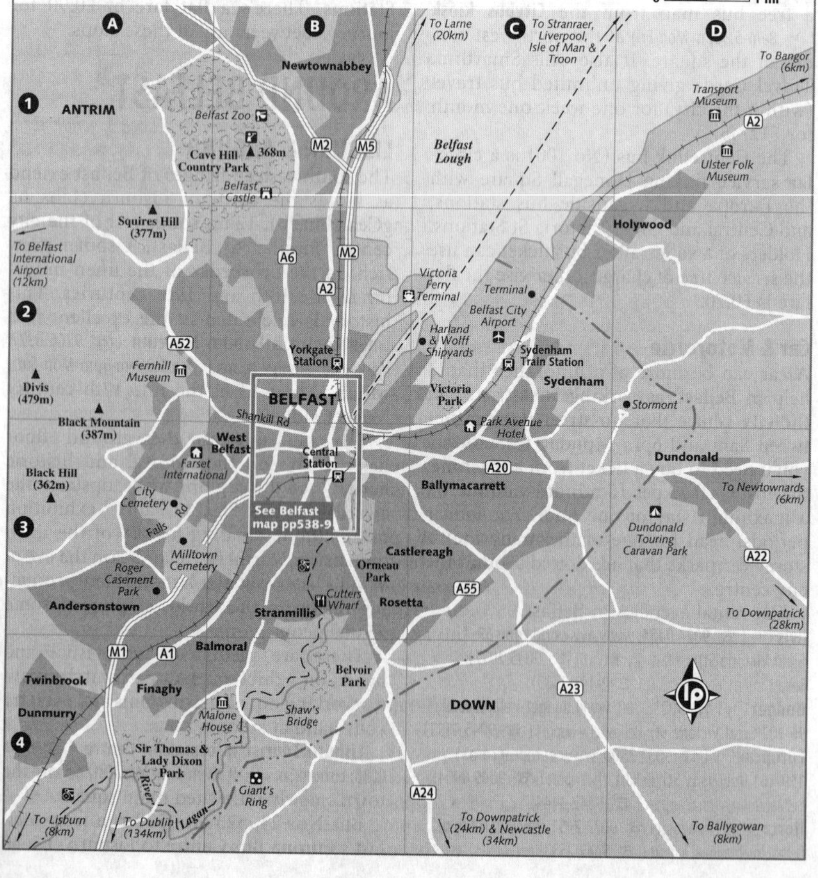

the world's first VTOL (vertical take-off and landing) aircraft made by the Belfast firm Shorts. The most popular gallery is the SS *Titanic* display, with photographs of the ship's construction and reports of its sinking.

Included in the automobile collection is the stainless-steel prototype of the famous but ill-fated DeLorean DMC, produced in Belfast in 1981, which achieved lasting fame as a time machine in the film *Back to the Future*.

The museums are 11km northeast of Belfast, off the A2 near Holywood. Buses to Bangor stop nearby. Cultra Station on the Bangor line is within a 10-minute walk. There are car parks at the rural, town and transport sections, but after that there's a lot of walking. You'll need at least half a day to do it justice.

Counties Down & Armagh

CONTENTS

County Down promotes itself as Northern Ireland's sun-kissed Riviera, boasting the lowest rainfall and the highest sunshine hours in the North. OK, so it's not the Mediterranean, but on a sunny summer weekend the traditional seaside resorts of Bangor and Newcastle pull in thousands of day trippers from nearby Belfast, and the sandy beaches of the Ards Peninsula become a bucket-and-spade paradise.

If you'd rather get away from it all, choose midweek in the spring or autumn and head for the picturesque harbour towns of Portaferry and Strangford, facing each other across the turbulent but scenic strait known as the Narrows. You'll find a handful of excellent hotels and restaurants, peaceful coastal walks and a lively pub culture.

The gentle landscapes around Strangford Lough are ideal for exploring by car or bike, or even on foot (the Ulster Way follows the lough's western shore), and offer plenty of historical interest in the form of Mount Stewart's stately home and gardens, Nendrum's ancient monastery, and the sites around Downpatrick associated with Ireland's patron saint.

Further south, but still only 1½ hours by bus from Belfast, the granite and heather peaks of the Mourne Mountains offer the best hill walking and the finest mountain scenery in the North.

Down's neighbour County Armagh is largely rural, from the low, rugged hills of the south, to the lush orchards and strawberry fields of the north. Its main attractions are the trim cathedral city of Armagh, seat of Ireland's most powerful clergy, and nearby Navan Fort, site of the ancient capital of Ulster.

HIGHLIGHTS

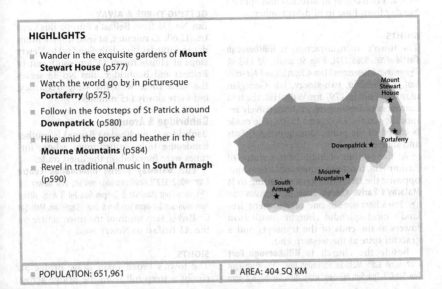

- Wander in the exquisite gardens of **Mount Stewart House** (p577)
- Watch the world go by in picturesque **Portaferry** (p575)
- Follow in the footsteps of St Patrick around **Downpatrick** (p580)
- Hike amid the gorse and heather in the **Mourne Mountains** (p584)
- Revel in traditional music in **South Armagh** (p590)

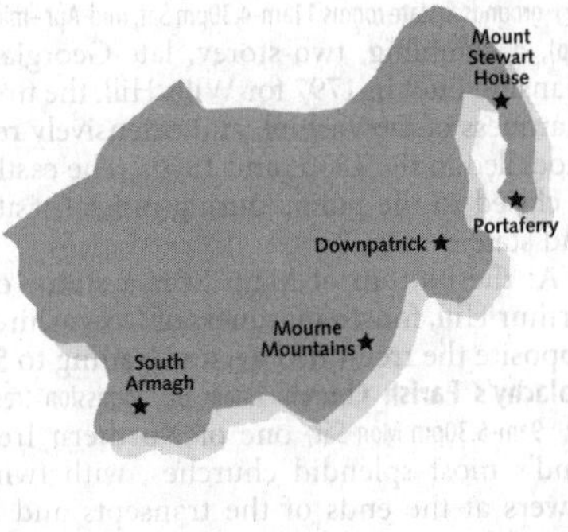

- POPULATION: 651,961
- AREA: 404 SQ KM

COUNTY DOWN

CENTRAL COUNTY DOWN

South of Belfast is pastoral countryside, with only the rough moorland of Slieve Croob, southwest of Ballynahinch, breaking the flatness of the terrain. The attractive towns of Hillsborough and Banbridge lie on the main A1 road from Belfast to Newry.

Hillsborough

pop 2400

Hillsborough is a name familiar to British ears as the official residence of the Secretary of State for Northern Ireland – it is used to entertain visiting heads of state (US president George W Bush and former president Bill Clinton have both enjoyed its hospitality) and it's also the Queen's official residence when she is in Northern Ireland.

The elegant little town of Hillsborough (Cromghlinn) was founded in the 1640s by Colonel Arthur Hill, who built a fort here to quell Irish insurgents. Fine Georgian architecture rings the square and lines Main St.

The **Hillsborough Tourist Information Centre** (☎ 9268 9717; hillsborough@nitic.net; The Square; ⏲ 9am-5.30pm Mon-Sat year-round, 2-6pm Sun Jul & Aug) is in the Georgian courthouse in the centre of the village. Walking tours (£2.50) leave here at 11am and 2pm Saturday and 3pm on Sunday from June to mid-September.

SIGHTS

The town's main attraction is **Hillsborough Castle** (☎ 9268 2244; Main St; adult/child £5/3.50; ⏲ grounds & state rooms 11am-4.30pm Sat, mid-Apr–mid-Sep), a rambling, two-storey, late-Georgian mansion built in 1797 for Wills Hill, the first marquess of Downshire, and extensively remodelled in the 1830s and 1840s. The castle is closed to the public during official visits and state events.

At the bottom of Main St is a statue of Arthur Hill, fourth marquess of Downshire, opposite the tree-lined avenue leading to **St Malachy's Parish Church** (Main St; admission free; ⏲ 9am-5.30pm Mon-Sat) one of Northern Ireland's most splendid churches, with twin towers at the ends of the transepts and a graceful spire at the western end.

Beside the church is **Hillsborough Fort** (☎ 9268 3285; Main St; admission free; ⏲ 10am-7pm Tue-Sat & 2-7pm Sun Apr-Sep, 10am-4pm Tue-Sat & 2-4pm Sun Oct-Mar). It was built as an artillery fort by Colonel Hill in 1650 and remodelled as a Gothic-style tower house in 1758.

SLEEPING & EATING

Fortwilliam Country House (☎ 9268 2255; www.fortwilliamcountryhouse.com; 210 Ballynahinch Rd; s/d £35/55; Ⓟ ⊠) If Hillsborough Castle puts you in the mood for a spot of country elegance, the Fortwilliam offers B&B in four luxurious rooms. Set on a stud farm just south of Hillsborough, this 300-year-old house is stuffed with antiques and period furniture, with the smell of home-baked cakes wafting from the Aga.

Plough Inn (☎ 9268 2985; 3 The Square; mains £5-10; ⏲ bar lunches noon-2.30pm, bistro noon-2.30pm Tue-Sat & 5-8pm Tue-Sun, restaurant 6-9.30pm Mon-Sat) This pub has been offering 'beer and banter' since 1758 and serves seafood, steaks and organic produce. Oysters are a speciality and the menu is truly global, with Indian, Scandinavian, Turkish, Chinese and Italian dishes.

Hillside Bar & Restaurant (☎ 9268 2765; 21 Main St; mains £5-9, 3-course dinner £22; ⏲ bar meals noon-2.30pm & 5-9pm, restaurant 7-9.30pm Tue-Sat) The Hillside is a homely real ale pub with a beer garden, serving excellent bar meals and offering more formal dining in the upstairs restaurant, with its crisp white table linen and sparkling crystal.

GETTING THERE & AWAY

Bus No 238 from Belfast's Europa Bus Centre (£2.60, 25 minutes, at least hourly Monday to Saturday, five daily Sunday) to Newry stops at Hillsborough (15km southwest of Belfast) and Banbridge. Bus No 38 serves the same route with the same frequency, but more slowly (45 minutes).

Banbridge & Around

Banbridge (Droíchead na Banna) is another handsome 18th-century town, whose fortunes were founded on the linen trade.

The **Gateway Tourist Information Centre** (☎ 4062 3322; tic@banbridge.gov.uk; 200 Newry Rd; ⏲ 9am-7pm Mon-Sat & 2-6pm Sun Jul & Aug, 10am-5pm Mon-Sat & 2-6pm Sun Jun & Sep, 10am-5pm Mon-Sat Oct-May) is 3km south of the town centre on the A1 Belfast to Newry road.

SIGHTS

The town's broad main drag, Bridge St, climbs a steep hill from the bridge across the River Bann (from which the town takes its name) to the unusual **Downshire Bridge** at the top of the hill. A cutting was made in the middle of the street in the 19th century to lower the crest of the hill and make the climb easier for the Royal Mail coaches, which had threatened to boycott the town because of the difficulty of scaling the incline.

On the opposite side of the river stands the **Crozier Monument**, adorned with four idiosyncratically sculpted polar bears. A native of Banbridge, Captain Francis Crozier (1796–1848) was commander of HMS *Terror* and froze to death in the Arctic during Sir John Franklin's ill-fated expedition in search of the elusive Northwest Passage. Crozier lived in the fine blue and grey Georgian house across the road from the statue.

Banbridge is the starting point for the **Brontë Homeland Drive**, a signposted route along the Bann valley to Rathfriland, 12km to the southeast. Patrick Brontë, father of the famous literary sisters, was born here and taught in a local school. The locals like to think that her father's tales of the Mourne Mountains inspired the bleak setting for Emily's classic *Wuthering Heights*. Milking this tenuous connection for all it's worth is **Brontë Homeland Interpretive Centre** (☎ 4063 1152; Ballyroney; adult/child £2/1; 🕑 11am-5pm Tue-Fri & 2-6pm Sat & Sun mid-Mar–Sep) in the former Drumballyroney School and Church, 13km southeast of Banbridge.

SLEEPING & EATING

Downshire Arms Hotel (☎ 4066 2638; www.downshirearmshotel.com; 95 Newry St; s/d £36/60; P) The Downshire Arms is a nicely restored Georgian coaching inn that once served the Belfast to Dublin stagecoach. It has nine elegant en-suite rooms and a good **restaurant** (mains £9-14; 🕑 12.30-2.30pm & 6-9pm) with a menu of modern Irish cuisine, including a couple of tasty veggie options.

Harry's Bar (☎ 4066 2794; 7 Dromore St; mains £7-10; 🕑 food served noon-3pm & 5.30-9pm Mon-Sat & 6-9pm Sun) Harry's is an unmissable local institution, a black and white Victorian pub done up like a law library, with legal tomes and lawyers' wigs scattered about the place. It serves hearty home-cooked bar meals, including house specialities such as roast venison and Louisiana blackened salmon.

GETTING THERE & AWAY

Bus No 238 from Belfast's Europa Bus Centre (£4.40, 50 minutes, at least hourly Monday to Saturday, five daily Sunday) to Newry stops at Hillsborough and Banbridge (15km southwest of Hillsborough). Bus No 38 serves the same route with the same frequency, but more slowly (1¼ hours).

Rowallane Garden

This **garden** (☎ 9751 0131; Crossgar Rd, Saintfield; adult/child £3.10/1.30 Mar-Oct, free Nov-Feb; 🕑 10am-8pm May-Sep, 10am-4pm Oct-Apr, closed 24 Dec–1 Jan) is renowned for its spectacular spring displays of rhododendrons and azaleas, which thrive behind a windbreak of Australian laurels, hollies, pines and beech trees. The walled gardens feature rare primulas, blue Himalayan poppies, plantain lilies, roses, magnolias and delicate autumn crocuses. Rowallane House was inherited in 1903 by Hugh Armitage Moore, a distinguished gardener who spent 25 years developing the 21-hectare garden.

The **Hypericum Tea Room** (🕑 1-5pm Jul & Aug, 12.30-5pm May & Jun, 2-6pm Sat & Sun Apr & Sep) serves hearty lunches, sandwiches, cakes and scones.

Rowallane Garden is 18km south of Belfast, signposted off the A7 Downpatrick road 2km south of Saintfield.

Legananny Dolmen

This is perhaps Ulster's most famous Stone Age monument. It's a strangely elegant tripod dolmen, looking as if the capstone has been dropped delicately on the three slim uprights. Its elevated position on the western slopes of Slieve Croob (532m) gives it an impressive view to the Mourne Mountains.

Legananny is a challenge to find without the aid of a 1:50,000 scale map. Heading south from Ballynahinch along the B7 to Rathfriland, go through the hamlets of Dromara and Finnis, then look out for a minor road on the left (signposted Legananny Dolmen). Continue for a further 3km, through a crossroads, and look for another road on the left (a signpost is there, but very difficult to spot). Continue over the hill for 2km, then turn left again at a farm. There's a parking place 50m along, and the dolmen is 50m uphill on the adjacent farm track.

COUNTIES DOWN & ARMAGH

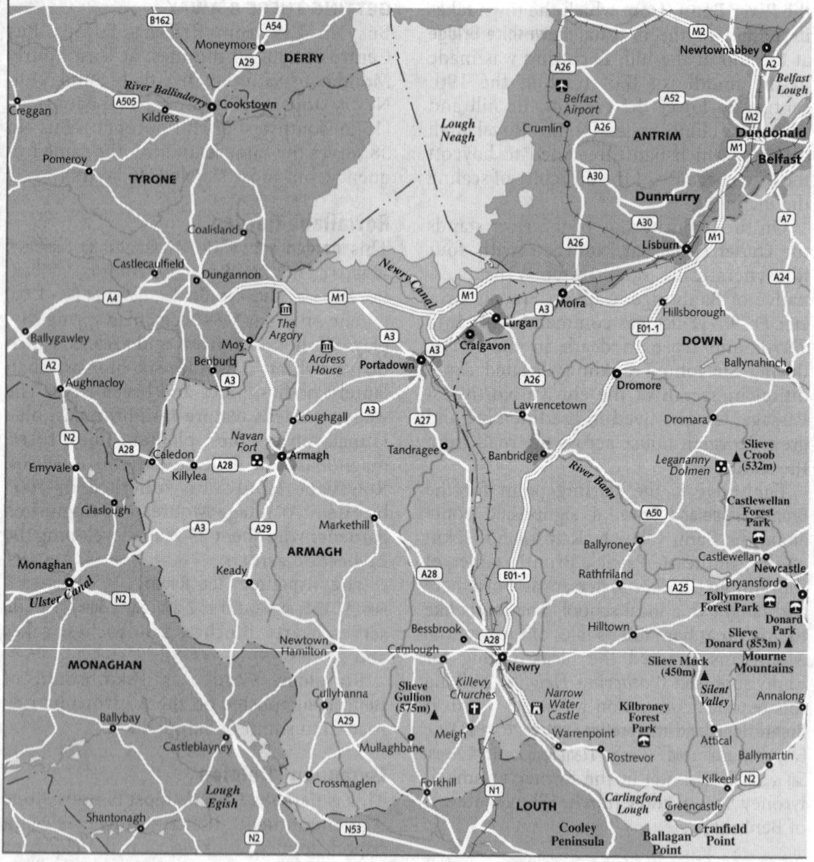

BELFAST TO BANGOR

The coastal region stretching east from Belfast to Bangor and beyond is commuter territory for the capital, and home to many of the North's wealthiest citizens – it's known locally as the 'Gold Coast'. The attractive **North Down Coastal Path** follows the shore from Holywood train station to Bangor Marina (15km), and continues east to Orlock Point.

See also the Ulster Folk and Transport Museums (p566).

Crawfordsburn Country Park

Just over 3km west of Bangor, off the B20 at Helen's Bay, **Crawfordsburn Country Park** (☎ 9185 3621; Bridge Rd S, Helen's Bay; admission free; 🕑 9am-8pm Apr-Sep, 9am-4.45pm Oct-Mar) offers a number of woodland and coastal walks. **Grey Point Fort** (admission free; guided tours 2-5pm Wed-Mon Apr-Sep, 2-5pm Sat & Sun Oct-Mar) is an early-20th-century gun emplacement with command post and lookout station. The large-calibre artillery has been trained on Belfast Lough since before WWI, though never fired in anger.

Access to the park is by the B2 Belfast to Bangor bus or by train to Helen's Bay Station, a wonderful little Victorian station dating from 1865 and built by the Marquess of Dufferin, who owned the surrounding estate.

BANGOR

pop 57,700

Bangor is to Belfast what Brighton means to London – a seaside resort and party town where the city slickers go to let their hair down. The Belfast to Bangor train

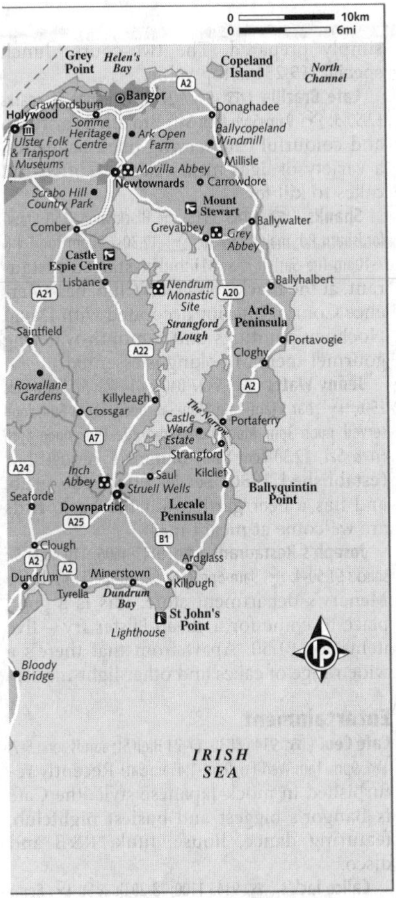

line was built in the late 19th century to connect the capital with the then flourishing resort. The opening of a huge marina and the emergence of a minor club scene have boosted the town's fortunes in recent years, though the kitsch tradition of British seaside towns survives in the Pickie Fun Park, with its swan-shaped pedalos and miniature railway.

Orientation & Information

The bus and train stations are together on Abbey St, at the top of Main St near the post office. At the bottom of Main St is the marina with B&Bs clustered to the east and west on Queen's Pde and Seacliff Rd. Unusually, Bangor has both a Main St and a High St, which converge at the marina.

The **Tower House Tourist Information Centre** (☎ 9127 0069; www.northdown.gov.uk; 34 Quay St; 🕑 10am-7pm Mon, 9am-7pm Tue-Fri, 10am-4pm Sat & noon-6pm Sun Jul & Aug, 10am-5pm Mon, 9am-5pm Tue-Fri, 10am-4pm Sat & 1-5pm Sun Jun & Sep, 10am-5pm Mon, 9am-5pm Tue-Fri & 10am-4pm Sat Oct-May) is adjacent to a tower built in 1637 as a fortified customs post.

Bangor Library (☎ 9127 0591; Hamilton Rd; 🕑 10am-8pm Mon-Wed, 10am-5pm Fri, 10am-1pm & 2-5pm Sat) has Internet access for £1.50 for 30 minutes.

Sights

Apart from strolling along the seafront, Bangor's main attraction is the **North Down Heritage Centre** (☎ 9127 1200; Castle Park Ave; admission free; 🕑 10.30am-4.30pm Tue-Sat & 2-4.30pm Sun year-round, to 5.30pm Jul & Aug), in the converted laundry, stables and stores of Bangor Castle. It contains an early-9th-century handbell, some ancient swords, a milepost with distances in Irish miles and a facsimile of *The Antiphonary of Bangor*, a small 7th-century prayer book and the oldest surviving Irish manuscript (the original is housed in Milan's Ambrosian Library). There's also an interesting section on the life of William Percy French (1854–1920), the famous entertainer and songwriter. The centre is in Castle Park, west of the train and bus stations.

The fishing village of Groomsport on the eastern edge of town has a picturesque harbour, overlooked by **Cockle Row Cottages** (☎ 9145 8882; admission free; 🕑 11.30am-5.30pm Tue-Sun Jul & Aug, 12.30-4.30pm Tue-Sun 16–30 Jun & 1–15 Sep, 12.30-4.30pm Sat & Sun 15 May–16 Jun & Sep-Oct), one of which is restored as a typical fisherman's home of 1910.

Sleeping

Accommodation can be hard to find so it's wise to book ahead.

Bangor Bay Inn (☎ 9127 0696; www.bangorbayinn.com; 10-12 Seacliff Rd; s/d £60/85; Ⓟ) This newly refurbished, 15-room hotel overlooking the marina is just around the corner from the tourist office. It has sea views, a friendly bar and a good restaurant.

Pierview House B&B (☎ 9146 3381; 28 Seacliff Rd; s/d £20/38; Ⓟ ⊠) Some of Pierview's five rooms have sea views; the nicest is on the 1st floor with a comfy sofa from which to watch the sea. There's one en-suite double (£44).

SOMETHING SPECIAL

Old Inn (☎ 9185 3255; www.theoldinn.com; 15 Main St, Crawfordsburn; r £65-90; P) The picturesque Old Inn, in the pretty village of Crawfordsburn, was established in 1614, making it Ireland's oldest hotel. The part-thatched hostelry has hosted many famous names through the centuries, including the young Peter the Great (tsar of Russia), Dick Turpin (highwayman), former US president George Bush Sr, and a veritable roll-call of literary figures including Swift, Tennyson, Thackeray, Dickens, Trollope and CS Lewis. The rooms, ranging in atmosphere from chintzy to antique, have bags of character, and the inn's **Restaurant 1614** (3-course dinner £25; noon-9.30pm) is one of Northern Ireland's best.

Cairn Bay Lodge (☎ 9146 7636; www.cairnbaylodge.com; s £30-35, d £50-60; P ⊠) This lovely seaside B&B villa overlooking Ballyholme Bay, east of the marina, oozes Edwardian elegance, with wood-panelled lounge and dining room, and three old-world bedrooms.

Clandeboye Lodge Hotel (☎ 9185 2500; info@clandeboyelodge.com; 10 Estate Rd; s £55-63, d £55-68; P ⊠) The Clandeboye is a modern, red-brick, country-house style hotel set amid quiet gardens on the southwest edge of town. Some of the rooms are wheelchair accessible.

Royal Hotel (☎ 9127 1866; www.royalhotelbangor.cs.com; 26 Quay St; s £63-73, d £60-85; P) A local landmark overlooking the marina, the refurbished Royal is Victorian on the outside, brisk and businesslike inside. Like most Bangor hotels, rates are cheaper at the weekend.

Eating

Genoa's (☎ 9146 9253; 1a Seacliff Rd; mains £9-17; 10.30am-2.30pm & 6-9.30pm Mon-Fri, 10.30am-10pm Sat, noon-8pm Sun) Genoa's is a cosy little nook of stone, brick and pine, tucked into the former Harbour Master's office across the street from the tourist office. The food is superb, especially the local seafood, and there's a separate vegetarian menu.

Avant-Garde (☎ 9145 4428; 132 Main St; lunch mains £5-7, dinner mains £8-13; café-bar 11.30am-11.30pm, food served 12.30-2.30pm & 5-9pm) This ultra-trendy café-bar at the top of Main St believes in serving quality local produce, simply prepared. The two-course lunch special (£5.25) is top value.

Cafe Brazilia (☎ 9127 2763; 13 Bridge St; snacks £2.50-5; 9am-5pm Mon-Sat) Brazilia is a stylish and colourful café serving filled baguettes, a variety of light meals, decent coffee and cakes to kill for.

Shanks (☎ 9185 3313; the Blackwood, 150 Crawfordsburn Rd; mains £16-36; 12.30-2.30pm Tue-Fri & 7-10pm Tue-Sat) This Michelin-starred restaurant, at the Blackwood Golf Club, has a Terence Conran interior decorated with David Hockney paintings and a mouth-watering gourmet menu. Booking is essential.

Jenny Watts (☎ 9127 0401; 41 High St; bar meals £5-6; bar 11am-1am Mon-Sat, noon-11pm Sun, food served noon-3pm Mon, noon-7pm Tue-Thu, noon-8pm Fri & Sat, 12.30-7pm Sun) Bangor's oldest bar (established 1780) serves good pub grub, and has a beer garden out the back. Kids are welcome at meal times.

Joseph's Restaurant (☎ 9147 4606; 110 Main St; snacks £1.50-4; 9am-5pm Mon-Sat, to 9pm Fri) Above Menary's department store, this is a good place to come for a cheap Ulster fry – five items for £1.50. Apart from that there's a wide range of cakes and other light meals.

Entertainment

Café Ceol (☎ 9146 8830; 17-21 High St; admission £5-7; 9pm-1am Wed-Fri, 9pm-1.45am Sat) Recently refurbished in mock-Japanese style, the Café is Bangor's biggest and busiest nightclub, featuring dance, house, funk, R&B and disco.

Calico Jack's (☎ 9145 1100; 18-20 Quay St; 8pm-1am Thu-Sun) Around the side of the Marine Court Hotel, Calico's is a pirate theme bar, and a busy pre-club venue. Live bands play on Thursday and a disco is held on the other nights.

Jenny Watts (☎ 9127 0401; 41 High St; 11am-1am Mon-Sat, noon-11pm Sun) This popular pub has folk music on Tuesday nights, easy listening on Thursday, clubbing (upstairs) on Friday and Saturday, and jazz on Sunday afternoons.

Getting There & Away

Ulsterbus Nos B1 and B2 run from Belfast's Laganside Bus Centre to Bangor (£2.60, 50 minutes, half-hourly Monday to Saturday, eight daily Sunday). From Bangor, bus No 3 goes to Donaghadee (£1.90, 25 minutes, hourly Monday to Saturday, five daily

Sunday), and bus No 6 heads for Newtownards (20 minutes, half-hourly).

There's a regular train service to Bangor from Belfast Central Station (£3.10, 30 minutes, half-hourly).

ARDS PENINSULA

The low-lying Ards Peninsula (An Aird) is the finger of land that encloses Strangford Lough, pinching against the thumb of the Lecale Peninsula at the Portaferry Narrows. The northern half of the peninsula has some of Ireland's most fertile farmland, with large expanses of wheat and barley, while the south is a landscape of neat fields, white cottages and narrow, winding roads. The eastern coast has some good sandy beaches.

Donaghadee

pop 4800

Until 1874 Donaghadee (Domhnach Daoi) was the main ferry port for Scotland – the 34km to Portpatrick was the shortest sea-crossing to Ireland. Its harbour walls were designed by John Rennie in 1819 and completed by his son, Sir John Rennie, who also designed several of London's bridges. Now it's fast becoming a commuter town for Belfast.

From June to September **Nelson's Boats** (☎ 9188 3403; www.nelsonsboats.co.uk) runs boat trips to **Copeland Island** (adult/child £3/2; 2pm), which was abandoned to the birds at the turn of the 20th century. They also offer **sea-angling trips** (£7 per person; 10.30am & 7pm), with all tackle and bait provided.

Grace Neill's (☎ 9188 4595; 33 High St) dates from 1611 and claims to be Ireland's oldest pub. Among its 17th-century guests was Peter the Great, tsar and later emperor of Russia, who stopped for lunch in 1697 on his grand tour of Europe. In the 19th century, John Keats found the place 'charming and clean' but was 'treated to ridicule, scorn and violent abuse by the local people who objected to my mode of dress and thought I was some strange foreigner'.

SLEEPING & EATING

Anathoth (☎ 9188 4004; sydneymcmaster@talk21.com; 9 Edgewater; s/d £18/32; P ⊠) About 1km out of town on the A2 Millisle road, this small, modern B&B has one room with shared bathroom.

Herdstown House (☎/fax 9188 3773; 9 Hogstown Rd; s/d £23/39; P ⊠) Herdstown is an old 18th-century farmhouse, offering family-friendly B&B in a country setting, 1.5km west of Donaghadee on the A48 towards Newtownards.

Pier 36 (☎ 9188 446; 36 the Parade; lunch mains £6-8, dinner mains £10-12; food served 11.30am-2.30pm & 7-11pm) An excellent pub with a big brick and terracotta dining room at the back, dominated by a yellow Raeburn stove that turns out home-baked bread and the daily roast. The hearty menu includes soups, stews, sausage and champ, barbecued meats, seafood specials and a good range of veggie dishes including tasty vegetarian fajitas.

Grace Neill's Bar & Grill (☎ 9188 4595; 33 High St; mains £5-12; food served noon-2.30pm & 6-9.30pm Tue-Sat) This bright and pleasant bistro in a new building at the back of the old pub serves up Italian- and French-influenced dishes. You can also enjoy bar meals in the modern Library Bar, with its bookshelves, gas fire and leather sofas.

East Coast

The A2 runs along the east coast of the peninsula through the seaside villages and permanent caravan parks of Millisle, Ballywalter and Ballyhalbert and the ugly fishing harbour of Portavogie. The best **beaches** are the Long Sand, immediately south of Ballywalter, and the seawater lagoon (enclosed by a stone dike for safe bathing) at Millisle.

About 1.5km northwest of Millisle (Oileán an Mhuilinn) is **Ballycopeland Windmill** (☎ 9181 1491; Moss Rd; admission free; 10am-1pm Wed & Thu & 2-6pm Tue & Fri-Sun Jul & Aug), a late-18th-century corn mill that remained in commercial use until 1915, and has been restored to full working order.

Portaferry

pop 2300

Portaferry (Port an Pheire), a neat huddle of streets around a medieval tower house, is the most attractive town on the Ards Peninsula, looking across the turbulent Narrows to the matching tower house of Strangford. A renowned marine biology station on the waterfront uses the lough as an outdoor laboratory; you can investigate the local marine life yourself at the nearby Exploris aquarium (see Sights & Activities on p576). There are some good coastal walks, and in fine weather you can sit outside the pubs on the waterfront and watch the comings and goings of yachts and the ferry.

The **Portaferry Tourist Information & Visitor Centre** (☎ 4272 9882; Castle St; 🕑 10am-5pm Mon-Sat, 2-6pm Sun Easter-Sep) is in a restored stable near the tower house.

SIGHTS & ACTIVITIES

You can take a look at **Portaferry Castle** (admission free; 🕑 10am-5pm Mon-Sat, 2-6pm Sun Easter-Sep), a small 16th-century tower house beside the visitor centre, which together with the tower house in Strangford used to control sea traffic through the Narrows.

Next to the tower house is the outstanding state-of-the-art aquarium, **Exploris** (☎ 4272 8062; www.ards-council.gov.uk/exploris/exploris.htm; Castle St; adult/child £5.40/3.20; 🕑 10am-6pm Mon-Fri, 11am-6pm Sat & 1-6pm Sun Mar-Aug, to 5pm Sep-Feb), with displays of marine life from Strangford Lough and the Irish Sea. Touch tanks allow visitors to stroke and hold rays, starfish, sea anemones and other sea creatures. Exploris also rehabilitates sick seals.

You can walk up to **Windmill Hill** above the town, topped by another old windmill tower, for a good view over the Narrows to Strangford. The Vikings named this stretch of water Strangfjörthr, meaning 'powerful fjord', because when the tide turns, as it does four times a day, 400,000 tonnes of water per minute churn through the gap at speeds up to eight knots (15km/h). You get some idea of the current's remarkable strength when you see the ferry being whipped sideways by the tide.

There are pleasant walks along the shore, north to Ballyhenry Island (accessible at low tide), and south to the National Trust nature reserve of Ballyquintin Point, good for bird-watching, seal-spotting, or just admiring the view of the Mourne Mountains.

Des Rogers (☎ 4272 8297) and **John Murray** (☎ 4272 8414) organise fishing and bird-watching trips, as well as pleasure cruises on the lough (around £150/75 a day/half-day) for up to six people.

SLEEPING

Barholm Hostel (☎ 4272 9598; www.barholmportaferry.co.uk; 11 the Strand; dm £10-11.50; 🕑 year-round; Ⓟ) Barholm has a superb seafront location opposite the ferry slipway, an excellent kitchen, laundry facilities and a big, sunny conservatory for breakfast (£3.75 extra). It's popular with groups, so be sure to book ahead.

Adair's B&B (☎ 4272 8412; 22 The Square; s/d £18/36; ☒) Mrs Adair's friendly and good-value B&B is an anonymous-looking house on the main square, without a sign to reveal its identity.

Fiddler's Green (☎ 4272 8393; www.fiddlersgreenportaferry.com; 10-12 Church St; s/d £30/50; Ⓟ) This popular pub and restaurant also offers excellent B&B accommodation in four rooms, one with a four-poster bed.

Narrows (☎ 4272 8148; www.narrows.co.uk; 8 Shore Rd; s/d £57.50/85; Ⓟ ☒; wheelchair accessible) The award-winning Narrows has 13 stylish but unfussy, not-quite-minimalist bedrooms, and every one of them has a sea view. One of the most pleasant places to stay in the whole of the North.

Portaferry Hotel (☎ 4272 8231; www.portaferryhotel.com; 10 the Strand; s/d £60/100; Ⓟ ☒; wheelchair accessible) Converted from a row of 18th-century terraced houses, this charming seafront hotel is as traditional and old-fashioned as the Narrows is hip and modern.

EATING & DRINKING

Cornstore (☎ 4272 9779; 2 Castle St; mains £5-7; 🕑 noon-7pm Wed-Thu & Sun, noon-8.30pm Fri & Sat) This bistro-style restaurant, across from the tourist office, specialises in local seafood.

Fiddler's Green (☎ 4272 8393; 10-12 Church St) Portaferry's liveliest pub, with traditional music sessions every Friday, Saturday and Sunday night, has a nautical-themed restaurant, the **Quarterdeck** (mains £7-12; 🕑 12.30-3pm & 5-9pm Fri & Sat, 12.30-8pm Sun), offering seafood specials, char-grilled steaks, roast lamb and a handful of Far Eastern dishes.

Narrows (☎ 4272 8148; 8 Shore Rd; lunch mains £5-9, dinner mains £12-15; 🕑 noon-2.30pm & 7-9pm) The restaurant at the Narrows is as relaxed and informal as the accommodation, with top-quality food simply prepared, home-baked bread, a good wine list and a view of the lough.

GETTING THERE & AWAY

Ulsterbus Nos 9A and 10 go from Belfast to Portaferry (£4.70, 1¼ hours, six daily Monday to Saturday, three Sunday) via Newtownards, Mount Stewart and Greyabbey. More frequent services begin from

Newtownards (some buses go via Carrowdore and don't stop at Mount Stewart and Greyabbey; check first).

The **ferry** (☎ 4488 1637) between Portaferry and Strangford sails every half-hour between 7.30am and 10.30pm Monday to Friday, 8am to 11pm Saturday and 9.30am to 10.30pm Sunday. The journey time is about 10 minutes. The single/same-day-return fares are £4.80/7.70 for a car and driver; £3.10/4.80 for motorcyclists and their bikes; and £1/1.60 for car passengers and pedestrians.

Greyabbey

pop 700

The village of Greyabbey is home to the splendid ruins of **Grey Abbey** (☎ 9054 6552; Church Rd; admission free; 10am-7pm Tue-Sat & 2-7pm Sun Apr-Sep, 10am-4pm & 2-4pm Sun Oct-Mar). The Cistercian abbey was founded in 1193 by Affreca, wife of the Norman John de Courcy (the builder of Carrickfergus Castle, see p629), in thanks for surviving a stormy sea-crossing from the Isle of Man. The abbey church, which remained in use as late as the 18th century, was the first in Ireland to be built in the Gothic style.

At the east end of the church is a carved tomb possibly depicting Affreca; her husband may be represented by the effigy in the north transept. The grounds, overlooked by 18th-century Rosemount House, are awash with trees and flowers on spreading lawns, making this an ideal picnic spot. The small visitor centre explains Cistercian life with paintings and panels.

Hoops Courtyard, off Main St in the village centre, has a cluster of 18 little shops selling antiques and collectables; opening times vary, but all are open on Wednesday, Friday and Saturday afternoons.

Hoops Coffee Shop (☎ 4278 8541; Hoops Courtyard, Main St; mains £4-5; 10am-5pm Wed, Fri & Sat, daily in Jul & Aug) is a traditional tearoom, with outdoor tables in the courtyard in fine weather. It serves good lunches (excellent roast beef with the works £4.95), wicked cream teas, and tea or coffee in antique silver teapots.

Wildfowler Inn (☎ 4278 8260; 1 Main St; mains £5-7.50; food served noon-2.30pm & 6-9pm) An atmospheric local pub crammed with wooden beams, copper jugs and ceramic tankards, the Wildfowler serves tasty bar meals – steaks, burgers, sausage and champ, grilled salmon, and huge smoking stir-fries.

Mount Stewart House & Gardens

The magnificent 18th-century **Mount Stewart** (☎ 4278 8387; house & gardens adult/child £4.95/2.35; house noon-6pm daily Jul & Aug, Wed-Mon Sep, 1-6pm Mon & Wed-Fri & noon-6pm Sat & Sun May & Jun, noon-6pm Sat, Sun & public hols 15 Mar–Apr & Oct) is one of Northern Ireland's grandest stately homes. It was the home of the marquess of Londonderry, and is decorated with lavish plasterwork, marble nudes and priceless artworks – the portrait of the racehorse Hambletonian by George Stubbs is one of the most important paintings in Ireland.

Much of the landscaping of the beautiful **gardens** (gardens only £3.90/2.10; 10am-8pm May-Sep, 10am-6pm Apr & Oct, 10am-4pm Nov-Mar)

LORD CASTLEREAGH

Mount Stewart was the childhood home of Robert Stewart, Lord Castlereagh (1769–1822), one of the most accomplished foreign secretaries in British history. As Irish chief secretary in the British government of William Pitt, he was responsible for quelling the 1798 Rising and for passing the Act of Union in 1800. Later he served as foreign secretary during the Napoleonic wars, and represented Britain at the Congress of Vienna in 1815, which re-drew the map of Europe, post-Bonaparte.

Castlereagh's father, the first marquess of Londonderry, primed his political career by buying him a place in the Irish parliament as member for County Down. The campaign cost a cool £60,000, leaving the marquess unable to afford various planned improvements to Mount Stewart.

Despite his political successes, Castlereagh was enormously unpopular with the British public who saw him as the spokesman for a violently repressive government. He was savagely attacked in print by liberal reformers, including the poets Percy Bysshe Shelley and Lord Byron. He eventually succumbed to mental illness, and committed suicide by slitting his throat with a penknife. Lord Byron's notorious *Epitaph for Lord Castlereagh* displayed little sympathy:

Posterity will ne'er survey
A nobler scene than this:
Here lie the bones of Castlereagh;
Stop, traveller, and piss!

was supervised in the early 1900s by Lady Edith, wife of the seventh marquess, for the benefit of her children – the Dodo Terrace at the front of the house is populated with unusual creatures from history (dinosaurs and dodos) and myth (griffins and mermaids), accompanied by giant frogs and duck-billed platypuses. The 18th-century **Temple of the Winds** (2-5pm Sat & Sun Apr-Oct) is a folly in the classical Greek style built on a high point above the lough.

Mount Stewart is on the A20, 3km northwest of Greyabbey and 8km southeast of Newtownards. Buses from Belfast and Newtownards to Portaferry pass the gate (see p576). The ground floor of the house and most of the gardens are wheelchair accessible.

NEWTOWNARDS

pop 27,800

Founded in the 17th century on the site of a 6th-century ecclesiastical centre, Newtownards (Baile Nua na hArda) today is a busy but unexceptional commercial centre. Unless you want to commission a guitar from Lowden's (see Sights following), there's little reason to hang around.

The **Ards Tourist Information Centre** (☎ 9182 6846; www.kingdomsofdown.com; 31 Regent St; 9.15am 5pm Mon-Fri, 9.30am-5pm Sat) is next to the bus station.

Sights

There's some fine 18th- and 19th-century architecture in the town, especially along Church St. Most striking of all is the 18th-century **Market House** (☎ 9181 0803; Conway Sq; admission free; 9am-4pm Mon-Sat), which once housed the town's prison – you can ask to see an original cell – and is now home to the local arts centre. In front of Market House a lively **market** takes place every Saturday and a traditional harvest fair in September. The **Market Cross** on High St dates back to the 17th century.

The remains of **Movilla Abbey** and its 13th-century church have been almost swallowed up by the forest of gravestones in Movilla Cemetery. There are some interesting Knights Templar grave slabs and Freemasonic memorials here.

The **Lowden Guitar Company** (☎ 9182 0542; 8 Glenford Way, Glenford Industrial Estate) has been creating guitars for the greats since the 1970s – Lowden owners include Eric Clapton, Van Morrison, Richard Thompson, Mark Knopfler and the Edge. Free 15- to 20-minute tours are available by prior arrangement 10am to 3.30pm Monday to Thursday and 10am to 1pm Friday.

Sleeping

Greenacres (☎ 9181 6193; 5 Manse Rd; s/d £25/40; P ⊠) A lovely stone villa set in spacious gardens overlooked by Scrabo Tower (see p578), Greenacres offers B&B in four large, en-suite rooms.

Strangford Arms Hotel (☎ 9181 4141; info@strangfordhotel.co.uk; 92 Church St; s/d £59/69; P ⊠) The newly refurbished Strangford Arms, on the western edge of town, is efficient and businesslike if a little lacking in character.

Getting There & Away

The Ulsterbus station is on Regent St, near the tourist office. Bus No 5 goes to Belfast (£2, 30 minutes; at least hourly Monday to Saturday, three daily Sunday), and Nos 9A and 10 run to Portaferry (six daily Monday to Saturday, three Sunday); some go via Mount Stewart and Greyabbey (check first).

AROUND NEWTOWNARDS

Scrabo Country Park

The superb viewpoint of Scrabo Hill, 2km southwest of town, was once the site of extensive prehistoric earthworks, but these were largely removed during construction of the 41m **1857 Memorial Tower** (☎ 9181 1491; admission free; 10.30am-6pm Sat-Thu Apr-Sep) in honour of the third marquess of Londonderry. Inside there's a slide show on Strangford Lough and a 122-step climb to the top of the tower. On a clear day you can see Scotland, the Isle of Man, and even Snowdon in Wales. The disused sandstone quarries nearby provided material for many famous buildings, including Belfast's Albert Memorial Clock Tower (see p543).

Somme Heritage Centre

This fascinating **heritage centre** (☎ 9182 3202; www.irishsoldier.org; 233 Bangor Rd; adult/child £3.75/2.75; 10am-5pm Mon-Fri & noon-5pm Sat & Sun Jul & Aug, 10am-4pm Mon-Thu & noon-4pm Sat & Sun Apr-Jun & Sep, 10am-4pm Mon-Thu Oct-Dec, Feb & Mar) vividly illustrates the horrors of the WWI Somme campaign of 1916 from the perspective of men of the 10th (Irish), 16th (Irish) and 36th

(Ulster) divisions. It's a high-tech show with short films and nothing celebratory about the exhibits, intended as a memorial to the men and women who died. A significant photographic display commemorates the suffragette movement and the part that women played in WWI.

The centre is 3km north of Newtownards on the A21 towards Bangor. The No 6 Bangor to Newtownards bus passes the entrance every half-hour or so.

Ark Open Farm

Opposite the Somme Heritage Centre, on the other side of the dual carriageway, is the **Ark** (☎ 9182 0445; 296 Bangor Rd; adult/child £2.90/2.10; 🕑 10am-6pm Mon-Sat & 2-6pm Sun), an open farm with displays of rare breeds of sheep, cattle and poultry, alongside a few llamas and a donkey or two.

STRANGFORD LOUGH

Connected to the open sea only by a 700m-wide strait (the Narrows) at Portaferry, Strangford Lough (Loch Cuan) is almost a lake. Its western shore is fringed by hump-backed islands – half-drowned mounds of boulder clay (called drumlins) left behind by ice sheets at the end of the last Ice Age. These show up well in the view from Scrabo Hill (see p578).

Large colonies of grey seals frequent the lough, especially at the southern tip of the Ards Peninsula where the exit channel opens out into the sea. Birds abound on the shores and tidal mudflats, including brent geese wintering from Arctic Canada, eider ducks and many species of wader. Strangford Lough oysters are a local delicacy.

Castle Espie Centre

About 2km southeast of Comber, off the Downpatrick road (A22), is the **Castle Espie Wildfowl and Wetlands Centre** (☎ 9187 4146; www.wwt.org.uk; Ballydrain Rd, Comber; adult/child £4/2.50; 🕑 10.30am-5pm Mon-Sat & 11.30am-5.30pm Sun Mar-Oct, 11.30am-4pm Mon-Sat & 11.30am-5pm Sun Nov-Feb). It's a haven for fledgling ornithologists and for large gatherings of geese, ducks and swans. Notably, it's a winter home for most of the world's population of light-bellied brent geese. The best time to visit is between May and June, when the grounds are overrun with goslings, ducklings and cygnets.

Sleeping

Anna's House B&B (☎ 9754 1566; anna@loughviewhouse.com; Loughview House, 35 Lisbarnett Rd, Lisbane; s/d £25/50; P ☒) Just west of the village of Lisbane, Anna's is a secluded country house set in a superb garden with views over a little lake. There are three en-suite rooms, and all the food is organic, even the coffee and tea.

Old School House Inn (☎ 9754 1182; www.theoldschoolhouseinn.com; Ballydrain Rd, Comber; s/d £45/65; P ☒) Just south of Castle Espie on the road to Nendrum, the characterful Old Schoolhouse has 12 luxurious rooms and one of the North's best **restaurants** (3-course dinner £18; 🕑 12.30-3pm Sun, 7-9.30pm daily). It serves fresh oysters from its own oyster farm, and game in winter.

Nendrum Monastic Site

The Celtic monastic community of **Nendrum** (admission free; 🕑 24 hr) was built in the 5th century under the guidance of St Mochaoi (St Mahee). It is much older than the Norman monastery at Grey Abbey on the opposite shore, and could not be more different. The scant remains provide a clear outline of its early plan. Foundations survive from a number of churches, a round tower, beehive cells and other buildings, as well as three concentric stone ramparts and a monks' cemetery, all in a wonderful island setting. A particularly interesting relic is the stone sundial that has been reconstructed with some of the original pieces. The minor road to Mahee Island from the lough's western shore crosses a causeway to Reagh Island and then a bridge guarded by the remains of 15th-century Mahee Castle.

The small **visitor centre** (☎ 9754 2547; admission free; 🕑 10am-7pm Tue-Sat & 2-7pm Sun Apr-Sep, 10am-4pm Sat & 2-4pm Sun Oct-Mar) screens an excellent video comparing Nendrum to Grey Abbey, and there's some interesting material about the concept of time and how we measure it, presented in child-friendly fashion.

The site is signposted from Lisbane, on the A20 5km south of Comber.

Lisbarnett House (☎ 9754 1589; 181 Killinchy Rd, Lisbane; lunch mains £6-10, dinner mains £11-16; 🕑 noon-2.30pm & 6.30-9.30pm Mon-Sat, 12.30-9.30pm Sun) restaurant has a good local reputation and serves traditional and modern Irish cuisine, including vegetarian options and a traditional roast on Sunday.

Killyleagh

pop 2200

Killyleagh (Cill O Laoch) is a fishing village dominated by the impressive **castle** (closed to the public) of the Hamilton family. Built originally by John de Courcy in the 12th century, the Scottish Baronial-style reconstruction of 1850 sits on the Norman motte and bailey. Outside the gatehouse, a plaque commemorates Sir Hans Sloane, the naturalist born in Killyleagh in 1660, whose collection was the basis for the founding of the British Museum (London's Sloane Square is named after him). The parish church houses the tombs of members of the Blackwood family (marquesses of Dufferin), who married into the Hamiltons in the 18th century.

SLEEPING & EATING

Killyleagh Castle Towers (☎ 4482 8261; rownhamilton.killyleaghcastle@virgin.net; High St; 4-person apt £230-280 per week; P) If you ever fancied staying in a castle, Killyleagh's three gatehouse towers (complete with spiral staircases and roof terraces) are available for weekly rental. The two smaller towers sleep four and the larger sleeps five.

Dufferin Coaching Inn (☎ 4482 8229; www.dufferincoachinginn.co.uk, 35 High St; s/d £37.50/65; ☒) The Dufferin has six spacious en-suite rooms, some with four-poster beds. The library-cum-reception has many books on the locale and Ireland. The inn has two bars – the comfortably old-fashioned **Dufferin Arms** (bar meals £6-10) and the larger **Stables Bar** downstairs – and the excellent, candle-lit **Kitchen Restaurant** (mains £9-14; 5.30-8.30pm Mon-Thu, 5.30-9.30pm Fri & Sat, 12.30-2.30pm Sat & Sun). Music nights (bands) are Thursday, Friday and Saturday, with traditional sessions on Saturday afternoon.

GETTING THERE & AWAY

Bus No 11 runs from Belfast to Killyleagh (£3.50, one hour, eight daily Monday to Friday, five Saturday, one Sunday) via Comber. No 14 continues from Killyleagh to Downpatrick (20 minutes, eight daily Monday to Friday, five Sunday).

DOWNPATRICK

pop 10,300

Downpatrick (Dún Pádraig) is named after Ireland's patron saint, who is associated with numerous places in this corner of Down, and on St Patrick's Day the town is crammed with crowds of pilgrims and revellers.

Downpatrick is County Down's administrative centre, 32km south of Belfast. It was settled long before the saint's arrival, his first church here being constructed inside the *dún* (fort) of Rath Celtchair, an earthwork still visible to the southwest of the cathedral. The place later became known as Dún Pádraig, anglicised to Downpatrick in the 17th century.

In 1176 the Norman John de Courcy is said to have brought the relics of St Colmcille and St Brigid to Downpatrick to rest with the remains of St Patrick, hence the local saying, 'In Down, three saints one grave do fill, Patrick, Brigid and Colmcille'. Later the town declined along with the cathedral until the 17th and 18th centuries, when the Southwell family developed the old town centre we see today. The best of its Georgian architecture is centred on English St and the Mall, which lead from the centre up to the cathedral.

The **Downpatrick Tourist Information Centre** (☎ 4461 2233; www.kingdomsofdown.com; 53a Market St; 9.30am-7pm Mon-Sat & 2-6pm Sun mid-Jun–Sep, 9.30am-5pm Mon-Fri & 10am-5pm Sat Oct–mid-Jun) is in the Saint Patrick Centre opposite the bus station.

Saint Patrick Centre

The Saint Patrick Centre houses a multimedia exhibition called **Ego Patricius** (I Am Patrick; ☎ 4461 9000; www.saintpatrickcentre.com; 53a Market St; adult/child £4.50/2.25; 9.30am-7pm Mon-Sat & 10am-6pm Sun Jun-Aug, 9.30am-5.30pm Mon-Sat & 1-5.30pm Sun Apr-May & Sep, 10am-5pm Mon-Sat Oct-Mar, 9.30am-7pm St Patrick's Day), charting the life and legacy of Ireland's patron saint. Occasionally filled with parties of school kids, the exhibition uses audio and video presentations to tell St Patrick's story, often in his own words (taken from his *Confession*, written in Latin around the year 450). At the end is a spectacular wide-screen film that takes the audience on a swooping, low-level helicopter ride over the landscapes of Ireland.

Down Cathedral

According to legend St Patrick died in Saul, where angels told his followers to place his body on a cart drawn by two untamed oxen, and that wherever the oxen halted, that was where the saint was to be buried.

They supposedly stopped at the church on the hill of Down, now the site of the Church of Ireland's **Down Cathedral** (☎ 4461 4922; the Mall; admission free; 9.30am-5pm Mon-Sat & 2-5pm Sun).

The cathedral is a conglomeration of 1600 years of building and rebuilding. Viking attacks wiped away all trace of the earliest churches, and the subsequent Norman cathedral and monasteries were destroyed by Edward Bruce in 1316. The rubble was used in a 15th-century construction, finished in 1512 but after the dissolution of the monasteries in 1541 it was razed to the ground. Today's cathedral dates largely from the 18th and 19th centuries, with a completely new interior installed in the 1980s.

In the churchyard immediately south of the cathedral is a slab of Mourne granite with the inscription 'Patric', placed there by the Belfast Naturalists' Field Club in 1900, marking the traditional site of St Patrick's grave.

To reach the cathedral, go up the stairs to the right of the Saint Patrick Centre and turn left at the top, opposite Down County Museum.

Down County Museum

Downhill from the cathedral is the **county museum** (☎ 4461 5218; the Mall; admission free; 10am-5pm Mon-Fri & 1-5pm Sat & Sun), housed in the town's restored 18th-century jail. In a cell block at the back are models of some of the prisoners incarcerated there, and details of their sad stories. The biggest exhibit of all is outside – a short signposted trail leads to the **Mound of Down**, a good example of a Norman motte and bailey.

The **Mall** itself is the most attractive street in Downpatrick, with some lovely 18th-century architecture, including Soundwell School built in 1733 and a courthouse with a finely decorated pediment.

Inch Abbey

This **abbey** (☎ 9023 5000; admission free; 24 hr), built by de Courcy for the Cistercians in 1180 on an earlier Irish monastic site, is visible across the river from the cathedral. The English Cistercians had a strict policy of nonadmittance to Irishmen and maintained this until the end in 1541. Most of the ruins are just foundations and low walls; the neatly groomed setting beside the marshes of the River Quoile is its most memorable feature.

To get here head out of town for about 1.5km on the A7 Belfast road, then take the first left after crossing the river.

Downpatrick Railway Museum

This working **museum** (☎ 4461 5779; www.downpatricksteamrailway.co.uk; Market St, museum 9am-4pm daily Jul–mid-Sep, 10am-4pm Sat year-round, trains 2-5pm Sat & Sun Jul–mid-Sep, St Patrick's Day, Easter & May Day) runs steam-hauled trains over a restored section of the former Belfast to Newcastle line. There is a western terminus at Ballydugan, and a northern one close to Inch Abbey. There is also a halt next to the **grave of King Magnus Barefoot**, a Norwegian king who died in battle on this spot in 1103.

Quoile Countryside Centre

A tidal barrier was built at Hare Island, 3km downstream from Downpatrick, in 1957 to control flooding. The waters enclosed by the barrier now form the Quoile Pondage Nature Reserve, whose ecology is explained at the **Quoile Countryside Centre** (☎ 4461 5520; www.ehsni.gov.uk; 5 Quay Rd; admission free; reserve 24 hr, visitor centre 11am-5pm daily Apr-Aug, 1-5pm Sat & Sun Oct-Mar). It's in a little cottage beside the ruins of **Quoile Castle**, a 17th-century tower house. There's a wheelchair-accessible **birdwatching hide** (10am-4pm) on Castle Island, downstream from the centre.

Sleeping & Eating

Hillside (☎ 4461 3134; 62 Scotch St; s/d £18/35; P ☒) Set in a listed Georgian town house, Hillside is a good-value, centrally located B&B.

Denvir's Hotel & Pub (☎ 4461 2012; fax 4461 7002; 14 English St; s/d £32.50/55; P) Denvir's is an old coaching inn dating back to 1642, offering B&B in six large, en-suite rooms with TV. The **restaurant** (mains £6-12; noon-2.30pm Mon-Sat, 7-9pm Fri & Sat) has an enormous, original fireplace and serves good wholesome dishes such as Irish stew, accompanied by fresh organic vegetables. There's live music in the bar on Thursday and Saturday with a folk club every Friday.

Mill at Ballydugan (☎ 4461 3654; www.ballyduganmill.com; Drumcullen Rd, Ballydugan; s/d £50/65; P) This giant, eight-storey, 18th-century mill building overlooking Ballydugan Lake was restored as a hotel and restaurant in the 1990s, and now offers 11 atmospheric, en-suite bedrooms with exposed beams and stone walls. It's 3km southwest of Downpatrick, off the A25.

Harry Afrika's (☎ 4461 7161; 102 Market St; mains £3-5; ⌚ 8.30am-5.30pm Mon-Sat & 10.30am-5.30pm Sun) In the shopping centre beside the bus station, this is an unremarkable cafeteria offering reasonably priced breakfasts, grills and daily specials, but one of the few eating places open on a Sunday.

Getting There & Away

Ulsterbus Nos 15 and 15A depart from the Europa Bus Centre in Belfast for Downpatrick (£4.10, one hour, at least hourly Monday to Saturday, five daily Sunday). There's also an express service, bus No 215 (45 minutes, seven daily Monday to Friday).

Bus No 240 runs from Downpatrick to Newry (£4.10, one hour, four daily Monday to Saturday, two Sunday) via Dundrum, Newcastle (£2.70, 25 minutes) and Hilltown.

AROUND DOWNPATRICK

According to popular tradition, the young St Patrick was kidnapped from Britain by Irish pirates and spent six years as a slave tending sheep (possibly on Slemish Hill in County Antrim) before escaping back home to his family. After religious training, he returned to Ireland to spread the faith and is said to have landed on the shores of Strangford Lough near Saul, northeast of Downpatrick. He preached his first sermon in a sheep shelter nearby, and eventually retired to Saul after some 30 years of evangelising.

Saul

On landing near this spot in 432, St Patrick made his first convert: Díchú, the local chieftain, who gave the holy man a sheep barn *(sabhal)* from which to preach. West of Saul village is the supposed site of the *sabhal*, with a replica 10th-century **church and round tower** built in 1932 to mark the 1500th anniversary of his arrival.

East of the village is the small hill of **Slieve Patrick** (120m), with stations of the cross along the path to the top and a massive 10m-high statue of St Patrick, also dating from 1932, on the summit.

Saul (Sabhal) is 3km northeast of Downpatrick off the A2 Strangford road.

Struell Wells

The well-preserved 17th-century bath-houses at these supposedly curative springs will induce a shiver – they look more likely to induce ill health than cure it! The wells are traditionally associated with St Patrick – it is said he scourged himself here, spending 'a great part of the night, stark naked and singing psalms' immersed in what is now the Drinking Well – but there is no proof of this. Nevertheless, the site has been venerated for centuries, although the buildings are all post-1600. Between the bathhouses and the ruined chapel stands the Eye Well, whose waters are reputed to cure eye ailments.

The wells are in a scenic, secluded glen 2km east of Downpatrick. Take the B1 road towards Ardglass, and turn left after passing the hospital.

LECALE PENINSULA

The low-lying Lecale Peninsula lies east of Downpatrick, isolated by the sea and Strangford Lough to the north, south and east, and the marshes of the Quoile and Blackstaff Rivers to the west. In Irish it is Leath Chathail, or Cathal's territory, a region of fertile farmland fringed by fishing harbours, rocky bluffs and sandy beaches.

Lecale is a place of pilgrimage for Van Morrison fans – Coney Island, immortalised in his song of the same name, is between Ardglass and Killough in the south of the peninsula.

Strangford

pop 550

Most of the picturesque fishing village of Strangford (Baile Loch Cuan) is a conservation area dominated by **Strangford Castle** (☎ 9023 5000; Castle St; admission free), a 16th-century tower house that faces its twin across the Narrows in Portaferry. To get inside, grab the keys from Mr Seed at 39 Castle St. At the end of Castle St is a footpath called the **Squeeze Cut** that leads over the hill behind the village, with a fine view of the lough, before looping back to Strangford via tree-lined Dufferin Ave (20 minutes), or continuing around the shoreline to Castle Ward Estate (one hour).

Strangford is 16km northeast of Downpatrick. See p577 for details of the car ferry between Strangford and Portaferry.

SLEEPING & EATING

Strangford Caravan Park (☎ 4488 1888; 87 Shore Rd; tent or campervan £6) The nearest place to camp is this waterside site 1km southwest of the ferry slip, on the A25 towards Downpatrick.

Castle Ward Estate Camp Site (☎ 4488 1680; 19 Castle Ward Rd; tent/caravan £6/11; mid-Mar–Sep) The entrance to this wooded, lough-shore National Trust site is separate from the main estate entrance, and closer to Strangford village.

Cuan (☎ 4488 1222; www.thecuan.com; The Square; s/d £45/80; P ⊠) The Cuan, just around the corner from the ferry slip, is a nice old hotel with nine modern en-suite rooms. It also has a **bar** (bar meals £5-7; food served noon-7pm), with traditional music on the last Friday of the month, and a **restaurant** (mains £10-13; 2-/3-course set dinner £16/20; 7-9.30pm Mon-Sat, noon-2.30pm & 5-9pm Sun) serving local seafood, lamb and beef.

Lobster Pot (☎ 4488 1288; 9-11 The Square; bar meals £5-10, restaurant mains £10-12; 11.30am-9pm Mon-Sat, 12.30-8pm Sun) This charmingly old-fashioned pub and restaurant overlooking the harbour is a local favourite, serving excellent seafood and a selection of vegetarian dishes. Their two-/three-course Sunday lunch (£11/15) is good value.

Castle Ward Estate

Castle Ward House, which enjoys a superb setting overlooking the bay to the west of Strangford, has a split personality. It was built in the 1760s for Lord and Lady Bangor – Bernard Ward and his wife, Anne – who were a bit of an odd couple. Their tastes started poles apart and continued to diverge, resulting in an eccentric country residence and a subsequent divorce. Bernard favoured the neoclassical Palladian style seen in the design of the front facade and the classical staircase. Anne leant towards Strawberry Hill Gothic, which she implemented on the rear façade and in her Gothic boudoir with its incredible fan vaulting. The rest of the house is an uneasy mixture of their contrasting tastes.

The house is now part of the National Trust's **Castle Ward Estate** (☎ 4488 1204; Park Rd; adult/child house & grounds £4.70/1.80, grounds only £3.10/1.30; house & wildlife centre noon-6pm daily Jun-Aug; noon-6pm Sat & Sun, 1-6pm Mon & Wed May, noon-6pm Sat, Sun & public hols mid-Mar, Apr, Sep & Oct, grounds 10am-8pm daily May-Sep, 10am-4pm daily Oct-Apr). In the grounds are a Victorian laundry museum, the Strangford Lough Wildlife Centre, Old Castle Ward (a fine 16th-century Plantation tower) and Castle Audley (a 15th-century tower house).

Kilclief Castle

Square-jawed and thick-set, **Kilclief Castle** (☎ 9023 5000; Kilclief; admission free; 2-6pm Tue & Fri-Sun, 10am-1pm Wed & Thu Jul & Aug) guards the seaward entrance to the Narrows. This is the oldest tower house in the county, built between 1413 and 1441 for John Cely, the adulterous bishop of Down. It has some elaborate details and is thought to have been the prototype for Ardglass, Strangford and other castles in Lecale.

Kilclief is on the A2, 4km south of Strangford.

Ardglass

Ardglass (Ard Ghlais) today is a small village with a busy fishing harbour, but in medieval times it was a major port and an important trading centre. A legacy of its importance is the seven tower houses, dating from the 14th to the 16th centuries, that punctuate the hillside above the harbour.

The only one open to the public is **Jordan's Castle** (☎ 9181 1491; Low Rd; admission free; 10am-1pm Tue, Fri & Sat, 2-6pm Wed & Thu Jul & Aug), a four-storey tower near the harbour. Like the others it was built by a wealthy merchant at the dawn of Ulster's economic development. The castle now houses a local museum and a collection of antiques accumulated by its last owner.

Ardglass is on the A2, 13km south of Strangford.

SLEEPING & EATING

Coneyisland Caravan Park (☎ 4484 1210; 75 Killough Rd; tent/campervan £5/9; Apr-Nov) The nearest camp site is just west of Ardglass on the way to Killough.

Margaret's Cottage (☎ 4484 1080; www.margaretscottage.com; 9 Castle Pl; s/d £20/40; P ⊠ ☐) Margaret's is a dinky little flower-bedecked 18th-century cottage (with a modern upper floor) squeezed between the Downs Restaurant and the ruins of Margaret's Castle. It now offers superb B&B accommodation, with four cosy rooms and an open fire in the lounge.

Downs Restaurant (Aldo's; ☎ 4484 1315; 7 Castle Pl; mains £9-11; 12.30-2pm Sun & 5-10pm Mon-Sun Jun-Aug, 12.30-2pm Sun & 5-10pm Thu-Sun Sep-May)

Aldo's is a local institution, a cosy Italian restaurant serving excellent seafood, pasta and vegetarian dishes.

Ardglass Golf Club (☎ 4484 1219; Castle Pl; bar meals £4-8, restaurant mains £10-15) The clubhouse bar and restaurant, housed in the medieval Ardglass Castle near the waterfront, are open to nonmembers.

For excellent, freshly landed fish and chips, head down to the **Quayside Restaurant** (☎ 4484 1444; the Harbour) beside the harbour.

Killough

The seaside village of Killough, 4km west of Ardglass, was planned by Castle Ward's Lord Bangor who constructed the dead-straight road between here and his estate, 12km to the north. The harbour has long since silted up and the village has a slightly run-down feel, but it is still picturesque, with several freshly painted cottages on tree-lined Palatine St and Palatine Square.

Across the bay from the village is the **Coney Island** made famous in Van Morrison's song of the same name. It's really a sandy peninsula, named for the coneys (an old word for rabbits) whose burrows once riddled the dunes.

There's a good walk south along the **Killough Coastal Path** to the 10th-century church ruins and nearby lighthouse of St John's Point, a return trip of about an hour.

SOUTH DOWN & THE MOURNE MOUNTAINS

Newcastle

pop 7200

The old-fashioned seaside resort of Newcastle (An Caisleán Nua) enjoys a superb setting on a 5km strand of golden sand at the foot of the Mourne Mountains. Nice surroundings, shame about the main street – on summer weekends it's a garish, traffic-choked strip of raucous amusement arcades and fast-food outlets. Nevertheless, the town is a good base for exploring the Mourne Mountains – on foot, by car or public transport – and in the quiet of winter it regains something of its Victorian composure.

ORIENTATION

As you exit the bus station, Main St stretches ahead towards the mountains, becoming Central Promenade (with the tourist office on the left) and then South Promenade. Turning left out of the bus station leads to a mini-roundabout; straight ahead is the beach, to the right is Downs Rd and the youth hostel, and to the left is the Slieve Donard Hotel.

INFORMATION

The **Tourist information Centre** (☎ 4372 2222; newcastle@nitic.net; 10-14 Central Promenade; 🕓 9.30am-7pm Mon-Sat & 1-7pm Sun Jul & Aug, 10am-5pm Mon-Sat & 2-6pm Sun Sep-Jun) sells local interest books and maps, and a range of traditional and contemporary crafts.

East Down Institute (☎ 4372 2451; newcastle@edifhe.ac.uk; Donard St; £1/30min; 🕓 9am-5pm Mon-Fri) has an Internet café in its single-storey college annex, a block north of the tourist office.

Mourne Heritage Trust (☎ 4372 4059; mht@mourne.co.uk; 87 Central Promenade; 🕓 9am-5pm Mon-Fri) sells books, maps and brochures on the Mourne region, and provides information on walking in the Mournes.

There's a **post office** (33-35 Central Promenade; 🕓 9.30am-12.30pm & 1.30-5.30pm Mon-Wed & Fri, 9.30am-12.30pm Thu & Sat) across the street from the tourist centre.

SIGHTS & ACTIVITIES

Newcastle's main attraction is the **beach**, which stretches 5km northeast to **Murlough National Nature Reserve** (admission free; 🕓 24 hr), where footpaths and boardwalks meander among the grassy dunes, with great views back towards the Mournes.

Back in town, **Tropicana** (☎ 4372 5034; Central Promenade; adult/child £2.50/2; 🕓 11am-7pm Mon & Wed-Fri, 11am-5.30pm Tue & Sat, 1-6pm Sun Jul & Aug) is a family entertainment centre with outdoor heated fun pools, giant water slides and paddling pools for toddlers.

Stretching north of town is the **Royal County Down Golf Course** (☎ 4372 3314; www.royalcountydown.org; green fees Mon-Fri £95, Sun £105 Apr-Oct, £47.50/52.50 Oct-Mar). The truly superb Championship Links is one of the world's top 10 golf courses, and is open to visitors on Monday, Tuesday, Thursday, Friday and Sunday.

SLEEPING

Tollymore Forest Park (☎ 4372 2428; 176 Tullybranigan Rd; tent or caravan £8-12; 🕓 year-round) The nearest camp site is 3km northwest of the town centre, amid the attractive scenery of

Tollymore Forest Park. You can hike there (along Bryansford Ave and Bryansford Rd) in 45 minutes.

Newcastle Youth Hostel (☎ 4372 2133; www.hini.org.uk; 30 Downs Rd; dm £9; 🕑 3 Jan–22 Dec) The hostel is only a few minutes' walk from the bus station, in a 19th-century villa close to the beach. It has 38 beds in four-, six- and seven-bed dorms, a kitchen, laundry and TV room.

Beach House (☎ 4372 2345; fax 4372 2817; 22 Downs Rd; s/d £35/60; P ⊠) Centrally located opposite the beach and just around the corner from the bus station, the Beach House is an elegant Victorian B&B with three rooms (two en suite).

Harbour House Inn (☎ 4372 3445; www.stoneboatrestaurant.com; 4 South Promenade; s/d £30/50; P ⊠) The Harbour House is a family-friendly guesthouse with four en-suite rooms, beside the harbour 2km south of the bus station. It also has a popular seafood restaurant.

Briers Country House (☎ 4372 4347; www.thebriers.co.uk; 39 Middle Tollymore Rd; s £25-40, d £40-55; P ⊠) The Briers is a wonderfully peaceful farmhouse B&B with seven en-suite rooms in a country setting with views of the Mournes, just 1.5km northwest of the town centre. Huge breakfasts – vegetarian if you like – and evening meals are available in its licensed restaurant.

Hastings Slieve Donard Hotel (☎ 4372 3681; www.hastingshotels.com; Downs Rd; s/d £120/170; P ⊠ 🏊) Established in 1897, the Slieve Donard is a grand, Victorian red-brick pile overlooking the beach, and claims Charlie Chaplin as a former guest. Add £20/35 to the room rate for a sea view, but ask for a discount in low season and you could get all that luxury for 60% of the full price.

EATING

Café Maud's (☎ 4372 6184; 106 Main St; mains £3-6; 🕑 9am-9.30pm) Maud's is a bright, modern café with picture windows allowing a view across the river to the Mournes. It serves good coffee, a range of tempting scones and sticky buns, and salads, crepes, pizza and pasta.

Seasalt (☎ 4372 5027; 51 Central Promenade; daytime mains £3-5; 2-/3-course dinner £14.95/19.50; 🕑 10am-6pm Tue-Sun, dinner at 7pm and 9pm Fri & Sat) This sunny bistro offers everything from organic soups to home-made beef-and-Guinness pie during the day. Dinner on Friday and Saturday is a bookings only, two sittings affair, with a superb Mediterranean/Asian fusion menu – easily the best place in town.

Percy French Bar & Restaurant (☎ 4372 3175; Downs Rd; mains £6-10; 🕑 food served 12.30-2.30pm & 5.30-9.30pm Mon-Fri, 12.30-9.30pm Sat & Sun) Themed after local composer William Percy French, this is an appealing, low-raftered barn of a place, with sea views in summer and a roaring log fire in winter. The menu includes steaks, salads, Mexican and Italian dishes, with the choice of bar meals or a sit-down restaurant.

Strand Restaurant & Bakery (☎ 4372 3472; 53-55 Central Promenade; mains £4-8; 🕑 8.30am-11pm Jun-Aug, 9am-6pm Sep-May) The Strand has been around since 1930, and dishes up great home-made ice cream and cakes, as well as serving breakfast, lunch and dinner in its traditional, seaside, chips-with-everything restaurant.

SHOPPING

Campers can stock up on provisions at the **Lidl Supermarket** (Railway St; 🕑 9am-7pm Mon-Wed & Fri, 9am-9pm Thu, 9am-6pm Sat, 1-6pm Sun) in the red-brick former train station beside the bus station.

Hill Trekker (☎ 4372 3842; 115 Central Promenade; 🕑 10am-5.30pm Tue-Sun), at the south end of town, sells hiking, climbing and camping equipment.

GETTING THERE & AROUND

The bus station is on Railway St. Ulsterbus Nos 18 and 20 run to Newcastle from Belfast (£5.30, 1¼ hours, 13 daily Monday to Friday, nine Saturday, six Sunday) via Dundrum. Most continue along the coast road to Annalong and Kilkeel (£2.60, 40 minutes).

Bus No 240 goes from Newry (£3.70, 40 minutes, four daily Monday to Saturday, two Sunday) to Newcastle (inland via Hilltown) and on to Downpatrick (£2.50, 40 minutes). You can also get to Newry along the coast road, changing buses at Kilkeel.

Wiki Wiki Wheels (☎ 4372 3973; 10b Donard St; 🕑 9am-6pm Mon-Sat & 2-6pm Sun) and **Ross Cycles** (☎ 4372 5525; Unit 9, Slieve Donard Shopping Centre, Railway St; 🕑 9am-5pm Mon-Sat), both near the bus station, rent out bikes for around £10/50 per day/week.

Around Newcastle

CLOUGH & AROUND

The village of Clough, 7km north of Newcastle on the A25 Downpatrick road, is unremarkable except for the ruins of **Clough Castle** (admission free; 24 hr), a good example of a 13th-century Norman motte and bailey with a small stone keep.

About 2km north of Clough on the A24 is the **Seaforde Tropical Butterfly House** (☎ 4481 1225; Newcastle Rd, Seaforde; adult/child £2.80/1.70 for butterfly house or gardens & maze, combined ticket £5/2.80; 10am-5pm Mon-Sat, 1-6pm Sun Easter-Sep). Set in a large walled garden, the butterfly house has hundreds of free-flying tropical butterflies and safely caged tropical insects and reptiles.

DUNDRUM

Second only to Carrickfergus as Northern Ireland's finest Norman fortress is **Dundrum Castle** (☎ 9181 1491; Dundrum; admission free; 10am-7pm Tue-Sat & 2-7pm Sun Apr-Sep, 10am-4pm Sat & 2-4pm Sun Oct-Mar). Founded in 1177 by John de Courcy of Carrickfergus, the original castle was made largely of timber. De Courcy's successor, Hugh de Lacy, added the massive circular keep in the first years of the 13th century, and the twin-towered gatehouse a few decades later. Occupied by the Maginnis family of Mourne from the 14th to the 17th centuries, it was finally captured by Cromwell who blew it up in 1652.

In mid-August, the streets of Dundrum fill with musicians, jugglers, fire-eaters and clowns for the annual **All Ireland Busking Competition** (☎ 4375 1412; www.dundrumfestival.com).

The **Buck's Head Inn** (☎ 4375 1868; 77-79 Main St; mains £7-9, 3-course dinner £24; noon-2.30pm, 5-6.45pm & 7-9.30pm Tue-Sun) is a cosy, traditional restaurant with a modern gourmet menu that features Dundrum oysters, Mourne lamb, Down beef and a selection of vegetarian dishes.

Dundrum is 4km south of Clough and 5km north of Newcastle. Bus No 17 from Newcastle to Downpatrick stops in Dundrum (£1.20, 12 minutes, 10 daily Monday-Friday, three Saturday, two Sunday) and Clough (17 minutes).

TOLLYMORE FOREST PARK

This scenic **forest park** (☎ 4372 2428; Bryansford; car/motorcycle £4/2; 10am-sunset), 3km west of Newcastle, has lengthy walks along the Shimna River and across the northern slopes of the Mournes. The **visitor centre** (noon-5pm daily Jun-Aug, noon-5pm Sat & Sun Sep-May), in 18th-century Clanbrassil Barn (it looks more like a church), has information on the flora, fauna and history of the park. Note: mountain-biking is not allowed in the park.

If the weather is wet, you can still go rock-climbing at **hot rock** (☎ 4372 5354; www.hotrockwall.com; adult/child £3.50/2; 10am-10pm Mon-Sat & 10am-6pm Sun), the indoor climbing wall at Tollymore Mountain Centre. The entrance is on the B180, 2km west of the Tollymore Forest Park exit gate.

CASTLEWELLAN FOREST PARK

A less rugged outdoor experience is offered by **Castlewellan Forest Park** (☎ 4377 8664; Main St, Castlewellan; car/motorcycle £4/2; 10am-dusk), with gentle walks around the castle grounds and trout fishing in its lovely lake (a daily permit costs £5).

Outside the park is **Mount Pleasant Horse Trekking Centre** (☎ 4377 8651; www.mountpleasantcentre.com; Bannonstown Rd, Castlewellan; adult/child £10/9 per hr), which caters for both experienced riders and beginners, and offers various guided treks into the park. Short rides, beach rides and pony trekking can also be arranged.

The Mourne Mountains

The granite peaks of the Mourne Mountains dominate the view as you head south from Belfast or Downpatrick towards Newcastle. This is one of the most beautiful corners of Northern Ireland, a distinctive landscape of yellow gorse and whitewashed cottages, grey granite and purple heather, with a neat patchwork of dry-stone walls on the lower slopes where farmers have cleared the fields of granite boulders.

The hills were made famous in a popular song penned by Irish songwriter William Percy French in 1896, whose chorus, 'Where the Mountains of Mourne sweep down to the sea', captures perfectly their scenic juxtaposition of sea, sky and hillside.

The Mournes offer the best hill walking and rock-climbing in the North. Specialist guidebooks include *The Mournes: Walks* by Paddy Dillon and *A Rock-Climbing Guide to the Mourne Mountains* by Robert

Bankhead. You'll also need an Ordnance Survey map, either the 1:50,000 Discoverer Series (Sheet No 29: *The Mournes*), or the 1:25,000 Outdoor Pursuits Series (*Mourne Country*).

HISTORY

The crescent of low-lying land on the south side of the mountains is known as the Kingdom of Mourne. Cut off for centuries by its difficult approaches (the main overland route passed north of the hills), it developed a distinctive landscape and culture. Neither St Patrick nor the Normans ventured here – their nearest strongholds were at Greencastle and Dundrum – and until the coast road was built in the early 1800s the only access was on foot or by sea.

Apart from farming and fishing, the region's main industry was the quarrying of Mourne granite. The quarried stone was carried down from the hills on special carts to harbours at Newcastle, Annalong and Kilkeel where fleets of 'stone boats' shipped it out; kerbstones of Mourne granite can be found in Belfast, Liverpool, London, Manchester and Birmingham.

Smuggling provided another source of income in the 18th century. Boats carrying French spirits would land at night and packhorses would carry the casks through the hills to the inland road, avoiding the excise men at Newcastle. The Brandy Pad, a former smugglers' path from Bloody Bridge to Tollymore, is today a popular walking route (see the boxed text below).

SIGHTS

At the heart of the Mournes is the beautiful **Silent Valley Reservoir** (☎ 9074 6581; Silent Valley; car/motorcycle £3/1.50; adult/child pedestrian £1.50/0.50; 🕒 10am-6.30pm May-Sep, 10am-4pm Oct-Apr), where the Kilkeel River has been dammed to provide water for Belfast. There are scenic, waymarked walks around the grounds, a **coffee shop** (🕒 11am-6.30pm daily Jun-Aug; 11am-6.30pm Sat & Sun Apr, May & Sep) and an information centre. From the car park a shuttle bus (adult/child return £1.50/0.90) will take you another 4km up the valley to the Crom Dam. It runs daily in July and August, weekends only in May, June and September.

The dry-stone **Mourne Wall** was built between 1904 and 1922 to provide work during a period of high unemployment, and to enclose the catchment area of the Silent Valley and the Annalong River, whose

CLIMBING SLIEVE DONARD

The rounded form of Slieve Donard (853m), the highest hill in Northern Ireland, looms above Newcastle like a slumbering giant. You can hike to the summit from various starting points in and around Newcastle, but remember – it's a stiff climb, and you shouldn't attempt it without proper walking boots, waterproofs and a map and compass.

On a good day the view from the top extends to the hills of Donegal, the Wicklow Mountains, the coast of Scotland, the Isle of Man and even the hills of Snowdonia in Wales. Two cairns near the summit were long believed to have been cells of St Donard, who retreated here to pray in early Christian times.

1. From Newcastle (9km, three hours)

This is the shortest but least interesting route. Begin at Donard Park car park, at the edge of town 1km south of the bus station. At the far end of the car park, turn right through the gate and head into the woods, with the river on your left. A gravel path leads up the Glen River valley to the saddle between Donard and Slieve Commedagh. From here, turn left and follow the Mourne Wall to the summit. Return by the same route.

2. From Bloody Bridge (10km, 3½ hours)

Start from the car park at Bloody Bridge on the A2 coast road 5km south of Newcastle (any bus to Kilkeel will drop you there). From here, an old smugglers' path called the Brandy Pad leads up the valley of the Bloody Bridge River past old granite workings to the saddle south of Slieve Donard. Turn right and follow the Mourne Wall to the summit; cross the wall first, as the best views are to your left. Return by the same route, or descend the Glen River (Route 1) to Newcastle.

waters are diverted to the reservoir via a 3.6km-long tunnel beneath Slieve Binnian (habitation and livestock are banned within the catchment). The spectacular wall, 2m high, a metre thick and over 35km long, marches across the summits of 15 of the surrounding peaks, including the highest, Slieve Donard (853m).

SLEEPING

Cnocnafeola Centre (☎ 4176 5859; www.cnocnafeolacentre.com; Bog Rd, Atticall; dm £10-14; Feb–22 Dec; P) This new, purpose-built hostel is 6km north of Kilkeel, off the B27 Hilltown road, and 3km west of the entrance to Silent Valley. It has a kitchen, laundry and restaurant.

Meelmore Lodge (☎ 4372 6657; www.meelmorelodge.co.uk; 52 Trassey Rd, Bryansford; camping per person £2; P) Set on the northern slopes of the Mournes, 5km west of Bryansford village, Meelmore has a basic camp site with hot showers and a coffee shop.

GETTING THERE & AWAY

In July and August only, the Ulsterbus No 34B Mourne Rambler service runs a circular route from Newcastle calling at a dozen stops around the Mournes, including Donard Park, Bloody Bridge (10 minutes), Silent Valley (25 minutes) and Tollymore Forest Park (50 minutes). It departs hourly from 10am to noon and 2pm to 5pm every day; a £4 all-day ticket allows you to get on and off as many times as you like.

Mournes Coast Road

The scenic drive south along the A2 coast road from Newcastle to Newry is the most memorable journey in Down. Annalong, Kilkeel and Rostrevor offer convenient stopping points from which you can detour into the mountains.

As in many parts of the North, someone has fixed signs bearing religious texts to many of the roadside telephone poles. Whoever it was has a sense of humour, though – one reading 'Prepare to meet thy God' appears just before a tricky S-bend.

See p585 and p590 for details of buses to Kilkeel.

ANNALONG

The harbour at the fishing village of Annalong (Áth na Long) desperately wants to be picturesque, with an early 19th-century **Corn Mill** (☎ 4376 8736; Marine Park; adult/child £1.85/0.95; 2-6pm Wed-Mon Apr-Oct) overlooking the river mouth on one side. The effect is spoiled a bit by graffiti and ugly buildings on the other side.

The attractive **Harbour Inn** (☎ 4376 8678; 6 Harbour Dr; bar meals £5-8; food served 12.30-2.30pm & 5-8pm Sun-Fri, 12.30-9pm Sat) has an upstairs dining room with a great view across the harbour to the Mournes.

KILKEEL

Kilkeel (Cill Chaoil, meaning 'church of the narrow place') takes its name from the 14th-century **Church of St Colman**, whose ruins stand in the graveyard across the street from the tourist office. The town has a busy commercial fishing harbour and a quayside fish market supplied by Northern Ireland's largest fishing fleet. The story of the fishing industry is told at the **Nautilus Centre** (☎ 4176 5555; Rooney Rd; admission free; 10am-9pm Mon-Sat, noon-6pm Sun Apr-Sep, 10am-6pm Mon-Sat Oct-Mar).

Kilkeel Tourist Office (☎ 4176 2525; kdakilkeel@hotmail.com; 28 Bridge St; 9am-1pm & 2-5.30pm Mon-Sat) is on the main road through town.

For a bite to eat, try the **Upper Deck Café** at the Nautilus Centre, or the deliciously fresh fish and chips at nearby **Neptune's Larder**.

GREENCASTLE

The square Norman keep of **Greencastle** (☎ 9181 1491; Cranfield Point; admission free; 2-6pm Tue & Fri-Sun, 10am-1pm Wed & Thu Jul & Aug) once guarded the entrance to Carlingford Lough. Built in 1261 as a companion to Carlingford Castle on the opposite side of the lough in County Louth, it later served as a royal garrison until it was destroyed by Cromwell's forces in 1652.

Greencastle is at the end of a minor road 6km southwest of Kilkeel.

ROSTREVOR

Rostrevor (Caislean Ruairi) is a pretty Victorian seaside resort famed for its lively pubs. Each year in late July folk musicians converge on the village for the **Fiddler's Green International Festival** (☎ 4173 9819; www.fiddlersgreenfestival.com).

To the east is **Kilbroney Forest Park** (☎ 4173 8134; Shore Rd; admission free; 9am-10pm Jun-Aug, 9am-5pm Sep-May). From the car park at the top of the forest drive, a 10-minute hike leads up to the **Cloughmore Stone**, a 30-tonne granite boulder inscribed with Victorian

RICHARD CUMMINS

Machinery, **Ulster Museum** (p546), Belfast

OLIVER STREWE

Kitchen Bar (p560), Belfast

Circle of Friendship **mural** (p550), Belfast

MARTIN MOOS

IAN CONNELL

Waterfront, **Portaferry** (p575)

Slieve Donard (p587), Mourne Mountains

GARETH MCCORMACK

Mount Stewart House and gardens (p577), near Greyabbey

RICHARD CUMMINS

graffiti, and a superb view over the lough to Carlingford Mountain.

There's a **camp site** (tent/campervan £6.20/11.25; Apr-Oct) in Kilbroney Forest Park. For B&B try the central **An Tobar** (4173 8712; 2 Cherry Hill; s/d £23/40; P), a modern house with grand views just northeast of the church.

The town is noted for its many pubs, most of which have regular live music. The best ones to eat in are the **Kilbroney** (4173 8390; 31 Church St) and the **Celtic Fjord** (4173 8005; 8 Mary St).

Warrenpoint

pop 13,500

Warrenpoint (An Pointe) is a Victorian resort at the head of Carlingford Lough, its seaside appeal somewhat diminished by the large industrial harbour at the west end of town. Its broad streets, main square and recently renovated prom are pleasant enough, though, and it has better sleeping and eating options than either Newry or Rostrevor.

The **Warrenpoint Tourist Information Centre** (4175 2256; Church St; 9am-5pm Jun-Aug, 9am-5pm Mon-Fri Oct-May) is in the town hall.

About 2km northwest of the town centre is **Narrow Water Castle** (9181 1491; admission free; 10am-1pm Tue, Fri & Sat, 2-6pm Wed & Thu Jul & Aug), a fine Elizabethan tower house built in 1568 to command the entrance to the Newry River.

Weather permitting, a passenger **ferry** (4177 2001) – OK, a small motor boat – crosses the lough to Omeath in County Louth every half-hour between 1pm and 6pm daily, June to September. It costs £2.50/1.50 per adult/child and takes 10 minutes.

SLEEPING & EATING

Mariann's Place (4175 2085; cooper.stuart@btconnect.com; 18 Upper Dromore Rd; s/d £22.50/35; P ⊠) Mariann's is a large modern B&B with views over the lough, about 500m north of The Square on the B7 Mayobridge road.

Boathouse Inn (41753743; www.boathouseinn.com; 3 Marine Parade; s/d £40/65; P ⊠) Overlooking Warrenpoint's tiny marina, the Boathouse has 12 luxury en-suite rooms. It also offers two excellent dining options: the **Boathouse Restaurant** (mains £8-13; 7-10pm), a chilled out, candle-lit bistro with a modern fusion menu, and the **Vecchia Roma** (mains £6-8; noon-2.30pm & 6-11pm), a traditional, checked-tablecloth-and-chianti-bottle Italian restaurant.

The **Whistledown & Finns** (4175 4174; www.whistledown.co.uk; 6 Seaview; s/d £30/55) This is another waterfront place that combines smart accommodation (four en-suite rooms, all with sea views) with a stylish bar and **restaurant** (mains £6-10; noon-5pm & 7-10pm Mon-Sat, 12.30-3.30pm Sun).

Café Siam (4175 3313; 1 Dock St, The Square; mains £7.50-10; 5-11pm Wed-Mon) Turn a blind eye to the slightly tacky décor and concentrate on the deliciously authentic Thai cuisine in this welcome addition to Warrenpoint's restaurant scene.

For snacks, there's the long-established **Genoa Cafe** (5 The Square), a fish and chip shop with old-style sit-in booths as well as a takeaway counter, and **Jenny Black's** (10 Church St), a trendy café-cum-art gallery.

For pub grub, try **Bennett's** (4175 2314; 21 Church St) or **Jack Ryan's** (18 The Square).

Newry

pop 22,975

Newry has long been a frontier town, guarding the land route from Dublin to Ulster through the 'Gap of the North', the pass between Slieve Gullion and the Carlingford hills, still followed by the main Dublin–Belfast road and railway. Its name derives from a yew tree (An tIúr) supposedly planted here by St Patrick.

The opening of the Newry Canal in 1742 – the first summit-level canal in the British Isles – linking the town with the River Bann at Portadown, made Newry into a busy trading port, exporting coal from Coalisland on Lough Neagh as well as linen and butter from the surrounding area.

Newry today is a major shopping centre, with a market on Thursday and Saturday, and makes a good base for exploring the Mourne Mountains, South Armagh and the Cooley Peninsula in County Louth.

INFORMATION

The **Newry Tourist Information Centre** (3026 8877; Town Hall; 9am-5pm Mon-Fri, to 8pm Jul & Aug, 10am-4pm Sat Jun-Sep) is off Kildare St and **Newry Library** (3026 4683; 79 Hill St; 9.30am-5pm Wed & Sat, 9.30am-6pm Mon & Fri, 9.30am-8pm Tue & Thu) has Internet access for £1 per 30 minutes.

SIGHTS

So fierce was the rivalry between Counties Down and Armagh in the 19th century, that when the new red-brick **town hall** was built in 1893 it was erected right on the border – on a three-arched bridge across the Newry River. The cannon outside was captured during the Crimean War (1853–56) and given to the town in memory of local volunteers who fought in the war.

The small **Newry & Mourne Museum** (☎ 3026 6232; Bank Pde; admission free; 🕑 10.30am-1pm & 2-4.30pm Mon-Fri) in the Arts Centre next to the town hall has an interesting display on the rediscovery of Bagenal's Castle.

Bagenal's Castle is the town's oldest surviving building, a 16th-century tower house built for Nicholas Bagenal, grand marshal of the English army in Ireland. Recently rediscovered, having been incorporated into more recent buildings, the castle is currently being restored and will house the Newry and Mourne Museum when the castle opens in late 2004 or 2005.

The **Newry Canal** runs parallel to the river through the town centre, and is a focus for the city's redevelopment. A cycle path runs 30km north to Portadown, following the route of the canal. **Newry Ship Canal** runs 6km south towards Carlingford Lough, where the Victoria Lock has been restored to working order as part of a long-term project to reopen the whole canal to leisure traffic. Designed by Sir John Rennie, the civil engineer who designed Waterloo, Southwark and London Bridges in London, the ship canal allowed large, sea-going vessels to reach Albert Basin in the centre of Newry.

SLEEPING & EATING

Marymount (☎ 3026 1099; kevin.ohare@talk21.com; Windsor Ave; s/d £23/36) Marymount is a modern bungalow in a quiet location up a hill off the A1 Belfast road, only a 10-minute walk from the town centre. One of the three rooms is en suite (single/double £25/40).

Belmont Hall (☎ 3026 2163; www.belmont-hall.co.uk; 18 Downshire Rd; s £30-42.50, d £60-70; P ⊠) Revel in Regency elegance at this lovingly restored Georgian villa, with 12 en-suite rooms, just 700m north of the town centre.

Canal Court Hotel (☎ 3025 1234; www.canalcourthotel.com; Merchants Quay; s/d £65/100; P ⊠ ♿) You can't miss this huge, yellow building overlooking the canal opposite the bus station. It's a pleasant, modern hotel with a deliberately old-fashioned feel, veering dangerously close to chintzy.

Café Krem (☎ 3026 6233; 14 Hill St; snacks £1.50-3; 🕑 8.30am-6pm Mon-Sat) In the middle of Newry's main shopping street, the Krem has good coffee, wicked hot chocolate, tasty panini and a couple of big, soft sofas to sink into.

Snaubs Coffee Shop (☎ 3026 5381; 15 Monaghan St; snacks £3.50-6; 🕑 9am-6pm Mon-Sat) Set in a women's clothing shop, Snaubs offers a range of vegetarian options as well as freshly baked bread and cakes.

Brass Monkey (☎ 3026 3176; 1-4 Sandy St; mains £5.50-7; 🕑 food served 12.30-2.30pm & 5-8pm) Newry's most popular pub, with Victorian brass, brick and timber décor, serves good bar meals ranging from lasagne and burgers to seafood and steaks.

GETTING THERE & AWAY

Newry Bus Centre is on the Mall, opposite the conspicuous Canal Court Hotel. Bus Nos 38, 45 and 238 run regularly to Newry from Belfast's Europa Bus Centre bus station (£5.90, 1¾ hours, hourly). Bus No 44 runs from Newry to Armagh (£3.40, 1¼ hours, twice daily Monday to Saturday), and No 295 from Newry to Enniskillen (£7.50, 2¾ hours, twice daily Monday to Saturday, July and August only) via Armagh and Monaghan. Bus No 39 departs at least hourly for Warrenpoint (15 minutes) and Rostrevor (25 minutes), with 10 a day continuing to Kilkeel (£2.80, one hour).

The train station is 2.5km northwest of the centre, on the A25; bus No 341 goes there hourly from the bus station. Newry is a stop on the train service between Dublin (£11.20, 1¼ hours, eight daily) and Belfast (£6.30, 50 minutes, seven daily).

COUNTY ARMAGH

SOUTH ARMAGH

Rural and staunchly republican, South Armagh is known to its inhabitants as 'God's Country'. But to the British soldiers stationed there from the 1970s on it had another, more sinister nickname – 'Bandit Country'. Although life now has regained some semblance of normality, here more than anywhere else in Northern Ireland you will be aware of the security forces' presence – the huge barracks at Bessbrook Mill and Crossmaglen, the hilltop watchtowers, the occasional foot patrol on village streets and the constant clatter of helicopters. And the insignia of republican resistance are everywhere – Irish tricolours, IRA signs nailed to telephone poles, and the notorious 'sniper at work' signs (mock road signs showing the silhouette of a masked gunman).

That said, like anywhere else in the North, there's no reason to stay away from what is a lovely part of Ireland.

Bessbrook

pop 3150

Bessbrook (An Sruthán) was founded in the mid-19th century by Quaker linen manufacturer John Grubb Richardson as a 'model village' to house the workers at his flax mill. Rows of pretty terraced houses made from local granite line the two main squares, Charlemont and College, each with a green in the middle, and are complemented by a town hall, school, bathhouse and dispensary. It is said that Bessbrook was the inspiration for Bournville (near Birmingham in England), the model village built by the Cadbury family for their chocolate factory. Sadly the village atmosphere is marred by the massively fortified Bessbrook Mill army base. The helipad on top of the former mill building is reputedly the busiest in Europe.

Just south of Bessbrook is **Derrymore House** (☎ 3083 8361; Bessbrook; adult/child £2.30/1.10; 🕑 house 2-5.30pm Thu-Sat May-Aug, ground 10am-8pm May-Sep, 10am-4pm Oct-Apr), an elegant thatched cottage built in 1776 for Isaac Corry, the Irish MP for Newry for 30 years. The Act of Union was drafted in the drawing room of the house in 1800. The surrounding parkland was laid out by John Sutherland (1745–1826), one of the most celebrated disciples of Capability Brown.

Bessbrook is 5km northwest of Newry. Bus No 41 runs from Newry to Bessbrook (15 minutes, hourly Monday to Saturday), while bus Nos 42 and 44 pass the entrance to Derrymore House on the A25 Camlough road.

Ring of Gullion

The Ring of Gullion is a magical region, steeped in Celtic legend, centred on Slieve Gullion (Sliabh gCuilinn; 575m) where the Celtic warrior Cúchulainn took his name after killing the dog *(cú)* belonging to the smith Culainn. The 'ring' is a necklace of rugged hills strung between Newry and Forkhill, 15km to the southwest, encircling the central whaleback ridge of Slieve Gullion. The unusual concentric formation is a geological structure known as a ring-dyke.

KILLEVY CHURCHES

Surrounded by beech trees, these ruined, conjoined **churches** (admission free; 🕑 24 hr) were built on the site of a 5th-century nunnery founded by St Moninna. The eastern church dates from the 15th century, and shares a gable wall with the 12th-century western one. The west door, with a massive lintel and granite jambs, may be 200 years older still. At the side of the churchyard a footpath leads uphill to a white cross, marking St Moninna's holy well.

The churches are 6km south of Camlough, on a minor road to Meigh. Look out for a crossroads with a sign pointing right to the churches and left to Bernish Rock Viewpoint.

SLIEVE GULLION FOREST PARK

A 13km scenic drive through this **forest park** (admission free; 🕑 10am-dusk) provides picturesque views over the surrounding hills. You can hike to the summit of Slieve Gullion, the highest point in County Armagh, topped by two early-Bronze Age cairns and a tiny lake, from the parking and picnic area at the top of the drive (1.5km round trip). The park entrance is 10km southwest of Newry on the B113 road to Forkhill.

MULLAGHBANE & FORKHILL

In the village of Mullaghbane (Mullach Bán), just west of Slieve Gullion, is **Thí Chulainn** (☎ 3088 8828; www.tichulainn.ie; Mullaghbane; admission free; 🕑 10am-4pm Mon-Fri & 10am-1pm Sat), a cultural activities centre that promotes the Irish language, local folklore, traditional music and storytelling.

The pubs in nearby **Forkhill** hold traditional music sessions on Tuesday nights and alternate Saturdays, and a **folk music festival** in October.

Crossmaglen

pop 1600

Crossmaglen (Crois Mhic Lionnáin) is a strongly republican village just 4km inside the border, ranged around one of Ireland's biggest market squares. At the height of the Troubles the barracks at 'Cross' was the most feared posting in the British Army. For today's visitors, however, it's a friendly place with a reputation for Gaelic football, horse breeding, and lively pubs known for their excellent music sessions.

You can get tourist information at **South Armagh Tourism Initiative** (☎ 3086 8900; www.south-armagh.com; 25-26 The Square; 9am-5pm Mon-Fri).

Creggans Visitor Centre (admission free; 3-5.30pm Sun Jun-Sep), in Creggans Churchyard 2km east of Crossmaglen, commemorates the three 18th-century Gaelic poets buried there.

Murtagh's Bar (☎ 3086 1378; aidanmurtagh@hotmail.com; 13 North St; s £20-25, d £40-50; ⊠) offers good craic, traditional music, bar meals, and B&B.

Ma Kearney's (☎ 3086 8944; 20 Newry St) serves bar meals all day and restaurant food for lunch and dinner Monday to Saturday. There's live music on Friday, Saturday and Sunday nights.

Bus No 42 runs from Newry to Crossmaglen (£2.80, 50 minutes, six daily Monday to Friday, four Saturday) via Camlough and Mullaghbane.

ARMAGH CITY

pop 14,600

Armagh (Ard Macha) is an attractive little cathedral city. It has been an important religious centre since the 5th century, and is today the ecclesiastical capital of Ireland, the seat of both the Anglican and Roman Catholic archbishops of Armagh and primates of all Ireland. In addition to its cathedrals and museums, Armagh offers pleasant strolling amid its Georgian streets and parks.

History

When St Patrick began his mission to spread Christianity throughout Ireland, he chose a site close to Emain Macha (Navan Fort), the nerve centre of pagan Ulster, for his power base. In 445 he built Ireland's first stone church on a hill nearby (now home to the Church of Ireland cathedral), and later decreed that Armagh should have pre-eminence over all the churches in Ireland.

By the 8th century Armagh was one of Europe's best-known centres of religion, learning and craftwork. The city was divided into three districts (called *'trians'*), centred around English, Scotch and Irish Sts. Armagh's fame was its undoing, however, as the Vikings plundered the city 10 times between 831 and 1013.

The city gained a new prosperity from the linen trade in the 18th century, a period whose legacy includes a Royal School, an astronomical observatory, a renowned public library and a fine crop of Georgian architecture.

Armagh is associated with some prominent historical figures. James Ussher (1580–1655), Archbishop of Armagh, was an avid scholar who is best known for pinning down the day of the Creation to Sunday, 23 October 4004 BC by adding up the generations quoted in the Bible, a date which was accepted as fact until the late 19th century. His extensive library became the nucleus of the great library at Trinity College, Dublin. Jonathan Swift (1667–1745), Dean of St Patrick's Cathedral, Dublin, and author of *Gulliver's Travels*, was a frequent visitor to Armagh, while the architect Francis Johnston (1760–1829), responsible for many of Dublin's finest Georgian streetscapes, was born in Armagh.

Information

The **Armagh Tourist Information Centre** (☎ 3752 1800; www.visit-armagh.com; 40 English St; 9am-5pm Mon-Sat, 1-5.30pm Sun Jul & Aug, 9am-5pm Mon-Sat, 2-5pm Sun Sep-Jun) is part of the St Patrick's Trian complex. **Eason** (☎ 3751 8280; 60 Scotch St; 9am-5.30pm Mon-Sat) sells books and maps.

St Patrick's Trian

The old Presbyterian church behind the tourist office has been turned into a heritage centre and visitor complex known as **St Patrick's Trian** (☎ 3752 1801; 40 English St; adult/child £4/2.25; 10am-5pm Mon-Sat & 2-5pm Sun). There are three exhibitions. The Armagh Story explores the history of Armagh from pagan prehistory to the present day, while Patrick's Testament takes an interactive look at the ancient *Book of Armagh*. For the kids there's the Land of Lilliput where Gulliver's adventures in Lilliput are recounted by a gigantic model of Jonathan Swift's famous creation.

St Patrick's Church of Ireland Cathedral

The city's **Anglican cathedral** (☎ 3752 3142; Cathedral Close; admission by donation; 10am-5pm Apr-Oct, 10am-4pm Nov-Mar; guided tours 11.30am &

2.30pm Mon-Sat Jun-Aug) occupies the site of St Patrick's original stone church. The present cathedral's ground plan is 13th century but the building itself is a Gothic restoration dating from 1834 to 1840. A stone slab on the exterior wall of the north transept marks the burial place of Brian Ború, the High King of Ireland who died near Dublin during the last great battle against the Vikings in 1014.

Within the church are the remains of an 11th-century **Celtic Cross** that once stood nearby, and the **Tandragee Idol**, a curious granite figure dating back to the Iron Age. In the south aisle is a **memorial to Archbishop Richard Robinson** (1709–94),

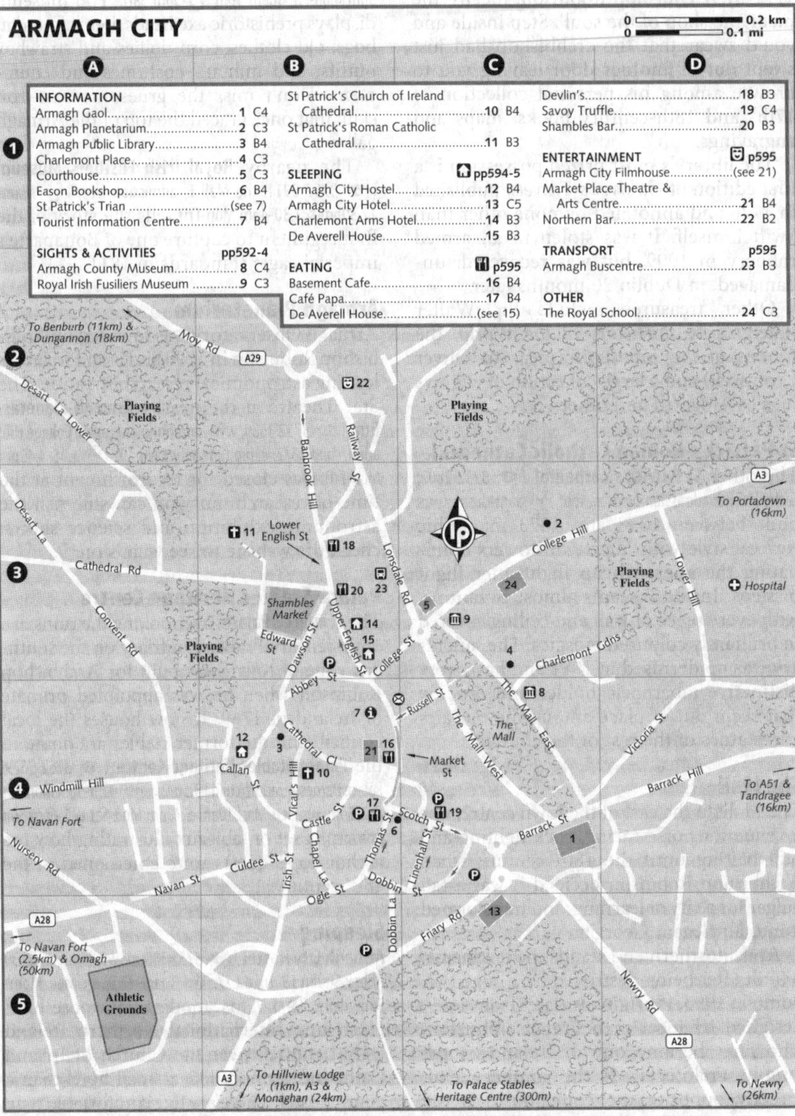

who founded Armagh's observatory and public library.

Armagh Public Library

The Greek inscription above the main entrance to **Armagh Public Library** (☎ 3752 3142; www.armaghlibrary.org; 43 Abbey St; admission free; ⌚ 10am-1pm & 2-4pm Mon-Fri), founded in 1771 by Archbishop Robinson, means 'the medicine shop of the soul'. Step inside and you'd swear that the archbishop had just swept out of another door leaving you to browse among his personal collection of 17th- and 18th-century books, maps and engravings.

The library's most prized possession is a first edition of *Gulliver's Travels*, published in 1726 and annotated by none other than Swift himself. It was stolen in an armed robbery in 1999, but was recovered, undamaged, in Dublin 20 months later.

Other treasures include Sir Walter Raleigh's 1614 *History of the World*, the *Claims of the Innocents* (pleas to Oliver Cromwell) and a large collection of engravings by Hogarth and others.

St Patrick's Roman Catholic Cathedral

The other **St Patrick's Cathedral** (☎ 3752 2802; Cathedral Rd; admission by donation; ⌚ 8am-dusk) was built between 1838 and 1873 in Gothic Revival style with huge twin towers dominating the approach up flight after flight of steps. Inside it seems almost Byzantine, with every piece of wall and ceiling covered in brilliantly coloured mosaics. The sanctuary was modernised in 1981 and has a very distinctive tabernacle holder and crucifix that seem out of place among the mosaics and statues of the rest of the church.

The Mall

The Mall, to the east of the town centre, was a venue for horse racing, cock fighting and bull baiting until the 18th century when Archbishop Robinson decided it was a tad vulgar for a city of learning, and transformed it into an elegant Georgian park.

At its northern end stands the **courthouse**, rebuilt after being destroyed by a huge IRA bomb in 1993. It originally dates from 1809, designed by local man Francis Johnston, who later became one of Ireland's most famous architects. At the southern end, directly opposite the courthouse, is the forbidding **Armagh Gaol**. Built in 1780 to the design of Thomas Cooley, it remained in use until 1988.

The east side of the park is lined with handsome Georgian terraces. **Charlemont Place** is another creation of Francis Johnston, as is the portico fronting **Armagh County Museum** (☎ 3752 3070; the Mall East; admission free; ⌚ 10am-5pm Mon-Fri, 10am-1pm & 2-5pm Sat). The museum displays prehistoric axe heads, items found in bogs, old clothes, corn dollies and strawboy outfits, and military costumes and equipment. Don't miss the gruesome cast-iron skull that once graced the top of the Armagh gallows.

The nearby **Royal Irish Fusiliers Museum** (☎ 3752 2911; the Mall E; admission free; ⌚ 10am-12.30pm & 1.30-4pm Mon-Fri) tells the story of the first regiment to capture one of Bonaparte's imperial eagle standards in 1811.

Armagh Planetarium

Armagh Observatory was founded by Archbishop Robinson in 1790 and is still Ireland's leading astronomical research institute. The Star Theatre at the nearby **Armagh Planetarium** (☎ 3752 3689; www.armaghplanet.com; College Hill; adult/child £3/2, exhibition only £1/0.50; ⌚ 1.45-4.45pm Mon-Fri) was closed for refurbishment at the time of research, but you can still visit the astronomy exhibition and science shows; check the website to see what's on.

Palace Stables Heritage Centre

The **Primate's Palace**, overlooking the ruins of a 13th-century Franciscan friary on the southern edge of town, was built for Archbishop Robinson when he was appointed primate of Ireland in 1769. It now houses the local council, and the former stables are home to the **Palace Stables Heritage Centre** (☎ 3752 9629; Palace Demesne; adult/child £3.50/2; ⌚ 10am-5pm Mon-Sat & 2-5pm Sun Sep-Mar, 10am-5.30pm Mon-Sat & 1-6pm Sun Apr-Aug), a set of tableaux illustrating how the archbishop's guests were entertained in the 18th century.

Sleeping

Armagh City Hostel (☎ 3751 1800; www.hini.org.uk; 39 Abbey St; dm £9-10, d £27; ⌚ 3 Jan–22 Dec, closed 11am-5pm daily; P) This modern, purpose-built Hostelling International Northern Ireland (HINI) hostel, near the Church of Ireland Cathedral, is more like a small hotel than a youth hostel. There are five comfortable twin rooms complete with en-suite bathroom, TV, and tea and coffee facilities, as well as 12 small dorms, a well-equipped kitchen, laundry, lounge and reading room.

De Averell House (☎ 3751 1213; www.deaverellhouse.com; 47 Upper English St; s/d £35/59; P ☒) The De Averell is a converted Georgian town house with four spacious en-suite rooms and a self-catering apartment, and is Armagh's best choice for comfort, friendliness and convenience.

Hillview Lodge (☎ 3752 2000; www.hillviewlodge.com; 33 Newtownhamilton Rd; s/d £30/50; P ☒) Just 1.5km south of Armagh, Hillview is a modern, family-run guesthouse with a self-contained accommodation block containing six appealing, en-suite rooms.

Charlemont Arms Hotel (☎ 3752 2028; www.charlemontarmshotel.com; 57-65 English St; s/d £45/70; P ☒ 💻) The hotel has been recently renovated, all rooms are en suite and there's a restaurant and wine bar.

Armagh City Hotel (☎ 3751 8888; www.mooneyhotelgroup.com; Friary Rd; s/d £69/80; P ☒ 🏊) Armagh's newest, shiniest hotel is aimed squarely at business travellers and the luxury end of the market, offering identikit international-hotel décor and free use of the fitness club, sauna and pool.

Eating

Armagh is not exactly a gourmet's paradise – there are only a few good places to eat, and even those are rarely open on weekday evenings. It's best to book to be sure of a table at the weekend.

Savoy Truffle (☎ 3751 8379; 37 Scotch St; mains £6-11; 🕑 9am-5.30pm Mon-Wed, 9am-9pm Thu-Sat) This modern bistro is a little lacking in atmosphere – it feels a bit like a stylish school canteen – but the home-made soups and burgers are tasty and filling.

Café Papa (☎ 3751 1205; 15 Thomas St; mains £4-8; 🕑 9am-5pm Mon-Thu, 9am-5pm & 6.30-9.30pm Fri & Sat) This café serves decent coffee and gourmet sandwiches, and does bistro dinners on Friday and Saturday evenings. You can bring your own wine.

Basement Cafe (☎ 3752 4311; Market Place; mains £3.50-5.50; 🕑 9am-5pm Mon-Sat) The trendy Basement, under the Market Place Art Centre, does good steak sandwiches and light meals.

De Averell House (☎ 3751 1213; 47 Upper English St; 🕑 noon-2.30pm daily, 6-9.30pm Thu-Sat) The basement restaurant at the De Averell is one of Armagh's best, and most popular, places to eat. Its Mediterranean-influenced menu includes daily seafood specials, and caters well for vegetarians.

The pubs along English St – notably the **Shambles Bar** (☎ 3752 4107; 9 Lower English St) and **Devlin's** (☎ 3752 3865; 23 Lower English St) – serve reasonable bar meals.

Entertainment

The **Market Place Theatre & Arts Centre** (☎ 3752 1820; www.marketplacearmagh.com; Market St) is Armagh's main cultural venue, with a 400-seat theatre, exhibition galleries, a restaurant, bar and café. Right next door is the **Armagh City Filmhouse** (☎ 3751 1033; Market St).

The **Shambles Bar** (☎ 3752 4107; 9 Lower English St) and **Devlin's** (☎ 3752 3865; 23 Lower English St) are good places to catch live bands on a Saturday night. Locals recommend the **Northern Bar** (☎ 3752 7315; 100 Railway St), better known as Hughes' Bar, which has DJs on Friday, live bands on Saturday, and traditional music sessions on Tuesday.

Spectator Sports

You may be lucky enough to catch a game of **road bowls**, a traditional game now only played in Armagh and Cork. Contestants hurl small metal bowls weighing 28oz (0.75kg) along quiet country lanes to see who can make it to the finishing line with the least number of throws. Games usually take place on Sunday afternoon, with championships held in May. Ask at the Tourist Information Centre.

Getting There & Away

Armagh Bus Centre is on Lonsdale Rd. Ulsterbus No 251 runs from Belfast (£5.90, 1¼ hours; hourly Monday to Friday, six daily Saturday, one Sunday) to Armagh. Bus No 44 runs from Armagh to Newry (£3.40, 1¼ hours, twice daily Monday to Saturday), and No 295 runs to Enniskillen (£5.40, two hours, twice daily Monday to Saturday, July and August only) via Monaghan.

There are no direct services from Armagh to Derry – the fastest route (3½ hours) is via Belfast (bus Nos 251 and 212).

Armagh is a stop on the once-daily (except Saturday) bus No 278 from Portrush to Dublin and the once-daily bus No 270 from Belfast to Galway.

AROUND ARMAGH CITY

Navan Fort

Perched atop a drumlin a little over 3km west of Armagh is Navan Fort (Emain Macha), the most important archaeological site in Ulster. It was probably a prehistoric provincial capital and ritual site, on a par with Tara in County Meath (see p512).

The Irish name Emain Macha means 'the twins of Macha', Macha being the same mythical queen or goddess after whom Armagh itself is named (from Ard Macha, 'the height of Macha'). The site is linked in legend with the epic tales of Cúchulainn, see 'The Táin Bó Cúalinge (Cattle Raid of Cooley)' boxed text p533, and named as the capital of Ulster and the seat of the legendary Knights of the Red Branch.

It was an important centre from around 1150 BC until the coming of Christianity; the discovery of the skull of a Barbary ape indicates trading links with North Africa. The main circular earthwork enclosure is no less than 240m in diameter, and encloses a smaller circular structure and an Iron Age burial mound. The circular structure has intrigued archaeologists. It appears to be some sort of temple, whose roof was supported by concentric rows of wooden posts, and whose interior was filled with a vast pile of stones. Stranger still, the whole thing was set on fire soon after its construction around 95 BC, possibly for ritual purposes. Unfortunately the nearby visitor centre remains closed due to lack of funding.

You can walk to the site from Armagh (45 minutes), or you can take the No 73 Ballygawley bus (10 minutes; seven daily Monday to Friday, three Saturday) to Navan village.

NORTH ARMAGH

North Armagh, 'the orchard of Ireland', is the island's main fruit-growing region, famed for its apples and strawberries.

Ardress House

Starting life as a farmhouse, **Ardress House** (☎ 3885 1236; 64 Ardress Rd; adult/child £2.80/1.40; 🕑 2-6pm Wed-Mon Jun-Aug, 2-6pm Sat, Sun & public hols mid-Mar–May & Sep) was upgraded to a manor house in 1760. Much of the original neoclassical interior remains and the farmyard still functions with a piggery and smithy. The walled garden has been planted with a selection of old apple varieties for which North Armagh's orchards are famous, and there are pleasant walks around the wooded grounds.

Ardress is 15km northeast of Armagh, on the B28 halfway between Moy and Portadown.

The Argory

A fine country house above the River Blackwater, the **Argory** (☎ 8778 4753; Derrycaw Rd; adult/child grounds & tour £4.10/2.10, grounds only £2.10 per car; 🕑 house noon-6pm daily Jul & Aug, 1-6pm Mon-Fri, noon-6pm Sat & Sun Jun, noon-6pm Sat, Sun & public hols mid-Mar–May & Sep) retains most of its 1824 fittings; some rooms are lit by acetylene gas from the house's private plant. There are two formal gardens featuring roses, Victorian clipped-yew arbours and a lime walk by the river.

The Argory is 3.5km northeast of Moy on the Derrycaw road (off the B28), and 5km northwest of Ardress.

Counties Derry & Antrim

CONTENTS

The historic city of Derry, nestled by a broad sweep of the River Foyle, is County Derry's chief attraction. It is the only walled city in Ireland whose ramparts have survived intact, and a walk around its city walls is one of the highlights of a visit to Northern Ireland. Derry's other draws include the powerful murals in the Bogside district and the lively music scene in its many pubs.

Northeast along the coast there are vast sandy beaches at Magilligan Point, Portstewart and Portrush, with good surfing and windsurfing at the latter two. The basalt escarpment of Binevenagh, which overlooks the coast here, offers superb views over Lough Foyle to the hills of County Donegal.

The coastal scenery of County Antrim ranks among the most beautiful and distinctive in Ireland – contrasting seacliffs of black basalt and white chalk, caves and rock pinnacles and broad, sweeping beaches, picturesque harbours and of course, the surreal geological centrepiece of the Giant's Causeway. And in summer you can test your nerve by teetering across the famous wire-rope bridge suspended high above the sea at Carrick-a-Rede.

East of Ballycastle, the dramatic cliffs of Fair Head offer fine walking with views over Rathlin Island to Scotland's Mull of Kintyre and the island hills of Islay and Jura. To the south lie the scenic Glens of Antrim, with the picture-postcard village of Cushendall and the picturesque old church of Layde, and south again the imposing castle of Carrickfergus, Northern Ireland's first and finest Norman fortress.

HIGHLIGHTS

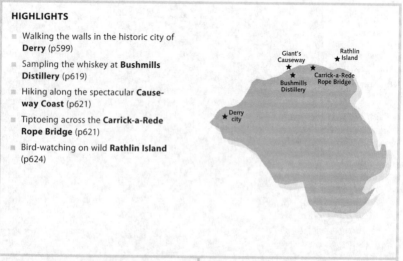

- Walking the walls in the historic city of **Derry** (p599)
- Sampling the whiskey at **Bushmills Distillery** (p619)
- Hiking along the spectacular **Causeway Coast** (p621)
- Tiptoeing across the **Carrick-a-Rede Rope Bridge** (p621)
- Bird-watching on wild **Rathlin Island** (p624)

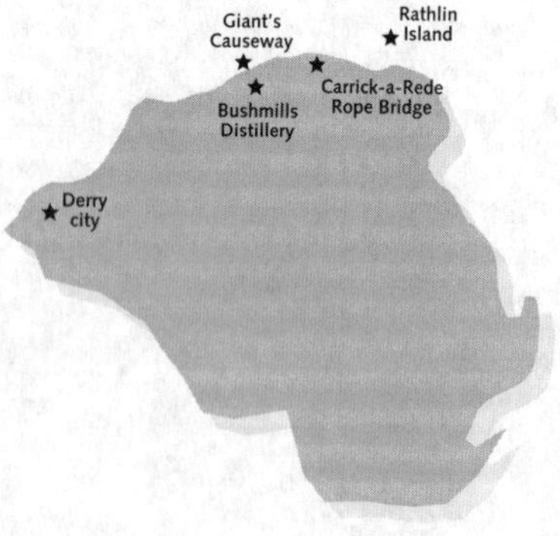

- POPULATION: 531,872
- AREA: 4696 SQ KM

TRANSPORT

Translink (☎ 9066 6630; www.translink.co.uk) operates several bus services specially designed for tourists visiting the popular Antrim coast and Giant's Causeway areas.

The Antrim Coaster (bus No 252) links Coleraine with Larne (£7, 3¼ hours, two daily) via Portstewart, Portrush, Bushmills, the Giant's Causeway, Ballycastle and the Glens of Antrim. In June to September one bus a day continues to/from Belfast's Europa Bus Centre (£7, 4½ hours), departing Belfast at 9am (June to September), and Larne at 10.15am and 3pm (year round). Southbound buses leave Coleraine at 9.40am (June to September ending in Belfast, October to April in Larne) and 3.40pm (Larne only).

From mid-June to mid-September the Causeway Rambler (bus No 376) links Bushmills Distillery and Carrick-a-Rede (£3.20, 25 minutes, seven daily) via the Giant's Causeway, Whitepark Bay and Ballintoy. The ticket allows unlimited travel in either direction for one day.

In July and August only the Bushmills Bus (No 177), an open-topped double-decker, runs (weather permitting) from Coleraine to the Giant's Causeway (single/day return £2.70/4, one hour, five daily) via Portstewart, Portrush, Portballintrae and Bushmills.

COUNTY DERRY

DERRY/LONDONDERRY

pop 83,100

The riverside city of Derry (or Londonderry – see the boxed text, p603), the fifth largest in Ireland, is a pleasant surprise to many visitors. There's lots of fascinating history to absorb – a stroll around the 17th-century city walls is a must, as is a visit to the Tower Museum – and the city has a well-founded reputation for musical excellence, from traditional to cutting-edge contemporary.

Derry is also a good base for exploring Donegal's Inishowen peninsula, and for an excursion to the Grianán of Aileách, a spectacular stone fort dating back to 1700 BC, just 6km over the border in Donegal.

History

Elizabeth I, determined to conquer Ulster, sent English troops to garrison Derry in 1566. In 1600 a second, more lastingly successful attempt to secure the town was made during the Nine Years' War (1594–1603) against the O'Neills and O'Donnells.

Sir Cahir O'Doherty attacked Derry in 1608 and virtually wiped it out but in 1609 James I, determined to settle matters for good, granted land to English and Scottish settlers. The wealthy London guilds were put in charge of 'planting' Derry and building the city walls.

During the Civil War the city backed parliament and supported William of Orange against James II. In December 1688 Catholic forces led by the earl of Antrim arrived on the other side of the Foyle. They sent emissaries into the city to discuss the crisis; in the meantime troops were being ferried across the river. Some apprentice boys on seeing this locked the city gates and the Great Siege of Derry began.

For 105 days the Protestant citizens of Derry withstood bombardment, disease and starvation. By the time a relief ship burst through and broke the siege, an estimated quarter of the city's 30,000 inhabitants had died.

In the 19th century Derry was one of the main emigration ports to the USA, a fact commemorated by the sculptures of an emigrant family standing in Waterloo Place. It also played a vital role in the transatlantic trade in linen shirts; supposedly, local factories provided uniforms for both sides in the American Civil War. To this day Derry still supplies the US president with 12 free shirts every year.

In the late 1960s, predominantly Catholic Derry became a flashpoint for the Troubles (see The Bogside, p604). In recent years, however, the Bogside and the inner city have been redeveloped. Major projects that reflect a new confidence in the future include the big Foyleside, Quayside and Richmond Shopping Centres and the Millennium Forum.

Orientation

The old centre of Derry is the small walled city on the western bank of the River Foyle. At its heart is the square called The Diamond, with Shipquay, Ferryquay, Butcher and Bishop Sts converging on it. The train station is on the eastern side of the River Foyle, the bus station on the western bank, just outside the walled city. Craigavon

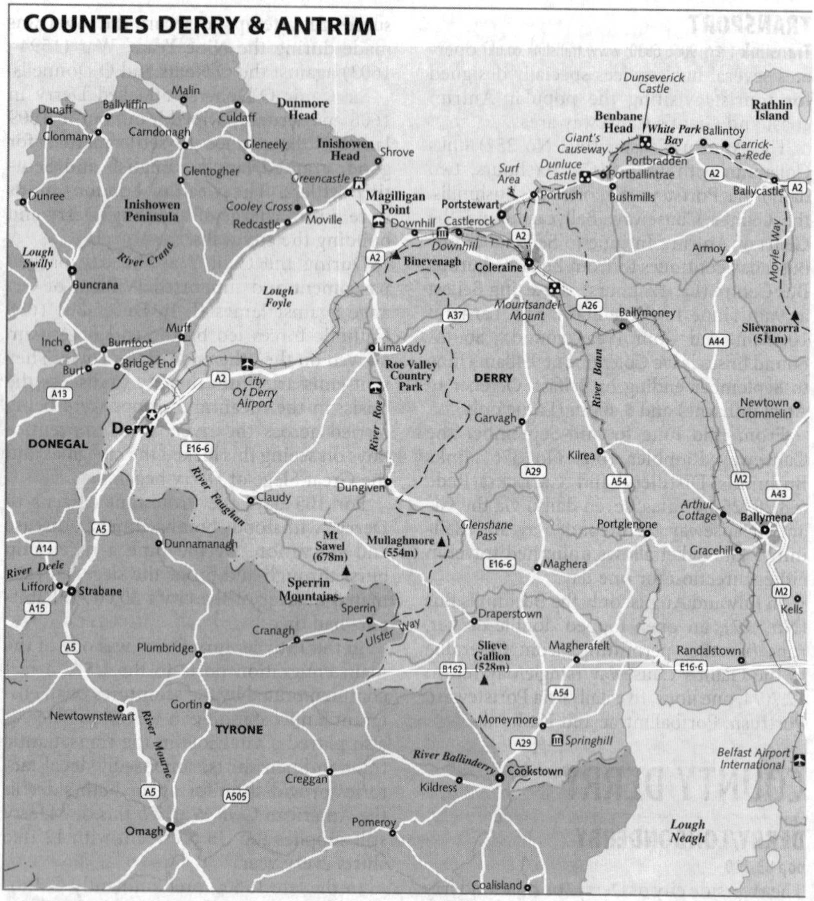

Bridge and, further downstream, the Foyle Bridge link the two banks of the river.

Information

BOOKSHOPS

Bookworm (Map p605; ☎ 7128 2727; 18-20 Bishop St Within) Good for books on Derry, the Troubles and Ireland generally. Has an in-store café.

Eason (Map p605; ☎ 7137 7133; Foyleside Shopping Centre, Foyle St) The city's biggest bookshop, on Level 3 of the shopping mall.

Foyle Books (Map p605; ☎ 7137 2530; 12a Magazine St) Stocks a good selection of second-hand books.

INTERNET ACCESS

bean-there.com (Map p605; ☎ 7128 1303; www.bean-there.com; 20 The Diamond; £1/2.50/4.50 for 8/30/60 min; 🕒 9am-7pm Mon-Wed & Sat, 9am-9pm Thu & Fri, noon-6pm Sun) Internet café serving good coffee and snacks.

Central Library (see Libraries following) Free Internet access until 1pm, thereafter at £1.25 per hour.

LIBRARIES

Central Library (Map p605; ☎ 7127 2300; 35 Foyle St; 🕒 9.15am-8pm Mon & Thu, 9.15am-5.30pm Tue, Wed & Fri, 9.15am-5pm Sat)

MONEY

Bank of Ireland (Map p605; 12 Shipquay St)

First Trust Bank (Map p605; 15-17 Shipquay St)

Thomas Cook (Map p605; ☎ 7185 2552; 34 Ferryquay St; 🕒 9am-5.30pm Mon-Wed, Fri & Sat, 10am-5.30pm Thu)

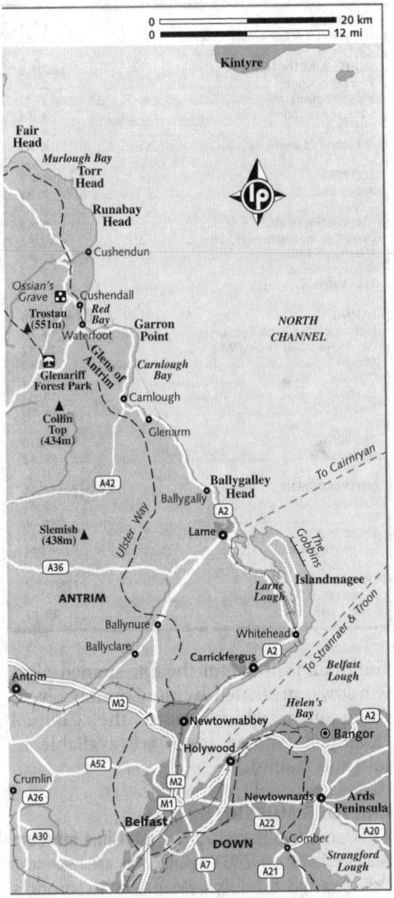

POST

Branch Post Office (Map p605; Bishop St Within; 9am-5.30pm Mon-Fri, 9am-12.30pm Sat) A convenient branch inside the city walls.

Main Post Office (Map p605; Custom House St; 8.30am-5.30pm Mon, 9am-5.30pm Tue-Fri, 9am-12.30pm Sat) Just north of the city walls.

TOURIST INFORMATION

Derry Visitor & Convention Bureau (Map p602; ☎ 7126 7284; www.derryvisitor.com; 44 Foyle St; 9am-7pm Mon-Fri, 10am-6pm Sat, 10am-5pm Sun Jul-Sep, 9am-5pm Mon-Fri, 10am-5pm Sat mid-Mar–Jun & Oct, 9am-5pm Mon-Fri Nov–mid-Mar) Covers all of Northern Ireland and the Republic as well as Derry. Books accommodation throughout Ireland and has a bureau de change.

TRAVEL AGENCIES

usit NOW (Map p605; ☎ 7137 1888; 4 Shipquay Pl; 9am-5pm Mon-Fri, 11am-4pm Sat)

Sights

Derry's walled city is Ireland's oldest example of town planning. It is thought to have been modelled on the French Renaissance town of Vitry-Le-François, designed in 1545 by Italian engineer Hieronimo Marino; both are based on the grid plan of a Roman military camp, with two main streets at right angles to each other, and four city gates at the ends.

CITY WALLS

Built between 1614 and 1619, Derry's **city walls** were the last to be constructed in Europe, and Ireland's only city walls to survive almost intact. They are about 8m high and 9m thick, and encircle the old city for 1.5km. The four original gates (Shipquay, Ferryquay, Bishop's and Butcher's) were rebuilt in the 18th and 19th centuries, while three new gates (New, Magazine and Castle) were added. Derry's nickname, the Maiden City, derives from the fact that the walls have never been breached by an invader.

See Walking Tour (p606) for a guided walk around the walls.

TOWER MUSEUM

Just inside the Magazine Gate is the award-winning **Tower Museum** (Map p605; ☎ 7137 2411; Union Hall Pl; adult/child £4.20/1.60; 10am-5pm Mon-Sat, 2-5pm Sun Jul & Aug, 10am-5pm Tue-Sat & bank hol Mon Sep-Jun), where well-thought-out exhibits and audiovisuals lead you through the history of Derry from the founding of St Colmcille's monastery in the 6th century to the Battle of the Bogside in the 1970s. Allow a good two hours to do the museum justice.

There's a wonderful eyewitness account of Shane O'Neill and his soldiers arriving at the court of Elizabeth I to pledge allegiance to the Crown in 1562 (he later reneged):

> ...armed with hatchets, all bare-headed, their hair flowing in locks on their shoulders, on which were yellow surplices dyed with saffron, or stained with urine, with long sleeves, short coats and thrum jackets, which caused as much staring and gaping among the English people as if they had come from China or America.

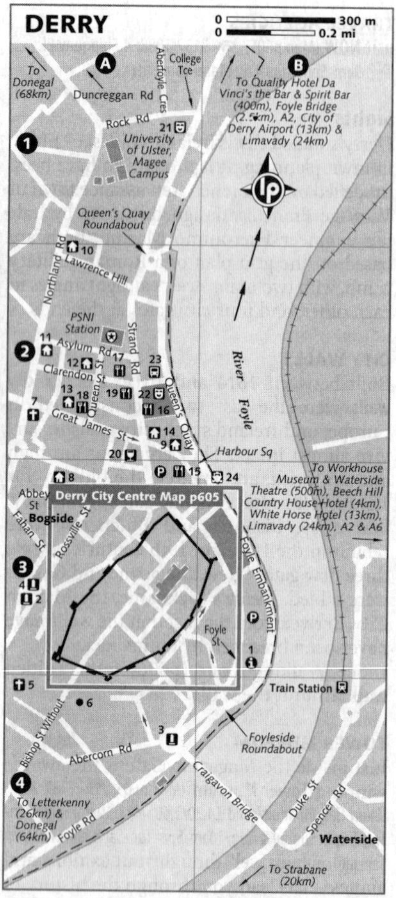

INFORMATION		p601
Derry Visitor & Convention Bureau	1	B3
SIGHTS & ACTIVITIES		pp601-6
Free Derry Corner	2	A3
Hunger Strikers' Memorial	3	A3
Long Tower Church	4	A4
Old Gaol	5	A4
St Eugene's Cathedral	6	A2
SLEEPING		pp608-9
Abbey B&B	7	A3
City Hotel	8	A2
Clarence House	9	A2
Derry City Independent Hostel	10	A2
Merchant's House	11	A2
Saddler's House	12	A2
Travelodge	13	A2
EATING		pp609-10
Exchange Wine Bar & Restaurant	14	A3
Lloyd's No 1 Bar/ The Ice Wharf	15	A2
Mange 2	16	A2
Ogmio's	17	A2
Sandwich Co	18	A2
Tesco		(see 21)
DRINKING		p610
Mullan's Bar	19	A2
ENTERTAINMENT		pp610-11
Café Roc	20	A1
Earth		(see 20)
Strand Multiplex	21	A2
Suzie's Piano Bar		(see 20)
TRANSPORT		pp611-12
Airporter Bus Service	22	A2
Foyle Cruises	23	B3

At the time of writing, a major new exhibition on the Spanish Armada in Ireland was being added to the Tower Museum, slated to open in December 2004.

GUILDHALL

Standing just outside the city walls opposite the Tower Museum, the red-brick **Guildhall** (Map p605; ☎ 7137 7335; Guildhall Sq; admission free; 🕐 9am-5pm Mon-Fri) was originally built in 1890, then rebuilt after a fire in 1908. As the seat of the old Londonderry Corporation, which institutionalised the policy of discriminating against Catholics over housing and jobs, it incurred the wrath of nationalists and was bombed twice by the Irish Republican Army (IRA) in 1972. The Guildhall is noted for the fine stained-glass windows, presented by the London Livery Companies, which adorn the Council Chamber. Guided tours are available in July and August.

HARBOUR MUSEUM

This small, old-fashioned **maritime museum** (Map p605; ☎ 7137 7331; Harbour Sq; admission free; 🕐 10am-1pm & 2-4.30pm Mon-Fri) with models of ships, a replica of a currach – an early sailing boat of the type that carried St Colmcille to Iona – and the bosomy figurehead of the Minnehaha, is housed in the old Harbour Commissioner's Building next to the Guildhall.

ST COLUMB'S CATHEDRAL

Standing at the southern end of the walled city, **St Columb's Cathedral** (Map p605; ☎ 7126 7313; London St; requested donation £1; 🕐 9am-5pm Mon-Sat Easter-Oct, 9am-1pm & 2-4pm Mon-Sat Nov-Easter), built between 1628 and 1633, was the first post-Reformation church to be built in Britain or Ireland, and is Derry's oldest surviving building.

In the **porch** (under the spire, by the St Columb's Court entrance) you can see the original foundation stone of 1633 that records the cathedral's completion, inscribed:

If stones could speake
Then London's prayse
Should sounde who
Built this church and
Cittie from the grounde

The smaller stone inset, inscribed '*In Templo Verus Deus Est Vereo Colendus*' (The True God is in His Temple and is to be truly worshipped), comes from the original Columban church built here in 1164.

Also in the porch is a hollow mortar shell fired into the churchyard during the Great Siege; inside were the terms of surrender. The neighbouring **chapter house** contains more historical artefacts, including paintings, old photos and the four huge padlocks used to secure the city gates in the 17th century.

The **nave**, built in a squat, solid style known as Planter's Gothic, shares the austerity of many Church of Ireland cathedrals, with thick walls, small windows, and an open-timbered roof (from 1823) resting on corbels depicting the heads of past bishops and deans. The bishop's throne, at the far end of the nave, is an 18th-century mahogany chair in ornate, Chinese Chippendale style.

The **chancel**, and the stained-glass east window depicting the Ascension, date from 1887. The flags on either side of the window were captured from the French during the Great Siege; although the yellow silk has been renewed several times since, the poles and gold wirework are original.

THE FIFTH PROVINCE

The **Fifth Province** (Map p605; ☎ 7137 3177; 4-22 Butcher St; adult/child £3/1; 9.30am-5pm Mon-Sat) has shows at 11.30am and 2.30pm Monday to Friday which take you on a multimedia trip with hunky Celtic warrior Calgach to discover the 'fifth province' of Ireland – the world of the Celts. After an introduction to the history of Derry (narrated by Irish actor Richard Harris) you sit in a moving 'time chariot' (the best bit) and listen

DERRY-STROKE-LONDONDERRY

Derry/Londonderry is a town with two names. Derry is derived from the Gaelic word *doíre*, meaning 'oak grove'. The settlement was originally named Doíre Calgaigh (Oak Grove of Calgach), after a pagan warrior-hero, then in the 10th century it was renamed Doíre Colmcille (Oak Grove of St Colmcille), in honour of the 6th-century saint who established the first monastic settlement here.

In the following centuries the name was shortened and anglicised to Derrie or Derry. Then in 1613, in recognition of the Corporation of London's role in 'planting' the city with Protestant settlers, the city's name was changed to Londonderry. However, people continued to call it Derry, except in official documents.

When nationalists gained a majority on the city council in 1984, they voted to change its name from Londonderry City Council to Derry City Council. This infuriated unionists, and the name became a touchstone for people's political views. Nationalists always use Derry, and extremists often deface the 'London' part of the name on road signs. Staunch unionists insist on Londonderry, which remains the city's (and county's) official name, used in government publications, Ordnance Survey maps, rail and bus timetables and Northern Ireland Tourist Board (NITB) tourist literature.

On radio and TV, to avoid giving offence to either side, some announcers use both names together – 'Derry-stroke-Londonderry' – while the BBC uses Londonderry at its first mention in a report, and Derry thereafter. Road signs in Northern Ireland point to Londonderry, those in the Republic point to Derry (or Doíre in Irish).

A move to change the city's official name to Derry failed in the 1980s, but in November 2002 Sinn Féin councillors again proposed a motion to make the name Derry official. However, this would take an act of parliament, and could only be done by the Queen on recommendation of the Westminster government.

Luckily, not everyone takes the Derry/Londonderry controversy too seriously. One local journalist opted instead for the simpler 'Stroke City'! In fact, the majority of the people in Northern Ireland, including unionists, still use 'Derry' in everyday speech, which is why we are using the shorter version in this book.

BLOODY SUNDAY

On Sunday 30 January 1972, some 20,000 civilians marched through Derry protesting against internment without trial. It now seems clear that soldiers of the 1st Battalion of the Parachute Regiment opened fire on unarmed marchers. Fourteen people were shot dead, some shot in the back. None of those who fired the 108 bullets, nor the officers in charge, have been brought to trial or even disciplined; records have disappeared and the weapons have been destroyed. The original Widgery Commission failed to find anyone responsible.

A new enquiry headed by Lord Saville, the Bloody Sunday Enquiry, has been underway since March 2000 and was still in process at the time of writing. It sits in the Guildhall in Derry (except for the witness statements of British soldiers, which are given in the Central Hall, Westminster, London) Monday to Friday. The public is able to attend.

Nearby is the **Bloody Sunday Trust** (Map p605; ☎ 7136 0880; 39 Shipquay St; admission by donation; 🕒 9am-5pm Mon-Fri), a community based history and education organisation that provides support for the families of Bloody Sunday. It is open to the public and has a range of photographic and audio exhibits on the events of that day.

to the handsome Calgach tell tales of Celtic Ireland; finally there's an over-the-top celebration of Irish culture that will convince you that everyone who emigrated ended up as an astronaut or president of the USA.

CONTEXT GALLERY

The **Context Gallery** (☎ 7126 8027; 5-7 Artillery St; admission free; 🕒 10am-5.30pm Tue-Fri, 10am-4.30pm Sat) is currently the city's only art gallery, hosting changing exhibitions of contemporary visual art.

THE BOGSIDE

The Bogside district, to the west of the walled city, developed in the 19th and early 20th centuries as a working-class, Catholic residential area. By the 1960s, its serried ranks of small, terraced houses had become an overcrowded ghetto of poverty and unemployment, a focus for the emerging civil rights movement and a hotbed of nationalist discontent.

In August 1969, the three-day 'Battle of the Bogside' – a running street battle between local youths and the police – prompted the UK government to send British troops into Northern Ireland. The residents of the Bogside and neighbouring Brandywell district – 33,000 of them – declared themselves independent of the civil authorities, and barricaded the streets to keep the security forces out. 'Free Derry', as it was known, was a no-go area for the police and army, its streets patrolled by IRA volunteers. In 1972, the area around Rossville St was the setting for the horrific events of Bloody Sunday (see the boxed text).

In recent years the area has been extensively redeveloped, the old houses and flats demolished and replaced with modern housing; the population is now down to 8000. All that remains of the old Bogside is **Free Derry Corner** (Map p602), at the intersection of Fahan and Rossville Sts, where the gable end of a terraced house painted with the famous 'You Are Now Entering Free Derry' slogan still stands. Nearby is the H-shaped **Hunger Strikers' Memorial** (Map p602).

The **Bloody Sunday Memorial** (Map p605), on Rossville St, is a simple granite obelisk that commemorates the 14 civilians who were shot dead by the British Army on 30 January 1972. The gable ends of the houses along Rossville St are decorated with murals painted by the Bogside Artists (see the boxed text, p606).

WORKHOUSE MUSEUM

The **Workhouse Museum** (☎ 7131 8328; 23 Glendermott Rd; admission free; 🕒 10am-4.30pm Mon-Sat Jul & Aug, closed Fri Sep-Jun) is across the river in the Waterside area, in Derry's original 1840–1946 workhouse. Daily life at the workhouse for the up to 800 inmates was designed to encourage them to leave as soon as possible. One of the few exhibits is the grisly horse-drawn hearse used to carry away the workhouse dead.

Other displays cover the Potato Famine, while the excellent Atlantic Memorial exhibition tells the story of the WWII Battle of the Atlantic and the major role that Derry played.

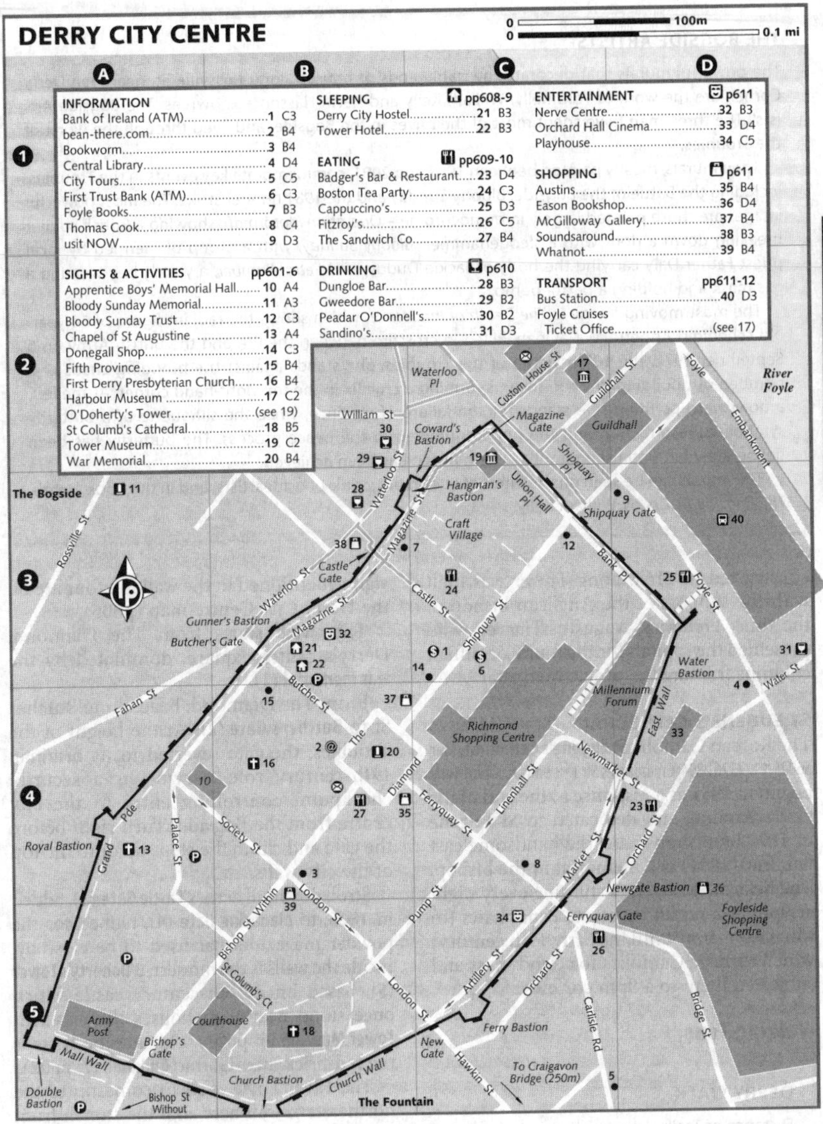

HANDS ACROSS THE DIVIDE

As you enter the city across Craigavon Bridge, the first thing you see is the **Hands Across the Divide** monument. The striking bronze sculpture of two men reaching out to each other symbolises the spirit of reconciliation and hope for the future; it was unveiled in 1992, 20 years after Bloody Sunday.

LONG TOWER CHURCH

Outside the city walls to the southwest is **Long Tower Church** (Map p602; ☎ 7126 2301; Long Tower St; admission free; ⌚ 9am-8.30pm Mon-Sat, 7.30am-7pm Sun), Derry's first post-Reformation Catholic church. Built in 1784 in neo-Renaissance style, it stands on the site of the medieval Tempull Mor (Great Church), which was

THE BOGSIDE ARTISTS

The powerful murals that decorate the gable ends of houses along Rossville St, near Free Derry Corner, are the work of Tom Kelly, William Kelly and Kevin Hasson – known as 'The Bogside Artists'. The three men have spent most of their lives in the Bogside, and lived through the worst of the Troubles.

Their murals, mostly painted between 1997 and 2001, commemorate key events in the Troubles, including the Battle of the Bogside, Bloody Sunday and the 1981 hunger strike. The most powerful images are those painted largely in monochrome – *Operation Motorman,* showing a British soldier breaking down a door with a sledgehammer; *Bloody Sunday,* with a group of men led by local priest Father Daly carrying the body of Jackie Duddy; and *Petrol Bomber,* a young boy wearing a gas mask and holding a petrol bomb.

The most moving image is *The Death of Innocence,* which shows the radiant figure of 14-year-old schoolgirl Annette McGavigan, killed in crossfire between the IRA and the British Army on 6 September 1971, the 100th victim of the Troubles. She stands against the brooding chaos of a bombed-out building, the roof-beams forming a crucifix in the top right-hand corner. At the left, a downward-pointing rifle stands for the failure of violence, while the silhouette of a butterfly symbolises resurrection and the hope embodied in the peace process. The butterfly has been deliberately left unfinished until a lasting peace has been achieved.

The murals can be seen on the Internet at cain.ulst.ac.uk/bogsideartists, and in the book *Murals: The Bogside Artists* by William Kelly.

constructed in 1164. Long Tower was built with the support of the Anglican bishop of the time, Frederick Augustus Harvey, who presented the capitals for the four Corinthian columns framing the ornate high altar.

ST EUGENE'S CATHEDRAL

The Roman Catholic **St Eugene's Cathedral** (Map p602; ☎ 7126 2894; Great James St; 🕑 9am-8.30pm) was begun in 1851 as a response to the end of the Great Famine, and dedicated to St Eugene in 1873 by Bishop Kelly; the handsome east window (1891) is a memorial to the bishop. The bells of St Eugene's still ring every night at 9pm as a reminder of the Penal Laws (in force from 1691 until the early 19th century) which forbade Catholics to attend mass and subjected them to a 9pm curfew.

Walking Tour

DERRY WALK

Distance of Trail: 3km
Duration: 30 to 40 minutes

You can make a complete circuit of Derry's walled city, walking along the top of the walls, in around 30 minutes. There are frequent sets of steps where you can get on and off. Unless otherwise indicated, all sights mentioned in the walking tour are on the Derry City Centre map (p605).

This walk starts from The Diamond, Derry's central square, dominated by the **war memorial** (**1**).

From The Diamond, head along Butcher St to **Butcher's Gate** (**2**). At the height of the Troubles, the gate reverted to its original, 17th-century role, serving as a security checkpoint controlling entry to the city centre from the Bogside. Turn right before the gate and climb the steps up onto the top of the city walls.

Stroll downhill across **Castle Gate** (**3**), added in 1865, to **Magazine Gate** (**4**), named for the powder magazine that used to be close by. Inside the walls is the modern **O'Doherty's Tower** (**5**), based on a 16th-century castle which once stood nearby. It houses the excellent **Tower Museum** (**6**; p601). Outside the walls is the red-brick, neo-Gothic **Guildhall** (**7**; p602).

The River Foyle used to come up to the northeastern wall here, and the stretch from Coward's Bastion to the Water Bastion (demolished 1844) once had ships moored just outside. In the middle is the **Shipquay Gate** (**8**) built in 1805 to link the port with the market area. Symbols above the arch show the cornucopia (horn of plenty) and the rod of Mercury (a symbol of trade and commerce).

The walls then turn southwest and begin a steep climb beside the modern **Millennium**

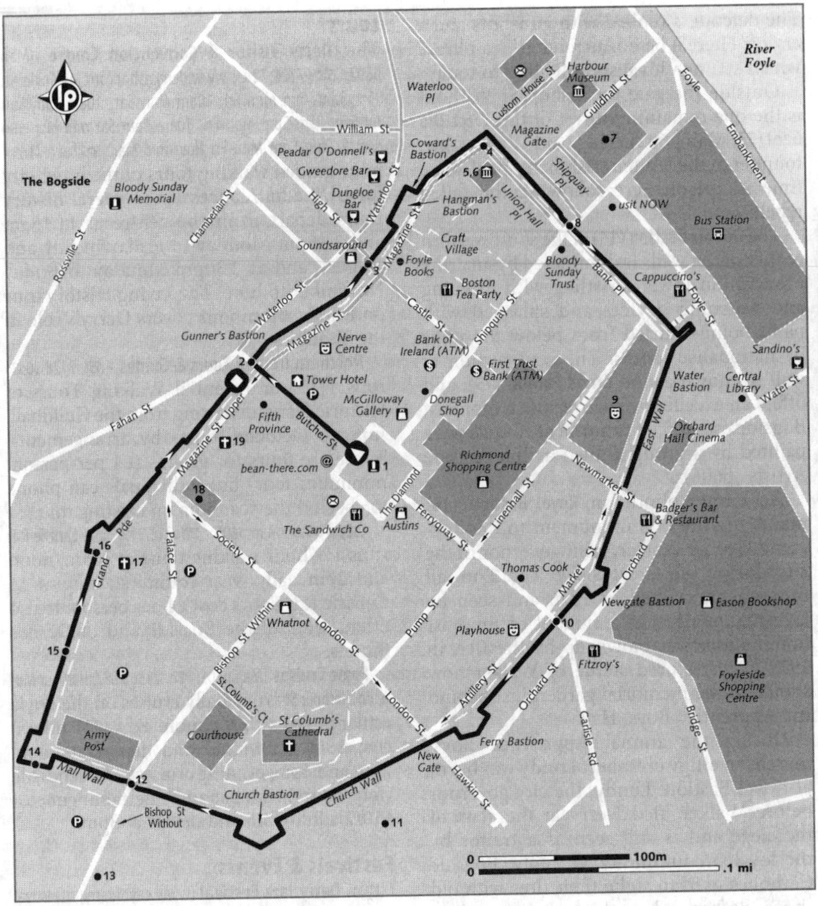

Forum (**9**) theatre and concert venue. At the top of the hill is the **Ferryquay Gate** (**10**), where the apprentice boys barred the gate at the start of the Great Siege of 1689. In those days there would have been a drawbridge as well as a padlock on the gate. Both padlock and key can be seen in the Chapter House of St Columb's Cathedral.

Above the gate is the image of the Reverend George Walker who was a city leader during the siege. Below in the arches to each side are metal rings. These were used to tether horses, which were not allowed into the inner city on market days.

The stretch of wall beyond overlooks the **Fountain** (**11**) housing estate, the last significant Protestant community on the western bank of the Foyle (the vast majority of Derry's Protestants have moved across the river to the Waterside area or further afield). A defiant mural proclaims 'Londonderry West Bank Loyalists Still Under Siege – No Surrender'. The round, brick-paved area on the ground outside New Gate is a bonfire site where a 10m-high bonfire is lit on the night before the annual Apprentice Boys march.

Bishop's Gate (**12**) which bisects the southern flank of the wall, was rebuilt in 1789 for the 100th anniversary of the siege. Bishop Harvey, a keen antiquarian, had a hand in the reconstruction and requested a triumphal arch in honour of King William III. During the Great Siege, it was here that King James II demanded the surrender of the city.

The defenders replied with gunshots and a cry of 'There'll be no surrender!' – a phrase which staunch loyalists still cling to today.

Outside the gate on Bishop St Without is the one remaining turret of the 1791 **Old Gaol** (**13**; Map p602). Theobald Wolfe Tone, founder of the United Irishmen, spent some time in prison here following the failed rebellion of 1798.

The **Double Bastion** (**14**) at the southwestern corner of the walls is dominated by an army observation tower, bristling with listening and watching devices and splashed with paint bombs hurled from below the walls by nationalist youths. The next section of wall is known as the **Grand Parade** (**15**), and offers an excellent view over the nationalist Bogside estate. The prominent murals were painted by a group known as the Bogside Artists (p606).

An empty plinth on **Royal Bastion** (**16**) marks the site of a monument to the Reverend George Walker, joint governor of the city during the Great Siege. The 27m-tall monument, erected in 1826 and seen by local nationalists as a symbol of unionist domination, was blown up by the IRA in 1973. The restored statue of Walker now stands in the memorial garden just behind the Apprentice Boys' Hall.

During the annual Apprentice Boys' march, an effigy of Robert Lundy was burnt at Royal Bastion. Lundy, the city governor before Walker, fled Derry at the start of the siege and is still seen as a traitor by the loyalist community. In reply, Bogside Catholics used to stoke their fires with old shoes, clothes and anything else to produce an obnoxious smoke, in the hope that the loyalists would be smoked out.

Behind the Royal Bastion is the 1872 Church of Ireland **Chapel of St Augustine** (**17**), built on the site of St Colmcille's 6th-century monastery. A little further along is the **Apprentice Boys' Memorial Hall** (**18**) its windows protected by steel grilles and, like the army observation tower, splashed with paint bombs, and the grand Corinthian temple of the **First Derry Presbyterian Church** (**19**).

Just past the church is the Butcher's Gate, from where you can return to The Diamond, head down Magazine St to the Tower Museum, or descend Fahan St to the Bogside and the haunting Bloody Sunday memorial.

Tours

The **Derry Visitor & Convention Centre** (Map p602; ☎ 7126 7284; www.derryvisitor.com; 44 Foyle St; 9am-7pm Mon-Fri, 10am-6pm Sat, 10am-5pm Sun Jul-Sep, 9am-5pm Mon-Fri, 10am-5pm Sat mid-Mar–Jun & Oct, 9am-5pm Mon-Fri Nov–mid-Mar) offers 1½-hour guided walking tours of the inner city for £4/3 adult/concession. General history tours depart from the centre at 11.15am and 3.15pm Monday to Friday in July and August, and at 2.30pm Monday to Friday November to June. The Living History tour on Friday afternoons covers Derry's role in the Troubles.

Northern Ireland Tours & Guides (☎ 7128 9051) runs 1¼-hour Essential Walking Tours of Historic Derry departing from the Guildhall, June to October (times by arrangement). These are tours for groups (£4 per person, minimum four) but individuals can phone to check if they can join an existing tour.

City Tours (Map p605; ☎ 7127 1996; 11 Carlisle Rd) runs 1½-hour walking tours at 10am, noon and 2pm daily, year round, starting at 11 Carlisle Rd. Tours cost £4 per person. It also offers tours of the Bogside and of Derry's murals.

Foyle Cruises (Map p605; ☎ 7136 2857; Harbour Museum, Harbour Sq) runs daily cruises on the Foyle estuary. Trips to Culmore Bay (1¼ hours) cost £6/4 adult/child and depart at noon, 2pm and 4pm; evening cruises to Greencastle (four hours) with bar and entertainment cost £10/7 adult/child and depart at 8pm.

Festivals & Events

City of Derry Jazz Festival (www.cityofderryjazzfestival.com; early May) Five days of jazz at various venues.

Gasyard Wall Féile (Aug) A cultural festival which features concerts, theatre and Irish-language events.

Féile na Samnha (31 Oct) The annual Halloween carnival, which has the entire city dressing up and partying in the streets.

Foyle Film Festival (www.foylefilmfestival.com; Nov) This week-long event is the North's biggest film festival.

Sleeping

It's best to book accommodation in advance during festival events.

BUDGET

Derry City Hostel (Map p605; ☎ 7128 0280; derrycitytours@aol.com; 4-6 Magazine St; dm £9-10, s/d £15/35; ; wheelchair access) This recently renovated, family-friendly hostel is inside the city walls near Butcher's Gate, a five-minute walk from the bus station. It has a 24-hour reception, kitchen, dining room and restaurant. Dorm and singles rates exclude breakfast; doubles/twins have en suite and include breakfast.

Derry City Independent Hostel (Steve's Backpacker's; Map p602; ☎ 7137 7989; 4 Asylum Rd; dm £8-10.50, d £24; ☒ 🖳) This small, friendly independent hostel is in a Georgian town house, just a short walk north of the walled city. Rates include a continental breakfast and 30 minutes of Internet access. There are laundry facilities, and a fifth night's stay is free. It's just more than a 10-minute walk from the bus station.

Magee Campus (Map p602; ☎ 7137 5283; gj.kennedy@ulster.ac.uk; University of Ulster, Northland Rd; s £14-16; Ⓟ) The university offers self-catering student rooms to individual travellers and groups by the night or week, from mid-June to mid-September.

MID-RANGE

Saddler's House (Map p602; ☎ 7126 9691; saddlershouse@btinternet.com; 36 Great James St; s/d £27.50/45; ☒) Centrally located within a five-minute walk of the walled city, this friendly place is set in a lovely, Victorian town house. Most rooms are en suite, and rates include a huge breakfast.

Merchant's House (Map p602; ☎ 7126 9691; merchantshouse@btinternet.com; 16 Queen St; s/d £25/45; ☒) Run by the same couple as the Saddler's House, this listed, Georgian-style town house is a gem of a B&B. It has an elegant lounge and dining room with marble fireplaces and antique furniture, TV and coffee-making facilities in all rooms, and home-made marmalade at breakfast. Singles with shared bathroom are only £20! Call at the Saddler's House first to pick up a key.

Abbey B&B (Map p602; ☎ 7127 9000; abbey.accom@ntlworld.com; 4 Abbey St; s/d £25/40; ☒) There's a warm welcome here, just a short walk from the walled city, on the edge of the Bogside. The brightly decorated rooms are mostly en suite.

Clarence House (Map p602; ☎ 7126 5342; clarencehouse@zoom.co.uk; 15 Northland Rd; s/d £25/50) A grand, red-brick Victorian town house, the Clarence opened as Derry's first ever B&B back in 1962. Popular with visiting TV crews (the BBC studio is across the road), the chintzy, en-suite rooms all have TV and phone.

Travelodge (Map p602; ☎ 0870 085 0950, from Republic of Ireland ☎ 1800 709 709; www.travelodge.co.uk; 22-24 Strand Rd; d £43; ☒) Central, comfortable and characterless, the Travelodge offers a flat rate for rooms that take up to two adults and two children.

TOP END

Tower Hotel (Map p605; ☎ 7137 1000; www.towerhotelderry.com; Butcher St; s £60-80, d £70-110; Ⓟ ☒; wheelchair access) The flashy new Tower is the only hotel within the old city walls, with plush rooms and business suites, a fitness centre and a good restaurant.

City Hotel (Map p605; ☎ 7136 5800; www.greatsouthernhotels.com; Queen's Quay; s/d £65/85; Ⓟ ☒ 🏊) The even newer City Hotel down by the river is modern, stylish and business oriented. It offers cheaper deals, especially over weekends, by booking online.

Quality Hotel Da Vinci's (☎ 7127 9111; www.davincishotel.com; 15 Culmore Rd; d £63-85, apt £67-93; Ⓟ ☒ 🖳) Da Vinci's is a boutique hotel located 1.5km north of the city centre, on the west bank of the Foyle. It also runs Da Vinci's Apartotel, a complex of 21 super-trendy, one- and two-bedroom serviced apartments closer to the city centre at College Terrace, on Strand Rd.

There are also a few places out of town.

Beech Hill Country House Hotel (☎ 7134 9279; www.beech-hill.com; 32 Ardmore Rd; s £75-85, d £120-160; Ⓟ ☒) The Beech Hill is an elegant 18th-century country house, 4km southeast of the centre, off the A6 road towards Belfast and Dublin. It's where Bill Clinton stays when he's in town.

White Horse Hotel (☎ 7186 0606; info@whitehorsehotel.biz; 68 Clooney Rd; s/d £60/70; Ⓟ ☒ 🏊) This Best Western hotel is near the airport, 8km northeast of the city centre on the Limavady road.

Eating

BUDGET

Boston Tea Party (Map p605; 15 The Craft Village; snacks £1-4; 🕒 9am-5.30pm Mon-Sat) Home-made soups, very tasty sandwiches, freshly baked cakes, friendly service – what more could you want from a café?

Cappuccino's (Map p605; ☎ 7137 0059; 31 Foyle St; mains £2.95; 🕒 8am-6pm Mon-Sat, 9am-1pm Sun) This cosy café does a decent fry-up for breakfast and offers local dishes like bacon, turnip and potatoes for lunch.

Sandwich Co The Diamond (Map p605; ☎ 7137 2500; sandwiches & salads £2.75; 🕑 9am-5pm Mon-Sat); Strand Rd (Map p605; 61 Strand Rd) White bread, brown bread, baguettes, paninis, ciabatta – this place offers good-value, choose-your-own sandwiches and salads.

Badger's Bar & Restaurant (☎ 7136 3306; 16-18 Orchard St; mains £4.50-5.50; 🕑 noon-6pm Mon, noon-7pm Tue & Thu, noon-9.30pm Fri & Sat, noon-4pm Sun) This convivial bar, decked out in stained glass and wood panelling, serves some of the best pub grub in town, including a superb steak-and-Guinness pie.

Lloyd's No 1 Bar/The Ice Wharf (Map p602; ☎ 7127 6610; 22 Strand Rd; snacks £3.50, mains £5-7; 🕑 10am-10pm Mon-Sat) Big, bustling Lloyd's is part of the Wetherspoon chain of pubs, and serves a meat or veggie breakfast fry (until noon), tasty bar snacks like nachos, veggie tempura and quesadillas, and hearty meals like steaks, burgers, pasta and a range of veggie dishes.

MID-RANGE

Exchange Wine Bar & Restaurant (Map p602; ☎ 7127 3990; Queen's Quay; lunch £5-6, dinner £9-11; 🕑 noon-2.30pm & 5.30-10pm Mon-Sat, 5.30-9pm Sun) Dripping designer chic in dark wood, stainless steel and leather, the Exchange sports a good-value international menu. No reservations – it's first-come first-served.

Fitzroy's (Map p605; ☎ 7126 6211; 2-4 Bridge St, 2nd entrance on Carlisle Rd; lunch £5-6, dinner £7-9; 🕑 10am-8pm Mon & Tue, 9.30am-10pm Thu-Sat, 10am-10pm Wed, noon-8pm Sun) Informal, bistro-style Fitzroy's does breakfast until 12.30pm, lunch to 5.30pm, and then dinner, or you can just drop in for a coffee anytime. There are good veggie dishes, and the three-course dinner for £10 (Wednesday and Thursday only) is excellent value.

Mange 2 (Map p602; ☎ 7136 1222; 2 Clarendon St; mains £11-14; 🕑 5.30-10pm) A candle-lit, Georgian-style dining room with pale green walls and dark wood furniture makes this an elegant venue for a splurge. The interesting fusion menu includes a handful of good veggie options.

SELF-CATERING

Tesco (Map p602; ☎ 7137 4400; Quayside Shopping Centre, Strand Rd; 🕑 9am-9pm Mon-Thu, 8.30am-9pm Fri, 8.30am-8pm Sat, 1-6pm Sun) Self-caterers can stock up at this big supermarket, just north of the walled city.

Drinking

Whatever you do in Derry, don't miss an evening in the city's lively pubs. They're friendly and atmospheric, mostly open until 1am, and are within easy walking distance of each other – there are six within dancing distance along Waterloo St.

Mullan's Bar (Map p602; ☎ 7126 5300; 13 Little James St) Mullan's is a good live-music venue, featuring jazz, blues and traditional sessions on Wednesday and Thursday nights. There's a DJ Friday to Sunday. The lavish interior, stuffed with stained glass, polished wood, brass rails and bronze figures, was rebuilt after a petrol bomb set the roof on fire during the Troubles.

Sandino's (Map p605; ☎ 7130 9297; 1 Water St) This is a Latin American-themed venue (named after Nicaraguan guerrilla leader Augusto Sandino), popular with up-and-coming local bands as well as visiting musicians. There's a live band on Friday and occasionally mid-week, and a traditional session on Sunday afternoon. A film club meets every Tuesday followed by a DJ. A DJ also plays on Saturday night. There are regular theme nights, fund-raising nights and political events. Check on www.wheretotonight.com for events.

Bar (☎ 7127 9111; 15 Culmore Rd) This award-winning bar at Quality Hotel Da Vinci's goes in for the monumentalism so loved by Irish bar designers – it sports a massive, polished wood bar topped with what can only be described as a triumphal arch. The mood is laid back, and food is available from noon to 5.30pm.

Peadar O'Donnell's (Map p605; ☎ 7126 2318; 63 Waterloo St) Peadar's goes for traditional music sessions every night starting about 11pm. It's done up as a typical Irish pub-cum-grocer down to shelves of grocery items, with a pig's head and hams hanging off the ceiling.

Other good bars in Waterloo St include:

Gweedore Bar (Map p605; ☎ 7126 3513; 59-61 Waterloo St) Live bands every night.

Dungloe Bar (Map p605; ☎ 7126 7716; 41 Waterloo St) Irish music Thursday night, live bands Friday and Saturday, karaoke on Sunday.

Entertainment

CINEMAS

Orchard Hall Cinema (Map p605; ☎ 7126 2845; Orchard St)

Strand Multiplex (Map p602; ☎ 7137 3900; Quayside Shopping Centre, Strand Rd)

NIGHTCLUBS

Earth (☎ 7136 0556; 1 College Terrace; admission free-£5) Derry's main nightclub and bar complex, close to the university, has music and moods to suit all tastes. The flagship Earth club has a student night on Thursdays, chart hits and dance anthems on Fridays, and guest DJs on Saturdays. Stylish **Café Roc** is the neighbouring pre-club bar, while the classical, candle-lit **Suzie's Piano Bar** offers the chance to relax with just a baby grand for background music.

Spirit Bar (☎ 7127 9111; 15 Culmore Rd) The Spirit Bar at Quality Hotel Da Vinci's is *the* place to sip cocktails and be seen among Derry's 20- and 30-something in-crowd (there's a strict 23-and-over age limit). There's a '60s and '70s night on Friday, chart hits and dance music on Saturday.

CONCERTS & THEATRE

Millennium Forum (Map p605; ☎ 7126 4455; www.millenniumforum.co.uk; Newmarket St) Ireland's biggest theatre auditorium is a major venue for dance, drama, concerts, opera and musicals.

Nerve Centre (☎ 7126 0562; www.nerve-centre.org.uk; 7-8 Magazine St) The Nerve Centre is a multimedia arts centre started in the late 1980s to encourage young, local talent in the fields of music and film. The centre has a performance area, theatre/cinema, bar and café.

Playhouse (Map p605; ☎ 7126 8027; 5 Artillery St) This community arts centre stages dance and theatre performances.

Waterside Theatre (☎ 7131 4000; The Ebrington Centre, Glendermott Rd) This theatre 500m east of the River Foyle stages concerts and plays about twice a week.

Magee College (Map p602; ☎ 7137 5679; www.ulster.ac.uk/culture; University of Ulster, Northland Rd) The college holds a variety of arts, theatrical and classical concert performances throughout the year.

Shopping

Craft Village (Map p605; entrances from Shipquay St, Magazine St & Tower Museum) is a little courtyard with a handful of craft shops selling Derry crystal, hand-woven cloth, ceramics, jewellery and other local craft items.

Other good places for crafts include the **Donegall Shop** (Map p605; ☎ 7126 6928; 8 Shipquay St), which sells garments, tweeds and souvenirs, and **Ogmios** (Map p602; ☎ 7126 4132; 34 Great James St), which stocks a good range of Irish-language books, traditional music CDs, musical instruments, pottery, prints and jewellery. **Soundsaround** (Map p605; ☎ 7128 8890; 22a Waterloo St) also has an excellent selection of traditional music on tape and CD.

McGilloway Gallery (Map p605; ☎ 7136 6011; 6 Shipquay St) is a commercial gallery that deals in modern Irish paintings, while the **What-not** (Map p605; ☎ 7128 8333; 22 Bishop St Within) is an interesting little antique shop crammed with jewellery and collectables. **Austins** (Map p605; ☎ 7126 1817; 2 The Diamond), Ireland's oldest department store, is a good place to shop for Irish linen.

Foyleside Shopping Centre (Map p605; ☎ 7137 7575; Orchard St) is a huge, four-level mall just outside the eastern city walls, which contains a Marks and Spencer, Virgin Megastore, Dixons and other high-street chain stores.

Getting There & Away

AIR

City of Derry Airport (☎ 7181 0784) is about 13km east of Derry along the A2 towards Limavady. There are direct flights daily to London Stansted (Ryanair), Dublin, Glasgow and Manchester (British Airways). For more information see p673.

BUS

The **bus station** (Map p605; ☎ 7126 2261) is on Foyle St, just northeast of the walled city.

Bus No 212, the *Maiden City Flyer*, is a fast and frequent service between Derry and Belfast (£9, 1¾ hours, hourly Monday to Saturday, six daily Sunday), calling at Dungiven. Other useful Ulsterbus services include No 273 to Belfast (three hours) via Omagh (£5.70, 1¼ hours, four or five daily); bus No 243 to Limavady and Coleraine (£5.60, one hour, three daily Monday to Saturday), continuing to Portstewart and Portrush in July and August only.

The **Airporter bus service** (Map p602; ☎ 7126 9996; www.airporter.co.uk; 3 Lower Clarendon St) runs direct from Lower Clarendon St in Derry to Belfast International (£14.50, 1½ hours) and Belfast City (£15, two hours) airports. There are six buses a day Monday to Friday, three on Saturday and four on Sunday.

Services to the Republic include bus No 274 to Dublin (£13.20, 4½ hours, five or six daily) and No 296 to Cork (10¼ hours, one daily Monday to Friday) via Enniskillen. The Cork bus leaves Derry at 9am, arriving at 7.15pm. The bus from Cork leaves at 9.15am and arrives in Derry at 8pm.

Bus Éireann (in Donegal ☎ 353-742 1309) operates a service from Derry to Galway (£12.50, 5¼ hours, three or four daily) via Letterkenny, Donegal and Sligo.

Lough Swilly (☎ 7126 2017) has an office upstairs at the bus station, and runs buses to Buncrana, Carndonagh, Dungloe, Letterkenny (£4.20, 10 daily Monday to Saturday) and Moville in County Donegal. The 10.15am bus to Carndonagh continues to Malin Head (£5.20, 1½ hours) on Monday, Wednesday, Friday and Saturday – a very scenic trip.

TRAIN

Derry's Waterside train station is on the eastern side of the River Foyle; a free shuttle bus (No 999) links with the bus station on Foyle St. Trains to Belfast (£8.20, 2¼ hours, eight daily) are slower but more comfortable than the bus, and the section of line between Derry and Coleraine is very scenic. There are also frequent trains to Coleraine (45 minutes, seven daily), with connections to Portrush (1¼ hours).

Getting Around

Bus No 143 to Limavady stops near the airport, otherwise a taxi costs about £10.

Local buses leave from Foyle St, outside the bus station, where there are also shareable black cabs to outlying suburbs such as Shantallow. The **Derry Taxi Association** (☎ 7126 0247) and **Foyle Taxis** (☎ 7126 3905) operate from the city centre to all areas.

The Foyle Valley cycle route passes through Derry on the way to Strabane.

LIMAVADY & AROUND

Enchanted by a folk tune played outside her window by a blind fiddler, Limavady resident Jane Ross (1810–79) jotted down the melody – O'Cahan's Lament, or the Londonderry Air. She had written down for the first time the tune that came to be known around the world as *Danny Boy* – probably the most famous Irish song of all time.

Limavady was granted to Sir Thomas Phillips, the organiser of the Plantation of County Londonderry (see p28), by James I in 1612, after the last ruling chief, Sir Donnell Ballagh O'Cahan, was found guilty of rebellion. Its original Gaelic name Léim an Mhadaidh means 'The Dog's Leap' and refers to one of the O'Cahans' dogs which jumped a gorge across the River Roe to bring warning of an unexpected enemy attack.

The **tourist office** (☎ 7776 0307; 7 Connell St; 🕑 9am-5pm Mon-Fri, 9am-5.30pm Sat Apr-Sep, 9am-5pm Mon-Fri Oct-Mar) is northeast of the town centre in the Limavady Borough Council Offices. Limavady holds a **jazz and blues festival** in early June.

Sights

Today Limavady is a quiet, prosperous small town. There's not much to see in town except the **blue plaque** on the wall at 51 Main St, opposite the Alexander Arms, commemorating the home of Jane Ross. The **town hall**, also on Main St, is being developed as a museum and arts centre.

The lovely **Roe Valley Country Park**, about 3km south of Limavady, has riverside walks stretching for 5km either side of the River Roe, a world-renowned trout and salmon river. The area is associated with the O'Cahans, who ruled the valley until the Plantation. The 17th-century settlers saw the flax-growing potential of the damp river valley and the area became an important linen-manufacturing centre.

The **Dogleap Centre** (☎ 7772 2074; 41 Dogleap Rd; admission free; 🕑 9am-6pm Apr-Sep, 9am-5pm Mon-Fri Oct-Mar) houses a visitor centre and tea room. Next door is Ulster's first domestic **hydroelectric power station**, opened in 1896; it opens on request at the visitor centre. The nearby **Weaving Shed Museum** (admission free; 🕑 1-5pm daily Jul-Aug, 1-5pm Sat & Sun May-Jun) contains old photographs and relics of the valley's flax industry. The scutch mill, where the flax was pounded, is a 20-minute walk away, along the river, past two watch towers built to guard the linen when it was spread out in the fields for bleaching.

The park is clearly marked off the B192 road between Limavady and Dungiven. Bus No 146 from Limavady to Dungiven will drop you on the main road, but there's no weekend service. The park is about a 30-minute walk from the main road.

Sleeping

Alexander Arms Hotel (☎ 7776 3443; 34 Main St; s/d £20/40; P ☒) A long-established, central hotel and pub dating from 1875, the Alexander Arms is now a friendly, family run B&B.

Gorteen House Hotel (☎ 7772 2333; info@gorteen.com; 187 Roe Mill Rd; s/d £42/44; P) A fine old country house off Roe Mill Rd, 1.5km south of Limavady town centre, the recently renovated Gorteen House is popular with golfers and sports a lovely conservatory-restaurant.

Eating

Lime Tree (☎ 7776 4300; 60 Catherine St; lunch £4-6, dinner £13-16; noon-2pm & 6-9pm Wed-Sun, noon-9.30pm Sat & Sun) Limavady's top restaurant serves up fresh local produce, with an emphasis on fish dishes like hot-smoked salmon with roasted red onion, fennel and coriander. There are good-value three-course lunches (£8.50) and dinners (£19.95).

Oven Door (☎ 7772 2411; 5 Market St; mains £3-5; 9am-5.30pm Mon-Sat) If you fancy a quick snack, this bakery has a comfy cafeteria at the back, serving good coffee, cakes and light meals.

Alexander Arms (☎ 7776 3443; 34 Main St) serves bar food and has a restaurant serving the usual pub-grub style meals.

Getting There & Away

Bus No 143 runs between Derry and Limavady almost hourly. There's no direct bus to Belfast from Limavady but connections can be made at Coleraine or Dungiven.

DUNGIVEN

The small market town of Dungiven (Dún Geimhin), 14km south of Limavady, has an interesting old priory and a good independent hostel. It's an easy stopoff if you're travelling between Belfast and Derry, and a better base than Limavady for exploring the Sperrin Mountains. The Ulster Way passes nearby.

There's a **tourist information** desk in Dungiven Castle (p613).

Dungiven Priory

The remains of this **Augustinian priory**, off the A6 on the eastern edge of town, date back to the 12th century when it replaced a pre-Norman monastery.

In the chancel of the church is the magnificent **tomb of Cooey-na-Gal**, a chieftain of the O'Cahans who died in 1385. It's difficult to see in the dark of the blocked-off chancel, but the tomb bears figures of six kilted 'gallowglasses' (armed retainers), Scottish mercenaries hired by Cooey O'Cahan as minders – they earned him the nickname 'na-Gal' ('of the Foreigners'). It's topped by a beautifully sculpted canopy of Gothic tracery.

Near the entrance to the churchyard is a **bullaun**, a mossy, hollowed stone originally used by the monks for grinding grain, but now collecting rainwater and used as a site of pilgrimage and prayer by people seeking cures for illnesses. A nearby tree is covered in prayer rags left by visiting pilgrims.

Sleeping

Dungiven Castle (☎ 7774 2428; www.dungivencastle.com; Main St; dm £12, s/d £15/30; P) Renovated Dungiven Castle provides good hostel-style accommodation in 10-bed dorms, and en-suite doubles, twins and family rooms. Facilities include laundry, kitchen and free tea and coffee. One room is wheelchair accessible. Don't be put off by the car park and ugly buildings on the street side – the other side looks out across beautiful gardens to the Sperrin Mountains.

Flax Mill Hostel (☎ 7774 2655; Mill Lane, Derrylane; tent sites £3.50, dm £5.80; P ☒) This converted 18th-century flax mill is 5km north of Dungiven, signposted off the B192 road to Limavady. The owners of this idyllic countryside retreat mill their own flour, grow their own veggies and generate their own electricity. There are 16 beds in three dorms and one double room. It's an extra £2 for breakfast. If you're travelling by bus, the owners will pick you up from Dungiven.

Getting There & Away

The hourly bus No 212 between Derry and Belfast stops on Main St in Dungiven. Goldline Express No 246 runs between Limavady and Dungiven (£2.20, 25 minutes, six daily Monday to Saturday, two Sunday).

INLAND COUNTY DERRY

Inland County Derry, southeast of Dungiven across the Glenshane Pass, is staunch Protestant territory occupied by Plantation towns like Draperstown, Magherafelt and Moneymore, established by the London guilds in the 17th century with grants of land from William of Orange.

Draperstown

pop 1400

Draperstown was founded in the early 17th century by, surprise surprise, the Worshipful Company of Drapers. Today it is a neat little market town, home to the **Ulster Plantation Centre** (☎ 7962 7800; 50 High St; adult/child £3/1.50; 10am-5pm Mon-Sat, 1-5pm Sun Easter-Sep, 10am-4pm Mon-Fri Oct-Easter), whose multimedia exhibits tell the story of the Plantation from the 'Flight of the Earls' in 1603 to the Potato Famine of the mid-19th century.

Draperstown can be reached from Dungiven by taking the Belfast bus No 212 to Glenshane Rd, Castledawson, then changing to No 182 (2¼ hours). Check the bus times locally.

Moneymore

pop 1200

Moneymore was also founded by the London Drapers, who installed Ulster's first piped water supply here in 1615. The country house of **Springhill** (☎ 8674 8210; 20 Springhill Rd; adult/child £3.65/1.80; noon-6pm daily Jul & Aug, noon-6pm Sat, Sun & hols mid-Mar–Jun & Sep), 1.5km south of Moneymore on the B18, is an interesting example of early Plantation architecture. The original house was built around 1695 by the Lenox-Conynghams, settlers from Scotland, and enlarged by the addition of the wings in the 18th century. Inside are antique weapons, an important collection of costumes dating from the 18th to the early 20th centuries, and a friendly ghost called Olivia.

Ulsterbuses Nos 110 and 210 between Belfast and Cookstown stop at Moneymore, a 20-minute walk from the house.

COASTAL COUNTY DERRY

Magilligan Point

The huge triangular spit of land that almost closes off the mouth of Lough Foyle is mostly taken up by a military firing range, and is home to a once-notorious prison. Still, it's worth a visit for its vast sandy beaches – **Magilligan Strand** to the west, and the 9km sweep of **Benone Strand** to the northeast. On the point itself, watching over the entrance to Lough Foyle, stands a **Martello tower**, built during the Napoleonic Wars in 1812 to guard against French invasion.

Benone Tourist Complex (☎ 7775 0555; 59 Benone Ave; tents £7.50, caravans £10.50-12; 9am-10pm Jul & Aug, 9am-dusk Apr-Jun & Sep, 9am-5pm Oct-Mar), adjacent to Benone Strand, has an outdoor heated pool, children's pool, tennis courts and putting green. Note that dogs are not allowed on the beach from May to September.

A car ferry goes between Magilligan Point and Greencastle in County Donegal (car/motorcycle/pedestrian £5/2.50/1, 15 minutes) every 30 minutes or so, all year round.

Downhill

In 1774 the eccentric Bishop of Derry and fourth Earl of Bristol, Frederick Augustus Hervey, built himself a palatial home, **Downhill**, on the coast west of Castlerock. It burnt down in 1851, was rebuilt between 1873 and 1876, and finally abandoned after WWII. The ruins of the house now stand forlornly on a cliff top.

The original demesne covered some 160 hectares, which is now part of the Forest Service's **Downhill Forest** (admission free; 10am-dusk). The beautiful landscaped gardens below the ruins of the house are the work of celebrated gardener Jan Eccles, who became custodian of Downhill at the age of 60 and created the garden over a period of 30 years. She died in 1997 aged 94.

The main attraction here is the little **Mussenden Temple** (admission free; parking at Lion's Gate car/motorbike £3.50/2; 11am-7.30pm daily Jun-Aug, 11am-6pm Sat, Sun & hols Mar-May & Sep, 11am-5pm Sat & Sun Oct), built by an energetic bishop to house his library or his mistress – opinions differ! He had an affair with the mistress of Frederick William II of Prussia well into his old age.

It's a pleasant, 15-minute walk to the temple from Castlerock, with fine views west to the beach at Benone and Donegal, and east to Portstewart and the shadowy outlines of the Scottish hills. On the beach below the temple, the bishop used to challenge his own clergy to horseback races, rewarding the winners with lucrative parishes.

On the main road 1km west of the temple, at the closed-down Downhill Hotel, the scenic **Bishop's Road** climbs steeply up through a ravine, and heads over the hills to Limavady. There are spectacular views over Lough Foyle, Donegal and the Sperrin Mountains from the **Gortmore** picnic area, and from the cliff top at **Binevenagh Lake**.

SLEEPING

Downhill Hostel (☎ 7084 9077; www.thedownhillhostel.com; 12 Mussenden Rd; dm/d/f £8/24/24 plus £5 per child) This beautifully restored late-19th-century house, tucked beneath the sea cliffs and overlooking the beach, offers very comfortable accommodation in three six-bed dorms and four double rooms. There's a well-stocked kitchen, laundry facilities and a big lounge with an open fire and a view of the sea. You can even paint your own mugs, plates and bowls in the neighbouring pottery. There are no shops in Downhill so bring supplies with you.

Castlerock

Castlerock is a small seaside resort with a decent beach. At the turn-off from the main coast road towards Castlerock is the late-17th-century **Hezlett House** (☎ 7084 8567; guided tour adult/child £3.50/2; noon-6pm Wed-Mon Jun-Aug, noon-6pm Sat & Sun mid-Mar–May & Sep), a thatched cottage noted for its cruck-truss roof gables of stone and turf strengthened with wooden crucks, or crutches. The interior decoration is Victorian.

GETTING THERE & AWAY

Bus No 134 between Limavady and Coleraine (six to eight daily Monday to Saturday) stops at Downhill and Castlerock, as does No 234 between Derry and Coleraine.

There are nine trains a day from Castlerock to Coleraine (10 minutes) and Derry (35 minutes) Monday to Saturday, and three on Sunday.

COLERAINE

pop 25,300

Coleraine (Cúil Raithin), on the banks of the River Bann, is an important transport hub and shopping centre for County Derry and the Causeway Coast. It was one of the original Plantation towns of County Londonderry, founded in 1613. The University of Ulster was established here in 1968, much to the chagrin of Derry, which had lobbied hard to win it.

Orientation & Information

The mostly pedestrianised town centre is on the east bank of the River Bann. From the combined train and bus station turn left along Railway Rd to find the **Tourist Information Centre** (☎ 7034 4723; colerainetic@btconnect.com; Railway Rd; 9am-5pm Mon-Sat) then turn right at King's Gate St for the main shopping area and **Coleraine Library** (☎ 7034 2561; Queen St; 10am-8pm Mon, Tue & Fri, 10am-5.30pm Wed & Thu, 10am-5pm Sat), which has public Internet access for £1.50 per 30 minutes.

Sights

The tourist office has a *Heritage Trail* leaflet that will guide you around what little remains of the original Plantation town, including **St Patrick's Church**, parts of which date from 1613, and fragments of the town walls.

Just 1.5km south of the town centre, on the east bank of the river, is **Mountsandel Mount**, a mysterious mound that may have been an Early Christian stronghold or a later Anglo-Norman fortification. Nearby, a 7th-millennium-BC Mesolithic site has been excavated, revealing post-holes, hearths and pits.

Sleeping

There's not much accommodation in the town centre; most B&Bs are on the fringes.

Town House (☎ 7034 4869; dale@townhouse.freeserve.co.uk; 45 Millburn Rd; s/d £20/36; P ⊠) The Town House B&B is a listed mid-19th-century terraced house with large bedrooms and a homely atmosphere. It's a 10-minute walk west of the train and bus station.

Camus Country House (☎ 7034 2982; 27 Curragh Rd, Castleroe; s/d £25/45; P ⊠) This lovely 17th-century house is on the site of an 8th-century monastery, and there's an old Celtic cross in the adjacent cemetery. The owner can organise fishing trips. It's signposted off the A54, west of the river and 5km south of town.

Getting There & Away

Ulsterbus No 218 links Coleraine to Portrush (£1.80, 20 minutes) and Belfast (£7, 1¾ hours, six daily Monday to Saturday, three Sunday). Bus No 234 goes to Derry (£5.60, one hour, seven daily Monday to Friday, two Sunday) via Limavady. See also Transport, p599.

There are regular trains from Coleraine to Belfast (£6.50, two hours) and Derry (see Getting There & Away, p612). A branch line links Coleraine to Portrush (£1, 12 minutes, hourly).

PORTSTEWART

pop 6500

When the English novelist Thackeray visited the seaside and golfing resort of Portstewart (Port Stíobhaird) in 1842, he noted the 'air of comfort and neatness'. His assessment still rings true, and the place has a slightly upmarket feel that distinguishes it from Portrush, 6km further east.

Orientation & Information

Central Portstewart consists of a promenade with a harbour at the north end. A coastal walk, paralleled by Strand Rd, continues south to the beach of Portstewart Strand.

The **Tourist Office** (☎ 7083 2286; Town Hall, The Crescent; ⌚ 10am-4pm Mon-Sat Jul & Aug) is in the library in the red-brick town hall at the south end of the promenade.

Sights & Activities

The broad, 2.5km-long beach of **Portstewart Strand** is a 20-minute walk south of the centre, or a short bus ride along Strand Rd. Parking (£4 per car) is allowed on the firm sand, which can accommodate over 1000 cars.

In early May the **North-West 200 motorcycle race** (www.northwest200.fm) is run on a road circuit taking in Portrush, Portstewart and Coleraine. This classic race is one of the last to be run on closed public roads anywhere in Europe, and attracts up to 70,000 spectators; if you're not one of them, it's best to avoid the area on the race weekend.

The **Port Path** is a 10.5km coastal footpath (part of the Ulster Way) that stretches from Portstewart Strand to White Rock, 2km east of Portrush.

Portstewart is within a few kilometres of three of Northern Ireland's top **golf courses** – Royal Portrush (green fees £85/95 weekday/weekend), Portstewart (£60/80) and Castlerock (£35/60).

Sleeping

Don't even think about turning up without a booking during the North-West 200 weekend in May.

BUDGET

Portstewart Holiday Park (☎ 7083 3308; 80 Mill Rd; tent site £12; ⌚ Mar-Oct) The nearest place to the promenade (a 15-minute walk away) that you can pitch a tent. Coming from Coleraine on the A2, turn right at the Mill Rd/Strand Rd roundabout.

Juniper Hill Caravan Park (☎ 7083 2023; 70 Ballyreagh Rd; tent site £12-15; ⌚ Apr-Sep) This fairly posh council-run park, 2.5km east of town on the way to Portrush, has space for half a dozen tents.

Causeway Coast Hostel (☎ 7083 3789; rick@causewaycoasthostel.fsnet.co.uk; 4 Victoria Terrace; dm £7.50-8.50, d £18-22) This terraced house just northeast of the harbour has four-, six- and eight-bed dorms plus three twin rooms. It has its own kitchen, laundry and a welcoming open fire in winter. Bus No 218 from Coleraine train and bus station stops nearby.

MID-RANGE

Anchorage Inn (☎ 7083 4401; info@theanchorbar.com; 87-89 The Promenade; s/d £40/60; P ⊠) The Anchorage's 20 en-suite rooms, some with sea views, provide comfortable, central B&B accommodation just a one-minute walk from the prom.

Cromore Halt Inn (☎ 7083 6888; www.cromore.com; 158 Station Rd; s/d £37.50/65; P ⊠) The Cromore has a dozen modern, businesslike rooms with satellite TV, phone and modem point, and a good restaurant. It's about 1km east of the harbour, on the corner of Station Rd and Mill Rd.

The following centrally located B&Bs are also recommended:

Akaroa (☎ 7083 2067; 75 The Promenade; s/d £25/50; ⊠)

Craigmore (☎ 7083 2120; 26 The Promenade; s/d £20/45; ⌚ Apr-Oct; ⊠)

Mount Oriel (☎ 7083 2556; 74 The Promenade; s/d £21/40; ⌚ Jun-Sep)

Eating

Morelli's (☎ 7083 2150; 53 The Promenade; ⌚ 9am-11pm) A local institution, Morelli's has been dispensing mouth-watering ice cream since 1911. This modern café dishes up pasta and pizza as well as good coffee and cakes, and has a great view across the bay to Mussenden Temple, Benone Strand and Donegal.

Harbour Café (☎ 7083 4103; 18 The Promenade; mains £2.50-4.50; ⌚ 9am-10pm, closed Mon Oct-Mar) The local 'greasy spoon' is the place for reasonably priced breakfast fry-ups, filled rolls and light meals.

Shenanigans Winebar & Restaurant (☎ 7083 6000; 78 The Promenade; lunch £6, dinner £9-12; ⌚ 12.30-2.30pm & 5-9.30pm Mon-Sat, 12.30-9.30pm Sun) Big, bright, brash and busy, Shenanigans has an international menu that ranges from Irish and Mexican through Indian to Chinese and Thai, with a fair selection of vegetarian dishes.

Ashiana (☎ 7083 4455; 12a The Diamond; mains £4.50-5.50; ⏲ 5-11pm) This place offers a mixed menu of Indian and European dishes, with a good vegetarian selection.

Drinking

Anchor Bar (☎ 7083 4401; 87-89 The Promenade) This bar at the Anchorage Inn is the liveliest of Portstewart's traditional pubs, and is hugely popular with students from the nearby University of Ulster. It serves decent pub food, opens till late, has live music Thursday to Monday, karaoke on Tuesday and a quiz on Wednesday.

Shenanigans (☎ 7083 6000; 78 The Promenade) In addition to a restaurant, the Shenanigans complex has two bars and a club. Rustic O'Haras Bar is another popular student venue, with standing room only at weekends, while Bar 7 is more relaxed, serving coffee, cocktails and shooters. Chaines 'niteclub' (Friday and Saturday only) is where Portstewart's teenagers go to get tanked on cheap drinks promos and (hopefully) pull.

Getting There & Away

Bus No 140 plies between Coleraine and Portstewart (£1.80, 17 minutes) roughly every half-hour (fewer on Sunday). Also see Transport, p599.

The nearest train station is at Portrush. See p618 for details.

COUNTY ANTRIM

PORTRUSH

pop 5700

The bustling seaside resort of Portrush (Port Rois) is bursting at the seams with holidaymakers in high season and, not surprisingly, many of its attractions are unashamedly focused on families. However, it is also one of Ireland's top surfing spots, and is home to the North's hottest nightclub.

Portrush Tourist Information Centre (☎ 7082 3333; portrush@nitic.net; Dunluce Centre, 10 Sandhill Dr; ⏲ 9am-7pm mid-Jun–Aug, 9am-5pm Mon-Fri, noon-5pm Sat & Sun Apr–mid-Jun & Sep, noon-5pm Sat & Sun Mar & Oct) books accommodation and has a bureau de change.

Sights & Activities

The **Dunluce Family Entertainment Centre** (☎ 7082 4444; 10 Sandhill Dr; admission £3-4; ⏲ 10.30am-7pm Sat & Sun Apr-May, 10am-5pm Mon-Fri, noon-7pm Sat & Sun Jun, 10.30am-7pm daily Jul & Aug, noon-5pm Sat & Sun Sep-Mar) is a hi-tech, indoor adventure playground for kids, with interactive games, a computerised treasure hunt and a 'turbo-tour' motion-simulator ride.

Waterworld (☎ 7082 2001; The Harbour; adult & child over 6/child 6 & under £4.50/1.50; ⏲ 10am-8pm Mon-Sat, noon-8pm Sun), by the harbour, has indoor swimming pools, waterslides and spa baths for children to play in (family tickets are available), and ten-pin bowling. The Health Suite (sauna, steam room and sunbeds) is included in the admission price.

Portrush Countryside Centre (☎ 7082 3600; Bath Rd; admission free; ⏲ 10am-6pm Jun-Sep) has even more activities for kids, including marine life exhibits, a touch pool, rock-pool rambles and fossil hunts.

In summer, boats depart regularly for **cruises** or **fishing trips**; the tourist office has a list of operators. For horse riding contact the **Maddybenny Riding Centre** (☎ 7082 3394; Maddybenny Farm, Atlantic Rd; lessons & hacking £10/hr); beginners are welcome.

Portrush is famous as a **surfing** centre. The friendly **Troggs** (☎ 7082 5476; www.troggs.com; 88 Main St; ⏲ 9am-5.30pm Tue-Sun) surf shop offers bodyboard/surfboard hire (£5/10 per day) and wetsuit hire (£5 per day), surf reports and general advice. A two-hour lesson including equipment hire costs £20.

Sleeping

Places fill up quickly during summer so it's advisable to book in advance.

BUDGET

MaCools (☎ 7082 4845; scilley@portrush.hostel.fsnet.co.uk; 5 Causeway View Terrace; dm £8; 💻) MaCools is a welcoming, independent hostel with 18 beds in single-sex dorms with sea views, and one private room. There's laundry and cooking facilities (with free tea, coffee, herbs and spices) and bicycles for rent (£5 per day). It's a 10-minute walk north of the train and bus station.

Carrick Dhu Caravan Park (☎ 7082 3712; 12 Ballyreagh Rd; tent site £12-15; ⏲ Apr-Sep) This is a small site with standard facilities, 1.5km west of Portrush on the A2 towards Portstewart.

MID-RANGE

Alexandra Town House (☎ 7082 2284; www.alexandratownhouse.com; 11 Landsdowne Cres; s £25, d £45-60; P ⊠) The Alexandra is an elegant, four-storey terraced town house dating from 1901, with lots of nice period features. The more expensive rooms have superb views along the coast.

Clarmont (☎ 7082 2397; www.clarmont.com; 10 Landsdowne Cres; s/d £25/50; ⊠) The Alexandra's next-door neighbour shares the great views, and has a décor that tastefully mixes period and modern.

Peninsula Hotel (☎ 7082 2293; www.peninsulahotel.co.uk; 15 Eglinton St; s/d/t £40/60/75; wheelchair access) A short walk from the train station, the rooms at the Peninsula are modern, functional and, well, pink. Rooms cost £10 more per person on Saturday nights.

There are a few B&Bs immediately opposite the train station in Eglinton St:

Glenshane (☎ 7082 4839; peterrosbb@aol.com; 113 Eglinton St; d £37-40; Apr-Sep; P ⊠)

Atlantic View (☎ 7082 3647; bandbni@aol.com; 103 Eglinton St; s £15-20, d £30-36)

TOP END

Magherabuoy House Hotel (☎ 7082 3507; www.magherabuoy.co.uk; 41 Magheraboy Rd; s/d £60/100; P) This plush country hotel is 1.5km south of the town centre; at the time of research it was undergoing a major renovation, and due to reopen by summer 2003. Reception can organise activities like water-skiing, horse riding, surfing, fishing and archery.

Eating

Coast (☎ 7082 3311; The Harbour; mains £5-8; 12.30-2.30pm & 5-10pm Mon-Sat, 12.30-10pm Sat & Sun) Offering a third harbour-side choice, Coast does stone-baked pizzas, pastas and a range of steak, chicken and fish dishes.

Harbour Bar & Bistro (☎ 7082 2430; The Harbour; mains £8-11; 12.30-2.15pm & 5.30-10pm Mon-Sat, 12.30-3pm & 5.30-9pm Sun) Quality grub – juicy steaks, home-made burgers, spicy chicken, oriental dishes and vegetarian meals – and a harbour-side location make the Harbour one of Portrush's most popular eating places.

Ramore Wine Bar (☎ 7082 4313; The Harbour; mains £6-12; 12.15-2.15pm & 5-10pm Mon-Sat, 12.30-3pm & 5-9pm Sun) The stylish Ramore, with a better view and a more upmarket menu offering the likes of Thai chicken and prawn tempura, is a posher alternative to the neighbouring Harbour Bar.

Don Giovanni's Ristorante (☎ 7082 5516; 9-13 Causeway St; mains £5-8; 5.30-11pm) Near the junction of Eglinton and Main Sts, Don Giovanni's is slightly tacky looking but serves authentic Italian grub, including steak, chicken and fish dishes as well as pasta and pizza.

Bread Shop (☎ 7082 3722; 21 Eglinton St; mains £3; 9am-5.30pm Mon-Sat) A bakery and café, the Bread Shop serves decent coffee, sandwiches, fish and chips and light meals.

Entertainment

Kelly's Complex (☎ 7082 6611; www.kellysportrush.co.uk; 1 Bushmills Rd) The North's top clubbing venue, regularly featuring DJs from London and Manchester, and attracting clubbers from as far afield as Belfast. Plain and small-looking from the outside, the Tardis effect takes over as you enter a wonderland of seven bars and three dance floors, with décor ranging from old-world wood and antiques to ultra-mod steel and mirrors. **Lush!@Kellys** (admission Wed/Sat £3/10; 9pm-2am Wed & Sat) is, quite simply, one of the best club nights in the UK and Ireland. Nuff said. Don't miss it.

The complex, which is on the A2 just east of Portrush, beside the Golf Links Holiday Park, includes a hotel and restaurant.

Other recommended venues in the town centre include:

Rogues (☎ 7082 2076; 54 Kerr St) Live music Monday, Wednesday, Thursday, Saturday and Sunday, disco on Friday. There is a £2 cover charge after 11pm.

Traks (☎ 7082 2112; www.traks-complex.com; Station Sq) Kellys' main competitor in the clubbing stakes.

Getting There & Around

The bus terminal is near the Dunluce Centre. Bus Nos 139 and 140 link Portrush with Coleraine (£1.80, 30 minutes) every half hour or so. Bus No 172 runs to Ballycastle (£4.10, one hour, five daily Monday to Saturday, three Sunday) via Portballintrae, Bushmills, Giant's Causeway and Ballintoy. Bus No 278 runs once daily, except Saturday, from Portrush to Dublin (five hours). Also see Transport, p599.

The train station is just south of the harbour. Portrush is served by trains from Coleraine (15 minutes, at least hourly), where there are connections to Belfast or Derry.

For taxis call **Andy Brown's** (☎ 7082 2223) or **North West Taxis** (☎ 7082 4446). Both are near the town hall. A taxi to Kelly's is around £5 and it's £10 to the Giant's Causeway.

DUNLUCE CASTLE

The views on the Causeway Coast between Portrush and Portballintrae are dominated by the romantic ruins of **Dunluce Castle** (☎ 2073 1938; 87 Dunluce Rd; adult/child £1.50/0.75; 🕓 10am-6pm Mon-Sat, noon-6pm Sun Jun-Aug, 10am-6pm Mon-Sat, 2-6pm Sun Apr & Sep, 10am-4pm Tue-Sat, 2-4pm Sun Oct-Mar), perched atop a dramatic basalt crag. In the 16th and 17th centuries it was the seat of the MacDonnell family (from 1620, the earls of Antrim), who built a Renaissance-style manor house within the walls. Part of the castle, including the kitchen, collapsed into the sea in 1639, taking seven servants and a night's dinner with it.

The landward wall has cannons salvaged from the *Girona*, a Spanish Armada vessel that foundered nearby. Below, a path leads down from the gatehouse to the Mermaid's Cave beneath the castle crag.

Dunluce is situated 5km east of Portrush, a one-hour walk away along the coastal path. All the buses that run along the coast also stop at Dunluce Castle; see Transport, p599.

PORTBALLINTRAE

pop 1100

During WWI Portballintrae was the only place in the UK to be shelled by a German submarine. And that's pretty much its only claim to fame. It's set around a sand-fringed, horseshoe bay with a tiny harbour, and the fine sandy beach of Bushfoot Strand stretching for 1.5km to the northeast. The village is an easy 30-minute walk from Bushmills, and 45 minutes from the Giant's Causeway.

There are two good places to eat here: **Sallie's Craft 'n' Coffee Shop** (☎ 2073 1328; 47 Beach Rd; snacks £2-3; 🕓 11am-6pm Fri-Sun Easter-Jun, 11am-6pm Tue-Sun Jul & Aug), and **Sweeney's Wine Bar** (☎ 2073 2405; 6b Seaport Ave; mains £5-10; 🕓 noon-9.30pm) in a converted 17th-century stable block just above the beach.

Bus No 138 runs regularly (except on Sunday) to Coleraine and Portrush, while bus No 172 operates several times daily to Portrush and Ballycastle. Also see Transport, p599.

SORLEY BOY & THE MACDONNELLS

Somhairle Buidhe (Sorley Boy) MacDonnell (1505–90) was 16th-century Antrim's top dog, a descendant of the Scottish Lords of the Isles, and inheritor of the title 'Lord of Dunyveg and the Glens of Antrim'. He was born at Ballycastle, which remained the principal MacDonnell stronghold until Sorley Boy (meaning 'yellow-haired Sorley') captured Dunluce Castle in 1584. He was made Constable of Dunluce by the English government, and extended and modernised the castle with gold and cannon salvaged from the Spanish Armada ship *Girona,* wrecked near the Giant's Causeway in 1588.

Sorley Boy's son Randal MacDonnell was created the first earl of Antrim in 1620, with an estate stretching from the River Bann round to Larne. Dunluce was abandoned in the late 17th century, when the second earl moved the family seat to nearby Ballymagarry House; in 1745 it was moved again to Glenarm Castle, where the 14th earl of Antrim, Rt Hon Alexander Randal Mark MacDonnell, now lives. Dunluce was given to the state in 1928.

Sorley Boy and other MacDonnell chiefs are buried in the MacDonnell vault at Bonamargy Friary at Ballycastle.

BUSHMILLS

pop 1350

The small town of Bushmills, off the A2 between Portrush and Ballycastle, has long been a place of pilgrimage for connoisseurs of Irish whiskey. A new youth hostel and a restored rail link with the Giant's Causeway have made it an attractive stop for hikers exploring the Causeway Coast.

Sights

Bushmills Distillery (☎ 2073 3218; Distillery Rd; adult/child £3.95/2; 🕓 9.30am-5.30pm Mon-Sat, noon-5.30pm Sun, last tour 4pm Apr-Oct; tours hourly 10.30am-3.30pm except 12.30pm Mon-Fri, 1.30pm-3.30pm Sat & Sun Nov-Mar) is the world's oldest legal distillery, having been granted a licence by King James I in 1608. Bushmills whiskey is made with Irish barley and water from St Columb's Rill, a tributary of the River Bush, and matured in oak barrels. During ageing, the alcohol content drops from around 60% to 40%; the spirit lost through evaporation is known, rather sweetly, as 'the angels' share'. After a tour of the distillery you're rewarded with a free sample (or a soft drink), and four lucky volunteers get a whiskey tasting session to compare Bushmills with other brands.

Giant's Causeway & Bushmills Railway (☎ 2073 2844; recorded timetable info ☎ 2073 2594; www.giantscausewayrailway.org; return adult/child £4.50/2.50) follows the route of a 19th-century tourist tramway for 3km from Bushmills to below the Giant's Causeway visitor centre. The narrow-gauge line and locomotives (two steam and one diesel) were bought from a private line on the shores of Lough Neagh. Trains run hourly between 11am and 4pm or 5pm, departing on the hour from Bushmills, the half-hour from the Causeway, from May to September, with some extra services in October and November.

Sleeping & Eating

Ballyness Caravan Park & B&B (☎ 2073 2393; www.ballynesscaravanpark.com; 40 Castlecatt Rd; tent site £8-10, campervans £10-11, B&B s/d £30/45; caravan park mid-Mar–Oct) This eco-friendly caravan park and farmhouse B&B is about 1km south of Bushmills town centre on the B66.

Mill Rest Youth Hostel (☎ 2073 1222; www.hini.org.uk; 49 Main St; dm £11-12.50, d £30; closed 11am-5pm Oct-Mar) This brand new, purpose-built hostel is just off The Diamond in the centre of town. Accommodation is mostly in four- to six-bed dorms, with one wheelchair-friendly, en-suite twin room. There's a kitchen, restaurant, laundry and bike shed.

Bushmills Inn (☎ 2073 2339; www.bushmillsinn.com; 9 Dunluce Rd; s £68-78, d £98-148; P ☒) One of Northern Ireland's most atmospheric hotels, the Bushmills Inn is an old coaching inn complete with peat fires, gas lamps and a round tower with a secret library. The rooms in the old part of the inn are small and cosy; there are larger, more expensive ones in the neighbouring Mill House. The inn's excellent **restaurant** (sandwiches £3.65-4.95, lunch £9, dinner £12-19; noon-9.30pm Mon-Sat, 12.30-9pm Sun), with intimate wooden booths, serves everything from sandwiches to full à la carte dinners.

Copper Kettle (☎ 2073 2560; 61 Main St; mains £2.50-4; 9am-5pm Mon-Sat, 10am-5pm Sun) A good place for a tea, coffee, cakes and light meals.

Getting There & Away

See Transport, p599.

GIANT'S CAUSEWAY

When you first see it you'll understand why the ancients thought the Causeway was not a natural feature. The vast expanse of regular, closely packed, hexagonal stone columns dipping gently beneath the waves looks for all the world like the handiwork of giants.

This spectacular rock formation – a Unesco World Heritage site and National Nature Reserve – is one of Ireland's most atmospheric sights, but it is all-too-often swamped by visitors. If you can, try to visit midweek or out of season to experience it at its most evocative.

Orientation & Information

The Causeway Tourist Office burnt down in April 2000. In April 2003 Moyle District Council announced plans for a competition to design a new one. Meanwhile, the council-run **Tourist Office** (☎ 2073 1855; causewaytic@hotmail.com; 10am-7pm Jul & Aug, 10am-6pm Jun, 10am-5pm Mar-May, Sep & Oct, 10am-4.30pm Nov-Feb) is housed in a wooden building beside the National Trust's gift shop and tea room.

Visiting the Giant's Causeway is free of charge but the overcrowded, council-run car park charges £5. It's a pleasant 1km walk from the car park down to the Causeway; minibuses with wheelchair access ply the route every 15 minutes (£0.60/1.20 one way/return). Guided tours of the site (June to August only) cost £2 per person.

Walking Tour

From the car park it's an easy 10- to 15-minute walk downhill on a tarmac road to the Giant's Causeway itself. However, a much better approach is to follow the clifftop path northeast for 2km to the Chimney Tops headland, which has an excellent view of the Causeway and the coastline to the west, including Inishowen and Malin Head. This pinnacled headland was bombarded by the Spanish Armada in 1588, who thought it was Dunluce Castle. Return towards the car park and about halfway back, above Port Noffer, descend to a lower-level footpath that leads to the Causeway. Allow 1½ hours for the round trip.

Sleeping & Eating

Causeway Hotel (☎ 2073 1226; 40 Causeway Rd; s/d £45/70) The National Trust's 19th-century Causeway Hotel is within spitting distance of the

DAVID TIPLING

Carrick-a-Rede Rope Bridge (p621), near the Giant's Causeway

GARETH MCCORMACK

Grazing sheep, **Causeway Coast** (p621)

Bogside Artists' mural (p606), Derry

MARTIN MOOS

RICHARD CUMMINS

Whiskey sign, **Bushmills Distillery** (p619)

MARTIN MOOS

Enniskillen Castle (p640), Enniskillen

GARETH MCCORMACK

Mt Sawel, **Sperrin Mountains** (p636)

Sunset, **Lower Lough Erne** (p645)

GARETH MCCORMACK

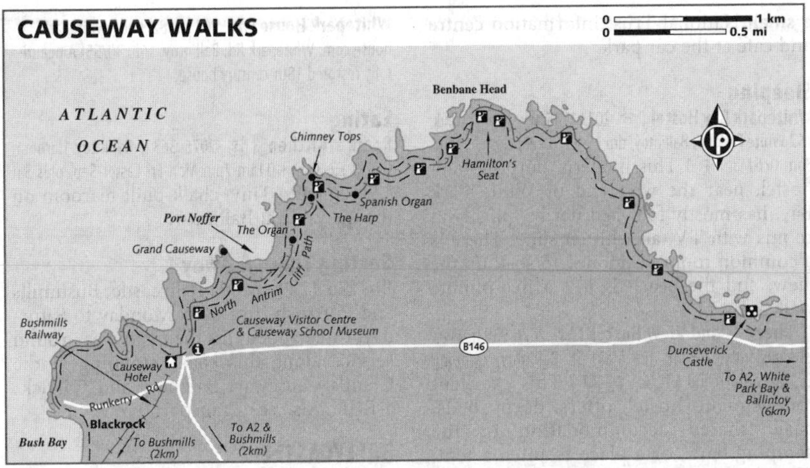

Causeway, and there are a few B&Bs nearby, but it's more pleasant staying in Bushmills or Ballintoy.

National Trust tearoom (⌚ 10am-7pm Jul & Aug, 10am-6pm Jun, 10am-5pm Sep & Oct, 10am-3pm Nov & Dec) The tearoom, above the Causeway car park, serves tea, coffee and light meals.

Getting There & Away

Bus No 172 from Portrush and Bushmills to Ballycastle passes the site year round. Also see Transport, p599.

GIANT'S CAUSEWAY TO BALLYCASTLE

Between the Giant's Causeway and Ballycastle lies the most scenic stretch of the Causeway Coast, with sea cliffs of contrasting black basalt and white chalk, rocky islands, picturesque little harbours and broad sweeps of sandy beach. It's best enjoyed on foot, following the 15km of waymarked **Causeway Coast Way** between the Giant's Causeway car park and Ballintoy, although the main attractions can also be reached by car or bus.

About 8km east of the Giant's Causeway is the meagre ruin of 16th-century **Dunseverick Castle** spectacularly sited on a grassy bluff. Another 1.5km on is the tiny seaside hamlet of **Portbradden**, with half a dozen harbourside houses and the tiny, blue-and-white St Gobban's Church, said to be the smallest in Ireland. Visible from Portbradden and accessible via the next junction off the A2 is the spectacular **White Park Bay** with its wide, sweeping sandy beach.

A few kilometres further on is **Ballintoy** (Baile an Tuaighe), another picture-postcard village, tumbling down the hillside to a scenic harbour. The restored limekiln on the quayside once made quicklime using stone from the chalk cliffs and coal from Ballymoney.

East of Ballintoy the Causeway Coast Way no longer sticks to the coast and follows the B15 road instead. The main attraction here is the famous **Carrick-a-Rede Rope Bridge** (☎ 2073 1582; admission free, car park £3.50; ⌚ 9.30am-7.30pm Jul & Aug, 10am-6pm mid-Mar–Jun & Sep). The 20m-long, 1m-wide bridge of wire rope spans the chasm between the sea-cliffs and the little island of Carrick-a-Rede, swaying gently 30m above the rock-strewn water.

The island has sustained a salmon fishery for centuries; fishermen stretch their nets out from the tip of the island to intercept the passage of the salmon migrating west along the coast to their home rivers. The fishermen put the bridge up every spring as they have done for the last 200 years – though it's not, of course, the original bridge.

Crossing the bridge is perfectly safe, but it can be frightening if you don't have a head for heights, especially if it's breezy (in high winds the bridge is closed). Once on the island there are good views of Rathlin Island and Fair Head to the east. There's a small National Trust information centre and café at the car park.

Sleeping

Whitepark Bay Hostel (☎ 2073 1745; www.hini.org.uk; 157 White Park Rd, Ballintoy; dm £9-11, d £26; closed 11am-5pm Oct-Mar; P) This modern, purpose-built hostel, near the west end of White Park Bay, has mostly four-bed dorms, plus twin rooms with TV, all with en suite. There is a common room positioned to soak up the view, and the beach is just a five-minute walk away.

Sheep Island View Hostel (☎ 2076 9391; www.sheepislandview.com; 42a Main St, Ballintoy; camping £5, dm adult/child £10/6; P) This excellent independent hostel offers dorm beds, basic shared accommodation in the camping barn, or a place to pitch a tent. There's a kitchen and laundry, a village store nearby, and a free pick-up service from the Giant's Causeway, Bushmills and Ballycastle. It's on the main coast road near the turn-off to Ballintoy harbour, and makes an ideal overnight stop if you're hiking between Bushmills and Ballycastle.

Good B&Bs in the area include:

Ballintoy House (☎ 2076 2317; 9 Main St, Ballintoy; s/d £20/34)

Whitepark House (☎ 2073 1482; bob@whiteparkhouse.com; Whitepark Rd, Ballintoy; s/d £30/55) A beautifully restored 18th-century house.

Eating

Roark's Kitchen (☎ 2076 3632; Ballintoy Harbour; snacks £2-3; 11am-7pm Mon-Fri Easter-Sep, plus Sat & Sun Oct-Easter) Tiny, chalk-built tearoom on the quayside at Ballintoy.

Getting There & Away

Bus No 172 between Ballycastle, Bushmills and Portrush (five daily Monday to Saturday, three Sunday) is the main, year-round service along this coast, stopping at the Giant's Causeway, Ballintoy and Carrick-a-Rede. Also see Transport, p599.

BALLYCASTLE

pop 4000

The harbour town and holiday resort of Ballycastle (Baile an Chaisil) marks the eastern end of the Causeway Coast. It's a pretty town with a good bucket-and-spade beach, but there's not a lot to see.

The **Tourist Information Office** (☎ 2076 2024; tourism@moyle-council.org; Moyle District Council, 7 Mary St; 9.30am-7pm Mon-Fri Jul & Aug, 9.30am-5pm Mon-Fri Sep-Jun) is in the council building at the east end of town. There's a First

MAKING OF THE CAUSEWAY

The Mythology

The story goes that the Irish giant, Finn MacCool, built the Causeway so he could cross the sea to fight the Scottish giant Benandonner. When he got there he found his rival asleep and, seeing that the Scot was far bigger than he, fled back to Ireland. Soon, Finn's wife heard the angry Benandonner come running across the Causeway, so she dressed Finn in a baby's shawl and bonnet and put him in a crib. When the Scottish giant came hammering at Finn's door, Mrs MacCool warned him not to wake Finn's baby. Taking a glance in the cot, Benandonner decided that if this huge baby was Finn's child, then MacCool himself must be immense, and fled in turn back to Scotland, ripping up the causeway as he went. All that remains are its ends – the Giant's Causeway in Ireland, and the island of Staffa in Scotland (which has similar rock formations).

The Geology

The more prosaic scientific explanation is that the Causeway rocks were formed 60 million years ago, when a thick layer of molten basaltic lava flowed along a valley in the existing chalk beds. As the lava flow cooled and hardened – from the top and bottom surfaces inward – it contracted, creating a pattern of hexagonal cracks at right angles to the cooling surfaces (think of mud contracting and cracking in a hexagonal pattern as a lake bed dries out). As solidification progressed towards the centre of the flow, the cracks spread down from the top, and up from the bottom, until the lava was completely solid. Erosion has cut into the lava flow, and the basalt has split along the contraction cracks, creating the hexagonal columns.

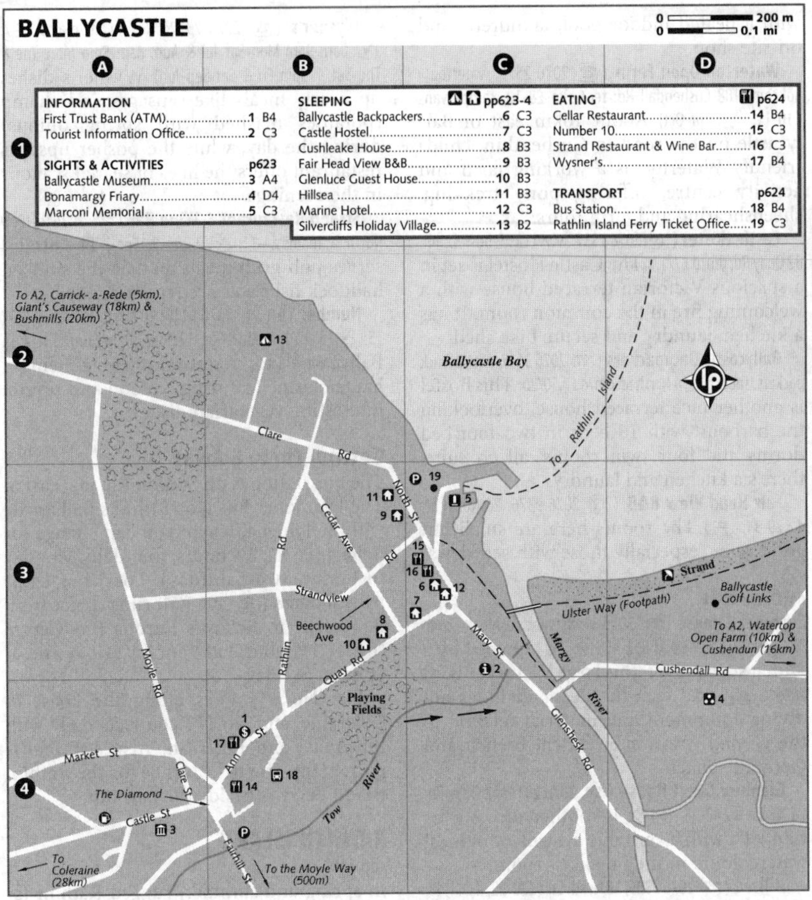

Trust Bank with an ATM on Ann St, near The Diamond.

Sights

The tiny **Ballycastle Museum** (☎ 2076 2942; 61a Castle St; admission free; noon-6pm Mon-Sat Jul & Aug), in the town's 18th-century courthouse, has a collection of Irish Arts and Crafts works. Near the harbour is the **Marconi Memorial**. Guglielmo Marconi's assistants contacted Rathlin by radio from Ballycastle in 1898 to prove to Lloyds of London that wireless communication worked.

Just east of town are the ruins of **Bonamargy Friary**, founded in 1485. The vault contains the tombs of MacDonnell chieftains, including Sorley Boy MacDonnell (p619).

Events

Ballycastle's **Ould Lammas Fair**, held on the last Monday and Tuesday of August, dates back to 1606. Thousands of people descend on the town for the market stalls and fairground rides, and to sample yellowman and dulse. Yellowman is a hard chewy toffee that's available from a few months before the fair. Dulse is dried edible seaweed. The fruit shop on The Diamond often stocks both delicacies.

Sleeping

BUDGET

Silvercliffs Holiday Village (☎ 2076 2550; 21 Clare Rd; tent & caravan sites £10-12) Silvercliffs is a big, posh family site on the clifftop above the harbour, with a heated indoor pool, laundrette and on-site shop.

Watertop Open Farm (☎ 2076 2576; watertop@aol.com; 188 Cushendall Rd; tent site £8-10, campervans £10-11; ⏲ Apr-Oct) About 10km east of Ballycastle on the road to Cushendun, child-friendly Watertop is a working farm and activity centre, offering pony trekking, sheepshearing and farm tours.

Castle Hostel (☎ 2076 2337; www.castlehostel.com; 62 Quay Rd; dm/d £7/17) The Castle Hostel is set in a spacious Victorian terraced house with a welcoming fire in the common room. It has a kitchen, laundry and secure bike shed.

Ballycastle Backpackers (☎ 2076 3612; am@bcbackpackers.fsnet.co.uk; 4 North St; dm/d £7.50/20) This hostel is another nice terraced house, overlooking the harbour, with 16 beds in two four-bed dorms and four twin rooms, all en suite; there's a kitchen and laundry.

Fair Head View B&B (☎ 2076 9376; 26 North St; d £29-34; Ⓟ) The rooms here are small but good value, especially those with sea views.

MID-RANGE

Cushleake House (☎ 2076 3798; www.cushleake.com; 32 Quay Rd; s £19-30, d £32-45; Ⓟ ⊠) Owned by a Dutch scuba diver, this large Victorian B&B has a nautical feel; the décor includes old diving equipment and material relating to the *Girona* wreck site. Dutch, French and German spoken.

Glenluce Guest House (☎ 2076 2914; 42 Quay Rd; s £18-35, d £40-45; Ⓟ ⊠) Another nice Victorian villa with a veritable art gallery of local watercolours in the breakfast room.

Hillsea (☎ 2076 2385; 28 North St; s £20-22, d £44-48; Ⓟ ⊠) Bigger than its neighbour Fair Head View, and with a better sea view, Hillsea's rooms are mostly en suite with TV and tea-making facilities.

Marine Hotel (☎ 2076 2222; www.marinehotel.net; 1 North St; s/d £50/75; Ⓟ ⊠ ♿) This newly refurbished hotel on the seafront is crisp and businesslike, with restaurant, fitness centre, sauna and steam room.

Eating

Cellar Restaurant (☎ 2076 3037; The Diamond; mains £8-13, pizza £6-8; ⏲ noon-11pm Mon-Sat, 5-10pm Sun Jun-Aug, noon-11pm Mon-Sat, noon-3.30pm Sun Sep-May) The Cellar is a cosy little basement restaurant with intimate wooden booths and a big fireplace, serving excellent steak, pork, chicken and fish dishes, as well as pizzas.

Wysner's (☎ 2076 2372; 16 Ann St; mains £5-7; ⏲ 8am-9pm Mon-Sat Jul & Aug, 8am-5pm Mon, Tue & Thu-Sat, 7-9pm Fri & Sat Sep-Jun) Wysner's dishes up hearty meals like sausages and champ (potatoes mashed with spring onions) during the day, while the posher upstairs restaurant offers the likes of seared scallops in the evenings.

Strand Restaurant & Wine Bar (☎ 2076 2349; 9 North St; mains £4-11; ⏲ 11am-9.15pm) The Strand serves pub-grub meals all day; the smoked haddock fishcakes are recommended.

Number 10 (☎ 2076 8110; 10 North St; mains £12-15; ⏲ 6-9.30pm Mon-Sat, 12.30-2.30pm Sun) This is Ballycastle's top restaurant, with a menu of haute cuisine featuring seafood and several interesting vegetarian dishes.

Getting There & Away

The bus station is on Station Rd, just east of The Diamond. Bus No 131 links Ballycastle with Ballymena, where you can change for Belfast (£6.50, 2¾ hours, four daily Monday to Friday, two Saturday). Local bus company **McGinns** (☎ 2076 3451) runs direct from Ballycastle to Belfast's Europa Bus Centre (£4.50, 1½ hours) at 4pm on Friday and at 8pm on Sunday.

Bus No 171 goes along the coast to Coleraine, and No 172 connects daily with Bushmills and Portrush. Also see Transport, p599. The ticket office for the Rathlin Island Ferry is beside the harbour.

RATHLIN ISLAND

pop 110

In spring and summer, rugged Rathlin Island (Reachlainn), 6km offshore from Ballycastle, is home to hundreds of seals and thousands of nesting seabirds. The island has a pub, a restaurant, two shops and a handful of accommodation options.

The island was raided by Vikings in AD 795 and suffered again in 1595 when Sorley Boy MacDonnell sent his family here for safety only to have them massacred by the English, along with most of the inhabitants. The island's most illustrious visitor was Robert the Bruce, who spent some time in 1306 in a cave on the northeastern point learning a lesson in perseverance. Watching a spider's resoluteness in repeatedly trying to spin a web gave him the courage to have another go at the English, whom he subsequently defeated at Bannockburn.

The chief attraction is the coastal scenery and birdlife of **Kebble National Nature Reserve** at the western end of the island. **RSPB West Lighthouse Viewpoint** (☎ 2076 3948; admission free; 🕒 by arrangement Apr-Aug) provides stunning views of the neighbouring sea stacks, thick with guillemots, kittiwakes, razorbills and puffins in spring and early summer. During the summer a minibus service runs there from the harbour.

The **Boathouse Visitor Centre** (☎ 2076 3951; admission £0.50; 🕒 11am-5pm Jul-Sep, noon-2pm Apr-Jun, on request Oct-Mar) south of the harbour details the history, culture and ecology of the island.

Sleeping & Eating

You can camp for free on the eastern side of Church Bay in a field not far from the harbour.

Soerneog View Hostel (☎ 2076 3954; Ouig; dm £8) Soerneog is a private house, a 10-minute walk south of the harbour, offering hostel-style accommodation in one double and two twin rooms. Advance booking is essential.

Kinramer Cottage (☎ 2076 3948; Kinramer; dm £5) This is a basic camping barn, a one-hour walk west from the harbour, where you bring your own food and bedding; book in advance. You might be able to get a lift on one of the minibuses; see the Getting There & Around section below for details.

Rathlin Guest House (☎ 2076 3917; The Quay; s/d £18/32; 🕒 Easter-Sep) The Rathlin overlooks Church Bay, just a five-minute walk from the ferry terminal. Evening meals are available for £8.50 per person.

Manor House (☎ 2076 3964; uravfm@smtp.ntrust.org.uk; Church Quarter; s £23-27, d £42) Restored and run by the National Trust, the 18th-century Manor House, on the north side of the harbour, is the island's biggest (11 rooms) and poshest place to stay. Evening meals are available by arrangement.

The Brockley Tearoom at Manor House serves soups, sandwiches, cakes and scones.

Getting There & Around

A **ferry** (☎ 2076 9299; www.calmac.co.uk) operates daily (adult/child/bicycle return £8.40/4.20/2, 45 minutes) from Ballycastle; advance booking is required.

From June to September ferries depart Ballycastle at 10am, noon, 4.30pm and 6.30pm (7pm on Friday), and leave Rathlin at 8.30am, 11am, 3.30pm and 5.30pm. In winter boats leave Ballycastle at 10.30am and 4pm (4.30pm on Friday) and from Rathlin at 9am and 3pm.

You can't take your car to Rathlin, but nowhere on the island is more than 6km (about 1½ hours' walk) from the ferry pier. You can hire a bicycle (£7 per day) from Soerneog View Hostel, or take a minibus tour with **Irene's** (☎ 2076 3949) or **McCurdy's** (☎ 2076 3909).

THE GLENS OF ANTRIM

The northeastern corner of Antrim is a high plateau of black basalt lava flows overlying beds of white chalk. Along the coast, between Cushendun and Glenarm, the plateau has been dissected by a series of scenic, glacier-gouged valleys known as the Glens of Antrim. In times past this region was a stronghold of the MacDonnells (see the boxed text, p619).

Two waymarked footpaths traverse the region: the Ulster Way sticks close to the sea, passing through all the coastal villages, while the 32km Moyle Way runs inland from Glenariff Forest Park to Ballycastle.

Torr Head Scenic Road

A few kilometres east of Ballycastle a minor road, signposted Scenic Route, branches north off the A2. This alternative route to Cushendun is not for the faint-hearted driver (nor for caravans), as it clings, precarious and narrow, to steep slopes high above the sea. Side roads lead off to the main points of interest – Fair Head, Murlough Bay and Torr Head. On a clear day, there are superb views across the sea to Scotland, from the Mull of Kintyre to the peaks of Arran.

The first turn-off ends at a parking area at Coolanlough. Here, a waymarked path leads north 1km to **Fair Head**, where the 180m-high basalt cliffs are split by a spectacular gully, bridged by a fallen rock, known as the Grey Man's Path. The trail then loops south along the cliff tops to the upper car park on the Murlough Bay road, from where you can return to Coolanlough (allow 1½ hours). Alternatively, you can descend the Grey Man's Path and follow the coast south to Murlough Bay.

The second turn-off leads steeply down to **Murlough Bay**. From the bottom parking area, you can walk north along the shoreline to some ruined miners' cottages (10 minutes);

coal and chalk were once mined in the cliffs above, and burned in a limekiln (south of the car park) to make quicklime.

The third turn-off leads past ruined coastguard houses to the rocky headland of **Torr Head**, crowned with a 19th-century coastguard station (abandoned in the 1920s). This is Ireland's closest point to Scotland – the Mull of Kintyre is a mere 19km away across the North Channel. In late spring and summer, a salmon fishery like the one at Carrick-a-Rede operates here, with a net strung out from the headland. The ancient ice house beside the approach road was once used to store the catch.

Cushendun

pop 350

The pretty seaside village of Cushendun is famous for its distinctive, Cornish-style cottages. Built between 1912 and 1925 at the behest of the local landowner, Lord Cushendun, they were designed by Clough Williams-Ellis, the architect of Portmeirion in North Wales. Much of Cushendun is now owned by the National Trust.

There's a nice sandy beach, and a footpath south of the river that leads along the shore to some caves, including a cave house carved out of the red sandstone cliffs.

SLEEPING & EATING

Cushendun Caravan Park (☎ 2176 1254; 14 Glendun Rd; tent site £6-10, campervan £13; Easter-Sep) The local council-run camping ground is just north of the village, a five-minute walk from the beach.

Cloneymore House (☎ 2176 1443; anne.cloneymore@btinternet.com; 103 Knocknacarry Rd; s/d £20/40; P ⊠) A traditional family B&B just south of Cushendun, Cloneymore has four en-suite rooms, equipped for visitors with limited mobility.

Villa Farmhouse (☎ 2176 1252; maggiescally@amserve.net; 185 Torr Rd; s £22-25, d £40-44; P ⊠) This luxurious farmhouse B&B, 1.5km north of the village, has great views over the bay. Evening meals are available for £12 per person.

Mullarts Apartments (☎ 2176 1221; anne@mullarts.fsnet.co.uk; 114 Tromra Rd; d per weekend/week £120/320) An unusual alternative, Mullarts has three luxury, self-catering apartments housed in a converted 19th-century church, 2.5km south of the village. There are two doubles, and one five-person apartment (£140/375).

Cushendun Tearoom (☎ 2176 1506; 1 Main St; mains £3-5; 11am-7pm daily Mar-Sep, 11am-7pm Mon-Fri Oct-Feb) The cosy village tearoom beside the bridge offers tea and cakes, hot snacks and salads.

Mary McBride's Pub (☎ 2176 1511; 2 Main St; mains bar/restaurant £3/10; food served noon-9pm) The original bar here is the smallest in Ireland (2.7m by 1.5m) but there's plenty of elbow-bending room in the rest of the pub, which serves locally caught seafood and home-made steak-and-Guinness pie.

GETTING THERE & AWAY

Ulsterbus No 254 runs from Cushendun to Belfast (£6.80, 2¼ hours), once a week, on Sunday evenings. Bus No 162 travels to Larne (£5.70, 1½ hours, three daily Monday to Friday, one Sunday), stopping at Cushendall, Carnlough and Glenarm; from Larne there are frequent trains and buses to Belfast. No 162A runs to Ballycastle (35 minutes, one daily Monday to Friday), departing from Cushendall at 9.25am and Cushendun at 9.36am; the return service leaves Ballycastle at 2.15pm.

Cushendall

pop 1400

The Glens of Antrim's biggest village is a holiday centre and traffic bottleneck at the mouth of the River Dall, overlooked by the flat-topped hill of Lurigethan. The beach is small and shingly, though; there are better ones at Waterfoot and Cushendun.

The **tourist office** (☎ 2177 1180; 24 Mill St; 10am-1pm & 2-5.30pm Mon-Fri, 10am-1pm Sat Jul-Sep, 10am-1pm Tue-Sat Oct-Jun) is run by the Glens of Antrim Historical Society, which also has public Internet access.

SIGHTS

The unusual red sandstone **tower** at the central crossroads was built in the early 19th century, based on a building the architect had seen in China. It was originally a prison 'for the confinement of idlers and rioters'.

From the car park beside the beach, a coastal path leads 1km north to the picturesque ruins of **Layde Old Church**, with views across to Ailsa Craig (a prominent island also known as 'Paddy's Milestone') and the Scottish coast. Founded by the Franciscans, it was used as a parish church from the early 14th century until 1790. The graveyard contains several grand MacDonnell memorials. Near the gate stands an ancient, weathered ring-cross (with the arms missing), much older than the 19th-century inscription on its shaft.

In Glenaan, 4km northwest of Cushendall, is **Ossian's Grave**, a Neolithic court tomb romantically, but inaccurately, named after the legendary 3rd-century warrior-poet. The site is signposted off the A2; you can park at the farm and walk up.

SLEEPING & EATING

Cushendall Caravan Park (☎ 2177 1699; 62 Coast Rd; tent site £6-10, campervan £13; 🕑 Easter-Sep) This camp site overlooks the sea, just over 1km south of the town centre.

Mountain View (☎ 2177 1246; 1 Kilnadore Rd; s/d £18/30; P ⊠) This is a good-value Victorian B&B with grand views, only a 10-minute walk uphill from the village.

Riverside (☎ 2177 1655; 14 Mill St; s/d £20/35; P ⊠) The Riverside is a centrally located B&B with two cosy rooms that have shared bathrooms.

Cullentra House (☎ 2177 1762; cullentra@hotmail.com; 16 Cloghs Rd; s/d £25/36; P ⊠) A modern bungalow with good views of the craggy Antrim coast, Cullentra has three en-suite rooms with TV.

Arthur's Tea & Coffee Warehouse (☎ 2177 1627; 1 Shore St; mains £2-3; 🕑 10am-5pm) This lively café serves good cakes and coffee, and home-made soups and snacks.

Harry's Restaurant (☎ 2177 2022; 10 Mill St; mains £8-11; 🕑 noon-9.30pm) With a cosy country house feel, Harry's is the village's top eating place, serving pub grub through the day, and an à la carte dinner from 6pm. Veggie dishes are available.

GETTING THERE & AWAY

See the Cushendun section (p626); the buses mentioned there also serve Cushendall.

Glenariff

About 2km south of Cushendall is the village of **Waterfoot**, with a 2km-long sandy beach. From here the A43 Ballymena road runs inland along Glenariff, the loveliest of Antrim's glens. Views of the valley led the writer Thackeray to exclaim that it was a 'Switzerland in miniature', a claim which makes you wonder if he'd ever been to Switzerland.

At the head of the valley is **Glenariff Forest Park** (☎ 2175 8232; cars/motorcycles/pedestrians £3/2/1.50; 🕑 10am-dusk) where the main attraction is **Ess-na-Larach Waterfall**, about a 30-minute walk from the visitor centre. There are various good walks in the park, not all clearly marked; the longest is a three-hour circular trail.

The park has a **camping & caravan site** (☎ 2175 8232; tent & caravan sites £6.50-10), across the main road from the entrance.

Manor Lodge (☎ 2175 8221; 120 Glen Rd; mains £7; 🕑 10.30am-9pm) is a restaurant and bar on a side road off the A43, 3km before the park entrance. The lodge serves grills, seafood and sandwiches in an interestingly decorated 1893 'Swiss-style' bungalow. You can hike uphill from here into the forest park.

You can reach Glenariff Forest Park from Cushendun (£2.80, 30 minutes, five daily Monday to Friday, three Sunday) and Ballymena (£2.80, 40 minutes) on Ulsterbus No 150.

Carnlough

pop 1500

Carnlough is an attractive little town with a pretty harbour and a fine beach. Many of the buildings, made of local limestone, were commissioned by the marquess of Londonderry in 1854. The limestone quarries were in use until the early 1960s; the white stone bridge across the main street carried a railway line that brought stone down to the harbour. The line is now a walkway that leads to the local beauty spot, Cranny Falls.

The **Tourist Information Centre** (☎ 2888 5236; 14 Harbour Rd; 🕑 10am-10pm daily Easter-Sep, 10am-8pm Mon-Sat Oct-Easter) is in McKillop's general store.

SLEEPING & EATING

Londonderry Arms Hotel (☎ 2888 5255; www.glensofantrim.com; 20 Harbour Rd; s £50-70, d £80-100; P ⊠) The marchioness of Londonderry built this atmospheric coaching inn in 1848. It was eventually inherited by a distant relation of hers, Winston Churchill, who sold it in 1921. The hotel restaurant serves locally caught fish, including lobster and wild salmon.

Harbour Lights (☎ 2888 5950; 11 Harbour Rd; mains £7-12; 🕑 noon-9pm Wed-Sun) This pleasant restaurant is set in the 19th-century building overlooking the harbour, with an outdoor terrace in summer.

GETTING THERE & AWAY

Bus No 162 runs from Larne to Glenarm and Carnlough (£2.80, 40 minutes, six daily Monday to Saturday, one Sunday); three buses a day on weekdays, and the Sunday bus, continue north to Cushendall and Cushendun. Bus No 128 travels to Ballymena (one hour, five daily Monday to Friday, four Saturday).

Glenarm

pop 600

Since 1750 Glenarm (Gleann Arma), the oldest village in the glens, has been the family seat of the MacDonnell family; the present 14th earl of Antrim lives in **Glenarm Castle**, on a private estate hidden behind the impressive wall that runs along the main road north of the bridge. It's normally closed to the public, but there is an annual open day in July.

Take a stroll into the old village of neat Georgian houses (off the main road, immediately south of the river). Where the street opens into the broad expanse of Altmore St, look right to see the **Barbican Gate** (1682), the entrance to Glenarm Castle grounds. Turn left and climb steeply up Vennel St, then left again at the Layde Path to the viewpoint, which has a grand view of the village and the coast.

The **tourist office** (☎ 2884 1705; 2 The Bridge; glenarm@nacn.org; ⏲ 9.30am-5pm Mon-Fri, 2-6pm Sun) is beside the bridge on the main road. It has Internet access for £2 per 30 minutes.

SLEEPING & EATING

Riverside House (☎ 2884 1474; elaine.boyle@talk21.com; 13 Toberwine St; s/d £20/36; ⊠) The Riverside B&B is a nicely restored Georgian house in the heart of the old village.

Drum na Greagh Hotel (☎ 2884 1651; drumnagreagh@nireland.com; 408 Coast Rd; s/d £40/54; P ⊠) This late-Victorian country house has 'location location location'; 5km south of Glenarm on the coast road, with fabulous views over the sea to Scotland from some rooms. The restaurant opens for lunch and dinner Monday to Saturday plus a Sunday lunch carvery.

GETTING THERE & AWAY

See the Carnlough section (above) for details of bus No 162, and also Transport (p599).

LARNE

pop 17,600

As a major port for ferries from Scotland, Larne (Lutharna) is one of Northern Ireland's main points of arrival. However, with its concrete overpasses and the huge chimneys of Ballylumford power station opposite the harbour, poor old Larne is a little lacking in the charm department. After a visit to the excellent tourist information centre, there's no real reason to linger.

Larne Harbour train station is in the ferry terminal. It's a short bus ride or a 15-minute walk from the ferry terminal to the town centre – turn right on Fleet St and right again on Curran Rd, then left on Circular Rd. At the big roundabout, Larne Town train station is to your left, the **Larne Tourist Information Centre** (☎ 2826 0088; larnetourism@btconnect.com; Narrow Gauge Rd; ⏲ 9am-5pm Mon-Sat Easter-Sep, 9am-5pm Mon-Fri Oct-Easter) is to the right, and the bus station is ahead (beneath the road bridge).

Sleeping

If you have to spend the night in Larne, there are plenty of accommodation options. The tourist information centre can book for you.

Curran Court Caravan Park (☎ 2827 3797; 131 Curran Rd; tent/campervan £5/8.50; ⏲ Apr-Sep) This site won't win any prizes for scenic setting, but it's less than a 10-minute walk from the ferry terminal.

Carnfunnock Country Park (☎ 2827 0541; Coast Rd; tent/campervan £8/14; ⏲ Apr-Oct) Although it's nearly 5km north of town, Carnfunnock is much more pleasantly situated than Curran Court.

Manor Guesthouse (☎ 2827 3305; www.themanorguesthouse.com; 23 Olderfleet Rd; s/d £22/40; P ⊠) The Manor is a beautifully restored mid-Victorian house with period décor, only a short walk from the ferry terminal.

Seaview Guest House (☎ 2827 2438; www.seaviewlarne.co.uk; 156 Curran Rd; s £18-25, d £36-44; P ⊠) The Seaview is another good choice within walking distance of the harbour.

Ballygally Castle Hotel (☎ 2858 3212; www.hastingshotels.com; 274 Coast Rd, Ballygally; s/d £75/100; P ⊠) Ballygally is situated 7km north of Larne on the Antrim Coast Road. This luxurious hotel is built around a genuine 17th-century castle.

Getting There & Away

BOAT

For information on ferries from Larne to Scotland and England, see the Sea section (p674).

BUS

Bus No 256 provides a direct service between the town centre and Belfast (£3.50, one hour, six daily Monday to Friday, five Saturday, two Sunday). Heading north to the Glens of Antrim, take bus No 162 (see the Carnlough Getting There & Away section opposite for details).

Also see Transport (p599) for information on the Antrim Coaster bus.

TRAIN

Larne has two train stations, Larne Town and Larne Harbour; there are more-frequent services from the former. Trains from Larne Town to Belfast Great Victoria St (£3.90, one hour) depart at least hourly; those from the harbour are timed to connect with ferries. All trains stop at Belfast's Central, Botanic and City Hospital stations.

ISLANDMAGEE

Islandmagee (Oileán Mhic Aodha) is the finger of land that encloses Larne Lough to the east. Access is by ferry from Larne or road from Whitehead to the south.

There's a popular sandy beach at **Brown's Bay** at the northern end of the peninsula. Nearby is the picturesque little harbour of **Portmuck** and, just 300m offshore, the North's second-largest seabird nesting colony on **Muck Island**.

On the east coast lie the rugged basalt seacliffs known as the **Gobbins**. The cliffs were developed as a tourist attraction in 1902, when a railway company engineer built a spectacular footpath along the coast from Whitehead, complete with steps, bridges and tunnels cut from the rock. By WWII the path had fallen into disrepair, and was closed for safety reasons. You can still see sections of it, but any exploring is entirely at your own risk.

The MV *North Irish Diver* (☎ 9338 2246) offers **boat trips** from Whitehead harbour to the Gobbins and Muck Island (adult/child £12/10, minimum six people).

A passenger **ferry** (☎ 2827 3785) runs between Larne Harbour and Ballylumford, Islandmagee (£1, five minutes, at least hourly).

CARRICKFERGUS

pop 28,000

Northern Ireland's most impressive medieval fortress commands the entrance to Belfast Lough from the rocky promontory of Carrickfergus (Carraig Fhearghais). It overlooks the harbour where William of Orange landed on 14 June 1690, on his way to the Battle of the Boyne; a blue plaque marks the site where he stepped ashore on the old harbour wall below the castle. The old town centre opposite the castle has some attractive 18th-century houses and you can still trace a good part of the 17th-century city walls.

Information

The **Tourist Information Centre** (☎ 9336 6455; touristinfo@carrickfergus.org; Heritage Plaza, Antrim St; 🕑 9am-6pm Mon-Fri, 10am-6pm Sat, noon-6pm Sun Jul & Aug, 9am-6pm Mon-Fri, 10am-6pm Sat Apr-Jun & Sep, 9am-5pm Mon-Fri Oct-Mar) has a bureau de change and books accommodation. The **Paradigm Internet Café** (☎ 9336 1531; 16 West St; 🕑 10am-4pm Mon-Sat) charges £1 for 15 minutes.

Sights

The central keep of **Carrickfergus Castle** (☎ 9335 1273; Marine Hwy; adult/child £3/1.50; 🕑 10am-6pm Mon-Sat, 2-6pm Sun Apr-Sep, 10am-4pm Mon-Sat, 2-4pm Sun Oct-Mar) was built by John de Courcy soon after his 1177 invasion of Ulster. The massive walls of the outer ward were completed in 1242, while the red-brick gun ports were added in the 16th century. Besieged by King John in 1210 and Edward Bruce in 1315 and briefly captured by the French in 1760, the castle also witnessed a successful attack on a British vessel in 1778 by John Paul Jones, founder of the US Navy, in the *Ranger*. The keep houses a museum and the site is dotted with life-sized figures illustrating the castle's history and adding colour to what is Ireland's first and finest Norman castle.

The glass-fronted Heritage Plaza on Antrim St was under redevelopment at the time of writing, but should have re-opened as **Carrickfergus Museum** and Civic Centre by summer 2003.

The parents of the seventh US president left Carrickfergus in the second half of the 18th century. His ancestral home was demolished in 1860, but the **Andrew Jackson**

Centre (☎ 9336 6455; Bonybefore; adult/child £1.20/0.60; ⏲ 10am-1pm & 2-4pm Mon-Fri, 2-4pm Sat & Sun Apr & May, 10am-1pm & 2-6pm Mon-Fri, 2-6pm Sat & Sun Jun-Sep) is housed in a replica thatched cottage complete with fireside crane and earthen floor. It has displays on the life of Jackson, the Jackson family in Ulster and Ulster's connection with the USA. Next door is the **US Rangers Centre**, with a small exhibition on the first US rangers, who were trained during WWII in Carrickfergus before heading for Europe. The centre is on the coast, 2km north of the castle.

Sleeping & Eating

Langsgarden (☎ 9336 6369; 72 Scottish Quarter; s/d £20/40; ⊠) This seafront B&B sits at the far end of the attractive Victorian terrace that stretches northeast from the old town.

Tramway House (☎ 9335 5639; 95 Irish Quarter South; s/d £23/36; P ⊠) The bright and cheerful Tramway, opposite the cinema and marina, has two good-value rooms with shared bathroom.

Dobbin's Inn Hotel (☎ 9335 1905; 6-8 High St; s £38-46, d £54-64; ⊠) Dobbin's Inn, in the centre of the old town, has been around for over three centuries, and has a priest's hole and an original 16th-century fireplace to prove it. The hotel restaurant serves dinner till 9pm nightly.

Courtyard Coffee House (☎ 9335 1881; 38 Scottish Quarter; snacks £2-4; ⏲ 9am-4.45pm Mon-Sat) This café serves light lunches as well as coffee and cakes, and has a second branch inside Carrickfergus Castle.

Wind Rose (☎ 9335 1164; Rodgers Quay; mains £6-11; ⏲ noon-9pm) The Wind Rose is a modern, stylish bar-bistro, with a posh restaurant upstairs, overlooking the marina about a five-minute walk west of the castle.

Getting There & Away

Ulsterbus Nos 163 and 166 go to Belfast's Laganside Bus Centre (£2.30, 30 to 40 minutes, twice hourly). Larne to Belfast trains (see Getting There & Away, p629) stop at Carrickfergus.

INLAND COUNTY ANTRIM

To the west of the high moorland plateau that backs the Glens of Antrim, the hills slope down to the agricultural lowlands of Lough Neagh and the broad valley of the River Bann. This region is rarely visited by tourists, who either take the coast road or speed through on the way from Belfast to Derry, but there are a few places worth seeking out if you have time to spare.

Antrim Town

pop 19,800

The town of Antrim (Aontroim) straddles the River Sixmilewater, close to an attractive bay on the shores of Lough Neagh. During the 1798 Rising, the United Irishmen fought a pitched battle along the length of the town's High St. Today Antrim is dominated by a bleakly modern shopping centre, but a few older buildings survive, including the fine **courthouse**, which dates back to 1762.

Antrim Tourist Information Centre (☎ 9442 8331; abs@antrim.gov.uk; 16 High St; ⏲ 9am-5pm Mon-Wed & Sat, 9am-6pm Thu & Fri Jul & Aug, 9am-5pm Mon-Fri & 9am-2pm Sat Easter-Jun & Sep, 9am-5pm Mon-Fri Oct-Easter) provides a free, self-guided heritage trail leaflet.

In **Pogue's Entry**, a narrow alley at the end of Church St, a blue plaque marks the tiny, mud-floored childhood home of Alexander Irvine (1863–1941), who was a missionary in New York's Bowery district. At the opposite end of High St, beyond the courthouse, is the **Barbican Gate** (1818) and a portion of the old castle walls.

Pass through the gate and the underpass beyond to reach **Antrim Castle Gardens** (admission free; ⏲ 9.30am-dusk Mon-Fri, 10am-5pm Sat, 2-5pm Sun). The castle burned down many years ago, but the grounds remain as one of the few surviving examples of a 17th-century ornamental garden.

Approximately 1.5km north of town, in Steeple Park, stands a 27m-tall, 10th- or 11th-century **round tower**, all that remains of a monastery that once stood on the site. Follow the signs for Steeple Industrial Estate, then for the Antrim Borough Council offices.

Lough Rd leads west from the town centre to **Antrim Bay**, where the vast size of Lough Neagh – the largest lake in the UK and Ireland – is apparent. **Waveriders Watersports Centre** (☎ 9442 8684, 0850 489 470) has jet-skiing (£20 for 20 minutes), canoeing (£10 per hour) and water-skiing (£15 per session).

Bus No 219 from Belfast to Ballymena stops in Antrim. Trains run more frequently (10 a day); Antrim is on the Derry to Belfast train line. See Getting There & Away (p611) for details.

Ballymena

pop 29,200

The predominantly Protestant town of Ballymena (An Baile Meánach) is the home turf of Ian Paisley, the founder and leader of the Free Presbyterian Church and the stridently antinationalist and anti-Catholic Democratic Unionist Party (DUP). The town council was the first to be controlled by the DUP in 1977 and voted unanimously to remove all mention of Darwin's theory of evolution from religious education in Ballymena's schools. The town is also the birthplace of the actor Liam Neeson, of *Schindler's List* and *Michael Collins* fame.

Ecos Environmental Centre (☎ 2566 4400; www.ecoscentre.com; Broughshane Rd; adult/child £4/3; 🕑 10.30am-5pm Mon-Sat, noon-5pm Sun Easter-Sep, noon-5pm daily Oct-Easter), on the eastern edge of town, is a visitor centre dedicated to issues like alternative energy sources and sustainable technology, with lots of hands-on exhibits to keep the kids amused.

Bus No 219 serves Ballymena from Belfast (£3.10, 35 minutes, five daily Monday to Friday, two Saturday). Bus No 128 goes to Carnlough on the coast (one hour, five daily Monday to Friday, four Saturday).

Trains run more frequently (10 daily); Ballymena is on the Derry to Belfast train line. See Getting There & Away (p611) for details.

Slemish

The skyline to the east of Ballymena is dominated by the distinctive craggy peak of Slemish (438m). The hill is one of many sites in the North associated with Ireland's patron saint – the young St Patrick is said to have tended goats on its slopes. On St Patrick's Day, thousands of people make a pilgrimage to its summit; the rest of the year it's a pleasant walk rewarded with a fine view (allow one hour return from the parking area).

Arthur Cottage

The ancestors of Chester Alan Arthur (1830–86), 21st president of the USA, lived in an 18th-century thatched **cottage** (☎ 2588 0781; Dreen, Cullybackey; adult/child £2/1; 🕑 10.30am-5pm Mon-Fri, 10.30am-4pm Sat Easter-Sep) in Cullybackey, about 6km northwest of Ballymena. Demonstrators in traditional costume bake and quilt on Tuesday, Friday and Saturday at 1.30pm throughout June, July (except on the 12th) and August.

Like Ballymena, Cullybackey is a stop on the Belfast to Derry railway line.

Gracehill

pop 700

In the mid-18th century many Protestants fled Moravia (now in the eastern Czech Republic) to escape religious persecution and some settled in Gracehill (Baile Uí Chinnéide), 2km west of Ballymena. The Georgian architecture of their elegant village square includes a **church** with separate entrances for men and women. If you'd like to see inside, visitors are welcome at 11am services on Sunday. Even the graveyard at the back of the church has separate areas, with men on the left and women on the right.

Bus No 127 from Ballymena stops at Gracehill (10 minutes, hourly Monday to Saturday). If you're driving, take the A42 towards Maghera; about 1km past the Gracehill roundabout, turn left at a brown sign with a church marked on it.

Galgorm Manor (☎ 2588 1001; www.galgorm.com; 136 Fenaghy Rd, Ballymena; s/d £99/119; Ⓟ), a 19th-century gentleman's residence, is one of Ireland's top country house hotels. **Gillie's Bar** (mains £6-10; 🕑 noon-11pm, food served noon-2.30pm & 6-9pm), in the former stables, is an atmospheric country pub that serves excellent bar meals. The hotel is 6km west of Ballymena – turn right at the Gracehill roundabout, signposted Cullybackey.

Counties Tyrone & Fermanagh

CONTENTS

County Tyrone – from *Tír Eoghain*, the Land of Owen, a legendary chieftain – is the ancient homeland of the O'Neill clan, dominated by the peaty moorlands of the Sperrin Mountains, whose southern flanks are dotted with prehistoric sites. Apart from the hiking opportunities offered by these heather-clad hills, the county's main attraction is the Ulster American Folk Park, a lively and interesting outdoor museum that celebrates Ulster emigrants' historic links with the USA.

The lush, green landscape of County Fermanagh is intimately entwined with the waters of Lough Erne – the surface area of the county is around one-third water. Local people like to say that for six months of the year the lakes are in Fermanagh; for the other six, Fermanagh is in the lakes. This watery wonderland makes the county a paradise for anglers, bird-watchers and boaters.

The pretty town of Enniskillen makes a good base for exploring Fermanagh's many and varied attractions, which include the contrasting stately homes of Florence Court and Castle Coole, the spectacular caves and underground river of Marble Arch, and the world-famous pottery at Belleek. It's also a good centre for activities such as hiking, cycling and canoeing.

Perhaps the most evocative of Fermanagh's sights are the mysterious ancient carved stones, some pagan, some Early Christian, that are found around the shores of Lower Lough Erne, from the curious stone figures of White Island to the 2000-year-old, two-faced Janus Figure of Boa Island.

HIGHLIGHTS

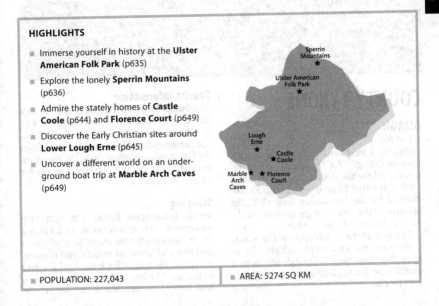

- Immerse yourself in history at the **Ulster American Folk Park** (p635)
- Explore the lonely **Sperrin Mountains** (p636)
- Admire the stately homes of **Castle Coole** (p644) and **Florence Court** (p649)
- Discover the Early Christian sites around **Lower Lough Erne** (p645)
- Uncover a different world on an underground boat trip at **Marble Arch Caves** (p649)

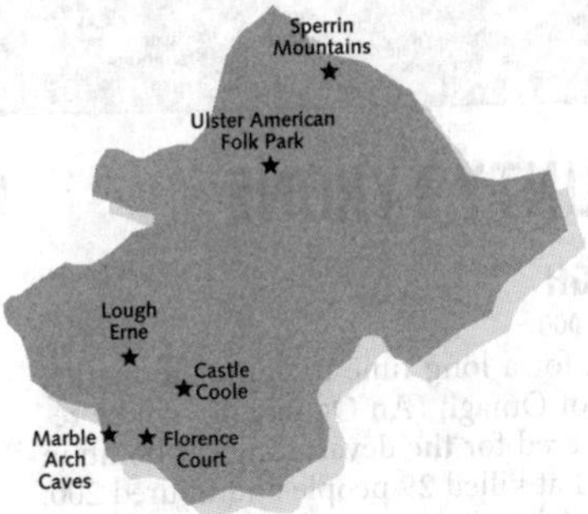

- POPULATION: 227,043
- AREA: 5274 SQ KM

COUNTIES TYRONE & FERMANAGH

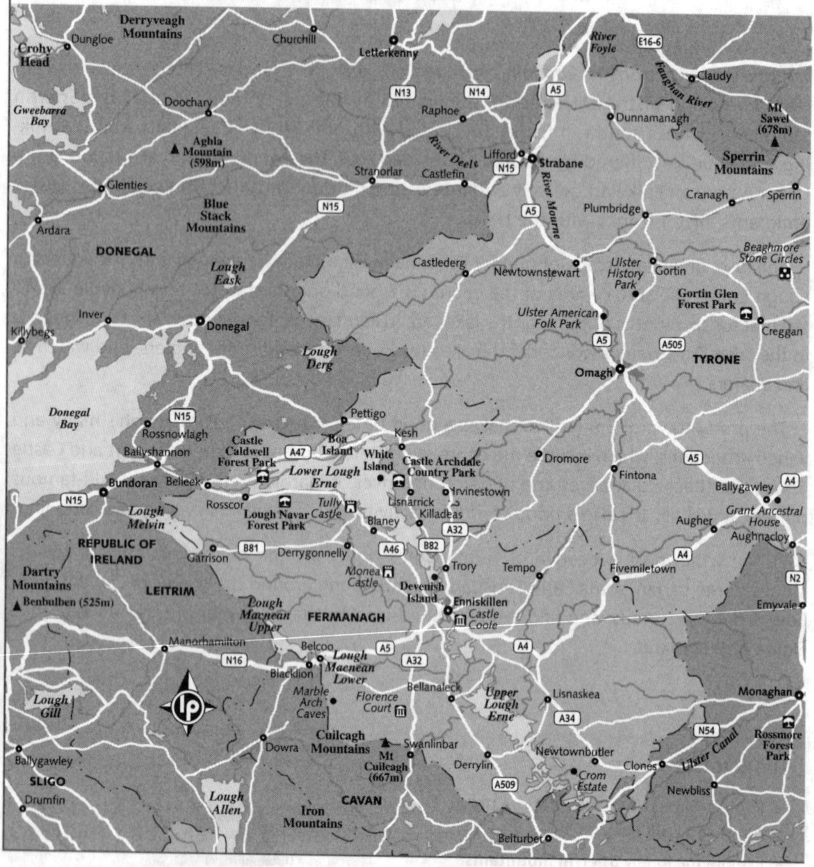

COUNTY TYRONE

OMAGH

pop 20,000

Sadly, for a long time to come the market town of Omagh (An Óghmagh) will be remembered for the devastating car bomb in 1998 that killed 29 people and injured 200. Planted by the breakaway Real IRA, the bomb was the worst single atrocity in the 30-year history of the Troubles.

Situated at the confluence of the Rivers Camowen and Drumragh, which join to form the River Strule, Omagh serves as a useful base for exploring the surrounding area by car.

Tourist Information

The **Omagh Tourist Information Centre** (☎ 8224 7831; omagh.tic@btconnect.com; 1 Market St; ⏲ 9am-5pm Mon-Sat Apr-Sep, 9am-5.30pm Mon-Sat Jul & Aug, 9am-5pm Mon-Fri Oct-Mar) is across the river from the bus station; go along Bridge St, then turn left onto High St. It has Internet access for £1 per 30 minutes.

Sleeping

Omagh Independent Hostel (☎ 8224 1973; www.omaghhostel.co.uk; 9a Waterworks Rd; dm £8, tent £7; ⏲ Mar-Nov; wheelchair access) This spacious and peaceful hostel, 4km northeast of town, is tucked away on a back road off the B48 to Gortin. The lovely, rural setting is awash with flowers in summer; if you prefer, you

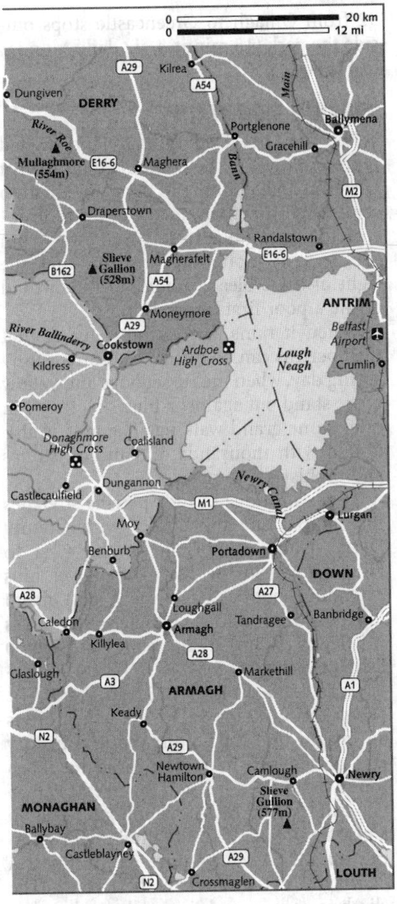

can pitch a tent outside. If you ring from the bus station someone will come and pick you up.

Ardmore (☎ 8224 3381; irismccann@hotmail.com; 12 Tamlaght Rd; s/d £17/34; P ⊠) This long-established family B&B has three rooms (shared bathroom) and is just a five-minute walk south of the town centre.

Arleston House (☎ 8224 1719; peterfox@btconnect.com; 1 Arleston Park; s/d £22/40; P ⊠) Arleston B&B is a large detached house with two en-suite rooms, off Cookstown Rd about 1km east of the town centre.

Dialinn Country House (☎ 8224 7974; 112 Doogary Rd; s/d £23/40; P ⊠) The Dialinn offers three spacious rooms (the double is best) in a detached modern house in the country, 3km south of Omagh on the A5 to Dublin.

Hawthorn House (☎ 8225 2005; www.hawthornhouse.co.uk; 72 Old Mountfield Rd; s/d £40/70; P ⊠) The five-room Hawthorn is a luxurious Victorian guesthouse with period décor and an excellent restaurant. All rooms have bathroom and TV, and rates include breakfast.

Eating

Riverfront Coffee Shop (☎ 8225 0011; 38 Market St; sandwiches £2.50; 9am-5.15pm Mon-Sat) The Riverfront offers excellent coffee, cakes, pastries, home-made soup, and roll-your-own sandwiches on baguette, panini or ciabatta.

Hawthorn House (☎ 8225 2005; www.hawthornhouse.co.uk; 72 Old Mountfield Rd; mains £12-16; noon-3pm & 7-10pm) The Hawthorn is easily Omagh's top restaurant, serving modern Irish cuisine. The menu includes at least one vegetarian main course.

Grant's of Omagh (☎ 8225 0900; 29 George's St; mains £9-14; noon-10.30pm) Round the corner from the courthouse, Grant's is an Omagh institution with a cosmopolitan menu of reasonably priced meals and bar snacks. Book ahead on weekends.

McElroy's (☎ 8224 4441; 30 Castle St; mains £4-10; food served noon-9pm) Of the town's many pubs this is the best for pub grub.

Getting There & Away

The bus station is on Mountjoy Rd, just north of the town centre along Bridge St.

Bus No 273 goes to Belfast (£7.80, 1¾ hours, eight daily Monday to Friday, six Saturday, one Sunday) and Derry (£5.70, 1¼ hours). Other frequent services run to Dungannon (No 78) and Enniskillen (No 94), where you change for Donegal.

Bus No 274 runs from Omagh, south to Dublin (£10.70, 3¼ hours, five or six daily) via Monaghan, and north to Derry (£5.70, one hour). Bus No 296 leaves Omagh for Cork (9¼ hours, one daily Monday to Friday).

AROUND OMAGH

Ulster American Folk Park

In the 18th and 19th centuries thousands of Ulster people left their homes to forge a new life across the Atlantic; 200,000 emigrated in the 18th century alone. Their story is told here at one of Ireland's best museums, the **Ulster American Folk Park** (☎ 8224 3292; www.folkpark.com; Mellon Rd; adult/child £4/2.50; 🕑 10.30am-6pm Mon-Sat, 11am-6.30pm Sun & public hols Apr-Sep, 10.30am-5pm Mon-Fri Oct-Mar). Most of the park is wheelchair accessible. Last admission is 1½ hours before closing.

The Exhibition Hall presents many of the close connections between Ulster and the USA – the American Declaration of Independence was signed by several Ulstermen – but the real appeal of the folk park is the outdoor museum, whose 'living history' exhibits include a forge, a weaver's cottage, a Presbyterian meeting house, a schoolhouse, a log cabin, a 19th-century Ulster street and a street from western Pennsylvania. Clever use is made of an emigrant ship to link the Ulster and USA exhibits.

Costumed guides and artisans are on hand to chat and explain the arts of spinning, weaving, candle making and so on, and there are regular theme events such as re-enactments of American Civil War battles. There's almost too much to absorb in one visit and at least half a day is needed to do the place justice.

The Appalachian and Bluegrass Music Festival is held at the park every September.

The park is 8km northwest of Omagh off the A5. Bus No 97 to Strabane stops outside the park (15 minutes). Buses depart Omagh at 7.55am, 10.55am and 1.25pm Monday to Friday, and return at 11.20am, 3.20pm and 4.50pm. On Saturday there's a bus at 1.25pm returning at 4.45pm.

Ulster History Park

The history of settlements in Ireland from the Stone Age to the 17th century is the theme of this **park** (☎ 8164 8188; Cullion, Lislap; adult/child £3.75/2.50; combined ticket with Folk Park £6.50/4; 🕑 10am-6.30pm daily Jul & Aug, 10am-5.30pm Mon-Sat & 11.30am-7pm Sun Apr-Jun & Sep, 10am-5pm Mon-Fri Oct-Mar). The self-guided tour allows you to stroll through reconstructions of a Mesolithic encampment, Neolithic houses, a late-Bronze Age *crannóg* (artificial island), a 12th-century monastic settlement complete with round tower, a Norman motte and bailey and a 17th-century Plantation town. The aim is to show what Ireland's ancient sites might have looked like in their own time. Last admission is one hour before closing.

The park is about 10km northeast of Omagh on the B48 road to Gortin. Bus No 92 from Omagh to Greencastle stops outside the park (15 minutes, six daily Monday to Friday).

SPERRIN MOUNTAINS

When the Lord Deputy of Ireland invited representatives of the London guilds to visit Ulster in 1609, hoping to persuade them to send English settlers to the region, he instructed their guide to stay well away from the Sperrin mountains, fearing that the sight of these bleak, moorland hills would create a poor first impression.

When it rains, there's no denying that the Sperrins can be dismal. But on a sunny spring day, when the russet bogs and yellow gorse stand out against a blue sky, they can offer some grand walking. The area is also dotted with thousands of standing stones and prehistoric tombs.

The main ridge of the Sperrins stretches for 30km along the border with County Derry, from Plumbridge in the west to Draperstown in the east, with lower hills extending south as far as the A505 Omagh to Cookstown road. The highest summit is Mt Sawel (678m), rising above the **Sperrin Heritage Centre** (☎ 8164 8142; 274 Glenelly Rd, Cranagh; adult/child £2.30/1.40; 🕑 11.30am-5.30pm Mon-Fri, 11.30am-6pm Sat & 2-6pm Sun Apr-Oct), which offers an insight into the culture, natural history and geology of the region. Gold has been found in the Sperrins, and for an extra £0.65 you can try your luck at panning for gold in a nearby stream. If you're thinking of walking up Mt Sawel, enquire at the Sperrin Heritage Centre about the best route. The climb is easy enough in good weather, but some farmers are not as accommodating as others about hikers crossing their land.

From Omagh, follow the B48 northeast through Gortin to Plumbridge. From there it's about 13km east on the B47 to Cranagh. Buses from Omagh go only as far as Plumbridge. From Cookstown take roads B162 and B47.

Gortin

The village of Gortin, 15km north of Omagh, lies at the foot of Mullaghcarn (542m), the southernmost of the Sperrin summits. Hundreds of hikers converge for a mass ascent of the hill on **Cairn Sunday** (the last Sunday in July), a revival of an ancient pilgrimage that petered out in the 19th century. There are several good walks around the village, and a scenic drive to **Gortin Lakes**, with views north over the main Sperrin ridge.

A few kilometres south of Gortin, towards Omagh, is **Gortin Glen Forest Park** (☎ 8167 0666; Gortin Rd; car/motorcycle £2.50/2; ⌚ 10am-dusk), whose dense conifer woodland is home to a herd of Japanese sika deer. The 8km scenic drive offers the chance to enjoy the views without breaking sweat.

There's a manageable day's walk (16km) from Gortin Glen Forest Park to the Ulster American Folk Park along a section of the Ulster Way, mostly on minor roads and forest tracks. From the folk park you can catch bus No 97 back to Omagh. A leaflet and map entitled *The Ulster Way: Northwest Section* is available from the tourist office in Omagh.

SLEEPING

Gortin Glen Caravan Park (☎ 8164 8108; 1 Lisnaharney Rd, Lislap; tent £4.50-9, campervan £9; ⌚ year round) The nearest official camp site is 10km northeast of Omagh on the B48 Gortin road. This council-run site is 4km south of Gortin, near the Ulster History Park, and a few minutes from the Ulster Way. Bus No 92 from Omagh (15 minutes, five daily Monday to Friday) to Gortin stops nearby.

Gortin Hostel (☎ 8164 8083; www.gortinhostel.com; 198 Glenpark Rd; dm £6.50) This hostel, set in a restored schoolhouse in the centre of the village, is popular with walkers and cyclists. It has kitchen and laundry facilities, and secure cycle storage.

Gortin Accommodation Suite (☎ 8164 8346; www.gortin.net; 62 Main St; dm £8.50) There is more hostel accommodation at this modern outdoor activity centre, also in the middle of Gortin village.

An Creagán

About halfway along the A505 between Omagh and Cookstown (20km east of Omagh) is **An Creagán Visitor Centre** (☎ 8076 1112; www.an-creagan.com; Creggan; adult/child £2/1; ⌚ 11am-6.30pm daily Apr-Sep, 11am-4.30pm Mon-Fri Oct-Mar), with an exhibition covering the ecology of the surrounding bogs and the archaeology of the region.

There are some 44 prehistoric monuments within 8km of the centre, including the **Beaghmore Stone Circles**. What this site lacks in stature – the stones are all less than 1m tall – it makes up for in complexity, with seven stone circles (one filled with smaller stones, nicknamed 'dragon's teeth') and a dozen or so alignments and cairns. The stones lie about 8.5km east of Creggan, and 4km north of the A505.

Getting Around

Ulsterbus No 182, known as the Sperrin Rambler, runs twice daily Monday to Saturday between Omagh and Castledawson, stopping at the Ulster History Park, Gortin, the Sperrin Heritage Centre and Draperstown (in County Derry). The morning bus leaves Omagh at 10.10am, arriving at the Sperrin Heritage Centre an hour later; the return bus leaves the centre at 2.40pm.

COOKSTOWN & AROUND

According to the tourist literature, Cookstown's greatest attraction is convenient parking, thanks to its 2km-long and 40m-wide, arrow-straight main street, the legacy of an over-ambitious 18th-century town planner. Today it's a modest market town and shopping centre for east Tyrone but, despite the ease of parking, there's little reason to stop. The main sights here are in the surrounding countryside.

Cookstown Tourist Information Centre (☎ 8676 7727; tic@cookstown.gov.uk; Burn Rd; ⌚ 9am-5pm Mon-Sat & 2-4pm Sun Jul & Aug, 9am-5pm Mon-Sat Jun & Sep, 9am-5pm Mon-Fri & 10am-4pm Sat Oct-May) is in the Burnavon Arts and Cultural Centre, west of the main street.

Wellbrook Beetling Mill

Beetling, the final stage of linen making, involved pounding the cloth with wooden hammers, or beetles, to give it a smooth sheen. In the 18th century there were six water-powered **beetling mills** (☎ 8675 1735; 20 Wellbrook Rd; adult/child £2.60/1.30; ⌚ noon-6pm daily Jul & Aug, noon-6pm Sat, Sun & public hols mid-Mar–Jun & Sep) at Wellbrook, and one has been preserved in working order by the National Trust.

Take the A505 Omagh road 5km west to Kildress and turn right at the church; the mill is 1km further on.

Ardboe High Cross

A 6th-century **monastic site** on the shores of Lough Neagh, now occupied by a ruined 17th-century church and graveyard, is home to one of Ireland's best-preserved

Celtic **high crosses**. The 10th-century Ardboe cross stands 5.5m tall, decorated with 22 carved panels depicting biblical scenes. The western side (facing the road) has New Testament scenes: (from the bottom up) the Adoration of the Magi; the Miracle at Cana; the miracle of the loaves and fishes; Christ's entry into Jerusalem; the arrest (or mocking) of Christ; and, at the intersection of the cross, the Crucifixion.

The more weathered eastern face (towards the lough) shows Old Testament scenes: Adam and Eve; the Sacrifice of Isaac; Daniel in the Lions' Den; the Three Hebrews in the Fiery Furnace; the panels above may show the Last Judgement, and/or Christ in Glory. There are further scenes on the narrow north and south faces of the shaft.

Ardboe is 16km east of Cookstown. Take the B73 through Coagh – ignore the first (white) road sign for Ardboe, and keep straight on until you find the (brown) sign for Ardboe High Cross.

Sleeping

Drum Manor Forest Park (☎ 8676 2774; Drum Rd, Oaklands; campervans £6.50-10) This is a pleasant site 4km west of Cookstown on the A505, with lakes, a butterfly farm and an arboretum.

Central Inn (☎ 8676 2255; 27 William St; s/d £20/36; P ⊠) If you have to spend the night in Cookstown, this pleasant pub offers B&B right in the centre of town.

Avondale (☎ 8676 4013; 31 Killycolp Rd; s/d £26/40; P ⊠) Avondale is a spacious detached house with a large garden, patio and sun lounge, offering B&B in two en-suite rooms with TV. It's 3km south of Cookstown, just off the A29 Dungannon road.

Greenvale Hotel (☎ 8676 2243; www.greenvalehotel.com; 57 Drum Rd; s/d £40/70; P ⊠) Set in its own grounds on the southern edge of town, a 10-minute walk from the centre, the 12-room Greenvale is a lovely, 19th-century mansion with a welcoming, country house feel.

Getting There & Away

The bus station is on Molesworth St, east of the main street. Bus No 210 connects Cookstown with Belfast via Antrim (£6.40, 1¾ hours, four daily Monday to Friday, two Saturday); bus No 110 (£6.40, 2¼ hours, two daily Monday to Friday, seven Saturday, one Sunday) plies the same route more slowly. Bus No 80 shuttles between Cookstown and Dungannon (£2.40, 45 minutes, 11 daily Monday to Friday, six Saturday).

DUNGANNON & AROUND

Until 1602, when the castle and town were burned to prevent them falling into the hands of the English, Dungannon (Dún Geanainn) was one of the chief seats of the O'Neill family. Planted with English and Scottish settlers in the 17th and 18th centuries, it became a centre of textile manufacture.

In August 1968 the town entered the history books when the Civil Rights Association, formed a year earlier to protest against the rampant social and political inequalities suffered by Catholics in Northern Ireland, organised its first march from Coalisland to Dungannon. The crowd of 4000 was met by a police cordon outside the town and, although there was no serious violence, it marked the beginning of a new era.

Today, Dungannon is an instantly forgettable market town halfway between Cookstown and Armagh, worth a brief stop in passing if you want to shop at the Tyrone Crystal factory.

Killymaddy Tourist Information Centre (☎ 8776 7259; killymaddy@nitic.net; 190 Ballygawley Rd; ⏲ 9am-5pm) is at a caravan site 10km southwest of Dungannon on the A4 road towards Enniskillen.

Tyrone Crystal

Ireland's first crystal factory was established in Dungannon in 1771 by Benjamin Edwards from Bristol. It closed down in 1870, but in 1968 Tyrone's crystal industry was revived by a local priest, Father Austin Eustace, who raised funding to establish a new factory to help relieve local unemployment.

Today, **Tyrone Crystal** (☎ 8772 5335; www.tyronecrystal.com; Coalisland Rd, Killybrackey; tours adult/child under 12 £2/free; ⏲ 9am-6pm Mon-Sat, 1-5pm Sun) continues to produce high-quality lead crystal (with more than 30% lead oxide content). The factory offers guided tours of the manufacturing process, from the furnace where molten glass is prepared, through hand-blowing and moulding to cutting and polishing. Admission to the showroom is free, and the tour price is reimbursed if you buy something.

The factory is 2.5km northeast of Dungannon on the A45 towards Coalisland – it is clearly signposted. Bus No 80 to Cookstown stops nearby.

Benburb

pop 280

The pretty village of Benburb, 13km south of Dungannon and 11km northwest of Armagh, clusters around **Benburb Castle** (☎ 3754 8241; www.servites-benburb.com; 10 Main St; admission free; 🕑 10am-5pm Mon-Sat Apr-Sep). Nothing remains of the original castle, founded by Shane O'Neill, but the impressive bawn added in 1611 by Sir Richard Wingfield still stands. Within the walls is a red-brick manor house built in 1887, which is now home to a Servite priory. The priory is used as a residential centre for cultural activities and courses in spiritual and human development, but the grounds, gift shop and café bar are open to all.

About 800m from the castle, across the River Blackwater (and therefore in County Armagh), is **Benburb Valley Heritage Centre** (☎ 3754 9885; 89 Milltown Rd; adult/child £2/1; 🕑 10am-5pm Mon-Sat Apr-Sep) a restored linen mill.

From Dungannon take the A29 south and turn right at Moy onto the B106. The centre is clearly marked; the castle is a short distance further along.

Donaghmore High Cross

The village of Donaghmore, 8km northwest of Dungannon on the B43 road to Pomeroy, is famed for its 10th-century **high cross**. It was cobbled together from two different crosses in the 18th century – note the obvious join halfway up the shaft – and now stands outside the churchyard. The carved biblical scenes are similar to those on the Ardboe Cross. On the eastern side are the Annunciation to the Shepherds, the Adoration of the Magi, the Miracle at Cana, the Miracle of the Loaves and Fishes, the Arrest of Christ and the Crucifixion. On the western side are Adam and Eve, Cain and Abel, and Abraham and Isaac. The nearby **heritage centre** (☎ 8776 7039; Pomeroy Rd; admission free; 🕑 9am-5pm Mon-Fri) is based in a converted 19th-century school.

Castlecaulfield

Not so much a castle as the remains of a substantial Jacobean house, **Castlecaulfield** (admission free; 🕑 24 hr) was built in the early 17th century by Sir Toby Caulfield on the site of an earlier fort belonging to the O'Donnellys.

Over the gatehouse, the Caulfield coat of arms can be made out, having survived the O'Donnellys' act of revenge in 1641 when the house was burned down. The house was rebuilt, and in 1767 it hosted a church service by John Wesley, the founder of Methodism.

The castle is 8km west of Dungannon. Take the A4 towards Enniskillen, and after about 6km look out for a small road on the right signposted to Castlecaulfield.

Grant Ancestral House

Ulysses Simpson Grant led Union forces to victory in the American Civil War and later served as the USA's 18th president for two terms from 1869–77. The **ancestral home** (☎ 8555 7133; 45 Dergina; adult/child £1.50/0.75; 🕑 noon-5pm Mon-Sat & 2-6pm Sun Apr-Sep) of his mother's family – the Simpsons – has been restored in the style of a typical 19th-century small farm. The furnishings are not authentic, but the original field plan of the farm survives together with various old farming implements.

The site is 20km west of Dungannon, south of the A4 just before the village of Ballygawley.

Sleeping & Eating

Dungannon Park (☎ 8772 7327; Moy Rd; tent/campervan £6/8) This council-run camp site is in a quiet, wooded location 2.5km south of Dungannon on the A29 towards Moy and Armagh.

Drumconnor House (☎ 8774 9102; drumconnorhouse@talk21.com; 96 Cookstown Rd; s/d £20/40; P ⊠) A modern bungalow offering B&B in two en-suite rooms with TV, Drumconnor is 6km north of Dungannon on the A29 to Cookstown.

Grange Lodge (☎ 8778 4212; grangelodge@nireland.com; 7 Grange Rd; s/d £55/78; P) The five-room Grange is a period gem set in its own 20-acre grounds. Parts of the house, which is packed with antiques, date from 1698, though most is Georgian with Victorian additions. It's 5km southeast of Dungannon, signposted off the A29 Moy road.

Viscounts Restaurant (☎ 8775 3800; 10 Northland Row; mains £6-14; 🕑 noon-9.30pm) Set in a converted church, Viscounts offers carvery lunches, snacks and á la carte dinners. You can feast on steaks, pasta, stir-fries and vegetarian dishes in a mock medieval setting of knights' armour, swords and jousting banners. Booking is advisable at weekends.

Stangmore Country House (☎ 8772 5600; 65 Moy Rd; 2-/3-course dinner £15.50/17.50; 🕒 7-9.30pm) Stangmore is an elegant, Georgian mansion whose restaurant offers a modern menu of Irish–Mediterranean–Asian fusion cuisine. It also has nine rooms offering B&B at £55/85 per single/double.

Getting There & Away

Dungannon's bus station is at the bottom of Scotch St, over the bridge and to the left. Bus No 261 runs from Belfast's Europa Bus Centre to Dungannon (£5.90, one hour, eight daily Monday to Saturday, two Sunday) and continues to Enniskillen (£6.40, 1½ hours). Bus No 273 travels from Belfast to Derry via Dungannon and Omagh (six daily Monday to Saturday, four Sunday).

Bus No 80 shuttles between Cookstown and Dungannon (£3.40, 45 minutes, 11 daily Monday to Friday, six Saturday). The No 278 service runs once or twice daily, Monday to Saturday, to Armagh (£2.80, 30 minutes) and on to Monaghan and Dublin (3½ hours).

COUNTY FERMANAGH

ENNISKILLEN

pop 11,500

Enniskillen (Inis Ceithleann) is an attractive town built on the roller-coaster back of a drumlin that commands the river passage between Upper and Lower Lough Erne. It's a pleasant place to stay, and makes a good base for exploring Fermanagh.

Oscar Wilde and Samuel Beckett were both pupils at the Portora Royal School northwest of the centre, but the town's name is sadly more familiar as the place where on Poppy Day (11 November 1987) an IRA bomb killed 11 innocent people during a service at the war memorial.

Orientation & Information

The town centre is on an island in the waterway connecting the upper and lower loughs. The main street changes name several times; the clock tower marks the centre. The other principal thoroughfare is Wellington Rd, south of and parallel to the main street, where you'll find the bus station and tourist office.

Fermanagh Tourist Information Centre (☎ 6632 3110; www.fermanagh-online.com; Wellington Rd; 🕒 9am-7pm Mon-Fri, 10am-6pm Sat & 11am-5pm Sun Jul & Aug, 9am-5.30pm Mon-Fri, 10am-6pm Sat & 11am-5pm Sun Easter-Jun & Sep, 9am-5.30pm Mon-Fri Oct-Easter) books accommodation, changes money, sells fishing licences and provides a postal and fax service.

There are ATMs and currency exchange facilities at the **Bank of Ireland** (7 Townhall St) and **Ulster Bank** (16 Darling St).

Enniskillen Library (☎ 6632 2886; Hall's Lane; 🕒 9.15am-5.15pm Mon, Wed & Fri, 9.15am-7.30pm Tue & Thu, 9.15am-1pm Sat) has public Internet access for £1 per 30 minutes.

Sights

Enniskillen Castle (☎ 6632 5000; Castle Barracks; adult/child £2/1; 🕒 10am-5pm Tue-Fri & 2-5pm Sat-Mon Jul & Aug, 10am-5pm Tue-Fri & 2-5pm Sat & Mon May-Jun & Sep, 10am-5pm Tue-Fri & 2-5pm Mon Oct-Apr), a former stronghold of the 16th-century Maguire chieftains, guards the western end of the town's central island, its twin-turreted **Watergate** looming over the fleets of passing cabin cruisers. Within the walls is the **Fermanagh County Museum**, with displays on the county's history, landscape and wildlife. The keep houses the **Regimental Museum of the Royal Inniskilling Fusiliers**, crammed full of medals, guns and uniforms.

In Forthill Park, at the eastern end of town, is **Cole's Monument** (adult/child £0.70/0.30; 🕒 2-6pm May-Sep). It commemorates the first earl of Enniskillen's son, Sir Galbraith Lowry-Cole (1772–1842), who was one of Wellington's generals. You can climb the 108 steps inside the column for a good view of the surrounding area.

Activities

Lakeland Canoe Centre (☎ 6632 4250; Castle Island) rents Canadian canoes (£18 per day) and bicycles (£10 per day). The centre is on an island west of the town centre – push the button on the edge of the jetty, south of the castle, to summon the free ferry.

The **Kingfisher Trail** is a waymarked, long-distance cycling trail that starts in Enniskillen and wends its way through the back roads of counties Fermanagh, Leitrim, Cavan and Monaghan. The full route is around 370km

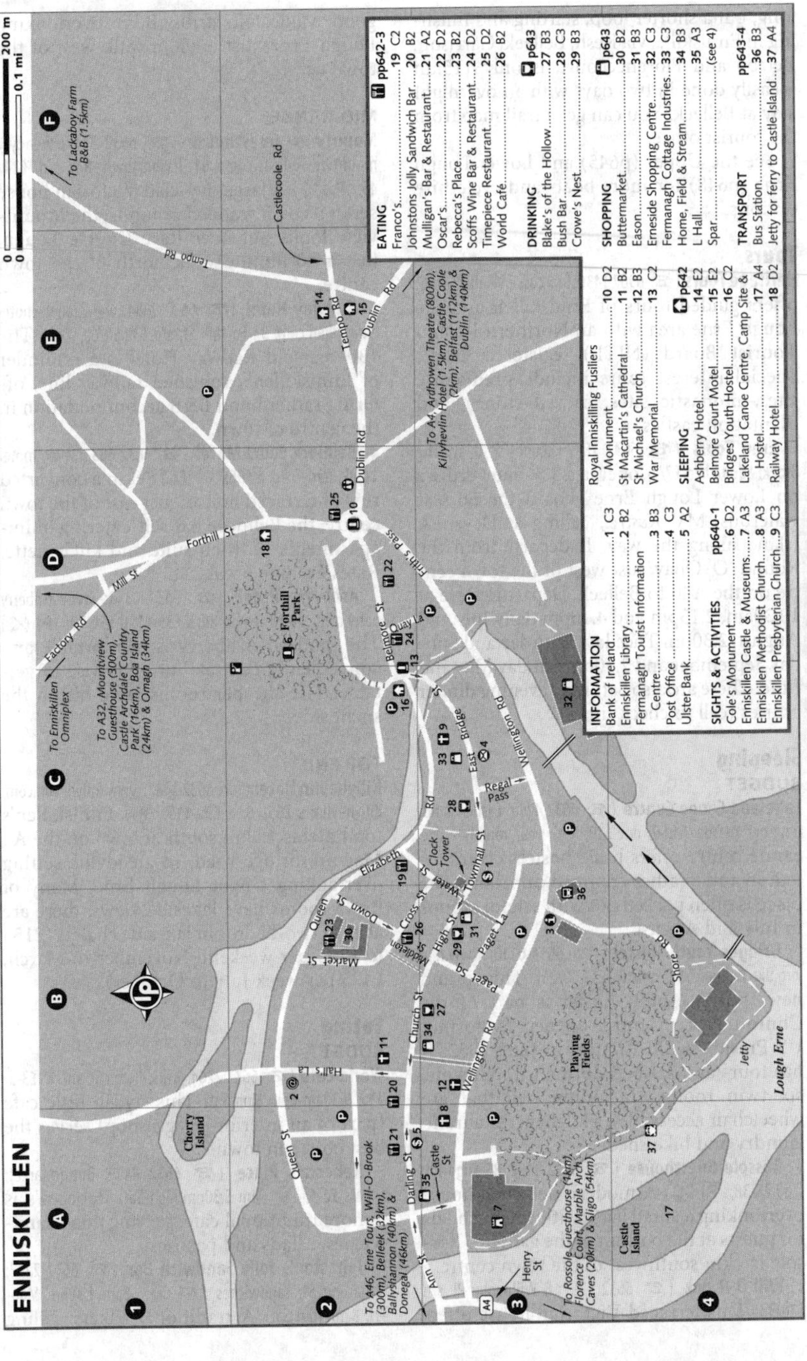
ENNISKILLEN
0 200 m
0 0.1 mi
To Lackaboy Farm B&B (1.5km)
To Enniskillen Omniplex
To A32, Mountview Guesthouse (300m), Castle Archdale Country Park (16km), Boa Island (24km) & Omagh (34km)
To A46, Erne Tours, Will-O-Brook (300m), Belleek (32km), Ballyshannon (40km) & Donegal (46km)
To Rossole Guesthouse (1km), Florence Court, Marble Arch Caves (20km) & Sligo (54km)
To A4, Ardhowen Theatre (800m), Killyhevlin Hotel (1.5km), Castle Coole (2km), Belfast (112km) & Dublin (140km)
Castlecoole Rd
Tempo Rd
Dublin Rd
Forthill St
Mill St
Factory Rd
Forthill Park
Frith's Pass
Belmore St
Quay La
Wellington Rd
East Bridge St
Regal Pass
Townhall St
Clock Tower
Water St
Elizabeth Rd
Queen Elizabeth Rd
Down St
Cross St
Middleton St
Market St
High St
Paget La
Paget Sq
Church St
Hall's La
Queen St
Darling St
Castle St
Ann St
Henry St
Shore Rd
Playing Fields
Jetty
Lough Erne
Cherry Island
Castle Island
EATING pp642-3
Franco's 19 C2
Johnstons Jolly Sandwich Bar 20 B2
Mulligan's Bar & Restaurant 21 A2
Oscar's 22 D2
Rebecca's Place 23 B2
Scoffs Wine Bar & Restaurant 24 D2
Timepiece Restaurant 25 D2
World Café 26 B2
DRINKING p643
Blake's of the Hollow 27 B3
Bush Bar 28 C3
Crowe's Nest 29 B3
SHOPPING p643
Buttermarket 30 B2
Eason 31 B3
Erneside Shopping Centre 32 C3
Fermanagh Cottage Industries 33 C3
Home, Field & Stream 34 B3
L Hall 35 A3
Spar (see 4)
TRANSPORT pp643-4
Bus Station 36 B3
Jetty for ferry to Castle Island 37 A4
INFORMATION
Bank of Ireland 1 C3
Enniskillen Library 2 B2
Fermanagh Tourist Information Centre 3 B3
Post Office 4 C3
Ulster Bank 5 A2
SIGHTS & ACTIVITIES pp640-1
Cole's Monument 6 D2
Enniskillen Castle & Museums 7 A3
Enniskillen Methodist Church 8 A3
Enniskillen Presbyterian Church 9 C3
Royal Inniskilling Fusiliers Monument 10 D2
St Macartin's Cathedral 11 B2
St Michael's Church 12 B3
War Memorial 13 C2
SLEEPING p642
Ashberry Hotel 14 E2
Belmore Court Motel 15 E2
Bridges Youth Hostel 16 C2
Lakeland Canoe Centre, Camp Site & Hostel 17 A4
Railway Hotel 18 D2

long, but a shorter loop, starting and finishing in Enniskille, via Kesh, Belleek, Garrison, Belcoo and Florencecourt, is only 115km – easily done in two days with an overnight stay at Belleek. You can get a trail map from the tourist office.

See the Upper (p645) and Lower Lough Erne (p648) for more boat- and cycle-hire options.

Tours

Heritage Tours (☎ 6962 1430; bmccusker@talk21.com) offers guided tours of Enniskillen and the Lough Erne area with an Northern Ireland Tourist Board (NITB)–registered guide. Special interest tours include prehistoric sites, monastic sites, carved stones, and Plantation castles.

Erne Tours (☎ 6632 2882; Round 'O' Quay, The Brook; adult/child £7/4) operates 1¾-hour cruises on Lower Lough Erne aboard the 56-seat waterbus, MV *Kestrel*, calling at Devenish Island along the way. It departs from the Round 'O' Quay, just west of the town centre on the A46 to Belleek. Departures are at 10.30am, 2.15pm and 4.15pm daily July and August, 2.30pm Tuesday, Saturday and Sunday September and 2.30pm Sunday May and June. There are also Saturday evening dinner cruises (call to check times).

Sleeping

BUDGET

Lakeland Canoe Centre (☎ 6632 4250; Castle Island; tent per person £4.50, dm £10; year round) The canoe centre offers basic hostel accommodation and a rather cramped camp site. The place is often packed out with school groups in July and August.

Bridges Youth Hostel (☎ 6634 0110; www.hini.org.uk; Belmore St; dm/tw £11.50/26) This brand new, purpose-built hostel is part of the Clinton Peace Centre, opened by former US President Bill Clinton in June 2002. It has four- and six-bed dorms with en suite, six twin rooms (including two that are wheelchair accessible), a kitchen, restaurant, laundry and bike shed.

Rossole Guesthouse (☎ 6632 3462; 85 Sligo Rd; s/d £25/38; P ⊠) A modern detached house overlooking a small lake (with rowing boats for guests at the bottom of the garden), Rossole is 1km southwest of the town centre.

Will-O-Brook (☎ 6632 5282; 8 Willoughy Pl; s/d £16/32) This terraced Victorian house offers good value, no frills B&B overlooking Lough Erne, just a 400m walk west of the town centre.

MID-RANGE

Mountview Guesthouse (☎ 6632 3147; wendy@mountviewguests.com; 61 Irvinestown Rd; s/d £34/45; P ⊠) A large, ivy-clad Victorian house set in its own wooded grounds, the Mountview looks out over Race Course Lough, just a 10-minute walk north of the town centre.

Railway Hotel (☎ 6632 2084; www.railwayhotelenniskillen.com; 34 Forthill St; s/d £32.50/60; ⊠) The 130-year-old Railway Hotel is a reminder of Enniskillen's vanished railway line, offering rather bijou B&B accommodation in the centre of town.

Belmore Court Motel (☎ 6632 6633; www.motel.co.uk; Tempo Rd; d £96; P) Set in a converted row of terraced houses just east of the town centre, the Belmore has self-catering 'mini-apartments' with en suite and kitchenette. Rates exclude breakfast.

Ashberry Hotel (☎ 6632 0333; www.ashberryhotel.com; 14-20 Tempo Rd; s £35-45, d £50-70; P ⊠) The modern Ashberry is comfortable and conveniently central, but otherwise forgettable. The cheaper rooms are a bit on the small side.

TOP END

Killyhevlin Hotel (☎ 6632 3481; www.killyhevlin.com; Killyhevlin; s £65-78, d £90-115; P) Enniskillen's top hotel is 1.5km south of town on the A4 Maguiresbridge road, in an idyllic setting overlooking Upper Lough Erne. Many of its 43 rooms have lakeside views; there are also 13 two-bedroom lakeside chalets (£155 to £195 per weekend November to March, £475 per week July to October).

Eating

BUDGET

World Café (☎ 6632 2264; 1 Middleton St; snacks £3-5; 9.30am-6pm Mon-Sat) This stylish little café (part of an interior design shop) serves the best coffee in town.

Rebecca's Place (☎ 6632 4499; Buttermarket; snacks £2-5; 9am-5.30pm Mon-Sat) Rebecca's is a more traditional café, serving good sandwiches, salads and pastries.

Johnston's Jolly Sandwich Bar (☎ 6632 2277; 3 Darling St; sandwiches £2-4; 8am-4.30pm Mon-Fri, 8am-4pm Sat) A traditional bakery selling excellent pick-and-mix sandwiches, soup, pies and cakes to take away or eat in.

Timepiece Restaurant (☎ 6632 5132; Forthill St; breakfast £2.75; ⌚ 9am-6pm Mon, Tue & Sat, 9am-9pm Wed-Fri, 1-6pm Sun) This self-service cafeteria in Dunnes Stores dishes up a good cooked breakfast.

MID-RANGE

Scoffs Wine Bar & Restaurant (☎ 6634 2622; 17 Belmore St; pasta dishes £5-6, mains £10-13; ⌚ 5pm-late) A trendy alternative to traditional Oscar's, Scoffs pulls in a younger crowd with an adventurous *nouvelle* Irish menu, and good value pasta and vegetarian dishes.

Oscar's (☎ 6632 7037; 29 Belmore St; pizzas £6-10, mains £8-13; ⌚ 5pm-10pm Wed-Mon) Named after former local schoolboy Oscar Wilde, this intimate restaurant has become an Enniskillen institution. Its wood-panelled, bookshop-style interior is decorated with the pithy sayings of the great man. The varied menu offers steak, fish, pizza and various vegetarian options.

Franco's (☎ 6632 4424; Queen Elizabeth Rd; pizzas £6.75-8.50, mains £11-16; ⌚ noon-11pm) Franco's is a bustling and noisy Italian place on the northern side of town, serving a range of seafood dishes as well as pizza and pasta.

Mulligan's Bar & Restaurant (☎ 6632 2059; 33 Darling St; mains £5-12; ⌚ noon-8pm) Mulligan's is a cosy, traditional Irish pub serving good bar meals as well as more formal á la carte restaurant dinners.

Drinking

Blake's of the Hollow (William Blake; ☎ 6632 2143; 6 Church St) Ulster's best pint of Guinness awaits you in this traditional Victorian pub, established in 1887, complete with marble-topped bar, sherry casks, brass lamp and a snug. There's traditional music at the weekend. Beyond the bar is a complex containing two modern theme bars, the Café Merlot wine bar, and the Number 6 restaurant.

Crowe's Nest (☎ 6632 5252; 12 High St) A lively bar with a conservatory and patio out back for those sunny summer afternoons, the Nest has live music nightly from 10.30pm in the back bar, and traditional music sessions on Monday during the summer.

Bush Bar (☎ 6632 5212; 26 Townhall St) The Bush has traditional Irish music sessions on Friday, Saturday and Sunday.

Entertainment

Ardhowen Theatre (☎ 6632 5440; Du office ⌚ 10am-4.30pm Mon-Fri, 10am-7pm performance, 11am-1pm, 2-5pm & 6-7pm Sat) Ardhowen's programme includes conce local amateur and professional drama an musical productions, pantomime and films. The theatre is about 2km south of the town centre on the A4.

Enniskillen Omniplex (☎ 6632 4777; Factory Rd) A seven-screen cinema, 700m north of the town centre on Race Course Lough.

Shopping

Buttermarket (☎ 6632 4499; Down St; ⌚ 9.30am-5.30pm Mon-Sat) The refurbished buildings in the old marketplace house a variety of craft shops and studios; ceramics and jewellery are the best buys.

Fermanagh Cottage Industries (☎ 6632 2260; 14 East Bridge St; ⌚ 9am-5.30pm Mon-Sat) Another craft shop, this is the place to go for linen, lace and tweed.

Erneside Shopping Centre (☎ 6632 5705; The Point; ⌚ 9am-5.30pm Mon-Wed, 9am-9pm Thu & Fri, 9am-6pm Sat, 1pm-6pm Sun) Erneside is a modern complex of shops, cafés and a supermarket. Millets stocks camping and outdoor equipment.

Eason (☎ 6632 4341; 10 High St; ⌚ 9am-5.30pm Mon-Sat) and **L Hall** (☎ 6632 2275; 34-36 Darling St) both stock local-interest books and maps.

Home, Field & Stream (☎ 6632 2114; 18 Church St; ⌚ 9am-5.30pm Mon-Sat) has a wide range of fishing tackle, and also sells fishing licences and permits.

The central **Spar** (13 East Bridge St; ⌚ 8am-10pm Mon-Sat, 9am-9pm Sun) is a handy, late-opening minimarket, and also houses a post office counter.

Getting There & Away

The bus station is opposite the tourist office on Shore Rd.

Ulsterbus No 261 runs from Enniskillen to Belfast (£8.20, two hours, eight daily Monday to Saturday, two Sunday) via Dungannon. Bus No 296 runs to Derry (£7.80, 2½ hours, one daily Monday to Friday) via Omagh (one hour) and, in the other direction, to Cork (8¼ hours) via Athlone (three hours). Bus No 99 goes from Enniskillen to Bundoran (1¼ hours, one or two daily) via Belleek (45 minutes).

Bus Éireann's No 66 service runs to Sligo (£6.20, 1½ hours, three daily Monday to

… and their bus No 30 … 80, 2¾ hours, five daily … day, four Sunday) and … urs) calls at Enniskillen.

… NISKILLEN

… tique Lace Museum

… um (☎ 6634 8052; www.irishlacemuseum … ellanaleck; adult/child £2.50/1; ⏲ 10am-6pm Mon-Sat) houses a collection of beautiful Irish lace dating from 1850 to 1900. Lace-making was an important cottage industry in the region both before and after the Famine – prior to WWI there were at least 10 lace schools in County Fermanagh. The museum shop has linen, lace and oil lamps for sale. The museum is just over 6km southwest of Enniskillen in the village of Bellanaleck.

Next to the museum, the 200-year-old thatched **Sheelin Restaurant** (☎ 6634 8232; Main St, Bellanaleck; mains £8-12; ⏲ noon-9pm) offers continental cuisine in a country cottage setting.

Castle Coole

When King George IV visited Ireland in 1821, the 2nd earl of Belmore had a bedroom at Castle Coole specially decorated in anticipation of a visit from the monarch. But the king was more interested in dallying with his mistress at Slane Castle (County Meath), and never turned up. The bedroom, draped in red silk and decorated with paintings depicting *The Rake's Progress* (the earl's sniffy riposte to the king's non-arrival), is one of the highlights of a visit to **Castle Coole** (☎ 6632 2690; Dublin Rd, Enniskillen; adult/child £4/2; ⏲ noon-6pm daily Jul & Aug, noon-6pm Wed-Mon Jun, noon-6pm Sat, Sun & public hols mid-Mar–May & Sep).

Designed by James Wyatt and built between 1789 and 1795 for Armar Lowry-Corry, the first earl of Belmore, this Palladian mansion is probably the purest expression of late-18th-century neoclassical architecture in Ireland. It is built of silvery-white portland stone, which was brought at great expense from southern England – by ship to Ballyshannon, then overland to Lough Erne, by boat again to Enniskillen, then by bullock cart for the last two miles.

The building costs of £70,000 nearly bankrupted the first earl, but that did not stop his son Somerset Lowry-Corry, the second earl, spending another £35,000 on exuberant Regency furnishings and decoration, best seen in the opulent, oval saloon where the family and friends would gather before dinner. The seventh earl of Belmore, John Armar Lowry-Corry, reserves part of the house for his private use, but most of the building is under the care of the National Trust.

The 600 hectares of landscaped **grounds** (car/pedestrian £2/free; ⏲ 10am-8pm May-Sep, 10am-4pm Oct-Apr) contain a lake that is home to the UK's only nonmigratory colony of greylag geese. It is said that if the geese ever leave, the earls of Belmore will lose Castle Coole.

Castle Coole is on the A4 Dublin road, 2.5km southeast of Enniskillen. You can easily walk there from Enniskillen town centre in 30 minutes – fork left beyond Dunnes Stores, and keep straight on along Tempo Rd and Castlecoole Rd.

UPPER LOUGH ERNE

About 80km long, Lough Erne is made up of two sections: the Upper Lough to the south of Enniskillen, and the Lower Lough to the north. The two are joined by the River Erne, which begins its journey in County Cavan and meets the sea at Donegal Bay west of Ballyshannon.

Upper Lough Erne is not so much a lake as a watery maze of islands (more than 150 of them), inlets, reedy bays and meandering backwaters. Birdlife is abundant, with flocks of whooper swan and goldeneye overwintering here, great crested grebes nesting in the spring, and Ireland's biggest heronry in a 400-year-old oak grove on the island of Inishfendra, just south of Castle Crom.

Crom Estate

Situated on the eastern shore of the Upper Lough, west of Newtownbutler, is National Trust's **Crom Estate** (☎ 6773 8118; Newtownbutler; car/pedestrian £4/free; ⏲ 10am-8pm Jul & Aug, 10am-6pm mid-Mar–Jun & Sep). The 760 hectares of woodland, parkland and wetlands offer numerous walking trails, the ruins of old Crom Castle, a boathouse and an island folly. There are boats for hire (£5 per hour), and camping facilities (£5 per night).

Doon Scenic Route

This signposted minor road leads west from Derrylin to the northern shoulder of Slieve Rushen (404m). The top of the ridge is occupied by a wind farm, but turn your back on it and enjoy the superb views over the

Upper Lough. If you're heading for Florence Court, you can continue down the far side.

Tours

The wheelchair accessible **Inishcruiser** (☎ 6772 2122; adult/child £7.50/6.50; 2.30pm Thu & Sun Jul & Aug, 2.30pm Sun Easter-Jun & Sep) offers 1½- to two-hour cruises from the Share Holiday Village southwest of Lisnaskea.

Activities

Day boats can be hired for fishing or exploring from **Carrybridge Boat Company** (☎ 6638 7034; Carrybridge, Lisbellaw), 12km south of Enniskillen, **Crom Estate** (☎ 6773 8118; Newtownbutler) and **Carrick Craft** (☎ 3834 4993; Knockninny Marina, Derrylinn), on the west shore of the lough. Rates are about £5/25 per hour/day for an open rowing boat with electric outboard, to £40/50 per half day/day for a six-seater with cabin and inboard diesel engine.

Guests at the **Share Holiday Village** (☎ 6772 2122; www.sharevillage.org) can take part in canoeing, windsurfing, dinghy sailing, archery, orienteering and other activities for £6.50 per person per 2½-hour session.

Sleeping

Lisnaskea Caravan Park (☎ 6772 1040; Gola Rd, Mullynascarty; tent/campervan £6/11) This local council-run site is about 2km northwest of Lisnaskea, on the B514 road towards Enniskillen.

Share Holiday Village (☎ 6772 2122; www.sharevillage.org; Smiths Strand, Lisnaskea; tent/campervan £8/12; Easter-Sep) Share is a charity that works towards the integration of disabled and nondisabled people through a range of activities and courses. The holiday village is mostly occupied by groups, but it also has a touring site with space for 18 caravans and 10 tents. Booking is strongly recommended. The village is 5km southwest of Lisnaskea, off the B127.

Donn Carragh Hotel (☎ 6772 1206; donncarraghhotel@btclick.com; Main St, Lisnaskea; s/d £35/60; P ⊠) There's not much in the way of hotel or B&B accommodation around Upper Lough Erne; this recently refurbished 18-room hotel in the middle of Lisnaskea is the best of what there is.

Getting There & Away

From Enniskillen, Ulsterbus No 95 runs along the east side of the lough to Lisnaskea (£2, 30 minutes, seven daily Monday to Friday, five Saturday, two Sunday), while No 58 goes down the west side to Derrylin (35 minutes, seven daily Monday to Friday, four Saturday), on the way to Belturbet in County Cavan.

LOWER LOUGH ERNE

Lower Lough Erne is a much more open expanse of water than the Upper Lough, with its 90-odd islands clustered mainly in the southern reaches. There are many ancient religious sites and other antiquities around its shores. In Early Christian times, when overland travel was difficult, Lough Erne was an important highway between the Donegal coast and inland Leitrim, and in medieval times the lough was part of an important pilgrimage route to Station Island in Lough Derg (County Donegal).

The following sights are described following anticlockwise around the lough from Enniskillen.

Devenish Island

Devenish Island (Daimh Inis) is the biggest of several 'holy islands' in Lough Erne. The remains of an Augustinian monastery, founded here in the 6th century by St Molaise, include a superb 12th-century round tower in near perfect condition, the ruins of St Molaise's Church and St Mary's Abbey, an unusual 15th-century high cross, and many fascinating old gravestones.

A **ferry** (☎ 6862 1588; adult/child return £2.25/1.20; 10am, 1pm, 3pm & 5pm daily Jul–mid-Sep, Sat, Sun & public hols Easter-Jun) crosses to Devenish Island from Trory Point landing. From Enniskillen, take the A32 towards Irvinestown and after 5km look for the sign on the left, just after a service station and immediately before the junction where the B82 and A32 part company.

Killadeas

Killadeas churchyard, 11km north of Enniskillen on the B82, contains several unusual carved stones. Most famous is the 1m-high **Bishop's Stone**, dating from between the 7th and 9th centuries, which has a Celtic head reminiscent of the White Island figures carved on its narrow western edge, and an engraving of a bishop with bell and crozier on the side. Located nearby is a slab set on edge, with several deep cup-marks (possibly bullauns) on one side, and a cross within a circle on the other. You will also find a broken phallic column and a large, perforated stone.

The **Lady of the Lake** (☎ 6862 2200), based at the Inishclare restaurant, offers cruises on the lough on Saturday and Sunday.

SLEEPING & EATING

Beeches (☎ 6862 8527; imeldabyrne@yahoo.com; Killadeas; s/d £25/40) This quiet, friendly and relaxing B&B is right on the shore of Lough Erne – two of the four rooms have superb views over the lough.

Manor House Country Hotel (☎ 6862 2211; www.manor-house-hotel.com; Killadeas; s £85-100, d £110-140; P ⊠) This grand, 19th-century neoclassical hotel overlooking Lough Erne has had a thorough makeover, complete with spa, sauna, pool and gym. The rooms, though luxurious, are disappointingly bland, but the restaurant is excellent.

Inishclare Bar & Restaurant (☎ 6862 8550; Killadeas; 2-/3-course dinner £19/25; noon-9pm) On the bay north of the Manor House (and under the same management), this place has a good bar, restaurant and bistro with great lough views.

Castle Archdale Country Park

This **park** (☎ 6862 1892; Lisnarick; admission free; 9am-dusk), 16km northeast of Enniskillen on the B82, has pleasant woodland and lakeshore walks in the former estate of 18th-century Archdale Manor. The island-filled bay was used in WWII as a base for Catalina flying boats, a history explained in the **visitor centre** (admission free; 11am-7pm Tue-Sun Jul & Aug, noon-6pm Sat & Sun Easter-Jun).

You can hire **bikes** for £3/6/10 per hour/half day/day, or swap two wheels for four legs – the park offers **pony trekking** (£12 per hour) and short rides (£4 per 15 minutes) for beginners, and hacking (£18 per hour) for experienced riders.

Ulsterbus No 194 from Enniskillen to Pettigo stops outside the park (35 minutes, two or three daily Monday to Saturday), from where the visitor centre is a 15-minute walk.

SLEEPING

Castle Archdale Caravan Park (☎ 6862 1333; www.castlearchdale.com; Castle Archdale Country Park; tent £10-15, campervan £15; Apr-Oct) This site is dominated by on-site caravans, but has good facilities, including a shop, launderette, kids' playground and restaurant.

Castle Archdale Youth Hostel (☎ 6862 8118; www.hini.org.uk; Castle Archdale Country Park; dm £9; Mar-Oct) This attractive and peaceful Hostelling International Northern Ireland (HINI) hostel is set in a converted 18th-century stable block, with separate male and female dorms, and a couple of family rooms.

White Island

White Island, in the bay to the north of Castle Archdale Country Park, is the most haunting of Lough Erne's monastic sites. At the eastern tip of the island are the ruins of a small 12th-century church with a beautiful Romanesque door on its southern side. Inside are six extraordinary Celtic stone figures, thought to date from the 9th century, lined up along the wall like miniature Easter Island statues.

This line-up is a modern arrangement; most of them were discovered buried in the walls of the church in the 19th century, where the medieval masons had used them as ordinary building stones. The six main figures, all created by the same hand, are flanked on the left by a *sheila-na-gig* (carved female figure with exaggerated genitalia), which is probably contemporary with the church, and flanked on the right by a scowling stone face. The age and interpretation pf these figures has been the subject of much debate; it has been suggested that the two central pairs, of equal height, were caryatids (pillars in human form) that once supported a pulpit, and that they represent either saints or aspects of the life of Christ.

The first figure is holding a book (Christ the Evangelist?), and the second holds a bishop's crozier and bell (Christ as Bishop?). The third has been identified as the young King David, author of the Psalms. The fourth is holding the necks of two griffins (symbols of Christ's dual nature as both human and divine?). The fifth bears a sword and shield (Christ's Second Coming?), and the sixth is unfinished.

A **ferry** (adult/child £3/2; 11am-6pm daily Jul & Aug, 11am-1pm Sat & Sun Apr-Jun) crosses to the island hourly from the marina in Castle Archdale Country Park. It takes 15 minutes.

Boa Island

Boa Island, at the northern end of Lower Lough Erne, is connected to the mainland at both ends – the main A47 road runs along its length. Spooky, moss-grown Caldragh graveyard, towards the western end of the island, contains the famous **Janus Stone**. Perhaps 2000 years old, this pagan figure is carved with two grotesque human heads, back to back. Nearby is a smaller figure, called the **Lusty Man**, brought here from Lusty More island. Their origin and meaning have been lost in the mists of time.

There's a small sign indicating the graveyard, about 1.5km from the bridge at the western tip of the island.

SLEEPING & EATING

Lakeland Caravan Park (☎ 6863 1578; mail@drumrush.co.uk; Boa Island Rd, Drumrush, Kesh; tent/campervan £10/14; 🕓 year round) This lakeshore site, on the A47 halfway between Kesh and Boa Island, has a sandy beach and water-sports centre.

Drumrush Lodge (☎ 6863 1578; mail@drumrush.co.uk; Boa Island Rd, Drumrush, Kesh; s/d £27/44; P ⊠) Under the same management as Lakeland Caravan Park, this guesthouse has 10 bright and cheerful en-suite rooms and located only a few paces from the lough shore.

Lusty Beg Island (☎ 6863 2032; www.lustybeg.com; Boa Island, Kesh; d £75) This private island retreat, reached by ferry from a jetty halfway along Boa Island, has self-catering chalets to let by the week but also offers B&B in its rustic Courtyard Motel. The informal **Island Lodge Restaurant** (☎ 6863 1342; bar meals £5-12, 4-course dinner £21; 🕓 1-9pm Jul & Aug) is open to all, and serves everything from baked potatoes to smoked Irish salmon. There's a telephone in a blockhouse on the slipway to summon the ferry.

Castle Caldwell Forest Park

Castle Caldwell, built between 1610 and 1619, is nothing but a ruin. The **park** (admission free; 🕓 24 hr), about 5km west of Boa Island along the A47, is a nature reserve full of birdlife and is a main breeding ground for the common scoter.

At the entrance to the park is the **Fiddler's Stone** (in the shape of a fiddle). The inscription, now too worn to read, commemorated a favourite musician who fell out of a boat while drunk:

> 'To the memory of Denis McCabe, Fiddler, who fell out of the St Patrick Barge belonging to Sir James Caldwell Bart and Count of Milan and was drowned off this point August ye 13 1770.'

Belleek

pop 550

Belleek's (Beal Leice) village street of colourful, flower-bedecked houses slopes up from a bridge across the River Erne, where it flows out of the Lower Lough towards Ballyshannon and the sea. The village is right on the border – the road south across the bridge passes through a finger of the Republic's territory for about 200m before leaving again.

The imposing Georgian-style building beside the bridge houses the world-famous **Belleek Pottery** (☎ 6865 9300; www.belleek.ie; Main St; adult/child £4/free; 🕓 9am-6pm Mon-Fri, 10am-6pm Sat & 2-6pm Sun Apr-Sep, 11am-6pm Sun Jul & Aug, 9am-5.30pm Mon-Fri, 10am-5.30pm Sat & 2-6pm Sun Oct, 9am-5.30pm Mon-Fri Nov-Mar). Founded in 1857 to provide local employment in the wake of the Potato Famine, it has been producing fine Parian china ever since, and is especially noted for its delicate basketware. There are guided tours every half-hour from 9.30am to 12.15pm and 2.15pm to 4.15pm (until 3.30pm on Friday) Monday to Friday, a small museum, showroom and restaurant.

On the far side of the river is the excellent **ExplorErne Exhibition** (☎ 6865 8866; Erne Gateway Centre, Corry; adult/child £1/0.50; 🕓 11am-5pm May-Sep), which tells the story of the Fermanagh lakelands' landscape and people.

Belleek hosts a **traditional music festival** each June.

SLEEPING & EATING

Hotel Carlton (☎ 6865 8282; www.hotelcarlton.co.uk; Main St; s/d £52.50/75; P ⊠) Though the rooms are plush and luxurious, the Carlton has a friendly and informal feel to it. It has a good restaurant, and there are frequent live music sessions in the hotel's Potters Bar.

Moohan's Fiddlestone (☎ 6665 8008; 15-17 Main St; s/d £20/40) The Fiddlestone is a traditional Irish pub offering B&B in five en-suite rooms. The lively bar downstairs is a popular venue for impromptu music sessions, so don't expect peace and quiet in the evenings.

Thatch Coffee Shop (☎ 6865 8181; 20 Main St; mains £3-9; 🕑 9am-5pm Mon-Sat) The Thatch may be Belleek's oldest building (late 18th century), but it serves a thoroughly modern cup of coffee.

Black Cat Cove (☎ 6865 8942; 28 Main St; mains £5-10; 🕑 noon-9pm) The Black Cat is a friendly, family-run pub that serves excellent bar meals. It also has music on Tuesday, Wednesday and Thursday nights from May to September.

South Shore

The lakeside A46 road leads along the south shore of Lower Lough Erne from Belleek to Enniskillen. **Lough Navar Forest Park** (car £2.50; 🕑 10am-dusk) boasts a superb viewpoint atop the Magho cliffs, overlooking the lough. The vehicle entrance is on the minor Glennasheevar road between Garrison and Derrygonnelly 20km, southeast of Belleek (take the B52 towards Garrison, and fork left after 2.5km). You can also hike to the viewpoint from a picnic site on the A46, 12km east of Belleek. It's a steep climb; allow 1½ hours there and back.

Tully Castle (☎ 9054 6552; admission free; 🕑 10am-6pm Wed-Sun Jun-Aug, 10am-6pm Sat, Sun & public hols Apr, May & Sep), off the A46 some 16km southeast of Belleek, was built in 1613 as a fortified home for a Scottish Planter's family, but was captured and burned by Roderick Maguire in 1641. The bawn (cattle enclosure) has four corner towers and retains a lot of the original paving.

Just south of the Tully Castle turn-off, the B81 leads south through Derrygonnelly for 10km to **Monea Castle** (admission free; 🕑 24 hrs). Another Scottish-style Plantation castle, built around the same time as Tully Castle, it too was captured in the 1641 rising but remained in use until the mid-18th century, when it was gutted by fire. A *crannóg* sits in the nearby lake.

SLEEPING

Blaney Caravan Park (☎ 6864 1634; info@blaneycaravanpark.com; Blaney; tent £6-8, caravan £10) This site is 3.5km south of Tully Castle on the A46 towards Enniskillen, and about 1km away from the lough shore.

Lakeview Guesthouse (☎ 6864 1263; Drumcrow, Blaney; s/d £22/40; 🕑 Jan-Nov; P ⊠) This farm guesthouse has panoramic views over the lough. It's off the A46 near Tully Castle.

Activities

FISHING

The lakes of Fermanagh are renowned for both coarse and game **fishing**; both require licences. The Lough Erne trout-fishing season runs from the beginning of March to the end of September. Salmon fishing begins in June and also continues to the end of September. The mayfly season usually lasts a month from the second week in May. There's no closed season for coarse fish.

Licences can be purchased from the **Fermanagh Tourist Information Centre** (☎ 6632 3110;

> **CRUISING HOLIDAYS ON LOUGH ERNE**
>
> If you fancy exploring Lough Erne as captain of your own motor cruiser, well, you can – and without any previous experience or qualification. Several companies in Fermanagh hire out self-drive, live-aboard cabin cruisers by the week, offering a crash course (not literally, you hope) in boat-handling and navigation at the start of your holiday. Weekly rates in high season (July and August) range from about £430 for a two-berth to £775 for a four-berth and £1300 for an eight-berth boat.
>
> The main cruiser hire companies in Fermanagh are:
>
> **Aghinver Boat Company** (☎ 6863 1400; abcboats@btinternet.com; Lisnarick)
>
> **Carrick Craft** (☎ 3834 4993; www.cruise-ireland.com; Knockninny Marina, Derrylinn, Upper Lough Erne)
>
> **Carrybridge Boat Company** (☎ 6638 7034; Carrybridge, Lisbellaw)
>
> **Corraquill Cruising** (☎ 6774 8712; Drumetta, Aghalane, Derrylinn)
>
> **Erincurragh Cruising** (☎ 6864 1737; www.boatingireland.ie; Blaney, Lower Lough Erne)
>
> **Erne Marine** (☎ 6634 8267; www.ernemarine.com; Bellanaleck Quay, Enniskillen)
>
> **Lochside Cruisers** (☎ 6632 4368; www.lochside.ie; Sligo Rd, Enniskillen)
>
> **Manor House Marine** (☎ 6862 8100; www.manormarine.com; Killadeas, Lower Lough Erne)
>
> See also the Shannon–Erne Waterway section on p456.

COUNTIES TYRONE & FERMANAGH

www.fermanagh-online.com; Wellington Rd) and **Home, Field & Stream** (☎ 6632 2114; 18 Church St) both in Enniskillen, and from the marina in Castle Archdale Country Park (see p646). A joint three-day game/coarse licence and permit for Lough Erne costs £10/8.

Most rivers in County Fermanagh are privately owned, and information on permits is available from the tourist information centre. It also has a list of ghillies (fishing guides).

BOAT HIRE

A number of companies rent out day boats at Enniskillen, Killadeas, Castle Archdale Country Park, Kesh and Belleek. Prices start at about £5/25 per hour/day for a rowing boat with electric outboard, and £40/50 per half day/day for a six-seater with front cabin and inboard diesel engine. The **Fermanagh Tourist Information Centre** (☎ 6632 3110; www.fermanagh-online.com; Wellington Rd) in Enniskillen has a full list of companies and costs.

WATER SPORTS

You can hire equipment for a range of water sports – dinghy sailing (£20 an hour), canoeing (£8 per hour), water-skiing (£15 to £30 per 30 minutes) and jet-skiing (£35 per 30 minutes) – from **Drumrush Watersports** (☎ 6863 1578; www.drumrush.co.uk; Lake Cottage, Drumrush, Kesh) and **Tudor Farm Watersports** (☎ 6863 1943; Boa Island Rd, Kesh).

Getting There & Away

On the eastern side of the lough, bus No 194 from Enniskillen to Pettigo via Irvinestown (two or three daily Monday to Saturday) stops at Castle Archdale (50 minutes) and Kesh (one hour); there's no service along the B82 south of Lisnarick. Bus No 99 goes from Enniskillen to Belleek (45 minutes, two daily Monday to Friday, one Saturday and Sunday) along the western shoreline via Blaney, Tully Castle and Lough Navar Forest Park.

Ulsterbus No 64 from Enniskillen to Bundoran runs twice on Thursday via Belleek (one hour), Belcoo and Garrison.

WEST OF LOUGH ERNE

Florence Court

Part of the first earl of Belmore's motivation in building Castle Coole was undoubtedly competition with his nearest aristocratic neighbour William Willoughby Cole, the first earl of Enniskillen. In the 1770s Cole oversaw the addition of grand, Palladian wings to the beautiful, baroque, mid-18th-century country house built by his father Sir John, and named after his Cornish grandmother, Florence Wrey.

Florence Court (☎ 6634 8249; Swanlinbar Rd, Florencecourt; adult/child £4/2; 🕑 noon-6pm daily Jul & Aug, noon-6pm Wed-Mon Jun, noon-6pm Sat, Sun & public hols mid-Mar–May & Sep) enjoys a superb setting, with open views over Lough Erne. Famous for its rococo plasterwork and antique Irish furniture, it feels more homely and lived-in than the rather cold and austere Castle Coole, especially since the family belongings of the sixth earl were returned. (The earl had a falling out with the National Trust in 1974 and stomped off to Scotland with all his stuff; it was returned after the death of his widow in 1998.)

In the **grounds** (cars/pedestrians £2.50/free; 🕑 10am-8pm May-Sep, 10am-4pm Oct-Apr) are a walled garden and, on the edge of Cottage Wood, southeast of the house, an ancient Irish yew tree. It's said that every Irish yew around the world is descended from this one.

The house is 12km southwest of Enniskillen. Take the A4 Sligo road and fork left onto the A32 to Swanlinbar. Ulsterbus No 192 will drop you about 1.5km from the entrance.

Marble Arch Caves

The limestone plateau to the west of Lough Erne is riddled with caves. The biggest of these is **Marble Arch** (☎ 6634 8855; www.enniskillen.com/marblearchcaves.html; Marlbank Scenic Loop, Florencecourt; adult/child £6/3; 🕑 10am-5pm Jul & Aug, 10am-4.30pm mid-Mar–Jun & Sep), first explored by the French caving pioneer Edouard Martel in 1895, but not opened to the public until 1985.

The guided tour of the caves starts with a short boat trip along the underground River Cladagh to Junction Jetty, where three subterranean streams meet. You continue on foot past the Grand Gallery, Stalactite Chamber and Pool Chamber. A man-made tunnel leads into the New Chamber, from which the route follows the underground River Owenbrean, through the Moses Walk (a pathway sunk into the river) to the Calcite Cradle, where the prettiest formations are found.

Unexpectedly severe flooding of the caves in 1989, just four years after they were opened to the public, was found to have been caused by mechanised peat-cutting in the blanket bog – one of Ireland's biggest – above the caves. This led to Fermanagh Council establishing the surrounding **Cuilcagh Mountain Park** to preserve the bog environment; the park's geology and ecology are explained in the caves' visitor centre.

The caves are very popular, so it's wise to phone ahead and book, especially if you're in a group of four or more.

The Marble Arch Caves are 16km southwest of Enniskillen, and some 4km from Florence Court (an hour's walk). They are reached via the A4 Sligo road and the A32. The site is well signposted.

Loughs Melvin & McNean

Lough Melvin and Lough McNean lie along the border with the Republic, on the B52 road from Belcoo to Belleek. Lough Melvin is famous for its salmon and trout fishing, and it is home to two trout species – the sonaghan, with its distinctive black spots, and the crimson-spotted gillaroo – which are unique to the lough, as well as brown trout, ferox trout and char.

Lough Melvin Holiday Centre (☎ 6865 8142; www.loughmelvinholidaycentre.com; Garrison; tent £8, caravan £12.50, dm £13, s/d £17/29) offers caving, canoeing, walking and fishing holidays, and also has a camp site, dorm accommodation, en-suite rooms, a restaurant and a coffee shop.

Corralea Activity Centre (☎ 6638 6668; www.activityireland.com; Belcoo), based on Lough McNean Upper, hires out bicycles (£8/13 per half day/day) and canoes (£12/18). It also offers instruction in activities such as caving, canoeing, climbing, windsurfing and archery from £25 per day.

Directory

CONTENTS

ACCOMMODATION

Our Sleeping entries are categorised by price and then preference. Rates are per *room* per night, unless otherwise stated: budget (less than €40/£20), mid-range (€40-75/£20-50) and top end (more than €85/£50), and high-season rates are given throughout. Where a range of prices is given, it refers to rates for different rooms during high season. Prices may be cheaper off-peak.

The majority of accommodations increase their rates by up to 10% on 'special' weekends, ie bank holidays or during major sporting events. Hotels will often offer packages, especially in low season, for more than one night's stay including dinner and it's also worth asking for a discount from the quoted rack rate (tourist board–approved rate) from Monday to Thursday. Ironically, in city hotels cheaper rates may apply at weekends, when their main corporate clients disappear.

In low season (November to March) you can simply call in or ring ahead in rural

PRACTICALITIES

- Use the metric system for weights and measures though watch out for speed limits and rural black-and-white road signs, given in miles.
- Use the PAL system for video recorders and players.
- Plug appliances into the three flat pin sockets for (220V, 50Hz AC) power supply.
- Get an insight into Irish life in one of the world's best newspapers the *Irish Times* or Ireland's biggest-selling *Irish Independent.*
- Relish Irish political satire in the fortnightly magazine *Phoenix,* brush up on current affairs in *Magill* magazine or multicultural issues and news in tabloid *Metro Eireann.*
- Check Northern Irish news from both sides of the fence with Protestant tabloid *News Letter* or the pro-Nationalist *Irish News.*
- Tune into *The Late Late Show* (RTE 1), the longest-running chat show in the world, hosted by Pat Kenny.
- Catch some great documentary on TG4, the national Irish language station. Subtitles are available!
- Tune into RTE Radio One (88–90 FM or 567/729 MW) with John Kelly's eclectic music show *The Mystery Train* (7pm to 8pm Monday to Friday), Lyric FM (96–99 FM) for nonstop classical music or Donal Dineen's indie music show *Here Comes The Night* (10pm to 1am Sunday to Thursday) on Today FM (100–100.3 FM).

areas. In peak season it's best to book ahead. Fáilte Ireland (Irish Tourist Board) or the Northern Ireland Tourist Board (NITB) will book serviced accommodation for a fee of €4 (£2) or €7 (£3) for self-catering.

Many accommodations close during Christmas and New Year, especially in rural areas, and most charge a single supplement.

B&Bs

The ubiquitous bed and breakfasts are small, family-run houses, farmhouses and period country houses with less than five bedrooms. Standards vary but most would have some en-suite bedrooms, at a cost of roughly between €33 to €38 per person per night, except in luxurious B&Bs where you can pay €55 or more per person. Remember, outside big cities most B&Bs only accept cash.

Camping & Caravan Parks

Camping and caravan parks aren't as common in Ireland as they are in Britain or on the continent. Some hostels have camping space for tents and offer house facilities, which makes them better value than the main camp sites. At commercial parks tent sites typically cost €6 to €15, depending on the size of tent and whether you arrive by bike or car. Caravan sites cost around €12 to €20. Most parks only open from Easter to the end of September or October.

WEBSITE RESOURCES

- **www.ireland.travel.ie** Gulliver, Fáilte Ireland and NITB's web-based accommodation reservation system.
- **www.everybody.co.uk** This website for Everybody's Hotel Directory lists accommodation suitable for disabled (and able-bodied) travellers in Northern Ireland.
- **www.irishlandmark.com** Hires self-catering properties of historical and cultural significance, such as castles, gate lodges and lighthouses.
- **www.elegant.ie** Specialises in self-catering castles, period houses and unique properties.
- **www.familyhomes.ie** Lists, you guessed it, family-run guesthouses and self-catering properties.
- **www.daft.ie** Online classified paper for short- and long-term rentals.
- **www.stayinireland.com** Lists guesthouses and self-catering.

Guesthouses

Guesthouses are larger than B&Bs, with as many as 30 bedrooms. Prices vary enormously according to the standard but the minimum you can expect to shell out is €35 per person (€40 in Dublin) up to about €100 in upmarket places. Unlike hotels, the majority of them are unlicensed but many have restaurants, good facilities and can take credit card payment.

Hostels

The prices quoted in this book for hostel accommodation are for those aged over 18. A dorm bed in high season generally costs €12 to €25.

An Óige and Hostelling International Northern Ireland (HINI) are the two associations that belong to Hostelling International (HI). About half of the hostels have family and smaller rooms. An Óige has 33 hostels scattered around the Republic and HINI has six in the North.

An Óige (☎ 01-830 4555; www.irelandyha.org; 61 Mountjoy St, Dublin 1; 🕑 9.30am-5.30pm Mon-Fri)
HINI (☎ 028-9031 5435, area code 048 if calling from Republic; www.hini.org.uk; 22-32 Donegall Rd, Belfast BT12 5JN)

Ireland also has a large number of independent hostels, some excellent, but many high on character and low on facilities.

The following associations do their best to offer reliable accommodation:

Hostelworld.com (www.hostelworld.com)
Independent Holiday Hostels of Ireland (IHH; ☎ 01-836 4700; www.hostels-ireland.com; 57 Lower Gardiner St, Dublin)
Independent Hostel Owners of Ireland (IHI; ☎ 073-30130; www.holidayhound.com/ihi; Dooey Hostel, Glencolmcille, Co Donegal)

Hotels

Hotels range from the local pub to medieval castles and prices fluctuate accordingly. It's often possible to negotiate better deals than the published rates, especially out of season and online. Payment usually includes breakfast and most have TV, and tea- and coffee-making facilities and phones. You may find that certain hotels will offer better rates than guesthouses.

House Swapping

House swapping has become a popular and affordable way to visit a country and enjoy a real home away from home. There are several agencies in Ireland that, for an annual fee, facilitate international swaps. The fee pays for access to a website and a book giving house descriptions, photographs and the owner's details. After that, it's up to you to make arrangements. Sometimes use of the family car is included.

Homelink International House Exchange (☎ 01-846 2598; www.homelink.ie; 95 Bracken Dr, Portmarnock, Co Dublin)

Intervac International Holiday Service (☎ 041-983 0930; www.intervac.ie; Drogheda, Co Dublin)

Rental Accommodation

Self-catering accommodation is often on a weekly basis and usually means an apartment or house where you look after yourself. The rates vary from one region and season to another. Fáilte Ireland publishes a guide for registered self-catering accommodation or you can check the website (www.ireland.travel.ie).

ACTIVITIES

Activities open up Ireland in a way that can be both cheap and relaxing, and offer a unique experience of the country.

Bird-Watching

The variety and size of the flocks that visit or breed in Ireland make it of particular interest to bird-watchers. It's also home to some rare and endangered species. For a description of some birds found in Ireland see p58.

There are more than 70 reserves and sanctuaries in Ireland, but some aren't open to visitors and others are privately owned, so you'll need permission from the proprietors before entering.

Information can be obtained from the tourist boards and the organisations listed following:

BirdWatch Ireland (☎ 01-280 4322; www.birdwatchireland.ie)

National Parks & Wildlife Service (☎ 01-661 3111)

Royal Society for the Protection of Birds (RSPB; ☎ 028-9049 1547; www.rspb.org.uk)

SOMETHING DIFFERENT

An alternative to normal caravanning is to hire a horse-drawn caravan with which to wander the countryside. In high season you can hire one for around €750 a week. Look at Fáilte Ireland's website www.ireland.travel.ie for a list of operators, or on www.horsedrawn-in-ireland.net.

Another unhurried and pleasurable way to see the countryside (with slightly less maintenance) is by barge on one of the country's canal systems. As above, contact Fáilte Ireland for a list of rental companies.

Another option is to hire a boat, which you can live aboard while cruising Ireland's inland waterways. One company offering boats for hire on the Shannon–Erne Waterway is **Emerald Star** (☎ 078-20234; www.emeraldstar.ie).

Birds of Ireland magazine (☎ 01-830 7364; www.birdsireland.com; 36 Claremont Ct, Glasnevin, Dublin11)

Some useful publications on bird-watching are *Where to Watch Birds in Ireland* by Clive Hutchinson and Dominic Couzens' *Collins Birds of Britain and Ireland.*

Cycling

Ireland is a great place for bicycle touring, despite bad road surfaces in places and inclement weather. If you intend to cycle in the west, the prevailing winds mean it's easier to cycle from south to north.

Bicycles can be transported by bus if there's enough room; the charge varies. By train the cost varies from €2 to €8 for a one-way journey, but bikes are not allowed on certain train routes, including the Dublin Area Rapid Transit (DART); check with **Iarnród Éireann** (☎ 01-836 3333).

Typical bicycle rental costs are €15 to €20 per day or €50 to €90 per week plus a deposit of around €80. Several dealers have outlets around the country:

Irish Cycle Hire (☎ 041-685 3772; www.irishcyclehire.com; Unit 6, Enterprise Centre, Ardee, Co Louth)

Raleigh Ireland (☎ 01-626 1333; www.raleigh.ie; Raleigh House, Kylemore Rd, Dublin) Ireland's biggest rental dealer.

Rent-a-Bike Ireland (☎ 061-416983; www.irelandrentabike.com; 1 Patrick St, Limerick, Co Limerick)

TRACING YOUR ANCESTORS

Many visitors come to Ireland purely to track down their Irish roots. Success in this activity is more likely if you have managed to obtain some basic facts about your Irish ancestors before leaving home. The name of your ancestor who left Ireland and his or her approximate date of birth is essential, but it's also helpful to know the ancestor's county and parish of origin in Ireland, their religious denomination, and their parent's and spouse's names.

Good starting points for research in Ireland are the **National Library** (☎ 01-603 0200; www.nli.ie; Kildare St, Dublin 2); the **National Archives** (☎ 01-407 2300; www.nationalarchives; Bishop St, Dublin 8); and the **Public Record Office of Northern Ireland** (☎ 028-9025 5905; http://proni.nics.gov.uk; 66 Balmoral Ave, Belfast). Other helpful resources include the **General Register Office** (☎ 01-635 4000; www.groireland.ie; Joyce House, 8-11 Lombard St East, Dublin 2) and **General Register Office Northern Ireland** (☎ 028-9025 2000; www.groni.gov.uk; Oxford House, 49/55 Chichester St, Belfast). These agencies hold records of births, deaths and marriages in Ireland.

There are also numerous agencies and individuals that will do the research for you for a fee. For information on these, contact the Association of Professional Genealogists in Ireland (APGI), c/o The Honorary Secretary, 30 Harlech Crescent, Clonskeagh, Dublin. In the North also contact the Association of Ulster Genealogists and Record Agents (Augra), c/o The Honorary Secretary, Glen Cottage, Glenmachan Rd, Belfast.

Dozens of books are available on Irish genealogy. Tony McCarthy's *Irish Roots Guide* is a good introduction to the subject, and John Grenham's *Tracing Your Irish Ancestors* is an excellent comprehensive guide. North Americans in particular benefit from *A Genealogists Guide to Discovering Your Irish Ancestors* by Dwight Radford and Kyle Betit.

There are also many local independent outlets. Regional and national tour operators organise cycling holidays and the tourist boards can supply you with a list of them.

Irish Cycling Safaris (☎ 01-260 0749; www.cyclingsafaris.com) organise tours for groups of cyclists in the southwest, the southeast and Connemara. **Go Ireland** (☎ 066-976 2094; www.goactivities.com; Old Orchard House, Killorglin, Co Kerry) provides cycling tours of the west and Donegal.

Fishing

Ireland is justly famous for its generally free coarse fishing, covering bream, pike, perch, roach, rudd, tench, carp and eels. Killing of pike over 6lb in weight is prohibited, anglers are limited to one pike and killing of coarse fish is frowned upon; anglers are encouraged to return coarse fish alive. Freshwater game fish include salmon, sea trout and brown trout. Some managed fisheries also stock rainbow trout.

The great western lakes of Corrib (p398), Mask and Conn (p420) have plenty of lakeshore B&Bs, good sturdy boats and knowledgeable boatmen. These lakes can be dangerous, as they tend to be littered with hidden rocks and shoals.

While Ireland is a land of opportunity for the angler, intensive agriculture and the growth of towns have brought about a general reduction in water quality in many areas, markedly so in some. Fáilte Ireland and the NITB produce several information leaflets on fishing, accommodation, events and licenses required.

Licences are available from the local tackle shop or direct from the **Central Fisheries Board** (☎ 01-837 9206; www.cfb.ie; Balnagowan House, Mobhi Boreen, Mobhi Rd, Dublin 9).

In the North, rod licences for coarse/game fishing are obtainable from the **Foyle Fisheries Commission** (☎ 028-7144 2100; 8 Victoria Rd, Derry) for the Foyle area, and from the **Fisheries Conservancy Board** (☎ 028-3833 4666; 1 Mahon Rd, Portadown, Co Armagh) for all other regions. You also require a permit from the owner, which is usually the **Department of Agriculture, Fisheries Division** (☎ 028-9052 3491; Annexe 5, Castle Grounds, Stormont, Belfast).

Golf

Contact Fáilte Ireland, the NITB, the **Golfing Union of Ireland** (☎ 01-269 4111; www.gui.ie; Glencar House, 81 Eglington Rd, Donnybrook, Dublin 4), or the **Irish Ladies Golf Union** (☎ 01-269 6244; 1 Clonskeagh Square, Clonskeagh Rd, Dublin 6) for information on golfing holidays.

Green fees, usually based on a per-day basis, start from around €25 on weekdays, but top-notch places charge up to €250. Courses are tested for their level of difficulty; many are playable year round.

Hang-gliding & Paragliding

Some of the finest hang-gliding and paragliding in the country is found at Mount Leinster in Carlow (p323), Great Sugar Loaf Mountain in Wicklow, Benone/Magilligan Beach in Derry (p614) and Achill Island in Mayo (p414). Check the Irish Hang Gliding and Paragliding Association (www.ihpa.ie) and Ulster Hang Gliding and Paragliding Club's (www.uhpc.co.uk) websites for local pilots.

Horse Riding

Not surprisingly this is a popular pastime and there are dozens of centres throughout Ireland offering possibilities ranging from hiring a horse for an hour (from €20) to fully packaged, residential equestrian holidays.

A recommended outfit is Canadian-based **Hidden Trails** (www.hiddentrails.com).

Walking

There are many superb walks in Ireland and over 30 'waymarked ways' or designated long-distance paths of varying length.

Ireland has a tradition of relatively free access to open country but the growth in the number of walkers and the carelessness of a few have made some farmers less obliging. Unfortunately it's not uncommon to find unofficial signs on gateways barring access or physical barriers blocking ways. If you come across this problem, refer to the local tourist office.

The maintenance and development of the ways is administered in the Republic by the **National Waymarked Ways Advisory Committee** (☎ 01-240 7717; www.irishwaymarkedways.ie; Irish Sports Council, 21 Fitzwilliam Sq, Dublin 2) and by **Countryside Access & Activities Network** (☎ 028-9038 1222; House of Sport, Upper Malone Rd, Belfast) in the North.

Some useful guides are Lonely Planet's *Walking in Ireland*, Michael Fewer's *Irish Long-Distance Walks* or *Best Irish Walks* by Joss Lynam. **EastWest Mapping** (☎ /fax 054-77835; eastwest@eircom.net) has good maps of long-distance walks in the Republic and the North.

Tim Robinson of **Folding Landscapes** (☎ 095-35886) produces superbly detailed maps of the Burren, the Aran Islands and Connemara. His and Joss Lynam's *Mountains of Connemara: A Hill Walker's Guide* contains a useful detailed map.

For mountain rescue call ☎ 999.

ORGANISED WALKS

If you don't have a travelling companion one option you could consider is joining an organised walking group.

Go Ireland (☎ 066-976 2094; www.goactivities.com; Old Orchard House, Killorglin, Co Kerry) Offers walking tours of the west, Donegal, Antrim and Fermanagh.

South West Walks Ireland (☎ 066-712 8733; www.southwestwalksireland.com; 40 Ashe St, Tralee, Co Kerry) Provides a series of guided and self-guided walking programmes around the southwest and northwest.

BEARA WAY

This moderately easy, 196km walk forms a loop around the delightful Beara Peninsula in West Cork (p222). The peninsula is relatively unused to mass tourism and makes a pleasant contrast with the Iveragh Peninsula to the north.

Part of the walk, between Castletownbere and Glengarriff, follows the route taken by Donal O'Sullivan and his band after the English took his castle following an 11-day siege in 1602. At Glengarriff, O'Sullivan met up with other families and set out on a journey north, hoping to reunite with other remaining pockets of Gaelic resistance. Of the 1000 or so men who set out that winter, only 30 completed the trek.

The Beara Way mostly follows old roads and tracks and rarely rises above 340m. There's no official start or finish point and the route can be walked in either direction. It could easily be reduced to seven days by skipping Bere and Dursey Islands, and if you start at Castletownbere you could reach Kenmare in five days or less.

BURREN WAY

This 35km walk traverses the Burren limestone plateau in County Clare (p356). It presents a strange, unique landscape to the walker. There's very little soil and few trees but a surprising abundance of flora. The way stretches between Ballyvaughan, on the northern coast of County Clare, and Liscannor to the southwest, taking in the village of Doolin, famous as a traditional-music centre. The trail south of Doolin to the dramatic

Cliffs of Moher is a highlight of the route. From the cliffs a new path is being developed inland towards Liscannor (though some maps may still show the old route along the cliffs, which has been closed).

The best time for this walk is late spring or early summer. The route is pretty dry, but walking boots are useful as the limestone can be sharp.

CAVAN WAY

In the northwest of County Cavan (p442) the villages of Blacklion and Dowra are the ends of the 26km Cavan Way. The way runs in a northeastwards or southwestwards direction past a number of Stone Age monuments – court cairns, ring forts and tombs – and this area is said to be one of the last strongholds of druidism. At the midpoint is the Shannon Pot, a pool on the boulder-strewn slopes of the Cuilcagh Mountains and the source of the River Shannon, which from there flows into Lough Allen. The Shannon Pot divides the walk into two parts: from Blacklion it is mainly hill walking; from Shannon Pot to Dowra it's mainly by road. The highest point on the walk is Giant's Grave (260m).

Dowra links up with the Leitrim Way (p456), which runs between Manorhamilton and Drumshanbo. Blacklion is also on the Ulster Way.

DINGLE WAY

This 168km walk in County Kerry loops round one of the most beautiful peninsulas in the country (see Dingle Peninsula, p255). It takes eight days to complete, beginning and ending in Tralee, with an average daily distance of 21km. The first three days offer the easiest walk but the first day, from Tralee to Camp, is the least interesting; it could be skipped by taking the bus to Camp and starting from there.

EAST MUNSTER WAY

This 70km walk travels through forest, open moorland, along small country roads and a river towpath. It's clearly laid out with black markers bearing yellow arrows, and could be managed in three days, starting at Carrick-on-Suir (p289) in County Tipperary and finishing at Clogheen in County Waterford. The first day takes you to Clonmel, the second to Newcastle and the last to Clogheen.

KERRY WAY

The 214km Kerry Way is the Republic's longest waymarked footpath and is usually walked anticlockwise. It starts and ends in Killarney (p230) and stays inland for the first three days, winding through the spectacular Macgillycuddy's Reeks (p237) and past 1039m Mt Carrantuohil, Ireland's highest mountain, before continuing around the Ring of Kerry coast through Cahirciveen, Waterville, Caherdaniel, Sneem and Kenmare (see p246).

You could complete the walk in about 10 days, provided you're up to walking a good 20km a day. With less time it's worth walking the first three days, as far as Glenbeigh, from where a bus or a lift could return you to Killarney.

Accommodation isn't a problem, but you need to book in July and August. In contrast, places to eat aren't common, so consider carrying your own food.

MOURNE TRAIL

The Mourne Trail is actually the southeastern section of the Ulster Way, south of Belfast, and runs from Newry (p589), around the Mourne Mountains (p586), to the seaside resort of Newcastle (p584) and then on to Strangford (p582), where you can take a ferry across to Portaferry (p575) and continue north to Newtownards (p578). From Newry to Strangford is a distance of 106km, which could probably be managed in four or five days.

There's gorgeous mountain, forest and coastal scenery along the way and, once you've left Newry, not much in the way of built-up towns to spoil the views. Provided you're reasonably fit and well shod this is not an especially difficult route to walk, although it does climb as high as 559m at Slievemoughanmore, the highest point on the Ulster Way.

SLIEVE BLOOM WAY

Close to the geographical centre of Ireland, the Slieve Bloom Way is a 77km waymarked trail through Counties Offaly and Laois, which does a complete circuit of the Slieve Bloom Mountains (p325) taking in most major points of interest. The trail follows tracks, forest firebreaks and old roads, and crosses the Mountrath–Kinnitty and Mountrath–Clonaslee roads. The trail's highest point is at Glendine Gap (460m).

The recommended starting point is the car park at Glenbarrow, 5km from Rosenallis.

Camping in state forests is forbidden, but there's plenty of open space outside the forest for tents; otherwise, accommodation en route is almost nonexistent. There is no public transport to the area, although buses do stop in the nearby towns of Mountrath and Rosenallis.

SOUTH LEINSTER WAY

The tiny village of Kildavin in County Carlow, just southwest of Clonegal on the slopes of Mt Leinster, is the northern starting point of the 100km South Leinster Way, which winds through Counties Carlow and Kilkenny. It follows remote mountain roads and river towpaths through the medieval villages of Borris (p322), Graiguenamanagh (p305), Inistioge (p305), Mullinavat and Piltown to the finish post at Carrick-on-Suir (p289) just inside the Tipperary border. The southerly section is not as scenic as the rest, but the low hills have their own charm and on a sunny day they offer fine views south over the Suir Valley and Waterford Harbour.

The way leads in a generally southwestwards direction but could easily be done the opposite way. It should take four or five days, depending on whether you stop over in Graiguenamanagh.

The route is marked so you should have no difficulty finding your way. Much of the trail is above 500m and the weather can change quickly. Good walking boots, outdoor gear and emergency supplies are essential.

ULSTER WAY: NORTHEASTERN SECTION

The Ulster Way makes a circuit around the six counties of Northern Ireland and Donegal. In total the footpath covers just more than 900km, so walking all of it might take five weeks. However, it can easily be broken down into smaller sections that could more realistically be attempted during a short stay. The scenery along the way varies enormously, encompassing dramatic coastal views, gentler lakeside country and the mountainous inland terrain of the Mourne Mountains.

Some of the most spectacular scenery lies along the northeastern section, which follows the Glens of Antrim (p625) and then the glorious Causeway Coastline (p621), a Unesco World Heritage site. The 165km northeastern section begins unpromisingly in Belfast's western suburbs, heads northeastwards to meet the coast at Glenarm, then follows the coast around to the Giant's Causeway; this can be completed in six or seven days. The stretch of coast immediately surrounding the Giant's Causeway is likely to be busy, especially in high summer, when you should book accommodation well ahead.

Walking this stretch of coast shouldn't be beyond most averagely fit and sensibly equipped people, but rockfalls along the coast can occasionally obstruct stretches of it. While some stretches of this walk can seem wonderfully wild, you're never going to be that far from civilisation.

ULSTER WAY: DONEGAL SECTION

The main Ulster Way crosses into Donegal at the small pilgrimage town of Pettigo on Lough Erne, but then circles straight back to Rosscor in Northern Ireland. A spur – also confusingly called the Ulster Way – cuts north across the central moorlands of Donegal to Falcarragh on the northern coast. In all, if you follow the spur, this stretch of walk is 111km long, which means it can be walked in four or five days. Bear in mind, however, that much of central Donegal is bleak, boggy terrain where walking can be tough going, especially if the weather's bad – which it often is! Although the walking-man symbol sometimes appears on markers, in general you'll be looking out for white-painted posts which simply tell you that you're heading in the right direction.

This stretch of the Ulster Way is intended for wilderness lovers. Some of the scenery en route is truly magnificent, as you pass the Blue Stack (p579) and Derryveagh Mountains and the 752m Mt Errigal (p483), Donegal's highest peak. The route also skirts the glorious Glenveagh National Park (p483), where you might want to divert and break your journey. There are few dramatic historic remains to distract you, but plenty of minor prehistoric burial sites en route.

WICKLOW WAY

Opened in 1982, the popular 132km Wicklow Way was Ireland's first long-distance trail. Despite its name it actually starts in southern Dublin and ends in Clonegal in County Carlow, although for most of the way it travels through Wicklow. From its beginnings in Marlay Park, Rathfarnham, in southern Dublin, the trail quickly enters a mountain wilderness (the highest point is White Hill at 633m). A mixture of forest walks, sheep paths, bog roads and mountain passes join up to provide a spectacular walk, which passes by Glencree (p140), Powerscourt (p138), Djouce Mountain, Luggala, Lough Dan, Glenmacnass (p141), Glendalough (p141), Glenmalure (p145) and Aghavannagh.

Some sections are desolate, especially south of Laragh, with much of the trail above 500m. The weather can change quickly, so good walking boots, outdoor gear and emergency supplies are essential. There are many worthwhile detours: up Glenmacnass to the waterfall or up to the summit of Lugnaquilla Mountain, for example.

For the entire trail, allow eight to 10 days, plus time for diversions. It's easy to pick up sections and it can be done in either direction, though most walkers start in Dublin. Breaking the journey at Laragh, just under halfway, would let you visit the monastic site at Glendalough and do some local walks. Because of the way's popularity, walking outside the busy June to August period is advisable. Camping is possible along the route, but you'll need to ask permission from local farmers. In peak season you should book accommodation in advance. If you're hostelling you'll need to carry food with you.

Rock Climbing

Ireland's mountain ranges aren't high – Mt Carrantuohil in Kerry's MacGillycuddy's Reeks is the tallest mountain in Ireland at only 1039m – but they're often beautiful and offer some excellent climbing possibilities (see p261). The highest mountains are in the southwest.

Adventure centres around the country run courses and organise climbing trips. For further information contact the **Mountaineering Council of Ireland** (☎ 01-450 7376; www.mountaineering.ie) which also publishes climbing guides and the quarterly magazine *Irish Mountain Log* or check www.climbing.ie.

Water Sports

Ireland's more than 3100km of coastline, its rivers and its numerous lakes provide plenty of opportunities for a range of water sports.

CANOEING

Ireland's indented coastline makes it ideal for exploring by canoe. The type of canoeing in Ireland and degree of difficulty varies from gentle paddling to white-water canoeing and canoe surfing. The best time for white water is winter, when the heavier rainfall swells the rivers.

Check out the **Irish Canoe Union** (☎ 01-450 9838; www.irishcanoeunion.com).

SAILING

There is a long history of sailing in Ireland and the country has more than 120 yacht and sailing clubs, including the Royal Cork Yacht Club at Crosshaven, which, established in 1720, is the world's oldest. The most popular areas for sailing are the southwestern coast, especially between Cork Harbour and the Dingle Peninsula; the Kerry coastline; the coast of Antrim; along the sheltered coast north and south of Dublin (see p129); and some of the larger lakes such as Lough Derg, Lough Erne and Lough Gill.

The **Irish Association for Sail Training** (☎ 01-605 1621; www.irishmarinefederation.com) watches over professional schools and the national governing body is the **Irish Sailing Association** (☎ 01-280 0239; www.sailing.ie). A recommended publication is *Irish Cruising Club Sailing Directions*, available from booksellers. It contains details of port facilities, harbour plans and coast and tidal information.

SCUBA DIVING

Ireland has some of the best scuba diving in Europe, almost entirely off the western coast among its offshore islands and rocks. The best period for diving is roughly March to October. Visibility averages more than 12m but can increase to 30m on good days. For more details about scuba diving in Ireland contact Comhairle Fó-Thuinn (CFT), The **Irish Underwater Council** (☎ 01-284 4601; www.scuba.ireland.com), Ireland's diving regulatory body, which publishes the dive magazine *SubSea*.

SWIMMING & SURFING

Ireland has some magnificent coastline and some great sandy beaches. A number of Irish beaches suffer from pollution, but the cleaner, safer ones have been awarded the EU Blue Flag. Get a list from the government agency **An Taisce** (☎ 01-454 1786; www.antaisce.org; Tailors' Hall, Back Lane, Dublin 8) or online at www.blueflag.org. Surfers should check www.surfingireland.net or www.victorkilo.com for beach reports and forecasts. Women should check out **Surf Honeys** (www.surfhoneys.com), which runs all-girl surfing, yoga, seaweed baths and reflexology safaris in Sligo.

The best months for surfing in Ireland, when the swells are highest, are September (when the water is warmest because of the Gulf Stream) and October. Some of the best locations are on the south and southwest coasts.

WATER-SKIING

There are water-ski clubs all over Ireland offering tuition, equipment and boats and a full list is available from the **Irish Water Ski Federation** (☎ 028-9260 3117).

WINDSURFING

The windsurfer has plenty of locations to indulge in this popular sport. Even the Grand Canal in Dublin is used by windsurfers. The western coast is the most challenging but is also less crowded. The bay at Rosslare in County Wexford is ideal for windsurfing (see p163). Get equipment and tuition there from the **Rosslare Windsurfing Centre** (☎ 053-32101). The **Irish Sailing Association** (☎ 01-280 0239; www.sailing.ie) is the sport's governing authority and has details of other centres.

BUSINESS HOURS

The standard business hours are generally the same for both the Republic and Northern Ireland and are shown below, with any variations noted:

Banks 10am-4pm (to 5pm Thu) Mon-Fri
Offices 9am-5pm Mon-Fri
Post Offices Northern Ireland 9am-5.30pm Mon-Fri, 9am-noon Sat; Republic 9am-6pm Mon-Fri, 9am-1pm Sat
Pubs Northern Ireland 11.30am-11pm Mon-Sat, 12.30-10pm Sun; pubs with late licences open until 1am Mon-Fri, midnight Sun; Republic 10.30am-11.30pm Mon-Thu, 10.30-12.30am Fri & Sat, noon-11pm Sun (30-min 'drinking up' time allowed), pubs with bar extensions open to 2.30am Thu-Sat; closed Christmas Day and Good Friday.
Restaurants noon-2.30pm & 6- 9pm (later at weekends and in cities); many close one day of the week.
Shops 9am-5.30pm or 6pm Mon-Sat (until 8pm on Thu & sometimes Fri), noon-6pm Sun; bigger towns only; shops and smaller post offices in rural towns may close at lunch and one day a week.
Tourist Offices 9am-5pm Mon-Fri, 9am-1pm Sat; extended hours in summer, less hours/days or may be closed Oct-Apr.

CHILDREN

Successful travel with young children requires effort, but can be done. Try not to overdo things and consider using some sort of self-catering accommodation. It's sometimes easier (or to at least have the option) to eat in, rather than be restricted by the relatively confined space of a hotel or B&B room. On the whole you'll find restaurants and hotels, especially in the countryside, will go out of their way to cater for you and your children – with the exception of a few places, generally in the capital, where children aren't allowed after 6pm. Children are allowed in pubs until 7pm.

You can often buy a family ticket for admission to attractions, and family passes are available on public transport. Ireland has one of the lowest rates of breastfeeding in the world, nevertheless you should be able to feed your baby in all but a few public places without jaws dropping. It's always a good idea to talk to fellow travellers with (happy) children and locals on the road for tips on where to go. For further general information see Lonely Planet's *Travel with Children* by Cathy Lanigan.

Practicalities

Most hotels will provide cots at no extra charge and restaurants will have high chairs. Car seats (€30 to €35 per rental) are mandatory for children in hire cars between the ages of nine months and four years. Bring your own seat for infants under about nine months as only larger forward-facing child seats are generally available. Remember not to place a baby seat in the front if the car has an airbag fitted.

Remarkably, nappy changing facilities are scarce, even in city centres.

Two great websites are www.eumom.ie for pregnant women and parents with young children, and www.babygoes2.com, which is a great travel site about family-friendly accommodation worldwide.

CLIMATE

Thanks to the moderating effect of the Atlantic Gulf Stream, Ireland's climate is relatively mild for its latitude, with a mean annual temperature of around 10°C. The temperature drops below freezing only

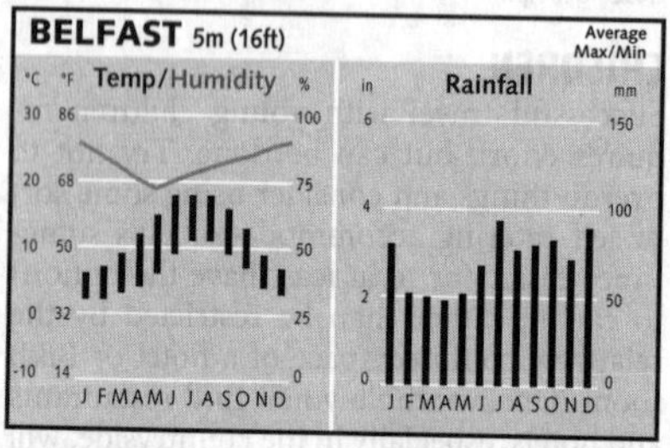

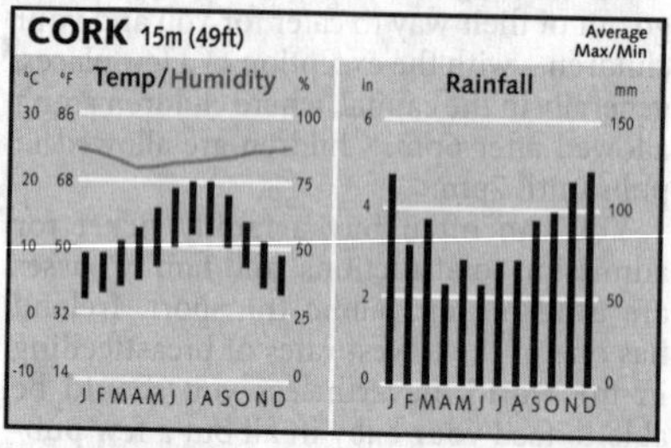

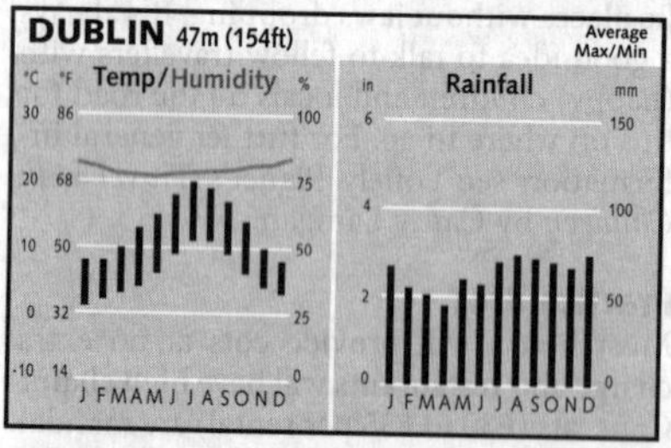

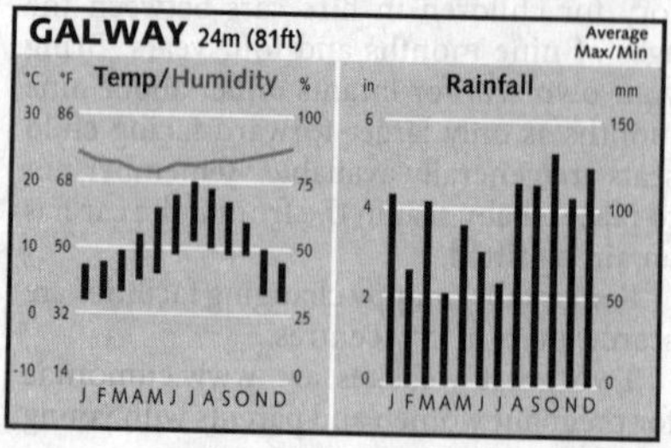

intermittently during winter, and snow is scarce – perhaps one or two brief flurries a year. The coldest months are January and February, when daily temperatures range from 4° to 8°C, with 7°C the average. In summer, temperatures during the day are a comfortable 15° to 20°C. During the warmest months, July and August, the average is 16°C. A hot summer's day in Ireland is 22 to 24°C, although it can sometimes reach 30°C. There are about 18 hours of daylight daily during July and August and it's only truly dark after about 11pm.

One thing you can be sure of about Irish weather is how little you can be sure of. It may be shirtsleeves and sunglasses in February but winter woollies in March and even during the summer.

And then there's the rain. Ireland receives a lot of rain, with certain areas getting a soaking as many as 270 days of the year, Kerry the worst affected. The southeast is the driest, enjoying something like a more continental climate.

Also see When to Go on p13.

COURSES

Irish Language

There are a number of courses in the Irish language and culture, particularly in the Gaeltacht (Irish-speaking areas). Contact Fáilte Ireland for information on other courses.

Intercelt (www.intercelt.com) Resource for Irish language-based holidays.

Oideas Gael (☎ 073-30248; www.oideas-gael.com; Foras Cultúir Uladh, Ulster Cultural Foundation, Glencolmcille, Donegal; 3-/7-day courses €90/170; ⏲ Mar-Oct) Courses in Irish and Irish culture, combined with outdoor activities.

English Language

Fáilte Ireland publishes a list of recognised schools for teaching English as a foreign language.

There are English-language schools in other parts of the country but most are in and around Dublin.

Centre of English Studies (☎ 01-671 4233; www.cesireland.ie; 31 Dame St, Dublin)

Dublin School of English (☎ 01-677 3322; www.dse.ie; 10-12 Westmoreland St, Dublin)

English Language Institute (☎ 01-475 2965; www.englishlanguage.com; 99 St Stephen's Green, Dublin)

Language Centre of Ireland (☎ 01-671 6266; www.lci.ie; 45 Kildare St, Dublin)

CUSTOMS

Duty-free sales are not available when travelling within the EU. Goods for personal consumption bought in and exported within the EU incur no additional taxes, if duty has been paid somewhere in the EU. Over certain limits you may have to show that they are for personal use. The amounts that officially constitute personal use are 800 cigarettes (or 400 cigarillos, 200 cigars or 1kg of tobacco) and either 10L of spirits, 20L of fortified wine, 60L of sparkling wine, 90L of still wine or 110L of beer. There's no customs inspection apart from those concerned with drugs and national security.

Travellers coming from outside the EU are allowed to import, duty free, 200 cigarettes, 1L of spirits or 2L of wine, 60ml of perfume and 250ml of toilet water.

Dogs and cats from anywhere outside Ireland and the UK are subject to strict quarantine laws. The EU Pet Travel Scheme, whereby animals are fitted with a microchip, vaccinated against rabies and blood tested six months *prior* to entry, will come into force in the Republic mid-2004. In the meantime, animals arriving into Ireland are quarantined for six months unless they first pass through the UK and meet British criteria for entry. Contact the **Department of Agriculture, Food & Rural Development** (☎ 01-607 2000) in Dublin for further details.

DANGERS & ANNOYANCES

Ireland is safer than most countries in Europe but normal precautions should be observed. In Dublin, drug-related crime is quite common and the city has its fair share of pickpockets and thieves (see p76).

Dublin is particularly notorious for car break-ins and insurance policies often don't cover losses from cars.

Obviously, there's a certain degree of violence due to the Troubles in Northern Ireland, but it's unusual to come across any personally, and if the peace process continues violence should diminish. Still, it's probably best to ensure your visit to Northern Ireland doesn't coincide with the climax of the Orange marching season on 12 July when even many Northern Irish leave the province.

DISABLED TRAVELLERS

If you have a physical disability, get in touch with your national support organisation (preferably the travel officer if there is one). It often has libraries devoted to travel and can put you in touch with travel agencies that specialise in tours for the disabled.

Guesthouses, hotels and sights in Ireland are gradually being adapted for people with disabilities. Fáilte Ireland's guide *Be Our Guest* and NITB's *Accessible Accommodation in Northern Ireland* indicate which places are wheelchair accessible.

Public transportation can be a nightmare: if you're using a wheelchair, forget about getting a bus. Trains are accessible with help. In theory, if you call ahead, an employee of Iarnród Éireann (Irish Rail) will arrange to accompany you to the train.

Further information on access for disabled travellers is available in the Republic from ☎ 1800 350150. **Comhairle** (The Access Service; ☎ 874 7503; www.comhairle.ie) or in Northern Ireland from **Disability Action** (☎ 028-9066 1252). Travellers to Northern Ireland can also check out the website www.everybody.co.uk.

DISCOUNT CARDS

Heritage Discounts

Heritage Card (☎ 01-647 3000; www.heritageireland.com; adult/child or student €20/€7.50; 51 St Stephen's Green, Dublin 2) Entitles you to free access to 65 sites for one year.

National Trust (☎ 0870 458 4000; www.nationaltrust.org.uk; adult/under 25/family £34/15.50/62.50; PO Box 39, Bromley BR1 3XL, UK) Entitles you to free admission to its properties, but there are fewer sites here so it only makes financial sense if you're touring Britain too.

Senior Cards

Senior citizens are entitled to many discounts in Ireland on things such as public transport and museum admission fees, provided they show proof of age. The minimum qualifying age is usually 60 to 65 for men and 55 to 65 for women. In your home country, a lower age may already entitle you to all sorts of interesting travel packages and discounts (on car hire, for instance).

Car rental companies usually won't rent to drivers aged over 70 or 75.

Student & Youth Cards

The International Student Identity Card (ISIC) gets discounts on transport commercial goods and services, and admission to museums and sights. The International Youth Travel Card (IYTC) and European Youth Card (Euro<26 card) offer similar discounts for nonstudents under 26. All these cards are issued by hostelling organisations, student unions and student travel agencies.

EMBASSIES & CONSULATES

Irish Embassies & Consulates

Irish diplomatic offices overseas:

Australia Embassy (☎ 02-6273 3022; irishemb@cyberone.com.au; 20 Arkana St, Yarralumla, Canberra, ACT 2615)

Canada Embassy (☎ 613-233 6281; 130 Albert St, Suite 1105, Ottawa, Ontario K1P 5G4)

France Embassy (☎ 01 44 17 67 00; 4 rue de Paris, 75116 Paris)

Germany Embassy (☎ 030-220 720; Friedrichstrasse 200, 10117 Berlin)

Italy Embassy (☎ 06 697 9121; Piazza di Campitelli 3, 00186 Rome)

Netherlands Embassy (☎ 070-363 09 93; Dr Kuyperstraat 9, 2514 BA The Hague)

New Zealand Embassy (☎ 09-302 2867; 2nd floor, Dingwall Bldg, Queen St, Auckland)

UK Embassy (☎ 020-7235 2171; 17 Grosvenor Place, London SW1X 7HR); Consulate (☎ 0131-220 8226; City Base, 1 St Colme St, Edinburgh EH3 6AA); Consulate (☎ 029-2023 0709; Jury's Hotel, Mary Ann St, Cardiff CF1 2EQ)

USA Embassy (☎ 202-462 3939; 2234 Massachusetts Ave, NW, Washington, DC 20008) There are also consulates in Boston, Chicago, New York and San Francisco.

UK (for Northern Ireland) diplomatic offices abroad:

Australia High Commission (☎ 02-6270 6666; Commonwealth Ave, Yarralumla, Canberra, ACT 2600)

Canada High Commission (☎ 613-237 1530; www.britain-in-canada.org; 80 Elgin St, Ottawa, Ontario K1P 5K7)

France Embassy (☎ 01 44 51 31 00; www.amb-grandebretagne.fr; 35 rue du Faubourg St Honoré, 75383 Paris)

Germany Embassy (☎ 030-204 570; www.britischebotschaft.de; Wilhelmstrasse 70, 10117 Berlin)

Italy Embassy (☎ 06 4220 0001; www.ukinitalia.it; Via XX Settembre 80a, 00187 Rome)

Netherlands Consulate (☎ 020-676 43 43; www.britain.nl; Koningslaan 44, 1007 AE Amsterdam)

New Zealand High Commission (☎ 04-472 6049; 44 Hill St, Wellington)

USA Embassy (☎ 202-588 6500; 3100 Massachusetts Ave NW, Washington, DC 20008)

Embassies & Consulates in Ireland

Your own country's embassy won't be much help if the trouble you're in is remotely your own fault. You are bound by the laws of the country you are in. In genuine emergencies you might get some assistance: a free ticket is exceedingly unlikely but embassies might assist you with getting a new passport.

Countries with diplomatic offices in Dublin include:

Australia Embassy (☎ 01-676 1517; www.australianembassy.ie; 2nd floor, Fitzwilton House, Wilton Terrace, Dublin 2)

Canada Embassy (☎ 01-417 4100; 4th floor, 65-68 St Stephen's Green, Dublin 2)

France Embassy (☎ 01-260 1666; 36 Ailesbury Rd, Dublin 4)

Germany Embassy (☎ 01-269 3011; 31 Trimleston Ave, Booterstown, Co Dublin)

Italy Embassy (☎ 01-660 1744; 63 Northumberland Rd, Dublin 4)

Netherlands Embassy (☎ 01-269 3444; 160 Merrion Rd, Dublin 4)

New Zealand Consulate (☎ 01-660 4233; 37 Leeson Park, Dublin 6)

UK Embassy (☎ 01-205 3700; www.britishembassy.ie; 29 Merrion Rd, Ballsbridge, Dublin 4)

USA Embassy (☎ 01-668 7122; aedublin@indigo.ie; 42 Elgin Rd, Dublin 4)

The following countries have consular representation in Northern Ireland:

Germany (☎ 028-7034 0403; Hillman's Way, Ballycastle Rd, Coleraine)

Netherlands (☎ 028-9077 9088; c/o All-Route Shipping Ltd, 14-16 West Bank Rd, Belfast)

USA (☎ 028-9032 8239; Queen's House, 14 Queen St, Belfast)

FESTIVALS & EVENTS

Following is a list of major annual events and festivals held around the island. Local tourist offices will have additional information. Also, the Association of Irish Festival Events (AOIFE) maintains a very useful website at www.aoifeonline.com; www.art.ie is worth perusing too. For regional festivals, see destination chapters.

MARCH

St Patrick's Day (17 March; ☎ 01-676 3205, www.stpatricksday.ie) The streets of Dublin reverberate to a cacophony of parades, fireworks and lightshows for three days around 17 March. Over 250,000 attend. Cork, Armagh and Belfast also have parades; elsewhere festivities are less ostentatious.

APRIL

Easter Parades Many small towns host an Easter parade. Ask the local tourist office for details.

World Irish Dancing Championships (☎ 01-475 2220) Four thousand dancers from all over the globe compete in early April. The location varies from year to year.

DECEMBER

Christmas This is a quiet affair in the countryside, though on 26 December the ancient practice of Wren Boys is re-enacted, most notably in Dingle, County Kerry, when groups of children dress up and go about singing hymns.

FOOD

Restaurant listings throughout the book appear in order of author preference with favourites appearing first. Please note though that this hierarchy is not written in stone as authors, like you readers, can crave for caviar on a Monday and cod and chips on a Friday! For explanations of peculiarities of Irish menus and further reading on Irish food and drink, see p61.

GAY & LESBIAN TRAVELLERS

Surprisingly for such an overwhelmingly Catholic country, Irish laws on homosexuality are among the most liberal and progressive in Europe. There is a common age of consent of 17, and neither gays nor lesbians (in the Republic) are excluded from the armed forces. Despite its dogma on the matter, the Catholic Church has maintained a silent neutrality on gay and lesbian issues.

Dublin (see p104), and to a lesser extent Belfast, Cork, Galway, Waterford and Limerick, have openly gay and lesbian communities, but elsewhere the scene is quiet. The monthly *Gay Community News* (www.gcn.ie) is a free publication of the **National Lesbian and Gay Federation** (☎ 01-671 9076; 2 Scarlett Row, Temple Bar, Dublin).

Check out the following online resources for the gay and lesbian community:

Channel Queer www.channelqueer.com
Gaire www.gaire.com
Gay Ireland www.gay.ie
Gay & Lesbian Youth Northern Ireland www.glyni.org.uk

Useful organisations:

Northern Ireland Gay Rights Association (Nigra; ☎ 028-9066 4111; PO Box 44, Belfast)
Outhouse (☎ 01-873 4932; www.outhouse.ie; 105 Capel St, Dublin 1) A gay, lesbian and transgender community centre.

The following helplines can be called from anywhere in Ireland:

Gay Men's Health Project (☎ 01-660 2189) Practical advice on men's health issues.
Gay Switchboard Dublin (☎ 01-872 1055; 🕑 8-10pm Sun-Fri, 3.30-6pm Sat)
Lesbian Line Belfast (☎ 028-9023 8668; 🕑 7.30-10pm Thu)
Lesbian Line Dublin (☎ 01-872 9911; 🕑 7-9pm Thu)
Mensline Belfast (☎ 028-9032 2023; 🕑 7.30-10.30pm Mon-Wed)

HOLIDAYS

Public Holidays

Public holidays in the Republic, Northern Ireland or both are:

New Year's Day 1 January
St Patrick's Day 17 March
Easter (Good Friday to Easter Monday inclusive) March/April
May Holiday 1 May
Christmas Day 25 December
St Stephen's Day (Boxing Day) 26 December

NORTHERN IRELAND

Spring Bank Holiday Last Monday in May
Orangeman's Day 12 July
August Holiday Last Monday in August

REPUBLIC

June Holiday 1st Monday in June
August Holiday 1st Monday in August
October Holiday Last Monday in October

St Patrick's Day, St Stephen's Day and May Day holidays are taken on the following Monday should they fall on a weekend. In the Republic, nearly everywhere closes on Good Friday even though it isn't an official public holiday. In the North, most shops open on Good Friday but close the following Tuesday.

School Holidays

In the Republic, school holidays are to be standardised in 2004 throughout primary and secondary schools as follows:

Mid-term break 27-31 Oct
Christmas 24 Dec-6 Jan
Mid-term 16-20 Feb (2 days only for primary schools)
Easter 5-16 Apr
Summer Jul & Aug (Jun also for secondary schools)

In the North, holidays for primary and secondary schools vary. Check out www.deni.gov.uk/schools/index.htm then click on school holidays for a comprehensive rundown.

INSURANCE

Insurance is important: it covers you for everything from medical expenses and luggage loss to cancellations or delays in your travel arrangements, depending on your policy.

If you're an EU citizen, an E111 form (available from health centres, or from post offices in the UK) covers you for most medical care. Other countries, such as Australia, also have reciprocal agreements with Ireland and Britain, but many countries do not.

If you do need health insurance, remember that some policies offer lower and higher medical-expense options, but the higher one is chiefly for countries such as the USA that have extremely high medical costs. Everyone should be covered for the worst possible case, such as an accident requiring an ambulance, hospital treatment or an emergency flight home. You may prefer a policy that pays healthcare providers directly rather than you having to pay on the spot and claim later.

See p681 for health insurance details and p678 for car insurance information.

INTERNET ACCESS

If you plan to carry your notebook or palmtop computer with you, remember that the power-supply voltage in Ireland may vary from that at home. To avoid frying your electronics, the best investment is a universal AC adapter and a plug adaptor, which will enable you to plug in anywhere. For more on travelling with portable computers visit www.teleadapt.com or www.roadwarrior.com.

Major Internet service providers (ISPs) such as **AOL** (www.aol.com), **CompuServe** (www.compuserve.com) and AT&T **Business Internet Services** (www.attbusiness.net) have dial-in nodes in Ireland. If you access your Internet email account at home through a smaller ISP, your best option is either to open an account with a global ISP, like those mentioned above, or to rely on Internet cafés. Armed with your incoming (POP or IMAP) mail server name, your account name and your password, you should be able to access your Internet mail account from any Net-connected machine in the world. Alternatively, you can open a free Web-based email account such as those provided by Hotmail (www.hotmail.com) or Yahoo! (mail.yahoo.com). Also see Internet Resources on p15.

You'll find Internet cafés in most major towns in Ireland and you can log on for €6 to €10 per hour in the Republic, or about £4 per hour in the North. Most public libraries have a free Internet access service but it may only be available (to a queue of people) at certain hours when connections may be slow.

LEGAL MATTERS

If you need legal assistance contact the **Legal Aid Board** (☎ 1890-615 200). It has a number of local law centres listed in the phone book.

The possession of small quantities of marijuana attracts a fine or warning, but harder drugs are treated more seriously. Public drunkenness is illegal and though police grant leeway, if matters get out of hand, you may receive a verbal caution. Fighting is treated a little more harshly: if you're involved in a fight you may spend a night in a cell, to 'cool off'.

MAPS

Many publishers produce good-quality maps of Ireland. Michelin's 1:400,000-scale Ireland map (No 923) is a good single-sheet map. The cartography is clear and comprehensive, and the map highlights most of the island's scenic roads. The four maps – North, South, East and West – that make up the Ordnance Survey Holiday map series at 1:250,000-scale are useful if you want more detail. Collins also publishes a range of maps covering Ireland.

FOR THE RECORD:

- The legal age to vote in Ireland is 18
- You can leave school when you're 16
- The legal drinking age is 18
- Smoking is legal at 18
- Heterosexual sex is legal when you turn 16
- The homosexual age of consent is 17
- You can ride a moped when you're 16
- You can drive a car when you're 17

For greater detail, the Ordnance Survey Discovery series covers the whole island in 89 maps at a scale of 1:50,000. They're available at the **National Map Centre** (☎ 01-476 0471; 34 Aungier St, Dublin 2) and many other bookshops around Ireland.

For details of Lonely Planet's *Dublin City Map* see p71.

MONEY

ATMs & Credit Cards

Plastic cards make the perfect travelling companions: they're ideal for major purchases and let you withdraw cash from selected banks and ATMs. ATMs are usually linked to international money systems such as Cirrus, Maestro or Plus. Bear in mind though, that each transaction incurs a currency conversion fee and credit cards can incur immediate and exorbitant cash advance interest rate charges.

Charge cards such as Amex and Diners Club don't have credit limits, but may not be accepted in smaller establishments. Visa and MasterCard are more widely accepted, though many B&Bs and some smaller or remote petrol stations take cash only.

Remember to keep a note of the telephone number to ring if your card is lost or stolen (your credit card company will supply you with it).

Cash & Travellers Cheques

Nothing beats cash for convenience – or risk. It's still a good idea, though, to arrive with some local currency (both euros and sterling, if travelling to the North) in cash, to tide you over.

Amex and Thomas Cook travellers cheques are widely recognised and offices don't charge commission for cashing their own cheques. Eurocheques can also be cashed in Ireland. Travellers cheques are rarely accepted outside banks or used for everyday transactions (as they are in the USA).

Take most cheques in large denominations. It's only towards the end of a stay that you may want to change a small cheque to make sure you don't get left with too much local currency.

Currency

In February 2002 the Republic bid adieu to the punt and adopted the euro; part of its ongoing commitment to greater European union.

The euro (€) is divided into 100 cents. The reverse side of the euro coins have a design particular to their country of issue (a Celtic harp in Ireland's case), but are legal tender in all countries that accept the euro (Austria, Belgium, Finland, France, Germany, Greece, Italy, Luxembourg, The Netherlands, Portugal and Spain). Remember that the UK is not a participant, so if you're travelling to Northern Ireland you'll have to change euros into UK pounds.

The British pound sterling (£) is used in Northern Ireland, where it is known as the Northern Irish pound. Northern Ireland notes, while equivalent in value to British pound notes, are not readily accepted in Britain, but British banks will swap them for you.

The best exchange rates are obtained at banks. Bureaus de change and other exchange facilities usually open for more hours but the rate and/or commission will be worse. Many post offices operate a currency-exchange facility and open on Saturday morning. Exchange rates at the time of writing are on the inside front cover.

International Transfers

The most practical way to receive money from overseas is by telegraphic transfer. There are two ways to do this. The first can take up to eight days through the banking system. Your bank sends money to an Irish bank nominated by you. You will need identification, most likely a passport, before the money is paid to you in euros, minus the transfer commission.

The quickest way to receive cash from home is to transfer it through Amex, Thomas Cook or Western Union.

It is not practical to receive money by bank draft. Irish banks are notorious sticklers about drafts and won't allow you to cash them unless you first open a bank account, a small bureaucratic nightmare. Even then, it can take three weeks to clear. If you're not planning a long stay, stick to telegraphic transfers.

Taxes & Refunds

Value-added tax (VAT) is a sales tax of 20% that applies to most goods and services in Ireland, excluding books and children's footwear. Visitors from non-EU countries can claim back the VAT on large purchases that are subsequently exported from the EU through the Cashback scheme. If you're a resident of a country outside the EU and buy something from a store displaying a Cashback sticker, you'll be given a Cashback voucher with your purchase which can be refunded in US, Canadian or Australian dollars, British pounds or euros at Dublin or Shannon airport.

If you reclaim more than €255 on any of your vouchers you'll need to get the voucher stamped at the customs booth in the arrivals hall at Dublin or Shannon airport before you can get your refund from the Cashback desk.

In Northern Ireland, shops participating in the refund scheme will give you a form/invoice on request to be presented to customs when you leave. After customs have certified the form, it will be returned to the shop for a refund.

PHOTOGRAPHY & VIDEO

Developing and printing a 24-exposure print film typically costs around €12 (£9 in Northern Ireland) for a one-hour service or from €6.50 to €8 (£4 to £5 in Northern Ireland) for a slower turnaround. Slide processing costs about €9 (£6 in Northern Ireland) per roll and takes up to a week in most places (an hour in Dublin).

Natural light in Ireland can be very dull, so to capture the sombre atmosphere use faster film, such as 400ASA but 200ASA should do in most situations. Lonely Planet's full-colour *Travel Photography: A Guide to Taking Better Pictures,* written by internationally renowned travel photographer Richard I'Anson, is full of handy hints and is designed to take on the road.

POST

Post offices in the Republic are operated by An Post, the Irish Postal Service, and in the North by Royal Mail.

Postcards and small airmail letters cost €0.41 within Ireland (£0.28 within Northern Ireland and Britain), €0.50 to Britain and €0.57 to continental Europe and the rest of the world (£0.38 and £0.42).

Letters sent by 1st-/2nd-class mail to Britain cost £0.28/0.20 as long as they weigh less than 60g. Airmail letters under 20g cost £0.38 to continental Europe and £0.67 to the rest of the world (under 10g to the rest of the world for £0.47).

You can also buy stamps from some newsagents and shops. All mail to Britain and Europe goes by air, so airmail envelopes and stickers are unnecessary.

Both postal services are efficient: over 95% of mail posted to destinations within Ireland is delivered the next working day. Mail to Britain and continental Europe takes three to five days, to Australasia a week to 10 days, and to North America about 10 days. If you want to send mail to a post office in Ireland to be held for collection, mark it 'Poste Restante: Hold for Collection'. The post office will officially only hold this post for two weeks; you will need photo identification to claim your post.

For post office opening hours see p659.

SHOPPING

Online shoppers can visit www.celticlinks.com for a wide selection of Irish goods.

Clothing

First made by Aran Island women for their husbands to wear in the harsh local climate, the famous Aran sweater is sold throughout Ireland, though it's found most in County Galway. The hand-knitted variety costs significantly more than its machine-manufactured counterpart.

County Donegal is famous for its tweeds; **Magee & Company** (☎ 073-31100; www.mageeshop.com; The Diamond, Donegal town) has a large selection. Tweed can be purchased in lengths or finished as jackets, skirts or caps. Counties Wicklow and Dublin also produce tweed.

Irish linen is of high quality and comes in the form of everything from blouses to handkerchiefs, with the main centres in the North. Irish lace is another fine product, at its best in Limerick, or Carrickmacross in County Monaghan. The Irish produce some high-quality outdoor-activities gear – they do have plenty of experience with wet and cold weather, after all. Hand-woven shawls and woollen blankets also make lovely presents.

Crystal

Waterford Crystal (☎ 051-73311; www.waterfordwedgwood.com; Kilbarry, Waterford) makes world-famous crystal that is available throughout Ireland, although the company has reduced its workforce in Waterford and moved some business overseas. Its main competitor is **Cavan Crystal** (☎ 049-433 1800; www.cavancrystaldesign.com; Dublin Rd, Cavan). Smaller manufacturers of crystal produce fine work and at more attractive prices. In the North, **Tyrone Crystal** (☎ 028-8772 5335; www.tyronecrystal.com; Killybrackey, Dungannon) hosts factory tours.

Food & Drink

Irish whiskey isn't just spelled differently: it also has its own distinctive taste. The big names are Paddy's, Jameson's, Power's, Bushmills and Tullamore Dew, and they're not always readily available in other parts of the world. Two well established Irish liqueurs are Irish Mist and Bailey's Irish Cream. Bailey's now also produce Irish coffee in a bottle, ready mixed.

Some excellent handmade cheeses are worth considering as a gift to take home. See p61 for cheese suggestions.

Pottery

All over the country there are small potteries turning out unusual and attractive work. The village of Belleek in County Fermanagh, which straddles the Northern Ireland border with Donegal, produces delicate bone china. In the Republic the area around Dingle in County Kerry has superb pottery. Enniscorthy in County Wexford, and Kilkenny and Thomastown in County Kilkenny also stand out in this regard. Generally, throughout West Cork and Kerry there are countless small workshops that open in the summer with their stocks of pottery and other craftwork. Stephen Pearce pottery, from Carrigaline in Cork, is available in gift shops all over Ireland.

Other Items

Other possibilities include Irish music; jewellery, especially Claddagh rings (see p378); enamel work; and baskets woven of willow or rush. Connemara marble is a natural green stone found in the west of Ireland; it is often fashioned into Celtic designs.

SOLO TRAVELLERS

Travelling alone in Ireland is easy. People are extremely sociable, especially in the countryside, and will be more than keen to chat with you in pubs or public places – whether you like it or not! Hostels and Internet cafés are always good stomping grounds to meet fellow travellers or you might consider combining independent travel with a short course or activity where you have more chance of meeting people. One disadvantage of solo travel is the extra cost of accommodation; many places charge per room or if they charge per person can also slap a (up to 30%) single supplementary charge on to the room rate.

TELEPHONE

For a small country, Ireland has a remarkably sophisticated phone service and was one of the first countries in the world to make the switch to high-speed fibreoptic cabling. Consequently, you shouldn't have any problems making phone calls to anyone, anywhere.

Eircom is Ireland's largest telephone service provider. Deregulation of the telephone industry has seen the arrival of a number of other providers to Ireland, all of which, however, rent their lines from Eircom. Eircom's main competitor is O2, which in 2001 launched its first land-line service. In the North most public phones are owned by British Telecom (BT).

Peak per-minute charges for international calls from Ireland to selected countries:

To	Republic	North
Australia	€0.85	£0.49
Canada	€0.19	£0.24
France	€0.39	£0.29
Germany	€0.38	£0.29
New Zealand	€0.85	£0.49
Italy	€0.48	£0.36
Netherlands	€0.38	£0.29
UK	€0.15	£0.08
USA	€0.19	£0.24

Prices are lower in the evening and at the weekend. The above prices are for calls placed from land-line phones to other land-line phones; international calls to mobiles can cost significantly more. Phone calls from hotel rooms cost at least double the standard rate. You can send and receive faxes from post offices (up to €2/£1 per page locally) or most hotels.

Rather than placing reverse-charge calls through the operator in Ireland, you can dial direct to your home-country operator and then reverse the charges or charge the call to a local phone credit card. To use the home-direct service dial the codes in the table below then the area code and, in most cases, the number you want. Your home-country operator will come on the line before the call goes through.

To call home from Ireland, dial the numbers outlined in the table below.

To	from the Republic	from the North
Australia	☎ 1800 550061 + number	☎ 0800 890061 + number
France	☎ 1800 551033 + number	☎ 0800 890033 + number
Italy	☎ 1800 550039 + number	☎ 0800 890039 + number
New Zealand	☎ 1800 550064 + number	☎ 0800 890064 + number
Spain	☎ 1800 550034 + number	☎ 0800 890034 + number
UK – BT	☎ 1800 550044 + number	n/a
USA – AT&T	☎ 1800 550000 + number	☎ 0800 890011 + number
USA – MCI	☎ 1800 551001 + number	☎ 0800 890222 + number
USA – Sprint	☎ 1800 552001 + number	☎ 0800 890877 + number

Local telephone calls from a public phone in the Republic cost €0.25 for around three minutes (around €0.50 to a mobile), regardless of when you call. In Northern Ireland a local call costs a minimum of £0.20.

Pre-paid phonecards by Eircom or private operators, available in newsagencies and post offices, work from all payphones and dispense with the need for coins.

Mobile Phones

Mobile phone usage in Ireland has skyrocketed. They're the most convenient – and expensive – way to keep in touch. Ireland uses GSM 900/1800, which is compatible with the rest of Europe and Australia but not with North American GSM 1900 or the totally different system in Japan (though some specially equipped North American phones do work here). There are three service providers in Ireland. Vodafone (087) is the most popular, followed by O2 (086) and the latest arrival, Meteor (085).

All three service providers are linked with most international GSM providers, which will allow you to 'roam' onto a local service once you arrive in Ireland. This means you can use your mobile phone to make local calls, but will be charged at the highest possible rate for all calls.

For around €50 you will get a Ready-to-Go pre-paid phone, your own number and anywhere up to €25 worth of airtime. As you use up your airtime, you simply buy more at newsagencies. The other service providers have variations on this scheme. Similar schemes exist in Northern Ireland.

Phone Codes

When calling the Republic of Ireland from abroad, dial your international access code, followed by 353, followed by the domestic number minus the initial '0'. When calling Northern Ireland from abroad, dial your international access code, then 44 28, and then the local number. To call Northern Ireland from Britain, simply dial 028, then the local number. This changes to 048 when calling from the Republic. The area code for the whole of Northern Ireland is 028, so domestic callers need only dial the eight-digit local number. To call UK numbers from the Republic dial 00 44, then the area code minus the initial '0', then the local number. Do the same for international calls, replacing 44 with the country code.

To call Britain from Northern Ireland dial the area code followed by the local number. To place an international call or to call the Republic from Northern Ireland dial 00 followed by the country code then the area code (dropping any leading '0') and the local number.

TIME

In winter, Ireland is on Greenwich Mean Time (GMT), also known as Universal Time Coordinated (UTC), the same as Britain. In summer, the clock shifts to GMT plus one hour. When it's noon in Dublin and London, it is 3am in Los Angeles and Vancouver, 7am in New York and Toronto, 1pm in Paris, 8pm in Singapore, and 10pm in Sydney.

TOURIST INFORMATION

Fáilte Ireland and the NITB each operate a separate network of tourist information offices throughout Ireland and co-produce publications and brochures.

Tourist offices can offer a variety of services including accommodation and attraction reservations, bureau de change services, map and guidebook sales and free publications.

Both national tourist boards feature a computerised tourist information and reservations service called **Gulliver** (www.ireland.travel.ie, www.discovernorthernireland.com) providing all kinds of tourist information. Telephone reservations can be made on ☎ 1800 668 668 (Ireland), ☎ 800 398 4376 (USA/Canada) or ☎ 0800 783 5740 (UK).

Fáilte Ireland's information service (in the Republic ☎ 1850 230 330; in the UK ☎ 0800 039 7000; www.ireland.travel.ie) and the **NITB** (head office ☎ 028-9023 1221; www.discovernorthernireland.com; 59 North St, Belfast) are a wealth of information.

Both Dublin and Belfast have Fáilte Ireland and NITB offices; Dublin and Belfast also have their own tourism agencies. Elsewhere in the Republic and the North there's a tourist office in almost every big town.

Tourist Offices Abroad

Fáilte Ireland offices abroad:

Australia (☎ 02-9299 6177; 5th level, 36 Carrington St, Sydney, NSW 2000) It also has information on Northern Ireland.

Canada (☎ 416-487 3335; 120 Eglinton Ave East, Suite 500, Toronto, Ontario M4P 1E2)

France (☎ 01 70 20 00 20; 33 rue de Miromesnil, 75008 Paris)

Germany (☎ 069-6680 0950; Untermain-anlage 7, 60329 Frankfurt-am-Main)

Ireland (☎ 028-9032 7888; 53 Castle St, Belfast)

Italy (☎ 02 4829 6060; Via Santa Maria Segreta 6, 20123 Milan)

Netherlands (☎ 020-504 0689; Spuistraat 104, 1012 VA Amsterdam)

New Zealand (☎ 09-379 8720; Dingwall Bldg, 2nd floor, 87 Queen St, Auckland)

UK (☎ 020-7493 3201; Ireland House, 150 New Bond St, London W1S 2AQ) Personal callers should go to the Britain Visitor Centre, 1 Regent St, London SW1Y 4PQ.

USA (☎ 800 223 6470; 345 Park Ave, New York, NY 10154)

NITB offices abroad:

Australia See Australia entry under Fáilte Ireland offices above.

Canada (☎ 416-925 6368; 2 Bloor St West, Suite 1501, Toronto, Ontario M5R 3J8)

France (☎ 01 49 39 05 77; Centre PO 166, 23 rue Lecourbe, 77015 Paris)

Germany (☎ 069-234 504; Westendstrasse 16-22, 60325 Frankfurt-am-Main)

Ireland (within the Republic ☎ 01-679 1977, 1850 230 230; 16 Nassau St, Dublin)

New Zealand (☎ 09-379 3708; 18 Shortland St, Private Bag 92136, Auckland)

UK London (☎ 0870 155 5250; 24 Haymarket, SW1 4DG); Glasgow (☎ 0141-572 4030; 98 West George St, G2 1PJ) Personal callers in London should go to the Britain Visitor Centre.

USA (☎ 212-922 0101; 551 5th Ave, Suite 701, New York, NY 10176)

VISAS

UK nationals don't need a passport to visit the Republic, but are advised to carry one (or some other form of photo identification) to prove that they *are* a UK national. It's also necessary to have a passport or photo ID when changing travellers cheques or hiring a car. EU nationals can enter Ireland with either a passport or a national ID card.

Visitors from outside the EU will need a passport, which should remain valid for at least six months after their intended arrival.

For citizens of EU states and most Western countries, including Australia, Canada, New Zealand and the USA, no visa is required to visit either the Republic or Northern Ireland, but citizens of India, China and many African countries do need a visa for the Republic. Full visa requirements for visiting the Republic are available online by checking out www.gov.ie/iveagh/services/visas; for Northern Ireland's visa requirements see http://visa.fco.gov.uk.

EU nationals are allowed to stay indefinitely, while other visitors can usually remain for three to six months. To stay longer in the Republic, contact the local garda (police) station or the **Department of Foreign Affairs** (☎ 01-478 0822; www.gov.ie/iveagh; 80 St Stephen's Green, Dublin 2). To stay longer in Northern Ireland contact the **Home Office** (☎ 0870-606 7766; Immigration and Nationality Department, Lunar House, Wellesley Rd, Croydon CR9 2BY, UK).

Although you don't need an onward or return ticket to enter Ireland, it could help if there's any doubt that you have sufficient funds to support yourself in Ireland.

WOMEN TRAVELLERS

Women travellers will probably find Ireland a blissfully relaxing experience, with little risk of hassle on the street or anywhere else. Nonetheless, you still need to take elementary safety precautions. Walking alone at night, especially in certain parts of Dublin, and hitching is probably unwise. Should you have serious problems, be sure to report them to the local tourist authorities.

There's little need to worry about what you wear in Ireland, and the climate is hardly conducive to topless sunbathing. Finding contraception is not the problem it once was, although anyone on the pill should bring adequate supplies.

The freefone number for the Rape Crisis Centre is ☎ 1800 77 88 88.

WORK

Lowly paid seasonal work is available in the tourist industry, usually in restaurants and pubs. Sometimes volunteer work is available in return for bed and board, for example from the **Burren Conservation Trust** (☎ 707 6105; jdmn@iol.ie; Admiral's Rest Seafood Restaurant, Fanore).

Citizens of other EU countries can work legally in Ireland. If you don't come from an EU country but do have an Irish parent or grandparent, it's fairly easy to obtain Irish citizenship without necessarily renouncing your own nationality, and this opens the door to employment throughout the EU. Obtaining citizenship isn't an overnight procedure, so enquire at an Irish embassy or consulate in your own country.

To work in the North, citizens of Commonwealth countries aged 17 to 27 can apply for a Working Holiday Entry Certificate that allows them to spend two years in the UK and to take work that's 'incidental' to a holiday.

Commonwealth citizens with a UK-born parent may be eligible for a Certificate of Entitlement to the Right of Abode, which entitles them to live and work in the UK free of immigration control. Commonwealth citizens with a UK-born grandparent, or a grandparent born before 31 March 1922 in what's now the Republic, may qualify for a UK Ancestry Employment Certificate, allowing them to work full time for up to four years in the UK.

Visiting full-time US students aged 18 and over can get a six-month work permit for Ireland and the UK through **Council Exchanges** (☎ 888 268 6245; www.councilexchanges.org/us; 633 3rd Ave, New York, NY 10017).

An excellent resource if passing through Dublin is the State-funded new **Work in Ireland** (☎ 01-677 0300; www.workinireland.ie; 26 Eustace St; noon-6pm Mon-Fri), a one-stop help centre which for €30 a year, will layout your CV, set up interviews, help find accommodation, recommend language courses and offer discounts on tours and phone calls.

Nixers (www.nixers.com) is another useful noticeboard site for those in search of casual labour.

Transport

CONTENTS

THINGS CHANGE...

The information in this chapter is particularly vulnerable to change. Check directly with the airline or a travel agent to make sure you understand how a fare (and ticket you may buy) works and be aware of the security requirements for international travel. Shop carefully. The details given in this chapter should be regarded as pointers and are not a substitute for your own careful, up-to-date research.

FARE GO

Travel costs throughout this book are for single (one-way) adult fares, unless otherwise stated.

GETTING THERE & AWAY

However you travel, be sure to take out travel insurance and photocopy all important documents before you leave home. Leave one copy with someone at home and keep another with you, separate from the originals. If your documents are lost or stolen, replacing them will be much easier.

ENTERING THE COUNTRY

Walking through the green or red channel at customs in Irish airports may not be quite as simple as before, for non-nationals. An increase in the numbers of foreign nationals seeking asylum over the last decade has meant often more rigorous questioning for those originating from African countries or Eastern Europe. For information on visa requirements see p669.

Passport

EU citizens can travel freely to and from Ireland if bearing official photo ID. Those from outside the EU, however must have a passport that remains valid for six months after entry.

AIR

The website of **Fáilte Ireland** (Irish Tourist Board; www.ireland.travel.ie) contains useful information on getting to Ireland from a number of countries.

Airports & Airlines

There are scheduled nonstop flights from Britain, continental Europe and North America to Dublin and Shannon, and good nonstop connections from Britain and continental Europe to Cork.

Cork (code ORK; ☎ 021-431 3131; www.corkairport.com)
Dublin (code DUB; ☎ 01-814 1111; www.dublinairport.com)
Shannon (code SNN; ☎ 061-712 000; www.shannonairport.com)

Other airports in the Republic with scheduled services from Britain are:

Kerry (code KIR; ☎ 066-976 4644; www.kerryairport.ie; Farranfore)
Knock (code NOC; ☎ 094-67222; www.west-irl-holidays.ie)
Waterford (code WAT; ☎ 051-875 589; www.flywaterford.com)

In Northern Ireland there are flights to **Belfast International** (code BFS; ☎ 028-9448 4848;

www.belfastairport.com) from Britain, continental Europe and the USA.

Other airports in Northern Ireland that operated scheduled services from Britain include:

Belfast City (code BHD; ☎ 028-9093 9093; www.belfastcityairport.com)

Derry (code LDY; ☎ 028-7181 0784; www.cityofderryairport.com)

Irish airlines include:

Aer Árann (☎ 01-814 5240; www.aerarann.ie) A small carrier that operates flights within Ireland and also to Britain.

Aer Lingus (☎ 01-886 8844; www.aerlingus.com) The Irish national airline, with direct flights to Britain, continental Europe and the USA.

Ryanair (☎ 01-609 7800; www.ryanair.com) Ireland's no-frills carrier with inexpensive services to Britain and continental Europe.

Airlines flying into and out of Ireland include:

Aer Árann (☎ 01-814 5240; www.aerarann.ie)
Aer Lingus (☎ 01-886 8844; www.aerlingus.com)
Aeroflot (☎ 01-844 6166; www.aeroflot.com)
Air Canada (☎ 01-679 3958; www.aircanada.ca)
Air France (☎ 01-605 0383; www.airfrance.com)
Air Malta (☎ 1800-397 400; www.airmalta.com)
Alitalia (☎ 01-844 6035; www.alitalia.com)
American Airlines (☎ 01-602 0550; www.aa.com)
Belavia (☎ 061-472 921; www.belaviashannon.com)
BMI British Midland (☎ 1332 854 854; www.flybmi.com)
British Airways (in UK ☎ 0845-773 3377; www.britishairways.com)
Continental (☎ 1890 925 252; www.continental.com)
CSA Czech Airlines (☎ 01-814 4625; www.csa.cz)
Delta Airlines (☎ 01-679 6755; www.delta.com)
EasyJet (☎ 048-9448 4929; www.easyjet.com)
Finnair (☎ 01-844 6565; www.finnair.com)
Iberia (☎ 01-407 3017; www.iberia.com)
Jetmagic (☎ 0870-1780 135; www.jetmagic.com)
KLM (☎ 01-663 6900; www.klm.nl)
Lufthansa (☎ 01-844 5544; www.lufthansa.com)
Malaysia Airlines (☎ 01-676 2131; www.malaysiaairlines.com)
Malev Hungarian Airlines (☎ 01-814 5830; www.malev.hu)
Qantas (☎ 01-407 3278; www.qantas.com.au)
Ryanair (☎ 01-609 7800; www.ryanair.com)
Scandinavian Airlines (☎ 01-844 5888; www.scandinavian.net)
Singapore Airlines (☎ 01-671 0722; www.singaporeair.com)
United Airlines (☎ 01-819 1760; www.ual.com)

> **DEPARTURE TAX**
>
> International departure tax is normally included in the price of your ticket.

Tickets

Fierce competition on most European routes has resulted in price wars between no-frills carriers and full-service airlines. Discounted web fares offer the best deals, and one-way tickets make it easy to fly into one city and out of another.

On transatlantic and long-haul flights your travel agent is still probably the best source of cheap tickets, though there are an increasing number of online booking agencies. Be sure to check the terms and conditions of the cheapest fares before purchasing.

ONLINE BOOKING AGENCIES

Best Fares (www.bestfares.com) American site offering discounted airfares and hotel rooms.

Cheap Flights (www.cheapflights.com) American- and British-based site that lists discounted flights and packages.

ebookers (www.ebookers.com) Irish web-based Internet travel agency.

Expedia (www.expedia.com) Microsoft's travel site, this is for the USA but has links for Canada, the UK and Germany.

Opodo (www.opodo.com) Joint booking service for nine European airlines.

Priceline (www.priceline.com) American web-based travel agency.

STA Travel (www.statravel.com) International student travel agency.

Travelocity (www.travelocity.com) American web-based travel agency.

COURIER FLIGHTS

Courier fares can present a good deal for travelling across the Atlantic; visit www.courier.org for more information. London is the biggest European hub – it's unlikely you'll find a courier fare direct to Dublin. **Now Voyager Travel** (in New York ☎ 212-459 1616; www.nowvoyagertravel.com) is one of the leading courier companies based in New York.

From Australia

There are no nonstop scheduled air services from Australia to Ireland; generally it's cheapest to fly to London or Amsterdam and continue from there. Most fares to European destinations can have a return flight to Dublin tagged on at little or no extra cost. Round-the-World (RTW) tickets are another good bet and are often better value than standard return fares.

The Saturday travel sections of the *Sydney Morning Herald* and Melbourne *Age* newspapers advertise cheap fares.

Recommended agencies:

Flight Centre (☎ 133 133; www.flightcentre.com.au)
Shamrock Travel (☎ 03-9602 3700; www.irishtravel.com.au)
STA Travel (☎ 1300-733 035; www.statravel.com.au)

From Canada

Air Canada is the only carrier flying directly to Ireland with its new daily Toronto–Shannon route. Your best bet for cheap fares may be to connect to transatlantic gateways in the USA or to fly to London and continue on to Ireland from there. Check the travel sections of the *Globe & Mail*, *Toronto Star*, *Montreal Gazette* or *Vancouver Sun* for the latest offers.

Recommended agencies:

Canadian Affair (www.canadian-affair.com) Cheap one-way fares to British cities.
Travel Cuts (☎ 866-246 9762; www.travelcuts.com)

From Continental Europe

Dublin and Belfast have good connections with all major centres in Europe including cheap deals with **Ryanair** (www.ryanair.com) and **EasyJet** (www.easyjet.com). Shannon is served by flights from Brussels, Frankfurt, Moscow and Paris; there are flights to Cork from Frankfurt, Malaga, Paris and Prague; and flights to Kerry from Frankfurt.

Alternatively, you could take a cheap flight with Ryanair, EasyJet, or Ryanair's recent acquisition, **Buzz** (www.buzzaway.com), to London, then pick up a connecting flight to Ireland. **Jetmagic** (www.jetmagic.com) operates flights from Cork to 12 European destinations. However, budget airlines tend to use secondary airports in or around major cities, which can make transfers expensive and time consuming. Check before you book.

Recommended agencies include:

France

Anyway (☎ 08 92 89 38 92; www.anyway.com)
Go Voyages (☎ 08 92 89 18 32; www.govoyages.com)
OTU Voyages (☎ 08 20 81 78 17; www.otu.fr)
Travelprice (☎ 08 92 35 05 00; www.travelprice.fr)

Germany

Just Travel (☎ 089-747 33 30; www.justtravel.de)
STA Travel (☎ 01805-456 422; www.statravel.de)

Italy

CTS Viaggi (☎ 199-50 11 50; www.cts.it)
Travelprice (☎ 199-40 02 00; www.travelprice.it)

Netherlands

Air Fair (☎ 020-620 51 21; www.airfair.nl)
Kilroy Travels (☎ 020-524 51 00; www.kilroytravels.nl)

From New Zealand

There are no nonstop scheduled air services from New Zealand to Ireland; generally it's cheapest to fly to London or Amsterdam and then continue with a connecting flight to Ireland. RTW fares can be real bargains. Check the *New Zealand Herald* travel section for the latest offers.

Recommended agencies:

Flight Centre (☎ 0800-243544; www.flightcentre.co.nz)
STA Travel (☎ 0508-782872; www.statravel.co.nz)

From the UK

There's a dizzying array of flights between Britain and Ireland. The best deals are available online, and it's not unusual for airport taxes to exceed the base price of the ticket on the lowest fares (generally early morning or late night flights during midweek).

Most regional airports in Britain have flights to Dublin and Belfast and some also have services to Shannon, Cork, Kerry, Knock and Waterford.

From the USA

In the USA discount travel agencies (consolidators) sell cut-price tickets on scheduled carriers. Aer Lingus is the chief carrier between the USA and Ireland, with flights from New York, Boston, Baltimore, Chicago and Los Angeles to Shannon, Dublin and Belfast. Heavy competition on transatlantic routes into London might make it cheaper to fly to there and then continue on to Ireland. The Sunday travel sections of the *New York Times*, *San Francisco Chronicle-Examiner*, *Los Angeles Times* or *Chicago Tribune* list cheap fares.

Some of the more popular travel agencies include:

Ireland Consolidated (☎ 212-661 1999; www.irelandair.com)

STA Travel (☎ 800-781 4040; www.statravel.com)

LAND

Eurolines (www.eurolines.com) has a three-times daily coach and ferry service from London's Victoria station to Dublin Busáras. For information on border crossings (see p677).

SEA

There are many ferry and fast-boat services from Britain and France to Ireland. Prices quoted throughout this section are one-way fares for a single adult on foot/up to four adults with a car during peak season.

To/From the UK

There are numerous services between Britain and Ireland but it's wise to plan ahead as fares vary considerably, depending on the season, day, time and length of stay. Some return fares don't cost much more than one-way fares and it's worth keeping an eye out for special offers. International Student Identity Card (ISIC) holders and Hostelling International (HI) members get a reduction on the normal fare.

Shipping lines operating between Britain and Ireland include:

Irish Ferries (☎ 0870-517 1717; www.irishferries.com) For ferry and fast-boat services from Holyhead to Dublin, and ferry services from Pembroke to Rosslare.

Isle of Man Steam Packet Company/Sea Cat (☎ 01624-661661; www.steam-packet.com) Ferry and fast-boat services from Liverpool to Dublin or Belfast, via Douglas (on the Isle of Man) and from Troon to Belfast.

Norse Merchant Ferries (☎ 0870-600 4321; www.norsemerchant.com) Ferry services from Liverpool to Belfast.

P&O Irish Sea (☎ 0870-242 4777; www.poirishsea.com) Ferry and fast-boat services from Cairnryan to Larne, and ferry services from Fleetwood to Larne, and Liverpool or Mostyn to Dublin.

Stena Line (☎ 0870-570 7070; www.stenaline.com) Ferry services from Holyhead to Dun Laoghaire and Stranraer to Belfast, and fast-boat services from Holyhead to Dublin, Fishguard to Rosslare, and Stranraer to Belfast.

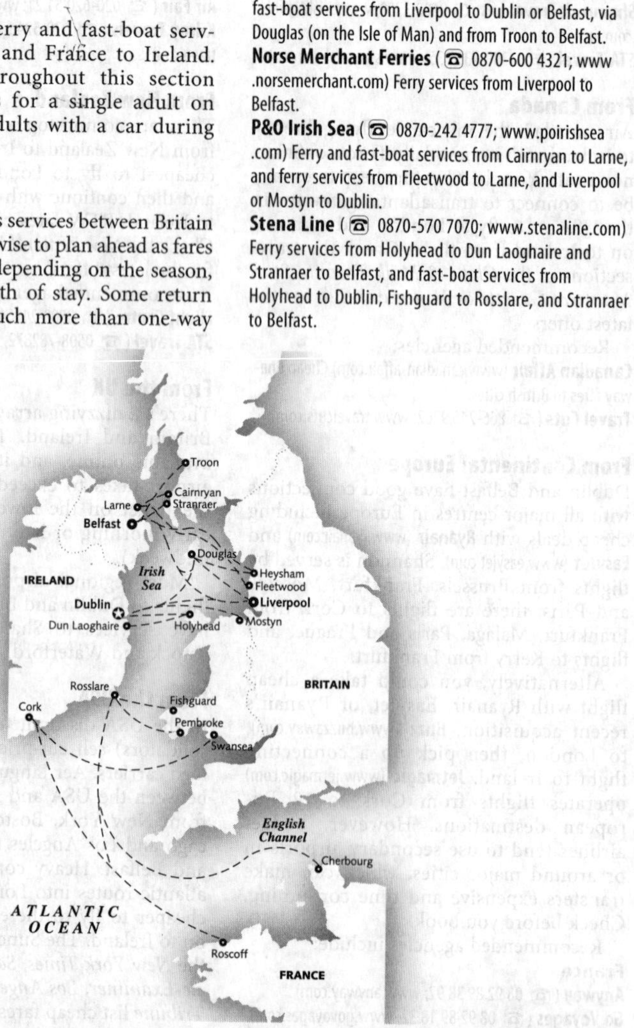

Swansea Cork Ferries (☎ 01792-456116; www.swansea-cork.ie) Ferry services from Swansea to Cork.

TO/FROM THE REPUBLIC OF IRELAND

The main routes from the UK to the Republic are:

Fishguard & Pembroke to Rosslare These popular, short ferry crossings take 3½ hours (from Fishguard) or four hours (from Pembroke) and cost around £22/130; the cost drops significantly outside peak season. The fast boat crossing from Fishguard takes just under two hours and costs around £29/146.

Holyhead to Dublin & Dun Laoghaire The ferry crossing takes just over three hours and costs around £22/145. The fast-boat service from Holyhead to Dun Laoghaire takes a little over 1½ hours and costs £29/160.

Liverpool & Mostyn to Dublin The ferry service takes seven hours from Mostyn or 8½ hours from Liverpool and costs £32/157. Cabins on overnight sailings cost more. The fast-boat service takes four hours and costs up to £40/250.

Swansea to Cork The 10-hour crossing costs around £35/180 but only operates from mid-March to early November.

TO/FROM NORTHERN IRELAND

The main routes from mainland Britain to the North are:

Liverpool to Belfast The 8½-hour crossing costs £30/160 (including meals) during the day and £40/255 (including cabin and meals) at night.

Stranraer to Belfast The fast boat takes 1¾ hours and costs £20/130. The ferry takes 3¼ hours and costs £13/90.

Troon to Belfast This fast-boat service takes 2½ hours and costs £30/210.

Cairnryan to Larne The fast boat takes one hour and costs £25/180. The ferry takes 1¾ hours and costs £20/149.

Fleetwood to Larne The eight-hour crossing costs £127; no foot passengers are carried.

It's possible to combine bus and ferry tickets from major UK centres to all Irish towns on the bus network, but with the availability of cheap flights it's hardly worth the hassle. The journey between London and Dublin takes about 12 hours and costs £27 one way. The London to Belfast trip takes 13 to 16 hours and costs £42 one way. For details in London contact **Eurolines** (☎ 0870-514 3219; www.eurolines.com).

Alternatively, you can combine a train and ferry ticket. The London–Dublin route takes eight to 10 hours via Holyhead and costs £90 return at peak times.

To/From France

Brittany Ferries (in Ireland ☎ 021-427 7801, in France ☎ 02 98 29 28 00; www.brittany-ferries.com) Weekly service from Roscoff to Cork from early April to late September. The crossing takes 14 hours and costs up to €85/498 without accommodation.

Irish Ferries (in Rosslare ☎ 053-33158, in Cherbourg ☎ 02-33 23 44 44, in Roscoff ☎ 02-98 61 17 17; www.irishferries.com) One to three times a week from Roscoff to Rosslare from late April to late September; the crossing time is 17½ hours. Ferries from Cherbourg to Rosslare sail two to four times per week year round except in late January and all of February; crossing time is 20½ hours. Both services cost €101/473 without accommodation.

GETTING AROUND

Travelling around Ireland should be simple – the distances are short and there's a network of roads and railways. In practice though, it's not always so simple – the public transport network can be expensive, infrequent or both and simply doesn't reach many interesting places. Having your own transport is a major advantage and it's worth considering car rental for at least part of your trip. However, delays on the roads, the narrow streets in towns and villages and poor road signs create their own problems.

If you opt not to drive, a mixture of buses, the occasional taxi, plenty of time, walking and sometimes hiring a bicycle will get you just about anywhere.

AIR

Airlines in Ireland

Ireland's size makes domestic flying unnecessary unless you're in a hurry, but there are flights between Dublin and Belfast, Cork, Derry, Donegal, Galway, Kerry, Shannon and Sligo, as well as a Belfast–Cork service. Most flights within Ireland take 30 to 50 minutes.

Domestic carriers include:

Aer Lingus (information & bookings ☎ 01-886 8844, flight information ☎ 01-705 6705, in Belfast ☎ 028-9442 2888; www.aerlingus.ie) The main domestic airline.

Aer Árann (☎ 1890-462726, in Dublin ☎ 01-814 5240, in Galway ☎ 091-593034, in Cork ☎ 021-814 1058; www.aerarann.ie) Operates flights from Dublin to Belfast, Cork, Derry, Donegal, Galway, Kerry, Knock and Sligo, as well as flights to the Aran Islands from Galway.

Jetmagic (in the Republic ☎ 0818-200 135, in the North ☎ 0870-1780 135; www.jetmagic.com) Operates flights from Belfast to Cork.

BICYCLE

Cycling is a popular, rewarding way to explore Ireland, both South and North. For information see p653.

BOAT

Ferry

There are many boat services to islands lying off the coast, including to the Aran and Skellig Islands to the west, the Saltee Islands to the southeast, and Tory and Rathlin Islands to the north. Ferries also operate across rivers, inlets and loughs providing useful short cuts, particularly for cyclists.

Cruises are very popular on the 258km-long Shannon–Erne Waterway and on a variety of other lakes and loughs. The tourist offices only recommend operators registered with them. Details of nontourist board–affiliated boat trips are given under the relevant sections throughout this book.

FERRY, BUS & TRAIN DISCOUNT DEALS

For travel across Europe

Eurail (www.eurail.com) passes are for non-Europeans who have been in Europe for less than six months. They are valid on trains in the Republic, but not in Northern Ireland, and offer discounts on Irish Ferries crossings to France. Passes are cheaper when bought outside Europe. In the USA and Canada phone (☎ 1888-667 9734). In London contact **Rail Europe** (☎ 0870-584 8848; 179 Piccadilly).

InterRail (www.interrail.com) passes give you a 50% reduction on train travel within Ireland and discounts on Irish Ferries and Stena Line services. Passes can be bought at most major train stations and student travel outlets.

For travel within Ireland

Travelsave stamps (€10 in the South, £7 in the North) entitle International Student Identity Card (ISIC) holders to a 50% discount on Irish trains and 15% off Bus Éireann services. Holders of an EYC (or EuroFairstamp) can get a 40% discount on trains with a Travelsave stamp. The stamps are available from usit offices (www.usitnow.ie).

Iarnród Éireann's Faircard (€10.15) gives up to 50% reductions on any intercity journey to people aged under 26, while the Weekender (€10.15) gives up to 30% off (Friday to Tuesday) to people aged 26 and over.

Unlimited-travel tickets for buses and trains

Irish Rambler tickets cover bus-only travel within the Republic. They cost €50 (for three days' travel out of eight consecutive days), €110 (eight days out of 15) or €160 (15 days out of 30).

Irish Rover tickets combine services on Bus Éireann and Ulsterbus. They costs €65 (for three days travel out of eight consecutive days), €145 (eight days out of 15) and €215 (15 days out of 30).

Iarnród Éireann Explorer tickets cover train travel in the Republic. They cost €105 (for five days travel out of 15 consecutive days) or €130 to include Northern Ireland.

Irish Explorer Rail and Bus tickets (€160) allow you eight days' travel out of 15 consecutive days on trains and buses within the Republic.

Freedom of Northern Ireland passes allow unlimited travel on NIR, Ulsterbus and Citybus services for £12 for one day, £30 (for three out of eight consecutive days), or £45 (for seven consecutive days).

Emerald Card gives you unlimited travel throughout Ireland on all Iarnród Éireann, NIR, Bus Éireann, Dublinbus, Ulsterbus and Citybus services. The card costs €180 (for eight days out of 15) or €310 (for 15 days out of 30).

Children aged under 16 pay half-price for all these passes and for all normal tickets. Children aged under three travel for free on public transport. You can buy the above passes at most major train and bus stations in Ireland. Although they're good value, many of them make economic sense only if you're planning to travel around Ireland at the speed of light.

BORDER CROSSINGS

Security has been progressively scaled down in Northern Ireland in recent years and all border crossings with the Republic are now open and generally unmanned. Permanent checkpoints have been removed and ramps levelled. On major routes your only indication that you have crossed the border will be a change in road signs and the colour of number plates and postboxes.

BUS

Bus Éireann (☎ 01-836 6111; www.buseireann.ie; Busáras, Store St, Dublin) is the Republic's bus line and offers an extensive network throughout the south. Private buses compete with Bus Éireann in the Republic and sometimes run where the national buses are irregular or absent. The larger companies will usually carry bikes for free but you should always check in advance to avoid surprises. **Ulsterbus** (☎ 028-9033 3000; www.ulsterbus.co.uk; Milewater Rd, Belfast) is the only service in Northern Ireland.

Bus Passes

Details of special deals and passes are given in the boxed text on p676.

Costs

Bus travel is much cheaper than train travel and private buses often charge less than Bus Éireann. Generally, return fares cost little more than a one-way fare.

Some sample single (one-way) bus fares include:

service	cost	duration (hrs)	frequency (Mon-Sat)
Belfast-Dublin	£13	3	7
Derry-Belfast	£9	1¾	10+
Derry-Galway	£17	5¼	4
Dublin-Cork	€20	4½	6
Dublin-Donegal	€23	4	5
Dublin-Rosslare	€14	3	12
Dublin-Tralee	€20	6	12
Dublin-Waterford	€10	2¾	7
Killarney-Cork	€11	2	12
Killarney-Waterford	€18.50	4½	12

Reservations

Bus Éireann bookings can be made online but you can't reserve a seat for a particular service.

CAR & MOTORCYCLE

Ireland's new-found affluence means there are far more cars on the road, and the building of new roads and the upgrading of existing ones just cannot keep pace. Be prepared for delays, especially at holiday weekends. **AA Roadwatch** (☎ 1550-131811) provides traffic information in the Republic.

In the North, speed-limit and distance signs are in miles. In the Republic, speed limits are shown in miles per hour but all new distance signs use kilometres. The older white road signs still give distances in miles.

You'll need a good road map and sense of humour to deal with the severe lack of signposts in the Republic, and on minor roads be prepared for lots of potholes.

Petrol is considerably cheaper in the Republic than in the North. Most service stations accept payment by credit card, but some small, remote ones may take cash only.

Parking in towns and cities is either by meter, 'pay and display' tickets or disc parking (discs, which rotate to display the time you park your car, are available from newsagents).

Bring Your Own Vehicle

It's easy to take your own vehicle to Ireland and there are no specific procedures involved but you should carry a vehicle registration document as proof that it's yours.

Automobile association members should ask for a Card of Introduction entitling you to services offered by sister organisations (maps, information, breakdown assistance, legal advice etc), usually free of charge.

Automobile Association (AA; www.aaireland.ie) Northern Ireland (☎ 0870-950 0600, breakdown assistance ☎ 0800-887 766); The Republic (in Dublin ☎ 01-617 9999, in Cork ☎ 021-450 5155, breakdown assistance ☎ 1800-667 788)

Royal Automobile Club (RAC; www.rac.ie) Northern Ireland (☎ 0800-029 029, breakdown assistance ☎ 0800-828 282); The Republic (☎ 1800-483 483)

Driving Licence

Unless you have an EU licence, which is treated like an Irish one, your driving licence is valid for 12 months from the date of entry to Ireland, but you should have held it for two years prior to that. If you don't hold an EU licence it's a good idea to obtain an International Driving Permit (IDP) from your

TRANSPORT

ROAD DISTANCES (KM)

	Athlone	Belfast	Cork	Derry	Donegal	Dublin	Galway	Kilkenny	Killarney	Limerick	Rosslare Harbour	Shannon Airport	Sligo	Waterford	Wexford
Athlone	---														
Belfast	227	---													
Cork	219	424	---												
Derry	209	117	428	---											
Donegal	183	180	402	69	---										
Dublin	127	167	256	237	233	---									
Galway	93	306	209	272	204	212	---								
Kilkenny	116	284	148	335	309	114	172	---							
Killarney	232	436	87	441	407	304	193	198	---						
Limerick	121	323	105	328	296	193	104	113	111	---					
Rosslare Harbour	201	330	208	397	391	153	274	98	275	211	---				
Shannon Airport	133	346	128	351	282	218	93	135	135	25	234	---			
Sligo	117	206	336	135	66	214	138	245	343	232	325	218	---		
Waterford	164	333	126	383	357	163	220	48	193	129	82	152	293	---	
Wexford	184	309	187	378	372	135	253	80	254	190	19	213	307	61	---

home automobile association before you leave. Your home-country licence is usually enough to hire a car for three months.

You must carry your driving licence at all times.

Hire

Car rental in Ireland is expensive, so you're often better off making arrangements in your home country with some sort of package deal. In July and August it's wise to book well ahead. Most cars are manual; automatic cars are available but they're more expensive to hire.

The international rental companies and the major local operators have offices all over Ireland. **Nova Car Hire** (www.rentacar-ireland.com) acts as an agent for Alamo, Budget, European and National and offers greatly discounted rates. In the Republic typical weekly high-season rental rates with Nova are around €150 for a small car, €190 for a medium-sized car, and €525 for a five-seater people carrier. In the North, similar cars are marginally more expensive.

When renting a car be sure to check if the price includes collision-damage waiver (CDW), insurance (eg, for car theft and windscreen damage), value-added tax (VAT) and unlimited mileage.

If you're travelling from the Republic into Northern Ireland it's important to be sure that your insurance covers journeys to the North. People aged under 21 aren't allowed to hire a car; for the majority of rental companies you have to be aged at least 23 and have had a valid driving licence for a minimum of one year. Some companies in the Republic won't rent to you if you're aged 74 or over; there's no upper age limit in the North.

You can't rent motorbikes and mopeds.

Insurance

All cars on public roads must be insured. If you are bringing your own vehicle check that your insurance will cover you in Ireland.

Purchase

It's more expensive to buy a car in Ireland than most other European countries. If you do buy a car (or intend to import one from another country) you must pay vehicle registration tax and motor tax, and take out insurance.

Road Rules

A copy of Ireland's road rules is available from tourist offices. The most basic rules are listed below:

- Drive on the left, overtake to the right.
- Safety belts must be worn by the driver and all passengers.
- Children aged under 12 aren't allowed to sit on the front seats.
- Motorcyclists and their passengers must wear helmets.
- When entering a roundabout, give way to the right.
- Speed limits are 70mph (112km/h) on motorways, 60mph (96km/h) on other roads, and 30mph (48km/h) or as signposted in towns.
- The legal alcohol limit is 80mg of alcohol per 100ml of blood or 35mg on the breath (roughly two units of alcohol for a man and one for a woman).

HITCHING

Lonely Planet doesn't recommend hitching. It's never entirely safe in any country: the local nutter doesn't carry an identifying badge. Travellers who decide to hitch should understand that they are taking a small but potentially serious risk. People who do choose to hitch are safer if they travel in pairs, travel during daylight hours and let someone know where they're planning to go. Women hitching on their own should be extremely careful when choosing lifts – if in any doubt, don't. Many local women may hitch alone without serious problems, but a tourist is likely to be more at risk.

That said, hitching in Ireland is generally easy, except in heavily touristed areas, where there may be competition from other hitchers and cars are often full with families.

LOCAL TRANSPORT

There are comprehensive local bus networks in Dublin (Bus Átha Cliath), Belfast (Citybus) and some other larger towns. The Dublin Area Rapid Transport (DART) line in Dublin is the only local train line. A new light rail system Luas (www.luas.ie) is planned to begin operating in Dublin in mid-2004. Taxis tend to be expensive.

TOURS

If your time is limited it might be worth considering an organised tour, though it's cheaper to see things independently and Ireland is small enough for you to get to even the most remote places within a few hours. Tours can be booked through travel agencies, tourist offices in the major cities, or directly through the tour companies themselves.

Bus Éireann (☎ 01-836 6111; www.buseireann.ie; 59 Upper O'Connell St, Dublin) Runs day tours to various parts of the Republic and the North.

CIE Tours International (☎ 01-703 1888; 35 Lower Abbey St, Dublin) Runs four- to 10-day coach tours of the Republic and the North, including accommodation and meals. Taste of Ireland tour (four days) takes in Blarney, the Ring of Kerry, Killarney, the Cliffs of Moher and the region around the River Shannon (€410 in high season).

Gray Line Tours (☎ 01-872 9010) Located in Dublin and offers half-day (€25), day and extended trips from Dublin to Newgrange, Glendalough, north Dublin and the Ring of Kerry.

Over the Top & Into the West Tours (☎ 01-869 0769; www.overthetoptours.com) Daily historical and heritage tours of Wicklow and the Boyne Valley (€27).

Paddywagon Tours (☎ 01-672 6007; www.paddywagontours.com) Activity-filled three- and six-day tours all over Ireland with friendly tour guides. Accommodation is in IHH hostels. Its Jump On Jump Off tour of Ireland (€129) allows you to stay in any place en route for as long as you like and pick up a later bus.

Ulsterbus Tours (☎ 028-9033 7004; www.ulsterbus.co.uk) Runs a large number of day trips throughout the North and the Republic.

It's worth checking **GoIreland.com** (☎ 074-23800; www.goireland.com) for an array of holiday packages.

For train enthusiasts, **Railtours Ireland** (☎ 01-856 0045; 58 Lower Gardiner St, Dublin 1) organises a series of one- and two-day train trips in association with Iarnród Éireann. A day trip from Dublin to Cork, Blarney Castle and Killarney costs €99.

TRAIN

Iarnród Éireann (Irish Rail; ☎ 01-836 2222; www.irishrail.ie; 35 Lower Abbey St, Dublin) operates trains in the Republic on routes that fan out from Dublin. The system is limited though: there's no north–south route along the western coast, no network in Donegal, and no direct connections from Waterford to Cork or Killarney. **Northern Ireland Railways** (NIR; ☎ 028-9089 9411; Belfast Central Station) runs four routes from Belfast. One links with the system in the Republic via Newry to Dublin; the other three go east to Bangor, northeast to Larne and northwest to Derry via Coleraine .

Costs

Train travel is more expensive than bus travel and one-way fares are particularly poor value – a midweek return ticket is often about the same as a one-way fare. First-class tickets cost around €5 to €10 more than the standard fare for a single journey.

Some sample one-way fares are:

service	cost	duration (hrs)	frequency (Mon-Sat)
Belfast-Dublin	£22	2	8
Dublin-Cork	€48.50	3¼	8
Dublin-Galway	€25	3¼	5
Dublin-Limerick	€36.50	2½	13
Dublin-Sligo	€22	3	3
Dublin-Tralee	€51.50	4½	8
Dublin-Waterford	€20	2½	7

Reservations

Iarnród Éireann takes reservations for all its train services. You need to fax your details (name, numbers of passengers, date and time of service, credit card number and expiry date) to 01-703 4136.

Health

CONTENTS

BEFORE YOU GO

While Ireland has excellent health care, prevention is the key to staying healthy while abroad. A little planning before departure, particularly for pre-existing illnesses, will save trouble later. Bring medications in their original, clearly labelled, containers. A signed and dated letter from your physician describing your medical conditions and medications, including generic names, is also a good idea. If carrying syringes or needles, be sure to have a physician's letter documenting their medical necessity. Carry a spare pair of contact lenses and glasses, and take your optical prescription with you.

Insurance

If you're an EU citizen, an E111 form, available from health centres or, in the UK, post offices, covers you for most medical care. E111 won't cover you for nonemergencies, or emergency repatriation home. Citizens from other countries should find out if there is a reciprocal arrangement for free medical care between their country and the country visited. If you do need health insurance, make sure you get a policy that covers you for the worst possible case, such as an accident requiring an emergency flight home. Find out in advance if your insurance plan will make payments directly to providers or reimburse you later for overseas health expenditures.

Recommended Vaccinations

No jabs are required to travel to Ireland. The World Health Organization, however, recommends that all travellers should be covered for diphtheria, tetanus, measles, mumps, rubella and polio, as well as Hepatitis B, regardless of their destination.

IN TRANSIT

Deep Vein Thrombosis (DVT)

Blood clots may form in the legs during plane flights, chiefly because of prolonged immobility. The longer the flight, the greater the risk. The chief symptom of deep vein thrombosis is swelling or pain of the foot, ankle, or calf, usually but not always on just one side. When a blood clot travels to the lungs, it may cause chest pain and difficulty breathing. Travellers with any of these symptoms should immediately seek medical attention.

To prevent the development of DVT on long flights you should walk about the cabin, contract the leg muscles while sitting drink plenty of fluids and avoid alcohol and tobacco.

Jet Lag & Motion Sickness

To avoid jet lag (quite common when crossing more than five time zones) try drinking plenty of nonalcoholic fluids and eating light meals. Upon arrival, get exposure to natural sunlight and readjust your schedule (for meals, sleep etc) as soon as possible.

Antihistamines such as dimenhydrinate (Dramamine) and meclizine (Antivert, Bonine) are quite often the first choice for treating motion sickness. A herbal alternative is ginger.

IN IRELAND

Availability & Cost of Healthcare

Excellent healthcare is readily available and for minor self-limiting illnesses pharmacists can give valuable advice and sell over-the-counter medication. They can also advise when more specialised help is required and point you in the right direction.

Travellers' Diarrhoea

If you develop diarrhoea, be sure to drink plenty of fluids, preferably in the form of an oral rehydration solution such as dioralyte. If diarrhoea is bloody, persists for more than 72 hours or is accompanied by fever, shaking, chills or severe abdominal pain you will need to seek urgent medical attention.

Environmental Hazards & Treatment

HEAT ILLNESS

Heat exhaustion (yes, even in Ireland it can still happen!) occurs following excessive fluid loss with insufficient replacement of fluids and salt. Symptoms include headache, dizziness and tiredness. Dehydration is already happening by the time you feel thirsty – aim to drink sufficient water to produce pale, diluted urine. To treat heat exhaustion drink water and/or fruit juice, and cool the body with cold water and fans.

COLD ILLNESS

Hypothermia occurs when the body loses heat faster than it can produce it. As ever, proper preparation will reduce the risks of getting it. Even on a hot day in the mountains, the weather can change rapidly, so carry waterproof garments, warm layers and a hat and inform others of your route.

Hypothermia starts with shivering, loss of judgment and clumsiness. Without re-warming, the sufferer deteriorates into apathy, confusion and coma. Prevent further heat loss by seeking shelter, warm dry clothing, hot sweet drinks and shared bodily warmth.

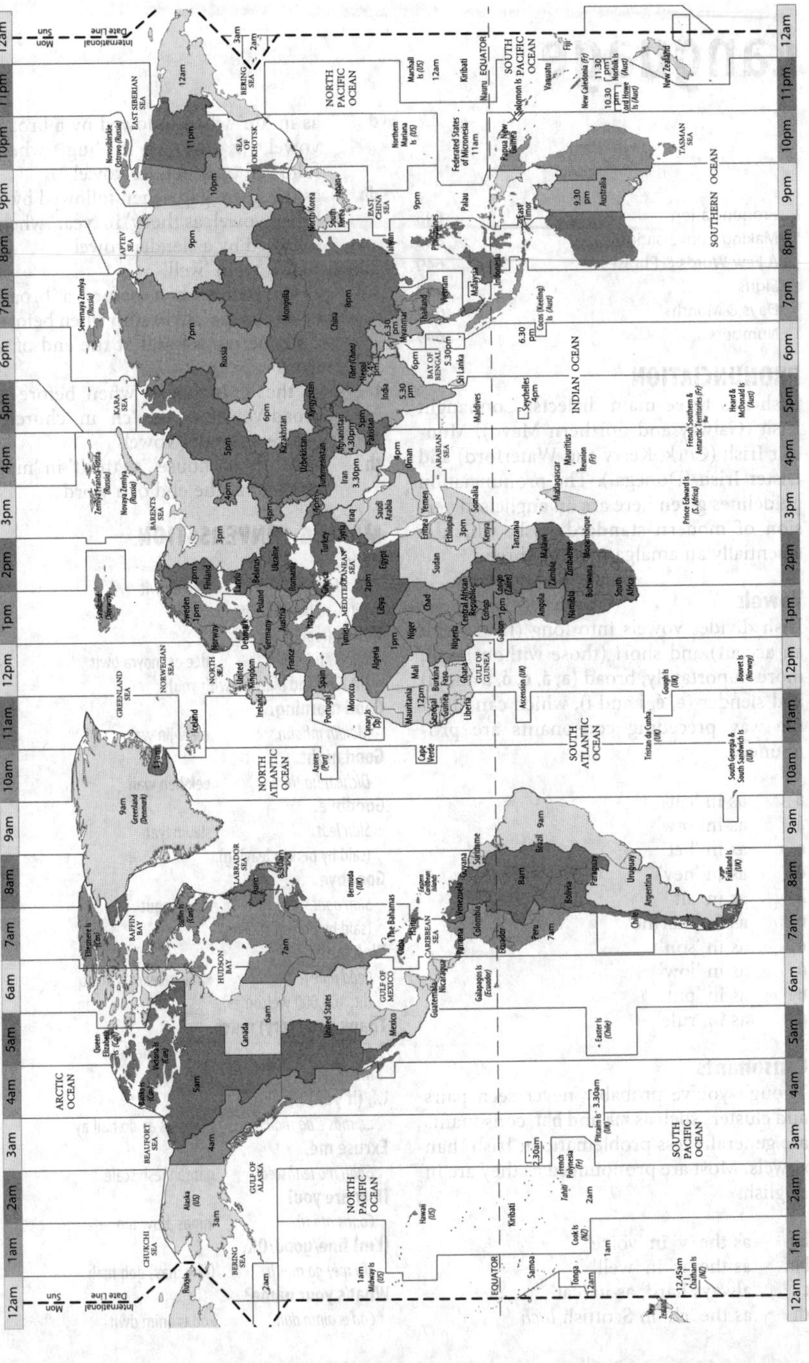
12am
1am
2am
3am
4am
5am
6am
7am
8am
9am
10am
11am
12pm
1pm
2pm
3pm
4pm
5pm
6pm
7pm
8pm
9pm
10pm
11pm
12am
International Date Line
Mon
Sun
ARCTIC OCEAN
NORTH PACIFIC OCEAN
SOUTH PACIFIC OCEAN
NORTH ATLANTIC OCEAN
SOUTH ATLANTIC OCEAN
INDIAN OCEAN
SOUTHERN OCEAN
EQUATOR
BERING SEA
GULF OF ALASKA
BEAUFORT SEA
HUDSON BAY
BAFFIN BAY
LABRADOR SEA
GULF OF MEXICO
CARIBBEAN SEA
GREENLAND SEA
NORWEGIAN SEA
NORTH SEA
MEDITERRANEAN SEA
BARENTS SEA
KARA SEA
LAPTEV SEA
EAST SIBERIAN SEA
SEA OF OKHOTSK
EAST CHINA SEA
ARABIAN SEA
BAY OF BENGAL
GULF OF GUINEA
TASMAN SEA
Alaska (US)
Canada
United States
Mexico
Greenland (Denmark)
Iceland
Brazil
Argentina
Chile
Peru
Bolivia
Colombia
Venezuela
Russia
China
Mongolia
India
Australia
New Zealand
Japan
Iran
Saudi Arabia
Egypt
Libya
Algeria
Sudan
Kazakhstan
Indonesia
Antarctica

Language

CONTENTS

PRONUNCIATION

Irish has three main dialects: Connaught Irish (Galway and northern Mayo), Munster Irish (Cork, Kerry and Waterford) and Ulster Irish (Donegal). The pronunciation guidelines given here are an anglicised version of modern standard Irish, which is essentially an amalgam of the three.

Vowels

Irish divides vowels into long (those with an accent) and short (those without) and, more importantly, broad (**a**, **á**, **o**, **ó**, **u** and **ú**) and slender (**e**, **é**, **i** and **í**), which can affect the way preceding consonants are pronounced.

a	as in 'cat'
á	as in 'saw'
e	as in 'bet'
é	as in 'hey'
i	as in 'sit'
í	as in 'marine'
o	as in 'son'
ó	as in 'low'
u	as in 'put'
ú	as in 'rule'

Consonants

Though you've probably never seen pairs and clusters such as **mh** and **bhf**, consonants are generally less problematic in Irish than vowels. Most are pronounced as they are in English.

bh	as the 'v' in 'voice'
bhf	as the 'w' in 'well'
c	always hard, as in 'cat'
ch	as the 'ch' in Scottish *loch*
d	as in 'do' when followed by a broad vowel, as the 'j' in 'jug' when followed by a slender vowel
dh	as the 'g' in 'gap' when followed by a broad vowel, as the 'y' in 'year' when followed by a slender vowel
mh	as the 'w' in 'well'
s	as in 'said' when before a broad vowel, as the 'sh' in ship when before a slender vowel and at the end of a word
t	as the 't' in 'toast' when before a broad vowel, as the 'ch' in 'church' before a slender vowel
th	as the 'h' in 'house', as the 't' in 'mat or silent at the end of a word

MAKING CONVERSATION

Hello.
Dia duit. — dee·a·gwit
(lit: God be with you)

Hello. (reply)
Dia is Muire duit. — dee·as moyra gwit
(lit: God and Mary be with you)

Good morning.
Maidin mhaith. — maw·jin wah

Good night.
Oíche mhaith. — eek·heh wah

Goodbye.
Slán leat. — slawn lyat
(said by person leaving)

Goodbye.
Slán agat. — slawn agut
(said by person staying)

Welcome.
Ceád míle fáilte. — kade meela fawltcha
(lit: 100,000 welcomes)

Thank you (very) much.
Go raibh (míle) maith agat. — goh rev (meeleh) mah agut

..., (if you) please.
..., más é do thoil é. — ... maws ay do hall ay

Excuse me.
Gabh mo leithscéal. — gamoh lesh scale

How are you?
Conas atá tú? — kunas ataw too

(I'm) fine/good/OK.
(Tá mé) go maith. — (taw may) goh mah

What's your name?
Cad is ainm duit? — kod is anim dwit?

My name is (Sean Frayne).

(Sean Frayne) is ainm dom.	(shawn frain) is anim dohm

Yes/It is.

Tá/Sea.	taw/sheh

No/It isn't.

Níl/Ní hea.	neel/nee heh

another/one more

ceann eile	kyawn ella

nice

go deas	goh dyass

A FEW WORDS & PHRASES

What is this/that?

Cad é seo/sin?	kod ay shoh/shin

I don't understand.

Ní thuigim.	nee higgim

I'd like to go to ...

Ba mhaith liom dul go dtí ...	baw wah lohm dull go dee ...

I'd like to buy ...

Ba mhaith liom ... a cheannach	bah wah lohm ... a kyanukh

here	*anseo*	onshoh
there	*ansin*	onshin
open	*oscailte*	uskawlta
closed	*dúnta*	doonta
big	*mór*	moor
small	*beag*	byawg
slowly	*go mall*	goh mohl
quickly	*go tapa*	goh topuh
fine (weather)	*go breá*	goh braw
awful (weather)	*go dona*	goh dohna
shop	*siopa*	shoppa
town	*baile*	bollyeh
town square	*lár an bhaile*	lawr an vallyeh

SIGNS

Leithreas	*lehrass*	Toilet
Fir	*fear*	Men
Mna	*m'naw*	Women
Gardaí	*gardee*	Police
Oifig An Phoist	*iffig ohn fwisht*	Post Office
Telefón	*taylayfon*	Telephone
An Lar	*an lawr*	Town Centre

DAYS & MONTHS

Monday	*Dé Luaín*	day loon
Tuesday	*Dé Máirt*	day maart
Wednesday	*Dé Ceádaoin*	day kaydeen
Thursday	*Déardaoin*	daredeen
Friday	*Dé hAoine*	day heeneh
Saturday	*Dé Sathairn*	day sahern
Sunday	*Dé Domhnaigh*	day downick

January	*Eanáir*	ann·ner
February	*Feabhra*	fiow·ra
March	*Márta*	mortha
April	*Aibreán*	ebb·rawn
May	*Bealtaine*	balthuna
June	*Meitheamh*	me·hiv
July	*Iúil*	ool
August	*Lúnasa*	loonassa
September	*Meán Fómhair*	mian fore
October	*Deireadh Fómhair*	djerru fore
November	*Samhain*	sowin
December	*Nollaig*	null·ig

NUMBERS

1	*haon*	hayin
2	*dó*	doe
3	*trí*	tree
4	*ceathaír*	kahirr
5	*cúig*	koo·ig
6	*sé*	shay
7	*seacht*	shocked
8	*hocht*	hukt
9	*naoi*	nay
10	*deich*	jeh
11	*haon déag*	hayin jague
12	*dó dhéag*	doe yague
20	*fiche*	feekhe
21	*fiche a haon*	feekhe uh hayin
30	*triocha*	tree·okha
40	*daichead*	day·khayd
50	*caoga*	kowga
60	*seasca*	shaska
70	*seachtó*	shocked·ow
80	*ochtó*	ukth·ow
90	*nócha*	nokha
100	*céad*	kade
1000	*míle*	meeleh

Glossary

A

An Óige – literally 'The Youth'; Republic of Ireland Youth Hostel Association
An Taisce – National Trust for the Republic of Ireland
Anglo-Norman – Norman, English and Welsh peoples who invaded Ireland in the 12th century
Apprentice Boys – *loyalist* organisation founded in 1814 to commemorate the Great Siege of Derry in August every year
ard – literally 'high'; Irish place name
ard rí – Irish 'high king'

B

bailey – outer wall of a castle
banshee – female spirit whose wailing warns of impending death
bawn – area surrounded by walls outside the main castle, acting as a defence as well as a place to keep cattle in times of trouble
beehive hut – circular stone building shaped like an old-fashioned beehive
Black and Tans – British recruits to the Royal Irish Constabulary shortly after WWI, noted for their brutality
Blarney Stone – bending over backwards to kiss this sacred rock in Blarney Castle, County Cork, is said to bestow the gift of the gab, or allow you to 'gain the privilege of telling lies for seven years'
bodhrán – *bore*-run; hand-held goatskin drum
boreen – see *botharin*
botharin – small lane or roadway; also known as boreen
Bronze Age – earliest metal-using period, around 2500 BC to 300 BC in Ireland, after the Stone Age and before the Iron Age
B-specials – Northern Irish auxiliary police force, disbanded in 1971
bullaun – stone with a depression, probably used as a mortar for grinding medicine or food and often found on monastic sites

C

CAC IRA – Continuity Army Council of the *IRA*, a breakaway group
caher – circular area enclosed by stone walls
cairn – mound of stones heaped over a prehistoric grave
camogie – women's hurling
cashel – stone-walled circular fort; see also *ráth*
cath – literally 'battle'; Irish place name
ceilidh – *kay*-lee; session of traditional music and dancing; also called ceili
Celts – Iron Age warrior tribes which arrived in Ireland around 300 BC and controlled the country for 1000 years
ceol – music
champ – a dish of mashed potatoes with spring onions or leeks
chancel – eastern end of a church, where the altar is situated, reserved for the clergy and choir
cill – literally 'church'; Irish place name; also known as kill
cillín – literally 'little cell'; a hermitage, or sometimes a small, isolated burial ground for unbaptised children and other 'undesirables'
Claddagh ring – ring worn in much of Connaught since the mid-18th century, with a crowned heart nestling between two hands; if the heart points towards the hand then the wearer is taken or married, towards the fingertip means he or she is looking for a mate
clochán – dry-stone beehive hut from the early Christian period
Connaught – one of the four ancient provinces of Ireland, made up of counties Galway, Leitrim, Mayo, Roscommon and Sligo
Continuity IRA – anti-Agreement splinter *republican* group, opposed to any deal not based on a united Ireland
control zone – area of a town centre, usually the main street, where parked cars must not, for security reasons, be left unattended
craic – conversation, gossip, fun, good times; also known as crack
crannóg – artificial island made in a lake to provide habitation in a good defensive position
creel – basket
crios – multicoloured woven woollen belt traditionally worn in the Aran Islands
cromlech – see *dolmen*
cú – dog
currach – rowing boat made of a framework of laths covered with tarred canvas; also known as cúrach

D

Dáil – lower house of the Republic of Ireland Parliament
dairtheach – oratory, a small room set aside for private prayer
DART – Dublin Area Rapid Transport train line
demesne – landed property close to a house or castle
diamond – town square
dolmen – tomb chamber or portal tomb made of vertical stones topped by a huge capstone, dating from around 2000 BC
drumlin – rounded hill formed by retreating glaciers

Dúchas – government department in charge of parks, monuments and gardens in the Republic; formerly known as the Office of Public Works
dún – fort, usually constructed of stone
DUP – Democratic Unionist Party; founded principally by Ian Paisley in 1971 in hard-line opposition to unionist policies. It publicly opposes the Good Friday Agreement but is willing to work with the other parties in the Assembly

E

Éire – Irish name for the Republic of Ireland
esker – gravel ridge

F

Fáilte Ireland – literally 'Welcome Board'; Irish Tourist Board
Fianna – mythical band of warriors who feature in many tales of ancient Ireland
Fianna Fáil – literally 'Warriors of Ireland'; a major political party in the Republic of Ireland, originating from the *Sinn Féin* faction opposed to the 1921 treaty with Britain
Fine Gael – literally 'Tribe of the Gael'; a major political party in the Republic, originating from the *Sinn Féin* faction that favoured the 1921 treaty with Britain. It formed the first government of independent Ireland
fir – literally 'men', singular *fear*; sign on men's toilets
fleadh – festival
fulacht fiadh – Bronze Age cooking place

G

gaelscoileanna – Irish-medium school
Gaeltacht – Irish-speaking area
gallery grave – tunnel-shaped burial chamber
gallóglí – mercenary soldiers of the 14th to 15th century; anglicised to gallowglasses
garda – Irish Republic police; plural *gardaí*
ghillie – fishing or hunting guide; also known as ghilly
gort – literally 'field'; Irish place name
Gothic – style of architecture characterised by pointed arches, common in Ireland from the late 12th to the 16th century

H

Hibernia – literally 'Land of Winter'; Roman name for Ireland; the Romans had confused Ireland with Iceland
hill fort – usually dating from the Iron Age, hill forts are formed by a ditch that follows the contour of the hill to surround and fortify the summit
HINI – Hostelling International of Northern Ireland
húicéir – traditional Galway vessel; also known as a hooker
hurling –Irish sport similar to hockey

I

Iarnród Éireann – Republic of Ireland Railways
INLA – Irish National Liberation Association; formed in 1975 as an *IRA* splinter group unhappy at the cease-fire; it has maintained its own cease-fire since 1998
IRA – Irish Republican Army; the largest republican paramilitary organisation founded 80 years ago with the aim to fight for a united Ireland. In 1969, the IRA split into the Official IRA and the Provisional IRA; the Official IRA is no longer active and the PIRA has become the IRA
IRB – Irish Republican Brotherhood; a secret society founded in 1858 and revived in the early 20th century. It believed in independence, through violence if necessary, and was a precursor to the *IRA*; also known as the Fenians
Iron Age – in Ireland this lasted from the end of the Bronze Age, around 300 BC (the arrival of the Celts), to the arrival of Christianity, around the 5th century AD

J

jarvey – driver of a *jaunting car*
jaunting car – Killarney's traditional horse-drawn transport

K

keep – main tower of a castle

L

Lambeg drum – very large drum associated with Protestant *loyalist* marches
Leinster – one of the four ancient provinces of Ireland, made up of counties Carlow, Dublin, Kildare, Kilkenny, Laois, Longford, Louth, Meath, Offaly, West Meath, Wexford and Wicklow
leithreas – toilets
leprechaun – mischievous elf or sprite from Irish folklore
lough – lake, long narrow bay or arm of the sea
loyalist – person, usually a Northern Irish Protestant, insisting on the continuation of Northern Ireland's links with Britain
loyalist orders – consists mainly of the *Orange Order* and the *Apprentice Boys* committed to the union with the UK
LVF – Loyalist Volunteer Force; an extreme *loyalist paramilitary* group opposed to the current peace process. It has been on cease-fire since 1998

M

marching season – *Orange Order* parades, which take place from Easter and throughout summer to celebrate the victory by Protestant King William II of Orange over Catholic James II in the Battle of the Boyne on 12 July 1690, and the union with Britain
Mesolithic – also known as the Middle Stone Age; time of the first human settlers in Ireland, about 8000 BC to 4000 BC
mná – literally 'women'; sign on women's toilets
motte – early Norman fortification consisting of a raised, flattened mound with a keep on top; when attached to a *bailey* it is known as a motte and *bailey* fort, many of which were built in Ireland until the early 13th century

Munster – one of the four ancient provinces of Ireland, made up of counties Clare, Cork, Kerry, Limerick, Tipperary and Waterford

N
naomh – holy or saint
nationalism – belief in a reunited Ireland through nonviolent means
nationalist – proponent of a united Ireland
Neolithic – also known as the New Stone Age; a period characterised by settled agriculture and lasting from around 4000 BC to 2500 BC in Ireland; followed by the Bronze Age
NIR – Northern Ireland Railways
NITB – Northern Ireland Tourist Board
NNR – National Nature Reserves
North, the – political entity of Northern Ireland, not the northernmost geographic part of Ireland

O
Ogham stone – Ogham (*o*-am) was the earliest form of writing in Ireland, using a variety of notched strokes placed above, below or across a keyline, usually on stone
Oireachtas – Parliament of the Republic, consisting of a lower and upper house, the *Dáil* and Senate
Orange Order – founded in 1795, the Orange Order is the largest Protestant organisation in Northern Ireland with a membership of up to 100,000. The name commemorates the victory of King William of Orange in the Battle of the Boyne
óstán – hotel

P
Palladian – style of architecture developed by Andrea Palladio (1508–80) based on ancient Roman architecture
paramilitaries – armed illegal organisations, either *loyalist* or *republican*, usually associated with the use of violence and crime for political and economic gain
Partition – division of Ireland in 1921
passage grave – Celtic tomb with a chamber reached by a narrow passage, typically buried in a mound
penal laws – laws passed in the 18th century forbidding Catholics from buying land, holding public office and so on
Plantation – settlement of Protestant migrants (sometimes known as Planters) in Ireland in the 17th century
poteen – *pot*-cheen; illegally brewed potato-based firewater
Prod – slang for Northern Irish Protestant
provisionals – Provisional IRA, formed after a break with the official *IRA*, who are now largely inconsequential; named after the provisional government declared in 1916, they have been the main force combating the British army in the *North*
PUP – Progressive Unionist Party; a small unionist party seen as a political front for the *UVF*, it is pro the Good Friday Agreement

R
ráth – circular fort with earth banks round a timber wall
Real IRA – splinter movement of the *IRA* and opposed to *Sinn Féin's* support of the Good Friday Agreement. The Real IRA was responsible for the Omagh bombing in 1998 in which 29 people died. It subsequently called a cease-fire but has been responsible for bombs in Britain and other acts of violence
Red Hand Commandos – illegal *loyalist paramilitary* group
Red Hand Defenders – breakaway *paramilitary loyalist* group formed in 1998 by dissident *UFF* and *LVF* members
Republic of Ireland – the 26 counties of the *South*
republican – supporter of a united Ireland
republicanism – belief in a united Ireland, sometimes referred to as militant nationalism
rí – petty kings
ring fort – circular habitation area surrounded by banks and ditches, used from the Bronze Age right through to the Middle Ages, particularly in the early Christian period
Romanesque – style of architecture seen in 12th-century Irish churches and monasteries, superseded by Gothic in the late 12th century; characterised by rounded arches and vaulting
round tower – tall circular tower dating from around the 9th to 11th centuries, built as a lookout and sanctuary during the period when monasteries were frequently subject to Viking raids
RUC – Royal Ulster Constabulary, the name for the armed Northern Irish police force at the time of writing

S
SDLP – Social Democratic and Labour Party; the largest nationalist party in the Northern Ireland Assembly and instrumental in achieving the Good Friday Agreement. Its goal is a united Ireland through nonviolent means; mostly Catholic
seisún – music session
sept – clan
shamrock – three-leafed plant said to have been used by St Patrick to illustrate the Holy Trinity
shebeen – from the Irish síbín; illicit drinking place or speakeasy
sheila-na-gig – literally 'Sheila of the teats'; female figure with exaggerated genitalia, carved in stone on the exteriors of some churches and castles; various explanations have been offered for the iconography, ranging from male clerics warning against the perils of sex to the idea that they represent Celtic war goddesses
shillelagh – stout club or cudgel, especially one made of oak or blackthorn
Sinn Féin – literally 'We Ourselves'; a *republican* party with the long-term aim of a united Ireland; seen as the political wing of the *IRA* but it maintains that both organisations are completely separate
slí – hiking trail or way

GLOSSARY

snug – partitioned-off drinking area in a pub
souterrain – underground chamber usually associated with ring and hill forts; probably provided a hiding place or escape route in times of trouble and/or storage space for goods
South, the – Republic of Ireland
standing stone – upright stone set in the ground, common across Ireland and dating from a variety of periods; usually the purpose is obscure, though some are burial markers
strawboy – traditional mummer who attended wakes or weddings in disguise (usually a hat, mask and skirt made of straw) to bring good luck to those involved

T

tánaiste – Republic of Ireland deputy prime minister
taoiseach – *tea*-shock; Republic of Ireland prime minister
TD – *teachta Dála*; member of the Republic of Ireland Parliament
teampall – church
Tinkers – derogatory term used to describe Irish gypsies, communities that roam the country; see also *Travellers*
trá – beach or strand
Travellers – the politically correct term used today to describe Ireland's itinerant communities
Treaty – Anglo-Irish Treaty of 1921, which divided Ireland and gave relative independence to the *South*; cause of the 1922–23 Civil War
trian – district
Tricolour – green, white and orange Irish flag designed to symbolise the hoped-for union of the green Catholic Southern Irish with the orange Protestant Northern Irish
turlough – from the Irish *turlach*; a small lake that often disappears in dry summers

U

UDA – Ulster Defence Association; the largest *loyalist paramilitary* group. It has observed a cease-fire since 1994
UDP – Ulster Democratic Party; a small fringe *unionist* party with links to the banned *loyalist UFF*
UFF – Ulster Freedom Fighters, aka the Ulster Defence Association; this group is pro the Good Friday Agreement and has been on cease-fire since 1994
Ulster – one of the four ancient provinces of Ireland; a term sometimes used to describe the six counties of the *North*, despite the fact that Ulster also includes counties Cavan, Monaghan and Donegal in the Republic
unionism – belief in the political union with Britain
unionist – person who wants to retain Northern Ireland's links with Britain
United Irishmen – organisation founded in 1791 aiming to reduce British power in Ireland; it led a series of unsuccessful risings and invasions
UUP – Ulster Unionist Party; the largest unionist party in Northern Ireland and the majority party in the Assembly, founded by Edward Carson. Once the monolithic unionist organisation but now under threat from the *DUP*
UVF – Ulster Volunteer Force; an illegal *loyalist* Northern Irish *paramilitary* organisation

V

Volunteers – offshoot of the *IRB* that came to be known as the *IRA*

Behind the Scenes

THIS BOOK

This is the 6th edition of *Ireland*. It all started back in January 1994 when the book was first published. The 1st edition was written by Jon Murray, Sean Sheehan and Tony Wheeler. The 2nd edition was updated by Tom Smallman, Sean Sheehan and Pat Yale. The 3rd edition was updated by Tom Smallman, Pat Yale and Steve Fallon, and the 4th by Tom Smallman, Fionn Davenport, Dorinda Talbot, Steve Fallon and Pat Yale. We sent Lou Callan, Fionn Davenport, Patrick Horton, Oda O'Carroll, Tom Smallman and David Wenk on the road to update the 5th edition.

THANKS FROM THE AUTHORS

Tom Downs Undying devotion to Fawn, Mai and Lana, of course. Eternal gratitude to Amanda Canning and Maria Donohoe for setting me up with this dream gig. A jovial punch in the arm to Joe Cleary and Gemma Murphy for pulling me out of the gutter when I needed it. Co-authors Fionn Davenport and Oda O'Carroll provided invaluable attitude adjustments. Thanks also to Garrett Kilroy for a grand time on Inishmaan, and to Sinead McPhillips for the pointers in Galway. I also want to tip the hat to Lynne Preston and Brian O'Neill for reassuring me that Galway is not Stab City.

Fionn Davenport A ton of people saw me through this update. Above all, I want to thank Anto Howard, Libby McCormack and the Ferriter clan, who answered all of my questions and poked and prodded me in the right direction. A big thank you to everyone at the various tourist offices I visited and to all those nameless locals whom I stopped in the street and in the pubs for directions, suggestions and advice. None of this would have been possible, however, without the help and understanding of LP GHQ in London, especially when my personal circumstances reached Def Con 4. Everyone, especially Amanda Canning, was absolutely terrific; *go raibh maith agat* to you all. Finally, a personal debt of gratitude to the staff at the Bon Secours and Mater Private hospitals in Dublin who saw me through the worst of an especially difficult situation, and to my family, who, as always, never let me down.

Des Hannigan My enduring gratitude to the scores of local people, tourism professionals and others who helped and advised me, always with good humour, wit and patience during my work in Ireland. A very big thank you to Cyril Guiney and Richard Costello of Adare, who know a thing or two about getting a travel-worn SRi back on the road. Thanks to Kay Harte in Cork, for wise words on what Irish food is all about, and to Sue Hill of Goleen for help and advice about the Mizen area. Retrospective thanks to my old Killarney mate Julian Behal for some great sport on the cliffs of Carrantuohil, Glendalough and Dalkey. Thanks also to my brother Kevin Hannigan for the inside track on Limerick and to my Dublin cousin, Eileen Denvir, for hearth and home. Special thanks to

THE LONELY PLANET STORY

The story begins with a classic travel adventure: Tony and Maureen Wheeler's 1972 journey across Europe and Asia to Australia. There was no useful information about the overland trail then, so Tony and Maureen published the first Lonely Planet guidebook to meet a growing need.

From a kitchen table, Lonely Planet has grown to become the largest independent travel publisher in the world, with offices in Melbourne (Australia), Oakland (USA), London (UK) and Paris (France).

Today Lonely Planet guidebooks cover the globe. There is an ever-growing list of books and information in a variety of media. Some things haven't changed. The main aim is still to make it possible for adventurous travellers to get out there – to explore and better understand the world.

At Lonely Planet we believe travellers can make a positive contribution to the countries they visit – if they respect their host communities and spend their money wisely. Since 1986 a percentage of the income from each book has been donated to aid projects and human rights campaigns, and, more recently, to wildlife conservation.

my fellow authors for helpful and entertaining e-conferences, and to Amanda Canning for holding it all together. Finally; total respect to all those superb Irish musicians and singers along the way, who proved yet again that when I tried my hand at Irish ballads many years ago, I was never, *ever*, close to the real thing.

Etain O'Carroll To all the people I met along the way and bombarded with questions, especially locals who provided the low down on where to go and where not to. Special thanks to Oliver Dempsey and Marguerite Osborne in Laois who fielded numerous requests for information. Thanks also to Amanda in the LP London office for all the support and good humour, and to Oda and Mark for seeing me through the mounds of paper.

Oda O'Carroll Thanks to Rosaleen and Caroline in Athlone and Mullingar tourist offices and Josephine in Carrick tourist office who was so helpful on her first day back, Josephine Murphy in Bord Fáilte, Mags O'Sullivan from the IFB, Vibeke at the Wicklow Film Commission, Sunniva and Antoinette at the Irish Film Archive, Jim Loughter at Outhouse, Sandra McCrann in Boyle, Clare Carthy in Tulsk, Breda in Monaghan, Shona Bushe, Clare, Kate, Charlotte and Orla for the company. Thanks to Isobel Stephenson, Edel O'Brien and Amanda's friend (you know who you are) for their insight into hidden Cavan. Thanks to Jackie Bourke for her tips on kids, Nora Mulligan whose farm I called into in search of telescopes in Frenchpark, Sarah Harte and Jay Burke for their infinite wisdom, Ashling Holohan for taking the dolly girls Esa and Mella from my lap, Mary and Brian O'Carroll at home on the range, Lisa and Etain O'Carroll whose contributions were immeasurable, fellow authors Fionn, Des, Neil, Etain and Tom for their goodwill and help and the unflappable Amanda Canning in the London office for her constant support and stellar sense of humour. And a big kiss to Zen veggieburgermeister Eoin, who makes me one with all.

Neil Wilson Thanks to the friendly and helpful tourist office staff all over Northern Ireland, to taxi driver Ken for his West Belfast insights, and to Carol Downie for a great weekend in Belfast and Portaferry.

CREDITS

This title was commissioned and developed in the London office by Amanda Canning. Cartography for this guide was developed by Mark Griffiths. Coordinating the production of this book from Lonely Planet's Melbourne office were Justin Flynn (editorial), an Irish name if ever you heard it, and Csanad Csutoros (cartography), a not-quite-so-Irish name. Craig Kilburn came off the bench at the last minute for a short stint to help with editorial layout. Eagle-eyed editorial assistance came from Andrea Baster, Bridget Blair, Emily Coles, Melanie Dankel, Stefanie Di Trocchio, Simone Egger, Victoria Harrison, Piers Kelly, Charlotte Keown, Stephanie Pearson, Kalya Ryan, Fiona Siseman, Katrina Webb and Gabbi Wilson. Steady-handed mapping assistance was provided by Hunor Csutoros, Daniel Fennessy, Huw Fowles, Joelene Kowalski, Valentina Kremenchutskaya, Adrian Persoglia, Helen Rowley, Jacqui Saunders, Andrew Smith, Chris Tsismetzis and the GIS unit.

Project manager Eoin Dunlevy (the Irishest of Irish names) made sure the ship stayed on course while Yvonne Bischofberger (the un-Irishest of un-Irish names) took care of layout and colour with assistance from Katherine Marsh. Thanks also to Quentin Frayne (language content coordinator) and Martin Hughes (Food & Drink) for their efforts. Pepi Bluck designed the cover and Brendan Dempsey was responsible for the artwork.

Series Publishing Manager Virginia Maxwell oversaw the redevelopment of the country guides series with help from Maria Donohoe. Regional Publishing Manager Katrina Browning steered the development of this title.

THANKS FROM LONELY PLANET

Many thanks to the hundreds of travellers who used the last edition and wrote to us with helpful hints, useful advice and interesting anecdotes:

A Joy Adams, Naomi Anders, Clare Anderson, Jocke Arfvidsson, Franck Asselman, Lydia Athmer, Jostein Austvik, Steven Aylward **B** Ted Baglin, Melanie Bale, Graham Banks, Helena Battdrill, Patricia Bernard, Kathrin Besse, Jude Billard, Tracey Berger, Pat Bode, Catherine Bonner, Stephanie Bradley, Jevan Brett, Jane Kantor Brickner, Baden Brown, John Buckwalter, Frank Bugeja, A G W Butler, Neil Byrne **C** Gerry Carden, John Carden, Katrina Cartwright, Brent Cassidy, Claire Caulton, Kristina Chamberlain, Maria Chamberlain, Edward Chambers, Simone Clark, Debbie Cleaveley, Liz Cochrane, Cathie Coles, Peter Collins, Ellen Connelly, Dan Conroy, Cathleen Conway, Noel Conway, Jean Cook, Alistair Craig, Marlene Crivello, Jennifer Cropley, Rodger Crowe, Shelagh Cullity, Andrea Curtis **D** Jayne D'Arcy, Janice Day, Flo & Paul De Beer, Antoine De Vermouthier, Niamh M Dempsey, Colm Dolan, Jeffrey Donnelly, Aline Doornhof, Mara d'Oriano, Kelly Douglas, M F Dowd, Shane Duffy, H Dunn **E** William Edwards, Sybil Ehrlich, Margaret Ellis, Robin Ellis, Tim Entwistle, Anthony Esposito, Caroline Evans **F** Aliza F, Rosemary Fairlain, Michael Falk, Rev Pat Farnham, Katja Fedrowitz, Arnold Fieldman, Kerstin Finkhaeuser,

Beth Ann Finlay, B Finnerty, Margaret Fitzherbert, Tim FitzPatrick, Joss Fitzsimons, Olivia Flynn, Sean Flynn, Karen For, Karen & Roberta For, Sally Forbes, Graham Ford, Rev John Fowler, Barbara Fraser, Sue Frezza, Anna Frith **G** Sarah Garrison, Jerry George, J M C Gibson, Stephen Gilmore, Susan Gilpin, Brad Gledhill, Grace Goh, Dominic Goodfellow, Kenneth Gordon, Marie Goss, Patricai E. Graham, Diana Green, Paul Green, Michel Gregoire, Ron Griep, Eberhard R Grosse, Torben Grue **H** Adrian Haas, John Hamilton, Jacki Hatnett, Henry Hauber, Erin Heffron, Lorenz A. Heinze, K G Hellyen, Ellie Henk, Irene Hennessey, Vincent Henry, Robert M Herbst, Nattanya Hewitt, Calvin Hilton Jr, Amber Hobson, Mairead Holt, Catherine Hovenden, Sabine Huba, Viktoria Huber, Lynn W Humeston, Josie Hunt, Terry Hunt, Jill Hunter, Jill & Rod Hunter **I** Yoel Izsak **J** Jan Jaap van Lomwel, Emma Jacobs, Fitzmaurice Joe, Betty Johnson, Danyane Johnston, Marina Josephs **K** Christine Kaegii, Daniel Kavanaugh, Victoria Kearns, Yorgos Kechagioglou, Rachel Kelly, Judith Kiddlo, William Kirwan, Andrew Knight, Frank Kohns, Jenifer Kooiman, Henry Koster, Anke Kuhner, S Brian Kyle **L** Abbi Lawrance, Tanya Lecut, Rob Lee, Evelyn Leeper, Jamie Lennahan, Tom R Linden, Par Longton Collis, Israel Luski, Marc Luthy-Gagliardo **M** Kathleen Madden, Valerie Maguire, Carolyn Mandersloot, Dan Manson, Tracey Marek, Chana Matzliach, Chana & Shabtai Matzliach, Jim and Pat McAtee, Mandy McCabe, Carmel Mccann, Jenny McCormick, Ian McGinley, Clare McGinness, Stephen McGinness, Karen McGlinchey, Mary McGreevy, Lisa McInnis, Carol McKay, Peter McKenna, Kylie McKernan, Jo McNicholas, Mary Medicus, J M Mellifont, David Monaghan, Christine Moon, Elaine Murphy, Hamish Murray, Beate Myran **N** John Naughton, Mary Naughton, Peter Neild, Victoria Newman Sumner, Christy Nickel, Melissa Nurczynski **O** Jean O Sullian, Kathy O'Brian, Con O'Conaill, John O'Connor, P Octay, Joe O'Dea, Tony Ogilvie, Giovanna Olivieri, Sharon O'Reilly, Stephen O'Reilly, Jen O'Shea **P** Aristea Parissi, Wendy Parnell, Derek Paterson, Ole P Pedersen, I Philips, Heike Phillips, Ben Pickett, D C Piper, Dorothee Podransky, Klaus Podransky, Robin Preece, Rosemarie Pundsack, Catherine Pyne **R** Geoff Ralph, Joel Rane, Anne Rasmusen, Petra Redelonghi, David Reid, Patricia Rensen, Robin Richards, Nancy Ristan, Katja Ritari, Cindy Roche, Marc Roede, Maik Roelofs, Ellen Roffey, Brittany Rogers, Christopher Romanet, Kris Rosar, Monica Rumpf, Nicky Rutherford, Emma Ryan **S** Roger Salinas, Patrick Samaey, Markus Schonherr, Larry Schwarz, Rebecca Scott, Dan Sharp, Laurie Sheldon, Ingrid Sinkunas, Tom William Skarre, Richard Smith, Richard & B Smith, Eugene Sobka, Mrs Cathleen Solms, P W Spencer, Helen Squires, Robert J Stagg, Robert Stanley, Lou Stephenson, Yvonne Sterling, Judy Stern, Paul Stewart, Kathryn Stokes **T** A Taylor, David Taylor, Veronica Teaman, Janice Teoh, Natalie T'Jampens, Mark Tottenham, Lisa Tremewan, Miguel Trevinto, Jean R Trimmer, Jackie Trott, Mike C Tucker, A.J. Turner **U** Chris Uphill **V** Sarann Forester Valentine, Monique Van Erp, Marieke van Riet, Hein Van Rossum, Sandra Van Tweel, Robert Vanover, Mirella Vaseley, Suzanne Vinci-Irwin, Rudy Volin **W** Sigrit Walloe, Aidan Walsh, J Walton, Dara Ward, Phil Waring, Richard Watson, Anthony Webb, Julie Webb, Robert Webb, Alison Weir, Shannon White, Daryl Williams, David Wilson, Johannes Woern, Zuzanna Wojcik, Jessica Wolf **Y** Leesa Yeo **Z** Bram Zandbelt

SEND US YOUR FEEDBACK

We love to hear from travellers – your comments keep us on our toes and help make our books better. Our well-travelled team reads every word on what you loved or loathed about this book. Although we cannot reply individually to postal submissions, we always guarantee that your feedback goes straight to the appropriate authors, in time for the next edition. Each person who sends us information is thanked in the next edition – and the most useful submissions are rewarded with a free book.

To send us your updates – and find out about LP events, newsletters and travel news – visit our award-winning website: **www.lonelyplanet.com**.

Note: We may edit, reproduce and incorporate your comments in Lonely Planet products such as guidebooks, websites and digital products, so let us know if you don't want your comments reproduced or your name acknowledged. For a copy of our privacy policy, email privacy@lonelyplanet.com.au.

ACKNOWLEDGMENTS

Many thanks to the following for the use of their content:

Mountain High Maps® Copyright © 1993 Digital Wisdom, Inc.

Index

C

000 Map pages
000 Location of colour photographs

000 Map pages
000 Location of colour photographs

INDEX

000 Map pages
000 Location of colour photographs

G

INDEX

000 Map pages
000 Location of colour photographs

N

000 Map pages
000 Location of colour photographs

000 Map pages
000 Location of colour photographs

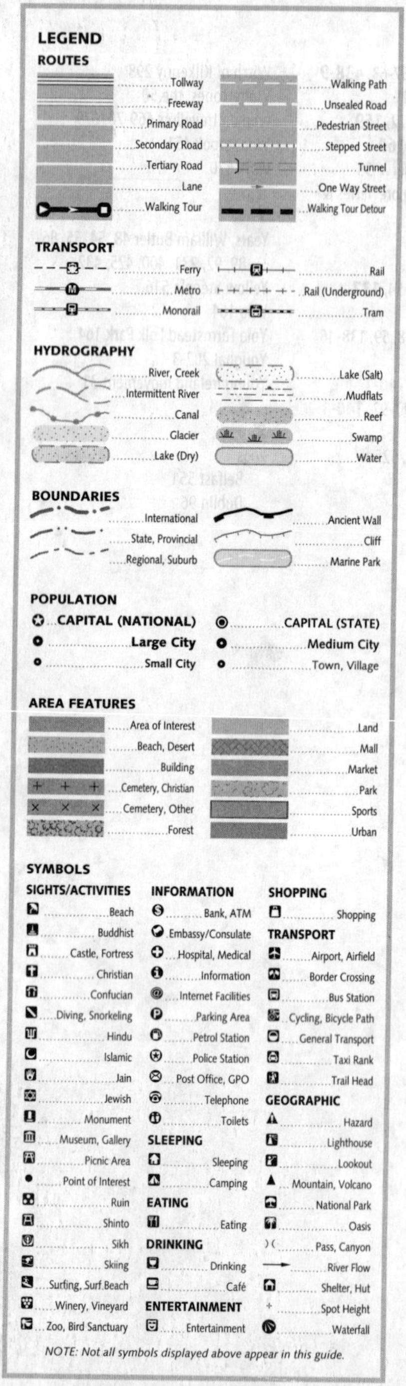

LONELY PLANET OFFICES

Australia
Head Office
Locked Bag 1, Footscray, Victoria 3011
☎ 03 8379 8000, fax 03 8379 8111
talk2us@lonelyplanet.com.au

USA
150 Linden St, Oakland, CA 94607
☎ 510 893 8555, toll free 800 275 8555
fax 510 893 8572, info@lonelyplanet.com

UK
72–82 Rosebery Ave,
Clerkenwell, London EC1R 4RW
☎ 020 7841 9000, fax 020 7841 9001
go@lonelyplanet.co.uk

France
1 rue du Dahomey, 75011 Paris
☎ 01 55 25 33 00, fax 01 55 25 33 01
bip@lonelyplanet.fr, www.lonelyplanet.fr

Published by Lonely Planet Publications Pty Ltd
ABN 36 005 607 983

Cover photographs: shamrocks, Charles W Campbell/CORBIS (front); The Temple Bar, Dublin, Richard Cummins (back). Many of the images in this guide are available for licensing from Lonely Planet Images: www.lonelyplanetimages.com.

Printed through Colorcraft Ltd, Hong Kong. Printed in China